ΟΟΥΝΝΟΜΟCΚΑΤΑΤωΝΕΠΑΓΓΕΛΙωΝΜΗΓΕ
ΝΟΙΤΟ ΕΙΓΑΡΕΔΟΘΗΝΟΜΟC ΟΔΥΝΑΜΕΝΟC
ΖωΟΠΟΙΗΘΗCΕΤΑΙ ΟΝΤωCΕΝΝΟΜωΗΝΑΝ
ΔΙΚΑΙΟCΥΝΗΑΛΛΑCΥΝΕΚΛΕΙCΕΝΗΓΡΑΦΗΤΑ
ΠΑΝΤΑΥΠΟΑΜΑΡΤΙΑΝΙΝΑΗΕΠΑΓΓΕΛΙΑ
ΕΚΠΙCΤΕωCΙΗΥ ΧΥ ΔΟΘΗΤΟΙCΠΙCΤΕΥΟΥCΙΝ
ΠΡΟΤΟΥΔΕΕΛΘΕΙΝΤΗΝΠΙCΤΙΝΥΠΟΝΟΜΟΝΕΦΡΟΥ
ΡΟΥΜΕΘΑCΥΝΚΛΕΙΟΜΕΝΟΙΕΙCΤΗΝΜΕΛΛΟΥCΑΝ
ΠΙCΤΙΝΑΠΟΚΑΛΥΦΘΗΝΑΙωCΤΕΟΝΟΜΟCΠΑΙΔΑ
...ΓΟCΗΜωΝΕΓΕΝΕΤΟ ΕΙCΧΝ ΙΝΑΕΚΠΙCΤΕ
ΚΑΙωΘωΜΕΝ ΕΛΘΟΥCΗCΔΕΤΗCΠΙCΤΕωCΟΥΚΕ
...ΠΑΙΔ... ...ΓΟΝ ΕCΜΕΝ ΠΑΝΤΕCΓΑΡΥΙΟΙΘΥ
...ΙΑΠΙCΤΕωCΧΡΥ ΙΗΥ ΟCΟΙΓΑΡΕΙCΧΡΝ ΕΒΑ
...ΗΤΕ ΧΝ ΕΝΕΔΥCΑCΘΕ ΟΥΚΕΤΙ ΙΟΥΔΑΙΟC
... ...ΚΕΤΙ ΔΟΥΛΟCΟΥΔΕΕΛΕΥΘΕΡ...
... ...ΤΕCΓ... ...CΕCΤΕ...
...ΡΑ... CΠΕ...

Galatians

A Commentary on
Paul's Letter
to the Churches in Galatia

by Hans Dieter Betz

Fortress
Press

Philadelphia

©1979 by Fortress Press

All rights reserved. No part of this publication may
be reproduced, stored in a retrieval system, or transmitted in any form or by any means, electronic,
mechanical, photocopying, recording, or otherwise,
without the prior permission of the copyright owner.

Library of Congress Catalog Card Number 77–78625
ISBN 0–8006–6009-9

Printed in the United States of America
Design by Kenneth Hiebert
Type set by Santype, Ltd., in the United Kingdom
6433G79   20–6009

iv

NEC DE POLITICA LIBERTATE
AGIMUS,
SED DE ALIA QUADAM,
QUAM DIABOLUS MAXIME ODIT ET
IMPUGNAT.
EA EST, QUA CHRISTUS NOS
LIBERAVIT, NON E SERVITUTE
ALIQUA HUMANA AUT VI
TYRANNORUM, SED IRA DEI
AETERNA.
UBI? IN CONSCIENTIA.

Martin Luther,
In epistolam S. Pauli
ad Galatas
Commentarius
(1535 WA 40/2, p. 3)

The Author

Hans Dieter Betz, born 1931 in Lemgo, Germany,
served several churches in Germany before coming to
the United States in 1963 as Professor of New Testament at the School of Theology at Claremont and the
Claremont Graduate School. He is now teaching at
the University of Chicago Divinity School. In addition
to his contributions to the study of New Testament
theology (*Nachfolge und Nachahmung Jesu Christi im
Neuen Testament, Paul's Concept of Freedom,* as well as
numerous articles and reviews in *Novum Testamentum,
Journal of Biblical Literature, Interpretation* and other
journals) his major interest has been the investigation
of the relationship of the New Testament to its religious
environment; this is reflected in several books on the
New Testament and Greco-Roman literature and in his
editorship of two volumes on *Plutarch and Early Christian
Literature* for the Corpus Hellenisticum Novi Testamenti.

Contents

The name *Hermeneia*, Greek ἑρμηνεία, has been chosen as the title of the commentary series to which this volume belongs. The word *Hermeneia* has a rich background in the history of biblical interpretation as a term used in the ancient Greek–speaking world for the detailed, systematic exposition of a scriptural work. It is hoped that the series, like its name, will carry forward this old and venerable tradition. A second, entirely practical reason for selecting the name lay in the desire to avoid a long descriptive title and its inevitable acronym, or worse, an unpronounceable abbreviation.

The series is designed to be a critical and historical commentary to the Bible without arbitrary limits in size or scope. It will utilize the full range of philological and historical tools including textual criticism (often ignored in modern commentaries), the methods of the history of tradition (including genre and prosodic analysis), and the history of religion.

Hermeneia is designed for the serious student of the Bible. It will make full use of ancient Semitic and classical languages; at the same time, English translations of all comparative materials—Greek, Latin, Canaanite, or Akkadian—will be supplied alongside the citation of the source in its original language. Insofar as possible, the aim is to provide the student or scholar with full critical discussion of each problem of interpretation and with the primary data upon which the discussion is based.

Hermeneia is designed to be international and interconfessional in the selection of its authors; its editorial boards were also formed with this end in view. Occasionally the series will offer translations of distinguished commentaries which originally appeared in languages other than English. Published volumes of the series will be revised continually, and, eventually, new commentaries will replace older works in order to preserve the currency of the series. Commentaries are also being assigned for important literary works in the categories of apocryphal and pseudepigraphical works of the Old and New Testaments, including some of Essene or Gnostic authorship.

The editors of *Hermeneia* impose no systematic–theological perspective upon the series (directly, or indirectly by its selection of authors). It is expected that authors will struggle to lay bare the ancient meaning of a biblical work or pericope. In this way the text's human relevance should become transparent, as is always the case in competent historical discourse. However, the series eschews for itself homiletical translation of the Bible.

The editors are heavily indebted to Fortress Press for its energy and courage in taking up an expensive, long–term project, the rewards of which will accrue chiefly to the field of biblical scholarship.

The present volume is the first commentary in this series which was commissioned by Fortress Press upon the recommendation of the editors. It opens thus a new phase in the development of *Hermeneia*. The editors are grateful to Professor Hans Dieter Betz for his work and for his gracious cooperation in the production of the book. Ms. Valerie Abrahamsen of Harvard Divinity School undertook the complex and time-consuming task of copyediting (assisted by Ron Cameron), helped in the proofreading, and composed the index. Her patient and untiring cooperation was invaluable.

Several members of the New Testament Editorial Board participated in the process of editing: James M. Robinson of the Claremont Graduate School in the early stages, George MacRae, S.J., of Harvard University in the final stages. The editor responsible for this volume is Helmut Koester of Harvard University.

June, 1978   *Frank Moore Cross*   *Helmut Koester*
For the Old Testament   for the New Testament
Editorial Board   Editorial Board

The commentary, friends and colleagues tell me, is at present not the most creative genre and format within which to work. It is true that after centuries of scholarly scrutiny spent on the Biblical texts one gets the impression that there are no problems left worth solving. In addition, the Biblical scholar today is under pressure to write quickly and popularly for an audience not interested in fine points of argumentation and careful documentation. Christendom is satisfied with the present state of its understanding of the Biblical literature. The main task still to be done, according to this line of reasoning, is to carry the message of the Christian faith to the millions of church members, non-believers, and no-longer believers.

The facts, however, point in a completely different direction. Strange as it may be after such long and intensive scholarly efforts, Paul's letter to the Galatians—to mention only this text among those that could be named—still presents the scholar with a most formidable challenge.

Everyone who studies Galatians must begin with Heinrich Schlier's monumental work. Currently, this commentary is regarded as "presently the best exegesis and interpretation of this letter." [1] During the investigations of the letter, however, it became clear that Schlier had completely, though ingeniously, misinterpreted the letter to the Galatians. Ironically, this misinterpretation was tied up, God only knows how, with Schlier's conversion to Roman Catholicism, of which it was supposed to render account.

Another challenge comes from Hans Joachim Schoeps' book on Paul. [2] In this work, which may very well be the most important book on Paul in this century, Schoeps had come to the conclusion that the apostle himself had also completely, though ingeniously, misunderstood the very issues about which he was writing. It is important to note that Schoeps' judgment is that of a Jew about a fellow-Jew. Substantiated by careful analyses of the texts and by arguments from the compara-

---

1   So Erich Dinkler in his review *VF* 1–3 (1953–55) 175, rep. in his *Signum Crucis: Aufsätze zum Neuen Testament und zur christlichen Archäologie* (Tübingen: Mohr, Siebeck, 1967) 270: "Der neue Galaterbrief–Kommentar von Heinrich Schlier . . . muss als die derzeit beste Exegese und Erläuterung dieses Briefes bezeichnet werden."

2   *Paul: The Theology of the Apostle in the Light of Jewish Religious History* (tr. Harold Knight; Philadelphia: Westminster, 1961; Tübingen: Mohr, Siebeck, 1959). Schoeps's work is really a study about Paul's understanding of the law, a concept fundamental to both Paul and Judaism. Schoeps came to the conclusion that Paul's doctrine of the law is "a fundamental misapprehension." He contends (*Paul*, 213) that "Paul succumbed to a characteristic distortion of vision which had its antecedents in the spiritual outlook of Judaic Hellenism. Paul did not perceive, and for various reasons was perhaps unable to perceive, that in the Biblical view the law is integral to the covenant; in modern terms it was the constitutive act by which the Sinai covenant was ratified, the basic ordinance which God laid down for His 'house of Israel'. . . . The maintenance of this ordinance, the proving of this constitutive act, is required of every member of the people in order that the covenant might be really embodied in Israelite life at all times and in all places." This criticism of Paul is the modern re-creation of the criticism of the ancient anti–Pauline opposition as we find it especially in the *Kerygmata Petrou*. Schoeps's book on Paul was written and rewritten at the same time when he also wrote his important work on Jewish Christianity. See his *Paul*, p. xi; also the Introduction below, 2. C.

tive study of religion, Schoeps' judgment basically reaffirms what the anti-Pauline opposition had contended in the first and second century, if not during the lifetime of the apostle himself.

Although coming from different angles, both Schlier and Schoeps have in fact destroyed the common belief that Paul's letter to the Galatians, and even his theology as a whole, are known entities. Therefore, Galatians is a mystery still to be unlocked. In other words, the conditions which arouse the curiosity of the historical and theological scholar still exist.

One of the areas almost entirely unexplored has been the formal and compositional structure of the letter to the Galatians. Of course nearly all introductions to the New Testament, commentaries, and studies provide outlines, tables of contents, or paraphrases of the argument. Yet no consideration is given to possible criteria for determining such an outline. This is astonishing because the letter is composed in accordance with the conventions of Greco-Roman rhetoric and epistolography. [3] The letter does contain an ongoing argument which can be analyzed in terms of conventional logic, a logic of course conforming to the time and circumstances of the author. [4]

These facts are startling and call for an explanation. If ancient and medieval exegesis was hampered, with rare exceptions, by unquestioned dogmatic presuppositions, modern scholarship has been and still is under the spell of the myth of Paul the non-thinker. During the nineteenth century the apostle Paul was more and more portrayed as the antitype of Jesus. Since Jesus was idealized, Paul was made almost a Satanic figure. This situation was summed up brilliantly by Friedrich Nietzsche: "The 'glad tidings' were followed closely by the absolutely *worst* tidings—those of St. Paul. Paul is the incarnation of a type which is the reverse of that of the Saviour; he is the genius in hatred, in the standpoint of hatred, and in the relentless logic of hatred." [5] In the English language world George Bernard Shaw agreed expressly with Nietzsche and went on to describe Paul as "the monstrous imposition upon Jesus." [6] Even at the end of this century this image of Paul is so widely believed that a Paul who was able to think clearly and write intelligently remains a stranger. The belief that Paul was a psychopath is often unconsciously behind the endless variety of notions implying that he was strangely "Jewish," had an "oriental temper" and was notoriously incompatible with Greco-Roman culture, of which we are of course the heirs. Thus he cannot have received a decent education. Having been brought up in Judaism and as a member of the Pharisaic sect, his language, style, and thought must be that of a barbarian. Why then should one even look for literary skills or thoughts which make sense to an intelligent and philosophic mind? Overwhelmed by this "myth," New Testament scholarship has largely been preoccupied with the study of Paul's "religion" and "theology." It is true, however, that the apostle Paul shows clear evidence that he took positions in the intellectual world in which he moved. In Galatians, his views on the law, on freedom, on ethics, to mention the most important themes, are more than esoteric Christian theology. They can be discussed

3   See the Introduction, § 5.

4   See the Introduction, § 7.

5   *Der Antichrist*, 42; Friedrich Nietzsche, *Werke* (Darmstadt: Wissenschaftliche Buchgesellschaft, 1963) 2.1204. The translation is by Anthony M. Ludovici, according to *The Writings of St. Paul* (ed. Wayne A. Meeks; New York: Norton, 1972) 290.

6   See the "Preface On the Prospect of Christianity," reprinted in *The Writings of St. Paul* (see n. 5, above) 296–302.

in terms of the philosophic traditions of his time, and, one must add, they are extremely interesting to study in the contemporary world of the end of the twentieth century. Translated into our world today, Paul's views seem to be still viable or even impressive. It is no longer a secret to this commentator why the letter to the Galatians has fascinated so many intellectuals over so many centuries.

Another strange fact from the history of scholarship deserves special comment. There is at least one commentary which in this commentator's opinion expresses an extraordinary and profound understanding of what Paul intended to say: Luther's commentary of 1535. Written after earlier attempts and including the entire range of scholarship available at the time, Luther's commentary is more than a scholarly commentary *upon* Galatians. It is a recreation *of* Galatians in the sixteenth century. Luther speaks as Paul would have spoken had he lived at the time when Luther gave his lectures. He often speaks in the first person singular, imitating the apostle. Surprisingly, Luther seems to be aware of Paul's rhetorical skills, so that he often appropriates his style and makes creative use of it for his own purposes.

Where does this leave the present writer? He started by accepting the honor of the assignment by the Editorial Board of the Hermeneia series, an act which now looks rather naive. The more he became involved in the work the more he became fascinated. His understanding of the letters and theology of Paul, and his methodological approaches to the material, changed to an extent difficult to comprehend. This experience only shows the text is still accomplishing its goals. What else would one expect given a text such as this? The present commentary, then, is intended to give account of a new reading of an old text. This commentary is the work of a historian whose goal is to understand a historical phenomenon with the help of the set of methods called the historical-critical method, and thus to prepare the ground for others who are interested in the phenomenon for perhaps other reasons. The commentary, however, is not and should not be a substitute for the reader's own encounter with the primary text. The experience of understanding should not be and cannot be anticipated by a commentator. The historian's work is to prepare the reader sufficiently for his own understanding, to provide a scientific basis of judgment, and to safeguard against arbitrariness, lack of perspective, or ideological prejudices.

The present commentator does not deny that his work is also that of a theologian, although he wishes to state clearly what he means by this often misunderstood term. It simply means that he is conscious of the fact that he knows what Paul is talking about. This awareness has been put to use to let Paul say what he wants to say. There is, however, no clear line of demarcation between one's intention to let Paul say what he wants to say and one's own saying it. The process of understanding quickly becomes a dialogue between author and commentator about the subject matter itself, if that subject matter really matters. This commentator, however, hopes to have avoided the danger of making Paul say what the commentator himself wants to say.

A word should be said about the method and presentation of the commentary. Paul's Galatians always stands in the center of interest. Parallel references are taken from Galatians first, then from other Pauline letters, then from Pauline tradition as it emerges in the deutero-Pauline literature. The attempt to harmonize Galatians with other Pauline letters has been resisted, and so has the attempt to interpret Galatians by interpreting "Paul's theology" into it. [7] Special attention is given to the other side of Galatians, the theology of the anti-Pauline opposition. To be sure, this other side is extremely difficult to reconstruct because of the scarcity of sources. The sources, however, which do exist should be used. Most of the sources which are important and perhaps not readily available have been included in the Appendices. Parallels from other Christian and non-Christian literature are adduced as they are needed to illustrate and explain a problem under discussion. General ideological preferences, e.g., of Biblical versus non-Biblical, or Jewish versus non-Jewish literature, have been avoided. The secondary literature has been listed as it contributes, in the view of the commentator, to the understanding of the text. The reader is directed either to places where the literature has been collected or to the more recent literature by title. A full discussion of the secondary literature has not been attempted. It would surpass the capacity and patience of any human being. Also, agreement or disagreement among scholars does not necessarily benefit the understanding of the problems of the text. When in doubt, this commentator has always preferred his own reading of the evidence. Careful attention has been paid to the translation, simply because Galatians is extremely difficult and at some places impossible to render into English. The notes on the translation take notice of how other modern scholarly translations render the text, but also here consideration had to be limited to those translations most commonly used: the *Revised Standard Version*, the *New English Bible*, and the *Jerusalem Bible*.

The present book has not been written in isolation. I am greatly indebted to a large number of people who have encouraged, criticized, and otherwise assisted me in my work, some of whom must be mentioned by name. Professor Gerhard Delling put at my disposal parallels from Philo of Alexandria which were collected for the *Corpus Hellenisticum Novi Testamenti* by Hans Windisch and Harald Hegermann; Professor Edward N. O'Neil allowed me to use the unpublished *Index Verborum Plutarcheus*; Professor Kurt Aland provided a list of textual changes in the 26th edition of the Nestle-Aland. [8] Several colleagues gave advice in their areas of competency: Rolf Knierim, Jane Dempsey Douglass, and James M. Robinson. Student assistants Ruth Dannemann, William Grese, Howard Jackson, Paul Terhune, and Marjorie Menaul shared the tedious work of checking references, compiling bibliographies, and—my "thorn in the flesh"—polishing my English. The editor of the volume, Professor Helmut Koester, and the other members of the Editorial Board demonstrated great care and love to make the manuscript conform to the *Hermeneia* format.

I should like to dedicate this volume to my colleagues, friends, and students who have enriched and stimulated my life and work during the past fifteen years at Claremont.

Claremont
May, 1978.

H. D. Betz

---

7   For this methodological problem, cf. my review of Ernst Käsemann, *An die Römer* (HNT 8a; Tübingen: Mohr, Siebeck, 1973, [3]1974) in *SEÅ* 40 (1975) 143–45. The difference between Käsemann and Schlier lies in the fact that Käsemann constructs Paul's theology basically from Rom, while Schlier does it from Eph, which he regards as Paul's work.

8   See the Introduction, § 4.

1. Abbreviations

Abbreviations used in this volume for sources and literature from antiquity are the same as those in the Theological Dictionary of the New Testament (vol. 1; eds. Gerhard Kittel and Gerhard Friedrich; tr. Geoffrey W. Bromiley; Grand Rapids: Eerdmans, 1964) xvi–xl. Some abbreviations are adapted from that list and can be easily identified. In addition, the list below is provided.

Unless indicated otherwise, texts and translations of Greek and Latin authors are taken from the Loeb Classical Library (LCL).

AAWLMG	Abhandlungen der Akademie der Wissenschaften und der Literatur in Mainz, Geistes- und sozialwissenschaftliche Klasse
Abot R. Nat.	*'Abot de Rabbi Nathan*
ABR	*Australian Biblical Review*
Acts Thom.	*Acts of Thomas*
ADAI	Abhandlungen des deutschen archäologischen Instituts, Kairo
ADAIK	— Koptische Reihe
ad loc.	*ad locum*
Aeschylus	Aeschylus
Agam.	*Agamemnon*
Eum.	*Eumenides*
Sept.	*Septem contra Thebas*
AGJU	Arbeiten zur Geschichte des antiken Judentums und des Urchristentums
AGSU	Arbeiten zur Geschichte des Spätjudentums und Urchristentums
AGWGPH	Abhandlungen der (königlichen) Gesellschaft der Wissenschaften zu Göttingen, Philologisch-historische Klasse
AHAWPH	Abhandlungen der Heidelberger Akademie der Wissenschaften, Philosophisch-historische Klasse
ALGHJ	Arbeiten zur Literatur und Geschichte des hellenistischen Judentums
Ammonius	Ammonius (grammaticus Alexandrinus)
De adfinium voc. diff.	*De adfinium vocabularum differentia*
AnBib	Analecta Biblica
ANTT	Arbeiten zur neutestamentlichen Textforschung
2 Apoc. Bar.	*Syriac Apocalypse of Baruch*

Ap. Jas.	*Apocryphon of James*
Apoc. Mos.	*Apocalypse of Moses*
APOT	R. H. Charles, ed., *Apocrypha and Pseudepigrapha of the Old Testament*
Apuleius	Apuleius
Met.	*Metamorphoses*
Aristides	Aristides
Or.	*Orationes*
Aristotle	Aristotle
EN	*Ethica ad Nicomachum*
Magna Mor.	*Magna Moralia*
Pol.	*Politica*
Rhet.	*Rhetorica*
Artemidorus	Artemidorus
Oneirocr.	*Oneirocriticon*
ARW	*Archiv für Religionswissenschaft*
As. Mos.	*Assumptio Mosis*
ASNU	Acta seminarii neotestamentici upsaliensis
AT	Altes Testament
ATD	Das Alte Testament Deutsch
AThANT	Abhandlungen zur Theologie des Alten und Neuen Testaments
Athenagoras	Athenagoras
Leg.	*Legatio*
ATR	*Anglican Theological Review*
auth.	author
AV	Authorized Version of the Bible (King James Version)
Barn.	*Epistle of Barnabas*
BBB	Bonner Biblische Beiträge
b. Ber.	*Babylonian Talmud, Berakot*
BDF	F. Blass, A. Debrunner, and R. W. Funk, *A Greek Grammar of the New Testament* (Chicago: University of Chicago, 1961)
BDR	F. Blass and A. Debrunner, *Grammatik des neutestamentlichen Griechisch* (ed. F. Rehkopf; Göttingen: Vandenhoeck & Ruprecht, 1976)
BEvTH	Beiträge zur Evangelischen Theologie
BFCTh	Beiträge zur Förderung christlicher Theologie
BHH	*Biblisch-historisches Handwörterbuch*
BHTh	Beiträge zur historischen Theologie
bib.	bibliography
Bib	*Biblica* (Rome)
BibS(F)	Biblische Studien (Freiburg, 1895)
BJRL	*Bulletin of the John Rylands Library*
BK	Biblischer Kommentar

BKP	Beiträge zur klassischen Philologie		*Did.*	*Didache*
BNTC	Black's New Testament Commentaries		*Didasc. Apost.*	*Didascalia Apostolorum*
			Dio Chrys.	Dio Chrysostom
BR	*Biblical Research*		*Or.*	*Orationes*
BT	Bibliotheca Teubneriana		Diodorus Sic.	Diodorus of Sicily
BU	Biblische Untersuchungen			
BWANT	Beiträge zur Wissenschaft vom Alten und Neuen Testament		Diog. Babyl.	Diogenes of Babylon
			Diog. L.	Diogenes Laertius
BZ	*Biblische Zeitschrift*		*Diogn.*	*Epistle to Diognetus*
BZAW	Zeitschrift für die alttestamentliche Wissenschaft, Beihefte		Dionysius Halic.	Dionysius of Halicarnassus
BZNW	Zeitschrift für die neutestamentliche Wissenschaft und die Kunde der älteren Kirche, Beihefte		Disc. 8–9	Discourse on the Eighth and the Ninth
			diss.	Dissertation
			ed(s).	editor(s), edited by
c.	*circa*, approximately		e.g.	*exempli gratia*, for example
CBQ	*Catholic Biblical Quarterly*		EKK	Evangelisch–katholischer Kommentar zum Neuen Testament
CChr	Corpus Christianorum			
CD	Cairo (Genizah text of the) Damascus (Document)		EKKV	— Vorarbeiten
			EncJud	*Encyclopaedia Judaica* (1971)
cent.	century		*1 Enoch*	*Ethiopic Enoch*
cf.	*confer*, compare with		*Ep.*	*Epistula, Epistle*
CG	(Codex) Cairensis Gnosticus		*Ep. Apost.*	*Epistula Apostolorum*
chap(s).	Chapter(s)		*Ep. Arist.*	*Epistula Aristeas*
Cicero	Cicero		*EphTheolLov*	*Ephemerides theologicae Lovanienses*
Amic.	*Laelius de amicitia*		*Epigr. Graec.*	*Epigrammata Graeca*, ed. Kaibel
De inv.	*De inventione*		Epiphanius	Epiphanius
De leg.	*De legibus*		*Adv. haer.*	*Adversus haereses (Panarion)*
De orat.	*De oratore*		*Anaceph.*	*Anacephalaiosis*
Fin.	*De finibus*		*Ep. Pet.*	*Epistula Petri* (ps.–Clementine)
Nat. deor.	*De natura deorum*		EPRO	Etudes préliminaires aux religions orientales dans l'empire romain
Off.	*De officiis*			
Tusc.	*Tusculanae disputationes*		esp.	especially
CII	*Corpus inscriptionum Iudaicarum*		ET	English translation
CJT	*Canadian Journal of Theology*		et al.	*et alii*, and others
1–2 Clem.	*1–2 Clement*		EtB	Etudes Bibliques
Clemens Alex.	Clement of Alexandria		Euripides	Euripides
			Andr.	*Andromeda*
Paed.	*Paedagogus*		*Hec.*	*Hecuba*
Quis dives	*Quis dives salvetur*		*Iph. Aul.*	*Iphigenia Aulidensis*
Strom.	*Stromateis*		*Iph. Taur.*	*Iphigenia Taurica*
ClR	*Classical Review*		*Med.*	*Medea*
CMC	Codex Manichaicus Coloniensis (cf. the Introduction n. 28, below)		*Or.*	*Orestes*
			Troad.	*Troades*
ConNT	*Coniectanea neotestamentica*		Eusebius	Eusebius
CNT	Commentaire du Nouveau Testament (Neuchâtel)		*De eccles. theol.*	*De ecclesiastica theologia*
			H.E.	*Historia ecclesiastica*
CNT(K)	Commentaar op het Nieuwe Testament (Kampen)		*Praep. ev.*	*Praeparatio evangelica*
			EvTh	*Evangelische Theologie*
Corp. Herm.	*Corpus Hermeticum*		*Exc. ex Theod.*	*Excerpta ex Theodoto*
CSEL	Corpus scriptorum ecclesiasticorum latinorum			
			Exeg. Soul	Exegesis On the Soul
DACL	*Dictionnaire d'archéologie chrétienne et de liturgie*		*ExpTim*	*Expository Times*
			ff	(and the) following (pages)
DB	*Dictionnaire de la Bible*		*FGH*	*Die Fragmente der griechischen Historiker*, ed. Jacoby
DBSup	*— Supplément*			
Demosthenes	Demosthenes		Firmicus Maternus	Firmicus Maternus
Exord.	*Exordia*			
Or.	*Orationes*		*De errore*	*De errore profanarum religionum*

Philops.	*Philopseudes*		Petr.	
Prom. es in verb.	*Prometheus es in verbis*		Mich.	Michigan
			par.	parallel(s)
Revivesc.	*Revivescentes*		*passim*	in various places
Rhet. praec.	*Rhetorum praeceptor*		PECL	*Plutarch's Theological Writings and Early Christian Literature* (ed. Hans Dieter Betz; SCHNT 3; Leiden: Brill, 1975)
Vit. auct.	*Vitarum auctio*			
LXX	Septuaginta			
MAMA	*Monumenta Asiae Minoris Antiqua*		*Pesiq. R.*	*Pesiqta Rabbati*
Mart. Polyc.	*Martyrdom of Polycarp*		Petronius	Petronius
Maximus Tyr.	Maximus of Tyre		*Sat.*	*Satyricon*
Diss.	*Dissertationes*		*PG*	*Patrologiae cursus completus. Accurante Jacques–Paul Migne. Series Graeca.*
Mek. Exod.	*Mekilta Exodus*		*PGL*	*Patristic Greek Lexicon* (ed. G. W. H. Lampe; Oxford: Clarendon, 1968)
Menander	Menander			
Comp.	*Comparationes*		*PGM*	*Papyri graecae magicae* (ed. Karl Preisendanz, new ed. Albert Henrichs; 2 vols.; Stuttgart: Teubner, 1973–74)
Pap.	*Papyri*			
Sent.	*Sententiae*			
MGWJ	*Monatsschrift für Geschichte und Wissenschaft des Judentums*		*Philologus*	*Philologus, Supplementband*
			Philo	Philo of Alexandria
MH	*Museum Helveticum*		*Abr.*	*De Abrahamo*
Midr.	*Midraš*		*Agr.*	*De agricultura*
Cant	*Canticles*		*Cher.*	*De cherubim*
Ps	*Psalms*		*Conf.*	*De confusione linguarum*
Qoh	*Qohelet*		*Cong.*	*De congressu eruditionis gratia*
MNTC	Moffatt New Testament Commentary		*Cont.*	*De vita contemplativa*
m.Sanh.	*Mišnah Sanhedrin*		*Decal.*	*De decalogo*
MT	Masoretic (Hebrew) Text		*Det.*	*Quod deterius potiori insidiari soleat*
MThS	Münchner theologische Studien		*Deus*	*Quod deus sit immutabilis*
MThZ	Münchener theologische Zeitschrift		*Ebr.*	*De ebrietate*
n.	note		*Flacc.*	*In Flaccum*
n.d.	no date		*Fug.*	*De fuga et inventione*
NEB	*New English Bible*		*Gig.*	*De gigantibus*
NF	Neue Folge, new series		*Her.*	*Quis rerum divinarum heres sit*
NHC	*Nag Hammadi Codices*		*Jos.*	*De Josepho*
NHS	Nag Hammadi Studies		*L.A.*	*Legum allegoriarum libri*
NICNT	New International Commentary on the New Testament		*Leg. Gai.*	*De legatione ad Gaium*
			Mig.	*De migratione Abrahami*
NKZ	*Neue Kirchliche Zeitschrift*		*Mos.*	*De vita Mosis*
no(s).	number(s)		*Mut.*	*De mutatione nominum*
NovT	*Novum Testamentum*		*Op.*	*De opificio mundi*
NovTSup	— Supplements		*Plant.*	*De plantatione*
NPNF	Nicene and Post–Nicene Fathers		*Post.*	*De posteritate Caini*
NRTh	*La Nouvelle revue théologique*		*Praem.*	*De praemiis et poenis*
NS	New Series		*Prob.*	*Quod omnis probus liber sit*
NT	New Testament, *Neues Testament*		*Q.Ex.*	*Quaestiones in Exodum*
NTAbh	Neutestamentliche Abhandlungen		*Q. Gen.*	*Quaestiones in Genesin*
NTD	Das Neue Testament Deutsch		*Sacr.*	*De sacrificiis Abelis et Caini*
NTS	*New Testament Studies*		*Somn.*	*De somniis*
Odes Sol.	*Odes of Solomon*		*Spec.*	*De specialibus legibus*
OLZ	*Orientalistische Literaturzeitung*		*Virt.*	*De virtutibus*
op. cit.	opere citato, in the work cited		Philostratus	Philostratus
Orac. Sib.	*Sibylline Oracles*		*Vita Apoll.*	*Vita Apollonii*
OT	Old Testament		Pindar	Pindar
Ovid	Ovid		*Ol.*	*Olympian Odes*
Ars am.	*Ars amatoria*		pl.	plural
p.	Palestinian Talmud		*PL*	*Patrologiae cursus completus. Accurante Jacques–Paul Migne. Series Latina*
p(p).	page(s)			
Pap.	Papyrus		Plato	Plato
Flind.	Flinders Petrie		*Apol.*	*Apologia*

Ep.	*Epistulae*
Euthyd.	*Euthydemus*
Euthyph.	*Euthyphro*
Gorg.	*Gorgias*
Leg.	*Leges*
Lys.	*Lysis*
Men.	*Meno*
Phaedr.	*Phaedrus*
Phileb.	*Philebus*
Polit.	*Politicus*
Prot.	*Protagoras*
Rep.	*Respublica*
Soph.	*Sophista*
Theaet.	*Theaetetus*
Tim.	*Timaeus*
Plautus	Plautus
Cas.	*Casina*
Mercat.	*Mercator*
Plutarch	Plutarch of Chaironeia
Adulat.	*Quomodo adulator ab amico internoscatur*
Adv. Colot.	*Adversus Colotem*
Aem. Paul	*Aemilius Paulus*
Alcib.	*Alcibiades*
Alex.	*Alexander*
Alex. magni fort.	*De Alexandri magni fortuna aut virtute*
Amic. mult.	*De amicorum multitudine*
An recte dictum	*An recte dictum sit latenter esse vivendum*
An vitiositas	*An vitiositas ad infelicitatem sufficiat*
Apophth.	*Apophthegmata regum et imperatorum*
Aquane an ignis	*Aquane an ignis sit utilior*
Aud.	*De recta ratione audiendi*
Cohib. ira	*De cohibenda ira*
Cup. div.	*De cupiditate divitiarum*
Defect. orac.	*De defectu oraculorum*
Fort. Rom.	*De fortuna Romanorum*
Frat. am.	*De fraterno amore*
Gen. Socr.	*De genio Socratis*
Glor. Athen.	*De gloria Atheniensium*
Herod. malig.	*De Herodoti malignitate*
Invid. et od.	*De invidia et otio*
Is. et Osir.	*De Iside et Osiride*
Laud. ips.	*De se ipsum citra invidiam laudando*
Lib. educ.	*De liberis educandis*
Mor.	*Moralia*
Mul. Virt.	*Mulierum virtutes*
Non posse	*Non posse suaviter vivi secundum Epicurum*
Pyrrh.	*Pyrrhus*
Praec. coniug.	*Coniugalia praecepta*
Praec. gerend.	*Praecepta gerendae reipublicae*
Prof. virt.	*Quomodo quis suos in virtute sentiat profectus*
Quaest. conv.	*Quaestiones convivalium*
Quaest. Gr.	*Quaestiones Graecae*
Quaest. Rom.	*Quaestiones Romanae*
Sera num.	*De sera numinis vindicta*
Superst.	*De superstitione*
Them.	*Themistocles*
Virt. et vit.	*De virtute et vitio*
Pol.	Polycarp
Phil.	*Epistle to the Philippians*
Porphyry	Porphyry
De abst.	*De abstinentia*
Prot. Jas.	*Protevangelium of James*
ps.–Aris.	pseudo–Aristotle
Rhet. ad Alex.	*Rhetorica ad Alexandrum*
ps.–Clem.	pseudo–Clementine
Hom.	*Homilies*
Recog.	*Recognitions*
ps.–Demetrius	pseudo–Demetrius
de eloc.	*De elocutione*
ps.–Libanius	pseudo–Libanius
Charact. Epistul.	*De charactere epistularum*
ps.–Longinus	pseudo–Longinus
De subl.	*De sublimitate*
ps.–Phocylides	pseudo–Phocylides
Sent.	*Sententiae*
ps.–Plato	pseudo–Plato
Alcib.	*Alcibiades*
ps.–Tertullian	pseudo–Tertullian
Adv. omn. haer.	*Adversus omnes haereses*
Pss. Sol.	*Psalms of Solomon*
PVTG	Pseudepigrapha Veteris Testamenti graece
PW	Pauly–Wissowa, *Real–Encyclopädie der classischen Alterthumswissenschaft*
PWSup	—Supplement
Q	Qumran documents
1QH	*Hôdāyôt* (*Thanksgiving Hymns*)
1QM	*Milhāmāh* (*War Scroll*)
1QpHab	*Pesher on Habbakuk*
1QpNah	*Pesher on Nahum*
1QS	*Serek hayyahad* (*Rule of the Community, Manual of Discipline*)
1QSa	*— Appendix A*
Quint.	Quintilian
	Institutio oratoria
RAC	*Reallexikon für Antike und Christentum*
RB	*Revue biblique*
RechSR	*Recherches de science religieuse*

REG	*Revue des études grecques*	*SVF*	*Stoicorum Veterum Fragmenta*, ed. von Arnim
rep.	reprinted		
RGG¹⁻³	*Die Religion in Geschichte und Gegenwart*	*t.*	Tosepta
Rhet. ad Her.	*Rhetorica ad Herennium*	TBAW	Tübinger Beiträge zur Altertumswissenschaft
RHPhR	*Revue d'histoire et de philosophie religieuse*		
RhM	*Rheinisches Museum für Philologie*	*TDNT*	*Theological Dictionary of the New Testament* (eds. Gerhard Kittel and Gerhard Friedrich; tr. Geoffrey W. Bromiley; 10 vols.; Grand Rapids: Eerdmans, 1964–76)
RSV	*Revised Standard Version* of the Bible		
RThom	*Revue thomiste*		
RVV	Religionsgeschichtliche Versuche und Vorarbeiten		
Šabb.	*Šabbat*	Tertullian	Tertullian
Sam. Targ.	*Samaritan Targum*	*Adv. Marc.*	*Adversus Marcionem*
SANT	Studien zum Alten und Neuen Testament	TextsS	Texts and Studies
		Tg.	*Targum*
SB	Sources bibliques	*Is.*	*of Isaiah*
SBL	Society of Biblical Literature	*Ps.–J.*	*of pseudo–Jonathan*
SBLDS	— Dissertation Series	*Yer.* I & II	*Yerušalmi* I & II
SBLMS	— Monograph Series	Theo-phrastus	Theophrastus
SBLSBS	— Sources for Biblical Study		
SBLSCS	— Septuagint and Cognate Studies	*Char.*	*Characteres*
SBM	Stuttgarter biblische Monographien	*De eloc.*	*De elocutione*
SBS	Stuttgarter Bibelstudien	ThExh	Theologische Existenz heute
SBT	Studies in Biblical Theology	ThF	Theologische Forschungen
sc.	*scilicet*, namely	ThHK	Theologischer Handkommentar zum Neuen Testament
SC	Sources chrétiennes		
SCHNT	Studia ad Corpus Hellenisticum Novi Testamenti	*ThLZ*	*Theologische Literaturzeitung*
		Thom. Cont.	*Thomas the Contender*
SEÅ	*Svensk exegetisk årsbok*	*ThQ*	*Theologische Quartalschrift*
Sextus	Sextus	*ThR*	*Theologische Rundschau*
Sent.	*Sententiae*	*ThViat*	*Theologia Viatorum*
SGDI	*Sammlung der griechischen Dialekt–Inschriften*, ed. Collitz	*ThZ*	*Theologische Zeitschrift* (Basel)
		T. XII	*Testamenta XII Patriarcharum*
Sipre Num	*Sipre Numeri*	*Jos.*	*Joseph*
SJTh	*Scottish Journal of Theology*	*t.r.*	*textus receptus*
SJThOP	— *Occasional Papers*	tr.	translation, translated by
SNTSMS	Society for New Testament Studies Monograph Series	*Treat. Res.*	*Treatise on the Resurrection*
		Tri. Trac.	*Tripartite Tractate*
SO	Symbolae osloenses	TThSt	Trierer Theologische Studien
Sophocles	Sophocles	*TThZ*	*Trierer Theologische Zeitschrift*
Oed. col.	*Oedipus coloneus*	TU	Texte und Untersuchungen zur Geschichte der altchristlichen Literatur
Sota	*Sota*		
Statius	Statius	*TWAT*	*Theologisches Wörterbuch zum Alten Testament* (eds. G. Johannes Botterweck and Helmer Ringgren; Stuttgart: Kohlhammer, 1970)
Theb.	*Thebais*		
STDJ	Studies on the Texts of the Desert of Judah		
StJud	Studia Judaica	UNT	Untersuchungen zum Neuen Testament
STK	*Svensk Theologisk Kvartalskrift*		
StNT	Studien zum Neuen Testament	v(v)	verse(s)
Stobaeus	Stobaeus	*VD*	*Verbum Domini*
Ecl.	*Eclogae*	*VF*	*Verkündigung und Forschung*
StPB	Studia post–biblica	Vg	Vulgate
Str–B	[H. Strack and] P. Billerbeck, *Kommentar zum Neuen Testament aus Talmud und Midrasch*	*VigChr*	*Vigiliae Christianae*
		viz.	*videlicet*, that is to say
		v.l.	*variae lectiones*, variant readings
StTh	*Studia Theologica*	VL	*Vetus Latina*
SUNT	Studien zur Umwelt des Neuen Testaments	*VT*	*Vetus Testamentum*
		WA	Martin Luther, Kritische Gesamtausgabe ("Weimarer" Ausgabe)
s.v.	*sub verbo* or *sub voce*, under the word (entry)		
		WMANT	Wissenschaftliche Mongraphien zum

	Alten und Neuen Testament
WuD	*Wort und Dienst*
WUNT	Wissenschaftliche Untersuchungen zum Neuen Testament
Xenophon	Xenophon
Anab.	*Anabasis*
Cyr.	*Cyropaedia*
Laced.	*Respublica Lacedaemoniorum*
Mem.	*Memorabilia*
y.	Jerusalem Talmud
YCS	Yale Classical Studies
YJS	Yale Judaica Series
ZAW	*Zeitschrift für die alttestamentliche Wissenschaft*
ZDPV	*Zeitschrift des deutschen Palästina-Vereins*
ZKG	*Zeitschrift für Kirchengeschichte*
ZKTh	*Zeitschrift für katholische Theologie*
ZNW	*Zeitschrift für die neutestamentliche Wissenschaft und die Kunde der älteren Kirche*
ZPE	*Zeitschrift für Papyrologie und Epigraphik*
ZRGG	*Zeitschrift für Religions- und Geistesgeschichte*
ZSTh	*Zeitschrift für systematische Theologie*
ZThK	*Zeitschrift für Theologie und Kirche*
ZWTh	*Zeitschrift für wissenschaftliche Theologie*

2. Short Titles of Commentaries, Studies, and Articles Often Cited

Commentaries on Galatians as well as a few basic reference works are cited by author's name only. Additional short titles are used within a specific sequence of footnotes for works cited only with reference to a single passage; full bibliographical information accompanies the first citation.

Aland, *Greek New Testament*
    Kurt Aland, *et al., The Greek New Testament* (Stuttgart: Württembergische Bibelgesellschaft, 1966).

Almqvist, *Plutarch*
    Helge Almqvist, *Plutarch und das Neue Testament* (ASNU 15; Uppsala: Almqvist & Wiksell, 1946).

Barnikol, *Zeit des Paulus*
    Ernst Barnikol, *Die vor– und frühchristliche Zeit des Paulus* (Kiel: Mühlau, 1929).

Barrett, "Paul and the 'Pillar' Apostles"
    C. K. Barrett, "Paul and the 'Pillar' Apostles" in *Studia Paulina in Honorem J. de Zwaan* (Haarlem: Bohn, 1953).

Bauer
    W. Bauer, W. F. Arndt, and F. W. Gingrich, *Greek–English Lexicon of the New Testament and Other Early Christian Literature.*

Bauer, *Orthodoxy and Heresy*
    Walter Bauer, *Orthodoxy and Heresy in Earliest Christianity* (eds. Robert Kraft and Gerhard Krodel; Philadelphia: Fortress, 1971).

Betz, "Composition"
    Hans Dieter Betz, "The Literary Composition and Function of Paul's Letter to the Galatians," *NTS* 21 (1975) 353–79.

Betz, "2 Cor 6:14–7:1"
    Hans Dieter Betz, "2 Cor 6:14–7:1: An Anti-Pauline Fragment?" *JBL* 92 (1973) 88–108.

Betz, *Lukian*
    Hans Dieter Betz, *Lukian von Samosata und das Neue Testament* (TU 76; Berlin: Akademie–Verlag, 1961).

Betz, *Nachfolge*
    Hans Dieter Betz, *Nachfolge und Nachahmung Jesu Christi im Neuen Testament* (BHTh 37; Tübingen: Mohr, Siebeck, 1967).

Betz, *Paulus*
    Hans Dieter Betz, *Der Apostel Paulus und die sokratische Tradition* (BHTh 45; Tübingen: Mohr, Siebeck, 1972).

Betz, "Spirit, Freedom, and Law"
    Hans Dieter Betz, "Spirit, Freedom, and Law: Paul's Message to the Galatian Churches," *SEÅ* 39 (1974) 145–60.

Beyer
    Wolfgang Beyer, *Der Brief an die Galater*, rev. Paul Althaus (NTD 8; Göttingen: Vandenhoeck and Ruprecht, [8]1962).

Blank, *Paulus und Jesus*
    Josef Blank, *Paulus und Jesus: Eine theologische Grundlegung* (SANT 18: Munich: Kösel, 1968).

Bligh
    John Bligh, *Galatians: A Discussion of St. Paul's Epistle* (Householder Commentaries 1; London: St. Paul, 1969).

Bohnenblust, *Beiträge*
    Gottfried Bohnenblust, *Beiträge zum Topos ΠΕΡΙ ΦΙΛΙΑΣ* (Diss. Bern; Berlin: Schade, 1905).

Bonnard
    Pierre Bonnard, *L'épître de Saint Paul aux Galates* (CNT 9; Neuchâtel and Paris: Delachaux & Niestlé, 1953, [2]1972).

Bornkamm, *Paul*
    Günther Bornkamm, *Paul* (tr. D. M. G. Stalker; New York: Harper & Row, 1971).

Bornkamm, *Studien*
    Günther Bornkamm, *Studien zu Antike und Urchristentum*; vol. 2 of his *Gesammelte Aufsätze* (BEvTh 28; Munich: Kaiser, 1959).

Borse, *Standort*
    Udo Borse, *Der Standort des Galaterbriefes* (BBB 41; Bonn: Hanstein, 1972).

Bousset
    Wilhelm Bousset, "Der Brief an die Galater," in *Die Schriften des Neuen Testaments* (Göttingen: Vandenhoeck & Ruprecht, [2]1908) 2.28–72.

Bousset, *Kyrios Christos*
    Wilhelm Bousset, *Kyrios Christos: A History of the Belief in Christ from the Beginning of Christianity to Irenaeus* (tr. John E. Steely; Nashville and New York: Abingdon, 1970).

Bousset–Gressmann, *Religion*
    Wilhelm Bousset, *Die Religion des Judentums im späthellenistischen Zeitalter* (ed. Hugo Gressmann; HNT 21; Tübingen: Mohr, Siebeck, [4]1966).

Brandenburger, *Fleisch und Geist*
    Egon Brandenburger, *Fleisch und Geist: Paulus und die dualistische Weisheit* (WMANT 29; Neukirchen–Vluyn: Neukirchener Verlag, 1968).

Braun, *Qumran*
    Herbert Braun, *Qumran und das Neue Testament* (2 vols.; Tübingen: Mohr, Siebeck, 1966).

Braun, *Radikalismus*
    Herbert Braun, *Spätjüdisch–häretischer und frühchristlicher Radikalismus* (2 vols.; BHTh 24; Tübingen: Mohr, Siebeck, 1957, [2]1969).

Braun, *Studien*
    Herbert Braun, *Gesammelte Studien zum Neuen Testament und seiner Umwelt* (Tübingen: Mohr, Siebeck, 1962, [2]1967).

Bring
    Ragnar Bring, *Commentary on Galatians* (tr. Eric Wahlstrom; Philadelphia: Muhlenberg, 1961).

Brun, *Segen und Fluch*
    Lyder Brun, *Segen und Fluch im Christentum* (Skriften utgit av det Norske Videnskaps–Akademi i Oslo, II, Hist.–Filos. Klasse 1932.1 [Oslo 1932]).

Brun and Fridrichsen, *Paulus*

Lyder Brun and Anton Fridrichsen, *Paulus und die Urgemeinde* (Giessen: Töpelmann, 1921).

Bultmann, *Exegetica*
Rudolf Bultmann, *Exegetica* (ed. Erich Dinkler, Tübingen: Mohr, Siebeck, 1967).

Bultmann, *John*
Rudolf Bultmann, *The Gospel of John: A Commentary* (tr. G. R. Beasley-Murray; Oxford: Blackwell, 1971).

Bultmann, *Stil*
Rudolf Bultmann, *Der Stil der paulinischen Predigt und die kynisch-stoische Diatribe* (FRLANT 13; Göttingen: Vandenhoeck & Ruprecht, 1910).

Bultmann, *Theology*
Rudolf Bultmann, *Theology of the New Testament* (2 vols.; tr. Kendrick Grobel; London: SCM; New York: Scribner's, 1951–55).

Burchard, *Der dreizehnte Zeuge*
Christoph Burchard, *Der dreizehnte Zeuge* (FRLANT 103; Göttingen: Vandenhoeck & Ruprecht, 1970).

Burton
Ernest de Witt Burton, *A Critical and Exegetical Commentary on the Epistle to the Galatians* (ICC; New York: Scribner's, 1920).

Chadwick, *Sextus*
Henry Chadwick, *The Sentences of Sextus: A Contribution to the Early Christian History of Ethics* (Cambridge: Cambridge University, 1959).

Conzelmann, *Apostelgeschichte*
Hans Conzelmann, *Die Apostelgeschichte* (HNT 7; Tübingen: Mohr, Siebeck, ²1972).

Conzelmann, *Outline*
Hans Conzelmann, *An Outline of the Theology of the New Testament* (tr. John Bowden; London: SCM, 1969).

Conzelmann, *1 Corinthians*
Hans Conzelmann, *1 Corinthians* (tr. James W. Leitch; ed. George W. MacRae; Hermeneia; Philadelphia: Fortress, 1975).

Cullmann, *Christology*
Oscar Cullmann, *The Christology of the New Testament* (tr. Shirley C. Guthrie and Charles A. M. Hall; Philadelphia: Westminster, ²1963).

Cullmann, *Peter*
Oscar Cullmann, *Peter: Disciple, Apostle, Martyr* (Philadelphia: Westminster, 1962).

Dahl, "The Atonement"
Nils A. Dahl, "The Atonement—An Adequate Reward for the Akedah" in his *The Crucified Messiah and Other Essays* (Minneapolis: Augsburg, 1974).

Dahl, "Widersprüche"
Nils A. Dahl, "Widersprüche in der Bibel, ein altes hermeneutisches Problem," *StTh* 25 (1971) 1–19.

Daube, *NT and Rabbinic Judaism*
David Daube, *The New Testament and Rabbinic Judaism* (London: Athlone, 1956).

Davies, *Gospel…Land*
W. D. Davies, *The Gospel and the Land* (Berkeley: University of California, 1974).

Davies, *Paul and Rabbinic Judaism*
W. D. Davies, *Paul and Rabbinic Judaism* (London: SPCK, ²1955).

Davies, *Sermon on the Mount*
W. D. Davies, *The Setting of the Sermon on the Mount* (Cambridge: Cambridge University, 1966).

Deissmann, *Licht vom Osten*
Adolf Deissmann, *Licht vom Osten* (Tübingen: Mohr, Siebeck, ⁴1923).

Dibelius–Greeven, *James*
Martin Dibelius, *James: A Commentary on the Epistle of James* (rev. Heinrich Greeven; tr. Michael A. Williams; Hermeneia; Philadelphia: Fortress, 1976).

Dieterich, *Mithrasliturgie*
Albrecht Dieterich, *Eine Mithrasliturgie* (Darmstadt: Wissenschaftliche Buchgesellschaft, 1966).

Dinkler, *Signum Crucis*
Erich Dinkler, *Signum Crucis: Aufsätze zum Neuen Testament und zur christlichen Archäologie* (Tübingen: Mohr, Siebeck, 1967).

Eckert, *Die urchristliche Verkündigung*
Jost Eckert, *Die urchristliche Verkündigung im Streit zwischen Paulus und seinen Gegnern nach dem Galaterbrief* (Münchener Universitäts-Schriften, Katholisch-theologische Fakultät; Regensburg: Pustet, 1971).

Elbogen, *Gottesdienst*
Ismar Elbogen, *Der jüdische Gottesdienst in seiner geschichtlichen Entwicklung* (Leipzig: Fock, 1913).

Fitzmyer, *Essays*
Joseph A. Fitzmyer, *Essays on the Semitic Background of the New Testament* (London: Chapman, 1971).

Foerster–Wilson, *Gnosis*
Werner Foerster, *Gnosis: A Selection of Gnostic Texts* (2 vols.; ed. Robert McL. Wilson; Oxford: Clarendon, 1972, 1974).

Furnish, *Theology and Ethics*
Victor P. Furnish, *Theology and Ethics in Paul* (Nashville and New York: Abingdon, 1968).

Georgi, *Kollekte*
Dieter Georgi, *Die Geschichte der Kollekte des Paulus für Jerusalem* (ThF 38; Hamburg-Bergstedt: Reich, 1965).

Gerhard, *Phoinix*
Gustav Adolf Gerhard, *Phoinix von Kolophon* (Leipzig and Berlin: Teubner, 1909).

Goodenough, *By Light, Light*
Erwin R. Goodenough, *By Light, Light: The Mystic Gospel of Hellenistic Judaism* (New Haven: Yale University, 1935).

Griffiths, *Apuleius of Madauros*
John G. Griffiths, *Apuleius of Madauros: The Isis-Book (Metamorphoses, Book XI)* (EPRO 39; Leiden: Brill, 1975).

Griffiths, *Plutarch*

John G. Griffiths, *Plutarch: De Iside et Osiride* (Cambridge: University of Wales, 1970).

Guthrie, *Sophists*
W. K. C. Guthrie, *The Sophists* (Cambridge: Cambridge University, 1971).

Güttgemanns, *Apostel*
Erhard Güttgemanns, *Der leidende Apostel und sein Herr* (FRLANT 90; Göttingen: Vandenhoeck & Ruprecht, 1966).

Hadot, *Seelenleitung*
Ilsetraut Hadot, *Seneca und die griechisch–römische Tradition der Seelenleitung* (Berlin: de Gruyter, 1969).

Haenchen, *Acts*
Ernst Haenchen, *The Acts of the Apostles* (tr. Bernard Noble *et al.*; Philadelphia: Westminster, 1971).

Harnack, *Marcion*
Adolf von Harnack, *Marcion: Das Evangelium vom fremden Gott. Neue Studien zu Marcion* (Darmstadt: Wissenschaftliche Buchgesellschaft, 1960).

Heinemann, *Philons Bildung*
Isaak Heinemann, *Philons griechische und jüdische Bildung: Kulturvergleichende Untersuchungen zu Philons Darstellung der jüdischen Gesetze* (Hildesheim: Olms 1962).

Hengel, *Judaism and Hellenism*
Martin Hengel, *Judaism and Hellenism* (2 vols.; tr. John Bowden; Philadelphia: Fortress, 1974).

Henrichs and Koenen, "Mani–Codex"
Albert Henrichs and Ludwig Koenen, "Ein griechischer Mani–Codex (P. Colon. inv. nr. 4780)," *ZPE* 5 (1970) 97–216.

Hilgenfeld
Adolf Hilgenfeld, *Der Galaterbrief übersetzt, in seinen geschichtlichen Beziehungen untersucht und erklärt* (Leipzig: Breitkopf & Härtel, 1852).

Holl, *Gesammelte Aufsätze*
Karl Holl, *Gesammelte Aufsätze zur Kirchengeschichte* (Darmstadt: Wissenschaftliche Buchgesellschaft, 1964).

HSW, *NT Apocrypha*
New Testament Apocrypha, ed. Edgar Hennecke, rev. Wilhelm Schneemelcher, tr. ed. Robert McL. Wilson (2 vols.; London: Lutterworth; Philadelphia: Westminster, 1963–65).

G. Jeremias, *Lehrer der Gerechtigkeit*
Gert Jeremias, *Der Lehrer der Gerechtigkeit* (SUNT 2; Göttingen: Vandenhoeck & Ruprecht, 1963).

Jeremias, *Abba*
Joachim Jeremias, *Abba: Studien zur neutestamentlichen Theologie und Zeitgeschichte* (Göttingen: Vandenhoeck & Ruprecht, 1966).

Jewett, "Agitators"
Robert Jewett, "The Agitators and the Galatian Congregation," *NTS* 17 (1971) 198–212.

Jewett, *Paul's Anthropological Terms*
Robert Jewett, *Paul's Anthropological Terms: A Study of Their Use in Conflict Settings* (AGJU 10;

Leiden: Brill, 1971).

Jonas, *Gnosis*
Hans Jonas, *Gnosis und spätantiker Geist* (FRLANT NF 33; Göttingen: Vandenhoeck & Ruprecht, ³1964).

Jonas, *Gnostic Religion*
Hans Jonas, *The Gnostic Religion* (Boston: Beacon, ²1963).

Jones, *Cities*
Arnold H. M. Jones, *Cities of the Eastern Roman Provinces* (Oxford: Clarendon, ²1971).

Käsemann, *Perspectives*
Ernst Käsemann, *Perspectives on Paul* (tr. Margaret Kohl; Philadelphia: Fortress, 1971).

Käsemann, *Römer*
Ernst Käsemann, *An die Römer* (HNT 8a; Tübingen: Mohr, Siebeck, 1973, ³1974).

Kautzsch, *De Veteris Testamenti Locis*
Aemilius F. Kautzsch, *De Veteris Testamenti Locis a Paulo Apostolo Allegatis: Dissertatio Critica* (Leipzig: Metzger & Wittig, 1869).

Kertelge, "*Rechtfertigung*"
Karl Kertelge, "*Rechtfertigung*" *bei Paulus* (NTAbh NF 3; Münster: Aschendorff, 1967).

Klein, *Rekonstruktion*
Günter Klein, *Rekonstruktion und Interpretation: Gesammelte Aufsätze zum Neuen Testament* (BEvTh 50; Munich: Kaiser, 1969).

Knox
John Knox, "Galatians, Letter to the," *IDB* (1962) 2.338–43.

Koskenniemi, *Studien*
Heikki Koskenniemi, *Studien zur Idee und Phraseologie des griechischen Briefes bis 400 n. Chr.* (Annales Academiae Scientiarum Fennicae; Ser. B; vol. 102.2; Helsinki: Suomalaisen Kirjallisuuden Kerjapaino, 1956).

Kramer, *Christ, Lord, Son of God*
Werner Kramer, *Christ, Lord, Son of God* (tr. Brian Hardy; SBT 1.50; London: SCM, 1966).

Kümmel, *Introduction*
Werner Georg Kümmel, *Introduction to the New Testament* (Nashville: Abingdon, 1975).

Kuss, *Römerbrief*
Otto Kuss, *Der Römerbrief* (2 Lieferungen [Rom 1:1–8:19]; Regensburg: Pustet, 1957, 1959).

Lagrange
Marie-Joseph Lagrange, *Saint Paul, Epître aux Galates* (Paris: Librairie Lecoffre, J. Gabalda, 1918, ²1925).

Lausberg, *Handbuch*
Heinrich Lausberg, *Handbuch der literarischen Rhetorik* (2 vols.; Munich: Hueber, 1960).

Lietzmann
Hans Lietzmann, *An die Galater* (HNT 10; Tübingen: Mohr, Siebeck, 1910, ²1923, ⁴1971).

Lietzmann, *Römer*
Hans Lietzmann, *An die Römer* (HNT 8; Tübingen: Mohr, Siebeck, ⁵1971).

Lightfoot

Joseph Barber Lightfoot, *Saint Paul's Epistle to the Galatians* (London: Macmillan, 1865, [10]1890).

Lipsius

Richard Adelbert Lipsius, *Briefe an die Galater, Römer, Philipper* (Freiburg: Mohr, Siebeck, [2]1892).

Lohse, *Colossians and Philemon*

Eduard Lohse, *Colossians and Philemon: A Commentary on the Epistles to the Colossians and to Philemon* (tr. William R. Poehlmann and Robert J. Karris; ed. Helmut Koester; Hermeneia; Philadelphia: Fortress, 1971).

Loisy

Alfred Loisy, *L'épître aux Galates* (Paris: Nourry, 1916).

Löning, *Saulustradition*

Karl Löning, *Die Saulustradition in der Apostelgeschichte* (NF 9; Münster: Aschendorff, 1973).

Lührmann, *Offenbarungsverständnis*

Dieter Lührmann, *Das Offenbarungsverständnis bei Paulus und in paulinischen Gemeinden* (WMANT 16; Neukirchen–Vluyn: Neukirchener Verlag, 1965).

Lütgert, *Gesetz und Geist*

Wilhelm Lütgert, *Gesetz und Geist: Eine Untersuchung zur Vorgeschichte des Galaterbriefs* (BFCTh 22.6; Gütersloh: Bertelsmann, 1919).

Luz, *Geschichtsverständnis*

Ulrich Luz, *Das Geschichtsverständnis des Paulus* (BEvTh 49; Munich: Kaiser, 1968).

Lyonnet

Stanislas Lyonnet, *Les Epîtres de Saint Paul aux Galates, aux Romains* (Paris: Cerf, 1953).

Magie, *Roman Rule*

David Magie, *Roman Rule in Asia Minor* (Princeton: Princeton University, [2]1971).

Martin, *Rhetorik*

Josef Martin, *Antike Rhetorik: Technik und Methode* (HKAW 2.3; Munich: Beck, 1974).

Mayser, *Grammatik*

Edwin Mayser, *Grammatik der griechischen Papyri aus der Ptolemäerzeit* (2 vols.; Berlin: de Gruyter, [2]1970).

Metzger, *Textual Commentary*

Bruce M. Metzger. *A Textual Commentary on the Greek New Testament* (London and New York; United Bible Societies, 1971).

Michel, *Paulus*

Otto Michel, *Paulus und seine Bibel* (BFCTh 2.18; Gütersloh; Bertelsmann, 1929; rep. Darmstadt: Wissenschaftliche Buchgesellschaft, 1972).

Mitteis–Wilcken, *Papyruskunde*

Ludwig Mitteis and Ulrich Wilcken, *Grundzüge und Chrestomathie der Papyruskunde* (rep. Hildesheim: Olms, 1963).

Molland, *Euangelion*

Einar Molland, *Das paulinische Euangelion* (Oslo: Dybwad, 1934).

Moore, *Judaism*

George Foot Moore, *Judaism in the First Three Centuries of the Christian Era* (3 vols.; Cambridge: Harvard University, 1927–30).

Moule, *Idiom Book*

C. F. D. Moule, *An Idiom Book of New Testament Greek* (Cambridge: Cambridge University, 1955).

Moulton–Milligan

James H. Moulton and George Milligan, *The Vocabulary of the Greek New Testament Illustrated from the Papyri and Other Non–literary Sources* (London: Hodder, 1930).

Munck, *Paul*

Johannes Munck, *Paul and the Salvation of Mankind* (tr. Frank Clarke; London: SCM, 1959).

Murray, *Symbols*

Robert Murray, *Symbols of Church and Kingdom: A Study in Early Syriac Tradition* (Cambridge: Cambridge University, 1975).

Mussies, *Dio Chrysostom*

G. Mussies, *Dio Chrysostom and the New Testament* (SCHNT 2; Leiden: Brill, 1972).

Mussner

Franz Mussner, *Der Galaterbrief* (HThK 9; Freiburg: Herder, 1974).

Nestle–Aland

Novum Testament Graece, cum apparatu critico curavit Eberhard Nestle, novis curis elaboraverunt Erwin Nestle et Kurt Aland (Stuttgart: Württembergische Bibelanstalt, [25]1963). On the 26th edition, see the Introduction to this commentary, §4.

Neusner, *Rabbinic Traditions*

Jacob Neusner, *The Rabbinic Traditions about the Pharisees before 70* (3 vols.; Leiden: Brill, 1971).

Niederwimmer, *Askese*

Kurt Niederwimmer, *Askese und Mysterium: Über Ehe, Ehescheidung und Eheverzicht in den Anfängen des christlichen Glaubens* (FRLANT 113; Göttingen: Vandenhoeck & Ruprecht, 1975).

Nilsson, *Geschichte*

M. P. Nilsson, *Geschichte der griechischen Religion* (HKAW 5.2.1–2; Munich: Beck, [2]1955–61).

Nock, *Essays*

Arthur Darby Nock, *Essays on Religion and the Ancient World* (2 vols.; ed. Zeph Stewart; Cambridge: Harvard University, 1972).

Oepke

Albrecht Oepke, *Der Brief des Paulus an die Galater* (ed. Joachim Rohde; ThHK 9; Berlin; Evangelische Verlagsanstalt, [3]1973 [[1]1937, [2]1957]).

Osten–Sacken, *Gott und Belial*

Peter von der Osten–Sacken, *Gott und Belial* (SUNT 6; Göttingen: Vandenhoeck & Ruprecht, 1969).

Pagels, *The Gnostic Paul*

Elaine H. Pagels, *The Gnostic Paul: Gnostic Exegesis of the Pauline Letters* (Philadelphia: Fortress, 1975).

Peter, *Brief*

Hermann Peter, *Der Brief in der römischen Literatur*

(Leipzig: Teubner, 1901; rep. Hildesheim: Olms 1965).

Pfitzner, *Agon Motif*
Victor C. Pfitzner, *Paul and the Agon Motif* (Nov. TSup 16; Leiden: Brill, 1967).

Preisigke, *Wörterbuch*
Friedrich Preisigke, *Wörterbuch der griechischen Papyrusurkunden mit Einschluss der griechischen Inschriften, Aufschriften, Ostraka, Mumienschilder usw. aus Ägypten* (vols. 1–3: 1924–31; vol. 4/1–4 rev. Emil Kiessling; *Supplement* 1.1–3: 1969–71; Berlin and Marburg: Selbstverlag, 1924–71).

Ramsay
William M. Ramsay, *A Historical Commentary on St. Paul's Epistle to the Galatians* (London: Hodder & Stoughton, 1899, ²1900; Grand Rapids: Baker. 1965).

Reitzenstein, *Mysterienreligionen*
Richard Reitzenstein, *Die hellenistischen Mysterienreligionen nach ihren Grundgedanken und Wirkungen* (Stuttgart: Teubner, ³1927).

Resch, *Agrapha*
Alfred Resch, *Agrapha: Ausserkanonische Schriftfragmente* (Leipzig: Hinrichs, ²1906).

Robinson and Koester, *Trajectories*
James M. Robinson and Helmut Koester, *Trajectories through Early Christianity* (Philadelphia: Fortress, 1971).

Schechter, *Rabbinic Theology*
Solomon Schechter, *Aspects of Rabbinic Theology* (New York: Schocken, 1961).

Schenk, *Segen*
Wolfgang Schenk, *Der Segen im Neuen Testament* (Theologische Arbeiten 25; Berlin: Evangelische Verlagsanstalt, 1967).

Schlier
Heinrich Schlier, *Der Brief an die Galater* (KEK 7; Göttingen: Vandenhoeck & Ruprecht, ¹⁴1971).

Schmithals, *Gnosticism*
Walter Schmithals, *Gnosticism in Corinth* (tr. John E. Steely; Nashville and New York: Abingdon, 1971).

Schmithals, *Paul and James*
Walter Schmithals, *Paul and James* (Naperville: Allenson, 1965).

Schmithals, *Paul and the Gnostics*
Walter Schmithals, *Paul and the Gnostics* (tr. John E. Steely; Nashville and New York: Abingdon, 1972).

Schoeps, *Jewish Christianity*
Hans Joachim Schoeps, *Jewish Christianity: Factional Disputes in the Early Church* (tr. Douglas R. A. Hare; Philadelphia: Fortress, 1969).

Schoeps, *Paul*
Hans Joachim Schoeps, *Paul: The Theology of the Apostle in the Light of Jewish Religious History* (tr. Harold Knight; Philadelphia: Westminster, 1961; Tübingen: Mohr, Siebeck, 1959).

Schoeps, *Theologie und Geschichte*

Hans Joachim Schoeps, *Theologie und Geschichte des Judenchristentums* (Tübingen: Mohr, Siebeck, 1949).

Schottroff, *Glaubende*
Luise Schottroff, *Der Glaubende und die feindliche Welt* (WMANT 37; Neukirchen: Neukirchener Verlag, 1970).

Schütz, *Authority*
John H. Schütz, *Paul and the Anatomy of Apostolic Authority* (SNTSMS 26; Cambridge: Cambridge University, 1975).

Schweizer, *Beiträge*
Eduard Schweizer, *Beiträge zur Theologie des Neuen Testaments* (Zurich: Zwingli, 1970).

Schwyzer, *Grammatik*
Eduard Schwyzer, *Griechische Grammatik* (3 vols.; HKAW 2.1–3; Munich: Beck, ²1959–60).

Sieffert
Friedrich Sieffert, *Der Brief an die Galater* (KEK 7; Göttingen: Vandenhoeck & Ruprecht, ⁶1880, ⁹1899).

Stolle, *Zeuge*
Volker Stolle, *Der Zeuge als Angeklagter, Untersuchungen zum Paulus–Bild des Lukas* (BWANT 102; Stuttgart: Kohlhammer, 1973).

Strecker, *Judenchristentum*
Georg Strecker, *Das Judenchristentum in den Pseudoklementinen* (TU 70; Berlin: Akademie–Verlag, 1958).

Stuhlmacher, *Evangelium*
Peter Stuhlmacher, *Das paulinische Evangelium. I: Vorgeschichte* (FRLANT 95; Göttingen: Vandenhoeck & Ruprecht, 1968).

Stuhlmacher, *Gerechtigkeit Gottes*
Peter Stuhlmacher, *Gerechtigkeit Gottes bei Paulus* (FRLANT 87; Göttingen: Vandenhoeck & Ruprecht, 1965).

Suhl, *Paulus*
Alfred Suhl, *Paulus und seine Briefe: Ein Beitrag zur paulinischen Chronologie* (StNT 11; Gütersloh: Mohn, 1975).

Tannehill, *Dying and Rising*
Robert Tannehill, *Dying and Rising with Christ: A Study in Pauline Theology* (BZNW 32; Berlin, Töpelmann, 1967).

Thraede, *Brieftopik*
Klaus Thraede, *Grundzüge griechisch–römischer Brieftopik* (Zetemata 48; Munich: Beck, 1970).

Thrall, *Greek Particles*
Margaret E. Thrall, *Greek Particles in the New Testament: Linguistic and Exegetical Studies* (NTTS 3; Leiden: Brill, 1962).

Vielhauer, *Geschichte*
Philipp Vielhauer, *Geschichte der urchristlichen Literatur* (Berlin: de Gruyter, 1975).

de Vogel, *Greek Philosophy*
Cornelia Johanna de Vogel, *Greek Philosophy* (3 vols.; Leiden: Brill, ³˒⁴1967–73).

Volkmann, *Rhetorik*

Richard Volkmann, *Die Rhetorik der Griechen in systematischer Übersicht* (Stuttgart: Teubner, ²1885).

Weber, *Jüdische Theologie*

Ferdinand Weber, *Jüdische Theologie auf Grund des Talmud und verwandter Schriften* (eds. Franz Delitzsch and Georg Schnedermann; Leipzig: Dörffling & Franke, ²1897).

Wegenast, *Tradition bei Paulus*

Klaus Wegenast, *Das Verständnis der Tradition bei Paulus und in den Deuteropaulinen* (WMANT 8; Neukirchen–Vluyn: Neukirchener Verlag, 1962).

Weiss, *Der erste Korintherbrief*

Johannes Weiss, *Der erste Korintherbrief* (KEK 5; Göttingen: Vandenhoeck & Ruprecht, 1910).

Wengst, *Christologische Formeln*

Klaus Wengst, *Christologische Formeln und Lieder des Urchristentums* (StNT 7; Gütersloh: Mohn, 1972).

Wettstein

Johann Jacob Wettstein, ʽΗ Καινὴ Διαθήκη. *Novum Testamentum graecum.... Tomus II, Continens epistolas Pauli, etc.* (Amsterdam: Ex officina Dommeriana, 1752).

Widengren, *Religionsphänomenologie*

Geo Widengren, *Religionsphänomenologie* (Berlin: de Gruyter, 1969).

Wikenhauser and Schmid, *Einleitung*

Alfred Wikenhauser and Josef Schmid, *Einleitung in das Neue Testament* (Freiburg: Herder, ⁶1973).

Winer

Georgius Benedictus Winer, *Pauli ad Galatas epistola latine vertit et perpetua annotatione illustravit* (Leipzig: Reclam, 1821, ⁴1859).

Wolf, *Griechisches Rechtsdenken*

Erik Wolf, *Griechisches Rechtsdenken* (4 vols.; Frankfurt: Klostermann, 1950–70).

Zahn

Theodor Zahn, *Der Brief des Paulus an die Galater* (KNT 9; Leipzig: Deichert, 1905, ³1922).

Zuntz, *Text*

Günther Zuntz, *The Text of the Epistles: A Disquisition upon the Corpus Paulinum* (London: British Academy/Oxford University, 1953).

The English translation of Paul's Epistle to the Galatians
was provided by the author; it reflects his exegetical
decisions. Other biblical texts are usually from the
Revised Standard Version. Quotations from Latin and
Greek authors follow the texts and translations of the
Loeb Classical Library or other standard editions.

The front endpaper in this volume is from P^{46}, one of the
Chester Beatty Papyri, the oldest manuscript of the
Pauline Epistles; it is reproduced by courtesy of the
Chester Beatty Museum, Dublin, Ireland. The text is that
of Galatians 3:16–29, folio 83 verso. The back endpaper is
a reproduction of the classical commentary of J. J.
Wettstein, *Novum Testamentum Graecum* (Amsterdam,
1752), volume 2, page 215, on Galatians 1:1.

1. The Author

The question of the authorship of Galatians does not present great difficulties. The epistolary preface (1:1) names the Apostle Paul as the author of the letter. Paul's authorship found unquestioned acceptance in antiquity. Comparison with other letters of Paul shows that the style of writing and the language are unmistakably Paul's. The theological argument made in Galatians (see below §7) is characteristically Pauline both in method and content.

For these reasons present New Testament scholars do not question Paul's authorship of the letter.[1] This situation should not, however, lead us to overlook some questions which arise because of facts stated in the letter itself.

First, the handwritten postscript (see on 6:11) presupposes that the preceding letter (1:1–6:10) has been written by an amanuensis, who was usually a professional. Was this amanuensis just a copyist, or did he have an influence on the composition of the letter itself? The very fact that Paul employed an amanuensis rules out a haphazard writing of the letter and presupposes the existence of Paul's first draft, or a sequence of draft, composition, and copy. The highly skillful composition of Galatians (see 5. below) leaves the choice of attributing this high degree of epistolographic expertise to Paul, to the amanuensis, or to a combination of both. I am inclined to attribute the composition to Paul himself, because the letter does more than simply conform to convention. While making use of convention, it is nevertheless a highly original creation. Nowhere in it is there any indication of a separation of form and content. This is even true of the personal postscript, which is well composed and fully integrated with the rest of the letter. Yet given the employment of an amanuensis and the common practices of letter-writing in Paul's time, the problem of authorship may be more complicated than we have previously imagined. If one adds to this the fact that there are co–senders named in the prescript (1:2) and that the "secretary" could be one of them,[2] the letter assumes more and more the character of an official document and less the character of a private letter.[3]

2. The Addressees

A. Galatia and the Galatians

When Paul addressed his letter "to the Galatians," he had in mind the inhabitants of the central plateau of Asia Minor.[4] This territory had passed through several turbulent centuries about which we are reasonably well–informed. There are, however, some questions

1 The Pauline authorship of Gal was denied by a number of scholars in the nineteenth century, beginning with Bruno Bauer, *Kritik der paulinischen Briefe* (Berlin: Hempel, 1852). The earlier history of this "radical criticism" is surveyed in Rudolf Steck, *Der Galaterbrief nach seiner Echtheit untersucht* (Berlin: Reimer, 1888); Carl Clemen, *Die Einheitlichkeit der paulinischen Briefe* (Göttingen: Vandenhoeck & Ruprecht, 1894) 100–25; Ernest de Witt Burton, *A Critical and Exegetical Commentary on the Epistle to the Galatians* (ICC; New York: Scribners, 1920) lxix–lxxi; Werner Georg Kümmel, *Introduction to the New Testament* (Nashville: Abingdon, 1975) 304. In the twentieth century the authenticity and integrity of Gal was denied by L. Gordon Rylands, *A Critical Analysis of the Four Chief Pauline Epistles* (London: Watts, 1929) 273–367; Frank R. McGuire, "Did Paul Write Galatians?" *Hibbert Journal* 66 (1967–68) 52–57; John C. O'Neill, *The Recovery of Paul's Letter to the Galatians* (London: SPCK, 1972), who also has a survey of the history of the question.

2 Cf. Rom 16:22, "I Tertius, the writer of this letter, greet you in the Lord." See also 1 Cor 16:21.

3 See Philipp Vielhauer, *Geschichte der urchristlichen Literatur* (Berlin: de Gruyter, 1975) 67f, 112f. The question of how Paul composed his letters needs fresh investigation. Perhaps a comparison with other ancient writers, especially Cicero and Seneca, would yield some clues. See, for this topic, Hermann Peter, *Der Brief in der römischen Litteratur* (Leipzig 1901; rep. Hildesheim: Olms, 1965) 32ff; Otto Roller, *Das Formular der paulinischen Briefe* (BWANT 4.6; Stuttgart: Kohlhammer, 1933) *passim*.

4 The basic study is by Felix Stähelin, *Geschichte der kleinasiatischen Galater* (Leipzig: Teubner, ²1907; Osnabrück: Zeller, 1973); see also Ludwig Bürchner, "Galatia, Galatike [chora], Gallo–graikia," *PW* 7 (1910) 519–34; G. Brandis, "ἡ Γαλατία," *PW* 7 (1910) 534–59; Arnold H. M. Jones, *The Cities of the Eastern Roman Provinces* (Oxford: Clarendon, ²1971); David Magie, *Roman Rule in Asia Minor* (Oxford: Clarendon, ²1971); Vielhauer, *Geschichte*, 104–05.

important for the letter of Paul that still await definitive answers. These questions pertain to the precise border-lines of that area which Paul had in mind, the ethnic identity of the churches in that area, and the social and cultural situation of those churches.

Nothing in Paul's letter points to the Celtic origin of the Galatians. Their name, οἱ Γαλάται, is derived from οἱ Γάλλοι (Latin *galli*),[5] that is, from those Celtic tribes who in 279 B.C. under Brennus pushed into the Balkans, Thrace, Macedonia, and Thessaly. Three tribes (the Trocmi, the Tectosages, and the Tolistobogii) crossed the Hellespont and settled down in the area around Ancyra in 278/77 B.C.[6] The subsequent history of the Galatians was violent and turbulent. Local potentates used them as mercenaries in their battles for territorial supremacy, and the Galatians took advantage of these opportunities to plunder cities and to gain land. This period ended when the Romans entered the area in 189 B.C. and defeated the Galatians in two devastating battles. From then on, the Galatians sided with the Romans and were of great help in the Roman effort to conquer areas in Asia Minor. The Galatians' loyalty, especially in the Roman war against Mithridates VI, was rewarded when, after Mithridates' defeat, Pompey reorganized the territory as a client kingdom under Galatian rulership. When the king Amyntas died in 25 B.C., Augustus created the Roman *Provincia Galatia*, which included the old country named Galatia as well as parts of Pisidia, Isauria, Pamphylia, Lycaonia, Paphlagonia, and Pontus Galaticus.

Culturally, the Galatians soon became Hellenized and then Romanized.[7] This must have happened primarily among the ruling aristocracy and the more prosperous city dwellers. The name Gallograeci, which some writers use, expresses this tendency toward Hellenization. Celtic personal names were dropped in favour of Greek names. On the other hand, some of the customs and institutional structures were perpetuated for a long time, and the Celtic language was spoken in rural areas as late as the time of Jerome.[8]

We do not know whether the Galatians whom Paul addressed were descendents of the old Celts, or whether they represented the ethnic mixture which was found in most Hellenistic–Roman towns. At any rate, these people must have belonged to the Hellenized town population and not to the rural people.[9]

This conclusion leads us to some sociological observations.[10] The fact that Paul wrote his well–composed and, both rhetorically and theologically, sophisticated "apology" forces us to assume that he founded the Galatian churches not among the poor and the uneducated but among the Hellenized and Romanized city population. These people also had some education and at least modest financial means. Paul's message of "freedom in Christ" must have found attentive ears among people interested in political, social, cultural,

5   On the names, see Bürchner, *PW* 7.519–20; Wilhelm Pape and G. Benseler, *Wörterbuch der griechischen Eigennamen* (Braunschweig: Vieweg, 1911) 1.238 *s.v.*

6   For sources and bib., see Paul Moraux, "L'établissement des Galates en Asie Mineure," *Istanbuler Mitteilungen, Deutsches Archäologisches Institut, Abteilung Istanbul* 7 (1957) 56–75; Jacques Moreau, *Die Welt der Kelten* (Stuttgart: Cotta, 1958).

7   On the hellenization of the Galatians, see Carl Schneider, *Kulturgeschichte des Hellenismus* (Munich: Beck, 1967) 1.810–14; Jones, *Cities*, 120f.

8   Jerome, *Commentarius in epistulam ad Galatas* (*PL* 26.357); Lucian *Alexander* 51. See Karl Holl, "Das Fortleben der Volkssprachen in Kleinasien in nachchristlicher Zeit," in *Gesammelte Aufsätze zur Kirchengeschichte* (Darmstadt: Wissenschaftliche Buchgesellschaft, 1964) 2.244; Leo Weisgerber, "Galatische Sprachreste," in *Natalicium: Johannes Geffcken zum 70. Geburtstag* (Heidelberg: Winter, 1931) 151–75.

9   See Clemens Bosch, "Die Kelten in Ankara," *Jahrbuch für kleinasiatische Forschung* 2 (1952/53) 283–93. Archaeological discoveries as well as inscriptions point in the same direction. See Ekrem Akurgal, *Treasures of Turkey* (Geneva: Skira, 1966) 45ff, 70ff; George E. Bean, *Turkey Beyond the Maeander* (London: Benn, 1971); Louis Robert, *Etudes anatoliennes: Recherches sur les inscriptions grecques de l'Asie Mineure* (rep. of the 1937 edition; Amsterdam: Hakkert, 1970); idem, *Documents de l'Asie Mineure méridionale, inscriptions, monnaies et géographie* (Paris: Minard, 1966); *Monumenta Asiae Minoris Antiqua* 1–8 (Manchester: Manchester University, 1928–62).

10   See the sociological observations made by Gerd Theissen, "Legitimation und Lebensunterhalt: Ein Beitrag zur Soziologie urchristlicher Missionare," *NTS* 21 (1975) 192–221.

and religious emancipation. Their Christian experience, what little Paul mentions of it, reflects this. Paul points out several changes which had occurred in the Galatians' way of life: they stopped worshipping the pagan gods and demons (4:8–10); their prayers were now addressed to a monotheistic deity, "the one God" (3:20; 4:6); and their abolishment of the old religion quite consistently led to the elimination of all religious, social, and cultural distinctions and discriminations based upon it and sanctioned by it. These changes were not simply considered "ideal" consequences of the gospel, but were actually carried out. Today we can only admire the incredible boldness of these people from Asia Minor—not to speak of Paul's even greater boldness—in doing away with the distinctions between Jews and Greeks, slaves and freemen, men and women (3:28). Being "barbarians" they may not have had great difficulty in rejecting the distinction between Greek and Jew, but to extend freedom to the slaves and equality to the women was as difficult at that time as it is at present. As members of the Christian community, the Galatians experienced the fulfillment of some old dreams of mankind, dreams of freedom which were very much alive at this time. They experienced the liberation from pagan superstition and the fear of Gods and demons—things for which the people in this area were notorious.[11] Instead they now endorsed "monotheism." For them the new religion represented "enlightenment" (cf. 4:8–10). For them, being members of the Christian community meant being cosmopolitans rather than "barbarians" and provincial "hicks" from an ungovernable and dangerous territory on the fringes of the Empire. Their world was now the Roman Empire. Also, throwing off social prejudices and acquiring a "liberated" way of life must have added to their self-consciousness and self-confidence. They

certainly must have approved when Paul, a Roman citizen himself, attributed to them the attitudes of adults and "mature" sons, as compared with "minors" who need constant supervision by tutors (4:1–3).

Paul's letter to the Galatians and his argument with them becomes even more intriguing, if his notion of "freedom in Christ" which sums up his gospel was not only a "religious" and "theological" notion, but pointed at the same time to a political and social experience. Perhaps it was for this reason that Paul chose to use the notion of freedom in his letter to the Galatians. A strange parallel in the *Gospel of Philip* from Nag Hammadi expresses vividly what may have been the Galatians' experience also: "If you say: 'I am a Jew,' nobody will be moved. If you say: 'I am a Roman,' nobody will be upset. If you say: 'I am a Greek, a barbarian, a slave, [a free man],' nobody will be disturbed. If you say: 'I am a Christian,' [the whole heaven] will shake."[12]

B. The Galatian Churches

Information about the Galatian churches, to which Paul sent his letter, is extremely scarce. He addresses them (1:2) as "the churches of Galatia" (αἱ ἐκκλησίαι τῆς Γαλατίας),[13] or simply (3:1) as "Galatians" (Γαλάται). The territorial name "Galatia" is found also in 2 Tim 4:10 and 1 Pet 1:1,[14] while the name "the Galatian country" (ἡ Γαλατικὴ χώρα) is used in Acts (16:6; 18:23). None of these passages say with any precision where these Galatian churches were located, when they were founded, or what type of people constituted them. Apart from Galatians itself, we have another bit of information in the "Marcionite Prologues to the Pauline Epistles," but the data on Galatians given there could have been concluded simply

---

11 Unfortunately Paul does not provide any clear information about the religious affiliations of the Galatians in their pre–Christian life. Therefore we cannot say whether they had been adherents of the old Celtic religion, perhaps in syncretistic transformations, or whether they had belonged to a variety of Hellenistic cults.

12 Section 49, tr. Martin Krause, in Werner Foerster, *Gnosis: A Selection of Gnostic Texts* (2 vols.; ed. Robert McL. Wilson; Oxford: Clarendon, 1972, 1974)

2.86. Cf. Gal 3:28.

13 The same name is used 1 Cor 16:1.

14 "To the exiles of the Dispersion in Pontus, Galatia, Cappadocia, Asia, and Bithynia...." See Karl Hermann Schelkle, *Die Petrusbriefe, Der Judasbrief* (Freiburg: Herder, 1970) 1–3.

from the letter itself.[15] The prologue to Galatians identifies the Galatians as "Greeks." They are said to have accepted "the word of truth" from the Apostle Paul, but after he left they were tempted by "false apostles" to turn to law and circumcision. In his letter, written from Ephesus, Paul called them back to the "true faith." This assessment looks accurate and, except for the location of Ephesus as the place of origin, it seems to be based upon the letter.[16] Ethnically, the Galatians were Gentiles (cf. 4:8; 5:2f.; 6:12f.).[17] Whether they were originally Greeks, Celts, or a mixture of diverse character is impossible to determine.[18]

Geographically, the name "Galatia" can refer to two adjacent territories in Asia Minor: to the "territory" in the central parts (the so-called "North Galatian" theory) or the "province" (the so-called "South Galatian" theory). Both theories have been discussed extensively, and today most commentators tend to favour the territory hypothesis, which would locate the Galatian churches in central Anatolia.[19] The province hypothesis has the advantage that the names found in Acts 13–14 (Antioch, Lystra, Derbe, Iconium, etc.) could be coordinated with Galatians. According to this theory, Paul would have founded these churches during the so-called "first missionary journey" and would have visited them again on the "second journey" (Acts 16:1–18:23).[20] The arguments in favor of the "province hypothesis," however, depend upon another hypothesis, the historical reliability of the itineraries in Acts, and upon the argument from silence. It is strange, however, that the Galatian churches are barely mentioned in Acts. There is no story telling about the founding of the churches. In fact, one may even doubt that Luke has a clear idea of whether and where they existed (see 16:6; 18:23, and 3A. below). Whether the author used actual information about the itineraries of Paul, or a source from which his itineraries came, is still an unsolved problem. There is no real need to think that the author of Acts always had reliable or complete information.

Therefore, even if he did not mention the Galatian churches at all, this silence does not mean much. Paul could have founded these churches during a journey not recorded by Acts. The argument that Jews must have been present in the Galatian churches, and that we know of no Jews in central Anatolia, is well-known but unfounded. Galatians does not presuppose Jews as resident members of the churches. In addition, recent

---

15   "Galatae sunt Graeci. hi verbum veritatis primum ab apostolo acceperunt, sed post discessum eius temptati sunt a falsis apostolis, ut in legem et circumcisionem verterentur. hos apostolus revocat ad fidem veritatis scribens eis ab Epheso." The Latin is quoted from Erwin Preuschen, *Analecta* vol. 2: *Zur Kanonsgeschichte* (Tübingen: Mohr, 1910) 86. The prologues are Marcionite in origin, probably from the 2nd century A.D. For a discussion and bib. see Karl Theodor Schäfer, "Marcion und die ältesten Prologe zu den Paulusbriefen," in *Kyriakon: Festschrift Johannes Quasten* (Münster: Aschendorff, 1970) 1.135–50.

16   See below § 3.D.

17   So most commentators, esp. Alfred Wikenhauser and Josef Schmid, *Einleitung in das Neue Testament* (Freiburg: Herder, [6]1973) 412; Kümmel, *Introduction*, 297; Vielhauer, *Geschichte*, 106; Gal 3:2–3, 13–14, 23–29; 4:2, 5; 5:1 do not imply that Jewish Christians are among the Galatians.

18   In the light of this, Gal 3:28 ("neither Jew nor Greek") expresses the intention of either giving up religious and cultural prerogatives or denying their desirability.

19   For a critical review of the arguments, see esp. Vielhauer, *Geschichte*, 105–08; also the detailed discussion by Wilhelm Michaelis, *Einleitung in das Neue Testament* (Bern: Haller, [3]1961) 183–87; Wikenhauser and Schmid, *Einleitung*, 411–13; Kümmel, *Introduction*, 296–98; Heinrich Schlier, *Der Brief an die Galater* (KEK 7; Göttingen: Vandenhoeck & Ruprecht, [14]1971) 17 n. 1; Franz Mussner, *Der Galaterbrief* (HThk 9; Freiburg: Herder, 1974) 3–9; John C. Hurd, *The Origin of 1 Corinthians* (London: SPCK, 1965), 303–05; F. F. Bruce, "Galatian Problems: 2. North or South Galatians?" *BJRL* 52 (1970) 243–66.

20   The province hypothesis was argued vigorously by William M. Ramsay in his various works, esp. in *St. Paul The Traveller and the Roman Citizen* (London: Hodder & Stoughton, [3]1897); idem, *The Cities of St. Paul* (London: Hodder & Stoughton, 1907; Grand Rapids: Baker, 1949); Valentin Weber, *Die Adressaten des Galaterbriefes: Beweis der rein-südgalatischen Theorie* (Ravensburg: Kitz, 1900); Wilhelm Michaelis, *Einleitung in das Neue Testament* (Bern: Haller, [3]1961) 183–87.

archeological discoveries have turned up Jewish inscriptions in the inner parts of Anatolia.[21] This new evidence removes one of the arguments against the territory hypothesis, but that argument was inconclusive anyway.

It is not necessary at this point to discuss fully the pros and cons of the two theories. The arguments used on both sides are mostly speculative. All we can say is this: it is more probable that the Galatian churches were located in central Anatolia. The arguments against this assumption, which were advanced by the defenders of the province hypothesis, have been shown to be inconclusive or built up on other unproven presuppositions. The author of Acts does not have, or does not want to provide, information concerning these churches. Hence, we are not in the position to say with certainty on which of his journeys Paul founded the churches.

C. The Anti-Pauline Opposition

Because they created the situation which caused Paul to write the letter, the question of the addressees of Galatians cannot be adequately discussed without considering the opponents' agitation against Paul.[22] Paul never addresses his opponents directly,[23] but he addresses the issues which they had introduced into the Galatian churches. The problem is that we have no primary evidence with regard to the origin, thoughts, and personalities that made up the opposition. Methodologically, therefore, we must reconstruct their views primarily on the basis of Galatians alone.[24] Other documents can only be supplementary; these include the Pauline[25] and deutero-Pauline epistles,[26] the book of Acts, and, to a certain degree, the anti-Pauline polemics in the Epistle of James and in other Jewish

21   See this introduction, § 2.A. On information about churches in Galatia, see Adolf von Harnack, *Die Mission und Ausbreitung des Christentums in den ersten drei Jahrhunderten* (Leipzig: Hinrichs, [4]1924) 764–69. On the tombstones, see Kurt Bittel, "Christliche und jüdische Grabsteine," in *Bogazköy 5* (Abhandlungen der Deutschen Orient–Gesellschaft 18; Berlin: Mann, 1975) 108–13.

22   Literature on the question of Paul's opponents in Galatia is to be found in Walter Schmithals, "The Heretics in Galatia," in *Paul and the Gnostics* (tr. John E. Steely; Nashville and New York: Abingdon, 1972) 13–64; idem, *Paul and James* (Naperville: Allenson, 1965) 103–17. For surveys of the history of research and for further bib., see Robert Jewett, "The Agitators and the Galatian Congregation," *NTS* 17 (1971) 198–212; Jost Eckert, *Die urchristliche Verkündigung im Streit zwischen Paulus und seinen Gegnern nach dem Galaterbrief* (Münchener Universitäts–Schriften, Katholisch–theologische Fakultät; Regensburg: Pustet, 1971); see my review in *JBL* 91 (1972) 566; John J. Gunther, *St. Paul's Opponents and Their Background* (Leiden: Brill, 1973); Alfred Suhl, *Paulus und seine Briefe: Ein Beitrag zur paulinischen Chronologie* (StNT 11; Gütersloh: Mohn, 1975) 15ff; Joachim Rohde, "Die Gegner des Paulus in Galatien nach der neueren Literatur" in Albrecht Oepke, *Der Brief des Paulus an die Galater* (ed. Joachim Rohde; ThHK; Berlin: Evangelische Verlagsanstalt, [3]1973) 30–36; John H. Schütz, *Paul and the Anatomy of Apostolic Authority* (SNTSMS 26; Cambridge: Cambridge University, 1975) 124ff; E.

Earle Ellis, "Paul and His Opponents: Trends in Research" in *Christianity, Judaism, and Other Greco-Roman Cults: Studies for Morton Smith at Sixty* (Leiden: Brill, 1975) 1.264–98. See also James M. Robinson and Helmut Koester, *Trajectories Through Early Christianity* (Philadelphia: Fortress, 1971) 120–23, 144–47; John G. Hawkins, *The Opponents of Paul in Galatia* (Ph.D. diss., Yale University, 1971). Of the older literature, see esp. Charles H. Watkins, *St. Paul's Fight for Galatia* (London: Clarke, 1914), originally a dissertation written under Johannes Weiss; Anton Fridrichsen, "Die Apologie des Paulus Gal. 1," in Lyder Brun and Anton Fridrichsen, *Paulus und die Urgemeinde* (Giessen: Töpelmann, 1921) 53–76. Of the recent introductions, see esp. Wikenhauser and Schmid, *Einleitung*, 415–17; Kümmel, *Introduction*, 298–301; Vielhauer, *Geschichte*, 113–24.

23   Cf. on Gal 1:6–7; 5:7, 10, 12; 6:12–13.

24   See Introduction, below § 6.

25   See my article "2 Cor 6:14–7:1: An Anti–Pauline Fragment?" *JBL* 92 (1973) 88–108.

26   A special problem is that of the relationship between the Colossian "heresy" and the opponents of Paul in Gal. See the articles and bib. in Fred O. Francis and Wayne A. Meeks, *Conflict at Colossae* (Missoula: Scholars, 1973).

Christian texts[27] of the post-apostolic period—even down to the newly published Mani biography.[28]

Moreover, references to Galatians must be used with methodological caution. Not everything that Paul denies is necessarily an accusation by his opposition, and not everything that he accuses his opponents of doing or thinking represents their actual goals and intentions. Paul's references must be interpreted in terms of their rhetorical origin and function before they can be used as the basis for conclusions about the opponents.[29]

With these caveats in mind, we best begin the discussion of the opponents by looking at the *peroratio* (6:12–17),[30] because in this section Paul attacks the opponents in the strongest possible terms. Much of 6:12 is Paul's polemic. Here, as elsewhere in the letter, it becomes clear that the opponents had pressured the Galatians into accepting Torah and circumcision. That they did so in order to "look good in the flesh" is Paul's caricature of the Jewish doctrine of meritorious works (cf. also 6:13). Whether the opponents made such demands because they wanted to escape from persecution because of the cross of Christ,[31] or whether this is another of Paul's sarcastic interpretations, remains unclear. Even less clear is 6:13, where Paul names the opponents "the circumcised" (οἱ περιτεμνόμενοι). Is this simply a name for "the Jews" (i.e. Jewish Christians), or does it point to Gentile Christians who have already undergone circumcision themselves (i.e. "Judaizers")?[32] When Paul claims that the opponents do not keep the Torah themselves, is this more than rhetoric? Is it conceivable that they demanded that others keep

---

27 Of special importance in this connection are the anti–Pauline polemics in the *Kerygmata Petrou* (ps.–Clem. *Hom.* 2.15–17; 11.35.3–6 [*Recog.* 4.34.5–4.35.2]; 17.13–19). See Appendix 3; *New Testament Apocrypha*, ed. Edgar Hennecke, rev. Wilhelm Schneemelcher, tr. ed. Robert McL. Wilson (2 vols.; London: Lutterworth; Philadelphia: Westminster, 1963–1965) 2.102ff, with further bib.; Georg Strecker, *Das Judenchristentum in den Pseudoklementinen* (TU 70; Berlin: Akademie-Verlag, 1958) 187ff; idem, "The Kerygmata Petrou Source of the pseudo–Clementines," in Walter Bauer, *Orthodoxy and Heresy in Earliest Christianity* (eds. Robert Kraft and Gerhard Krodel; Philadelphia: Fortress, 1971) 257–71. The discovery of the Nag Hammadi Codices has made it clear that the works of Hans Joachim Schoeps have not yet been given adequate consideration; see his *Theologie und Geschichte des Judenchristentums* (Tübingen: Mohr, Siebeck, 1949); idem, *Jewish Christianity: Factional Disputes in the Early Church* (tr. Douglas R. A. Hare; Philadelphia: Fortress, 1969) with further bib.; idem, *Paul,* esp. 74–87; idem, *Urgemeinde, Judenchristentum, Gnosis* (Tübingen: Mohr, Siebeck, 1956). Research on the relationship between Jewish–Christian movements, Nag Hammadi, and anti–Paulinism is still in the beginning stages; see Alexander Böhlig, *Mysterion und Wahrheit* (Leiden: Brill, 1968); *Judéo-Christianisme; Recherches historiques et théologiques offerts en hommage au Cardinal Jean Daniélou* (RechSR 60 [1972]); A. F. J. Klijn and G. J. Reinink, *Patristic Evidence for Jewish-Christian Sects* (NovTSup 36; Leiden: Brill, 1973).

28 See Albert Henrichs and Ludwig Koenen, "Ein griechischer Mani–Codex (P. Colon. inv. nr. 4780)," *ZPE* 5 (1970) 97–216. The first 72 pages of the codex have been published by Henrichs and Koenen, "Der Kölner Mani–Kodex (P. Colon. inv. nr. 4780)," *ZPE* 19 (1975) 1–85. See also Albert Henrichs, "Mani and the Babylonian Baptists: A Historical Confrontation," *Harvard Studies in Classical Philology* 77 (1973) 23–59; Kurt Rudolph, "Die Bedeutung des Kölner Mani–Codex für die Manichäismusforschung," in *Mélanges d'histoire des religions offerts à Henri-Charles Puech* (Paris: Presses universitaires de France, 1974) 471–86. This Mani–Codex presents Mani not only as an imitator of the apostle Paul, but as a congenial interpreter of Paul's Gal; Mani uses Gal and its theology to justify his break with the Elchasaite sect, a Jewish–Christian group, just as Paul justifies his break with Judaism.

29 At this point, serious methodological objections must be raised against the work of Schmithals (see n. 22, above) and those who follow him.

30 In the following only the passages from Gal are cited; for further information and interpretation see the Introduction § 5 and the commentary.

31 Jewett ("Agitators," esp. 204ff) argues that the opponents of Paul were stimulated by the threat of persecution by Zealots in Palestine, and that they tried to avert this persecution by circumcizing Gentile Christians in Asia Minor. Jewett builds his case mainly on Acts, but Zealots are not mentioned in the passages he refers to.

32 On this interpretation, see Schmithals, *Paul and the Gnostics*, 27ff; Jewett, "Agitators," 202f.

the Torah, while not keeping it themselves (cf. 2:14)?[33] Did they only keep part of the Torah? Did they have their own "special" Torah?[34] Does Paul allude to "libertinistic tendencies"?[35] All of these questions remain possibilities for which some evidence can be produced. A clear decision is, however, hardly possible.

Galatians does, however, yield some facts. The opponents of Paul must have come into contact with the Galatian churches after Paul founded them.[36] The gospel which the opponents proclaimed was, in Paul's view, "another gospel."[37] In some way, this gospel was associated with observance of the Jewish Torah and with the ritual of circumcision.[38] The opponents had, in Paul's words, "confused" the churches.[39] Paul also puts the opponents in a historical perspective. He names as their historical predecessors the dissenting faction at the Jerusalem conference,[40] "the men from James,"[41] and the Cephas group at Antioch.[42] This arrangement is, however, made for apologetic reasons. Perhaps the opponents had their own version of the historical developments.[43] It is noteworthy that "the men from James" (2:12) did not criticize Paul but Cephas.[44] On the other hand, Paul accused Cephas, not "the men from James," of compulsive "judaizing" of the Gentiles.

These are the data which Galatians provides. They permit us to assume that the opponents of Paul were Jewish–Christian missionaries rivaling Paul. Contrary to the agreement reached in Jerusalem (2:1–10), they

had transcended the borderlines of Judaism for their mission and had turned to making converts among the Gentile Christian churches founded by Paul. Except for the demand of obedience to the Torah and acceptance of circumcision, their "gospel" must have been the same as Paul's. Otherwise it would be difficult to understand why Paul is so eager to demonstrate that they are so radically different from him. There is no real reason to believe that these anti-Paulinists were morally dishonest or theologically deficient.[45] Their message must have made good sense to the Galatians and to others, and they must have been quite serious about the salvation of the Galatians. How else could one understand the fact that Paul had been pushed against the wall?

Finally, we must discuss the hypothesis advanced by several scholars that the opponents were characterized by "gnostic" traits.[46] The fact is that no passage in Galatians yields any data which clearly point to those gnostic traits. This lack of unambiguous evidence is obvious. But one must also realize that Paul has no intention of describing his opponents' views with any degree of accuracy and completeness. The argument (see 7. below; also 3.) shows that there are Jewish–Christian issues and that if there are "gnostic" traits they were represented by Paul himself rather than by his opponents. Nevertheless, the possibility that the opponents also had gnostic tendencies cannot be automatically excluded; later Jewish–Christian

---

33   This question arises because of the apparent contradiction between Gal 5:3 and 6:13. It is the starting point for Schmithals' hypothesis, that Paul's Jewish–Christian–gnostic opponents propagate the ritual of circumcision as a magic–gnostic symbol, but that they have no interest in keeping the Jewish Torah. Cf. Hans Dieter Betz, *Nachfolge und Nachahmung Jesu Christi im Neuen Testament* (BHTh 37; Tübingen: Mohr, Siebeck, 1967) 148ff; Jewett, "Agitators," 199f. For a critique of Schmithals, cf. Vielhauer, *Geschichte*, 118–24.

34   See the commentary on 5:3.

35   For this interpretation, see Schmithals, *Paul and the Gnostics*, 46ff; cf. Vielhauer, *Geschichte*, 114f.

36   See Gal 1:6; 4:13–14; 5:7.

37   See 1:6–9; cf. 2:7–9, and the notion of "the gospel of the circumcision."

38   See 2:15–21; 3:2–5; 4:21; 5:2–12; 6:12–17.

39   See 1:7; 5:10.

40   See 2:4–5.

41   See 2:12.

42   See 2:11–14.

43   Cf. Schoeps's hypothesis of the "Ebionite party-history" in the ps.–Clementines, esp. in his *Jewish Christianity*, 15ff.

44   The *Kerygmata Petrou* defends Peter against Paul's attack at Antioch (ps.–Clem. *Hom.* 17.19; HSW, *NT Apocrypha* 2.123). See the commentary on 2:11 and Appendix 3.C.

45   See 1:6–7; 4:17; 5:7–12; 6:12–13.

46   The main proponent of this hypothesis is Schmithals. Cf. the critique by Robert McL. Wilson, "Gnostics—in Galatia?" *Studia Evangelica* 4 (Berlin: Akademie–Verlag, 1968) 358–64; idem, *Gnosis and the New Testament* (Oxford: Blackwell, 1968) 43, 54f, 58; Vielhauer, *Geschichte*, 120–24.

sources do show gnostic traits. The question, therefore, can only be whether the anti-Paulinists had gnostic tendencies already by the time of Galatians. Given the scarcity of sources, this question cannot be conclusively answered either way.

The question must also be raised how it was possible for the anti-Pauline forces to get a foothold among the Galatian Christians.[47] The Galatians, to be sure, did not admit them out of their "foolishness" (3:1), so they must have had solid reasons. Can we say anything about those reasons?

By the time Paul wrote his letter, the period of initial enthusiasm which had characterized the life of the Galatian Christians was over. We do not know how much time had passed or precisely what had happened in the meantime, but it is evident that the situation had changed. Indeed, Paul's letter was the reaction to the fact that the Galatians had changed their mind about him, about his message, and about themselves. They were, in Paul's view, ready to betray the gospel to which they had converted, to become apostates, to desert him, and to go over to the opposition.[48] The reasons for this shift seem to have been the following.

After a period of initial enthusiasm, the Galatians apparently ran into problems which they could not handle under the terms with which they were familiar through Paul's teaching. Consequently they had listened to other Christian missionaries who impressed them to such a great extent that they expected from them a solution to their problems. We can assume that the Galatians knew about these opponents, and that they understood their theological conceptions and concerns. It must have been the persuasiveness[49] of the opponents' theology which turned them away from

their Apostle. The opponents must have made sense in terms of the problems the Galatians had with themselves. A number of passages in Galatians suggest that they had a concrete problem with the "flesh" ($\sigma\acute{\alpha}\rho\xi$):[50]

5:13   "only let not this freedom become an opportunity for the flesh . . ." ($\mu\acute{o}\nu o\nu$ $\mu\grave{\eta}$ $\tau\grave{\eta}\nu$ $\grave{\epsilon}\lambda\epsilon\upsilon\theta\epsilon\rho\acute{\iota}\alpha\nu$ $\epsilon\grave{\iota}\varsigma$ $\grave{\alpha}\phi o\rho\mu\grave{\eta}\nu$ $\tau\hat{\eta}$ $\sigma\alpha\rho\kappa\acute{\iota}$ . . .)

5:16   ". . . walk by the Spirit and you will not carry out the desire of the flesh" (. . . $\pi\nu\epsilon\acute{\upsilon}\mu\alpha\tau\iota$ $\pi\epsilon\rho\iota\pi\alpha\tau\epsilon\hat{\iota}\tau\epsilon$ $\kappa\alpha\grave{\iota}$ $\grave{\epsilon}\pi\iota\theta\upsilon\mu\acute{\iota}\alpha\nu$ $\sigma\alpha\rho\kappa\grave{o}\varsigma$ $o\grave{\upsilon}$ $\mu\grave{\eta}$ $\tau\epsilon\lambda\acute{\epsilon}\sigma\eta\tau\epsilon$)

5:17   ". . . for the flesh sets its desire against the Spirit, and the Spirit against the flesh . . ." ($\grave{\eta}$ . . . $\sigma\grave{\alpha}\rho\xi$ $\grave{\epsilon}\pi\iota\theta\upsilon\mu\epsilon\hat{\iota}$ $\kappa\alpha\tau\grave{\alpha}$ $\tau o\hat{\upsilon}$ $\pi\nu\epsilon\acute{\upsilon}\mu\alpha\tau o\varsigma$, $\tau\grave{o}$ $\delta\grave{\epsilon}$ $\pi\nu\epsilon\hat{\upsilon}\mu\alpha$ $\kappa\alpha\tau\grave{\alpha}$ $\tau\hat{\eta}\varsigma$ $\sigma\alpha\rho\kappa\acute{o}\varsigma$ . . .)

5:19   the list of vices and virtues (5:19–23), lifted from an original baptismal context and reiterated in the exhortational part of the letter, includes a list called "the works of the flesh" ($\tau\grave{\alpha}$ $\grave{\epsilon}\rho\gamma\alpha$ $\tau\hat{\eta}\varsigma$ $\sigma\alpha\rho\kappa\acute{o}\varsigma$)

6:12   the opponents want the Galatians to "look good in the flesh" ($\epsilon\grave{\upsilon}\pi\rho o\sigma\omega\pi\hat{\eta}\sigma\alpha\iota$ $\grave{\epsilon}\nu$ $\sigma\alpha\rho\kappa\acute{\iota}$)

6:13   the opponents themselves want "to boast in your flesh" ($\grave{\epsilon}\nu$ $\tau\hat{\eta}$ $\grave{\upsilon}\mu\epsilon\tau\acute{\epsilon}\rho\alpha$ $\sigma\alpha\rho\kappa\acute{\iota}$ $\kappa\alpha\upsilon\chi\acute{\eta}\sigma\omega\nu\tau\alpha\iota$)

Thus in their midst "transgressions" have occurred and the claim to live "in the Spirit" ($\grave{\epsilon}\nu$ $\pi\nu\epsilon\acute{\upsilon}\mu\alpha\tau\iota$)[51] came into conflict with the realities of daily life. From Paul's words we may conclude that the problem with which the Galatians felt they were confronted was this: how can the "pneumatic" ($\grave{o}$ $\pi\nu\epsilon\upsilon\mu\alpha\tau\iota\kappa\acute{o}\varsigma$) live with "trespasses" in his daily life?[52]

At this point Paul's opposition had concrete help to offer. According to the opponents' theology, Christian existence takes place within the terms of the Jewish

---

47   The ideas set forth below were first presented in my paper "Spirit, Freedom and Law: Paul's Message to the Galatian Churches," *SEÅ* 39 (1974) 145–60, esp. 153ff.

48   See Gal 1:6–9; 4:9, 17, 21; 5:4, 17; 6:12–13.

49   See Gal 3:1; 5:7–8.

50   In Gal Paul advocates a strict dualism of "Spirit" and "flesh" (see 3:3; 5:16–24; 6:8; also 1:6; 2:16, 20; 3:5; 4:13, 14, 23, 29; 5:4–5, 13; 6:12, 13).

51   ($\grave{\epsilon}\nu$) $\pi\nu\epsilon\acute{\upsilon}\mu\alpha\tau\iota$ is a theological "abbreviation" (see below § 6).

52   See 6:1. The terminology of "sin" occurs in 1:4; 2:15, 17; 3:19, 22; 6:1 (cf. 4:12, 14). All passages

refer to situations which, according to Paul's theology, no longer exist for Christians. Cf. the similar doctrine in *Gos. Phil.* 110 (Foerster–Wilson, *Gnosis* 2.96). On this problem see Paul Wernle, *Der Christ und die Sünde bei Paulus* (Freiburg and Leipzig: Mohr, 1897) esp. 75f; Hans Windisch, *Taufe und Sünde im ältesten Christentum bis auf Origenes* (Tübingen: Mohr, Siebeck, 1908) 154–63.

Torah covenant. [53] Christ is understood as the decisive force opposing evil ("Beliar") both cosmically and upon earth. As long as they stand firmly in the Torah covenant, the Christians are under the protection of Christ. The goal of Christian life is to obtain a state of "holiness" and thus become acceptable to God as "his sons and daughters." For this reason, the Christians must keep themselves pure from all the defilement that is brought about by "Beliar" and his forces.

Paul's words suggest that the opponents have urged the Galatians to accept the Torah and circumcision in order to become partakers of the Sinai covenant. [54] Presumably they were told that outside the Torah there is no salvation. [55] In the view of the opponents, Paul and his mission are illegitimate and an embodiment of everything they abhor and warn against. His "freedom from the law" must have seemed to them to be committing those who followed Paul to the realm of "Beliar" and turning Christ into a "servant of sin." [56] Faced with such a peculiar dilemma, the Galatians must have taken very seriously what these opponents of Paul had to say. Compared with them the Apostle had indeed little to offer. [57] In his conception, the familiar means for dealing with man's transgressions were eliminated. The Galatians had been given the "Spirit" and "freedom," but they were left to that Spirit and freedom. There was no law to tell them what was right or wrong. [58] There were no more rituals to correct transgressions. [59] Under these circumstances, their daily life came to be a dance on a tightrope! Left with only "Spirit" and "freedom," how could they face the world of hostility, in particular the evil world whose destructive forces were working within, in the human "flesh"? The occurrence of transgressions,

therefore, could not have come as a surprise, but rather was predictable. [60]

In conclusion, it was quite understandable that the Galatians more or less decided to accept the recommendations of Paul's opponents, to have themselves circumcised, to become conscientious observers of the Torah and thereby "heirs" of the security that this included.

3. The Date of the Letter

A. The Historical Situation

The historical situation which gave rise to the letter to the Galatians can be determined only generally (see 2.C above). Vielhauer has suggested that the original letter was dated in accordance with the conventions of letter-writing, but that address and date were cut off by the editor. [61] This is the reason why the present letter does not drop any hint at all as to the date of the situation. In fact, the cause of the letter (1:6–7) could have occurred at almost any time after Paul's departure. A date *post quem* can be established, however, because Paul mentions a number of historical events which preceded his letter and in fact led up to its writing:
1. General events of the history of Christianity:
   Jesus' crucifixion (1:1; 2:21; 3:1, 13; 5:11; 6:14)
   Paul's pre-Christian period (1:13–14, 23)
   Paul's "call" (1:1, 11–12, 15–16)
   Paul's journey to Arabia and his return to Damascus (1:17)
   Paul's first journey to Jerusalem "after three years" (1:18)
   Paul's journey to Syria and Cilicia (1:21)

---

53 For the following see my article on 2 Cor 6:14–7:1, cited above, n. 25; also Appendix 2.
54 See Gal 4:21–31; 5:2; 6:12–13.
55 See Acts 15:1 (quoted in the commentary on 2:2, n. 259).
56 See Gal 2:17.
57 Cf. the anti–Pauline polemic ps.–Clem. *Hom.* 2.17.3 (HSW, *NT Apocrypha* 2.122): "he who follows this order can discern by whom Simon (i.e. Paul), who as the first came before me to the Gentiles, was sent forth, and to whom I (i.e. Peter) belong who appeared later than he did and came upon him as light upon darkness, as knowledge upon ignorance,

as healing upon sickness."
58 See Gal 3:25; 5:18; also 5:6; 6:15.
59 Cf. 4:9–11.
60 Cf. the *Ep. Pet.* 2.3 (ps.–Clem. *Hom.*; also HSW, *NT Apocrypha* 2.112): "for some from among the Gentiles have rejected my [sc. Peter's] lawful preaching and have preferred a lawless and absurd doctrine of the man who is my enemy [sc. Paul]" (τινὲς γὰρ τῶν ἀπὸ ἐθνῶν τὸ δι' ἐμοῦ νόμιμον ἀπεδοκίμασαν κήρυγμα, τοῦ ἐχθροῦ ἀνθρώπου ἄνομόν τινα καὶ φλυαρώδη προσηκάμενοι διδασκαλίαν). See Appendix 3.A.
61 *Geschichte*, 66, 71.

The conference at Jerusalem "after fourteen years" (2:1–10)
The conflict at Antioch (2:11–14)
The beginning of the collection for the poor in Jerusalem (2:10)
2. Specific events related to the Galatian churches:
The founding of the churches (1:6–9; 4:13–14, 19)
The invasion of the churches by the opponents (1:6–9; 4:17; 5:7–12; 6:12–13)

Paul himself argues that his letter was necessitated by the previous events in the congregation and that this letter is his response to this situation. Within the letter itself we can distinguish between three periods: the beginning period of the Galatian enthusiasm (see 3:1–5; 4:13–15); the end of that period (4:15) and the appearance of the opponents; finally, Paul's struggle to regain the confidence of his churches. How long these periods lasted we do not know. One may venture to suggest that Paul did not wait long in responding to the threat by the opposition.[62]

Although none of the events mentioned in Galatians can be dated accurately,[63] scholars have tried their best to establish some dates.[64] All these attempts, however, depend upon the hypotheses that the itinerary of Paul's missionary journeys in Acts gives historically reliable information about Paul's journeys and that there were no other journeys which Paul undertook but which Acts does not report.[65] Yet it has been demonstrated that the accounts in Acts cannot be harmonized with the Galatian information supposedly referring to the same events.[66] Moreover, events decisive for the Galatian churches are not mentioned by Acts: the founding of the churches and Paul's struggle against the opponents.[67] Therefore, the attempts to find a place for Galatians in Acts rest upon very fragile foundations.

If Acts 18:23[68] had the Galatian churches in mind, Paul's visit must have been his second. "Strengthening the disciples" presupposes that the churches[69] were founded at an earlier visit. The earlier visit can be

62 Nothing can be made chronologically of the phrase in Gal 1:6, "so quickly you have changed." See the commentary.

63 Paul's visit in Corinth is at least identifiable (Acts 18:11–17). As we know from the inscription found in Delphi, the Roman proconsul Gallio mentioned in Acts 18:12 was in office in the spring of 52/53 or 51/52. For this inscription, see the new edition by André Plassart, *Fouilles de Delphes 3.4* (Paris: de Boccard, 1970) no. 286, pp. 26ff; idem, "L'inscription de Delphes mentionnant le proconsul Gallion," *REG* 80 (1967) 372–78; James H. Oliver, "The Epistle of Claudius which Mentions the Proconsul Junius Gallio," *Hesperia* 40 (1971) 239f. For discussion, see also C. K. Barrett, *The New Testament Background: Selected Documents* (London: SPCK, 1958) 48f; George Ogg, *The Chronology of the Life of Paul* (London: Epworth, 1968) 104–11; Suhl, *Paulus*, 324–27; Klaus Haacker, "Die Gallio–Episode und die Paulinische Chronologie," *BZ* 16 (1972) 252–55; Hans Conzelmann, *Die Apostelgeschichte* (HNT 7; Tübingen: Mohr, Siebeck, ²1972) on Acts 18:12; idem, *1 Corinthians* (tr. James W. Leitch; ed. George MacRae; Hermeneia; Philadelphia: Fortress, 1975) 12f; Vielhauer, *Geschichte*, 72f.

64 Recently scholars have tried to break the deadlock. See esp. Vielhauer, *Geschichte*, 70–81; John C. Hurd, "Pauline Chronology and Pauline Theology," in *Christian History and Interpretation: Studies Presented to John Knox* (Cambridge: Cambridge University,

1967) 225–48; idem, "The Sequence of Paul's Letters," *CJT* 14 (1968) 89–200; Kümmel, *Introduction*, 252–55; Robert Jewett, *Paul's Anthropological Terms: A Study of Their Use in Conflict Settings* (AGJU 10; Leiden: Brill, 1971) 11ff; idem, *A Chronology of Paul's Life and Letters* (unpublished manuscript which the author was kind enough to let me see); Suhl, *Paulus*.

65 On the itinerary, see Ernst Haenchen, *Acts of the Apostles* (Philadelphia: Westminster, 1971) 84ff; Vielhauer, *Geschichte*, e.g., 71f, 76ff, 108, 388ff.

66 For a critical discussion, see esp. Vielhauer, *Geschichte*, 70–81.

67 Martin Dibelius (*Studies in the Acts of the Apostles* [London: SCM, 1956] 148f) and Vielhauer (*Geschichte*, 74–81, 108, 125) assume that the author of Acts has shortened the itinerary at several points. Due to his tendency he may have omitted information about Paul's struggle, or even about the Galatian churches.

68 "... he departed and went from place to place through the region of Galatia and Phrygia, strengthening all the disciples."

69 As Vielhauer (*Geschichte*, 108) correctly points out, "the disciples" is a Lucan term and refers to churches (see Acts 14:22–23).

identified with the one mentioned in Acts 16:6. [70] This first visit can then be related to Gal 4:13 and to the hypothesis that Acts' statement about the Holy Spirit preventing Paul from proclaiming the word in Asia refers *de facto* to Paul's illness as the cause for his stay in Galatia. [71] We are asked to believe that Paul stayed in Galatia contrary to his original plans, and, since he had nothing to do while he was sick, founded the churches. Equally imaginative is the attempt by some to find a place for a second visit in Galatians with which the second visit in Acts 18:23[72] can be identified. Such a possibility is opened up by the term $\tau\grave{o}\ \pi\rho\acute{o}\tau\epsilon\rho\sigma\nu$ (Gal 4:13), which can mean "the only earlier time" or "the former time." The latter meaning would leave room for a second visit and is favored by those who want a second visit. They then declare the former meaning "completely superfluous." [73] The question is, however, whether anyone would find two visits in Gal 4:13 if he were not looking for them because of Acts 18:23. [74] There is also the problem of relating 4:13 and 1:9: if $\tau\grave{o}\ \pi\rho\acute{o}\tau\epsilon\rho\sigma\nu$ (4:13) has a second visit in mind, the same must be assumed for the term $\pi\rho\sigma\epsilon\iota\rho\acute{\eta}\text{-}\kappa\alpha\mu\epsilon\nu$ ("as we have said before") which refers to the issuing of the curse against apostasy. There can be little doubt, however, that the whole section 1:6–9 has Paul's first visit in mind when he preached the gospel to the Galatians and they "received" it (1:9). Therefore, Galatians alone does not suggest a second visit of

Paul in Galatia between founding the churches and writing the letter.

B. The Chronology of Paul's Letters

Establishing an internal chronological order among the extant letters of Paul is another unresolved problem. With regard to Galatians, there is little evidence to go on. [75] Since Romans was Paul's last letter, sent probably from Corinth before his final journey to Jerusalem, [76] it is almost certain that Galatians was written prior to Romans. More could be said if it were possible to determine relationships between Galatians and other Pauline letters. Such attempts have been made recently, but in our view unsuccessfully. [77] The references to the collection for the poor in Jerusalem in Gal 2:10 and 1 Cor 16:1–4 provide no basis for a sequential order of the letters. [78] Developments of thought can be shown to have taken place between Galatians and Romans, [79] but not between Galatians and other Pauline letters. Similarities between Galatians and 2 Corinthians 10–13 do exist, but they prove neither any sequential order nor even temporal closeness. [80]

C. The Date of Galatians

The result of the previous points of discussion is that Galatians can be dated only approximately. Among scholars, all possibilities from early to late are repre-

---

70 Vielhauer (*ibidem*, 79, 108ff) proposes as dates for the so–called "second missionary journey" (Acts 15:40–18:22) the period from spring 48 to summer/fall 51, and for the founding of the Galatian churches c. 49 (p. 110).

71 So now also Vielhauer, *ibidem*, 79.

72 "And they went through the region of Phrygia and Galatia, having been forbidden by the Holy Spirit to speak the word in Asia."

73 Kümmel, *Introduction*, 302; cf. also Vielhauer, *Geschichte*, 109f.

74 Vielhauer (*Geschichte*, 79f) proposes the spring of 52 as the beginning of the so–called "third missionary journey" (Acts 18:23–21:17), and for the second visit to the Galatian churches 52 or 53 at the earliest (p. 110).

75 Cf. Vielhauer, *Geschichte*, 110f; Kümmel, *Introduction*, 313f.

76 See Rom 15:25; Acts 20:2–3. Cf. Kümmel, *Introduction*, 311. However, the composite nature of Rom

creates additional problems; see Walter Schmithals, *Der Römerbrief als historisches Problem* (Gütersloh: Mohn, 1975).

77 See the recent studies by Charles Buck and Greer Taylor, *Saint Paul: A Study of the Development of His Thought* (New York: Scribner, 1969) esp. 82ff; Udo Borse, *Der Standort des Galaterbriefes* (Köln: Hanstein, 1972); Mussner, pp. 9–11; Suhl, *Paulus*, 217ff.

78 Cf. the systematic attempt by Borse (ibidem, 32ff) whose method is, however, highly speculative.

79 Cf. Borse, ibidem, 120ff.

80 Cf. Borse, ibidem, 84ff; followed by Mussner, p. 10.

sented.[81] It should be noted that the guesses are mostly speculative and are based upon other, unproven hypotheses or upon arguments from silence. On the whole, an early date is more commendable than a late date. Paul's theological position is different from the later letter to the Romans. As a matter of fact, it closely resembles the "enthusiastic" or even "gnostic" position.[82] Paul does not find it necessary to protect himself against misunderstandings, but emphasizes the "Spirit" without any qualification. The letter seems to belong to the beginning of his difficulties with his opponents, rather than to an advanced stage. The most likely date would fall into the beginning of the middle period of his mission in Asia Minor, the first period being that of the founding of the Galatian churches. The years between 50–55 as the date of writing may be accepted as a reasonable guess.[83]

D. The Place from which Galatians was Sent

There is not the slightest hint in Galatians itself as to the place from which it was sent. This situation gives ample room for speculation. The Marcionite Prologues have the letter sent from Ephesus, and most scholars tend to agree.[84] The source of the information in the Prologues is not known. Equally unknown is the source of the statement in the *subscriptio* contained in many manuscripts especially of the 𝔐 tradition and Syriac versions, according to which Rome was the place from which Galatians was sent.[85] On the basis of Paul's itineraries in Acts, scholars argue for Ephesus,[86] Macedonia,[87] or Corinth.[88] All of these places are possible, but so are others.

4. The Text of Galatians

The commentary is based upon the 26th edition of Erwin Nestle and Kurt Aland, *Novum Testamentum Graece*.[89] There are not many changes as compared with the 25th edition. A list of the changes is provided below; for their discussion, see the respective sections of the commentary.

81 For a discussion of the various hypotheses see the introductions, esp. Wikenhauser and Schmid, *Einleitung*, 417–19 (A.D. 54–58); Kümmel, *Introduction*, 304 (A.D. 54–55); furthermore John Knox, "Galatians, Letter to the," *IDB* 2 (1962) 342f; Jewett, *Chronology* (winter of 53; above n. 64); Günther Bornkamm, *Paul* (tr. D. M. G. Stalker; New York: Harper & Row, 1971) 241 (A.D. 54); Borse, *Standort*, 175 (A.D. 57–58); Suhl, *Paulus*, 217ff, 343 (A.D. 54).

82 See my article in *SEÅ* 39 (1974) 155–60; also Kurt Niederwimmer, "Die Freiheit des Gnostikers nach dem Philippusevangelium. Eine Untersuchung zum Thema: Kirche und Gnosis," in *Verborum Veritas: Festschrift für Gustav Stählin zum 70. Geburtstag* (Wuppertal: Brockhaus, 1970) 361–74.

83 Vielhauer (*Geschichte*, 110f) also rejects a late date for Gal. He assumes that Paul wrote it "during the two or three years of his residence at Ephesus" (52–54/55). See also Herbert Braun, "Christentum I. Entstehung," *RGG*³ 1.1693–94.

84 See above, n. 15.

85 See the *apparatus criticus* in *Novum Testamentum Graece* . . . curavit Eberhard Nestle, . . . Erwin Nestle et Kurt Aland (Stuttgart: Württembergische Bibelanstalt, ²⁵1963); Bruce M. Metzger, *A Textual Commentary on the Greek New Testament* (London and New York: United Bible Societies, 1971) 599.

86 So, e.g., Schlier, p. 18; Bornkamm, *Paul*, 241; Wikenhauser and Schmid, *Einleitung*, 418f; Suhl, *Paulus*, 217f; Vielhauer, *Geschichte*, 111; Kümmel, *Introduction*, 304: Ephesus or Macedonia.

87 So Borse, *Standort*, 79f, 175; Mussner, pp. 9f.

88 So Burton, p. xlvii; Pierre Bonnard, *L'épître de Saint Paul aux Galates* (CNT 9; Neuchâtel and Paris: Delachaux & Niestlé, ²1972) 14. According to Werner Foerster ("Abfassungszeit und Ziel des Galaterbriefes," in *Apophoreta: Festschrift für Ernst Haenchen* [BZNW 30; Berlin: Töpelmann, 1964] 135–41), Gal was written during the journey from Corinth to Jerusalem.

89 For the list regarding the changes in the 26th edition I am indebted to Kurt Aland.

	Nestle-Aland 25th ed.	*Nestle-Aland 26th ed.*
1:6	ἐν χάριτι Χριστοῦ	ἐν χάριτι [Χριστοῦ]
1:15	εὐδόκησεν	εὐδόκησεν [ὁ θεός]
1:18	τρία ἔτη	ἔτη τρία
2:14	οὐκ Ἰουδαϊκῶς	οὐχὶ Ἰουδαϊκῶς
2:16	εἰδότες δέ	εἰδότες [δέ]
2:16	Χριστοῦ Ἰησοῦ	Ἰησοῦ Χριστοῦ
3:14	Ἰησοῦ Χριστῷ	Χριστῷ Ἰησοῦ
3:19	ἄχρις ἄν	ἄχρις οὗ
3:21	ζωοποιῆσαι	ζωοποιῆσαι
4:9	δουλεῦσαι	δουλεύειν
4:23	ἀλλ' ὁ [μέν]	ἀλλ' ὁ μέν
4:23	διὰ τῆς ἐπαγγελίας	δι' ἐπαγγελίας
4:24, 25	Σινά	Σινᾶ
5:7	ἀληθείᾳ	[τῇ] ἀληθείᾳ
5:24	Χριστοῦ Ἰησοῦ	Χριστοῦ ['Ιησοῦ]
6:12	Χριστοῦ [Ἰησοῦ]	Χριστοῦ

The text of Galatians must be discussed in conjunction with the tradition of the entire *Corpus Paulinum*.[90] The most important witnesses are:

1. Papyri

P[46] (c. 200), missing is Gal 1:9; 2:10–11; 3:1; 4:1, 19; 5:18–19; 6:9[91]

P[51] (c. 400), contains Gal 1:2–10, 13, 16–20[92]

2. Codices containing Galatians or parts of it[93]

א Codex Sinaiticus (4th cent.)

A Codex Alexandrinus (c. 5th cent.)
B Codex Vaticanus (4th cent.)
C Codex Ephraemi Syri Rescriptus (5th cent.)
D Codex Claromontanus (6th cent.)
F Codex Augiensis (9th cent.), bilingual
G Codex Boernerianus (9th cent.), with interlinear Latin
H Codex Euthalianus (6th cent.)
I Codex Freerianus (5th/6th cent.)
K Codex Mosquensis (9th/10th cent.)
L Codex Angelicus (9th cent.)
P Codex Porphyrianus (10th cent.)
Ψ Codex Athous Laurae (8th/9th cent.)
049 (8th/9th cent.)
056 (10th cent.)
062 (5th cent.), contains Gal 4:15–5:14
075 (10th cent.)
0122 (9th cent.), contains Gal 5:12–6:4
0142 (10th cent.)
0158 (5th/6th cent.), contains Gal 1:1–13
0174 (5th cent.), contains Gal 2:5–6
0176 (4th cent.), contains Gal 3:16–25
0254 (5th cent.), contains Gal 5:13–17
0261 (5th cent.), contains Gal 1:9–12, 19–22; 4:25–31

3. The Old Latin Versions[94]

The tradition includes the bilingual uncials, D, F, the interlinear Latin translation in G, the Freising frag-

---

90 On the textual history of the Pauline letters, see Hans Lietzmann, "Einführung in die Textgeschichte der Paulusbriefe," in *An die Römer* (HNT 8; Tübingen: Mohr, Siebeck, [5]1971) 1–18; Bruce M. Metzger, *The Text of the New Testament* (Oxford: Oxford University, [2]1968); Kümmel, *Introduction*, 511–54; Kurt Aland, *Kurzgefasste Liste der griechischen Handschriften des Neuen Testament* (Berlin: de Gruyter, 1963); idem, "Die griechischen Handschriften des Neuen Testament: Ergänzungen zur 'Kurzgefassten Liste'," in *Materialien zur neutestamentlichen Handschriftenkunde* (Berlin: de Gruyter, 1969) 1–53. See also Burton, pp. lxxiv–lxxxii; Mussner, pp. 33f.

91 See Günther Zuntz, *The Text of the Epistles: A Disquisition upon the Corpus Paulinum* (London: British Academy/Oxford University, 1953); Aland, *Liste*, 31f; idem, "Das Neue Testament auf Papyrus," in *Studien zur Überlieferung des Neuen Testaments und seines Textes* (Berlin: de Gruyter, 1967) 91–136; Metzger, *Text*, 252; Kurt Aland (ed.), *Repertorium der griechi-*

schen christlichen Papyri, I: Biblische Papyri (Patristische Texte und Studien 18; Berlin: de Gruyter, 1976) 273–76.

92 See Aland, *Liste*, 32; Metzger, *Text*, 252; Aland, *Repertorium*, 281.

93 See Aland, *Liste*, 37ff; idem, *Materialien* 1.7ff, 22ff; Metzger, *Text*, 42ff.

94 See Metzger, *Text*, 72ff; Karl Theodor Schäfer, *Die Überlieferung des altlateinischen Galaterbriefes* (Braunsberg, 1939 [*non vidi*]); Bonifazius Fischer, "Das Neue Testament in lateinischer Sprache: Der gegenwärtige Stand seiner Erforschung und seine Bedeutung für die griechische Textgeschichte," in Kurt Aland (ed.), *Die alten Übersetzungen des Neuen Testaments: die Kirchenväterzitate und Lektionare* (Arbeiten zur neutestamentlichen Textforschung 5; Berlin: de Gruyter, 1972) 1–92, esp. 67–73.

ments, and the quotations in Marcion, Tertullian, and Cyprian.

4. Quotations of Galatians in the Patristic Literature. [95]

5. The Literary Composition and Function of Galatians[96]

Paul's letter to the Galatians can be analyzed according to Greco-Roman rhetoric and epistolography. [97] This possibility raises the whole question of Paul's relationship to the rhetorical and literary disciplines and culture, a question which has not as yet been adequately discussed.

German scholarship at the end of the nineteenth and the beginning of the twentieth century was sharply divided on the question of how to classify Paul's letters, whether to classify them as literary or non-literary, and whether or not to assume influence of Hellenistic rhetoric. Although men like Ulrich von Wilamowitz-Moellendorff[98] and Martin Dibelius[99] included Paul among the great letter writers of antiquity, it seems that the strong opposition against such a judgment expressed by scholars like Franz Overbeck, [100] Paul Wendland[101] and Eduard Norden[102] has prevailed. When one reads their arguments today, however, the heavy influence of ideology arouses suspicion. Scholars of the later twentieth century seem in basic agreement that Paul's letters are "confused," disagreeing only about whether the confusion is caused by emotional disturbances, "*Diktierpausen*," or "Rabbinic" methodology. [103]

Paul's letter to the Galatians is an example of the "apologetic letter" genre. The evidence for this hypothesis must, of course, be derived from an analysis of the composition of the letter, but before we turn to this subject at least a few remarks on the literary genre of the apologetic letter are necessary. [104] The emphasis on the interrelationships between various literary genres is one of the major contributions of Arnaldo Momigliano's 1968 lectures at Harvard University on "The Development of Greek Biography". [105] The genre of the apologetic letter which arose in the fourth century

---

95 See *Biblia Patristica: Index des citations et allusions bibliques dans la littérature patristique* (Paris: Editions du Centre National de la Recherche Scientifique, 1975) 481–89; also Metzger, *Text*, 86ff; Kümmel, *Introduction*, 538–40.

96 The ideas presented here were first published in my article, "The Literary Composition and Function of Paul's Letter to the Galatians," *NTS* 21 (1975) 353–79. See also Hans Dieter Betz, "Galatians, Letter to the," *IDBSup* 352f.

97 This fact was apparently not recognized before, although Luther at least, in his commentary of 1535, shows great interest in compositional and rhetorical matters. Joseph Barber Lightfoot, in his still valuable commentary on Gal (*Saint Paul's Epistle to the Galatians* [London: Macmillan, 1865, [10]1890]), has an outline in which he uses the term "narrative" for the first two chapters, "argumentative" for chapters 3–4, and "hortatory" for 5:1–6:10. These are indeed proper terms if we analyze the letter according to Greco–Roman rhetoric, but Lightfoot never betrays whether he was aware of this fact. Professor Gerhard Ebeling (letter of July 17, 1975) has called my attention to the fact that Melanchthon analyzed Rom according to rhetorical criteria. See his *Commentarii in epistolam Pauli ad Romanos* (Wittenberg, 1532), ed. Rolf Schäfer, in *Melanchthons Werke in Auswahl* 5 (Gütersloh: Mohn, 1965); see esp. the description, 373–78; also Rolf Schäfer, "Melanchthons Hermeneutik im Römerbrief-Kommentar

von 1532," *ZThK* 60 (1963) 216–35.

98 "Die Griechische Literatur des Altertums," in *Die Kultur der Gegenwart* (Teil 1; Abteilung 8; Berlin und Leipzig: Teubner, [2]1907) 159f.

99 *Geschichte der urchristlichen Literatur* (Munich: Kaiser, [2]1975) 95–100; see also on Gal, 105f.

100 "Über die Anfänge der patristischen Literatur," *Historische Zeitschrift* 48 (1882) 417–72.

101 *Die urchristlichen Literaturformen* (HNT 1.2–3; Tübingen: Mohr, Siebeck, [2–3]1912) 342ff. In regard to Gal, Wendland says (349): "An exegesis which wants to comprehend the content of the letter according to a carefully designed outline and as a logically conceived whole will go astray."

102 *Die antike Kunstprosa* (Darmstadt: Wissenschaftliche Buchgesellschaft, [5]1958) 492ff.

103 An example of this is Wilhelm Koepp, "Die Abraham–Midraschimkette des Galaterbriefes als das vorpaulinische heidenchristliche Urtheologumenon," *Wissenschaftliche Zeitschrift der Universität Rostock*, 2. Jg.; H.3.; Reihe Gesellschafts– und Sprachwissenschaften (1952–53) 181–87.

104 See also my book *Der Apostel Paulus und die sokratische Tradition* (BHTh 45; Tübingen: Mohr, Siebeck, 1972) chap. 2.

105 *The Development of Greek Biography* (Cambridge: Harvard University, 1971); idem, "Second Thoughts on Greek Biography," *Mededelingen der Koninklijke Nederlandse Akademie van Wettenschappen*, Afd. *Letterkunde, nieuwe reeks* (deel 34; no. 7; [1971]).

B.C.[106] presupposes not only the existence of the letter form but also the genres of autobiography and apologetic speech, which are also older forms of literary expression. In Greek literature all of these genres are represented by famous examples, of which we need to mention only Plato's pseudo-autobiography of Socrates; its imitation in Isocrates' Περὶ ἀντιδόσεως, an authentic apologetic autobiography; and Demosthenes' self-apology, *De corona*. These examples inspired later writers who imitated them, e.g., Cicero in his *Brutus* or Libanius in his "Autobiography" (*Oratio* 1).[107]

Momigliano also makes the Socratics responsible for creating the genre of the apologetic letter,[108] the most famous example of which is Plato's *Ep.* 7. The authenticity of this letter and of the other Platonic letters is presently very much a matter of scholarly debate[109] but is of no substantive importance for the genre itself. "In any case it is a remarkable attempt to combine reflections on eternal problems and personal experiences."[110] The subsequent history of the genre is difficult to trace, since most of the pertinent literature did not survive:[111]

"We cannot, therefore, see the exact place of Plato's letter in the history of ancient autobiographical production. But one vaguely feels the Platonic precedent in Epicurus, Seneca, and perhaps St. Paul."[112]

Momigliano's last words—"and perhaps St. Paul"—come rather unexpectedly and without any further explanation. However, the literary analysis of this letter demonstrates that whatever reason may have caused his remark, it is certainly correct, and that the cautious "perhaps" is no longer necessary.

The epistolary framework of the Galatian letter can be easily recognized and separated from the body—in fact it separates so easily that it appears almost as a kind of external bracket for the body of the letter. However, several interrelations between the epistolary framework and the body of the letter indicate that both elements are part of one and the same composition.[113] The postscript (6:11–18) must not only be examined as an epistolographic convention, but also as a rhetorical feature. Rhetorically, it serves as the *peroratio* or *conclusio* ("conclusion") of the apologetic speech which forms the body of the letter and which is composed according to the traditional structure (see the discussion in the commentary on 6:11–18). In the following an attempt has been made to present an analysis of the composition of Galatians. This analysis shows the surface structure of the letter. In addition, the function of the letter, the "traditions and doctrinal presuppositions" (6.) and the "argument" (7.) should be taken into account. Further discussion and bibliography regarding the sections of the letter may be found in the paragraphs of the commentary introducing these sections.

---

106 Momigliano, *Biography*, 62.
107 Ibidem, 58–60, with further bib.
108 Ibidem, 60–62.
109 Ibidem, 60 n. 16, with the literature mentioned there. In addition see Ludwig Edelstein, *Plato's Seventh Letter* (Leiden: Brill, 1966); furthermore, the papers by N. Gulley and G. J. D. Aalders, in *Pseudepigrapha 1: Entretiens sur l'antiquité classique* 18 (Vandoeuvres–Geneva: Fondation Hardt, 1972); Jonathan A. Goldstein, *The Letters of Demosthenes* (New York: Columbia University, 1968) chap. 7: "The Forms of Ancient Apology and Polemic, Real and Fictitious."
110 Momigliano, *Biography*, 62.
111 Momigliano does not mention the so–called "Cynic Epistles," a body of epistolary literature which deserves to be carefully studied with regard to early Christian letters. See the editions by Rudolf Hercher, *Epistolographi Graeci* (Paris: Didot, 1873) 208–17, 235–58; Franz H. Reuters, *Die Briefe des Ana-charsis, griechisch und deutsch* (Berlin: Akademie–Verlag, 1963); Rodolfo Mondolfo and Leonardo Tarán, *Eraclito: Testimonianze e imitazioni* (Florence: "La Nuova Italia," 1972) with bib.; furthermore, John Strugnell and Harold Attridge, "The Epistles of Heraclitus and the Jewish Pseudepigrapha: A Warning," *HTR* 64 (1971) 411–13; Rudolf Kassel, "Der siebente pseudoheraklitische Brief auf Pergament und Papyrus," *ZPE* 14 (1974) 128–32.
112 Momigliano, *Biography*, 62.
113 It is precisely at the points of expansion where we find close relations between the prescript and various parts of the body of the letter: the title and its definition (Gal 1:1), and the christological–soteriological statements (1:4).

I. Epistolary Prescript
1:1–5

1:1a	A. Name and title of the principle sender
1:1b	B. Definition of the title "apostle"
	1. Negatively: "not from men, nor through man"
	2. Positively: "but through Jesus Christ and God the Father"
	3. Interpretation of "through" by a christological statement: "who raised him from the dead"
1:2a	C. Stating of co–senders
1:2b	D. Naming of the addressees
1:3–4	E. Salutation
	1. The salutation
	2. Interpretation of "Lord Jesus Christ"
	a. A christological statement (formula of self–sacrifice): "who gave himself for our sins"
	b. Two soteriological statements
	1) With regard to Christ's death: "to deliver us from the present evil age"
	2) With regard to God's will: "according to the will of our God and Father"
1:5	F. A doxology, with the concluding "amen"

II. Exordium
1:6–11

1:6–7	A. The statement of the *causa*
1:6	1. A preliminary, ironic statement of the cause
1:7a	2. A self–correction
1:7b	3. A corrected restatement of the cause
1:8–9	B. The issuing of a double curse
1:8	1. Issuing of a conditional curse
1:9a	2. Formula of repetition
1:9b	3. Reissuing of the curse
1:10–11	C. The *transitus* or *transgressio*
1:10	1. A denial in form of two rhetorical questions (v 10ab) and a hypothetical conclusion (v 10c)
1:11	2. An introduction of the point of contention of the following "statement of facts" (1:12–2:14)
	3. Address: "brothers"

III. Narratio
1:12–2:14

1:12	A. Thesis to be demonstrated in the "statement of facts"
1:12a	1. Negatively: "For I did not receive it [*sc.* the gospel] from (a) man, nor was I taught it…"
1:12b	2. Positively: "but [I received it] through a revelation of Jesus Christ."
1:13–24	B. First part: From Paul's birth to the mission in Asia Minor
1:13–14	1. Paul's conduct as a Jew before his conversion to the Christian faith
1:13a	a. Reference to information known to the Galatians: "You have heard…"
1:13b	b. Reference to Paul's persecution of the Church
1:14	c. Reference to Paul's standing in Judaism
1:15–17	2. Paul's conduct as a Christian from his conversion to Christianity to his visit with Cephas at Jerusalem
1:15a	a. Reference to Paul's election by God
1:15b–16	b. Reference to Paul's vocation by God
1:15b	1) The vocation by God
1:16a	2) The revelation of Christ in Paul
1:16b	3) The commission
1:16c–17	c. Reference to Paul's conduct immediately following his conversion
1:16c	1) No conferring "with flesh and blood"
1:17a	2) No visiting with the other apostles in Jerusalem
1:17b–c	3) The journey to Arabia and the return to Damascus
1:18–19 (20)	3. Paul's first visit in Jerusalem
1:18a	a. Reference to time period prior to the visit in Jerusalem
	b. Reference to person visited
1:18b	c. Reference to length of visit
1:19	d. Additional remark about persons visited
	1) Denial of visits with other apostles
	2) Exception: visit with James
1:20	e. Oath: affirmation of the truth
1:21	4. Paul's conduct after the visit in Jerusalem: the beginning of the mission in Syria and Cilicia
1:22–24	5. Evaluation of Paul's relationship with the churches in Judea
1:22	a. Statement of the fact that he is unknown to them personally

cerned: it was the "collection for the poor."

2:10c   (2) Affirmation of Paul's present concern to comply with the additional agreement (does he imply that only this part is still in force?)

2:11–14   D. Third part: the conflict at Antioch

2:11   1. Reference to the facts concerning the incident

2:11a   a. Reference to the occasion of the incident

       b. Reference to the name of the person causing the incident

2:11b   c. Reference to the action taken by Paul

2:11c   d. Reference to the reason for Paul's action

2:12–14   2. Account and evaluation of the incident

2:12   a. Account of Cephas' conduct

2:12a   1) Before the arrival of the "men from James"

2:12b   2) Change of his conduct after the arrival of the "men from James"

2:12c   3) Reason for his change of conduct

2:13   b. Account of the other Jews' conduct

2:13a   1) Their complicity with Cephas' change of conduct

2:13b   2) The effect upon Barnabas, and his change of conduct

       3) The reason for Barnabas' change of conduct

2:14   c. Account of Paul's confrontation with Cephas

2:14a   1) Paul's theological evaluation of the conduct of the Jewish Christians opposed to him

2:14b   2) Statement of his public opposition to Cephas

2:14c   3) Statement of Cephas' self-contradiction (a 'dilemma' in form of a question)

        a) Protasis, stating Cephas' religious status in Judaism and his non–Jewish way of life

        b) Apodosis, stating Cephas' demand upon the Gentile Christians as a contradiction of his own conduct

IV.   Propositio
2:15–21

2:15–16   A. The point of agreement: the doctrine of justification by faith

2:15   1. A self–definition of Jewish Christians as Jews

      a. Self–designation as "Jews"

      b. Stating the basis for being Jews: "birth"

      c. Stating their distinctiveness in contrast to non–Jews ("not 'sinners' from the Gentiles")

2:16a   2. A self–definition of Jewish Christians as Christians: Stating the basis for being Christians

      a. Naming the type of basis: "theological conviction"

      b. Stating the content of the theological conviction

       1) A negative eschatological judgment about man

       2) An exception to that negative judgment

2:16b–c   c. Stating the consequence of the theological conviction

2:16b   1) Reference of the past act of becoming Christian believers

2:16c   2) Statement of the purpose of becoming Christian believers

2:16d   d. Citation of the theological presupposition, with an allusion to Scripture

2:17–18   B. The point of disagreement: the consequence for Gentile Christians

2:17   1. Hypothetical statement of the consequence for the Gentile Christians

2:17a.1   a. First (correct) presupposition

2:17a.2   b. Second (false) presupposition

2:17b   c. (False) inference

2:17c   d. Rejection of the false argument

2:18   2. Critique of the second (false) presupposition

2:18a   a. Implied presupposition of a legal definition (the definition is cited in Rom 4:15b)

      b. Application of the definition to the present case

       1) Statement of present hypothetical presuppositions

        a) Reference to previous action: "I have dissolved"

        b) Reference to present reversal of the previous action: "I establish again"

This formal analysis of the letter to the Galatians also permits us to arrive at some conclusions with regard to its *function*. We must of course distinguish between the general function of the letter as letter,[114] and the specific function of the letter to the Galatians. As a

114 Research in the field of epistolography has long been neglected and has only recently regained attention. For an introduction, see William G. Doty, *Letters in Primitive Christianity* (Philadelphia: Fortress, 1973); Vielhauer, *Geschichte*, 58–70. The major studies to be mentioned here are: Hermann Peter, *Der Brief in der römischen Litteratur* (Lepizig: Teubner, 1901; Hildesheim: Olms, 1966); Heikki Koskenniemi, *Studien zur Idee und Phraseologie des griechischen Briefes bis 400 n. Chr.* (Helsinki, 1956); Gustav Karlsson, *Idéologie et cérémonial dans l'épistolographie byzantine* (Uppsala: Almqvist & Wiksell, [2]1962); Klaus Thraede, *Grundzüge griechisch-römischer Brieftopik* (Munich: Beck, 1970); Gregor Maurach, *Der Bau von Senecas Epistulae Morales* (Heidelberg: Winter, 1970).

letter Galatians is a means of communication, carrying a certain message which is part of an ongoing debate. This debate includes a past history, in which issues as well as positions with regard to these issues were formed. The debate also includes prospective future developments and options which the partners believe are open or closed to them. The participants in the debate include primarily the senders and the addressees,[115] and secondarily the opponents,[116] who have contributed to the cause of the original writing of the letter. Because of the fundamental issues under discussion, the readers do not simply include the Galatian churches but all churches. What the Apostle has to say, he has to say to the whole of Christianity: Jewish and Gentile Christians, Paulinists and anti-Paulinists. In principle, therefore, even the present readers of the letter are participants in the debate.[117]

The function of the letter as letter implies also that the sender and the addressee are unable to have an oral conversation. The letter is a necessary substitute for such an oral exchange. By necessity, therefore, the letter is reductive. The letter represents its author, yet cannot act and react as its author might in person. Thus, the sender expresses himself *in absentia* and without the full range of communicative devices which an oral conversation can provide. The letter represents its author, without being able to act and react as an author.

The apologetic letter, such as Galatians, presupposes the real or fictitious situation of the court of law, with jury, accuser, and defendant. In the case of Galatians, the addressees are identical with the jury, with Paul being the defendant, and his opponents the accusers. This situation makes Paul's Galatian letter a self-apology,[118] delivered not in person but in a written form. If one looks at the letter from the point of view of its function, i.e., from the rhetorical point of view, this substitution is indeed a poor one. Since it is simply a lifeless piece of paper, it eliminates one of the most important weapons of the rhetorician, the oral delivery. The actual delivery of the speech includes a whole range of weapons relating to modulation of voice and to gestures, all of which a letter makes impossible.[119] In his remarks Paul is fully aware of these disadvantages, as shown in 4:18–20.[120]

Far more serious problems arise from the nature of the defense speech itself. The apologetic letter is by definition a part of rhetoric and, for that reason, limits its writer to the devices of the "art of persuasion." In its written form such a letter can persuade its addressees only by its rational arguments.[121] The "art of persuasion"[122] has its proper place in the court of law, but it is obviously inadequate for the defense case Paul must make. As antiquity saw it, the law court rhetoric is beset with a number of unpleasant characteristics which impinge upon the very things Paul wants to accomplish. Rhetoric, as antiquity understood it, has little in common with the truth, but it is the exercise of those skills which make people believe something to be true. For this reason, rhetoric is preoccupied with demonstrations, persuasive strategy, and psychological exploration and exploitation of the audience, but it is not interested in establishing the truth itself. Consequently, people who are interested in the truth itself must be distrustful of the "art of persuasion," because they know of its capacity for intellectual manipulation, dishonesty, and cynicism. The effectiveness of rhetoric depends primarily upon the naiveté of the hearer, rather than upon the soundness of the case. Rhetoric works only as long as one does not know *how* it works.

115 See Gal 1:2, and this Introduction, § 2.B.
116 See this Introduction, § 2.C.
117 This provides, it seems, an internal justification for the collection of Paul's letters and for their inclusion in the canon of Christian Holy Scriptures. The question is whether it also provided the editor(s) of the *Corpus Paulinum* with a criterion as to what to include and what to omit.
118 On the self–apology, see Fritz Loheit, *Untersuchungen zur antiken Selbstapologie* (Rostock: Adlers Erben, 1928); Betz, *Paulus, passim.*
119 On the *pronunciatio*, see Heinrich Lausberg, *Handbuch der literarischen Rhetorik* (2 vols.; Munich, Hueber, 1960) § 1091; Josef Martin, *Antike Rhetorik: Technik und Methode* (HKAW 2.3; Munich: Beck, 1974) 351–55.
120 See also Gal 3:1; 4:13–15.
121 On the argument, see this Introduction, § 7.
122 On rhetoric and its definitions, see Martin, *Rhetorik,* 1–12.

The need to use this rather suspect form of logical argumentation becomes even more questionable when one realizes that *no* kind of rational argument can be adequate with regard to the defense Paul must make. In effect his defense amounts to a defense of the "Spirit" which was given to the Gentile Galatians outside of the Torah. How can an irrational experience like the ecstatic reception of the divine Spirit be defended as legitimate if the means of such a defense are limited to those available in the apologetic letter?

It must be for this reason that the Galatian letter has still another function. Galatians begins with a conditional curse, very carefully constructed, cursing every Christian who dares to preach a gospel different from that which Paul had preached and still preaches, different from the gospel which the Galatians had accepted.[123] At the end, the letter pronounces a corresponding conditional blessing upon those who remain loyal to the Pauline gospel.[124] What does this imply for the literary function of the letter? It means that as the carrier of curse and blessing the letter becomes a "magical letter." This category is well-known from ancient epistolography.[125] In other words, Paul does not simply rely on the "art of persuasion" and its system of rational argumentation, although this system is used to yield as much as it can. He does not leave things to be decided by the reasonableness of the Galatians, although their reason is supposedly being informed by the Spirit of God. He also introduces the dimension of magic, that is, the curse and the blessing, as inescapable instruments of the Spirit, in order to confront the Galatians with the choice between salvation and condemnation. Reading the letter will automatically produce the "judgment." The readers will either go free—be acquitted—or they will be sent back to the cosmic "prison" guarded by the "elements of the world" ($\tau\grave{\alpha}$ $\sigma\tau o\iota\chi\epsilon\hat{\iota}\alpha$ $\tauο\hat{\upsilon}$ $\kappa\acute{o}\sigma\muου$).[126]

By including this dimension of magic, Paul *repeats* the Galatians' initial confrontation with the gospel. His letter is not merely a piece of rhetoric, but it is composed in such a way that it functions at the same time as an efficacious display of the divine Spirit and Power ($\mathring{\alpha}\pi\acute{o}\delta\epsilon\iota\xi\iota\varsigma$ $\pi\nu\epsilon\acute{\upsilon}\mu\alpha\tauο\varsigma$ $\kappa\alpha\grave{\iota}$ $\delta\upsilon\nu\acute{\alpha}\mu\epsilon\omega\varsigma$).[127] The letter simultaneously functions as a *reminder* of the Galatians' history. Not only are they informed about events of the past, but having read the letter they see themselves transferred back into the moment when they first encountered the gospel, so that suddenly Paul's defense of the Spirit coincides with the proclamation of the gospel of freedom through the crucified Jesus Christ. Only as this happens can Galatians, as a letter, fully represent Paul, the Apostle of Christ.[128] If one takes the perspective of the readers seriously, one must go even further. Since Paul understands himself as the Apostle and representative of the Lord Jesus Christ, and then as a representative of God, his letter amounts to a "heavenly letter," a term signifying another category of letters.[129] This must have been true for the readers especially after Paul's death, and may therefore be an internal reason for Paul's letter becoming Holy Scripture.

123 Gal 1:8–9.
124 Gal 6:16.
125 No satisfactory investigation of the genre exists. Johannes Sykutris mentions it in his article "Epistolographie," PWSup 5 (1931) 207; also Johannes Schneider, "Brief," *RAC* 2 (1954) 572f. Both authors refer to the *Papyri Graecae Magicae: Die griechischen Zauberpapyri* (2 vols.; eds. Karl Preisendanz and Albert Henrichs; Stuttgart: Teubner, 1973–74) for examples. Actually, the oldest letter in the Greek language is a magical letter (Homer *Il.* 6.167ff). For further discussion, see below on Gal 1:8–9.
126 See Gal 3:23ff; 4:8–10.
127 1 Cor 2:4.
128 See Robert W. Funk, "The Apostolic *Parousia*: Form and Significance," in *Christian History and Interpreta-tion: Studies Presented to John Knox* (Cambridge: Cambridge University, 1967) 249–68; Klaus Thraede, *Grundzüge griechisch-römischer Brieftopik* (Zetemata 48: Munich: Beck, 1970) 146ff.
129 Cf. the "angel from heaven" (Gal 1:8); the "Letters to the Seven Churches" in Rev 2–3; furthermore Rev 10:9–10; 14:6. In *Herm. Vis.* 2.2.1–2.3.4 a "heavenly book" is revealed, which contains a curse and a blessing. See also the studies by Rudolf Stübe, *Der Himmelsbrief* (Tübingen: Mohr, Siebeck, 1918); Klaus Berger, "Apostelbrief und apostolische Rede: Zum Formular frühchristlicher Briefe," *ZNW* 65 (1974) 190–231.

6. Traditions and Doctrinal Presuppositions

To a considerable degree, Galatians is made up of a variety of traditions and doctrinal presuppositions which have been extracted and classified in the following. They do not constitute Paul's argument itself, but are presuppositions of the argument. The letter serves as a "reminder" of these presuppositions, which Paul then uses to build his "argument" (see below §7).

I. Scripture
   A. Reference to the call of the prophets: 1:15
   B. Reference to God's impartiality: 2:6
   C. Interpretation of the Abraham tradition: 3:6–18
   D. Interpretation of the Sinai tradition: 3:19–25
   E. Interpretation of the Sarah–Hagar allegory: 4:21–31
   F. Reference to the love–command (Lev 19:18): 5:14

II. Proverbs
   A. 4:16—ἐχθρὸς ὑμῶν γέγονα ἀληθεύων ὑμῖν
   B. 4:18—καλὸν δὲ ζηλοῦσθαι ἐν καλῷ πάντοτε
   C. 5:9—μικρὰ ζύμη ὅλον τὸ φύραμα ζυμοῖ
   D. 6:7—θεὸς οὐ μυκτηρίζεται
   E. 6:7—ὃ ... ἐὰν σπείρῃ ἄνθρωπος τοῦτο καὶ θερίσει

III. Illustrations from the common law
   A. The illustration of the "testament": 3:15
   B. The illustration of legal "guardianship": 4:1–2

IV. Liturgical Material
   A. Epistolary formulae (secondary *Sitz im Leben*)
      1. Salutation: 1:3
      2. Doxology: 1:5
      3. Curse: 1:8–9
      4. Blessings: 6:16, 18
      5. Oath: 1:20
      6. Amen: 1:5; 6:18
   B. Hymnic or credal phrases and formulae
      1. Referring to God
         a. Epithets: θεὸς (καὶ) πατήρ: 1:1, 3, 4
         b. Acclamation: ἀββὰ ὁ πατήρ: 4:6
         c. Creed: ὁ θεὸς εἷς ἐστίν: 3:20
         d. Act of sending the Son: 4:4
         e. Act of raising Jesus Christ from the dead: 1:1
         f. Act of sending the Spirit: 4:6
      2. Referring to Christ
         a. The death of Christ
            1) τοῦ δόντος ἑαυτὸν ὑπὲρ τῶν ἁμαρτιῶν ἡμῶν: 1:4
            2) τοῦ ἀγαπήσαντός με καὶ παραδόντος ἑαυτὸν ὑπὲρ ἐμοῦ: 2:20
            3) Χριστὸς ... γενόμενος ὑπὲρ ἡμῶν κατάρα: 3:13
         b. The resurrection of Christ: τοῦ ἐγείραντος αὐτὸν ἐκ νεκρῶν: 1:1

      3. Referring to soteriology
         a. ὅπως ἐξέληται ἡμᾶς ἐκ τοῦ αἰῶνος τοῦ ἐνεστῶτος πονηροῦ: 1:4
         b. Χριστὸς ἡμᾶς ἐξηγόρασεν ἐκ τῆς κατάρας τοῦ νόμου γενόμενος ὑπὲρ ἡμῶν κατάρα: 3:13
         c. ὅτε δὲ ἦλθεν τὸ πλήρωμα τοῦ χρόνου, ἐξαπέστειλεν ὁ θεὸς τὸν υἱὸν αὐτοῦ, γενόμενον ἐκ γυναικός, γενόμενον ὑπὸ νόμον, ἵνα τοὺς ὑπὸ νόμον ἐξαγοράσῃ, ἵνα τὴν υἱοθεσίαν ἀπολάβωμεν: 4:4–5
   C. Christological titles
      1. ὁ κύριος: 1:3, 19; 5:10; 6:14, 18
      2. ὁ υἱὸς τοῦ θεοῦ: 1:16; 2:20; 4:4, 6
   D. Baptismal formulae
      1. A "macarism": 3:26–28
      2. A "list of vices and virtues": 5:19–23

V. Doctrinal Material
   A. From Jewish Christianity
      1. Citation of a Jewish–Christian view of Paul's conversion: 1:23–24
      2. Reference to the Jewish–Christian doctrine of Justification by Faith: 2:15–16
      3. Citation of an anti–Pauline polemic (Χριστὸς ἁμαρτίας διάκονος): 2:17
      4. Citation (?) of a Jewish–Christian (?) concept of the "Law of Christ": 6:2
      5. Citation of Jewish–Christian self–designations (?)
         a. ἡ ἐκκλησία τοῦ θεοῦ: 1:13
         b. αἱ ἐκκλησίαι τῆς Ἰουδαίας αἱ ἐν Χριστῷ: 1:22
         c. οἱ πτωχοί (?): 2:10
         d. οἱ υἱοὶ Ἀβραάμ: 3:7; cf. 3:26, 29; 4:5, 6, 28
         e. ὁ Ἰσραὴλ τοῦ θεοῦ: 6:16
      6. Citation of Jewish–Christian "titles"
         a. οἱ ἀπόστολοι: 1:17, 19; cf. 2:8
         b. ὁ ἀδελφὸς τοῦ κυρίου: 1:19
         c. οἱ στῦλοι: 2:9
   B. From the agreements made at Jerusalem
      1. Reference to the two gospels: τὸ εὐαγγέλιον τῆς ἀκροβυστίας, τὸ εὐαγγέλιον τῆς περιτομῆς: 2:7; cf. 1:6–7; 2:8–9
      2. Reference to the theological foundation of the agreements: 2:8
      3. Reference to the missionary strategy: ἡμεῖς εἰς τὰ ἔθνη, αὐτοὶ εἰς τὴν περιτομήν: 2:9; cf. 2:8
      4. Reference to the collection: 2:10
   C. From Paul's own theology
      1. Pharisaic doctrines once held and now rejected
         a. The doctrine of δικαιοσύνη: διὰ νόμου δικαιοσύνη (2:21c; 3:21b; 5:4a)
         b. The doctrine of κληρονομία: ἐκ νόμου ἡ κληρονομία (3:18a)

c. The doctrine of νόμος: ἐδόθη νόμος ὁ δυνάμενος ζῳοποιῆσαι (3:21a)

d. The doctrine of περιτομή: every circumcised man is ὀφειλέτης ... ὅλον τὸν νόμον ποιῆσαι
(5:3b; cf. 6:13a)

2. Paul's apostolic office

a. His titles

1) ἀπόστολος, with a definition :1:1; cf. 1:17

2) Χριστοῦ δοῦλος (1:10)

b. His vocation and mission

1) His "call": 1:1, 12, 15–16

2) His mission: 1:6–7, 11, 16, 23; 2:2, 5,
7, 14; 3:1–5; 4:13–14, 19; 5:8

3) His representation of Christ: 1:1, 10, 12,
16; 2:20a; 4:14; 6:14, 17b

c. The history of Paul's struggle up to the
present: 1:12–2:14; 3:1–5; 4:9–11, 12–20,
21a, 29; 5:1–6:10; 6:12–14, 17

3. Paul's definition of his gospel

a. A definition of its nature and origin:
1:11–12

b. Definitions of the content

1) The doctrine of justification by faith:
2:15–16; cf. 2:17, 21; 3:6–25; 5:5

2) The definition of the gospel as Ἰησοῦς
Χριστὸς ἐσταυρωμένος: 3:1; cf. 5:11, 24;
6:12, 14

3) The definition of the gospel as ἐλευθερία:
2:4; 5:1a, 13a; cf. 3:26–28; 4:1–10, 22, 23,
26, 30, 31

c. Definitions of Christian existence

1) Four definitions of Christian existence:
2:19–20

a) As freedom from the Torah: 2:19a;
cf. 2:4–5, 15–21; 3:1–5, 6–18, 19–25;
4:5, 21; 5:1–12; 6:13

b) As crucifixion together with Christ:
2:19b; cf. 5:24; 6:14, 17

c) As indwelling of Christ: 2:20a; cf. the
doctrine of the Spirit (see V.C.3.d.)

d) As life in faith: 2:20b; cf. the doctrine
of sonship (see below V.C.3.c.2–3)

2) Definition of Christian existence as "sonship of Abraham": 3:7, 29; 4:7, 31

3) Definition of Christian existence as "sonship of God": 3:26–28; 4:4–6, 7

4) Definition of Christian existence as that
of οἱ πνευματικοί: 6:1 (see V.C.3.d.5)

d. Definitions of the basis of Christian existence

1) References to God's will: 1:4; cf. 1:1, 15;
3:8, 18; 4:4, 6, 7, 9

2) References to christology and soteriology
(see IV.B. 2–3)

3) References to πίστις: 3:2, 5, 23, 25

4) References to the proclamation of the
gospel (see V.C.2.b)

5) References to the gift of the Spirit: 3:2,
3, 5, 14; 4:6, 29; 5:5, 16, 17, 18, 22–23, 25;
6:1, 8, 18

6) References to the "putting on of Christ"
in baptism: 3:27

7) References to eschatological "hope":
5:5; cf. 1:4; 2:15–16, 19 [ἵνα θεῷ ζήσω];
6:7–9

e. The manifestations of Christian existence

1) References to Paul himself and his experiences: 1:1, 10–11, 12, 13–2:14, 15–16,
19–20; 4:12–20; 5:10–11; 6:14, 17

2) References to the Galatians' experiences:
3:1–5, 26–28; 4:1–10, 12–15; 5:1a, 5–6, 7a,
13a, 18a, 19–23, 25a

f. Guide–lines for Christian existence in the
future ("exhortation")

1) The "canon": 6:15; cf. 5:6

2) The rebuttal against the opponents:
5:2–12; cf. 2:3–5; 2:17–18, 21; 6:12–13

3) Exhortation against the temptations of
the "flesh": 5:13–24

4) Exhortation to "follow the Spirit":
5:25–6:10

a) A series of gnomic sentences: 5:25–6:6

b) An eschatological warning: 6:7–9

c) A general ethical rule: 6:10

4. Theological "Abbreviations"

The letter contains a considerable number of brief
expressions, most of them prepositional phrases. All
of them are abbreviations of theological doctrines.
Their origin is unknown, but they can be most likely
explained as coming from the oral transmission of
Paul's theology.

δι' ἀγάπης: 5:6; 5:13: διὰ τῆς ἀγάπης

ἐξ ἀκοῆς πίστεως: 3:2, 5

ἀπ' ἀνθρώπων: 1:1

δι' ἀνθρώπου: 1:1

κατὰ ἄνθρωπον: 1:11; 3:15

παρ' ἀνθρώπου: 1:12

δι' ἀποκαλύψεως: 1:12

κατὰ ἀποκάλυψιν: 2:2

εἰς δικαιοσύνην: 3:6

δι' ἐπαγγελίας: 3:18 (cf. 4:23)

ἐξ ἐπαγγελίας: 3:18

κατ' ἐπαγγελίαν: 3:29

ἐξ ἔργων νόμου: 2:16; 3:2, 5, 10

κατὰ τὸ θέλημα τοῦ θεοῦ: 1:4

διὰ θεοῦ: 1:1; 4:7

ἐνώπιον τοῦ θεοῦ: 1:20

ἐν κυρίῳ: 5:10

διὰ νόμου: 2:19, 21

ἐκ νόμου: 3:18, 21

ἐν νόμῳ: 3:11, 21; 5:4; cf. 2:19: νόμῳ
ὑπὸ νόμον: 3:23; 4:4, 5, 21; 5:18; cf. 3:25: ὑπὸ
   παιδαγωγόν
ἐκ περιτομῆς: 2:12
διὰ (τῆς) πίστεως: 2:16; 3:14, 26
ἐκ πίστεως: 2:16; 3:7, 8, 9, 11, 12, 22, 24; 5:5
ἐν πίστει: 2:20
πνεύματι: 3:3; 5:5, 16, 18, 25
ἐκ πνεύματος: 6:8
κατὰ πνεῦμα: 4:29
(τῇ) σαρκί: 3:3; 5:13; 6:12; cf. 1:16: σαρκὶ καὶ
   αἵματι
ἐκ τῆς σαρκός: 6:8
ἐν σαρκί: 2:20; 4:14; 6:13
κατὰ σάρκα: 4:23, 29
διὰ τῆς χάριτος: 1:15
ἐν χάριτι: 1:6
διὰ Ἰησοῦ Χριστοῦ: 1:1; cf. 6:14: δι' οὗ ἐν Χριστῷ
   (Ἰησοῦ): 1:22; 2:4, 17; 3:14, 26, 28; 5:6

7. The Theological Argument in Galatians

It took the movement which began with Jesus of
Nazareth only a generation to rush through the world
of both the Jews and the gentiles and to establish itself
as a separate and self–conscious new religion. In our
judgment today, Paul's letter to the Galatians is one of
the earliest documents testifying to this development.
To the early Christians themselves, however, these
developments were far from clear. The separation of
the new movement from the mother religion, Judaism,
was a painful struggle which preoccupied Christianity
for a long time. Only in retrospect did it become clear
that a new religion had entered the scene of history.[130]
The letter to the Galatians also documents another
fact: already at this early stage the Christian movement
was confronted with a crisis of the most serious nature.

While the apostle Paul had been the pioneer of expansion, he was not spared the disappointment of
seeing the validity, legitimacy, and viability of his
gospel message questioned by his own converts to the
Christian faith. Paul's letter to the Galatians is the
historic document which testifies to the first radical
questioning of the Pauline gospel by Christians themselves. Hence it presents the first systematic apology of
Christianity,[131] not to outsiders, but to Christians
themselves. In Galatians Paul defends what he calls
"the truth of the gospel."[132]

What does he mean by this expression, and what is
the goal of his defense? Most commentaries argue that
the Apostle defends his apostolic office and his gospel.
The literary analysis has shown that he defends primarily his gospel,[133] that is, "the gospel of uncircumcision."[134] This gospel is of course intimately connected
with his own vocation and apostolic office, so that his
apostolic authority depends entirely upon the outcome
of the defense of his gospel. But how can the Pauline
gospel be defended? In his defense Paul goes directly to
the root of the matter. As his strategy of defense he has
chosen to defend the gift of the Spirit to the Galatians.[135] At first sight, this strategy seems hazardous, if
not absurd. Nevertheless, in the final analysis Paul's
strategy must be judged as highly skillful, well–conceived, and in the terms of his time, successful.[136]
Paul had preached among the Galatians the same
gospel he had preached and was still preaching among
all the gentiles.[137] The Galatians had heard and
accepted the message.[138] They had become Christian
believers and had been baptized.[139] They had come to
regard themselves as "sons of God,"[140] as "people

---

130 For this development see my contribution "The
     Rise of Christianity: B. From the Greek Side," in
     The Cambridge History of Judaism (Cambridge:
     Cambridge University, [forthcoming]).

131 See on this subject my lecture "In Defense of the
     Spirit: Paul's Letter to the Galatians as a Document
     of Early Christian Apologetics," in *Aspects of Reli-
     gious Propaganda in Judaism and Early Christianity* (ed.
     Elisabeth Schüssler Fiorenza; Notre Dame: Univer-
     sity of Notre Dame, 1976) 99–114.

132 The notion occurs in Gal 2:5, 14.

133 See the analysis in § 5 above, esp. sections I B; D 2;
     II C.2 a; 4 b 2; IV; VII B.

134 See Gal 2:7; also 1:6; 5:6; 6:15.

135 For Paul's doctrine of the Spirit in Gal, see 3:2.

136 This should not be taken to mean that we have any
     information about the result of Paul's argument
     among the Galatians. The bare fact that primitive
     Christianity found the letter worth preserving is
     about the only indication as to how they felt in re-
     gard to Paul's argument. For an excellent discussion
     of this point see Vielhauer, *Geschichte*, 125.

137 See 1:16; 2:2; 4:13.

138 See 1:6–9; 3:1–5.

139 See 3:27.

140 See 3:26; also 3:7; 4:6–7.

belonging to Christ,"[141] and as "heirs" of God's promised salvation.[142] All of this was made possible by the divine gift of the Spirit. Most likely the Galatians had experienced this gift of the Spirit in the form of an ecstatic manifestation.[143] On account of this experience they seemed to have regarded themselves as "the people of the Spirit" (οἱ πνευματικοί),[144] a self–designation which betrays high religious claims and expectations.

The concept which best sums up the Galatians' basic self–understanding is the concept of "freedom" (ἐλευθερία).[145] To them the Christian faith meant that the age–old dream of human freedom had become a reality. For them "freedom" was not merely a theological notion, but they regarded themselves as free from "this evil world" with its repressive social, religious, and cultural laws and conventions. They had left behind the cultural and social distinctions between Greeks and non–Greeks, the religious distinctions between Jews and non–Jews, the social systems of slavery and the subordination of women. They had overcome their "ignorance of God," and their barbaric superstition. These Galatians were no longer the "hicks" of that rough and ungovernable area in central Anatolia. They were the avant–garde, a "new creation" (καινὴ κτίσις). All these accomplishments, Paul reminds the Galatians, make up their μακαρισμός ("blessing").[146]

Opening the door to the anti–Pauline opposition implied that the Galatians had come to doubt the validity, legitimacy, and viability of Paul's version of Christianity.[147] As we have seen, this doubt was most probably the result of the end of the initial enthusiasm and of problems with the "flesh." When "transgressions" had occurred in their community they found themselves unprepared to deal with them. Paul's opponents, however, had the means which seemed to be adequate and effective: Torah and circumcision. The Christian faith coupled with the safeguards provided by the Jewish religion appeared to be a better way to protect the new Christian life from deterioration and destruction than Paul's concept of "freedom."

For Paul to present his defense of the gospel as a defense of the Spirit seems to be at once logical and absurd. The Spirit was believed by early Christians to be God's self–manifestation among and within human beings. This Spirit is by definition outside of human control.[148] It cannot be manipulated or averted. "The wind blows where it wills, and you hear the sound of it, but you do not know whence it comes and whither it goes; so it is with everyone who is born of the Spirit."[149] But how can this Spirit be defended? As an ecstatic experience, any experience of the Spirit is by definition irrational, that is, it is not subject to rational control and comprehensions. An attempt to defend such an irrational phenomenon by the means of a rational argument appears absurd. Still, this is precisely Paul's strategy of defense.

Paul's approach provides him with a number of strategic advantages which he would have had difficulty obtaining in other ways. (1) The *factum* to be defended is identical with the experience of the "jury," the Galatians. Paul is thus able to discuss the issues in terms of the Galatians' own experience. He can call upon them as first-hand witnesses who hold the evidence in their own hands.[150] (2) Paul can avoid casting himself in the haughty and unconvincing position of an expert and authority figure who explains the inexplicable to the ignorant. Instead he can appeal to the Galatians as experts in matters of the Spirit.[151] (3) By speaking in terms of the Spirit, Paul can appeal to reason—not only the common–sense reason basic to all arguments, but to that "reason" which is especially

141 See 3:28, 29; 5:24.
142 See 3:29; 4:1, 7, 30.
143 See 3:2, 5.
144 See 6:1.
145 See 2:4–5; 4:22–31; 5:1, 13.
146 It should be noted that Paul's concept of freedom in Gal has a strange parallel in the *Gospel of Philip* from Nag Hammadi. See Kurt Niederwimmer, "Die Freiheit des Gnostikers nach dem Philippusevangelium. Eine Untersuchung zum Thema: Kirche und Gnosis," in *Verborum Veritas: Festschrift für Gustav Stählin zum 70. Geburtstag* (Wuppertal; Brockhaus, 1970) 361–74.
147 For the opponents, see this Introduction, § 2.C.
148 On the notion of "spirit" see Geo Widengren, *Religionsphänomenologie* (Berlin: de Gruyter, 1969) 111–13.
149 John 3:8.
150 See 3:1–5.
151 See 4:21–31; 6:1.

endowed by the Spirit. The Galatians' claim to possess the Spirit forces them to expose themselves to rational arguments. At this point, Paul is then able to activate and utilize the full forces of "the art of persuasion."[152]

As an argument, Paul's defense assumes that "the truth of the gospel" can be defended by rational logic. This approach, in terms of ancient thought, included both discursive thinking and the arsenal of rhetorical devices provided by Greco–Roman rhetoric, "the art of persuasion." As we have discussed previously,[153] "the art of rhetoric" was considered to be irreconcilably opposed to the discussion of theological "truth" questions. The composition of Galatians has shown that Paul was aware of this limitation and had found ways to overcome it.[154] Nevertheless, Paul does have room for rational arguments. As a matter of fact, the body of the letter contains nothing but one strictly rational argument.[155] Of course one must keep in mind that Paul's rationality is conditioned by his time and its intellectual traditions and conventions. "Logic" is certainly not above historical relativity! The fact that Paul enters into a rational argument does not imply a failure on Paul's part to realize the problematic nature of such an approach, nor does it imply a contradiction of his own principles. The composition of the letter shows that he first provides a theological basis for his rational argument, and then lets the argument take its course. Certainly Paul was more than a rhetorician.[156] Defending the "truth of the gospel" requires making room for an irrational phenomenon par excellence, the defense of the Spirit. Paul demonstrates by the way he deals with this phenomenon that he is a theologian, one who is able to handle irrational phenomena in terms of rational thought. His major arguments can be summarized[157] as follows:

1. The most important argument, which runs through the entire letter, is the argument of *experience*. In terms of force, this is an argument of undeniable evidence and authority, belonging to what the rhetoricians called the *genus inartificiale*. In 3:1–5 he uses the interrogative method and forces the readers to admit as witnesses that they themselves experienced the Spirit without having done any "works of the Torah." Therefore, "works of the Torah" cannot have been a precondition for their salvation in Christ, a fact which is contrary to what the anti-Pauline opposition now wants the Galatians to accept. This argument is backed up by the subservient argument of historical consistency and inconsistency. Paul makes this argument especially in the *narratio* section (1:13–2:14), demonstrating that the Galatians' experience of salvation has happened outside of normal expectation, but that this role of the outsider has always been the trademark of Christianity. The opponents are doubtless correct: what happened to the Galatians should never have happened.[158] Yet it did happen. The same is true of the Christian faith as such. Salvation in Christ should never have happened according to normal Jewish standards, but it did happen through God's resurrection of Jesus, whose death on the cross God accepted as a propitiatory self–sacrifice.[159] Paul's own conversion to the Christian faith and his call to apostleship should, by human standards, never have occurred. But through God's grace it did occur.[160] The gospel which Paul preached should, by normal standards, never have been recognized as valid. But it was officially approved even by the authorities of the church in Jerusalem—Peter, James, and John.[161] Jewish Christians should never have agreed to establish table-fellowship with gentile Christians, but it was done at Antioch under the leadership of Peter himself.[162] In sum: the role of the "outsider" and the appearance of "illegitimacy" has always been the mark of Christianity. It is the way God works in his-

---

152 See Günther Bornkamm, "Glaube und Vernunft bei Paulus," in his *Studien zu Antike und Urchristentum*, vol. 2 of his *Gesammelte Aufsätze* (BEvTh 28; Munich: Kaiser, 1959) 119–37.

153 See this Introduction, § 5.

154 On Gal as a magical letter and as, in a sense, a "heavenly" letter, see this Introduction, § 5.

155 See this Introduction, § 5.

156 Cf. Paul's denials in 1:10.

157 For more discussion, see the commentary on the passages mentioned.

158 See the phrase εἰς κενὸν τρέχω ("I run in vain," 2:2); and the term εἰκῇ ("in vain," 3:4; 4:11).

159 For the christology of Gal, see this Introduction, § 6 (IV.B.2–4).

160 See 1:13–24.

161 See 2:1–10.

162 See 2:11–14.

tory.[163] This shows that the Galatians' experience of the Spirit, and hence the manifestations of God's salvation among them, was consistent with God's work. It was granted against human expectation, in disregard of human standards, without human merits —by grace alone,[164] as "new creation" (καινὴ κτίσις 6:15c).

The other side of this argument is, as Paul points out, the inconsistency of the opponents. It began at Jerusalem, when the "false brothers" (i.e., Jewish Christians opposed to Paul's mission to the gentiles) demanded that gentile Christians submit to the Jewish ritual of circumcision as a sign of obedience to the Torah.[165] At Antioch Cephas first had table fellowship with gentile Christians, but then he reversed himself when an oppositional delegation ("the men from James") arrived and criticized him. Cephas and other Jewish–Christian missionaries, but not Paul, "withdrew" from the table fellowship. Doubtless this withdrawal from fellowship with other Christians served to uphold the Jewish dietary and purity laws, an act which Paul termed "hypocrisy."[166] The anti–Pauline opposition at work in Galatia[167] denied in the name of Christ that "faith in Christ" is sufficient for salvation and demanded submission to the Jewish ritual of circumcision and the observance of the Jewish Torah. In addition to this inconsistency, they made such demands without applying the same standards to themselves. The inconsistencies of the opponents are summed up in Paul's question to Cephas: "If you, being a Jew, live like a gentile and not like a Jew, how can you compel the gentiles to live like Jews?"[168] Or as Paul points out in the *propositio*,[169] the Jewish Christians, although born as Jews, had become believers in Christ because they had come to recognize that Jewish "works of the Torah" would not lead to their justification before God; it makes no sense to demand submission to a Jewish ritual by non–Jews who have also become believers in Christ.[170] And yet this is precisely the demand that the anti–Pauline opposition was making.[171]

2. The second major argument is proof from Scripture. In 3:6–14, 18 especially, Paul interprets the Abraham tradition in order to show that God made his promise to Abraham and his offspring as those who "believe" instead of as those who are circumcised observers of the Torah. What rabbinic tradition held together, Paul rigorously separates: Abraham was a "believer"[172] but he knew neither Torah nor circumcision because the Torah only came 430 years later.[173] The sons of the "believer" Abraham are the Christians who believe like Abraham. The dualistic wedge between the "believers" and the "observers of the Torah" is then translated as the juxtaposition of the people "according to the Spirit" and the people "according to the flesh," a juxtaposition found in Paul's interpretation of the Sarah–Hagar allegory.[174] Again, Paul separates what Judaism joined together: possession of the Spirit and observance of the Torah. While the Abraham tradition shows that circumcision and observance of the Torah are not necessary preconditions for the promise of God's salvation, the Sarah–Hagar allegory shows that the fulfillment of God's promise, the gift of the Spirit, is irreconcilably opposed to the observance of the Torah. Instead of making the gift of the Spirit complete and perfect by the acceptance of circumcision and Torah, as the opponents most likely wanted to have it, Paul contends that the former is destroyed by the latter.[175]

3. Between these powerful arguments, Paul has inserted an excursus on the Torah[176] which supports the argument made by the interpretation of the Abraham tradition. Four "definitions" of the Torah (see on 3:19) prove that God himself did not intend the

---

163 See the references to God's will in 1:4; 1:15–16; also 1:1; 3:6–8, 17, 18, 22–25; 4:4, 7, 21–23; 6:7, 16.

164 For the doctrine of "grace" see 1:6, 15; 2:9, 21; 5:4.

165 2:4–5.

166 2:11–14.

167 See this Introduction, § 2.C.

168 2:14.

169 2:15–16.

170 2:17–18.

171 6:12–13.

172 3:6–13.

173 3:17.

174 4:21–31.

175 See 5:1–6; cf. also 2:5, 21; 3:3–5; 4:9–11.

176 3:19–25.

Torah to be a precondition of salvation. Instead its true purpose was to make salvation by grace necessary.

4. Following the excursus on the Torah, Paul presents a "reminder," in which he recalls what the Galatians were told at baptism and what they then accepted as their state of salvation. Since the composition in 3:26–28, which is most probably quoted from the baptismal liturgy, attributes to the gentile Galatians the blessings of the divine salvation without Torah and circumcision, the Galatians' acceptance of the doctrines of the anti–Pauline opposition would necessitate revoking those statements and thus cancelling the very foundation of their existence as Christian converts. Such a step would, in effect, imply turning away from the Christian faith to Judaism, that is, to a pre-Christian situation and thereby to a situation equal to paganism.[177]

5. An argument which is not so heavy and more emotional, but no less effective, is the string of friendship *topoi* in 4:12–20. Again, it is introduced as a "reminder," recalling to the Galatians the time when Paul first came to them and brought them the gospel. He reminds his churches of the extraordinary sacrifices they would have made on his behalf and of the untroubled good relationships they have so far enjoyed. A friendship which has lasted and which has withstood temptations should not be broken lightly. Paul does not hesitate to point out in very emotional terms what this friendship means to him, and what the consequences of its end would be for him as well as for them.

6. The final argument, and the cutting edge of the letter, is identical with Paul's exhortation and with his theory of ethics.[178] The central concept of this argument is freedom.[179] This notion of freedom also underlies the other parts of the letter, but only in the "exhortation" is it fully used as an argumentative weapon. If the Galatians' situation can be described as freedom, this situation should not be taken for granted. The Galatians' freedom is not a state of deprivation in the sense that they lack something important which they ought to have. Freedom exists only for people who have been enabled to be free. In the case of the Galatians, it was Christ who liberated them.[180] Moreover, the Spirit which is identical with Christ's Spirit[181] has enabled them to shake off the forms of "slavery" and to accomplish all the changes of which at one time they were so proud.[182] The opponents cannot understand an existence in freedom because they themselves have never been liberated from their slavery and have not been given the chance to exist in freedom. To them Paul's notion of freedom appears as a dangerous lack of the protection without which no one can survive in this evil world. To them such freedom means libertinism, naked exposure of frail human beings to the multiple attacks of the forces of evil.[183]

According to Paul, "freedom in Christ" is a gift of God, but a delicate one. It is a gift, but it is not to be taken for granted. Freedom exists only insofar as people live in freedom. Freedom is given only as a task, and this task is nothing but the preservation of freedom.[184] How can freedom be preserved? It is at this point that Paul applies his dialectic of "indicative" and "imperative."[185] According to Paul, it is hopeless and fruitless to expect the preservation of freedom by those who are not free themselves. It is fully understandable why the opponents have recommended ending that freedom and coming under the yoke of the Torah.[186] If the Galatians' "freedom in Christ" is to be preserved, it can be done only by the same means by which their freedom was created: the work of Christ and the Spirit. Those who were liberated by the Spirit can protect their freedom only by "walking by the Spirit," by "being led by the Spirit," and by "following the Spirit."[187]

If the Galatians have problems with their life in the "freedom of Christ," they should not expect solutions from people who neither share nor understand that

---

177 4:8–10.

178 5:1–6:10.

179 See above, n. 145, and § 2.A.

180 1:4; 4:5; 5:1, 13.

181 4:6.

182 4:15.

183 Cf. 2:4–5; 4:17; 5:7–12; 6:12–13.

184 See 5:1b, 13b; cf. 2:4–5; 4:9–11.

185 For this terminology, see the commentary on 5:25, n. 9.

186 See 2:5; 4:9; 5:1b; 6:12. But nothing concretely is said about the opponents' real motives.

187 5:16, 18, 25.

freedom. Instead, they should rely on the same forces that liberated them in the first place. The way of the opponents does not secure their salvation in Christ, but destroys it by replacing it with the Jewish concept of salvation. Up to this point Paul's argument is consistent and not too difficult to understand. [188] But the final test of his argument is his own theory of ethics, which spells out how the Galatians should solve their problems with freedom by relying on freedom. [189]

We must realize that Paul's ethics is quite unlike the common Greek and Roman philosophical ethics of this period. He does not share the philosophical concept of the Logos dwelling in the human soul, nor does he advocate the process of education ($\pi\alpha\iota\delta\epsilon\acute{\iota}\alpha$) by which human life is developed from raw nature to ethical and psychological refinement, with the "virtues" as the ethical ideals in this educational process. Paul's ethics is also unlike the Jewish ethical concept of obedience to the Torah, which has a historical-mythical foundation and functions basically as a system of religious rituals, with ethics being more a by-product than the primary objective.

In Paul's ethics, the good and the evil figure as manifestations of forces operating in human life. These forces and their manifestations are conditioned historically. This means that human life is conditioned in different ways for different people. For the Christian community, manifestations of the good occur as part of the process of divine salvation. The decisive events of the past are Christ's meritorious self-sacrifice and death on the cross and his resurrection from the dead. At the same time, Paul understands the entire "Christ event" as a historical-mythical manifestation of the good. [190] The Christian participates in this event as a member of the church community. In baptism, every Christian learns that all Christians "have put on Christ" and that all are "one with Christ." [191] This unity between the Christian community and the process of divine redemption rests in the presence of the Spirit among and

within the members of the Christian community. This Spirit makes the "Christ event" a present reality by letting manifestations of the good occur. These manifestations Paul calls the "fruit of the Spirit." [192] They include: "Love, joy, peace, magnanimity, kindness, goodness, faithfulness, humility, self-control." Although Paul, with the exception of love ($\dot{\alpha}\gamma\acute{\alpha}\pi\eta$), uses the conventional terms of Greek philosophical ethics, they do not represent "virtues" in the traditional sense, but "manifestations" of divine redemption. They occur in the Christian community as manifestations of Christ's presence in the church by means of the Spirit. The individual Christians participate in them as members of the "body of Christ" and "people of the Spirit" ($o\dot{\iota}\ \pi\nu\epsilon\upsilon\mu\alpha\tau\iota\kappa o\acute{\iota}$). Having been given the Spirit and having been seized by it, they become agents through whom the "fruit of the Spirit" manifests itself. [193] The set of three times three manifestations of the Spirit, [194] with "love" ($\dot{\alpha}\gamma\acute{\alpha}\pi\eta$) at the beginning and "self-control" ($\dot{\epsilon}\gamma\kappa\rho\acute{\alpha}\tau\epsilon\iota\alpha$) at the end, represents perfection and completeness. Where all these manifestations occur, they "fill out" the life of the church as well as of the individual Christian. There is no room left for the opposite, the manifestations of evil ("the works of the flesh"). [195]

Paul's ethics is, in the final analysis, quite simple. The Christian is asked to let the "fruit of the Spirit" happen. The "virtues" are there to manifest themselves and the Christian is enabled to allow this. As they occur, evil and its chaos have no room. The connection between this concept of ethics and the notion of freedom is also clear: the "fruit of the Spirit" and its virtues are at the same time manifestations of freedom. Where they occur no law is required. [196] No law can force people to bring them about. If they occur it is because people let them occur voluntarily. Therefore, Paul is quite logical when he sums up his argument in the *peroratio*: "Circumcision is nothing; uncircumcision is nothing; the only thing that counts is new creation!" [197]

---

188 See 2:18, 21; 5:2, 4.
189 Paul's ethics can here be only summarized; for discussion of individual points, see the commentary on 5:1–6:10.
190 See above, n. 159.
191 See on 3:26–28.

192 See on 5:22–23.
193 See also on 5:6, 13–14; 6:1, 8–10.
194 5:22–23.
195 See 5:16–17.
196 See 2:19–21; 5:6, 18, 23–24.
197 6:15 (*NEB*); cf. 2:3; 5:6.

Galatians

1

1   Paul,[1] an apostle not from men nor
through [a?] man,[2] but through[3] Jesus
Christ and God the Father who raised
him from the dead, 2/ and all the
brothers who are with me,[4] to the
churches of Galatia: 3/ Grace be to you
and peace from God our Father and
(our) Lord Jesus Christ, 4/ who gave
himself up[5] for our sins, in order that
he might rescue us[6] from the present
evil age, according to the will of our
God and Father, 5/ to whom be the
glory for ever and ever. Amen.

Analysis

The epistolary prescript of the Galatian letter can be
recognized easily and then separated from the letter. It
is also interesting that at several points there are interrelations between the preface and the body of the letter.
It is at these points that the theological tendencies and
the purpose of the letter can be observed.[7] The basic
pattern of the prescript is the same as in other Pauline
letters, the sequence of *superscriptio*, *adscriptio*, and
salutatio.[8] This pattern has been called "oriental" in
character and origin, but the Hellenistic and even
Pauline developments should not be overlooked.[9] The
Galatian prescript shows several expansions, notably at
the very points where we also find close relationships
between the prescript and various other parts of the
body of the letter: the title and its definition (1:1), and
the christological-soteriological statements (1:4).

Interpretation

■1 At the beginning of the letter stands the name of the
principal sender, Paul.[10] As he usually does in his
epistolary prefaces, he gives only his Roman surname.
Provided that the information is reliable,[11] we know
from Acts that his Jewish name was Saul (Hebrew:
שָׁאוּל, Greek: Σαῦλος, Σαούλ). The name is followed by

1   *NEB*, *JB* have "from Paul," signifying Paul as the
sender. Note that *JB*'s paraphrase destroys the careful composition of the prescript.

2   *NEB* paraphrases: "not by human appointment or
human commission. . . ."

3   *NEB* paraphrases: "by commission from Jesus
Christ. . . ."

4   Cf. *NEB*: "I and the group of friends now with me
send greetings. . . ." This paraphrase has changed
the text and has assimilated it to Greek style and
culture.

5   *NEB*, *JB* have "sacrificed himself"—a correct interpretation.

6   So *NEB*, *JB*; cf. *RSV*: "deliver."

7   See Hans Dieter Betz, "Composition," 353–79, esp.
355–56.

8   For the bib. on the subject, see Conzelmann, *1 Corinthians*, 19 nn. 6, 7. In addition, see Joseph A. Fitzmyer, "Some Notes on Aramaic Epistolography,"
JBL 93 (1974) 201–25; Klaus Berger, "Apostelbrief und apostolische Rede: Zum Formular frühchristlicher Briefe," *ZNW* 65 (1974) 190–231, esp.
191–207; Vielhauer, *Geschichte*, 64–66.

9   The formal similarity between the Galatian preface,
esp. vv 3–5, and Rev 1:4b–6 shows that Paul did
not create the pattern. Certainly the prescript of
Rev is not based on Gal 1. (So also Nils A. Dahl, in
a letter dated July 19, 1974.)

10   See Str–B 3.1; Bauer, *s.v.* Παῦλος, 2; Σαούλ, 2;
Σαῦλος; Bornkamm, *Paul*, 3f.

11   Acts 13:9: "Saul who is also called Paul." The
author of Acts does not betray where he received
this information. See G. A. Harrer, "Saul who is
also called Paul," *HTR* 33 (1940) 19–33; Henry
Cadbury, *The Book of Acts in History* (London: Black,
1955) 69ff; Haenchen, *Acts*, on 13:9; Christoph
Burchard, *Der driezehnte Zeuge*, (FRLANT 103; Göttingen: Vandenhoeck & Ruprecht, 1970); Karl
Löning, *Die Saulustradition in der Apostelgeschichte*
(NTAbh NF 9; Münster: Aschendorff, 1973) *passim*.

the official title, without the article: [12] ἀπόστολος ("apostle"). [13] The genitive Χριστοῦ Ἰησοῦ ("of Christ Jesus") found elsewhere is missing here. [14] Instead the title is supplemented, no doubt purposefully, by a carefully composed definition of the concept of apostle. [15] The definition itself is composed of a negative and a positive part. The negative[16] part denies twice[17] that Paul's apostleship is human in origin and nature: it is not "from men" nor "through [a?] man." [18] While these statements use nouns only, the positive part uses also a verb which describes God's raising of Jesus Christ from the dead (see 1:4; 1:11–16a). Parallels connected with the call of the prophet[19] in the Hebrew tradition and the poet[20] in Greek tradition suggest that the definition has a history. Lack of sources prevents a clear decision whether the definition itself came from a tradition or whether Paul himself made it up. Parallels also suggest that the definition has a connection with the motif of

12 It is difficult to say whether or not a comma should be placed before or after "apostle." Theodor Zahn, *Der Brief des Paulus an die Galater* (KNT 9; Leipzig: Deichert, 1905; ³1922) 34 n. 2; Schlier, 26 n. 2; Mussner, p. 43; cf. 45, prefer it before "apostle" and consider the entire following passage an apposition belonging to the name. Nestle–Aland has it after "apostle."

13 On the notion of "apostle," see the excursus below on Gal 1:17.

14 Cf. 1 Cor 1:1; 2 Cor 1:1. Eph 1:1; Col 1:1; 1 Tim 1:1; 2 Tim 1:1; Titus 1:1 are imitations of the Pauline style.

15 This particular definition is unique in Paul. Other, similar statements occur in Rom 1:1–5; 1 Cor 1:1; 2 Cor 1:1. The definition of Galatians seems to be imitated by the ps.–Pauline *Epistle to the Laodiceans*: Paulus apostolus non ab hominibus neque per hominem, sed per Ihesum Christum, fratribus ("Paul the apostle not from men nor through [a?] man, but through Jesus Christ, to the brothers"). See HSW, *NT Apocrypha* 2. 128ff.

16 Cf. the parallel statements in Gal 1:11, 12. *CMC* 60.18–23 quotes Gal 1:1 in a combination with 2 Cor 12:2–5; Gal 1:11–12.

17 Since the double negation is found also in Amos 7:14, the question is whether a sharp distinction should be made between ἀπ᾽ ἀνθρώπων ("from men") and δι᾽ ἀνθρώπου ("through [a?] man"). See Burton; Hans Lietzmann, *An die Galater* (HNT 10; Tübingen: Mohr, Siebeck, ⁴1971); Oepke; Schlier. Zahn has suggested that the references point to different concrete personalities, a suggestion taken up by Mussner, p. 45. The formulaic character does not necessarily exclude this possibility.

18 ἄνθρωπος ("man, human being") signifies the sphere of the human in general (see Gal 1:10, 11, 12; 2:6; 3:15), in contrast to the divine revelation ἀπὸ θεοῦ ("from God"). For the latter see 1:3, and various combinations with the preposition διά ("through") in 1:1, 12; 4:7; 6:14.

19 An early parallel is Amos 7:14–15: "I am no prophet (נביא) nor am I a prophet's son, for I am a herdsman. . . . But the Lord took me. . . ." Cf. also Jer 1:5–6 (see on Gal 1:15); 14:14; 23:16, 21, 26, 31–32; 1 Kgs 22:1–38. In Philo *Virt.* 63, Moses states in regard to himself: "I did not of my own free–will choose to superintend and preside over public affairs, nor did I receive the office through appointment by some other of mankind, but when God by plain oracles . . . made clear to me His will. . . ." See also *Mos.* 1.175, 201, 277, 281, 286; *Her.* 69, 74, 85, 265; *Spec.* 1.65, 315; 4.50–52; *L.A.* 3.28–31, 32–33, 36, 41, 43; *Mig.* 22. From the NT, see Mark 6:1–6, par.; 11:30–33. See Hermann Schult, "Amos 7:15a und die Legitimation des Aussenseiters," in *Probleme biblischer Theologie: Gerhard von Rad zum 70. Geburtstag* (ed. Hans Walter Wolff; Munich: Kaiser, 1971) 462–78. It is noteworthy that much later, R. Hanina ben Dosa has applied Amos 7:14 to himself in connection with a miracle *b. Ber.* 34b; cf. Str–B 3.13.

20 See Hesiod *Theog.* 21–34; *Erga* 1–10. On the subject, see Kurt Latte, "Hesiods Dichterweihe," in his *Kleine Schriften* (Munich: Beck, 1968) 60–75; Herwig Maehler, *Die Auffassung des Dichterberufs im frühen Griechentum bis zur Zeit Pindars*, Hypomnemata 3 (Göttingen: Vandenhoeck & Ruprecht, 1963) 19f, 32, 41, 45. The subject was often treated, e.g., by Plato *Ion* 534E, who defines inspired poems in this way: "that these fine poems are not human nor the work of men, but divine and the work of Gods." Implied is of course that the poems are not the poet's own work. See also Lucian *Hes.* 4; Dio Chrys. *Or.* 77/78.1 (see A. Mussies, *Dio Chrysostom and the New Testament* [SCHNT 2; Leiden: Brill, 1972] on Gal 1:12); 1.10, 57f; 12.23; 36.35; 55.1f.

the self-defense for the "outsider."[21] At any rate, the Apostle himself provides further explanation of how the definition must be understood in Gal 1:12–16.

Frequently, the definition in 1:1 has been used to reconstruct the charge made against Paul by his opponents. The charge would criticize Paul because his apostolic office is human in nature and origin and, because of this, inferior compared with that of the other apostles. Hence, it is concluded that they claim a right to supervise and control the apostle Paul.[22] This method of reconstructing the charge is, however, questionable. Formally, the charge against Paul is contained in Gal 2:17. From the anti–Pauline *Kerygmata Petrou* (see Appendix 3, below), we know that this opposition criticized Paul because he had "only" a vision but no personal contact with the historical Jesus. Notably Acts has avoided such criticism by letting Paul have both a vision and personal, direct contacts with the Jerusalem and the Damascus churches.

The positive, second part is constructed as a chiasm[23] and refers to the two[24] authorities approving Paul's apostleship: ἀλλὰ διὰ ᾽Ιησοῦ Χριστοῦ[25] καὶ θεοῦ πατρός ("but through Jesus Christ and God the Father").[26] "Through Jesus Christ" stands juxtaposed with "through [a] man" as "God the Father" is contrasted with "through men."[27]

The relationship between Christ and God is defined by a christological formula stating that God raised Christ from the dead. Since Jesus' crucifixion is not expressly mentioned, one may call this phrase a "resurrection formula."[28] It occurs only here in Galatians, but it has parallels elsewhere in Paul.[29] Paul does not spell out here how his apostleship is related to Christ's resurrection. At any rate, the Christ who appeared to him (1:12, 16) is the resurrected Christ.[30]

■ 2 As the Apostle does in most of his other letters,[31]

21 Cf. Socrates in Plato *Apol.* 20E, who explains how he came to believe that his wisdom is more than human (κατ᾽ ἄνθρωπον): "for the word which I speak is not mine. . . . For of my wisdom—if it is wisdom at all—and of its nature, I will offer you the god of Delphi as a witness." He goes on telling the story about the oracle given to Chairemon at Delphi. Cf. also Ignatius' compliment about a bishop (Ign. *Phld.* 1): "not from himself, nor through men" (οὐκ ἀφ᾽ ἑαυτοῦ οὐδὲ δι᾽ ἀνθρώπων).

22 Differently, Mussner, pp. 46f.

23 John Bligh (*Galatians: A Discussion of St. Paul's Epistle* [Householder Commentaries 1; London: St. Paul, 1969] 61f) suggests that because of the chiasm the preposition "from" should be supplemented before "God the Father" as in 1:3. This arbitrariness is characteristic of Bligh's method in general; cf. my review in *JBL* 89 (1970) 126f. Paul can use other phrases like "through God" (Gal 4:7), "through his grace" (1:15), "through his will" (1 Cor 1:1; 2 Cor 1:1; Rom 15:32; also cf. 2 Cor 8:5).

24 Paul intends to underscore his appointment as an apostle by God and Christ. Cf. also Gal 1:15–16; 4:14; Rom 15:15–16; 2 Cor 5:20. See Gerhard Delling, "Zusammengesetzte Gottes– und Christusbezeichnungen in den Paulusbriefen," in his *Studien*, 417–24.

25 διὰ ᾽Ιησοῦ Χριστοῦ ("through Jesus Christ") is an abbreviation used elsewhere in Paul, but in prescripts it is found only here and in Rom 1:5 (δι᾽ οὗ ["through whom"]). See Werner Kramer, *Christ, Lord, Son of God* (tr. Brian Hardy; SBT 1.50; London: SCM, 1966) 146f. Gal 1:12 interprets the phrase further: "through a revelation of Christ." See also 1:16; 1 Cor 9:1; 15:8, and the term "called" (κλητός) Rom 1:1; 1 Cor 1:1.

26 καὶ θεοῦ πατρός ("and God the Father") is omitted by Marcion who also changed αὐτόν ("him") to αὑτόν ("himself"). See Adolph von Harnack, *Marcion: Das Evangelium vom fremden Gott. Neue Studien zu Marcion* (Darmstadt: Wissenschaftliche Buchgesellschaft, 1960) *67f. But the phrase is Pauline; see Gal 1:3; Rom 1:7; 15:6; 1 Cor 1:3; 8:6; 15:24; 2 Cor 1:2, 3; 11:31; Phil 1:2; 2:11; 4:20; 1 Thess 1:1, 3; 3:11, 13; Phlm 3.

27 "God the Father" plays a special role in Gal (see 1:3, 4; 4:2, 6) because of the concept of adoption (see 3:7, 26; 4:4–7, 22–31).

28 On this formula see Kramer, *Christ, Lord, Son of God,* 20ff, 58ff; Klaus Wengst, *Christologische Formeln und Lieder des Urchristentums* (StNT 7; Gütersloh: Mohn, 1972) 27ff; Martin Rese, *VF* 15 (1970) 89ff; Delling (see n. 24 above) 407.

29 Rom 4:24; 8:11; 10:9, 1 Cor 6:14; 15:15; 2 Cor 4:14; 1 Thess 1:10; etc.

30 Cf. Rom 1:4–5; 1 Cor 9:1; 15:8.

31 See 1 Cor 1:1 (καὶ Σωσθένης ὁ ἀδελφός ["and Sosthenes the brother"]); 2 Cor 1:1 (καὶ Τιμόθεος ὁ ἀδελφός ["and Timothy the brother"]); Phlm 1 (same as 2 Cor 1:1); Phil 1:1; 1 Thess 1:1; also Col 1:1; 2 Thess 1:1. The lists of greetings must be related: cf. Phil 4:21; Col 4:10; 1 Cor 16:19–20; 2 Cor 13:12; Rom 16:21–23.

he includes as co–senders his companions and fellow missionaries: "and all the brothers who are with me" (καὶ οἱ σὺν ἐμοὶ πάντες ἀδελφοί). Paul does not name them, but we can assume that he refers to fellow missionaries[32] known to the Galatians, and not to the whole church from where he sent the letter.[33] The emphatic "all" is unique in Paul[34] and indicates that he wanted to write as the spokesman of a group which is solidly behind him and the letter.[35] If the secretary who actually wrote the letter (see on 6:11–18) is included among the "brothers," which may well be, Paul does not indicate it.[36] In v 2b the addressees are named: "to the churches of Galatia" (ταῖς ἐκκλησίαις τῆς Γαλατίας). This address is rather brief, lacking the usual epithets and polite compliments in references to churches.[37] The fact that Paul writes to several churches[38] raises the question of their organization. They must have been close geographically.[39] The same problems must apply to them. Also, they must have been connected in some organizational way unknown to us.

■ 3 The salutation, "Grace be to you and peace from God our Father and the Lord Jesus Christ," is the same as in other letters of Paul.[40] The salutation is a form of prayer. Here it implicitly expresses Paul's wish that the Galatians remain partakers of God's redemption in Christ (1:4). The salutation also confirms the apostle's position of a mediator who had first brought that redemption to them (cf. 1:6–9).[41] The terms "grace and peace" (χάρις καὶ εἰρήνη) are found also as part of other epistolary blessings.[42] "Grace" may have developed out of the Greek form of greeting (χαίρειν).[43] It is not found in Jewish blessings and salutations, which usually have "peace" (שלום, εἰρήνη) and "mercy" (ἔλεος).[44] The omission of the article has been explained as due to the "liturgical" origin of the saluta-

---

32 So, e.g., Adolf Hilgenfeld, *Der Galaterbrief übersetzt, in seinen geschichtlichen Beziehungen untersucht und erklärt* (Leipzig: Breitkopf & Härtel, 1852); Lightfoot; Richard Adelbert Lipsius, *Briefe an die Galater, Römer, Philipper* (Freiburg: Mohr, Siebeck, ²1892); Friedrich Sieffert, *Der Brief an die Galater* (KEK 7; Göttingen: Vandenhoeck & Ruprecht ⁶1880, ⁹1899); Burton; Oepke; Bligh; Borse, *Standort*, 43f; Mussner. See E. Earle Ellis, "Paul and His Co-Workers," *NTS* 17 (1971) 437–52; Eduard Lohse, "Die Mitarbeiter des Apostels Paulus im Kolosserbrief," in *Verborum Veritas: Festschrift G. Stählin* (Wuppertal: Brockhaus, 1970) 189–94.

33 So, e.g., Zahn, Bousset, Ramsay, Lietzmann.

34 Cf. Schlier (pp. 28f) with references to Ambrosiaster and Chrysostom.

35 Contra Schlier (p. 29) who suggests that Paul considered himself the representative of the one Christian brotherhood, an assumption which presupposes the later concept of the one church (cf. Eph 3:1–13). Mussner (p. 48 n. 27) suggests that "all" is said in contrast to "a few" in 1:7. Cf. also Vielhauer, *Geschichte*, 67.

36 Cf. Rom 16:22, where the secretary Tertios names himself in the greetings. See Betz, "Composition," 356; also the Introduction above, § 1.

37 Cf. Rom 1:7; 1 Cor 1:2; 2 Cor 1:1; Phil 1:1; 1 Thess 1:1.

38 ἐκκλησία is the name for the local "church" (cf. 1 Cor 1:2; 2 Cor 1:2; 1 Thess 1:1; Phlm 2). For further discussion and bib. see Conzelmann, *1 Corinthians*, 21f; Klaus Berger, "Volksversammlung und Gemeinde Gottes: Zu den Anfängen der christlichen Verwendung von 'ekklesia'," *ZThK* 73 (1976) 167–207.

39 These churches are also mentioned in 1 Cor 16:1; 2 Tim 4:10; 1 Pet 1:1. See Introduction, § 2. B.

40 Cf. Rom 1:7; 1 Cor 1:3; 2 Cor 1:2; Phil 1:2; 1 Thess 1:1; Phlm 3; also Eph 1:2; Col 1:2; 2 Thess 1:2; Titus 1:4. Different forms occur 1 Tim 1:2; 2 Tim 1:2; 1 Pet 1:2; 2 Pet 1:2; Rev 1:4; *1 Clem. inscr.*; Pol. *Phil. inscr.*; see Lyder Brun, *Segen und Fluch im Christentum* (Skrifter utgitt av det Norske Videnskaps–Akademi i Oslo, II. Hist.–Filos. Klasse 1932.1 [Oslo 1932]) 35ff.

41 This is emphasized by Schlier, p. 30.

42 But there they are separated. Cf. Gal 6:16, 18; Rom 2:10; 15:33; 16:20, 24; 1 Cor 16:23; 2 Cor 13:11, 13; Phil 4:9, 23; 1 Thess 5:23, 28; 2 Thess 3:16, 18; Eph 6:23, 24; Col 3:15–16; 4:18; 1 Pet 5:14; Heb 13:20–21, 25; etc.

43 This was suggested by Johannes Weiss, *Der erste Korintherbrief* (KEK 5; Göttingen: Vandenhoeck & Ruprecht, 1910) 4f; see also Koskenniemi, *Studien*, 162.

44 Cf. Dan 3:98 (4:1); *2 Apoc. Bar.* 78.2: "thus says Baruch, son of Neriah, to the brethren carried into captivity: mercy and peace be with you." On the Bar Kokhba letters, see Fitzmyer, *JBL* 93 (1974) 214–16; Berger, *ZNW* 65 (1974) 193ff. On rabbinic literature, see Str–B 1.154; 2.94f; 3.1, 25.

tion.[45] Given the fact that as a prayer the salutation is "liturgical," the omission of the article may be a result of the rendering of *shalom* ("peace") which has no article either. "Grace and peace" have their origin in God and Christ. The sequence differs here from 1:1 but is probably more original. In 1:1 God is named second, because of the following formula "who raised him from the dead." 1:3 not only conforms to the other Pauline salutations,[46] but also establishes the proper hierarchical order[47] of the Father, God, and his Son, the "Lord Jesus Christ."[48]

■ **4** In analogy to the christological statement in 1:1,

which states what God has done to Jesus, Paul attaches another christological formula to the salutation. This formula (v 4a) and its interpretation (v 4b) sum up what Christ has done "for us." Its formulaic character is apparent from its close parallels elsewhere in Paul.[49] These parallels can take three basic forms: "Christ gave himself up,"[50] or "God gave him up,"[51] or "Christ was given up."[52] Only the first of these is used in Galatians (cf. 2:20). "Christ gave himself up for our sins" implies an old christology which understood Jesus' death as an expiatory self–sacrifice.[53] This christology is likely to have originated in Judaism.

45 For a discussion of this problem and the literature, see Conzelmann, *1 Corinthians*, 23f; also Eduard Lohse, *Colossians and Philemon: A Commentary on the Epistles to the Colossians and to Philemon* (tr. William R. Poehlmann and Robert J. Karris; ed. Helmut Koester; Hermeneia; Philadelphia: Fortress, 1971) 10f.

46 "Grace" in the specific sense refers of course to the Christ–event; cf. Gal 1:6; 2:21; 5:4; 6:17, and often in Paul; see Bauer, *s.v.*; Hans Conzelmann, "χάρις κτλ.," *TDNT* 9.393–96; Berger, "Apostelbrief und apostolische Rede," *ZNW* 65 (1974) 191–231. "Peace" (εἰρήνη) is, at least in the Greek tradition, originally a political term. For Paul, however, it sums up God's whole redemptive work in the world. Cf. Rom 15:33; 16:20; 2 Cor 13:11; Phil 4:7, 9; 1 Thess 5:23. "Peace" is the basis for Christian existence (cf. Rom 5:1; 8:6; 1 Cor 7:15; 14:33; Gal 5:22; 1 Thess 5:3; etc.). See Gerhard von Rad and Werner Foerster, *TDNT* 2, *s.v.* εἰρήνη κτλ.; Heinrich Gross, *Die Idee des ewigen und allgemeinen Weltfriedens im Alten Orient und im Alten Testament* (TTSt 7; Trier: Paulinus–Verlag, ²1967); Walter Eisenbeis, *Die Wurzel שׁלם im Alten Testament* (BZAW 113; Berlin: de Gruyter, 1969); Hans H. Schmid, *Šalôm: "Frieden" im Alten Orient und im Alten Testament* (SBS; Stuttgart: Katholisches Bibelwerk, 1971); Erich Dinkler, *Eirene: Der urchristliche Friedensgedanke* (AHAWPH 1973.1).

47 This consideration makes the different sequence πατρὸς καὶ κυρίου ἡμῶν ("of our Father and Lord"), represented by many witnesses (P⁴⁶,⁵¹ B D G H K 88 614 1739 *et al.*), a secondary alteration. See Metzger, *Textual Commentary*, 589. See Phil 2:6–11; 1 Cor 8:6; 11:3; 15:23–28; and Conzelmann, *1 Corinthians*, on these passages.

48 The acclamation "Lord [is] Jesus Christ" (κύριος Ἰησοῦς Χριστός) is reflected here. Cf. 1 Cor 12:3; Phil 2:11; Rom 10:9. See Wengst, *Christologische*

Formeln, 131ff. The Christological title "Lord" (κύριος) is frequent in Paul; for Gal see 1:3, 19; 5:10; 6:14, 18. On the title, see Oscar Cullmann, *The Christology of the New Testament* (tr. Shirley C. Guthrie and Charles A. M. Hall; Philadelphia: Westminster, ²1963) 195ff; Herbert Braun, *Gesammelte Studien zum Neuen Testament und seiner Umwelt* (Tübingen: Mohr, Siebeck, 1962, ²1967) 243ff; Ferdinand Hahn, *The Titles of Jesus in Christology* (Cleveland: World, 1969) 68ff; Kramer, *Christ, Lord, Son of God*, 65ff; Joseph A. Fitzmyer, "Der semitische Hintergrund des neutestamentlichen Kyriostitels," in *Jesus Christus in Historie und Theologie: Neutestamentliche Festschrift für Hans Conzelmann zum 60. Geburtstag* (ed. Georg Strecker; Tübingen: Mohr, Siebeck, 1975) 267–98.

49 For this formula and other passages, see Kramer, *Christ, Lord, Son of God*, 115ff; Wengst, *Christologische Formeln*, 55ff. Gal 1:4 shows that the formula was not always connected with the title "Son of God." See also Wiard Popkes, *Christus Traditus: Eine Untersuchung zum Begriff der Dahingabe im Neuen Testament* (AThANT 49; Zurich: Zwingli, 1967); Ernst Käsemann, "Formeln II. . . . im Neuen Testament," *RGG*³ 2.995; Mussner, p. 50 n. 38.

50 Gal 1:4; 2:20; also Eph 5:2, 25; 1 Tim 2:6; Titus 2:14. Cf. *CMC* 16.4–7; 64.20–65.3.

51 Rom 8:32.

52 Rom 4:25.

53 See Rudolf Bultmann, *Theology of the New Testament* (2 vols.; tr. Kendrick Grobel; London: SCM; New York: Scribner's, 1951–55) § 7, 3; Hans Conzelmann, *An Outline of the Theology of the New Testament* (tr. John Bowden; London: SCM, 1969) 69–71; Harald Riesenfeld, "ὑπέρ," *TDNT* 8.507; Nils A. Dahl, "The Atonement—An Adequate Reward for the Akedah," in his *The Crucified Messiah* (Minneapolis: Augsburg, 1974) 146–60.

Jewish theology could have interpreted the death of Jesus in this way because according to Jewish belief the righteous man, when he suffered martyrdom, would expiate the sins of others. [54] We may suppose that in the pre–Pauline period Jewish Christianity interpreted Jesus' death in this manner, so that we have here one of the oldest christologies of the New Testament, perhaps the oldest one of all. [55] Verse 4b then interprets the formula v 4a soteriologically: "in order that he might rescue us from the present evil age." [56] The phrase "for our sins" (plural!) suggests a pre–Pauline concept of sins as individual transgressions of the Torah. But it must be read also in conjunction with Paul's concept of the demonic power of "sin," by which mankind is "enslaved" [57] in the present evil aeon[58] and from which mankind must be rescued. [59] This is accomplished through Christ's redemptive self–sacrifice (cf. 2:19–20; 3:13; 3:22–25; 4:5). The conjunction ὅπως ("in order that") refers to the present reality of salvation. It does not say that the coming aeon has already begun. [60] Rather, while the present evil aeon continues, Christ's coming and the gift of the Spirit (cf. 3:23–4:10) have granted freedom to the believers in Christ (cf. 5:1, 13). Paul, therefore, speaks of the liberation "out of" the evil aeon and not of the change of the aeons themselves.

The phrase "according to the will of our God and

---

54 Cf. 2 Macc 7:32, 37–38; 4 Macc 6:27–29; 17:21–22. See George Foot Moore, *Judaism in the First Three Centuries of the Christian Era* (3 vols.; Cambridge: Harvard University, 1927–30) 546–49; Wilhelm Bousset, *Die Religion des Judentums im Späthellenistischen Zeitalter* (ed. Hugo Gressmann; HNT 21; Tübingen: Mohr, Siebeck, [4]1966) 198f; Str–B 2.275–82, 537, 740; Eduard Lohse (*Märtyrer und Gottesknecht* [FRLANT 64; Göttingen: Vandenhoeck & Ruprecht, 1955, [2]1963]), who wants to derive the concept from Palestinian Judaism, whereas Wengst (*Christologische Formeln*, 62ff) opts for Hellenistic Judaism and syncretism. Important for the whole problem is Sam K. Williams, *Jesus' Death as Saving Event: The Background and Origin of a Concept* (HDR 2; Missoula: Scholars, 1975).

55 The plural "sins" is not typical for Paul and points to a Jewish (Christian) concept of sin. Cf. 1 Cor 15:3; Rom 4:25; 5:6, 7, 8; 14:15; 1 Cor 1:13; 11:24. Whether the reading ὑπέρ, "in behalf of" (P[51] B H 33 1611 *pm*) or περί, "concerning" (P[46] ℵ* A ℜ D G *al*) is to be preferred is difficult to decide; there is no difference in meaning (cf. BDF, § 229, 1; 231; BDR, § 229, 1; 231, 1; Schlier, p. 32 n. 2; Conzelmann, *1 Corinthians*, 253 n. 48; Wengst, *Christologische Formeln*, 56 n. 6). Uncertain is also the question of the possible influence of Isa 53, because that passage does not have the concept of self–sacrifice (cf. Isa 53:6, 12). See Conzelmann, *1 Corinthians*, 253; Joachim Jeremias, *Abba: Studien zur neutestamentlichen Theologie und Zeitgeschichte* (Göttingen: Vandenhoeck & Ruprecht, 1966) 199ff; Popkes, *Christus Traditus*, 36, 253; Norman Perrin, *A Modern Pilgrimage in New Testament Christology* (Philadelphia: Fortress 1974) 103.

56 So Wengst, *Christologische Formeln*, 61.

57 Cf. Gal 3:22; 4:3, 7, 8, 9, 24; 5:1.

58 The concept of "the present evil aeon" (ὁ αἰὼν ὁ ἐνεστὼς πονηρός) stems from Jewish apocalypticism, where we have the juxtaposition of "this aeon" (ὁ αἰὼν οὗτος) and the "aeon to come" (ὁ αἰὼν μέλλων). Cf. for parallel expressions Rom 12:2; 1 Cor 1:20; 2:6, 8; 3:18–19; 2 Cor 4:4; Eph 2:1–2, 7; 5:16; 1 John 5:19; Mark 16:14 (W). On the origin, see Moore, *Judaism* 1.270; 2.378f; Bousset–Gressmann, *Religion*, 242ff; Str–B 4.799ff, esp. 844–57; Hermann Sasse, *TDNT* 1, *s.v.* αἰών; idem, "Aion," *RAC* 1.193–204; Otto Kuss, *Der Römerbrief* (2 Lieferungen [Rom 1:1–8:19]; Regensburg: Pustet, 1957, 1959) 275ff; Herbert Braun, *Qumran und das Neue Testament* (2 vols.; Tübingen: Mohr, Siebeck, 1966) 1.205; Kertelge, "*Rechtfertigung*," 35–37, 134–58. For a parallel from the Mithras cult, see Betz, *NovT* 10 (1968) 77f.

59 The term ἐξαιρεῖσθαι ἔκ τινος ("to rescue [someone] from something") is a Pauline *hapax legomenon*. See Bauer, *s.v.*, 2a. Cf. the interesting parallel in ps.–Crates *Ep.* 19 (p. 212, ed. Hercher), for which I am indebted to Dr. Ronald Hock. The reference is to Diogenes who τὸν πολλοὺς καὶ ὅτε ἔζη ἐξελόμενον ἐκ κακίας εἰς ἀρετὴν καὶ ὅτε τέθνηκε δι' ὧν κατέλιπεν ἡμῖν λόγων ("while he was alive saved many from evil to virtue and since he died does so through the words which he has left us").

60 Differently, W. D. Davies, *Paul and Rabbinic Judaism* (London: SPCK, [2]1955) 36; Burton, 15f; and Schlier (p. 34), who speaks both of the beginning of the coming aeon and also of the anticipation of the coming aeon. If Paul has connections with the apocalyptic terminology, he has modified it. The ὅπως sentence is parallel to the more frequent ἵνα sentences (cf. Gal 1:16; 2:16, 19; 3:14, 22, 24, 4:5). See BDF, § 369; BDR, § 369.

Father"[61] confirms the previous references to God the Father in 1:1, 3. It underscores that the salvation through Christ did not occur apart from, but in complete harmony with the will of God.

■ **5** Differing from other Pauline prescripts, the Galatian prescript concludes with a doxology:[62] "To whom be the glory for ever and ever. Amen." The language indicates that the doxology must have originated in liturgical contexts of a Jewish background.[63] Here, however, it has become part of the epistolary style of early Christianity. Why did Paul feel such a doxology is appropriate at this point? Perhaps it was caused by Paul's deep concern that the redemption through Christ would be replaced by "the other gospel." One will have to admit that the usual thanksgiving at the end of the prescript would be out of place in Galatians.[64] Only after the letter had been received could one have known, through the consequent actions of the recipients, whether there was a reason for a thanksgiving.

---

61   This statement is also unique in Paul. Cf. Eph 1:5; 1 Pet 4:19; Justin *Dial.* 116. It must be distinguished from the formula διὰ θελήματος θεοῦ ("through [the] will of God"), which occurs as part of the prescript in 1 Cor 1:1; 2 Cor 1:1; Eph 1:1; Col 1:1; 2 Tim 1:1; in these passages it is related to Paul's apostleship and not to Christ's self–sacrifice. Cf. also Rom 1:10; 2:18; 12:2; 15:32; 2 Cor 8:5; 1 Thess 4:3; 5:18. On the whole problem, see Kasimierz Romaniuk, *L'amour du Père et du Fils dans la sotériologie de S. Paul* (AnBib 15; Rome: Pontifical Biblical Institute, 1961) 158ff; Wilhelm Thüsing, *Per Christum in Deum* (NTAbh 1; Münster: Aschendorff, ²1969).

62   A doxology at the end of the prescript occurs also in Rev 1:6. For other doxologies, all of which end with "amen," cf. Rom 11:36; 16:27; Phil 4:20; Eph 3:21; 1 Tim 1:17; 2 Tim 4:18; Heb 13:21; etc.

       For literature on doxologies, see Johannes Hempel, "Doxology," *IDB* 1.867; Ernst Käsemann, "Liturgische Formeln," *RGG*³ 2.993–96; Erhard Kamlah, *Traditionsgeschichtliche Untersuchungen zur Schlussdoxologie des Römerbriefes* (diss., Tübingen, 1955); Alfred Stuiber, "Doxologie," *RAC* 4.210–26.

63   On the concept of "glory" (δόξα) as an attribute of God see Gerhard von Rad and Gerhard Kittel, *TDNT* 2, s.v.; Bauer, s.v., 1a; Kuss, *Römerbrief*, 608–18; Heinrich Schlier, "Doxa bei Paulus als heilsgeschichtlicher Begriff," in his *Besinnung auf das Neue Testament* (Freiburg: Herder, 1964) 307–18. On the acclamation "amen" see Heinrich Schlier, *TDNT* 1, s.v.; Bauer, s.v.; Alfred Stuiber, "Amen," *JAC* 1 (1958) 210–16; Alfred Jepsen, "אמן," *TWAT* 1.345–48.

64   So also Zahn; Burton; Lietzmann; Schlier.

1

Exordium

6 I am astonished that you are so quickly deserting him who called you[1] in [the] grace of Christ[2] [and turning] to a different gospel—7/ not that there is another [gospel], but there are some who disturb you and want to pervert the gospel of Christ.
8/ But even if we or an angel from heaven should proclaim to you a gospel contrary to that which we proclaimed to you, let him be accursed.[3]
9/ As we have said before, so now I say again: if anyone is proclaiming to you a gospel contrary to[4] that which you have received, let him be accursed.
10/ For am I now persuading men or God?[5] Or am I seeking to please men? If I were still pleasing men, I would not be Christ's slave. 11/ For I would have you know, brothers, that the gospel preached by me is not human in nature.[6]

Analysis

Generally speaking the first part of the "body" of the Galatian letter conforms to the customary *exordium* ("introduction"), which is otherwise known as the *prooemium* or *principium*.[7] In the treatment of the *exordium* in Aristotle's *Rhetorica*,[8] the *Rhetorica ad Herennium*,[9] Cicero's *De inventione*,[10] and Quintilian,[11] there is considerable agreement in regard to the definition, composition, and function of the *exordium*. This includes the understanding that various types of *exordia* must be distinguished and applied in accordance with the nature of the case. There is also disagreement and development among these authors in determining what the various types are and how they can best be applied.

Aristotle advises that if the audience is already attentive, the speaker may start his speech by directly introducing a summary of the "facts."[12] The *Rhetorica ad Herennium*[13] names the summary of the *causa* as a means for making the hearers attentive and receptive. The handbook sets forth four methods for making the hearers well disposed: "by discussing our own person, the person of our adversaries, that of our hearers, and the facts themselves."[14] But in 1:6–7, Paul does more than simply present the bare facts. He also discredits

---

1 So *RSV*. Cf. *NEB*: "I am astonished to find you turning so quickly away from him who called you . . ."

2 So *RSV*. Cf. *NEB*: "by grace;" *JB* omits the phrase.

3 *RSV*: "let him be accursed;" *NEB*: "let him be outcast;" *JB*: "he is to be condemned."

4 So *RSV*. Cf. *NEB*: "at variance with;" *JB*: "a different version of the Good News."

5 Cf. *RSV*: "am I now seeking the favor of men, or of God?" *NEB*: "does my language now sound as if I were canvassing for men's support? Whose support do I want but God's alone?"

6 Cf. *RSV*: "not man's gospel;" *NEB*: "no human invention."

7 For most of the following discussion see also Betz, "Composition," 353–79, esp. 359–62. On the *exordium*, see especially Richard Volkmann, *Die Rhetorik der Griechen in systematischer Übersicht* (Stuttgart:

Teubner, [2]1885) § 12; Lausberg, *Handbuch*, § 263–88; Martin, *Rhetorik*, 60–75.

8 1.1.9 (p. 1354b); 3.14.1ff (p. 1414b19ff); cf. *Rhet. ad Alex.* 28ff (p. 1436a32ff).

9 1.4.6–7.11.

10 1.15.20–17.25.

11 4.1.1–79.

12 *Rhet.* 3.14.8 (p. 1415b). Cf. *Rhet. ad Alex.* 29 (p. 1437b35ff).

13 1.4.7: "Dociles auditores habere poterimus, si summam causae breviter exponemus et si adtentos eos faciemus . . ." ("we can have receptive hearers if we briefly summarize the cause and make them attentive . . ."; tr. Harry Caplan, LCL).

14 1.4.8: "Benivolos auditores facere quattuor modis possumus: ab nostra, ab adversariorum nostrorum, ab auditorum persona, et ab rebus ipsis." Cf. Aristotle *Rhet.* 3.14.7 (p. 1415a); Cicero *De inv.* 1.16.22.

his adversaries by using the language of demagoguery[15] and expresses his disappointment and disapproval of the Galatians for changing over to the side of the opposition.[16] Speaking in the terms of the *Rhetorica ad Herennium*, Paul's statement of the *causa* is a mixture of two types of *exordia*, the *principium* ("direct opening") and the *insinuatio* ("subtle approach"). The former, the *principium*, is appropriate in addressing an audience where attention, receptivity, and a favorable disposition can be obtained directly and without difficulty,[17] while the *insinuatio* should be used in cases where, for example, the audience has been won over by the previous speech of the opponent.[18]

Paul's case stands in the middle: he can be certain of having the attention and receptivity of the Galatians at once, but they have almost been won over, though not quite.[19] This mixture of the *principium* and the *insinuatio* may be peculiar, but it conforms precisely to the situation with which Paul sees himself confronted. It also gives the Galatians another chance to think over the whole question of their faith, and perhaps to reverse their decision, if indeed they have already made it.

Cicero's treatment in his *De inventione* is very similar to the treatment in the *Rhetorica ad Herennium*. Without fully going into the problems of the relationship between the two works,[20] it may suffice to mention that Cicero has a greater tolerance of variability and mixture of cases and types. He places great emphasis upon discrediting the opposition. In comparison with Paul, it is noteworthy that he recommends the expression of astonishment and perplexity as one of the means to regain the goodwill of an audience which has been won over by the opposition.[21]

The next section of the Galatian *exordium* (1 : 8–9) contains a double curse, issued conditionally upon those who preach a gospel different from the Pauline gospel.[22] The way Paul states this curse indicates that he merely repeats (cf. v 9a) a curse which had been issued at some earlier occasion (cf. v 8), so that what appears now as a double curse is really the reissuing of a previous curse. Also, this curse must be seen in connection with the conditional blessing in the postscript (see 6 : 16). How does this curse fit into the *exordium*? In his treatment of the *exordium* Quintilian discusses devices to be employed in cases where the judge is influenced by prejudice, most likely through the previous speech of

15 Cf. *Rhet. ad Her.* 1.5.8: "Ab adversariorum persona benivolentia captabitur si eos in odium, in invidiam, in contemptionem adducemus. In odium rapiemus si quid eorum spurce, superbe, perfidiose, crudeliter, confidenter, malitiose, flagitiose factum proferemus. In invidiam trahemus, si vim, si potentiam, si factionem, divitias, incontinentiam, nobilitatem, clientelas, hospitium, sodalitatem, adfinitates adversariorum proferemus, et his adiumentis magis quam veritati eos confidere aperiemus. In contemptionem adducemus si inertiam, ignaviam, desidiam, luxuriam adversariorum proferemus" ("from the discussion of the person of our adversaries we shall secure goodwill by bringing them into hatred, unpopularity, or contempt. We shall force hatred upon them by adducing some base, highhanded, treacherous, cruel, impudent, malicious, or shameful act of theirs. We shall make our adversaries unpopular by setting forth their violent behaviour, their dominance, factiousness, wealth, lack of self–restraint, high birth, clients, hospitality, club allegiance, or marriage alliances, and by making clear that they rely more upon these supports than upon the truth. We shall bring our adversaries into contempt by presenting their idleness, cowardice, sloth, and luxurious habits").

16 Cf. Aristot. *Rhet.* 3.14.2 (p. 1414b), who names as the sources of epideictic *exordia* ἔπαινος ἢ ψόγος (cf. 3.14.4 [p. 1415a]).

17 *Rhet. ad Her.* 1.4.6: "Principium est cum statim auditoris animum nobis idoneum reddimus ad audiendum. Id ita sumitur ut adtentos, ut dociles, uti benivolos auditores habere possimus" ("the Direct Opening straightway prepares the hearer to attend to our speech. Its purpose is to enable us to have hearers who are attentive, receptive, and well–disposed").

18 1.6.9: "There are three occasions on which we cannot use the Direct Opening, and these we must consider carefully: (1) when our cause is discreditable, that is, when the subject itself alienates the hearer from us; (2) when the hearer has apparently been won over by the previous speakers of the opposition; (3) or when the hearer has become wearied by listening to the previous speakers."

19 Note the present tense in Gal 1 : 6–7; 4 : 9, 21; cf. also 4 : 11, 12–20; 5 : 1, 4, 7–12, 13; 6 : 12–16.

20 See Joachim Adamietz, *Ciceros de inventione und die Rhetorik ad Herennium* (Marburg: Mauersberger, 1960) 21ff.

21 *De inv.* 1.17.25.

22 For details, see below.

an opponent.[23] One effective method, for which Cicero is cited as an example, is to frighten the judge by threats. Most popular was the move to threaten the judge with the displeasure of the Roman people, or more brutally, with prosecution for bribery.[24] Quintilian regards such threats as extreme measures which should be used only as a last resort, since in his view they lie outside of the art of oratory.[25] Such threats, a form of which must have been the curse, may have been used more often than Quintilian would like. It is significant that one of the greatest masterpieces of Greek rhetoric, Demosthenes' *De corona*, has as its *peroratio* a prayer to the gods which includes a curse upon the enemies of Athens.[26] Demosthenes has the curse in the end, the *peroratio*, while Paul has it as part of the *exordium*, but since *exordium* and *peroratio* were considered intimately related, the difference is insignificant.[27]

The conclusion is apparently reached in v 9, while the next major section, the *narratio*, begins in v 12. This leaves us with the question what to do with vv 10–11. Scholars have been divided in their opinions on whether v 10 should be connected with the preceding or with the following, and whether the following section begins with v 11 or v 12. A clear decision seems impossible unless one recognizes that, according to the rhetoricians, there should be a smooth transition between the *exordium* and the *narratio*.[28]

The most extensive discussion on this point is found in Quintilian,[29] who calls this transitional part *transitus*[30] or *transgressio*.[31] The purpose of this *transitus* is to provide an end to the *exordium*, which is distinguishable but in harmony with the beginning of the *narratio*.[32] An abrupt change from one part to the next is to be avoided, as well as the complete smoothing out of any differences.[33] In addition, the transition may contain an announcement of the major topic of the *narratio*.[34]

Verses 10–11 meet these requirements very well. The two rhetorical questions and the assertion in v 10 put a clear end to the *exordium*. They deny that Paul is a rhetorical "flatterer," "persuading" or "pleasing" men, or a magician, trying to "persuade God."[35] Verse 11 then introduces[36] what is going to be Paul's contention in the *narratio*.[37]

Interpretation

■ 6 Immediately following the epistolary prescript (1:1–5), Paul states the cause for writing the letter to the Galatians. This cause is not an uncomplicated matter. Moreover, Paul does not want to spend time on explanations and declarations. Therefore he states the cause without any further ado, and does it in an ironic and polemic way. The cause is the present state of the Galatian churches. They are in the process of shifting their allegiance away from Paul, their founder, and away from the Pauline form of the gospel to his Jewish–Christian competitors and enemies. His reaction to this shift is one of ironic astonishment: θαυμάζω ("I am

---

23 Quint. 4.1.20–22.
24 4.1.21.
25 4.1.22.
26 18.324.
27 On the *peroratio*, see below on Gal 6:12–17.
28 See Lausberg, *Handbuch*, § 288.
29 4.1.76–79.
30 4.1.77.
31 4.1.78.
32 4.1.76.
33 4.1.79.
34 4.1.79.
35 See below on 1:10.
36 See below on 1:11. *Rhet. ad Her.* 4.26.35 provides examples for *transitio*, in which what follows next is set forth, e.g.: "Mea in istum beneficia cognoscitis; nunc quomodo iste mihi gratiam rettulerit accipite" ("my benefactions to this defendant you know; now learn how he has requited me").

37 So also Luther (1535) who takes 1:11–12 together: "Haec est propositio praesentis loci quae dabit confutationem et Apologiam usque ad finem 2. cap., Estque historia perpetua quaedam quam Paulus hic recitat" (WA 40/1. 126; "this is the central proposition of this chapter, down to the end of the second chapter; it is a refutation and a defense. Here Paul is reciting a sort of perpetual history" [tr. from *Luther's Works* 26.61]).

astonished").[38] Reacting in this way, Paul makes use of a device which was used in the rhetoric of law courts and politics. It is a device of indignant rebuttal and attack of things the opposition party has done and is about to do.[39] It is important for understanding what Paul means that the rhetorical background of his language be taken into consideration.[40] The same is true of the rest of the sentence. Paul describes the actions taken by the Galatians with these words: "you are so quickly deserting him who called you in [the] grace of Christ [and turning] to another gospel." The term μετατίθημι ("desert") comes from political language and is here applied to "desertion" from God in the sense of a shifting away from the Pauline gospel.[41] As a political term,

μετατίθημι is intended to express a partisan point of view, to cast a negative judgment on the Galatians, to question their stability and loyalty, and to characterize their plans as typical "party politics." All this is said not in the face of mere hypothesis, but in the face of facts. The present tense of the verbs in 1:6–7 indicates that the Galatian maneuvers are still in progress.[42] By writing his letter Paul hopes to be able to still influence and perhaps reverse the decision of the Galatians.[43] The phrase οὕτως ταχέως ("so quickly") is also rhetorical in origin.[44] It should not be used too quickly to date the letter. The words would make little sense, to be sure, if a considerable length of time had passed since the founding of the churches, but that is about all one can

---

38 For a thoughtful discussion of the rhetorical *artificium et ingenium Pauli* with regard to this beginning, see Luther (1535). Luther observes that Paul's letter conforms to his own rule set forth in 6:1 (WA 40/1, 100). Differently, Mussner (p. 53), who takes it at face value: Paul is incredulous in view of the quick pace of the Galatians' apostasy. But Mussner (p. 53 nn. 53–54) also refers to the rhetorical and epistolary cliché.

39 The rhetorical θαυμάζω ("I am astonished") occurs often in Demosthenes, Antiphon, and Lysias. See Siegmund Preuss, *Index Demosthenicus* (Leipzig: Teubner, 1892) *s.v.*; David H. Holmes, *Index Lysiacus* (Bonn: Cohen, 1895) *s.v.* See also Plato *Apol.* 17A, 24A; *Crito* 50C. For the epistles see, e.g., Isocrates *Ep.* 2.19; 9.8. Examples are to be found also in John L. White, "Introductory Formulae in the Body of the Pauline Letter," *JBL* 90 (1971) 91–97, esp. 96; Nils A. Dahl, "Paul's Letter to the Galatians: Epistolary Genre, Content, and Structure" (unpublished paper, 1974). For the term in connection with the *exordium*, see Lausberg, *Handbuch*, § 270.

40 Related to it is the epistolary complaint. Cf., e.g., Pap. Mich. 479.4f: "I am astonished . . . that you have not written to me" (θαυμάζω πῶς . . . οὐκ ἀντέγραψάς μοι . . .). For examples, see also Koskenniemi, *Studien*, 66f. Cf. White, *ibidem*, 96: "the object of Paul's dissatisfaction is not the Galatians' failure to write but their apparent rejection of the gospel."

41 On μετατίθημι (middle) see Bauer, *s.v.*, 2b: "change one's mind, turn away, desert, turn apostate." The political meaning is obvious in Polybius 5.111.8; 24.9.6 (see furthermore *Polybios-Lexikon* [ed. Arno Mauersberger; Berlin: Akademie–Verlag, 1975] 1/4, *s.v.*); Diodorus Sic. 11.4.6. Closer to Paul is the nickname ὁ μεταθέμενος ("the turncoat") for Dionysius of Heraclea (c. 330–250 B.C.) because "he de-

serted the doctrines of the Stoa and went over to Epicurus," Athenaeus 7.281D–E; cf. 10.437E; Diog. L. 7.23, 166f; 5.92; Hierocles 7 (*Fragmenta Philosophorum Graecorum* [ed. Friedrich W. A. Mullach; Paris: Didot, 1860] 1.429); Philo *Praem.* 58. For the religious meaning, see Plutarch *Is. et Osir.* 358C; 2 Macc 7:24, 11:24; Jos. *Ant.* 20.38 (see Appendix 1, below). The anti–Pauline passage in ps.–Clem. *Recog.* 1.70.2 is interesting: After a speech by James, Saul [i.e., Paul!] comes running into the temple of Jerusalem, shouting: "what are you doing, O men of Israel? Why are you so easily snatched away? Why are you led headlong by the most miserable men who are deceived by a magician?" (Quid facitis, O viri Israhelitae? cur vobis tamen facile subripitur? cur praecipites ducimini ab hominibus infelicissimis et a mago decepti?). See also Schlier, p. 36 n. 1; Christian Maurer, "μετατίθημι," *TDNT* 8. 161–62; *PGL, s.v.*, B. 4.

42 Cf. Burton, pp. 18f: "The present tense of the verb μετατίθεσθε indicates clearly that when the apostle wrote the apostasy of the Galatians was as yet only in process. They were, so to speak, on the point, or more exactly in the very act, of turning."

43 Cf. Burton, p. 19: "The mind of the apostle wavers while he writes between hope and fear as to the outcome (4:20, 5:10)."

44 Cf. Mussner (p. 53 n. 54) who refers to the LXX: Exod 32:8; Deut 9:16 (A); Judg 2:17. There seems to be no intention by Paul to allude to the proverbial instability of the Galatians (as noted by Jerome; Johann Jacob Wettstein, Ἡ Καινὴ Διαθήκη. *Novum Testamentum graecum . . . Tomus II, continens epistolas Pauli, etc.* [Amsterdam: Ex officina Dommeriana, 1752], 2.216).

say.[45] The time reference seems to be the founding of the churches, and not a later visit of the apostle. The expression "from him who called you" can, according to grammar, refer to God or Christ.[46] Pauline usage elsewhere suggests that God be regarded as the primary agent of the calling.[47] In actuality it was of course Paul who did the calling. The words ἐν χάριτι Χριστοῦ ("in [the] grace of Christ") designate the Galatians' present state of salvation. The words are synonymous with "in Christ Jesus" (see especially 3:26–28), or the "body of Christ."[48] Contrary to many commentaries, ἐν ("in") should not be taken as the "means by which"[49] but as a definition of the situation before God enjoyed by those who were called.[50] It was because of God's call, delivered through Paul, that the Galatians are now "in Christ Jesus,"[51] "in peace,"[52] "in hope,"[53] and in the state of "holiness."[54] The genitive Χριστοῦ ("of Christ") is certainly in conformity with Paul's christology; it refers to the grace of God which Christ represents. There is, however, reason to doubt the genitive "of Christ" textually.[55] The direction in which the Galatians are moving is indicated by the words εἰς ἕτερον εὐαγγέλιον ("to a different gospel").[56] In Paul's judgment the Galatians' move is a move away from grace, the essence of the Pauline message of faith. What was this "other gospel?" This question has often been discussed in New Testament scholarship.[57] The apostle seems to deny here the existence of "another gospel," but it should be noted that he himself mentions the "other gospel" in Gal 2:7 as the "gospel of circumcision."[58]

---

45 Other commentators take οὕτως ταχέως to mean "so soon." See Oepke. But the difference is not great; cf. Borse, *Standort*, 45; Eckert, *Verkündigung*, 169 n. 1; Erich Grässer, "Das eine Evangelium: Hermeneutische Erwägungen zu Gal 1, 6–10," *ZThK* 66 (1969) 306–44, esp. 314f. Some manuscripts omit οὕτως (G 1 *al*); cf. Luther (1535); Sieffert; Burton; Schlier.

46 In this case one would have to translate: "from Christ who called you in grace." Older commentaries taking this position are listed in Sieffert, p. 42; Zahn, pp. 44–46; Burton, p. 19.

47 See Gal 1:15; 5:8, 13; Rom 4:17; 8:30; 9:12, 24; 11:29; 1 Cor 1:9, 26; 7:15, 17, 18–24; Phil 3:14; 1 Thess 2:12; 4:7; 5:24; also 2 Thess 1:11; 2:14; 2 Tim 1:9. See Burton, pp. 19f; Schlier, p. 37; Mussner, pp. 54f; Grässer, "Das eine Evangelium," 323 n. 57 (see n. 45 above).

48 For the concept of χάρις ("grace") in Paul, see Bultmann, *Theology*, §§ 32–34; Conzelmann, *Outline*, 213f; Hans Conzelmann and Walther Zimmerli, *TDNT* 9, *s.v.*, esp. 393–96; Grässer, *ibidem*, 328ff.

49 Cf. Mussner (p. 55 n. 62) who assumes an hebraism and an adverbial meaning of the phrase. For the expression, see also 2 Cor 1:12; 8:7; 2 Tim 2:1, and Conzelmann, *TDNT* 9.395 n. 186.

50 Cf. Rom 3:24; 5:1–2, 15, 17, 20; 6:1, 14–15; also Gal 3:18; 5:1, 13.

51 For this formula, see Gal 1:22; 2:4, 17; 3:26, 28.

52 ἐν εἰρήνῃ ("in peace"): 1 Cor 7:15; cf. Gal 5:22; 6:16; Rom 5:1.

53 ἐν μιᾷ ἐλπίδι ("in one hope"): Eph 4:4; cf. Gal 5:5; Rom 5:2; 8:24.

54 ἐν ἁγιασμῷ ("in holiness"): 1 Thess 4:7; cf. 1 Cor 1:30.

55 A number of good witnesses do not have it (P[46 vid] G H[vid] it[g] Marcion Tertullian Ambrosiaster *al*), but others do have it (P[51 vid] ℵ A B Ψ 4 *al*). Also, the genitive varies between Χριστοῦ ("of Christ") and Ἰησοῦ Χριστοῦ ("of Jesus Christ"). For more discussion, see Zuntz, *Text*, 47; Lietzmann; Schlier, p. 37 n. 2; Mussner, p. 55 n. 63; Metzger, *Textual Commentary*, 589f. Nestle–Aland 26th edition now doubts its authenticity (see the Introduction, § 4, above).

56 On the term "gospel" (εὐαγγέλιον) cf. Gal 1:7, 8, 11, 16, 23; 2:2, 5, 7, 14; 4:13. See Str-B 3.4–11; Gerhard Friedrich, *TDNT* 2, *s.v.*; Peter Stuhlmacher, *Das paulinische Evangelium, I: Vorgeschichte* (FRLANT 95; Göttingen: Vandenhoeck & Ruprecht, 1968); Petr Pokorný, *ThLZ* 95 (1970) 202–04; Erhardt Güttgemanns, "Literatur zur Neutestamentlichen Theologie," *VF* 15 (1970) 71–74.

57 Cf. the conditions for salvation stated in Col 1:23: "if indeed you continue in faith, firmly established and steadfast, and if you are never dissuaded from the hope of the gospel which you have heard." Cf. also *Ep. Apost.* 1; 7 (HSW, *NT Apocrypha* 1.191f, 194).

58 Cf. also 2 Cor 11:4. See F. F. Bruce, "Galatian Problems: 3. The 'Other' Gospel," *BJRL* 53 (1970/71) 253–71; the article by Erich Grässer cited above (see n. 45). Interestingly, the *Ap. Jas.* from Nag Hammadi has James make the prediction: "another (faith) that is better than mine" will come in the future; this "other faith" seems to be the faith held by the gnostic author of the epistle (p. 16 lines 17–18; ed. Michel Malinine *et al.* [Zurich and Stuttgart: Rascher, 1968] 130). Also interesting are Luther's comments at this point (1535, WA 40/1. 108–13).

■ **7** Paul gives the impression that the statement of the cause in v 6 is not adequate. He starts again, first correcting himself. [59] If he said that the Galatians were turning to "another gospel," this is misleading because there is no other gospel ($\hat{o}$ $o\mathring{v}\kappa$ $\check{\epsilon}\sigma\tau\iota\nu$ $\check{\alpha}\lambda\lambda o$). [60] More precisely: what his opponents proclaim is not a "gospel" because, as we must conclude, it lacks grace as its content. Hence apostasy from Paul's gospel is apostasy from the gospel as such. This is no doubt Paul's own theological judgment. [61] But his Jewish–Christian opponents will no doubt have disagreed with it. [62] There is also a strange disagreement here compared with Gal 2 : 7, where Paul distinguishes between "the gospel of uncircumcision" ($\tau\grave{o}$ $\epsilon\mathring{v}\alpha\gamma\gamma\acute{\epsilon}\lambda\iota o\nu$ $\tau\hat{\eta}s$ $\mathring{\alpha}\kappa\rho o\beta v\sigma$-$\tau\acute{\iota}\alpha s$) and "the gospel of circumcision" ([$\tau\grave{o}$ $\epsilon\mathring{v}\alpha\gamma\gamma\acute{\epsilon}\lambda\iota o\nu$] $\tau\hat{\eta}s$ $\pi\epsilon\rho\iota\tau o\mu\hat{\eta}s$). He seems to hesitate in calling the latter a "gospel" and we must supplement what is left out. He also connects only the "gospel of uncircum-

cision" with the notion of grace. [63] But the whole context of the conference in Jerusalem presupposes that there were two gospels. What the conference agreed upon was that there is no material difference between the two gospels and that both are the work of God (see on 2 : 1–10). Therefore, Paul would not have denied the quality of "grace" to the "gospel of circumcision" at the time of the Jerusalem conference. In the meantime, however, things have changed (since Antioch, 2 : 11–14). Now Paul and his opponents deny each other the salvific power of their gospels (see on Gal 2 : 17, 21).

After the self–correction in v 7a, Paul now restates the cause in a different form. If he blamed the situation before on the Galatians (v 6), he now blames it on the opponents. [64] False teachers [65] have confused the minds of the Galatians. Again Paul uses "political" language: $\tau\alpha\rho\acute{\alpha}\sigma\sigma\epsilon\iota\nu$ ("disturb") describes the destructive work of political agitators who cause confusion and turmoil. [66]

59   On the *correctio*, see Lausberg, *Handbuch*, § 784–86; Martin, *Rhetorik*. 279f; BDR, § 495 n. 12.

60    $\check{o}$ ("which") refers to $\check{\epsilon}\tau\epsilon\rho o\nu$ $\epsilon\mathring{v}\alpha\gamma\gamma\acute{\epsilon}\lambda\iota o\nu$ ("another gospel") and not to "gospel" alone, nor to the entire clause introduced by $\check{o}\tau\iota$. Cf. Burton, p. 22: "the clause is thus a qualification of the preceding statement, intended to exclude the possible implication that what the Galatians were urged to accept was really a gospel which might legitimately be substituted for that which Paul preached." There is no material difference between $\check{\epsilon}\tau\epsilon\rho o\nu$ ("another") and $\check{\alpha}\lambda\lambda o$ ("other"); see for a discussion of this point Burton, pp. 22–24; BDF, § 306, 4; BDR, § 306, 4; James K. Elliott, "The Use of $\check{\epsilon}\tau\epsilon\rho o s$ in the New Testament," *ZNW* 60 (1969) 140f; Schlier, p. 38 n. 1; Mussner, pp. 56f. See also Gal 2 : 2, 5, 20b; 1 Cor 15 : 10, 2 Cor 11 : 4.

61   Cf. the parallel in 2 Cor 11 : 4, where Paul speaks of "another Jesus" whom the opponents proclaim, "another Spirit" and "another gospel" which the Corinthians have received and accepted. Cf. Mussner, p. 56 n. 64.

62   Cf. also Einar Molland, *Das paulinische Euangelion* (Oslo: Dybwad, 1934) 42f; Mussner, pp. 55f; and the article of Grässer on Gal 2 : 6, mentioned above n. 45.

63   Cf. also Gal 1 : 6, 15; 2 : 9, 21; 5 : 4; furthermore Rom 3 : 24 and often in Paul. The concept became part of the Pauline tradition, as Eph 2 : 5, 8; Col 1 : 6; 3 : 16; etc. show.

64    $\epsilon\mathring{\iota}$ $\mu\acute{\eta}$ ("except that") has an exceptive, not merely an oppositive force; it does not limit the preceding

but restates it. Cf. Lightfoot's ironical paraphrase: "only in this sense it is another gospel, in that it is an attempt to pervert the one true Gospel." See also Burton, pp. 23f; Schlier, p. 38 n. 2; Mussner, p. 57; BDF, § 376; 448, 8; BDR, § 376, 1; 448, 8.

65    $\tau\iota\nu\acute{\epsilon}s$ $\epsilon\mathring{\iota}\sigma\iota\nu$ ("certain ones are") is the phrase by which Paul refers to the opponents, thus avoiding the use of names and the providing of free publicity. The practice was common. So the *Ep. Pet.* 2.3 (see Appendix 3) calls the Paulinists "some from among the Gentiles." Ign. *Smyrn.* 5.3 gives this reason for not mentioning the names of his opponents: "their names, since they are unbelievers, I have decided not to write down, but may I not even remember them until they repent about Christ's suffering, which is our resurrection" (tr. Goodspeed). Cf. also Gal 2 : 6, 12; 4 : 17; 5 : 7, 10, 12; 6 : 12–13; Rom 3 : 8; 1 Cor 4 : 18; 15 : 12, 34; 2 Cor 3 : 1; 10 : 2; 1 Tim 1 : 3, 6, 19; 5 : 15; 6 : 10, 21; 2 Pet 3 : 9; Acts 15 : 1, 5; Ign. *Smyrn.* 2.1; 5.1; *Trall.* 10. See Bauer, *s.v.* $\tau\grave{\iota}s$ 1, a, β. Mussner's conclusion (p. 57) that the opponents are few in number, and that their names are not known or worth mentioning, is precisely what the rhetorical device intends to foster. See also C. F. D. Moule, *An Idiom Book of New Testament Greek* (Cambridge: Cambridge University, 1955) 106 n. 1.

66   For references see LSJ, *s.v.*; Bauer, *s.v.*, 2. The special meaning with reference to the agitation of "heretics" is found also Gal 5 : 10; Acts 15 : 24.

These opponents attempt "to pervert the gospel of Christ." Paul's language is of course biased. If the agitators had to express their goals, they would no doubt use language more favorable to themselves.[67]

The term μεταστρέφω ("turn things upside down") is again originally political and suggests revolutionary activities.[68] It is here that, so far as we know, for the first time Paul claims to represent Christian orthodoxy,[69] i.e., "the gospel of Christ."[70] Consequently, if the Galatians were to go over completely to the opposition, they would become, in the Pauline sense, apostates.

Excursus:
The Curse in 1:8–9

As the text now stands, vv 8–9 form a double curse. The two curses in v 8 and v 9 are parallel in formulation: the protases (vv 8a, 9c) state the conditions under which the curse will become effective, while the apodoses (vv 8b, 9d) are magical imperatives. For details see the analysis below. Strictly speaking, however, what appears to be a double curse is only the reissuing of a previous curse. For that reason, v 8 seems to be a (non-literary) "citation" from an earlier occasion, and v 9 its "application." The "application" in v 9 is given in the form of a reissuing of the previous curse, with special attention to the present situation as described in 1:6–7. The original occasion

of the first curse remains unclear. However, we can assume that the original curse had a similar purpose compared with its reissuing. We may also supplement what we know from phenomenology of religion about the general background and significance of the phenomenon.

One of the special features of Paul's Galatians is that the curse (1:8–9) must be seen in its connection with the conditional blessing in the *peroratio* (see on 6:16). As a result the entire "body" of the letter is bracketed in by this conditional curse and blessing. This composition has important consequences for the form and content of the letter. The letter to the Galatians is more than the carrier of an apologetic argument, but in addition it assumes the power of a magical letter.[71] The combination of curse and blessing also places the entire document in the context of "sacred law." In a manner analogous to that of other religious and quasi–religious communities, Paul treats the Galatian churches as religious societies, which have their own constitutive law and which sanction them by curse and blessing. Hereby, he places the entire content of the letter at the high level of "sacred law." Thus, obedience becomes a matter of life or death. Furthermore, the employment of curse and blessing presupposes a situation of legal conflict. In this conflict the letter provides the opportunity for the final and non–negotiable decision (see on the concept of κανών ["rule"] in 6:16).

This phenomenon is known from the traditions of "sacred law" in the ancient Near East, the Old Testa-

---

67   On the intention of the opponents see the notion of θέλειν ("want") in Gal 4:17; 6:12–13; implicitly also 4:9, 21; 5:17.

68   μεταστρέφω ("turn about, turn around") corresponds to μετατίθημι ("turn away") in 1:6. The meaning comes close to "misrepresent." See LSJ, *s.v.*; Bauer, *s.v.*; Georg Bertram, "μεταστρέφω," *TDNT* 7.729. Cf. similar notions, like μετασχημα-τίζομαι ("change the form of," 2 Cor 11:13–15); μετακινέομαι ("shift," Col 1:23).

69   τὸ εὐαγγέλιον τοῦ Χριστοῦ ("the gospel of Christ") is a concept often attested in Paul; it refers both to the content and the preaching of the gospel message. See Rom 15:19; 1 Cor 9:12; 2 Cor 2:12; 9:13, 10:14; Phil 1:27; 1 Thess 3:2; furthermore Rom 1:1–3, 9; 2 Cor 4:4; 2 Thess 1:8. For Paul, it is identical with the "gospel of the uncircumcision" (Gal 2:7) as he preached it (1:8, 9, 11, 16, 23; 2:2, 5, 14; 4:13). On the concept, see Kramer, *Christ, Lord, Son of God*, 50ff; Stuhlmacher, *Evangelium*, 266ff. The genitive "of Christ" is both objective and subjective. Cf. the phrase "through a revelation of

Jesus Christ" (1:12) and the genitive constructions in 1:6; 2:16; 3:22; 5:24.

70   See on this problem my essay "Orthodoxy and Heresy in Primitive Christianity," *Int.* 19 (1965) 299–311, esp. 306–09; Bauer, *Orthodoxy and Heresy*, 312.

71   On the magical letters, see the Introduction, §5.

ment, Judaism, Greek religions, Roman religions, and primitive Christianity.[72]

The most interesting examples include the great curse in Qumran's 1QS 2.5–17:

> "and the Levites shall curse all the men of the lot of Satan, saying: 'Be cursed because of all your guilty wickedness! May He deliver you up for torture at the hands of the vengeful Avengers! May He visit you with destruction by the hands of all the Wreakers of Revenge! Be cursed without mercy because of the darkness of your deed! Be damned in the shadowy place of everlasting fire! May God not heed when you call on Him, nor pardon you by blotting out your sin! May He raise His angry face towards you for vengeance! May there be no "Peace" for you in the mouth of those who hold fast to the Fathers!' And after the blessing and the cursing, all those entering the Covenant shall say, 'Amen, Amen!'
>
> "And the Priests and the Levites shall continue, saying: 'Cursed be the man who enters his Covenant while walking among the idols of his heart, who sets up before himself his stumbling–block of sin so that he may backslide! Hearing the words of this Covenant, he blesses himself in his heart and says, 'Peace be with me, even though I walk in the stubborness of my heart' (Deut 29: 18–19), whereas his spirit, parched (for lack of truth) and watered (with lies), shall be destroyed without pardon. God's wrath and His zeal for His precepts shall consume him in everlasting destruction. All the curses of the Covenant shall cling to him and God will set him apart for evil. He shall be cut off from the midst of all the sons of light, and because he has turned aside from God on account of his idols and his stumbling–block of sin, his lot shall be among those who are cursed for ever.' And after them, all those entering the Covenant shall answer and say, 'Amen, Amen!'"[73]

As a parallel from the Greek side, the "Hippocratic Oath" may be singled out. The "Oath" provides the ground rules for the (or: a) professional guild of the physicians in the form of a covenant made before the gods "Apollo the Physician and Asclepius and Hygeia." It concludes with this statement: "If I fulfil this oath and do not violate it, may it be granted to me to enjoy life and art, being honored with fame among all men for all time to come; if I transgress it and swear falsely, may the opposite of all this be my lot."[74]

---

72 For bibliographical and textual material see Willy Schottroff, *Der altisraelitische Fluchspruch* (WMANT 30; Neukirchen–Vluyn: Neukirchener Verlag, 1969); Gerhard Liedke, *Gestalt und Bezeichnung alttestamentlicher Rechtssätze* (WMANT 39; Neukirchen–Vluyn; Neukirchener Verlag, 1971) esp. 153 n. 3; Dennis J. McCarthy, *Old Testament Covenant: A Survey of Current Opinions* (Richmond: John Knox, 1972) 39ff; Volkmar Wagner, *Rechtssätze in gebundener Sprache und Rechtssatzreihen im israelitischen Recht* (BZAW 127; Berlin: de Gruyter, 1972); Kurt Latte, *Heiliges Recht: Untersuchungen zur Geschichte der sakralen Rechtsformen in Griechenland* (Tübingen: Mohr, Siebeck, 1920) 61ff; Franciszek Sokolowski, *Lois Sacrées de l'Asie Mineure* (Paris: de Boccard, 1955) no. 48, 49, 50, 58; *MAMA* VII, pp. xxxivff; Claus–Hunno Hunzinger, *Die jüdische Bannpraxis im neutestamentlichen Zeitalter* (diss. Göttingen, 1954 [unpublished; *non vidi*]); Wolfgang Wiefel, "Fluch und Sakralrecht," *Numen* 16 (1969) 211–33; Brun, *Segen und Fluch;* Göran Forkman, *The Limits of the Religious Community: Expulsion from the Religious Community within the Qumran Sect, within Rabbinic Judaism, and within Primitive Christianity* (Lund: Gleerup, 1972). Rich collections of material are found in the following articles: Johannes Behm, "ἀνάθεμα," *TDNT* 1.354–56; Wolfgang Schrage, "ἀποσυνάγωγος," *TDNT* 7.848–52; Helmut Koester, "Segen und Fluch III. Im Neuen Testament," *RGG³* 5.1651f;

W. Doskocil, "Exkommunikation," *RAC* 7.1–22; Wolfgang Speyer, "Fluch," *RAC* 7.1160–1288; Karl Preisendanz, "Fluchtafel," *RAC* 8.1–29.

73 Tr. Geza Vermes, *The Dead Sea Scrolls in English* (Baltimore; Penguin, 1962) 73–74. See also the strongly anti–Pauline *Contestatio*, ps.–Clem. *Hom.*, pp. 2–4; tr. HSW, *NT Apocrypha*, 2.112–15.

74 ὅρκον μὲν οὖν μοι τόνδε ἐπιτελέα ποιέοντι καὶ μὴ ξυγχέοντι εἴη ἐπαύρασθαι καὶ βίου καὶ τέχνης δοξαζομένῳ παρὰ πᾶσιν ἀνθρώποις ἐς τὸν ἀεὶ χρόνον, παραβαίνοντι δὲ καὶ ἐπιορκοῦντι τἀναντία τουτέων. Text and tr. of Ludwig Edelstein, *The Hippocratic Oath* (Supplement to the Bulletin of the History of Medicine 1; Baltimore: Johns Hopkins, 1943) 2–3; see also M. P. Nilsson, *Geschichte der griechischen Religion* (HKAW 5.2.1–2; Munich: Beck, ²1955–61) 2.291.

The Nag Hammadi texts include a hermetic writing without title, at the end of which we find a long oath with blessing and cursing.[75]

■ **8** The situation of the Galatian churches, as the apostle had described it in 1:6–7, calls for his immediate reaction. This reaction, without any further explanation, takes the form of what appears now as a double curse. The sentence beginning with the $\dot{\epsilon}\dot{\alpha}\nu$ *eventuale* (with the aorist subjunctive) defines the conditions under which the curse is to become effective. In principle the curse is directed against any reader of the letter who falls under the conditions stated in vv 8a, 9c.[76] In actuality of course, Paul has his opponents and, potentially, the Galatians in mind—should they go over to the opponents. Furthermore, it is significant that the curse is presented as a "self-curse." The relationship

between the two curses in vv 8 and 9 is more subtle than a mere parallelism. The conditional clause in v 8a ("even if we or an angel from heaven should proclaim a gospel to you contrary to that which we proclaimed to you. . .")[77] includes first a "self–curse" of Paul himself; the plural "we" refers certainly to Paul himself, in which case we would translate "I", but more likely other persons are to be included.[78] Certainly, within the present context, the co–senders of the letter are to be included (cf. 1:2). But if Paul cites an earlier curse, persons present at the earlier occasion would have to be included as well. The curse then extends to the "angel from heaven" which might appear and "preach a gospel"[79] different from and thus contrary to[80] the gospel, which Paul preaches and which the Galatian churches have accepted when they were founded. Usually commentators believe that these references

75 *Disc. 8–9*, ed. Martin Krause and Pahor Labib, *Gnostische und hermetische Schriften aus Codex II und Codex VI* (Glückstadt: Augustin, 1971) 63 lines 16–32. In a conversation with Dr. Jan Bergman of Uppsala it became apparent that there may be yet unexplored connections with ancient Egyptian funerary inscriptions. See Henry Sottas, *La préservation de la propriété funéraire dans l'ancienne Egypte avec le recueil des formules d'imprécation* (Paris: Champion, 1913); André Parrot, *Malédictions et violations de tombes* (Paris: Geuthner, 1939); Eberhard Otto, *Die biographischen Inschriften der ägyptischen Spätzeit: ihre geistesgeschichtliche und literarische Bedeutung* (Leiden: Brill 1954) 53ff. These inscriptions are like magical letters from the dead, addressing the potential visitor of the tomb, and threatening him with a curse, if he is a graverobber; for those who perform the correct ritual there is a blessing. See further, Alan H. Gardiner and Kurt Sethe, *Egyptian Letters to the Dead Mainly from the Old and Middle Kingdoms* (London: The Egypt Exploration Society, 1928) nos. 4, 5; Paul Moraux, *Une Imprécation Funéraire à Néocésarée* (Paris: Maisonneuve, 1959); Rudolf G. Björck, *Der Fluch des Christen Sabinus: Papyrus Upsaliensis 8* (Uppsala: Almqvist & Wiksell, 1938); Rudolf Egger, *Von Römern, Juden, Christen und Barbaren* (Österreichische Akademie der Wissenschaften, phil. hist. Kl., Sitzungsberichte, Band 247, Abh. 3, 1965).

76 For the formulation of such conditions in curses see Schottroff, *Der altisraelitische Fluchpruch*, 36ff, 92ff, 104ff (above n. 72).

77 The textual tradition is divided at this point: part of it reads $\epsilon\dot{v}\alpha\gamma\gamma\epsilon\lambda\dot{\iota}\sigma\eta\tau\alpha\iota$ (א* A lat Marcion Cyprian), part $\epsilon\dot{v}\alpha\gamma\gamma\epsilon\lambda\dot{\iota}\zeta\eta\tau\alpha\iota$ (P⁵¹ B D* G H K P). See Nestle-Aland and Kurt Aland, *et. al.*, *The Greek New Testament* (Stuttgart: Württembergische Bibelanstalt, 1966); Metzger, *Textual Commentary*, 590. The position of $\dot{v}\mu\hat{\iota}\nu$ is also disputed: some witnesses have it before, some after the verb (see also the discussion by Burton, p. 26). On $\dot{\epsilon}\dot{\alpha}\nu$ with the subjunctive, see BDF § 373; BDR § 373.

78 Paul's usage of the first person singular and plural allows for both possibilities; see BDF § 280; BDR § 280; Bauer, *s.v.* $\dot{\epsilon}\gamma\dot{\omega}$; Roller, *Formular*, 169ff; Mussner, p. 59 n. 84. On the "self–curse" which Paul uses also Rom 9:3 (cf. Mark 14:71; Matt 26:74; Acts 23:12–13, 14, 21; ps.–Clem. *Hom.*, *Contestatio* 4.3) see Brun, *Segen und Fluch*, 126ff; Speyer, "Fluch," *RAC* 7.1208f, 1211, 1217 (n. 72 above).

79 $\epsilon\dot{v}\alpha\gamma\gamma\epsilon\lambda\dot{\iota}\zeta o\mu\alpha\iota$ ("proclaim the gospel") is a technical term of primitive Christian missionary language. Cf. Gal 1:9, 11, 16, 23; 4:13; Rom 1:15; 10:15; 1 Cor 1:17; 9:16; 15:1–2; 2 Cor 10:16; 11:7; 1 Thess 3:6. See on the concept Gerhard Friedrich, *TDNT* 2.707ff; Bauer, *s.v.*; Stuhlmacher, *Evangelium*; Otto Michel, "Evangelium," *RAC* 6.1107–60.

80 $\pi\alpha\rho'$ $\ddot{o}$ is adversative ("against, contrary to"). Cf. Rom 16:17: $\pi\alpha\rho\dot{\alpha}$ $\tau\dot{\eta}\nu$ $\delta\iota\delta\alpha\chi\dot{\eta}\nu$ ("against the teaching"); Acts 18:13; Rom 1:25, 26; 4:18; 11:24; 1 Cor 3:10–15. See the discussion about other interpretations in Burton, pp. 26f; Schlier, p. 40 n. 3; Mussner, p. 59. In Gal 1:8, 9 especially (cf. 2:4–5, 11–14; 6:12–14; etc.), Paul takes the message of the opponents as diametrically opposed to his own.

are "a highly improbable supposition,"[81] since the Apostle appears so convinced of his message that he could not conceive of himself as a "heretic."[82] However, if the curse were issued at an earlier occasion, the point was precisely to envision the seemingly unthinkable, and thus to include all forms of heresy. Also, the conditional "self–curse" avoids the outright act of cursing others, and thus respects the early Christian prohibition of cursing.[83] A wealth of material from antiquity makes it virtually certain that Paul has in mind actual cases of "angelic revelations."[84] It is possible—to say more would be speculation—that the opponents derived their message from such angelic revelations. In any case, the characteristic differences between v 8 and v 9 show that Paul deals with real situations, not with improbabilities. The earlier occasion, when the curse was first (or repeatedly?) pronounced, certainly was directed at real possibilities. This would be especially true if the curse functioned in a liturgical context. Therefore, there can be no doubt that the present application points to the real situation in the Galatian churches, not to hypothetical situations or to Paul's desire to be rhetorically impressive (cf. 1:10).[85]

The imperative ἀνάθεμα ἔστω ("let him be accursed") implies the magical concept according to which the curse as it is set down in writing becomes automatically effective whenever the conditions of v 8a are fulfilled.[86]

The Greek term ἀνάθεμα (in classical Greek ἀνάθημα,[87] in Hebrew חרם)[88] signifies something which has been withdrawn from profane use and consecrated to the deity, either as a votive offering or for its destruction.[89] Paul means it in the latter sense of the term.[90]

■ 9 The second curse repeats the first curse and thereby applies the latter to the present situation: "As we have said before so now I say again: If anyone preaches to you a gospel contrary to that which you have received, let him be accursed." The phrase ὡς προειρήκαμεν ("as we have said before") refers to something preceding v 8,[91] or to the first visit, another earlier visit,[92] or an

81 Lightfoot, p. 77; cf. Burton, p. 26; Schlier, p. 40 n. 4; Mussner, p. 60.
82 Cf. Mussner, p. 60.
83 Cf. Rom 12:14; Luke 6:27; Matt 5:44; Jas 3:9; *Did.* 1.3.
84 Revelations through angels were common in antiquity. See the collections of material by Walter Grundmann et al. "ἄγγελος," *TDNT* 1.74–76; Johann Michl, "Engel," *RAC* 5.53ff (pagan), 60ff (Jewish), 97ff (gnostic), 109ff (Christian). Cf. also Col 2:18, and on this passage Lohse, *Colossians and Philemon*, 117ff; Ign. *Smyrn.* 6.1. Whether Paul has specifically Gal 3:19 in mind or wants to contrast himself with an angel of revelation (cf. 4:14) remains uncertain. See Schlier, p. 40 n. 1.
85 The transition would then be provided by ἀλλὰ καί. On this see Bauer, *s.v.* ἀλλά, 3; BDF, § 448, 6; BDR, § 448, 6.
86 On the logical subject of curses see Schottroff, *Fluchspruch*, 50ff; Speyer, "Fluch," *RAC* 7.1160ff.
87 Cf. the concluding *ANEΘEMA* (=ἀνάθεμα) on the curse tablets from Megara (1–2 c. A.D.); cf. *Inscriptiones Graecae* 3/3, p. xiiif; Adolf Deissmann, "Anathema," *ZNW* 2 [1901] 342; idem, *Licht vom Osten* (Tübingen: Mohr, Siebeck, ⁴1923) 74, 258), and from Cnidus. See James H. Moulton and George Milligan, *The Vocabulary of the Greek New Testament Illustrated from the Papyri and Other Non-literary Sources* (London: Hodder, 1930) 33; LSJ, *s.v.*; Speyer, *RAC* 7.1213; Preisendanz, *RAC* 8.1–29.
88 So Johannes Behm, *TDNT* 1.354; Bauer, *s.v.*; Schlier, p. 40; Schottroff, *Fluchspruch*, 27 n. 4.
89 Cf. Karl Hofmann, "Anathema," *RAC* 1.427–30; Behm, *ibidem*, 1.354f.
90 Cf. 1 Cor 5:5: παραδοῦναι τὸν τοιοῦτον τῷ σατανᾷ εἰς ὄλεθρον τῆς σαρκός ("to hand him over to Satan for the purpose of the destruction of his flesh"); Acts 8:20; 13:10–11; 1 Tim 1:19–20. Also Paul's other references to curses should be compared (Rom 9:3; 1 Cor 12:3; 16:22). See Günther Bornkamm, "Das Anathema in der urchristlichen Abendmahlsliturgie," in his *Das Ende des Gesetzes* (Gesammelte Aufsätze vol. 1; BEvTh 16; Munich: Kaiser, 1952) 123–32; ET "The Anathema in the Early Christian Lord's Supper Liturgy," in *Early Christian Experience* (tr. Paul L. Hammer; London: SCM; New York: Harper & Row, 1969) 169–76, 178f; Ernst Käsemann, "Sätze heiligen Rechts im Neuen Testament," in his *Exegetische Versuche und Besinnungen* (2 vols.; Göttingen: Vandenhoeck & Ruprecht, 1960, 1964) 2.69–82; ET "Sentences of Holy Law in the New Testament," in *New Testament Questions of Today* (tr. W. J. Montague; London: SCM, 1969) 66–81.
91 So Chrysostom; Schlier, p. 40.
92 So Bauer, *s.v.* προεῖπον, 2a. Cf. also the parallels in Gal 5:21; 2 Cor 13:2; 1 Thess 4:6; etc.

earlier letter. Strangely, Paul then changes from the first person plural to the first person singular. This cannot simply be an awkward expression. [93] There are two other peculiarities: the phrase καὶ ἄρτι πάλιν λέγω ("so now I say again") places a temporal distance between the two occurrences. In addition, the protasis now has εἰ with the indicative of reality, [94] pointing to a concrete instance. These changes seem to indicate that the two curses are related in such a way that the second actualizes the first (λέγω = "I say now"). [95] The application of the curse is then justified by a reference to the fact (cf. 1:6–7) that the opponents [96] have introduced into the churches a gospel which is contrary to that which they had "received" in the beginning. [97] The whole act of the curse has strong legal overtones and amounts to a ban or excommunication,—in fact Gal 1:8–9 is the first instance of Christian excommunication. [98] In this sense, the passage can be compared with the *Birkat ha-minim*, the excommunication ban which is spoken against the heretics in the *Shemoneh Esreh*. [99]

■ **10** The curse in vv 8–9 has ended the *exordium* rather abruptly. In terms of composition this makes a transition to the next section desirable. Such a transition (*transitus*) seems to be provided in vv 10–11. [100] In v 10 Paul raises and answers two different questions which have kept commentators puzzling. [101] They have been recognized as rhetorical, as parallel, and as interpreting each other. [102] If the questions express the same idea in different ways, and if v 10c implies a negative answer to the second question (v 10b), this negative answer must apply also to the first question (v 10a). In addition, the negative answer is apparent from the questions themselves: "For am I now persuading men or God?" may reject one of the alternatives or both. The decision depends upon the meaning of the phrases "persuade men" and "persuade God." The former, "persuade men (ἀνθρώπους πείθω) is, as the parallels show, a definition of rhetoric. [103] Since Plato philosophers and others have regarded the "art of persuasion" (ἡ πιθανουργικὴ τέχνη) as something rather negative and

---

93 προείρηκα ("I have said before") (א*, *pc* syᵖ) seems to be a harmonization with λέγω ("I say").

94 See on this BDF § 372; BDR § 372.

95 In this respect, Gal 1:8–9 is different from the real double curses, e.g., in Judg 5:23: "curse Meroz, says the angel of the Lord, curse bitterly its inhabitants"; Mal 2:2: ". . . I will send the curse upon you, and I will curse your blessings, indeed I have already cursed them" (*RSV*).

96 For the meaning of τις in v 9 cf. τινές in v 7.

97 παραλαμβάνω ("receive [*sc.* a tradition]) is a technical term, often corresponding to παραδίδωμι ("transmit"). The pair occurs in Greek as well as in Hebrew (= מסר ל / קבל מן). Paul uses it also in Gal 1:12; 1 Cor 11:23; 15:1, 3; Phil 4:9; 1 Thess 2:13; 4:1; see also Col 2:6; 2 Thess 3:6. On the terms, see Bauer, *s.v.*, 2, b, γ; Gerhard Delling, "παραλαμβάνω," *TDNT* 4.11–14; Klaus Wegenast, *Das Verständnis der Tradition bei Paulus und in den Deuteropaulinen* (WMANT 8; Neukirchen–Vluyn: Neukirchener Verlag, 1962) 30ff, 132ff; Conzelmann, *1 Corinthians*, 195f.

98 On later developments, see Speyer, "Fluch," *RAC* 7.1262f; *PGL*, *s.v.* ἀνάθεμα; also Birger A. Pearson, "Anti–heretical Warnings in Codex IX from Nag Hammadi," in *Essays on the Nag Hammadi Texts* (NHSt 6; Leiden: Brill, 1975) 145–54, where Gal 1:8 is mentioned (p. 154).

99 On the Birkat ha–minim, see Ismar Elbogen, *Der jüdische Gottesdienst in seiner geschichtlichen Entwicklung*

(Leipzig: Fock, 1913) 37f, 252ff; Emil Schürer, *A History of the Jewish People in the Time of Jesus Christ* (2d ed.; Edinburgh: Clark, 1896) 2/2, 88f; Moore, *Judaism* 1.292, 294; Hofmann, *RAC* 1.427–30; Schrage, *TDNT* 7.848–50; Doskocil, *RAC* 7.11ff.

100 For the analysis of form, see the introduction to this section. The ἄρτι ("now") is emphatic, as it is in 1:9; γάρ ("for") is not so much connected with the preceding, but introduces another matter. Cf. Zahn; Sieffert; Burton; Schlier, p. 41 nn. 2–3; Mussner, p. 63.

101 Cf. the discussion by Rudolf Bultmann, "πείθω," *TDNT* 6.2–3.

102 Cf. Sieffert, pp. 48f; Burton, pp. 30–32; Bultmann, ibidem.

103 See the definition (by Gorgias?) in Plato *Gorg.* 452E: "I call it the ability to persuade [τὸ πείθειν] with speeches either judges in the law courts or statesmen in the council chamber or the commons in the Assembly or an audience in any other meeting that may be held on public affairs." The orator is one who is able "to speak and to persuade the multitude" (λέγειν καὶ πείθειν τὰ πλήθη). See also 458E, 462C, 453A, 454E; *Prot.* 352E (πείθειν τοὺς ἀνθρώπους); *Theaet.* 201A; in the NT, see Matt 27:20; 28:14; Acts 12:20; 14:19; 19:26; 18:4. Cf. Lausberg, *Handbuch*, § 257; Martin, *Rhetorik*, 2–4.

unfitting. [104] Rhetoric became identified with deception, [105] slander, and even sorcery. [106] Paul as well as other Christian writers share this view. [107] The other expression, "persuade God" turns out to be a polemical definition of magic and religious quackery. [108] This background means that we should take the questions as ironical[109] and should expect an emphatic denial. [110]

Verse 10b is parallel to v 10a: "Or am I seeking to please men?" (ἢ ζητῶ ἀνθρώπους ἀρέσκειν;). Persuading men by pleasing them is of course one of the notorious strategies of political rhetoric and demagoguery. [111] The "man pleaser" was a familiar figure already in antiquity,[112] especially his most appalling variety, "the flatterer. [113] Thus, Paul's rhetorical questions imply an emphatic denial that he has anything in common with the "man pleasers." [114] Whether or not

---

104 See Plato *Soph.* 222C; and Martin, *Rhetorik*, 4ff.

105 Cf. the rhetorical strategy as part of the accusation against Socrates (Plato *Apol.* 19B): "making the weaker argument the stronger" (τὸν ἥττω λόγον κρείττω ποιεῖν). See on this Thomas Meyer, *Platons Apologie* (TBAW 42; Tübingen: Mohr, Siebeck, 1962) 133ff. The method was believed to be an invitation to deception, slander, and lies. Cf. Plato *Apol.* 17A, 18D; *Theaet.* 201C; and Meyer, *Apologie*, 115ff.

106 Cf. Plato *Euthyd.* 289D–290A.

107 See Gal 5:7–8; 1 Cor 2:4 ("not by persuasive words of wisdom"); 2 Cor 5:11; Col 2:4: πιθανολογία ("art of persuasive speech"); Ign. *Rom.* 3.3; "Christianity is not the work of persuasion (πεισμονή) but of greatness." See also Justin *Dial.* 47.1 (see Appendix 4, below) and many parallels in Philo which show how this language entered into Hellenistic Judaism. Only the "inspired" person is able to persuade in the real sense (*Virt.* 217; *Fug.* 139; *Plant.* 10; *L.A.* 3.80; *Det.* 131; *Somn.* 1.191; also *Ep. Arist.* 266), while the persuasive techniques of the common orators equal deception (*Post.* 55; *Det.* 131; *Op.* 165; *Agr.* 13).

108 See Plato's polemical comparison of the "sophists" with soothsayers and charlatans who by means of incantations, expiation rituals, and magic claim they can "persuade the gods to serve them" (τοὺς θεούς, ὥς φασιν, πείθοντές σφισιν ὑπηρετεῖν) *Rep.* 364C. See Walter Burkert, "ΓΟΗΣ: Zum griechischen Schamanismus," *RhM* 102 (1962) 36–55, esp. 55; Betz, *Paulus*, 33f, 113. The phrase is also part of a sarcastic proverb, quoted by Plato (probably from Hesiod) *Rep.* 390E: δῶρα θεοὺς πείθει, δῶρ' αἰδοίους βασιλῆας ("gifts move the gods, gifts move worshipful princes"). Cf. Euripides *Med.* 964: πείθειν δῶρα καὶ θεοὺς λόγος ("Gifts persuade even the gods, as the saying goes"). See also Ovid *Ars am.* 3.653; Pindar *Ol.* 2.144; Josephus *Ant.* 4.123; 8.256. For passages cf. August Otto, *Die Sprichwörter und sprichwörtlichen Redensarten der Römer* (Leipzig, 1890; rep. Hildesheim: Olms, 1968) 233. The proverb may also be behind the words of R. Yohanan ben Zakkai, when he says this about God: ". . . whom I cannot appease with words or bribe with money"

(*b. Ber.* 28b). For a different interpretation, see André Feuillet, "Chercher à persuader Dieu (**Gal.** 1, 10a)," *NovT* 12 (1970) 350–60.

109 Not sarcasm, as Schlier (pp. 41f) proposes.

110 Differently also Bultmann, "πείθω," *TDNT* 6.2. Cf. the apophthegm ascribed to Antisthenes (*Gnom. Vatic.* 7): "when he [Antisthenes] was asked by someone what he should teach his son he answered: if you want him to live together with the gods, a philosopher; if, however, with men, a rhetorician."

111 See the definition of rhetoric in Plato *Gorg.* 462D as "something to gratify people" (χαρίζεσθαι οἷόν τ' εἶναι ἀνθρώπους). The matter became a topos, as can be seen from ps.–Longinus *De subl.* 1.4: "for the effect of genius is not to persuade the audience but to transport them out of themselves. Invariably what inspires wonder casts a spell upon us and is always superior to what is merely convincing and pleasing. For our convictions are usually under our own control, while such passages exercise an irresistible power of mastery and get the upper hand with every member of the audience." See also Demosthenes *Ep.* 3.27; Plato *Ep.* 4, 321B; Diodorus Sic. 13.53.3; 17.115.

112 On the figure of ὁ ἄρεσκος see Aristotle *EN* 2.7.13; 4.6.1; 9.10.6; Theophrastus *Char.* 5; Plutarch *Lib. educ.* 4D; 6A.

113 Cf. Aristotle *EN* 4.6.1; Athenaeus 6.255A–B; Philo *Mig.* 111; Plutarch *Adulat.* 48E ff. See Werner Foerster, "ἀρέσκω, κτλ.," *TDNT* 1.455–57; Johannes Schneider, "κολακεύω," *TDNT* 3.817f; Bauer, *s.v.*

114 A parallel is 1 Thess 2:4: οὐχ ὡς ἀνθρώποις ἀρέσκοντες ("not as pleasing men"), and 2:5: οὔτε γάρ ποτε ἐν λόγῳ κολακείας ἐγενήθημεν ("for we never spoke in words of flattery"). Cf. 1 Cor 10:33; Eph 6:6; Col 3:22: ὡς ἀνθρωπάρεσκοι ("as manpleasers").

anybody has actually accused him of being a "man pleaser" cannot be concluded from this reference.[115]

Verse 10c confirms[116] the meaning of the preceding questions: "If I were still pleasing men, I would not be Christ's slave." The word ἔτι ("still") refers to Paul's pre–Christian existence and to his call to apostleship,[117] thus characterizing "man pleasing" as an attitude unfitting for the Christian life.[118] It is incompatible with being a "slave of Christ" (Χριστοῦ δοῦλος),[119] a concept describing Christian existence.[120]

■ 11 The introductory words "For I would have you know, brothers. . ." (γνωρίζω γὰρ ὑμῖν, ἀδελφοί. . .) open up a new section of the epistle.[121] It points forward to the *narratio* ("statement of facts") which begins in 1:12 and announces the argument Paul is going to prove in the "statement of facts" and in the rest of the letter. The rather formal tone of this announcement underscores the significance of his thesis.[122] The content cannot have been new to the Galatians;[123] they were no doubt familiar with it. Paul pretends to introduce new information, but in reality he reminds them of what they knew very well, but would at present rather forget. The thesis is very concise, but it does contain the whole basis upon which Paul's gospel, as well as his own mission, and indeed his defense in the letter, rest. Therefore, we can conclude that it is precisely this point that the Galatians have come to doubt. His defense, we can further conclude, will concentrate on the very center of the argument. It is "the gospel which is being proclaimed by me" (τὸ εὐαγγέλιον τὸ εὐαγγελισθὲν ὑπ᾽ ἐμοῦ). Apparently the opponents are criticizing this gospel, and the Galatians are about to reject it in favor of that "other gospel."[124] Paul's line of defense looks simple: his gospel "is not human in nature" (οὐκ ἔστιν κατὰ ἄνθρωπον).[125]. As we shall see, this line of defense stands in a long tradition. Already the prophets of the Old Testament as well as Socrates in the Greek tradition have used it. Most impressive is the example of Socrates in Plato's *Apology*, his defense speech, in which he denies that his wisdom is merely human, and claims that he has it from the god Apollo himself.[126]

---

115 Not every rhetorical denial is an accusation turned around! Cf. Wilhelm Lütgert, *Gesetz und Geist: Eine Untersuchung zur Vorgeschichte des Galaterbriefes* (BFCTh 22.6; Gütersloh: Bertelsmann, 1919), 42ff; 92f; Zahn; Lightfoot; Lietzmann; Burton; Oepke; Schlier; Bligh; Schmithals, *Paul and the Gnostics*, 56–58. Sieffert (p. 50), who rejects such a conclusion, is correct.

116 The γάρ supported by 𝕸 *pm* sy, makes this clearer, but the tradition is too weak.

117 So correctly Sieffert, p. 51; Schlier, p. 42; Mussner, p. 64.

118 On the form ἤμην see BDF § 98; BDR § 98.

119 Paul uses this title in reference to himself also in Rom 1:1; Phil 1:1 (cf. Tit 1:1), but not exclusively to himself; cf. Rom 6:16; 1 Cor 7:22; Col 4:12. On the title and its origin, see Karl Heinrich Rengstorf, *TDNT* 2, *s.v.*; Gerhard Sass, "Zur Bedeutung von δοῦλος bei Paulus," *ZNW* 40 (1941) 24–32; Bauer, *s.v.*, 4.

120 "Manpleasing" and being Christ's "slave" do not go together. See Eph 6:6; 1 Cor 7:22–23; Col 3:25. In Gal 2:6; 5:11 the same matter is expressed in different ways. The ἔτι ("still") stands in contrast to ἄρτι ("now") in v 10a. Cf. the οὐκέτι ("no longer") Gal 2:20; 3:25; 4:7.

121 See the introduction to the section 1:6–11 (with the parallels in n. 36); also John L. White, "Introduc-

tory Formulae in the Body of the Pauline Letter," *JBL* 90 (1971) 91–97, esp. 94 (listing Gal 1:11; Rom 1:13; 1 Thess 2:1; Phil 1:12; 2 Cor 1:8; and examples from papyrus letters); Bultmann, "γνωρίζω," *TDNT* 1.718. For similar instances in Paul, see 1 Cor 12:3; 15:1; 2 Cor 8:1.

122 The textual tradition wavers between γνωρίζω γάρ (𝕏ᵃ B D* G *al*) and γνωρίζω δέ (P⁴⁶ 𝕏* A 𝕸 *al*). See Zuntz, *Text*, 204; Mussner, p. 65 n. 110. The δέ would certainly be correct Pauline style (cf. 1 Cor 15:1; 2 Cor 8:1); γάρ as pointing forward to the next issue is a possibility; see BDF § 448, 6; BDR § 448, 6. Gal 1:11–12 is quoted textually differently in *CMC* 61.16–22.

123 See also Gal 1:10, 12.

124 See Gal 1:6–7, 8–9.

125 For this phrase, see also Gal 3:15; Rom 3:5; 1 Cor 3:3; 9:8; 15:32; 1 Pet 4:6. See Bauer, *s.v.* ἄνθρωπος, 1, c. The phrase declares something inferior compared with the divine.

126 Cf. Socrates in Plato *Apol.* 20D–E, who contrasts the divine wisdom (ἡ ἀνθρωπίνη σοφία, or: ἡ κατ᾽ ἄνθρωπον σοφία) with the higher wisdom of the god of Delphi, Apollo (20F–21A). "The merely human wisdom is of little or no value" (ἡ ἀνθρωπίνη σοφία ὀλίγου τινὸς ἀξία ἐστι καὶ οὐδενός [*Apol.* 23A]). See also above on Gal 1:1.

1

12 For I did not receive it[1] from [a ?] man, nor was I taught [it], but [I received it] through a revelation of Jesus Christ. 13/ For you have heard of my former way of life in Judaism, that I vigorously persecuted the Church of God and tried to destroy it, 14/ and that I advanced in Judaism beyond many among my people who were of the same age, since I was far more zealous for the traditions of my forefathers. 15/ But when it pleased him[2] who had set me aside from my mother's womb and called me through his grace, 16/ to reveal his son in me,[3] in order that I might preach him [=Christ] among the gentiles, immediately[4] I did not confer with 'flesh and blood,' 17/ nor did I go up to Jerusalem, to those who were apostles before me, but I went away to Arabia, and again I returned to Damascus. 18/ Then after three years I went up to Jerusalem to visit[5] Cephas, and I stayed with him for 15 days. 19/ But I saw none of the other apostles,[6] but only James the brother of the Lord.—20/ Now, what I am writing to you, behold, before God, I am not lying! 21/ After that I went into the regions of Syria and Cilicia. 22/ But I remained personally unknown[7] to the churches of Judea which are 'in Christ.'[8] 23/ They only heard that "the one who once persecuted us now preaches the faith he formerly tried to destroy"; 24/ and they praised God because of me.

2:1 Then after 14 years I went again up to Jerusalem, together with Barnabas, taking along also Titus. 2/ But I went up according to a revelation. And I laid before them the gospel which I preach among the gentiles,—but privately before the 'men of eminence'[9]—, so that I might not run or have run in vain. 3/ However, not even Titus who was with me and who was a Greek was compelled to be circumcised.

4 But because of the false brothers secretly brought in, who had infiltrated in order to spy out our freedom which we have in Christ Jesus, so that they might enslave us,—5/ to those we did not yield by submission for a moment, in order that the truth of the gospel might remain with you.

6 But as for the 'men of eminence'[9]—what they were makes no difference to me: 'God does not show partiality!'—these 'men of eminence'[9] did not make any

1. That is, the gospel.
2. That is, God.
3. So *JB*; cf. *RSV*, *NEB*: "to me."
4. *RSV* omits "immediately;" *NEB* connects it differently: "I went off at once to Arabia." Similarly *JB*.
5. So *RSV*, *JB*; cf. *NEB*.
6. So *RSV*; similarly *NEB*, *JB*.
7. Cf. *RSV*, *JB*: "still not known by sight;" *NEB*: "unknown by sight."
8. Cf. *RSV*, *JB*: "the churches of Christ in Judea;" *NEB*: "Christ's congregations in Judaea."
9. Cf. *RSV*: "those who were of repute." *NEB* has "men of repute;" *JB's* translation is from v 6 and reads: "the leading men," or "people who are acknowledged leaders."

demand upon me.[10] 7/ On the contrary, when they saw that I had been entrusted with the 'gospel of the uncircumcision,' just as Peter with the ['gospel'] of the circumcision'—8/ for he who worked through Peter for the apostolate of the circumcision also worked through me for the Gentiles[11]— 9/ and when they recognized the grace which was given to me, James and Cephas and John, the reputed 'pillars', gave to me and to Barnabas the right hand of partnership, [agreeing] that 'we [go] to the Gentiles, and they to the circumcision.' 10/ [They] only [requested] that we should remember the poor, which request I have made my special concern to fulfill.

11   But when Cephas came to Antioch, I opposed him to his face because he stood condemned. 12/ For until certain people came from James he ate with the Gentiles, but when they arrived he drew back and separated himself,[12] because he was afraid of the men of the circumcision. 13/ And also the other Jews committed the same hypocrisy with him,[13] so that even Barnabas was carried away through their hypocrisy.[14] 14/ However, when I saw that they did not act consistently[15] with the truth of the gospel, I said to Cephas before all of them: 'If you, being a Jew, live like a Gentile and not like a Jew, how can you compel the Gentiles to live like Jews?'

10   Cf. *RSV*: "added nothing to me;" similarly *JB*. *NEB* has: "did not prolong the consultation," with the alternative: "gave no further instructions."

11   *NEB* makes Paul an apostle at this point: "also made me an apostle to the Gentiles." *RSV* is more accurate in not promoting Paul. *JB* introduces another unknown person: "The same person whose action had made Peter the apostle of the circumcised had given me a similar mission to the pagans." For the problems of this sentence, see the commentary below.

12   That is, from the Gentiles.

13   Cf. *RSV*: "acting insincerely;" *NEB*: "showed the same lack of principle;" *JB*: "joined him in his pretence."

14   Cf. *RSV*: "insincerity;" *NEB*: "played false;" *JB*: "Barnabas felt himself obliged to copy their behavior."

15   Cf. *RSV*: "that they were not straightforward about the truth of the gospel." *NEB*: "that their conduct did not square with the truth of the Gospel," with the alternative: "that they were not making progress towards...." *JB* loses the metaphor: "they were not respecting the true meaning of the Good News."

Analysis

As the Greco–Roman rhetoricians recommend, Paul's *exordium* ("introduction" [1:6–11]) is followed by the "statement of facts" (διήγησις, *narratio*).[16] In discussing Paul's *narratio*, which extends over the entire section 1:12–2:14, Quintilian's remark should be kept in mind: "there is no single law or fixed rule governing the method of defense. We must consider what is most advantageous in the circumstances and nature of the case ..."[17] Consequently the handbooks contain wide-ranging discussions which leave room for considerable differences of opinion going back to the various schools of rhetorical theory.

Cicero's treatment of the subject in *De inv.* 1. 19. 27–31. 30 contains what may be regarded as a summary of the *communis opinio*. He starts by providing a general definition of "narrative": "the narrative is an exposition of events that have occurred or are supposed to have occurred."[18] He then distinguishes between three types (*genera*) of narrative, the first of which

16   On the *narratio* see Anton Schäfer, *De rhetorum praeceptis quae ad narrationem pertinent* (Dissertation; Freiburg i.B., 1921); Fritz Loheit, *Untersuchungen zur antiken Selbstapologie* (Dissertation; Rostock: Adlers Erben, 1928); Volkmann, *Rhetorik*, § 13; Lausberg, *Handbuch*, §§ 289–347; Martin, *Rhetorik*, 75–89.

17   Quint. 4.2.84: "Neque enim est una lex defensionis certumque praescriptum: pro re, pro tempore in-

tuenda quae prosint, ..." The tr. is that of Butler, LCL.

18   *De inv.* 1.19.27: "Narratio est rerum gestarum aut ut gestarum expositio." The tr. is by Hubbel, LCL. Cf. Quint. 4.2.31 (see n. 37, below). For other definitions, see Lausberg, *Handbuch*, § 289; Martin, *Rhetorik*, 75f.

applies to Galatians: "that form of narrative which contains an exposition of a case of law."[19] Nearly all writers of the period agree that such a narrative ought to possess three necessary qualities (*virtutes necessariae*): "it should be brief, clear, and plausible."[20] In Cicero,[21] the *Rhetorica ad Herennium*,[22] and especially Quintilian,[23] we find extensive discussions about how such qualities can best be achieved. Several points in Quintilian's discussion of the *narratio* are directly relevant to an understanding of Paul. The first of these points addresses the question of whether or not the *narratio* is dispensable in certain cases.[24] Contrary to others, Quintilian takes the position that the *narratio* should not be omitted even when the accused simply denies the charge.[25] Indeed, in Galatians we have strong denials (see on 1:11–12; 2:17, 21) but also a longer *narratio* (1:12–2:14).

Quintilian's explanation, for which he cites the highest authorities,[26] makes clear why the short sentence of a denial is not an adequate "statement of facts."[27] The denial must not simply contradict the charge made by the opponent. Instead, the denial should introduce the subject matter on which the defense wishes to be judged.[28] It is part of the defense strategy. The *narratio*, on the other hand, is more than simply a narrative form of the denial.[29] In fact, the *narratio* may not even explicitly mention the charge. Its purpose is to deal with the facts that have a bearing on the case, in order to make the denial plausible.[30]

If this has a bearing on Paul, one should exercise caution and not simply conclude from v 11 that the charge against Paul was in fact that his gospel was "according to man." Rather this denial is part of his defense strategy. In v 12, the simple denial of v 11 is made more explicit: "it is not according to man" means negatively, "I did not receive it from [a?] man nor was I taught [it]," and positively, "I received [it] through a revelation of Jesus Christ" (v 12).[31] The *narratio* proper begins in v 13, substantiating the claims made in v 12 by appropriate facts. However, neither the denial nor the charge is explicitly mentioned in 1:13–2:14. The reason for this can only be that the facts of 1:13–2:14 serve to make the denial of 1:11–12 credible in the eyes of the addressees of the letter.

Another point of relevance concerns the beginning of the *narratio*, which intends "not merely to instruct, but rather to persuade the judge."[32] Quintilian recommends beginning the *narratio* with a statement, the *propositio*,[33] which will influence the judge in some way, even though he may be well-informed about the case.[34] He mentions examples like these: "I know that you are aware. . . "; "You remember . . . "; "You are not ignorant of the fact . . . "; etc.[35] Which of these one chooses depends entirely upon how one can best influence the judge.

Paul announces his *narratio* with the words (v 11): γνωρίζω γὰρ ὑμῖν, ἀδελφοί ("I want you to know, brothers"), thus conforming to Quintilian's advice. We must conclude, therefore, that the term γνωρίζω ("know") does not simply announce information, but by pretending to tell the Galatians something new in fact reminds them of something they no doubt know,

19 *De inv.* 1.20.28. "nunc de narratione ea quae causae continet expositionem dicendum videtur." See Lausberg, *Handbuch*, § 290, 1.

20 *De inv.* 1.20.28. "Oportet igitur eam tres habere res: ut brevis, ut aperta, ut probabilis sit." See Lausberg, *Handbuch*, §§ 294–334.

21 *De inv.* 1.20.28–21:30.

22 1.8.12–10.16.

23 4.2.2–132.

24 4.2.4ff. See Martin, *Rhetorik*, 79–81.

25 4.2.9.

26 4.2.9ff.

27 4.2.12. " 'Non occidi hominem': nulla narratio est; . . . "

28 4.2.1. ". . . res de qua pronuntiaturus est indicetur."

29 Cf. 4.2.10.

30 4.2.11; examples are given in 4.2.12–18.

31 Cf. Gal 1:1.

32 4.2.21. "Neque enim narratio in hoc reperta est, ut tantum cognoscat iudex, sed aliquanto magis ut consentiat." See Lausberg, *Handbuch*, §§ 300–01, 308.

33 Cf. Quint. 3.9.5; 4.2.7, 30; its purpose is defined 3.9.2: "proponere quidem quae sis probaturus necesse est." Cf. Lausberg, *Handbuch*, § 289.

34 4.2.21.

35 4.2.21–23.

but would at this time rather forget.[36] As to the "facts" themselves, Quintilian provides a more explicit definition than Cicero, saying: "the statement of facts consists in the persuasive exposition of that which either has been done, or is supposed to have been done, or, to quote the definition by Apollodorus, is a speech instructing the audience as to the nature of the case in dispute."[37] Consequently, the facts themselves, as well as their delivery, are subjected to partisan interest.[38] The three qualities of lucidity, brevity, and plausibility serve no other purpose.[39] This does not mean that the facts are necessarily false. On the contary, a statement which is wholly in our favor is most plausible when it is true.[40] But truth is not always credible, nor is the credible always true. In short, whether the "facts" are true or fictitious, the effort required to make them believable is the same.[41]

Most of the discussion of the *narratio* by the rhetoricians is devoted to the explanation of the three qualities.[42] Quintilian begins with lucidity or clarity.[43] This quality is ensured by first choosing "words appropriate, significant and free from meanness" and by avoiding the "farfetched or unusual"; secondly, by the "distinct account of facts, persons, times, places and causes."[44] The delivery must conform to this quality,

so that the judge will readily accept it.[45] At this point Quintilian wants to eliminate all rhetorical tricks and gimmickry normally employed to evoke the applause of the crowds.[46] It is when the speaker gives the impression of absolute truth that his rhetoric is best.[47] One would have to say that Paul's *narratio* conforms to these requirements.[48]

The quality of brevity[49] will be achieved, "if in the first place we start at the point of the case at which it begins to concern the judge, secondly avoid irrelevance, and finally cut out everything the removal of which neither hampers the activities of the judge nor harms our own case."[50] As Quintilian sees it, brevity should not be misunderstood as the excision of the necessary information: "I mean not saying less, but not saying more than occasion demands."[51] If brevity is misunderstood as excessive abridgement, the *narratio* loses its power of persuasion and becomes meaningless.[52] If the case requires a longer statement, various means of avoiding tediousness should be employed.[53] Among the measures Quintilian recommends is the division of the statement into several sections, thereby creating the impression of several short statements instead of one long one.[54]

---

36 On the *transitio*, the beginning of the *narratio*, see the introduction to the section 1.6–11, above. Cf. the beginning of the *narratio* in Demosthenes *De corona* (*Or.* 18.17): "It is necessary, men of Athens, and not improper, to remind you of the position of affairs in those days (ὡς κατ' ἐκείνους τοὺς χρόνους εἶχε τὰ πράγματ' ἀναμνῆσαι), so that you may consider each transaction with due regard to its occasion" (tr. C. A. and J. H. Vince, LCL).

37 4.2.31: "Narratio est rei factae aut ut factae utilis ad persuadendum expositio, vel, ut Apollodorus finit, oratio docens auditorem quid in controversia sit."

38 Cf. 4.2.33.

39 Cf. 4.2.31–33. See Lausberg, *Handbuch*, § 294.

40 4.2.34: "... quod proposuerim eam quae sit tota pro nobis debere esse veri similem cum vera sit." Cf. Jack T. Sanders, "Paul's 'Autobiographical' Statements in Galatians 1–2," *JBL* 75 (1966) 335–43.

41 4.2.34.

42 See Lausberg, *Handbuch*, §§ 294–334; Martin, *Rhetorik*, 82–84.

43 4.2.31, 36; see Lausberg, *Handbuch*, § 315–21.

44 4.2.36.

45 Ibidem.

46 4.2.37–39.

47 4.2.38: "tum autem optime dicit orator cum videtur vera dicere."

48 See, esp., Gal 1:10, and the oath 1:20.

49 See Lausberg, *Handbuch*, §§ 297–314.

50 Quint. 4.2.40: "Brevis erit narratio ante omnia si inde coeperimus rem exponere unde ad iudicem pertinet, deinde si nihil extra causam dixerimus, tum etiam si reciderimus omnia quibus sublatis neque cognitioni quicquam neque utilitati detrahatur; ..."

51 Ibidem, 43: "Nos autem brevitatem in hoc ponimus, non ut minus sed ne plus dicatur quam oporteat." See Lausberg, *Handbuch*, §§ 298–308.

52 Ibidem, 41–47.

53 Ibidem, 47–51.

54 Ibidem, 49–50: "Et partitio taedium levat: ... ita tres potius modicae narrationes videbuntur quam una longa." See Lausberg, *Handbuch*, §§ 299–307, 311; Martin, *Rhetorik*, 81f.

It is apparent that Paul follows this recommendation. His case requires a long statement of facts, since he has to cover his entire history from his birth on. He begins with his birth because it is relevant to the case. Then he covers the history of the problem, which one must know in order to understand the *causa* (1:6), by subdivisions. His *narratio* has three parts, a method of division which seems to have been popular.[55] The first section (1:13–24) covers a long period of time and is divided into several subsections. The middle section is somewhat shorter, reporting on the so-called Apostolic Council (2:1–10). The final section contains just a brief episode, the conflict at Antioch (2:11–14). In this way Paul is able to cover the long history of the problem, saying all that is necessary to know for the case, while leaving out all unrelated material. The account is brief, but not excessively concise. It is a lively and dramatic narrative, but there is no superfluous embellishment or ornament. The information given has no other purpose than to support the proposition (1:12).

The most difficult task is, of course, to make the *narratio* credible.[56] In principle Quintilian suggests that this quality will be achieved, "if in the first place we take care to say nothing contrary to nature, secondly if we assign reasons and motives for the facts on which the inquiry turns (it is unnecessary to do so with the subsidiary facts as well), and if we make the characters of the actors in keeping with the facts we desire to be believed."[57] Among the specific devices Quintilian recommends, we notice that it is "useful to scatter some hints of our proofs here and there, but in such a way that it is never forgotten that we are making a *statement of facts* and not a *proof*."[58] Simple and brief

arguments may be thrown in, but these should be taken as only preparatory for the arguments to be developed in the *probatio*.[59] Such remarks should remain part of the *narratio*, since they are most effective when they are not recognizable as arguments.[60] Again, Paul's *narratio* seems to obey the main rules of theory. Motivation and reason are provided for the major facts (revelations in 1:15–16; 2:1–2; "because he stood condemned" in 2:11), but not for the subsidiary ones (1:17, 18, 21). Persons are characterized in conformity with the events (the "false brothers" in 2:4; the "men of eminence" in 2:6; the "hypocrisy" of Cephas, Barnabas, and "the other Jews" in 2:11–14). Scattered throughout the *narratio* but remaining subject to it are hints of proofs and small arguments (e.g., 1:13: "you have heard"; 1:23: "they had heard"; 1:20: an oath; 2:3, 4, 5, 6, etc.). The entire *narratio* is so designed that it makes the introductory statement (1:11–12) credible. Among the further points in Quintilian's discussion, two deserve special attention as far as Paul is concerned. First, Quintilian disagrees with the general rule that the order of the events in the *narratio* should always follow the actual order of events.[61] He himself wants to subject the order of events in the *narratio* to the rationale of expediency, which seems logical. But his example shows that if he changed the order, he would indicate to the judge the order in which the events occurred.[62] With this exception, Quintilian reaffirms that "this is no reason for not following the order of events as a general rule."[63] If we apply this to Paul, it would seem he follows the natural order of events in 1:13–2:14, since there is no indication that he does not.[64] The other remark pertains to the

---

55   See Lausberg, *Handbuch*, § 338.

56   Ibidem, §§ 322–34.

57   4.2.52: "Credibilis autem erit narratio ante omnia si prius consuluerimus nostrum animum ne quid naturae dicamus adversum, deinde si causas ac rationes factis praeposuerimus, non omnibus, sed de quibus quaeritur, si personas convenientes iis quae facta credi volemus constituerimus. . . ." See Lausberg, *Handbuch*, § 328.

58   Ibidem, 54: "Ne illud quidem fuerit inutile, semina quaedam probationum spargere, verum sic ut narrationem esse meminerimus, non probationem."

59   See Lausberg, *Handbuch*, § 324.

60   4.2.57: "Optimae vero praeparationes erunt quae

latuerint."

61   4.2.83: "Namque ne iis quidem accedo qui semper eo putant ordine quo quid actum sit esse narrandum, sed eo malo narrare quo expedit."

62   Cf. ibidem, 83–85.

63   Ibidem, 87: "Neque ideo tamen non saepius id facere oportebit ut rerum ordinem sequamur." See Lausberg, *Handbuch*, § 317.

64   This rhetorical argument goes against the hypothesis of Zahn (pp. 110ff) that the Antioch episode took place before the Jerusalem meeting. Cf. Johannes Munck, *Paul and the Salvation of Mankind* (tr. Frank Clarke; London: SCM, 1959) 74f, 100f.

conclusion of the *narratio*. Quintilian again goes against the practice of the majority of the rhetoricians. The majority rule says that the *narratio* should "end where the issue to be determined begins."[65] It cannot be accidental that at the end of the *narratio* in Gal 2 : 14, when Paul formulates the dilemma which Cephas is in, this dilemma[66] is identical with the issue the Galatians themselves have to decide: "why do you compel the Gentiles to judaize?"[67]

Interpretation

■12 Paul sets forth as the "thesis" he is going to defend what he had stated before in a more concise form in 1 : 1: "for I did not receive it [*sc.*, the gospel] from [a?] man, nor was I taught [it], but [I received it] through (a) revelation of Jesus Christ." The sentence is less concise than 1 : 1, but it is also made up of abbreviations. The exegetical problem is how to decode the abbreviations. It should be noted that there is an im-

portant commentary on the section in ps.-Clem. *Hom.* 17. 13–19 (see Appendix 3, below). Presented as a discussion between Simon Magus and Peter, it really is a discussion of Paul's claim made in Gal 1 : 12–2 : 14, and a rejection of that claim by Peter. The section in the ps.-Clementine *Homilies* shows how Paul's claim was understood in anti-Pauline circles. To that extent it is most relevant to Gal 1 : 12–2 : 14.

Paul claims that his gospel is more than human because of its origin.[68] In this regard, the Apostle is in a different position than the Galatians who have received the gospel from him (cf. 1 : 8–9, 11; 3 : 1–2; 4 : 13–14; 5 : 8). Paul denies that he received the gospel from any merely human source—in general or by specific persons. He also denies that he received it through the medium of teaching (οὔτε[69] ἐδιδάχθην ["nor was I taught"]).[70] In stating this denial, Paul stands in older traditions, according to which truth in the authentic sense cannot be obtained through teaching,[71] but only

---

65 Quint. 4.2.132: "De fine narrationis cum iis contentio est qui perduci expositionem volunt eo unde quaestio oritur. . . ."

66 On the dilemma (*complexio*) see Cicero *De inv.* 1 : 29 : 45 with good examples. See also Lausberg, *Handbuch*, § 393.

67 The connection of this question with the *causa* (1 : 6f) of the *exordium* and with the *peroratio* of the *post-scriptum* (6 : 12–16) should be noted because it also conforms to rhetorical theory (cf. Lausberg, *Handbuch*, § 431–42). Cf. also 2 : 3 (*narratio*) and 5 : 2 (beginning of the *exhortatio*). Paul's own position is antithetical: cf. 1 : 7 (*causa*); 2 : 3, 5 (*narratio*) 2 : 15–21 (*propositio*); 4 : 9, 11, 19–21 (*probatio*); 5 : 1–12, esp. 6 (*exhortatio*); 6 : 15 (*recapitulatio*).

68 Cf. also Gal 1 : 9. On the tradition behind Gal 1 : 12, see Plato *Phaedr.* 244D: "The ancients . . . testify that in proportion as prophecy is superior to augury . . . in the same proportion madness, which comes from God, is superior to sanity, which is of human origin" (. . . οἱ παλαιοὶ μανίαν σωφροσύνης τὴν ἐκ θεοῦ τῆς παρ' ἀνθρώπου γιγνομένης). See also 245A.

69 οὔτε is read by P[46] B 𝔐 *pm*, οὐδέ by 𝔖 D* G 69 *al.* Cf. BDF, § 445, 2; BDR, § 445 n. 3; Burton, pp. 40f; Bauer, *s.v.*

70 Cf. ps.-Clem. *Hom.* 17.18.2–3: τὸν δὲ μακαρίσαντά με μηνῦσαί μοι τὸν ἀποκαλύψαντα πατέρα εἶναι, ἐμὲ δὲ ἔκτοτε μαθεῖν ὅτι τὸ ἀδιδάκτως ἄνευ ὀπτασίας καὶ ὀνείρων, μαθεῖν ἀποκάλυψίς ἐστιν ("But He, pronouncing me blessed, pointed out to me that it was the Father who had revealed it to me; and from this

time I learned that revelation is knowledge gained without instruction, and without apparition and dreams"). The speaker is Peter, commenting upon his revelation Matt 16 : 16. See also Appendix 3.c, below. On the whole see Strecker, *Judenchristentum*, 192. One should note also that the terminology of teaching is conspicuously scarce in the letters of Paul. See Karl Heinrich Rengstorf, "διδάσκω," *TDNT* 2.146; Schlier, pp. 46f. Rom 16 : 17; 1 Cor 4 : 17 may even be interpolations (see Rudolf Bultmann, *Exegetica* [ed. Erich Dinkler; Tübingen: Mohr, Siebeck, 1967] 283f; Weiss, *Der erste Korintherbrief*, p. XLI; Erich Dinkler "Korintherbriefe," *RGG* 4.17ff).

71 Since Plato, "teaching" has taken on the negative connotations of the work of the sophists. See the famous reference to the testing of the Delphic oracle by his student Chaeremon, which led Socrates to his wisdom, rather than "being taught" (*Apol.* 19Eff; 20Dff; 33A–D; *Laches* 200Eff). See Thomas Meyer, *Platons Apologie* (TBAW 42; Tübingen: Mohr, Siebeck, 1962) 133ff. See also Heracleitus, according to Diogenes Laert. 9.5 (cf. Diels–Kranz 12 B 101); Epicurus disliked learning (see Cornelia Johanna de Vogel, *Greek Philosophy* [3 vols.; Leiden: Brill, [3, 4]1967–73] 3. nos. 811, 816, 879d). Philo also stands in this tradition, when for him the true wise man does not need to be taught by others but is himself "autodidact" (αὐτοδίδακτος and αὐτομαθής); cf. *Abr.* 6; *Fug.* 21, 168f, 172; *Conf.* 59; *Mig.* 140; *Her.* 295; *Som.* 1.160; *Mut.* 85f, 88; *Cong.* 70; *Plant.* 110;

62

through direct revelation.[72] Therefore, the opposite of the "merely human" is "through revelation." The abbreviation δι' ἀποκαλύψεως Ἰησοῦ Χριστοῦ ("through revelation of Jesus Christ") restates 1:1 δι' Ἰησοῦ Χριστοῦ ("through Jesus Christ") and anticipates 1:16a ἀποκαλύψαι τὸν υἱὸν αὐτοῦ ἐν ἐμοί ("reveal his son in me"). The problem often raised in commentaries is whether "of Jesus Christ" is a subjective or objective genitive construction. The answer must be given from the context, because grammatically it can be either.[73] Strictly speaking, we do not have in 1:12 a "self-revelation" of Christ[74] because God does the revealing (1:16a). But the revelation itself must be understood as an appearance of Christ "in Paul" (1:16a; cf. 2:20a). This in turn is identical with the revelation of the gospel to Paul.[75]

In discussing the content of the passage one must realize that the abbreviations point back to a fuller account of Paul's conversion and commission which we do not have, but which also underlies the statements in 1:16. There are also other passages, especially 1 Corinthians 15, which refer to Paul's vision of Christ and his commissioning by him to preach the gospel. The author of Acts has presented the matter in chapter 9 and, making Paul himself the speaker, in chapters 22 and 26. These parallel texts cannot be harmonized with Galatians 1.

Furthermore, we have parallel accounts of the appearance of Christ and the commissioning of Peter,[76] of James the brother of Jesus,[77] of the Twelve,[78] and of Thomas.[79] Related are accounts about the transfer of authority and "powers" from James to Clement,[80] and from James to the pseudepigraphical author of the *Apocryphon of James*[81] from Nag Hammadi. The complexities of traditional and literary relationships between these accounts require new investigation.

Mos. 1.21; *Animal.* 7. See furthermore, Mayer, *Index Philoneus*, *s.v.* αὐτοδίδακτος, αὐτομαθής; also Ludwig Bieler, ΘΕΙΟΣ ΑΝΗΡ (Darmstadt: Wissenschaftliche Buchgesellschaft, 1967) 1.35f, 2.34; Hans Dieter Betz, *Lukian von Samosata und das Neue Testament* (TU 76; Berlin: Akademie–Verlag, 1961) 106; Gerd Petzke, *Die Traditionen über Apollonius von Tyana und das Neue Testament* (SCHNT 1; Leiden: Brill, 1970) 166f; Herwig Maehler, *Die Auffassung des Dichterberufs im frühen Griechentum bis zur Zeit Pindars* (*Hypomnemata* 3; Göttingen: Vandenhoeck & Ruprecht, 1963) 22f. The NT has applied the concept to Jesus (Mark 6:1–6 par; Luke 2:47; John 7:15f) and the apostles (Acts 4:13).

72 See the phrase "the truth of the gospel" Gal 2:5, 14; also cf. 5:7.

73 Most important is the imitation of the Galatian passage in the Mani biography *CMC* 64.1–15.

74 Against Oepke; idem, "ἀποκαλύπτω," *TDNT* 3:583; Schlier, p. 47.

75 The line of thought was continued by later Paulinists. See "Paul's" statement in Eph 3:3: κατὰ ἀποκάλυψιν ἐγνωρίσθη μοι τὸ μυστήριον [*sc.* τοῦ Χριστοῦ] ("how the mystery [of Christ] was made known to me by revelation"). Cf. Eph 1:9, 17; 3:4–6; Col 1:26f; 2:2. See Karl M. Fischer, *Tendenz und Absicht des Epheserbriefes* (FRLANT 111; Göttingen: Vandenhoeck & Ruprecht, 1973) 98ff. Cf. also the discussion about "revelation of Jesus Christ," in Justin *Dial.* 116.

76 Matt 16:13–20; John 21:15–19. See the studies by Jacques Dupont, "La Révélation du Fils de Dieu en faveur de Pierre (Mt 16, 17) et de Paul (Gal 1, 16)," *RechSR* 52 (1964) 411–20; Anton Vögtle, "Zum Problem der Herkunft von 'Mt 16, 17–19'," in *Orientierung an Jesus, Festschrift für J. Schmid* (Freiburg: Herder, 1972) 372–93; Franz Leenhardt, "Abraham et la conversion de Saul de Tarse, suivi d'une note sur 'Abraham dans Jean VIII,'" *RHPhR* 53 (1973) 331–51; Sten Lundgren, "Ananias and the Calling of Paul in Acts," *StTh* 25 (1971) 117–22; Karl Kertelge, "Apokalypsis Jesou Christou (Gal 1, 12)," in *Neues Testament und Kirche, Festschrift für R. Schnackenburg* (Freiburg: Herder, 1974) 266–81.

77 *Gos. Heb.* (*KlT* 8 = *Apocrypha* II, p. 8 no. 21; tr. in HSW, *NT Apocrypha* 1.165).

78 *Kerygma Petrou*, according to Clemens Alex. *Strom.* 6.6.48 (*KlT* 3 = *Apocrypha* I, p. 15; tr. in HSW, *NT Apocrypha* 2.101). See also John 20:19–23; Matt 28:19f; Acts 1:8; Mark 16:15–20; *Asc. Isa.* 11.22; etc.

79 *Gos. Thom.* 13, p. 34 line 30–p. 35, line 14.

80 *Ep. of Clement to James*, ps.–Clementine *Hom.*, GCS vol 1, pp. 5–22.

81 *Ap. Jas.* Codex Jung F. Iʳ–F. VIIIᵛ (p. 1–16), ed. Michel Malinine *et al.* (Zurich and Stuttgart: Rascher, 1968) 16 lines 12ff.

Excursus:
Conversion, Revelation, and Tradition

In the exegetical literature dealing with Gal 1:12–2:14 there are extensive discussions with regard to Paul's so-called conversion to Christianity. The problems include the revelation of Christ "in Paul" and of the gospel of Jesus Christ to Paul, and the relationship between these specific revelations and the preceding tradition of the church. Since these issues are complicated, they ought to be held separately. Also, the account of Galatians must be taken by itself, before other texts are brought in to supplement it.

(1) Paul's so-called conversion to Christianity is still an unresolved problem.[82] Strictly speaking, however, we cannot speak at all of a "conversion" of Paul. As Galatians reports, Paul was "called" to be a missionary to the Gentiles, and he changed parties within Judaism from Pharisaism to Jewish Christianity. At the time of this shift, Jewish Christianity was still a movement within Judaism, so that one should not call it a "conversion" from Judaism to Christianity. His switch is comparable to the present Galatian plans to change from Pauline Christianity to another rival faction of Christianity. Paul's "call" can be accounted for within the terms of Judaism, so that there is no need to relate it to a breaking away from Judaism. Paul himself sees his "call" in analogy to that of a prophet like Jeremiah, and there is no reason to doubt the appropriateness of that analogy.

Paul's account in Gal 1:12–2:14[83] is extremely concise and points to a fuller narrative, in which more details would be given. Of course, we do not possess this fuller account but only the concise version. In addition, one must consider the fact that Paul's account is given long after the event as a reaction of defense against attacks by opponents. This has analogies in the Old Testament vocation accounts.[84] Thus, Gal 1:12–2:14 must be interpreted in conformity with the limitations prescribed by its literary purpose and function.

(2) According to Gal 1:1, 11–16, Paul has received the gospel as he preaches it among the Gentiles through a revelation of Christ in him.[85] Paul does not explain the relationship between this revelation of Christ in him and the gospel message which he was ordered by Christ to proclaim. At this point, one should be careful not to create artificial problems. Certainly, the revelation of Christ in Paul points to a visionary experience of some sort, while the order to proclaim the gospel among the Gentiles implies a verbal revelation. Ample evidence from the religious literature shows that the visionary experience and the verbal revelation do not exclude each other. Most interesting in this regard is the brief remark in the ps.–Clem. *Hom.* 17.19.4 (see Appendix 3.c), that Christ has stayed with Paul for an hour and has instructed him. This information, which comes from a tradition prior to the *Homilies*, tries to explain away the conflict, but it thereby shows also that this conflict is artificial to the ancient mind. It is probably only the modern reader who finds these statements difficult to relate. At any rate, Paul sees this revelation to be exclusively his own, unalterable, and final (cf. 1:6–9; 3:1;

---

82 On Paul's conversion the literature is enormous. For surveys and bib., see Eduard Pfaff, *Die Bekehrung des heiligen Paulus in der Exegese des 20. Jahrhunderts* (Rome: Officium Libri Catholici, 1942); Munck, *Paul*, 11–35; Schoeps, *Paul*, 51ff; Ernst Benz, *Paulus als Visionär* (Wiesbaden: Steiner, 1952); Paul Aubin, *Le problème de la 'conversion'* (Paris: Beauchesne, 1963) 70ff; Dietrich Wiederkehr, *Die Theologie der Berufung in den Paulusbriefen* (Freiburg, Switzerland: Universitätsverlag, 1963); Johannes Lindblom, *Gesichte und Offenbarungen* (Lund: Gleerup, 1968); Ulrich Wilckens, "Die Bekehrung des Paulus als religionsgeschichtliches Problem," *ZThK* 56 (1959) 273–93, rep. in his *Rechtfertigung als Freiheit* (Neukirchen-Vluyn: Neukirchener Verlag, 1974) 11–32; Bornkamm, *Paul*, 13ff; Jacques Dupont, "The Conversion of Paul, and its Influence on his Understanding of Salvation by Faith," in *Apostolic History and the Gospel, Biblical and Historical Essays Presented to F. F. Bruce on His Sixtieth Birthday* (ed. Ward Gasque and Ralph P. Martin; Grand Rapids: Eerdmans, 1975) 176–94.

83 See, esp., Dieter Lührmann, *Das Offenbarungsverständnis bei Paulus und in paulinischen Gemeinden* (WMANT 16; Neukirchen–Vluyn: Neukirchener Verlag, 1965) 74f and *passim*; Schütz, *Authority*, 131ff; Gerhard Lohfink, *Paulus vor Damaskus* (SBS 4; Stuttgart: Katholisches Bibelwerk, 1965) 88f; Josef Blank, *Paulus und Jesus: Eine theologische Grundlegung* (SANT 18; Munich: Kösel, 1968) 208–14; Willi Marxsen, *The Resurrection of Jesus of Nazareth* (London: SCM, 1970) 98–111; C. F. D. Moule, *The Significance of the Message of the Resurrection for Faith in Jesus Christ* (London: SCM, 1968); Burchard, *Der dreizehnte Zeuge*; Xavier Léon-Dufour, *Resurrection and the Message of Easter* (London: Chapman, 1974) 47–51; Karl Löning, *Saulustradition*, 48ff; Volker Stolle, *Der Zeuge als Angeklagter, Untersuchungen zum Paulus-Bild des Lukas* (BWANT 102; Stuttgart: Kohlhammer, 1973) 155ff.

84 Cf. Rolf Knierim, "The Vocation of Isaiah," *VT* 18 (1968) 47–68.

85 See Conzelmann, *1 Corinthians*, 249ff, and the excursus "The Christ Formula" (251–54).

6:12–16). He contrasts it with receiving the gospel by way of human intermediaries (cf. 1:1, 11, 12). This seems to rule out any possibility of Paul's having received instruction by other early Christian missionaries. It seemingly contradicts Paul's own statement in 1 Cor 15:1–11. As a matter of fact, the relationship between 1 Cor 15:1–11 and Galatians 1 is far more complicated. In 1 Cor 15:8 Paul adds his own vision of Christ to the visions of the other apostles and Christians mentioned. To be sure, none of these visions presuppose human intermediaries, but their association with Paul's vision must have been a provocation (see the excursus on "apostle" following the discussion of Gal 1:17). The "kerygma" of the church which Paul says he has "received," i.e., as "tradition" (1 Cor 15:3), is not identical with either vision or the gospel to the gentiles, so that there is no real contradiction of content between the vision of Christ, the order to proclaim the gospel to the Gentiles (Gal 1:16), and the "kerygma" of the church formulating the salvation event(s) (1 Cor 15:3–8).

(3) Paul himself becomes one of the most important transmitters of the tradition of the church and to the church. As an apostle he stands as a mediator between Christ (God) and his Gentile Christian churches and, beyond them, the Gentile world as a whole. He received the gospel from God and Christ, and he proclaims it to the Gentiles (cf. 1:6–9, 11, 12, 23; 2:2, 7–9; 3:1; 4:13–14; Eph 3:1–21; Col 1:9–23; etc.). He "represents" the crucified Christ upon earth (cf. Gal 2:20; 4:14; 5:11; 6:17).[86] He formulates the "tradition" (cf. the Introduction, §6). He defends the "truth of the gospel" (cf. the Introduction, §7) against misunderstanding and misinterpretation ("heresy"). He creates "tradition" (cf. especially the "canon" in 6:15–16; 5:6). One of the challenges he faces is the coordination of his gospel with the message of other apostles before him. His contention in Galatians and Romans is that his gospel is consistent with the kerygma of the church and that it was recognized as such by the authorities of the church at Jerusalem. A large part of Paul's theology is devoted to reconciling the conflicts between his gospel and the gospel

preached by "the apostles before me" (cf. 1:17). In Paul's view, which is of course rejected by his Jewish–Christian opponents (cf. 2:4–5, 11–14), there is no material conflict between his gospel and the tradition of the church. In fact, in his view his gospel is the fulfilment even of the tradition of Judaism, "the Israel of God" (cf. 6:16). It is interesting that the same problem existed much later for Mani, whose "autobiography" was written to prove that there is no difference between his revelation and vision and those of "the earlier apostles" (CMC 71.1–72.7).

(4) "Tradition" itself is for Paul not a given fact, but a matter of controversy.[87] There are always conflicting traditions, and all traditions are in need of interpretation. The clearest case of this is his discussion of the Abraham tradition as over against the Sinai tradition (3:6–25). Galatians as a whole was written to be a defense of Paul's gospel as his reading of the tradition, contrasted with the way his opponents understood and interpreted it. Transmitting tradition for Paul does not mean the transferral of fixed dogmas, but the critical evaluation of Christian expressions of faith (cf., e.g., 2:11–14), the affirmation of certain traditions while rejecting others, and the formulation of new traditions (see the Introduction §6).

If this point of view is assumed, we have to discuss briefly other explanations found in the scholarly literature. Walter Schmithals[88] and others[89] have suggested that in Gal 1:12 Paul indirectly refers to an accusation made by his opponents, according to which Paul depended upon the human authorities at Jerusalem rather than upon a revelation by Christ himself. There is no real reason, however, to assume that 1:12 contains an accusation against Paul. He is using traditional concepts, in order to defend his position as an outsider (see on 1:1, 12). Also, the anti–Pauline discussion in ps.–Clem. Hom. 17.17–18 does not doubt that Paul received the gospel by vision, but criticizes precisely this fact (see Appendix 3.c). More probable, therefore, is Dieter Georgi's[90] view, that Paul is out of touch with tradition. It is interesting to see how

86   See Betz, Nachfolge, esp. 137ff; Erhard Güttgemanns, Der leidende Apostel und sein Herr (FRLANT 90; Göttingen: Vandenhoeck & Ruprecht, 1966) 126–35 and passim; Schütz, Authority, 226ff.

87   On the concept of tradition in Paul, see Klaus Wegenast, Tradition bei Paulus; Schütz, Authority, 114ff and passim.

88   Schmithals, Paul and the Gnostics, 19ff, 24f, 29f.

89   See Ragnar Bring, Commentary on Galatians (tr. Eric Wahlstrom; Philadelphia: Muhlenberg, 1961) 37f. Jeremias (Abba, 286) thinks that Paul was accused

of having received his gospel from Peter, but having perverted it. Cf. also Eduard Meyer, Ursprung und Anfänge des Christentums (3 vols.; Stuttgart and Berlin: Cotta, 1923) 3.347f; Stuhlmacher, Evangelium, 66f.

90   Dieter Georgi, Die Geschichte der Kollekte des Paulus für Jerusalem (ThF 38; Hamburg–Bergstedt: Reich, 1965) 36 n. 113.

Heinrich Schlier[91] tries to solve the problem. He strictly distinguishes between the receiving and the handing down of tradition as compared with the formal process of "teaching." While ordinary Christians become members of the church through other Christians giving to them the "kerygma" of the church, Paul received his gospel directly by a self-revelation of Jesus Christ. This event, according to Schlier, was an anticipation of Christ's eschatological revelation, which was granted to Paul as a charismatic figure.[92] Schlier sees no contradiction between this revelation and formulated tradition or the preaching of the word. The "kerygma" as a "fixed λόγος ["word"] (1 Cor 15:2) of the gospel is "in origin and in principle" ("*seinem Ursprung und seiner Substanz nach*") identical with the appearance of Christ. The kerygmatic formulae are revelations that have assumed the form of human languages and have been used by the church even before Paul, just as Paul himself uses them.[93] The gospel, which was revealed to him, was non–verbal, but in substance the same as the doctrinal formulae.

A different view is that held by Oscar Cullmann.[94] For him "tradition" includes not only a summary of the Christian faith (= "kerygma") but also words of Jesus and gospel narratives. Cullmann rejects the idea that in Galatians one can separate the "facts," which Paul would have obtained from human sources, from the "meaning" of these facts, which would have been revealed to him by Christ.[95] Facts and interpretation belong together. For Cullmann, all tradition goes back to the apostles, and all of them received it from Christ. "Transmission by the apostles is not affected by men, but by Christ the Lord himself who thereby imparts the revelation. All that the Church knows about words of Jesus, about stories of his life, or about their interpretation, comes from the apostles." Cullmann's solution is this: every apostle received his own revelation, and he passed on what he had received. "But since everything has not been revealed to each individual apostle, each must first pass on his testimony to another (Gal 1:18; 1 Cor 15:11), and only the entire *paradosis*, to which all the apostles contribute, constitutes the *paradosis* of Christ."[96] There cannot be any "antithesis between apostolic tradition and direct revelation," because "the *Kyrios* himself controls its transmission."[97] The antithesis is one between legitimate "tradition of the apostles" and of the Lord, and illegitimate "traditions of men." Paul's gospel, then, includes not only his own revelation, but also the entire tradition of the church.[98] This thesis, however, interprets away the entire problem, and one no longer understands why there ever was a Galatian crisis. These and other discussions[99] of the problem between revelation and tradition do not really conform to the situation presented in the letter to the Galatians.[100] They are more expressions of the theological situation of today and are intended to take a position in the context of these modern theological concerns.

■13 Paul begins the *narratio* proper by referring to his pre-Christian life in Judaism (1:13–14). This reference is needed because it shows the radical change which took place as a result of his vision of Jesus Christ.[101] As Paul tells it, his pre-Christian life rules out the

91 Schlier, pp. 44–48; idem, "Kerygma und Sophia," in his *Die Zeit der Kirche* (Freiburg: Herder, 1962) 216f; Blank, *Paulus and Jesus*, 208ff.
92 Schlier, p. 47.
93 Ibidem, 48.
94 Oscar Cullmann, "Paradosis et Kyrios. Le problème de la tradition dans le paulinisme," *RHPhR* 30 (1950) 12–30; idem, "'Kyrios' as Designation for the Oral Tradition concerning Jesus," *SJTh* 3 (1950) 180–97; idem, *Die Tradition als exegetisches, historisches und theologisches Problem* (Zurich: Zwingli Verlag, 1954); idem, "The Tradition: the exegetical, historical, and theological problem," in *The Early Church* (Philadelphia: Westminster, 1966) 55–99. See also Lucien Cerfaux, "La tradition selon saint Paul," in *Recueil Lucien Cerfaux* (Louvain: Duculot, 1954) 2.253–63; idem, "Les deux points de départ de la tradition chrétienne," in *Recueil Lucien Cerfaux* 2.265–82; idem, *Jésus et les origines de la tradition* (Louvain: Desclée de Brouwer, 1968) 214ff.

95 Cullmann, *The Early Church*, 60, 66, 72.
96 Ibidem, 73.
97 Ibidem, 74.
98 Ibidem, 78, 80.
99 See also Leonhard Goppelt, "Tradition bei Paulus," *KD* 4 (1958) 213–33; Wegenast, *Tradition bei Paulus*, 43f; Stuhlmacher, *Evangelium* 1.70f; Erich Dinkler, "Tradition V. Im Urchristentum," *RGG* 6.970–74, who regards the problem as insoluble.
100 Especially Scandinavian scholars have kept insisting that Paul's gospel is in conflict with other gospels. See Olaf Moe, *Paulus und die evangelische Geschichte* (Leipzig: Deichert, 1912) 14; Anton Fridrichsen, "Die Apologie des Paulus Gal. 1," in Brun and Fridrichsen, *Paulus*, 55f; Molland, *Euangelion*, 90ff; Schoeps, *Paul*, 70–74. The point is also made by Robert M. Hawkins, "The Galatian Gospel," *JBL* 59 (1940) 141–46.
101 γάρ ("for") refers to v 12. So correctly Schlier, Mussner.

assumption that he was in any way prepared for the change or that he had developed gradually towards Christianity.[102] Rather, all developments pointed in the opposite direction. The Galatians "have heard" (ἠκούσατε) about this,[103] so that Paul merely needs to remind them.[104] In his pre-Christian life Paul was not only a Jew, but he was a faithful and zealous observer of "the Jewish religion and way of life" (ἐν τῷ Ἰουδαϊσμῷ).[105] His former[106] conduct[107] as a Jew was extraordinary for two main reasons,[108] the first of which is told in v 13, the second in v 14. Most importantly, he engaged in excessive[109] persecutions[110] of the Christians, "the church of God" (ἡ ἐκκλησία τοῦ θεοῦ),[111] with the goal "to destroy it" (ἐπόρθουν αὐτήν).[112]

■ **14** The second reason for these anti-Christian activities was, Paul explains, his deep devotion and commitment to the Jewish religion. His standing in Judaism

102 The anti–Pauline opposition circulated stories about the "real" reasons for Paul's conversion: unfulfilled ambitions and failure of marriage plans. For the sources, see HSW, *NT Apocrypha* 2.71; Strecker, *Judenchristentum*, 187ff. See the quotation below on Gal 1:14, note 124.

103 Paul only rarely talks about his past (cf. 1 Cor 15:9f; Phil 3:5f). Rumors spread outside of the Pauline churches (Gal 1:22f). Later his persecutions of the church became part of the Paul legend (Acts 8:3; 9:1, 21; 22:4f; 26:9–11). On Paul's self–descriptions, see Günter Klein, *Die Zwölf Apostel: Ursprung und Gehalt einer Idee* (FRLANT 77; Göttingen: Vandenhoeck & Ruprecht, 1961) 127–44; Blank, *Paulus und Jesus*, 238–48. On Acts, see Burchard, *Der dreizehnte Zeuge*, 40–51; Löning, *Saulustradition*, 43–61; Stolle, *Der Zeuge als Angeklagter*, 200–06. On Paul's pre–Christian life generally, see Ernst Barnikol, *Die vorchristliche und frühchristliche Zeit des Paulus* (Kiel: Mühlau, 1929); Schoeps, *Paul*, 51ff; Willem C. van Unnik, *Tarsus or Jerusalem* (London: Epworth, 1962) with further literature.

104 Cf. Demosthenes *De corona* 17, at the beginning of the *narratio*: ". . . to remind you of the position of affairs in those days, so that you may consider each transaction with due regard to its occasion" (tr. Vince, LCL).

105 Ἰουδαϊσμός ("Judaism") is a Hellenistic–Jewish term. See 2 Macc 2:21; 8:1; 14:38; 4 Macc 4:26; also the inscriptions from Stobi (CII 2, No. 694); cf. Martin Hengel, "Die Synagogeninschriften von Stobi," *ZNW* 57 [1966] 145–83); and Rome (*CII* 2, No. 537). See Karl Georg Kuhn, "Ἰσραήλ," *TDNT* 3.359–69. The term describes the Jewish religion and way of life as a whole as it is distinct from that of other religions. In the NT the term is found only in Gal 1:13, 14; cf. 2:14; Ign. *Mag.* 8.1; 10.3; Ign. *Philad.* 6.1, where it appears opposite Χριστιανισμός ("Christianity").

106 ποτέ ("formerly") belongs with ἀναστροφή. Cf. Gal 1:23, and BDF, § 269, 1; BDR, § 269, 1.

107 ἀναστροφή means "way of life, conduct, behavior." See Bauer, *s.v.*; Georg Bertram, "ἀναστρέφω,"

TDNT 7.715–17, where the passages are listed.

108 The sentence beginning with ὅτι ("that") describes that conduct.

109 καθ᾿ ὑπερβολήν ("excessively") expresses Paul's emphasis. See for this expression also Rom 7:13; 1 Cor 12:31; 2 Cor 1:8; 4:17; *Barn.* 1.2. See also Bauer, *s.v.* ὑπερβολή; Gerhard Delling, "Zum steigernden Gebrauch von Komposita mit ὑπέρ bei Paulus," *NovT* 11 (1969) 127–53; Arland J. Hultgren, "On Translating and Interpreting Galatians 1.13," *Bible Translator* 26 (1975) 146–48.

110 On the persecution, see 1 Cor 15:9; Phil 3:6; 1 Tim 1:13; Acts 8:1–3; 9:1–2, 4–5; 22:4–5, 7, 8; 26:9–11, 14, 15. See Burchard, *Der dreizehnte Zeuge*, 40–51; Löning, *Saulustradition*, 116–20; Arland J. Hultgren, "Paul's Pre–Christian Persecutions of the Church: Their Purpose, Locale, and Nature," *JBL* 95 (1976) 97–111. The term διώκειν ("persecute") seems to have become already "technical" as referring to the persecution of the church (cf. Gal 1:23; 4:29; 5:11; 6:12; etc.). See Albrecht Oepke, "διώκω," *TDNT* 2. 229–30.

111 This name seems to be used by the Pauline churches. Cf. 1 Cor 15:9; 1:2; 10:32; 11:16, 22; 2 Cor 1:1; 1 Thess 2:14; 2 Thess 1:4; 1 Tim 3:5, 15; Acts 20:28; etc. The problem of the origin of the name is still unsolved. For the present state of the debate and for bib., see Klaus Berger, "Volksversammlung und Gemeinde Gottes. Zu den Anfängen der christlichen Verwendung von 'ekklesia,'" *ZThK* 73 (1976) 167–207, esp. 198ff.

112 Bauer's tr. uses the imperfect *de conatu*: "I tried to destroy." So also BDR, § 326. Cf. the same term Gal 1:23; Acts 9:21, in the same context. The term is common as a description of political oppression. See 4 Macc 4:23; 11:4; Philo *Flacc.* 54; Josephus *BJ* 4.405; *Ant.* 10.135. For passages see also LSJ, *s.v.*, and Philippe–H. Menoud, "Le sens du verbe πορθεῖν," in *Apophoreta, Festschrift für E. Haenchen* (BZNW 30; Berlin: Töpelmann, 1964) 178–86. G reads ἐπολέμουν ("I attacked") instead, perhaps an influence of the Latin *expugnabam*.

was unblemished.[113] He "made progress"[114] in its practice and thought. Among his people[115] he surpassed many of his own age.[116] He did more than merely fulfill the duties and expectations of a faithful Jew. The "excessive" nature of his persecutions of Christianity demonstrates the high degree ($\pi\epsilon\rho\iota\sigma\sigma\sigma\tau\acute{\epsilon}\rho\omega s$)[117] of "zeal", which he had for "the traditions of his forefathers."[118] When Paul says he was a $\zeta\eta\lambda\omega\tau\acute{\eta}s$[119] he does not suggest that he was a member of the party of the "zealots,"[120] but rather "an ardent observer of the Torah."[121] Such conduct was not extremist or a form of mindless fanaticism, but was in conformity with the contemporary expectations of what a faithful Jew ought to have been.[122] The fact that Paul was a Pharisee agrees with this activity.[123] In his defense Paul wants to make sure that as far as his standing in Judaism was concerned he had a clean record of integrity. There was development, to be sure, but development away from and not towards Christianity.[124] As a Jew he had no reason to leave Judaism.

113 The same point is made in other autobiographical statements, all apologetic in tendency. See 2 Cor 11:22; Phil 3:5f; Rom 11:1; Acts 22:3–5; 23:6; 26:4f.

114 $\pi\rho o\kappa\acute{o}\pi\tau\epsilon\iota\nu$ plays a prominent role in popular philosophy, and has entered early Christian language through the medium of Hellenistic Judaism. See also Phil 1:12, 25; 2 Tim 2:16; 3:9, 13; 1 Tim 4:15; Luke 2:52; *2 Clem.* 17.3. See Gustav Stählin, "$\pi\rho o\kappa o\pi\acute{\eta}$," *TDNT* 6.703–19.

115 $\epsilon\nu$ $\tau\hat{\omega}$ $\gamma\acute{\epsilon}\nu\epsilon\iota$ $\mu o\upsilon$ ("among my people") similarly 2 Cor 11:26; Phil 3:5; Acts 7:19; cf. 4:36; 18:24. The phrase does not refer, as Theodor Mommsen ("Die Rechtsverhältnisse des Apostels Paulus," *ZNW* 2 [1901] 85) had suggested, to "my homeland (Tarsus)," or, as Barnikol (*Zeit des Paulus*, 31–46) proposed, to the Pharisaic movement.

116 $\sigma\upsilon\nu\eta\lambda\iota\kappa\iota\acute{\omega}\tau\eta s$ ("a person of one's own age, a contemporary") is a *hapax legomenon* in the NT. See Bauer, *s.v.*

117 The adverb should be taken as an "elative." It is part of what elsewhere is called "boasting" (cf. 2 Cor 11:23; 1 Cor 15:10; Phil 1:14, 2 Cor 10:8; 1:12; 2:4; 12:15; 1 Thess 2:17).

118 $a\acute{\iota}$ $\pi a\tau\rho\iota\kappa a\grave{\iota}$ $\pi a\rho a\delta\acute{o}\sigma\epsilon\iota s$ here refers to the Jewish tradition of the Torah as a whole, not specific family traditions of Paul (contra Zahn, p. 61; Gottlob Schrenk, *TDNT* 5.1022). The concept is frequent in Hellenistic Judaism. For passages see Schrenk, ibidem, *TDNT* 5.1014f, 1021f. For rabbinic Judaism, see Str–B 1.691–94; for the NT, see Matt 15:2, 3, 6; Mark 7:3, 5, 8, 9, 13. The concept is also common in antiquity; see Schrenk, "$\pi a\tau\rho\hat{\omega}os$, $\pi a\tau\rho\iota\kappa\acute{o}s$," *TDNT* 5.1015 n. 1, 1021; LSJ, *s.v.* $\pi a\tau\rho\iota\kappa\acute{o}s$, $\pi\acute{a}\tau\rho\iota os$.

119 Paul claims the term only here, but cf. Acts 22:3: $\zeta\eta\lambda\omega\tau\grave{\eta}s$ $\acute{\upsilon}\pi\acute{a}\rho\chi\omega\nu$ $\tau o\hat{\upsilon}$ $\theta\epsilon o\hat{\upsilon}$ ("I was zealous for God"); Phil 3:6: $\kappa a\tau\grave{a}$ $\zeta\hat{\eta}\lambda os$ ("with zeal"); 2 Cor 11:2.

120 Against Lightfoot. Cf. the different use of the concept in Luke 6:15; Acts 1:13. On the whole question of the Zealots, see Morton Smith, "Zealots and Sicarii: Their Origins and Relations," *HTR* 64

(1971) 1–19; Martin Hengel, "Zeloten und Sikarier. Zur Frage nach der Einheit und Vielfalt der jüdischen Befreiungsbewegung 6–74 nach Christus," in *Josephus-Studien*, . . . *Otto Michel zum 70. Geburtstag* . . . (Göttingen: Vandenhoeck & Ruprecht, 1974) 175–96.

121 Cf. Acts 21:20 of the Jewish Christians: $\pi\acute{a}\nu\tau\epsilon s$ $\zeta\eta\lambda\omega\tau a\grave{\iota}$ $\tau o\hat{\upsilon}$ $\nu\acute{o}\mu o\upsilon$ $\acute{\upsilon}\pi\acute{a}\rho\chi o\upsilon\sigma\iota\nu$ ("they are all strict observers of the Torah"); of Paul himself 22:3. Zeal for the Torah is a general ideal of the time: see Josephus *Ant.* 12.271 of the call of Mattathias: $\epsilon\acute{\iota}$ $\tau\iota s$ $\zeta\eta\lambda\omega\tau\acute{\eta}s$ $\acute{\epsilon}\sigma\tau\iota\nu$ $\tau\hat{\omega}\nu$ $\pi a\tau\rho\acute{\iota}\omega\nu$ $\acute{\epsilon}\theta\hat{\omega}\nu$ $\kappa a\grave{\iota}$ $\tau\hat{\eta}s$ $\tau o\hat{\upsilon}$ $\theta\epsilon o\hat{\upsilon}$ $\theta\rho\eta\sigma\kappa\epsilon\acute{\iota}as$, $\acute{\epsilon}\pi\acute{\epsilon}\sigma\theta\omega$ . . . $\acute{\epsilon}\mu o\acute{\iota}$ ("Whoever is zealous for our ancestral laws and the worship of God, let him follow . . . me!"). Philo *Spec.* 1.30, 2.253; *Abr.* 60; *Virt.* 175; 1 Macc 2:26, 27, 50; 2 Macc 4:2; 4 Macc 18:12. See A. Stumpff, "$\zeta\hat{\eta}\lambda os$," *TDNT* 2.877–88; Herbert Braun, *Spätjüdisch-häretischer und frühchristlicher Radikalismus* (2 vols.; BHTh 24; Tübingen: Mohr, Siebeck, 1957, ²1969) 1.71 n. 1; 31 n. 3; index, *s.v.* קנא; 2.57 n. 1; Martin Hengel, *Judaism and Hellenism* (2 vols.; tr. John Bowden; Philadelphia: Fortress, 1974) 1.114, 287, 300, 305, 312, 314. Beyond Judaism, the concern for the ancestral traditions was a common ideal; see Isocrates 1.11; Plato *Prot.* 343A; Diogenes L. 9.38; Philo *Mos.* 2.161; etc.

122 Cf. Acts 22:3; 24:14; 28:17. Hengel, *ZNW* 57 (1966) 178f points to tomb inscriptions, where the ideal is expressed (*CII* 1, no. 509; 537).

123 Cf. Phil 3:5f; Acts 22:3; 23:6; 26:5.

124 A "Freudian" interpretation of Paul's conversion was anticipated by his opponents. Cf. HSW, *NT Apocrypha* 2.71, quoting from the Jewish Christian *Anabathmoi Iakobou* (Epiphanius *Pan.* 30.16): "Paul was a man of Tarsus and indeed a Hellene (i.e. Gentile), the son of a Hellenist mother and a Hellenist father. Having gone up to Jerusalem and having remained there a long time, he desired to marry a daughter of the (high) priest and on that account submitted himself as a proselyte for circumcision. When nevertheless he did not obtain that girl, he became furious and began to write against circum-

This situation is of course emphasized in order to underscore the miraculous nature of his conversion.[125]

■ **15** Paul's conversion to Christianity was entirely the work of God. This is the tenor of his account of his call by God to be an apostle. It is important for the understanding of the passage vv 15–16 that we realize the limited and purposeful character of Paul's remarks. The account is biographical, no doubt, but it is part of the apologetic *narratio*. For this reason, there are no long narratives as in Acts.[126] Probably for the same reason, Paul's "conversion" to the Christian faith disappears behind his vocation to the apostolate. It is extremely difficult—if not altogether impossible—to extract from Paul's words the facts as they really happened. We can understand, in the light of the present context of his defense, what Paul sees as having happened to him back then. One should not simply take for granted that Paul had a conversion experience in

the sense that he was converted from Judaism to Christianity. At the time of his conversion the two religions were still one and the same, so that the most one could say is that he was converted from one Jewish movement, the Pharisees, to another, the Christians.[127] Even after so many years, when Christianity was recognized as different from "Judaism" (1:13, 14), Paul still speaks only with caution of his call to apostleship. This call was an act of God.[128] It was not his own decision, or any human decision–making. It happened suddenly, but was the result of God's longstanding plans. It is of course intentional that Paul casts his call to apostleship into the language belonging to the call of the Old Testament prophets.[129] The vocation occurred when it "pleased God" and when he had determined it ($\H{o}\tau\epsilon$ $\delta\grave{\epsilon}$ $\epsilon\grave{v}\delta\acute{o}\kappa\eta\sigma\epsilon\nu$).[130] Although Paul does not name God as the author,[131] it is clear that this is what he

---

cision, the sabbath, and the law." Modern scholars have also tried time and again to explain Paul's "conversion" to Christianity in psychological terms. See Schoeps (*Paul*, 54f) who rightly rejects these attempts. Schoeps himself has a somewhat different explanation: Paul was prepared for Christianity by his failure to understand the Jewish concept of the Torah, a "fundamental misapprehension" he inherited from his Hellenistic Jewish background (*Paul*, 213ff, 219ff).

125 Such miraculous conversions are features of the biographical literature. See Olof Gigon, "Antike Erzählungen über die Berufung zur Philosophie," *MH* 3 (1946) 1–21. The complicated problem of Jesus' "conversion" and baptism by John the Baptist should not be overlooked. Related are the NT narratives of the call of the disciples. See Lyder Brun, "Die Berufung der ersten Jünger Jesu in der evangelischen Tradition," *SO* 11 (1932) 35–54. Cf. the different explanation in the Mani biography (*CMC* 5.3–11).

126 Paul's hesitation to make long statements about himself has its theological reason in the fact that it is part of improper "boasting." Cf. Georg Eichholz, *Tradition und Interpretation* (Munich: Kaiser, 1965) 174–79; Betz, *Paulus*, 70ff.

127 Cf. Gal 1:12 with the *excursus*; Phil 3:7f. See on this point Akira Satake, "Apostolat und Gnade bei Paulus," *NTS* 15 (1968/69) 96–107.

128 See Gal 1:1, 11f, and the excursus on 1:17, the concept of "apostle." See furthermore Rom 1:1–7; 1 Cor 15:10; Eph 3:1–21; Col 1:9–23; etc.

129 Research on prophetic vocation in the OT is in progress. See Johannes Lindblom, *Prophecy in Ancient Israel* (Philadelphia: Fortress, 1962) 182ff. Henning Graf Reventlow, *Liturgie und prophetisches Ich bei Jeremias* (Gütersloh: Mohn, 1963) 24ff; Wolfgang Richter, *Die sogenannten vorprophetischen Berufungsberichte* (FRLANT 101; Göttingen: Vandenhoeck & Ruprecht, 1970), with more bib.; also Mussner, p. 82 n. 24. One question is whether Paul can be understood as following a particular tradition, e.g. Deutero–Isaiah (so Traugott Holtz, "Zum Selbstverständnis des Apostels Paulus," *ThLZ* 91 [1966] 321–30). For the concept of divine election in the Hellenistic mystery cults, see Widengren, *Religionsphänomenologie*, 222f.

130 $\epsilon\grave{v}\delta\acute{o}\kappa\eta\sigma\epsilon\nu$ refers to the divine decision. See Ps (LXX) 39:14; 67:17; Luke 12:32; 1 Cor 1:21; Col 1:19. Gal 1:15 is used several times in the Mani biography: *CMC* 19.8–9; 68.16; 69.10. See Gottlob Schrenk, "$\epsilon\grave{v}\delta o\kappa\acute{\epsilon}\omega$," *TDNT* 2.738–42.

131 Cf. the same ambiguity in Gal 1:6; 2:8; 3:5; 5:8; Rom 8:11; Phil 1:6; 1 Thess 5:24. See Lightfoot. p. 83; Schlier, p. 53.

means.[132] The vocation has two stages:[133] the "setting aside" ($\dot{a}\varphi o\rho \dot{\iota}\zeta\epsilon\iota\nu$)[134] of the person for the special divine assignment.[135] This was done, Paul says, "from my mother's womb."[136] Then there is the "call" ($\kappa a\lambda\epsilon\hat{\iota}\nu$)[137] itself, which Paul emphasizes occurred "through God's grace" ($\delta\iota\dot{a}\ \tau\hat{\eta}\varsigma\ \chi\dot{a}\rho\iota\tau o\varsigma\ a\dot{\upsilon}\tau o\hat{\upsilon}$).[138] It is interesting that Paul understands his appointment to proclaim the gospel of Christ in line with the tradition of the prophetic vocation.[139] He took this appointment to be part of his Jewishness. Indeed, Romans 9–11 shows that even at the end of his career Paul had not ceased to formulate his task in the terms of a Jewish eschatological universal mission.[140]

■16 While 1:15 uses predominantly Jewish categories, v 16 now introduces specifically Christian ideas. More descriptively than in 1:1, 12 Paul claims that his vocation[141] took the form of a revelation of Christ: God called him by "revealing his son" ($\dot{a}\pi o\kappa a\lambda\dot{\upsilon}\psi a\iota\ \tau\dot{o}\nu\ \upsilon\dot{\iota}\dot{o}\nu\ a\dot{\upsilon}\tau o\hat{\upsilon}$) in him.[142] The language which Paul uses at this point raises difficult questions and has caused much speculation. We do not know why Paul here introduces the christological title "Son of God" ($\dot{o}\ \upsilon\dot{\iota}\dot{o}\varsigma\ \tau o\hat{\upsilon}\ \theta\epsilon o\hat{\upsilon}$). Does this indicate that Paul cites a traditional phrase?[143] Is the title "Son of God" firmly attached to accounts of visions of Christ? At any rate, the title here refers to the crucified and risen Lord Jesus Christ who

---

132 The variant reading in 𝕳 𝕽 D pl of $\dot{o}\ \theta\epsilon\dot{o}\varsigma$ is probably a gloss (correctly) explaining the matter. P[46] B G pc lat sy Irenaeus do not read it. For the change in Nestle–Aland, 26th edition, see the Introduction, § 4, above. See Metzger, *Textual Commentary*, 590; Sieffert, p. 60; Burton, pp. 51f; Mussner, p. 81 n. 21.

133 Cf. Jer 1:5: "Before I formed you in the womb I knew you, and before you came out of your mother I consecrated you, I appointed you a prophet to the nations." See also Isa 42:6; 49:1, 5–6. For the later period, see the Qumran texts (1QH 9.29f).

134 $\dot{o}\ \dot{a}\varphi o\rho\dot{\iota}\sigma a\varsigma\ \mu\epsilon$ ("he who set me aside") has parallels in Jer 1:5 (Hebrew הקדשתיך; LXX $\dot{\eta}\gamma\dot{\iota}a\kappa\dot{a}\ \sigma\epsilon$); Rom 1:1; Acts 13:2; 26:16; see Schlier, p. 53 n. 1. See also *CMC* 65.4f; 70.5–8. The term $\dot{a}\varphi o\rho\dot{\iota}\zeta\epsilon\iota\nu$ refers to the setting aside as "holy" in contrast to the "profane." It is used often also in Greek literature (cf. e.g., Plato *Tim.* 24A; Aristotle *Pol.* 1322b26). For the LXX see Exod 19:23; 29:24, 26, 27; Lev 10:15; 20:25, 26; 27:21 etc. For rabbinic literature, see Str–B 3.4. In the NT, see Gal 2:12; 2 Cor 6:17 (Isa 52:11; cf. Appendix 2, below; Hans Dieter Betz, "2 Cor 6:14–7:1: An Anti–Pauline Fragment?" *JBL* 92 [1973] 96). Some scholars suggest that Paul may have alluded by the term to the Hebrew פרוש (Aram. פרישא), and thereby to his having been a Pharisee. So Zahn, p. 33; Schlier, p. 53 n. 3; Jan W. Doeve, "Paulus der Pharisäer und Galater 1:13–15," *NovT* (1963) 170–81; critical is Hans Friedrich Weiss, "φαρισαῖος," *TDNT* 9.46 n. 211. There is no evidence that Paul knew of the linguistic relationship.

135 Cf. Gal 1:16.

136 $\dot{\epsilon}\kappa\ \kappa o\iota\lambda\dot{\iota}a\varsigma\ \mu\eta\tau\rho\dot{o}\varsigma$ is a "septuagintism" (cf. BDF, §259, 1; BDR, § 259, 1). For a collection of passages see Johannes Behm, "$\kappa o\iota\lambda\dot{\iota}a$," *TDNT* 3.786–89; also Philo *Leg.* 56; *L.A.* 3.88; cf. *CMC* 33.1.

137 On $\kappa a\lambda\dot{\epsilon}\sigma a\varsigma$ cf. Isa. 41:9; 42:6, 11; 43:1; 45:3;

48:12, 15; 49:1; 50:2; 51:2, and often. Cf. Paul's self–designation as $\kappa\lambda\eta\tau\dot{o}\varsigma\ \dot{a}\pi\dot{o}\sigma\tau o\lambda o\varsigma$ ("called apostle") in Rom 1:1; 1 Cor 1:1. See also *CMC* 18.12f; 64.18.

138 $\delta\iota\dot{a}\ \tau\hat{\eta}\varsigma\ \chi\dot{a}\rho\iota\tau o\varsigma\ a\dot{\upsilon}\tau o\hat{\upsilon}$ is a Pauline expression. See Rom 1:5; 12:3; 15:15; 2 Cor 9:14; Gal 1:6; 2:9. It is equal to $\delta\iota\dot{a}\ \dot{\prime}I\eta\sigma o\hat{\upsilon}\ X\rho\iota\sigma\tau o\hat{\upsilon}$ ("through Jesus Christ") Gal 1:1; cf. 1:12. The whole phrase $\delta\iota\dot{a}\ \tau\hat{\eta}\varsigma\ \chi\dot{a}\rho\iota\tau o\varsigma\ a\dot{\upsilon}\tau o\hat{\upsilon}$ is not read by P[46] Origen. Cf. *CMC* 18.13f; 64.19; 65.4.

139 One should, however, avoid simply interpreting ideas of Second Isaiah into Paul, cf. Holtz, *ThLZ* 91 (1966) 321–30; André–Marie Denis, "L'apôtre Paul, prophète 'messianique' des gentils," *Eph Theol Lov* 33 (1957) 245–318; Stuhlmacher, *Evangelium* 1.72f; Mussner, p. 82 n. 26.

140 See esp. Schoeps, *Paul*, 219ff.

141 This event presumably is the same as the one connected with Damascus (cf. Gal 1:17). Other commentators wish to separate the conversion (1:15) and the vocation (1:16) as two events (Sieffert, p. 62; Loisy, p. 73; Lietzmann, p. 7; Bonnard). Cf. Stuhlmacher, *Evangelium* 1.73 n. 1; 82 n. 2; Mussner, p. 84.

142 On this Christological title see Gal 2:20; 4:4, 6; Rom 1:3f, 9; 5:10; 8:3, 29, 32; 1 Cor 1:9; 15:28; 2 Cor 1:19; 1 Thess 1:10. See Cullmann, *Christology*, 270ff; Ferdinand Hahn, *The Titles of Jesus in Christology* (Cleveland: World, 1969) 279ff; Kramer, *Christ, Lord, Son of God*, 108ff; 183ff; Eduard Schweizer, "$\upsilon\dot{\iota}\dot{o}\varsigma$," *TDNT* 8.383; Braun, *Studien*, 255ff; Lührmann, *Offenbarungsverständnis*, 76ff.

143 If so, this does not mean, however, that the term can be interpreted as "Jewish apocalyptic." Visions of this kind were known to antiquity generally. Paul had the vision as a Jew, but having such a vision of Christ was considered typically "Christian." Whether this experience has a connection with apo-

is also the present Christ, and whose presence is identical with the content of the Pauline gospel.[144] Furthermore, which form of revelation Paul has in mind is unclear. The term ἀποκαλύπτω ("reveal") can mean many things.[145] Most commentators interpret the concept in analogy to 1 Cor 9:1; 15:8, where Paul also talks about his revelation. But in 1 Corinthians the terminology is different. In 1 Cor 9:1 ("Have I not seen Jesus our Lord?") and 15:8 ("he [sc. Christ] appeared also to me"), the terms are forms of ὁρᾶν ("see"), once active (9:1) and once passive (15:8). Both suggest external visions rather than internal experiences.[146] This raises the other question of how to interpret "in me" (ἐν ἐμοί). Does this refer to a "mystical" experience[147] or is the reference simply equal to a dative (= "to me")?[148] The "mystical" interpretation once had many supporters, but has nowadays fallen into disrepute. Also, the interpretation as a dative makes it easier to reconcile Gal 1:16 with 1 Cor 9:1; 15:8 and the accounts in Acts (9:1–19; 22:3–16; 26:9–18).[149] But we must avoid deciding the matter by way of outside influences or apologetic interests. We should not suppose that Paul feels he contradicts himself in Gal 1:16 and 1 Cor 9:1; 15:8. Apparently for him the two forms

of visions (external and internal) are not as distinct as they may be for some commentators. Paul can use a variety of concepts and languages when he describes his vocation, which in any case he does only rarely. There are indications, however, that we should take his words seriously. The "in me" corresponds to Gal 2:20 ("Christ . . . lives in me")[150] and 4:6 ("God has sent the Spirit of his Son into our hearts").[151] Paul does not explain how the three passages are related to each other, but we may assume that they complement each other. This would mean that Paul's experience was ecstatic in nature, and that in the course of this ecstasy he had a vision (whether external or internal or both— "I do not know, God knows" [cf. 2 Cor 12:2, 3]). This interpretation is supported by the debate about Paul's vision in the ps.-Clem. *Hom.* 17. 13–19.[152]

The purpose and result (ἵνα ["so that"])[153] of Paul's vision of Christ was his commission "to preach the gospel among the Gentiles" (εὐαγγελίζωμαι . . . ἐν τοῖς ἔθνεσιν).[154] Again, we must not expect at this point more than Paul is willing to tell us. Therefore, it is rather useless to ask how he could have known im-

---

calypticism is another question: we find visions in apocalypticism, but they are not exclusively apocalyptic. A vision of Christ falls outside of apocalypticism, and for this reason Eduard Schweizer wants to see behind Gal 1:16 an older "apocalyptic Son of Man" tradition (*TDNT* 8.383); also Ulrich Wilckens, "Der Ursprung der Überlieferung der Erscheinungen des Auferstandenen," in *Dogma und Denkstrukturen. Festschrift für Edmund Schlink* (Göttingen: Vandenhoeck & Ruprecht, 1963) 56–95, 83f.

144 Cf. Gal 1:1, 4, 11; 3:13; 4:4–6.

145 Cf. Gal 1:12; 2:2; 3:23; 1 Cor 9:1; 15:1ff; Phil 3:8ff, 12ff. See Albrecht Oepke, "ἀποκαλύπτω κτλ.," *TDNT* 3.563–592; Lührmann, *Offenbarungsverständnis*, 79 n. 1; Stuhlmacher, *Evangelium* 1.72ff.

146 The distinctions between the two forms of vision have been pointed out especially by Alfred Wikenhauser, *Die Christusmystik des Apostels Paulus* (Freiburg: Herder, ²1956) 88–90; idem, *Pauline Mysticism: Christ in the Mystical Teaching of St. Paul* (New York: Herder, 1960) 134–36; Albert Schweitzer, *The Mysticism of Paul the Apostle* (New York: Macmillan, 1956) *passim*; Lietzmann, pp. 7–8; Schlier, p. 55. See also Ernst Benz, *Die Vision* (Stuttgart: Klett, 1969).

147 See also Richard Reitzenstein, *Die hellenistischen Mysterienreligionen nach ihren Grundgedanken und Wirkungen* (Stuttgart: Teubner, ³1927) 371; Béda Rigaux, *Letters of Saint Paul* (ed. and tr. Stephen Yonick; Chicago: Franciscan Herald, 1968) 51–55.

148 See on the philological question BDF, § 220, 1; BDR, § 220, 1; Bauer, *s.v. ἐν*, IV, 4, a; Lührmann, *Offenbarungsverständnis*, 79 n. 1; Stuhlmacher, *Evangelium* 1.82 n. 1; Oepke, pp. 60f; Mussner, pp. 86f.

149 The accounts in Acts do not seem to be informed by Paul's own letters. Neither can both be harmonized, nor are they altogether contradictory.

150 See also Gal 4:19; 2 Cor 4:6; 11:10; 13:3; Rom 8:9; Col 3:16.

151 See also Rom 8:9, 11, 15f; 1 Cor 3:16; 6:19; 2 Cor 6:16 (on this, see Appendix 2, below; Betz, "2 Cor 6:14–7:1," 93–95); Eph 3:16ff; 2 Tim 1:14. On the whole concept, see Johannes Haussleiter, "Deus Internus," *RAC* 3.794–842; Eduard Schweizer, "πνεῦμα," *TDNT* 6.424–34.

152 See Appendix 3, c, below.

153 On the "redemptive" ἵνα see also Gal 2:16, 19; 3:14, 22, 24; 4:5.

154 P⁴⁶ D* read εὐαγγελίσωμαι, a grammatical correction.

mediately what the meaning of the vision was.[155] Paul speaks very concisely, whereas in Acts the stories indulge in details. The phrase εὐαγγελίζεσθαι αὐτόν ("proclaim as the gospel him [sc. Christ]") is remarkable. After 1:11 we would expect a neuter object to the verb, instead of the personal object Christ.[156] But Paul also elsewhere identifies "gospel" and "Christ": the content of the gospel is Jesus Christ,[157] or "Jesus Christ crucified."[158] Paul's commission to preach is clearly limited to the Gentiles.[159] The formulation "among the Gentiles" suggests that Paul's mission includes the entire world population apart from the Jews.[160]

The last part of the verse (v 16c) really belongs to v 17, so that its treatment will be found there.

■17 In vv 16c–17 Paul describes his reaction to the vision and commission. Strangely, he does it first of all negatively, saying what he did *not* do: "immediately I

did not confer with 'flesh and blood.'"[161] Commentators differ whether the adverb εὐθέως ("immediately")[162] should go with the preceding sentence,[163] with the negative statement in v 16c,[164] or with the whole following sentence up to "into Arabia."[165] It is obvious that Paul wants to underscore his immediate reaction to the call. Why does he not simply state his obedience as he does in Acts 26:19–20? The negative statement is indeed mysterious. The adverb "immediately" seems to belong to the "call narratives,"[166] but here in v 17 it has been given a special twist. What Paul denies having done is προσανατίθεσθαι ("consult with," "confer with").[167] There is no object, about which such consultation could have taken place.[168] The phrase "flesh and blood" (σὰρξ καὶ αἷμα) refers to human beings generally, not to specific names.[169] It expresses the same concerns as in 1:1, 11, 12. The

---

155 Speculations at this point were provoked by the differing accounts in Acts, where careful distinction is made between Paul's conversion near Damascus (9:1ff; 22:3ff; 26:9ff), his period as a missionary (13:1ff), and his final commission in a special vision in the Temple at Jerusalem (22:17–21). But Acts presents first of all Luke's construction, and Paul only reports in Gal 1:16 what is to him at this time the most important outcome. Cf. Barnikol, *Zeit des Paulus*, 18ff; Schoeps, *Paul*, 54, 72, 168; Mussner, pp. 87f. Burchard, *Der dreizehnte Zeuge, passim*; Löning, *Saulustradition*, 126ff; Stolle, *Zeuge*, 155ff.

156 Cf. also Gal 1:8, 9, 23; 4:13; furthermore 2:2. See Eduard Schweizer, "υἱός," *TDNT* 8.384f.

157 See Rom 1:2–5; 15:18f; 16:25–27; 2 Cor 1:19; Phil 1:15. See also Molland, *Euangelion*, 40, 64ff.

158 See Gal 3:1; 1 Cor 1:23; 2:2; also 1:17f; 2:8; 2 Cor 13:4; Gal 5:11, 24; 6:12, 14; Phil 2:8; 3:18; etc.

159 Paul's commission to preach the gospel among the Gentiles was approved at the conference at Jerusalem (Gal 2:1–10). Later Paul calls himself τῶν ἐθνῶν ἀπόστολος ("apostle of the Gentiles") in Rom 11:13; cf. also Rom 1:1, 5, 13; 15:16, 18; 1 Thess 2:16, and often. This notion then becomes part of the Pauline tradition: see Eph 3:1, 8; 1 Tim 2:7; 3:16; 2 Tim 4:17; cf. Col. 1:23; Acts 9:15; 22:15, 21; 26:17f, 20; 28:28. See Edward P. Blair, "Paul's Call to the Gentile Mission," *BR* 10 (1965) 19–33.

160 Cf. the quotation of Deut 32:21 in Rom 10:19.

161 Usually, translations tend to smooth out the awkwardness of expression: *RSV* omits the adverb. Cf. *NEB*: "When that happened, without consulting any human being, . . ." Too free is *JB*: "I did not

stop to discuss this with any human being, nor. . . ."

162 On the form of εὐθέως see BDF, § 102, 2; BDR, § 102 n. 2; Bauer, *s.v.*

163 See the informative discussion in Sieffert, pp. 63–65.

164 So Zahn, Sieffert, Oepke, Schlier; cf. Mussner, p. 89 n. 56.

165 So, e.g., Lightfoot; Burton; Lietzmann.

166 See Mark 1:18; Matt 4:20, 22. Cf. Acts 26:19f: "Wherefore, O King Agrippa, I was not disobedient to the heavenly vision, but declared first to those at Damascus, then at Jerusalem and throughout all the country of Judea, and also to the Gentiles, that they should repent . . ." (*RSV*). Cf. *CMC* 44.2 (παραχρῆμα).

167 The term is rare. See LSJ, *s.v.*; Bauer, *s.v.*; Friedrich Preisigke, *Wörterbuch der griechischen Papyrusurkunden mit Einschluss der griechischen Inschriften, Aufschriften, Ostraka, Mumienschilder usw. aus Ägypten* (vol. 1–3: 1924–31; vol. 4, 1–4 rev. Emil Kiessling; *Supplement* 1.1–3: 1969–71; Berlin and Marburg: Selbstverlag, 1924–71) *s.v.* The meaning of the term in Gal 2:6 is different.

168 Cf. ἀνατίθημι ("present for consideration") in Gal 2:2. Paul only hesitantly admits that he did this later; his denial in v 16c might have the same thing in mind. See also Acts 25:14; 2 Macc 3:9. What Paul may mean is what Luke tells us in Acts 15:6ff.

169 Speculation has tried to fill in names. See on those possibilities Bonnard, pp. 31f. On the phrase "flesh and blood" see Matt 16:17; 1 Cor 15:50; Eph 6:12; Heb 2:14. For the background, see Str–B 1.730f; Eduard Schweizer, "σάρξ," *TDNT* 7.109f, 124, 128f; Jewett, *Paul's Anthropological Terms*, 95ff.

question is, of course, why does Paul feel compelled to make these statements of denial? Is v 16c a refutation of contrary accounts which claim that he has received his gospel from a human teacher? The narratives of Acts (especially Acts 9:6, 20) would substantiate this version because, according to Acts, Paul was directed back into Damascus in order to receive the Holy Spirit through Ananias (9:10–19). In Gal 1:16c he apparently denies such stories in order to defend the independence of his commission.[170]

Paul refers in v 17 either to the concrete instance he had in mind in v 16c, or to another and even more important instance like it:[171] "nor did I go up to Jerusalem, to those who were apostles before me." The city of Jerusalem,[172] important as it was for Judaism, must have figured highly in the minds of the Galatians because the Pauline opponents derived their authority from there (cf. Gal 2:4–5, 11–14; 4:25, 26). By not going there,[173] Paul demonstrates that he has re-

mained independent from these highest but human authorities in the church (cf. on 2:6). We must remember at this point that Paul makes his remark as part of the evidence needed for his contention in 1:11–12. Within reason (2:6) Paul does not deny "authority" to the mother church in the Holy City. Nor is it Paul's intention to deny that before him[174] there were other apostles. But his gospel did not originate with them. The Apostle goes on to say that he went away "to Arabia." This incidental remark is highly puzzling. Paul does not say precisely where he went nor for what purpose. We can assume, however, that he went to the cities of the Kingdom of Nabataea (called "*provincia Arabia*"),[175] rather than to the desert east and southeast of the Gulf of Aqaba. Recent excavations have brought to light a prosperous civilization in that territory, which was at its peak by the time of Paul's visit.[176] Buildings and inscriptions show strong Hellenistic influences.[177] The centers of this culture were the cities

---

170 See Lütgert, *Gesetz und Geist*, 46; Zahn, p. 67; Schlier, p. 57.

171 The οὐδέ is climactic. So Schlier, p. 58.

172 The spelling Paul uses most often is Ἰερουσαλήμ (Gal 4:25, 26; Rom 15:19, 25, 26, 31; 1 Cor 16:3), but in Gal 1:17, 18; 2:1 he spells Ἰεροσόλυμα. For this problem, see BDF, § 56, 1; BDR, § 56, 1; Bauer, *s.v.*; Joachim Jeremias, "ΙΕΡΟΥΣΑΛΗΜ / ΙΕΡΟ-ΣΟΛΥΜΑ," *ZNW* 65 (1974) 273–76; Ben Zion Wacholder, *Eupolemus* (Cincinnati: Hebrew Union College, 1974) 87. On the city of Jerusalem in the NT, see Joachim Jeremias, *Jerusalem in the Time of Jesus* (Philadelphia: Fortress, 1969); Georg Fohrer and Eduard Lohse, "Σιών," *TDNT* 7.292–338; Hans Kosmala, *BHH* 2.820–850; James C. De Young, *Jerusalem in the New Testament* (Kampen: Kok, 1960); Emil Schürer, *The History of the Jewish People in the Age of Jesus Christ* (tr. T. A. Burkill; ed. M. Black and others; Edinburgh: Clark, 1973) 1. § 2.

173 Because of the position of the city on the hill one must go "up." The term ἀνέρχομαι ("go up") occurs only in Gal 1:17, 18, while the synonym ἀναβαίνω is more common (see Gal 2:1, 2 and Bauer, *s.v.* for the passages elsewhere). The variant reading ἀπῆλ-θον ("he went away") read by P⁵¹ B D G *al* is probably due to a confusion with the following verb.

174 For similar expressions, see Rom 16:7; 1 Cor 9:5; 15:7, 9; cf. also *CMC* 71.18f. But Paul does not identify these apostles with the Twelve or any other group. There was no definition of apostleship which

all could agree upon. See the excursus on "apostle" below, and also Conzelmann, *1 Corinthians*, on 1 Cor 9:1f; Walter Schmithals, *The Office of the Apostle in the Early Church* (tr. John E. Steely; Nashville and New York, 1969) 82ff. Differently Mussner, p. 91 n. 64.

175 On Arabia, see Schürer, *History* 1.574–86 (n. 172 above). The older works are still very valuable: Félix–Marie Abel, *Géographie de la Palestine* (Paris: Lecoffre, ³1933–38) 1.288–98; Rudolf E. Brünnow and Alfred von Domaszewski, *Die Provincia Arabia* (3 vols.; Strassburg: Trübner, 1904–09); René Dussaud, *La pénétration des Arabes en Syrie avant l'Islam* (Paris: Geuthner, 1955); Franz Altheim, *Die Araber in der Alten Welt* (5 vols.; Berlin: de Gruyter, 1964–69).

176 For bib. and surveys of the current state of research, see Jean Starcky, "Pétra et la Nabatène," *DB Sup* 7 (1966) 886–1017; Glen W. Bowersock, "A Report on Arabia Provincia," *JRS* 61 (1971) 219–42; Schürer, *History* (n. 172 above) 575–86.

177 See Frederic V. Winnett and William L. Reed, *Ancient Records from North Arabia* (Toronto: University of Toronto, 1970); Joseph T. Milik, *Recherches d'épigraphie proche-orientale. I: Dédicaces faites par des dieux* (Paris: Geuthner, 1972). Current events are reported in the "Bulletin d'épigraphie sémitique," *Syria* 44 [1967] and subsequent vols.

of Petra and Bostra, but more cities have been discovered between Bostra and the Gulf of Aqaba, and in the Negev between Petra, Gaza, and El-'Arīsh.[178] Inscriptions show that the Nabataean influences reached into the Sinai peninsula and into the northern parts of the Arabian desert. To the west some of the cities of the Decapolis were included: Philadelphia ('Ammān), Gerasa (Jerash), Dium (n.i.), and Adraa (Der'ā).[179] By the time of Paul the Nabataeans were ruled by King Aretas IV (8 B.C.–A.D. 40), a fact which Paul himself mentions 2 Cor 11:32. In A.D. 106 the kingdom became a Roman province with the name Arabia.[180] Contacts between Arabs and Jews must have been manifold and different at times.[181] The recently discovered papyri from En-Geddi are valuable documents, although they belong to the period of the Bar Kokhba revolt.[182] Although Paul does not say why he went to Arabia, we can assume that he did so for the purpose of mission. It would be interesting to know whether at that time there were Christian congregations already there or whether or not Paul's mission was successful. Paul's silence proves neither option. At any rate, Gal 1:17 is the oldest reference to Christian activity in Arabia.[183]

From Arabia Paul "returned to Damascus": καὶ πάλιν ὑπέστρεψα εἰς Δαμασκόν.[184] This brief remark reveals that he had been in Damascus before he went to Arabia. Acts also reports that Paul went to Damascus after his conversion.[185] We may assume that Paul did not consider Damascus as part of the Nabataean kingdom.[186] There is some ambiguity, however. By the time of Paul, Damascus was under Roman rule, a city of great beauty and wealth.[187] Culturally it was a Hellenistic city, but it had a large Jewish community.[188] If the information in 2 Cor 11:32 is correct, the city must have been under the supervision of the Nabataean King Aretas IV. At any rate, the Christian congregation in Damascus was one of the oldest, preceding even Paul's "conversion."[189]

Excursus:
Apostle (ἀπόστολος).

"At present the question as to the origin and the idea of the apostolate is one of the most intricate and difficult problems of New Testament scholarship." This judgment, made by Erich Haupt in 1896 and restated by Wilhelm Schneemelcher in 1964 (in HSW, *NT Apocrypha* 2.25), is still true today. The main problems are caused by our limited sources, which do not sufficiently illuminate the earliest period of Christianity and with it the beginning of the Christian

178 See the reports by Abraham Negev in *IEJ* 17 (1967) and subsequent vols.

179 See Hans Bietenhard, "Die Dekapolis von Pompeius bis Trajan," *ZDPV* 79 (1963) 24–58; S. Thomas Parker, "The Decapolis Reviewed," *JBL* 94 (1975) 437–41.

180 A survey of the history is found in Bowersock, "*Arabia*," 228ff.

181 Cf. 1 Macc 5:25, 39; 9:35; 12:31; 2 Macc 12:10.

182 See Yigael Yadin, *The Finds from the Bar-Kokhba Period in the Cave of Letters* (JDS 1; Jerusalem: Israel Exploration Society, 1963); idem, *Bar-Kokhba* (Jerusalem: Weidenfeld & Nicolson, 1971).

183 In primitive Christian literature Arabia is mentioned, apart from Gal 1:17, also 4:25; Acts 2:11; *1 Clem.* 25.1, 3 (cf. Rom 15:19). See also Adolf von Harnack, *Die Mission und Ausbreitung des Christentums in den ersten drei Jahrhunderten* (Leipzig: Hinrichs, ⁴1924) 699ff; Bornkamm, *Paul*, 27; Mussner, p. 92 n. 66. Strange is a remark by Ambrosiaster about the purpose of Paul's visit (CSEL 81/3, p. 15).

184 So Schlier, p. 58f. The πάλιν ("again") is pleonastic, as in Gal 4:9; Acts 18:18. See BDF, § 484; BDR, § 484.

185 See Acts 9:3ff; 22:5ff; 26:12ff, 20.

186 Differently Justin *Dial.* 78.10.

187 On the city of Damascus at the time of the NT, see Carl Watzinger and Karl Wunzinger, *Damaskus, die antike Stadt* (Berlin and Leipzig, 1921); Louis Jalabert, "Damas," *DACL* 4 (1920) 119–45; A. Legendre, "Damas," *DB* 2 (1912) 1213–32; A. Barrois, "Damas," *DB Sup* 2 (1934) 277–87; Jean Sauvaget, *Les monuments historiques de Damas* (Beyrouth: Imprimerie Catholique, 1932); idem, "Esquisse d'une histoire de la ville de Damas," *Revue des études islamiques* 8 (1934) 421–80; N. Elisséeff, "Dimashk," *Encyclopedia of Islam* 1 (1965) 277–91.

188 See Josephus *BJ* 2.559–61; 7.368. Whether the "Damascus Scroll," of which fragments were found also in Qumran, had any real connection with Damascus is unknown. See Joseph A. Fitzmyer, *The Dead Sea Scrolls: Major Publications and Tools for Study* (Missoula: Scholars, 1975).

189 See Acts 9:10ff. Cf. Harnack, *Mission und Ausbreitung*, 553, 622, 633, 655ff. That Paul has had any contact with the Damascus branch of the Qumran sect has been suggested, but there is no evidence for it. See Braun, *Qumran*, 1.206.

concept of apostleship. The New Testament sources are reflections of an already advanced stage of the development, but this powerful later picture has determined the historical investigations up to the present.

One of the fundamental problems of the concepts of apostleship is part of the Galatian controversy. In the address of the letter Paul calls himself "apostle" (see on 1:1). In Gal 1:17 he speaks about those "who were apostles before me," but he does not name them. In 1:18 he names Cephas as one of them, but he has another title for James (the "brother of the Lord"), which seems to indicate that he was not an apostle (see on 1:19). When reporting on the conference at Jerusalem, Paul names the "pillars" James, Cephas and John (2:9), but he does not say they are also called "apostles." Then in 2:8 he reports that the "apostleship of the circumcision" was given to Peter (!), while Paul and Barnabas were sent to the gentiles —but there is no mentioning of a parallel "apostleship of the uncircumcision." If this picture is correct, the "pillars" were those who stayed at Jerusalem as the "authorities" of the church (2:3, 6–9), while "apostle" was the title of Peter when he was charged with the mission to the Jews in the diaspora (!). Yet Peter was not the only one who was called "apostle" (cf. 1:17). At that stage, however, Paul and Barnabas were evidently not called "apostles"; neither was their "apostleship" nor specifically Paul's "apostleship" a point of discussion at Jerusalem (see the *excursus* and interpretation of 2:1–10). Later Paul called himself "apostle of the Gentiles" ($\ldots\epsilon\iota\mu\iota\ \epsilon\gamma\grave{\omega}\ \epsilon\theta\nu\hat{\omega}\nu\ \alpha\pi\acute{o}\sigma\tauo\lambda o\varsigma$ [Rom 11:13]). This peculiar concept is more presupposed than explained in Gal 1:1, 12–16. It is, however, carefully defined in Rom 1:1–7. Paul's claim was, as he frequently admits, hotly disputed in primitive Christianity (cf. 1 Cor 9:1–27; 15:1–11; 2 Cor 10–13; etc.). Paul himself concedes that his "apostleship" is a "miscarriage" ($\epsilon\kappa\tau\rho\omega\mu\alpha$ [1 Cor 15:8]), a term perhaps borrowed from his adversaries. Jewish Christianity did not recognize "the apostle of the Gentiles" even in the second century (cf. Irenaeus, *Adv. haer.* 1.26.2; 3.15.1; etc.; for the sources and a survey, see Walter Bauer in HSW, *NT Apocrypha* 2.71–74).

In the light of this evidence it is unlikely that the Christian concepts of apostleship, as we find them in the New Testament, are derived from one origin. (1) Paul's own concept of apostleship has its closest parallels, and most probably its antecedents, in Syriac gnosticism. With this hypothesis we follow the studies of Geo Widengren. (2) The concept of "apostle" as it was used with reference to Jesus' disciples during his life-time may have its roots in Judaism, but there the question remains as to what branch of Judaism this

may have been and whether that branch had any connections which would later be regarded as anormative Judaism. At any rate, there seem to be two roots of the concept of apostle, both of which suddenly appeared in the dark zones of the origins of primitive Christianity. The Pauline concept of apostle, as he develops it in Gal 1:1, 12–2:10, became very popular among the gnostics, who regarded Paul as "the apostle" par excellence. This and the fact that Paul appears phenomenologically close to figures like Mani and Muhammad may not be accidental, but a reflection of the possible origin of the Pauline concept.

Bibliography: Karl Heinrich Rengstorf, *TDNT* 1 *s.v.* "$\alpha\pi\acute{o}\sigma\tauo\lambda o\varsigma$"; Harald Riesenfeld, "Apostel," *RGG* 1.497–99; Günter Klein, "Apostel," *BHH* 1.111–12; HSW, *NT Apocrypha* 2.35–89, and index, *s.v.*; Walter Schmithals, *Office;* idem, *Paul and the Gnostics;* Elaine H. Pagels, *The Gnostic Paul.* Research has not paid adequate attention to the investigations by Geo Widengren: see his *The Great Vohu Manah and the Apostle of God: Studies in Iranian and Manichaean Religion* (Uppsala: Almqvist & Wiksell, 1945); idem, *The Ascension of the Apostle and the Heavenly Book* (Uppsala: Almqvist & Wiksell, 1950); idem, *Muhammad, the Apostle of God, and His Ascension* (Uppsala: Almqvist & Wiksell, 1955); idem, *Religionsphänomenologie,* 503ff, 506, 548, 555, 564, 566, 628f; idem, *The Gnostic Attitude* (tr. and ed. Birger A. Pearson; Santa Barbara: University of California, 1973) 28ff and *passim. CMC* has the concept throughout (see especially 17.7; 45.5f; 60.13–63.1; 63.2ff; 66.5; 71.17ff). See also Foerster and Wilson, *Gnosis* 2.325, *s.v.* "Apostle(s)," and 2.347, *s.v.* "Messenger."

More in the traditional line of thought are the surveys by Karl Kertelge, "Das Apostelamt des Paulus, sein Ursprung und seine Bedeutung," *BZ* 14 (1970) 161–81; Joseph Eckert, "Die Verteidigung der apostolischen Autorität im Galaterbrief und im zweiten Korintherbrief," *Theologie und Glaube* 65 (1975) 1–19.

■ 18 It was only two or three[190] years later[191] that Paul went to Jerusalem for the first time: "then after three years I went up to Jerusalem." Paul's remarks are kept brief and contain only what is needed for the purpose of his defense, which means that he stresses those words he actually uses. "After three years" makes the "immediately" ($\epsilon\dot{v}\theta\dot{\epsilon}\omega\varsigma$) of v 16c (cf. v 17a) specific: Paul did not go up to Jerusalem at once, but only after a considerable period of time. "Then" ($\ddot{\epsilon}\pi\epsilon\iota\tau\alpha$) indicates that he considers this visit to be part of another period,[192] and not part of the reaction to the vision of Christ. The importance of the visit is played down further by the fact that Paul visited only with Cephas,[193] staying with him for the short period of two weeks.[194] His visit had no official character or purpose. For describing the visit Paul chooses the non-committal phrase $\iota\sigma\tau\rho\rho\hat{\eta}\sigma\alpha\iota$ $K\eta\phi\hat{\alpha}\nu$ ("pay Cephas a visit").[195] Much speculation has been spent on the term $\iota\sigma\tau\rho\rho\epsilon\hat{\iota}\nu$, usually without considering the literary context and function of the passage. To be sure, Paul wants to rule out that it was at this occasion that he received instruction (cf. 1:12) about the gospel or Jesus.[196] An informal "visit" to the famous Cephas by

the Apostle is quite understandable after all these years, and it does not put into question the contention that he received the gospel from divine revelation and not from human sources.[197]

Excursus: Cephas

Paul mentions Cephas (Peter) as a leading Christian personality several times in Galatians. When he first traveled to Jerusalem, it was for the purpose of visiting Cephas (1:18). Cephas appears at that time to have been the leading man among the apostles (1:19). At the so-called Apostolic Council (2:1–10) Cephas appears behind James and before John as one of the "pillars" who concluded the agreement with Paul and Barnabas (2:9). This agreement charged him with the responsibility for the mission to the Jews (2:7–8, where his name is Peter [on this problem see below on 2:7]). Later at Antioch (2:11–14) Paul confronted Cephas in that severe conflict which led to their separation. Cephas' influence is further attested by the existence of a Cephas group in Corinth (1 Cor 1:12; on this see the article by Vielhauer mentioned below). The figure of Cephas–Peter in other parts of primitive Christian literature is informed mostly by

---

190   Since the first year counts as a full year, it is not possible to determine the time period with precision. See Schlier, p. 59.

191   The point of reference is left unclear; was it three years after his vision of Christ or after his return to Damascus? The hopeless problem of coordinating this first visit of Paul in Jerusalem with Acts cannot be discussed here. See recently Charles H. Talbert, "Again: Paul's Visits to Jerusalem," *NovT* 9 (1967) 26–40; D. R. De Lacey, "Paul in Jerusalem," *NTS* 20 (1974) 82–86, where further literature can be found.

192   The $\ddot{\epsilon}\pi\epsilon\iota\tau\alpha$ ("then") indicates the beginning of the second period of the first part of the *narratio* (cf. 1:21; 2:1).

193   $K\eta\phi\hat{\alpha}\varsigma$ is the Greek transcription of the Aramaic surname כֵּיפָא ("rock"). Paul nearly always uses Cephas as a name (Gal 1:18; 2:9, 11, 14; 1 Cor 1:12; 3:22; 9:5; 15:5), with the exception of Gal 2:7f, where $\Pi\dot{\epsilon}\tau\rho\rho\varsigma$ ("Peter") is used. The problem of textual tradition is difficult because in part of the manuscript tradition "Cephas" has been replaced by "Peter," probably because "Peter" later became the preferred name. So Metzger, *Textual Commentary*, 591. On "Cephas" see also Joseph A. Fitzmyer, "The Contribution of Qumran Aramaic to the

Study of the New Testament," *NTS* 20 (1974) 382–407, 401.

194   $\dot{\eta}\mu\dot{\epsilon}\rho\alpha\varsigma$ $\delta\epsilon\kappa\alpha\pi\dot{\epsilon}\nu\tau\epsilon$ ("fifteen days"). See Bauer, *s.v.* $\delta\epsilon\kappa\alpha$.

195   See, e.g., George D. Kilpatrick, "Galatians 1:18 $I\Sigma TOPH\Sigma AI$ $KH\Phi AN$," in *New Testament Essays, Studies in Memory of T. W. Manson* (Manchester: Manchester University, 1959) 144–49; Oscar Cullmann, *Peter: Disciple, Apostle, Martyr* (Philadelphia: Westminster, ²1962) 40.

196   Kilpatrick's interpretation of $\iota\sigma\tau\rho\rho\dot{\epsilon}\omega$ as "getting information from," though possible philologically, runs counter to Paul's defense. See also W. D. Davies, *The Setting of the Sermon on the Mount* (Cambridge: Cambridge University, 1966) 453–55; Ernst Haenchen, "Petrus–Probleme," *NTS* 7 (1961) 187–97, 187–89.

197   This was well understood by Chrysostom, Jerome, Augustine, Ambrosiaster (see the quotations excerpted by Mussner, pp. 94f). Differently Jürgen Roloff (*Apostolat–Verkündigung–Kirche* [Gütersloh: Mohn, 1965] 67f, 86), who also thinks Paul used the visit to get trustworthy information about Jesus and his life on earth, and to coordinate his theology with Peter's.

legend, and reliable historical data are scarce. John 1:35–42, a section which perhaps depends on reliable sources, gives his name as "Simon the son of John" (*v.l.* "the son of Jona"),[198] and his and his brother's home village as Bethsaida.[199] The two brothers, Simon and Andrew, are said to have been disciples of John the Baptist before they became disciples of Jesus. Simon was married (Mark 1:29–31; 1 Cor 9:5), and owned a house at Capernaum (Mark 1:29), which may have been found by recent excavations. His profession may have been that of a fisherman (Mark 1:16 par.; Luke 5:2; John 21:3). "Cephas" is an honorific name (Aramaic כֵּיפָא "rock"; Greek πέτρα, transcribed as Κηφᾶς and rendered into Greek as Πέτρος, Latin *Petrus*, English "Peter"). When and why Simon received this name is described by the legend of his vocation (Matt 16:16–19).[200] After Jesus' death Cephas may have been the first to see the risen Jesus in a vision (1 Cor 15:5; Luke 24:34). He appears as the first leader of the church in Jerusalem (Gal 1:18; Acts 1:15, and *passim*). His death as a martyr is attested in the New Testament (cf. John 21:18–19; 1 Pet 5:1 [?]; 2 Pet 1:14; see also *1 Clem.* 5.1–7). The tradition has Rome as the place of martyrdom (most probable), but it could be also Asia Minor and Syria (less probable). Whether the "tomb of Peter" found under the Vatican is historical, or what is historical about it, is still doubtful in spite of all the publicity. The date of Cephas' death is also uncertain. The anti-Pauline literature included in the pseudo-Clementines show Peter, together with James, as the main opponents of Paul. This situation is consciously seen in harmony with Galatians, and indeed it may be historical.

Bibliography: Oscar Cullmann, *Peter: Disciple, Apostle, Martyr* (tr. Floyd v. Filson; Philadelphia: Westminster, ²1962); idem, *TDNT* 6, *s.v.* "Πέτρος, Κηφᾶς", with further bibliography; Karl Heussi, *Die römische Petrustradition in kritischer Sicht* (Tübingen: Mohr, Siebeck,

1955); Kurt Aland, "Wann starb Petrus? Eine Anmerkung zu Gal. II 6," *NTS* 2 (1955/56) 267–75; Gerhard Schulze–Kadelbach, "Die Stellung des Petrus in der Urchristenheit," *ThLZ* 81 (1956) 1–14; Erich Dinkler, "Die Petrus–Rom–Frage," *ThR* 25 (1959) 189–230, 289–335; 27 (1961) 33–64; Erik Peterson, "Das Martyrium des Hl. Petrus nach der Petrus–Apokalypse," in his *Frühkirche, Judentum, Gnosis* (Freiburg: Herder, 1959) 88–91; Ernst Haenchen, "Petrus–Probleme," *NTS* 7 (1960/61) 187–97; Klein, *Rekonstruktion*, 11ff, 49ff, 99ff; Paul Gächter, *Petrus*; Béda Rigaux, "Der Apostel Petrus in der heutigen Exegese: Ein Forschungsbericht," *Concilium* 3 (1967) 585–600; Rudolf Pesch, "Die Stellung und Bedeutung Petri in der Kirche des NT," *Concilium* 7 (1971) 240–45; John K. Elliott," Κηφᾶς: Σίμων Πέτρος: ὁ Πέτρος: An examination of NT Usage," *NovT* 14 (1972) 241–56; HSW, *NT Apocrypha* 2, index; Raymond E. Brown (ed.), *Peter in the New Testament* (Minneapolis: Augsburg, 1973); Philipp Vielhauer, "Paulus und die Kephaspartei in Korinth," *NTS* 21 (1975) 341-52; Daniel W. M. O'Connor, "Peter in Rome: A Review and Position," in *Christianity, Judaism and other Graeco–Roman Cults: Studies for Morton Smith at Sixty* (Leiden: Brill, 1975) 2.146–60; Michael Mees, "Das Petrusbild nach ausserkanonischen Zeugnissen," *ZRGG* 27 (1975) 193–205.

■ **19** Paul must admit that he has seen at least one other person in Jerusalem, but this does not change the private character of the visit. First he denies to have seen another of the apostles: ἕτερον δὲ τῶν ἀποστόλων οὐκ εἶδον ("but I saw none of the other apostles").[201] Obviously, Paul counts Cephas among the apostles who were also at Jerusalem and whom he could have seen if he had chosen to do so. Who these "other apostles" were and why Paul did not visit them we do not

---

198 The name in Matt 16:17 is Σίμων Βαριωνᾶ; in John 1:43 it is Σίμων ὁ υἱὸς Ἰωάννου; John 21:15, 16, 17: Σίμων Ἰωάννου; 2 Pet 1:1: Συμεών. See Samuel Sandmel, "John," *IDB* 2.930.

199 John 1:44; 12:21. On the problem of the location see Bauer, *s.v.*; Michael Avi-Yonah, "Beth-Saida," *IDB* 1.396f, with bib.

200 Matt 16:16–18; John 1:42; see also *PGL, s.v.* πέτρα. On Matt 16:16–19 as a parallel to Paul's vocation see above on Gal 1:15f. On 1 Cor 15:3–5, see Conzelmann, *1 Corinthians*, 248–57.

201 See L. Paul Trudinger ("*ΕΤΕΡΟΝ ΔΕ ΤΩΝ ΑΠΟΣΤΟΛΩΝ ΟΥΚ ΕΙΔΟΝ ΕΙ ΜΗ ΙΑΚΩΒΟΝ*: A Note on Galatian i 19," *NovT* 17 [1975] 200–

202), who proposes to translate: "Other *than* the apostles I saw no one except James, the Lord's brother." For such a denial, see also the parallel in *Herm. Vis.* 1.1.2.—D* G lat read εἶδον οὐδένα, P⁵¹ᵛⁱᵈ E read οὐκ εἶδον οὐδένα. These variants may be secondary attempts to clarify the text. Cf. Zahn, p. 71, n. 86.

know.[202] G. Klein[203] has shown convincingly that there is no reason to identify these apostles with the group called "the Twelve" (οἱ δώδεκα). But Paul is forced to admit that he has seen also James, Jesus' brother: εἰ μὴ Ἰάκωβον τὸν ἀδελφὸν τοῦ κυρίου ("except James, the brother of the Lord"). The question has been extensively debated whether or not Paul considers James to be one of the apostles.[204] The answer depends on the question whether εἰ μή should be rendered inclusively ("apart from") or exclusively ("but"); in the first instance James would be regarded as one of the "other apostles," while in the latter case he would fall into another category. Philologically both are possibilities. It is clear from other passages that James had a special position[205] in primitive Christianity, which was expressed by his title: "the brother of the Lord" (ὁ ἀδελφὸς τοῦ κυρίου).[206] Apparently, he was not regarded as an "apostle"[207] nor as one of "the Twelve." The question also arises, why does Paul mention the names of Cephas (v 18) and James? He most likely does so because of the fact that the opposition derives its authority from these two men.[208]

Excursus:
James

James, "the brother of the Lord,"[209] must not be confused with other New Testament figures bearing the name: James, the son of Zebedee, and James, the son of Alphaeus. Mark 6:3 (= Matt 13:55) mentions James as one of Jesus' brothers. During Jesus' lifetime James was not a member of his movement (cf. Mark 3:21, 31–35, and par.; John 7:3–5). Like Paul, James was converted by a vision of Jesus (1 Cor 15:7).[210] He became a member of the Jerusalem church (Acts 1:14) and rose to prominence quickly (Gal 1:18–19; 2:1–10; Acts 15:13; 21:18–19). After Peter's departure (Acts 12:17) he became the leading figure of Jewish Christianity. His death as a martyr is attested by Josephus as having occurred in A.D. 62.[211] He bore the title ὁ δίκαιος ("the Just") because of his piety.[212] Nothing is known about James' theology, but after his death he became an important figure

202 See Gal 1:17a. Zahn (pp. 70f) points out that Paul says the direct opposite of what one reads in Acts 9:26–30—as if Paul wants to deny such a version of the story. Acts also gives the reasons for Paul's difficulties: the church does not trust him, the Jews are hostile. Perhaps this is the truth (so Lietzmann, p. 9; Oepke). Far–fetched is Ramsay's (pp. 283f) and Sieffert's (p. 70) suggestion that the other apostles may have been out of town at the time.

203 Klein, *Zwölf Apostel*, 44ff (above n. 103); cf. Schmithals, *Office*, 82ff. Most commentators do not count James among the Twelve (e.g., Zahn, Schlier, Oepke, Bonnard, Mussner).

204 See Lightfoot, pp. 252–91; Josef Blinzler, *Die Brüder und Schwestern Jesu* (SBS 21; Stuttgart: Katholisches Bibelwerk, 1967) 119ff.

205 1 Cor 9:5 distinguishes between the apostles, the brothers of the Lord, and Cephas.

206 This title is given to James also in the *Kerygmata Petrou* (ps.–Clem. *Hom.* 11.35.4 [cf. Appendix, 3. b]). See Strecker, *Judenchristentum*, 194f.

207 Zahn, pp. 70f.

208 Cf., esp., Gal 2:11–14, and the anti–Pauline *Kerygmata Petrou* (see below, Appendix, 3. c).

209 This is his title (see Hegesippus, in Eusebius *H.E.* 2.23.4; Epiphanius *Adv. haer.* 78.13; etc.).

210 The vision is told at greater length in the *Gospel according to the Hebrews* (in Jerome *Vir. inl.* 2; cf. HSW, *NT Apocrypha* 1.165).

211 Josephus *Ant.* 20.200; Hegesippus, in Eusebius *H.E.* 2.23.10–18; *1 and 2 Apoc. Jas. NHC* V.3, pp. 42.20–44.6; V.4, p. 61, 1–63, 29. See Nils Hyldahl, "Hegesipps Hypomnemata," *StTh* 14 (1960) 70–113, esp. 103ff; Alexander Böhlig, *Mysterion und Wahrheit* (Leiden: Brill, 1968) 102–11; Kurt Rudolph, "Gnosis und Gnostizismus," *ThR* 34 (1969) 157ff; 36 (1971) 118f; Karlmann Beyschlag, "Das Jakobusmartyrium und seine Verwandten in der frühchristlichen Literatur," *ZNW* 56 (1965) 149–83; Donald H. Little, *The Death of James the Brother of Jesus* (Ph.D. diss.; Houston: Rice University, 1971).

212 On the titles of James, see Charles H. Torrey, "James the Just, and His Name Oblias," *JBL* 63 (1944) 93–98; Klaus Baltzer and Helmut Koester, "Die Bezeichnung des Jakobus als ΩΒΛΙΑΣ," *ZNW* 46 (1955) 141f; Hyldahl, ibidem, 103ff.

in Jewish Christianity and was made the author or addressee of pseudepigraphical writings.[213] The opposition against Paul made him their leader, a process which begins in Gal 2:11–14 and continues in the Jewish–Christian groups of the second century.[214]

Bibliography: Sources are collected by Theodor Zahn, *Forschungen zur Geschichte des neutestamentlichen Kanons und der altchristlichen Literatur* (6.2; Leipzig: Deichert, 1900). Reference Works: Kurt Aland, *RGG*³ 3.525–26; William A. Beardslee, *IDB* 2.790–94; Karl–Heinrich Rengstorf, *BHH* 2.800; Schürer (1973) 1.428–41: "Excursus II: Josephus on Jesus and James." Studies: Franz Mussner, *Jakobusbrief* §1–2; Hugo Koch, "Zur Jakobusfrage Gal 1:19," *ZNW* 33 (1934) 204–09; Hans von Campenhausen, "Die Nachfolge des Jakobus: Zur Frage eines urchristlichen Kalifates," *ZKG* 63 (1950/51) 133–44; Ethelbert Stauffer, "Zum Kalifat des Jakobus," *ZRGG* 4 (1952) 193–214; Paul Gächter, *Petrus*, 258–310; William K. Prentice, "James the Brother of the Lord," in *Studies in Roman Economic and Social History in Honor of A. C. Johnson* (ed. Paul R. Coleman–Norton; Princeton University, 1951) 144–52; Munck, *Paul, passim;* Ethelbert Stauffer, "Petrus und Jakobus in Jerusalem," in *Begegnung der Christen* (ed. Maximilian Roessle and Oscar Cullmann; Stuttgart and Frankfurt: Evangelischer Verlag, 1960) 361–72; Joseph Blinzler, *Die Brüder und Schwestern Jesu* (SBS 21; Stuttgart: Katholisches Bibelwerk, 1967) 119ff; Schmithals, *Paul and James, passim;* Schoeps, *Theologie und Geschichte, passim;* idem, *Jewish Christianity, passim.*

■ **20** A solemn oath[215] concludes the preceding account.[216] Paul employs the oath formula in order to assure that he had written the truth: ἃ δὲ γράφω ὑμῖν, ἰδοὺ ἐνώπιον τοῦ θεοῦ ὅτι οὐ ψεύδομαι ("Now, what I am writing to you, behold before God, I am not lying!"). The function of such oaths in rhetoric is to provide a kind of "proof" to cover what is in doubt.[217] But Paul's words are too concise to conclude from them precisely what was in doubt and why. We can say that Acts 9:26–30 shows a different version of the story which supports the doubts rather than Paul's assurances. But we do not know whether Acts has included traditions which were unfavorable to Paul, or which turned out to be unfavorable later, or which were used by the opponents of Paul against him.[218]

■ **21** The next phase of Paul's activity was far away from and out of the reach of Jerusalem:[219] ἔπειτα ἦλθον εἰς τὰ κλίματα τῆς Συρίας καὶ τῆς Κιλικίας ("Then I went to the regions of Syria and Cilicia."). It is not entirely clear which territories[220] Paul has in mind, but

---

213 On the Epistle of James, see the commentaries and introductions to the NT; on the NT Apocrypha, see HSW, *NT Apocrypha*, index; on the ps.–Clem. literature, see Strecker, *Judenchristentum, passim.* The Nag Hammadi Codices include the *Ap. Jas.* (Codex Jung, 1 [=2, according to a recent discovery. James M. Robinson]) and two *Apoc. Jas.* (see n. 211 above).

214 See Strecker, *Judenchristentum*, 187ff; Schoeps, *Jewish Christianity, passim.*

215 For other instances of the oath, see Rom 1:9; 9:1; 1 Cor 15:31; 2 Cor 1:23; 11:31; Phil 1:8; 1 Thess 2:5, 10; 1 Tim 5:21; 2 Tim 2:14; 4:1. See Theodor Klauser, "Beteuerungsformeln," *RAC* 2.219–24.

216 Commentaries vary as to which text is considered covered by the oath. Burton (p. 61) wants to include everything from v 13 or v 15 on; Sieffert (p. 71) only vv 18f; Schlier (p. 62) only v 19. I would tend to agree with Burton, but the decision is intuitive.

217 For the function of the oath in rhetoric, see ps.–Aristotle *Rhet. ad Alex.* 17, p. 1432a33. On the subject, see Kurt Latte, *Heiliges Recht* (Tübingen: Mohr, 1920) chap. 1; Volkmann, *Rhetorik*, 184–86; Lausberg, *Handbuch*, § 351; Martin, *Rhetorik*, 98, 100.

218 These suggestions have been made by many scholars; cf. Zahn, p. 74; Bligh, p. 142; Eckert, *Die urchristliche Verkündigung*, 181; Mussner.

219 Gal 1:21 agrees with Acts 9:30, where Paul is sent to Tarsus, in order to get him out of the reach of Jews of Jerusalem who are about to kill him. There is further agreement between Gal 1:21 and Acts 15:23, the address of an apostolic letter that may be a pre-Lukan source. This letter is addressed to "those in Antioch and Syria and Cilicia." The regions are the same as in Gal 1:21, and the names do not conform to Luke's normal understanding of Syria as the Roman province.

220 τὰ κλίματα refers to "regions" and not to the Roman provinces. Cf. the use of the term in Rom 15:23; 2 Cor 11:10. See Ramsay, *A Historical Commentary on St. Paul's Epistle to the Galatians* (Grand Rapids: Baker, 1965) 278ff; Bauer, *s.v.*

it is safe to assume that "Syria"[221] refers to the area south of the Taurus, around Antioch, and Cilicia to the area around his home town Tarsus.[222]

■ 22 The result of Paul's departure to Syria and Cilicia was that he remained[223] personally[224] unknown to the Jewish-Christian churches of Judea: ἤμην δὲ ἀγνοούμενος τῷ προσώπῳ ταῖς ἐκκλησίαις τῆς Ἰουδαίας ταῖς ἐν Χριστῷ ("But I remained personally unknown to the churches of Judea which are 'in Christ'"). In other words, Paul could not have appeared in their meetings and received instruction from them.[225] What kind of churches were these Christian churches,[226] and why does Paul mention them here? Judea[227] was the territory south of Samaria, north of the Negev, its border in the west being the Mediterranean Sea and in the east the Jordan River and the Dead Sea. Where precisely these churches were located, we do not know. Probably Jerusalem was counted as one of them; at least Paul does not make a distinction between them.[228] Gal 1:22 is one of the oldest[229] references to these churches, which must have been the oldest in Christendom.[230] Religiously, they were Jewish-Christian and faithful observers of the Torah.[231] The later anti-Pauline opposition had its roots in these churches. From there the invaders in Galatia[232] must have come. This may be the reason why Paul mentions them here. Their knowledge about Paul was not first-hand; they did not

221 Gal 1:23 shows that Paul does not regard Judea as part of Syria, which means that he does not have the province in mind which would include Judea. Cf. Matt 4:24; Luke 2:2; Acts 18:18; 20:3; 21:3. On Syria see René Dussaud, *Topographie historique de la Syrie antique et médiévale* (Paris: Geuthner, 1927); Ernst Honigmann, "Syria" *PW* 2. Reihe 4 (1932) 1549–1727, bib.; Jean Lassus, "Syrie," *DACL* 15. 2 (1953) 1855–1942, with bib.; Helmuth Th. Bossert, *Alt-Syrien* (Tübingen: Wasmuth, 1951); Philip K. Hitti, *History of Syria, Including Lebanon and Palestine* (London: MacMillan, ²1957); Henri Seyrig, *Antiquités syriennes* (5 vols.; Paris: Geuthner, 1934–58); Georges Tchalenko, *Villages antiques de la Syrie du Nord* (3 vols.; Paris: Geuthner, 1953–58); Jones, *Cities*, 226–94, with notes; Magie, *Roman Rule* 1.360ff and index, *s.v.* Syria.

222 The repetition of the article before Κιλικίας is unusual; only ℵ* 33 1611 pc omit it; in Acts 15:41 some MSS insert the article (see Burton, p. 62). Cilicia was a Roman province since 66 B.C.: its Jewish community is mentioned in Acts 6:9. On Cilicia, see Ruge, "Kilikia," *PW* 11 (1921) 385–90; Konrat Ziegler, *KP* 3 (1969) 208f; Jones, *Cities*, 191–214, with bib.; Magie, *Roman Rule*, 266ff, and index; Machteld J. Mellink, "Cilicia," *IDB* 1.426–28.

223 ἤμην ἀγνοούμενος is a periphrastic construction. See BDF, § 352f. Lagrange translates, together with the following ἀκούοντες ἦσαν (1:23), as imperfect of continuity: "*Or je n'était point connu . . .*".

224 τῷ προσώπῳ ("by face, personally"), with the dative of relation (cf. BDF, § 197; BDR, § 197), stands in contrast to 1:23 "they had only heard." Cf. also 1 Thess 2:17; 3:10; Col. 2:1, and Bauer, *s.v.*, 1, b.

225 Paul's statement contradicts Acts 9:26–30, where it is assumed that Paul preached in Jerusalem and moved freely in and out of the city. For older attempts to harmonize the passages, see Sieffert, p. 73.

226 For the elaborate name of the churches cf. 1 Thess 2:14: αἱ ἐκκλησίαι τοῦ θεοῦ αἱ οὖσαι ἐν τῇ Ἰουδαίᾳ ἐν Χριστῷ Ἰησοῦ ("the churches of God which are in Judea in Christ Jesus"). See also 1 Thess 1:1; 2 Thess 1:1; Acts 9:31; 10:37; 11:1, 29. See Klaus Berger, "Volksversammlung und Gemeinde Gottes. Zu den Anfängen der christlichen Verwendung von 'ekklesia'," *ZThK* 73 (1976) 167–207, 187f.

227 On Judea, see Georg Beer, *PW* 9 (1916) 2458–60; Hans W. Hertzberg, *RGG* 3.964f; Kenneth Clark, "Judea," *IDB* 2.1011f; Jones, *Cities*, 233, 235, 248f, 251–58, 269–81; Schürer, *History* 1, *passim* (n. 172 above); M. Stern, "The Province of Judaea," *Compendium Rerum Judaicarum ad Novum Testamentum* (Assen: Gorcum, 1974) 1.308ff.

228 So most modern commentators: Burton, Oepke, Schlier, Mussner. See the discussion in Eckert, *Die urchristliche Verkündigung*, 182f.

229 The other reference could be a later interpolation. See Birger A. Pearson, "1 Thess 2:13–16: A deutero–Pauline Interpolation," *HTR* 64 (1971) 79–94.

230 See Harnack, *Mission und Ausbreitung*, 50ff; Leonhard Goppelt, *Apostolic and Post–Apostolic Times* (London: Black, 1970) 25ff; Hans Conzelmann, *History of Primitive Christianity* (tr. John E. Steely; Nashville and New York: Abingdon, 1973) 62ff.

231 In this point Paul (cf. Gal 2:1ff) and Acts (cf. 2:46; 3:1ff; 5:12, 20f, 42; 15:1ff; 21:26; etc.) agree. Paul does not say that at that early time he preached the gospel free from the Law. If he had done this, the Judean Christians would hardly have approved of it.

232 Again, Paul (cf. Gal 2:1ff, 12; Rom 15:31) and Acts (cf. 20:23; 21:10ff) agree. Perhaps, these churches turned against Paul, when he began preaching his gospel without the Torah.

know him personally. What they had was hearsay (v 23).[233]

■ **23–24** If the present opposition against Paul derived its authority from these Judean churches, this was unjustified, as Paul documents by their past testimony.[234] At the beginning, when Paul was converted to Christianity, his preaching of the faith[235] was acknowledged positively by them.[236] He quotes verbatim[237] what at that time they spread about concerning Paul: ὁ διώκων ἡμᾶς ποτε νῦν εὐαγγελίζεται τὴν πίστιν ἥν ποτε ἐπόρθει ("Our former persecutor is now preaching the faith which he once tried to destroy").[238] The churches had accepted this turnabout of events[239] as God's work, and they praised him for it: καὶ ἐδόξαζον ἐν ἐμοὶ τὸν θεόν ("and they glorified God in me").[240] Ernst Bammel[241] has tried to show that the "quotation" contains pre-Pauline ideas which come from the Judean churches themselves, so that we would have here in fact one of the oldest theological statements of Christianity. The pre-Pauline ideas present Paul's conversion in terms of the Jewish martyrdom ideology, where the conversion of the persecutor by a miraculous act of God is a topos.[242] The language is Pauline, though this does not invalidate Bammel's suggestion.

Excursus:
The Conference at Jerusalem

Paul's second journey to the Holy City was undertaken to attend the conference which is often called the Apostolic Council. Familiar as this name is, it is misleading. Paul and Barnabas did not attend as apostles. The type of meeting which took place must not be confused with the later ecclesiastical councils. Nevertheless, the Jerusalem conference was an event of enormous importance for the history of primitive Christianity.

The facts are not easy to determine. It is true that we possess two fairly detailed accounts of the event in Gal 2:1–10 and Acts 15:1–29. Paul's own account in Galatians 2 is that of a first-hand witness and it must have priority in case of doubt, but the circumstance and function of the defense in his letter to the Galatians have colored his account. The purpose of his report was not to give an objective eye-witness account, but to use it as proof in his defense. This must have led to a certain selectivity and tendency in his account, but does not necessarily render the facts reported unreliable. Acts 15:1–29 is based upon second-hand data, perhaps from a source of Antiochean origin. The author of Acts is a historical writer, interested in historical detail, but he writes from a later perspective, and his information is limited. He

---

233 1:23: μόνον δὲ ἀκούοντες ἦσαν ὅτι. . . .

234 Paul does not say that he personally persecuted the *Judean* churches, but Acts assumes it (cf. 7:58; 8:1, 3; 9:1; 26:10). See Burton, p. 65: "The satisfaction which the churches of Judea found in Paul's missionary activity in this period is in sharp contrast with the opposition to him which later developed in Jerusalem." Differently, Goppelt, *Apostolic and Post-Apostolic Times*, 73. If the Jewish Christians of Judea were obeying the Torah, Paul would have had no reason to persecute them. See also Walther Schmithals, *Paul and James*, 24; Bligh, p. 143; Eckert, *Die urchristliche Verkündigung*, 182f.

235 πίστις ("faith") here in the absolute state (as 3:23–25; 6:10) is understood as the content of faith (*fides quae creditur*) rather than the act of believing. See Rudolf Bultmann, "πιστεύω," *TDNT* 6.209ff. It is not clear whether the term is exclusively Pauline or generally Christian, but one should not overstress the point (as Ernst Bammel does, "Galater 1, 23," *ZNW* 59 [1968] 108).

236 See BDF, § 134, 2; BDR, § 134, 2 for the problem of connecting the masculine participle with a feminine noun.

237 The ὅτι is recitative. See BDF, § 470; BDR, § 470.

238 Cf. also on Gal 1:13. Also here G reads ἐπολέμει instead of ἐπόρθει.

239 The Judean Christians do not indicate the end of their persecutions. Therefore, ἡμᾶς ("us") does not specify who the persecuted were, especially so if we have before us a "wandering message." Cf. for a different view Oepke, p. 38.

240 This phrase is also found in Rom 1:21; 15:6, 9; 1 Cor 6:20; 2 Cor 9:13, and often in the Gospels and Acts. Cf. the doxology Gal 1:5. A parallel is the prayer of the Jews after the arrest of Flaccus (Philo *Flacc.* 123f).

241 "Galater 1, 23," *ZNW* 59 (1968) 108–12. See Barnikol, *Zeit des Paulus*, 57–59. Cf. Burchard, *Der dreizehnte Zeuge*, 49 n. 34.

242 The ἐν ἐμοί ("in me") refers to Paul. Cf. 1 Cor 15:10. On this meaning of ἐν see Bauer, *s.v.*, III. 3. The martyrological material has been collected by Bammel (see above, n. 241). See the NT passages Mark 15:39 par.; Acts 16:27ff; also 26:28; 27:3, 42f.

adds his tendencies to whatever tendencies may have already been contained in his source material. None of these considerations, however, necessarily renders the data unreliable.

Problems raised by the accounts in Galatians 2 and Acts 15 have been widely discussed (see the bibliography below). They include (1) the question related to the date of the conference, (2) the causes that led to it, (3) the course of the negotiations, and (4) the agreements that were reached.

The problem of the date (1) can only be solved approximately; for the complicated problems see Kümmel, *Introduction* §13 (he dates it A.D. 48); Bornkamm, *Paul*, 31 (c. A.D. 48); Vielhauer, *Geschichte*, 77–78 (A.D. 44). The reasons (2) for convening the meeting can be concluded from Acts 15. The Christian mission to the gentiles had resulted in a large number of converted Christians who were not subjected to the Jewish Torah and were not circumcised. This development increasingly became a dilemma for Jewish Christianity, groups of which became more and more irritated. It seems that no principal decision was made until things had developed into a crisis. The question that now had to be decided was this: are Torah and circumcision peculiar customs of Judaism only, and irrelevant for Gentile Christianity, or is the whole Christian church as "the Israel of God" obligated to observe the Jewish Torah and to become circumcised? If the "yoke of the Torah" was of no consequence for the Christian understanding of salvation, why should Jewish Christians, especially those living in the diaspora, be bound any longer by it? If Gentile Christians live outside of the protection of the Torah, how can they be considered ritually pure and acceptable members of the community?

Things came to a head when conservative Jewish Christians arrived in Antioch to demand the circumcision of all Gentile Christians. As a result of the conflict, a delegation was formed and sent to Jerusalem. The leaders of the delegation were Paul and Barnabas. The objective this delegation wished to achieve was the recognition that the gospel as it was preached among the Gentiles, that is, the gospel without implied submission to the Jewish Torah and to circumcision, was valid and that salvation for the Gentile Christians was ensured. The delegation included Titus, a Gentile Christian missionary, who returned to Antioch uncircumcised and a living example of what was agreed in Jerusalem.

The negotiations (3) took place between three factions: the delegation from Antioch (headed up by Paul and Barnabas), the leaders at Jerusalem (James, Cephas, and John), and a third group of conservative Jewish Christians whom Paul calls the "false brothers" (2:4). The debates must have been fierce.

The final agreements (4) which were reached show that the delegation from Antioch had reached their goal and that the conservative faction was defeated. But the price was high. The agreements to which Paul refers in 2:7–9 (see below) represent a compromise of two factions at the expense of the third. The mission to the world is divided into two thrusts, one directed toward the Jews with Peter as the leader, and one toward the Gentiles with Paul as the leader. This division of labor was made possible by the concept of two gospels, the "gospel of uncircumcision" and the "gospel of circumcision" (2:7), held together by the one God who works the salvation of mankind through both (2:8). The agreement must have recognized Peter's apostleship, but left Paul without a specific title. Whether or not Paul had at that time demanded to be recognized as the apostle of the Gentiles seems uncertain and is, at least, not suggested by the texts. If he did in fact make such a demand, it was ignored in the agreements. Whatever happened, this situation made it possible later to question Paul's apostleship altogether (see the excursus on "Apostle" at Gal 1:17). The agreement also meant the sacrifice of the unity of the church, if such unity ever existed.

The third faction was excluded and continued its agitation against Paul, parts of which were the conflict at Antioch (2:11–14) and the present crisis in Galatia. Another concession made by the Gentile Christians was the financial collection for the poor in Jerusalem (2:10). Paul seems to be right that this request had nothing to do with the main issues of the conference, but was an additional request which the Gentile Christians, especially Paul himself, committed themselves to fulfill.

The "pillar apostles" seem to have taken a position in the middle between the delegation from Antioch and the conservative Jewish Christians. Whether this position was theologically distinctive or a mere willingness to be broad-minded, we do not know. At any rate, it was a compromise and a gamble. The compromise was fragile and did not survive the turbulent changes of history. The middle position proved untenable, and the Jerusalem leaders must have changed their position afterwards. Gal 2:11–14 shows that James may at that time have already changed, and that he, or others in his name, forced others to change. Peter had to flee from Jerusalem; James died as a martyr. By the time of his letter to the Galatians, Paul is the only leader who had kept his position, but the Galatian crisis shows that even he is in danger of losing his congregations in Galatia.

In spite of the failure of the agreements made in Jerusalem, the conference marked an important point in the history of early Christianity. The right of Gentile Christianity and its theological message to exist was formally acknowledged by the "men of eminence." Paul was established as leader of the Gentile Christians. Thereby the future course of the church was determined. The acknowledgment of the gospel without the Jewish Torah and of the independent mission to the Gentiles resulted in an enormous expansion of Gentile Christianity during the latter part of the century. The ultimate result of the conference is the fact that the Christian churches today are culturally Gentile and not Jewish. On the other hand, Jewish Christianity was more and more driven into isolation. The middle group broke up and their position eroded, so that Jewish Christianity came under the control of the anti-Pauline opposition. It would be interesting to know whether the middle position survived in some form in some of the writings of the New Testament, perhaps Matthew or James, but there is no evidence of such a connection. In any case, the gap between Jewish and Gentile Christianity continued to widen. The final historical result was the practical extinction of Jewish Christianity as a branch of the church.

Bibliography: Eduard Meyer, *Ursprung und Anfänge*, 3.64ff; Johannes Weiss, *Das Urchristentum* (Göttingen: Vandenhoeck & Ruprecht, 1917) 192ff; = *Earliest Christianity* (New York: Harper & Row, 1959) 1. 258ff; Wilfred L. Knox, *St. Paul and the Church at Jerusalem* (Cambridge: Cambridge University, 1925); Martin Dibelius, "Das Apostelkonzil," in his *Aufsätze zur Apostelgeschichte* (Göttingen: Vandenhoeck & Ruprecht, 1957) 84–90; = *Studies in the Acts of the Apostles* (New York: Scribner's, 1956) 93–101; Johannes Munck, *Paul*, 93ff; 231ff; 282ff; and *passim*; cf. Morton Smith, "Pauline Problems: Apropos of J. Munck, *Paulus und die Heilsgeschichte*," *HTR* 50 (1957) 107–31; Ernst Haenchen, *Acts*, 464–68; Walter Schmithals, *Paul and James*, chap. 2; Schoeps, *Paul* 63ff; Georg Strecker, "Christentum und Judentum in den ersten beiden Jahrhunderten," *EvT* 16 (1956) 458–77; idem, "Die sogenannte zweite Jerusalemreise des Paulus (Act. 11, 27–30)," *ZNW* 53 (1962) 67–77; Bo Reicke, "Der geschichtliche Hintergrund des Apostelkonzils und der Antiochia–Episode, Gal. 2,

1–14," in *Studia Paulina in honorem J. de Zwaan* (Haarlem: Bohn, 1953) 172–87; Olof Linton, "The Third Aspect: A Neglected Point of View, a Study in Gal. I–II and Acts IX and XV," *StTh* 3 (1949/50) 79–95; Dieter Georgi, *Kollekte*, 13–30; Jack T. Sanders, "Paul's 'Autobiographical' Statements in Gal 1–2," *JBL* 58 (1966) 335–43; Günter Klein, "Galater 2, 6–9 und die Geschichte der Jerusalemer Urgemeinde," *ZThK* 57 (1960) 275–95; = *Rekonstruktion*, 99–118; 118–28: *addendum*; Martin Hengel, "Die Ursprünge der christlichen Mission," *NTS* 18 (1971/72) 15–38; Traugott Holtz, "Die Bedeutung des Apostelkonzils für Paulus," *NovT* 16 (1974) 110–48; Bauer, *Orthodoxy and Heresy*, *passim*; Robinson and Koester, *Trajectories*, 120–21; Conzelmann, *History*, 82ff; Leonhardt Goppelt, *Apostolic and Post–Apostolic Times*, 61ff; Schlier, 64–81; Mussner, 127–32.

■ **1** Gal 2:1–10 contains the second part of the *narratio* (see above, the analysis of 1:12–2:14). For the interpretation we must bear in mind the principles which are operative in this as well as in the other parts of the "statement of facts." The episode is told for the purpose of Paul's defense and not for its own sake. The next occasion which in his view demonstrates that he has received his gospel from God (cf. 1:11–12) is his second journey to Jerusalem: "then after 14 years I again went up to Jerusalem." The "then" ($\check{\epsilon}\pi\epsilon\iota\tau\alpha$) continues the naming of the events of the narratio (cf. 1:16: $\epsilon\vartheta\theta\acute{\epsilon}\omega\varsigma$ ["immediately"]; 1:18, 21: $\check{\epsilon}\pi\epsilon\iota\tau\alpha$).[243] Again, we are left in the dark whether we should begin counting the 14 years[244] with the last "then" (1:21, the visit to Syria and Cilicia),[245] with the first journey to Jerusalem (1:18),[246] or with Paul's vision of Christ (1:15).[247] The question is whether "then" ($\check{\epsilon}\pi\epsilon\iota\tau\alpha$) is used simply to divide up the narrative, or whether it serves as a historical connection. The ambiguity does not allow a clear decision, but 1:21 seems to be the most probable point of connection. This connection, to be sure, increases the difficulty of using the 14 years for an estab-

---

243 For further discussion of the chronological problem see Kümmel, *Introduction*, § 13; Suhl, *Paulus*, 46ff; J. van Bruggen, *"Na veertien jaren:" De datering van het in Galaten 2 genoemde overleg te Jeruzalem* (Kampen: Kok, 1973). Cf. the review by A. F. J. Klijn, *ThLZ* 100 (1975) 201f.

244 On διά with the genitive ("after") see BDF, § 223 (1); BDR, § 223 n. 4; Bauer, *s.v.* A. II. 2; Moule, *Idiom Book*, 56. On the conjecture τεσσάρων

("four"), proposed by Grotius, see Sieffert, p. 77n; Burton, p. 69.

245 See Sieffert, pp. 77f.

246 See Sieffert; Zahn; Marie–Joseph Lagrange, *Saint Paul, Epître aux Galates* (Paris: Gabalda, 1918, ²1925); Burton; Lietzmann, p. 9; Oepke; Schlier.

247 See Ramsay; Alfred Loisy, *L'épître aux Galates* (Paris: Nourry, 1916); Georgi, *Kollekte*, 13; Suhl, *Paulus*, 46f.

lishment of a Pauline chronology.[248] Also, Paul does not reveal how long he stayed in Syria and Cilicia. At any rate, the expression "again I went up" ($\pi \acute{a} \lambda \iota \nu$[249] $\grave{a} \nu \acute{\epsilon} \beta \eta \nu$) is said in view of 1:18, the first visit in Jerusalem. It should be clear that the two visits of which we read in Galatians cannot be harmonized with Acts, where several visits precede Paul's and Barnabas' journey to the 'Apostolic Council' at Jerusalem (cf. Acts 22:3; 8:3; 9:1–2, 26–29; 11:27–30; 12:25; 15:2).[250] No information is given in Galatians about the events that preceded the journey to Jerusalem, although this journey appears to be the result of those decisions. It included Paul and Barnabas who at the time seem to have been of equal rank (cf. 2:9).[251] For a specific purpose (cf. 2:3) and perhaps at Paul's request, Titus, a Gentile–Christian fellow missionary, was "taken along."[252] Paul does not specify what the cause or purpose of the journey was, nor where it began, but we can safely assume that it was the mission of an official delegation from Antioch.[253]

Excursus:
Barnabas

Barnabas was one of the most important Christian missionaries. He is mentioned in Gal 2:1 for the first time (see also Gal 2:9, 13; 1 Cor 9:6). According to Acts his name was Joseph, while Barnabas (= "son of consolation") was the name given to him by the apostles (4:36–37). He was a Jew from Cyprus who had moved to Jerusalem, had become a Christian,

and had supported the church by selling a piece of land. Barnabas became Paul's mentor and introduced him to the apostles (9:27). He went to Antioch as a Christian missionary (11:22) and became the leading personality there (see 11:30; 12:25; 13:1–3; 14:12, 14; 15:2, 25; also 13:7, 43, 46, 50; 15:22, 35). After the conflict at Antioch (Gal 2:11–14; cf. Acts 15:33–41; Col 4:10) Paul and Barnabas worked separately. Acts 14:4, 14 calls Barnabas an "apostle" (old source?). Later information is probably legendary.

Bibliography: Bauer, *s.v.*; Montgomery J. Schreyer, *IDB* 1.356–57; Conzelmann, *History*, 158–60; HSW, *NT Apocrypha* 2, index.

Excursus:
Titus

Titus was a Greek (Gal 2:3) and a fellow missionary of Paul. He may have been converted by Paul (cf. Titus 1:4). According to 2 Cor 2:13; 7:6, 13, 14; 8:6, 16, 23; 12:18 Titus was a chief organizer of the collection for Jerusalem. Acts never mentions him. 2 Tim 4:10 has him at work in Dalmatia; Titus 1:5 has him in Crete, where according to later tradition he was a bishop.

Bibliography: Howard C. Kee, *IDB* 4.656–57; Conzelmann, *History*, 160–61; C. K. Barrett, "Titus," *Neotestamentica et Semitica: Studies in Honour of Matthew Black* (Edinburgh: Clark, 1969) 1–14; HSW, *NT Apocrypha* 2, index.

■ **2** Paul does not provide us with specific historical information concerning the circumstances which led

248 See Georgi, *Kollekte*, 91–96; and the Introduction, § 3 above.

249 $\pi \acute{a} \lambda \iota \nu$ is missing in several versional and patristic sources, probably as a result of the contradiction with Acts. Cf. Metzger, *Textual Commentary*, 591.

250 See Georg Strecker, "Die sogenannte zweite Jerusalemreise des Paulus (Act. 11, 27–30)" *ZNW* 53 (1962) 67–77; Georgi, *Kollekte*, 13 n. 3.

251 So Haenchen, *Acts*, p. 464; Georgi, *Kollekte*, 14 n. 9; 16 n. 20.

252 $\sigma \upsilon \mu \pi \alpha \rho \alpha \lambda \alpha \mu \beta \acute{a} \nu \omega$ ("take along as an adjunct or assistant") (LSJ, *s.v.*). The term is also used in Acts 12:25; 15:37f. It suggests a lower rank for Titus. See also Bauer, *s.v.* Georgi, *Kollekte*, 16 has suggested that Titus was taken along as a living test for the question to be decided at the meeting—whether or not Gentile Christians must undergo circumcision. This interpretation is found already in Luther, 1519

(*Luther's Works* 27.200): ". . . by presenting himself with both of them [*sc.* Barnabas and Titus] he intended to make it clear that he was at liberty to be a Gentile with Titus and a Jew with Barnabas. Thus he would prove the freedom of the Gospel in each case, namely, that it is permissible to be circumcised and yet that circumcision is not necessary, and that this is the way one should think of the entire Law."

253 The information provided in Acts 15:1ff must of course be taken with great caution, but it is remarkable how much seemingly reliable historical information the passage contains. See on this problem Haenchen, *Acts*, pp. 443f, 464ff; Conzelmann, *Apostelgeschichte*, 81f; idem, *History of Primitive Christianity*, 82ff (above n. 230); Bornkamm, *Paul*, 31f; Suhl, *Paulus*, 57ff.

up to the meeting in Jerusalem. In the context of his defense he merely mentions the points which support his claim made in 1:11–12. The phrase "but I went up because of a revelation" (ἀνέβην δὲ κατὰ ἀποκάλυψιν) places the whole matter in the same category as the reception of the call and commission, and the nature of the gospel (cf. 1:1, 12, 16).[254] The ancient practice of relying on revelations when a decision must be made, e.g., whether or not to undertake a journey,[255] is shared by Paul.[256] He does not indicate, however, what kind of revelation he has in mind.[257] On the other hand, such revelations did not *ipso facto* exclude very down-to-earth circumstances and considerations. The information in Acts 15:1–2 (cf. 15:24) about the extended ecclesiastical intrigue which led up to the journey to Jerusalem[258] is by no means incompatible with such a revelation. According to Acts, a delegation "from Judea" had come to Antioch and had presented the demand that Gentile Christians must submit to circumcision.[259] After considerable debate between the Jewish–Christian delegation from Judea on the one side and Paul and Barnabas on the other, the church in Antioch decided to send Paul and Barnabas, and also other members of the church, to the apostles and presbyters at Jerusalem in order to settle the controversy.[260]

The information given in Acts agrees remarkably well with Paul's own account about the purpose of the journey: "and I laid before them the gospel which I preach among the Gentiles . . . , so that I might not run or have run in vain." This way of putting it presupposes that Paul's gospel was the point of the controversy because he did not prescribe circumcision, while other Jewish Christians did demand it.[261] If this is assumed, the delegation sent to Jerusalem knew these reasons[262] and was prepared to face the opposition, which Paul characterizes in Gal 2:4 as the "false brothers." Taking along Titus as a living test case also fits into this picture (cf. 2:1).[263] The question arises, however, why Paul submits his gospel only at this time, after he has preached it—apparently without opposition—for so many years. Why is it that his law-free gospel has become a subject of controversy so lately? Several possibilities exist. The anti-Pauline opposition may have been formed only at a later stage, while at the beginning everybody was in agreement. This is the situation as Paul presents it on behalf of his defense in Galatians 2. But it is by no means clear that he began by preaching his gospel as including freedom from Torah and circumcision. All he says is that he always preached the law-free gospel to the Gentiles. How he had preached it to Jews we do not know. Clearly, the concept of a gospel free from Torah and circumcision must have been a secondary development. Only when this concept was developing could the opposition to it have developed. It is also clear that for this law-free gospel Paul was not depending upon the authorities in Jerusalem. Once the controversy had heated up, those authorities in Jerusalem were forced to deal with it.

---

254 Paul speaks here only about himself because his collaboration with Barnabas had ended after the Antioch episode (cf. 2:13), so that Barnabas is not included in the present defense.

255 See, e.g., Xenophon *Anab.* 3.1.5ff; Philo *Mos.* 1.268; Plutarch *Gen. Socr.* 579E (*PECL* 1.254).

256 See also 1 Thess 2:18; Rom 1:13; 15:22.

257 Looking at Acts, it could have been a dream revelation (16:9; 18:9; 23:11; 27:23), an ecstatic seizure (22:17), a sign of the Spirit (16:6f; 19:21; 20:22–23), a sign given by a prophet (11:28; 21:4, 10f). See Schlier, p. 66; Lührmann, *Offenbarungsverständnis*, 41f. The phrase κατὰ ἀποκάλυψιν ("according to a revelation") occurs also Rom 16:25; Eph 3:3; *Mart. Pol.* 22.3 also *Epilogus Mosquensis* 5; cf. κατ' ὄναρ ("according to a dream") Matt 1:20; 2:12, 13, 19, 22; 27:19.

258 So in agreement with Georgi, *Kollekte*, 15f. Cf. Haen-

chen, *Acts*, 464ff; Bornkamm, *Paul*, 31ff; Conzelmann, *History of Primitive Christianity*, 82–84 (above n. 230); Suhl, *Paulus*, 57ff. On Schmithals' thesis that the cause was difficulties of the *Jerusalem* church which they had with their Jewish "supervisors," see Suhl, ibidem, 52–56.

259 Acts 15:1 has preserved even the legal formulation of such a demand: "Unless you become circumcised according to the custom of Moses, you cannot be saved." See also Appendices 1 and 4, below.

260 Acts 15:2; cf. 11:30.

261 See Gal 2:3–4. The present opposition makes the same demand on the Galatians (Gal 5:2, 3; 6:12, 13).

262 See Acts 15:5, and on this point Georgi, *Kollekte*, 15f.

263 See Georgi, ibidem, 16.

Paul no doubt would have preferred to avoid the encounter if he had been able to do so. When he admits that he presented his gospel for approval, he must have been under some higher compulsion to make such a concession. The same was probably true for the authorities in Jerusalem. What then was the purpose of the meeting?

Paul himself admits that the delegation was sent to Jerusalem in order to get some kind of belated approval[264] by the authorities for Paul's and Barnabas' gospel, that is, the gospel which was free from Torah and circumcision. Other reasons are sometimes mentioned by commentators, such as the preservation of the unity of the church,[265] or the establishment of consistency between the mission to the Gentiles and the historical Jesus.[266] But these considerations have no basis in the text.

Paul emphasizes that he did not go to Jerusalem as a petitioner, and he may be right. Apparently the matter at stake was to force the church authorities in Jerusalem to give *post factum* approval to the Pauline gospel in the face of heated opposition,[267] and thereby help to defeat the anti-Pauline forces in Asia Minor. Such an objective requires considerable political leverage. Thus Paul did not go as a humble petitioner, but as a tough negotiator who forced the Jerusalem authorities to make a decision which one can imagine they made only with great reluctance.

Paul describes the events at the conference with considerable detail. The use of official political language shows that the event had an official and legally binding character. The task of the delegation was to "submit for consideration"[268] the gospel message as it was preached to Gentile Christians by Paul and his fellow missionaries.[269] This same gospel Paul had of course preached to the Galatians, so that in Paul's argument the Jerusalem conference and its outcome have the importance of a *praeiudicium*.[270]

The Apostle does not name with any degree of clarity the specific group which was to receive the presentation. He seems to have two events[271] in mind: one event included "them" ($\alpha\dot{\upsilon}\tau o\hat{\iota}\varsigma$),[272] whoever they may have been; at another occasion he met "separately" ($\kappa\alpha\tau$' $\dot{\iota}\delta\dot{\iota}\alpha\nu$)[273] with the "men of reputation" ($o\dot{\iota}$ $\delta o\kappa o\hat{\upsilon}\nu\tau\epsilon\varsigma$),[274] that is, the "pillars" ($o\dot{\iota}$ $\sigma\tau\hat{\upsilon}\lambda o\iota$), James, Cephas, and John (cf. 2:9). The expression $o\dot{\iota}$ $\delta o\kappa o\hat{\upsilon}\nu\tau\epsilon\varsigma$ ("the men of

---

264 Cf. Schlier (pp. 65f), who takes the Jerusalem authorities to be the highest authorities ("the old and regular apostles") of the entire church, who must give approval to Paul's ("the new and extraordinary apostle") special preaching. Schmithals (*Paul and James*, 42f) rightly objects that Paul would have needed approval at the beginning if the Jerusalem leaders had such a universal authority.

265 The fact is that the unity was not preserved, because the so-called "false brothers" remained in opposition to the agreement. Differently Schlier, pp. 65f; also Conzelmann, *History of Primitive Christianity*, 84–87 (above n. 230).

266 Differently C. K. Barrett, "Paul and the 'Pillar' Apostles," *Studia Paulina in Honorem J. de Zwaan* (Haarlem: Bohn, 1953) 18; Wolfgang Beyer, *Der Brief an die Galater* (rev. by Paul Althaus; NTD 8; Göttingen: Vandenhoeck and Ruprecht, ⁸1962) 15–16.

267 So Georgi, *Kollekte*, 27ff; differently Schmithals, (*Paul and James*, 42ff) who, contrary to Paul's intention, separates between the present interpretation of the meeting and its historical purpose.

268 For the official tone of the term $\dot{\alpha}\nu\alpha\tau\dot{\iota}\theta\eta\mu\iota$ $\tau\iota\nu\iota$ $\tau\iota$ see parallels in Acts 25:14; and LSJ, *s.v.*; Bauer, *s.v.* 2; PGL, *s.v.*; Polybios-Lexikon, *s.v.*; Index Verborum Plu-

tarcheus, *s.v.*; Preisigke, *Wörterbuch* 4/1.142f, *s.v.*

269 Cf. Gal 1:2, 6–9, 11, 16; 6:14f. It is identical with the "gospel of the uncircumcision" (cf. 2:7); The term $\kappa\eta\rho\dot{\upsilon}\sigma\sigma\omega$ ("proclaim") is technical. Cf. 5:11 $\pi\epsilon\rho\iota\tau o\mu\dot{\eta}\nu$ $\kappa\eta\rho\dot{\upsilon}\sigma\sigma\omega$ ("proclaim circumcision"). See Gerhard Friedrich, "$\kappa\eta\rho\dot{\upsilon}\sigma\sigma\omega$," *TDNT* 3.703–14. For Paul, to "proclaim the gospel" and to "proclaim Christ" (1:16) or "the cross of Christ" (3:1; 6:14) is the same.

270 See also Gal 2:4–5.

271 The particle $\delta\dot{\epsilon}$ in 2:2c indicates a distinction between two events.

272 Was the first a "plenary session"? For this suggestion see Schlier, p. 66; Mussner, pp. 104f.

273 The practice is known from the political life. Cf. Josephus *BJ* 2.199: "he held . . . private conferences with the aristocracy, and public meetings with the people" ($\tau o\dot{\upsilon}\varsigma$ $\delta\upsilon\nu\alpha\tau o\dot{\upsilon}\varsigma$ $\kappa\alpha\tau$' $\dot{\iota}\delta\dot{\iota}\alpha\nu$ $\kappa\alpha\dot{\iota}$ $\tau\dot{o}$ $\pi\lambda\hat{\eta}\theta o\varsigma$ $\dot{\epsilon}\nu$ $\kappa o\iota\nu\hat{\omega}$ $\sigma\upsilon\lambda\lambda\dot{\epsilon}\gamma\omega\nu$). Also, Plutarch *Romulus* 20.4 (Helge Almqvist, *Plutarch und das Neue Testament* [ASNU 15; Uppsala: Almqvist & Wiksell, 1946] 109). See also LSJ, *s.v.* $\dot{\iota}\delta\iota o\varsigma$ VI. 3; Bauer, *s.v.* 4; Schlier, p. 67 n. 1; BDR, § 241 n. 9; § 286.

274 The term is found with this meaning in the NT only Gal 2:2, 6, 9. Cf. Mark 10:42.

influence and reputation") is familiar from political rhetoric,[275] where it is used both positively[276] and negatively (derogatorily or ironically).[277] Most interesting is the ironic usage in Plato's *Apology*,[278] where the term serves a purpose comparable to Paul's: as a rhetorical device the expression "men of eminence" avoids the confusion of *pro forma* recognition of authority in court and the acceptance of authority in the sincere philosophical sense. In analogy, the expression enables Paul to recognize the *de facto* role which "the men of reputation" play, without compromising his theological stance that God and Christ are the only authority

behind his gospel (cf. 1:1, 12, 15–16).[279]

On this basis the difficult phrase 2:2c must be interpreted: "that perhaps I may be running or might have run in vain" ($\mu\dot{\eta}\pi\omega\varsigma$ $\epsilon\dot{\iota}\varsigma$ $\kappa\epsilon\nu\dot{o}\nu$ $\tau\rho\dot{\epsilon}\chi\omega$ $\ddot{\eta}$ $\ddot{\epsilon}\delta\rho\alpha\mu\omega\nu$).[280] Combined with a subjunctive, the $\mu\dot{\eta}$ in $\mu\dot{\eta}\pi\omega\varsigma$ ("lest") usually expresses apprehension.[281] Applied to the sentence here, the question is whose apprehension may be expressed. Paul could mean that he had presented his gospel to the Jerusalem church because he was really concerned that this gospel might not be genuine and valid.[282] However, such an admission would undo

---

275 See LSJ, *s.v.* δοκέω II.5; Bauer, *s.v.* 2, b; Werner Foerster, "Die δοκοῦντες in Gal. 2," *ZNW* 36 (1937) 286–92; Barrett, "Paul and the 'Pillar' Apostles," 1–19; Schlier, p. 67; Mussner (p. 104 n. 25) mentions the "men of the name" (אנושי השם) in 1QSa II 2, 8, 11, 13.

276 See e.g., Xenophon *Cyr.* 7.1.41; Euripides *Hec.* 295; Plutarch *Superst.* 166B; *Mul. virt.* 244E; *Quaest. Rom.* 282A; *Quaest Gr.* 296F; *Isid. et Os.* 363D; *Frat. am.* 488B.

277 See, e.g., Demosthenes *Or.* 21.213; Josephus *C. Apion.* 1.67; Philo *Mos.* 2.241; Plutarch *Aud.* 47E; *Adulat.* 72A; *Invid. et od.* 538D; *Laud. ips.* 540A, 544D, 546, and often.

278 *Apol.* 21B, C, D, E; 22A, B; 29A; 36D; 41E. Socrates speaks of "those who are reputedly the wisemen" (τῶν δοκούντων σοφῶν εἶναι, 21B), recognizing that claim and at the same time distancing himself from it. See also *Gorg.* 472A; *Euthyd.* 303C. See also Barrett, "Paul and the 'Pillar' Apostles," 2–4; Edouard Des Places, *Lexique de la langue philosophique et religieuse de Platon*, in *Platon. Oeuvres complètes* 14.1 (Paris: Les belles lettres, 1970) 143. Epictetus shows how the concept functions later on: "When you are about to meet somebody, in particular when it is one of those men who are held in very high esteem (τῶν ἐν ὑπεροχῇ δοκούντων), propose to yourself the question, 'What would Socrates or Zeno have done under these circumstances?' and then you will not be at a loss to make proper use of the occasion" (*Ench.* 33.12).

279 So Joseph Klausner, *From Jesus to Paul* (tr. William F. Stinespring; London: Allen & Unwin, 1946) 581; also, with caution, Barrett, "Paul and the 'Pillar' Apostles," 4; against irony in Paul's term are Lightfoot; Burton; Lietzmann, pp. 9–10; Oepke; Gerhard Kittel, "δόγμα," *TDNT* 2.232f; Karl Ludwig Schmidt, "ἐκκλησία," *TDNT* 3.508; by implication also Mussner, pp. 104f.

280 The tr. is that in Bauer, *s.v.* μήπως 2.

281 τρέχω is subjunctive, in dependence upon the will of the subject; ἔδραμον as the unalterable past is indicative. See BDF, § 370 (2); BDR, § 370 n. 4; Edwin Mayser, *Grammatik der griechischen Papyri aus der Ptolemäerzeit* (2 vols.; Berlin: de Gruyter, ²1970) 2/2.549. For other interpretations see Oepke, p. 74; Schlier, p. 67.

282 This is Schlier's view (pp. 67–69). He concludes that Paul himself was not convinced that the revelation of Christ was sufficient basis for his apostleship. Schlier does not hesitate to read into the text the basic structures of his Roman Catholic doctrine of the authority of the church, that (1) "the true gospel and the legitimate apostolic mission carry in them the tendency towards catholicity. For the church is built only through the *one* gospel, mediated through the *one* apostolate. But this unity must become visible. It cannot merely be presupposed." Furthermore, the fact that Paul goes to Jerusalem instead of the Jerusalem apostles coming to him demonstrates that (2) "the decisive authority is represented by the *earlier* gospel and the *earlier* apostolate." Paul, in Schlier's opinion, affirms this "principle of the connection with the tradition" "not on the basis of his own insight and will" but "because of a revelation." The fact that (3) the unity of the gospel and the apostolate, and thereby of the church, was "not achieved by a theoretical or practical compromise about fundamental issues, but by the official recognition of the Pauline gospel and the apostolate by the Jerusalem authorities" shows this principle: "The unity of the church comes about through the judgment of the authorities of the church, and by their common discovery and acknowledgment of the truth of the gospel and of the one apostolate." This interpretation misses Paul's intention by a wide margin. Different from Schlier, and also from the remarkably similar view of Klaus Wengst, ("Der

his defense[283] by suggesting that he himself had felt the need for approval of his gospel. Thus Paul himself would admit dependence upon the authorities of the church in Jerusalem. We must, therefore, take the context of the apology into account.[284] "To run in vain" must reflect the present concern of the Galatians who because of this concern are considering circumcision and obedience to the Torah. It is also the concern of the opposition who would have told the Galatians that without circumcision and Torah they are "running in vain." Paul takes this concern up in order to disprove it. His account of the events at Jerusalem provides him with the opportunity to report that at that meeting his presently proclaimed gospel was recognized as not in vain,[285] so that the Galatians' present doubts are unfounded.[286] The term τρέχω ("run") is metaphorical and may be related to the "*agon* motif" which Paul uses elsewhere to describe his missionary work.[287] Indeed, he would run "in vain"[288]

if the Galatians' acceptance of the gospel and their faith in Christ were not sufficient for their eschatological redemption.

Paul's remark throws an interesting light upon the present evaluation of Paul's gospel by the Galatians. Influenced by the anti-Pauline opposition, they have come to doubt whether Paul's gospel has any salvific validity and power. To show that his gospel is "sufficient" is also the central point of Paul's defense.[289]

■ 3 The continuation with ἀλλά ("but") suggests an intermittent rejection of the concern to have "run in vain" (2:2).[290] Paul, however, at once points to the evidence,[291] the case of Titus, which shows that he was and is "running well" (cf. 5:7). Since he was a Greek[292] and an uncircumcised Christian, Titus had been taken along to Jerusalem as a living piece of evidence (cf. 2:1).[293] The result of the test was that he was not forced[294] to submit to circumcision (. . . οὐδὲ Τίτος . . . ἠναγκάσθη περιτμηθῆναι).[295] He proved fully acceptable

---

Apostel und die Tradition," *ZThK* 69 [1972] 155f) is Mussner (pp. 102f) who attributes the opinion expressed in the indirect question to the "false brothers" of 2:4–5. Remarkably, Schlier's position agrees with that expressed in the anti–Pauline *Kerygmata Petrou*. See the regulation ps.-Clem. *Hom.* 11.35.4; *Recog.* 4.34–35; (see Appendix 3, below), that no apostle, teacher, or prophet is to be admitted, unless he has submitted his kerygma to James "the . . . brother of the Lord, to whom the congregation of the 'Hebrews' in Jerusalem is entrusted."

283 Georgi (*Kollekte*, 17 n. 27) rightly says that in this case Paul would have written the first chapter of Gal in vain.

284 Cf. Gal 4:11: "I am afraid that in vain I have bestowed my labor upon you."

285 See 2:7–9.

286 See 2:4; 5:7a: "You were running well."

287 See Rom 9:16; 1 Cor 9:24, 26; Phil 2:16; Pol. *Phil.* 9.2; also Gal 5:7; 2 Thess 3:1; Heb 12:1. On the term see Otto Bauernfeind, "τρέχω," *TDNT* 8.225–35; Victor C. Pfitzner, *Paul and the Agon Motif* (NovTSup 16; Leiden: Brill, 1967) 99ff.

288 Cf. also Phil 2:16; 1 Thess 3:5; 2 Cor 6:1; furthermore 1 Cor 15:10, 14; 1 Thess 2:1; Eph 5:6. See Bauer, *s.v.*; Moule, *Idiom Book*, 70.

289 See the *propositio* Gal 2:15–21.

290 See BDF, § 448 (6); BDR, § 448 n. 7.

291 On the level of the apology, Titus functions as the prototype for the Galatians themselves (see 3:1–5; 5:2–12; 6:12f).

292 Ἕλλην ὤν. See Moule, *Idiom Book*, 102. Cf. 3:28, where the contrast is "Jew" (Ἰουδαῖος). The difference is marked by circumcision and uncircumcision (cf. 5:6; 6:15). According to Jewish thought, at least of the rigorous group (cf. 2:4–5), this difference marks also the partakers vs. the non–partakers in the Torah covenant, so that those outside the Torah covenant are called "sinners" (cf. 2:15, 17). According to Paul, however, Christians are not equal to "sinners" because of the salvation in Christ (cf. 1:4; 2:15, 17f; 3:19–25). Titus shows how a Gentile can be a partaker of God's salvation without being a partaker of the Jewish Torah covenant. See Hans Windisch, "Ἕλλην," *TDNT* 2.504–16.

293 The οὐδέ ("not even") indicates the evidential value of Titus' case: if it is true for him, it is true in principle.

294 ἠναγκάσθη (cf. 2:14; 6:12). Oepke, p. 75; Georgi (*Kollekte*, 17) assume with good reason that the demand was in fact made, even if we can only speculate that the rigorous party (2:4–5) made it. Cf. also below on Gal 6:12, n. 9; and Appendix 4.

295 As a consequence, the present opponents' demand for circumcision is rejected by Paul (see 5:1–12; 6:12–16). What this means for the Galatians is pointed out by Ambrosiaster, CSEL 81.3, p. 19.

as a member of the Christian church. Undoubtedly, this result was achieved only after fierce debates among the groups represented at the conference (cf. 2:4–5). Moreover, the present situation which forces Paul to write his letter to the Galatians shows that the struggle had not ended with the conference, but continued increasingly to haunt the Apostle.[296] While the so-called "false brothers" (2:4–5) had demanded that Titus be circumcised, the other Jewish Christians had rejected their demand. For them circumcision was not indispensible for salvation. We know that in Paul's time Judaism was not unanimous as to whether or not proselytes must without exception undergo circumcision.[297] Thus, the internal Jewish debate had become an internal Christian conflict. Attempts have always been made by New Testament scholars to reconcile Gal 2:3 with Acts 16:3, where Paul is reported to have circumcised Timothy.[298] But Timothy represents a different case because he had a Jewish mother and a Gentile father, and thus would be counted as a Jew. The contrast is not that Paul had resisted Jewish pressure in Gal 2:3,

while he had yielded in Acts 16:3, but that Titus was a Gentile and Timothy could be regarded as a Jew. Paul himself did not deny the Jews their Jewish rites, even when they were Christians; so both accounts can be true.

■ 4 In 2:4–8 Paul's account of the events at the Jerusalem conference is at several points interrupted by digression and parenthesis.[299] The first digression (2:4–5) is a grammatical anacoluthon.[300] After Paul had reported the outcome of the confrontation in 2:3, the digression in 2:4–5 returns to that confrontation and gives a more detailed account of it. The Apostle begins by a description of his opponents, using, as he did before (cf. 1:6–7), the language of political demagoguery. First he introduces and names the opposition: διὰ δὲ τοὺς παρεισάκτους ψευδαδέλφους. The translation of the statement is difficult because the introductory prepositional construction has no connection (except for the δέ ["but"]) with the preceding or the following. But the meaning of the statement is clear: it is descriptive of the circumstances which had caused the whole

296 The subject of circumcision is mentioned by Paul also in Gal 2:7, 8, 9, 12; 5:1–11; 6:12, 13, 15; Rom 2:25–29; 3:1, 20; 4:9–12; 15:8; 1 Cor 7:19; Phil 3:3–5.
297 On this problem see Karl Georg Kuhn and Hartmut Stegemann, "Proselyten," *PW*Sup 9 (1962) 1248–83; Folker Siegert, "Gottesfürchtige und Sympathisanten," *JJS* 4 (1973) 109–64; Neil J. McEleney, "Conversion, Circumcision and Law," *NTS* 20 (1974) 319–41; Heinz–Wolfgang Kuhn, "Jesus als Gekreuzigter in der frühchristlichen Verkündigung bis zur Mitte des 2. Jahrhunderts," *ZThK* 72 (1975) 1–46, esp. 32. On the ritual of circumcision generally, see Str–B 4/1.23–40; Rudolf Meyer, "περιτέμνω," *TDNT* 6.72–84; Friedrich Stummer, "Beschneidung," *RAC* 2.159–69; J. Philipp Hyatt, "Circumcision," *IDB* 1.629–31; Leonard V. Snowman, "Circumcision," *EncJud* 5 (1971) 567–76; Erich Isaac, "Circumcision As a Covenant Rite," *Anthropos* 59 (1964) 444–56; Jack M. Sasson, "Circumcision in the Ancient Near East," *JBL* 85 (1966) 473–76.
298 Haenchen, (*Acts*, 482) and Conzelmann (*Apostelgeschichte*, 88f) suggest that there may have been rumors that Paul occasionally had agreed to circumcision (cf. also Gal 5:11; Acts 21:20ff), and that these rumors translated into the tradition Luke readily takes up in Acts 16:3 because it proves his theory that Paul was a faithful Jew. A number of commentators have interpreted the "he was not

forced" as meaning "he did it voluntarily," but this is an artificial construction. See on this Francis C. Burkitt, *Christian Beginnings* (London: University of London, 1924) 118; Johannes Weiss, *Das Urchristentum* (Göttingen: Vandenhoeck & Ruprecht, 1917) 202–204 (ET *The History of Primitive Christianity* [New York: Wilson, Erickson, 1937] 1.271–73); Burton, pp. 75–86; Bligh, pp. 160f; Haenchen, *Acts*, 478–82.
299 On the analysis of the passage, see the Introduction, § 5, above.
300 With good reasons Schlier, Mussner, and most modern exegetes. See the careful analysis of the grammatical options by Herman Ljungvik, "Aus der Sprache des Neuen Testaments," *Eranos* 66 (1968) 24–51, 30–34; also Bernard Orchard, "Ellipsis Between Gal 2:3, 2:4," *Bib* 54 (1973) 469–81; A. C. M. Blommerde, "Is There an Ellipsis Between Gal 2:3 and 2:4?" *Bib* 56 (1975) 100–102; BDR, § 467 n. 2.

affair,[301] and can be translated as, "Now this happened because of the false brothers secretly brought in." The name "false brothers"[302] expresses of course Paul's negative judgment upon them and his personal feelings of disgust and disrespect. But this must not be confused with the understanding of the "false brother" themselves, who undoubtedly thought they were orthodox and conscientious Christians, and who simply understood the nature of their Christian existence in different terms.[303] In Paul's view, however, these Jewish Christians are "pseudo-Christians" and hence as far as the Gentile Christians are concerned, "pseudo-brothers." They deny that the Gentile Christians are saved by God's grace (cf. 2:21). They cannot accept Gentile Christians as "brothers" unless they first become Jews; as Gentile Christians they are not "brothers." But even for Paul the Jew, these opponents are pseudo-brothers

because they deny God's universal plan of salvation which, in his view, includes the salvation of the Gentiles through Christ (cf. especially Rom 9–11).

It should also be clear that whatever Paul says about his opponents in Jerusalem applies also to his present opposition in Galatia.[304] He misses no opportunity to discredit the present agitators in the eyes of the Galatian readers. Discrediting is the function of his characterization of their activities. For this reason, he uses the language of political demagoguery, that is, military language turned into political metaphors. This is also to be applied by the readers to the present agitators in Galatia. These agitators are "secretly smuggled in" (παρεισάκτοι),[305] like undercover agents and conspirators. Their activity is the "infiltration" (παρεισέρχεσθαι)[306] and "spying out" (κατασκοπεῖν)[307] of what Paul calls "our freedom which we have in Christ Jesus"

301   Schlier, Mussner, and most modern commentaries rightly take διὰ δέ as the beginning of a new sentence. The preposition can introduce an explanatory remark. Cf. Acts 16:3 διὰ τοὺς Ἰουδαίους ("because of the Jews"). On διά see Bauer, s.v. B. II. 1; Mayser, *Grammatik* 2/2.426; Mussner, p. 107 n. 37. δέ is omitted by Marcion (see Harnack, *Marcion*, *70).

302   The name can of course be applied to all kinds of people, but there can be no doubt that Paul refers here to his Jewish Christian opponents at Jerusalem. Cf. 2 Cor 11:26; Pol. *Phil.* 6.3; also the related "false apostle" (ψευδαπόστολος) 2 Cor 11:13. Paul (Rom 9:3) calls *non*–Christian Jews ἀδελφοὶ κατὰ σάρκα ("brothers according to the flesh"), a fact which was pointed out by Wegenast (*Tradition bei Paulus*, 47) against Schmithals (see n. 303). See also BDR, § 119, 5; Georgi, *Kollekte*, 16 n. 19; Stuhlmacher, *Evangelium*, 1.90 n. 1; Schmithals, *Paul and James*, 108 n. 16. On the whole question of the opponents of Paul, see the Introduction, § 2. C.

303   Differently Schmithals, *Paul and the Gnostics*, 14f; idem, *Paul and James*, 38ff, 109ff. He argues from silence that we know nothing of the status of the Law in Jerusalem Christianity and that only non–Christian Jews could have had an interest in it. Therefore, the "false brothers" must have been non–Christian Jews who after the persecution of the "Hellenists" (Acts 8:1, 4) had been appointed by the Jewish authorities as supervisors of the Jerusalem Christians.

304   Against Munck (*Paul*, 86f) who assumes that the "false brothers" are not in Jerusalem but in Galatia; similarly A. S. Geyser, "Paul, the Apostolic Decree

and the Liberals in Corinth," in *Studia Paulina in Honorem J. de Zwaan* (Haarlem: Bohn, 1953) 124–38. However, one possibility does not exclude the other. Paul talks about the opposition in Jerusalem for the precise purpose of discrediting his present opponents. Schlier (p. 71) denies that there is an identity of the present and the past opponents except for the insistence upon circumcision. What else is needed?

305   The expression is found only here in the NT. Originally, the term describes a military or political conspiracy (see, e.g., Polybius 1.18.3; 2.7.8; Diodorus Sic. 12.41.4; Plutarch *Mor.* 261B and often [see *Index Verborum Plutarcheus, s.v. παρεισάγω*]). In Christian literature it is often applied to "heretics" (e.g., 2 Pet 2:1; for later references see *PGL, s.v.*). Vg renders: sed propter subintroductos falsos fratres. Cf. Ambrosiaster, CSEL 81/3.20 lines 14–15: subinductos dicit, quia cum dolo intraverunt, ostendentes se fratres, cum essent inimici.

306   Cf. Polybius 1.7.3: παρεισελθόντες δ' ὡς φίλοι ("after being admitted as friends"); 2.55.3; Plutarch *Mor.* 596A, 964C, 980B; etc. (see *PECL*, 284; *Index Verborum Plutarcheus, s.v.*); ps.–Lucian *Asinus* 15; Philo *Op.* 150; *Ebr.* 157; *Abr.* 96; *T. Judah* 16.2. Cf. also synonyms, e.g., παρεισπορεύομαι (2 Macc 8:1); παρεισδύ(ν)ω (Jude 4); παρείσδυσις (*Barn.* 2.10; 4.10); Philo *L.A.* 116, 200, etc.: παρεισφθείρομαι. Schlier (p. 71) points to instances of such behavior in Gal 2:11–14; Acts 15:1, 24. See LSJ, *s.v.*; Bauer, *s.v.*; *PGL, s.v.*; Vg renders: *subintroierunt.* Cf. Ambrosiaster, CSEL 81/3.20 lines 16–17: fingentes amicitiam.

($\tau\grave{\eta}\nu$ $\grave{\epsilon}\lambda\epsilon\upsilon\theta\epsilon\rho\acute{\iota}\alpha\nu$ $\mathring{\eta}\nu$ $\check{\epsilon}\chi o\mu\epsilon\nu$ $\grave{\epsilon}\nu$ $X\rho\iota\sigma\tau\mathring{\omega}$ $\rq I\eta\sigma o\hat{\upsilon}$). Of course Paul's statement is meant positively and defines the Gentile Christian "indicative of salvation" as Paul understands it.[308] But the opposition no doubt saw this as lawlessness and judged its religious status as leading to eternal condemnation.[309] The goal of the opponents, to use Paul's defamatory language, was to get him and the Gentile Christians under control: "so that they might enslave us."[310] What they really intended was to ensure the Gentile Christians' salvation by subjecting them to circumcision and thus making them partakers of the Torah covenant.[311] In Paul's view, however, such a move would end up in "enslavement" under the "elements of the world" ($\tau\grave{\alpha}$ $\sigma\tau o\iota\chi\epsilon\hat{\iota}\alpha$ $\tau o\hat{\upsilon}$ $\kappa\acute{o}\sigma\mu o\upsilon$), a return to their pre-Christian existence.[312]

■ **5** Following the description of the opponents, their activities, and their goals (v 4), Paul recalls his reaction of unbending resistance against their demands (v 5a) and his own objectives (v 5b). Verse 5a contains a much discussed textual problem.[313] But it seems clear that the variant readings are secondary and that the reading of Nestle-Aland is to be preferred: $o\hat{\iota}\varsigma$ $o\grave{\upsilon}\delta\grave{\epsilon}$ $\pi\rho\grave{o}\varsigma$ $\mathring{\omega}\rho\alpha\nu$ $\epsilon\check{\iota}\xi\alpha\mu\epsilon\nu$ $\tau\hat{\eta}$ $\grave{\upsilon}\pi o\tau\alpha\gamma\hat{\eta}$ ("to those we did not yield by submission for a moment"). A number of witnesses[314] omit $o\hat{\iota}\varsigma$ $o\grave{\upsilon}\delta\acute{\epsilon}$, thereby expressing the view that Paul did in fact yield for a moment—by consenting to the circumcision of Titus.[315] Such a reading would dissolve the possible conflict between Gal 2:3–4 and Acts 16:3. Indeed, it may reflect a tradition according to which Paul at times did agree to circumcision.[316] Marcion omits $o\hat{\iota}\varsigma$,[317] so that Paul made no concession either to the "false brothers" or to the apostles, who in his view (and Paul's own later experience) were not much different from the former.[318] In any case, these theological tendencies show the variant readings to be secondary. The structure of the statement in v 5a is parallel to v 4a ($\delta\iota\grave{\alpha}$ $\delta\grave{\epsilon}$ $\tau o\acute{\upsilon}\varsigma$ ...). Paul's emphasis that he did not "yield[319] by submission"[320] even "for a

---

307   The term is a NT *hapax legomenon.* Vg renders *explorare*; cf. Ambrosiaster, CSEL 81/3.20 line 19: explorare est sic intrare, ut aliud fingat et aliud quaerat .... See *LSJ, s.v.*; Bauer, *s.v.*; *PGL, s.v.*, $\kappa\alpha\tau\alpha$-$\sigma\kappa o\pi\acute{\epsilon}\omega$, $\kappa\alpha\tau\acute{\alpha}\sigma\kappa o\pi o\varsigma$; Ernst Fuchs, "$\kappa\alpha\tau\alpha\sigma\kappa o\pi\acute{\epsilon}\omega$," *TDNT* 7.416f; for further instances, see *Index Verborum Plutarcheus, s.v.*; *Polybios–Lexicon* (ed. Arno Mauersberger; Berlin: Akademie–Verlag, 1966) 1.1337f, *s.v.* The suggestion was made by Karl Holl ("Der Kirchenbegriff des Paulus in seinem Verhältnis zu dem der Urgemeinde," in his *Gesammelte Aufsätze zur Kirchengeschichte* 2 [Tübingen: Mohr, Siebeck, 1928] 44–67, 57) that Paul argues against the claim by the Jerusalem apostles that they have a right of supervision. But this hypothesis is derived from Acts; cf. also *PGL, s.v.* $\kappa\alpha\tau\acute{\alpha}\sigma\kappa o\pi o\varsigma$; Georgi, *Kollekte*, 15 n. 18; Schlier (p. 71) who suggests that the opponents may claim a right to "inspection."

308   See on Gal 5:1, 13; cf. Jas 1:25; 2:12, where "freedom" is related to the Torah in a positive (anti–Pauline?) way. On the meaning of "in Christ Jesus" see Gal 2:17; 3:14, 28; 5:6.

309   See Gal 2:17, also 2:15.

310   Again the term is originally "political." See LSJ, *s.v.*; Bauer, *s.v.*; *Index Verborum Plutarcheus, s.v.*; *Polybios–Lexikon* (see n. 307) 1.1299, *s.v.* The expression occurs also 2 Cor 11:20 in a similar polemic. Vg renders Gal 2:4c: ut nos in servitutem redigerent. G adds a denial ($\mu\acute{\eta}$) before $\grave{\eta}\mu\hat{\alpha}\varsigma$, probably because in connection with 2:5.

311   So correctly Ambrosiaster, CSEL 81/3.20 line 25:

cogentes nos subici legi circumcisionis.

312   Cf. Gal 4:1–11; 5:1–12.

313   See the critical apparatus of Nestle–Aland and Aland, *Greek New Testament;* Metzger, *Textual Commentary*, 591f. For a full discussion, see Zahn, pp. 91f, 289–98; Lagrange; Burton; Oepke; Schlier; Mussner; Benjamin W. Bacon, "The Reading $o\hat{\iota}\varsigma$ $o\grave{\upsilon}\delta\acute{\epsilon}$ in Gal. 2:5," *JBL* 42 (1923) 69–80.

314   D* it^d Marius Victorinus and Latin manuscripts. See Metzger, *Textual Commentary*, 591.

315   This we conclude with Mussner.

316   On this problem, see on Gal 2:3; 5:11.

317   See Harnack, *Marcion*, 71*. The same omission is found in sy^p Ephraem. See also Ambrosiaster, CSEL 81/3.20–22.

318   For Marcion's criticism of the Jerusalem apostles, and for related passages, see Harnack, *Marcion*, 37–39.

319   $\epsilon\check{\iota}\kappa\omega$ ("yield") is a NT *hapax legomenon*. See Bauer, *s.v.*; BDR, § 67, 1a.

320   $\tau\hat{\eta}$ $\grave{\upsilon}\pi o\tau\alpha\gamma\hat{\eta}$. The dative is associative, see BDF, § 198; BDR, § 198. As a pleonasm the expression is emphatic. The article raises the question whether a formal demand was in fact made. See Lyder Brun, in Brun and Fridrichsen, *Paulus*, 30 n. 1 (following Anton Fridrichsen); Burton, p. 84; Schlier, pp. 72f; Gerhard Delling, "$\tau\acute{\alpha}\sigma\sigma\omega$ ($\grave{\upsilon}\pi o\tau\alpha\gamma\acute{\eta}$)," *TDNT* 8.46f.

moment"[321] stands of course in contrast to the Galatians' present readiness to accept the demands of the anti-Pauline opposition.[322]

Verse 5b formulates Paul's goals in antithesis to v 4c and in view of the present situation in Galatia: "so that the truth of the gospel might continue with you." Paul argues that, if he had yielded at Jerusalem, the "truth of the gospel" would have been compromised, and the Galatians would not have received any gospel at all.[323] Now they are about to make the very mistake which Paul had avoided at Jerusalem. As a result, they will thereafter be without gospel.[324] The expression "the truth of the gospel" ($\dot{\eta}$ ἀλήθεια τοῦ εὐαγγελίου)[325] is peculiar. It can mean the "true gospel" versus the "false gospel" (cf. 1:6–9),[326] or the "real consequences of the gospel,"[327] or the "integrity of the gospel."[328] Most likely, Lightfoot[329] is correct: "Paul's language denotes the doctrine of grace." Yielding to the opposition would have eliminated grace from the gospel. The same would be true of the Galatians' present plans.[330]

■ 6 Paul's narrative account of the conference with the authorities of the church in Jerusalem (2:6–10) is one of the most intriguing, historically fascinating, and textually complicated sections of New Testament literature. The entire section v 6–10 appears to be one convoluted sentence, a strange phenomenon in the otherwise so well-composed letter. Detailed analysis, however, reveals that the section is by no means carelessly composed. On the contrary, it is simply more complex. The enormous care which the author has apparently devoted to this section can only be explained if the event on which he reports constitutes the center of his "statement of facts." If this is the case, then there must be a relationship between the events at Jerusalem and the present crisis in Galatia. Then the present agitators and their theological position must in some way be related to the authorities in Jerusalem. This relationship probably existed not only in Paul's mind, but in the minds of the agitators and the Galatians as well. The relationship should be viewed as parallel to that between the "men from James" (cf. 2:11–14) and the present crisis.

Paul begins this section (2:6–10) with a characterization of the Jerusalem authorities analogous to the characterization of the opponents (2:4).[331] Notably, the characterization is much more objective and also less hostile. Of course one will have to assess this difference in tone not only with reference to Paul's later relationship with the men leading the Jerusalem church, but also by taking into account his present defense situation. If Paul did not receive his gospel and commission from the Jerusalem authorities but from God himself (cf. 1:1, 12), he must come to terms with the question of what role these authorities should play for him. More specifically, why did he and Barnabas even go to Jerusalem? What really did happen at that conference? If this conference did not prove Paul's dependence on Jerusalem, what did the meeting prove?

Paul deals first with the question of how he related then and now to the Jerusalem apostles. The name which he gives to them is important for his answer (cf. already 2:3): he calls them "men of eminence" (οἱ δοκοῦντες εἶναί τι). This expression, when it occurs in an apologetic context,[332] allows Paul both to acknowledge the fact that these men possess authority and power and to remain at a distance with regard to his own subservience to such authority.[333]

In the parenthesis v 6b–c Paul explains further how

321 For this expression see 2 Cor 7:8; Phlm 15; 1 Thess 2:17; John 5:35; *Mart. Pol.* 11.2. See also Mayser, *Grammatik*, 2/2.499.

322 See Gal 3:1–5; 4:8–11, 21; 5:1, 7–12. What Paul refused to do, was done by Cephas, Barnabas and other Jewish Christians at Antioch (Gal 2:11–14).

323 διαμένω πρός τινα is a *hapax legomenon* in the NT; cf. however, Acts 10:48 D. Bauer, *s.v.* renders "remain continually with someone." See LSJ, *s.v.*; Preisigke, *Wörterbuch* 4/3, *s.v.*

324 Cf. Gal 1:7a; 5:2, 4.

325 The expression occurs only here and Gal 2:14. See also Col 1:5; 2 Cor 11:10.

326 Rudolf Bultmann, "Untersuchungen zum Johannesevangelium," *ZNW* 27 (1928) 129; idem, *Exegetica*, 139, 143.

327 Schlier, p. 73. Cf. Mussner, p. 111 n. 58: "the logic of the gospel."

328 Lightfoot, p. 107; similarly Burton, p. 86.

329 Ibidem.

330 See Gal 2:21, also 1:6–9, 15; 2:9; 5:4; 6:18.

331 The beginning of v 6 is parallel to the beginning of v 4. For the analysis of the section, see the Introduction, § 5.

332 See on Gal 2:3.

333 That the "men of eminence" are really nothing is

he evaluates these authorities. His evaluation includes a statement on the nature of their status, the present argumentative value of their status, and the theological reason for Paul's evaluation. The parenthesis includes these words: "what they were makes no difference to me: 'God does not show partiality'." The first words ὁποῖοί ποτε ἦσαν can be taken as one expression ("what kind of people they were"),[334] or separately with an emphasis on ποτέ ("what kind of people [they] once [were]").[335] The more difficult problem is why Paul put the verb in the imperfect tense of ἦσαν ("they were") instead of the present tense, which would be consistent with the following present of οὐδὲν διαφέρει ("it makes no difference").[336] The discrepancy between the tenses is grammatically awkward and makes one suspect that Paul created it intentionally, because he wanted to distinguish between the past and the present. At this point a number of hypotheses have been suggested. Karl Heussi[337] defended in many publications his hypothesis that the ἦσαν ("they were") points to the death of Peter, James, and John at the time when Paul wrote his letter. The discussion, how-

ever, has shown that this hypothesis is improbable.[338]

Other scholars have taken the ἦσαν ("they were") as references to positive qualities which the apostles once had, but which they at present no longer have. Schlier[339] sums up the position of a long line of scholars who believe that Paul means to refer to the life of the apostles before Pentecost: "they may have had fellowship with the historical and, in particular, with the resurrected Jesus-Messiah; they themselves or others may base their reputation upon that fellowship; or James may even be a relative of the Χριστὸς κατὰ σάρκα ["Christ according to the flesh"] (cf. 2 Cor 5:16), [yet] God did not pay attention to these historical qualifications when he called Paul. Therefore, Paul does not pay attention to them either, when apostolic decisions must be made." Again, others believe the phrase "they were" refers to an advantageous situation that existed only at the time of the conference,[340] or prior to the proclamation of the Pauline gospel.[341] Again, general positive qualities could be relativized.[342] Another approach is characterized by having "they were" refer to negative qualities, such as the apostles' lack of educa-

---

made clear in Plato's *Apol.* 41E. Cf. Gal 6:3: "If anyone thinks he is something, when he is nothing, he deceives himself." Cf. Schlier (p. 76) who recognizes that Paul does not wish to discredit the apostles, but he fails to see that for Paul the apostles' authority is limited for theological reasons.

334 So BDF, § 303; Bauer, *s.v.* Burton (p. 87) points out that here the term refers to rank or standing.

335 Cf. Gal 1:13, 23. Schlier notes that there is no real difference in meaning: because of ἦσαν the past tense is meant.

336 The problem has been pointed out especially by Barrett, "Paul and the 'Pillar' Apostles," 19 n. 1; Günter Klein, "Galater 2, 6–9 und die Geschichte der Jerusalemer Urgemeinde," *ZThK* 57 (1960) 275–95 (now in his *Rekonstruktion und Interpretation: Gesammelte Aufsätze zum Neuen Testament* [BEvTh 50; Munich: Kaiser, 1969] 99–128, with a supplement); Eckert, *Die urchristliche Verkündigung*, 188f; Schütz, *Authority*, 136ff.

337 His final assessment of the matter is stated in his book *Die römische Petrustradition in kritischer Sicht* (Tübingen: Mohr, Siebeck, 1955). There also Heussi's numerous other publications on the subject are listed. For further material, see Erich Dinkler, "Die Petrus-Rom-Frage," *ThR* 25 (1959) 189–230, 289–335; 27 (1961) 33–64.

338 See Kurt Aland, "Wann starb Petrus? Eine Bemerkung zu Gal. II. 6," *NTS* 2 (1955/56) 267–75; Gerhard Schulze-Kadelbach, "Die Stellung des Petrus in der Urchristenheit," *ThLZ* 81 (1956) 1–14, esp. 8ff; Klein, *Rekonstruktion*, 100ff; Schlier, p. 75 n. 4; Mussner, p. 113 n. 67.

339 Schlier, pp. 75f. Actually, this argument is found already in the anti-Pauline passage in ps.-Clem. *Hom.* 17.18, where Peter insists that he has a better understanding of "revelation" than Paul, because Paul must rely only on a vision while Peter has learned it in Jesus' lifetime (see Appendix 3, below). According to Schlier, Paul does not intend to deny the authority of the Jerusalem apostles, but only a false justification of that authority. In this way, Schlier avoids the conclusion that Paul would reject in principle that the church has authority in matters of doctrine. Similarly also Lightfoot; Barrett, "Paul and the 'Pillar' Apostles," 18f. For a critique, see Klein, *Rekonstruktion*, 101f.

340 See, e.g., Zahn; Sieffert; Oepke; and, for a critique of these, Klein, ibidem, 103.

341 See Aland, "Wann starb Petrus?" *NTS* 2.274f, n. 338 above.

342 See, e.g., Lagrange; Lietzmann; Morton Smith, "Pauline Problems," *HTR* 50 (1957) 107–31, 120f; for a critique, Klein, *Rekonstruktion*, 103f.

tion,[343] or their unfaithfulness during the passion of Jesus.[344]

A somewhat new solution was presented by Günter Klein,[345] who has also delivered the most incisive critique of previous attempts to solve the problem. With Erich Dinkler[346] he assumes that Gal 2:7–9 contains a quotation from the "protocol" of the Apostolic Council. These verses, accordingly, contain information about the situation at the Council. This agrees with 1:18–19: Peter was responsible for the apostolate to the Jews. At Paul's second visit 2:7–8 this situation had not changed. At both visits we hear nothing of the "men of eminence" or the "pillars" (except for James, who is mentioned as the brother of Jesus, 1:19). Hence, Klein argues, the reference to the "men of eminence" and the "pillars" only reflects the situation at the time of Paul's writing of Galatians, but not the situation at the Council itself. In the meantime a shift of power has occured. The different order of the names shows that James' influence has increased while that of Peter has decreased.[347] At the first visit in Jerusalem Peter seemed to be in full control (1:19), but later other men gained the upper hand, and this process was not completed by the time of the Council. Peter was still in power at that time, but the up–and–coming men were James and John. Yet looking back (2:3, 9), it is more important for Paul that those who at the Council were the up–and–coming men and who have in the meantime taken over completely, did in fact agree to the terms of the agreement. At the present time, James, Peter, and John form a triumvirate, with James being the chairman who also shares in the charge of the mission to the Jews. Therefore, between the protocol of the Council (2:7–8) and the time when Galatians was written (2:9), a shift of power from Peter to the triumvirate of the "pillars" has taken place. This shift is expressed by the past tense of ἦσαν ("they were").

The problem, however, of the interpretation of ἦσαν ("they were") not only involves the meaning of the present tense of 2:6b, οὐδέν μοι διαφέρει ("it makes no difference to me"), but the whole parenthesis whose elements must all be related to it. As was already mentioned, the phrase "it makes no difference to me" is stated in the present tense. This present tense can refer, as Klein has it, to a condition which exists at present, but did not exist previously. The type of statement and the parallels in Greek literature,[348] however, suggest a "proverbial present."[349] In connection with the "men of eminence" this statement more than anything else declares their authority to be an *adiaphoron*. According to the Stoic doctrine of the *adiaphora* ("matters of indifference"),[350] things like δόξα versus ἀδοξία ("fame" versus "absence of fame") or εὐδοξία and εὐγένεια versus ἀδοξία and δυσγένεια ("good reputation" and "nobility" versus "lack of reputation" and "low descendence")[351] relativize the "authority" of the "men of eminence" at Jerusalem. Paul subscribes to this doctrine of *adiaphora* also in other passages and contexts.[352] Therefore, one may conclude that he uses it as a principle here for the purpose of relativizing the authority of the Jerusalem apostles.

If we assume this, 2:6c provides the theological

343 So Werner Foerster, "Die δοκοῦντες in Gal 2," *ZNW* 36 (1937) 288; Munck, *Paul*, 99 (with implicit reference to Acts 4:13). Cf. Smith, ibidem, 120f; Klein, *Rekonstruktion*, 105; Schlier, p. 76 n. 2; Eckert, *Die urchristliche Verkündigung*, 188 n. 3.

344 So Ethelbert Stauffer, "Zum Kalifat des Jakobus." *ZRGG* 4 (1952) 193–214, 203 n. 11a.

345 Klein, *Rekonstruktion*, 109ff.

346 For references, see on Gal 2:7–9.

347 See Klein, *Rekonstruktion*, 112f, 124f.

348 See for the phrase *Antipho* 5.13; Plato *Prot.* 316B, 358E; *Phaedo* 89C; *Leg.* 887B. Further instances are given in LSJ, *s.v.* διαφέρω III. 2; Bauer, *s.v.* 2. c; Konrad Weiss, "φέρω (διαφέρω)," *TDNT* 9.62–64.

349 See Eduard Schwyzer, *Griechische Grammatik* (3 vols.; HKAW 2.1–3; Munich: Beck, ²1959–60) 2.270f. Differently, Berthold Haesler, "Sprachlich–gram-

matische Bemerkungen zu Gal II, 6," *ThLZ* 82 (1957) 393f; Mussner, p. 114.

350 On this subject, see Johannes Stelzenberger, "Adiaphora," *RAC* 1.83–87.

351 See, e.g., Zeno *SVF* 1.190; de Vogel, *Greek Philosophy* 3, nos. 1012 b, c; 1018–22; 1030 b; 1034 b; 1050 a; 1087 a; 1088 b. Philo shows that the doctrine was adopted by Hellenistic Judaism (*Det.* 122; *Post.* 81; *Mos.* 2.240f; *L.A.* 2.17; *Op.* 74; *Sac.* 99; *Fuga* 152; *Her.* 253; *Praem.* 70; *Spec.* 2.46; *Prob.* 61; 83).

352 The phrase itself is a NT *hapax legomenon*; for the subject matter, see 1 Cor 1:26–29; Phil 3:7–8; etc. See Braun, "Die Indifferenz gegenüber der Welt bei Paulus und bei Epiktet," in *Studien*, 159–67: Betz, *Paulus*, 97.

rationale for the principle: πρόσωπον [ὁ] θεὸς ἀνθρώπου οὐ λαμβάνει ("God shows no partiality to man"). This dogmatic statement recalls an old theological doctrine, according to which "God is a judge who cannot be corrupted and has no regard for persons."[353] The Hebrew idiom נשא פנים[354] has a wide range of applications already in the Old Testament, but it is conspicuously used with reference to judges[355] and to God.[356] The dogma was generally held in Judaism[357] and was then taken over by early Christianity.[358] Paul applies it here to the proper status of the "men of eminence." We must also consider the fact that the present tense of λαμβάνει is the same as that of διαφέρει, both being "proverbial presents." This means that there is no real discrepency between the statements, but that they evaluate the past status of the Jerusalem apostles ("they were") as having no argumentative value in the present. In other words, Paul is not interested in a shift of historical circumstances of the men then and now, but in the principle that their past status at the conference cannot now be used as an argument. At present a theological question is to be decided, and for this decision one must not be unduly influenced by considerations of external status. It is, however, proper to render judgment upon the existing status of people, past or present, while applying the rule of God's impartiality.

After the completion of the parenthesis, Paul turns in v 6d to the results of the conference which he reports in v 6d–10. He repeats the beginning of the sentence (cf. v 6a), and first states the most important result of the conference: "upon me these 'men of eminence' did not make any demand." The verb προσανατίθημι ("add something to someone")[359] has a different meaning here than in 1:16.[360] Paul uses it here in the active voice, not in the middle,[361] so that its meaning is not different from ἀνατίθημι.[362] What kind of "addition" does Paul have in mind? It can only be the kind of request which his opponents had made (cf. 2:3–4) and which the present opponents are in fact making: to subject the Gentile Christians to Torah and circumcision (cf. 4:9; 5:1b). It is most decisive for Paul's defense that he is able to report and substantiate that at the Jerusalem conference his gospel was approved as is and that no additional requests, such as the opponents are now making, were made.[363] Thereby the present demands of the opponents are declared illegitimate.

■ **7** Having stated the most important and negative

353 See Eduard Lohse, "πρόσωπον (προσωπολημψία)," *TDNT* 6.779f; Schlier, p. 75; Klein, *Rekonstruktion*, 105; David M. Hay, "Paul's Indifference to Authority," *JBL* 88 (1969) 36–44.

354 See Ludwig Köhler and Walther Baumgartner, *Lexicon in Veteris Testamenti Libros* (Leiden: Brill, 1953), s.v. נשא, 4. נשא פנים is rendered by the LXX as λαμβάνειν πρόσωπον or θαυμάζειν πρόσωπον. Synonymous is הכיר פנים (LXX: γινώσκειν ἄνθρωπον).

355 See, esp., LXX Lev 19:15; Deut 1:17; 16:19; Ps 81:2; Prov 18:5; Job 13:10; Mal 2:9; 2 Chr 19:7.

356 See LXX Gen 32:21; Deut 10:17; Sir 35:13; *Ps. Sol.* 2:18; *Jub.* 5:16; *Abot* 4.22; etc.

357 See Str–B 3.79–83; Lohse, "πρόσωπον," *TDNT* 6.779f.

358 Apart from Gal 2:6, see Rom 2:11; Eph 6:9; Col 3:25; Acts 10:34; 1 Pet 1:17; *Barn.* 4.12. Of man it is used Jas 2:1 (cf. 2:9); *Barn.* 19.4; *Did.* 4.3; *1 Clem.* 1.3; Pol. *Phil.* 6.1; of Jesus Luke 20:21 par.; of heretics Jude 16.

359 The term used with this meaning is a NT *hapax legomenon*. See Bauer, s.v. 1; Johannes Behm, "ἀνάθεμα," *TDNT* 1.353f.

360 So rightly Oepke, pp. 78f; Schlier, p. 74 n. 2; differently Zahn.

361 "Take an additional burden on oneself" (LSJ, s.v. I); LSJ renders Gal 2:6 as "contribute of oneself" (sc. to another).

362 So with Schlier, p. 74; cf. LSJ, s.v. ἀνατίθημι B. I. Burton has a lengthy note on the term (pp. 89–91); he renders "for to me the men of eminence taught nothing new," in the sense that the apostles imposed on Paul no new burden of doctrine or practice.

363 So also Schlier, pp. 74f; Mussner, pp. 114f. Georgi (*Kollekte*, 19f) suggests that Paul has specifically in mind the so–called "Apostolic Decree" (Acts 15:24–29), which in the meantime had been issued without Paul's consent by others. This suggestion, however, does not fit the Galatian argument. Whether Paul knew of the "Decree" or not is impossible to establish. Notably, it does not include the demand of circumcision. Acts regards it as an organic part of the Jerusalem agreements, not as its violation and not as an "additional demand" (cf. Acts 15:10, 19, 28). On the whole problem, see August Strobel, "Das Aposteldekret in Galatien: Zur Situation von Gal I und II," *NTS* 20 (1974) 177–90.

result of the conference in v 6, Paul now turns to the positive result.[364] As in v 6, it is stated in a long and difficult sentence (vv 7–9). In his view, the positive result consists of the fact that his gospel and mission were officially acknowledged by the Jerusalem apostles. This fact is no doubt the most precarious part of Paul's argument, because it seems to support the notion that at the conference Paul had at least implicitly honored the Jerusalem apostles as a court of higher authority. Consequently, his defense must demonstrate the opposite, namely that no such acknowledgement had taken place at that time. Therefore, Paul argues that he did not recognize the Jerusalem apostles, but they recognized him. Verse 7 begins by identifying the reason why Paul was recognized: "on the contrary, when they saw that I had been entrusted with the 'gospel of the uncircumcision', just as Peter with the [sc. 'gospel] of the circumcision', . . . " The type of reason was "theological insight" (ἰδόντες).[365] Paul does not indi-

cate how and when this insight had occurred, but we may not go wrong in assuming that it had happened at the conference and only after heated debates.[366] Interesting is also the fact that non-Pauline language is used for the description of the content of the insight.[367] Erich Dinkler[368] emphasized that the notions of the "gospel of the uncircumcision"[369] as well as the "gospel of the circumcision"[370] are not Paul's language and that these concepts contradict his statement in Gal 1:6–7.[371] Surprising is also the name "Peter,"[372] instead of the usual "Cephas,"[373] in this passage. Karl Holl[374] and Adalbert Merx[375] proposed a solution of the problem of the name by textual emendation, assuming that "Peter" was inserted by later redactors for whom this was the standard name. Ernst Barnikol[376] thought of a later gloss which intended to put Peter and Paul on an equal level. Holl[377] assumed that "Peter" was the name of the missionary, while "Cephas" was

---

364 Note the emphatic "But on the contrary" (ἀλλὰ τοὐναντίον).

365 Cf. Gal 2:14; Matt 27:3, 24; Acts 12:3.

366 In this point Acts 15 reflects historical reality.

367 This is not true, however, of πεπίστευμαι ("I was entrusted"), which is a Pauline expression. See Rom 3:2; 1 Cor 9:17; 1 Thess 2:4; also 1 Tim 1:11; Tit 1:3; Ign. *Mag.* 6.1; Ign. *Phld.* 9.1. See Rudolf Bultmann, "πιστεύω," *TDNT* 6.177f; 203.

368 *Signum Crucis*, 282; Klein, *Rekonstruktion*, 118 n. 3 agrees.

369 It is the gospel of the Gentiles. On ἀκροβυστία ("foreskin") see 1 Cor 7:18f; *Barn.* 9.5; it is the opposite of περιτομή ("circumcision"), see Gal 5:6, 6:15; Rom 2:25, 26; 4:10; Eph 2:11; Col 3:11. The former serves as an abbreviation of "the heathen" (cf. Rom 3:30; 4:9; Eph 2:11; Col. 3:11; Ign. *Phld.* 6.1). See Karl Ludwig Schmidt, "ἀκροβυστία," *TDNT* 1.225f; Rudolf Meyer, "περιτέμνω," *TDNT* 6.72ff.

370 "Circumcision" is an abbreviation for "the Jews" (see Gal 2:12; Rom 3:30; 4:9, 12; 15:8; Eph 2:11; Col 3:11; 4:11; Tit 1:10; Acts 10:45; 11:2). Cf. the concept τὸ νόμιμον κήρυγμα used by the anti–Pauline *Kerygmata Petrou, Ep. Petr.* 3.3 (see Appendix 3, below).

371 Differently Schlier (p. 76) who quotes Tertullian, *De praescriptione haereticorum* 23: "Inter se distributionem officii ordinaverunt, non ut separationem evangelii, nec ut aliud alter sed ut aliis alter praedicarent." ("Between them they ordained the distri-

bution of the office, not with the purpose of the separation of the gospel, nor that one would proclaim this and the other that, but that one would preach to the ones, and the other to the others").

372 This name occurs in Paul only Gal 2:7, 8.

373 Gal 1:18; 2:9, 11, 14; 1 Cor 1:12; 3:22; 9:5; 15:5.

374 "Der Kirchenbegriff," 45 n. 3.

375 *Die vier kanonischen Evangelien nach ihrem ältesten bekannten Texte, 2:1: Das Evangelium des Matthäus* (Berlin: Reimer, 1902) 161ff. For a critique, see Schulze–Kadelbach, *ThLZ* 81 (1956) 10 n. 48; Schlier, p. 77 n. 2.

376 *Der nichtpaulinische Ursprung des Parallelismus der Apostel Petrus und Paulus (Gal 2, 7–8)* (Forschungen zur Entstehung des Urchristentums, des Neuen Testament und der Kirche, Heft 5; Kiel: Mühlau, 1929). For a critique, see Johannes Behm, *ThLZ* 58 (1933) 29; Hans Lietzmann, *ZNW* 33 (1934) 93; idem, *Galater*, p. 13; Schlier, p. 77 n. 2; Dinkler, *Signum Crucis*, 279f; Klein, *Rekonstruktion*, 106, n. 37.

377 Against Holl ("Der Kirchenbegriff," 45) Dinkler, *Signum Crucis*, 278f; idem, "Die Petrus–Rom–Frage," 198.

the name of the apostle at Jerusalem. Others[378] expressed doubt that the two names refer to the same person. John Chapman[379] argued that Paul formulated Gal 2:7 under the influence of Matt 16:16–19.

More convincing is another hypothesis advanced by Erich Dinkler,[380] who cites Ernst Barnikol[381] and Oscar Cullmann[382] as predecessors. Barnikol had observed that the passage 2:7–8 separates the two participles of ἰδόντες (v 7) and γνόντες (v 9), and that the intermediate section can be taken out without destroying the sentence. Cullmann suggested that Paul "here cites an official document, in the Greek translation in which the form *Petros* was used."[383] Dinkler attempted to prove this hypothesis and to actually reconstruct the quotation. He assumed that the conference had issued an official "decree," which was contained in the minutes in a Greek and an Aramaic[384] version. Paul, according to Dinkler, quoted verbatim from the Greek version as evidence for this argument. The actual quotation which Dinkler reconstructs requires only slight alterations to make it fit into the Pauline context: "the pillars saw that Paul had been entrusted with the gospel of the uncircumcision, just as Peter with that of the circumcision, for he who worked through Peter for the apostolate of the circumcision worked also through Paul for the Gentiles . . .". Unfortunately, however, this hypothesis collapses when examined critically. The formulation of v 7 is on the whole Paul's own: the first person plural cannot have been part of the "minutes" and is here part of a good Pauline phrase.[385] Verse 7, therefore, is Paul's own evaluation of an agreement as it pertains to his own position. But the non-Pauline notions of the "gospel of circumcision" and "of uncircumcision" as well as the name "Peter" may very well come from an underlying official statement. One also notes that in v 7 Paul mentions himself first (his own formulation), while v 8 mentions Peter first and Paul second. In conclusion, Dinkler's reconstruction does not work for v 7 as a whole, but it does for certain concepts and the name Peter. Rather than "quoting" from the written protocol, Paul reminds the readers of the agreements by using the terms upon which the parties had agreed.

■ **8** The parenthetical[386] statement of v 8 is very strange indeed: "for he who worked through Peter for [the] apostolate of the circumcision worked also through me for the Gentiles." The introductory γάρ ("for") provides a connection with the preceding, but the statement is complete in itself without that connection. It is in some sense parallel to v 9d: "we to the Gentiles, they to the circumcision." As in v 7, also in v 8 non-Pauline language is employed, and again the name of Peter is used instead of the usual Cephas.[387] The expression "apostolate of the circumcision" is non-

---

378 Kirsopp Lake, "Simon, Kephas, Peter," *HTR* 14 (1921) 95–97; Donald W. Riddle, "The Cephas–Peter Problem, and a Possible Solution," *JBL* 59 (1940) 169–80; Clemens M. Henze, "Cephas seu Kephas non est Simon Petrus!" *Divus Thomas* 61 (1958) 63–67; Joseph Herrera, "Cephas seu Kephas est Simon Petrus," *Divus Thomas* 61 (1958) 481–84. Cullman (*Peter*, 20 n. 7) mentions patristic representatives of the hypothesis.

379 "St. Paul and Revelation to St. Peter, Matt XVI. 17," *Revue Bénédictine* 29 (1912) 133–47. For a critique, see Munck, *Paul*, 63 n. 2; Klein, *Rekonstruktion*, 106 n. 37.

380 "Der Brief an die Galater," *VF* 1953–55, 182f; now in his *Signum Crucis*, 279ff; idem, "Die Petrus–Rom–Frage," 198. In agreement are Klein, *Rekonstruktion*, 106ff; 118ff; Schlier, p. 77 n. 2. Cf. also Munck, *Paul*, 61f.

381 See above, n. 376.

382 *Peter*, 20; idem, "Πέτρος, Κηφᾶς," *TDNT* 6.100 n. 6.

383 *Peter*, 20.

384 Dinkler, *Signum Crucis*, 280. In the supplement to the original article, 281f, Dinkler tries to support his thesis by a reconstruction of the "protocol" on the basis of the Peshitta.

385 See above, n. 367. There is no evidence, of course, for an Aramaic version of the document. Other linguistic objections must be raised against the Greek "text" of the supposed document. Cf. the inadequate defense against Ulrich Wilckens by Klein, *Rekonstruktion*, 118 n. 3. For criticism against Dinkler and Klein, see also Georgi, *Kollekte*, 14 n. 10; Haenchen, *Acts*, 466–67; idem, "Petrus–Probleme," *NTS* 7 (1961) 187–97, 192ff; rep. in his *Gott und Mensch* (Tübingen: Mohr, Siebeck, 1965) 63ff.

386 So with Schlier, p. 77, and most commentators. See BDF, § 465; BDR, § 465.

387 See above on 2:7, nn. 372 and 373. The datives Πέτρῳ and ἐμοί may be *dativi commodi* (so with Schlier, p. 78 n. 1; see BDF, § 188; BDR, § 188), or *instrumentalis* (see BDF, § 195; BDR, § 195).

Pauline[388] and corresponds to the "gospel of the circumcision" (v 7); it is a New Testament *hapax legomenon*. Most surprisingly, the statement does not contain the parallel notion of Paul's "apostolate of the Gentiles" (ἡ ἀποστολὴ τῶν ἐθνῶν). Characteristically, in describing Paul's mission the statement omits the term.[389] Taken by itself the sentence appears to be a summary or quasi-legal definition[390] of the relationship between the apostolate of Peter and the new mission of Paul. The definition states the competencies in terms of a division of labor. Although the apostolate of Peter is named first, the two missionary strategies are recognized as equal. They are equal because they share the same soteriological basis: it is the same God[391] who "works"[392] through both. The difference is that only Peter's mission is called "apostolate" (ἀποστολή),

while Paul's mission is not given a specific name but only equal status. Different is also the direction of the work: Peter is charged with the responsibility for the mission to the Jews, and Paul with that to the Gentiles.[393] This summary statement may very well be a quotation from the agreement made at Jerusalem. It is not really necessary to assume that it was taken from a written document. It could be an oral quotation, i.e., a quasi-legal rule which is easy to remember and which can be easily applied in different contexts. If this is true, the statement would indeed provide the evidence for Paul's claim that he did not receive the gospel message from the apostles at Jerusalem. In fact, the apostles recognized his gospel as equal with theirs, but they never recognized him as an "apostle."[394] This fact, that only he himself acknowledged his claim to the title of apostle,

---

388 Notably, Paul's account about the revelation of Christ Gal 1:15f does not mention his appointment as "apostle." For Paul's claim of the apostolate see Gal 1:1, 17; Rom 1:5; 1 Cor 9:1ff; 15:9; 2 Cor 11:5; 12:11f.

389 Against Schlier (p. 78 n. 2) and Mussner (p. 116 n. 91), who take it as an instance of *comparatio compendiaria*. For this construction, see Schwyzer, *Grammatik* 2.99 n. 1; BDF, § 479, 483; BDR, § 479, 483. This hypothesis is, however, by no means necessary. While Mussner (p. 116 n. 91) regards it as a "matter of no consequence," this matter in fact decides the question of what actually happened at the Jerusalem meeting.

390 Extensive search may produce form-critical parallels. Lightfoot and Schlier (p. 78 n. 2) mention a strange statement in *Acta Pauli et Theclae*, 40 (eds. Lipsius and Bonnet, *Acta Apostolorum Apocrypha* [Darmstadt: Wissenschaftliche Buchgesellschaft, 1959] 1.266 lines 8–10), where Thecla says to Paul: Ἔλαβον τὸ λουτρόν, Παῦλε· ὁ γὰρ σοὶ συνεργήσας εἰς τὸ εὐαγγέλιον κἀμοὶ συνήργησεν εἰς τὸ λούσασθαι ("I have taken the bath, Paul; for he who worked with thee for the Gospel has also worked with me for baptism," tr. HSW, *NT Apocrypha* 2.364). Similar is the peculiar doctrine which formulates the relationship between Jews and Christians in the ps.–Clem. *Hom.* 8.5–7.

391 The subject of the sentence is God. Cf. Gal 1:6, 15; 3:5; 5:8.

392 The term ἐνεργέω is difficult to translate. Bauer renders "be at work, be effective." It refers to God's redemptive activity as a whole. See 1 Cor 12:6: "It is the same God who works (ὁ ἐνεργῶν) all in

all." Cf. ps.–Clem. *Hom.* 17.7.3: πανταχόθεν γὰρ ἀκούει, νοεῖ, κινεῖ, ἐνεργεῖ, ποιεῖ ("for from every direction he [i.e., God] hears, thinks, moves, works, acts"). Cf. Xenophanes, according to Diog. L. 9.19. See furthermore 1 Cor 12:11; Gal 3:5; Phil 2:13; 1 Thess 2:13; Eph 1:11, 20; 3:20. Schlier interprets on the basis of 1 Thess 2:13: God lets his word be effective by providing power to the preaching of the apostles. But 1 Thess 1:5; Rom 15:19; 1 Cor 2:4; 2 Cor 12:12; Rom 1:16f show that the term must be understood in an inclusive sense. See also Kenneth W. Clark, "The Meaning of ΕΝΕΡΓΕΩ and ΚΑΤΑΡΓΕΩ in the New Testament," *JBL* 54 (1935) 93–101; Georg Bertram, "ἐνεργέω," *TDNT* 2.652–54.

393 See Gal 1:16; 2:2, 7, 9. Cf. the Mani Codex (*CMC* 87.19–21), where the expression "he wants to go to the Gentiles and eat Greek bread" (εἰς τὰ ἔθνη βούλ- [εται πο] ρευθῆναι καὶ Ἑλ [ληνικὸν] ἄρτον φαγεῖν) becomes identical with "being an enemy of the Law" (87, 16–19), i.e., an apostate from the Elchasaite sect (cf. also 80, 16–18; 89, 13f). The language appears in the mouths of the Elchasaites against Mani who imitates Paul in freeing himself from his parents' religion. The references are taken from Henrichs and Koenen, "Mani–Codex," *ZPE* 5 (1970) 139; cf. 145, 157. See the Introduction, n. 28, above.

394 Here most modern commentators present different conclusions. Representative are Schlier (pp. 76–81) and Mussner (pp. 117f), who assume that one of the main results of the Jerusalem conference was the recognition of Paul's apostolic grace and office. That such recognition is not to be found in the text

was of course used against him by the opponents, as we know from Paul's letters themselves and from Acts.[395]

■9 From the summary of the agreement of recognition (v 8) we move to the formal act concluding the meeting. The structure of the sentence is again peculiar. Detailed information with regard to the official act is packed into a very concise statement. In spite of its first appearance, the statement is clearly structured. The reason for being so meticulous at this point is related to the defense argument. The recalling of the specific acts and agreements serves as a control device in the apology. There can be no doubt that v 9 reached into the nerve center of the present debate.

(1) The statement first returns to the participle ἰδόντες ("they saw [= recognized]") in v 7 and evaluates it in Paul's own terms: "and recognizing the grace that was given to me" (καὶ γνόντες τὴν χάριν τὴν δοθεῖσάν μοι). The terms are Pauline, especially the term "grace"

(χάρις). In the context of the letter, "grace" is the content of the Pauline message of the gospel.[396] It is important to see that at this crucial point Paul does not identify, as he later does,[397] this "grace" with his apostolic office. Furthermore, the reason for the official act was not "church politics" (cf. the supplementary agreement of v 10!), but the "theological insight"[398] of God's redemptive work as "grace." This means that the apostles at Jerusalem understood and approved Paul's message and his theology.[399]

(2) The leaders of the Jerusalem side are identified by their names and by their titles. James is now named first,[400] then Cephas (!),[401] and finally John. As has often been observed by scholars, James appears now as the leading figure (cf. 1:19),[402] while Cephas is second in order and importance.[403] The Jerusalem leaders make up a triumvirate, carrying the title of "the pillars" (οἱ στῦλοι).[404]

---

was correctly pointed out by Lipsius, and also by Rudolf Bultmann, *History of the Synoptic Tradition* (tr. John Marsh; New York: Harper & Row, ²1968) 289. The matter has an interesting parallel in the Mani Codex (see n. 393 above). *CMC* 71.1–20 states as the apologetic purpose of the biography, that Mani's opponents are forced to admit the identity of Mani's revelations with those of the preceding apostles.

395 For the problem of Paul's apostleship, see at Gal 1:17, the excursus on "Apostle." Gal 2:8 shows that by the time of the Jerusalem conference Paul was not called and did not call himself "apostle," but apparently (Gal 1:1) claimed this title only later. The Jerusalem conference should, therefore, not be called "Apostolic Council."

396 Paul can use the term with reference to God's redemption in general (Gal 1:6, 15; 2:21; 5:4; etc.) or specifically to his apostolic office (see esp. Rom 1:5 ["through whom we have received grace *and* apostleship"]; 12:3; 15:15; 1 Cor 3:10; 10:30; 15:10; Phil 1:7; cf. also Eph 3:2, 7, 8).

397 See Gal 1:1, 17.

398 For the phrase "to recognize the grace" see 2 Cor 8:9; cf. Phil 3:10; Acts 15:11; 2 Cor 13:6; etc.

399 Against many commentators, esp. Schlier, p. 78. He takes "grace" to refer to the "grace of the apostolic office ("Apostelgnade")" and fills in the content from Rom and Eph. For Schlier this office is an established ecclesiastical position ("das Amt der Gnade"). But Schlier interprets the concept of apostolic office too much from the perspective of the later

Ancient Church. At the time of the Jerusalem conference the apostles were not the representatives of the whole church but only of one of the parties, and there existed no "unity of the apostolic office" which they had to guarantee. A "unity of the church" never existed either before or after the conference. Schlier is followed by Mussner, p. 118; Akira Satake, "Apostolat und Gnade bei Paulus," *NTS* 15 (1968/69) 96–107. Cf. also Schütz, *Authority*, 147ff.

400 Cf. Gal 1:18f.

401 Instead of Cephas, the Greek name Peter is read by a number of witnesses: P⁴⁶ D F G it^{d, g, r} goth Ambrosiaster *et al.* (cf. on 1:18). Some of the witnesses also prefer the order of Peter, James, John. But these clearly are secondary readings. See Metzger, *Textual Commentary*, 592; differently James N. Sanders, "Peter and Paul in the Acts," *NTS* 2 (1955/56) 133–43, 137.

402 See on this point Klein, *Rekonstruktion*, 107–09, 123ff; Mussner, pp. 118–20.

403 Cf. Gal 1:18; 2:7–8.

404 Paul's formulation combines two things, the expression "men of eminence" (cf. on 2:2, 6) and the honorific title "the pillars," into "those who are reputed to be 'the pillars'" (οἱ δοκοῦντες στῦλοι εἶναι). In the NT, the title "pillar" is mentioned only here, but in *1 Clem.* 5.2 Peter and Paul are named as "the greatest and most righteous pillars" (οἱ μέγιστοι καὶ δικαιότατοι στῦλοι). To be sure, this title is an honorific epithet similar to what we find in Judaism. See also 1 Tim 3:15, Rev 3:12. There is, however, no evidence that the epithet is con-

(3) Paul then states the official act of agreement: "they gave me and Barnabas the right hand of fellowship." Ordinarily merely an expression of fellowship,[405] the gesture of the handshake here formally concludes an agreement.[406] Its implications should be clear, but unfortunately they are not. As an implication, any recognition of subjugation by Paul and Barnabas can be ruled out.[407] The handshake does not automatically imply a recognition of supremacy as far as the Jerusalem apostles are concerned.[408] On the contrary, it is clear that the agreement was made between equal partners.[409] But what was meant by "equal," is not clear. The genitive "of fellowship" (κοινωίας) can imply that the fellowship has existed before and is simply extended to Paul and Barnabas, or it can mean that the fellowship was first established at that point. The "right hand of fellowship" can mean that the act makes apparent what has been implicit.[410] Finally, "fellowship" can include various forms of relationship, anything from unity to separation.[411]

(4) The next reference names the Gentile–Christian leaders, Paul and Barnabas. Paul names himself first, perhaps because he may have been the more important of the two, or perhaps because he now is primarily concerned with his own defense. It is also interesting that, contrary to our expectation, Paul and Barnabas are not given any titles. In a legal context this omission cannot be accidental (cf. on 2:8).

(5) Finally, Paul includes a summary statement, much like that in v 8. Its formula-like character states the content of the agreement: "so that: 'we to the Gentiles, they to the Jews'" (ἵνα ἡμεῖς εἰς τὰ ἔθνη, αὐτοὶ δὲ εἰς τὴν περιτομήν). Surprisingly, this formulation of the agreement is different from the one reported in v 8. Now Paul refers to himself and Barnabas (= "we") first, to the "pillars" second. While vv 7–8 had juxtaposed Peter and Paul, in v 9 Paul and Barnabas are juxtaposed with the three "pillars," James, Cephas, and John. Yet the relationship between the two situations seems clear. The first act (vv 7–8) was a recognition of Paul and his gospel as theologically valid. The second act (v 9) is the consequence of the first, and divides up the mission field.[412] The preposition εἰς ("to")[413] points to two ethnic divisions, not geographic territories.[414] By implication, the agreement sets up two cooperative but independent missionary efforts.[415] The old mission to the Jews is continued under the authority of the "pillars." The new mission to the Gentiles is integrated as equally valid and as a logical extension of the former. The division of labor is necessary because of the cultural barriers between Jews and Gentiles, not because of a disunity in the understanding of God, his redemption of mankind, and the gospel of Jesus Christ.

The formula also reflects a historic compromise which had to be made. It was *not* possible to preserve

---

nected with the notion of the church as a spiritual temple. See Ulrich Wilckens, "στῦλος," *TDNT* 7.732–36; Schlier, pp. 78f; Barrett, "Paul and the 'Pillar' Apostles," 5f; Mussner, pp. 120f. On the use of Judaism, see also Str-B. 1.208f; 3.537; Braun, *Qumran* 1.207f.

405 On the meaning of the gesture, see Carl Sittl, *Die Gebärden der Griechen und Römer* (Leipzig: Teubner, 1890) 27–31, 135–38; 276f, 363, 368; Gerhard Neumann, *Gesten und Gebärden in der griechischen Kunst* (Berlin: de Gruyter, 1965) 49ff; Walter Grundmann, "δεξιός," *TDNT* 2.37–40; Mussner, p. 121.

406 See Otto Eger, *Rechtsgeschichtliches zum Neuen Testament* (Basel: Reinhardt, 1919) 40f; Schlier, p. 79.

407 Cf. 1 Chr 29:24; 2 Chr 30:8; Lam 5:6.

408 So rightly Schlier, p. 79.

409 Cf. Xenophon *Anab.* 1.6.6; 2.5.3; Diodorus Sic. 16.42.3; on the Jewish side 2 Kgs 10:15; Ezra 10:19; 1 Macc 6:58; 11:50, 62, 66; 13:45, 50; 2 Macc 4:34; 11:26; Josephus *Vita* 30; *Ant.* 18.326,

328. Further parallels are collected in Wettstein, 2, pp. 220f.

410 Cf. Schlier, p. 79.

411 Cf. Homer *Il.* 2.341; Euripides *Med.* 21: δεξιᾶς πίστις μεγίστη ("that mightiest pledge of the right hand"); Xenophon *Anab.* 7.3.1; Statius *Theb.* 1.470; Livy 1.1.8; etc. On κοινωνία as "treaty" see Eger, *Rechtsgeschichtliches*, 40 n. 97.

412 On this statement, see Klein, *Rekonstruktion*, 107–09, 121ff; Mussner, pp. 122f.

413 See the use of propositions in Gal 2:7–8; 1:16; 2:2; 3:14; Rom 1:5; 15:16, 18; (16:26). Cf. Schlier, pp. 79f; Georgi, *Kollekte*, 21f.

414 So correctly Schmithals, *Paul and James*, 45f; Bonnard; Mussner, p. 122 (not entirely clear, however); differently, Oepke; Schlier.

415 Georgi, *Kollekte*, 21f.

the unity of the church.[416] Apparently, Paul's opposition, the "false brothers" (cf. 2:4–5), did not approve of the agreement, so that of the original three parties only two made the agreement, while the third is not mentioned and, we conclude, remained in opposition. The third party is, of course, behind Paul's present opponents. It is also noteworthy that the formula uses no titles, but only concerns itself with missionary strategy.

Excursus:
John, the Apostle

The third person named among the "pillars" (2:9) is the so-called apostle John, a mysterious figure of whom we know little as far as reliable historical information is concerned, and too much as far as legends are concerned. While in Gal 2:9 he shares the responsibilities for the mission to the Jews, the parallel account in Acts 15 does not mention him at all. Where he is mentioned in connection with Peter, he is mentioned second; he was of lesser significance. From the gospel tradition we know that John was the son of Zebedee and the brother of James (see Mark 1:16–20; 3:17; 10:35–45; 14:33; also Matt 27:56; John 21:2; Acts 1:13; 3:1, 3, 4, 11; 4:13, 19; 8:14; 12:2). Later tradition interpreted the prophecy Mark 10:39 as a prophecy (*ex eventu*!) of the martyrdom of the sons of Zebedee. If this were historical, it must have happened after what is told in Gal 2:9; Acts 12:2. Characteristic of the later tradition are also identifications: John was identified with the "Beloved Disciple" of the Fourth Gospel (John 13:23; etc.), and he became the author of the Johannine literature (John, the Epistles of John, Revelation). Whether in these traditions historical information has been preserved is an open question.

Bibliography: Gerhard Delling, *RGG*[3] 3.803–04; Floyd V. Filson, *IDB* 2.953–55; HSW, *NT Apocrypha*, 2.51–56, and index; Rudolf Schnackenburg, *Das Johannesevangelium* (HThK 4.1; Freiburg: Herder, 1967) 60–88; Kümmel, *Introduction*, 234–46; Conzelmann, *History*, 138–40.

■ **10** The third result of the conference is supplementary: "only that we should remember the poor." The adverb μόνον ("only") at the beginning separates the following from the preceding matter under discussion.[417] At the same time it expresses a concession. Paul had insisted in v 6d that no additional demand was made upon him. Now he seems to concede that such a demand had been made after all. How do we deal with this inconsistency? Paul clearly plays down this additional request, saying that there was only this one, and it was supplementary, unrelated to the main points of the debate, and immaterial to the present crisis in Galatia. From Paul's words it appears that what had been requested and granted was a kind of philanthropic gesture. Yet one must also see that Paul's concession in fact strengthens his defense.

The Galatians of course know about this collection for the poor because they themselves have become involved in it.[418] In this way they have become executors of the Jerusalem agreement. This changes their position from mere readers about past events to active participants in the implementation of the Jerusalem agreements. The collection, however, in which they have become involved would never have been requested or granted, if the other parts of the agreement, including the recognition of Paul, had not also been made. In other words, the Galatians are no longer asked simply to believe what Paul tells them, but instead they are now considering hard evidence in which they themselves have had a share. The object "the poor" (οἱ πτωχοί) is anticipated, leaving ἵνα ("so that") in postposition.[419] The verb μνημονεύω ("remember") here

---

416 See, e.g., Ferdinand Christian Baur, *Paulus* (Stuttgart: Becher & Müller, 1845) 1.142f; Loisy; Albert Schweitzer (*Die Mystik des Apostels Paulus* [Tübingen: Mohr, Siebeck,[2]1954] 199) who put the emphasis on the division of the two missionary enterprises. Cf. the other line of thought, which includes Lagrange, Schlier (pp. 79f), Mussner (pp. 122f), who assume that the purpose was to preserve the peace and the unity of the church. Mussner's critique of Baur (122, n. 118) fails to distinguish clearly enough between the situation at the Jerusalem conference and his own present perspective.

417 See Bauer, *s.v.* μόνος, 2, b; Schlier, p. 80 n. 2. Cf. the parallels Phil 1:27; 2 Thess 2:7; Ign. *Rom.* 5.3.

418 See 1 Cor 16:1–4, cited below.

419 See BDF, § 475, 1; BDR, § 475 n. 1; Moule, *Idiom Book*, 144; Schlier, p. 80 n. 3; Mussner, p. 124 n. 122.

refers to a specific, ongoing[420] financial subsidy.[421]

The receivers of this financial subsidy are called by the ancient honorific name "the poor." Scholars have for some time debated certain important questions, such as whether these "poor" are identical with the Jerusalem church or with a group within that church, whether these people are merely financially poor, or whether "poor" is the name of a special kind of piety, the "*anawim* piety."[422] Elsewhere, the members of the Jerusalem church are called "the saints" (οἱ ἅγιοι).[423] Rom 15:26 calls them even more fully "the poor of the saints in Jerusalem" (οἱ πτωχοὶ τῶν ἁγίων τῶν ἐν Ἱερουσαλήμ). Perhaps they were both,[424] economically "poor" by the standards of Hellenistic–Gentile Christians, but also exponents of the Jewish "*anawim* piety," naturally of a Jewish–Christian variety.[425] Nothing is known about the reason for their poverty. That they had become poor because of the sharing of their goods in the beginning is a speculation based upon Acts.[426] There is no compelling reason to assume that they have suffered particularly from oppression and persecution, although this may have been a cause.[427] The economic and social conditions in Jerusalem were less fortunate than in other Hellenistic cities of Greece and Asia Minor. In addition to this economic and social condi-

tion, poverty was embraced by many Jews and Christians as an expression of personal piety. That in the end such piety must rely on outside help is a well-known religious phenomenon elsewhere.[428]

In the second part of the sentence (v 10c) Paul affirms his concern to comply with this supplementary agreement: "which request I have made my special concern to fulfill." In the meantime, between the Jerusalem conference and the writing of Galatians, Paul and Barnabas have separated,[429] and this may account for Paul's changing from the first person plural to the first person singular. It is interesting that in spite of the separation from Barnabas and the other Jewish Christians, Paul has continued to implement the supplementary agreement.[430] In addition, the general conditions under which the agreements were made have in the meantime drastically changed. Possibly the main agreements are no longer valid, and only the supplementary one is. Then Paul must have new reasons for keeping the financial collection going.

In the context of the present argument, Paul's "zeal" (σπουδάζειν)[431] serves as evidence that the agreement had in fact been concluded and that he had never stopped honoring its terms. The Galatians themselves are witnesses to this, because they participate in the

---

420 μνημονεύωμεν is a present subjunctive and points to an ongoing activity; so correctly Georgi, *Kollekte*, 27ff, and the title of his book: "The History of Paul's Collection for Jerusalem."

421 In this sense the term occurs only here in the NT. See Bauer, *s.v.*, 1, a. For the term "remember," see the basic study by Willy Schottroff, "*Gedenken*" im Alten Orient und im Alten Testament (WMANT 15; Neukirchen: Neukirchener Verlag, ²1967) 160ff.

422 See Holl, *Gesammelte Aufsätze* 2.58f; Lietzmann, *Römer*, on Rom 15:25; Bauer, *s.v.* πτωχός, 1; Friedrich Hauck and Ernst Bammel, "πτωχός," *TDNT* 6.885–915; Leander Keck, "The Poor Among the Saints in the New Testament," *ZNW* 56 (1965) 100–29; idem, "The Poor Among the Saints in Jewish Christianity and Qumran," *ZNW* 57 (1966) 54–78.

423 Georg Strecker, in Bauer (*Orthodoxy and Heresy*, 272) emphasizes that only in Rom 15:25f is the expression "the poor of the saints" used, and that Paul says at other places simply "the saints" (see Rom 15:25, 31; 1 Cor 16:1; 2 Cor 8:4; 9:1, 12; Acts 11:29; 24:16f).

424 Bammel ("πτωχός," *TDNT* 6.908f) retranslates the

name into the Hebrew אביונים ועניים בירושלים. But as a self-designation, this combination looks odd. On the background of the "*anawim* piety" see Jacques Dupont, *Les Béatitudes* 2 (Paris: Gabalda, ²1969); Johannes Botterweck, *TWAT* 1, *s.v.* אביון.

425 See also Franz Mussner, *Der Jakobusbrief* (Freiburg: Herder, ²1967) 76ff, with further bib.

426 Acts 2:44f, 4:32.

427 See Georgi, *Kollekte*, 22ff.

428 See Rom 15:27: "They [*sc.* Macedonia and Achaia] were pleased to do it [*sc.* the collection], and indeed they are in debt to them, for if the Gentiles have come to share in their spiritual blessings, they ought also to be of service to them in material blessings" (*RSV*). Cf. 15:25f; 2 Cor 8:9.

429 See Gal 2:13; Acts 15:39.

430 Note the emphatic αὐτὸ τοῦτο ("this very item"). Cf. BDF, § 297; BDR, § 290; Schlier, p. 81 n. 1.

431 See Rom 15:26f; 1 Cor 16:3; 2 Cor 9:1ff; Acts 24:17. On the term σπουδάζω ("be zealous, make every effort") see Bauer, *s.v.*, 2; Günther Harder, "σπουδάζω," *TDNT* 7.559–68, esp. 565. Cf. Gal 1:14; 4:17, 18.

collection. There is no reason to believe, as Georgi has suggested,[432] that they have discontinued their participation. On the contrary, switching to the anti-Pauline opposition would make it all the more plausible for the Galatians to collect money for Jerusalem. Nevertheless, they are contributing to Paul's collection activity, not to the opponents', sending contributions to no other recipients than the Jerusalem church itself. This is "living" evidence that Paul was approved by the Jerusalem church. After all, the Jerusalem church must accept Paul if they accept his money![433]

That the Galatians participated in the collection, we know from 1 Cor 16:1–4:[434] "now concerning the collection for the saints, you should do as I have appointed for the churches in Galatia. On the first day of the week let each of you put aside and store up whatever he can spare, so that collections are not made only when I come. After my arrival, I shall send people of your choice with letters to bring your gift to Jerusalem. If it is your mind that I should also go, then they shall go with me." The early form of a collection of financial contributions must have been instituted in Galatia earlier than in Corinth, and it must have worked well among the Galatian churches, so that Paul could recommend the adoption of the method to the Corinthians. There can be little doubt that the collection was still in process when Galatians was written.

Excursus:
The Collection For Jerusalem

Acting as representatives of the church of Antioch, Paul and Barnabas committed themselves to a financial collection on behalf of the poor of the church in Jerusalem. For the name "the poor" see the notes on 2:10. It has been suggested by scholars (see Nickle, 74–99, in the bibliography below) that the original agreement was a kind of "tax," a regular ecclesiastical assessment to which the Jerusalem church felt entitled on account of their unique position in salvation history, and because of the analogy of the Jewish "temple tax." This analogy, however, and with it the hypothesis, fails. Not all Christians contributed, but only certain Gentile churches, and those because of Paul's urging. It was not an annual assessment, but a one–time collection extended over a long period of

time. Its installation was felt to be a new venture without analogies. The reason was not cultic, but social. Its reason was not a legal obligation, but a voluntary charity by the relatively wealthy new Gentile churches (see 2 Cor 8:9, 14–15). It was an act of gratitude towards the mother church in Jerusalem (cf. Rom 15:28).

The voluntary act of charity demonstrated visibly the self-consciousness and increasing importance of Gentile Christianity. It was also a demonstration of independence on the part of Paul's churches. Paul's commitment had grave consequences for himself personally; the collection took a great amount of his time and energy. See especially Rom 15:25–29; 1 Cor 16:1–4; 2 Corinthians 8 and 9 (these last two are probably fund-raising letters). His last journey to Jerusalem was designed to deliver the collection, but as he had feared (see Rom 15:30–32) his arrival led to unrest and trouble. The collection, it appears, was refused by the recipients. In the course of the trouble, Paul was arrested and transported to Rome (cf. Acts 11:29; 24:16–28:31).

Bibliography: Charles H. Buck, "The Collection for the Saints," *HTR* 43 (1950) 1–29; Keith F. Nickle, *The Collection: A Study in Pauline Strategy* (Naperville: Allenson, 1966), with further bibliography; Dieter Georgi, *Kollekte*, with bibliography; see the review of Georgi by Walter Schmithals, *ThLZ* 92 (1967) 668–72; idem, *Paul and James*, 79–84; Klein, *Rekonstruktion*, 81–83; Käsemann, *Römer*, 381ff; Suhl, *Paulus*, 57ff; David Hall, "St. Paul and Famine Relief," *ExpTim* 82 (1971) 399–411.

Excursus:
The Conflict At Antioch

In Gal 2:11–14 Paul reports the last episode of the *narratio* (see the introduction to the section, and the Introduction, §5, above). As in the case of the other episodes, careful distinction must be made between Paul's tendencies, which are due to his apologetic argument, and the facts. In terms of his defense strategy, the final episode serves several purposes. Most importantly, the episode should bring the pre-history of the problem up to the point where it meets with the present situation. This connection is made by Paul in the dilemma formulated in v 14c. At present, the Galatians must face the same dilemma as Peter at Antioch, only from the opposite side. They are Gentiles who are under pressure to enter into a Jewish

---

432 Georgi, *Kollekte*, 30ff. Cf. Borse, *Standort*, 144f; Mussner, p. 124 n. 125.

433 Cf. Acts 24:17.

434 See on this passage Conzelmann, *1 Corinthians*, 295f.

way of life (see also 2:4–5, 17; 4:8–11; 5:1–12; 6:13–14). The account of the episode also demonstrates how the initially good relationships between Paul and the Jerusalem authorities had deteriorated, and this not through Paul's fault. The relationship between the three parts of the *narratio* is climactic: the first section (1:13–24) demonstrates how Paul the outsider was accepted into the Jewish–Christianity community; the second section (2:1–10) shows how Paul's gospel and mission were officially recognized by the Jerusalem authorities against the opposition; the third section shows how the original agreements were broken, partly as the result of historical developments, partly by human failure, especially of Peter. Paul contends that he has faithfully maintained the same position which he had always defended and which had been approved by the Jerusalem authorities and indeed by God himself.

The facts are simple: for reasons not spelled out Cephas had come to Antioch and taken up table fellowship with the Gentile Christians, and perhaps even the Gentile way of life altogether. For whatever reason, this was considered proper by all people present. Then, again for reasons unknown, a delegation of "men from James" arrived. Pressured by them, Cephas and the other Jewish Christians reversed themselves and withdrew from the fellowship with their Gentile fellow Christians. They took up again the Jewish way of life, especially the part of ritual separation from the unclean. Paul did not follow the other Jewish Christians' action, but stayed with the Gentiles and confronted Cephas in an open debate. The result of this confrontation is unknown. It appears that the break between Paul and the other Jewish–Christian missionaries, including his former mentor Barnabas, was irreparable. The event seems to have been well-known in the early church. Especially important is the defense of Peter's position at Antioch in the *Kerygmata Petrou* (see Appendix 3, below). The author of Acts avoids a report, but admits the separation of Paul and Barnabas (Acts 15:36–39).

Paul's account shows the developments after the conference at Jerusalem. The middle group (James, Cephas, John) is in the process of dissolution. The "men of James" now represent the same position as the "false brothers" at Jerusalem, although the issue is not circumcision but purity. Most Jewish Christians, when forced to choose, opt for the Jewish position; only Paul is left with the new converts. The decision was awesome but tragic. The Jewish Christians no doubt had good reasons to support their decision. But those reasons were derived from Jewish theology rather than Christian theology. They decided in favor of safe tradition and religious conservatism, but they decided against the course of history.

Bibliography: Franz Overbeck, *Über die Auffassung des Streits des Paulus mit Petrus in Antiochien (Gal. 2, 11ff.) bei den Kirchenvätern* (Basel: 1877; rep., Darmstadt: Wissenschaftliche Buchgesellschaft, 1968); Lightfoot, 128–32; Theodor Zahn, "Petrus in Antiochien," *NKZ* 5 (1894) 434–48; Benjamin W. Bacon, "Peter's Triumph at Antioch," *JR* 9 (1929) 204–23; Paul Gächter, "Petrus in Antiochien," *ZKTh* 72 (1950) 177–212; idem, *Petrus*, 213–57; Munck, *Paul, passim*; Ernst Haenchen, "Petrus–Probleme," *NTS* 7 (1960/61) 195–96; Georgi, *Kollekte*, 31ff; Bornkamm, *Paul*, 43–48; Schmithals, *Paul and James*, 63–78; Klein, *Rekonstruktion*, 83; Conzelmann, *History*, 89–90; Mussner, 146–67.

Excursus:
Antioch–on–the–Orontes

Paul refers to the city of Antioch–on–the–Orontes in northwestern Syria (= modern Antakya [Turkey]). The city is a Hellenistic foundation of Seleucus I Nicator in 300 B.C., who named it after his father Antiochus. From its beginning, the city was Hellenistic in character, populated by a mixture of Macedonians, Greeks, Syrians, and a contingent of Jewish war veterans (see Kraeling in the bibliography below). The Jews had been given land around Antioch as a reward for their service in Seleucus' army. As it was a cosmopolitan center with regard to population, its fortunate location and nearby seaport helped the city to become prosperous and cultured. Antioch became the third most important city after Rome and Alexandria. As the political capital of the Seleucids and, since 64 B.C., the residence of the Roman governor of the province of Syria, the city had great influence politically. The architectural and artistic splendor must have been impressive. By the time of Paul, Antioch was at its peak.

Many religious cults were represented in the city, among them a sizable Jewish community. About the origin of the Christian church we have some information in Acts which may be reliable. According to Acts 11:19–30 some of the followers of Stephen fled to Antioch after his martyrdom. Jewish–Christian refugees from Cyprus and Cyrene began to preach the Christian message to Gentiles in Antioch, and gathered a group which was called οἱ Χριστιανοί ("the Christians"). The church of Jerusalem had sent Barnabas to Antioch, who in turn brought Paul to that church. Other names of Antiochean Christians are mentioned in Acts 6:5; 13:1. Acts views Antioch as the main center of missionary activity among the Gentiles in Syria and Asia Minor. The oldest information about the church at Antioch is found in Gal 2:11–14 (see below). After the meeting, nothing certain is known until Ignatius, the bishop of Antioch (martyred in Rome soon after A.D. 110). Whether Paul was forced out of Antioch altogether, as many scholars assume, cannot be established beyond doubt. The sources which we have do not say that he returned to Antioch after the conflict reported in Gal 2:11–14. Acts, however, ignores the incident, although the author may have had access to Antiochean sources, if he was not from Antioch himself. Ignatius professes to be a Paulinist, but ignores the incident too. That Peter was the "first bishop" of Antioch is a later legendary tradition (see Oscar Cullmann, *Peter: Disciple, Apostle, Martyr* [tr. Floyd V. Filson; Philadelphia: Westminster,² 1962] 54). Ignatius also refers to a Jewish–Christian opposition, apparently existing at the "fringe" of the church in conventicles, but this may be his own polemic (cf. Ign. *Mag.* 8–11; *Phld.* 6.1–2; *Smyrn.* 2. 4–7). That this opposition continues the earlier opposition against Paul is probable. Throughout the history of the ancient church Antioch remained a major center of Christian life in the eastern mediterranean.

Bibliography: Victor Schultze, *Altchristliche Städte und Landschaften* (vol. 3; Gütersloh: Bertelsmann, 1930); *Antioch-on-the-Orontes* (vols. 1–5; Princeton: Department of Art and Archaeology, 1934–52); Glanville Downey, *A History of Antioch in Syria: From Seleucus to the Arab Conquest* (Princeton University, 1961), with further bibliography; André J. Festugière, *Antioche païenne et chrétienne* (Paris: Boccard, 1959); Arnold H. M. Jones, *The Cities of the Eastern Roman Provinces* (Oxford: Clarendon,² 1971); John H. W. G. Liebeschütz, *Antioch: City and Administration in the Later Roman Empire* (Oxford: Clarendon, 1972), with further bibliography.

On the Christian church in Antioch, see Harnack,

Mission und Ausbreitung, 57ff, 660ff; Ernst Bammel, "Zum jüdischen Märtyrerkult," *ThLZ* 78 (1953) 119–26; Bauer, *Orthodoxy and Heresy*, index, *s.v.* Antioch; Robinson and Koester, *Trajectories*, index, *s.v.* Antioch; Carl H. Kraeling, "The Jewish Community at Antioch," *JBL* 51 (1932) 130–60; Robert M. Grant, "Jewish Christianity at Antioch in the Second Century," in *Judéo–Christianisme, Recherches historiques et théologiques offerts en hommage au Cardinal Jean Daniélou* (= *RechSR* 60 [1972] 97–108); Sherman E. Johnson, "Asia Minor and Early Christianity," in *Christianity, Judaism and other Greco–Roman Cults: Studies for Morton Smith at Sixty* (Leiden: Brill, 1975) 2.77–145; C. K. Barrett, "Pauline Controversies in the Post–Pauline Period," *NTS* 20 (1974) 229–45; August Strobel, "Das Aposteldekret in Galatien: Zur Situation von Gal I und II," *NTS* 20 (1974) 177–90.

■ **11** As in the other parts of the *narratio*, Paul begins the last episode by briefly stating the facts concerning the incident.[435] It happened "when Cephas came to Antioch." The reason why Paul tells about the incident is this: κατὰ πρόσωπον αὐτῷ ἀντέστην, ὅτι κατεγνωσμένος ἦν ("I opposed him to his face because he stood condemned"). No date is given as to when the incident took place,[436] only the location at Antioch (see the excursus on "Antioch–on–the–Orontes"). Nor does Paul provide the reason for Cephas'[437] coming to Antioch. Probably, the incident was well-known to the readers. What kind of visit would have brought Cephas to Antioch? It could have been an occasional visit,[438] perhaps a stop-over on the way to some other place. Or it could have been a final move from Jerusalem to Antioch because of unfavorable circumstances in

---

435 δέ ("but") sets the episode off from the preceding (cf. 1:15; 2:12; 4:4).

436 ὅτε ("when") is indeterminate. Cf. Gal 1:15; 2:11, 12, 14; 4:3, 4. The Antioch episode occurred *after* the conference in Jerusalem. Some scholars, however, have tried to reverse the order, but this has no good reasons to commend it. Cf. Zahn, pp. 110f, with the older literature; Munck, *Paul*, 74f, 100ff; Schoeps, *Jewish Christianity*, 19; Henricus M. Féret, *Pierre et Paul à Antioche et à Jérusalem: Le "conflict" des deux apôtres* (Paris: Cerf, 1955); for a decisive critique, see Jacques Dupont, "Pierre et Paul à Antioche et à Jérusalem," *RechSR* 45 (1957) 42–60, 225–39. See also Betz, "Composition," 367, and the Introduction, § 3, above.

437 The name is again Cephas (see 1:18; 2:9, 14; cf. 2:7, 8), which is attested by the better witnesses,

while the *Textus Receptus* D G minuscules, it^d,g vg^mss syr^h goth *al* again read Πέτρος. See Metzger, *Textual Commentary*, 593.

438 Acts suggests that there were frequent visitations between Jerusalem and Antioch (see Acts 11:19–27; 14:26; 15:1ff, 22, 30; 18:22). This picture conforms to Jewish sources. See Carl H. Kraeling, "The Jewish Community at Antioch," *JBL* 51 (1932) 130–60.

Jerusalem.[439] There are also questions with regard to the situation in Antioch. Clearly, the arrival of Cephas must have occurred prior to Paul's confronting him.[440] Was there one church made up of Gentiles and Jewish Christians? Or were there two churches, one Gentile and one Jewish Christian?[441] If the latter, which of them did Cephas join? Was the act of table fellowship with the Gentile Christians (v 12) his own personal decision or did it include others? Did the meal include Cephas and the Gentile Christians, or a Gentile– as well as a Jewish–Christian party? Was the meal some kind of demonstrative act or an unplanned incidental event? Although one can only raise these questions, some information can be extracted from Paul's account.

Prior to the arrival of the "men from James" (v 12), all participants in the event seem to have agreed that their table fellowship was proper. Indeed, it seems consistent with the presuppositions of the Jerusalem agreements (2 : 7–9). On the other hand, it also seems to have been understood that Cephas' participation was extraordinary. And again, this can be interpreted in the light of the Jerusalem agreements. When Cephas came to Antioch he came as the representative of Jewish Christianity.[442] Eating with Gentile Christians implied the crossing of the line drawn by the Torah

covenant as understood by Jews (and Jewish Christians). Taking up table fellowship was consistent with Paul's understanding of the agreements made at Jerusalem; withdrawing from the table fellowship was in line with the conservative Jewish understanding of these agreements. Paul's emphasis was on unity of the salvation in Christ; the Jews' emphasis was on cultic separation. Both interpretations have roots in the Jerusalem agreements. It was Cephas' vacillation between the two options that caused Paul to "oppose him to his face."[443] This confrontation must have been the very opposite of that for which the meeting had originally been planned. That Cephas "stood condemned" ($\kappa\alpha\tau\epsilon\gamma\nu\omega\sigma\mu\acute{\epsilon}\nu\sigma\varsigma\ \mathring{\eta}\nu$)[444] should not be taken as Paul's triumph, but as the result of the failure of the meeting and, indeed, as the end of the Jerusalem agreements.

■ 12 After providing general information of the incident as a whole (v 11), Paul turns to a more detailed account of the events and his own evaluation of them. He begins with the account of Cephas' conduct. Three stages of development can be distinguished: (1) "for until certain men from James came, he ate with the Gentiles" (v 12a); (2) the change of conduct: "but when they came he withdrew and separated himself" (v 12b);

---

439 The legend told in Acts 12 : 1–17, which probably comes from some kind of source, may describe Peter's last days in Jerusalem before coming to Antioch. Does the phrase in 12 : 17 "and leaving [sc. Jerusalem] he went to another place" have Antioch in mind? After Peter's departure James remained in Jerusalem as the only leader of the church (Acts 12 : 17). See Haenchen, *Acts*, 380ff; Conzelmann, *Apostelgeschichte*, 69ff; Wolfgang Dietrich, *Das Petrusbild der lukanischen Schriften* (Stuttgart: Kohlhammer, 1972) 296–306.

440 On συνήσθιεν, see v 12.

441 No conclusion can be drawn on the basis of Acts because of the author's tendency to present a harmonious picture of primitive Christianity. Later, Ignatius of Antioch is engaged in fights with Jewish-Christian opponents, but he leaves it unclear whether they belong to his congregation or to separate conventicles. On the problem of Christianity in Antioch, see the excursus "Antioch–On–the–Orontes."

442 Of course, Cephas is the same as Simon Peter, and not, as some commentators (following Clement *Hypotyposes* [according to Eusebius *H.E.* 1.12.2]) see it,

another disciple. On the attempts to exonerate Peter, see the Appendix 3, below; also Cullmann, *Peter*, 48f; Schlier, p. 82 n. 1. A curiosity is Hermann Grosch, *Der im Galaterbrief Kap. 2, 11–14 berichtete Vorgang in Antiochia: Eine Rechtfertigung des Verhaltens des Apostels Petrus* (Leipzig: Deichert, 1916).

443 What Paul did is explained in v 14. The verb ἀνθίστημι ("oppose") is originally a military and political term; see its connection with the exposure of "heretics" and "charlatans" (Acts 13 : 8; 2 Tim 3 : 8; for further passages, see Bauer, *s.v.*). The same is true for κατὰ πρόσωπον ("face to face"). See 2 Cor 10 : 1; Acts 25 : 16; etc. See Bauer, *s.v.*, 1, c, δ; Eduard Lohse, "φέρω (διαφέρω)," *TDNT* 6.769, 777; Mussner, p. 137 n. 15.

444 Again, the term comes from the political life. See Josephus *BJ* 2.135: "For they say that one who is not believed without an appeal to God stands condemned already" (ἤδη γὰρ κατεγνῶσθαι); Plutarch *Quaest. Rom.* 280E; *Alcib.* 22 (202F); Mauersberger, *Polybios–Lexikon*, 1295 *s.v.*; LSJ, *s.v.*, II; Bauer, *s.v.*; BDF, § 312, 1; BDR, § 312 n. 1. The *Kerygmata Petrou* (ps.–Clem. *Hom.* 17.19) explicitly cite the term (see Appendix 3, below).

finally (3), Paul gives his own reason for Cephas' change of conduct: "because he was afraid of the men of the circumcision" (v 12c). In other words, Cephas shifted his position, and this must have become one of the preconditions for the Galatians' own plans to shift (cf. 1:6–7).

The situation was this: after Cephas had come to Antioch, he agreed to have table fellowship with "the Gentiles" (τὰ ἔθνη),[445] i.e., Gentile Christians who, however, had also included Jewish Christians like Paul and Barnabas. In other words, Cephas had adopted the same way of life as Paul and Barnabas. To them this no doubt appeared natural, because it was understood to be the proper consequence of formulas like "neither Jew nor Greek" (3:28) or "roles" like those found in 6:15; 5:6. The imperfect form of συνήσθιεν[446] ("he ate with someone") suggests that he did so repeatedly and almost habitually.[447] Nothing is said whether these meals were ordinary meals,[448] or celebrations of the Lord's Supper,[449] or both.[450]

The point of concern is the Jewish purity requirements which must be observed whatever meals were involved. The issue at stake was not Cephas' breaking of fellowship by first participation in and subsequent withdrawal from the meal, but his shifting attitude with regard to the Jewish dietary and purity laws. In the beginning Cephas and the others had agreed that Christian Gentiles are non-Jews, but that because of their faith in Christ they are not to be regarded as "sinners out of the Gentiles" (cf. 2:15). For the conscientious Jew, therefore, they could not be regarded as impure. It must have been for this reason that Cephas ate with them.

Who the "men from James" were and what had caused them to travel to Antioch is a problem much discussed in New Testament scholarship.[451] Because they were his opponents, Paul does not give their names (cf. 1:7), but leaves them as "certain people" (τινές).[452] The readers know, and Paul knows, but there is no point in providing free advertisement! Were these "men from James" sent by James, the brother of the Lord,[453] or did they belong to a group that used his name (rightly or wrongly)?[454] Did they come from Jerusalem, or if not, from where did they come? What was the relationship between the "men from James"

445 By this term Paul refers to Gentile Christians; see also Gal 1:16; 2:14, 15–16; 3:8, 14; Rom 15:16; 16:4.

446 συνήσθιον ("they ate together") is clearly an "improvement" read by P[46].

447 So with Burton, Schlier, Mussner.

448 From the Jewish point of view, the issue is that of κοινοφαγία ("eating of unclean food"). See Josephus Ant. 11.346. For a discussion, see Jan N. Sevenster, The Roots of Pagan Anti-Semitism in the Ancient World (NovTSup 41; Leiden: Brill, 1975) 139. Cf. the Cornelius story (Acts 10:1–11:18), in the course of which (11:3) "those of the circumcision" (οἱ ἐκ περιτομῆς) raise criticism against Peter: "You went in with the uncircumcised and ate with them (συνέφαγες αὐτοῖς)." The whole story has the purpose of justifying Peter's action (cf. esp. 10:9–16). In the gospel tradition, συνεσθίω ("eat together with") and synonyms refer to Jesus' table fellowship with the "sinners and tax collectors" (Mark 2:16 par.; Luke 15:2, 30; 19:1–10) and with his disciples (Mark 14:14, 18, 20 par.; Matt 8:11; 24:49; Luke 7:36; John 12:2; 13:18). See also Pap. Egerton 2 (λεπροῖς . . . συνεσθίων ["eat with lepers"]); 1 Cor 5:11).

449 See Acts 10:41: "We ate together with him [sc.

450 See 1 Cor 11:20–34. This option is favored by Schlier, p. 83. He downgrades the "private meals," saying that there was no reason for Cephas to eat private meals with gentile Christians, while withdrawal from the eucharist was a denial and breaking up of the unity of the church. . . . See also Bornkamm, Paul, 45.

451 See Sieffert, pp. 127f; Oepke; Schmithals, Paul and James, 66ff; Mussner, pp. 139f; Jewett, "Agitators," 198–212.

452 τινα instead of τινας is read by P[46vid] it[d,r] Irenaeus; it is perhaps a scribal error. See Metzger, Textual Commentary, 592.

453 Obviously influenced by Acts, Schlier (p. 83) thinks that James may have sent them, but they were not "James' adherents." Schlier cannot imagine that James could initiate such official "visitations." Following Burton, Oepke, and others, Schlier believes that rumors had reached Jerusalem and James had sent the men out to get more information. This, however, could not have caused Cephas' "fear" (v 12c).

454 Cf. Schmithals, Paul and James, 66ff.

Christ] and drank together with him after his resurrection from the dead." See also Luke 24:30; John 21:13.

and the "false brothers" (2:4–5)?[455] Their actions are indeed parallel, but they must not be identical. Paul no doubt sets them up as people continuing the old opposition of the "false brothers."[456] It should be remembered that the "false brothers" at the Jerusalem conference did not approve of the agreements made there. But the "men from James" do approve and in fact insist on the carrying out of the agreements.

There is little reason to doubt that James himself was behind the "men from James." It is only because of Acts 15 that scholars have doubted this.[457] In the apostolic letter of Acts 15:24 there is a denial which must be regarded as "apologetic": "since we have heard that some persons from us [τινὲς ἐξ ἡμῶν] have disturbed you with words, confusing your souls, whom we did not instruct . . ." Why then would the historical James object to Cephas' eating with Christian Gentiles? Paul reports that, when the "men from James" came,[458] Cephas broke off the table fellowship with his Gentile–Christian brothers. This abrupt change must have been his reaction to demands made by the "men from James."[459]

The terminology used by Paul to describe the shift is highly polemical and is taken from the arsenal of military and political language. The verb ὑποστέλλω ("withdraw") occurs as a description of military and political maneuvers of retreating to an inconspicuous or sheltered position.[460] The term takes Cephas' move to have been a tactical maneuver: he had the same theological convictions as Paul, but he did not dare to express them.[461] This kind of double-dealing must have been part of Cephas' image, because in the anti-Pauline *Kerygmata Petrou* Peter explicitly defends himself against it.[462] The second verb is more concrete: ἀφορίζειν ἑαυτόν ("separate oneself") is a Jewish technical term describing cultic separation from the "unclean."[463] If Cephas' shift of position resulted in "separation," this must have been the demand made by the "men from James." If they made this demand, it was made because of their understanding of the implications of the Jerusalem agreement (cf. 2:7–9). The separation of the mission to the Jews from that to the Gentiles would imply that Peter would retain his Jewish way of life, and this included first of all the dietary and purity laws. As a result, cultic separation would have to be observed also during table fellowship with Gentile Christians. This was especially important in the diaspora, where defilement was most likely to occur.[464]

If we take this as a possible scenario of the situation, the "men from James" simply had insisted on the terms of the Jerusalem agreement. Their criticism must have been that Cephas had violated those

---

455 Schoeps (*Paul*, 67f, 74f) identifies "the false brothers" with "the men from James" and with the "ardent law–observers" of Acts 15:5. They are, in his view, the forerunners of the later Ebionites.

456 Cf. Schmithals, *Paul and James*, 67.

457 See on this passage the commentaries by Haenchen and Conzelmann.

458 ἦλθεν instead of ἦλθον is read by a number of good witnesses (P[46 vid] ℵ B D* 33 330 *al*), but the plural must be correct (A C D[c] H[vid] K P Ψ 81 614 *al*). See Metzger, *Textual Commentary*, 592f.

459 Against Schlier, pp. 84f; also Burton, p. 107.

460 The term can be used with or without ἑαυτόν. In this sense it is used only here in Paul. For the military and political usage, see passages in Polybius (1.16.10; 6.40.14; 7.17.1; 10.32.3; 11.21.2); Plutarch *Demetrius* 47, 912 E (with the "fear" motif); *Crassus* 23, 557D; 26, 559F; *Lucullus* 38, 518A; *Aratus* 47, 1049B; *Adulat.* 60C; Philo *Leg.* 71 and often. See LSJ, *s.v.*; Bauer, *s.v.*, 1; Karl Heinrich Rengstorf, "ὑποστέλλω," *TDNT* 7.597f.

461 Against Schlier, pp. 84f.

462 See Appendix 3, below.

463 The same meaning as here is found 2 Cor 6:14. See Appendix 2, below; and Betz, "2 Cor 6:14–7:1," 96. On cultic separation, see the passages in Bauer, *s.v.* ἀφορίζω; Karl Ludwig Schmidt, "ἀποδιορίζω," *TDNT* 5.455; Braun, *Radikalismus* 1.31 n. 1; idem, *Qumran* 1.202, 2.288f; Wilfried Paschen, *Rein und Unrein* (StANT 24; Munich: Kösel, 1970) 44; Jacob Neusner, *The Idea of Purity in Ancient Judaism* (SJLA; Leiden: Brill, 1973) 59 (on Paul); idem, *A History of the Mishnaic Law of Purities* (11 Vols.; SJLA 6.1–11; Leiden: Brill, 1974–76); Lawrence H. Schiffman, *The Halakhah at Qumran* (SJLA 16; Leiden: Brill, 1975) esp. 123f.

464 See esp. Acts 11:3 (cited n. 448, above). For the diaspora view, see esp. Dan 1:8ff; Esth 4:17x [14:17 vg] LXX; Tob 1:10, 11; *Jub.* 22.16; 3 Macc. 3:4; 7:11; Josephus *Ant.* 4.137; 13.243; etc.; Philo *Jos.* 202; *Jos. et As.* 7.1; see Edgar W. Smith, *Joseph and Aseneth and the Early Christian Literature* (Ph.D. Diss.;

terms.[465] Cephas then must have reached the conclusion that they were right in criticizing him, and he drew the logical consequences and withdrew. In Paul's view, of course, this step was disastrous. The reason which he attributes to Cephas in v 12c is phrased highly polemically: "he feared the Jews" (*φοβούμενος τοὺς ἐκ περιτομῆς*). In other words, Cephas did not act on the basis of his own theological convictions, but irrationally out of fear.[466] This judgment has caused much speculation. Why was Cephas afraid? Whom did he fear? What did he fear would happen if he did not yield? Whatever the answers may be, "fear" itself was an absurd motive in the eyes of Paul, and indeed a mark of the superstitious mind-set (cf. Rom 8:15; Gal 4:9–10). Yet in spite of the polemical rhetoric Paul may be right, because Acts (10:45; 11:2) reports that Peter was accused by Christian believers from Judaism (*οἱ ἐκ περιτομῆς πιστοί*). In Acts 16:3, Paul yields to Jewish (=Jewish–Christian?) pressure to circumcise Timothy (cf. on Gal 2:3–5). In sum, Cephas may have concluded that given the theological presuppositions of the Jewish Christians he was expected to represent,[467] his table fellowship was indefensible. In Paul's terms, Cephas "feared" the "political" consequences of losing his position of power. Peter chose the position of power and denied his theological convictions.[468]

■ **13** Another reason why Cephas' separation from the table of the Gentiles must have been based upon sound reasons is that "the other Jews" ([*καὶ*][469] *οἱ λοιποὶ Ἰουδαῖοι*) followed his example: "also the other Jews committed the same 'hypocrisy' with him, so that even Barnabas was carried away through their 'hypocrisy'." In describing this "victory"[470] of Cephas, Paul again uses highly polemical language. Most difficult is the phrase *συνυπεκρίθησαν αὐτῷ*, because it is almost impossible to translate.[471] Parallels in Greek literature, however, help to understand it. The backgronnd is most likely the political sphere. Polybius, in this context, makes an interesting observation about human nature: "for all men are given to adapt themselves and assume a character suited to the times, so that from their words and actions it is difficult to judge of the principles of each, and in many cases the truth is quite overcast."[472] In Paul's opinion, Cephas' action must

Claremont Graduate School, 1974) 92; Justin *Dial.* 47 (see Appendix 4, below). On the subject, see Bousset–Gressmann, *Religion*, 93f; Moore, *Judaism* 2.75; Str–B. 3.421f; 4.374ff.

465 Differently Schmithals (*Paul and James*, 65), who does not think that the table fellowship at Antioch violated the Torah and the agreements of 2:7–9; in the Jewish view, according to Schmithals, Peter had misused the meal, in order to start the full emancipation of Jewish Christianity.

466 Cullmann ("*Πέτρος*," *TDNT* 6.110) thinks this is what happened in reality. But John 7:13; 9:22; 19:38; 20:19; Acts 16:3, etc., show that the motive was common.

467 See terminologically Gal 2:7, 8, 9, 12; 5:6, 11; 6:15—all referring to Jewish Christians. Differently Bauer, *s.v.*; for Munck (*Paul*, 87ff) Paul has circumcised *Gentiles* in mind; cf. Bo Reicke, "Der geschichtliche Hintergrund des Apostelkonzils und der Antiochia–Episode, Gal. 2, 11–14," *Studia Paulina in honorem J. de Zwaan* (Haarlem: Bohn, 1953) 172–87, 176ff; Schmithals, *Paul and James*, 67f; Klein, *Rekonstruktion*, 83 n. 205; Mussner, pp. 141f.

468 Schlier (p. 84 n. 4.) rejects earlier attempts to exonerate Cephas, but he himself is not free from this either. Agreeing with Alphons Steinmann, he sees in "the men from James" dangerous propagandists who spread defamations against Peter, so that Peter's fear is well justified; Peter himself did not change his mind, but became uncertain whether his approach was practically feasible.

469 *καί* ("also") is read by many good witnesses (𝔊 𝔎 D G it sy *al*), but omitted in P^{46} B 1739 vg Origen. Cf. Burton, p. 109: "Neither external nor internal evidence is decisive. . . ."

470 See Benjamin W. Bacon, "Peter's Triumph at Antioch," *JR* 9 (1929) 204–23.

471 The term *συνυποκρίνομαι* is a *hapax legomenon* in the NT. LSJ, *s.v.* renders: "accommodate oneself by pretending." Bauer, *s.v.*: "join in pretending" or "playing a part," "join in playing the hypocrite" (with the dative of the person one joins). See also Ulrich Wilckens, "*ὑποκρίνομαι κτλ.*", *TDNT* 8.568f; *PGL*, *s.v.*, which points to Chrysostom's commentary on Gal 2:13.

472 Polybius 3.31.7: *πρὸς μὲν γὰρ τὸ παρὸν ἀεί πως ἁρμοζόμενοι καὶ συνυποκρινόμενοι τοιαῦτα καὶ λέγουσι καὶ πράττουσι πάντες ὥστε δυσθεώρητον εἶναι τὴν ἑκάστου προαίρεσιν καὶ λίαν ἐν πολλοῖς ἐπισκοτεῖσθαι τὴν ἀλήθειαν.* (tr. W. R. Paton, LCL). See also Polybius 3.52.6; 3.92.5; etc.; Plutarch *Marius* 14.8, 413A; 17.3, 415B; *Ep. Arist.* 267.

be understood in terms of political compromise, and the shift of "the other Jews"[473] as conformism. The other element in the term is that of "role-playing." Epictetus has a proverbial sentence which almost completely expresses what Paul wants to say: "for example, whenever we see a man halting between two faiths, we are in the habit of saying, 'He is not a Jew, he is only acting the part'." Such people he calls "ostensibly Jews, but in reality something else, not in sympathy with our [i.e., their] own reason, far from applying the principles which we [i.e., they] profess, yet priding . . . upon them as being men who know them."[474] When we apply this language to the situation in Antioch, Cephas' act of withdrawal was a case of ὑπόκρισις ("play-acting"). Moreover, taking the phrase συνυπεκρίθησαν αὐτῷ ("they committed the same hypocrisy with him") in this sense, it was an act of manipulation: Cephas managed to get "the other Jews" to join him in the withdrawal. Of course, this is the evaluation which Paul presents as part of his self-defense. It is highly subjective and polemical. In reality, "the other Jews" had simply arrived at the same conclusions as Cephas. They were not convinced by Paul's reasoning. Therefore, there is no reason for us today to condemn "the other Jews" as morally and spiritually corrupt. In v 13b, Paul is compelled to admit that Cephas' decision had caused even Barnabas,[475] his former mentor and companion, to go along with "the other Jews" rather than with him. Again, Paul's explanation is that this happened "through their 'hypocrisy'" (τῇ ὑποκρίσει). Barnabas was "carried away with them" (συναπήχθη). The verb συναπάγομαι τινί ("be carried away with someone") has a strong connotation of irrationality,[476] implying that Barnabas was carried away by emotions. Barnabas was thus a different case compared with Cephas and "the other Jews"; he did not manipulate, but was the victim of manipulation. The dative τῇ ὑποκρίσει is most likely a dative of instrumentality or modality.[477] It refers again to manipulative "role-playing" as well as theological inconsistency.[478] We can only speculate as to what rationale Barnabas had for joining the anti-Pauline group. Paul indicates that his position was not the same as the others' and that he must have hesitated before joining the Cephas party. The fact that a man like Barnabas decided against his former student and fellow worker Paul shows how difficult a question the Antioch meeting had to decide.

■ 14 Paul now turns to his own intervention[479] and the confrontation with Cephas.[480] First of all, he evaluates the situation created by the actions of the Jewish–Christian group led by Cephas: "however, when I saw that they did not act in consistency with the truth of the gospel . . . ." Paul presupposes that at some point had come to the conclusion that he had to intervene and to confront Cephas publicly. That

---

473 The expression "the other Jews" refers to other Jewish Christians at Antioch, men like Cephas, Barnabas, and Paul. Beyond these, does Paul refer to a Jewish Christian congregation or to other individuals like those mentioned by name? At any rate, these people must have been the same as those of v 12 ("those of the circumcision"). The term Ἰουδαῖος ("Jew") occurs in Gal only 2:13, 14, 15; 3:28, as the opposite of Ἕλλην ("Greek") as in Rom 1:16; 2:9, 10; 3:9; 10:12; 1 Cor 1:24; 10:32; 12:13; etc. See Walter Gutbrod, "Ἰσραήλ," TDNT 3; Paul Gaechter, Petrus und seine Zeit: Neutestamentliche Studien (Innsbruck: Tyrolia, 1958) 235; Mussner, p. 143 n. 39.

474 Epictetus Diss. 2.9.20: καὶ ὅταν τινὰ ἐπαμφοτερίζοντα ἴδωμεν, εἰώθαμεν λέγειν "οὐκ ἔστιν Ἰουδαῖος, ἀλλ' ὑποκρίνεται." 2.9.21: . . . λόγῳ μὲν Ἰουδαῖοι, ἔργῳ δὲ ἄλλο τι, ἀσυμπαθεῖς πρὸς τὸν λόγον, μακρὰν ἀπὸ τοῦ χρῆσθαι τούτοις ἃ λέγομεν, ἐφ' οἷς ὡς εἰδότες αὐτὰ ἐπαιρόμεθα (tr. Oldfather, LCL).

475 See Gal 2:1, 9. The reasons for conflict between Paul and Barnabas given here and in Acts 15:36–39 are completely different.

476 See 2 Pet 3:17; Rom 12:16; also Gal 5:18; Rom 8:14; 1 Cor 12:2. See LSJ, s.v.; Bauer, s.v.; PGL, s.v.

477 See Burton, p. 109; Schlier, p. 85 n. 1.

478 Wilckens ("ὑποκρίνομαι κτλ.," TDNT 8.563ff) points to the use of the term in diaspora Judaism, where ὑποκριτής is a rendering of חנף ("apostate"), describing someone who pretends orthopraxy. Cf. Schmithals (Paul and James, 71f) who points to ὀρθοποδέω ("walk straight") in 2:14.

479 ἀλλά ("but") indicates the turning point. Cf. Mussner, p. 143 n. 43.

480 Κηφᾷ ("to Cephas") is read by P⁴⁶ ℵ A B C H 33 88 al vg sy: cop^{sa,bo} arm eth, while the Textus Receptus, following D F G K L P, most minuscules, it^{d,g} vg^{mss} sy^h goth al read Πέτρῳ ("to Peter"). See on Gal 1:18, and Metzger, Textual Commentary, 593.

moment had come when Paul "saw" ($\epsilon\hat{\iota}\delta o\nu$)[481] that the course of action which the Jewish Christians around Cephas were about to take was inconsistent with what he perceived to be "the truth of the gospel."[482] The phrase $o\dot{\upsilon}\kappa\ \dot{o}\rho\theta o\pi o\delta o\hat{\upsilon}\sigma\iota\nu\ \pi\rho\dot{o}\varsigma\ \tau\dot{\eta}\nu\ \dot{a}\lambda\dot{\eta}\theta\epsilon\iota a\nu\ \tau o\hat{\upsilon}\ \epsilon\dot{\upsilon}a\gamma\gamma\epsilon\lambda\dot{\iota}o\upsilon$ presents difficulties especially because of the term $\dot{o}\rho\theta o\pi o\delta\dot{\epsilon}\omega$. In the present context, it describes "orthodoxy," or rather the lack of it.[483] The metaphor may come from colloquial language, for in some instances its contrast is $\chi\omega\lambda\epsilon\dot{\upsilon}\omega$ ("go lame").[484] It can mean "go straight toward a goal" or "proceed on the right road." In the present context, it is not a moral term, but describes "orthodoxy."[485]

The contrast with 2:4–5 is obvious: if Paul had yielded to the pressures of the "false brothers" at Jerusalem, he would have ended up in the same situation in which he now sees Cephas and his group. He did, however, withstand in Jerusalem, as they should have done now in Antioch. The same is, of course, true now of the Galatians (see 4:8–10). It also may have been the case that it was not clear to everybody what "the truth of the gospel" was, and that it had to be progressively comprehended.[486] On the other hand, since they all "knew" (see 2:15–16)[487] the doctrinal principles which should determine their decisions, the

outcome should have been clear. Yet obviously the situation was confused. Paul then decided to confront Cephas, the leader of the new Cephas party, "before all" ($\check{\epsilon}\mu\pi\rho o\sigma\theta\epsilon\nu\ \pi\acute{a}\nu\tau\omega\nu$). This occasion must have been a kind of plenary assembly, perhaps parallel to the one in Jerusalem (2:2).[488] Was this assembly called together for this special purpose? Or was it in session at that time? Did it include all members of one church, or the members of a Gentile–Christian and a Jewish–Christian church? We do not know. The impression one gets is that there was only one congregation within which different parties were debating issues. What happened after the meeting? Did the church continue to exist in the same way, did it break up into two churches, or was Paul forced out like the "false brothers" at Jerusalem (2:4–5)? The high regard for Paul in Acts and in the letters of Ignatius, the bishop of Antioch, is difficult to understand if such an expulsion should have occurred.

Paul's objection against Cephas is formulated as a dilemma in the form of a question: it states Cephas' situation as one of self-contradiction.[489] It is obvious that this dilemma is Paul's own evaluation. Also interesting is the literary formulation.[490] "If you, being a Jew, live like a Gentile and not like a Jew, how can you

---

481 See the parallel in 2:7.

482 See this concept as used in 2:5; cf. also 5:7.

483 The term is a NT *hapax legomenon*. See George D. Kilpatrick, "Gal 2:14 $\dot{o}\rho\theta o\pi o\delta o\hat{\upsilon}\sigma\iota\nu$," *Neutestamentliche Studien für Rudolf Bultmann* (BZNW 21; Berlin: Töpelmann, 1957) 269–74; Bauer, *s.v.*; idem, *Orthodoxy and Heresy*, 63, 114f, 263f, 312; Hans Dieter Betz, "Orthodoxy and Heresy in Primitive Christianity," *Int* 19 (1965) 299–311, 305–08. Cf. the parallel in Qumran (1QH 7.14): "directing my steps into the paths of righteousness" (פעמי לנתיבות לישר צדקה). Similar is 2 Tim 2:15: $\dot{o}\rho\theta o\tau o\mu o\hat{\upsilon}\nu\tau a\ \tau\dot{o}\nu\ \lambda\acute{o}\gamma o\nu\ \tau\hat{\eta}\varsigma\ \dot{a}\lambda\eta\theta\epsilon\dot{\iota}a\varsigma$ (Bauer: "guide the word of truth along a straight path").

484 Apart from Kilpatrick (see previous n.), see Charles H. Roberts, "A Note on Galatians 2:14," *JTS* 40 (1939) 55f; John G. Winter, "Another Instance of $\dot{o}\rho\theta o\pi o\delta\epsilon\hat{\iota}\nu$," *HTR* 34 (1941) 161f; LSJ, *s.v.*; Suppl., *s.v.*; Herbert Preisker, "$\dot{o}\rho\theta o\pi o\delta\dot{\epsilon}\omega$," *TDNT* 5.451; *PGL*, *s.v.*; Mussner, p. 144.

485 For a different assessment, see Schlier (pp. 85f) who wants to reduce the confrontation to a merely personal disagreement between Cephas and Paul; both agree on the principles, and only disagree on strat-

egy. Schlier defends Paul by saying: "Within the church there is no silent deed and, strictly speaking, no deed which is an adiaphoron" (p. 85).

486 See Bauer, *s.v.* $\dot{o}\rho\theta o\pi o\delta\dot{\epsilon}\omega$.

487 So with Mussner, p. 144.

488 See on 2:2; also 1 Cor 11:18, 20; 14:23; 1 Tim 5:20; Ign. *Phld.* 7–8. Cf. also the *Moshab ha-rabbim* at Qumran, for which see Edmund F. Sutcliffe, "The General Council of the Qumran Community," *Bib* 40 (1959) 971–83; Lawrence H. Schiffman, *The Halakhah at Qumran* (SJLA 16; Leiden: Brill, 1975) 68ff.

489 For parallels, see Gal 3:3; 4:9. Paul himself guards against such a possibility in 1 Cor 9:27: "that I do not preach to others and become corrupted myself." Cf. also 2 Cor 13:5–7; Gal 5:26; 6:1–10; Jas 1:22f; Tit 1:16; Matt 23:3–4; etc. See also Betz, *Lukian*, 114f; idem, *Paulus*, passim.

490 Technically, it is a quotation of himself. On the dilemma as a literary form see n. 66 above. Similar questions, introduced by $\pi\hat{\omega}\varsigma$ ("how") occur Gal 4:9; Rom 10:14, 15; 1 Cor 15:12; Matt 12:34; 22:12; John 3:4; 4:9; 7:15; 9:16.

compel the Gentiles to live like Jews?" The implied answer is, of course, that Cephas cannot do that. In the protasis Paul defines Cephas' present religious status as being a Jew ('Ιουδαῖος ὑπάρχων)[491] who has given up his Jewish way of life. He lives like a Gentile (ἐθνικῶς),[492] that is, no longer in observati on of Jewish customs and law (οὐκ Ἰουδαϊκῶς).[493] The present tense of ζῇς ("you are living") implies much more than an act of table fellowship with Christian Gentiles.[494] It suggests that the table fellowship was only the external symbol of Cephas' total emancipation from Judaism. The apodosis presupposes Cephas' recent change of conduct as a self-contradiction: "how can you compel the Gentiles to live like Jews?"

This formulation, however, presents several problems. In itself, the dilemma does not expressly state Cephas' return to Judaism, nor are we prepared for Cephas' demand that the Gentiles submit to circumcision and Jewish law.[495] Paul's evaluation was made *post factum* and assumes a number of intermediate considerations. By changing back to the observance of Jewish custom and law, the Jewish Christians have not only reversed their emancipation from Judaism. When they gave up the observance of the Torah, they also admitted that as a Christian one can be saved without the Torah. Returning to the Torah cannot simply eliminate that first step of denying the necessity of Torah observance. In addition, the return to the observance of the Torah expresses the judgment that living outside the Torah even for Christians is the same as living like "sinners from the heathen" (see 2:15-16). Therefore, Cephas had explicitly or implicitly made a demand upon the Gentiles to become partakers of the Torah covenant. In effect, Cephas had done the same as the "false brothers" at Jerusalem (2:4-5). The term "compel" (ἀναγκάζω)[496] must be seen in parallelism with 2:3, the demand to circumcise Titus, and the demand of the present agitators in Galatia to accept Torah and circumcision (see 6:13). In Paul's view, ιουδαΐζειν ("judaize")[497] includes more than submitting to Jewish dietary laws; it describes forcing one to become a Jewish convert obliged to keep the whole Torah (cf. 5:3). Ironically, therefore, by attempting to preserve the integrity of the Jewish Christians as Jews, Cephas destroys the integrity of the Gentile Christians as believers in Christ. Instead of welcoming them as converts to Christianity, he wants to make them into converts of Judaism. This contradicts the principles of the doctrine of justification by faith, which had been the basis of the faith thus far (see 2:15-16).

491 See also Gal 2:13, 15; Rom 11:1; 2 Cor 11:22; Phil 3:5. On ὑπάρχων cf. Bauer, *s.v.* ὑπάρχω, 2.

492 The term is a *hapax legomenon* in the NT. Cf. the adjective ἐθνικός Matt 5:47; 6:7; 18:17; 3 John 7. See Bauer, *s.v.* ἐθνικός, ἐθνικῶς; Karl Ludwig Schmidt, *TDNT* 2.72, *s.v.*; *PGL, s.v.*

493 The words καὶ οὐκ Ἰουδαϊκῶς ζῇς are textually uncertain: ℵ D vg^{cl}, have another word-order; P[46] 917 d Ambrosiaster Marius Victorinus omit the first three words; a minor matter is the change between οὐκ, οὐχ or οὐχί. For a detailed discussion see Sieffert, pp. 133f n.; Burton, pp. 114f. The adverb ιουδαϊκῶς ("according to Jewish custom") is a NT *hapax legomenon*. See Bauer, *s.v.*; Walter Gutbrod, "'Ισραήλ," *TDNT* 3.381; *PGL, s.v.*

494 So correctly Burton, p. 112; Schlier, p. 86.

495 See Lagrange; Schlier, p. 86 n. 6.; Mussner, p. 145 n. 52.

496 In Maccabees the term plays a significant role in the Jewish struggle against compulsory hellenization (cf. e.g., 1 Macc 2:25; 2 Macc 6:1, 7, 18; 4 Macc 5:2, 27; 8:1; 18:5; Josephus *BJ* 1.34; etc.; Philo *Leg.* 293). See also Justin *Dial.* 47.1 (see Appendix 4).

497 The term is a *hapax legomenon* in the NT; it is not quite synonymous with ιουδαϊκῶς ζῆν ("live as a Jew"), but it seems to describe the somewhat artificial behavior of new converts. Cf. Esth 8:17 LXX: "... and many of the people had themselves circumcised and practiced Judaism because of their fear of the Jews" (καὶ πολλοὶ τῶν ἐθνῶν περιετέμνοντο ιουδάϊζον διὰ τὸν φόβον τῶν Ἰουδαίων). According to Josephus *BJ* 2.454, the Roman officer Metilius saved his life by promising to become a Jew and even to submit to circumcision (καὶ μέχρι περιτομῆς ιουδαΐσειν). Josephus *BJ* 2.463, seems to distinguish between οἱ ιουδαΐζοντες ("the Judaizers") and οἱ Ἰουδαῖοι ("the Jews"); similarly, the term is used by Plutarch *Cicero* 7.5, 864C, of a freedman who is suspected of practicing Judaism. In Christian literature, the term characterizes Christians engaged in Jewish practices, e.g., Ign. *Mag.* 10.3: "It is absurd to say 'Jesus Christ' and to practice Judaism" (ἄτοπόν ἐστιν, Ἰησοῦν Χριστὸν λαλεῖν καὶ ιουδαΐζειν). For further material, see *PGL, s.v.*

2

15 We who are Jews by birth and not sinners from [the] Gentiles[1] know that a human being[1] is not justified by works of [the] Law but [only] through faith in Christ Jesus. So we also have come to believe in Christ Jesus, in order that we might be justified by faith in Christ and not by works of the Law,[2] since it is not by works of [the] Law that all flesh will be justified.[3]
17/ If, however, we who are seeking to be justified in Christ are also found to be sinners, is Christ then a servant of sin? This can never be!
18/ For [only] if I establish again what I have dissolved, [do] I set myself up[4] as a transgressor.
19/ For through [the] Law I died to [the] Law, in order that I might live for God. I have been crucified with Christ;
20/ and, it is no longer I who live, but Christ lives in me; and, what[5] I now live in [the] flesh I live in [the] faith in the Son of God who loved me and gave himself up for me.
21/ I do not nullify the grace of God. For [only] if justification [came] through [the] Law has Christ died in vain.

Analysis

Since antiquity the question has been discussed whether Paul's account of the episode at Antioch ends with 2:14, or whether it includes 2:15–21 as a summary of the speech he made at Antioch.[6] Those who assume that 2:14–21 is a restatement of what Paul had said to Cephas and the church at Antioch have also discussed the question whether it is historically accurate, a summary, a free paraphrase, or simply an invention for rhetorical purposes. Otto Bauernfeind[7] called attention to the need to consider the literary form, which he thought was that of a "report about a speech" ("*Redereferat*"). In present New Testament scholarship the whole question is unresolved. Most scholars take a

1 *RSV, NEB, JB* render ἄνθρωπος ("a human being") as "man."
2 *NEB* is slightly misleading: ". . . not through deeds dictated by law."
3 Usually translations turn the sentence positive: "because of works of the law shall no one be justified" (*RSV*).
4 Cf. *RSV*: "prove myself;" *NEB*: "show myself up." *JB* here as well as in the entire passage has a very free but, as far as the meaning is concerned, correct paraphrase.
5 *RSV, NEB, JB* supplement: "the life I now live. . . ."
6 On the positions taken by older commentators, see Friedrich Zimmer, "Paulus gegen Petrus," *ZWTh* 25 (1882) 129–88; Sieffert, pp. 139f; Zahn, pp. 119f; Franz Overbeck, *Über die Auffassung des Streits des Paulus mit Petrus in Antiochen (Gal. 2, 11ff) bei den Kirchenvätern* (Basel 1877; rep.: Darmstadt: Wissenschaftliche Buchgesellschaft, 1968). For modern positions see the commentaries, and Otto Bauernfeind, "Der Schluss der antiochenischen Paulusrede," in *Theologie als Glaubenswagnis, Festschrift für Karl Heim* (Hamburg: Furche–Verlag, 1954) 64–78; Rudolf Bultmann, "Zur Auslegung von Galater 2:15–18," in his *Exegetica*, 394–99; Gaechter, *Petrus und seine Zeit*, 251–54; Schmithals, *Paul and James*, 72–78; Klein, *Rekonstruktion*, 181–202; Werner Georg Kümmel, "'Individualgeschichte' und 'Weltgeschichte' in Galater 2, 15–21," in *Christ and Spirit in the New Testament, In Honour of C. F. D. Moule* (eds. Barnabas Lindars and Stephen S. Smalley; Cambridge: Cambridge University, 1973) 157–73.
7 Bauernfeind (see n. 6 above), 71.

middle position, saying that Paul addresses Cephas formally, and the Galatians materially.[8]

Between the *narratio* and the *probatio*[9] ancient rhetoricians insert the *propositio* (the name Quintilian uses).[10] Quintilian has the fullest account of this part of the speech, but again he takes a special position in applying it. We find the general view in the *Rhetorica ad Herennium* and in Cicero's *De inventione*, although there is also considerable difference between them. The *Rhetorica ad Herennium* provides for two kinds of statements after the *narratio*: "the division of the cause falls into two parts. When the statement of facts has been brought to an end, we ought first to make clear what we and our opponents agree upon, if there is agreement on the points useful to us, and what remains contested...."[11] Then comes the *distributio* in two parts, the *enumeratio* and the *expositio*, the former announcing the number of points to be discussed, the latter setting forth these points briefly and completely.[12] The function of the *propositio* is two-fold: it sums up the legal content of the *narratio* by this outline of the case and provides an easy transition to the *probatio*.[13]

Gal 2:15–21 conforms to the form, function, and requirements of the *propositio*. Placed at the end of the last episode of the *narratio* (2:11–14), it sums up the *narratio's* material content. But it is not part of the *narratio*,[14] and it sets up the arguments to be discussed later in the *probatio* (chapters 3 and 4).[15] The points of presumed agreement are set forth first (2:15–16). This passage is a summary of the doctrine of justification by faith. It is thoroughly Pauline, but Paul's claim that he shares this doctrine with Jewish Christianity should be taken seriously. The summary is made to appear as the logical conclusion one would draw from the *narratio* as a whole. Verses 17–18 contain the point of disagreement. Here especially, language from the opposition is borrowed. Verses 19–20 contain the exposition in form of four theological theses, to be elaborated upon later. Verse 21 concludes with a *refutatio*, a sharp denial of a charge.[16] Paul does not use *partitio* or *enumeratio* because there is only one[17] point against which the whole defense has to be made (2:17).[18] The *propositio* is extremely concise and consists largely of dogmatic abbreviations, i.e., very short formulaic summaries of doctrines.

---

8 So Oepke; Lietzmann; Lightfoot; Burton; Schlier, pp. 87f, 104.

9 See above, on Gal 3:1–4:31, and the Introduction, § 5.

10 Quint. treats the forms and possibilities of the *propositio* in 4.4.1–4.5.28 (see also 3.9.2, 5; 3.11.27). See Cicero *De inv.* 1.22.31–23.33, who calls it *partitio*, while the *Rhet. ad Her.* 1.10.17 uses *divisio*. See Volkmann, *Rhetorik*, § 15; Lausberg, *Handbuch*, § 346; Joachim Adamietz, *Ciceros de inventione und die Rhetorik ad Herennium* (Marburg: Mauersberger, 1960) 36ff; Martin, *Rhetorik*, 91–95.

11 *Rhet. ad Her.* 1.10.17: "Causarum divisio in duas partes distributa est. Primum perorata narratione debemus aperire quid nobis conveniat cum adversariis, si ea quae utilia sunt nobis convenient, quid in controversia relictum sit. . . ." Cf. Cicero *De inv.* 1.22.31.

12 The *propositio* should have the following characteristics: *brevitas, absolutio, paucitas* ("brevity, completeness, conciseness"). So Cicero *De inv.* 1.22.32; similarly *Rhet. ad Her.* 1.10.17; Quint. 4.5.26–28. See Lausberg, *Handbuch*, § 671, 1; Martin, *Rhetorik*, 94.

13 Quint. 4.4.1: "Mihi autem propositio videtur omnis confirmationis initium, quod non modo in ostendenda quaestione principali sed nonnunquam etiam in singulis argumentis poni solet . . ." ("But it seems to me that the beginning of every *proof* is a *proposition*, such as often occurs in the demonstration of the main question and sometimes even in the enunciation of individual arguments . . ."). See Lausberg, *Handbuch*, § 343–45.

14 This formal argument would then also decide the old controversy whether or not vv 15–21 must be regarded as part of Paul's speech at Antioch. See above, n. 6.

15 This was recognized, without the formal considerations, by Schlier, pp. 87f.

16 For examples of such refutations in a *propositio*, see Quint. 4.4.6–8; 4.5.11–13. Cf. the connections with the *exordium* (1:6f), and the *recapitulatio* (6:12–16).

17 See Quint. 4.5.8: "Itaque si plura vel obiicienda sunt vel diluenda, et utilis et iucunda partitio est ut, quid quaque de re dicturi simus, ordine appareat; at si unum crimen varie defendemus, supervacua." ("Consequently if we have to prove or refute a number of points *partition* will be both useful and attractive, since it will indicate in order what we propose to say on each subject. On the other hand, if we are defending one point on various grounds *partition* will be unnecessary"). See Lausberg, *Handbuch*, § 347.

18 See below, on 2:17.

Interpretation

■ **15** Paul begins the *propositio* by stating what he assumes is common ground between him and Jewish Christianity. He sets forth a "self-definition" of Jewish Christians,[19] beginning by considering them, including Paul himself,[20] as Jews:[21] "we who are Jews by birth." Here Jewishness is determined by birth.[22] This also separates the Jews from the Gentiles[23] who are called in Jewish terms "sinners from [the] Gentiles." At this point we find the first of Paul's doctrinal abbreviations: the expression "sinners from [the] Gentiles"[24] presupposes the Jewish concept of human sinfulness,[25] according to which sinners within Judaism must be distinguished from sinners who come from the non-Jewish population and who wish to partake of salvation.[26] Jews commit sins when they transgress the Torah, and they can obtain forgiveness by various cultic means or by vicarious suffering, that is, by the Torah. Gentiles, however, are "sinners" as Gentiles, and outside of the Torah covenant there is no salvation.[27]

■ **16** The second part of the "self-definition" defines the status before God which Jewish Christians claim as Christians. This part contains what is traditionally called Paul's doctrine of justification by faith: "(we) know that a human being is not justified by works of [the] Law but only through faith in Christ Jesus." There are two important considerations which one must bear in mind when one approaches this famous doctrine. First of all, in this context the doctrine of justification by faith is part of a Jewish-Christian theology.[28] It is based upon the self-definition of Jewish Christians as Jews (see v 15), and v 16 is an addition to what is stated in v 15.[29]

The second consideration relates to the entire *propositio* and other parts of the letter: it is composed of a great deal of doctrinal "abbreviations." These abbreviations are difficult to translate. Commenting upon them means that they must be dissolved into the doctrinal statements which they intend to abbreviate (see the Introduction, §6. 4).

---

19 Cf. the self-definition 2 Cor 6:16b: "For we are the temple of the living God." See Appendix 2, below; also Betz, "2 Cor 6:14–7:1," 92. See also Rom 2:17ff; 3:1ff; 9:4f; Phil 3:5f. Cf. Oepke (p. 58) who emphasizes the "thetical" character of the statement; Schlier (p. 88) believes it to be a *captatio benevolentiae*.

20 The "we" (ἡμεῖς) which we find in vv 15–17 includes all Jewish Christians. Cf. Oepke, Schlier.

21 Ἰουδαῖοι ("Jews"); see on 2:13, 14; 3:28.

22 On the meaning of φύσει see Rom 2:27; Eph 2:3; also Gal 1:13f. See Bauer, *s.v.* φύσις, 1; Helmut Koester, "φύσις κτλ.," *TDNT* 9.272; Schlier, p. 88 n. 2.

23 See Gal 1:16; 2:2, 8, 9, 12, 14; 3:8, 14 for other occurrences of τὰ ἔθνη ("the Gentiles"), a name which of course includes the Galatian churches.

24 The phrase ἐξ ἐθνῶν ("from [the] Gentiles") also occurs Rom 9:24; 2 Cor 11:26.

25 The concept of sin here is Jewish. See Str-B. 3.537. The reason why the Gentiles are sinners is that they do not possess the Torah (cf. Rom 2:14) and that because of this defect they cannot achieve righteousness (cf. Rom 9:30, 31; 3:1f; 1 Cor 6:1; 9:21; 12:2; 1 Thess 1:9f; 4:5; Phil 3:6). See also Str-B. 3.36ff; Lightfoot, p. 115; Oepke, p. 90; Schlier, pp. 88f; Karl Heinrich Rengstorf, "ἁμαρτωλός," *TDNT* 1.332–33; differently Burton, p. 119. For Paul's own concept, see Rom 5:12ff and Walter Grundmann, "ἁμαρτάνω," *TDNT* 1.308–13.

26 Cf. the term "judaize" in Gal 2:14.

27 2 Macc 6:12–17 states the Jewish position with regard to the sinfulness of Jews in distinction to non-Jews. The sins of the Gentiles are punished with the goal of destruction (πρὸς ὄλεθρον), while Jewish sinners are merely disciplined (πρὸς παιδείαν).

28 The doctrine of justification by faith was not only a doctrine of Paul, but was to an extent shared by Jewish Christianity. Reflections of non-Pauline, Jewish-Christian presentations of the doctrine are to be found in Jas 2:14–26; ps.-Clem. *Hom.* 8.5–7; probably also Heb and Justin *Dial.* 116. See also Rom 3:21–31; Acts 15:10f; Matt 12:37; Luke 15:11–32; 16:15; 18:11–14; Acts 13:39; Justin *Dial.* 46.1; 47.1 (see below, Appendix 4). See Georg Strecker, "Befreiung und Rechtfertigung. Zur Stellung der Rechtfertigungslehre in der Theologie des Paulus," in *Rechtfertigung, Festschrift für Ernst Käsemann zum 70. Geburtstag* (Tübingen: Mohr, Siebeck; Göttingen: Vandenhoeck & Ruprecht, 1976) 479–508.

29 δέ points to the contrast between φύσει ("by birth" v 15) and εἰδότες ("we know" v 16). It is not attested by P^{46} A 𝔎 *al* syr. Nestle-Aland, 26th edition, doubts its authenticity. See also Sieffert, p. 142 n.

The first word of v 16 states the basis for being a Christian in distinction from being a Jew. This basis is "theological conviction" ($\epsilon i\delta \acute{o}\tau\epsilon\varsigma$ ["we know"])[30] over against birth (v 15).

Next we are given the content of that conviction, again in the form of doctrinal principles. It is the denial of the orthodox Jewish (Pharisaic) doctrine of salvation.[31] This doctrine states that $\mathring{a}\nu\theta\rho\omega\pi\sigma\varsigma$ ("a [=any] human being")[32] is in need of $\delta\iota\kappa\alpha\iota o\mathring{v}\sigma\theta\alpha\iota$ ("being justified")[33] at the eschatological judgment of God, and that this "justification" can be obtained by doing and thus fulfilling the ordinances of the Torah).[34] This is the full meaning of the abbreviation $\mathring{\epsilon}\xi\,\mathring{\epsilon}\rho\gamma\omega\nu\,\nu\acute{o}\mu\sigma\upsilon$ ("on the basis of [the] works of [the] Torah").[35] This Jewish (Pharisaic) doctrine is denied by Paul (as he assumes, in conformity with Jewish Christianity).[36] Instead,

---

30   See the use of this concept in Gal. 4:8, 13; Rom 2:2; 3:19; 5:3; 6:9, 16; 7:15; etc. See Justin *Dial.* 46.20 (see below, Appendix 4). For the relationship of "faith" and "knowledge" in Paul's theology, see Wilhelm Mundle, *Der Glaubensbegriff bei Paulus* (Leipzig: Heinsius, 1932) 18f; Bultmann, *Theology*, § 36, 2; Günther Bornkamm, "Glaube und Vernunft bei Paulus," in his *Studien*, 119–37; idem, "Faith and Reason in Paul," in his *Early Christian Experience* (tr. Paul L. Hammer; London: SCM; New York: Harper & Row, 1969) 29–46.

31   Principle formulations of a similar kind are to be found also in Rom 3:20: $\mathring{\epsilon}\xi\,\mathring{\epsilon}\rho\gamma\omega\nu\,\nu\acute{o}\mu\sigma\upsilon\,o\mathring{v}\,\delta\iota\kappa\alpha\iota\omega\theta\acute{\eta}\sigma\epsilon\tau\alpha\iota\,\pi\mathring{a}\sigma\alpha\,\sigma\mathring{a}\rho\xi\,\mathring{\epsilon}\nu\acute{\omega}\pi\iota\sigma\nu\,\alpha\mathring{v}\tau o\mathring{v}$ ("by works of [the] law all flesh will not be justified before him"). Gal 3:11: $\mathring{\epsilon}\nu\,\nu\acute{o}\mu\omega\,o\mathring{v}\delta\epsilon\mathring{\iota}\varsigma\,\delta\iota\kappa\alpha\iota o\mathring{v}\tau\alpha\iota\,\pi\alpha\rho\mathring{a}\,\tau\mathring{\omega}\,\theta\epsilon\mathring{\omega}$ ("by [the] law nobody is justified before God"). For similar statements see Rom 3:28; 4:5; 10:5f; 11:6; Phil 3:6–9. Cf. Gal 2:21; 5:4; and contrast Jas 2:24–26.

32   For the meaning of $\mathring{a}\nu\theta\rho\omega\pi\sigma\varsigma$ ("human being") see Gal 1:1, 10, 11, 12; 2:6, 16; 3:15; 5:3; 6:1, 7.

33   In Gal the verb $\delta\iota\kappa\alpha\iota\acute{o}\omega$ ("justify") is found also in 2:17; 3:8, 11, 24; 5:4; cf. Rom 2:13; 3:4, 20, 24, 26, 28, 30; 4:2, 5; 5:1, 9; 6:7; 8:30, 33; 1 Cor 6:11. See J. A. Ziesler, *The Meaning of Righteousness in Paul* (SNTSMS 20; Cambridge: Cambridge University, 1972) esp. 172–74.

    The noun $\delta\iota\kappa\alpha\iota o\sigma\acute{v}\nu\eta$ ("righteousness") occurs in Gal 2:21; 3:6, 21; 5:5; Rom 1:17; 3:5, 21, 22, 26, and often. The literature is vast: see Gottlob Schrenk, "$\delta\iota\kappa\alpha\iota o\sigma\acute{v}\nu\eta$," *TDNT* 2.202–10; Bultmann, *Theology*, §§ 28–30; Conzelmann, *Outline*, § 25 (II); Peter Stuhlmacher, *Gerechtigkeit Gottes bei Paulus* (FRLANT 87; Göttingen: Vandenhoeck & Ruprecht, 1965); Karl Kertelge, *"Rechtfertigung" bei Paulus* (NTAbh NF 3; Münster: Aschendorff, 1967); idem, "Zur Deutung des Rechtfertigungsbegriffs im Galaterbrief," *BZ* 12 (1968) 211–22; Hans Conzelmann, *Theologie als Schriftauslegung: Aufsätze zum Neuen Testament* (Munich: Kaiser, 1974) 200ff; Dieter Zeller, *Juden und Heiden in der Mission des Paulus* (Forschung zur Bibel, 1; Stuttgart: Katholisches Bibelwerk, 1973) 163ff; Günter

Klein, "Gerechtigkeit Gottes als Thema der neuesten Paulusforschung," *VF* 12 (1967) 1–11; Georg Eichholz, *Glaube und Werk bei Paulus und Jakobus* (Munich: Kaiser, 1961) 215–36; Herman Ridderbos, *Paul: An Outline of His Theology* (tr. John R. de Witt; Grand Rapids: Eerdmans, 1975) 159–81; Ernst Käsemann, *Perspectives on Paul* (tr. Margaret Kohl; Philadelphia: Fortress, 1971) *passim*; idem, *An die Römer* (HNT 8a; Tübingen: Mohr, Siebeck, 1973, ³1974) esp. 18ff. The *Käsemann Festschrift* contains a number of articles dealing with a wide range of implications of the doctrine: *Rechtfertigung, Festschrift für Ernst Käsemann zum 70. Geburtstag* (ed. Johannes Friedrich, *et al.*; Tübingen: Mohr, Siebeck; Göttingen: Vandenhoeck & Ruprecht, 1976).

34   On the doctrine of justification in Rabbinic theology, see Str–B 3.160–64; Ferdinand Weber, *Jüdische Theologie auf Grund des Talmud und Verwandter Schriften* (eds. Franz Delitsch and Georg Schredermann; Leipzig: Dörffling, ²1897) §§ 55–72; Solomon Schechter, *Aspects of Rabbinic Theology* (New York: Schocken, 1961 [rep. of the 1909 edition]); Moore, *Judaism* 1.445ff, 2.180; Schoeps, *Paul*, 168ff.

35   This abbreviation occurs only in Pauline theology (Gal 2:16; 3:2, 5, 10; Rom 3:20; 4:2; 9:11f, 32; 11:6; for the Pauline tradition, see Eph 2:9; Tit 3:5; Pol. *Phil.* 1.13). On the notion of "works of the Torah" see Str–B 3.160–62; Georg Bertram, "$\mathring{\epsilon}\rho\gamma\sigma\nu$," *TDNT* 2.643–48; Ernst Lohmeyer, "Gesetzeswerke," in his *Probleme paulinischer Theologie* (Stuttgart: Kohlhammer, n.d.) 31–74; Schlier, pp. 91f; Joseph B. Tyson, " 'Works of Law' in Galatians," *JBL* 92 (1973) 423–31. On Paul's understanding of $\nu\acute{o}\mu\sigma\varsigma$ ("law"), see 3:19–25.

36   Also implicitly anti–Pharisaic is the Jewish–Christian doctrine of works and faith in James (see esp. Jas 2:14–26). See Martin Dibelius, *James: A Commentary on the Epistle of James* (rev. Heinrich Greeven, tr. Michael A. Williams; Hermeneia; Philadelphia: Fortress, 1976) 149–80; Franz Mussner, *Der Jakobusbrief* (HThK 13.1; Freiburg: Herder, ²1967) 127–57. The same is true in a different way of the Qumran community, which has a doctrine of justification by grace remarkably similar to Paul. See Her-

justification before God can be obtained[37] "only" (ἐὰν μή)[38]—and now follows another abbreviation— "through [the] faith of [= in] Christ Jesus." This abbreviation must be old, and it is easy to interpret it in pre-Pauline, Jewish-Christian terms. "Faith" is not "the basis" like meritorious works of the Torah[39] which then "earn" eschatological justification, but such justification is mediated "through [the] faith" (διὰ πίστεως).[40] This "faith"[41] has a distinct content: it is πίστις Ἰησοῦ Χριστοῦ ("[the] faith of [= in] Christ Jesus").[42] Also this strange abbreviation must be dissolved: it is the faith (*fides quae creditur*) the content of which is "Christ Jesus," or better: "The Christ is Jesus." This abbreviation seems to be old and retains the character of Χριστός as a messianic title.[43] Believing (*fides qua creditur*) that the Messiah is Jesus becomes the channel which mediates "justification" before the throne of God, instead of "doing" the works of the Torah. This understanding, to be sure, would be pre-Pauline. For the Apostle, "faith in Christ Jesus" is faith in the crucifixion and resurrection of Christ (see

Gal 1:1, 4; 2:20; 3:1, 13; 4:4–6), that is, "being in Christ" (see Gal 2:19–21; 3:26–28; 5:5–6, 24; 6:14). In view of the controversy in Galatia, it should be noted that the denial does not imply that "the works of the Torah" do not need to be done. Denied is only that they produce justification before God.

For the Jewish Christians, this "theological conviction" has had consequences. It was the reason why Jews had come to believe in Christ (v 16b). Paul of course refers to the fact that all Jewish Christians, including himself, had at one point become Christian believers: "also we have come to believe in Christ Jesus." The reason was—Paul now applies the previous statement—"in order that we might be justified by faith in Christ and not by works of [the] Law."[44] Paul uses the same doctrinal abbreviations as in the beginning of v 16, but the shift towards polemic is obvious. The phrase ἡμεῖς εἰς Χριστὸν Ἰησοῦν ἐπιστεύσαμεν ("we have come to believe in Christ Jesus") interprets the genitive in the previous phrase "[the] faith of Christ Jesus" (πίστις Ἰησοῦ Χριστοῦ). This interpreta-

bert Braun, "Römer 7, 7–25 und das Selbstverständnis des Qumranfrommen," in his *Studien*, 100–19; Siegfried Schulz, "Zur Rechtfertigung aus Gnaden in Qumran und bei Paulus," *ZThK* 56 (1959) 155–85; Kertelge, "*Rechtfertigung*," § 3; Ziesler, *Righteousness*, 93ff; Otto Betz, "Rechtfertigung in Qumran," in the *Käsemann Festschrift* (see above, n. 33) 17–36. A special problem is that of the relationship between the Pauline doctrine and the OT: see D. H. van Daalen, "Paul's Doctrine of Justification and its OT Roots," *Studia Evangelica* 6 (TU 112; Berlin: Akademie–Verlag, 1973) 556–70; Rafael Gyllenberg, *Rechtfertigung und Altes Testament bei Paulus* (Stuttgart: Kohlhammer, 1973).

37   So with Schlier, p. 92 n. 6.
38   See εἰ μή in Gal 1:7. On the grammatical problems, see BDF, § 376; BDR, § 376.
39   Cf. the expression χωρὶς νόμου ("without [the] Torah") in Rom 3:21; χωρὶς ἔργων νόμου ("without works of [the] Torah") in Rom 3:28; cf. 4:6.
40   The expression occurs as διὰ πίστεως ("through faith") Gal 2:16; Rom 3:22, 30; Phil 3:9; cf. Eph 2:8; ἐκ πίστεως ("out of, on the basis of faith") Gal 2:16; 3:8, 22, 24; Rom 3:26, 30; 5:1; 9:30; 10:6; πίστει ("by faith") Rom 3:28. Still other forms are used in Rom 4:5, 9, 11, 13; 10:11; Phil 3:9. See Kertelge, "*Rechtfertigung*," 161f.
41   On the concept of "faith" in Paul, see Rudolf Bultmann, "πιστεύω κτλ.," *TDNT* 6.209–28, 217ff;

idem, *Theology*, § 35–37; Conzelmann, *Outline*, § 20; idem, *Theologie als Schriftauslegung*, 191–206, 215–28; Henrik Ljungman, *Pistis* (Lund: Gleerup, 1964); Kertelge, "*Rechtfertigung*," 162ff; Dieter Lührmann, *Glaube im frühen Christentum* (Gütersloh: Mohn, 1976).
42   The abbreviation occurs in slightly different forms (πίστις Χριστοῦ Ἰησοῦ or Ἰησοῦ Χριστοῦ [so now Nestle–Aland]; the order of the names varies, see the *apparatus criticus*) in Gal 2:16; 3:22; Rom 3:22; with Ἰησοῦ ("Jesus") Rom 3:26; with Χριστοῦ ("Christ") in Phil 3:9; with τοῦ υἱοῦ τοῦ θεοῦ ("the son of God") Gal 2:20. See Bultmann, "πιστεύω κτλ.," *TDNT* 6.210 n. 267. The interpretation of the doctrine is still disputed. See the older literature in Erwin Wissmann, *Das Verhältnis von ΠΙΣΤΙΣ und Christusfrömmigkeit bei Paulus* (FRLANT NF 23; Göttingen: Vandenhoeck & Ruprecht, 1926); Rudolf Bultmann, "πιστεύω κτλ.," *TDNT* 6.209ff; Fritz Neugebauer, *In Christus* (Göttingen: Vandenhoeck & Ruprecht, 1961) 150ff; Kertelge, "*Rechtfertigung*," 162ff.
43   See on this problem Walter Grundmann, "χρίω κτλ.," *TDNT* 9.540–80.
44   For parallels in Gal 2:16, see Rom 3:20, 28; 4:5; 11:6; Phil 3:7–10; Eph 2:8; the verb πιστεύω with the preposition εἰς occurs also Rom 10:10, 14; Phil 1:29; cf. Rom 6:8; 1 Thess 4:14. See Kertelge, "*Rechtfertigung*," 172.

tion rules out the often-proposed but false idea that the genitive refers to the faith which Jesus himself had.[45] The preposition εἰς ("in") stands for an entire christology and soteriology which explains why the Christian can expect justification through his faith relationship with God "through Christ." The sentence v 16c, beginning with ἵνα ("so that"), reveals that becoming a Christian was a step done for theological purposes. Jews who believed they needed justification before God, but did not accept the doctrine of meritorious works of the Torah, became believers in Christ[46] because they believed that in this way they could obtain what they needed. The contrast between the abbreviations ἐκ πίστεως Χριστοῦ ("on the basis of [the] faith of [=in] Christ") and ἐξ ἔργων νόμου ("on the basis of [the] works of [the] Torah") is emphasized by Paul polemically, because in a non-Pauline context both do not necessarily exclude each other; in Paul's formulation, however, the first abbreviation is taken to exclude the second. The clause also indicates that justification remains a matter of hope, and is not in any way a present guarantee.[47]

The final clause (v 16d) cites the theological presupposition which undergirds the whole rejection of the doctrine of meritorious "works of the Torah." "Because all flesh shall not be justified by works of [the] Law." The statement consists of a Pauline interpretation of Scripture, Ps 143:2 (= 142:2 LXX).[48] It is introduced by what appears to be a quotation formula (ὅτι ["that"]).[49] The statement itself contains both a quotation from Scripture and Paul's interpretation which is made part of the quotation, so that the whole forms a statement of theological doctrine.[50] A comparison of the elements shows the composition of the statement: MT: כי לא יצדק לפניך כל־חי; LXX: ὅτι οὐ δικαιωθήσεται ἐνώπιόν σου πᾶς ζῶν ("For every living being will not be justified before you"); Gal 2:16: ὅτι ἐξ ἔργων νόμου οὐ δικαιωθήσεται πᾶσα σάρξ ("For all flesh will not be justified on the basis of works of [the] Law").

Paul's exegesis[51] points out that "every living being" (πᾶς ζῶν) means "all flesh" (πᾶσα σάρξ),[52] for "the works of the Torah" are "done" by "the human being" (ἄνθρωπος [v 16a]) who is "flesh" (σάρξ). Paul then

---

45 The older literature is discussed by Kertelge, "*Rechtfertigung*," 164–66. Recently, this interpretation has been revived by Erwin R. Goodenough, "Paul and the Hellenization of Christianity," in *Religion in Antiquity. Essays in Memory of E. R. Goodenough* (Leiden: Brill, 1967) 47ff; Greer M. Taylor, "The Function of ΠΙΣΤΙΣ ΧΡΙΣΤΟΥ in Galatians," *JBL* 85 (1966) 58–76; George Howard, "On the 'Faith of Christ,'" *HTR* 60 (1967) 459–65. Because of the grammatical ambiguity the problem must be decided by context analysis, a methodical principle which these authors violate.

46 What becoming a believer meant, is spelled out in Rom 10:9–10: ἐὰν ὁμολογήσῃς ἐν τῷ στόματί σου κύριον Ἰησοῦν, καὶ πιστεύσῃς ἐν τῇ καρδίᾳ σου ὅτι ὁ θεὸς αὐτὸν ἤγειρεν ἐκ νεκρῶν, σωθήσῃ ("If you confess with your mouth 'Lord [is] Jesus,' and if you believe with your heart 'God raised him from the dead,' you will be saved"). For the interpretation of this passage, see Conzelmann, *Theologie als Schriftauslegung*, 109–14, 120–30; idem, *Outline*, § 9; Klaus Wengst, *Christologische Formeln und Lieder des Urchristentums* (StNT 7; Gütersloh: Mohn, 1972) 27ff; Martin Rese, "Formeln und Lieder im Neuen Testament," *VF* 15 (1970) 75–96, 87ff.

47 See the eschatological passages in Gal 5:6; 6:7–9; also 1:8–9.

48 The same quotation is found in a similar context in Rom 3:20. The positive counterpart is Gal 3:11; Rom 1:17 (Hab 2:4); Gal 3:6; Rom 4:3 (Gen 15:6).

49 ὅτι, cf. Rom 3:20: διότι.

50 For this type of Scripture exegesis, see Otto Michel, *Paulus und seine Bibel* (BFCTh 2.18; Gütersloh: Bertelsmann, 1929; rep. Darmstadt: Wissenschaftliche Buchgesellschaft, 1972) 73ff; Betz, "2 Cor 6:14–7:1," 92ff.

51   See also Ulrich Wilckens, "Was heisst bei Paulus: 'Aus Werken wird kein Mensch gerecht'?" *EKKV* 1 (1969) 51–77; idem, *Rechtfertigung als Freiheit: Paulusstudien* (Neukirchen–Vluyn: Neukirchener Verlag, 1974) 77–109.

52 The phrase "all flesh" is Jewish. It occurs also in Rom 3:20; 1 Cor 1:29. On the concept of σάρξ ("flesh") see Gal 1:16; 2:16, 20; 3:3; 4:13, 14, 23, 29; 5:13, 16, 17, 19, 24; 6:8, 12, 13. See Bultmann, *Theology*, § 22; Conzelmann, *Outline*, 178f; Jewett, *Paul's Anthropological Terms*, 49f; Eduard Schweizer et al., *TDNT* 8, s.v. σάρξ; Egon Brandenburger, *Fleisch und Geist: Paulus und die dualistische Weisheit* (WMANT 29; Neukirchen–Vluyn: Neukirchener Verlag, 1968) 42; Alexander Sand, *Der Begriff "Fleisch" in den paulinischen Hauptbriefen* (Regensburg: Pustet, 1967) 125, 149ff, 232.

interprets the phrase "justified before you" of the Psalm verse. The future of δικαιωθήσεται ("will be justified") is taken to refer to the eschatological judgment, an interpretation which renders "before you" a redundancy.[53] More important is that the question why there is no justification for the "flesh" is answered. Justification of the "flesh" can only mean justification "by works of the Torah" (ἐξ ἔργων νόμου), so that Paul has added this abbreviation. The flesh cannot be justified on its own terms and through its own efforts, because that would be "through works of the Torah."[54]

Finally, it should be noted that Paul has succinctly introduced the two major types of evidence he is going to use in the *probatio* section (3:1–4:31): eye-witness evidence ("we have come to believe" [v 16b]) and proof from Scripture.

■ 17 From the statement of the assumed agreement (v 15–16) we now move on to the disagreement. The disagreement does not pertain to the doctrine of justification by faith for Jewish Christians, but to the implications of that doctrine for Gentile Christians. This means, of course, that the entire doctrine of justification by faith in Christ Jesus is at stake. In Paul's view, the implications of this doctrine show what the doctrine itself means. His statement is extremely complicated and raises a number of questions, a fact that no commentator fails to mention.[55] Is the entire sentence a question[56] or a factual statement,[57] answered by the μὴ γένοιτο ("by no means!") ? Is the first conditional clause an *irrealis*[58] or a *realis*? In what sense can Christ be misunderstood as "a servant of sin"? Does v 17 contain a charge made by opponents, which Paul takes up and disproves?

Paul's statement of the disagreement has two parts. First, he constructs a false argument. This argument seems hypothetical, but in fact it contains the real argument of the opponents. The false argument is, of course, constructed only to be criticized and refuted (vv 18, 21). Paul builds the false argument upon two presuppositions, the first of which is correct and the second false: "if, however, we who are seeking to be justified in Christ..." and: "are also found sinners...." The first, correct presupposition takes up the statement of definition in v 16, now emphasizing that "justification by faith" is an eschatological hope of "seeking to be justified (ζητεῖν δικαιωθῆναι)[59] and that this "seeking to be justified" (which is the same as "believing in Christ Jesus" [v 16b]) takes place "in Christ" (ἐν Χριστῷ).

This last phrase is another abbreviation, which says that this "seeking to be justified" is done by participation in the "body of Christ."[60] For this reason the

---

53   It is kept in Rom 3:20, however.

54   This amounts to "boasting in the flesh" (see on this concept Gal 6:13f and further passages there). Paul's rejection of boasting is shared by parts of Judaism. See Str-B 3.156f, 162; 4/2.1108; Davies, *Paul and Rabbinic Judaism*, 11 n. 3; for Qumran, see 1QS 11.2ff, 9ff; 1QH 4.29–31; and Braun, *Qumran* 1.173, 209.

55   For detailed analysis of the various positions which were taken by scholars in the past, see the commentaries, esp. Sieffert, pp. 146ff; Burton, pp. 125ff; Schlier, pp. 95f; and the studies by Wilhelm Mundle, "Zur Auslegung von Gal 2:17, 18," *ZNW* 23 (1924) 152f; Rudolf Bultmann, "Zur Auslegung von Galater 2, 15–18," in his *Exegetica*, 394–99; Klein, *Rekonstruktion*, 185ff.

56   This understanding is present in Nestle–Aland, and Aland, *Greek New Testament*. Oepke (p. 92) points out that the following denial (μὴ γένοιτο) is usually preceded by a question (cf. Rom 3:3f, 5f; Gal 3:21; Rom 3:31; 6:2, 15; 7:7, 13; 9:14; 11:1, 11; 1 Cor 6:15). On the whole question, see Klein, *Rekonstruk-*

tion, 186–89; BDF, § 440, 2; BDR, § 440 n. 3.

57   So Bultmann (*Exegetica*, 394f), who interprets v 17a in parallelism with Gal 2:21 and 1 Cor 15:17 ("If however, Christ has not been raised, your faith is futile, [for] you are still in your sins"). The statements construct, in Bultmann's view, theological "absurdities." Against Bultmann, Klein argues that v 17 and v 21 cannot be parallel.

58   So Bultmann (*Exegetica*, 395f), following many older commentaries.

59   The "seeking" (ζητέω) is a conclusion from v 16. See for this term also 1 Thess 2:6; Rom 2:7; 3:11; 1 Cor 1:22; Col 3:1. Cf. Bauer, *s.v.*

60   The question is whether Paul refers to the formula "in Christ" (for which see on Gal 1:22; 2:4; 3:14, 26–28; 5:6; etc.) or whether he formulates in contrast to ἐν νόμῳ ("through [the] law"), thereby making the phrase instrumental ("through Christ"). The latter option is preferred by Oepke (p. 92 n. 228), who sees the phrase in analogy to Gal 3:11; Rom 5:9. Cf. also 1 Cor 6:11: ἐν τῷ ὀνόματι Ἰησοῦ Χριστοῦ ("through the name of Jesus Christ").

second presupposition must be false: those[61] who are members of the "body of Christ" cannot be regarded[62] as "sinners" in the Jewish sense of the term, i.e., as living outside of the realm of God's salvation.[63] For Paul there is no possibility of conceiving of Christians as living outside of the realm of God's grace. This must then be applied to v 15 and the concept of "sinners from the Gentiles." If Jewish Christians are not "sinners from the Gentiles," which of course they are not, the same must be true of the Gentile Christians because they, in the same way, are "seeking to be justified 'in Christ'." The fact that one is a Jew or a Gentile is irrelevant, if salvation comes through faith in Christ. "For in Christ Jesus neither circumcision nor uncircumcision means anything . . ." (5:6; 6:15). Gentile Christians, therefore, can no longer be regarded as existing in the situation of "sinners from the Gentiles," even though they are not circumcised and have not become part of the Torah covenant (in the Jewish sense of the term).

On this basis, Paul raises a strange question (v 17b): Χριστὸς ἁμαρτίας διάκονος; ("Is Christ then a servant of sin?") The statement is presented as a conclusion from the preceding two presuppositions, one correct and one false, so that for this logical reason alone it must be false. Being false, however, does not simply mean that the conclusion is absurd. If the Gentile Christians—as the opposition maintains—are as Christians still sinners until they come under the Torah, then Christ has in fact become "a servant of sin."

The question is whether Paul himself has merely invented this idea or whether he has adopted a slogan from his opponents.[64] A decision is difficult, but the phrase itself has the appearance of a kind of slogan, to be sure a polemical one: Χριστὸς ἁμαρτίας διάκονος ("Christ servant of sin").[65] The slogan contains an absurd antithesis to similar formulations like "Christ servant of circumcision" (Χριστὸς διάκονος περιτομῆς) in Rom 15:8, or "the service of righteousness" (ἡ διακονία τῆς δικαιοσύνης) in 2 Cor 3:9. The parallel in v 21c poses a similar problem. It is quite conceivable and even probable that the absurd christological formulation in 2:17b comes from the opponents. But Paul himself has taken it up and has turned it into a self-caricature which sums up what the opponents think of his christology.[66] Whether or not this explanation is correct, one thing should be clear: "this can never be!" (μὴ γένοιτο).[67]

■18 Paul supplies an explicit legal critique of the previous false argument (v 17). The critique shows that the entire problem was recognized and treated by Paul as one of religious law.[68] His critique presupposes a legal principle which he explicitly cites in Rom 4:15b: "where there is no law, there is no transgression."[69] Applied to the present context, this principle calls for

---

61 αὐτοί ("they themselves") does not refer to v 15, but to those who seek to be justified in Christ.

62 For the meaning of εὑρίσκω ("find"), see Rom 7:10; 1 Cor 4:2; 15:15; 2 Cor 5:3; 11:12; Phil 2:8; 3:9. See Bauer, s.v., 2.

63 The meaning of ἁμαρτωλός ("sinful") is the same as in 2:15. See also Rom 6:1 ("Shall we remain in sin?").

64 Cf. the anti–Pauline designations of Paul as ἄνομος ("lawless"), ὁ ἐχθρὸς ἄνθρωπος ("the inimical man") in the ps.–Clem. literature (Ep. Petr. 2.3; Recog. 1.70.1; Hom. 2.15.5: "collaborator of the weak left"). Cf. also Matt 5:17–20; Jas 2:9f; 2 Cor 6:14–7:1 (see Appendix 2, below). Interestingly, the accusation "This man is the enemy of our law" (οὗτ [ός ἐ]στιν ὁ ἐχθρὸς το[ῦ νόμου] ἡμῶν) was used by the Baptists against Mani (see Henrichs and Koenen, "Mani–Codex," 139; cf. the Introduction, § 2. C).

65 Cf. also Helmut Feld ("'Christus Diener der Sünde'; Zum Ausgang des Streites zwischen Petrus und Paulus," ThQ 153 [1973] 119–31) who believes that v 17 is what Cephas said in Antioch.

66 For a parallel, see Philo Spec. 2.10f. Cf. Paul's own self-understanding in 2 Cor 5:18: ἡ διακονία τῆς καταλλαγῆς ("the ministry of reconciliation"). Remarkable is also the parallel in Odes Sol. 10.5, where Christ says: "And the Gentiles who had been dispersed were gathered together, but I was not defiled by my love (for them) . . ." (tr. Charlesworth).

67 The expression is common in Hellenistic diatribe literature. In Paul it is found, apart from Gal 2:17, in 3:21; Rom 3:4, 6, 31; 6:2, 15; 7:7, 13; 9:14; 11:1, 11; 1 Cor 6:15. See Rudolf Bultmann, Der Stil der paulinischen Predigt und die kynisch-stoische Diatribe (FRLANT 13; Göttingen: Vandenhoeck & Ruprecht, 1910) 33, 68; BDF, § 384; BDR, § 384; Bauer, s.v. γίνομαι, I. 3. a.

68 So Bultmann, Exegetica, 397f; Schlier, pp. 96–98.

69 Cf. also Gal 4:1–2; Rom 3:20; 7:1–3, 7.

two hypothetical presuppositions: "I have dissolved"[70] the Torah in the sense that, for Paul, the difference between a "sinner" and a "righteous" is not determined by the existence or non-existence of "works of the Torah." Consequently, nobody can be regarded as a transgressor of a law[71] which he is not required to obey. Turned the other way around, the other presupposition is presented: "only if I again institute"[72] the law, I can become a transgressor[73] of that law. In other words: if I[74] want to regard the Gentile Christians as "transgressors" of the Torah and "sinners" in the Jewish sense of the term, I have to first reinstate the Torah as the law which then the Gentiles would be obliged to obey. Why, however, should anyone make such a demand, if not for the reason that the Gentile Christians need "the works of the Torah" for their justification at the last judgment?[75] If this should be the reason, the point of agreement, i.e., the doctrine of

justification by faith (v 15f), collapses (cf. v 21b–c).

■19 In vv 19–20 Paul presents the basic elements of his own theological position. Rhetorically this passage conforms to the "exposition" (*expositio*). The elements are set forth as four "theses." These theses are not only Paul's answers to the question raised in vv 17–18: how can the Christian who seeks to be justified before God by faith in Christ and not by "works of the Torah" escape being "a sinner"? They are also to be elaborated in the rest of the letter. But the form in which the theses are presented is peculiar; Paul uses the first person singular, i.e., himself as the prototypical example of what applies to all Pauline Christians.[76] Rhetorically there is no difficulty with this form,[77] but the analogy to the aretalogical statements[78] and even to the *synthemata*[79] of the mystery cults is remarkable. The four statements are as follows:

19a]   1. ἐγὼ διὰ νόμου νόμῳ ἀπέθανον ἵνα θεῷ ζήσω

---

70 The term καταλύω ("do away with, annul, make invalid, repeal" [Bauer, *s.v.*]) is used here in the legal sense. See LSJ, *s.v.*; Bauer, *s.v.*, 1.c; Friedrich Büchsel, "λύω," *TDNT* 4.335–36; idem, "καταλύω, κατάλυμα," *TDNT* 4.338; Str–B 1.241, 3.537f. In the NT the term is used in this sense only in Matt 5:17. If the term is not used in this sense already in Matt 5:17, it became a catchword in the accusations against Paul (cf. Rom 3:31; Acts 18:13; 21:28; *Ep. Petr.* 2.4 [see Appendix 3, below]). Paul defends himself against this charge in Rom 3:31; 6–8; cf. also Acts 21:24–26; 22:3; 24:14; 25:8.

71 The term παραβάτης ("transgressor") is also a legal term, here with special application to the Jewish Torah. Cf. Rom 2:25, 27; Jas 2:9–11; Luke 6:5 D. See Johannes Schneider, "παραβάτης," *TDNT* 5.740–41; Schlier, pp. 97f; differently Oepke, p. 93.

72 οἰκοδομέω ("build") is of course a metaphor. Cf. Philo *Somn.* 2.284f: οἰκοδομεῖν δόγμα ("build up doctrine"); see also Otto Michel, "οἰκοδομέω," *TDNT* 5.138–44; cf. the legal overtones in the use of ἐνοικοδομέω in Plutarch *Cup. div.* 526C. For rabbinic parallels, see Str–B 3.537f; Michel, "οἰκοδομέω," *TDNT* 5.140–41, 146–47.

73 The rendering of συνιστάνω is difficult. Bauer (*s.v.*, *l. c.*) translates: "I demonstrate that I am a wrong-doer." Schlier (p. 97 n. 3) suggests that it comes close to "institute myself as someone." The legal meaning is obvious. See also LSJ, *s.v.*; Wilhelm Kasch, "συνίστημι κτλ.," *TDNT* 7.896–98. Cf. the simplex ἵστημι Rom 3:31.

74 In v 18 Paul changes from the first person plural to

the first person singular. This shift has caused much discussion, for which see esp. Burton, pp. 130f; Oepke, p. 93; Schlier, pp. 96f; Mussner, pp. 177f; Klein, *Rekonstruktion*, 195ff. One should not deny that it is a rhetorical feature, by which Paul uses himself as the example. The change also indicates that this and the following were not shared by Jewish Christianity.

75 Cf. the Galatians' present plan to accept Torah and circumcision (see Gal 4:21).

76 Cf. Gal 6:14, 17b; 1:10, 11, 12ff; 4:12–20; 5:2, 10, 11; 1 Cor 15:10; 2 Cor 10:1; 12:1–10; etc.

77 See Betz, *Paulus*, 64, 73ff, and *passim*; also idem, "Eine Christus–Aretalogie bei Paulus (2 Kor 12, 7–10)" *ZThK* 66 (1969) 288–305.

78 See, e.g., *Corp. Herm.* 1.30; 13.11. Cf. the commentary in William Grese, *Corpus Hermeticum XIII and Early Christian Literature* (Ph.D. dissertation, Claremont Graduate School, 1977 [unpubl.]). Other parallels are found in the presentations of themselves by the philosophers in Lucian's "Philosophies for Sale" (*Vit. auct.*).

79 For a collection of the synthemata see Albrecht Dieterich, *Eine Mithrasliturgie* (Darmstadt: Wissenschaftliche Buchgesellschaft, 1966) 213ff. See furthermore, Günter Zuntz's new edition and commentary of the Orphic Gold Tablets in his *Persephone* (Oxford: Oxford University, 1971); John G. Griffiths, *Apuleius of Madauros: The Isis-Book (Metamorphoses Book XI)* (EPRO 39; Leiden: Brill, 1975) 294ff.

19b]	2. Χριστῷ συνεσταύρωμαι
20a]	3. ζῶ οὐκέτι ἐγώ, ζῇ δὲ ἐν ἐμοὶ Χριστός
20b]	4. ὃ νῦν ζῶ ἐν σαρκί, ἐν πίστει ζῶ
	τῇ τοῦ υἱοῦ τοῦ θεοῦ
	τοῦ ἀγαπήσαντός με
	καὶ παραδόντος ἑαυτὸν ὑπὲρ ἐμοῦ
19a]	1. "through [the] Law I died to [the] Law, in order that I might live for God"
19b]	2. "I have been crucified with Christ"
20a]	3. "it is no longer I who live, but Christ lives in me"
20b]	4. "what I now live in [the] flesh, I live in [the] faith
	in the Son of God
	who loved me and gave himself up for me"

(1) Verse 19a contains the first thesis: "through the Torah I died to the Torah, in order that I might live for God." The difficulty of interpreting this *crux interpretum* comes from its nature of "abbreviation," which must be "decoded." The "I" (ἐγώ) to which Paul refers is not so much the personal "I" but the paradigmatic "I," which had occurred already in v 18. The content of the statement is expanded in the *probatio* section, especially 3:19–25. "Through the Torah" is explained in 3:19–25 by attributing to the Torah an active role in salvation (3:22), while "I died to the Torah" refers to the end of that role of the Torah (3:25; cf. Rom 7:4; 10:4).[80] The aorist ἀπέθανον ("I have died") in a metaphorical way points to some kind of death experience, which is clarified by the following thesis: "I have been crucified together with Christ." The purpose and goal is stated in this sentence: ἵνα θεῷ ζήσω ("in order that I might live for God").[81] "Death to the Torah" is the presupposition for the "life for God," but as the parenesis (5:1–6:10) shows, "life for God" does not happen automatically. "To live for God" sums up Paul's concept of Christian existence, soteriology as well as ethics.[82] Perhaps one may call it Paul's "telos formula," analogous to those found in the philosophical literature.[83]

(2) The second thesis (v 19b) is also very concise: Χριστῷ συνεσταύρωμαι ("I have been crucified together with Christ"). A similar statement occurs in the *exhortatio* (5:24) and in the *peroratio* (6:14).[84] But the main

---

80 The "I" stands in juxtaposition to the "we are found" in v 17, but Paul has more in mind than his "own experiences" (Burton, p. 132). See also C. F. D. Moule, "Death 'to Sin', 'to Law,' and 'to the World': A Note on Certain Datives," in *Mélanges Bibliques en hommage au R. P. Béda Rigaux* (Gembloux: Duculot, 1970) 367–75.

81 On the soteriological meaning of ἵνα ("in order that") see Gal 2:16; 3:22, 24; 4:5; Rom 5:20; 6:1, 4, 6; 7:4; 8:17; 11:32; 2 Cor 5:15; Phil 3:8; 1 Thess 5:10. See also Ethelbert Stauffer, *TDNT* 3, *s.v.* ἵνα.

82 The concept occurs also Rom 6:10, 11 (where it is supplemented by "in Christ Jesus"). The opposite is "live for oneself" (ζῆν ἑαυτῷ), cf. Rom 14:7; 2 Cor 5:15. Related expressions are: "live for the Lord" Rom 14:8; 2 Cor 5:15; "live with Christ" Rom 6:8; 2 Cor 7:3; 13:4; 1 Thess 5:10; (2 Tim 2:11); cf. Phil 1:21f; "live by the Spirit" Gal 5:25; cf. Rom 8:13; "live out of faith" Gal 3:11; Rom 1:17; "live in faith" Gal 2:20. See furthermore Luke 20:38; Heb 9:14; 1 Pet 2:24; 4:6; *Herm. Mand.* 3.5. See Rudolf Bultmann, *TDNT* 2, *s.v.* ζάω κτλ., esp. 863 n. 263.

83 Cf. esp. *Sent. Sextus* 201 (in Henry Chadwick, *The Sentences of Sextus: A Contribution to the Early Christian History of Ethics* [Cambridge: Cambridge University, 1959] 34): τέλος ἡγοῦ βίου τὸ ζῆν κατὰ θεόν ("Consider as the goal of life living in accordance with God."). Cf. also Pyth. *Sent.* 30 (ibidem, 87). For Jewish parallels, see 4 Macc. 6:18; 7:19; 16:25; Philo *Her.* 111; *Mut.* 213; cf. *Her.* 57; *Post.* 73; *Det.* 48. On the subject of the "telos formulae" see Gerhard Delling, "Telos-Aussagen in der griechischen Philosophie," *ZNW* 55 (1964) 26–42; now in his *Studien zum Neuen Testament und zum hellenistischen Judentum: Gesammelte Aufsätze 1950–1968* (ed. Ferdinand Hahn *et al.*; Göttingen: Vandenhoeck & Ruprecht, 1970) 17–31.

84 Other formulaic statements about "dying with Christ" are found in Rom 6:3–10; 8:17; Phil 3:10, 21; Col 2:12–14, 20; 3:3–4; Ign. *Eph.* 9.1; Ign. *Trall.* 11.2; Ign. *Smyr.* 1.1; 7.2. On the whole concept see Bultmann, *Theology*, § 33; Conzelmann, *Outline*, 209, 281; Betz, *Nachfolge*, 169–85; Robert C. Tannehill, *Dying and Rising with Christ* (BZNW 32; Berlin: Töpelmann, 1967), esp. 55–61; Eduard Schweizer, "Die 'Mystik' des Sterbens und Auferstehens mit Christus bei Paulus," in his *Beiträge zur Theologie des Neuen Testaments* (Zurich: Zwingli, 1970) 183–203; idem, "Dying and Rising with Christ," *NTS* 14 (1967) 1–14; Rudolf Schnackenburg, *Baptism in the Thought of St. Paul* (New York: Herder, 1964); idem, "Todes- und Lebensgemein-

passage to compare is 3:26–28. A more detailed interpretation is found in Rom 6:1–10. At this point, however, the methodological problem arises, whether or not Gal 2:19–20 should be interpreted on the basis of Romans 6. Is Gal 2:19–20 a condensation of Romans 6?[85] Most interpreters answer affirmatively and, therefore, interpret Romans 6 into Gal 2:19–20.[86] To be sure, Paul mentions baptism only once, in Gal 3:27, where it may be part of a pre-Pauline baptismal formula. Strangely, in 3:27 Paul does not mention the dying together with Christ, while in 5:24; 6:14, when he speaks of the death together with Christ he does not mention baptism. In none of the passages does he mention Christ's resurrection, or any of the other concepts of Romans 6. This difference cannot be accidental. Galatians seems to express a similar restraint with regard to baptism as we find in 1 Cor 1:13–17. It is only in Romans 6 that Paul interprets the ritual of baptism in terms of death and resurrection together with Christ. That interpretation must be secondary and cannot be tied entirely to baptism in the way Schlier does. In fact, it may be just the other way around; Gal 2:19 may contain the theological principle by which Paul interprets the ritual of baptism in Romans 6.

■ **20** The (3) third of the four "theses" (see v 19) follows in v 20a, connected by δέ ("but"): "it is no longer I who live, but Christ lives in me." In terms of content, there are of course many connections between this statement and the rest of the letter. Surprisingly, Paul declares the "I"[87] to be dead; if he speaks of "living for God" as the goal of Christian existence, that "life" must be different from the "life" of the "I". "Crucifixion together with Christ" implies not only "death to the Law" (2:19), but also "death to the 'I.'" The "I" belongs to the sinful "flesh with its passions and desires" (5:24), and thus to "the world." For Paul, "crucifixion together with Christ" also means "crucifixion to the world" (6:14), and for that reason he can declare the "I" to be "dead."

One should not confuse this doctrine about the "I" with the more elaborate and different treatment of the subject in Rom 7:9–25:[88] before the "coming" of the Torah the "I" lived (Rom 7:9), but when Torah and sin entered into human existence, the "I" died (7:10); pre–Christian humans have an "I," but it is defunct

schaft mit Christus: Neue Studien zu Röm 6, 1–11," in his *Schriften zum Neuen Testament* (Munich: Kösel, 1971) 361–90, with extensive bib.; Peter Siber, *Mit Christus Leben* (AThANT 61; Zurich: Theologischer Verlag, 1971) esp. 192, 196, 222ff. Since most authors find the concept of baptism in Gal 2:19f, literature on baptism usually discusses the passage. See Mussner (pp. 179ff) with bib.

85 See the conclusions reached by Blank, *Paulus und Jesus*, 298f.

86 This is done systematically by Schlier (pp. 99f) who follows patristic commentators and interprets the event of death as "an objective event which happens to the baptizant in the act of baptism." This act is "a growing together with the death of Christ," and it implies "a real, even if invisible elimination of 'the old man' and his basis of life which was entirely controlled by sin." It also includes "the creation of a new basis of life in which man in Christ Jesus is opened up for God." Most recent commentators follow Schlier, esp. Blank, *Paulus und Jesus*, 298f; Kertelge, "*Rechtfertigung*," 239–42. For a critique of this sacramentalism, see Schulz, "Katholisierende Tendenzen in Schliers Galater–Kommentar," *KD* 5 (1959) 33–41; Betz, "2 Cor 6:14–7:1," 106 n. 111.

87 On the meaning of ἐγώ ("I") in Gal, see on 2:19, n. 76. Strangely, no satisfactory investigation of the notion in Paul exists. See, for further literature, Ethelbert Stauffer, "ἐγώ," *TDNT* 2.356–62; Rudolf Bultmann, "Römer 7 und die Anthropologie des Paulus," in his *Exegetica*, 198–209; Werner Georg Kümmel, *Römer 7 und das Bild des Menschen im Neuen Testament* (Munich: Kaiser, 1974).

88 We differ here especially from Schlier (pp. 101f) who interprets Gal 2:20 by a mixture of Rom 8:9f and Col 3:3f: "Christ is our life," and we who have died with him in baptism also live with him in a hidden way in God. He lives in us through the indwelling Spirit (Rom 8:9f). "Justification in Christ has not only killed the old man and thereby removed him from the Law, but it has also created in us the new hidden man in Christ who becomes strong through the Spirit and the faith, and who 'takes shape'... (Gal 4:19)." The "Christ in us" is "the inner man," which we have "put on" in baptism (Eph 3:16f; Col 3:9f). According to Schlier, all expressions correlating "Christ" and "us" (e.g., "we in Christ," and "Christ in us") are baptismal formulae. Similarly, Kertelge, "*Rechtfertigung*," 240. On Rom 7:9ff, see Käsemann (*Römer*, 183ff) with further bib.

and its place is occupied by "sin" (Rom 7:14, 17), as is the entire "flesh" (σάρξ). When we compare Gal 2:20 with Romans, the "I" in Gal 2:20 can be compared with the concept of "our old man" (ὁ παλαιὸς ἄνθρωπος ἡμῶν) in Rom 6:6, who dies with Christ in baptism. Also different from Galatians is the introduction of the concept of "the inner man" (ὁ ἔσω ἄνθρωπος) in Rom 7:22.[89] Paul does not say in Romans, as he does in Galatians, that the "I" is evil as such, but he makes new distinctions: "our old man" which is identical with the "flesh" and the "sinful body" (τὸ σῶμα τῆς ἁμαρτίας) dies together with Christ, but according to Rom 7:22–23 one part of the "I", the "inner man" with its "mind" (νοῦς) wills the good but is hindered from achieving it "by the law of sin which resides in my members."[90] In other words, not all of the "I" is dead—the "mind" (νοῦς) of the "inner man" is still alive even though it is imprisoned and prevented from its activities.

To return to Galatians, since the "I" is dead, another agent must do the "living in me" if the statement "I shall live for God" (v 19) is to be accepted.[91] Paul's thesis specifies that "Christ lives in me" (ζῇ δὲ ἐν ἐμοὶ Χριστός). This statement must be seen in connection with Gal 1:16 ("God revealed his son in me") and 4:6 ("God has sent the Spirit of his son into our hearts"). The underlying assumption is that the resurrected Christ (1:1) is identical with the "Spirit" (2 Cor 3:17a) which is given to the Christians, and which dwells in them and provides "life for God" for them.[92] There can be no doubt that Paul speaks here in "mystical" terms.[93] The doctrine of the indwelling Christ is developed in the *probatio* section in those passages which deal with the Spirit (3:2–5; 4:6 especially), and in the *exhortatio* section in the passages dealing with "life in the Spirit" (especially 5:5, 16, 17, 18, 22–23, 25; 6:1, 8.)

(4) Verse 20b contains the fourth and concluding "thesis": "what I now live in the flesh, I live in the faith in the Son of God who loved me and gave himself up for me." Again, this thesis is simply added to the previous ones (δέ ["and"]). In terms of content, it further interprets what is meant by "Christ lives in me" (v 20a). Paul's understanding that life has some kind of object is strange:[94] ὅ ("what") can be understood to simply refer to "life,"[95] it can be taken to limit that

---

89 For this concept, see 2 Cor 4:16; also Eph 3:16, where the notion is used differently. See Conzelmann, *Outline*, 180; Jewett, *Paul's Anthropological Terms*, 391ff.

90 Note the different meaning in Rom 7:24a ("I" is simply "sinful man") and 7:24b, probably a post-Pauline gloss, where the "I" is split. See Bultmann, *Exegetica*, 278f; Käsemann, *Römer*, 190ff, with further literature.

91 Cf. Phil 1:21: ἐμοὶ γὰρ τὸ ζῆν Χριστός ("for me living means Christ"). See Bultmann, "ζάω," *TDNT* 2.866–70.

92 Rom 8:2–11 provides a more systematic and slightly different interpretation. In Rom 8:9f the "Spirit of God," "the Spirit of Christ," and the indwelling Christ are all one. If Christ dwells in the Christian, it means that "the body is dead because of sin" and that "the spirit is life because of righteousness." The same Spirit raised Jesus from the dead and makes the mortal bodies of the Christians alive (8:11). Schlier (pp. 101–03) interprets Rom into Gal and goes further in systematizing Paul, saying that in baptism the "new man" is created sacramentally as the "objective basis" upon which the Christian life rests. "Spirit" and "faith" are the means by which "the new life based upon Christ in baptism" be-

comes real in the concrete life of the Christian. Schlier explicitly rejects all "mysticism" as "subjectivism" and favors sacramental objectivism. Similarly Kertelge, "*Rechtfertigung*," 240.

93 Cf. the close parallel *Odes Sol.* 10.2: "And He [God] has caused to dwell in me His immortal life, and permitted me to proclaim the fruit of the peace" (tr. Charlesworth). The concept of a deity indwelling in man was held widely in different religions in antiquity, including Christianity. The literature on the subject is vast. See Widengren, *Religionsphänomenologie*, 516ff; Reitzenstein, *Mysterienreligionen*, 361 and *passim*; Hermann Kleinknecht, "πνεῦμα, πνευματικός," *TDNT* 6.339–59; Brandenburger, *Fleisch und Geist*, 136ff, 216ff; Johannes Haussleiter, "Deus Internus," *RAC* 3.794–842; Hans Dieter Betz, "The Delphic Maxim ΓΝΩΘΙ ΣΑΥΤΟΝ in Hermetic Interpretation," *HTR* 63 (1970) 465–84; *PECL*, index, *s.v.* ἐνθουσιασμός, "Inspiration."

94 Cf. the parallel in Rom 6:10.

95 So Schlier, p. 102 n. 4. Many commentators refer to the parallel in Plutarch *Virt. et vit.* 100F: καὶ γὰρ ὁ καθεύδουσι τοῦ σώματος ὕπνος ἐστὶ καὶ ἀνάπαυσις ... ("For what sleep there is, it is sleep and repose for the body . . .").

life ("to the extent that I have life"),[96] or it can point to the following "in the faith." [97] A decision is difficult. At any rate, Paul's concept of life requires not only a subject which lives the life, but also a content–object: those who live, live something, i.e., a life. What the Apostle means is clear: Christian life takes place "in the flesh" (ἐν σαρκί).[98] This statement, simple as it is, may be polemical. It rejects widespread enthusiastic notions, which may have already found a home in Christianity, according to which "divine life" and "flesh" are mutually exclusive, so that those who claim to have divine life also claim that they have left the conditions of mortality.[99] The Christian life "in the flesh" is at the same time a life "in faith" (ἐν πίστει ζῶ).[100] In other words, the "divine life" which the Christian receives through the indwelling of Christ expresses itself as "faith." [101] This faith is of course "faith in Christ Jesus" (2:16).[102] The full interpretation of this "thesis" is to be found in the entire *probatio* section (3:1–4:31) and in the *exhortatio* section (5:1-6:10).

In 2:20 Paul defines[103] "faith" by a further statement combining the christological title "Son of God" [104] with a christological formula. The title "Son of God" is well–attested in Paul.[105] The following christological formula combines two participial expressions, both of which occur elsewhere, together[106] or separately:[107] "who loved me and gave himself up for me." The formula refers to Christ's death on the cross as an act of

---

96   So, e.g., Lightfoot, p. 119: "So far as I live now in the flesh. . . ." This understanding takes into account that "life in the flesh" is not yet the full life to come in the afterlife.

97   So Bauer, *s.v.* ὅς, 7. c.

98   The adverb νῦν ("now") is related to the οὐκέτι ("no longer") in v 20a and points to the Christian existence in contrast to the pre–Christian (see Gal 3:3; 4:9, 29, and often in Paul). On the whole concept, see Peter Tachau, *"Einst" und "Jetzt" im Neuen Testament* (FRLANT 105; Göttingen: Vandenhoeck & Ruprecht, 1972).

99   Also 2 Cor 10:3 is polemical: "for we are walking in the flesh" (ἐν σαρκὶ γὰρ περιπατοῦντες). See Betz, *Paulus*, 140f. Cf. also Gal 6:12–17; 4:13f; 5:1-6:10; Phil 1:22, 24; 2 Cor 4:11; Phlm 16; etc. Differently, Rom 8:8f contrasts the "life according to the Spirit" with the "life according to the flesh" and concludes: "But you are not in the flesh, but in the Spirit" (ὑμεῖς δὲ οὐκ ἐστὲ ἐν σαρκὶ ἀλλὰ ἐν πνεύματι . . .). The dualism between "flesh" and "Spirit" is clearly expressed in Gal 5:16ff.

100   Cf. 1 Cor 16:13: στήκετε ἐν τῇ πίστει ("stand in the faith"); 2 Cor 1:24; 13:5. See Bauer, *s.v.* πίστις, 2. b. β.

101   For Schlier (p. 102) the "earthly existence" of the Christian occurs "in a new mode of being: ἐν πίστει." This "new mode of being" is granted to the Christian in baptism: "Christ has entered into our being, insofar as we were implanted in the being of Christ" (pp. 101f). This sacramental grace is received in baptism and continued in faith. Cf. the critique of Schlier by Kertelge, "*Rechtfertigung*," 241f.

102   Cf. Eph 3:17, where what Paul means is stated: κατοικῆσαι τὸν Χριστὸν διὰ τῆς πίστεως ἐν ταῖς καρ-

δίαις ὑμῶν ("Christ dwells, through the faith, in your hearts").

103   For other instances of such "definitions" see Burton, p. 139.

104   Instead of υἱοῦ τοῦ θεοῦ, P⁴⁶ B D* G itᵈ·ᵍ Marius Victorinus Pelagius read θεοῦ καὶ Χριστοῦ. But "faith in God and Christ" is not a Pauline phrase and must be due to later theology. See Metzger, *Textual Commentary*, 593.

105   On this title, see on Gal 1:16.

106   Cf. Eph 5:2: ". . . as also Christ loved us and gave himself for us as an offering and sacrifice to God for a fragrance of pleasant odor" (. . . καθὼς καὶ ὁ Χριστὸς ἠγάπησεν ἡμᾶς καὶ παρέδωκεν ἑαυτὸν ὑπὲρ ἡμῶν προσφορὰν καὶ θυσίαν τῷ θεῷ εἰς ὀσμὴν εὐωδίας). For the textual question see Metzger, *Textual Commentary*, 606. A similar formula is found Eph 5:25.

107   For the christology of self–sacrifice see Gal 1:4; 3:13; Rom 4:25; 8:32; 1 Tim 2:6; Tit 2:14; also Phil 2:6f; 1 Cor 11:23f; etc. References to the "love of Christ" are in form of the aorist participle (see Rom 8:37; also Eph 5:2, 25; 2 Thess 2:16) or the noun ἀγάπη (see Rom 8:35, 39; 2 Cor 5:14; Eph 3:19; Col 1:13). Christ's love and God's love are related in Rom 8:32, 39 (cf. 5:5; 2 Cor 13:11; Eph 2:4; 2 Thess 2:13, 16; 3:5; and often in Ign.).
    The variant reading ἀγοράσαντος by Marcion, Rufinus, is probably taken from Gal 3:13, and is thus secondary (see Nestle–Aland, *apparatus criticus, ad loc.*).

love[108] and self–sacrifice on behalf of the Christian.[109]

■ **21** The concluding statement of the *propositio* is the refutation[110] of a charge: "I do not nullify the grace of God." Of course, this refutation rests upon the preceding statements in the *propositio* (2:15–20) and anticipates what the Apostle will prove and defend in the following sections of the letter. Paul denies that his theology, which he had set forth in the four "theses" (v 19–20), amounts to a corruption of God's grace. The concept of "the grace of God" (ἡ χάρις τοῦ θεοῦ)[111] describes the entire process of salvation in Christ; the term ἀθετέω ("nullify")[112] is rather strong and has legal overtones. The implication is that the denial rejects a charge actually made by Paul's opponents. It is conceivable that the charge "Paul annuls the grace of God" was actually made against him by his opponents.[113] They could make such a charge if their concept of divine redemption ("grace of God") would include the Torah covenant.[114] But it could also be Paul himself who draws the conclusion from whatever his opponents say against him, and denies it.[115]

Why is the refutation justified? Because the accusation is false. The accusation rests upon a false presupposition and a false conclusion. "For if righteousness [came] through [the] Torah, then Christ has died in vain." The abbreviation "through [the] Torah" (διὰ νόμου)[116] is equal to "through [the] works of [the] Torah" (ἐξ ἔργων νόμου) in 2:16–17 and stands in contrast to "through [the] faith in Christ Jesus." The noun "righteousness" (δικαιοσύνη)[117] describes what the act of justification (δικαιοῦσθαι) is expected to produce: the status of righteousness before God. The conditional clause, therefore, states the opposite of what Paul had formulated in v 16 as the common agreement. For this reason it must be a false presupposition.[118] If it were accepted, however, it would simply amount to the affirmation of Jewish (non-Christian) doctrine, and in that case[119] the death of Christ would be deprived of its salvific character. His death would have been a death "in vain" (δωρεὰν ἀπέθανεν).[120] In other words, the charge against Paul would be justified only if he did

---

108 On the notion of ἀγαπάω ("love") see also Robert Joly, *Le vocabulaire chrétien de l'amour est-il original? Φιλεῖν et ἀγαπᾶν dans le grec antique* (Université libre de Bruxelles, Institut d'histoire du christianisme; Brussels: Presses Universitaires, 1968); Conzelmann, *1 Corinthians*, 218–31.

109 Joachim Jeremias (*Abba*, 206f) has tried to show that Gal 2:20 contains a "ὑπέρ–formula," which is derived from Isa 53. See also his somewhat different views in "παῖς θεοῦ," *TDNT* 5.706–07. Against Jeremias, Kramer (*Christ, Lord, Son of God*, 30ff) attributes Gal 2:20 to an older stage of a formula, which is not influenced by Isa 53. For the whole, largely speculative discussion, see Wengst, *Christologische Formeln*, 55ff; furthermore, Harald Riesenfeld, "ὑπέρ," *TDNT* 8.507–16; Hermann Patsch, "Zum alttestamentlichen Hintergrund von Römer 4, 25 und I. Petrus 2, 24," *ZNW* 60 (1969) 273–79.

110 On the *refutatio*, see, e.g., Rom 3:31; 6:1; 7:7; Matt 5:17; John 7:28; 8:42; 12:49; 15:16.

111 On the notion of "grace" see Gal 1:3, 6, 15; 2:9; 5:4; 6:18.

112 On this concept, see Gal 3:15; 1 Cor 1:19; 1 Tim 5:12; Ign. *Eph.* 10.3. See also Bauer, *s.v.*; Wilhelm Maurer, "τίθημι," *TDNT* 8.155–59.

113 Schlier (p. 104) considers the possibility that Paul was actually accused of doing away with God's grace.

114 For the unity of "grace" and "Torah" in Judaism, see Hans Conzelmann, "χάρις, κτλ.," *TDNT* 9.387–91; Heinrich Gross, "Tora und Gnade im Alten Testament," *Kairos* 14 (1972) 220–31; R. J. Zwi Werblowski, "Tora als Gnade," *Kairos* 15 (1973) 156–63; Mussner, pp. 185f.

115 Cf. the charge in 2:17.

116 Cf. 2:19a.

117 On this concept, see Gal 3:6, 21; 5:5. For the literature, see on 2:16.

118 See 2:19; 3:21. On the unreal indicative in conditional sentences without ἄν in the apodosis cf. BDF, § 360; also Reitzenstein, *Mysterienreligionen*, 375f.

119 On the particle ἄρα, cf. 2:17; 3:29; 5:11. See Margaret E. Thrall, *Greek Particles in the New Testament: Linguistic and Exegetical Studies* (NTTS 3; Leiden: Brill, 1962) 36.

120 On "in vain" see 2:2; 3:4; 4:11.

the opposite of what he is in fact doing. In fact, his opponents are those who argue a theology diametrically opposed to Paul's, so that—here the refutation turns into an accusation—the charge of "invalidation of God's grace" must be raised against his opponents. In Paul's view, the "false brothers" at Jerusalem had denied God's grace (2:4–5), Cephas had denied it in Antioch (2:11–14), the present opponents deny it, and the Galatians themselves are about to reject the grace of God.[121]

If our interpretation is correct, we should expect the refutation to recur in the *peroratio*. And it does recur, but not as the refutation of the charge, because Paul disproves it fully in the *probatio* and the *exhortatio* sections. What he repeats in the *peroratio* is the accusation against the opponents (6:12–13).

---

121 See Gal 1:6f; 5:4, 11; 6:12–14.

3

Probatio: The First Argument

1   You foolish Galatians! Who has
bewitched you, before whose eyes
'Jesus Christ [the] crucified'[1] was so
vividly portrayed?[2] 2/ This only do I
want to learn from you: did you
receive the Spirit by 'works of [the]
Law' or by [the] 'proclamation[3] of [the]
faith'? 3/ Are you so foolish? Having
begun 'in [the] Spirit,' are you now
finishing up 'in [the] flesh'?[4] 4/ Have
you experienced such things in vain?
If so, it really was in vain![5] 5/ Does he,
therefore, who supplies the Spirit to
you and who works miracles among
you [do so] by 'works of [the] Law' or
by [the] 'proclamation of [the] faith'?

Analysis

3:1–5 contains the introduction to and first part of the
probatio section of the epistle (3:1–4:31). In a speech,
the *probatio* section is the most decisive of all because in
it the "proofs" are presented.[6] This part determines
whether or not the speech as a whole will succeed.
Exordium and *narratio* are only preparatory steps leading
up to this central part. The purpose of the *probatio* (as
Quintilian[7] calls it) or the *confirmatio* (as Cicero[8] and
the *Rhetorica ad Herennium*[9] call it) is to establish credibility for the defense by a system of arguments.[10]
Because of the importance of the *probatio*, the Greco-
Roman rhetoricians have devoted the major portions
of their works to it. Understandably, there is also considerable difference of opinion in regard to the classification, distribution, and effectiveness of individual
forms and types of arguments.

---

1   For this abbreviation of the kerygma see on 5:1.
2   Cf. *RSV*: "…Who has bewitched you before whose
     eyes Jesus Christ was publicly portrayed as cruci-
     fied?" *NEB* makes the statement an exclamation:
     "…You must have been bewitched—you before
     whose eyes Jesus Christ was openly displayed upon
     his cross!" *JB* translates in the light of 1 Cor 15:3f:
     "Has someone put a spell on you, in spite of the
     plain explanation you have had of the crucifixion
     of Jesus Christ?"
3   The translation of ἀκοή unavoidably shifts the em-
     phasis from the hearing to the preaching of the
     message.
4   Cf. *RSV*: "Having begun with the Spirit, are you
     now ending with the flesh?" *NEB* introduces "ideal-
     istic" concepts: "You started with the spiritual; do
     you now look to the material to make you perfect?"
     JB points to the Judaizers' demand of circumcision
     and translates accordingly: "Are you foolish enough
     to end in outward observances what you began in
     the Spirit?"
5   Cf. *RSV*: "Did you experience so many things in
     vain?—if it really is in vain." *NEB*: "Have all your
     great experiences been in vain—if vain indeed they
     should be?" *JB*: "Have all the favors you received
     been wasted? And if this were so, they could most
     certainly have been wasted."

6   On the *probatio* see, esp., Volkmann, *Rhetorik*, §§ 16ff;
     Lausberg, *Handbuch*, §§ 348–430; Martin, *Rhetorik*,
     95ff.
7   Quint. 5, *prooemium* 5. The Greek term is πίστις
     (Aristotle *Rhet*. 3.13.4, p. 1414b), which Quint.
     thinks is best translated by the Latin *probatio* (5.10.8)
     rather than the literal *fides*. See Lausberg, *Handbuch*,
     §§ 348–49.
8   Cicero *De inv*. 1.24.34.
9   *Rhet. ad Her*. 1.10.18.
10   See the definition given by Cicero *De inv*. 1.24.34:
     "Confirmation or proof is the part of the oration
     which by marshalling arguments lends credit,
     authority, and support to our case" (Confirmatio
     est per quam argumentando nostrae causae fidem
     et auctoritatem et firmamentum adiungit oratio).
     Rhet. ad Her. 1.10.18: "The entire hope of victory
     and the entire method of persuasion rest on proof
     and refutation, for when we have submitted our
     arguments and destroyed those of the opposition,
     we have, of course, completely fulfilled the speaker's
     function" (Tota spes vincendi ratioque persuadendi
     posita est in confirmatione et in confutatione. Nam
     cum adiumenta nostra exposuerimus contrariaque
     dissolverimus, absolute nimirum munus oratorium
     confecerimus). See Lausberg, *Handbuch*, § 348.

Viewing Galatians from a rhetorical perspective suggests at once that chapters 3 and 4 must contain the *probatio* section. Admittedly, an analysis of these chapters in terms of rhetoric is extremely difficult. One may say that Paul has been very successful—as a skilled rhetorician would be expected to be—in disguising his argumentative strategy. This is to say that, in spite of the apparent confusion, there is to be expected a clear flow of thought. What makes these chapters look so confusing is the frequent interruption of the argumentative sections by dialogue, examples, proverbs, quotations, etc. But this is in conformity with the requirements of Hellenistic rhetoric. In fact, for the rhetoricians of Paul's time, there could be nothing more boring than a perfect product of rhetorical technology.[11] Therefore, the appearance of an argument as a dead system of inescapable and preformed syllogisms had to be avoided; instead, the arguments were to be presented in a lively way. Quintilian's advice is to "diversify by a thousand figures."[12] Paradoxically, extremely perfected logic was thought to create suspicion and boredom, not credibility, while a carefully prepared mixture of some logic, some emotional appeal, some wisdom, some beauty, and some entertainment was thought to conform to human nature and to the ways in which human beings accept arguments as true. Galatians 3 and 4 are such a mixture.

The beginning of the *probatio* section (3:1–5) reveals interesting aspects. The particular "case" in which Paul is involved is constituted by two components. First, there is agreement on the *factum* itself but disagreement on the question of whether the *factum* is right or wrong. Therefore, the argument pertains not to the *factum* itself, but to its *qualitas*. Thus the defense must try to prove that the *factum* was legal (*iure, recte*).[13] This includes also a defense of the *auctor* of that *factum*.[14] In the case of Galatians, the *factum* is not disputed because the founding of the Galatian churches by Paul is not questioned by any of the parties.[15] The question is rather whether this foundation was done rightfully or "in vain."[16]

Secondly, the addressees of the letter, that is, the hearers of the arguments, are also the eye-witnesses of the evidence.[17] This situation provides the writer of the letter with the possibility of proceeding as if the eye-witnesses are "in court."[18] Paul makes full use of this opportunity in 3:1–5; by applying the "inductive method," which rhetoricians traced back to Socrates,[19]

---

11   See Quint. 5.14.27–35.

12   Ibidem, 32; see Lausberg, *Handbuch*, § 257.

13   On the *status qualitatis* see Volkmann, *Rhetorik*, § 7; Lausberg, *Handbuch*, §§ 89, 123–130, 134–138, 171–196; Martin, *Rhetorik*, 36–41.

14   Lausberg, *Handbuch*, §§ 126, 175. He refers to Quint. 3.6.79: "...we...should differentiate between two kinds of quality, one of which comes into play when both the accused person and his act are defended, and the other when the accused person alone is defended" (...qualitatis duplex ratio facienda sit, altera qua et factum defenditur, altera qua tantum reus).

15   See Gal 1:6–9, 11; 3:1–5; 4:13–15.

16   See εἰκῆ Gal 3:4; 4:11; cf. also 2:2, 15–21; 5:2–12; 6:12–16.

17   Cf. 3:1:.. οἷς κατ᾽ ὀφθαλμοὺς Ἰησοῦς Χριστὸς προεγράφη ἐσταυρωμένος. This statement also uses a rhetorical *topos*; see Lausberg, *Handbuch*, § 810; index *s.v. oculus, conspectus*.

18   Cf. Aristotle *Rhet.* 1.15.15f (p. 1376a); Quint. 5.7.1ff, and Lausberg, *Handbuch*, § 354; Martin, *Rhetorik*, 99f.

19   See Cicero *De inv.* 1.31.51: "*Induction* is a form of argument which leads the person with whom one is arguing to give assent to certain undisputed facts; through this assent it wins his approval of a doubtful proposition because this resembles the facts to which he has assented. For instance, in a dialogue by Aeschines Socraticus, Socrates reveals..." (Inductio est oratio quae rebus non dubiis captat assensiones eius quicum instituta est; quibus assensionibus facit ut illi dubia quaedam res propter similitudinem earum rerum quibus assensit probetur; velut apud Socraticum Aeschinen demonstrat Socrates...). 53: "Socrates used this conversational method a good deal, because he wished to present no argument himself, but preferred to get a result from the material which the interlocutor had given him—a result which the interlocutor was bound to approve as following necessarily from what he had already granted" (Hoc modo sermonis plurimum Socrates usus est propterea quod nihil ipse afferre ad persuadendum volebat, sed ex eo quod sibi ille dederat quicum disputabat, aliquid conficere malebat, quod ille ex eo quod iam concessisset necessario approbare deberet). Cf. Quint. 5.11.3–5, and Lausberg, *Handbuch*, §§ 419–421.

he enters into his first argument by an *interrogatio* of these witnesses.[20] In every case the answers to the questions are self-evident and need not be recorded. Paul is not only fortunate in being able to question the eye-witnesses themselves,[21] but he also compels them to produce the strongest of all possible defense arguments—undeniable evidence.[22] This undeniable evidence is the gift of the Spirit, which the Galatians themselves have experienced. The gift of the Spirit was an ecstatic experience.[23] Together with the miracles which are being performed at present among the Galatians,[24] this constitutes evidence of supernatural origin and character which is, for ancient rhetoric, evidence of the highest order.[25]

If, as Paul presumes, the evidence is accepted, his readers will have to make a necessary concession: the experience of the Spirit and the occurrence of miracles did not come about "by works of [the] Law" (ἐξ ἔργων νόμου) but "by [the] proclamation of faith" (ἐξ ἀκοῆς πίστεως).[26] This is evident because at the time of this experience the Galatians had no doubt heard the proclamation of the gospel,[27] but being outside of the Torah they could not have produced "works of [the] Law." This, Paul argues, proved his main point, "justification by faith" instead of "by works of [the] Torah" (cf. 2:16). The *interrogatio* thus also prepares the ground for the next argument, the argument from Scripture (see 3:6–14).

Interpretation

■1 Paul's opening address is no longer as friendly as before (1:11), but biting and aggressive: "O, you foolish Galatians!" (ὦ ἀνόητοι Γαλάται). This insult, however, should not be taken too seriously. Such addresses were commonplace among the diatribe preachers of Paul's day.[28] Paul does not want to say that the Galatians distinguished themselves by their low intelligence.[29] Rather, in his view, they ought to act as "pneumatics" who "know" (cf. 4:8–9; 6:1).

---

20 On the *interrogatio* see the treatment by Quint. 5.7.8–37; also Lausberg, *Handbuch*, § 354; Martin, *Rhetorik*, 100.

21 Cf. Quint. 5.7.1: "It is, however, the evidence that gives the greatest trouble to advocates. Evidence may be given either in writing or orally by witnesses present in court" (Maximus tamen patronis circa testimonia sudor est. Ea dicuntur aut per tabulas aut a praesentibus).

22 Cf. Cicero *De inv.* 1.32.53: "In argumentation of this kind I think the first rule to lay down is that the statement which we introduce as a basis for analogy ought to be of such a kind that its truth must be granted" (Hoc in genere praecipiendum nobis videtur primum, ut illud quod inducemus per similitudinem eiusmodi sit ut sit necesse concedere). See also Quint. 9.2.8.

23 See on Gal 3:2–5.

24 Gal 3:5 ...ἐνεργῶν δυνάμεις ἐν ὑμῖν....

25 Cf. Quint. 5.7.35: "If to this kind of evidence anyone should wish to add evidence of the sort known as supernatural, based on oracles, prophecies and omens, I would remind him that there are two ways in which these may be treated. There is the general method, with regard to which there is an endless dispute between the adherents of the Stoics and the Epicureans, as to whether the world is governed by providence. The other is special and is concerned with particular departments of the art of divination, according as they may happen to affect the question

at issue" (His adiicere si qui volet ea, quae divine testimonia vocant, ex responsis oraculis, ominibus duplicem sciat esse eorum tractatum; generalem alterum, in quo inter Stoicos et Epicuri sectam secutos pugna perpetua est regaturne providentia mundus; specialem alterum circa partis divinationis, ut quaeque in quaestionem cadit). Quint. also has comments about the ambiguity of such divine testimonies (5.7.36). See Lausberg, *Handbuch*, § 176; Volkmann, *Rhetorik*, 239; Martin, *Rhetorik*, 98.

26 Gal 3:2, 5.

27 Cf. Gal 1:6–9; 2:5; 3:2, 5; 4:13; 5:7–10.

28 For examples from the diatribe literature see Bultmann, *Stil*, 13f, 32f, 55, 60ff, 85ff; Bauer, *s.v.*, 1; in the NT see Luke 24:25; Gal 3:3; Rom 1:14; 1 Tim 6:9; Titus 3:3; also *1 Clem.* 21.5; *2 Clem.* 11.3; *Herm. Mand.* 10.2.1.

29 So Jerome, on Gal 3:1 (*PL* 26.372). The right understanding follows from Dio Chrys. 11.1: "I am almost certain while all men are hard to teach, they are easy to deceive. They learn with difficulty—if they learn anything—from the few that know, but they are deceived only too readily by the many who do not know, and not only by others but by themselves as well. For the truth is bitter and unpleasant to the unthinking, while falsehood is sweet and pleasant. They are, I fancy, like men with sore eyes...." The passage is noted by Mussies, *Dio Chrysostom*, 184, on Gal 4:16. Cf. Gal 5:7–10.

The following question is ironic or even sarcastic:[30] "who has bewitched you?" (τίς ὑμᾶς ἐβάσκανεν...;) The term βασκαίνω is used figuratively ("bewitch someone"),[31] a usage common at least since Plato.[32] Its purpose was to characterize opponents and their sophistic[33] strategies.[34] Also Paul's next remark is taken from the rhetorical tradition:[35] "before whose eyes 'Jesus Christ [the] crucified' was portrayed" (οἶς κατ' ὀφθαλμοὺς Ἰησοῦς Χριστὸς προεγράφη ἐσταυρωμένος).

One of the goals of the ancient orator was to deliver his speech so vividly and impressively that his listeners imagined the matter to have happened right before their eyes.[36] All kinds of techniques were recommended to achieve the effect, including impersonations and even holding up painted pictures.[37] Paul, in a case of self-ironic exaggeration, makes use of this topos, reminding[38] the Galatians of his initial efforts to proclaim[39] the gospel of "Jesus Christ [the] crucified"

---

30 Oepke, p. 100.

31 Lightfoot, p. 133; Burton, pp. 143f. Originally, the term is related to magic, especially "the evil eye" (cf. Plutarch *Quaest. conv.* 680C–683B). See Wettstein, on Gal 3:1; Gerhard Delling, "βασκαίνω," *TDNT* 1.594–95; Ernst Kuhnert, "Fascinum," *PW* 6 (1909) 2009–14; Bernhard Kötting, "Böser Blick," *RAC* 2 (1954) 474–82; Preisigke, *Wörterbuch* 4/2 (1958) 353; Dov Noy, "Evil Eye," *EncJud* 6 (1971) 997–1000.

32 In Plato *Phaedo* 95B Socrates says: "My friend,...do not be boastful, lest some evil eye put to rout the argument that is to come" (ὦ 'γαθέ,...μὴ μέγα λέγε, μή τις ἡμῶν βασκανία περιτρέψῃ τὸν μέλλοντα λόγον ἔσεσθαι). Cf. also *Apol.* 17A; *Gorg.* 452Eff.

33 On the idea of rhetorical "enchantment" see Walter Burkert, "ΓΟΗΣ," *RhM* 105 (1962) 36–55, 42f; 55; Betz, *Paulus*, 113 (with reference to 2 Cor 11:4, 13–15, 19–20).

34 See, e.g., Demosthenes 8.19; 16.19; 18 (*De corona*). 108, 132, 139, 189, 242, 252, 307, 317; 20.24; 21.209; *etc.*; *Exord.* 32.3; Libanius (ed. R. Foerster, BT), *Ep.* 1403, vol. 11, 446; Philostratus *Vita Apoll.* 6.12; Lucian *Philops.* 35; Philo *Mos.* 1.4; Hesychius *Lex.* (ed. Latte), s.v. βάσκανος: καὶ ὁ συκοφάντης παρὰ τοῖς ῥήτορσιν ("also the sycophant among the rhetoricians"). Luther, in his commentary of 1535 on 3:1, impressively describes the "magic" of false teaching and illusionary beliefs. Schlier (cf. p. 119) does not recognize the rhetorical background and as a result overemphasizes the magical element; he assumes that in Paul's opinion the Galatians have in fact fallen into the hands of a strange magician and his demonic spells.

35 The matter was correctly understood by those witnesses who add after ἐβάσκανεν the words from Gal 5:7: τῇ ἀληθείᾳ μὴ πείθεσθαι (the *Textus Receptus*, following C D^c K L P Ψ, most minuscules, vg^mss syr^h goth eth, *al*. So Metzger, *Textual Commentary*, 593; cf. Nestle–Aland, *apparatus criticus*).

36 Cf. Aristotle (*Rhet.* 3.11, p. 1411b) where the term is πρὸ ὀμμάτων ποιεῖν (for other instances, see Hermann Bonitz, *Index Aristotelicus* [Berlin: Reimer, 1870] s.v. ὄμμα, 8); *Rhet. ad Her.* 4.47.60; 4.48.61; 4.49.62; Cicero *De orat.* 3.40.160ff; Quint. 4.5.22, 10.2.26; esp. 6.2.29–36. See already Wettstein, on Gal 3:1; also Lausberg, *Handbuch*, § 2, index, *s.v. oculus, conspectus*. It should be noted that the motif is also part of the NT miracle–stories; see e.g. Mark 2:12; cf. 4:12; 8:18.

37 So Quint. 6.1.32: "Still I would not for this reason go so far as to approve a practice of which I have read, and which indeed I have occasionally witnessed, of bringing into court a picture of the crime painted on wood or canvas, that the judge might be stirred to fury by the horror of the sight" (...depictam in tabula sipariove imaginem rei, cuius atrocitate iudex erat commovendus). For other means of reaching the effect see Quint. 6.1.29–36: among the *realia* he mentions blood–stained swords and garments, fragments of bones, wounds stripped of their bandages, and scourged bodies.

38 The epistle makes all of this present again. Cf. Gal 4:13f; 6:17. See on this point Thraede, *Brieftopik*, 157ff; Karlhans Abel, *Bauformen in Senecas Dialogen* (Bibliothek der Klassischen Altertumswissenschaft NF 2.18; Heidelberg: Winter, 1967) 31f.

39 προγράφω can here mean "portray publicly" or "proclaim publicly." See LSJ, *s.v.*; Gottlob Schrenk, "προγράφω," *TDNT* 1.770–72; Bauer, *s.v.*, 2. Modern commentators usually prefer the second option (Lightfoot; Burton; Oepke; Schlier; Mussner; Betz, *Nachfolge*, 178), but the rhetorical material lends support also to the first (Chrysostom, Erasmus, Luther, Calvin; see the list in Sieffert, pp. 162f). The *Textus Receptus*, following D E F G K L, many minuscules, it^{d, g} syr^h goth *al*, add ἐν ὑμῖν (so Metzger, *Textual Commentary*, 593f). This indicates that these witnesses probably understood "προ-" in the sense of "at the beginning (cf. Gal 4:13)." *AV* translates "crucified among you," which agrees with Luther's interpretation, that Paul preached Christ as the one who through their apostasy is being crucified among the Galatians now (*In Epist. ad Gal.* [1535], on Gal 3:1). Cf. Schlier, p. 120 n. 4; Mussner, p. 207 n. 11.

(Ἰησοῦς Χριστὸς ἐσταυρωμένος) to them.[40] But what can he do against the spells and charms his opponents have cast upon the Galatians! Something "irrational" must have happened to them, or else one cannot explain why they so quickly abandon the original kerygma in which they had believed thus far (cf. 1:6–7; 5:7–10).

■ **2** The second rhetorical question introduces the main point of Paul's defense. Rather than presenting it himself,[41] Paul wants to hear it from the Galatians, and thus uses a dialogical device:[42] "this only I want to learn from you..." (τοῦτο μόνον θέλω μαθεῖν ἀφ' ὑμῶν). Paul's reason for asking the question is that he can expect their answer to come from their own experience.[43] This experience is an undeniable fact and contradicts their present inclination to accept circumcision and Torah. "Did you receive the Spirit on the basis of 'works of [the] Law' or on the basis of 'proclamation of [the] faith'?" The answer to this question is self-evident; since the Galatians are only presently considering coming under the Torah, they must have received the Spirit at the beginning after hearing Paul's proclamation of the Christian gospel, that is, outside of the Torah. We can conclude that "receiving the Spirit"[44] meant an enthusiast's or ecstatic experience.[45] The basis for making this assumption is certainly hypothetical, since nothing is said at least in this passage.[46] But in 6:1 Paul calls the Galatians, certainly with their approval, by the technical term "pneumatics" (οἱ πνευματικοί).

In 4:6 his description of the gift of the Spirit of God's son into the hearts of the believers suggests ecstasy; it is the Spirit of the believers which cries out "Abba,

40 This abbreviated form of the "kerygma" is found also 1 Cor 1:23; 2:2; cf. 1 Cor 1:13, 17, 18; 2:8; 2 Cor 13:4; Gal 5:11, 24; 6:12, 14, 17; Phil 2:8; 3:18; Col 1:20; 2:14; Eph 2:16; Ign. *Eph.* 16.2; Ign. *Trall.* 9.1; etc. See Johannes Schneider, "σταυρός κτλ.," *TDNT* 7.575–76; Bultmann, *Theology*, § 33; Conzelmann, *Outline*, § 24; Ernst Käsemann, "The Saving Significance of the Death of Jesus in Paul," in his *Perspectives*, 32–59; Heinz–Wolfgang Kuhn, "Jesus als Gekreuzigter in der frühchristlichen Verkündigung bis zur Mitte des des 2. Jahrhunderts," *ZThK* 72 (1975) 1–46, esp. 31–37.

41 Cf. Rom 1:13; 11:25; 16:19; 1 Cor 10:1; 11:3; 12:1; 2 Cor 1:8; 1 Thess 4:13.

42 Other examples are to be found in Sophocles *Oed. Col.* 505; Euripides *Iph. Taur.* 493: τόδε μαθεῖν πρῶτον θέλω ("This I want to learn first." [A question precedes.]); *Troad.* 63; Dionysius Halic. 3.60.1: ἐν τοῦτο μόνον ἔφη παρ' αὐτῶν βούλεσθαι μαθεῖν... ("This one thing only, said he, he wanted to learn from them..."); 3.3.4, 5.54.3. See also Plato *Phaedr.* 262 D; *Phaedo* 63 E; *Gorg.* 494 D; Philo *Her.* 33; *Fuga* 8; 164; *Decal.* 59; *Spec.* 1.36, 42; *Flacc.* 363; and *Corp. Herm.* 1.3.

43 So with most exegetes Schlier (p. 121). See esp. Luther (1535) on Gal 3:2, who recognized that Paul's argument in 3:1–5 is based on experience (*argumentum ab experientia*, WA 40/1.328, cf. 359).

44 The expression "receive the Spirit" (τὸ πνεῦμα λαμβάνειν) occurs also Gal 3:14 (τὴν ἐπαγγελίαν τοῦ πνεύματος λαμβάνειν, "receive the promise of the Spirit"); Rom 8:15; 1 Cor 2:12; 2 Cor 11:4. It is a common Christian term: cf. John 20:22; Acts 2:38; 8:15, 17, 19; 10:47; 19:2. The doctrine of the divine Spirit plays a very important role in Gal; the term used is usually τὸ πνεῦμα ("the Spirit"), see 3:2, 3, 5, 14; 4:6, 29; 5:5, 13 *v.l.*, 16, 17, 18, 22, 25; 6:1, 8, 18. On Paul's pneumatology in general, see Bultmann, *Theology*, §§ 37, 38; Eduard Schweizer, "πνεῦμα, πνευματικός," *TDNT* 6.413–51, with a large bib.; Ingo Hermann, *Kyrios und Pneuma: Studien zur Christologie der paulinischen Hauptbriefe* (StANT 2; Munich: Kösel, 1961); Brandenburger, *Fleisch und Geist, passim*; Willibald Pfister, *Das Leben im Geist nach Paulus. Der Geist als Anfang und Vollendung des christlichen Lebens* (Studia Friburgensia NF 34; Freiburg, Switzerland: Universitätsverlag, 1963); Max Alain Chevallier, *Esprit de Dieu, paroles d'hommes. Le rôle de l'esprit dans les ministères de la parole selon l'apôtre Paul* (Neuchâtel: Delachaux & Niestlé, 1966); Béda Rigaux, "L'anticipation du salut eschatologique par l'Esprit," in *Foi et salut selon S. Paul* (AnBib 42; Rome: Pontifical Biblical Institute, 1970) 101–35; Johannes S. Vos, *Traditionsgeschichtliche Untersuchungen zur paulinischen Pneumatologie* (Assen: Van Gorcum, 1973); Martin Winter, *Pneumatiker und Psychiker in Korinth* (Marburger Theologische Studien 12; Marburg: Elwert, 1975); James D. G. Dunn, *Jesus and the Spirit* (Philadelphia: Westminster, 1975) esp. 199–342.

45 See the section on the spirit in Widengren, *Religionsphänomenologie*, 111–13. For parallels from Hellenistic religions, see Conzelmann, *1 Corinthians*, 204ff; *PECL*, index, *s.v.* "Spirit."

46 Paul's remarks are, however, confirmed by Acts (cf. 10:44, 45, 47; 11:12, 15; 15:8; 19:1–5).

Father." 3:2–4 uses terminology familiar from other religions, in particular the mystery cults: ἐνάρχεσθαι ["begin"] and ἐπιτελεῖν ["finish"][47] and also the word pair μαθεῖν / παθεῖν ("learn / experience"). It remains unclear how baptism is related to this experience.[48] At any rate, it cannot be denied that the experience of the Spirit occurred outside of the Torah covenant, that is, not as a result of "works of the Torah" (ἐξ ἔργων νόμου) now.[49] If the experience of the Spirit was not based on the "works of the Torah" it could only be based on the "proclamation of faith" (ἐξ ἀκοῆς πίστεως).[50] If this were sufficient then, why not now?

■ 3 Paul repeats his biting attack[51] upon the readers (cf. 3:1) by asking again "are you so foolish?" (οὕτως ἀνόητοί ἐστε;) "Foolish" they are because they are contradicting themselves when they, as they presently plan, come under the Torah (cf. 4:21). Paul formulates what he perceives as their self-contradiction in the form of a dilemma and a chiastic antitheton:[52] "having

begun 'in [the] Spirit,' are you now finishing up 'in [the] flesh'?" (ἐναρξάμενοι πνεύματι νῦν σαρκὶ ἐπιτελεῖσθε;) Paul's antitheton which has parallels in 2:14; 4:8–9 uses several opposites to characterize the inconsistencies of the Galatians: beginning and end,[53] imperfect beginning and climactic perfection,[54] Spirit and flesh.[55] The beginning "in the Spirit" ought to continue "in the Spirit":[56] "if we live by the Spirit, let us also follow the Spirit" (5:25). In the context of the dualism of the Spirit and flesh, it only makes sense to move out of the sphere of the flesh into that of the Spirit, but not the other way around. "For he who sows into his flesh will from the flesh harvest corruption; but he who sows into the Spirit will from the Spirit harvest eternal life" (6:8). It is equally absurd to regard the gift of the divine Spirit as an imperfect beginning and to expect the climax and perfection from something done to the human "flesh." It is important to hear the cultic overtones[57] in Paul's language. Perhaps one of the terms

---

47 See Widengren, *Religionsphänomenologie*, 494.

48 Gal 3:27 presupposes the initiation rite of baptism, but the Spirit is not mentioned in the composition 3:26–28. Cf. Acts 10:47–48; 11:16–18. Paul's reservations with regard to baptism are apparent from 1 Cor 1:14–17. Perhaps Paul hesitated to say simply that the Spirit is "mediated" through baptism (cf. Schlier, p. 123; Kertelge, "*Rechtfertigung*," 248f).

49 For this concept, see on Gal 2:16.

50 This concept comes from missionary language (see Gal 3:5; Rom 10:16–17; 1 Thess 2:13; Heb 4:12; John 12:38). On the concept see Albrecht Oepke, *Die Missionspredigt des Apostels Paulus* (Leipzig: Hinrichs, 1920) 40ff; Gottfried Quell, "ἀγαπάω," *TDNT* 1.22–23; Burton, p. 147; Oepke, p. 67; Schlier, pp. 121f; Mussner, p. 207. The term ἀκοή implies that a message which was received by divine revelation is being proclaimed orally and heard. When heard in the sense of "accepted" it creates faith because it carries with it a divine power—the "power of the word" (cf. Rom 1:16; 1 Cor 1:18, 24; 2:4f; 4:19f; 1 Thess 1:5). The phrase ἐξ ἀκοῆς πίστεως may be constructed in antithesis to ἐξ ἔργων νόμου; while the Torah requires man to do "works of [the] law," the Christian message "gives" Spirit and faith to man (cf. 3:21f; Rom 10:8–18). Paul does not reflect upon the difference between himself and the Galatians; his conversion was the result of a vision of Christ and not, as it is for them, of the hearing of the Christian message (cf. 1:12–16a).

51 In rhetoric this type of invective would fall under "frankness of speech" (παρρησία, *oratio libera, licentia*). See *Rhet. ad Her.* 4.36.48, and Lausberg, *Handbuch*, § 761; Martin, *Rhetorik*, 279.

52 On this figure of speech, see Lausberg, *Handbuch*, § 796.

53 The temporal meaning is expressed by ἐνάρχομαι ("begin") and νῦν ("now"). Cf. Gal 6:9; Phil 1:6; 2 Cor 8:6. For a philosophical parallel, see Plutarch *Prof. virt.* 77A–B.

54 ἐπιτελέομαι has a qualitative connotation ("completion," "perfection"). Cf. Phil 1:6; Rom 15:28; 2 Cor 8:6, 11. For the older literature, see Bauer, *s.v.*, 1: "either as mid.: *you have begun in the Spirit, will you now end in the flesh?* or as pass: *will you be made complete in the flesh?*"; Oepke, Schlier, Sieffert (p. 167).

55 The juxtaposition of "Spirit" (πνεῦμα) and "flesh" (σάρξ) occurs also Gal 5:16f, and 4:23, 29; 5:19–23; 6:8. On Paul's doctrine of "flesh" cf. on 2:16.

56 The dative πνεύματι ("in" or "by" [the] Spirit") appears throughout Gal (cf. 5:5, 16, 18, 25; also Rom 8:13, 14; 12:11; 1 Cor 14:2, 15, 16; 2 Cor 12:18; Phil 3:3). See Bauer, *s.v.*, 5, d, β.

57 ἐνάρχομαι ("begin") can have cultic overtones. Cf. its usage at the beginning of the sacrifice in Euripides *Iph. Aul.* 1470; in magic *PGM* 4.509 (vol. 1, p. 90). See LSJ, *s.v.*; Paul Stengel, *Die griechischen Kultusaltertümer* (HKAW 5.3; Munich: Beck, 1920) 109f; Walter Burkert, *Homo Necans* (RVV 32; Berlin: de Gruyter, 1972) 11f, 19f. If the initial experience of the Galatians had cultic overtones,

played a role for the opponents.[58] In any case, by adding σαρκί ("in" or "through the flesh")[59] the gift is turned into an absurdity.[60] Ultimately, of course, Paul alludes to the rite of circumcision considered at present by the Galatians.[61] The real reason for this step may be revealed in Jas 2:22, where "works" are the goal and perfection of "faith." This Jewish–Christian concept, which is diametrically opposed to Paul's, may have been shared by the anti-Pauline opposition in Galatia.

■ 4 Paul acts as if he is at the end of his wits.[62] He exclaims seemingly in despair and also in anger: "have you experienced such things in vain? If so, it really was in vain!" (τοσαῦτα ἐπάθετε εἰκῇ; εἴ γε καὶ εἰκῇ.) The translation of this passage is difficult and dis-

puted.[63] The experiences Paul refers to must be those connected with the Spirit (cf. 3:3).[64] The term πάσχω can be taken in a more neutral sense ("experience") or negatively, as often in the New Testament ("suffer").[65] Again, the possibility exists that Paul plays with terminology known to us especially from the context of the mystery religions.[66] This becomes possible not only because of the experiences of ecstasy and miracles, but also because of the association of παθεῖν ("experience") with μαθεῖν ("learn," 3:2). This word pair has had a long history in Greek thought[67] and seems to be brought in by Paul here to make his point. Gift of the Spirit, enthusiasm, miracles[68]—was it all in vain? The next sentence can be interpreted in several ways. It can be taken as another question, or it can be an exclamation,

---

they did not by necessity include notions of "sacrifice" (contra Lightfoot, p. 135). The term ἐπιτελέω was used for all kinds of rituals. See passages listed in LSJ, *s.v.*; Bauer, *s.v.*, 2; Gerhard Delling, "ἐπιτελέω," *TDNT* 8.61–62; Franciszek Sokolowski, *Lois sacrées des cités grecques* (Paris: de Boccard, 1969) index, *s.v.* Cf. Epiphanius *Pan.* 2.2 about "Ebion" and his adherence to the Jewish Law: "the sabbath and circumcision and all the other things which are performed (ἐπιτελεῖται) by Jews and Samaritans."

58 Note the importance of the term in 2 Cor 7:1 (see below, Appendix 2). This must be the result of observing the precepts for purity (2 Cor 6:17) and the "cleansing of the flesh and the spirit from all pollution" (2 Cor 7:1). See also Betz, "2 Cor 6:14–7:1," 98f. That the term comes from Paul's opponents has been suggested before (see Sieffert, p. 168; Oepke, p. 68). Note also the importance of similar concepts in James: τελέω Jas 2:8; τέλειος 1:4, 17, 25; 3:2; τελειόω 2:22.

59 This form has no precise parallel elsewhere in Paul; it seems to be created in juxtaposition to πνεύματι (see above, n. 56); for other meanings cf. Gal 1:16; 5:13; Rom 7:25; 8:12; 1 Cor 7:28; 2 Cor 12:7. That man lives "in [the] flesh" (ἐν σαρκί) is part of human existence in this "evil eon" (1:4). Cf. 2:16, 20; 4:13f; 5:13, 16, 17, 19, 24; etc.

60 See the parallel in Gal 6:12: "those who want to make a good showing in the flesh." See Eduard Schweizer, "σάρξ," *TDNT* 7.129–30; Brandenburger, *Fleisch und Geist*, 45.

61 See on this Gal 5:2–12; 6:12–16; also 2:3, 7, 8, 9, 12; Phil 3:3f. Differently Rom 2:28.

62 It may be a case of *dubitatio*; cf. Lausberg, *Handbuch*, §§ 776–78.

63 See the n. on the tr. On the meaning of the particles see BDF, § 439; BDR, § 439; Bauer, *s.v.* γέ, 3, a; John D. Denniston, *The Greek Particles* (Oxford: Clarendon, ²1954) 126; Thrall, *Greek Particles*, 86f.

64 Contra Lightfoot (p. 135) who thinks Paul refers to persecutions endured by them. This interpretation goes back as far as Chrysostom (see Sieffert, p. 168); it is shared by Zahn; Lütgert, *Gesetz und Geist*, 97. But nowhere else does Paul say that the Galatians have been persecuted (cf. 6:12).

65 See Bauer, *s.v.*, 1; Wilhelm Michaelis, "πάσχω," *TDNT* 5.904–39, esp. 912; Burton, Oepke, Schlier, Mussner.

66 Cf. Aristotle, Περὶ φιλοσοφίας, 15 (ed. Ross): "as Aristotle thinks that those who are initiated [into the mysteries] should not simply learn something, but should experience and be put into a certain disposition, that is, they should become suitable" (καθάπερ Ἀριστοτέλης ἀξιοῖ τοὺς τελουμένους οὐ μαθεῖν τι δεῖν ἀλλὰ παθεῖν καὶ διατεθῆναι, δηλονότι γενομένους ἐπιτηδείους). See Nilsson, *Geschichte*, 1.654. Plutarch *Frag.* 178: "…but when that time comes, it [the soul] has an experience like that of men who are undergoing initiation into [? the] great mysteries" (τότε δὲ πάσχει πάθος οἷον οἱ τελεταῖς μεγάλαις κατοργιαζόμενοι). See Nilsson, *Geschichte*, 2.680; *PECL* 1.322.

67 See Mario Untersteiner, *Le origini della tragedia e del tragico dalla preistoria a Eschilo* (Turin: Einaudi, 1955) 572–81; Heinrich Dörrie, *Leid und Erfahrung. Die Wort- und Sinnverbindung παθεῖν–μαθεῖν im griechischen Denken* (AAWLMG, Jg. 1956, No. 5; Wiesbaden: Steiner, 1956) with many references. From the NT Dörrie cites only Heb 5:8 (39f).

68 Cf. Gal 3:5.

either emphatically denying or indeed threatening that it was "in vain."[69] Paul does entertain elsewhere the idea that his efforts in Galatia may have been in vain.[70] Also the Galatians inadvertently admit that they think Paul's mission was "in vain" and that they must turn to his opponents for that very reason.[71] In rhetoric the exclamatory "in vain" seems to have been a popular device for threatening people who enter into dubious political deals and maneuvers.[72] Therefore, it is most probably a rhetorical exclamation and Paul himself provides the answer: "if so, it really was in vain!"

■ 5 Paul concludes[73] the section by now confronting the Galatians with the main argument of his defense.[74] More than merely repeating the question of v 2 he gives it another twist by further interpreting some of its elements and by including the substance of v 3. He also continues to use the form of the question because the answer to be given by the Galatians must inevitably be affirmative, and thus must support Paul's argument: "therefore, does he who supplies the Spirit to you and who works miracles among you [do so] by 'works of [the] Law', or by 'proclamation of [the] faith'?" Instead of merely naming the experience as he had done in v 2, Paul now goes on to identify its source: "he who grants you the Spirit" (ὁ... ἐπιχορηγῶν ὑμῖν τὸ πνεῦμα) is of course no one else but God,[75] as the Spirit is his gift.[76] Also, this experience is not limited to the initial period, but there are even at present manifestations of the Spirit among them.[77] "Miracles" (δυνάμεις)[78] can be named as evidence for the fact that the Spirit is "at work" (ἐνεργῶν)[79] among them.[80] Consequently, God must now be at work among them.

69 εἴ γε καὶ εἰκῆ can be understood as an encouragement, that it cannot have been in vain (so Chrysostom, Ambrosiaster, Luther, Calvin, etc.; see the list in Sieffert, pp. 170f), or as a threat (so Sieffert, Oepke, Burton, Schlier, Mussner). Lightfoot (p. 135) seems to grasp Paul's strategy best: "It is hard to believe this; the Apostle hopes better things of his converts. Εἴ γε leaves a loophole for doubt, and widens this, implying an unwillingness to believe on the part of the speaker." On εἰκῆ see also BDF, § 26; BDR, § 26.

70 Cf. Gal 4:11, 15a; 2:2, 5, 14, 21; 1 Cor 15:2.

71 Cf. Gal 1:6–9; 2:4, 14; 5:10; 1 Cor 15:2, 14, 17; 16:22; 2 Cor 11:3f; 13:5. Differently Schlier (pp. 124f) for whom the Spirit given in baptism is an indestructible gift. Cf. Mussner, p. 210.

72 εἰκῆ occurs often in the rhetoricians and the diatribe philosophers. Especially close is Epictetus Diss. 2.23.3: "Did God give you eyes to no purpose [εἰκῆ], did He to no purpose [εἰκῆ] put in them a spirit so strong...?" See also 3.23.3; 4.3.3 (εἰ δὲ μή, ...εἰκῆ...), and often; Demosthenes 27.54, 28.5, 30.20, 33.1, 48.43; Isocrates Ep. 1.10; 2.9, 22; 6.11; Paneg. 12, 136; Eir. 30; Antid. 157, 209, and often; Isaeus 1.9. Parallels may be found also in Plato Gorg. 506 D; Alcib. 2.141 C.

73 On this meaning of οὖν ("therefore"), see Bauer, s.v., 1, c; Schlier (p. 125 n. 2).

74 This may be what Paul calls in 1 Cor 2:4 ἡ ἀπόδειξις πνεύματος καὶ δυνάμεως ("the proof of Spirit and power"). See also Lausberg, Handbuch, §§ 358–72.

75 Cf. esp. Gal 4:6; also 1:1, 4, 15; 2:21, passages which underscore that God is the source of Paul's concept of salvation. Cf. furthermore 1 Thess 4:8;

76 Cf. Phil 1:19: διὰ τῆς...ἐπιχορηγίας τοῦ πνεύματος Ἰησοῦ Χριστοῦ ("through the ...gift of the spirit of Jesus Christ").

77 The participle ἐπιχορηγῶν ("provide") suggests a continuous supply rather than an initial and momentary "outpouring" (cf. the use of the term in 2 Cor 9:10; Col 2:19; Eph 4:16; 1 Clem. 38.2; Herm. Sim. 2.5, 6, 7).

78 δύναμις in connection with ἐνεργεῖν points to the occurrence of miracles. See Mark 6:14; Matt 14:2; Eph 2:2; also 1 Cor 12:10, 28f; 2 Cor 12:12; 2 Thess 2:9; Acts 2:22. See Walter Grundmann, "δύναμαι, δύναμις," TDNT 2.304–17; Bauer, s.v., 4; Betz, Paulus, 95. It remains unclear what kind of miracles Paul has in mind. Schlier (p. 126) thinks of exorcisms because it would provide a contrast to v 1: "The Galatians whom God gave the power over the evil demons, so that they can drive them out, are themselves fascinated and taken captive by them, when they appear as preachers of the law." This is, however, over–interpretation. Schmithals (Paul and the Gnostics, 47) thinks of ecstatic phenomena; Mussner (p. 211) of charismatic gifts.

79 On God's ἐνεργεῖν see Gal 2:8; also 1 Thess 2:13; Phil 2:13; 1 Cor 12:6, 10, 11 ("Spirit"); Phil 3:21 ("Christ"). On the term see Kenneth W. Clark, "The meaning of ἐνεργέω and καταργέω in the New Testament," JBL 54 (1935) 93–101; Georg Bertram, "ἔργον κτλ.," TDNT 2.652–54; Eduard Schweizer, "πνεῦμα, πνευματικός," TDNT 6.421–22; Bauer, s.v.; Bultmann, Theology, § 14; Käsemann, Römer, 19ff.

80 ἐν ὑμῖν ("among you"), so Burton, Schlier, Mussner, and most commentators, but Lightfoot (p. 136)

76 2 Cor 1:22; Rom 5:5; 8:15.

The rest of the sentence is elliptical,[81] so that we must supplement the missing link—something like "does he do so...?" The argument is clear. If the preceding is assumed, what does this mean for the alternative introduced in v 2: did these things happen "on the basis of works of [the] Law" (ἐξ ἔργων νόμου) or "on the basis of proclamation of [the] faith" (ἐξ ἀκοῆς πίστεως)? The answer is obvious because the Galatians were not "under the Torah" at the beginning of their Christian life, nor are they law observers now. God gave the Spirit and lets the miracles happen as a result of Paul's preaching of the Christ crucified, that is, apart from any observation of the Torah. This means that the proclamation of the Christian faith alone is sufficient for God's grace, and therefore suffi-

cient for the Galatians' salvation. This is no doubt Paul's position. But is it the only conceivable position? Presumably, the opponents of the Apostle see the matter differently, and as a result of their influence the Galatians must have come to look at themselves differently. It is hardly possible to say more and remain free from sheer speculation. But at least in v 3 there could be a hint that Paul's missionary efforts were taken as merely the first step, and that the opponents claimed to provide the necessary and final measures to bring salvation to completion and perfection. Paul would then defend himself by saying that the first step was all that was needed, and that his gospel is in no way deficient, premature, or illegitimate.[82]

renders "in you" (cf. also Sieffert, p. 171). The same problem exists in Gal 4:19–20.

81   See for this BDF, § 479, BDR, § 479.

82   Schlier (p. 126) sees it differently: Paul does not dwell for long on this first argument, because "he must speak more basically." The argument from Scripture, to which Paul turns next, is "of still greater weight both for the Galatians and for Paul's opponents." Mussner (p. 211) does not regard v 5 as an answer at all: "And yet, there is an answer, not an answer which the Galatians give on the basis of their Christian experience or which Paul himself gives, but an answer which Scripture gives."

3

Probatio: The Second Argument

6 As [it is written], "Abraham believed, and this was credited to him as righteousness." 7/ Recognize, therefore, that the men of faith,[1] these are sons of Abraham. 8/ But Scripture, foreseeing that God justifies the Gentiles through faith, proclaimed the gospel beforehand to Abraham, "In you shall all the Gentiles be blessed." 9/ Therefore, the men of faith[1] are blessed together with Abraham the believer. 10/ By contrast, those who are men of works of [the] Law[2] are under a curse. For it is written, "Cursed is everyone who does not stay with everything that is written in the book of the Law, to do it." 11/ It is, then, obvious that nobody is justified before God by Law, because "The righteous shall live by faith." 12/ Also, the Law is not by faith,[3] but "He who does them shall live by them." 13/ Christ has redeemed us from the curse of the Law by becoming a curse for us,[4] for it is written, "Cursed is everyone who hangs on a tree." 14/ [The purpose was] that the blessing of Abraham might come upon the Gentiles through Jesus Christ, and that we might receive the promise of the Spirit through faith.

Analysis

The section 3:6–14 contains the second part of the *probatio*, an argument from the Scripture which makes use of the *exemplum* of Abraham.[5] There is agreement among the exegetes that Paul's argument in this section is extremely difficult to follow. To the readers of today, especially to those trained in the methods of historical-critical Scripture interpretation, Paul's way of arguing appears arbitrary in the highest degree. Thus it is understandable that a critical mind like Alfred Loisy called it "*une fantaisie ingénieuse.*"[6]

As a matter of methodological principle, however, one will have to analyze both the quotations from Scripture and the meaning Paul finds in terms of *his*, and not simply our modern, methodology. This requires that we distinguish between his reading of the quotations and what the same quotation meant to other authors, and of course what they meant originally and historically.[7] We cannot expect more from Paul's method than what was expected in his own time. It was expected that a proof could demonstrate by some agreed method that one's ideas and notions were

1 So *RSV, NEB. JB* translates: "those who rely on faith."
2 Cf. *RSV:* "all who rely on works of the law;" *NEB:* "those who rely on obedience to the law;" *JB:* "those who rely on the keeping of the law."
3 Cf. *RSV:* "the law does not rest on faith;" *NEB:* "law is not at all a matter of having faith;" *JB:* "the Law is not even based on faith."
4 Cf. *NEB:* "Christ bought us freedom from the curse of the law by becoming for our sake an accursed thing...."
5 So correctly Luther (1535): "Now Paul adds the example of Abraham and recites testimonies from Scripture" ("Iam addit exemplum Abrahae et recitat testimonia Scripturae." WA 40/1.359).
6 Loisy, p. 151.
7 Differently Peter Jung, "Das paulinische Vokabular in Gal 3:6–14," *ZKTh* 74 (1952) 439–49. If I understand him correctly, Jung tries to show that the consistency of Paul's argument derives from the fact that he extracts his vocabulary from the Scripture quotations, in order then to regard it as the prototype of his concept of salvation.

attested by or contained in the passage referred to as evidence.[8] The basic skill, therefore, was to find passages in the Scriptures which had the same terminology one was using in the argument.[9] If we keep this methodology in mind, it can be shown that Paul's argument is consistent.[10]

Paul starts out (3:6) by quoting that Scripture passage which he claims as the proof text for the entire argument in 3:6–14. This is followed by the presentation of his exegetical thesis (3:7). The main section (3:8–13) includes a set of five Scripture proofs which are intended as evidence for the thesis in 3:7. They show that 3:7 is the correct interpretation of the Scripture passage quoted in 3:6. The section 3:8–13 mixes in a peculiar way quotations and exegetical conclusions,

leaving unexplained most of the methods by which Paul arrives at his conclusions. Usually the exegetical conclusions precede the Scripture quotations; only in the first proof (3:8–9) does a dogmatic presupposition precede (3:8a) and a conclusion follow (3:9) the actual quotation (3:8b). The first and the last of the five proofs are positive (3:8–9, 13), focusing upon "Scripture" and "Christ" as God's agents—the last proof (3:13) being formulated as a christological dogma. The second, third, and fourth proofs are negative, serving to exclude the opposite alternatives, especially the Torah, as a way to salvation. There are two conclusions to the section (3:14). The first (3:14a) states the result of the discussion of 3:6–13, the second (3:14b)

---

8 Following Gottlieb Klein (*Studien über Paulus* [Stockholm: Bonniers, 1918] 67f), Schoeps (*Paul*, 177f) has suggested that in 3:11–12 Paul makes use of the 13th middah of R. Ishmael. Hab 2:4: "The righteous one shall *live by faith*," and Lev 18:5: "He who *does* them [*sc.* the commandments of the Torah], shall *live by them*" are to be taken as contradictions of Scripture, posing the problem: Does one live by faith or by works? According to Schoeps, Paul solves this rabbinic problem by applying the 13th middah of R. Ishmael (the שני כתובים): "Two verses contradict one another until a third verse reconciles them." This third verse is then identified as Gen 15:6: "Abraham believed and this was reckoned to him as righteousness" (3:6). This intriguing hypothesis, however, cannot be accepted for the following reasons: (1) the 13th middah is not attested before R. Ishmael who died ca. A.D. 135 and who is believed to have created it. See on this, Adolf Schwarz, *Die hermeneutische Antinomie der talmudischen Literatur* (Vienna and Leipzig: Hölder, 1913), and the corrections by Vigdor Aptowitzer, "Die talmudische Literatur der letzten Jahre," *MGWJ* 60 (1916) 174–81; cf. also Louis Jacobs, "Hermeneutics," *EncJud* 8 (1971) 366–72; Shmuel Safrai, "Ishmael Ben Elisha," *EncJud* 9 (1971) 83–86 for further bib. (2) The "third verse" does not *follow* as would be required by the 13th middah, but according to Schoeps is anticipated already in Gal 3:6.

A variation of Schoeps' hypothesis was proposed by Nils A. Dahl, "Motsigelser i Skriften et gammelt hermeneutisk problem," *STK* 45 (1969) 22–36; rep. as "Widersprüche in der Bibel, ein altes hermeneutisches Problem," *StTh* 25 (1971) 1–19. Dahl sees that Ishmael's 13th middah, as it was traditionally

understood, does not apply in Paul's case. But he wants to go back to Hillel's older understanding of the rule, according to which both related but contradictory passages must be upheld as equally valid through relating them to their respective contexts. The rule would of course apply to Gal 3:11f only if Paul were in fact concerned with the problem of two contradicting passages. In Paul's argument, however, this is not the case. According to Pauline theology, Scripture says that the *concepts* of "faith" and "law" are opposites. This is different from the rabbinic problem of two Scripture *texts* opposing each other. For Paul, Hab 2:4 and Lev 18:5 do not contradict each other, but prove separate points in a consecutive argument. Against Dahl see also Ragnar Bring, "Tosrättfärdighet och lagens fullgörande," *STK* 45 (1969) 101–15.

9 This leads also to the rejection of the hypothesis offered by Wilhelm Koepp, "Die Abraham-Midraschimkette des Galaterbriefes als das vorpaulinische heidenchristliche Urtheologumenon," *Wissenschaftliche Zeitschrift der Universität Rostock*, 2, 3 (1952/53) 181–87. Koepp takes Gal 3–4 and divides it up into five "midrashim," which he thinks Paul has taken over from the church in Antioch. But Koepp makes no attempt to prove any of the many links of his chain of suppositions.

10 The other side of this argument can be seen in the strongly anti–Pauline *Kerygmata Petrou*, where it is argued that the written text of the OT was falsified by "forgers" who inserted "false pericopes" for the purpose of proving doctrine opposed to the *Kerygmata Petrou*. See on this HSW, *NT Apocrypha* 2.111–15, 118–21; Strecker, *Judenchristentum*, 166ff. See also the Introduction, § 2. c, and Appendix 3.

relates this result to the first argument (3:2, 5), and also introduces the catch word "promise" to be taken up in the following section.

Excursus:
Abraham

The role Abraham played in Judaism is clearly outlined in the "praise of the Fathers" Sir 44:19–21 (*NEB*): "great Abraham was the father of many nations; no one has ever been found to equal him in fame. He kept the law of the Most High; he entered into covenant with him, setting upon his body the mark of the covenant; and when he was tested, he proved faithful. Therefore, the Lord swore an oath to him, that nations should find blessing through his descendants, that his family should be countless as the dust of the earth and be raised as high as the stars, and that their possessions should reach from sea to sea, from the Great River to the end of the earth." Cf. *Jub.* 23.10 (tr. Charles): "for Abraham was perfect in all his deeds with the Lord, and well-pleasing in righteousness all the days of his life." Abraham, says God to Isaac, "obeyed My voice, and kept My charge and My commandments, and My laws, and My ordinances, and My covenant" (24.11).

Jewish haggadah developed this model at greater length and with more detail. It was especially the sacrifice of Isaac which was taken to be the most difficult of Abraham's temptations—all the more proving his faithfulness ($\epsilon \dot{\upsilon} \rho \acute{\epsilon} \theta \eta \ \pi \iota \sigma \tau \acute{o} \varsigma$ ["he was found faithful"] [Sir 44:19–21; 1 Macc 2:52]). Abraham's faith is, according to Jewish theology, in no way opposed to his deeds; rather, it is this unyielding trust in God's promise and his steadfastness in all his temptations that make up his works, and thus qualify him for the reward of righteousness. Consequently Philo is right when he names $\pi \acute{\iota} \sigma \tau \iota \varsigma$ ("faithfulness") as Abraham's greatest virtue.

In regard to the New Testament, this interpretation of Abraham is shared by Jas 2:21–23 (see also *1 Clem.* 10), but contradicted by Paul. Paul separates Abraham's faith in God's promise from his obedience to the Jewish Torah. He denies the existence of the Torah at the time of Abraham on the ground that the Jewish Torah was revealed only 430 years later (cf. Gal 3:17). Therefore, Abraham's faith cannot have been anything but his belief in God's promise. This "faith" is then set up in opposition of the "works of the law," i.e., the obedience to the Jewish Torah. As a result, Abraham becomes the prototype of the Gentile–Christian believer, as opposed to the Jewish (and Jewish–Christian) observer of the Torah. The question is whether this contrasting of Abraham with the

Torah of Moses is Paul's own invention or whether there were antecedents. Hengel, *Judaism and Hellenism* 1.277ff; and his "Zwischen Jesus und Paulus: Die 'Hellenisten', die 'Sieben' und Stephanus (Apg 6, 1–15; 7, 54–8, 3)" *ZThK* 72 (1975) 151–206, following Elias Bickermann (*Der Gott der Makkabäer* [Berlin: Schocken, 1937] 126ff) has called attention again to the "Hellenistic reformers" in Jerusalem prior to the Maccabean revolt who wanted to end Jewish particularism. Apparently these reformers wanted to abolish the Torah of Moses as the legal basis of Jewish theocracy and to retain it only as a code of religious customs and practices. This change would allow Judaism to fully integrate with its Hellenistic environment. In justifying the reform, its proponents may have used the theory of Posidonius about "origin and degeneration" (see Hengel, *Judaism and Hellenism* 1.300ff). If this theory is applied to the history of Judaism, the Mosaic Torah could be presented as a "later addition" (cf. below on 3:19b). It is interesting that one of the primal heroes of the reformers seems to have been Abraham: "*Abraham* above all seems to have been of interest to them, especially as the most remarkable reports about him were current: Berossos had already mentioned him: he was said to have joined friendship with the Pergamenes and to have ruled for a certain time as king of Damascus. He is also said to have gone to Egypt to hear the priests there and to compare his views about the gods with theirs. This is not to say that these scattered reports all come from the 'Hellenists' in Jerusalem from the time about 175 *B.C.*, but they show that in early Hellenistic Judaism, perhaps in connection with proselytism, there was a view of Abraham and the other fathers which in its cosmopolitan breadth fundamentally differed from the one which Ben Sira puts in the foreground..." (Hengel, *Judaism and Hellenism* 1.302). Does Paul have anything to do with these "Hellenists"? Perhaps their ideas were not altogether eliminated, contrary to what the extant sources wish us to believe. Perhaps attention should be paid to the mysterious polemic in *m. Sanh.* 10.1, eliminating from the world to come these people: "he that says there is no resurrection of the dead prescribed in the Law, and [he that says] that the Law is not from Heaven, and the Epicurean" (tr. Danby; cf. Henry Fischel, *Rabbinic Literature and Greco–Roman Philosophy* [Leiden: Brill, 1973] 35ff). Philo has other statements directed against opponents of the Torah (see below, on Gal 3:19). Perhaps it is no accident that the speech by Stephen—one of the "Hellenists" (cf. Acts 6:1; 9:29; 11:20 *v. l.*)—begins with Abraham and ends with a polemic against the Torah (cf. Acts 7:2–53). The statement about the Torah (Acts 7:53), which leads to Stephen's martyrdom, has two verbal parallels to

Galatians: "you received the Law as delivered by angels [cf. Gal 3:19d] and did not keep it [cf. Gal 6:13]." Because of the scarcity of the sources we can only propose as a suggestion that Paul's contrasting of the Torah with Abraham may have its origin with the so-called movement of the "Hellenists."

Bibliography; The sources are collected in Bernhard Beer, *Leben Abraham's nach Auffassung der jüdischen Sage* (Leipzig: Leiner, 1859); Ginsberg, *Legends*, 1.183–308; 5.207–69; Str–B, 4.1213 *s.v.* Abraham. For studies and bibliography, see Otto Schmitz, "Abraham im Spätjudentum und Urchristentum," in *Aus Schrift und Geschichte: Theologische Abhandlungen Adolf Schlatter zu seinem 70. Geburtstage dargebracht...* (Stuttgart: Calwer Vereinsbuchhandlung, 1922) 99–123; Geza Vermes, *Scripture and Tradition in Judaism* (Leiden: Brill,² 1973) 66–126; Samuel Sandmel, *Philo's Place in Judaism* (Cincinnati: Hebrew Union College, ²1972); Nahum M. Sarna *et al.* "Abraham," *Enc. Jud.* 2 (1971) 111–25; Goodenough, *By Light, Light*, chap. 5; Hengel, *Judaism and Hellenism, passim*; Günter Mayer, "Aspekte des Abrahambildes in der hellenistisch–jüdischen Literatur," *EvT* 32 (1972) 118–27; Ben Zion Wacholder, *Eupolemus* (Cincinnati: Hebrew Union College–Jewish Institute of Religion, 1974) 76; John Van Seters, *Abraham in History and Tradition* (New York and London: Yale University, 1975). Important *excursus* are found in Lietzmann, *Römer*, on Rom 4:21; Dibelius–Greeven, *James*, 168–74.

On Paul's interpretation of Abraham, see Christian Dietzfelbinger, *Paulus und das Alte Testament: Die Hermeneutik des Paulus, untersucht an seiner Deutung der Gestalt Abrahams* (*ThExh* NF 95; Munich: Kaiser, 1961); Luz, *Geschichtsverständnis*, 177–82; Klaus Berger, "Abraham in den paulinischen Hauptbriefen," *MThZ* 17 (1966) 47–89, with extensive bib.; Ronald Clements, *Abraham and David* (London: SCM, 1967) 87f, pointing to Old Testament antecedents between the Abraham tradition and the Sinai tradition; Kertelge, *Rechtfertigung*, 185ff; Käsemann, *Römer*, 99ff; *idem*, "The Faith of Abraham in Romans 4," *Perspectives*, 79–101; Ulrich Wilckens, "Die Rechtfertigung Abrahams nach Römer 4," in his *Rechtfertigung*, 33–49; Dieter Zeller, *Juden und Heiden in der Mission des Paulus* (Forschung zur Bibel 1; Stuttgart: Katholisches Bibelwerk, 1973) 79ff; Nils A. Dahl, "The Atonement—An Adequate Reward for the Akedah?" in his *The Crucified Messiah and Other Essays* (Minneapolis: Augsburg, 1974) 146–66; Davies, *Gospel... Land*, 168–79.

Interpretation

■ **6** Paul begins his second argument by quoting Gen 15:6, a passage famous in both Jewish[11] and Christian[12] interpretation of Scripture. The quotation is marked by an introductory formula, καθώς ("as [*sc.* it is written])"[13] and agrees almost word for word with the LXX,[14] the name of Abraham at the beginning being the only addition:[15] "Abraham believed God,

11 For Gen 15:6 in Jewish literature see the material in Str–B 3.199–201; Philo *Mut.* 177; 186 (cf. 181f; 218); *L.A.* 3.228; *Mig.* 44; *Her.* 90–95 (cf. 101); *Abr.* 262–274; cf. also *Deus* 4; *Virt.* 216–218; *Praem.* 27–30. Unfortunately, the Genesis Apocryphon from Qumran breaks off just before coming to Gen 15:6 (see Joseph A. Fitzmyer, *The Genesis Apocryphon of Qumran Cave 1, A Commentary* [Biblica et Orientalia 18; Rome: Pontifical Biblical Institute, ²1971] 164).

12 Other passages include Rom 4:3, 9, 22, 23; Jas 2:23; *1 Clem.* 10.6; *Barn.* 13.7; Justin *Dial.* 23.4; 92.3; 119.6. Marcion has eliminated Gal 3:6–8 from the letter (see Harnack, *Marcion*, *72). For further references, see *Biblia Patristica: Index des citations et allusions bibliques dans la littérature patristique, des origines à Clément d'Alexandrie et Tertullian* (Paris: Editions du Centre National de la Recherche Scientifique, 1975) 79f. On the NT, see Ferdinand Hahn, "Genesis 15, 6 im Neuen Testament," in *Probleme biblischer Theologie, Festschrift für Gerhard von Rad zum 70. Geburtstag* (Munich: Kaiser, 1971) 90–107, esp. 97–100.

13 This abbreviated formula occurs only here in Paul. See Michel, *Paulus*, 72; E. Earle Ellis, *Paul's Use of the Old Testament* (Edinburgh: Oliver & Boyd; Grand Rapids: Eerdmans, 1957) 22ff. It does not occur in the Qumran texts; see Joseph A. Fitzmyer, "The Use of Explicit Old Testament Quotations in Qumran Literature and in the New Testament," *NTS* 7 (1961) 297–333, rep. in his *Essays on the Semitic Background of the New Testament* (London: Chapman, 1971) 3–58. In Gal 3:6, G Ambrosiaster vg^clem have an added γέγραπται probably taken from Rom 4:3, where the longer formula is used (as it is in Jas 2:23; *1 Clem.* 10.6); see Zahn, p. 146 n. 90. Cf. *RSV*, *NEB*, which seem to indicate more a reference to an example than a quotation formula.

14 LXX reads: καὶ ἐπίστευσεν 'Αβρὰμ τῷ θεῷ καὶ ἐλογίσθη αὐτῷ εἰς δικαιοσύνην. The difference from the MT is minimal; והאמין ביהוה ויחשבה לו צדקה. See Aemilius F. Kautzsch, *De Veteris Testamenti locis a Paulo Apostolo allegatis* (Leipzig: Metzger & Wittig, 1869) 25.

15 So also Philo *L.A.* 3.228. Rom 4:3 is in literal agreement with the LXX.

and this was credited to him as righteousness" (᾽Αβραὰμ ἐπίστευσεν τῷ θεῷ, καὶ ἐλογίσθη αὐτῷ εἰς δικαιοσύνην.).

By quoting this passage, Paul claims not only Scripture as an argument, but also the figure of Abraham, who according to Jewish tradition was the greatest example of the Jewish "faith." [16] In opposition to Judaism, however, Paul interprets the concept of "faith" not in the Jewish sense, but in terms of his own theology. [17] In his view, the example of Abraham is not one that shows faithfulness and trust in the Jewish sense, but faith in the Pauline sense. Therefore his contention that Gen 15:6 proves his understanding of "justification by faith" as opposed to "by works of the Torah" can convince only those who share his theological and methodological presuppositions. This is not a case of naiveté on the part of Paul. He wishes, as he shows more fully in Romans 4, to demonstrate in all seriousness that his concept of faith is true because it is found in the Scriptures. The possibility of doing this comes from the fact that in Jewish tradition there is an uneasy union between Abraham's "faith" and his "works." [18] Paul dissolves the union and argues that not his works justified Abraham (Rom 4:2) but his faith (Rom 4:16). This faith is not the faith of one who is righteous, but that of one who believes in the God who justifies the unrighteous (Rom 4:5), who makes the dead alive, and who calls things that do not yet exist as if they do exist (Rom 4:17). It is a faith by which one moves "from hope to hope" (παρ᾽ ἐλπίδα ἐπ᾽ ἐλπίδι), trusting God's promise against the evidence which the eye can see (Rom 4:18–20). This faith is then "reckoned by God as righteousness" (Rom 4:4),[19] not as a meritorious "work" (κατὰ ὀφείλημα), but according to God's grace (κατὰ χάριν).

■ 7 The quotation of Gen 15:6 is followed by Paul's exegetical "thesis": "recognize, therefore, that the men of faith, these are sons of Abraham" (γινώσκετε ἄρα ὅτι οἱ ἐκ πίστεως, οὗτοι υἱοί εἰσιν ᾽Αβραάμ).[20] The introductory γινώσκετε can be taken as an indicative ("you know")[21] or as an imperative ("recognize");[22] the latter is preferable because it conforms to the parallels in didactic literature.[23] What the Galatians are asked to recognize is not obvious, but is the result of the following argument here anticipated.[24] The "thesis" is more fully discussed by Paul in Romans 4, but contrary to Romans 4, in Gal 3:6–14 Paul does not discuss the figure of Abraham first,[25] but immediately focuses upon the "sons of Abraham" and their faith. The οἱ ἐκ πίστεως ("the men of [the] faith") are those whose existence before God is based upon (ἐκ) faith. The phrase occurs only here in Paul[26] and seems to be created by him, perhaps in contrast to οἱ ἐξ ἔργων νόμου

---

16 On Abraham see the excursus above.

17 On "faith" in Paul's theology, see above on 2:16. Note Luther's remarkable statement about the significance of "faith" in Paul, WA 40/1. 360ff.

18 The Jewish position is notably maintained in Jas 2:20–26.

19 This originally prominent Jewish concept is used by Paul also in Rom 4:3, 9, 22, 23 (cf. 2:3, 26; 3:28; 4:4, 5, 6, 8, 10, 11, 24; 6:11; etc.). Cf. Jas 2:23. On the concept see the material in Str–B 3.201 (also 121–23); Hans Wolfgang Heidland, *Die Anrechnung des Glaubens zur Gerechtigkeit* (BWANT 4.18; Stuttgart: Kohlhammer, 1936); idem, "λογίζομαι," *TDNT* 4.286–92; Bauer, *s.v.*, 1; Gerhard von Rad, 'Die Anrechnung des Glaubens zur Gerechtigkeit," *ThLZ* 76 (1951) 129–32; Kertelge, "*Rechtfertigung*," 185–95. Luther (1535) develops at this point his famous doctrine of the Christian as simultaneously righteous and a sinner: "Sic homo Christianus simul iustus et peccator, Sanctus, prophanus, inimicus et filius Dei est" (WA 40/1.368). On the concept of "righteousness" (δικαιοσύνη) see above on Gal 2:16, 21.

20 ℵc A C 𝕾 D G *pl* have υἱοί after εἰσιν, but the text given in Nestle–Aland is to be preferred (P46 ℵ* B *pc*). See Sieffert, p. 173.

21 So many older commentators, e.g., Cyprian (see the list in Sieffert, p. 173).

22 So most modern commentators, also Lightfoot, Zahn, Lagrange, Burton, Oepke, Schlier, Mussner. Of the older ones: Ambrosiaster, Vg, Luther, Calvin (see the list in Sieffert, p. 174).

23 Cf., e.g., *2 Clem.* 5.5; 16.3 (γινώσκετε); 9.2 (γνῶτε); also *Corp. Herm.* 1.6. More common is μάθετε (*Barn.* 5.6, 6.9 and often; cf. Philo *Sac.* 8; *L.A.* 3.51; *Deus* 4; and often).

24 On this type of "knowledge" see Jas 2:20; *Barn.* 1.5; 6.9; 7.1; 13.7; 14.7; 16.2; *1 Clem.* 32.1; 40.1; 41.4; etc. See Rudolf Bultmann, "γινώσκω," *TDNT* 1.708.

25 Only at the end of Rom 4 does Paul turn to the "believers" (4:23–25, cf. 16).

26 Cf. Rom 4:16: τῷ ἐκ πίστεως ᾽Αβραάμ.

("the men of [the] works of [the] Torah")[27] and οἱ ἐκ περιτομῆς ("the men of [the] circumcision").[28] These "men of [the] faith" are identified with the "sons of Abraham"[29] because they believe the same way as Abraham did.[30] To be sure, this identification is intentionally anti-Jewish.[31] In the following section (3:8–13) Paul presents five proofs from Scripture in order to substantiate his thesis.

■ 8 The first proof is an interpretation of the famous "blessing of Abraham." The words are clearly marked as a quotation, although they cannot precisely be identified with any LXX passage in which the blessing is found. Paul's words may therefore be his own: ἐνευλογηθήσονται ἐν σοὶ πάντα τὰ ἔθνη ("In you shall all the nations [or: Gentiles] be blessed.")[32] In Jewish theology the ἐν σοί attracts most of the attention and is interpreted to mean "because of the works of Torah obedience."[33] Paul, however, is mostly interested in the phrase πάντα τὰ ἔθνη, which in his view means "all the

Gentiles."[34] To be sure, in the Old Testament God had promised to Abraham that he would have a plentiful offspring and a land in which for them to live (see Gen 12:1–2, 7; 13:14–18; 15:5–6, 18; 17:4–8, 16–21; 18:18; 22:17). Based on this was the covenant which God made with Abraham and his offspring (see Gen 17:7–14; 18:19; 22:16–17). Paul's question, however, goes beyond the Old Testament: how could God bless the Gentiles? This question is familiar to us from the Judaism[35] of his time, which knows of certain blessings given to all the nations because of Abraham: the creation of the world and its continuance in spite of mankind's sinfulness; and the existence of grace, monotheism, penitence, proselytism, scientific knowledge, cultural achievements, etc. Paul no doubt goes much further when he simply identifies the blessing with God's[36] "grace" (χάρις)[37] and his "justification by faith" (ἐκ πίστεως δικαιοῖ τὰ ἔθνη ὁ θεός ["God justifies the Gentiles through faith"]).[38] Did Abraham, to

27 See Gal 3:10.
28 For this and similar expressions see Gal 2:12; Rom 4:12; Acts 10:45; 11:2; also Rom 2:8: οἱ ἐξ ἐριθείας.
29 The concept of the "sons of Abraham" is also part of the final argument Gal 4:22–31, but prior to that Paul has identified the "sons of Abraham" with the "sons of God" (3:26; 4:6, 7). Identical is also the "seed of Abraham" (3:16, 19, 29; cf. Rom 4:13, 16, 18; 9:7, 8, 29; 11:1; 2 Cor 11:22; etc.). Cf. also the expression "Abraham our father" (Rom 4:1, 12). Originally the concepts were Jewish and may have been part of the theology of the opposition; see Burton, pp. 153f; cf. Betz, "2 Cor 6:14–7:1," 97f, commenting on 2 Cor 6:18 (see Appendix 2, below). For the concept of the "sons of Abraham" see the material in Str–B. 3.263ff; Eduard Schweizer, "υἱός κτλ.," TDNT 8.365 with further references; E. Jacob, "Abraham et sa signification pour la foi chrétienne," RHPhR 42 (1962) 148–56; Franz Leenhardt, "Abraham et la conversion de Saul de Tarse, suivi d'une note sur Abraham dans Jean VIII," RHPhR 53 (1973) 331–51.
30 The question of whether every Jew could claim "we have Abraham as our father" (cf. Matt 3:9; Luke 3:8; 16:24; John 8:33f) or whether "not all who stem from Israel are Israel" (Rom 9:6; cf. 2:28f) was discussed both in Christianity and in Judaism. Cf. the honorific name Ἀβραμιαῖοι of the martyrs 4 Macc 9:21; 18:23; Philo Virt. 195–97; see the rabbinic material in Str–B 3.263f, 535; on

Jewish esoterism in general see Braun, Qumran 2.235ff.
31 For an extensive defense of Paul's position see Rom 9–11.
32 The blessing of Abraham is quoted in various forms, none of which completely agrees with Gal 3:8 (cf. Gen 12:3; 18:18; 22:18; 26:4; 28:14; Ps 71:17 LXX; Sir 44:21 LXX; Acts 3:25; see also Rom 4:13ff). On the textual problem, see Kautzsch, De Veteris Testamenti locis, 60f. On the history of Abraham's blessing, see Josef Scharbert, Solidarität in Segen und Fluch im Alten Testament und in seiner Umwelt (BBB 14; Bonn: Hanstein 1958) chap. 1; Josef Schreiner, "Segen für die Völker in der Verheissung an die Väter," BZ 6 (1962) 1–31, esp. 7f; Wolfgang Schenk, Der Segen im Neuen Testament (Theologische Arbeiten 24; Berlin: Evangelische Verlagsanstalt, 1967) 42ff; Gerhard Wehmeier, Der Segen im Alten Testament (Basel: Reinhardt, 1970) 177–79.
33 Cf. for the Jewish material Str–B 3.539–41.
34 Cf. Gal 1:16; 2:2, 8, 9, 12, 14, 15; 3:14.
35 For passages, see Str–B 3.539–41.
36 The passive in ἐνευλογηθήσονται ("they will be blessed") is a Semitism and expresses God's activity. Cf. δικαιωθῆναι ("be justified") in Gal 2:16, and the christology in 3:13f.
37 Cf. Gal 1:6; 2:21; 5:4.
38 Cf. Gal 2:15–21. To be sure, faith is not a condition to be met by the nations, and thus a new kind of work (against Mussner, p. 200 n. 41).

whom this promise was given, understand it also in this sense? Paul concludes he did. The Apostle thereby attributes to Abraham a unique role:[39] he was the only person before Christ[40] who actually knew the gospel and believed in it.[41] How can this be? Paul explains this by the reference to his concept of Scripture: "Scripture foresaw [it]" (προϊδοῦσα δὲ ἡ γραφή)[42] and "proclaimed [it] before to Abraham" (προευηγγελίσατο τῷ ᾿Αβραάμ).[43]

■ **9** This statement concludes the first proof (3:8–9).[44] If the interpretation suggested in v 8 is carried out, the result is this: "therefore, the men of faith are blessed together with Abraham the believer." The phrase (v 8) πάντα τὰ ἔθνη ("all the nations [or: Gentiles]") must be taken to mean those of the Gentiles who believe like Abraham. They are "the men of faith" (οἱ ἐκ πίστεως).[45]

Abraham's traditional attribute ὁ πιστός can now be understood in the sense of "being a believer" like the Christians.[46] Abraham who in Judaism is the prototype of "righteousness through obedience to the Torah" now has become the prototype of the "men of faith." They are "blessed together with him"[47] because they share in the same faith. It is noteworthy that Paul does not replace the εὐλογοῦνται ("they are blessed") with a δικαιοῦνται ("they are justified")[48] because he still needs it for his next Scripture proof (3:10).[49] The conclusion in v 9, however, shows already that the thesis of v 7 is exegetically correct. What is still to be done is the elimination of those who base their salvation upon the "works of the Torah." Furthermore, the christological and soteriological interpretation of the

---

39 In this Paul agrees with the Jewish tradition. Cf. Bernhard Beer, *Leben Abrahams nach Auffassung der jüdischen Sage* (Leipzig, 1859) 86–92.

40 Cf. Gal 3:22f.

41 Schlier (p. 130) questions Sieffert's statement (p. 175): "That promise was a gospel before the gospel." Schlier wants to take it in the sense that the promise made to Abraham, that he will become the blessing of the Gentiles, was the *beginning* of the gospel. But there is little room for a development of the gospel because no material difference seems to exist between Abraham's faith and the Christian faith. How this situation can or cannot be reconciled with christology is a problem in Paul's theology. See Hendrikus W. Boers, *Theology out of the Ghetto* (Leiden: Brill, 1971) 74–82; Betz, "2 Cor 6:14–7:1," 104. Mussner (p. 222) has tried to solve the problem for Paul by introducing the concept of "corporate personality": "in Abraham" the nations were blessed because they were spiritually included "in Him" (cf. ἐν σοί) as a "corporate personality." The concept of "corporate personality," however, is employed by Paul only with reference to Adam (see Rom 5:15) and Christ (on "in Christ" see Gal 2:17).

42 Paul treats "Scripture" (ἡ γραφή) almost like a hypostasis which acts like a human being (see also Gal 3:22; 4:30; Rom 4:3; 9:17; 10:11; 11:2; and on the subject Gottlob Schrenk, "γραφή," *TDNT* 1.754–55). The idea that Scripture "foresees" (cf. also Rom 9:29; Acts 2:31) is rabbinic, as the expression "What has the Torah seen?" shows (for the material see Str–B. 3.538; Wilhelm Michaelis, "προοράω, προεῖδον," *TDNT* 5.381–82). Cf. also Philo *L. A.* 3.118: εἰδὼς γοῦν ὁ ἱερὸς λόγος ("the

Sacred Word knew"); *Cont.* 78 about the Therapeutae: "For to these people the whole law book seems to resemble a living creature with the literal ordinances for its body and for its soul the invisible mind laid up in its wording."

43 Προευαγγελίζομαι is a *hapax legomenon* in the NT; it is found also in Philo *Op.* 34; *Mut.* 158. See Bauer, *s.v.*; Gerhard Friedrich, "προευγγελίζομαι," *TDNT* 2.737. On the problem of the temporal meaning, see Peter Stuhlmacher, "Erwägungen zum Problem von Gegenwart und Zukunft in der paulinischen Eschatologie," *ZThK* 64 (1967) 423–50, 434; Ulrich Luz, *Das Geschichtsverständnis des Paulus* (BEvTH 49; Munich: Kaiser, 1968) 111f.

44 For the function of ὥστε ("therefore") in Scripture exegesis, see also Gal 3:24; 4:7.

45 For this concept, see Gal 3:7.

46 ὁ πιστός ("the faithful") as an eponym of Abraham occurs in the NT only here; see also *1 Clem.* 10.6. In Hellenistic Jewish literature it is found often: Sir 44:20; 1 Macc 2:52; 2 Macc 1:2; Philo *Post.* 173. See Rudolf Bultmann, "πιστεύω κτλ.," *TDNT* 6.175, 201–02, 214–15; Bauer, *s.v. πιστός*; Roy B. Ward, "The Works of Abraham," *HTR* 61 (1968) 283–90; idem, "Abraham Traditions in Early Christianity," *SBLCS* 2 (1972) 165–79; Dieter Lührmann, "Pistis im Judentum," *ZNW* 64 (1973) 19–38; idem, *Glaube im frühen Christentum* (Gütersloh: Mohn, 1976) 31ff.

47 The "in you" (ἐν σοί) in v 8 is now interpreted as "together with" Abraham.

48 Cf. Gal 2:16f; 3:8, 11, 24.

49 Cf. εὐλογία ("blessing") Gal 3:14.

concept "through faith" which is to follow in 3:10–13 is still lacking.

■10 Paul introduces[50] his second proof from Scripture. Again, he states his conclusion first: "those who are of [the] works of [the] Torah are under a curse" (ὅσοι γὰρ ἐξ ἔργων νόμου εἰσίν, ὑπὸ κατάραν εἰσίν). Paul arrives at his conclusion by way of a negative inference: if—as stated in v 9—the "men of faith" are blessed together with Abraham, those who are not "men of faith" must be "men of [the] Torah" (οἱ ἐκ νόμου), and they must be "under a curse."[51] Not being blessed is the same as being cursed. Not belonging to the "men of faith" is the same as belonging to the "men of the Torah"—these two types of people were mentioned in the previous discussion.[52] Furthermore, the "men of the Torah" are those who for their salvation rely on the works of the Torah (οἱ ἐξ ἔργων νόμου).[53] Consequently all who are of this type are "under a curse."[54] This includes the Jews and also those Jewish Christians who, as Paul's opponents do, regard the observation of the Torah as a condition for salvation. It would include also the Galatians if they would carry out their present plans to come under the Torah.[55] Thus this curse must be connected with Paul's own curse in Gal 1:8–9. The logic behind Paul's words, therefore, is simply that exclusion from "blessing" (cf. 6:16) equals "curse."[56] The problems to be considered in the following are how this curse is related to the curse which Christ himself has become[57] and how Paul's conclusion is grounded in Scripture.

The Scripture passage assumed to support[58] Paul's thesis is taken from Deut 27:26. The quotation is marked by the formula γέγραπται... ὅτι ("it is written... that")[59] and reads: ἐπικατάρατος πᾶς ὃς οὐκ ἐμμένει πᾶσιν τοῖς γεγραμμένοις ἐν τῷ βιβλίῳ τοῦ νόμου τοῦ ποιῆσαι αὐτά ("cursed is everyone who does not remain in everything that is written in the book of the Law, in order to do it").[60] The text, however, does not

---

50 γάρ should best be taken as inferential ("certainly, so, then") or as marking another step in the argument. Cf. Bauer, s.v., 3–4.

51 This conclusion is contained already in the *propositio* Gal 2:15–21.

52 Cf. Gal 2:16; 3:2, 5, 7, 8, 9.

53 Cf. Rom 4:4–5.

54 ὑπὸ κατάραν ("under the curse") occurs only here in the NT. Cf. synonyms in 3:22: "under sin" (ὑπὸ ἁμαρτίαν); 4:2, 3, 8, 9: "under tutors and administrators" (ὑπὸ ἐπιτρόπους καὶ οἰκονόμους) equaling "under the 'elements of the world'" (ὑπὸ τὰ στοιχεῖα τοῦ κόσμου).

55 ὑπὸ νόμον ("under the Torah"). Cf. Gal 4:4, 5; 5:18; also Rom 6:14. On ὑπό with an accusative, see Bauer, s.v., 2, b; Mayser, *Grammatik* 2/2.514.

56 So also Sieffert, p. 178; Peter Jung, "Das paulinische Vokabular in Gal 3, 6–14," *ZKTh* 74 (1952) 446; Schlier, p. 133; Burton, pp. 164f. Differently, Mussner (p. 223) who denies that Paul argues by any logic except "Scripture."

57 The discrepancy between Gal 4:4–5 and 3:13 may be noted here: Christ came "under the law" when he was sent by God into the world and after he was born by a woman, in order to redeem those who are "under the law" (4:4–5); in 3:13 it was on the cross that he became a curse "for us," in order to redeem us from the curse of the law. The differences seem to have their origin in different pre-Pauline christologies and were not smoothed out by the Apostle.

58 γάρ ("for") here introduces the reason for the preceding statement. See Bauer, s.v., 1.

59 This form of the quotation formula occurs also Gal 4:22; cf. Rom 12:19; 14:11; 1 Cor 1:19; 3:19. See Michel, *Paulus*, 72; Ellis, *Paul's Use of the Old Testament*, 22ff (n. 13, above); Fitzmyer, *Essays*, 9.

60 ἐμμένει + ἐν is read by A C 𝔐 D G *pm* Origen, but it is most likely a correction on the basis of Deut 27:26 LXX. The majority of witnesses read ἐμμένει + dative, which is acceptable Koine Greek. See BDF, § 202; BDR, § 202 n. 3. A number of scholars have suggested that an official legal formula consisting of ἐμμένειν + dative of a participle (with or without ἐν) has caused the change from (LXX) ἐν πᾶσιν τοῖς λόγοις τοῦ νόμου to (ἐν) πᾶσιν τοῖς γεγραμμένοις ἐν τῷ βιβλίῳ τοῦ νόμου. See Adolf Deissmann, *Bible Studies* (tr. Alexander Grieve; Edinburgh: Clark, 1931) 248f; idem *Neue Bibelstudien* (Marburg: Elwert, 1897) 76f; Moulton–Milligan, *s.v.*; Friedrich Hauck, "ἐμμένω," *TDNT* 4.576–77; Raphael Kühner and Bernhard Gerth, *Ausführliche Grammatik der griechischen Sprache* (Hannover: Hahn, ³1890–1904) 1.443 n. 1; Mayser, *Grammatik* 2/2.287; Adolf Berger, *Die Strafklauseln in den Papyrusurkunden* (Leipzig and Berlin: Teubner, 1911) 3f; Preisigke, *Wörterbuch* 4.776 *s.v.*; idem, *Fachwörter des öffentlichen Verwaltungsdienstes Ägyptens in den griechischen Papyrusurkunden der ptolemäisch-römischen Zeit* (Göttingen: Vandenhoeck & Ruprecht, 1915) 74 *s.v.*; Otto Eger, "Rechtswörter und Rechtsbilder in den paulinischen

fully correspond to the LXX[61] or the MT.[62] Does Paul quote from a LXX version unknown to us, or from memory, or does he intentionally change the text? Since the differences are not limited to Paul but are found elsewhere in the manuscript tradition,[63] Paul's text may have contained what he quoted, or he may have quoted from memory.[64]

The crux of the passage, however, is the question of how Paul could have thought Deut 27:26 proves his conclusion. On the surface, Deut 27:26 says the opposite of what he claims it says. Scholars have made several important attempts for solving the problem: (1) Martin Noth[65] has tried to show that Paul understands Deuteronomy correctly, with the exception of the generalizing of the curse and the change of the LXX text from the original "this Torah" (= the 12 curses in Deut 27:15–26) to the entire "book of the law." According to Noth, Paul interprets Deuteronomy correctly when he assumes that in the beginning Yahweh blessed the forefathers and promised to give them the land. The "covenant" was made at Mount Sinai, and the Torah was given with the expectation that Israel would keep it faithfully and would thus retain the promises of Yahweh. The transgression of only one law would imply apostasy and the breaking of the entire covenant, whereupon the curse would become effective. According to Noth, for the author of Deuteronomy all this has in fact happened, so that for him Israel is presently under the curse. Whether Noth has in fact interpreted Deuteronomy adequately is a question not to be discussed here. In any case, Paul's position is different; for him the Torah was not given to be faithfully obeyed as the covenant, but for the purpose of breaking it and generating sin (cf. 3:19–25).[66] (2) Hans Joachim Schoeps[67] assumes that Paul's intention is to show the unfulfillable nature of the Torah from the Torah itself: everybody is under the curse of the law because nobody is able to keep *the whole law*.[68] Paul does not state this explicitly because for him it is self-evident.[69] Paul shares his idea with some rabbinic teachers who have been aware of the problem that it might not be possible for the whole Torah to be fulfilled.[70] However, this argument *e silentio* is not convincing: Paul not only fails to say what Schoeps thinks is self-evident, but in fact he says the opposite.[71] The Law was given to generate sin; sin is not the result of

Briefen," *ZNW* 18 (1917) 94; LSJ, *s.v.*; Bauer, *s.v.*, 2; Schlier, p. 132 n. 7.

61 Except for a few variants, LXX reads: ἐπικατάρατος πᾶς ἄνθρωπος, ὃς οὐκ ἐμμενεῖ ἐν πᾶσιν τοῖς λόγοις τοῦ νόμου τούτου τοῦ ποιῆσαι αὐτούς. ("Cursed be every man who does not abide by all the words of this law, in order to do them.")

62 MT reads: אָרוּר אֲשֶׁר לֹא־יָקִים אֶת־דִּבְרֵי הַתּוֹרָה־הַזֹּאת לַעֲשׂוֹת אוֹתָם ("Cursed is he who does not keep the words of this law, in order to do them"). The "all" ("all the words") which is read by LXX (cf. also Deut 28:58, 30:10) and Gal 3:10 is found also in the *Sam. Tg., Lev. Rab.* 25 (123a), *p. Sota* 21d6. See Rudolf Kittel, *Biblia Hebraica, ad loc.*; Str–B 3.541f. The passage is also quoted and discussed in Justin *Dial.* 95.1; *Didasc. Apost.* 55.15–17(ed. Tidner).

63 Paul's quotation at least comes close to LXX readings A and Ambrosius. See Kautzsch, *De Veteris Testamenti locis*, 61f.

64 So Kautzsch, ibidem, 60.

65 "For all who rely on works of the law are under a curse," in his *The Laws in the Pentateuch and Other Studies* (tr. D. R. Ap–Thomas; Philadelphia: Fortress, 1966) 118–31; idem (German): "Die mit des Gesetzes Werken umgehen, die sind unter dem

Fluch," *Gesammelte Studien zum Alten Testament* (Munich: Kaiser, 1957) 155–71. Critical is Walther Zimmerli, *Das Gesetz und die Propheten* (Göttingen: Vandenhoeck & Ruprecht, 1963) 78, 81–93; for the meaning of Deut 27:26, see also Willy Schottroff, *Der altisraelitische Fluchspruch* (WMANT 30; Neukirchen: Neukirchener Verlag, 1969) 26, 74ff, 220ff.

66 For other reasons, see Rom 2:13ff; 5:12ff; Phil 3:6–8.

67 *Paul*, 175–77.

68 The "all" (πᾶσιν) is then more than a "formal" addition (cf. above, n. 13); against Oepke, p. 105. Schoeps (*Paul*, 175–77) thinks Paul refers to the 613 prescriptions and prohibitions of the Torah, "all" of which nobody can fulfill, as Paul says in Gal 5:3. See also Luz, *Geschichtsverständnis*, 149f; Hans Hübner, "Gal 3, 10 und die Herkunft des Paulus," *KD* 19 (1973) 215–31.

69 So also already Lietzmann, on 3:10; Oepke, p. 105.

70 Schoeps, *Paul*, 177. See also Moritz Löwy, "Die paulinische Lehre vom Gesetz," *MGWJ* 47 (1903) 417–22; Moore, *Judaism* 3.150 n. 209.

71 See Gal 1:13f; 3:19–25; Phil 3:6–8; 2 Cor 11:18ff. For the correct view, see Bultmann, *Theology*, § 27; Schlier, p. 133.

man's inability to keep it but the necessary presupposition for salvation.

(3) Schlier[72] explains Paul's position as saying that those who *do* the Torah are under the curse. Thus, the emphasis is on "doing" ($\pi o\iota\epsilon\hat{\iota}\nu$),[73] instead of on "believing" and, for that reason, is the opposite of the "faith" of Abraham.

(4) Mussner,[74] following Luz, remarks that "not the doing is under the curse, but the not doing" of the Torah. Then he combines the explanations given by Schoeps and by Schlier, saying that the principle of "doing" the Torah is ineffective as far as salvation is concerned because nobody is capable of fulfilling (= doing) the demands of the Law. It is noteworthy that Mussner bases this explanation not on Galatians but on Rom 3:19–20 (combined with Gal 6:13).

Since none of the preceding solutions is satisfactory, it can be said, however, that Galatians itself sufficiently presents Paul's view of the matter. For Paul, salvation in Christ and the fulfilling of the Torah undoubtedly go together (cf. 5:14, 19–23; 6:2). The question is only whether the *Jewish* concept of "works of the Torah" can lead to the fulfillment of the Torah. This Paul denies. The *Jewish* Torah given on Mount Sinai was an inferior entity, not intended to provide eternal life (3:21) but given "because of transgressions" ($\tau\hat{\omega}\nu\ \pi\alpha\rho\alpha\beta\acute{\alpha}\sigma\epsilon\omega\nu\ \chi\acute{\alpha}\rho\iota\nu$). As he explains in his excursus on the Jewish Torah (3:19–22), the establishment of the Law leads to the breaking of the Law (cf. 2:18). The accumulation of transgressions made sin so overwhelming that "everything was confined under sin" (3:22).

"Not abiding in everything which is written in the book of the Law" means "transgressing" it, and those who are "under sin" are "under the curse."

■ 11 The third Scripture proof continues in the line of v 10, but the conclusion v 11a stands on its own: $\acute{o}\tau\iota\ \delta\grave{\epsilon}$ $\acute{\epsilon}\nu\ \nu\acute{o}\mu\omega\ o\grave{\upsilon}\delta\epsilon\grave{\iota}\varsigma\ \delta\iota\kappa\alpha\iota o\hat{\upsilon}\tau\alpha\iota\ \pi\alpha\rho\grave{\alpha}\ \tau\hat{\omega}\ \theta\epsilon\hat{\omega}\ \delta\hat{\eta}\lambda o\nu$ ("it is, then, obvious that nobody is justified before God by Law"). The $\delta\acute{\epsilon}$ introduces a matter in addition to a previous one ("furthermore"), so that v 11 is more than simply a "parallel" to v 10.[75] The phrase $\delta\hat{\eta}\lambda o\nu\ \acute{o}\tau\iota$ ("it is obvious that") is often found in the context of Scripture interpretation.[76] As in other such Scripture proofs it should be connected with the following quotation from Hab 2:4. That "nobody" is justified before God "by Law" (i.e., by the Jewish Torah)[77] had been stated before in the *propositio* in other terms (2:16). Instead of "by works of [the] Law" in 2:16,[78] Paul now has the brief "by Law"[79]—perhaps because of v 12 $\zeta\acute{\eta}\sigma\epsilon\tau\alpha\iota\ \acute{\epsilon}\nu\ \alpha\grave{\upsilon}\tauo\hat{\iota}\varsigma$ ("he shall live by them") and v 10 ("abide *in* everything that is written in the book of the Law"). Although the conclusion is drawn from Hab 2:4, v 11 at the same time continues the argument of v 10: if the "men of the Law" are under the curse, it is obvious that by that Law no one can be justified before God.[80]

The Scripture passage which is adduced to prove Paul's point is from Hab 2:4, introduced this time without the usual quotation formula:[81] $\acute{o}\ \delta\acute{\iota}\kappa\alpha\iota o\varsigma\ \acute{\epsilon}\kappa$ $\pi\acute{\iota}\sigma\tau\epsilon\omega\varsigma\ \zeta\acute{\eta}\sigma\epsilon\tau\alpha\iota$ ("the righteous shall live by faith"). Paul cites the passage in the same form as in Rom

---

72 Schlier, pp. 132f, 134f; see also Bonnard, pp. 67, 149; Luz, *Geschichtsverständnis*, 149f (unclear).

73 This position is emphatically argued in James; see esp. 1:22–27, and on the passage Dibelius–Greeven, *James*, 114–23. Luz (*Geschichtsverständnis*, 149 n. 56) correctly points out that Schlier interprets Rom 7:7ff into Gal 3:10.

74 Mussner, pp. 224–26.

75 Against Schlier, p. 133.

76 See also 1 Cor 15:27; 1 Tim 6:7 *v. 1.*; Ign. *Eph.* 6.1. A collection of material is found in Hermann Hanse, "*ΔΗΛΟΝ* (Zu Gal 3, 11)," *ZNW* 34 (1935) 299–303; Rudolf Bultmann, "δηλόω," *TDNT* 2.61–62; Bauer, *s.v.* δῆλος.

77 Against Mussner (p. 228) who takes ἐν νόμῳ not as a reference to the Jewish Torah, but: "The Torah in a certain sense becomes the universal law." For the Jew, this distinction is of course artificial; for Paul the "universal law" would be the "will of God" itself which is identical with salvation as a whole (cf. 1:4; 5:14) and different from the Jewish Torah.

78 Cf. Gal 3:2, 5, 10.

79 Cf. Gal 5:4; Rom 2:12, 20, 23; 3:19; Phil 3:6. Different is the usage in 1 Cor 9:9; 14:21.

80 Cf. Gal 3:19, 21; differently Rom 2:13.

81 The quotation formula can be omitted, as Gal 3:12b; Rom 9:7; 1 Cor 15:27; Heb 10:37f show. On the same phenomenon in Qumran, see Fitzmyer, *Essays*, 14. The quotation of Hab 2:4 in Rom 1:17 is prefaced by a quotation formula, so that the reason for the omission in Gal 3:11 given by Schlier (p. 133) does not apply.

146

1:17.[82] He interprets it in accordance with his own theology, that is, differently from the LXX[83] as well as the MT.[84] Paul's interpretation is different also from Jewish[85] and other Christian[86] interpretations. He omits the μου ("my") and understands the phrase ἐκ πίστεως ("by faith") as a theological formula "by faith in Christ Jesus" (cf. 2:16).[87] Accordingly, Scripture says that a person who is to be called "righteous" is called by that term because of faith, and this person has access to eternal life here and in the hereafter "by faith" (cf. 2:20; 6:8). Conversely, those who seek to become righteous "by Law" must be regarded as "under a curse" (v 10a) ending in destruction (φθορά 6:8; cf. 5:10) and exclusion from eternal salvation.

■ **12** Paul sets forth another[88] exegetical conclusion: ὁ δὲ νόμος οὐκ ἔστιν ἐκ πίστεως ("also, the Law is not 'by faith'"). The previous conclusion (v 11a) had stated that nobody can be justified before God "by Law" (= by the Jewish Torah) because Scripture (Hab 2:4) declares that the "righteous lives by faith" (ἐκ πίστεως).[89] Now, Paul infers from Lev 18:5 that

"by faith" cannot include, as it does in Judaism, the Torah.[90] Rather, "by faith" excludes the Torah. Presupposed here, of course, is Paul's contrast between "doing" and "believing." It is not the doing of the Law that can make the "men of faith" partakers of the promise made to Abraham. Certainly, Paul argues at this point not only against Judaism in general, but also against the Galatians' expectation, introduced by the anti-Pauline opposition, that "doing" of the Torah is the prerequisite for becoming partakers in the salvation to be had through Christ.

The passage Paul quotes, again without a quotation formula,[91] is taken from Lev 18:5: ὁ ποιήσας αὐτὰ ζήσεται ἐν αὐτοῖς ("He who does them shall live by them").[92] The meaning of the words is clear from the full text of the LXX passage: "and you shall observe all my commandments and all my decrees and do them; the man who does them shall live by them. I am the Lord your God." Those who live ἐν νόμῳ ("by Law") are those who actually do it, i.e. do the "works

---

82   On the quotation of Hab 2:4 in the NT see Kertelge ("*Rechtfertigung*," 89–95, 115, 150) with further bib.; August Strobel, *Untersuchungen zum eschatologischen Verzögerungsproblem auf Grund der spätjüdisch-urchristlichen Geschichte von Habakuk 2, 2ff.* (NovTSup 2; Leiden: Brill, 1961); Gerhart Herold, *Zorn und Gerechtigkeit Gottes bei Paulus. Eine Untersuchung zu Röm 1: 16–18* (Europäische Hochschulschriften 23.14; Bern and Frankfurt: Lang, 1973) 170–84; Käsemann, *Römer*, 18f, 28f.

83   LXX reads: ὁ δὲ δίκαιος ἐκ πίστεώς μου ζήσεται ("The righteous shall live by my [God's] faithfulness"). Some MSS, in addition to Paul (Gal 3:11; Rom 1:17), omit μου ("my"). See Joseph Ziegler, *Duodecim prophetae* (Septuaginta 13; Göttingen: Vandenhoeck & Ruprecht, 1943) 264; Kautzsch, *De Veteris Testamenti locis*, 71–73.

84   MT reads: וצדיק באמונתו יחיה ("The righteous shall live because of his faithfulness"). See Kertelge, "*Rechtfertigung*," 89f; Mussner, p. 226. The passage was also quoted in 1QpHab 7.17–8.3, but the text unfortunately is lost.

85   See Str-B 3.542–44. In 1QpHab 8.1–3 the "righteous" is defined as the one who does the Torah (עושה התורה) and who is faithful to the "Teacher of Righteousness." For further bib., see Braun, *Qumran* 1.169–71, 209, 2.169, 171f; Gert Jeremias, *Der Lehrer der Gerechtigkeit* (SUNT 2; Göttingen:

Vandenhoeck & Ruprecht, 1963) 142–44; Herold, *Zorn*, 152ff. See also Mussner, p. 227 n. 74.

86   Cf. Heb 10:38–39. A number of scholars assume that Paul depends upon a general Christian familiarity with Hab 2:3–4; so Zahn, p. 153; C. H. Dodd, *According to the Scriptures* (London: Nisbet, 1952) 51; Ellis, *Paul's Use of the Old Testament*, 120; Schlier, p. 133; Strobel, *Untersuchungen* (see above n. 82), 79f; Kertelge, "*Rechtfertigung*," 91ff; Käsemann, *Römer*, 28f.

87   Against Schlier (p. 133) who interprets ἐκ πίστεως ("by faith") more in the sense of the OT as "faithfulness to God's word" (similarly Kuss, *Römerbrief*, 25; Kertelge, "*Rechtfertigung*," 90). For the correct interpretation, see Käsemann, *Römer*, 8f. On the meaning of the OT concepts, see Alfred Jepsen, *TWAT*, s.v. אמן, esp. VII, 1.

88   δέ stands juxtaposed to ὅτι δέ v 11a and can therefore be translated as "also."

89   For this theological formula, see Gal 2:16; 3:7, 8, 9, 11.

90   οὐκ ἔστιν is an interpretive expression ("is not the equivalent of"). See Bauer, s.v. εἰμι, II, 3.

91   See on Gal 3:11b.

92   The quotation does not follow LXX precisely: ἄνθρωπος which is read by LXX is attested only by 𝔐 pm Clement. Paul quotes the same text in Rom 10:5. See Kautzsch, *De Veteris Testamenti locis*, 44.

of the Torah."[93] This way of life is structured by "doing"[94] and not by "believing" (ἐκ πίστεως).[95]

The passage contains one of the fundamental doctrines of the Old Testament[96] and of Judaism.[97] It affirms not only the centrality of the Torah, but also the significance of the "doing" of it. The whole of the Jewish literature confirms this. It is summed up in the *Pirqe 'Abot*, which has at its beginning (1.2) a saying by Simon the Just:[98] "by three things is the world sustained: by the Law, by the [Temple] service, and by deeds of loving kindness." The last chapter of *'Abot* (chap. 6, called "The Acquisition of the Torah") contains a praise of the Torah (6.7) which begins: "great is the Law, for it gives life to them that practice (עשה) it in this world and the world to come." Christian literature, especially the Epistle of James, upholds the principle by emphasizing the "doing" as over against mere "believing": "but someone who looks into 'the perfect law of freedom' and perseveres, and is not a forgetful hearer, but an obedient doer (ποιητὴς ἔργου), such a person will be blessed in his doing (ἐν τῇ ποιήσει)."[99]

■**13** Without interruption Paul now comes to his fifth and most important Scripture proof. It is also the most difficult one for us to understand.

In 3:10 Paul had shown that those who base their salvation upon "works of the Torah" are "under a curse." The observance of the Jewish Torah does not lead to "justification before God" (3:11). Law and faith must be radically separated (3:12). How, then, can Paul say that as Christians "we" share the blessing of Abraham (cf. 3:9, 14)?[100] Who are the "we"? According to the context Paul means by "we" those who through Christ were delivered from the "curse of the Law," that is, Jewish Christians[101] who were "under the curse" described in 3:10.[102] The Galatian Gentile Christians were not under *this* curse, because before they converted to Christianity they were not "under the Torah" but "under the 'elements of the world'" (ὑπὸ τὰ στοιχεῖα τοῦ κόσμου).[103] Paul assumes, however, that being under the Torah is only another way of being "under the 'elements of the world'." Only if the Galatians should decide to accept circumcision and Torah, would they also come under this

---

93 Cf. Gal 2:16; 3:2, 5, 10, 11.
94 So Schlier (p. 134): "the law does not exist 'by faith,' it is not based upon faith as its principle of life."
95 In Rom 10:5–6 the contrast is between ἡ δικαιοσύνη ἡ ἐκ τοῦ νόμου ("righteousness based upon the law") and ἡ ἐκ πίστεως δικαιοσύνη ("righteousness based upon faith"). Both exclude each other (Rom 10:4). See on this passage Käsemann, *Römer*, 273ff. Cf. also Rom 2:13: "For it is not the hearers of the law who are righteous before God, but the doers of the law who will be justified." See also Herbert Braun, "ποιέω κτλ.," *TDNT* 6.479–84.
96 On the "doing" of the Torah in the OT and collections of passages, see Walter Gutbrod, *TDNT* 4, *s.v.* νόμος, B; Braun, *TDNT* 6, *s.v.* ποιέω κτλ., B II 5.
97 On Judaism, see Philo's interpretation *Cong.* 86f and the material in Str–B 3.126–33, 277f (on Lev 18:5); Gutbrod, *TDNT* 4, *s.v.* λόγος, C; Braun, *TDNT* 6, *s.v.* ποιέω κτλ., B III–IV; Meinrad Limbeck, *Die Ordnung des Heils* (Düsseldorf: Patmos, 1971).
98 For this saying and Simon the Just, see Jacob Neusner, *The Rabbinic Traditions about the Pharisees before 70* (3 vols.; Leiden: Brill, 1971) 1.29, 41–44.
99 Jas 1:25. See the entire section 1:22–25, and Dibelius–Greeven, *James*, 114–20; also Matt 7:21–

23, 24–27; *Ep. Petr.* 2.3 (see Appendix 3, below).
100 Paul had outlined his position already in the *propositio* 2:15–21: Jewish Christians who seek justification before God no longer "by works of the Torah" but "by faith in Christ Jesus" do not become "sinners" like the Gentiles. In 3:13 he demonstrates why they are no longer "under the curse of the Torah."
101 ἡμᾶς ("us") refers back to 2:15 (cf. also 3:10, 22–24; 4:3–5). So correctly Zahn, Sieffert, Burton, Lietzmann, Lagrange. Differently, Friedrich Büchsel, "ἐξαγοράζω," *TDNT* 1.126–27, 450; Oepke; Schlier; Klein, *Rekonstruktion*, 207f; Kertelge, "*Rechtfertigung*," 210; Luz, *Geschichtsverständnis*, 152f; Mussner; and others, who systematize Paul by interpreting Rom 1:18ff; 2:12ff; 3:23; 5:12ff into Gal. However, the universal reign of law and sin over both the Jew and the Gentile is stated clearly only in Rom, not in Gal. In Gal both Jews and Gentiles are "under the elements of the world" (τὰ στοιχεῖα τοῦ κόσμου), part of which is the Jewish Torah (see Gal 3:19–25; 4:1–3, 8–10). Notably, Paul does not repeat this conceptuality in Rom.
102 Cf. also Gal 2:16; furthermore, Phil 3:4–11.
103 See Gal 4:8–11.

curse of the Law (cf. 1:8–9).[104]

The concept of "curse of the Law" is strange and occurs only here in Paul.[105] What does he mean by it? In the context of the letter, he certainly assumes that the Law becomes a curse for those who seek justification before God "by works of the Law," because by doing so they deprive themselves of the blessing of Abraham given to "men of faith" (3:9). The question is, however, whether Paul does not go further, calling the Law itself a curse.[106] 3:19–25 indeed comes close to saying that;[107] the only positive thing Paul can say about the Torah is that it was limited in time and function. Compared with the blessing of Abraham it is certainly inferior. The concept of the Law as παιδαγωγὸς εἰς Χριστόν ("custodian up until Christ"), keeping everybody imprisoned and being no different than the enslavement under the "elements of the world," comes very close to being a curse. "The curse of the Law is the curse which the Law brings and which, in this sense, the Law itself is."[108] And yet, the Law is not contrary to the promise made to Abraham, but remains a tool of God to realize those promises (3:21, 22–24).[109]

The liberation from the "curse of the Torah" is taken to be a benefit of Christ's death on the cross.[110] Paul affirms this by a reference to a christological-soteriological dogma: Χριστὸς ἡμᾶς ἐξηγόρασεν ἐκ τῆς κατάρας τοῦ νόμου ("Christ has redeemed us from the curse of the Law").[111] The very concise formulation of this doctrine employs several concepts which were brought together to define what is meant by "redemption."[112] Presupposed is a situation of humanity before redemption: unredeemed humanity is "enslaved" by "the elements of the world"[113] which for the Jew specifically means "being under the curse of the Torah." In order to redeem humanity from its terrible fate, God sent his son Jesus Christ into this world. By becoming a human being ("born by a woman") and by having "come under the Law" (Gal 4:4) Christ "purchases"[114] the freedom of those "under the law" (4:5a) and makes available to those "under the elements of the world" (4:9b) the adoption as "sons of God."[115] For the Apostle, the adoption as sons and the granting

---

104 See Gal 4:21; 5:4, 10b; 6:7–8, 12–16.

105 On this concept, see Moritz Löwy, "Die paulinische Lehre vom Gesetz, I: Der Fluch des Gesetzes," *MGWJ* 47 (1903) 417–22; Schoeps, *Paul*, 175–83; Friedrich Büchsel, "κατάρα," *TDNT* 1.450–51; Kertelge, "*Rechtfertigung*," 207–10.

106 The parallel passage in Rom 7:7–12 reveals a different position compared with Gal; in Rom Paul does not repeat what he said in Gal 3:19–25, but emphasizes the positive role of the Torah. In Gal, this positive role remains implicit (cf. 5:14; 6:2).

107 Cf. Schoeps, *Paul*, 182f: "In the last analysis this means that the law springs not from God but from the angels."

108 Schlier, p. 136.

109 In Jewish Christianity, Cerinthus may have been the first to take the step of coordinating the angels which gave the Torah with the god of the Jews (ps.-Tertullian *Adv. omn. haer.* 3 [CSEL 47, 219]). Epiphanius attributes to Cerinthus the view that the angels which gave the Torah also created the world (*Anaceph.* 28.1.3 [GCS 1, 313]). This doctrine is, of course, shared by other gnostics and Marcion. See Adolf Hilgenfeld, *Die Ketzergeschichte des Urchristentums* (Leipzig: 1884; rep. Darmstadt: Wissenschaftliche Buchgesellschaft, 1963) 412f; Harnack, *Marcion*, 97–118; *73 (on Gal 3:13–14).

110 See Gal 3:13b below.

111 For other christological statements, see the Introduction, § 6. On Χριστός without article, see Conzelmann, *1 Corinthians*, 253f.

112 "Redeem" is the English equivalent of ἐξαγοράζω. See *PGL*, *s.v.*; Carl Andresen, "Erlösung," *RAC* 6.59.

113 See Gal 4:1, 3, 7, 8, 9, 24, 25; 5:1; also 2:4–5. Cf. *CMC* 69.17–20: ὡς ἂν ἐξαγοράση [ι] με καὶ λυτρώσαιτο [ἐκ] τῆς πλάνης τῶν τοῦ [νό] μου ἐκείν⟨ου⟩ ("in order that he might redeem me and liberate (me) from the error of the people of that law [i.e., the Elchasaites]).".

114 ἐξαγοράζω is here not a technical term describing the purchasing of freedom for slaves. Cf. Diodorus 15.7.1 about Plato who was sold into slavery by Dionysius: "but the philosophers joined together, purchased him (his freedom) and sent him to Greece" (...ἐξηγόρασαν καὶ ἐξαπέστειλαν...). So also Diodorus 36.2.2, but most of the instances are simply business language (e.g., Polybius 3.42.2; Plutarch *Crassus* 2.4; Dicaearchus 1.22 [*Geogr. graeci min.* 1, p. 104]). See Stanislaus Lyonnet, "L'emploi paulinien de ἐξαγοράζειν au sens de 'redimere' est–il attesté dans la littérature grecque?," *Bib* 42 (1961) 85–89; Elpidius Pax, "Der Loskauf," *Antonianum* 37 (1962) 239–78.

115 See Gal 3:26–28, 29; 4:1–7, 21–31.

of freedom amount to the same: both become manifest in the gift of the Spirit.[116] This concept implies that the language of purchasing freedom for the slave is used as a religious metaphor, a transposition known also from other sources.[117] The application of this religious language[118] to christology is probably pre-Pauline in origin.[119] Most likely, this christological and soteriological doctrine comes from Jewish Christianity.[120]

This becomes apparent from the next component, according to which Christ accomplished that redemption by "becoming a curse for us" ($\gamma\epsilon\nu\acute{o}\mu\epsilon\nu o\varsigma\ \acute{v}\pi\grave{\epsilon}\rho\ \acute{\eta}\mu\tilde{\omega}\nu\ \kappa\alpha\tau\acute{\alpha}\rho\alpha$).[121] This statement presupposes sacrificial ideas which are, however, not spelled out. Does Paul mean that Christ became the *object* of the curse in place of us,[122] or a "curse offering" as a means of propitiation "for us"? Is the notion derived from Judaism,[123]

---

116 See Gal 3:2, 5; 4:4–6, 7, 21–31; 5:1, 13.

117 Deissmann (*Licht vom Osten*, 270–78) had proposed that Paul makes use of an ancient institution of sacred law, through which the deity could purchase a slave for freedom. There are, in fact, only a few known cases of this procedure, where "the god himself" is buying the slave. Most impressive is a Delphic inscription containing these words (*SGDI* 2, No. 2116): ... $\dot{\epsilon}\pi\rho\acute{\iota}\alpha\tau o\ \acute{o}\ \H{}A\pi\acute{o}\lambda\lambda\omega\nu\ \acute{o}\ \Pi\acute{v}\theta\iota o\varsigma\ \pi\alpha\rho\grave{\alpha}$ $\Sigma\omega\sigma\iota\beta\acute{\iota}o\upsilon\ \H{}A\mu\varphi\iota\sigma\sigma\acute{\epsilon}o\varsigma\ \dot{\epsilon}\pi'\ \dot{\epsilon}\lambda\epsilon\upsilon\theta\epsilon\rho\acute{\iota}\alpha\iota\ \sigma\tilde{\omega}\mu[\alpha]\ \gamma\upsilon\nu\alpha\iota$-$\kappa\epsilon\tilde{\iota}o\nu\ \tilde{\alpha}\iota\ \check{o}\nu o\mu\alpha\ N\acute{\iota}\kappa\alpha\iota\alpha\ \tau\grave{o}\ \gamma\acute{\epsilon}\nu o\varsigma\ \H{}P\omega\mu\alpha\acute{\iota}\alpha\nu,\ \tau\iota\mu\tilde{\alpha}\varsigma$ $\dot{\alpha}\rho\gamma\upsilon\rho\acute{\iota}o\upsilon\ \mu\nu\tilde{\alpha}\nu\ \tau\rho\iota\tilde{\omega}\nu\ \kappa\alpha\grave{\iota}\ \acute{\eta}\mu\mu\nu\alpha\acute{\iota}o\upsilon$ ("The Pythian Apollo bought from Sosibios of Amphissa, for freedom, a woman by the name of Nicaia, of Roman nationality, for the price of $3\frac{1}{2}$ silver minas").

The more common formula, however, presumes that the slave–owner sells the slave to the deity for an amount of money. The former owner receives the purchase price, and the slave is then set free. The differences between this concept and Paul's christology are great indeed and have often been pointed out. See Friedrich Büchsel, "$\dot{\epsilon}\xi\alpha\gamma o\rho\acute{\alpha}\zeta\omega$," *TDNT* 1.126–28; Werner Elert, "Redemptio ab hostibus," *ThLZ* 72 (1947) 265–70; Pax, "Loskauf," 254–59 (n. 114 above); Conzelmann, *1 Corinthians*, 127–29. The discussion is continuing. See the important investigation and critique of Deissmann by Franz Bömer, *Untersuchungen über die Religion der Sklaven in Griechenland und Rom, Teil 2: Die sogenannte sakrale Freilassung in Griechenland und die* ($\delta o\tilde{\upsilon}\lambda o\iota$) $\iota\epsilon\rho o\acute{\iota}$ (AAWLMG 1; Wiesbaden: Steiner, 1960); and the review by Louis Robert, *REG* 75 (1962) 135–37; Lienhard Delekat, *Katoche, Hierodulie und Adoptions-freilassung* (Münchener Beiträge zur Papyrusforschung und antiken Rechtsgeschichte 47; Munich: Beck, 1964) 118ff; S. Scott Bartchy, "*MAΛΛON XPHΣAI*": *First Century Slavery and the Interpretation of 1 Corinthians 7:21* (SBLDS 11; Missoula: Scholars, 1973).

118 See for other, rather speculative hypotheses Elert, ibidem, 265–70 (see n. 18); Pax (ibidem) who

follows Stanislaus Lyonnet, "De notione emptionis seu acquisitionis," *VD* 36 (1958) 257–69.

119 In Gal 4:4–5, which probably contains a pre–Pauline christology, Christ's death and the "curse" are not mentioned. Cf. also 1 Cor 7:23 (6:20): $\tau\iota\mu\tilde{\eta}\varsigma\ \acute{\eta}\gamma o\rho\acute{\alpha}\sigma\theta\eta\tau\epsilon$ ("you were bought for a price"); 2 Pet 2:1; Rev 5:9; 14:3f; *Mart. Pol.* 2.3. Cf. Bultmann, *Theology*, 1.297f; Conzelmann, *Outline*, 69f, 205; Käsemann, *Perspectives*, 36, 43f.

As a result, Gal 3:13 and 4:4–5 must be kept separate. Differently Luz (*Geschichtsverständnis*, 283), who tries to harmonize by taking 4:5a to be an insertion into pre–Pauline material, done by Paul and based upon 3:13.

120 This doctrine seems to be preserved, independently of Paul, in the *Ap. Jas.* (ed. Michel Malinine *et al.*, Codex Jung F. 1ʳ–F. VIIIᵛ; Zurich & Stuttgart: Rascher, 1968) 13 lines 23–25, with n., p. 71; Hans–Martin Schenke ("Der Jakobusbrief aus dem Codex Jung," *OLZ* 66 [1971] 117–30, 126) renders: "I have given myself up for you under the curse, in order that you might be saved." The speaker is Christ.

121 For analogous formulations, see 1 Cor 1:30: "who became our wisdom from God, righteousness and sanctification and redemption;" Rom 3:24–26; 8:3f; 9:3; 1 Cor 4:9, 13; 5:7; 11:25; 15:3–5; 2 Cor 5:21; cf. 1 Tim 2:6. In every case, the interpretation is difficult and disputed. See the commentaries.

122 Schlier (p. 138) interprets in analogy with 2 Cor 5:21: Christ took upon himself the curse for our benefit, so that he represented the curse which was upon him and which wholly covered him. Hartwig Thyen (*Studien zur Sündenvergebung im Neuen Testament und seinen alttestamentlichen und jüdischen Voraussetzungen* [FRLANT 96; Göttingen: Vandenhoeck & Ruprecht, 1970] 188f) shows that this concept comes close to that of the scapegoat. See for an explicit scapegoat christology *Barn.* 7.

123 For the concept of the vicarious atonement death in Judaism, see Eduard Lohse, *Märtyrer und Gottesknecht* (FRLANT NF 46; Göttingen: Vanden-

from the pre-Pauline tradition in Gal 4:4–5,[124] or is it a formulation *ad hoc*?[125] A definitive answer cannot be given. Most likely, the statement is based upon a pre-Pauline interpretation of Jesus' death as a self-sacrifice and atonement (see also Gal 1:4; 2:20). Due to Christ's incarnation (4:4–5) he suffered his death as a human being. Since he was free of sin (cf. 2 Cor 5:21), his death was, in Jewish terms, uniquely meritorious.[126] The result is that "we"[127] are free from the "curse of the Law" and indeed from the Law itself. Therefore, Paul can say that Christ is the "end of the Law" (Rom 10:4; Gal 2:19–20; 3:25; 5:6; 6:15). Although this last conclusion was drawn most likely only by Paul,[128] one can still see an underlying concept of Jesus' death interpreted by means of the Jewish concept of the meritorious death of the righteous and its atoning benefits.[129]

In order to support his christology, Paul again quotes a passage from Scripture. The introductory formula is ($\ddot{o}\tau\iota$) $\gamma\acute{e}\gamma\rho\alpha\pi\tau\alpha\iota$ ("for it is written").[130] The quotation is taken from Deut 21:23, although it does not fully conform to the LXX: $\dot{e}\pi\iota\kappa\alpha\tau\acute{a}\rho\alpha\tau\sigma\varsigma\ \pi\hat{a}\varsigma\ \dot{o}\ \kappa\rho\epsilon\mu\acute{a}\mu\epsilon\nu\sigma\varsigma\ \dot{e}\pi\grave{\iota}\ \xi\acute{\upsilon}\lambda\sigma\upsilon$ ("cursed be everyone who hangs on a tree").[131] Deut 21:22–23 contains a legal regulation for the hanging of criminals:[132] "when someone is convicted of a capital crime and is put to death, you shall hang him on a gibbet; his body shall not remain on the gibbet overnight, but you shall bury him on the same day, for 'cursed by God is everyone who hangs on the gibbet' ($\kappa\epsilon\kappa\alpha\tau\eta\rho\alpha\mu\acute{e}\nu\sigma\varsigma\ \dot{\upsilon}\pi\grave{o}\ \theta\epsilon\sigma\hat{\upsilon}\ \pi\hat{a}\varsigma\ \kappa\rho\epsilon\mu\acute{a}\mu\epsilon\nu\sigma\varsigma\ \dot{e}\pi\grave{\iota}\ \xi\acute{\upsilon}\lambda\sigma\upsilon$). And you shall not pollute the land which the Lord your God gave you as your inheritance." The words Paul quotes look like a quotation in Deuteronomy itself. The considerable difference between Paul's quotation and LXX can be explained in several ways. Paul may have used a different *Vorlage*,[133] or he

---

hoeck & Ruprecht, 1955) esp. 9ff; Weber, *Jüdische Theologie*, § 69–70; Str–B 2.274ff, 3.260ff; Schechter, *Rabbinic Theology*, 304–12; Moore, *Judaism* 1.546–52; Rudolf Mach, *Der Zaddik in Talmud und Midrasch* (Leiden: Brill, 1957) 124–33.

124 In this case, "getting under the law" is the same as "becoming a curse." This view is held by Kramer, *Christ, Lord, Son of God*, 25; Schweizer, *Beiträge*, 94, 104, 202; idem, "$\upsilon\iota\acute{o}\varsigma\ \kappa\tau\lambda$.," *TDNT* 8.383 n. 358.

125 So Lohse, *Märtyrer und Gottesknecht*, 155.

126 Cf., esp. Phil 2:8; 1 Cor 15:3–5, also the quotation above in. n. 120; and the discussion of the material in Lohse, ibidem 113ff. Differently, Dahl ("The Atonement," 153f) wants to interpret Gal 3:13–14 on the basis of Gen 22 and parallel to Rom 8:32, where God is the agent.

127 On the formula "for us" ($\dot{\upsilon}\pi\grave{e}\rho\ \dot{\eta}\mu\hat{\omega}\nu$) see Gal 1:4; 2:20; and the material in Harald Riesenfeld, "$\dot{\upsilon}\pi\acute{e}\rho$," *TDNT* 8.509ff.

128 Cf. also Col 2:13–15; and Lohse, *Colossians and Philemon*, 106ff; Eph 2:14–18. On Paul's doctrine of reconciliation, see Ernst Käsemann, "Erwägungen zum Stichwort Versöhnungslehre im Neuen Testament," in *Zeit und Geschichte, Dankesgabe für Rudolf Bultmann* (Tübingen: Mohr, Siebeck, 1964) 47–59; idem, *Perspectives*, 36, 43f; Peter Stuhlmacher, "Das Ende des Gesetzes," *ZThK* 67 (1970) 14–39, 29; Dieter Lührmann, "Rechtfertigung und Versöhnung," *ZThK* 67 (1970) 437–52; Thyen, *Studien*, 152–94 (n. 122 above).

129 For Paul's own self-sacrifice, see Rom 9:3, and the interpretation of Paul's suffering and death in Col 1:24; Eph 3:1, 13; 4:1; 2 Tim 2:10. See Karl-

Martin Fischer, *Tendenz und Absicht des Epheserbriefes* (FRLANT 111; Göttingen: Vandenhoeck & Ruprecht, 1973) 104–08.

130 This type of formula is used only here in Paul. See Michel, *Paulus*, 72; Ellis, *Paul's Use of the Old Testament*, 22ff (n. 13 above); Fitzmyer, *Essays*, 9.

131 The double–composite $\dot{e}\pi\iota\kappa\alpha\tau\acute{a}\rho\alpha\tau\sigma\varsigma$ may come from Deut 27:26 quoted by Paul in Gal 3:10. Differently from LXX, Paul has the article after $\pi\hat{a}\varsigma\ (\dot{o})$; $\dot{\upsilon}\pi\grave{o}\ \theta\epsilon\sigma\hat{\upsilon}$ is omitted by Paul. See Kautzsch, *De Veteris Testamenti locis*, 92f; Hans Vollmer, *Die alttestamentlichen Citate bei Paulus* (Freiburg and Leipzig: Mohr, Siebeck, 1895) 29; Str–B 3.544f; Georg Bertram, "$\kappa\rho\epsilon\mu\acute{a}\nu\nu\upsilon\mu\iota$," *TDNT* 3.917–19; Friedrich Büchsel, "$\kappa\alpha\tau\acute{a}\rho\alpha$," *TDNT* 1.450–51. The MT is even shorter: כִּי־קִלְלַת אֱלֹהִים תָּלוּי. It corresponds to part of the LXX tradition ($A\Theta$): $\kappa\alpha\tau\acute{a}\rho\alpha\ \theta\epsilon\sigma\hat{\upsilon}\ \kappa\rho\epsilon\mu\acute{a}\mu\epsilon\nu\sigma\varsigma$.

132 The concept of $\xi\acute{\upsilon}\lambda\sigma\upsilon$ ("gallows," "cross") occurs often in the OT: cf., e.g., Gen 40:19, 22; 41:13; Jos 8:29; 10:26; 2 Sam 4:12; Jdt 14:1, 11; 2 Macc 15:33. See for further passages Georg Bertram, "$\kappa\rho\epsilon\mu\acute{a}\nu\nu\upsilon\mu\iota$," *TDNT* 3.917–18; Johannes Schneider, "$\xi\acute{\upsilon}\lambda\sigma\upsilon\ \kappa\tau\lambda$.," *TDNT* 5.39–40; Bauer, *s.v.* $\xi\acute{\upsilon}\lambda\sigma\upsilon$, 2, c.

133 So, e.g., Vollmer, *Citate*, 29 (n. 131 above); Michel, *Paulus*, 54, 75. Cf. the form of the quotation in Josephus *Ant.* 4.202; Philo *Spec.* 3.151f; *Post.* 26f; cf. *Som.* 2.213. Deut 21:23 is now also attested and interpreted in the "Temple Scroll" from Qumran, col. 64, lines 6–13. See Yigael Yadin, "Pesher Nahum (4QpNah) Reconsidered," *IEJ* 21 (1971) 1–12, 7f; Joseph M. Baumgarten, "Does *tlh* in the

may have made the changes himself.[134] The problem is far from clear. Whatever the origin, the passage proves for Paul that Christ's death on the cross fulfilled Scripture.[135] It does not mean that Christ was a criminal, but that a curse became effective through the act of hanging on the cross.[136]

■ **14** Two clauses, both beginning with ἵνα ("in order that") conclude the section 3:6–14 and state the results. The first clause states a general benefit: ἵνα εἰς τὰ ἔθνη ἡ εὐλογία τοῦ Ἀβραὰμ γένηται ἐν Ἰησοῦ Χριστῷ ("in order that the blessing of Abraham might come to the Gentiles through Jesus Christ"). If οἱ ἐξ ἔργων νόμου ("those who base their salvation upon works of the Torah") are under a curse (3:10), if they cannot obtain justification before God by the Torah (3:11), if they are not ἐκ πίστεως ("men of faith" [3:12]), but if, on the other hand, Christians are saved by Christ's atoning death (3:13), the "men of works of the Torah"

cannot be those who inherit Abraham's blessing. If they are not Abraham's heirs, then the heirs must be those Gentiles (τὰ ἔθνη) who have received their salvation "through Jesus Christ" or "in Christ Jesus."[137] These are they who are the "men of faith." Consequently, as the proof-texts show, Scripture has indeed foreseen and foretold that the Gentiles who come to believe are those blessed together with Abraham (cf. 3:8–9).

The second conclusion presupposes[138] the first and is not simply parallel to it: ἵνα τὴν ἐπαγγελίαν τοῦ πνεύματος λάβωμεν διὰ τῆς πίστεως ("in order that we might receive the promise of the Spirit through [the] faith"). From the doctrinal discussion concluded in v 14a Paul can now return to the argument from experiential evidence (cf. 3:2, 5); he changes to the first person plural. The new element in v 14b is that the promise God made to Abraham is now called

Temple Scroll Refer to Crucifixion?" *JBL* 91 (1971) 472–81; Heinz–Wolfgang Kuhn, "Jesus als Gekreuzigter in der frühchristlichen Verkündigung bis zur Mitte des 2. Jahrhunderts," *ZThK* 72 (1975) 1–46, 33–36.

134 See, e.g., Zahn, pp. 156f; Sieffert, pp. 186f; Schlier, p. 138.

135 This is in agreement with Christian apologetics (cf. Acts 5:30; 10:39; 13:29; *Barn.* 5.13; 7.7, 9; Pol. *Phil.* 8.1 [1 Pet 2:24]; *Gos. Pet.* 2 [HSW, *NT Apocrypha* 1.183]). Schoeps (*Paul*, 178–80) thinks that Paul interprets the תלוי in its double meaning of the "hanged" and the "elevated" (cf. Phil 2:8f). Schoeps takes this suggestion up from Klein, *Studien über Paulus*, 62–67 (n. 8 above). However, there is no linguistic indication that Paul knew Hebrew (cf. 2 Cor 11:22; Phil 3:5f). See Schlier, p. 139 n. 2.

136 In Rabbinic theology, for the most, the "curse of God" is taken as a "blasphemy against God." See the material collected in Str–B 1.1012f, 1034, 3.544f; *Tg. Yer.* I, II to Num 25:4; 4QpNah I, 7f; and Symmachus' translation. Apparently, this has become the starting point for an old Jewish anti-Christian polemic (cf. 1 Cor 1:23); see Jeremias (*Lehrer der Gerechtigkeit*, 133–35); Peter Stuhlmacher ("Das Ende des Gesetzes," 29 n. 32; n. 128 above); Hans Hübner ("Gal 3, 10 und die Herkunft des Paulus," *KD* 19 [1973] 215–30); Kuhn ("Jesus als Gekreuzigter," 21, 35f), who regard the connection between Deut 21:23 and Christ's cross as stemming from Paul's own pre–Christian period (so already Klein, *Studien*, 62f). The Jewish (Christian) origin

may be reflected also in Ariston of Pella *Altercatio*, in Jerome's commentary, on Gal 3:13 (*PL* 26.361f; also in *Writings of the Ante-Nicene Fathers* 8.749); Justin *Dial.* 32.1, 89.2, 90.1, 94.5. For further references see *Biblia Patristica*, 117f, 484 (above n. 12). The matter was well understood by the Ambrosiaster commentary. See also Luther (1535) on 3:13.

137 The difference in the word order implies a difference also in meaning. If ἐν Ἰησοῦ Χριστῷ (B ℵ) is to be preferred, the phrase refers to Christ's saving death ("through Jesus Christ"); if one reads with P⁴⁶ A C 𝔐 D G *pl* ἐν Χριστῷ Ἰησοῦ, the phrase refers to the "in Christ" formula (cf. on 1:22; 2:4, 17; 3:26, 28; 5:6). Both forms are Pauline and, therefore, possible. The former, however, is more probable: it refers to v 13, stands in opposition to ἐν νόμῳ ("through the law" [v 11]), and is parallel to διὰ πίστεως ("through faith" [v 14b]). Cf. also the discussion in Burton (p. 176); Schlier (p. 140) advocates an understanding of ἐν as "in his person."

138 Cf. the two ἵνα–clauses in Gal 4:5, which are parallel in form and meaning. See also 1 Cor 4:6; 2 Cor 12:7; Eph 5:26f. Differently, Mussner (pp. 234–36), who takes both sentences to depend upon v 13. This also enables him to carry "the Gentiles" over into v 13, so that in his view the "curse of the law" includes the Gentiles. Cf. on 3:13, above.

"the promise of the Spirit."[139] He arrives at this conclusion for these reasons: the Gentile Christians did receive the Spirit (3:2, 5),[140] and they did so "through [the] faith" (διὰ τῆς πίστεως).[141] If this is the fulfillment of the promise God made to Abraham (3:8), the blessing which is the content of the promise must be the gift of the Spirit. When the Galatians received the Spirit, this could not have been an illegitimate, premature, or deficient event; they must have experienced nothing less than the fulfillment of the solemn promise God had made to Abraham.

---

139   Instead of ἐπαγγελίαν ("promise") P⁴⁶ D* Fᵍʳ G 88* 489 itᵈ· ᵍ Marcion Ambrosiaster *al* read εὐλογίαν ("blessing"). This, however, must be a secondary development, caused by v 14a. See on the textual situation Metzger, *Textual Commentary*, 594; also Schlier, p. 140 n. 2; Schenk, *Segen*, 42ff.

The term "promise" will be in the center of interest in the following sections (3:16, 17, 18, 19, 21, 22, 29; 4:23, 28). See Julius Schniewind and Gerhard Friedrich, "ἐπάγγελμα, προεπαγγέλλομαι," *TDNT* 2.576–86. Paul's opponents would of course disagree; cf. 2 Cor 7:1 and Betz, "2 Cor 6:14–7:1," 98; 103ff. See Appendix 2, below.

140   The expression does not mean "receive a (mere) promise of the Spirit" but "receive the Spirit which has been promised." See Acts 2:33; John 7:39; also Acts 2:38; 1 Cor 2:12; 2 Cor 11:4; Eph 1:13; etc. See Bauer, *s.v.* ἐπαγγελία, 2, b; Burton, p. 176; Schlier, pp. 140f.

141   See Gal 2:16; 3:2, 5, 7, 9, 11, 12. Schlier (p. 141), tries to distinguish between Abraham's faith and the Christian faith: the faith of Abraham is faith in the promise; the Christian faith is faith in the fulfillment of that promise. Paul, however, does not make such a distinction: the faith of the Christians also remains faith in a promise (Gal 5:5). See also Rom 4:17, 24: both Abraham and the Christians believe in God who makes the dead alive.

3

Probatio: The Third Argument

15 Brothers, I draw an example from common human life: likewise,[1] nobody annuls or adds a codicil to a testament of a man, once it has been ratified. 16/ Now, the promises were spoken to Abraham "and to his seed."[2] It does not say "and to his seeds," as about many, but as about one: "and to your seed"—which is Christ. 17/ But this is what I mean: the Law which came 430 years later does not make void a testament[3] previously ratified by God, in order to nullify the promise. 18/ Hence, if the inheritance comes through [the] Law,[4] it no longer comes through [the] promise. However, by promise God has granted it to Abraham as a gift of grace.

Analysis

Paul's third argument (3:15–18) is taken, in his own words, from common human practice.[5] According to Greco–Roman rhetoric, this type of argument would have to be classified under the general rubric of *exempla* (Greek: παραδείγματα).[6] Since Paul's "example" is taken from the field of law, it falls into the more specific category of *similitudo* (Greek: παραβολή).[7] The argumentative value is not as high as the first two arguments in 3:1–5 and 3:6–14, because the *exempla* belong to the *genus artificiale*, but within the *genus* the argumentative value is relatively high. The legal example has evidence in itself,[8] and its application to a quasi-legal argument such as Paul's draws its strength simply from analogy.[9]

Interpretation

■ **15** Paul introduces his example from the practice of law by addressing the Galatian readers again as "brothers" (ἀδελφοί)[10] and by announcing that his example is taken from ordinary human life: κατὰ ἄνθρωπον λέγω (Burton: "I draw an illustration from common human practice").[11] Although the phrase is clearly understandable, its origin is to some degree still in doubt.

---

1 So Bauer. Cf. *RSV*: "even a man's will;" *NEB*: "Even in ordinary life...." See on 3:15.

2 Cf. *RSV*: "offspring;" *NEB*: "issue." *JB* destroys Paul's argument by translating "and to his descendants" the first time and "to his posterity" the second time.

3 *RSV* changes from "will" in v 15 to "covenant" in v 17, with the marginal n. to v 15: "or 'covenant' (as in verse 17)." *NEB* has "will and testament" in v 15, and "testament, or covenant" in v 17. *JB* keeps the same term by rendering "will" in all instances.

4 Cf. *NEB*: "by legal right;" *JB*: "as a legal right."

5 See on 3:15a. The rhetorical nature of the argument was correctly stated by Luther (1535): "...Paul adds another [argument], one that is based on the analogy [*a similitudine*] of a man's will; this seems to be a rhetorical argument."

6 See on this subject, Lausberg, *Handbuch*, §§ 410–26; Martin, *Rhetorik*, 119–24. A general definition of the "example" is found in Quint. 5.11.6: "...ex-

ample, that is...the adducing of some past action real or assumed which may serve to persuade the audience of the truth of the point which we are trying to make" ("...exemplum, id est rei gestae aut ut gestae utilis ad persuadendum id quod intenderis commemoratio").

7 See on this Lausberg, *Handbuch*, §§ 422–425.

8 On the *exempla ex iure* see Quint. 5.11.32–35, with good examples.

9 Paul uses another example from law in Gal 4:1–2.

10 For this address in Gal see 1:11; 4:12, 28, 31; 5:11, 13; 6:1, 18.

11 Zahn (p. 161) remarks that κατὰ ἄνθρωπον ("the way human beings do things") usually implies a contrast to God or revelation. But here, this does not seem to be in the mind of Paul. Cf. also Sieffert, p. 190.

While it also occurs in Rom 3:5; 1 Cor 9:8, and in a different form in Rom 6:19,[12] it is found nowhere else in primitive Christian literature.[13] Yet the Pauline usage suggests that we have here a somewhat technical expression.[14] The strange fact remains, however, that neither the Jewish[15] nor the Greek[16] literature have *precise* parallels.

The example itself comes from the practice of law, but here also difficulties exist. Paul describes a legal procedure: ὅμως ἀνθρώπου κεκυρωμένην διαθήκην οὐδεὶς ἀθετεῖ ἢ ἐπιδιατάσσεται ("likewise, nobody annuls or adds to a testament of a man, once it has been ratified"). While it is clear that Paul refers to the legal institution of the "testament,"[17] it is far from obvious which kind of testament he has in mind. According to Greek[18] and Roman[19] law a testament can be changed at any time. In order to explain the problem, Ernst Bammel[20] has called attention to the Jewish institution

of the מתנת בריא (*mattenat bari'*), which, in distinction to the דייתיקי (*diyathiki*), cannot be changed.[21] The "*mattenat bari'*" designates a transaction of property from donor to donee, which takes place at once and is not conditional upon the donor's death, although he may retain his right to usufruct during his lifetime. The disposition, however, cannot be canceled or changed. If Bammel is correct, Paul's term διαθήκη ("testament") would in reality refer to the legal institution of the "*mattenat bari'*". This possibility cannot be denied, but it raises further questions. If this is a purely Jewish institution, how can the Gentile Galatians be expected to understand this illustration?[22] A way to overcome this problem is to assume that its use was more widespread than we know from the sources.[23] This possibility may be enhanced by several other typically Greek legal terms in the sentence: κυρόω

---

12 David Daube (*The New Testament and Rabbinic Judaism* [London: Athlone, 1956] 394) correctly criticizes Str–B 3.136 for overstating the differences in meaning in those passages.

13 Cf. also 1 Tim 3:1 *v.l.*; 1:15 *v.l.*

14 This was recognized by Daube, *NT and Rabbinic Judaism*, 394f.

15 Comparable Jewish material is discussed by Str–B 3.136–39; Daube, ibidem, 394–400; Carl J. Bjerkelund, "'Nach menschlicher Weise rede ich': Funktion und Sinn des paulinischen Ausdrucks," *StTh* 26 (1972) 63–100. Bjerkelund has called attention to the phrase "I want to prove it to you not from Scripture, nor from the Mishnah, but from daily life" (מדרך ארץ).

16 For similar expressions, cf. Aeschylus *Agam.* 351; *Sept.* 425; *Eum.* 310; Sophocles *Ajax* 761, 777; *Oed. Col.* 598; Plato *Phileb.* 62 A–B; Aristides *Or.* 19 (vol. 2, p. 16; ed. Keil); Athenaeus 10.444B; Diodorus Sic. 16.11.2; Porphyry *De abst.* 2.2. See also Wetstein on Rom 3:5; Lietzmann, *Römer*, on 3:5.

17 So now most commentaries, except Burton (pp. 178f, 496–505) who prefers "covenant." See also Johannes Behm and Gottfried Quell," διατίθημι, διαθήκη," *TDNT* 2.104–34 (with further bib.); Erich Bernecker, "Diatheke," *KP* 1.1514–17.

18 See, esp., Raphael Taubenschlag, *The Law of Graeco-Roman Egypt in the Light of the Papyri, 332 B.C.–640 A.D.* (Warsaw: Państwowe Wydawnictwo Naukowe, ²1955) 190ff, with many passages and bib.

19 See Max Conrat [Cohn], "Das Erbrecht im Galaterbrief (3:15–4:7)," *ZNW* 5 (1904) 204–27; Boaz

Cohen, *Jewish and Roman Law* (New York: The Jewish Theological Seminary of America, 1966) 1.35f; Max Kaser, *Das Römische Privatrecht* (HKAW 10.3.3.1; Munich: Beck, 1971) §§ 160, 163, 165.

20 Ernst Bammel, "Gottes ΔΙΑΘΗΚΗ (Gal. III 15–17) und das jüdische Rechtsdenken," *NTS* 6 (1959/60) 313–19, with further bib.

21 See on this the basic study by Reuven Yaron, *Gifts in Contemplation of Death* (Oxford: Clarendon, 1960) 19ff, 49ff; also Walter Selb, "Διαθήκη im Neuen Testament: Randbemerkungen eines Juristen zu einem Theologenstreit," *JJS* 25 (1974) 183–96. The discussion in Str–B 3.545–53 must be revised accordingly.

22 Otherwise, Schoeps's protest (*Paul*, 181 n. 5) that Paul's example is "lame" and his attempt "abstruse" is still in order.

23 A more widespread usage is suggested by the material from Egypt discussed by Yaron (*Gifts*, 46ff). Professor Yaron, in a letter of April 17, 1975, agrees with this suggestion: "...I have little doubt that arrangements akin to *mattenat bari'* were widespread in the Near East in NT times. In my book... I put special stress on the Egyptian material.... The reason for this is that, due to the dry climate, Egypt is our primary, almost exclusive source for legal papyri. However, these legal institutions tend to become disseminated—especially if they are well formulated and answer social needs in a satisfactory manner."

("confirm," "validate," "ratify"),[24] and its opposite ἀθετέω ("declare invalid," "nullify"),[25] and finally ἐπιδιατάσσομαι ("add a codicil to a testament").[26] Grammatically difficult is also the word ὅμως.[27] Bauer is probably right in preferring the older meaning of "equally," "likewise," rather than "nevertheless" (which would amount to this: "even though only a man's will, nevertheless...").[28] In spite of all these difficulties, however, the meaning of Paul's words is fairly clear: according to legal practice, once a testament has been ratified, nobody has the right to cancel it or add a codicil to it.[29]

■16 The application of the illustration (3:15) clarifies what Paul has in mind. He is thinking of the promises made[30] to Abraham: τῷ δὲ Ἀβραὰμ ἐρρέθησαν αἱ ἐπαγγελίαι καὶ τῷ σπέρματι αὐτοῦ ("now the promises were spoken to Abraham and to his seed"). The notion of "promise" (ἐπαγγελία)[31] was mentioned first in 3:14, and is now taken up for further interpretation. For the Apostle, the promises made to Abraham are identical with the blessing of Abraham discussed in 3:6–14. Paul again interprets the Abraham tradition (cf. Gen 12:2–3, 7; 13:15–16; 15:4–6; 17:1–11; 22:16–19; 24:7–9; etc.). In fact, Gen 17:1–11 (LXX) has the terms all coordinated:[32]

" and when Abraham was ninety-nine years old, the Lord appeared to Abraham and said to him, 'I am your God, live a life acceptable before me and be blameless, and I will set my covenant [διαθήκη] between myself and you and multiply you greatly.' And Abraham fell upon his face, and God spoke to him and said, 'And I, behold, my covenant [διαθήκη] with you, and you shall be a father of a host of nations. And...your name shall be Abraham, for I have made you a father of many nations, and I will greatly increase you, and I will make you into nations, and kings shall go out from you. And I will fulfill my covenant [διαθήκη] which is between me and you and your seed [σπέρμα] after you, for their generations, for an eternal covenant [διαθήκη], to be your God and the God of your seed [σπέρμα] after you. And I shall give to you and to your seed after you the land in which you now live as strangers, all the land of Canaan, as an everlasting possession, and I shall be their God.' And God said to Abraham: 'But you shall keep my covenant [διαθήκη], you and your seed [σπέρμα] after you, from generation to generation. And this is the covenant [διαθήκη] which you shall keep, between me and you and your seed [σπέρμα] after you, from generation to generation: circumcised shall be every male among you, and you shall circumcise the flesh of your foreskin, and this shall be the sign of the covenant [διαθήκη] between me and you.'"

---

24 In this sense the term is used only here in the NT. See Johannes Behm, "κυρόω, ἀκυρόω, προκυρόω," *TDNT* 3.1098–99; Bauer, *s.v.*, 1; Schlier, p. 143 n. 8; LSJ, *s.v.*; *Suppl.*, *s.v.*, Manfred Hässler, *Die Bedeutung der Kyria-Klausel in den Papyrusurkunden* (Berliner Juristische Abhandlungen 3; Berlin: Duncker & Humbolt, 1960).

25 See also Gal 2:21; Mark 7:9; Luke 7:30; Heb 10:28, 1 Tim 5:12. See Bauer, *s.v.* 1; Christian Maurer, "ἀθετέω κτλ.," *TDNT* 8.158–59; Preisigke, *Wörterbuch*, 4/1 (1944) 51, *s.v.*

26 The term is a NT *hapax legomenon*. See LSJ, *s.v.*; Conrat, "Das Erbrecht im Galaterbrief (3:15–4:7)," *ZNW* 5 (1904) 215f (see above n. 19); Otto Eger, "Rechtswörter," *ZNW* 18 (1917) 92f; Schlier, p. 143 n. 8; Gerhard Delling, "διατάσσω, διαταγή," *TDNT* 8.34–36; Preisigke, *Wörterbuch*, 4/3 (1966) 557, *s.v.* διατάσσω; *PGL*, *s.v.*, lists the Anonymous in Eusebius *H.E.* 5.16.3: ἐπισυγγράφειν ἢ ἐπιδιατάσσεσθαι τῷ τῆς εὐαγγελίου καινῆς διαθήκης λόγῳ, ᾧ μήτε προσθεῖναι μήτε ἀφελεῖν δυνατόν...("to write something in addition or add a provision to the word of the new covenant of the gospel, to which it is not possible to add or take away some-

27 Cf., esp., Burton, pp. 178f; Schlier, p. 143 n. 4.

28 See Bauer, *s.v.*; BDF, § 450, 2; BDR, § 450, 2; Joachim Jeremias, "ΟΜΩΣ (I Cor 14, 7; Gal 3, 15)," *ZNW* 52 (1961) 127f; Rudolf Keydell, "ΟΜΩΣ," *ZNW* 54 (1963) 145f; Schwyzer, *Grammatik* 2.582f.

29 It is not clear whether "nobody" refers to the donor (ἄνθρωπος) or to somebody else. See Schlier, pp. 143f.

30 ἐρρέθησαν ("they were spoken" [by God]) refers to the setting up of the testament; this corresponds in Rabbinic law to אמר or כתב (cf. Bammel, "Gottes ΔΙΑΘΗΚΗ," *NTS* 6.316 n. 2; Schlier, p. 144 n. 2). See the formal parallels in Philo *Conf.* 169; *Mut.* 145.

31 The term ἐπαγγελίαι ("promises") does not occur in Gen and is brought in here by Paul; the plural is found in Gal 3:16, 21; the sing. 3:14, 17, 18, 22, 29; 4:23, 28. Probably the concept is important in the polemic against the opponents; cf. 2 Cor 7:1 (see below, Appendix 2), and Betz, "2 Cor 6:14–7:1," 92–99, 104f; Jas 1:12; 2:5; etc.

32 So with Zahn, pp. 166f; Schlier, pp. 144f; Mussner, pp. 237f.

It is important for Paul that the covenant includes the promises (the multiplication of offspring, the gift of the land, the inclusion of the offspring), and that these are made to Abraham and to his "seed." This is what he calls the "inheritance" (κληρονομία).[33] Paying no attention to the content of the promises, he moves on directly with the phrase "and to his seed,"[34] naming the recipients. In Paul's view, this phrase is so important because it has a deeper meaning. On the basis of the singular σπέρμα ("seed") he first rejects the traditional[35] interpretation: οὐ λέγει· καὶ τοῖς σπέρμασιν, ὡς ἐπὶ πολλῶν ("it[36] does not say 'and to the seeds,' as about many"). To Paul, the singular points to one heir, whom he then identifies[37] as Christ: ἀλλ᾽ ὡς ἐφ᾽ ἑνός· καὶ τῷ σπέρματί σου, ὅς ἐστιν Χριστός ("but as about one: 'and to your seed,' who is Christ"). The argument must be seen on two levels: the argument as a whole is designed to show that the "men of faith," whom he had demonstrated to be blessed together with Abraham and to be identical with the believers in Christ (3:6–14), are also the heirs of the covenant and of the promises. This is done merely in preparation to the discussion to follow later. In this passage, Paul takes advantage of the singular "seed," in order to exclude the traditional Jewish interpretation[38] and to reserve the role of the heir for Christ. To be sure, this identification is Christian, but it was made possible by the LXX text,[39] and perhaps even by Jewish thought.[40]

■ 17 Paul now sets forth the real issue on account of which he had used the illustration in v 15. The phrase τοῦτο δὲ λέγω ("but this is what I mean") alerts the reader to pay attention to the following.[41] The "testament"[42] Paul had in mind is the promise God made to Abraham, calling it: διαθήκην προκεκυρωμένην ὑπὸ τοῦ

---

33 In Gen the verb is found in 15:3, 4, 7, 8; cf. Gal 3:18, 29; 4:30; 5:21.

34 Nestle–Aland mark καὶ τῷ σπέρματι as a quotation from LXX. As Kautzsch (*De Veteris Testamenti locis*, 20f) and more recently Daube (*NT and Rabbinic Judaism*, 438) have pointed out, the phrase "and to your seed" is found only in connection with the promise of the land (cf. Gen [MT] 13:15; 17:8; Gen [LXX] 13:15; 17:8; 24:7), while in connection with Abraham's offspring the words read "in your seed" (Gen 22:18); cf. Str–B 3.553, with references to Gen 13:15; 17:8; 22:18.

35 See Ps 105:8ff and the material in Str–B 3.211. In Paul, this interpretation is found in Rom 4:16f (Gen 17:5); 9:4ff; 15:8f; furthermore in Eph 3:6; Heb 4:1ff; 11:9, 11; Acts 13:22; 26:6f. In Judaism, of course, the heirs include the Jews and, to a certain degree, the proselytes. Cf. *Ps. Sol.* 12.6; *T. Jos* 20; Wis 12:21, and the material in Str–B 3.207–09; Schlier, p. 145 n. 2; Gottfried Quell and Siegfried Schulz, "σπέρμα κτλ.," *TDNT* 7.536–47.

36 The subject of λέγει may be God (as in ἐρρέθησαν [cf. n. 30, above]) or Scripture (cf. Gal 3:8; Rom 15:10, and Bauer, *s.v.* λέγω, I, 7). See BDR, § 130, n. 7.

37 ὅ instead of ὅς is read by D* 81 Irenaeus[lat] Tertullian Ambrosiaster Augustin. ὅ ἐστιν would be an explanatory phrase (cf. Heb 7:2, Col 1:24; Eph 5:5; other examples in Bauer, *s.v.* ὅς, 7); ὅς ἐστιν looks like a stylistic improvement (so Schlier, p. 145 n. 5). G reads οὗ. No clear decision can be made.

38 Improving on Str–B. 3.553, Daube (*NT and Rabbinic Judaism*, 438–44), has presented material for showing Paul's agreement with midrashic teaching, where the generic singular can be interpreted as a specific one.

39 σπέρμα can be used in the Greek to designate "offspring." So especially in LXX (cf. Gen 4:25; 21:13; Deut 25:5; etc.); for passages, see Quell and Schulz, "σπέρμα κτλ.," *TDNT* 7.539–41.

40 See above, n. 38. Some scholars have suggested that the Pauline interpretation of "seed" as Christ may reflect a Christian adaptation of the so-called *Akedat Jishaq* in the form of an Isaac–Christ typology. The "seed" could then be taken to refer to the sacrifice of Isaac/Christ. The problem with this hypothesis, however, is that (1) no indication in Gal 3:16 points to Isaac, (2) Rom 8:32, which is the text usually discussed in this connection, cannot simply be taken as a basis for interpreting Gal 3:16. Cf. Schoeps, *Paul*, 147f; Daube, *NT and Rabbinic Judaism*, 443f; Dahl, "The Atonement," 146–60; idem, "Widersprüche," 13. For further bib., see J. Edwin Wood, "Isaac Typology in the New Testament," *NTS* 14 (1967/68) 583–89; Mussner, p. 240 n. 147.

41 On this form of reference, see Bauer, *s.v.* λέγω, I, 7; Boaz Cohen (*Jewish and Roman Law* [New York: The Jewish Theological Seminary of America, 1966] 1.35f) and Mussner (p. 240) assume that Paul employs here the conclusion *a minore ad maius*.

42 Schlier (p. 146 n. 4) is correct in saying that one should not render διαθήκη in 3:17 differently from 3:15, as Burton (pp. 182f) had proposed.

θεοῦ ("the testament previously ratified by God").[43] It is obviously Paul's method to apply the language of the legal example v 15 to the issue he wants to argue, the promise to Abraham. Again the language is technical: the term προκυρόω ("ratify previously")[44] is rare; the προ- ("previously") stands in contrast to μετά ("after"). This "testament" cannot have been nullified by the Torah because the Torah was only given 430 years later on Mount Sinai.[45] To be sure, the ἀκυροῦν ("making void, nullifying")[46] would result in the cancellation[47] of the promise made to Abraham, an absurd assumption. It is absurd because of the legal parallel (v 15) reflected also in the Rabbinic rule that anyone who precedes in Scripture also precedes in reality.[48] Paul's chronology, according to which the Torah was given 430 years after the promise to Abraham, is based upon Exod 12:40 (LXX): "the dwelling of the Israelites, during which they dwelled in Egypt in the land of Canaan, lasted 430 years...".[49] However, the chronology itself is of no particular interest to Paul.[50] He intends to render impossible the assumption that the revelation of the Torah on Mount Sinai could imply a cancellation of the promise made to Abraham.[51]

Who would ever think of such an absurd possibility? According to normative Jewish tradition,[52] Abraham kept the Torah, even though it was given only much later. How he could do so is explained in various ways: he knew the Torah "out of himself,"[53] or from secret writings,[54] or through a special revelation by God.[55] Therefore, it may be Paul himself who introduces the alternative as part of his polemic against the opponents. Perhaps his position had some connection with the "Hellenistic reformers" of the Maccabean revolt (see the excursus on "Abraham" above on 3:6). If the opponents, along with Judaism, based salvation exclusively upon the revelation of the Torah on Mount Sinai, Paul is interested exclusively in the promise to

---

43 After θεοῦ the *Textus Receptus*, following later uncials and many minuscules (D^gr G^gr 1^vid K 0176 88 *al*) read εἰς Χριστόν. This seems to be an interpretative gloss based upon 3:16 (cf. 3:24). P^46 א A B C and other good witnesses support the shorter text. See Metzger, *Textual Commentary*, 594.

44 The legal meaning is clear from the existing instances. See *Suppl. Epigr. Graec.* 3.674 A, lines 29, 31 (Rhodes, 2nd c. *A.D.*): ἐν τῷ προκεκυρωμένῳ ψαφίσματι ("in the decree ratified before"); Eusebius *Praep. ev.* 10.4 (*PG* 21.780 C); etc. See LSJ, *s.v.*; *PGL*, *s.v.*; Johannes Behm, "ἀκυρόω, προκυρόω," *TDNT* 3.1099–1100; Bauer, *s.v.*; Bammel, "Gottes ΔΙΑΘΗΚΗ," *NTS* 6.316 (n. 20 above).

45 ὁ νόμος refers to the "Torah" revealed to Moses on Mount Sinai. See Gal 3:19–25; Rom 4:15; 5:13f; 20; 10:5; 2 Cor 3:7, 12.

46 This legal term is rare; in this sense it occurs only here in the NT. See LSJ, *s.v.*; *Suppl. s.v.* ἀκυρισμός; Preisigke, *Wörterbuch* 4/1 (1944) *s.v.*; Eger, "Rechtswörter," *ZNW* 18 (1917) 92; Johannes Behm, "ἀκυρόω, προκυρόω," *TDNT* 3.1098–99; Bauer, *s.v.*

47 The term καταργέω ("make ineffective, nullify") is rare, but Paul uses it many times with several meanings. Cf. Gal 5:4, 11; Rom 3:3, 31; 4:14; 7:2, 6; etc.; also Eph 2:15. See Gerhard Delling, "καταργέω," *TDNT* 1.453–54; Bauer, *s.v.*, 1, b; Schlier, p. 148 n. 2. The closest parallel is Rom 4:14: "If the 'men of the law' are the heirs, the faith is empty and the promise is destroyed" (κεκένωται ἡ πίστις καὶ κατήργηται ἡ ἐπαγγελία).

48 *Sipre Num.* § 73. See Karl Georg Kuhn, *Der tannaitische Midrasch Sifre zu Numeri* (Rabbinische Texte 2.3; Stuttgart: Kohlhammer, 1959) 188.

49 Cf. Exod 12:41 (B* reads 435 years). Gen 15:13 (cf. 15:16) has 400 years. Rabbinic exegesis explains the difference with the help of the rule שני כתובים. This solution must be old and already presupposed in LXX; cf. also *Mek. Exod.* 12.40 (19ᵃ); *Tg. Yer. I* Exod 12:40f; *Gen. Rab.* 63 (39c); Josephus *Ant.* 2.15.2. On the whole, see Str-B 2.668–71; Daube, *NT and Rabbinic Judaism*, 440; Dahl, "Widersprüche," 11 n. 18. It is noteworthy that Acts 7:6 follows the tradition of Gen 15:13, counting 400 years.

50 So Philipp Vielhauer, "Paulus und das Alte Testament," in *Studien zur Geschichte und Theologie der Reformation, Festschrift für E. Bizer* (Neukirchen: Neukirchener Verlag, 1969) 33–62, 45.

51 On the notion of "promise" (ἐπαγγελία), see on Gal 3:18.

52 For a collection of the sources, see Str-B 3.204–06.

53 So, e.g., R. Shimeon (ca. 150), *Gen. Rab.* 61 (38b): "A father did not teach him, and a teacher he did not have. Wherefrom did he learn the Torah?" Shimeon explains by reference to Ps 16:7: God used the kidneys to teach Abraham the Torah. Cf. Philo *Abr.* 275f, and other passages in Str-B 3.205.

54 So, e.g., *Jub.* 21.10, with reference to "the words of Enoch and Noah."

55 So, e.g., R. Nathan in *Mek. Exod.* 20, 18 (78b); *Gen. Rab.* 44 (27d); see Str-B 3.206.

Abraham. To make his point, he takes advantage of the problem presented by the sources.[56] Paul polemically separates what Judaism tries to hold together.[57] In order to break up the Jewish concept, he emphasizes that Abraham did *not* know the Torah and did *not* gain his righteousness by keeping its ordinances, but that he was regarded as righteous as a result of his "faith." In other words, Paul turns the traditional Jewish view upside down: instead of attributing to Abraham a foreknowledge of the Torah, Paul deprives the Sinai Torah of any significance. If Abraham could obtain righteousness without the knowledge of the Torah, the revelation of the Torah 430 years later cannot have cancelled that promise, and consequently cannot render invalid Abraham's way of obtaining righteousness before God without the Torah and through faith.[58]

■ **18** Here Paul sums up the argument in 3:15–17. Where did the "inheritance" ($\kappa\lambda\eta\rho\text{ovo}\mu\text{i}\alpha$) come from: "from the Torah" ($\dot{\epsilon}\kappa\ \nu\text{ó}\mu\text{ov}$)[59] of Moses or "from the promise" ($\dot{\epsilon}\xi\ \dot{\epsilon}\pi\alpha\gamma\gamma\epsilon\lambda\text{i}\alpha\varsigma$) to Abraham? The Apostle presents this as an alternative without room for compromise:[60] "if, then, the inheritance comes from the Torah [of Moses], it no longer comes from the promise [made to Abraham]." It should be noticed that a new term, "inheritance,"[61] has now been introduced; it will play a major role from here on. "Inheritance" includes all the benefits of God's work of salvation. Paul's conclusion is that the insistence with which Judaism bases this inheritance upon the Torah of Moses in effect cancels out the promise made to Abraham. Judaism, to be sure, would not accept this conclusion, arguing that Abraham somehow had a preview

---

56 As I have pointed out in my article, "2 Cor 6:14–7:1," the fragment 2 Cor 6:14–7:1 presupposes a Jewish–Christian theology based solidly upon the Sinai covenant (see Appendix 2, below). Schlier (pp. 148f) assumes that the anti–Pauline opponents combined both, promise to Abraham and Sinai Torah; this would represent the normative Jewish position. Mussner (p. 241) thinks the opponents made the Sinai Torah a mere codicil to the Abraham promise or wanted even to nullify it—a difficult hypothesis.

57 The normative Jewish position was that both belong together. See, e.g., 2 Macc 2:17f: "God has saved his whole people and gave us all the inheritance ($\kappa\lambda\eta\rho\text{ovo}\mu\text{i}\alpha$), the kingship, the priesthood, and the consecration, as he had promised by the law ($\kappa\alpha\theta\dot{\omega}\varsigma\ \dot{\epsilon}\pi\eta\gamma\gamma\epsilon\text{i}\lambda\alpha\tau\text{o}\ \delta\iota\dot{\alpha}\ \tau\text{o}\hat{\text{v}}\ \nu\text{ó}\mu\text{ov}$)." See also *Apoc. Bar.* 57.2; *Jub.* 24.11; etc. For a collection of material see Str–B 3.204–09.

59 So also Rom 4:13ff: the promise was given to Abraham and to his offspring not "through the Torah" ($\delta\iota\dot{\alpha}\ \nu\text{ó}\mu\text{ov}$) but "through faith–righteousness" ($\delta\iota\dot{\alpha}\ \delta\iota\kappa\alpha\iota\text{o}\sigma\acute{v}\nu\eta\varsigma\ \pi\text{i}\sigma\tau\epsilon\omega\varsigma$).

59 The concept $\dot{\epsilon}\kappa\ \nu\text{ó}\mu\text{ov}$ occurs also Gal 3:21; Rom 2:18; 4:14, 16; 10:5; Phil 3:9. The meaning in Paul is different from the Greek notion; Greek rhetoric has $\dot{\epsilon}\kappa\ \tau\hat{\omega}\nu\ \nu\text{ó}\mu\omega\nu$ or $\dot{\epsilon}\kappa\ \tau\text{o}\hat{\text{v}}\ \nu\text{ó}\mu\text{ov}$ as signifying "in accordance with the laws or the law" (see Erik Wolf, *Griechisches Rechtsdenken*, [4 vols.; Frankfurt: Klostermann, 1950–70] 3.2, 428, index *s.v.*). Paul's concept is Jewish; it is an abbreviation for "based upon the Torah of Moses." P[46] reads $\delta\iota\dot{\alpha}\ \nu\text{ó}\mu\text{ov}$ ("through law"), probably under the influ-

ence of Rom 4:13 and in clear juxtaposition with $\delta\iota'\ \dot{\epsilon}\pi\alpha\gamma\gamma\epsilon\lambda\text{i}\alpha\varsigma$ (Gal 3:18b).

60 Any compromise is even more sharply rejected in Rom 4:13ff. (see above, on 3:17).

61 The noun $\kappa\lambda\eta\rho\text{ovo}\mu\text{i}\alpha$ ("inheritance") occurs in Gal 3:18; $\kappa\lambda\eta\rho\text{ovó}\mu\text{o}\varsigma$ ("heir") in Gal 3:29; 4:1, 7; Rom 4:13, 14; 8:17; the verb $\kappa\lambda\eta\rho\text{ovo}\mu\acute{\epsilon}\omega$ ("inherit") in Gal 4:30 (citing Gen 21:10 LXX); for verb cf. also 1 Cor 6:9–10; 15:50; Gal 5:21. If Paul did not receive the terminology directly from the LXX (cf. Gen 15:3, 4, 7, 8; 21:10; 22:17; 24:60; etc.), he received it from the Jewish tradition. See Werner Foerster and Johannes Herrmann, "$\kappa\lambda\eta\rho\text{ovó}\mu\text{o}\varsigma$," *TDNT* 3.767–85; Paul L. Hammer, "A Comparison of *kleronomia* in Paul and Ephesians," *JBL* 19 (1960) 267–72; James D. Hester, "Paul's Concept of Inheritance," *SJTh* (Occasional Papers 14; Edinburgh: Oliver & Boyd, 1961); idem, "The 'Heir' and Heilsgeschichte: A Study of Gal 4:1ff," in *Oikonomia, Festschrift für Oscar Cullmann* (Hamburg–Bergstedt: Reich 1967) 118–25; Luz, *Geschichtsverständnis*, 182ff.

of the Torah. If Abraham, as Paul sees it, were promised the inheritance without the Torah, upon what was the promise based? Paul's conclusion is that it was a gift of grace made to Abraham by God: δι᾽ ἐπαγγελίας κεχάρισται ὁ θεός. The term χαρίζομαι ("make a gift") correlates the promise made to Abraham with God's present work of salvation[62] and, through it, with the salvation of the Galatians.[63]

---

62 The term, especially in its perfect form, is related to God's "grace" (χάρις), i.e., the work of salvation *in toto*; cf. Gal 1:3, 6, 15; 2:9, 21; 5:4; 6:18; Rom 4:4, 16 (κατὰ χάριν, "according to grace"). See BDF, § 342; BDR, § 342, 5; Moule, *Idiom Book*, 14f; Mussner, pp. 242f. Paul may still be playing with legal language, where the term is also important ("make a gracious gift"). See LSJ, *s.v.*, II; Preisigke, *Wörterbuch*, 2 (1927) 720f; Ludwig Mitteis and Ulrich Wilcken, *Grundzüge und Chrestomathie der Papyruskunde* (rep.; Hildesheim: Olms, 1963) 2/2.305 line 25ff; Bauer, *s.v.*; Schlier, p. 149 n. 3; Walther Zimmerli, "χάρις κτλ.," *TDNT* 9.365 line 16–366 line 6; 9.379 lines 19f; 386–87 n. 193. Cf. also Philo *Mut.* 53f who speaks about Gen 17:2 and makes this remark: "Now covenants are drawn up for the benefit of those who are worthy of the gift, so that a covenant is a token of the grace which God has set between Himself who proffers it and man who receives" (διαθῆκαι δὲ ἐπ᾽ ὠφελείᾳ γράφονται τῶν δωρεᾶς ἀξίων, ὥστε σύμβολον εἶναι διαθήκην χάριτος, ἣν μέσην ἔθηκεν ὁ θεὸς ἑαυτοῦ τε ὀρέγοντος καὶ ἀνθρώπου λαμβάνοντος). It should be noted that the ambiguities are similar to Paul's.

63 Cf. Rom 11:6: "But if it is by grace (χάριτι), it is no longer on the basis of works (ἐξ ἔργων); otherwise grace would no longer be grace."

3

A Digression on the (Jewish) Torah

19 What then is the Law?—Because of the transgressions it was given in addition,[1] till the offspring should come to whom the promise had been made,[2] ordained through angels, through a mediator.[3] 20/ But the mediator is not of one, but God is one.[4] 21/ Is the Law, then, contrary to the promises (of God)?—By no means! For if a law had been given which was capable of making alive, then righteousness would indeed come from [the] Law.[5] 22/ But Scripture has confined everything[6] under sin, in order that the promise, by faith in Jesus Christ, might be given to those who believe.[7] 23/ Before the faith came, we were kept in custody under [the] Law, confined until the coming faith was to be revealed. 24/ Therefore, the Law has been our guardian until Christ, in order that we might be justified by faith. 25/ But since the faith has come, we are no longer under a guardian.[8]

---

1 *NEB* translates: "It was added to make wrong-doing a legal offence." As an alternative this rendering is given by *NEB*: "added because of offences." This translation is based upon Rom 4:15; 5:13, 20; Gal 2:18; etc. Cf. *JB*'s paraphrase: "What then was the purpose of adding the Law? This was done to specify crimes...." Also this is based upon Rom, and it destroys the sentence structure.

2 So *RSV*. *NEB* paraphrases correctly: "It was a temporary measure pending the arrival of the 'issue' to whom the promise was made." *JB* paraphrases in light of Gal 3:6–18: "until the posterity came, to whom the promise was addressed."

3 *RSV* combines the third and the fourth definition: "and it was ordained by angels through an intermediary...." *JB* goes further: "The Law was promulgated by angels, assisted by an intermediary."

4 So Burton. Cf. *RSV*: "Now an intermediary implies more than one; but God is one." *NEB*: "but an intermediary is not needed for one party acting alone, and God is one." *JB*: "Now there can only be an intermediary between two parties, yet God is one." These translations try to spell out the definition of a mediator, which is the background of Paul's statement.

5 The translation of *NEB* seems to look upon Gal 2:15f: "then indeed righteousness would have come from keeping the law."

6 Cf. *RSV*: "all things." *NEB*: "the whole world."

7 *NEB*'s paraphrase renders the meaning well: "so that faith in Jesus Christ may be the ground on which the promised blessing is given, and given to those who have such faith."

8 *NEB*'s rendering expresses well what Paul has in mind: "Thus the law was a kind of tutor in charge of us until Christ should come, when we should be justified through faith; and now that faith has come, the tutor's charge is at an end." The alternative given, however, considers "a kind of tutor to conduct us to Christ."

Analysis

The question in 3:19 "What then is the Law?" ($\tau\iota$ $o\hat{\upsilon}\nu$ $\dot{o}$ $\nu\acute{o}\mu o\varsigma$;)[9] introduces a new and extraordinary section in Paul's argument. Following this question,[10] we should expect the Apostle to enter into the discussion of the subject "On the Law" ($\pi\epsilon\rho\grave{\iota}$ $\nu\acute{o}\mu ov$), a topic common for the philosophers and theologians of the Greco–Roman world.[11]

In view of the ongoing argument, such a discussion is certainly in order. If the blessing of Abraham and the promise to Abraham include the believers in Christ,

that is, those who are $\dot{\epsilon}\kappa$ $\pi\acute{\iota}\sigma\tau\epsilon\omega\varsigma$ ("men of faith"), but excludes those who are $\dot{\epsilon}\xi$ $\ddot{\epsilon}\rho\gamma\omega\nu$ $\nu\acute{o}\mu ov$ ("men of the works of the Torah"), and if neither the "promise" nor the "inheritance" comes "from the Torah," the Torah itself seems to be deprived of its traditional role in Judaism.[12] Therefore, the argument requires at this point an answer to the following questions: after all that has been said by Paul about the Torah, how can the Torah be defined? What is the function and purpose of the Torah? Paul is confronted with the "Marcionite" possibility, that the Torah becomes an entirely negative

---

9   This is the correct form of the question. Differently, P[46] G Irenaeus Ambrosiaster read: $\tau\acute{\iota}$ $o\hat{\upsilon}\nu$ $\dot{o}$ $\nu\acute{o}\mu o\varsigma$ $\tau\hat{\omega}\nu$ $\pi\rho\acute{\alpha}\xi\epsilon\omega\nu$; ("What then is the law of deeds?"). This and other variants try to eliminate the offense of Paul's statement (so rightly Oepke, p. 115; cf. also Zahn, p. 173). On the elliptic form of the question see BDF, § 480, 5; BDR, § 480 n. 9. For parallels in Paul, see 1 Cor 3:5: $\tau\acute{\iota}$ $o\hat{\upsilon}\nu$ $\dot{\epsilon}\sigma\tau\iota\nu$ $'A\pi o\lambda\lambda\hat{\omega}\varsigma$; ("What then is Apollos?") and Rom 3:1: $\tau\acute{\iota}$ $o\hat{\upsilon}\nu$ $\tau\grave{o}$ $\pi\epsilon\rho\iota\sigma\sigma\grave{o}\nu$ $\tau o\hat{\upsilon}$ $'Iov\delta\alpha\acute{\iota}ov$; ("What then is the advantage of the Jew?").

10   Paul's question has important predecessors. The ps.–Platonic Minos, a tractate "On the Law" ($\pi\epsilon\rho\grave{\iota}$ $\nu\acute{o}\mu ov$), begins with this question asked by Socrates: $\dot{o}$ $\nu\acute{o}\mu o\varsigma$ $\dot{\eta}\mu\hat{\omega}\nu$ $\tau\acute{\iota}$ $\dot{\epsilon}\sigma\tau\iota\nu$; ("Tell me, what is the law?"). Cf. also Minos 313BC, 314 B, 316 E. See Wolf, Griechisches Rechtsdenken 4/1, 81ff. Also Cicero introduces the subject matter of his De leg. (1.4.14) with the words: "sed iam ordire explicare, quaeso, de iure civili quid sentias" ("But kindly begin without delay the statement of your opinions on the civil law"). Cf. the following deliberations (1.4.15ff). In Hellenistic Judaism the question functions in connection with the defense of the Torah. Cf. Ep. Arist. 128–171; and passim; Philo Decal. 2, etc.; Josephus C. Apion., etc. See on this subject Moriz Friedländer, Geschichte der jüdischen Apologetik als Vorgeschichte des Christenthums (Zurich: Schmidt, 1903) 441 ff; Paul Krüger, Philo und Josephus als Apologeten des Judentums (Leipzig: Dürr, 1906) 51ff; Juda Bergmann, Jüdische Apologetik im neutestamentlichen Zeitalter (Berlin: Reimer, 1908) 94ff, 110ff; Adolf Schlatter, Die Theologie des Judentums nach dem Bericht des Josefus (BFCTh 2.26; Gütersloh: Bertelsmann, 1932) 62ff; Isaak Heinemann, Philons griechische und jüdische Bildung: Kulturvergleichende Untersuchungen zu Philons Darstellung der jüdischen Gesetze (Hildesheim: Olms, 1962) § 10; Ehrhard Kamlah, "Frömmigkeit und Tugend. Die Gesetzesapologie des Josephus in c.Ap. 2, 145–295," in Josephus-Studien, . . . O. Michel zum 70. Geburtstag gewidmet (eds. O. Betz et al.; Göttingen:

Vandenhoeck & Ruprecht, 1974) 220–32; Hengel, Judaism and Hellenism 1.267ff; Willem C. van Unnik, "Josephus' Account of the Story of Israel's Sin with Alien Women in the Country of Midian (Num. 25: 1ff.)," in Travels in the World of the Old Testament, Studies Presented to Professor M. A. Beek (Assen: van Gorcum, 1974) 241–61.

11   See the older works, esp. Plato Leg.; ps.–Plato Minos; ps.–Demosthenes Or. 25.15ff (see on this speech, W. K. C. Guthrie, The Sophists [Cambridge: Cambridge University, 1973] 75ff). See on the whole Wolf, ibidem, 1–4/2. Furthermore: Chrysippus, Frag. 314 (SVF 3.77); Cicero De leg. (on this, Ada Hentschke, "Zur historischen und literarischen Bedeutung von Ciceros Schrift 'De legibus,'" Ph. 115 [1971] 118–30); Epictetus Diss. 1.26; Dio Chrys. Or. 75; Stobaeus Ecl. 4, chap. 2 (rep. in Stobaeus Anthol., 4/1, 115–83 [eds. Curt Wachsmuth and Otto Hense; Berlin: Weidmann, [2]1958]). For collections of sources, see Auguste Bill, La morale et la loi dans la philosophie antique (Paris: Alcan, 1928) 265–99. For the state of research, see Hermann Kleinknecht, "$\nu\acute{o}\mu o\varsigma$," TDNT 4.1022–35; J. Walter Jones, The Law and Legal Theory of the Greeks (Oxford: Clarendon, 1956); Jacqueline de Romilly, La loi dans la pensée grecque des origines à Aristote (Paris: Les Belles Lettres, 1971) with full bib.

12   The normative Jewish view is stated by Simeon the Righteous at the beginning of 'Aboth (1.2): "The world is based upon three things: the Torah, (Temple) service, and deeds of loving kindness." This view is carried out in Aboth, passim; see esp. 3.21; 6.1, 6, 7, 9; see also 'Aboth R. Nat. B, 18, with Saldarini's commentary, 55–59; Charles Taylor, Sayings of the Jewish Fathers (New York: KTAV, [2]1969) 12. Similarly Josephus (C. Apion. 1.42), who affirms that, although long periods have passed since the Torah was given, no Jew "has ventured either to add or to remove, or to alter a syllable; and it is an instinct with every Jew, from the day of

entity and that those who accuse him of being an
enemy of the law are proven right.[13]

In terms of rhetoric, 3:19–25 is an extremely concise
"digression" (*digressio*).[14] It does not add a new argument to the defense, but prevents a wrong conclusion
the readers might reach on the basis of the preceding.[15]

Interpretation

■ **19** Paul's digression on the (Jewish) Torah starts out
with the question, "What then is the meaning of the
Torah?"[16] This question is then followed by a set of
four definitions, summing up Paul's view on the ques-

tion.[17] The definitions are set forth *seriatim*, as a sequence of very concise and unconnected statements.[18]
Parallels show that this form of definition seems to
have been common in related literature.[19] In the
following, each of the statements will be discussed
separately, since each of them contains specific doctrines related to the Law:

3:19b   (1) τῶν παραβάσεων χάριν προσετέθη
3:19c   (2) ἄχρις ἂν ἔλθῃ τὸ σπέρμα ᾧ ἐπήγγελται
3:19d   (3) διαταγεὶς δι' ἀγγέλων
3:19e   (4) ἐν χειρὶ μεσίτου

---

his birth, to regard them [*sc.* the statutes of the
Torah] as the decrees of God, to abide by them,
and, if need be, cheerfully to die for them." On the
Jewish position, see Weber, *Jüdische Theologie*, 14ff
and *passim*; Schechter, *Rabbinic Theology*, chaps.
8–13; Bousset-Gressmann, *Religion*, chap. 4; Moore,
Judaism 1.251–80; Walter Gutbrod, "νόμος," *TDNT*
4.1036–59; Warren Harvey, "Torah," *EncJud* 15
(1971) 1235–46; Meinrad Limbeck, *Die Ordnung
des Heils: Untersuchungen zum Gesetzesverständnis des
Frühjudentums* (Düsseldorf: Patmos, 1971). On
Qumran, see Braun, *Qumran*, 2, § 12; idem, *Radikalismus*. The most recent study on Jesus' understanding of the law is by Robert Banks, *Jesus and the
Law in the Synoptic Tradition* (SNTSMS 28; Cambridge: Cambridge University, 1975).

13   The accusation against Paul that he is an enemy of
the law begins in the NT itself, with Paul's allusion
Gal 2:17. See also 5:23; Rom 3:5–8; 6:1f; 1 Cor
9:19–23. Acts defends Paul against it (18:13;
21:21, 24; 24:5, 13ff; 25:7f). For the continuation
in later anti-Pauline Jewish Christianity see the
Introduction, § 2.c; Appendix 3; and the commentary on Gal 2:17.

14   On the *digressio* (excursus) in Graeco-Roman rhetoric, see Lausberg, *Handbuch*, §§ 340–42; Martin,
Rhetorik, 89–91.

15   Paul's doctrine of the law cannot be treated here in
full. Brief surveys are to be found in Bultmann,
Theology, § 27; Conzelmann, *Outline*, § 26; W. D.
Davies, "Law," *IDB* 3.95–102, esp. 99f. A survey of
the literature is contained in Otto Kuss, "Nomos
bei Paulus," *MThZ* 17 (1966) 172–227. Still useful
is the article by Hermann Kleinknecht and Walter
Gutbrod, *TDNT*, *s.v.* νόμος κτλ.; the studies by
Eduard Grafe, *Die paulinische Lehre vom Gesetz nach
den vier Hauptbriefen* (Freiburg and Leipzig: Mohr,
Siebeck, ²1893); Christian Maurer, *Die Gesetzeslehre
des Paulus nach ihrem Ursprung und in ihrer Entfaltung*

dargelegt (Zollikon–Zürich: Evangelischer Verlag,
1941). See also Charles E. B. Cranfield, "St. Paul
and the Law," *SJTh* 17 (1964) 43–68; Ragnar
Bring, *Christus und das Gesetz* (Leiden: Brill, 1969);
Andrea van Dülmen, *Die Theologie des Gesetzes bei
Paulus*, (SBM 5; Stuttgart: Katholisches Bibelwerk,
1968) esp. 39ff; Luz, *Geschichtsverständnis*, 186–222;
Eckert, *Die urchristliche Verkündigung*, 106–30; and
the commentaries by Schlier (pp. 176–88) and
Mussner (pp. 277–90). Important for the under-
standing of the anti-Pauline opposition is Schoeps
(*Paul*, esp. 168–218).

16   See on the nature of the question above nn. 9 and
10.

17   The same formal sequence of question and brief
definitions is found in Epictetus *Diss.* 2.16.28: τίς
δ' ὁ νόμος ὁ θεῖος; τὰ ἴδια τηρεῖν, τῶν ἀλλοτρίων μὴ
ἀντιποιεῖσθαι, ἀλλὰ διδομένοις μὲν χρῆσθαι, μὴ διδό-
μενα δὲ μὴ ποθεῖν, ἀφαιρουμένου δέ τινος ἀποδιδόναι
εὐλύτως καὶ αὐτόθεν, χάριν εἰδότα οὗ ἐχρήσατο χρόνου
…("And what is the law of God? To guard what is
his own, not to lay claim to what is not his own, but
to make use of what is given him, and not to yearn
for what has not been given; when something is
taken away, to give it up readily and without delay,
being grateful for the time in which he had the use
of it…". See also Plato *Prot.* 326D, 337D; *Leg.* 9.880
DE; Aristotle *Pol.* 3.11.4 (p. 1287a lines 25ff); ps.–
Demosthenes *Or.* 25.16; Cicero *De leg.* 1.6.18; Dio
Chrys. *Or.* 75.1.

18   That these statements represent a definition was
emphasized by Luther: "Paulus ergo hic novo
capite incipit tractare legem et definit, quid sit…"
WA 40/1.490, line 25 ("here, then, Paul begins to
discuss the Law under a new heading and to define
what it is," *Luther's Works* 26. 316).

19   See *Gnomol. Vatic.* 427: Πλάτων πυθομένου τινὸς τί
ἐστι νόμος εἶπε· "ψυχὴ πόλεως [ἢ δόγμα ἀθάνατον καὶ
κοινόν]" ("When someone asked what the law is,

3:19b (1) "because of the transgressions it was given in addition"

3:19c (2) "until the offspring should come to whom the promise had been made"

3:19d (3) "ordained through angels"

3:19e (4) "through [the hand of] a mediator"

(1) The first statement of the definition (3:19b) determines that the Torah "was given in addition, because of the transgressions" (τῶν παραβάσεων χάριν προσετέθη).[20] This statement, taken by itself, can be interpreted in several ways. If the definition were to state the *necessity* of the Law, Greco–Roman legal thought would agree. Understood in these terms, it would reaffirm the general Hellenistic concept that the law is a divine gift to man and must be regarded as an indispensable instrument for controlling criminal acts. This affirmation of the validity of the law is itself a reaction against the moral relativism which began with the sophists.[21] This means that it is also a reaffirmation: "without law no city can be administered."[22] As the Greco–Roman sources reveal, this affirmation intends to support the need for law generally, but it can be accompanied by the understanding that the wiseman and philosopher does not need such law. An example of the first option is Dio Chrysostom's *Oratio* 75, a eulogy on the law, which unrestrictedly affirms Pindar's famous dictum of νόμος βασιλεύς ("Law is king.")[23] This dictum applies to the administration of cities as well as to one's individual life: "If one expels the laws from his life, just as he has lost his mind, I believe he will be brought into a state of utter madness and confusion."[24]

The second option is also part of Greco–Roman thought, especially among the Cynic and Epicurean schools. While the Cynics were famous for their disregard for the law in principle,[25] the Epicureans formed a combination of both. Epicurus[26] declared: "the laws are established because of the wisemen, not that they do not commit injustice, but that they do not suffer injustice" (οἱ νόμοι χάριν τῶν σοφῶν κεῖνται, οὐχ ὅπως μὴ ἀδικῶσιν ἀλλ᾽ ὅπως μὴ ἀδικῶνται). The wiseman himself does not need any law to prevent him from

Plato said: 'Soul of the city [or immortal and common decree]'"). Cf. Plato *Leg.* 1.644 D. Also *Gnom. Vatic.* 507: Σόλων ἐρωτηθεὶς ὑπό τινος τί ἐστι νόμος εἶπε· "τῶν μὲν δειλῶν φόβος, τῶν δὲ τολμηρῶν κόλασις" ("When Solon was asked by someone what the law is, he said: 'Fear of the cowards, but punishment of the reckless'").

20 Instead of παραβάσεων ("transgressions") a number of witnesses read πράξεων ("deeds"): P[46] F[gr] G it[d.g] Irenaeus[lat] Ambrosiaster Marius Victorinus *Speculum*; or: παραδόσεων ("traditions"): D*. See Metzger, *Textual Commentary*, 594.

21 See, esp., Plato *Prot.* 326 D, and on that Wolf, *Griechisches Rechtsdenken*, vol. 2; 3/1; 4/1–2; furthermore Aristotle *EN* 5.1, 1129a lines 32ff; *Pol.* 7.12.3, 1332a lines 8–18. This interpretation was applied to Gal by Jerome, Chrysostom, *et al.* (see the list in Sieffert, p. 202). Also Calvin remarks that this is the way philosophers speak about the law. Cf. Schlier, p. 153 n. 1. Philosophers discuss the issue in terms of φύσις/νόμος ("nature/law"); see Felix Heinimann, *Nomos und Physis* (Schweizerische Beiträge zur Altertumswissenschaft 1; Basel: Reinhardt, 1945); J. Walter Jones, *The Law and Legal Theory of the Greeks*, 35ff (n. 11 above); Guthrie, *Sophists*, 55ff.

22 The quote is from Dio Chrys. *Or.* 75.2, but it is commonplace. Cf. Heraclitus in Diog. L. 9.2: "The people must fight for the law as for city-walls." Cf.

Diogenes in Diog. L. 6.72.

23 Pindar *Frag.* 169: νόμος ὁ πάντων βασιλεὺς θνατῶν τε καὶ ἀθανάτων ἄγει δικαιῶν τὸ βιαιότατον ὑπερτάτᾳ χειρί ("Law, the lord of all, mortals and immortals, carrieth everything with a high hand, justifying the extreme of violence"). Usually, only the first part of the statement is quoted. This dictum has had an enormous impact on the legal theory of the Greeks. See, with further literature, Marcello Gigante, *ΝΟΜΟΣ ΒΑΣΙΛΕΥΣ* (Naples: Glaux, 1956), and the review by Hans Volkmann, *Gnomon* 30 (1958) 474–75; de Romilly, *La loi*, 62–69; Guthrie, *Sophists*, 131–34.

24 Dio Chrys. *Or.* 75.10.

25 So already Antisthenes, according to Diog. L. 6.11: "that the wise man will be guided in his public acts not by the established laws, but by the law of virtue." The concept of "the perfect law of freedom" (νόμος τέλειος ὁ τῆς ἐλευθερίας) in Jas 1:25 (see the excursus in Dibelius–Greeven, *James*, 116–20) may be intentionally opposite.

26 *Frag.* 530, ed. Usener (according to Stobaeus *Flor.* 43.139; the version in Prophyry *Ad Marcell.* 27 is different).

27 Cf. Aristippus (Diog. L. 2.68): "Being once asked what advantage philosophers have, he replied: 'Should all laws be repealed, we shall go on living as we do now.'" See also the accusation made

wrongdoing because he is guided by his own insight into good and evil, and thus he is law to himself.[27]

The situation in Judaism with regard to the Law is not altogether different. The Jewish definition would say that the Torah was given because of Israel.[28] As a gift of God the Torah provides an impenetrable "fence" of protection around Israel. "Now our Lawgiver being a wise man and especially endowed by God to understand all things, took a comprehensive view of each particular detail, and fenced us round with impregnable ramparts and walls of iron, that we might not mingle at all with any of the other nations, but remain pure in body and soul, free from all vain imaginations, worshipping the one Almighty God above the whole creation."[29] Or: "therefore lest we should be corrupted by any abomination, or our lives be perverted by evil communications, he hedged us round on all sides by rules of purity...".[30] This concept of the "fence" was of special importance in the diaspora.[31]

How does Paul's position with regard to the Law fit into this picture? According to him, the Torah was not given for the purpose of providing righteousness and life as Judaism generally assumed. In this regard, Paul takes a decidedly non–Jewish position: "for the purpose of the transgression" is to be taken in a wholly negative way. But strangely enough, Paul also knows of the

necessity of the Jewish Torah, even if this necessity consists of the negative role which this Torah plays. He points out that the Jewish Torah served to "enclose everything under sin" (Gal 3:22) and to "keep it imprisoned" (3:23). Until the coming of Christ, the Torah served as a custodian (3:24–25). In Romans Paul goes even further: the power of sin is regarded as an almost personal entity of demonic dimensions; it existed even before the Torah was given (Rom 5:13) and used the Torah in order to "multiply sin" which in turn multiplied God's grace (Rom 5:20). Since without the Law there are no transgressions, the gift of the Torah produced those transgressions (Rom 4:15) and intensified them to a point where God's interference with grace became necessary (Rom 5:20; cf. 3:20; 7:4–13; 8:3; 1 Cor 15:56; 2 Cor 3:6–9). Rather than preventing transgressions,[32] Paul's view is that the purpose of the Torah was to "produce" them.[33] The coming of Christ put an end to this role of the Torah (Gal 3:24–25; Rom 10:4).

How did Paul, a former Pharisaic Jew, reach such a radically un-Jewish position with regard to the Torah?[34] This problem is still very much disputed among New Testament scholars. The fact that Paul interpreted the Christ–event as the end of the Law is not in itself a

---

against Socrates that he despises the law (Xenophon *Mem.* 1.2.9), his defense (ibidem 1.2.34), and the debate about law and justice (ibidem 4.4.12–25). See on the whole Ragnar Höistad, *Cynic Hero and Cynic King* (Uppsala: Blom, 1948) 113–15. See Rom 2:14: "they are law to themselves."

28   See R. Aqiba in *'Aboth* 3.15 (tr. Danby): "Beloved are Israel, for to them was given the precious instrument; still greater was the love, in that it was made known to them that to them was given the precious instrument by which the world was created, as it is written, *For I give you good doctrine; forsake ye not my Law.*" The "precious instrument" is of course the Torah. For further passages, see Str–B 3.115–18, 126–33.

29   *Ep. Arist.* 139 (*APOT* 2.107f). See also the explanation by Chrysostom, in his commentary on 3.19.

30   *Ep. Arist.* 142 (*APOT* 2.108); cf. also 130–133; 3 Macc 3:4, 7. See the material in Str–B 3.126–33, 587f.

31   See, e.g., Philo *Decal.* 2, 15, 17, 32, 36, 44, 50, 52; Josephus *Ant.* 4.198, where he mentions that he

wants to write a book on "Customs and Causes," i.e., on the law; 3.84, 88, 213, 4.180–193, 196, 210, 16. 31–43; *C. Apion.* 2.147–150, 151, 174, 218, 291f. A different matter is the rabbinic concept of the "fence *around* the Torah" (see *'Abot* 1.1; *'Abot R. Nat. A*, 1).

32   Most commentators (including Lightfoot, Zahn, Sieffert, Lietzmann, Oepke, Schlier, Mussner) rightly reject the older interpretation, that the law's purpose was to make possible "the recognition of the sinfulness of the deeds, which otherwise might have passed without recognition" (Burton, p. 188). This interpretation is based on Rom 3:20. For the older commentaries, see Sieffert's list, p. 201.

33   παράβασις ("transgression") is a legal term. See also Rom 2:23; 4:15; 5:14; παραβάτης ("transgressor") Gal 2:18; Rom 2:25, 27; furthermore Rom 5:20; 7:7ff; 8:3; 11:32; Jas 2:9, 11. See Johannes Schneider, "παραβαίνω, παράβασις, παραβάτης," *TDNT* 5.736–42.

34   This problem has correctly been formulated by Schoeps (*Paul*, 182f).

sufficient explanation.[35] How did he arrive at this explanation?

We must mention in this connection that the radical devaluation of the Jewish Torah is juxtaposed with the high regard for what might be called Paul's notion of the Torah of God, which is identical with the Torah of Christ (cf. Gal 6:2; 5:14; Rom 7:12). Is there any connection between this downgrading of the Jewish Torah and the radical devaluation of the city laws in the Greek philosophical tradition?[36] While in the Socratic tradition we find the combination of a devaluation of the city laws with a high estimation of the "law of nature" or "unwritten law" (ἄγραφος νόμος), Philo reflects applications of this concept to the Torah.[37] He himself downgrades the city laws in favor of the Torah revealed by God in the desert. In fact, he has taken over much of the philosophical tradition in expressing his distrust in human laws and, especially,

the city laws.[38] He speaks of the "law of nature" and finds Abraham to be the Jewish example of a wiseman who is a "living law" all by himself.[39] Philo develops his position against Jewish opponents who are altogether hostile to the Torah and abandon it. "Persons who cherish a dislike of the institutions of our fathers and make it their constant study to denounce and decry the Laws" are quoted as saying: "can you still... speak gravely of the ordinances as containing the canons of absolute truth? For see your so–called holy books contain also myths, which you regularly deride when you hear them related to others. And indeed... it is needless to collect the numerous examples scattered about the Law–book, as we might had we leisure to spend in exposing its failings."[40]

Whether there is any connection between Paul's stance against the Torah and Philo's "antinomists" remains only a possibility.[41] In any case, Paul repre-

35 See Gal 2:19–21; 3:24f; Rom 10:4; 2 Cor 3:4ff, and on the problem Schoeps (*Paul*, 168ff), Luz (*Geschichtsverständnis*, 139ff). Paul's conclusion that Christ's death and resurrection brings in the new messianic age can explain why the Torah comes to its end, but not why the Torah *before* Christ's coming is so radically devaluated.

36 The concept of νόμος τύραννος ("law is a despot") seems to have been developed first by Hippias of Elis (5th c. B.C.). Plato refers to it in *Prot.* 337 C/D. The dictum of Hippias appears to be nothing but a negative interpretation of Pindar's verse (cf. above, n 23). See Wolf, *Rechtsdenken* 2.76ff; 3/1.75ff; Horst–Theodor Johann, "Hippias von Elis und der Physis–Nomos–Gedanke," *Phronesis* 18 (1973) 15–25; Guthrie, *Sophists*, 70, 138, 142ff, 280ff.

37 See Philo *Ebr.* 198: "Now I for my part do not wonder that the chaotic and promiscuous multitude who are bound in inglorious slavery to usages and customs [ἐθῶν καὶ νόμων] introduced anyhow [or: whatever their source], and who are indoctrinated from the cradle with the lesson of obedience to them, as to masters and despots (δεσποτῶν ἢ τυράννων), with their souls buffeted into subjection and incapable of entertaining any high or generous feeling, should give credence to traditions delivered once and for all...." Colson and Whitaker (LCL Philo 3.508) refer as a parallel to ps.–Longinus *Subl.* 44.3.4. See also Philo *Decal.* 2ff; and for the whole problem, see Heinemann, *Philons Bildung*, 448ff. Willem C. van Unnik (see n. 10, above) has called attention to some passages in Josephus, esp. to *Ant.*

4.145–49, where the apostate Zambrias calls the law of Moses "tyrannical" (τυραννικῶς) and the life under that law "living under a tyranny" (ἐν τυραννίδι ζῆν).

38 See, esp. *Mos.* 2.4, 6; *Jos.* 29; *Agr.* 45–46; *Spec.* 1.319–325.

39 See Philo *Abr.* 4–5, 276. Colson (LCL Philo 6.605) refers to Erwin Goodenough, *The Political Philosophy of Hellenistic Kingship* (YCS 1, 1929) 56–101. The more general view that the wise men are "living law" is cited *Abr.* 4–5; *Virt.* 194; *Spec.* 4.150. See Dibelius–Greeven, *James*, 116–20.

40 Philo *Conf.* 2–3; cf. *Migr.* 89–93.

41 See also the prayer, probably Jewish in origin, in *Apost. Const.* 8.12.23: "Thou art He who didst deliver Abraham from the impiety of his forefathers, and didst appoint him to be the heir of the world and didst discover to him Thy *Christ*.... 25. And when men had corrupted the Law of Nature, and had sometimes esteemed the creation to be self-caused (αὐτόματον), and sometimes honoured it more than they ought, and made it the equivalent of Thee, the God of the universe, thou didst not, however, suffer them to go astray, but didst raise up Thy holy servant Moses, and by him didst give the written Law for the assistance of the Law of Nature..." (tr. Erwin R. Goodenough, *By Light, Light: The Mystic Gospel of Hellenistic Judaism* [New Haven: Yale University, 1935] 323). Cf. *Apost. Const.* 8.9.8 (Goodenough, *By Light, Light*, 331). The origin of Jewish antinomism is obscure. See the excursus on Abraham, above on Gal 3:6. For traces in the rabbinic

sents a position which is implicitly rejected by Philo. Philo programmatically identifies the Jewish Torah with the "law of nature" and juxtaposes it with the man–made city laws, while Paul equates the particularistic Jewish Torah with only those inferior laws, contrasting it with the universal Torah of God.

Puzzling is also the verb $προσετέθη$ ("it was given in addition").[42] In the present context, this must refer to the giving of the Torah 430 years after God's promise to Abraham (Gal 3:17). But the reference may also come from a pre–Pauline context. The passive form implies that God gave the Torah, an implication that contradicts Paul's own statement later in the verse (v 19d).[43] Moreover, Philo has an intriguing interpretation of the allegorical meaning of the Jewish Lawbook. He declares that with the Hebrews the matter of the Law is called by the name of Joseph, which he says means "addition of a lord" ($κυρίου$ $πρόσθεσις$): "thus naturally particular polities are rather an addition to the single polity of nature, for the laws of the different states are additions to the right reason of nature, and the politician is an addition to the man whose life accords with nature."[44]

This type of doctrine no doubt has a connection with the Stoic concept of good origin and later degeneration in history. This concept was applied to Judaism perhaps as early as Posidonius, and showed that in the begin-

ning the Jews under Moses had developed an almost ideal state. Then things deteriorated: "his successors for some time abided by the same course, acting righteously and being truly pious toward God; but afterwards, in the first place, superstitious men were appointed to the priesthood, and then tyrannical people; and from superstition arose abstinence from flesh, from which it is their custom to abstain even today, and circumcisions and excisions [i.e., of the females] and other observances of the kind...." (Strabo 16.2. 37). There is a high probability that the so-called "Hellenizers" at the beginning of the Maccabean revolt had applied these theories to their own program of ridding Judaism of its particularistic laws and policies and of integrating it with Hellenistic culture.[45]

Therefore, the formulation in 3:19b that the Torah "was given in addition" may come from a pre-Pauline tradition, where it expressed the view that the introduction of the Torah was due to a later state of depravation in the Jewish religion. Unfortunately we do not have the sources that would allow us to investigate whether Paul has had any connection with these "Hellenizers." Philo at least shows that they were still active at his time, so that such a connection is entirely within the range of possibility.

(2) The second part of the definition (v 19c) limits the validity of the Torah to the period from its revela-

---

literature, see Schoeps, *Paul*, 173–75. For the later history, cf. Gershom Sholem, *Sabbatai Sevi, The Mystic Messiah* (Princeton: Princeton University, 1973).

42 $προστίθημι$ ("add") is used here with a temporal meaning, but it could originally be the legal term ("add articles to legal documents"). See LSJ, *s.v.* A, III, 1; Preisigke, *Wörterbuch, s.v.*; Moulton–Milligan, *s.v.*; Bauer, *s.v.*, 1; Christian Maurer, "$προστίθημι$," *TDNT* 8.167–68. The reading $ἐτέθη$ by D* G it Clement Origen Irenaeus Ambrosiaster Vg *et al.* is clearly secondary; the intention is to remove a possible conflict with Gal 3:15. See Zahn, p. 173 n. 31; Sieffert, p. 201 n.; Burton, p. 188; Schlier, p. 151 n. 4.

43 Oepke (p. 115) has pointed out that the origin of the law remains obscure as it does in Rom 5:20, where the verb in $νόμος$ $δὲ$ $παρεισῆλθεν$ reminds him of Gal 2:4, and he concludes: "Also the law sneaked in from behind." This interpretation, however, goes too far in the Marcionite direction.

44 *Jos.* 31; cf. 28–36. Colson (LCL 6.600) refers to the Stoics Zeno (*SVF* 1.262) and Chrysippus (*SVF* 3.322); see also Heinemann, *Philons Bildung*, 449.

45 See Karl Reinhardt, *Poseidonios über Ursprung und Entartung* (Orient und Antike 6; Heidelberg: Winter, 1928); idem, "Poseidonios," *PW* 22/1 (1953) 639f; Isaak Heinemann, *Poseidonios' metaphysische Schriften* 1 (Breslau: Marcus, 1921) 97ff; 2 (1929) 72ff; *FGH* II C, 196ff; Elias Bickerman, *Der Gott der Makkabäer* (Berlin: Schocken, 1937) 126ff; Arthur Darby Nock, *Essays on Religion and the Ancient World* (2 vols.; ed. Zeph Stewart; Cambridge: Harvard University, 1972) 2.864f; John G. Gager, *Moses in Greco-Roman Paganism* (SBLMS 16; Nashville: Abingdon, 1972) esp. 38–47; Ben Zion Wacholder, *Eupolemus: A Study of Judaeo-Greek Literature* (Cincinnati: Hebrew Union College–Jewish Institute of Religion, 1974) 71ff; Menahem Stern, *Greek and Latin Authors on Jews and Judaism* (Jerusalem: The Israel Academy of Sciences and Humanities, 1974) 1.261ff.

tion on Mount Sinai to the coming of Christ:[46] "till the offspring should come to whom the promise had been made."[47] To be sure, such a temporal limitation for the Torah is contrary to orthodox Judaism, where the Torah is regarded as eternal[48] and, in some traditions, even pre-existent.[49] By contrast, Paul implies that Christ's coming is the end of the Torah. There is no mentioning here of a new Torah to be given in the messianic age.[50] Paul's statement simply recalls Gal 3:16, where it was said that Christ is the "seed" ($\tau\grave{o}$ $\sigma\pi\acute{\epsilon}\rho\mu\alpha$), i.e., the offspring to whom the promise was made.[51] This does not mean, however, that the statement in 3:19c was formulated *ad hoc* on the basis of 3:16. In both places Paul seems to go back to pre-Pauline tradition, which contained the doctrine that Christ was the seed of which the promise to Abraham speaks.[52]

(3) The third part of the definition also has its roots in Judaism: the Torah "was ordained through angels." The contrast to the promise to Abraham, which was spoken by God himself (cf. Gal 3:8 [Scripture!], 16) is of course intended. The verb $\delta\iota\alpha\tau\acute{\alpha}\sigma\sigma\omega$ ("ordain, order") again is a legal term,[53] used here in the context of revelation.[54] Perhaps we have here another allusion to the supplement made to a testament.[55] The preposition $\delta\iota\acute{\alpha}$ ("through") implies either that the angels, not God, are regarded as the originators of the Torah,[56] or that they act on behalf of God as his mediators.[57] The term "angels" can refer to good or evil angels,[58] qualifying the Torah itself as divine or demonic. Deciding the problem in which way Paul understood the matter depends not only on the Pauline context, but also on the Jewish tradition used here.[59]

In the Old Testament narratives about the revela-

---

46   See Gal 3:22–25; cf. Acts 7:52.

47   $\mathring{\alpha}\chi\rho\iota\varsigma$ $\mathring{\alpha}\nu$ ("as long as") is read by B *pc* Clement, while $\mathring{\alpha}\chi\rho\iota\varsigma$ $o\mathring{\upsilon}$ is preferred by P[46] 𝕳 𝕽 D G *pl*, Irenaeus Theodorus Mops. Since Paul has $\mathring{\alpha}\chi\rho\iota$ $o\mathring{\upsilon}$ also in Rom 11:25; 1 Cor 11:26; 15:25; while $\mathring{\alpha}\chi\rho\iota\varsigma$ $\mathring{\alpha}\nu$ is found only in Gal 3:19, the choice is whether one prefers the usual Pauline way or the *lectio difficilior* (which may be pre-Pauline). Nestle–Aland, 26th edition, changes from $\mathring{\alpha}\chi\rho\iota\varsigma$ $\mathring{\alpha}\nu$ to $\mathring{\alpha}\rho\chi\iota\varsigma$ $o\mathring{\upsilon}$. See BDF, § 21; 383; 455, 3; BDR § 21; 383; 455, 3; Bauer, *s.v.* $\mathring{\alpha}\chi\rho\iota$, 2.

48   On the eternity of the Torah, see Sir 24:9; Wis 18:4; 2 Esdr 9:37; *1 Enoch* 99.2; *As. Mos.* 1.11ff; Jos. *C. Apion* 2.38; Philo *Mos.* 2.14; for the Jewish material see Str–B 1.244ff; Weber, *Jüdische Theologie*, 14–18; Moore, *Judaism* 1.263–80; Hengel, *Judaism and Hellenism* 1.169ff. Parts of early Christianity continue this line of tradition: cf. Matt 5:17–19, and especially the anti–Pauline *Kerygmata Petrou*, *Ep. Petr.* 2.5 (see Appendix 3. A).

49   See the collection of passages in Str–B 2.353–57.

50   Cf. Schlier, pp. 155, 272f. The concept of the new Torah is complex in itself. See Weber, *Jüdische Theologie*, 378f; Str–B 4/2.919; 1146; 1152f; W. D. Davies, *Torah in the Messianic Age and/or the Age to Come* (SBLMS 7; Philadelphia: SBL, 1952); idem, *Paul and Rabbinic Judaism*, 131ff, 147ff; idem, *The Setting of the Sermon on the Mount* (Cambridge: Cambridge University, 1966) 363ff; idem, "Torah and Dogma: A Comment," *HTR* 61 (1968) 87–105; Jacob Jervell, "Die geoffenbarte und die verborgene Tora. Zur Vorstellung über die neue Tora im Rabbinismus," *StTh* 25 (1971) 90–108.

51   The perfect passive of $\mathring{\epsilon}\pi\alpha\gamma\gamma\acute{\epsilon}\lambda\lambda o\mu\alpha\iota$ is found only here in Paul. See BDR, § 311 n. 1.

52   The origin may be in Judaism itself. Dahl ("Widersprüche," 14) believes that it is a messianic interpretation of the Judah oracle in Gen 49:10. He also points to Jewish legal language, where phrases like "until somebody comes" mark the provisional nature of a decree. See, e.g., Ezra 2:63; Neh 7:65; 1 Macc 4:46; 14:41. There are parallels also in Qumran (1QS 9.10f; CD 6.10f; 12.23f; 20.1f). See also Jeremias, *Lehrer der Gerechtigkeit*, 284, 312.

53   See other instances in Paul: 1 Cor 7:17; 9:14; 11:34; 16:1; cf. also Acts 7:44; Titus 1:5. See furthermore Bauer, *s.v.*; Gerhard Delling, "$\delta\iota\alpha\tau\acute{\alpha}\sigma\sigma\omega$," *TDNT* 8.34–35; Preisigke, *Wörterbuch* 4/3 (1966) 557, *s.v.*

54   This is of course to be contrasted with the revelation of the gospel through Christ (Gal 1:1, 12).

55   Cf. Gal 3:15, 19b. Schlier (p. 155) makes this suggestion and refers to the parallel in Plutarch *An recte dictum*, 1129 A. Parallels from papyri are now collected in Preisigke, *Wörterbuch* 4/3 (1966) 557 *s.v.*, 4.

56   See Bauer, *s.v.* $\delta\iota\acute{\alpha}$, III, 2, b.

57   Ibidem, III, 2, a, with reference to Heb 2:2.

58   See Bauer, *s.v.* $\mathring{\alpha}\gamma\gamma\epsilon\lambda o\varsigma$, 2.

59   The sources for this doctrine are collected in Str–B 3.554–56; Johann Michl, "Engel II (jüdisch)," *RAC* 5.60–97. See also Schoeps, *Paul*, 182f.

tion of the Torah on Mount Sinai no angels are present.[60] But the cosmic phenomena accompanying the revelation were later interpreted to have been caused by the "angels of the elements."[61] In the LXX the presence of angels is assumed.[62] Most important, however, is a passage of Josephus (*Ant.* 15.136) where Herod says in a speech: "...and we have learned the noblest of our doctrines and the holiest of our laws through angels sent by God."[63] This view is also reflected in the New Testament (Acts 7:38, 53 [see above on 3:6, *excursus* on "Abraham"]; Heb 2:2). It is continued and further developed in primitive Christianity. In *Hermas* (*Sim.* 8.3.3), the archangel Michael is said to

have been the one who "put the law into the hearts of those who believe." In Jewish Christianity and early Christian gnosticism these doctrines were expanded. The angels which gave the Torah became evil demons and were identified with the evil powers that created the world.[64] Paul certainly did not go this far, but doctrines like this[65] paved the way for the "Marcionite" solution.[66] For Paul himself, the Jewish Torah plays a limited "positive" role in God's redemptive work. Neither the Torah itself nor the angels which gave it are evil. But the Torah of Moses is inferior to the promise of Abraham. Drawing upon certain Jewish traditions, Paul proves this point by showing that the Torah

---

60 See Exod 19:9, 16ff; 24:15ff; Deut 4:11ff; 5:22ff; 2 Esdr 3:17ff.

61 LXX Ps 102:20; 103:4; *Jub.* 2.2ff; *1 Enoch* 60.1ff.

62 See Deut 33:2 LXX: Κύριος ἐκ Σινὰ ἥκει,... ἐκ δεξιῶν αὐτοῦ ἄγγελοι μετ' αὐτοῦ ("The Lord comes from Sinai,... on his right side are angels with him.") Later rabbinic traditions explain in various ways what the purpose of these angels was. See Str–B. 3.554–56; Peter Schäfer, *Rivalität zwischen Engeln und Menschen: Untersuchungen zur rabbinischen Engelvorstellung* (StJud 8; Berlin: de Gruyter, 1975) 43ff.

63 Following an objection made by Louis Ginzberg (*The Legends of the Jews* [tr. Henrietta Szold; Philadelphia: Jewish Publication Society, 1909–38] 6.47), saying that it is impossible for Josephus to have made such attribution of the Torah to angels, Ralph Marcus (LCL *Josephus* 8.67) translates δι' ἀγγέλων as "from the messengers," meaning prophets or priests. This view is also held by W. D. Davies ("A note on Josephus, Antiquities 14.136," *HTR* 47 [1954] 135–40) and Francis A. Walton ("The Messenger of God in Hecataeus of Abdera," *HTR* 48 [1955] 255–57). However, Jewish traditions rule out Ginzberg's "impossible," and although ἄγγελος can mean "messenger," it does not decide the translation of the Josephus passage. See also the polemic in 'Abot R. Nat. B, 2 (tr. Anthony J. Saldarini, *The Fathers according to Rabbi Nathan* [Leiden: Brill, 1975] 25): "'Moses received Torah from Sinai.' Not from the mouth of an angel and not from the mouth of a Seraph, but from the mouth of the King over the Kings of Kings, the Holy One..."; *Jub.* 1.27ff; 2.1ff; 6.22; 30.12, 21; 50.1f; *Apoc. Mos.* 1; *Pesiq. R.* 21 (103b): Two myriads of the אלפי שנאן among the angels descended together with God upon Mount Sinai, in order to give the Torah to Israel. See the parallels in *Pesiq. R.*

107b and *Midr. Ps.* 68 § 10 (160a).

64 This doctrine may begin with Cerinthus (Epiphanius *Pan.* 28.1.3; ps.–Tertullian *Adv. omn. haer.* 3 [CSEL 47.219]) and is held by many gnostics, e.g. Marcion (cf. Harnack, *Marcion*, 97ff). For passages, see *PGL*, s.v. νόμος, 921f; Johann Michl, "Engel III (gnostisch)," *RAC* 5.97–109. On the subject, see Ludwig Diestel, *Geschichte des Alten Testaments in der christlichen Kirche* (Jena: Mauke, 1869); Viktor E. Hasler, *Gesetz und Evangelium in der alten Kirche bis Origenes* (Zurich and Frankfurt: Gotthelf–Verlag, 1953); Pieter G. Verweijs, *Evangelium und neues Gesetz in der ältesten Christenheit bis auf Marcion* (Utrecht: Demplein, 1960).

65 See already *Barn.* 9.4, where an evil angel is said to have taught circumcision to Israel; cf. also Epiphanius *Pan.* 28.2.1.

66 Schoeps (*Paul*, 182) thinks that the angels in Gal 3:19 "were obviously hostile to the Jewish people." But there is no indication that Paul holds this view. The rabbinic tradition interpreting the angels as hostile against the Israelites is late (see Str–B. 3.555 No. 3). A gnostic interpretation of Gal 3:19, which is quoted, is found in *Exc. ex Theod.* 53.2 (Foerster–Wilson, *Gnosis* 1.149). See Elaine H. Pagels, *The Gnostic Paul: Gnostic Exegesis of the Pauline Letters* (Philadelphia: Fortress, 1975) 107.

of Moses was not given by the one God directly but only through subaltern divine beings.[67]

(4) The fourth part of Paul's definition is also taken from the Jewish tradition: "through [the hand of] a mediator" (ἐν χειρὶ μεσίτου). There can be no doubt[68] that the mediator Paul has in mind is Moses[69] and that the mediation is identical with the revelation of the Torah on Mount Sinai.[70] Lev 26:46 (LXX) sums it up in these words: "these are the judgments and the ordinances and the law, which the Lord gave between him and the Israelites on Mount Sinai through Moses" (ἐν χειρὶ Μωυσῆ). The expression ἐν χειρί is a rendering of the Hebrew ביד ("through" or literally "through the hand of"),[71] but it is noteworthy that in LXX ἐν χειρὶ Μωυσῆ has become almost a formula,[72] while according to Billerbeck[73] "through a mediator" is found only in p. Meg. 4.74d.9.

Paul's statement, therefore, also comes from Jewish tradition and does not as such imply a negative evaluation of Moses. Especially in Hellenistic Judaism, Moses was regarded as a "divine man"[74] or even an angelic figure[75] precisely because of his role as a mediator of the Torah.

How then did Paul arrive at his negative evaluation of the mediator Moses? Schlier (p. 161) raises the question: "should it be that behind the Pauline μεσίτης ['mediator'] of Gal 3:19 is a hidden concept of Moses as akin to the ἄγγελοι ['angels'] and as representing them as the ἄγγελος ['angel' or 'messenger']?" If this were true, one could understand why the angels who ordain the Law are associated with Moses as a mediator. Schlier also points to the generic singular of "a mediator." However possible this certainly is, there is no indication that the third and the fourth part of the definition have inner connections of a specific nature. More likely, all four statements are independent of

---

67   Cf. Philo *Decal.* 61, where he makes this remark in his polemic against deification of the elements (53ff): "So just anyone who rendered to the subordinate satraps the honours due to the Great King would have seemed to reach the height not only of unwisdom but of foolhardiness, by bestowing on servants what belonged to their master, in the same way anyone who pays the same tribute to the creatures as to their Maker may be assured that he is the most senseless and unjust of men in that he gives equal measure to those who are not equal, though he does not thereby honour the meaner many but deposes the one superior." Cf. Rev 19:10, 22:8f.

68   Older commentaries often took Christ to be the mediator (see Sieffert, pp. 205f), but modern scholarship is unanimous in preferring Moses. See also Joachim Jeremias, "Μωυσῆς," *TDNT* 4.869–70; Albrecht Oepke, *TDNT* 4.598–624, *s.v. μεσίτης κτλ.* esp. 618f.

69   On Moses generally, see Josef Scharbert, *Heilsmittler im Alten Testament und im Alten Orient* (Freiburg: Herder, 1964) 82–92, 242–44; Israel Abrahams *et al.*, "Moses" *Enc Jud* 12 (1971) 371–411; Siegfried Herrmann, "Mose," *EvTh* 28 (1968) 301–28, with further bib.

70   See Exod 19:7, 9, 21ff; 20:19; 24:3, 4, 12; 31:18; 32:16, 19, 30; 34:1ff; Deut 4:14; 5:4f; etc.

71   So most commentaries. See esp. Zahn, pp. 175f. Sieffert (p. 205) wants to take it more literally; so also Burton, p. 189; Schlier, pp. 155, 158–61; furthermore, Bauer, *s.v.*, 1; Eduard Lohse, "χείρ," *TDNT* 9.430–31.

72   See LXX Num 4:37, 41, 45, 49; 9:23; 10:13; 15:23; 17:5; 33:1; 36:13; Jos 21:2; 22:9; Judg 3:4; 1 Chr 16:40; 2 Chr 33:8; Ps 76:21; Bar 2:28.

73   Str-B 3.556; cf. also 3.512, 515f.

74   This may be an apologetic reaction. See John G. Gager, *Moses in Graeco-Roman Paganism* (SBLMS 16; Nashville: Abingdon, 1972); David Lenz Tiede, *The Charismatic Figure as Miracle Worker* (SBLDS 1; Missoula: SBL, 1972) 101–240. Hengel, *Judaism and Hellenism, passim*; Wacholder, *Eupolemus*, 71ff.

75   Especially Philo needs to be mentioned. See his assessment in *Spec.* 1.116: "For the law desires him to be endured with a nature higher than the merely human and to approximate to the Divine, on the border line, we may truly say, between the two, that men may have a mediator through whom they may propitiate God and God a servitor to employ in extending the abundance of his boons to men." See for more material Jeremias, "Μωυσῆς," *TDNT* 4.848–73; Goodenough, *By Light, Light*, 199–234; Wayne A. Meeks, "Moses as God and King," in *Religions in Antiquity* (ed. Jacob Neusner; Leiden: Brill, 1968) 354–71; idem, "The Divine Agent and His Counterfeit in Philo and the Fourth Gospel," in *Aspects of Religious Propaganda in Judaism and Early Christianity* (Notre Dame: Notre Dame University, 1975) 43–67; Tiede, ibidem, 101–37; Burton L. Mack, *Logos und Sophia: Untersuchungen zur Weisheitstheologie im hellenistischen Judentum* SUNT 10; Göttingen: Vandenhoeck & Ruprecht, 1973) *passim*.

each other, coming from pre-Pauline Jewish traditions. Also, there is nothing in the words of v 19e that devaluates the Torah. Such negative evaluation is only the result of v 20.

■ 20 Paul provides a general definition[76] of the concept of "mediator." This definition then explains the reason for his regarding the Jewish Torah as inferior (3:19). The definition has two parts, a negative (v 20a) and a positive (v 20b):

v 20a: ὁ δὲ μεσίτης ἑνὸς οὐκ ἔστιν,

"But the mediator is not of one,"

v 20b: ὁ δὲ θεὸς εἷς ἐστιν.

"but God is one."[77]

Scholarship has clarified this extremely difficult statement sufficiently, and further suggestions will be provided here—but there is no need to report on the host of solutions which were proposed in the past.[78] The chief remaining problem is the relationship of the definition to the context: does it refer to the "duality of the persons, between whom the mediator acts,"[79] or is the plurality implied in the mediator concept then contrasted with the oneness of God?

It can be concluded that in any case Paul regards the mediator and the one God as mutually exclusive concepts. Grammatically, the rule is[80] that the negation οὐ ("not") belongs to the following verb. But in v 20a the negated verb has attracted to itself the negative,[81] so that ἑνός ("of one") must be a masculine form.[82] Instead, as a go-between related to two parties, the mediator is defined merely in contrast with the oneness of God, that is, as the representative of a plurality. It is not at all necessary to identify this plurality as the angels in 3:19d,[83] or as the people in the Sinai tradition.[84] Paul argues that anything that stands in contrast to the oneness of God is inferior. Since the concept of mediator presupposes by definition a plurality of parties, it is inferior and, consequently, renders the

---

76   So rightly Luther, WA 40/1.501, line 17; Burton, p. 190. The sentence structure has led some scholars to believe that 3:20 is a gloss later inserted, but the definition is needed for the argument and must have been part of the text from the beginning. Cf., for theories making v 20 a gloss, Sieffert, pp. 209f; Burton, pp. 191f.

77   The difficulty of the sentence is reflected in the translations. See the notes on the translation, above. Cf. also Bauer, *s.v.* εἷς 2, b.

78   Older commentaries report large numbers of hypotheses: Georgius Benedictus Winer, *Pauli ad Galatas epistola latine vertit et perpetua annotatione illustravit* (Leipzig: Reclam, 1821) 250; August Friedrich Christian Vilmar, *Praktische Erklärung des Neues Testaments* (Vol. 2; Gütersloh: Bertelsmann, 1880), more than 400; Lightfoot, 250 or 300; Burton, 300; Oepke, 430 (this number may reflect Gal 3:17 more than scholarship!). See the surveys in Sieffert, pp. 209–18; Burton, pp. 191f; Oepke, p. 117; Marc-François Lacan, "Le dieu unique et son médiateur Galates 3, 20," in *L'homme devant dieu, Mélanges Henri de Lubac* (Paris: Aubier, 1964) 1.113–125; Ragnar Bring, "Der Mittler und das Gesetz. Eine Studie zu Gal. 3, 20," *KD* 12 (1966) 292–309; idem, *Christus und das Gesetz* (Leiden: Brill, 1969) chap. 3.

79   So Burton, p. 190, Lightfoot, Luther, etc.

80   See Schwyzer, *Grammatik*, 2.596

81   See BDF, § 433, 1; BDR, § 433, 1.

82   See Burton, p. 191.

83   So especially Oepke, pp. 118f; idem, "μεσίτης κτλ.,"

TDNT 4.618–19; Lietzmann; Mussner; and others. On Schlier's position cf. above on 3:19.

84   So especially Zahn (pp. 176f), who refers to Exod 20:19; Deut 5:19–25; 18:16; Acts 7:38. Philo (*Som.* 1.142f; *Spec.* 1.116 [quoted above on 3:19 n. 75]; *Her.* 205f) and the Church Fathers could also support this interpretation. See the definition given by Clement of Alexandria (*Paed.* 3.1.2.1, ed. Stählin, GCS 1.236f): μεσίτης γὰρ ὁ λόγος ὁ κοινὸς ἀμφοῖν, θεοῦ μὲν υἱός, σωτὴρ δὲ ἀνθρώπων... ("For the Logos is a mediator common to both, being the Son of God, and the savior of men..."); see *PGL*, *s.v.* μεσιτεία, μεσιτεύω, μεσίτης.

Torah inferior.[85] The true revelation of the one God does not need this concept.[86]

This rationale is implied in the second, positive part of the definition, which is nothing but a citation of the famous acclamation $\epsilon\hat{\iota}\varsigma$ $\theta\epsilon\acute{o}\varsigma$ ("God is one").[87] It is introduced here as the dogma of monotheistic religion and therefore carries the argument in itself.[88] The implication is that the process of divine redemption

85 At this point Paul may be in agreement with a Jewish tradition emerging at several points, e.g. in Qumran, provided the restoration of 1QH 6.13f by Menahem Mansoor is correct (*The Thanksgiving Hymns* [STDJ 3; Leiden: Brill, 1961] 143f): "And there is no intercessor [to Thy holy ones]...an (angel) announ[cer]...And they shall return to Thy glorious word." Schlier sees a connection with Isa 63:9 (*NEB*): "It was no envoy, no angel, but he himself that delivered them." Living together with the heavenly being (1QH 3.22f) directly, the Qumran community does not need intermediaries. Cf. Heinz–Wolfgang Kuhn, *Enderwartung und gegenwärtiges Heil* (Göttingen: Vandenhoeck & Ruprecht, 1966) 146f. Cf. the parable of R. Abbahu, said in the name of R. Johanan, *Pesiq. R.* 21.5, which ends thus: "In giving His children the Torah, He is committing His commandments, fully explained, directly to Israel His son (tr. William G. Braude, *Pesikta Rabbati* [New Haven: Yales University, 1968] 1.420)." One should also note the apologetic remarks by Clement of Alexandria (*Paed.* 1.7.60.1–2, 125, line 19) who argues that the law was given through Moses, but by the Logos; or Eusebius *De eccles. theol.* 2.14 (ed. Klostermann, GCS 4, 116, line 5): the law comes from God ($\dot{\epsilon}\kappa\ \tau o\hat{v}\ \theta\epsilon o\hat{v}$) while Moses was only a servant ($\delta\iota\acute{a}\kappa o\nu o\varsigma\ \kappa a\grave{\iota}\ \dot{v}\pi\eta\rho\acute{\epsilon}\tau\eta\varsigma$). The opposite conclusion was drawn by Simon Magus (according to ps.-Clem. *Hom.* 3.2.2–3 [cf. 18.12.1; Epiphanius *Pan.* 21.4, p. 243, line 15]): "Two deities, of which one was the one who created the world, while the other one gave the law" ($\delta\acute{v}o...\theta\epsilon o\acute{v}\varsigma$, $\dot{a}\phi'\ \hat{\omega}\nu\ \dot{o}\ \mu\grave{\epsilon}\nu\ \epsilon\hat{\iota}\varsigma\ \dot{\epsilon}\sigma\tau\iota\nu\ \dot{o}\ \kappa\acute{o}\sigma\mu o\nu\ \kappa\tau\acute{\iota}\sigma a\varsigma$, $\dot{o}\ \delta\grave{\epsilon}\ \dot{\epsilon}\tau\epsilon\rho o\varsigma\ \dot{o}\ \tau\grave{o}\nu\ \nu\acute{o}\mu o\nu\ \delta o\acute{v}\varsigma$).

86 In the revelation of the gospel, Christ does not figure for Paul as a "mediator." Cf. 1 Tim 2:5; Heb 8:6; 9:15; 12:24.

87 The basic study is by Erik Peterson, *ΕΙΣ ΘΕΟΣ: Epigraphische, formgeschichtliche und religionsgeschichtliche Untersuchungen* (FRLANT NF 24; Göttingen Vandenhoeck & Ruprecht, 1926); see also Theodor Klauser, "Akklamation," *RAC* 1.230; Ethelbert Stauffer, "$\epsilon\hat{\iota}\varsigma$," *TDNT* 2.434–42; Hermann Kleinknecht, "$\theta\epsilon\acute{o}\varsigma$," *TDNT* 3.71–79; Bauer, *s.v.* $\epsilon\hat{\iota}\varsigma$, 2, b; Preisigke, *Wörterbuch* 4/4 (1971) 678; *PGL*, *s.v.* $\epsilon\hat{\iota}\varsigma$ and $\theta\epsilon\acute{o}\varsigma$; André Feuillet, *Le Christ Sagesse de Dieu d'après les épîtres pauliniennes* (Paris: Gabalda, 1966) 71ff; Wengst, *Christologische Formeln*, § 12; *PECL*, index *s.v.* $\epsilon\hat{\iota}\varsigma$ $\theta\epsilon\acute{o}\varsigma$. The formula is Greek, most probably

Orphic, in origin (see *Orphicorum Fragmenta*, ed. Kern, *Frag.* 31, line 23; 168, lines 6–7; 239; 245 line 8; 247 line 10). Hellenistic Judaism adapted it and connected it with the Jewish monotheistic "creed" of Deut 6:4. This was done probably as early as Aristobulus (according to Eusebius *Praep. ev.* 13.12); the connection with the "law" is noteworthy (see also Eusebius *Praep. ev.* 13.13.5; 13.13.40, and on this Nikolaus Walter, *Der Thoraausleger Aristobulos* [TU 86; Berlin: Akademie-Verlag, 1964] 103–15, 140f; cf. Hengel, *Judaism and Hellenism* 1.163ff). The similarity of the formula with Deut 6:4 is striking (cf. also Exod 20:2–3; Deut 5:6f; 2 Chr 32:12) and the identification predictable. See Gottfried Quell, "$\kappa\acute{v}\rho\iota o\varsigma$," *TDNT* 3.1079–81; Gerhard Lohfink and Jan Bergman, *TWAT* 1, *s.v.* אחד (with further bib.). In Hellenistic Judaism the formula is connected also with the decalogue (see Josephus *Ant.* 3.91; 4.200; Philo *Op.* 170–172), but other "one–only" derivations were made: Philo has "One God, one temple, one city, one altar" (*Spec.* 1.67, and cf. Leisegang's index, *s.v.* $\epsilon\hat{\iota}\varsigma$). The process continues in Christianity. Cf. Mark 12:29; Matt 23:9 (cf. Str–B 2.28–30); Gal 3:20; 1 Cor 8:4, 6; Rom 3:30; 1 Tim 2:5 ("One God, one mediator [*sc.* Christ]"); Eph 4:6 ("One God, one Lord, one faith, one baptism"); Ign. *Magn.* 8.2; *Herm. Mand.* 1.1; *Kerygma Petrou*, Frag. 2 (*Apocrypha I* [ed. Erich Klostermann; KlT 3; Bonn: Marcus & Weber, 1921] 13); *Diogn.* 3.2; Athenagoras *Leg.* 4.2ff, 8.1; Clemens Alex. *Paed.* 1.8, 1.10 ("One God, one church"); ps.-Clem. *Hom.* 13.15 ("One God, one wife"). Clemens Alex. (*Strom.* 1.29, ed. Stählin, GCS 2, 111, line 19) then takes up consciously "Plato": One God, one law, one lawgiver, one Logos.

88 The ramifications are many, ranging into the religious and the political arena. See Samuel S. Cohon, "The Unity of God: A Study in Hellenistic and Rabbinic Theology," *HUCA* 26 (1955) 425–79; Erik Peterson, "Der Monotheismus als politisches Problem," in his *Theologische Traktate* (Munich: Wild, 1951) 46–147; Guthrie, *Sophists*, 247–49; Erik Hornung, *Der Eine und die Vielen. Ägyptische Gottesvorstellungen* (Darmstadt: Wissenschaftliche Buchgesellschaft, 1971). In Gal, the religious and social implications are to be discussed in connection with 3:26–28.

requires conformity to the oneness of God.[89] If the argument is to make sense, we must supply as the presupposition the ancient rule τὸ ὅμοιον τῷ ὁμοίῳ φίλον ("like is the friend of like" [translation of LCL]).[90] A good example of how this argument is made is supplied by Josephus (*C. Apion.* 2.193):[91] Εἷς ναὸς ἑνὸς θεοῦ, φίλον γὰρ ἀεὶ παντὶ τὸ ὅμοιον, κοινὸς ἀπάντων κοινοῦ θεοῦ ἀπάντων ("We have but one temple for the one God [for like ever loveth like], common to all as God is common to all"). It should be noted, however, that Paul's argument is convincing only so long as one does not subscribe to the Stoic concept of associating the "one law" with the one God.[92]

If Paul knew about this Stoic concept, which is at least probable,[93] he avoided it by focussing upon the concept of the mediator rather than upon the Torah itself. Paul's own soteriology conforms throughout to the principle of oneness: one God, one redeemer Christ (3:16), one gospel (1:6–7; 2:5), one church (3:28; cf. 5:14), one "fruit of the Spirit" (5:22).

■ **21** If Paul's definition of the Torah (3:19–20) is accepted, the question arises as to which consequences[94] are to be drawn from it with regard to the promises made by God to Abraham: ὁ οὖν νόμος κατὰ τῶν ἐπαγγελιῶν [τοῦ θεοῦ];[95] ("is the law, then, contrary to the promises [of God]?") The matter of God's promises to Abraham had been discussed before (3:6–18), but was interrupted by the digression on the Torah (3:19–25). Therefore, the question in v 21a simply takes up the former discussion, now applying to it the results of the definitions in v 19–20. The question is hypothetical but by no means unreal.[96] The total separation between Torah of Moses and promise to Abraham lies within the range of possibilities, but Paul's strong denial μὴ γένοιτο ("by no means")[97] shows that he wants to avoid such separation. To be sure, Marcion drew this conclusion; he probably omitted the entire section 3:15–25 from his text of Galatians.[98]

In order to avoid the Marcionite conclusion Paul proposes another hypothetical case.[99] This case, however, is not really hypothetical at all, but is identical with one of the fundamental ideas of Judaism: εἰ γὰρ ἐδόθη νόμος ὁ δυνάμενος ζωοποιῆσαι, ὄντως ἐκ νόμου ἂν ἦν

---

89 Cf. Paul's argumentation in 1 Cor 8:4, 6; Rom 3:30. See Conzelmann, *1 Corinthians*, 142 n. 26; Daube, *NT and Rabbinic Judaism*, 443; Charles H. Giblin, "Three Monotheistic Texts in Paul," *CBQ* 37 (1975) 527–47, esp. 537–43, with further literature.

90 See Aristotle *EN* 1165b17, 1155a34; Plato *Gorg.* 510b. The basic study is by Carl Werner Müller, *Gleiches zu Gleichem: Ein Prinzip frühgriechischen Denkens* (Klassisch–philologische Studien 31; Wiesbaden: Harrassowitz, 1965); Müller thinks Paul uses the principle in Rom 12:15 (160 n. 30). See, especially, 1 Cor 2:11, 13, and the discussion in Conzelmann, *1 Corinthians*, 66f.

91 See Thackeray's note in LCL, *ad loc.*, where reference is made to Sir 13:15 (19); Daube (*NT and Rabbinic Judaism*, 443) points to Sir 27:9 in addition. Cf. also Philo *Gig.* 9.

92 See, especially, Marcus Aurelius 7.9: κόσμος τε γὰρ εἷς ἐξ ἁπάντων καὶ θεὸς εἷς διὰ πάντων, καὶ οὐσία μία, καὶ νόμος εἷς, λόγος κοινὸς πάντων τῶν νοερῶν ζῴων, καὶ ἀλήθεια μία· εἴγε καὶ τελειότης μία τῶν ὁμογενῶν καὶ τοῦ αὐτοῦ λόγου μετεχόντων ζῴων ("For there is both one Universe, made up of all things, and one God, immanent in all things, and one Substance and one Law, one Reason common to all intelligent creatures, and one Truth: if indeed

there is also one perfecting of living creatures that have the same origin and share the same reason)". This doctrine goes back to Zeno (*SVF* No. 162 [1.42f] etc.; see also index *s.v.* νόμος); cf. Clemens Alex. *Strom.* 1.29 (cited above, n. 87).

93 Cf. also the "rule" of the anti–Pauline *Ep. Petr.* 2.1: "One God, one law, one hope" (see Appendix, 3. A).

94 οὖν ("then") indicates the conclusion. Cf. Gal 3:5; 4:15; 5:1; 6:10. See BDF, § 451; BDR, § 451.

95 The words τοῦ θεοῦ ("of God") are read by most witnesses, but a few good and early witnesses do not have them (P[46] B it[d] Ambrosiaster Marius Victorinus). The words are Pauline (cf. Rom 4:20; 2 Cor 1:20). It is possible that they were supplemented from Gal 3:20, or that they were dropped by accident. See Metzger, *Textual Commentary*, 594f.

96 Cf. the similar question in Rom 7:7: ὁ νόμος ἁμαρτία; ("Is the law sin?"). See also Rom 8:2–4; Gal 2:17.

97 On this negation, see above on 2:17.

98 See Harnack, *Marcion*, *73.

99 Cf. Gal 1:10; 2:21; 3:18; 5:11.

ἡ δικαιοσύνη[100] ("for if a law had been given which was capable of making alive, then righteousness would indeed come from [the] Law").

It is one of the principal doctrines of Judaism[101] that God gave[102] the Torah[103] for the purpose of providing a way for Israel into eternal life.[104] We can safely conclude that Paul's opponents agreed with the Jewish position, or they would never have required the Galatians to accept circumcision and Torah.[105] Also, it is obvious that Paul himself denies the doctrine. For him, life is given through the Spirit.[106] Indeed, according to Paul it is false to expect life from the Torah, since it was never given for that purpose. If, however, life does not come from the Torah, neither does righteousness.[107] It may be that this argument is directed against accusations made by opponents against the Apostle. These accusations would object to Paul's construct of a total dualism between the Torah of Moses and the promise to Abraham.[108] Paul defends himself by an attack: a contradiction between the Torah of Moses and the promise to Abraham can be perceived only if the Torah retains its traditional Jewish role. This is done by his opponents, not by Paul himself. If, therefore, there is such an objection against him, it is based upon a misunderstanding of his theology.[109]

■ 22 After having rejected in v 21 the false concept of the Torah and the false consequences of the relationship of the Torah of Moses to the promise to Abraham, Paul now presents his positive interpretation of the definition (3:19). This part includes v 22–25. First we learn: ἀλλὰ συνέκλεισεν ἡ γραφὴ τὰ πάντα ὑπὸ ἁμαρτίαν... ("but Scripture has confined everything under sin").

---

100 There are several textual variants, which, however, do not change the meaning: instead of ὄντως ("really") G reads ἀληθείᾳ ("truly"), possibly an influence from the Latin (so Nestle–Aland). Also, the position of ἄν varies (א *al*, 𝔐 *pm*), or it is omitted altogether (D* *al*, G). Instead of ἐκ νόμου (A C), some have ἐν νόμῳ (P⁴⁶ B Clement). All these seem to be scribal confusion of ἄν and ἦν, ἐκ and ἐν. See Zahn, p. 178 n. 43; Sieffert, p. 218 n.; Burton, pp. 194f. Paul himself can alternate between ἐκ νόμου (3:18) and ἐν νόμῳ (3:11; 5:4).

101 Note Hillel's statement ('*Abot* 2.8): "...the more Torah, the more life...." Cf. '*Abot* 6.1ff. So already the OT: Deut 30:15–20; 32:47, etc. For a collection of texts see Rudolf Bultmann, "ζάω," *TDNT* 2.855–72; Str–B 3.129–31, 498f. "Life" is both divine and human, which is emphasized in particular in Wisdom literature. See, e.g., Prov 3:1f; Sir 17:11: "He endowed them with the life–giving law" (νόμον ζωῆς); similarly Bar 3:9; 4:1. From the NT, see especially Mark 10:17–20; Matt 5:17–20 and 7:13f.

102 The passive in ἐδόθη ("it was given") indicates God as the giver. See on Gal 3:16, 19, 22.

103 νόμος ("law") here without the article refers to the Jewish Torah. Cf. on Gal 2:21. See BDF, § 258, 2; BDR, § 258, 2.

104 ζωοποιέω ("make alive, give life to") is a soteriological term in Paul. See Rom 4:17; 8:11; 1 Cor 15:22, 36, 45; 2 Cor 3:6; furthermore John 5:21; 6:63; 1 Pet 3:18; *Barn.* 6.17; 7.2; 12.5, 7; *Herm. Mand.* 4.3.7; *Sim.* 9.16.2, 7. See Rudolf Bultmann, "ζωοποιέω," *TDNT* 2.874–75; Bauer, *s.v.*; *PGL*, *s.v.*

105 Cf. the implications of 2 Cor 6:16: "we are the temple of the living God." See on this Appendix 2; and Betz, "2 Cor 6:14–7:1," 92–95.

106 Cf. 2 Cor 3:6: τὸ δὲ πνεῦμα ζωοποιεῖ ("but the Spirit makes alive"). Paul's strange concept in Rom 8:2 ὁ νόμος τοῦ πνεύματος τῆς ζωῆς ("the law of the Spirit of life") has been the subject of much discussion. See Eduard Lohse, "ὁ νόμος τοῦ πνεύματος τῆς ζωῆς. Exegetische Anmerkungen zu Röm 8, 2," in *Neues Testament und christliche Existenz, Festschrift für Herbert Braun* (eds. Hans Dieter Betz and Luise Schottroff; Tübingen: Mohr, Siebeck, 1973) 279–87.

107 See Gal 2:21; Rom 3:20–26; 4:6, 13; 8:10; 9:31; 10:3–10; 14:17; Phil 3:6, 9.

108 Cf. Gal 2:15–21. Contrast 2 Cor 6:14–7:1, where law and promises are identical and lead to righteousness (6:14, 18). See Appendix 2.

109 But in Rom Paul takes a different position: according to Rom 7:7–10, the law was originally given εἰς ζωήν ("to give life"), but because of the interference of sin it turned out to be εἰς θάνατον ("to give death"). In Gal this active role of sin is not mentioned (see also 1 Cor 15:56b). In Rom 7:14ff; 8:2ff, Paul speaks about two laws: the law of sin and death, and the law of Spirit and life. This distinction is also absent in Gal. Did Paul change his position between the two letters, in order to avoid "Marcionite" ("gnostic"?) consequences? Cf. Schlier (p. 163) who again interprets Rom into Gal.

The sudden change from the Torah to Scripture is not accidental.[110] After what Paul had said about the Torah in v 21, it can no longer be regarded as a subject but only as an object in the process of salvation.[111] It can no longer be taken as God's agent of salvation. This role, then, is given to Scripture (ἡ γραφή). An entity working almost like Fate,[112] Scripture confines[113] everything "under sin."[114] At this point, Paul shares the extreme pessimism prominent in some of the Jewish traditions, especially among the apocalypticists.[115] But the universal confinement under sin[116] is only a transitory period before the coming of the redeemer Christ. Since Christ has come, this entire period can be relegated to the past. The implication is that the Torah becomes a mere tool in the hands of Scripture. Its purpose is to generate transgression and all-pervasive sin up to the coming of Christ (cf. 3:19b–c, 23–25). When that period was completed (cf. 4:4–5), Christ came as Scripture had foreseen (cf. 3:8), and God fulfilled the promise made to Abraham (cf. 3:6–18 and 3:1–5). Therefore, although the Torah does not give

life (cf. 3:21), it does have a positive part in the process of salvation: ἵνα ἡ ἐπαγγελία ἐκ πίστεως Ἰησοῦ Χριστοῦ δοθῇ τοῖς πιστεύουσιν ("in order that the promise, on the basis of faith in Jesus Christ, might be given to those who believe"). This statement contains a number of key theological concepts, all of which were discussed before. Therefore, it simply sums up the preceding argument in 3:6–18 (cf. especially 3:14b, 18b).[117]

■ 23 Paul applies[118] what he had said in v 22 about the notion "under sin" to the Torah and to the Christian faith; this is still part of the explanation of the definition 3:19 b–c: πρὸ δὲ τοῦ ἐλθεῖν τὴν πίστιν ὑπὸ νόμον ἐφρουρούμεθα συγκλειόμενοι εἰς τὴν μέλλουσαν πίστιν ἀποκαλυφθῆναι ("before faith came, we were kept in custody under the Law, confined until the coming faith was to be revealed"). It must be said that in spite of his explanations the Apostle leaves things rather ambiguous. His extremely concise statements do not allow us to answer all the questions which we may raise. It is clear, however, that two mythico–historical periods are to be distinguished:[119] the period of the

110 On Paul's concept of Scripture see Gal 3:8; 4:30; Rom 1:2; 4:3; 9:17; 10:11; 11:2; 15:4; 16:26; 1 Cor 15:3–4. Schlier (pp. 164f) points out that Paul distinguishes between law and Scripture; differently Oepke (p. 119), who identifies them; Burton (p. 195), who thinks of a specific passage (Deut 27:26 = Gal 3:10). For the history of exegesis see Sieffert (p. 221).

111 Cf. Rom 7:5, 10, 13; 8:2.

112 Cf. Polybius 3.63.3: "Fortune...has brought you to a like pass, she has shut you in on a like listed field of combat...." See also 2.60.4; 11.2.10; 11.20.7; Diodorus Sic. 15.63.1. In gnosticism it is the "archons" which imprison man into matter; for passages, see Foerster–Wilson, Gnosis 2.325, s.v. "Archon, Archons;" furthermore Hans Jonas, The Gnostic Religion (Boston: Beacon, ²1963) 62–65; idem, Gnosis 1.105f; Pagels, The Gnostic Paul, 107. See the passages assembled by Otto Michel, "συγκλείω," TDNT 7.744–47; Schlier, p. 164 n. 2.

113 See also Gal 3:23, and the close parallel in Rom 11:32, where God himself acts: συνέκλεισεν γὰρ ὁ θεὸς τοὺς πάντας εἰς ἀπείθειαν ἵνα τοὺς πάντας ἐλεήσῃ ("God has confined all of them into disobedience, in order to show mercy to all of them").

114 For this expression, see Rom 3:9; 7:14; cf. also 11:32 (above n. 113); also 3:12, 19f; 5:12; 8:3.

115 See, e.g., 2 Esd 7:46: "For who among the living is there that has not sinned, or who among men that

has not transgressed thy covenant?" (tr. RSV, The Apocrypha [Oxford: Oxford University, 1965] 38). See the collection of passages in Str–B 3.155–57, 1.166f, 815f. For Qumran, see Braun, Qumran 1.177f, 2.166–72.

116 τὰ πάντα ("everything") and Rom 11:32 τοὺς πάντας ("all mankind") must be identical, but no attempt is made in Gal to demonstrate the universal rule of the law. Paul only takes this step in Rom and puts also the Gentiles under the law (cf. Rom 2:14f); see Rom 2:1–3:20; 5:12.

117 On the formula ἐκ πίστεως Ἰησοῦ Χριστοῦ ("by faith in Jesus Christ") see Gal 2:16; 3:7, 8, 9, 11, 12, 24; 5:5. On δοθῇ ("it might be given"), cf. 3:21.

118 δέ stands third in place, pointing to the next step of the argument. See BDF, § 475, 2; BDR, § 475, 2; Schlier, p. 166 n. 1.

119 On the whole problem see also Luz, Geschichtsverständnis, 153f, 191ff; Eberhard Jüngel, "Das Gesetz zwischen Adam und Christus: Eine theologische Studie zu Röm 5, 12–21," ZThK 60 (1963) 42–74; Peter Stuhlmacher, "'Das Ende des Gesetzes': Über Ursprung und Ansatz der paulinischen Theologie," ZThK 67 (1970) 14–39.

Law and the period of the faith.[120] The former ends and the latter begins with the coming of Christ (v 24) and the revelation of faith.[121] Before Christ's coming, faith existed only exceptionally in Abraham and in Scripture as a promise. It became a general possibility for mankind[122] only when God sent his son and the Spirit of his son (4:4–6; 3:2, 5).[123] In other words, faith was not generally available to mankind before Christ's coming, but was a matter for the future.[124] During this time the Jews were kept imprisoned[125] "under the Torah" (ὑπὸ νόμον).[126] This gives a very negative interpretation of the "fence" around Israel, which according to Jewish understanding the Torah is supposed to be.[127]

The period of the Law kept the Jews confined in sinfulness (3:22) and under the curse of the Law (3:10), a situation not different from the slavery under the "elements of the world" (4:1–10).[128] Several questions,[129] however, remain open: When did the period of the Law begin? How is the period related to the history of Judaism? Is it identical with the entire history of Judaism, or only a part of it? What does the end through Christ mean for those Jews who remain non-believers? What about the Gentiles? Were they not under the Torah? How is the beginning of the period of faith related to the conversion of the Galatians? Paul deals only with the principal doctrines and does not here answer all of these questions. Some of them he has tried to answer in Romans, but we must be very careful not to simply harmonize Galatians with Romans. In Rom 1:18–3:20 the Apostle demonstrates that both Jews and Gentiles are "under sin" (3:9, 19, 23; 5:12, 14, 16). This period begins with Adam's transgression (5:12–21), so that even prior to Moses sin and death ruled, but they were not counted because there was no Law (cf. 5:14). Also, the question of how the pre-Christian situation ends for the Christian is much more carefully discussed in Romans

---

120 πίστις ("faith") describes the occurrence of a historical phenomenon, not the act of believing of an individual (cf. Gal 1:23; 3:25; 5:6; 6:10; also CMC 70.4). Käsemann (Perspectives, 83) speaks of "the manifestation of faith in personified form." Wilhelm Mundle, (Der Glaubensbegriff bei Paulus [Leipzig: Heinsius, 1932] 93) and Lietzmann (on 3:23) take it to mean "Christianity." See Stuhlmacher, Gerechtigkeit Gottes, 81; Luz, Geschichtsverständnis, 153 n. 73. Schlier (p. 167) distinguishes between Christ as the "ground" of faith, faith as the objective means and principle of salvation, and the "actualization" of that potential faith by the individual believer. He concludes that faith is for Paul more than the "subjective" act of faith (cf. Schlier, pp. 94f).

121 The term ἀποκαλύπτω ("reveal") does not here refer to the revelation of the faith to Paul (cf. Gal 1:12, 16), but in the general sense of the revelation of the gospel (see Rom 1:16f). See Albrecht Oepke, "ἀποκαλύπτω," TDNT 3.582–87.

122 Differently Schlier (p. 166) who assumes "believers" even before Christ's coming, although "faith as a clearly formed phenomenon as concrete faith in Jesus Christ is," could not exist. Schlier constructs here an analogy to the existence of the Torah before Moses (Rom 5:13f), which then came with Moses (Gal 3:15ff). However, nothing in Gal suggests that the Torah existed prior to Moses, and one would have to supply this idea from Rom.

123 This sending, of course, includes Christ's death and resurrection (see Gal 1:1, 4; 2:20f; 3:13; 4:5).

124 Cf. the parallel temporal statements in Rom 8:18: πρὸς τὴν μέλλουσαν δόξαν ἀποκαλυφθῆναι ("for the coming glory that is to be revealed"). Cf. Gal 3:24: εἰς Χριστόν ("until Christ"). On this meaning of εἰς, see Bauer, s.v., 2, a, α; on μέλλουσαν, cf. also 1 Pet 5:1, and BDF, § 474, 5; BDR, § 474, 5.

125 "We were kept in custody, confined...." C 𝔐 pl Clement read the perfect συγκεκλεισμένοι. The expression of φρουρέω strongly emphasizes the element of imprisonment (cf. Gal 3:22; 4:1–10); see also LSJ, s.v.; Bauer, s.v. For the figurative meaning, cf. Aeschylus Eum. 218: "For marriage appointed by fate 'twixt man and woman is mightier than an oath and Justice is its guardian" (...τῇ δίκῃ φρουρουμένῃ). See also Wis 17:15; Plutarch Defect. orac. 426B with reference to the Stoic treatment of Gods: φρουρεῖν συγκλείσαντας τῇ ὕλῃ ("keep them imprisoned by enclosing them with matter"); Diogn. 6.4, 7. The term is used in the literal sense in 2 Cor 11:32, and with a positive meaning in Phil 4:7; 1 Pet 1:5.

126 For this expression, see Gal 4:4f, 21; 5:18; Rom 6:14, 15; 1 Cor 9:20; also Rom 3:9; 7:14; Gal 3:10, 22, 25; 4:2, 3; 1 Cor 15:56. The expression "under the Torah" corresponds to the "yoke of the Torah." Cf. Gal 5:1; 2 Cor 6:14 (see Appendix 2).

127 On this concept, see above on 3:19b.

128 "Death" is not mentioned in Gal. Cf. Rom 1:32; 5:12, 14, 17, 21; 6:9, 16, 21, 23; 7:5, 10, 13, 24; 8:2, 6; 1 Cor 15:21, 56. Differently Schlier, p. 167.

129 Cf. Luz, Geschichtsverständnis, 153ff, 191ff.

5–8. The same is true for Paul's discussion of the situation of the non-Christian Jew after Christ's coming, a question which is not taken up at all in Galatians, but treated especially in Romans 9–11.

■ **24** In vv 24–25 Paul sets forth his conclusion[130] of the section 3:19–25; this conclusion contains his final answer to the question about the Torah (3:19a): ὥστε ὁ νόμος παιδαγωγὸς ἡμῶν γέγονεν εἰς Χριστόν, ἵνα ἐκ πίστεως δικαιωθῶμεν ("therefore, the Law has been our guardian until Christ, in order that we might be justified by faith"). Most important and also most puzzling is Paul's description of the Torah as our παιδαγωγός ("pedagogue"). The concept seems to have been familiar to his readers. We associate pedagogues with the well-established teaching profession. In antiquity,[131] however, the term "pedagogue" does not refer to the "teacher" (διδάσκαλος), but to the slave who accompanied the school boy to the school and back, and carried his books and writing utensils. The task of this slave was to protect the child against molesters and accidents, and also to make sure he learned good manners. These pedagogues had the bad image of being rude, rough, and good for no other business. The school boy remained under the supervision of this pedagogue until the time of puberty. Understandably, the public did not have much respect for this pedagogue, although there are witnesses of a life-long affection between pupil and pedagogue. On the stage, the pedagogue could be seen as a comic type, recognizable by his rod.

The question arises, then, as to how this figure of the pedagogue could have become associated with the Law.[132] This association was made at least since Plato, who connected παιδεία ("education") and law. When describing the self-controlled man, Aristotle compares him with a boy living "in obedience to his tutor."[133] Of course, there is nothing negative about such παιδεία εἰς ἀρετήν ("education with the goal of obtaining virtue").[134] In the Hellenistic period, including Judaism, this view was commonplace.[135] The figure of the pedagogue is looked upon as a hard but necessary instrument in bringing a person to achieve and realize virtue. Clearly, however, this view does not suffice to explain Paul's concept, which presupposes a radical devaluation of the Law and a denial that the Law could accomplish something like virtue. On account of this devaluation, the pedagogue becomes an ugly figure, comparable to Fate. It is remarkable, and may point to the background from which Paul's concept came, that Philo comes close to this view. This is the case in spite of the fact that he does not devalue the Torah. But for him the symbol of παιδεία ("education") is the rod. His explanation is: "for there is no way of taking to heart warning and correction, unless for some offences one is chastised and brought to a sense of shame."[136] Philo then speaks about everything coming "under the rod."[137] At least in one place the rod appears in the company of instruments belonging to Fate: "whose is the ring, the pledge of faith, the seal of the universe, the archetypal idea by which all things

---

130 ὥστε ("therefore") in the concluding sense. See Gal 3:9; 4:7. Cf. BDF, § 391, 2; BDR, § 391, 2; Bauer, *s.v.*, 1, a.

131 See the typical description in Plato *Lysis* 208C–D. On the whole, see Martin P. Nilsson, *Die hellenistische Schule* (Munich: Beck, 1955); Henri–Irenée Marrou, *A History of Education in Antiquity* (New York: Mentor, 1964) 220–22. The most important texts are to be found in E. Schuppe, "Paidagogos," PW 18 (1942) 2375–85; Harald Fuchs, "Enkyklios Paideia," *RAC* 5.366–91; Georg Bertram, "παιδεύω," *TDNT* 5.596–625; Oepke, pp. 120–22; Schlier, pp. 168f. Alfred Stückelberger, *Senecas 88. Brief: Über Wert und Unwert der freien Künste* (Heidelberg: Winter, 1965) 31ff, 60ff; Hengel, *Judaism and Hellenism* 1.65ff.

132 See esp. Plato *Leg.* 5.730B, 7.808E–810C. On the subject, see de Romilly, *Loi*, 226ff (n. 11 above).

133 *EN* 3.12.8, p. 1119b13: "the appetitive part of us should be ruled by principle, just as a boy should live in obedience to his tutor." Cf. also *Pol.* 3.11.4, p. 1287a25; Plutarch *Quaest. conv.* 645B (Helge Almqvist, *Plutarch und das Neue Testament* [ASNU 15; Uppsala: Almqvist & Wiksell, 1946] 110 no. 230).

134 Ps.–Plato *Minos* 319C; cf. 320B.

135 So esp. 4 Macc 1:17: ἡ τοῦ νόμου παιδεία, also 5:34. For rabbinic theology, see Str–B 3.557, 339f; the term παιδαγωγός has become a loanword; see Samuel Krauss, *Griechische und lateinische Lehnwörter im Talmud, Midrasch und Targum* (Berlin: Calvary, 1899) 2.421; Schoeps, *Paul*, 30f.

136 Philo *Post.* 97; cf. also *L.A.* 2.89f; *Spec.* 3.182; *Sac.* 63; *Fug.* 150; *Det.* 145; *Deus* 111–116.

137 *Cong.* 94.

without form or quality before were stamped and shaped? Whose is the cord, that is, the world order, the chain of destiny, the correspondence and sequence of all things, with their ever-unbroken chain? Whose is the staff [ῥάβδος], that is the firmly planted, the unshaken, the unbending; the admonition, the chastening, the discipline; the sceptre, the kingship? Whose are they? Are they not God's alone?"[138]

Paul's concept presupposes not only the radical devaluation of the Law, but also a grim concept of παιδεία ("education") in addition to the rather ugly type of the pedagogue. All of these elements are attested in the Cynic-Stoic diatribe literature, and there can be no doubt that the notions come from that source.[139] Paul must have received them from Hellenistic Judaism, which had adapted them.[140] For the Apostle, existence "under the pedagogue" equals "slavery" "under the 'elements of the world'"[141] and amounts to "imprisonment," absence of "freedom" and "maturity." Thus the situation comes to the very opposite of the Christian existence: a curse and not a blessing.[142]

For these reasons, we must reject an interpretation according to which εἰς Χριστόν ("unto Christ") would imply the idea of a positive educational development from Judaism to Christianity.[143] In this view, by psy-chology and education the Torah would have "prepared the way" towards acceptance of the Christian message. Rather, εἰς Χριστόν must be taken in the merely temporal sense ("until Christ").[144] The "coming of Christ" ended the period of the Torah, like the task of the pedagogue ends when the boy has reached the age of maturity (cf. 3:19c, 23, 25; 4:1–3, 7).[145]

Therefore, for the Christian this period of the Torah is a matter of the past.[146] The Torah has fulfilled its role "in order that we might be justified by faith."[147] What this means was discussed before and does not need to be explained again. Negative as it certainly is, the Torah remains part of God's salvation. There is no ultimate abolition of the Torah. The Torah represents the negative backdrop, without which the positive divine redemption would never have come.[148]

■ 25 The final sentence of the section (3:19–25) and its conclusion (3:24–25) brings us up to the present situation: ἐλθούσης δὲ τῆς πίστεως οὐκέτι ὑπὸ παιδαγωγόν ἐσμεν ("but since the faith has come we are no longer under a guardian"). As was noted earlier in connection with v 23, the coming of the faith is identical with that of Christ (cf. 3:19c, 24; 4:4). For the Christian this implies that he is "no longer" (οὐκέτι)[149] "under the

---

138 *Mut.*135.

139 See Otto Hense, ed., *Teletis Reliquiae* (Freiburg, 1889) 6 lines 2f; 24 line 5; 50 lines 3–9; Epictetus *Diss.* 3.19.5; 3.22.7; 3.26.3f; 1.11.22; 2.22.26; Dio Chrys. *Or.* 75.1, 8, 9 (see Mussies, *Dio Chrysostom*, 183); Marcus Aurelius 5.9.1; 10.25.1. See Bultmann, *Stil*, 35f, 89.

140 See also 1 Cor 4:15, 21.

141 See Gal 2:4; 3.23; 4:1–10; 5:1.

142 See Gal 3:8–14; 4:4f.

143 This view was expressed in a variety of ways. See Zahn, pp. 184–86; Sieffert, pp. 224f; Ramsay, pp. 381ff; Georg Bertram, "παιδεύω," *TDNT* 5.619–25.

144 Cf. Xenophon *Laced.* 3.1: "When a boy ceases to be a child, and begins to be a lad, others release him from his moral tutor and his schoolmaster: he is then no longer under a ruler and is allowed to go his own way."

145 See also Burton, p. 200; Oepke, pp. 122f; Schlier, p. 170; Mussner, pp. 256–60.

146 γέγονεν ("it was"). P⁴⁶ B Clement^pt read ἐγένετο ("became"). See Zahn, p. 185 n. 54. Cf. the οὐκέτι ("no longer") in Gal 3:25; 4:7.

147 On the sentences beginning with ἵνα ("in order that"), see Gal 2:16, 19; 3:14, 22; 4:5; furthermore 2:17; 3:8, 11.

148 This interpretation is accepted by most commentators; see, e.g., Burton, pp. 200f; Oepke; Schlier, pp. 168–71; Luz, *Geschichtsverständnis*, 191–93; Mussner. See also Krister Stendahl, "Lagen som övervakare intill Kristus," *SEÅ* 18–19 (1953–54) 161–73.

149 Cf. 2:20; Gal 4:7; Rom 6:9; 11:6; also Eph 2:19. Noteworthy is the parallel in *Corp. Herm.* 13.9.

Torah,"[150] because τέλος γὰρ νόμου Χριστὸς εἰς δικαιοσύνην παντὶ τῷ πιστεύοντι ("for Christ is the end of the Torah, for [the] righteousness of everyone who believes").[151] This is first of all true for the Jew; we may simply recall what Paul had stated in Gal 2:16–17, 19: "I have died through the Torah to the Torah." But it is also true for the Gentiles, in the sense that there is no longer any reason for them to come under the Torah— a step the Galatians are at present considering.[152]

A problem of consequence is the word ἐσμέν ("we are"). Schlier (pp. 170f) interprets it to mean "that the rule of the law, fundamentally and rightly understood, has been broken in principle." According to Schlier, Christ has *de facto* become its end for the entire cosmos (Rom 10:4). If in contrast to this, the Law still operates in the world as a very real force even after the coming of faith, this does not disprove Paul's contention that the Law has come to its end, but only proves that the world has not yet recognized and taken hold of the principal abolishment of the Law in Christ and the triumph of faith over it. Therefore, the Law merely poses as an unbroken power, giving itself the appearance of real power—so far Schlier's interpretation. This betrays Schlier's interest in the "objective" nature of the salvation in Christ as over against the merely "subjective" faith of the believer. He also relates the matter directly to the doctrine of the sacrament of baptism. However, in Gal 3:25 Paul does not speak about the rule of the Law over the cosmos in general, but over those who very specifically were "under the Torah" (cf. 2:15, 16, 17; 3:13, 14, 23, 24; 4:4–5). Paul is not concerned with the general metaphysical dimensions of law, but with the role of the Christian faith with respect to the Jewish Torah. Although he can speak of his death to the Law (Gal 2:19) in the same way as of his death to the cosmos (6:14; cf. 5:24), the contention in Galatians is that "faith in Jesus Christ" is the constitutive basis for Christian existence.[153]

Paul's argument in chapters 3 and 4 leads to the conclusion that he regards the Torah observance of the Jews as the equivalent of serving the "elements of the world" (see 4:8–10), but this contention has its purpose primarily in disproving the theology of the Jewish-Christian opposition, which holds that even for the Christian the Jewish Torah is still the indispensable basis for salvation.

If this argument is seen in terms of history of religions, Paul draws a line between being a Jew and being a Christian.[154] Of course, this line of demarcation is polemical, but, as Romans shows (Rom 9–11), it was in no way intended to establish a new religion. Yet the establishment of a new religion is in effect what happened. If the validity of the Jewish Torah ends for the Jew when he becomes a Christian, there is no point or basis for Gentiles as well as for Jews to adhere to the Jewish religion. Since those Christians no longer regard themselves as pagans, a new religion has *de facto* come into existence.

It must also be recognized that Paul does not mean to declare the end of all law, as Schlier proposes. He would not be able to speak of the "fulfillment of the Law" (5:14) and the "law of Christ" (6:2), if he held such a view. For Paul, the will of God is not identical with and expressed by the Jewish Torah, which he understands in terms of his former Pharisaism (see 5:3), but God's will is identical with the salvation in Christ (see 1:4). The point about God's demands is that they are fulfilled—not that they "rule"—and that fulfilled, they will be part of the salvation in Christ (see 5:14, 19–23, 24; 6:2, 10).

Furthermore, one must keep in mind that the problem of the Torah continues to be discussed by Paul. In Romans, the Apostle must face up to the fact that other parts of Christianity have a more positive relationship to Judaism, and that Christian as well as non-Christian Judaism as a whole has rejected the Galatian position, adhering to the Torah as ever before (cf. Romans 2–4; 9–11). In the course of this discussion, Paul has apparently modified his position; these rather far-reaching changes, however, cannot be the subject of this commentary. It seems that a generation later the problem

---

150 Gal 5:18; Rom 6:14, 15; 7:24–25a; cf. 7:14; 1 Cor 9:20.

151 Rom 10:4. See on this Kertelge, "*Rechtfertigung*," 202ff; Luz, *Geschichtsverständnis*, 136ff, 139ff. Cf. the literature noted above, on 3:23 n. 119.

152 See Gal 1:6f; 3:1–5; 4:9, 21; 5:4.

153 See Gal 1:23; 2:16, 20; 3:2, 5, 7, 9, 11, 12, 14, 22, 23, 24, 26; 5:5, 6; 6:10; Rom 1:16f; etc.

154 See Gal 1:13f; 2:4f, 11–14, 15; 3:26–28; 5:2–12; 6:10.

has altogether disappeared. The author of Ephesians, who was a Paulinist of considerable potential, could take the step which Schlier[155] had assumed already for Paul himself. Eph 2:11–22 declares the end of the Law as a cosmic demonic force. Through the salvation in Christ this Law was abolished and replaced by another cosmic force. "love" ($\dot{\alpha}\gamma\dot{\alpha}\pi\eta$).[156]

---

155 It should be noted that Schlier assumes Pauline authorship of Eph: *Der Brief an die Epheser* (Düsseldorf: Patmos, ²1958) 22–28.

156 See Joachim Gnilka, *Der Epheserbrief* (Freiburg: Herder, 1971) 17f. He considers Eph to be pseudepigraphical, and the Jewish question a matter of the past. See furthermore, Karl Martin Fischer, *Tendenz und Absicht des Epheserbriefes* (FRLANT 111; Göttingen: Vandenhoeck & Ruprecht, 1973) 79–94; Lohse, *Colossians and Philemon* 108–13 (on Col 2:14f); Hans–Martin Schenke, "Das Weiterwirken des Paulus und die Pflege seines Erbes durch die Paulusschule," *NTS* 21 (1975) 505–18. See also the texts discussed in Appendices 2–4, below.

3

26 For you are all sons of God through [the]
faith in Christ Jesus.[1]
27/ For as many of you as were baptized
into Christ[2] have put on Christ.[3]
28/ There is neither[4] Jew nor Greek;
there is neither slave nor freeman;
there is no male and female.[5]
For you are all one in Christ Jesus.
29/ If, however, you belong to Christ,[6]
then you are Abraham's offspring,
heirs according to [the] promise.

Analysis

The section 3:26–28 stands apart and seems to form
the centre of the *probatio* section (3:1–4:31). Following
the discussion of the situation of the Jewish Christians
which is concluded in 3:25, 3:26–28 turns to the Gentile Christians and defines their status before God. This
is the goal toward which Paul has been driving all
along.

A most interesting phenomenon is the formal aspect
of the section, its composition and structure. Form–
critical analysis shows that the structure is complex.
Parallels in other literature suggest that we have before
us a form of a saying, made up of a number of components, which must have had its place and function in
early Christian baptismal liturgy. The analysis shows
that the section is composed of 6 lines:

3:26] 1. πάντες γὰρ υἱοὶ θεοῦ ἐστε διὰ τῆς πίστεως
ἐν Χριστῷ Ἰησοῦ

3:27] 2. ὅσοι γὰρ εἰς Χριστὸν ἐβαπτίσθητε, Χριστὸν
ἐνεδύσασθε

3:28a] 3. οὐκ ἔνι Ἰουδαῖος οὐδὲ Ἕλλην

3:28b] 4. οὐκ ἔνι δοῦλος οὐδὲ ἐλεύθερος

3:28c] 5. οὐκ ἔνι ἄρσεν καὶ θῆλυ

3:28d] 6. πάντες γὰρ ὑμεῖς εἷς ἐστε ἐν Χριστῷ Ἰησοῦ

3:26] 1. "For you are all sons of God, through [the]
faith, in Christ Jesus.

3:27] 2. For as many of you as were baptized into
Christ have put on Christ.

3:28a] 3. There is neither Jew nor Greek;

3:28b] 4. there is neither slave nor freeman;

3:28c] 5. there is no male and female.

3:28d] 6. For you are all one in Christ Jesus."

Lines 1 and 6 are clearly parallel, with the exception
of the phrase διὰ τῆς πίστεως ("through the faith"),
which seems to be an interpretive addition by Paul;[7]
this phrase occurs only in line 1 and has no parallel in
line 6. Line 2 is an explanatory statement which connects the composition with the ritual of baptism. The
language presupposes doctrines about baptism which
may be pre-Pauline in origin.

Gal 3:27 raises the question as to what role baptism
plays in Paul's letter. This verse is the only explicit
reference to baptism in the entire letter. Even in the
argument the sacrament of baptism is never adduced
except here. On the other hand, we know that the
Spirit in which Paul is primarily interested was connected with baptism in some important way. If the
whole composition were lifted from the baptismal
liturgy, the ritual of baptism would assume quite a
distinctive role in Paul's argument.

The three lines in the center (3, 4, 5) are peculiar.
They are meant to be parallel, although line 5 differs

---

1 *NEB* translates this formula by "in union with
Christ Jesus."

2 Cf. *NEB*: "Baptized into union with him...."

3 *NEB* and *JB* emphasize the putting on of Christ "as
a garment" (*NEB*). *JB* has: "you have clothed
yourselves in Christ."

4 The translation of *JB* ("and there are no more distinctions between Jew and Greek...") is based upon
Rom 10:12.

5 *RSV, NEB* and *JB* eliminate the change of words

6 The translation "one person" by *NEB* is misleading.

7 P⁴⁶ gig Clement read διὰ πίστεως. Paul uses the
formula elsewhere either without (Gal 2:16; cf.
Rom 3:22, 27; 4:13; 2 Cor 5:7; Phil 3:9; Eph 2:8)
or with the article (Gal 3:14; Rom 1:12; 3:25 [cf.
v.l.], 30, 31; 1 Thess 3:7; cf. Col 2:12; Eph 2:8
v.l.; 3:12, 17). P⁴⁶ has the whole phrase differently:
διὰ πίστεως Χριστοῦ Ἰησοῦ ("through faith in Christ
Jesus"); 1739 *pc* have the names reversed.

and make the three lines v 28a–c parallel.

somewhat from line 3 and 4: line 5 is connected by καί ("and") and stands in the neuter, while lines 3 and 4 are masculine and connected by οὐδέ ("nor"). Thus line 5 appears to be a secondary addition to an earlier version; it is not found in the parallels in 1 Cor 12:13 and Col 3:11. Of the lines 3, 4, and 5, only 3 has a function in the argument, while the others appear "redundant" for the argument Paul is making.

While the composition of Gal 3:26–28 raises many intriguing questions, light can be shed on some of them—especially the problem of the origin in baptismal liturgy and the problem of form-critical classification. Both of these considerations help to clarify the function of the saying and its meaning. There are several interesting parallels in primitive Christian literature which shed light on the origin of the saying:

1 Cor 12:13

1. καὶ γὰρ ἐν ἑνὶ πνεύματι ἡμεῖς
πάντες εἰς ἓν σῶμα ἐβαπτίσθημεν
2. εἴτε Ἰουδαῖοι εἴτε Ἕλληνες
3. εἴτε δοῦλοι   εἴτε ἐλεύθεροι
4. καὶ   πάντες (εἰς)[8] ἓν πνεῦμα ἐποτίσθημεν

1. "For in one Spirit we were
all baptized into one body,
2. whether Jews or Greeks,
3. whether slaves or freemen,
4. and   we were
all embued with one Spirit."

Lines 1 and 4 are parallel; in line 1 the γάρ ("for") may have been added to connect the passage with the context, and ἐν ἑνὶ πνεύματι ("in one Spirit") may be Paul's interpretive addition,[9] parallel to the phrase "through [the] faith" in Gal 3:26. Lines 2 and 3 are parallel and correspond to Gal 3:28a, b, although the formulations are in the first person, instead of the second person plural.

Col 3:11

A second close parallel is found in Col 3:11. Its formulation is, however, more divergent; it is also more integrated with its context. Yet the connections with Gal 3:26–28 can still be recognized: there is the reference to baptism and the "putting on" of Christ (Col 3:9–10). The middle section is similar to Gal 3:28, especially because of the οὐκ ἔνι ("there is not"); but it is expanded, and after the first lines (3, 4) the contrasts change to simple listing (5–6). The concluding line is different from Gal 3:28 (7).[10]

1. ἀπεκδυσάμενοι τὸν παλαιὸν ἄνθρωπον σὺν ταῖς
πράξεσιν αὐτοῦ,
2. καὶ ἐνδυσάμενοι τὸν νέον τὸν ἀνακαινούμενον εἰς
ἐπίγνωσιν κατ᾽ εἰκόνα τοῦ κτίσαντος αὐτόν,
3. ὅπου οὐκ ἔνι Ἕλλην καὶ Ἰουδαῖος
4.   περιτομὴ καὶ   ἀκροβυστία
5.   βάρβαρος Σκύθης
6.   δοῦλος ἐλεύθερος
7. ἀλλὰ πάντα καὶ ἐν πᾶσιν Χριστός.

1. "Put off the old man with his practices,
2. and put on the new (man) who is being renewed in knowledge according to the image of his creator,
3. where there is no Greek and Jew
4.   circumcision   and uncircumcision
5.   barbarian, Scythian
6.   slave, freeman
7. but Christ is all in all."

A later but extraordinary parallel has surfaced in one of the Nag Hammadi Codices. It seems to reflect the baptismal *Sitz im Leben* most clearly. It also shows how sayings like these were composed. It looks as if Galatians and Colossians had been merged and expanded to bring out the specifically gnostic concept of the new life in Christ:

For (γάρ) when we confessed (ὁμολογεῖν) the Kingdom which is in Christ (Χριστός) they were liberated from all this multiplicity of moods and the inequality and the change. For (γάρ) the end will receive again the essence of a single one, even as the beginning (ἀρχή) is a single one, the place where there is no male and female, nor (οὐδέ) angel (ἄγγελος) nor (οὐδέ) man, but (ἀλλά) Christ (Χριστός) is all in all.[11]
The problem of the form critical classification can

---

8   εἰς is read by only a few witnesses. See Nestle–Aland, *apparatus criticus*; Weiss, *Der erste Korintherbrief*, 304 n. 1.

9   Cf. 1 Cor 12:4, 8, 9, 11.

10   Cf. 1 Cor 15:28; also Lohse, *Colossians and Philemon*,

143–46.

11   *NHC* I, 4.132, lines 16–28, from the *Tri. Trac.* (Codex Jung F. 52ᵛ–70ᵛ; ed. Rodolphe Kasser *et al.*; Bern: Francke, 1975).

be clarified to a sufficient extent by comparison with other similar sayings in Paul and in other Christian literature. Some of these parallels may be quoted here:

1 Thess 5:5

πάντες γὰρ ὑμεῖς υἱοὶ φωτός ἐστε καὶ υἱοὶ ἡμέρας.

"For you are all sons of [the] light and sons of [the] day."

Matt 23:8[12]

εἷς γάρ ἐστιν ὑμῶν ὁ διδάσκαλος, πάντες δὲ ὑμεῖς ἀδελφοί ἐστε.

"For one is your teacher, but you are all brothers." The formal analysis of these sayings in the Pauline letters and in the Gospel tradition[13] raises the question of their origin, form, and function. Since no investigation of these problems exists, preliminary explanations must suffice for the time being.[14] In the wider sense of comparative history of religions material, a statement like Gal 3:26-28 at least permits some observations. The saying addresses a group of people in the second person plural, defining their religious status before God. Such a statement must somehow be related to the form of the beatitude ("macarism"). The typical beatitude is stated in the third person singular ("blessed is the one who..."), but there are also a number of beatitudes in the second person plural ("blessed are you who...").[15] The real difference is indicated by the introductory term "blessed" (μακάριος), which is typical of the beatitude[16] but which is not found in Gal 3:26-28. The question is how decisive the difference really is. Common elements, however, include the eschatological nature of the sayings. They are strictly speaking anticipated eschatological judgments. There is the element of "eschatological reversal": the beatitudes of the Sermon on the Mount (Matt 5:3-11 // Luke 6:20-22) turn the natural order upside down by praising the unfortunate, while Gal 3:26-28 declares the abolishment of social, cultural, and religious prerogatives (3:28a-c). Is the μακαρισμός ("macarism") to which Paul refers in Gal 4:15 identical with 3:26-28?

Outside the New Testament,[17] we find similar sayings beginning with the words "You are..." in a variety of contexts and forms: in the Old Testament,[18]

---

12 Cf. also John 13:35.

13 See esp. also Matt 5:13, 14; John 13:10; 15:3; 1 John 2:14; 4:4; Eph 2:8. See furthermore Rom 1:6; 6:16; 15:14; 1 Cor 1:30; 3:3, 9, 16f; 5:2, 7; 6:2; 9:2; 12:27; 14:12; 15:17; 2 Cor 1:7; 2:9; 3:2f; 7:3; Gal 3:29; 4:28; Eph 5:2, 19; Col 2:10; 1 Thess 2:20; 4:9. Related are polemic statements against the Jews (Matt 23:28, 31; Luke 11:44, 48; 16:15; John 8:23-44; Acts 3:25; 1 Cor 2:17ff), as well as forms in the negative (e.g., Matt 10:20) or questions (e.g., 1 Cor 4:8).

14 See also my article, "Spirit, Freedom and Law," 147-51; Michel Bouttier, "*Complexio Oppositorum*: sur les Formules de I Cor. xii. 13; Gal. iii. 26-8; Col. iii. 10, 11," *NTS* 23 (1976) 1-19.

15 For similar macarisms in the second person plural, see e.g., Matt 5:11; Luke 6:22; 10:23; John 13:17; *Herm. Vis.* 2.2.7; *Sim.* 9.29.3.

16 Among the recent literature on the beatitudes, see Walter Käser, "Exegetische Erwägungen zur Seligpreisung des Sabbatarbeiters Lk 6, 5 D," *ZThK* 65 (1968) 414-30; Georg Strecker, "Die Makarismen der Bergpredigt," *NTS* 17 (1971) 255-75; Eduard Schweizer, "Formgeschichtliches zu den Seligpreisungen Jesu," *NTS* 19 (1973) 121-26; also, Jacques Dupont, *Les Béatitudes* (Paris: Gabalda, ²1969); Siegfried Schulz, *Q—Die Spruchquelle der Evangelisten* (Zurich: Theologischer Verlag, 1972) 76ff. Background material is collected in the studies by Jacques Dupont, "Béatitudes égyptiennes," *Bib* 47 (1966) 185-222; E. Lipinski, "Macarismes et Psaumes de congratulations," *RB* 75 (1968) 321-67. The dissertation by Christian H. Maahs, *The Macarisms in the NT* (Tübingen 1965 [unpubl.]), has a large collection of passages but little analysis.

17 See also the Oxyrhynchus Pap. 654 no. 3 (Coptic *Gos. Thom.* logion 3), according to Jacques-E. Ménard, *L'Evangile selon Thomas* (NHS 5; Leiden: Brill, 1975) 80-82.

18 See already Deut 14:1 (LXX): υἱοί ἐστε κυρίου τοῦ θεοῦ ὑμῶν...("You are sons of the Lord, your God..."); Lev 25:23; Deut 1:10; 7:7; 1 Esdr 8:57 (LXX); Ps 81:6 (LXX); Amos 9:7; Isa 57:4; Jer 18:6; Ezra 34:31; etc.

in Judaism,[19] in the Hellenistic mystery religions,[20] in the diatribe literature,[21] and in gnosticism.[22] A saying like Gal 3:26–28 could easily have had its *Sitz im Leben* in the baptismal liturgy.[23] Later Christian liturgies do contain statements similar to the passage from Galatians.[24] One may therefore venture the suggestion that Paul has lifted Gal 3:26–28, in part or as a whole, from a pre-Pauline liturgical context. In the liturgy, the saying would communicate information to the newly initiated, telling them of their eschatological status before God in anticipation of the Last Judgment[25] and also informing them how this status affects, and in fact changes their social, cultural, and religious self-understanding, as well as their responsibilities in the here–and–now.[26]

Therefore, Paul's use of the saying in his letter is

---

19 The Jewish–Hellenistic novel *Joseph and Aseneth* which shows strong influences of mystery–cult language has at its center an initiation ceremony and a beatitude pronounced by an angel (16.7): μακαρία εἶ σύ, ᾿Ασενέθ, ὅτι ἀπεκαλύφθη σοι τὰ ἀπόρρητα τοῦ θεοῦ μυστήρια…("Blessed are you, Aseneth, because the secret mysteries of God have been revealed to you…"). See the discussion in Edgar W. Smith, *Joseph and Aseneth and Early Christian Literature* (Ph.D. dissertation; Claremont Graduate School, 1974) 190f; also Christoph Kähler ("Zur Form- und Traditionsgeschichte von Matth. xvi. 17–19," *NTS* 23 [1976] 36–58) who discusses the beatitude in *Joseph and Aseneth*, 48–50.

20 Cf. the "macarism" which, according to Firmicus Maternus, *De errore prof. rel.* 22.1, a priest whispered into the ears of the initiates of a mystery cult: θαρρεῖτε μύσται, τοῦ θεοῦ σεσωσμένου, ἔσται γὰρ ὑμῖν ἐκ πόνων σωτηρία ("Rejoice, initiates, because the god has been saved, salvation from afflictions will be yours"). On the form of the "macarism" see Eduard Norden, *Agnostos Theos: Untersuchungen zur Formengeschichte religiöser Rede* (Leipzig and Berlin: Teubner, 1913) 100f; Reitzenstein, *Mysterienreligionen*, 400f; Nock, *Essays*, 1.83f; Nilsson, *Geschichte*, 2.639. The formal similarity with Eph 2:8 is striking: "For by grace you are saved through faith." Cf. also the last beatitude of the Sermon on the Mount, Matt 5:12, cf. Luke 6:23. André–Marie–Jean Festugière (*La révélation d'Hermès Trismégiste* [Paris: Librairie Lecoffre, 1944–54] 3.155 n. 1) refers also to Firmicus Maternus *De errore prof. rel.* 19.1.

21 See, e.g., Epictetus *Diss.* 3.22:4–8.

22 Festugière (*Révélation* 3.155 n. 1) mentions *Corp. Herm.* 13.8, where the accomplished salvation is stated: χαῖρε λοιπόν, ὦ τέκνον, ἀνακαθαιρόμενος τοῖς τοῦ θεοῦ δυνάμεσιν, εἰς συνάρθρωσιν τοῦ Λόγου ("Rejoice now, my child, cleansed you are by the powers of God, for the building up of the Logos"). See also *Corp. Herm.* 1.28; 7.1–3; the "Hymn of the Pearl" (*Acts Thom.* 110; cf. 94, 121); Valentinus, according to Clemens Alex. *Strom.* 4.13, § 89, 2–3 (tr. Foerster–Wilson, *Gnosis* 1.242): "From the beginning you are immortal and children of eternal life. You wished to take death to yourselves as your portion in order that you might destroy it and annihilate it utterly, and that death might die in you and through you. 3. For when you destroy the world and you yourselves are not destroyed, then you are lords over the whole creation and over all decay." Cf. *Exc. ex Theod.* 78.2. A large number of interesting parallels could be collected from the *NHC*. See, e.g., *Gos. Truth* 32.32: "you are the perfect day"; 33.10: "you are the wisdom" (Foerster–Wilson, *Gnosis* 1.64); *Gos. Phil.* 112 (Foerster–Wilson, *Gnosis* 1.96): "you who are with the Son of God…"; *Gos. Phil.* 44; *Thom. Cont.*, 138 lines 5ff; 145 lines 2ff; *Hyp. Arch.*, 96 lines 18ff.

23 Pre-Pauline origins have been suggested before; cf. Georg Braumann, *Vorpaulinische christliche Taufverkündigung bei Paulus* (BWANT 82; Stuttgart: Kohlhammer, 1962) 24f, 64f; Hubert Frankemölle, *Das Taufverständnis des Paulus* (SBS 47; Stuttgart: Katholisches Bibelwerk, 1970) 14, 50. Wayne A. Meeks ("The Image of the Androgyne: Some Uses of a Symbol in Earliest Christianity," *HR* 13 [1974] 165–208) calls the passage a "baptismal reunification formula" (180ff).

24 On this subject, see Hugh M. Riley, *Christian Initiation* (Washington: Catholic University of America, 1974); Robert Murray, "The Exhortation to Candidates for Ascetical Vows at Baptism in the Ancient Syriac Church," *NTS* 21 (1974) 59–80.

25 On this point, see Murray (ibidem, 64f) who quotes a baptismal macarism from Ephraem's *Epiphany Hymns* (13.14):
"(You) baptized, who have found
the Kingdom in the womb of baptism,
Come down, put on the Only One,
who is the Lord of the Kingdom.
Blessed are you who are crowned."
See also the material from Syriac sources quoted in Robert Murray, *Symbols of Church and Kingdom: A Study in Early Syriac Tradition* (Cambridge: Cambridge University, 1975) 162f.

26 The question of the origin of Gal 3:26–28 has been related by some scholars to the *berakot* opening the Jewish morning prayers, in which the Jew renders

secondary in function. In the context of the present argument it serves as a "reminder"[27] and as the cardinal proof. Again, Paul can activate the Galatians' situation of eye-witnesses: they themselves know the things of which Paul is reminding them; they have heard them before and have agreed to them in the decisive ceremony which had made them members of the Christian church. What has become of their "macarism"?[28]

Interpretation

■ **26** The first of the "definitions" contained in 3:26–28 is presented in v 26: "for you are all sons of God, through the faith, in Christ Jesus." The statement is very concise and includes a number of theological formulae which must be recognized and then related to their respective contexts. There is, in addition, a most important change from the first person to the second person plural.[29] The implication is that from 2:15–3:25 Paul has discussed the situation of the Jewish Christians, with whom he himself belongs. Having concluded that part of the argument in v 25, he now turns to the situation of the Gentile–Christian Galatians.[30] What he has to say to them is of course the consequence of the preceding discussion of the situation of Jewish Christianity.[31] The Gentile Galatians, that is, all [32] Gentile Christians, are told that before God they are "sons of God." It is understood that this honorific designation[33]

thanks to God that he did not create him a Gentile, an ignorant person, a slave, a woman. See on this prayer, David Kaufmann, "Das Alter der drei Benedictionen von Israel, vom Freien und vom Mann," *MGWJ* 37 (1893) 14–18; Bousset–Gressmann, *Religion*, 426f; Elbogen, *Gottesdienst*, 89f; Albrecht Oepke, "γυνή," *TDNT* 1.776; Meeks, "Androgyne," *HR* 13 (1974) 67f. J. J. Meuzelaar (*Der Leib des Messias: Eine exegetische Studie über den Gedanken vom Leib Christi in den Paulusbriefen* [Assen: van Gorcum, 1961] 84f) even believes that Gal 3:28 is based upon the prayer—an improbable suggestion. Analogous statements of gratitude are extant for the Greek (Plutarch *Marius* 46.1; Diog. L. 1.33; Lactantius *Inst.* 3.19.17) and for the Persian; the Persian praises Ormuzd for having created his faithful as Iranians and of the right religion, freemen and not slaves, men and not women (see James Darmesteter, *Une Prière Judéo-Persane* [Paris: Cerf, 1891]). As this type of prayer is still an unresolved problem, so is the relationship between the previous material and certain cultic laws, e.g., the temple law of Philadelphia in Lydia (1st c. B.C.), where it is said of Zeus: ...π[ρόσοδον διδόν] τ᾿ εἰς τὸν ἑαυτοῦ οἶκον ἀνδρά[σι καὶ γυναιξὶν] ἐλευθέροις καὶ οἰκέταις ("he grants access to his temple to men [and women], freemen and slaves"). The temple law was revealed in a dream–vision and grants admission to people normally excluded from the worship. The quotation is according to Wilhelm Dittenberger, *Sylloge Inscriptionum Graecarum a Guilelmo Dittenbergero condita et aucta* (4 vols.; Leipzig: Hirzel, ³1915–21) no. 985, lines 5–7; see also Franciszek Sokolowski, *Lois sacrées de l'Asie Mineure* (Paris: de Boccard, 1955) no. 20; a tr. of the inscription is found in Frederick C. Grant, *Hellenistic Religions* (Indianapolis and New York: Bobbs–Merrill, 1953) 28–30. Another example is the Hippocratic Oath, which contains the vow: "Whatever houses I may visit, I will come for the benefit of the sick, remaining free of all intentional injustice, of all mischief and in particular of sexual relations with both female and male persons, be they free or slaves" (tr. Ludwig Edelstein, *The Hippocratic Oath* [Supplement to the Bulletin of the History of Medicine 1; Baltimore: Johns Hopkins, 1943] 3); cf. 34f.

27 See the parallel in Philo *Cher.* 48, where Philo "reminds" his readers with these words: "These thoughts, ye initiated, whose ears are purified, receive into your souls as holy mysteries indeed...." See also the Hymn of the Pearl (*Acts Thom.* 110.44 [in HSW, *NT Apocrypha* 2.500]): "remember that thou art a son of kings."

28 Gal 4:15. The question should at least be raised whether a connection exists between Gal 3:26–28 and the Synoptic pericope on baptism, Mark 1:9–11 par; cf. also *Acts Thom.* 121.

29 The change is usually noted by commentaries, e.g., Lightfoot, Zahn, Burton, Sieffert, Mussner.

30 So correctly Burton, p. 202.

31 Burton (p. 202) takes γάρ ("for") to mean: "And this applies to all of you."

32 The emphasis on "all" can be noted throughout Gal (see 2:16; 3:8, 10, 13, 22, 26, 28; 4:1, 26 (*v.l.*); 5:3; 6:10); it corresponds to the monotheistic εἷς ("one") in 3:16, 20, 28.

33 On the title "son of God" see Eduard Schweizer, ("υἱός κτλ.," *TDNT* 8.389ff, esp. 391f) with further literature.

is normally reserved for Jews, and that even Jews will receive this status only at the Last Judgment from God himself.[34] Thus, it is exceptional and extraordinary that Paul attributes this status to Gentiles now.[35] The question is how this designation can be explained. The explanation is contained in the formulae of the statement, which must be understood in the general context of Paul's theology. One must also recall the argument following the "thesis" in 3:7. It is Christ as the "Son of God"[36] who makes adoption as "sons"[37] available through the gift of the Spirit.[38] Two formulae state the conditions for this adoption: "through [the] faith" ($\delta\iota\grave{\alpha}\ \tau\hat{\eta}\varsigma\ \pi\acute{\iota}\sigma\tau\epsilon\omega\varsigma$)[39] and through incorporation in the "body of Christ," i.e., "in Christ Jesus."[40] This definition is clearly polemical and must be seen in contradiction to the doctrine of Paul's opponents. The present tense of $\grave{\epsilon}\sigma\tau\epsilon$ ("you are") really refers to an event in the past of which Paul reminds his readers. This event combined the aspects of myth, ritual, and experience in the ceremony of baptism (cf. 3:27). Through this event, the Galatians have become, and now are, "sons of God."[41]

■ **27** In the formal composition of 3:26–28, v 27 stands out as an explanatory insertion of great significance:[42] $\check{o}\sigma o\iota\ \gamma\grave{\alpha}\rho\ \epsilon\grave{\iota}\varsigma\ X\rho\iota\sigma\tau\grave{o}\nu\ \grave{\epsilon}\beta\alpha\pi\tau\acute{\iota}\sigma\theta\eta\tau\epsilon,\ X\rho\iota\sigma\tau\grave{o}\nu\ \grave{\epsilon}\nu\epsilon\delta\acute{\upsilon}\sigma\alpha\sigma\theta\epsilon$ ("for as many of you as were baptized into Christ, have put on Christ"). As we have suggested before, this is Paul's only explicit reference to baptism in Galatians. It serves to connect 3:26–28, and thereby the letter as a whole, with the Christian ritual of baptism. What this connection implies is, however, a question. At any rate, we can assume that at some point in the course of the ceremony, the candidates for baptism were officially informed that they now had the status of "sons of God." It would be important to know whether Paul is the author of v 27, or whether it was part of the tradition he has taken over. Although we cannot be sure, indications speak in favor of the tradition. The function of v 27 is that of a reminder of the ceremony and its meaning. The $\check{o}\sigma o\iota$ ("as many of you") is not intended to limit the "all" of v 26, but identifies what is meant by "all."[43] Included are all Christians because they were all baptized. The baptismal theology which is reflected in Paul's remark appears to antedate Paul's own theology. The problem presented here is a rather difficult one. The phrase "baptized into Christ" can be and actually was interpreted in different ways, even by Paul himself.[44] At some points Paul does not hesitate to accept the language (as in 3:27), but in other instances he seems to have trouble with it. We know that early Christian baptismal theology presented serious problems to the Apostle. In 1 Thessalonians he does not

34   Cf. in this regard 2 Cor 6:18, where those who are faithful to the "covenant" are promised to become "sons and daughters of God" in heaven. See Appendix 2, below; and Betz, "2 Cor 6:14–7:1," 97f. For "sonship" as a Jewish prerogative, cf. Rom 9:4, 26; on the whole question, see Str–B 3.15ff; Georg Fohrer *et al., TDNT* 8, *s.v.* υἱός, sections B.5; C.I; C.II, 3–4; D.IV.

35   See Gal 3:7, 29; 4:6, 7, 22, 30; also 4:19, 25, 27, 28, 31; Eph 1:5; John 1:12; 1 John 3:1f; etc. The extraordinary and controversial nature of this statement can still be seen in Justin *Dial,* 123–24. See also the interesting parallels in Philo *Conf.* 144f; *Odes Sol.* 36; *Acts Thom.* 47f.

36   See Gal 1:16; 2:20; 4:4, 6.

37   See Gal 4:4–6; Rom 8:3f, 14–17, 29.

38   See Gal 3:1–5; 4:6; Rom 8:2–29; etc.

39   On this formula, see the introduction of this section, above n. 7. In an important but misleading interpretation Schlier (pp. 171f) deemphasizes the role of faith in favor of baptism, saying that in v 26 Paul refers not so much to the personal faith of the believer, as to faith as an objective *factum* which "came"

(3:25). The act of individual faith is reduced to a "medium" ("*Mittel*"). For Oepke (p. 124) it is salvation history, not the "subjective" apperception of faith, which enables Paul to look with such confidence at the congregation. It is clear, however, that the formula in v 26 takes up the previous concept from the *propositio* (2:16): "through faith in Christ Jesus" as opposed to "through works of the law."

40   On this formula, see Gal 1:22; 2:4, 17; 3:14, 28; 5:6. See Bultmann, *Theology,* § 34, 3; Ernest Best, *One Body in Christ* (London: SPCK, 1955) 1ff; Walter Grundmann, "χρίω," *TDNT* 9.550–52; Conzelmann, *Outline,* 265; idem, *1 Corinthians,* 21.

41   See on the meaning of the ritual the article by Meeks, "Androgyne," 180–97.

42   See the introduction to this section, above.

43   See Rom 6:3: ὅσοι ἐβαπτίσθημεν εἰς Χριστὸν Ἰησοῦν ...("as many as we were baptized into Christ Jesus...").

44   Paul has quite a variety of interpretations of the preposition εἰς ("into"); apart from Rom 6:3f, see 1 Cor 1:13–17; 10:2; 12:13; 15:29; also Col 2:12.

mention baptism at all; in 1 Corinthians he has to struggle with unacceptable interpretations of baptism (1 Cor 1:13–17); in Romans he does accept the concept of "baptism into Christ," but only after interpreting it in terms of his own concept of "dying and rising with Christ."[45] Because of these varieties in Paul's baptismal language, it is not advisable simply to harmonize the passages. In Galatians, Paul refers to the doctrine of "dying and rising with Christ" elsewhere, but he does so without reference to the baptismal rite.[46] We ought not, therefore, to interpret baptism into these passages. Moreover, in Gal 3:27 Paul makes use of another concept when he identifies the expression "into Christ" with "putting on Christ" ($X\rho\iota\sigma\tau\dot{o}\nu$ $\dot{\epsilon}\nu\delta\dot{\nu}\epsilon\iota\nu$).[47] This concept, which has a powerful and long tradition in ancient religions, describes the Christian's incorporation into the "body of Christ" as an act of "clothing," whereby Christ is understood as the garment.[48] Before this concept is given further consideration, it should be stated with Schlier[49] that this phrase presupposes the christological–soteriological concept of Christ as the heavenly garment by which the Christian is enwrapped and transformed into a new being. The language is certainly figurative, but it goes beyond the dimension of merely social and ethical inclusion in a religious community;[50] it suggests an event of divine transformation.

For Schlier and those who agree with him, this reference is decisive for the interpretation of the letter as a whole. As he sees it, the Apostle reminds the Galatians, as people whose *subjective* faith is wavering, of the *objective* basis of their Christian existence.[51] This objective basis is, according to Schlier, the sacrament of baptism. Thus, the Christian situation can be described

in terms of Being (*Sein*) and Existence (*Existenz*) on the one hand, and Roman Catholic sacramentalism on the other hand. This combination constitutes the core of Schlier's interpretive efforts.

The question is, however, whether or not this interpretation applies to Paul's theology. This question is extremely complicated, for Schlier is both right and wrong, and ultimately quite wrong. Schlier is right insofar as Paul has to deal with people whose faith is wavering. Paul indeed reminds them of the ceremony of baptism as the objective basis of their Christian existence. This basis is objective in the sense that the baptismal ceremony constitutes the legal act of joining the Christian religion. One may also name the magic ideas implied in the *ritus* itself, although these magic ideas are very compatible with Schlier's sacramentalism. Schlier is wrong, however, because Paul's categories are quite different from Schlier's. The objective basis upon which the Christian existence rests and of which Paul reminds the Galatians is the official declaration of adoption, a legal act which took place at baptism. But this legal basis is only the conclusion of previous events: the christological–soteriological events named in Gal 1:4; 2:20; 3:13; 4:4–5; the gift of the Spirit (3:2–5; 4:6); and the faith of the Galatians in Christ. Of all this Paul reminds the Galatians. In other words, the objective basis of which Paul speaks is faith in Christ, but not the sacrament as a *ritus ex opere operato*. Faith in Christ can only be grounded in Christ himself, not in a reality outside of him. Paul does not share and would even oppose calling the ritual of baptism "sacramentally objective" and faith in Christ "subjective." If one wants to employ these categories at all, Paul would call "faith in Christ" the objective basis, because it is

---

45 See Betz, *Nachfolge*, 174f; Tannehill, *Dying and Rising*; Eduard Schweizer, "Dying and Rising with Christ," *NTS* 14 (1967) 1–14; idem, "Die Mystik des Sterbens und Auferstehens mit Christus bei Paulus," in Beiträge, 183–203.
46 Cf. Gal 2:19; 5:24; 6:14.
47 In Gal, this concept occurs only here.
48 For further explanations, see below.
49 Schlier, pp. 173f. One should be aware that Schlier works with a baptismal theology which interprets a combination of Rom, Eph, and Col in terms of Roman Catholic sacramental dogma. Schlier then interprets this doctrinal complex into Gal. Although

this approach must be rejected for reasons of method, it should be noted that Col/Eph may reflect the same pre–Pauline baptismal theology as in Gal 3:27—of course at a later stage and in a different context.
50 This is true even for 1 Cor 12:13: $\epsilon\dot{\iota}\varsigma$ $\dot{\epsilon}\nu$ $\sigma\hat{\omega}\mu\alpha$ $\beta\alpha\pi\tau\iota\sigma\theta\hat{\eta}\nu\alpha\iota$ ("be baptized into one body"). On "ritual and community" see Meeks, "Androgyne," 189–97.
51 Schlier's views have been widely accepted—a strange case of ecumenical consensus. Also Oepke (p. 124) thinks Paul stresses "objectivity" and does so "sacramentally, but not magically."

predicted by Scripture and because it has become a historical reality through Christ's coming (3:23, 25; 4:4–5) and his self-sacrifice on the cross (1:4; 2:20; 3:13). The individual Christian existence was brought into contact with salvation by the preaching of the word and the gift of the Spirit (see especially 3:2–5; 4:6). Also these factors would be named by Paul as "objective." The Christian's subjectivity, in Paul's view, cannot be separated from this whole process, but is woven into it.[52]

The fact must be stated, therefore, that Schlier's presentation of Paul's theology of baptism in Galatians is a misrepresentation. Perhaps Schlier has more in common with the pre–Pauline baptismal theology than he has with Paul himself.[53] Paul himself seems to have been aware of the danger of "cultic formalism" inherent in pre–Pauline baptismal theology, and seems to argue against that background in Romans.[54]

The concept of "putting on Christ" is extremely interesting.[55] In the early Christian literature, we must distinguish between "putting on Christ" in baptism,[56] as a phrase used in parenesis,[57] and as a hope to be realized in the hereafter.[58] The figurative language of clothing is found already in the Old Testament,[59] but the "putting on" of a redeemer figure has parallels only in the mystery religions[60] and in gnosticism.[61] Geo Widengren[62] has strongly emphasized the Iranian background of the idea. Also impressive are the parallels from ethnology and primitive religions.[63]

The connection between "putting on" Christ and

52 See on this point also Meeks, "Androgyne," 182.

53 So also Meeks, ibidem, 181f.

54 This concern lies behind the long discussion of baptism in Rom 6–8.

55 On this concept and collections of parallel material see Bauer, *s.v.* ἐνδύω, 2, b; *PGL, s.v.*; Albrecht Oepke, "ἐνδύω," *TDNT* 2.319–21; idem, pp. 124f; Schlier, pp. 173f; Lohse, *Colossians*, 141f; Joachim Gnilka, *Der Epheserbrief* (Freiburg: Herder, 1971) 231f; Jacob Jervell, *Imago Dei. Gen: 1,26f im Spätjudentum, in der Gnosis und in den paulinischen Briefen* (FRLANT 76; Göttingen: Vandenhoeck & Ruprecht, 1960) 231–56; Kertelge, "*Rechtfertigung*," 238f; Meeks, "Androgyne," 183–89. Cf. Hermann–Joseph Venetz, "Christus anziehen," *Freiburger Zeitschrift für Philosophie und Theologie* 20 (1973) 3–36.

56 Gal 3:27; Col 3:10; Eph 4:24; *Gos. Phil.* 101 (*NHC* II, 75, 21–25). See also Meeks, ibidem, 187f.

57 See Rom 13:12, 14; Col 2:12; 3:9f; Eph 4:22–24; 6:11, 14; 1 Thess 5:8; etc. See Meeks, ibidem, 184, with more references.

58 See 1 Cor 15:53f; 2 Cor 5:3; also Rev 15:6; 19:14.

59 Cf. the material in Albrecht Oepke, "ἐνδύω," *TDNT* 2.320.

60 See Ephippus in Athen. 12.53, p. 537 E (quoted in Bauer [see n. 55, above]); Plutarch *Is. et Osir.* 352 B; Apuleius *Met.* 11.24; Philo *Fug.* 110. See Reitzenstein, *Mysterienreligionen*, 42f, 60–62, 266, 350f; idem, *Die Vorgeschichte der christlichen Taufe* (Leipzig and Berlin: Teubner, 1929) 42f; Goodenough, *By Light, Light*, 265f, 328f, 351, 367; Nilsson, *Geschichte*, 2.632ff; Geo Widengren, "Heavenly Enthronement and Baptism: Studies in Mandean Baptism," in *Religions in Antiquity, Essays in Memory of E. R. Goodenough* (ed. Jacob Neusner; Leiden: Brill, 1968) 551–82; Murray, *Symbols*, 69f, 310–12; J. Gwyn

Griffiths, *Plutarch: De Iside et Osiride* (Cambridge: University of Wales, 1970) 267f; idem, *Apuleius of Madauros*, 308–10, 313f.

61 The language of "putting off" and "putting on" salvation or the redeemer, often in connection with baptism, is common in gnostic texts. See "Hymn of the Pearl" (*Acts Thom.* 108–113); *Gos. Thom.*, log. 36–37; *Gos. Phil.* 24 (*NHC* II, 57, 19–24); *Gos. Truth* 20.30ff; *Thom. Cont.*, p. 143, 37 (Foerster–Wilson, *Gnosis* 2.117); for further passages see Foerster–Wilson, *Gnosis* 2, indices, *s.v.* "Coat," "Garb"; "Garments"; HSW, *NT Apocrypha* 2, index, *s.v.* "garment"; Fitzmyer, *Essays*, 405–08 (on Pap. Oxyr. 655); Jonathan Z. Smith, "The Garments of Shame," *HR* 5 (1965) 217–38. Most interesting are the passages in the *Odes Sol.* (e.g., 7.4; 25.8; 33.12; 39.8), the Mandaic literature (see Kurt Rudolph, *Die Mandäer* [FRLANT NF 57; Göttingen: Vandenhoeck & Ruprecht, 1961] 2.181–88), and the Church Fathers (see Hugh M. Riley, *Christian Initiation* [Washington: The Catholic University of America and Consortium, 1974] esp. 413–51).

62 Geo Widengren, "Der iranische Hintergrund der Gnosis," *ZRGG* 4 (1952) 105–14; idem, *Religionsphänomenologie*, 434, 483, 485, 495ff; cf. Hans Jonas, *Gnosis*, 1.102, 320ff; idem, *Gnostic Religion*, 118f, 122f; Jervell, *Imago Dei*, 168. For different views, cf. Eduard Schweizer, "σῶμα κτλ.," *TDNT* 7.1070–74; Ernest Best, *One Body in Christ*, 67ff (n. 40 above); Meuzelaar, *Der Leib des Messias*, 87ff, 92 (n. 26 above); Pieter W. van der Horst, "Observations on a Pauline Expression," *NTS* 19 (1972/73) 181–87; cf. Meeks, "Androgyne," 184 n. 83.

63 See Hermann Baumann, *Das doppelte Geschlecht* (Berlin: Reimer, 1955) 14ff; Marie Delcourt, *Hermaphrodite* (London: Studio Books, 1961) 9ff; Mircea

baptism is found in Gal 3:27; Col 3:10; Eph 4:24 and in gnosticism, especially in *Gos. Phil.* 101.[64] Considering this background, we may assume that the concept implies the "putting off" of "the old man" and the "putting on" of "the new man." This would explain why Paul can refer to the act also as "new creation" (Gal 6:15).

The connection of this concept with that of "dying and rising with Christ" is not as fully developed in Galatians as it is in Romans 6–8. In Galatians Paul uses the concepts of "putting on Christ" and "dying and rising together with Christ" at different places, while only in Romans 6–8 does he identify them both (but he also extends the "dying and rising with Christ" beyond the act of baptism into the life of the Christian, which as a whole takes on the character of "imitation of Christ").[65] The simple identity of the "putting on" of Christ and the ritual of baptism seems to present as many difficulties for Paul as the concept of baptism "in the name" of Christ, which he discussed rather critically in 1 Cor 1:13–17.[66]

■ **28** Surprisingly, v 28 leads to the field of political and social ideals and practices. The first part (v 28a–c) contains three parallel statements in the present tense, which define the religious, cultural, and social conse-

quences of the Christian baptismal initiation. The three statements, extremely concise as they are, name the old status of the baptized and declare this old status abolished. By implication a new status[67] is claimed, but no further explanation is given at this point. It is significant that Paul makes these statements not as utopian ideals or as ethical demands, but as accomplished facts. The question is, therefore, how the present tense of the phrase "you are" is to be understood. Why does Paul make such claims? How are they related to baptism? What is the reality of these claims?

Strangely enough, the commentaries pass over these odd statements rather quickly.[68] But recently Wayne Meeks has seen the phenomenon and has correctly related the phrases to "performative language," the function of which he describes in this way: ". . . a resident of one of the cities of the province Asia who ventured to become a member of one of the tiny Christian cells in their early years would have heard the utopian declaration of mankind's reunification as a solem ritual pronouncement. Reinforced by dramatic gestures (disrobing, immersion, robing), such a declaration would carry—within the community for which its language was meaningful—the power to assist in shaping the symbolic universe by which that group dis-

Eliade, *Shamanism: Archaic Techniques of Ecstasy* (Bollingen Series 76; New York: Bollingen Foundation, 1964).

64 "The living water is a body. It is fitting for us to put on the living man. Therefore when he comes to descend into the water, he strips, in order that he may put on this one" (tr. Foerster–Wilson, *Gnosis* 2.94). On the passage, see Hans–Georg Gaffron, *Studien zum koptischen Philippusevangelium unter besonderer Berücksichtigung der Sakramente* (Diss.; Bonn: Universität, 1969) 126ff, with notes; Meeks, "Androgyne," 187f.

65 See above, n. 45.

66 See Conzelmann, *1 Corinthians*, 35f; cf. also the discussion and further literature in Lars Hartman, "Baptism 'Into the Name of Jesus' and Early Christology," *StTh* 28 (1974) 21–48; idem, "Into the name of Jesus," *NTS* 20 (1974) 432–40.

67 Cf. Gal 6:15b: "new creation."

68 Commentators have consistently denied that Paul's statements have political implications. Cf. Burton, pp. 206f: "The passage has nothing to do directly with the merging of nationalities or the abolition of slavery.... Yet that the principle has its indirect

social significance is shown by the implications of the Antioch incident 2:11–14...." Reading Oepke's commentary on this passage is a painful experience. According to the second edition (1957; pp. 90f) it is "impossible" for Paul to have in mind an emancipation of slaves and women, and "a pale internationalism." In the third edition (1973), the political jargon has been brought up to date, but even now Paul is said to speak "purely religiously" (p. 126), which amounts to the opposite of what Paul actually says: "Because of this, there is room in the congregation for ethnic differences, as well as for the social distinctions between slaves and freemen, man and woman." Schlier (p. 174) declares that for the Christians "all metaphysical, historical and natural distinctions stemming from the old eon are abolished sacramentally, i.e., in a hidden but real way." With this, Schlier (p. 175) can do both: emphasize strongly "the reality of equality" and deny that any conclusions can be drawn from this in regard to the ecclesiastical offices (!) and the political order.

tinguished itself from the ordinary 'world' of the larger society."[69]

There can be no doubt that Paul's statements have social and political implications of even a revolutionary dimension.[70] The claim is made that very old and decisive ideals and hopes of the ancient world have come true in the Christian community.[71] These ideals include the abolition of the religious and social distinctions between Jews and Greeks, slaves and freemen, men and women. These social changes are claimed as part of the process of redemption and as the result of the ecstatic experiences which the Galatians as well as other Christians have had. Being rescued from the present evil aeon (Gal 1:4) and being changed to a "new creation" implies these radical social and political changes. The Christian's relationship to the social and political structures of "this world" follows the rule set forth in 6:14: "through whom [= Christ] the world is crucified to me and I to the world." The Christian is now "dead" to the social, religious, and cultural distinctions characteristic of the old world–order (cf. Gal 2:19).

Arnold A. T. Ehrhardt[72] once spelled out clearly what must also be applied to Paul's statements in Gal 3:28: "it is a fact all too often overlooked by political theory that revolutions should not be judged according to the terror they spread around, but according to the question, whether or not they are capable of presenting a political alternative to the system which they fight. If the new political ideas cannot be integrated into the existing order which they fight, if at best they may be balanced out over a period of time, if every single and even the most prudential measure of the ruling principle is thoroughly criticized by the representatives of the new order, . . . then the movement which proclaims these revolutionary principles is truly revolutionary. In this sense Christianity in the first centuries was a radical revolution . . .".

(a) The first of the parallel statements declares that in the Christian church the religious, cultural, and social distinctions between Jews and Greeks are abolished: "there is neither Jew nor Greek." The expression οὐκ ἔνι stands for οὐκ ἔνεστιν (ἔνι = ἐν) and means "there is not."[73] The phrase "neither Jew nor Greek" is a slogan which occurs also elsewhere in Paul.[74] From Rom 10:12 we may conclude that Paul has in mind the removal of the distinctions which customarily separate the Jew and the non–Jew: "there is no distinction between Jew and Greek" (οὐ γάρ ἐστιν διαστολὴ Ἰουδαίου τε καὶ Ἕλληνος). According to Rom 3:1–20; 9:3–5, this abolition pertains to the religious prerogatives claimed by the Jews and symbolized by the ritual of circumcision (cf. Gal 5:6; 6:15; Rom 2:25–29;

69 Meeks, "Androgyne," 182. See also Karlmann Beyschlag, "Christentum und Veränderung in der Alten Kirche," *KD* 18 (1972) 26–55; Gerd Theissen, "Soteriologische Symbolik in den paulinischen Schriften," *KD* 20 (1974) 282–304.

70 On the political and social significance of the early Christian church see especially Widengren, *Religionsphänomenologie*, § 21; Arnold Ehrhardt, *Politische Metaphysik von Solon bis Augustin*, vol. 2: *Die christliche Revolution* (Tübingen: Mohr, Siebeck, 1959); Francis Dvornik, *Early Christian and Byzantine Political Philosophy* (2 vols.; Dumbarton Oaks Studies 9; Washington, D.C.: Dumbarton Oaks Center, 1966).

71 The old ideals are summarized in Zeno's *Politeia*, according to Plutarch, *De Alex. Magni Fort.* 329 A–B: "...that all the inhabitants of this world of ours should not live differentiated by their respective rules of justice into separate cities and communities, but that we should consider all men to be of one community and one polity, and that we should have a common life and an order common to us all, even as a herd that feeds together and shares the pasturages of the common field." For further material see John Ferguson (*Utopias of the Classical World* [Ithaca: Cornell University, 1975]), who mentions Paul and quotes Phil 3:20 (pp. 68f). For the reception of the ideas in Hellenistic Judaism see Erwin R. Goodenough, *The Politics of Philo Judaeus, Practice and Theory* (New Haven: Yale University, 1938); idem, *The Political Philosophy of Hellenistic Kingship* (YCS 1, 1929) 55–102.

72 Ehrhardt, *Politische Metaphysik* 2.19.

73 See also 1 Cor 6:5; Col 3:11; Jas 1:17. See BDF, § 98; BDR, § 98; Bauer, *s.v.* ἔνι.

74 Cf. 1 Cor 12:13. The formula is related to the other, Ἰουδαῖος πρῶτον καὶ Ἕλλην "Jew first and then Greek" (Rom 1:16; 2:9f; 3:9; cf. also 1 Cor 1:24; 10:32; Acts 14:1; 18:4; 19:10; 20:21; *Kerygma Petrou* 2, 15 line 7 [ed. Erich Klostermann, *Apocrypha* I; KlT 3; Bonn: Marcus & Weber, 1921]; Ign. *Smyrn.* 1.2, etc.; for references see also Bauer, *s.v.* Ἰουδαῖος, 2, c).

4:9–12; 1 Cor 7:19; Phil 3:3; also Col 2:11; 3:11; Eph 2:11–22). By implication then, elimination of the Jewish religious and cultural distinctions leads to equality between Jews and Greeks, i.e., to the emancipation of the Jews. Naming the Jews first seems to indicate that Jews on their own initiative gave up their prerogatives.[75] A clear instance of this kind of self–abnegation was the behavior of Peter at Antioch, when he took up table fellowship with Christian Gentiles (Gal 2:11–14). By contrast, Col 3:11 names the Greeks first,[76] thus implying the self–abnegation by Greeks of their socio–cultural supremacy.[77] The formula "neither Jew nor Greek" seems to point to Hellenistic Judaism as its origin. It programatically proclaims both a universalizing and a hellenizing of Judaism.[78] This program seems to have been taken over by primitive Christianity, where in its mission the formerly exclusively Jewish prerogatives were extended to Gen-

tile believers by simultaneously removing the Jewish external religious and social distinctions. In this program "mission" and "Hellenization" must necessarily have become one and the same thing, a fact which may have been a reason for the early opposition against Paul and his missionary efforts.[79] If this hypothesis of the Hellenistic–Jewish origin of the formula is accepted,[80] it must have been known to the Galatians from the time they were converted to Christianity.[81] At that time they must have welcomed it as the great opportunity to become included in God's salvation without being subjected to the external norms of Judaism. Now, however, they must have become suspicious that this freedom is in effect an obstacle to their salvation.

The formula "neither Jew nor Greek" is most likely a variation of the well–known Hellenistic political slogan "Greeks and barbarians" (Ἕλληνες καὶ βάρβαροι).[82] This slogan had been circulating for several

---

75 This is what Paul himself has done (see Gal 4:12; 1:13ff; 2:11–14; 2:15–21; Rom 1:5, 14; 2–4; 9–11; Phil 3:3–10).

76 See also Acts 14:5; furthermore Acts 2:10f, 14; 9:22.

77 Cf. also 1 Cor 1:18–24, where the cultural supremacy of the Greeks is denied.

78 See especially Hans Windisch, "Ἕλλην," *TDNT* 2.504–16; the basic study is by Julius Jüthner, *Hellenen und Barbaren* (Leipzig: Dieterich, 1923) 27ff. Cf. 2 Macc 4:10ff, where a vivid description is given of what happened when Jason made the Jews conform to the Greek way of life; also 2 Macc 6:1ff. Josephus (*C. Apion.* 1.180) characterizes a hellenized Jew: "Now this man...not only spoke Greek, but had the soul of a Greek." See also the Introduction, §2.C.

79 See Gal 2:7–9. As such the formula leaves open whether the Christians should all be regarded as Jews or as Gentiles, or as it was later understood, as the "third race" (cf. *Kerygma Petrou*, Frag. 2 [ed. Erich Klostermann, *Apocrypha I*; KlT 3; Bonn: Marcus & Weber, 1921] 15 lines 7–8; tr. in HSW, *NT Apocrypha* 2.100). This ambiguity may be behind the present inclination of the Galatians to come under the Torah (cf. 4:21). Cf. furthermore, Paul's concepts of the "Israel of God" (Gal 6:16), the "true Jew," "true circumcision," etc. (Rom 2:28f).

80 In this we follow Windisch, "Ἕλλην," 513–14 (n. 78 above).

81 The formula is certainly related also to the "mis-

sionary maxim" in 1 Cor 9:20ff: "To the Jews I became like a Jew, in order that I might win Jews; to those under the Law like one under the Law...in order that I might win them that are under the law; to those outside of the Law like one outside of the Law...in order that I might win those outside of the Law." See on this Daube, *NT and Rabbinic Judaism*, 336ff; Conzelmann, *1 Corinthians*, 159ff.

82 Paul knows this formula (Rom 1:14). Both formulae seem to be combined and expanded in Col 3:11: "there is neither Greek nor Jew, circumcision nor uncircumcision, barbarian, Scythian, slave, freeman..." (see the Introduction to this section, above). See also Justin *Apol.* 1.5.4; 7.3; 46.3; Tatian 1.1; 21.3; 29.1; 30.1 (see furthermore *PGL, s.v.*); *Gos. Phil.* 49 (*NHC* II, 62, 26–35). Noteworthy are also other variations: "Jews and Christians" (Aristides *Apol.* 2.1); attributed to gnostics are these variations: "no longer Jews, not yet Christians" (Irenaeus *Adv. haer.* 1.24.6); "no longer Jews, no longer Christians" (Epiphanius *Pan.* 24.5.5). Luther (1535; WA 40/1, 542, lines 16–17) continues: "Non est magistratus neque subditus, non est doctor neque auditor, Non est paedagogus neque discipulus, Non est Hera neque ancilla, etc." ("There is neither magistrate nor subject, neither professor nor listener, neither teacher nor pupil, neither lady nor servant;" *Luther's Works* 26.353f).

centuries before Paul.[83] It promises or proclaims the unity of mankind through the abolition of the cultural barriers separating Greeks and non–Greeks.[84] The Jews seem to have appropriated this slogan, correctly assuming that they themselves belong to the barbarians.[85] By turning the order of the terms around, they claimed that they were realizing the old political ideal.[86] When it first took over the slogan, Christian mission must have been a part of that political program, claiming that in their midst it has become a fact.[87] Paul also shares the view with Judaism and Stoicism that the unity of mankind corresponds to the oneness of God.[88] Characteristic of Paul is that the unity has been accomplished through Christ and the gift of the Spirit.[89]

(b) The second statement declares the institution of slavery[90] abolished in the church: "there is neither slave nor freeman." Taken alone the statement can be

83   See Jüthner, *Hellenen und Barbaren* (n. 78 above); idem, "Barbar," *RAC* 1.1173–76, with bib.; Heinrich Greeven, *Das Hauptproblem der Sozialethik in der neueren Stoa und im Urchristentum* (Gütersloh: "Der Rufer," 1935) chap. 1; *Grecs et Barbares* (Entretiens sur l'antiquité classique 8; Vandoeuvres–Genève: Fondation Hardt, 1961); Harold C. Baldry, "Zeno's Ideal State," *JHS* 79 (1959) 3–15; idem, *The Unity of Mankind in Greek Thought* (Cambridge: Cambridge University, 1965), with the review by Oswyn Murray, *ClR* 80 (1966) 368–71; John M. Rist, *Stoic Philosophy* (Cambridge: Cambridge University, 1969) 64ff; Joseph Vogt, *Kulturwelt und Barbaren: Zum Menschheitsbild der spätantiken Gesellschaft* (AAWLMG 1967.1; Wiesbaden: Steiner, 1967).

84   Cf. the inscription of Antiochus I of Commagene: "Persians and Greeks" (Wilhelm Dittenberger, *Orientis graeci inscriptiones Selectae* [2 vols.; Leipzig: Hirzel, 1903–05] no. 383, line 30); similar material associating Greeks and Egyptians is listed in Preisigke, *Wörterbuch* 3 (1931) 269, *s.v.* Ἕλλην. For the history and variants of the formula, see Jüthner, *Hellenen und Barbaren, passim.* Cf. also Felix Stähelin (*Geschichte der Kleinasiatischen Galater* [Leipzig: Teubner, ²1907] 105–107), who points to the pro-Roman, anti–Greek sentiments of the Galatians.

85   Cf. Philo's usage of the pair "Greeks and barbarians" in *Ebr.* 193–205; *Mos.* 2.12, 20; *Spec.* 2.44f, 165; *Op.* 128; *Joseph.* 28, 29, 30f; *Cont.* 48; *Decal.* 153; *Leg.* 145, 162, 292.

86   Cf. Philo *Mos.* 2.18–20, arguing that the Gentile nations all reject each other's customs and institutions: "It is not so with ours. They attract and win the attention of all, of barbarians, of Greeks, of dwellers on the mainland, and islands, of nations of the east and the west, of Europe and Asia, of the whole inhabited world from end to end (20)." Philo also calls Adam, Moses, and the sages of Judaism "cosmopolitans" (*Op.* 3, 142; *Conf.* 106; *Spec.* 2.44f).

87   Apart from the Jewish mission, the Stoics claimed to have realized the old ideal. Most likely, the Sophists had first demanded that one should end the separation between Greeks and non–Greeks (see Guthrie, *Sophists*, 153, 160–63). The Cynics had attacked society and had practiced the demand in a provocative fashion individually; they called Diogenes the first "cosmopolitan." But only the Roman Stoics tried to turn Zeno's ideal into a political reality. On the subject, see the more recent studies, in which older literature may also be found: Greeven, *Das Hauptproblem der Sozialethik in der neueren Stoa und im Urchristentum* (see n. 83, above) 6ff; Hans–Rudolf Neuenschwander, *Mark Aurels Beziehungen zu Seneca und Poseidonios* (Bern: Haupt, 1951); Baldry, *Unity of Mankind*, 151ff; Arthur Bodson, *La morale sociale des derniers stoïciens, Sénèque, Epictète et Marc Aurèle* (Paris: Les belles lettres, 1967).

88   See Plutarch's summary of Zeno's *Politeia* (*De Alex. Magni Fort.* 329A): εἷς βίος καὶ κόσμος ("One life and world order"). In 329 C/D he describes Alexander the Great as a redeemer figure who came from the gods in order to realize the ideal in his empire. Very similar to Plutarch is what Philo has to say about Joseph (*Jos.* 28–31). For further passages, see *SVF* 3, no. 333–339.

89   See Gal 3:1–18, 20, 28d; 4:6, etc.; 1 Cor 8:6; Rom 11:36; etc. See also D. W. B. Robinson, "The Distinction Between Jewish and Gentile Believers in Galatians," *ABR* 13 (1965) 29–48; Dieter Zeller, *Juden und Heiden in der Mission des Paulus* (Forschung zur Bibel 1; Stuttgart: Katholisches Bibelwerk, 1973).

90   The number of works on the institution of slavery in antiquity is immense. See for further bib. and basic information: William L. Westermann, PW Sup. 6 (1935) 894–1068; idem, *The Slave Systems of Greek and Roman Antiquity* (Philadelphia: The American Philosophical Society, 1955); Joseph Vogt, *Sklaverei und Humanität im klassischen Griechentum* (AAWLMG 4; Wiesbaden: Steiner, 1953); idem, "Die Sklaverei im utopischen Denken der Griechen," *Rivista Storica dell' Antichità* (1971) 19–32; idem, *Ancient Slavery and the Ideal of Man* (Cambridge:

understood in two ways: (a) as a declaration of the abolishment of the social institution of slavery, or (b) as a declaration of the irrelevancy of that institution, which would include the possibility of its retainment.[91] In the New Testament itself, and indeed in Paul's own letters, we find both positions in regard to slavery. The overwhelming evidence in early and later Christianity seems to recommend only the second option as viable, a view taken by most commentators.[92] The first option is then usually taken as a "misunderstanding." But it is important to bear in mind that Paul's views cannot always be harmonized. Gal 3:28, 1 Cor 7:21–24, or Philemon may express different positions on the same subject. In 1 Corinthians and Philemon Paul advises the Christian slaves to retain the social status in which they find themselves, since to the Christians it makes no difference whether socially they are slaves or freemen. 1 Cor 12:13, which is a parallel to Gal 3:28, must be interpreted in the context of 1 Cor 7:21–24: whether Jews or Greeks, slaves or freemen, we all have the same

one Spirit and are members of the same one "body of Christ." Even in Col 3:11, where the form of Gal 3:28 is reflected, it is coupled with exhortation to the slaves to remain obedient to their masters (Col 3:22–25). And yet there are indications which suggest that Gal 3:28 represents a different standpoint with regard to the institution of slavery: its probable pre-Pauline origin,[93] the connection with the ecstatic experience of the Spirit, the absence elsewhere in Galatians of any exhortation that slaves should remain in slavery, the analogy of the other statements in v 28—all this represents a different situation when compared with 1 Corinthians. In addition, Paul's statement is in conformity with a long tradition of social criticism against the institution of slavery in the Hellenistic world (Sophists, Cynics, Jews).[94]

The social criticism of the institution of slavery seems to have begun with the Sophists.[95] Alcidamas, a student of Gorgias, is said to have taught: "God has set

---

Harvard University, 1975); Moses I. Finley, *Slavery in Classical Antiquity* (New York: Barnes & Noble, ²1968); Dieter Nestle, "Freiheit," *RAC* 8.269–306; Herbert Rädle, *Untersuchungen zum griechischen Freilassungswesen* (Augsburg: Blasaditsch, 1969); idem, "Selbsthilfeorganisationen der Sklaven und Freigelassenen in Delphi," *Gymnasium* 77 (1970) 1–5; *Forschungen zur antiken Sklaverei* (eds. Joseph Vogt and Hans Ulrich Instinsky; vols. 1–4; Wiesbaden: Steiner, 1967–71); Henneke Gülzow, *Christentum und Sklaverei in den ersten drei Jahrhunderten* (Bonn: Habelt, 1969); Siegfried Schulz, *Gott ist kein Sklavenhalter* (Zurich: Flamberg, 1972); S. Scott Bartchy, *ΜΑΛΛΟΝ ΧΡΗΣΑΙ: First-Century Slavery and 1 Corinthians 7:21* (SBLDS 11; Missoula: Scholars, 1973).

91   See also 1 Cor 7:21f; 12:13; Gal 4:1; Eph 6:8; Col 3:11; Rev 6:15; 13:16; 19:18; Ign. *Rom.* 4.3.

92   Chrysostom, however, clearly expressed the possibility of a revolutionary interpretation, but he shied away from it. On Gal 3:28 (tr. Philip Schaff, *A Select Library of the Nicene and Post-Nicene Fathers of the Christian Church* 13 [Grand Rapids: Eerdmans, 1956] 30) he says: "What can be more awful than these words! He that was a Greek, or Jew, or bondman yesterday, carries about with him the form, not of an Angel or Archangel, but of the Lord of all, yea displays in his own person the Christ." In the *argumentum* prefaced to his commentary on Philemon (tr. Schaff, ibidem, 546), he

admits that there is a revolutionary interpretation of the matter: "But now many are reduced to the necessity of blasphemy, and of saying Christianity has been introduced into life for the subversion of everything, masters having their servants taken from them, and it is a matter of violence."

93   See the introduction to this section, above.

94   On the Jewish attitude toward slavery, see Str–B 3.562f, 4/2. 698–744; Solomon Zeitlin, "Slavery During the Second Commonwealth and the Tannaitic Period," *JQR* 53 (1962/63) 185–218; Haim H. Cohn, "Slavery," *EncJud* 14 (1971) 1655–60; Hengel, *Judaism and Hellenism*, index, *s.v.* "slaves"; Bartchy, *Slavery*, 30ff (n. 90 above).

95   Cf. the sophistic position as reported by Aristotle *Pol.* 1.2.3, p. 1253b20–24: "others however maintain that for one man to be another man's master is contrary to nature (παρὰ φύσιν), because it is only convention (νόμῳ) that makes the one a slave and the other a freeman and there is no difference between them by nature (φύσει), and that therefore it is unjust, for it is based on force." See Guthrie, *Sophists*, 24, 155–60.

all men free, nature has made no man a slave."[96] This criticism then became part of the Cynic and Stoic philosophy.[97] Zeno's *Politeia* included equality for the slaves.[98] It must be said, however, that this criticism did not carry much weight, since the philosophers lacked the power to implement their ideas. It is, therefore, also understandable that the idea became "internalized."[99] The result of this "internalizing" was the concept that only the "wise man" is really free, while the "fool" becomes the real slave. This view implies that for the Cynic–Stoic philosophy, the social class distinctions were indeed irrelevant;[100] a slave who is a philosopher may be called "free," whereas a freeman who is a slave to his passions cannot be called free. This internalization also made sure that the matter continued to be discussed throughout antiquity.[101] Philo quotes the old doctrine against slavery with approval.[102] He points out that among the Jewish sects of the Therapeutae and the Essenes there are no slaves.[103] One must conclude, therefore, that by the time of the

New Testament the old utopian dream of abolishing slavery was still alive, although the possibilities for implementation were extremely limited.[104] There can be no doubt that the slaves themselves never ceased to regard freedom as their first priority and that they sought to attain freedom by whatever means they could.[105] To some degree, religion was such a means.[106] Some mystery cults practiced equality among the members.[107] In later Christianity, it was the gnostics who put Paul's words into practice. The gnostic work "On Righteousness," which Clement of Alexandria attributes to the gnostic Epiphanes, affirms the old dream: "God . . . does not make any distinction between rich or poor, people or ruler, fools and wise, female, male, freemen, slaves."[108] H. Bellen has called attention to the monastic movement, where Gal 3:28 was taken literally. In addition, radical movements such as that of Eustathius in Asia and of the Circumcelliones in North Africa in the fourth century should be mentioned.[109] Even the famous *Regula Benedicti*

96 ἐλευθέρους ἀφῆκε πάντας θεός, οὐδένα δοῦλον ἡ φύσις πεποίηκεν (Frag. 1, eds. Georg Baiter and Hermann Sauppe, *Oratores Attici* 2 [Zurich: Impensis S. Hoehrii, 1850] 154). See Franz Bömer, *Untersuchungen über die Religion der Sklaven in Griechenland und Rom. Teil 2: Die sogenannte sakrale Freilassung in Griechenland und die (δοῦλοι) ἱεροί* (AAWLMG 1; Wiesbaden: Steiner, 1960) 36f.

97 See Baldry, *Unity of Mankind*, 101ff.

98 See Plutarch *Alex. Magni Fort.* 329A–B (quoted above nn. 71 and 88); Baldry, ibidem, 107f; Ragnar Höistad, *Cynic Hero and Cynic King* (Uppsala and Lund: Bloms, 1948) *passim*.

99 A typical example is Crates' parody in his poem about the city of Pera (Diog. L. 6.85). The name of the city means "Knapsack," a part of the equipment of the philosopher which contains all the philosopher needs; the content amounts to freedom from slavery to passions and vanities.

100 See the sources contained in *SVF* 3, no. 349–366; de Vogel, *Greek Philosophy* 3, no. 1069–1076; also Bodson, *Morale sociale*, 112ff (n. 87 above).

101 See Baldry, *Unity of Mankind*, 135ff.

102 Philo *Spec.* 2.69: "For nobody is by nature a slave." See also 2.122; cf. *Prob.* 48. At the same time, Philo shares the view that "the sage alone is free" (*Post.* 138; cf. *Prob.*, *passim*). See also Goodenough, *By Light, Light*, 70; Heinemann, *Philons Bildung*, 329–45.

103 See Philo *Cont.* 9, 70; *Prob.* 79; Josephus *Ant.* 18.21.

104 See, e.g., Epictetus *Diss.* 2.2.12–13; 4.1–11; 3.22.40.

105 See, e.g., Philo *Spec.* 2.84, about the setting free of a slave: "...grant his freedom to him who is naturally free and grant it without hesitation, my friends, and rejoice that you have found an opportunity of benefitting the highest of living creatures, man, and his chief interest. For a slave can have no greater boon than freedom." On the whole question see Heinz Bellen, *Studien zur Sklavenflucht im römischen Kaiserreich* (Forschungen zur antiken Sklaverei 4; Wiesbaden: Steiner, 1971) 80 n. 566; Bartchy, *Slavery*, 82ff.

106 See for this esp. Bömer, *Freilassung* (cf. n. 96 above); Bellen, *Sklavenflucht* (cf. n. 105 above); Bartchy, ibidem, 121ff and *passim*.

107 See Widengren, *Religionsphänomenologie*, 611.

108 Clemens Alex. *Strom.* 3.2.6.2 (ed. Stählin 2.198): . . . μὴ διακρίνει πλούσιον ἢ πένητα, δῆμον ἢ ἄρχοντα, ἄφρονάς τε καὶ τοὺς φρονοῦντας, θηλείας ἄρσενας, ἐλευθέρους δούλους. Cf. 3.2.7.1, and Adolf Hilgenfeld, *Die Ketzergeschichte des Urchristentums* (Leipzig, 1884; rep. Darmstadt: Wissenschaftliche Buchgesellschaft, 1963) 402ff. See also *Gos. Phil.* 49 (*NHC* II, 62, 26–35; Foerster–Wilson, *Gnosis* 2.86); 73 (*NHC* II, 69, 1–4; Foerster–Wilson, *Gnosis* 2.90).

109 *Sklavenflucht*, 80f, 147ff.

included a provision regarding the emancipation of slaves joining the order, and in that provision allusion to Gal 3:28 seems to be made.[110]

The question is to what extent we can assume such a tendency for Paul's own time and even for Paul himself. Usually it is assumed that his real attitude is expressed in his retention of the social institution in 1 Cor 7:21–24 and in Philemon, and that the literal understanding of Gal 3:28 is a later misunderstanding. It is more likely, however, that Gal 3:28 was the cause of the confusion, rather than a confusion of the cause. Taken at face value when heard by Christian slaves at the ceremony of their baptism, the message could hardly be misunderstood. The running away of Christian slaves from their masters may have been one result of such preaching, and the case of Onesimus in Paul's letter to Philemon may be a typical instance of this.[111] Paul's reaction in Philemon, sending the slave Onesimus back to his master, shows that the baptismal message created social problems with unforeseeable consequences. Paul's elaborate recommendations to protect Onesimus show how painful it must have been for him to take such action.[112] On the other hand, Paul shied away from the alternative of social rebellion which no doubt would have been suppressed violently. Taking the Stoic option of internalizing, therefore, was the most logical way to solve the problem. His recommendations in 1 Cor 7:21–24 and in Philemon appear to take this way out, but the question of how to interpret the Corinthian passage is far from settled.[113] Later, this option (1 Cor 7:21–24; Philemon) was emphasized as the only one and was used to suppress the slave problem for centuries.[114] In spite of the weight of this tradition, however, Gal 3:28 was never completely forgotten: the gnostics, the monks, and even secular legislation remained under its influence.[115]

(c) The strangest of the three statements occurs in v 28c: "there is no male and female." There are several ways in which the statement can be interpreted, but in every interpretation the claim is made that in the Christian church the sex distinctions between man and woman have lost their significance. It is important to recognize that, analogous to the previous statement about slaves and freemen, this statement as well is not actually used in Paul's argument—an indication that we have pre–Pauline material before us.

In contrast with the preceding statements, this one names the sexes in the neuter,[116] which indicates that not only the *social* differences between man and woman ("roles") are involved but the *biological* distinctions. There are no parallels to this statement elsewhere in the New Testament,[117] but an abundance of them is found

---

110 Benedict *Regula* 2.20 (ed. Rudolphus Hanslik, *CSEL* 75.22f): "...quia sive servus sive liber omnes in Christo unum sumus et sub uno domino aequalem servitutis militiam baivlamus, quia non est apud deum personarum acceptio" ("because, whether a slave or freeman, we are all one in Christ and under one Lord we bear equal obligations of service, since with God there is no partiality"). Cf. Gal 3:28; 2:6.

111 See, esp., Bellen, *Sklavenflucht*, 78ff.

112 Bellen (ibidem, 79) thinks that sending Onesimus back to his master was Paul's way of preventing a massive desertion of Christian slaves from their masters προφάσει εὐλαβείας ("under the pretext of religion"), as it was later called. If Bellen is right, this may also be the reason why the Philemon letter was incorporated among the letters of Paul in the NT. It serves the same function as the admonitions to the slaves in the "Haustafeln." On Philemon, see Peter Stuhlmacher, *Der Brief an Philemon* (EKK; Neukirchen: Neukirchener Verlag, 1975) esp. also his chapter on the history of interpretation (58–66).

113 See Conzelmann, *1 Corinthians*, 126–29; and Bartchy, *Slavery, passim*. For admonition to the slaves to "endure slavery to the glory of God" see Ign. *Pol.* 4.3, where it is explicitly stated: "Let them not desire to be set free at the Church's expense, that they be not found slaves of (evil) desire." Less frank are the admonitions to slaves in Col 3:22; Eph 6:5–8; 1 Tim 6:1–2; Tit 2:9–10; 1 Pet 2:18; *1 Clem.* 55.2; *Herm. Sim.* 1.8. See also Dieter Lührmann, "Wo man nicht mehr Sklave oder Freier ist. Überlegungen zur Struktur frühchristlicher Gemeinden," *WuD* 13 (1975) 53–83.

114 See Bellen, *Sklavenflucht*, 81, 147ff.

115 Idem, 81–92, with references.

116 See BDF, § 34, 2; BDR, § 34, 2; Bauer, *s.v.* ἄρσην, θῆλυς.

117 The parallels 1 Cor 12:13; Col 3:11 (see the introduction to this section, above) do not have the line. Cf., however, Matt 19:12; Mark 12:25 par; Rev 14:4f.

in gnosticism,[118] in particular in the apocryphal gospels,[119] in other gospel material from Nag Hammadi,[120] and in *2 Clem.* 12.[121] Often these parallels are presented as sayings of Jesus. As far as Gal 3:28 is concerned we must choose between several options. Paul's statement can be interpreted in parallelism to the others as references to the *social* emancipation of women. Or if we interpret Paul in the context of the apocryphal and gnostic parallels, "neither male nor female" would claim the metaphysical removal of the *biological* sex distinctions as a result of the salvation in Christ. In the latter case, we must then speak not merely of social emancipation but of androgyny.[122] Another, but less probable interpretation would suggest that Paul has adopted Stoic anthropology. The Stoics did teach that women, like all human beings, have the same "nature" as men.[123] However, Paul does not seem to make use of this Stoic doctrine—at least not directly.

Looking at the social situation of women in antiquity, little help is gained for the interpretation of Gal 3:28. General abolition of sexual differences, understood in

118 The Naassenes, according to Hippolytus *Ref.* 5.7.15, have combined various concepts, some of which come from Gal: "For...Attis was castrated, that is, (cut off) from the earthly parts of the creation (here) below, and has gone over to the eternal substance above where...there is neither female nor male [cf. Gal 3:28], but a new creature [cf. Gal 6:15], 'a new man' [cf. Eph 2:15; 4:24], which [*sic*] is bisexual..." (ὅπου...οὐκ ἔστιν οὔτε θῆλυ οὔτε ἄρσεν, ἀλλὰ καινὴ κτίσις, καινὸς ἄνθρωπος, ὅ ἐστιν ἀρσενόθηλυς, tr. Foerster–Wilson, *Gnosis* 1.266, slightly altered).

119 Cf. *Gos. Eg.* 2 (Clemens Alex. *Strom.* 3.92.2 [ed. Stählin, 238 lines 24–26]): ὅταν τὸ τῆς αἰσχύνης ἔνδυμα πατήσητε καὶ ὅταν γένηται τὰ δύο ἓν καὶ τὸ ἄρρεν μετὰ τῆς θηλείας οὔτε ἄρρεν οὔτε θῆλυ ("When you have trampled on the garment of shame and when the two become one and the male with the female [is] neither male nor female"; tr. HSW, *NT Apocrypha* 1.168).

120 Especially close is the parallel in *Gos. Thom.* 22 (tr. Bruce Metzger, in Kurt Aland, *Synopsis Quattuor Evangeliorum, locis parallelis evangeliorum apocryphorum et patrum adhibitis* [Stuttgart: Württembergische Bibelanstalt, 1964] 520f): "When you make the two one, and make the inside like the outside and the outside as the inside and the upperside like the underside and when you make the male and the female into a single one, so that the male will not be male and the female [not] be female,...then you shall enter [the Kingdom]." On this saying, see Jacques–E. Ménard, *L'Evangile selon Thomas* (Leiden: Brill, 1975) 113–15. See also *Gos. Phil.* 78 (*NHC* II, 70, 9–17): "If the woman had not separated from the man, she would not die with the man. His separation became the beginning of death. Therefore Christ came that he might set right again the separation which arose from the beginning and unite the two, and give life to those who died in the separation and unite them." This unification takes place in the sacrament of the "bridal chamber." See also *Gos. Phil.* 73 (*NHC* II, 69, 1–4): "There is no bridal chamber for the beasts, nor for slaves, nor for women who are defiled, but it is (only) for free men and virgins" (tr. Foerster–Wilson, *Gnosis* 2.90f). See further *Gos. Phil.* 71, 79, 103 (*NHC* II, 68, 22–26; 70, 17–22; 76, 6–9; Foerster–Wilson, *Gnosis* 2.90f, 95). On the sayings see Richard A. Baer, *Philo's Use of the Categories Male and Female* (AGSU 3; Leiden: Brill, 1970) 72–74; Ernst Haenchen, "Die Anthropologie des Thomasevangeliums," in *Neues Testament und christliche Existenz, Festschrift für Herbert Braun* (Tübingen: Mohr, Siebeck, 1973) 213f; Kurt Niederwimmer, *Askese und Mysterium: Über Ehe, Ehescheidung und Eheverzicht in den Anfängen des christlichen Glaubens* (FRLANT 113; Göttingen: Vandenhoeck & Ruprecht, 1975) 176ff.

121 *2 Clem.* 12 quotes sayings of Jesus which are similar to those transmitted in the apocryphal gospels (see above, nn. 119, 120) and provides an interpretation. The saying (12.5) about "the male with the female neither male nor female" is said to mean: "he means this, that when a brother sees a sister he should have no thought of her as female, nor she of him as a male."

122 This understanding is presented with good reasons by Meeks, "Androgyne," (n. 23 above) 165–208.

123 See *SVF* 3, no. 254; Plutarch *Praec. coniug.* 34, p. 142E–143A; Clemens Alex. *Strom.* 4.58.2–59.5 (ed. Stählin, 275).

whatever way, is not found in Greco–Roman sources.[124] Strong ascetic tendencies are common, but these do not lead to the abolition of sex distinctions. Some philosophical schools favor equality of women among the members, but this remains exceptional.[125] The situation in Judaism is similar.[126] Thus, Gal 3:28 is the first occurrence of a doctrine openly propagating the abolition of sex distinctions.[127]

It is, moreover, important to take into consideration that the abolition of the differences in all three statements of Gal 3:28 is tied to the "unity in Christ." The question arises, therefore, whether the concept of an *androgynous* Christ–figure lies in the background. To be sure, in the New Testament we do not have explicit references to such a christology, but in gnostic texts it is well–attested. Such a doctrine was also held by several older religious traditions in antiquity.

The old *Orphic doctrine* that Zeus is both male and female played an extraordinary role in Hellenistic times. The old hymn preserved in ps.–Aristotle *De mundo* 401b2 (= *Orphicorum Fragmenta*, Frag. 21a, ed. Otto Kern) contains this line: $Z\epsilon\dot{v}\varsigma\ \ddot{a}\rho\sigma\eta\nu\ \gamma\acute{\epsilon}\nu\epsilon\tau o,\ Z\epsilon\dot{v}\varsigma\ \ddot{a}\mu\beta\rho\sigma\tau\sigma\varsigma\ \ddot{\epsilon}\pi\lambda\epsilon\tau o\ \nu\acute{v}\mu\phi\eta$ ("Zeus is a man, Zeus an immortal maid"). Known already to Plato (*Leg.* 4.715a), this hymn becomes important to the Stoics (cf. Diog. Babyl., Frag. 33 [= *SVF* 3, no. 33]). Later, in Neoplatonism, we find the concept of $\dot{a}\rho\sigma\epsilon\nu\acute{o}\theta\eta\lambda\nu\varsigma\ \mu\acute{o}\nu\alpha\varsigma$ ("male–female monad" [Nicomachus of Gerasa]). As one can expect, this doctrine becomes very important in the Stoic–Neoplatonic monism.[128] Diogenes Laertius (1.3) may sum up what seems to have been a wider understanding: "that all things proceed from unity and are resolved again into unity."

Hellenistic Religions were also familiar with the famous myth in Plato *Symposium* 189 D–193 D, which Aristophanes relates. According to this myth, there were in the beginning three kinds of human beings, not merely the two sexes of male and female. The "third sex" was

---

124 The literature on women in antiquity is of course vast. See for surveys and bib. Johannes Leipoldt, *Die Frau in der antiken Welt und im Urchristentum* (Leipzig: Koehler & Amelang, ²1962); Joseph Vogt, *Von der Gleichwertigkeit der Geschlechter in der bürgerlichen Gesellschaft der Griechen* (AAWLMG 2; Wiesbaden: Steiner, 1960); Carl Schneider, *Kulturgeschichte des Hellenismus* (Munich: Beck, 1967) 1.78–117; Walter K. Lacey, *The Family in Classical Greece* (London: Thames & Hudson, 1968); Klaus Thraede, "Frau," *RAC* 8 (1970) 197–269.

125 Diogenes' demand that sex relations should be a matter of mutual consent does not imply emancipation of women. Epictetus has some strange polemics against "confusing ($\sigma\nu\gamma\chi\epsilon\hat{\iota}\nu$) the sexes" (*Diss.* 1.6.9; 1.16.10–14; 3.1.31ff). See also John M. Rist, *Stoic Philosophy* (Cambridge: Cambridge University, 1969) 54–80; Daniel Babut, "Les Stoïciens et l'amour," *REG* 76 (1973) 55–63; C. E. Manning, "Seneca and the Stoics on the Equality of the Sexes," *Mnemosyne* 4.26 (1973) 170–77.

126 The differences between man and woman in Judaism are the result of their different position in regard to the Torah. See the material in Str–B 3.558–62; Meeks, "Androgyne," 174ff, 185ff (n. 23 above). Philo does not attribute equal status to men and women even among the Therapeutae (*Cont.* 32f, 68, 80, 85–90). The role of women in Qumran is still a matter of controversy (see Braun, *Qumran* 1.40–42, 2.288; Meeks, ibidem, 178f).

127 On the NT in particular see Albrecht Oepke,

"$\gamma\nu\nu\acute{\eta}$," *TDNT* 1.776–89; Gerhard Delling, "$\pi\alpha\rho\theta\acute{\epsilon}\nu\sigma\varsigma$," *TDNT* 5.826–37; Greeven, *Das Hauptproblem der Sozialethik in der neueren Stoa und im Urchristentum*, 123ff (n. 83 above); Krister Stendahl, *The Bible and the Role of Women* (Philadelphia: Fortress, 1966); Thraede, "Frau," 238–69; Meeks, ibidem, 197ff; Robin Scroggs, "Paul and the Eschatological Woman," *JAAR* 40 (1972) 283–303; idem, "Paul and the Eschatological Woman: Revisited," *JAAR* 42 (1974) 532–37; Elaine H. Pagels, "Paul and Women: A Response to Recent Discussion," *JAAR* 42 (1974) 538–49; William O. Walker, "1 Corinthians 11:2–16 and Paul's Views Regarding Women," *JBL* 94 (1975) 94–110; Niederwimmer, *Askese, passim* (n. 120 above).

128 Kern in his edition notes other parallels in Greek and Latin literature. See also Festugière, *Révélation* 4.43ff (n. 20 above). On androgynous deities see *Wörterbuch der Mythologie* (ed. Hans W. Haussig; Stuttgart: Klett, 1973) 1.179f, 190, 200f, 498, 548; Marie Delcourt, *Hermaphrodite* (London: Studio Books, 1961); eadem, *Hermaphroditea* (Bruxelles: Latomus, 1966); Mircea Eliade, *Patterns in Comparative Religion* (New York: Sheed & Ward, 1958) §§ 160–61; idem, *Shamanism: Archaic Techniques of Ecstasy* (New York: Bollingen Foundation, 1964); idem, *Mephistopheles and the Androgyne* (New York: Sheed & Ward, 1966) 78–124; Hermann Baumann, *Das doppelte Geschlecht: Ethnologische Studien zur Bisexualität in Ritus und Mythos* (Berlin: Reimer, 1955).

androgynous: "for 'man–woman' was then a unity in form no less than name, composed of both sexes and sharing equally in male and female" (ἀνδρόγυνον γὰρ ἐν τότε μὲν ἦν καὶ εἶδος καὶ ὄνομα ἐξ ἀμφοτέρων κοινὸν τοῦ τε ἄρρενος καὶ θήλεος . . .).[129]

This myth then goes on to explain the sexual love between the sexes as the result of their separation into two halves and their desire to regain the primordial state of unity, which is accomplished in the sexual cohabitation as the healing of the old wound (ποιῆσαι ἓν ἐκ δυοῖν καὶ ἰάσασθαι τὴν φύσιν τὴν ἀνθρωπίνην ["make one out of two and heal human nature"] [191 D]). The myth in Plato is a parody of older oriental concepts of anthropogony.[130] This myth was known also to Judaism[131] and to the gnostics.[132]

In *Judaism* the situation appears complex. Probably under the influence of the Greek and oriental myths of androgyny, the statement in Gen 1:27 that God created man "male and female" (MT: זכר ונקבה; LXX: ἄρσεν καὶ θῆλυ) was subjected to a flurry of speculative interpretations in Judaism, gnosticism, and in Christianity.[133] The LXX translation of Gen 1:27 was ready-made for interpreting into it, if indeed it is not already contained in it, the myth of the primordial man

(*Urmensch*) who is androgynous. This is done, e.g., in Philo, who may depend upon a middle–Platonic version of the myth (*Op.* 134ff). At the beginning God created a primordial man: "he that was after the (Divine) image was an idea or type or seal, an object of thought (only), incorporeal, neither male nor female, by nature incorruptible" (ὁ δὲ κατὰ τὴν εἰκόνα ἰδέα τις ἢ γένος ἢ σφραγίς, νοητός, ἀσώματος, οὔτ' ἄρρεν οὔτε θῆλυ, ἄφθαρτος φύσει). Man, as we now find him on earth, is different from the primordial prototype, because he exists, among other things, as man or woman.[134] As long as he was by himself, i.e., "as long as he was one, he imitated the oneness of God" (μέχρι μὲν γὰρ εἷς ἦν, ὡμοιοῦτο κατὰ τὴν μόνωσιν κόσμῳ καὶ θεῷ).[135]

Then he met a woman, love overcame them—here we have an allusion to the myth in Plato's *Symposium*[136]—"that pleasure which is the beginning of wrongs and violation of law, the pleasure for the sake of which men bring on themselves the life of mortality and wretchedness in lieu of immortality and bliss."[137] When Philo describes redemption, the overcoming of the sex distinctions is one of the results: man is to become one again. Philo has several ways of description,[138] but it is

---

129 *Symp.* 189 E.

130 On this myth see Perceval Frutiger, *Les Mythes de Platon* (Paris: Alcan, 1930) 196f, 237ff; Richard Batey, "The μία σάρξ Union of Christ and the Church," *NTS* 13 (1967) 270–81; Niederwimmer, *Askese*, 45ff (n. 120 above).

131 Philo refers to the myth in *Op.* 151–152 with approval, while in *Cont.* 63 he rejects it. See Baer, *Philo's Use* (see above n. 120) 38 and *passim*; Niederwimmer, ibidem, 46ff. The myth was also known to rabbinic Judaism. *Gen. Rab.* 8.1 cites probably old tradition which is, however, derived from the Greek tradition because of the loan-word אנדרוגינוס: "R. Jeremiah b. Leazar said: When the Holy One, blessed be He, created Adam, He created him an hermaphrodite, for it is said 'Male and female created He them and called their name Adam' (Gen. V, 2). R. Samuel B. Nahman said: When the Lord created Adam He created him double-faced, then He split him and made in him two backs, one back on this side and one back on the other side" (tr. Harry Freeman, *Midrash Rabbah: Genesis* [London: Soncino, ²1951] 1.54). See also Daube, *NT and Rabbinic Judaism*, 441–44.

132 Most probably the myth is used in the *Exeg. Soul*,

NHC II, p. 131–132 (tr. in Foerster–Wilson, *Gnosis* 2.105f). See William C. Robinson, Jr., "The Exegesis on the Soul." *NovT* 12 (1970) 102–17, 114–16.

133 The basic study on this topic is by Jervell, *Imago Dei: Gen 1,26f im Spätjudentum, in der Gnosis und in den paulinischen Briefen* (FRLANT 76; Göttingen: Vandenhoeck & Ruprecht, 1960) esp. 107ff, 161ff. See also Peter Schwanz, *Imago Dei als christologisch-anthropologisches Problem in der Geschichte der Alten Kirche von Paulus bis Clemens von Alexandrien* (Arbeiten zur Kirchengeschichte und Religionswissenschaft 2; Halle: Niemeyer, 1970); Suso Frank, ΑΓΓΕΛΙΚΟΣ ΒΙΟΣ: *Begriffsanalytische und begriffsgeschichtliche Untersuchung zum "engelgleichen Leben" im frühen Mönchtum* (Beiträge zur Geschichte des alten Mönchtums und des Benediktinerordens 26; Münster: Aschendorff, 1964); Niederwimmer, *Askese*, *passim*.

134 *Op.* 134.

135 *Op.* 151; cf. *QGen* 1.42.

136 See above, n. 131.

137 *Op.* 152.

138 See especially *Mos.* 2.288; *Mut.* 33f; *Som.* 2.70; *QEx* 2.29.

noteworthy that he does not return to the Anthropos myth[139] and does not describe man's redemption as the returo to the *status quo ante*.[140]

The myth of the androgynous Anthropos is of course known to us in a variety of forms from many gnostic sources. Here, androgyny can be attributed to the highest god, to the Anthropos or to the "inner man," and to a number of other divine figures.[141]

How much Paul may have known of these religious traditions is difficult to say. He does not directly appeal to any one of the mythical doctrines mentioned, but this silence does not necessarily mean that he was unaware of them. He may merely mention it, without making use of it. After all, Paul does have a Christ–Anthropos. He also conceives of unity as a sign of redemption, which he envisions as the return of all things into God.[142] Paul makes use of the Christ–Anthropos in 1 Corinthians and in Romans,[143] but not in Galatians. Where he does use the concept, however, he never mentions the questions of androgyny. This situation may explain why the origin of the concept of the Christ–Anthropos and its possible usage by Paul is still so much a matter of dispute.[144]

The possibility, however, that the Christ–Anthropos myth lies behind Gal 3:28 cannot be excluded.[145] In addition, Paul's silence in other places may be explainable, if the whole formula is pre–Pauline in origin. The deutero–Pauline epistles seem to affirm the concept. If the assumption is made that behind Gal 3:28c lies a doctrine of an androgynous Christ–redeemer, the implication would be that the dissolution of the sexual distinctions is coupled with a christology in which Christ figures as the androgynous Anthropos. Being "one in Christ Jesus" (Gal 3:28d) would then be a form of "imitation of Christ" and would follow from the inclusion of the Christian into the "body of Christ."[146] Since Christ is androgynous, his "body" would be also, and so would the Christians who are the members of that "body."[147]

Thus, the hypothesis can be proposed that this doctrine lies behind Gal 3:28, although definite proof is impossible for lack of sources. This doctrine of an androgynous nature of the redeemed Christian seems to be pre–Pauline.[148] Paul never repeats it elsewhere

---

139 Baer, ("Philo's Use," 45ff [see above n. 120]), has shown that the Anthropos myth is used to a limited extent by Philo, but he overstates Philo's reluctance towards myth and the difference between asexuality and bisexuality. On Philo see also J. M. Wedderburn, "Philo's 'Heavenly Man,'" *NovT* 15 (1973) 301–26; Meeks, "Androgyne," 183ff.

140 Philo considers also "Sophia" and "Arete" as androgynous, but he is not eager to discuss the matter (*fuga* 51f). See Goodenough, *By Light, Light*, 18f, 201f, 248f; Baer, ibidem, 62f; Niederwimmer, *Askese*, 137ff.

141 See besides the literature in the preceding notes Ernst Ludwig Dietrich, "Der Urmensch als Androgyn," *ZKG* 58 (1939) 297–345; Widengren, *Religionsphänomenologie*, 83ff.

142 See, especially 1 Cor 15:20–28 and its connection with Col 3:11; also 1 Cor 8:6; 12:6; Rom 11:36. In Gal, cf. 3:20, 22, 26, 28d; 5:14. More explicit are Col 1:15–20; Eph 2:14–18; 4:3–7; etc.

143 See 1 Cor 15:21f, 45–50; Rom 5:12–21; again the deutero–Pauline literature is more explicit (Eph 2:15; 3:16–19; 4:22–24; etc.).

144 See Carsten Colpe, *Die Religionsgeschichtliche Schule* (FRLANT 78; Göttingen: Vandenhoeck & Ruprecht, 1961); idem, *TDNT* s.v. ὁ υἱὸς τοῦ ἀνθρώπου

(8.400ff); Geo Widengren, "Die religionsgeschichtliche Schule und der iranische Erlösungsglaube," *OLZ* 58 (1963) 533–48; Egon Brandenburger, *Adam und Christus* (WMANT 7; Neukirchen: Neukirchener Verlag, 1962); Luise Schottroff, *Der Glaubende und die feindliche Welt* (WMANT 37; Neukirchen: Neukirchener Verlag, 1970); Conzelmann, *1 Corinthians*, 284–86; Käsemann, *Römer*, 131ff.

145 A similar question arises in connection with 2 Cor 5:17: ὥστε εἴ τις ἐν Χριστῷ, καινὴ κτίσις· τὰ ἀρχαῖα παρῆλθεν, ἰδοὺ γέγονεν καινά ("Therefore, if one is in Christ, [one is a] new creation: the old things have passed away, behold the new have occurred"). What does this mean for human sexuality?

146 See also 1 Cor 4:8.

147 Note the contrast to 2 Cor 6:18, where the sexual differences are retained: "and you shall be my sons and daughters" (see Appendix 2, below; also Betz, "2 Cor 6:14–7:1," 98, 106).

148 Is there any relation with the quotation in 1 Cor 7:1 (καλὸν ἀνθρώπῳ γυναικὸς μὴ ἅπτεσθαι, "It is good for a man not to touch a woman")? Cf. Conzelmann, *1 Corinthians*, 115; Niederwimmer, *Askese*, 83ff.

in his letters.[149] Analogous to its answer to the slave question, 1 Corinthians is different and emphasizes the subordination of the woman. The parallel to Gal 3:28 in 1 Cor 12:13 does not contain this line;[150] instead we find the woman "under man" in a hierarchy of beings (1 Cor 11:2–16).[151] The question arises, furthermore, whether the extraordinary space given to the women's issues in 1 Corinthians, especially with regard to the so–called "virgins" (1 Cor 7:25–40), reflects difficulties which arose from the emancipation of the women proclaimed in Gal 3:28c.[152] This may imply that in 1 Corinthians Paul has retracted the Galatian position. 1 Cor 11:11–12 may still use similar words, but in fact Paul argues in the opposite direction compared with Gal 3:28c.

If Paul had any knowledge of an androgynous Christ–Anthropos, he seems to avoid the discussion of the point of androgyny.[153] Perhaps this is parallel to Philo's reluctance to describe salvation in terms of androgyny.[154] If we do not presuppose Paul's knowledge of the myth, however, it is difficult to see how he can have used the language and the concepts without knowing which religious traditions he had thereby introduced. In fact, we may assume that Gal 3:28 lets us take a glimpse into the otherwise hidden beginnings of Christianity in Galatia. These beginnings may have been connected with teachings which later appear only in gnostic circles.[155] While Paul admits the radical implications in Galatians, he has obviously changed his position in 1 Corinthians, and it may not be accidental that the whole matter is dropped in Romans.

(d) The last line (v 28d) of the composition 3:26–28 is remarkably parallel to the first line (v 26).[156] But there are also differences. In v 26 the Galatians were told, "for you are all sons of God," and in v 28a–c the claim was made that all forms of discrimination are abolished. These changes are now justified by the final line: "for you are all one in Christ Jesus" ($\pi\acute{a}\nu\tau\epsilon\varsigma$ $\gamma\grave{a}\rho$ $\acute{v}\mu\epsilon\hat{\imath}\varsigma$ $\epsilon\hat{\imath}\varsigma$ $\acute{\epsilon}\sigma\tau\epsilon$ $\acute{\epsilon}\nu$ $X\rho\iota\sigma\tau\hat{\omega}$ $\mathrm{'I}\eta\sigma o\hat{v}$).[157] While in v 26 the inclusiveness is emphasized, v 28d stresses the oneness. Clearly this "oneness" corresponds to the oneness of God (3:20), the oneness of Christ (3:16), the one apostle (1:1, 10–12), and the one gospel (see 1:6–9; 2:7–8; 5:14). Paul does not explain in detail what he means by being "one in Christ Jesus,"[158] but we can infer this from Rom 10:4 ("the many of us are one body in Christ" [$o\acute{\iota}$ $\pi o\lambda\lambda o\grave{\iota}$ $\acute{\epsilon}\nu$ $\sigma\hat{\omega}\mu\acute{a}$ $\acute{\epsilon}\sigma\mu\epsilon\nu$ $\acute{\epsilon}\nu$ $X\rho\iota\sigma\tau\hat{\omega}$]). Paul does not use the concept of $\sigma\hat{\omega}\mu a$ $X\rho\iota\sigma\tau o\hat{v}$ ("body

---

149 This has been shown convincingly by Jervell, *Imago Dei*, 293f, 310ff. However, he wants to restrict the women's equality in Corinth to their "religious status" and rules out social emancipation (293 n. 405, 298f). This limitation is certainly artificial. See also Thraede, "Frau," *RAC* 8.238–39.

150 Neither does it occur in Col 3:11.

151 The deutero–Pauline epistles affirm the women's subordination (Col 3:18; Eph 5:21–33 [Christ is the bridegroom, the church the bride, and the institution of marriage is its imitation on earth]; Tit 2:5). See also Thraede, "Frau," *RAC* 8.239ff; Meeks, "Androgyne," 197ff; Niederwimmer, *Askese*, 124ff.

152 See esp. 1 Cor 6:12–20; 7:1–40; 11:2–16; 14:33–35. Cf. Niederwimmer, ibidem, 74ff.

153 A special problem arises because of the concept of Christ as the bridegroom (2 Cor 11:2–4; also Eph 5:22–33); see Niederwimmer, ibidem, 58ff, 134f.

154 See above n. 139.

155 See Walter Schmithals (*Gnosticism in Corinth* [tr. John C. Steely; Nashville and New York: Abingdon, 1971] 239f), who assumes that Gal 3:26–28 is "a liturgical piece of gnostic origin" (239 n. 162); Niederwimmer, *Askese*, 177, 178, 183 n. 83.

156 See the introduction to this section above.

157 The formal composition speaks against the textual variants. ℵ A read $\ddot{a}\pi a\nu\tau\epsilon\varsigma$ instead of $\pi\acute{a}\nu\tau\epsilon\varsigma$. The reading $\acute{\epsilon}\sigma\tau\epsilon$ $X\rho\iota\sigma\tau o\hat{v}$ $\mathrm{'I}\eta\sigma o\hat{v}$ ("you belong to Christ Jesus") which is represented by P⁴⁶ (ℵ*) A may be a harmonization with Gal 3:29.

158 Cf. Justin *Dial.* 116.3: "we who through the name of Jesus have become as one man..." ($\acute{\omega}\varsigma$ $\epsilon\hat{\imath}\varsigma$ $\ddot{a}\nu\theta$-$\rho\omega\pi o\varsigma$); cf. also *Odes Sol.* 41.13–15; the unidentified quotation in Carl Schmidt's edition of the *Unbekanntes altgnostisches Werk* (GCS, *Koptisch-gnostische Schriften* 1), chap. 11, 351 lines 5–6: "Und sie wurden alle eins, wie geschrieben steht: 'Sie wurden alle eins in dem Einzigen Alleinigen'" ("And they all became one, as it is written: 'They all became one in the One and Only'"). On the formula "in Christ" see above on 2:17.

of Christ")[159] in Galatians, but he seems to presuppose it here, as also in the parenetical section.[160]

■ **29** Paul now draws the conclusion from 3:26–28 with regard to the whole argument which began in 3:6: "if, however, you belong to Christ, then you are Abraham's offspring, heirs according to [the] promise" (εἰ δὲ ὑμεῖς Χριστοῦ, ἄρα τοῦ Ἀβραὰμ σπέρμά ἐστε, κατ' ἐπαγγελίαν κληρονόμοι). Generally, on the basis of 3:26–28 Paul is now able to say that "Christ" includes all those who belong to Christ, because they constitute the "one body of Christ."[161] In 3:29, the conditional protasis sums up 3:26–28 by now using the genitive construction "to be Christ's" instead of the expression "in Christ Jesus." This shows that the two phrases are not different in meaning.[162] The apodosis consists of two conclusions,[163] the first of which confirms the thesis presented in 3:16, that Scripture refers to Christ when it refers to "Abraham's seed," to a unity (εἷς) and not to a plurality.[164] Therefore, the second conclusion can state that as believers in Christ the Galatians are indeed "the heirs according to the promise." God's promise to Abraham has come to fulfillment in them, and they are "the sons of Abraham" (see 3:6–14, 18, 22).[165] The last conclusion also leads to the opening of the next section, with the term κληρονόμος ("heir") serving as the link (see 4:1, 7, 23, 28, 30, 31).

---

159 See for this concept also Rom 12:4f; 1 Cor 10:17; 12:4–31; etc. On the whole see also Eduard Schweizer, "σῶμα κτλ.," *TDNT* 7.1064–74. Bultmann, *Theology*, § 15, 4e; § 34, 2–3; Conzelmann, *Outline*, 260–65. Robert H. Gundry, *Sōma in Biblical Theology, with Emphasis on Pauline Anthropology* (SNTSMS 29; Cambridge: Cambridge University, 1976) 223ff.

160 Cf. Gal 5:13f; 6:2, 10, 15.

161 Perhaps those witnesses (F G 33 *al*) which read v 28 the neuter ἕν instead of the masculine εἷς think of ἓν σπέρμα v 29 (3:16). See Burton, p. 208.

162 The concept of Χριστοῦ εἶναι ("be Christ's, belong to Christ") is Pauline. Cf. Gal 5:24; 1 Cor 1:12; 3:23; 15:23; 2 Cor 10:7; Rom 8:9. See Schmithals *Gnosticism*, 199ff; Dieter Georgi, *Die Gegner des Paulus im 2. Korintherbrief* (WMANT 11; Neukirchen-Vluyn: Neukirchener Verlag, 1964) 227ff; Betz, *Nachfolge*, 172f; Walter Grundmann, "χρίω," *TDNT* 9.547–52.

163 Cf. for conclusions with ἄρα Gal 2:17, 21; 5:11. See also the conclusions in 3:14, 18, 24f; 4:7, 31.

164 Cf. also Gal 3:20, 28d.

165 Schlier (p. 175) interprets the genitive "to be Christ's" on the basis of Rom 8:8f (1 Cor 3:16; 12:16; Gal 5:24f) as "the possession of the sacramental πνεῦμα Χριστοῦ" ("Spirit of Christ"), or also the being of Christ "in us." Although Paul does not mention the Spirit at this point, the underlying thought is of course that the experience of the Spirit (cf. 3:1–5), "being in Christ" and "belonging to Christ," point to one and the same thing.

4

Probatio: The Fourth Argument—Proofs

1   I tell [you this as an illustration]: as long
     as he is a minor, the heir is no different
     than a slave, although he is lord of all,[1]
     2/ but he is under guardians and
     administrators until the time fixed by
     the father. 3/ So with us also: when
     we were minors, we were enslaved
     under the "elements of the world."[2]
     4/ When, however, the fullness of the
     time[3] had come, God sent his son, born
     by [a] woman, put under [the] Law, 5/
     in order that he might redeem those
     who are under [the] Law, in order that
     we might receive the adoption as sons.
     6/ And, since you are sons, God sent
     the spirit of his son into our hearts,
     crying out "Abba! Father!" 7/
     Therefore, you are no longer a slave
     but a son, and if a son [then] also an
     heir through God.

Analysis

The section 4:1–7 contains a discussion of what Paul
had set forth in 3:26–28 (29). First, he draws on an
illustrative comparison from the practise of law (4:1–2).
In 4:3–7, he applies the comparison to the present
situation of the Galatians. This application is further
justified by christological and soteriological "formulae"
(4:4–6). A conclusion (4:7) connects this section with
3:29 and, through 3:29, with 3:1–28 (see especially
3:2–5, 14). Equally manifold are the connections
between 4:1–7 and the following sections of the letter.
The theme of "freedom" is implicitly introduced in
4:3, 5, 7 (cf. 4:22–31; 5:1, 13), while the emphasis on
experience prepares for the emotional appeal in 4:12–
20.

Interpretation

■1 Paul begins his discussion of the situation of the
Gentile Galatians before God (4:1–11) by making use
of a comparison from the legal practice[4] of guardianship. The introductory phrase λέγω δέ ("I tell [you as
an illustration]") is almost parenthetical.[5] The illustration itself is not without its difficulties. Certainly it is
taken from the legal practice as it was known to Paul
and his readers. Paul refers to a practice in Roman law
called *tutela impuberis* ("guardianship for a minor"),
specifically the *tutela testamentaria* ("guardianship established by testament").[6] According to this institution
the *paterfamilias* appoints one or more guardians for his
children who are entitled to inherit his property after
his death. During the period of time[7] in which the heir

---

1   I.e.: "the inheritance." Cf. *RSV, NEB* which supple-
     ment "the estate."

2   Translations use paraphrases to render the technical
     expression. *RSV, NEB*: "the elemental spirits of the
     universe." *NEB* suggests as alternatives: "the ele-
     ments of the natural world," or "elementary ideas
     belonging to this world." *JB* has "the elemental
     principles of this world."

3   *JB* conforms the translation to v 2: "when the
     appointed time came." Cf. *NEB*: "when the term
     was completed."

4   See, for other comparisons from law, Gal 3:15,
     Rom 7:1–4.

5   Cf. Gal 3:17; 5:16; also 3:15; 5:2; 1 Cor 1:12; 7:8.
     See BDF, § 465 (2); BDR, § 465.

6   On this legal institution and for further literature,
     see Erich Sachers, "Tutela," PW 2 (Reihe 7 [1948])

1497–1599; Mitteis–Wilcken, *Papyruskunde*, 2.1,
231–56; 2.2, 340–83; Raphael Taubenschlag, *The
Law of Greco-Roman Egypt in the Light of the Papyri
332 B.C.–640 A.D.* (Warsaw: Pánstwowe Wydawnictwo Naukowe, ²1955) 157ff; Max Kaser, *Das
Römische Privatrecht* (HKAW 10.3.3.1; Munich:
Beck,² 1971) 1.83ff, 352ff; Alan Watson, *The Law of
Persons in the Later Roman Republic* (Oxford: Clarendon, 1967) 114ff.

7   Cf. Gal 4:4 (τὸ πλήρωμα τοῦ χρόνου); on ἐφ' ὅσον
     χρόνον see Rom 7:1; 1 Cor 7:39; and Bauer, *s.v.*
     ἐπί, III, 2, b.

(δ $\kappa\lambda\eta\rho o\nu\delta\mu o\varsigma$)[8] is a minor ($\nu\eta\pi\iota o\varsigma$)[9] he is potentially the legal owner (δ $\kappa\upsilon\rho\iota o\varsigma$)[10] of the inheritance,[11] but he is for the time being prevented from disposing of it. Although he is legally (potentially) the owner of it all, he appears not to be different from a slave ($o\upsilon\delta\epsilon\nu$ $\delta\iota\alpha$-$\phi\epsilon\rho\epsilon\iota$ $\delta o\upsilon\lambda o\upsilon$). To be sure, this comparison must be taken *cum granu salis*.[12] The similarity between the minor and the slave is one of appearance only. The point Paul wants to make is, however, clear: both, the minor and the slave, lack the capacity of self–determination.[13]

■ **2** As a minor, the heir is under the tutelage of "tutors [= English 'guardians'] and administrators" ($\upsilon\pi\delta$ $\epsilon\pi\iota\tau\rho\delta\pi o\upsilon\varsigma$ $\kappa\alpha\iota$ $o\iota\kappa o\nu\delta\mu o\upsilon\varsigma$), to whom the inheritance is

entrusted, and who conduct business affairs for him. This situation lasts to a point fixed by the father in his testament, at which the guardianship is to be terminated. At this time the heir is given free access to the inheritance, and the *tutor* is to him like any other person.

The difficulties with this illustration are minor and are perhaps caused by the influence which the application (4:3–4) has exerted upon it.[14] That the heir is given more than one *tutor* is legally possible,[15] but the association of $\epsilon\pi\iota\tau\rho o\pi o\varsigma$ and $o\iota\kappa o\nu\delta\mu o\varsigma$ is somewhat awkward; the former is the legally required term for "tutor"[16] while the latter is simply an administrative term with no legal connotations ("administrator").[17] If Paul had wanted to name the two existing legal

---

8   On this legal term see Gal 3:29; 4:7; and Werner Foerster, "$\kappa\lambda\eta\rho o\nu\delta\mu o\varsigma$," *TDNT* 3.767–85; Bauer, *s.v.* 1; Taubenschlag, *Law*, 181ff; James Hester, "The 'Heir' and Heilsgeschichte: A Study of Galatians 4:1ff," in *Oikonomia: Heilsgeschichte als Thema der Theologie, Oscar Cullmann zum 65. Geburtstag gewidmet* (Hamburg–Bergstedt: Reich, 1967) 118–25.

9   This legal term (Gal 4:1; 1 Cor 13:11) is used in the NT mostly in a figurative way in parenetical contexts (see Gal 4:3; Rom 2:20; 1 Cor 3:1; 1 Thess 2:7; Eph 4:14; etc.). See Walter Bauer, "Mündige und Unmündige bei dem Apostel Paulus" (1902, now in *Aufsätze und kleine Schriften* [Tübingen: Mohr, Siebeck, 1967] 122–54); Bauer, *s.v.*, 2; Georg Bertram, "$\nu\eta\pi\iota o\varsigma$," *TDNT* 4.912–23; Walter Grundmann, "Die *NHΠIOI* in der urchristlichen Paränese," *NTS* 5 (1959) 188–205; S. Légasse, *Jésus et l'enfant: "enfants," "petits" et "simples" dans la tradition synoptique* (Paris: Gabalda, 1969) 168ff.

10   On this legal term, see Bauer, *s.v.*, 1; Taubenschlag, *Law*, 230ff.

11   $\pi\alpha\nu\tau\omega\nu$ ("of all") refers to $\kappa\lambda\eta\rho o\nu o\mu\iota\alpha$ ("inheritance"). Cf. the parallel in Mitteis–Wilcken, *Papyruskunde* 2.2, 211 lines 33–34 (quoted by Schlier, p. 189 n. 1).

12   Paul's claim that there is *no* difference is hyperbolic, since legally there is a vast difference between a free person and a slave. Paul coordinates the terms because of his equation of the pre–Christian situation of Christians with slavery (see Gal 2:4; 3:23–25; 4:3, 7, 9, 21–31; 5:1). On the legal situation of the slave, see Taubenschlag, *Law*, 66ff; Watson, *Law of Persons*, 173ff (n. 6 above).

13   See Str–B 3.564.

14   So Schlier, p. 188; Bonnard, p. 83; Mussner, p. 267.

15   See above on 4:1 (n. 6) for the literature.

16   This technical term occurs only here in the NT, but see *CMC* 16.8. See Theodor Thalheim,"'$E\pi\iota\tau\rho o\pi o\varsigma$," PW 6 (1907) 224f; Friedrich Preisigke, *Fachwörter des öffentlichen Verwaltungsdienstes Ägyptens in den griechischen Papyrusurkunden der ptolemäisch-römischen Zeit* (Göttingen: Vandenhoeck & Ruprecht, 1915) 93; Mitteis–Wilcken, *Papyruskunde* 2.1, 248–51; Otto Eger, "Rechtswörter und Rechtsbilder in den paulinischen Briefen," 105–08; Bauer, *s.v.*, 3; Taubenschlag, *Law*, 153, 154, 157ff. The Latin equivalent is *tutor impuberis* ("guardian of the minor"), for which see Erich Sachers, "Tutela impuberum," PW 2. Reihe 7 (1948) 1503–88. In Rabbinic law there is the loan–word אפיטרופוס; see Str–B 3.564–69; Moses Bloch, *Die Vormundschaft nach mosaisch-talmudischem Rechte* (Budapest and Pressburg: Alkalay, 1904); Marcus Cohn, "Jüdisches Waisenrecht," *Zeitschrift für vergleichende Rechtswissenschaft* 37 (1920) 417–45; idem, "Vormund," *Jüdisches Lexikon* 5 (1930) 1248–50; Ben–Zion Schereschewsky, "Apotropos," *EncJud* 3 (1971) 218–22.

17   The term has nothing to do with guardianship, but can designate various court officials. See Preisigke, *Fachwörter*, 132f; idem, *Wörterbuch* 3.137f; Taubenschlag, *Law*, index, *s.v.*; Bauer, *s.v.*, 1; Mitteis–Wilcken, *Papyruskunde* 1.1, 150f; Otto Michel–, "$o\iota\kappa o\nu\delta\mu o\varsigma$," *TDNT* 5.149–51; John Reumann, *The Use of* oikonomia *and Related Terms in Greek Sources to about A.D. 100, as a Background for Patristic Applications* (Diss. University of Pennsylvania, 1957); idem, "'Stewards of God'—Pre–Christian Religious Application of *OIKONOMOS* in Greek," *JBL* 77 (1958) 339–49; Gerd Theissen, "Soziale Schichtung in der korinthischen Gemeinde," *ZNW* 65 (1974) 232–272, esp. 237ff.

institutions for guardianship, he should have used as the second term, κουράτωρ ("curator").[18] Probably, Paul's association of the two terms came about because of the mention of slavery (4:3; also 4:1), since οἰκονόμος ("administrator") can designate the supervisor of slaves.[19]

Another problem arises from the stipulation that the guardianship lasts only ἄχρι τῆς προθεσμίας τοῦ πατρός ("until the time set by the father").[20] Normally, however, guardianship of orphans ends automatically when the child reaches the age of maturity. This date was fixed by the government, not by the father, because the institution of guardianship was regarded as a public office.[21] There are, however, some examples from provincial legal practice in which the testator expressly sets the end of the guardianship at a certain age of the ward.[22] This would imply that Paul was influenced more by legal practice in the provinces than by the standards of Roman law. Another possibility is to assume that Paul was more interested in the application than in the illustration itself, and that the application caused him to make the illustration conform to it.[23] In either case, the meaning of the illustration is fairly clear: the guardianship comes to an absolute end at the date fixed by the law.

■3 Paul applies the comparison in vv 1–2 to the present situation of the Christians: οὕτως καὶ ἡμεῖς, ὅτε ἦμεν νήπιοι ("so with us also: when we were minors"). It should be noted that Paul changes here to the first person plural;[24] what he has to say applies to *all* Christians, whether Jewish or Gentile in origin.[25] In their pre–Christian situation they were all in the situation of minors[26] in the sense: "we were enslaved under 'the elements of the world'" (ὑπὸ τὰ στοιχεῖα τοῦ κόσμου ἤμεθα δεδουλωμένοι). Oepke (p. 129) has pointed out correctly that this association of Judaism and paganism under the common denominator of "slavery under the elements of the world" has programmatic significance. This description of the pre–Christian situation as one of slavery[27] is, of course, to be contrasted with the liberation through Christ.[28] Most important, however, is Paul's concept of τὰ στοιχεῖα τοῦ κόσμου ("the elements of the world"),[29] by which he designates the "slaveholders." A large number of scholarly investigations have arrived at the conclusion that these "elements of the world" represent demonic forces which constitute and control "this evil aeon" (1:4).[30] The Greco-Roman (and Jewish) syncretism of the time of Paul is characterized by a very negative view of the world; the κόσμος ("world") was thought to be composed of

---

18 The term is a loanword in Greek. See Taubenschlag, *Law*, 178, 180, 181.

19 Wilhelm Dittenberger (*Orientis graeci inscriptiones selectae* [Leipzig: Hirzel, 1903–05] 2, no. 669, pp. 395f) has an inscription from Egypt where both terms are conjoined: ἐπίτροπος τοῦ κυρίου ἢ ⟨ι⟩ οἰκονόμος.

20 The technical term προθεσμία ("appointed day, fixed time") is a *hapax legomenon* in the NT. See LSJ, *s.v.*; Bauer, *s.v.*; Preisigke, *Fachwörter*, 147; idem, *Wörterbuch* 2.370f; Schlier, p. 189 n. 6; Giuseppe Flore, "*ΜΕΤΑ ΠΡΟΘΕΣΜΙΑΝ* e *ΤΗ ΠΡΟΘΕΣ-ΜΙΑ* nelle *ΑΠΟΓΡΑΦΑΙ* alla *ΒΙΒΛΙΟΘΗΚΗ ΤΩΝ ΕΓΚΤΗΣΕΩΝ*" (*Studi in Onore di Edoardo Volterra* [Rome: E. Giuffrè, 1971] 1.733–42).

21 See Sachers, "Tutela impuberum," 1587 (see n. 16 above); Taubenschlag, *Law*, 167f; Watson, *Law of Persons*, 139; Kaser, *Privatrecht*, 1.362f; Str-B 3.569f.

22 Taubenschlag (*Law*, 167 n. 56) lists from the Papyri: Pap. Oxyr. 487 (A.D. 156); 491 (A.D. 126); 495 (A.D. 181–89); Fouad 28 (first c. A.D.). He also has further bib.

23 Cf. Gal 3:19–25, 4:4.

24 See Gal 3:26. ἤμεθα is read by P⁴⁶ ℵ D* G 33 *pc*; ἦμεν by 𝕳 𝕸 *pl*, Clement. There is no difference in meaning. Cf. BDF, § 98; BDR, § 98. On the periphrastic conjugation, see BDF, § 353; BDR, § 353.

25 So with many other commentators, e.g., Sieffert, Bousset, Ropes (pp. 37f), Lagrange, Lightfoot, Burton, Oepke, Schlier, Mussner. Others (Zahn, following Chrysostom, Ambrosiaster, and medieval commentators) limit the "we" to former Jews because they say vv 8–10 could not have been applied to Jews.

26 Note that νήπιος ("minor") is now used figuratively. See on 4:1.

27 Cf. Gal 2:4; 3:23–25; 4:7, 8, 9, 24, 25; 5:1.

28 Cf. Gal 2:4; 4:22, 23, 26, 30, 31; 5:1, 13.

29 The concept occurs also Gal 4:9; Col 2:8, 20; 2 Pet 3:10–12. Cf. also *CMC* 16:1–16.

30 The secondary literature is collected in Gerhard Delling, "στοιχεῖον," *TDNT* 7.670–87; Adolf Lumpe, "Elementum," *RAC* 4.1073–1100; Lohse, *Colossians and Philemon*, 96–98 (excursus); Heinz Schreckenberg, *Ananke* (Zetemata 36; Munich: Beck, 1964); Braun, *Qumran* 1.228ff; Alfred Adam,

four or five "elements," which are not simply material substances, but demonic entities of cosmic proportions and astral powers which were hostile towards man.[31] In Judaism, these forces were integrated in the world of "angelic beings."

The common understanding was that man is hopelessly and helplessly engulfed and oppressed by these forces. They play capricious games with man from the time of his entering into the world until his departure. While working inside of man, they make up the body, yet they also encounter him from the outside, in that he has terrible and traumatic experiences of whatever "Fate" (*Tyche*—this word would normally be used by the Greeks) has in store. Under such conditions life is not life at all but a daily death.[32] In many ancient cults, cultic measures were developed in order to soothe and pacify the demonic forces. These included prayers, rituals, sacrifices, astrology, magic, and theurgy.[33]

The concept of "slavery under the elements of the world" can also be illustrated by reference to the context. There the "elements" are identical with those beings named in 4:8 which "in nature are not gods" ($\tau o \hat{\imath} s \ \phi \acute{\upsilon} \sigma \epsilon \iota \ \mu \grave{\eta} \ o \hat{\upsilon} \sigma \iota \nu \ \theta \epsilon o \hat{\imath} s$); they are the "tutors and administrators" of 4:2, the masters of the slaves (4:3).[34] Being "under them" is not different from being "under the Law" (3:22–25).[35] "Slavery" is nothing but the scrupulous observation of cultic requirements (4:9–10; cf. Col 2:8, 16–23).[36] Brief as it is, Gal 4:3 contains Paul's thought about man's situation before God prior to the redemption in Christ, seen of course from the point of view of Christian faith.[37]

■ 4 In describing redemption from slavery Paul seems to make use of traditional christological statements. These appear to be formulaic in nature and can be found elsewhere in Paul[38] and in John.[39] Recent

"Die sprachliche Herkunft des Wortes Elementum," *NovT* 6 (1963) 229–32; Andrew J. Bandstra, *The Law and the Elements of the World* (Kampen: Kok, 1964); Eduard Schweizer, "Die 'Elemente der Welt' Gal 4, 3.9; Kol 2, 8.20," in *Verborum Veritas, Festschrift für G. Stählin* (Wuppertal: Brockhaus, 1970) 245–59 (also in *Beiträge*, 147–63); Gerhard Münderlein, *Die Überwindung der Mächte: Studien zu theologischen Vorstellungen des apokalyptischen Judentums und bei Paulus* (Zurich: Selbstverlag, 1971) 90–96; Johannes Lähnemann, *Der Kolosserbrief* (StNT 3; Gütersloh: Mohn, 1971) 89ff. Alf Thomas Kraabel, *Judaism in Asia Minor Under the Roman Empire* (Th.D. Thesis; Harvard Divinity School, 1968) 145; Mussner, pp. 291–303.

31   Schlier, p. 191 n. 3; Delling, "$\sigma \tau o \iota \chi \epsilon \hat{\imath} o \nu$," *TDNT* 7.676–77; Schweizer, Münderlein, Herman Ridderbos (*Paul: An Outline of His Theology* [tr. John R. de Witt; Grand Rapids: Eerdmans, 1975] 148f) express doubts that the "elements" were thought to be "personal," and prefer a materialist explanation of those "elements." See also Eckert, *Die urchristliche Verkündigung*, 126ff. But insofar as the term "personal" can be attributed to demons, they certainly were. See also the material in Hans Dieter Betz, "On the Problem of the Religio-Historical Understanding of Apocalypticism," *JTC* 6 (1969) 134–56; Griffiths, *Apuleius of Madauros*, 301–303.

32   See Rom 7:24; 2 Cor 4:11f; 7:10. On the subject see Rudolf Bultmann, "$\theta \acute{\alpha} \nu \alpha \tau o s, \theta \alpha \nu \alpha \tau \acute{o} \omega, \theta \nu \eta \tau \acute{o} s$," *TDNT* 3.7–22; idem, *Theology*, §§ 21–27; Conzelmann, *Outline*, 23; Güttgemanns, *Apostel, passim*;

Betz, *Nachfolge*, esp. 169ff.

33   Still unsurpassed is the compendium of matters related to these subjects by Theodor Hopfner, *Griechisch-ägyptischer Offenbarungszauber* (2 vols.; Leipzig: Haessel, 1921, 1924; republished Amsterdam: Hakkert, 1974). See also Jonas, *Gnosis*, 1, 2.1; idem, *Gnostic Religion*.

34   Cf. 1 Cor 8:4–6; Conzelmann, *1 Corinthians*, 142–45.

35   Cf. Gal 3:10, 4:5. Paul's position, however, is different from gnostics like Cerinthus, according to whom the world was not created by the supreme God, but by inferior angels which also gave the law (Irenaeus *Adv. haer.* 1.26.1; Epiphanius *Anaceph.* 28.1.3).

36   In Col 2:8, the word is "ensnare" ($\sigma \upsilon \lambda \alpha \gamma \omega \gamma \epsilon \hat{\imath} \nu$). See the commentary by Lohse, *Colossians and Philemon*, 94, 114–31; also the parallels noted in *PECL* 1.17, 33, 239, 294, 300. The relationship between Gal and Col is a problem in itself; cf. Vielhauer, *Geschichte*, 115f, 192–95.

37   It should be noted that Paul has discussed these ideas in greater detail in Rom, esp. 5:12–7:24.

38   A longer statement, probably also pre-Pauline in origin and containing an entire christology and soteriology, is found in Rom 8:3–4; cf. also Rom 8:14–17, 23; Mark 12:1–12 par. For other christological formulae in Gal, see 1:4; 2:20; 3:13 (for the relationship between 3:13 and 4:4f, see the discussion above on 3:13).

39   John 3:16f; 1 John 4:9 (cf. 4:10, 14).

investigations[40] have tried to establish the nature and origin of these formulae. Taken by itself, the formula in Gal 4:4–5 is dogmatic and christological in structure. Still unclear is whether Paul has included the formula in the present text with or without change, how far the pre–Pauline formula extends, whether it belonged together with 4:6, and from which original context it came.[41] The following can be stated with some degree of probability:[42]

The statement vv 4–5 is a highly complex entity. It begins with a temporal clause (4a) and then states God's act of sending his son (4b). This is followed by two parallel statements, in form of attached participles, providing a kind of "definition" of the son (4c–d). Verse 5 adds two parallel ἵνα–clauses, containing soteriological doctrine.

The temporal clause (4a) now specifies what Paul had meant by the "time fixed by the father" (4:2; cf. also 3:23, 25): ὅτε δὲ ἦλθεν τὸ πλήρωμα τοῦ χρόνου ("when, however, the fullness of time had come"). The phrase "the fullness of time" is found only here in Paul, but belongs to the Jewish and Christian eschatological language[43] which Paul shared.[44]

God's redemptive act is described by the phrase "God sent his son" (ἐξαπέστειλεν ὁ θεὸς τὸν υἱὸν αὐτοῦ). This act, however, is only the first of two: God's sending of his son, and then of the spirit of his son (cf. v 6).[45] Generally speaking, the concept of a deity sending his or her representative as a "redeemer" into the world is widely known in various forms and by various religious cults in antiquity.[46] These concepts do not automatically presuppose a "preexistence" idea,[47]

40   See Kramer, *Christ, Lord, Son of God*, § 25; Eduard Schweizer, "Zum religionsgeschichtlichen Hintergrund der 'Sendungsformel' Gal 4:4f; Rom 8:3f; John 3:16f; 1 John 4:9," *ZNW* 57 (1966) 199–210; (also in *Beiträge*, 83–95); idem, "υἱός κτλ.," *TDNT* 8.374ff; Luz, *Geschichtsverständnis*, 282f, following with some skepticism; Blank, *Paulus und Jesus*, 260ff; Mussner, pp. 271–74. Klaus Wengst (*Christologische Formeln*, 59) denies the existence of the formula, but fails to explain the undeniable similarities.

41   Eduard Schweizer has suggested it originated in a combination of Jewish Hellenistic wisdom speculation and christology. See, apart from the article mentioned in n. 40 above, his "Zur Herkunft der Präexistenzvorstellung bei Paulus," in *Neotestamentica* (Zurich and Stuttgart: Zwingli–Verlag, 1963) 105–09; idem, "Aufnahme und Korrektur jüdischer Sophia–Christologie im Neuen Testament (ibidem, 110–21); idem, "υἱός κτλ.," 374–76; also André Feuillet, *Le Christ, Sagesse de Dieu d'après les épîtres pauliniennes* (Paris: Gabalda, 1966) with extensive bib.; Felix Christ, *Jesus-Sophia. Die Sophia-Christologie bei den Synoptikern* (AThANT 57; Zurich: Zwingli–Verlag, 1970); Burton L. Mack, *Logos und Sophia. Untersuchungen zur Weisheitstheologie im hellenistischen Judentum* (SUNT 10; Göttingen: Vandenhoeck & Ruprecht, 1973).

42   A possible *formal* origin may be indicated by the doxology at the end of *2 Clem.* (20.5). See Karl P. Donfried, *The Setting of Second Clement in Early Christianity* (NovTSup 38; Leiden: Brill, 1974) 187–89.

43   Cf. Eph 1:10; Mark 1:15; 16:14 (*v.l.*); John 7:8; Heb 1:2. See Str–B 3.570; Gerhard Delling, "πλήρης," *TDNT* 6.283ff, esp. 303–04; Mussner

(p. 269 n. 114) notes parallels from Qumran (1QS 4.18f; 1QM 14.14; 1QpHab 7.13).

44   See Gal 1:4, 15; 1 Cor 10:11; 1 Thess 5:1ff.

45   So also Rom 8:3. Different is the pre–Pauline hymn Phil 2:6–11, where the redeemer Christ himself makes the decision to descend to earth and where the Spirit plays no role.

46   For bib. on Paul's concept of "redeemer" see Philipp Vielhauer, "Erlöser II. im Neuen Testament," *RGG*³ 2.579–84; Schottroff, *Glaubende*, *passim*; Widengren, *Religionsphänomenologie*, index, *s.v.* "Erlöser."

47   So correctly Wilhelm Bousset, *Kyrios Christos: A History of the Belief in Christ from the Beginning of Christianity to Irenaeus* (tr. John E. Steely; Nashville and New York: Abingdon, 1970) 208–10; Schweizer, *Beiträge*, 90. To be sure, Paul does have a preexistence christology (1 Cor 8:6; 2 Cor 8:9; Rom 8:3; Phil 2:6–11; different is Rom 1:3f). See Schweizer's articles noted above n. 41; idem, "Ökumene im Neuen Testament: Der Glaube an den Sohn Gottes," in *Beiträge*, 97–111; John Macquarrie, "The Preexistence of Jesus Christ," *ExpTim* 77 (1966) 199–202; Fred B. Craddock, *The Pre-existence of Christ in the New Testament* (Nashville: Abingdon, 1968); Conzelmann, *Outline*, 199–203.

nor are they necessarily connected with specific honorific titles, like "son of God."[48] Therefore, we must
treat these subjects by themselves. In the context of
Galatians, we were told about Christ's "coming" in
3:19, 23, 25, but only the christological statement in
4:4–5 tells us more about this coming. Christ's appearance is described and defined in two extremely concise
statements in v 4b. The statements are formally parallel, but, like the two ἵνα–clauses in 4:5, sequential in
meaning: γενόμενον ἐκ γυναικός ("born by a woman"),
γενόμενον ὑπὸ νόμον ("put under the Law"). The term
γίνεσθαι ἐκ refers to the birth of a human being "out of"
a human mother,[49] while γίνεσθαι ὑπό defines the
conditions of existence of a human being.[50] This statement is puzzling in many respects. Only the second
part of the statement ("put under the Law") fits the

argument in Galatians,[51] while the first ("born by a
woman") is never discussed in the letter. This suggests
that it was part of the pre–Pauline material, taken up
here by Paul in full and without regard to its usability
in the argument. Even if the whole statement reflects an
essentially pre–Pauline christology, its contours are
clearly visible.

This christology emphasizes Christ's existence as a
human being, in particular his being a Jew.[52] As a
parallel to "born by a woman" the phrase "put under
the law" must have originally had a positive meaning,[53]
in contrast to the Pauline context, where it is viewed
negatively.[54] Originally, the statement is not even one
of christology, but anthropology: it is a definition of
human life.[55] A human being is a being born by a

48 Schweizer, *Beiträge*, 91. It is Paul who connects the
concept of "sending" with the pre-existence of
Christ and the title "son of God." On the title "son
of God" see Gal 1:16; 2:20; 4:6.

49 Cf. Rom 1:3, and Moulton–Milligan, *s.v.*; Bauer,
s.v. γίνομαι. I, 1, a; Schweizer, "υἱός κτλ.," *TDNT*
8.383f, 386; Mussner, pp. 269f.

50 Cf. Luke 2.22–24, 39. See Bauer, *s.v.* γίνομαι, II, 4,
a; Schlier, p. 196 n. 3.

51 Cf. Gal 3:13: both passages cannot be harmonized.
In 3:13 Christ becomes a curse at the cross, in order
to redeem those who are under the curse of the law.
In 4:4 Christ becomes man and lives under the law,
and thus redeems those under the law (v 5). How
the two passages relate to each other doctrinally and
historically is difficult to say. Schweizer ("υἱός κτλ.,"
383) assumes that 4:4 and 3:13 are related by the
latter being a "development" of the former; this,
however, is hardly plausible.

52 Difficult to understand for antiquity (cf., e.g.,
Jerome's and Luther's commentaries), the dogma of
the virgin birth of Jesus was unknown to Paul as
well as to his tradition in 4:4. So correctly Schlier,
p. 196; Mussner, p. 270. See also Emile de Roover,
"La maternité virginale dans l'interprétation de
Gal 4:4," in *Studiorum Paulinorum Congressus Inter-
nationalis Catholicus* (AnBib 17–18; Rome: Pontifical
Biblical Institute, 1963) 2:17–37; Heikki Räisänen,
"Die Mutter Jesu im Neuen Testament," *Acta
Academiae Scientiarum Fennicae*, 158 (Helsinki, 1969)
3–217, 17–20.

53 Cf. Rom 8:3, which may reflect also pre–Pauline
ideas. See Käsemann, *Römer*, 8ff.

54 The phrase "under the law" is found also in Gal
3:23 (cf. also 4:5, 21; 5:18; 1 Cor 9:20; Rom

6:14f), but this Pauline usage does not preclude a
pre–Pauline origin and context (against Luz,
Geschichtsverständnis, 282 n. 67).

55 So rightly Schlier, p. 196; Bonnard. On traces of
matriarchal law, see Victor Aptowitzer, "Spuren
des Matriarchats im jüdischen Schrifttum," *HUCA*
4 (1927) 207–40; 5 (1928) 261–97; Joachim Jeremias, *Jerusalem in the Time of Jesus* (Philadelphia:
Fortress, 1969) 351. Cf. Str-B 3.570; also the parallels from Qumran noted by Mussner, pp. 269f
(1QS 11.20f; 1QH 13.14; 18.12f, 16), esp. 1QS
11.20f (tr. Vermes): "Who can contain Thy glory,
and what is the son of man in the midst of Thy
wonderful deeds? What shall one born of woman be
accounted before Thee? Kneaded from the dust,
his abode is the nourishment of worms." See from
gnosticism *Exc. ex Theod.* 80.1: "He whom the
Mother generates is led into death and into the
world, but he whom Christ regenerates is transferred
to life into the Ogdoad." (tr. Robert P. Casey, *The
Excerpta ex Theodoto of Clement of Alexandria* [London:
Christophers, 1934]). Cf. also *Exc. ex Theod.* 67–68;
PGM IV. 518–20.

human mother[56] and subjected to human law—"law" applies of course to the Jewish Torah.[57]

This anthropological definition is given a christological purpose, indicating that Christ's appearance was that of a human being in the full sense of the term. This christology shows characteristic differences with other Pauline christological passages, but it is acceptable to Paul.

■ **5** The purpose and goal of Christ's coming into the world was the redemption of both Jews and Gentiles.[58] It is interesting that the cross of Christ[59] is not mentioned in this passage. The soteriology is stated in the form of two consecutive sentences, each beginning with ἵνα ("so that"), and related to 4:4 chiastically. This kind of sentence is known from other Pauline parallels.[60] The doubling of the sentences is strange and needs explanation.[61] The first sentence refers to the redemption of those "under the Law", i.e., the Jews:[62] ἵνα τοὺς ὑπὸ νόμον ἐξαγοράσῃ ("in order that he might redeem those who are under the Law"). Paul has used the term ἐξαγοράζω ("redeem") before

in 3:13, in order to describe Christ's redemptive work.[63] If the first ἵνα–sentence refers to the Jews, the subject of the last remains an open question. The relationship is probably not one of parallelism,[64] but one of sequence, reflecting the sequence of "Jew first and then Greek"—a formula which Paul uses elsewhere.[65] In the context of Galatians, the two ἵνα–sentences summarize the sequence of Gal 2:15–3:25 and 3:26–29.[66] If this is the case, the question may still be raised, even if it cannot be answered, whether v 5 was part of the pre–Pauline material or whether it was formulated *ad hoc* by Paul.[67]

The second ἵνα–clause in v 5b includes all Christians: ἵνα τὴν υἱοθεσίαν ἀπολάβωμεν ("in order that we may receive the adoption as sons"). Paul had explained before, especially in 3:14–29, how this second clause is based upon the first. The term "adoption" (υἱοθεσία)[68] itself is originally a legal term referring to adoption[69] as sons of those who are not kin by birth. In the New Testament, the notion is always used in the religious

---

56   Cf. Plutarch *Frag.* 177 (LCL 15.314–16) where the birthday signifies "the beginning of great trials and tribulations" (ἄθλων καὶ πόνων μεγάλων ἀρχή). See *PECL*, 321.
57   See the circumcision and presentation of Jesus in Luke 2:21, 22–24. For the significance of Jesus' circumcision in gnosticism and Jewish Christianity, see Walter Bauer, *Das Leben Jesu im Zeitalter der neutestamentlichen Apokryphen* (Tübingen: Siebeck, Mohr, 1909) 74.
58   See Gal 3:26–28.
59   Cf. Gal 1:4; 2:19f; 3:1, 13; 5:24; 6:14.
60   For the references, see the commentary on Gal 2:16; 3:14, 22, 24.
61   The same phenomenon is found also in Gal 3:14; Rom 15:31f; 1 Cor 4:6; 2 Cor 11:12; 12:7. Cf. BDR, § 369, n. 8.
62   Against Burton (p. 219) and Schlier (pp. 196f) who take it to refer to all mankind. But the presupposition that also the Gentiles are "under the law" is unproven, or rather it is a construction on the basis of Rom 2:14f. Paul does not regard the worshiping of the "elements of the world" as observance of the Torah, but observance of the Torah as a form of veneration of the "elements of the world" (cf. 4:9f; 5:1). So rightly Lagrange and others listed by Schlier (p. 196 n. 4).
63   This does not, however, mean that Paul "took" the

term "from" 3:13 (against Luz, *Geschichtsverständnis*, 283).
64   Against Schlier (pp. 196f), who takes v 5a to be the negative, and v 5b the positive parallel. See also on Gal 4:4.
65   So also Mussner, pp. 270f. See Rom 1:16; 2:9, 10; 3:9; 1 Cor 1:24; 9:20f; 10:32. Cf. also Gal 2:1–10; 3:14. Luz (*Geschichtsverständnis*, 283) sees a tension between "individual history" in v 3 and "world history" in v 4f, but these notions are alien to Paul.
66   See above, on this passage.
67   Cf. Schweizer ("υἱός κτλ.," *TDNT* 8.383f) who offers a rather speculative interpretation: the pre-Pauline formula speaks of Jesus' incarnation only, so that Paul supplements it by his doctrine of Christ's "substitutionary death on the cross, 3.13b."
68   On "sonship" see Peter Wülfing von Martitz, *et al*, *TDNT* 8, *s.v.* υἱός, υἱοθεσία, esp. 391f, with a large bib.; Nock, *Essays* 1.85ff, 2.928ff; Werner Schlisske, *Gottessöhne und Gottessohn im Alten Testament* (Stuttgart: Kohlhammer, 1973).
69   On adoption in Greco–Roman law, see Taubenschlag, *Law*, 133ff; Kaser, *Privatrecht*, 1. § 15, and index, *s.v. adoptio*.

sense describing adoption as sons by God.[70] This concept of adoption was widely known in antiquity, where various religions employed it, most notably the mystery cults.[71] In Galatians, "receiving sonship" occurs in the ritual of baptism.[72] Paul also speaks of "receiving the Spirit," without saying, however, that both are one and the same.[73] "Sonship" appears to be some kind of a link between baptism and the gift of the Spirit, which Paul tends to keep apart here and also in Romans.[74] This is evident also from the next statement (v 6).

■ **6** The sending of God's son is followed by a second act, again initiated by God: "and because you are sons, God sent the spirit of his son into our hearts" (ὅτι δέ ἐστε υἱοί, ἐξαπέστειλεν ὁ θεὸς τὸ πνεῦμα τοῦ υἱοῦ αὐτοῦ εἰς τὰς καρδίας ἡμῶν).

Clearly, the ὅτι is causal[75] ("because") and refers back to 3:26. Commentators have argued whether "sonship" is first and the gift of the Spirit second, or the other way around. Additional problems are gener-

ated when dogmatic and philosophical categories are brought in to determine the proper relationship. Schlier[76] interprets the first act, the sending of the son (4:4–5), as the new, *objective* basis for Christian existence, which then is to be followed by the sending of the Spirit (4:6) as the *subjective* experience. Differently, Lietzmann[77] assumes a linguistic awkwardness and translates: "that you are really sons [of God] you can see from this: God has sent . . .". By this translation, Lietzmann has Paul say that the adoption as sons of God occurs through the gift of the Spirit.[78] The conflict of opinions is difficult to resolve, not only because of a scarcity of parallel passages,[79] but also because of the dogmatic–philosophical principles involved. These external categories determine Schlier's Roman Catholic and Lietzmann's liberal Protestant positions.

What can be determined apart from these categories is this:[80] (1) the meaning of ὅτι is causal and refers

---

70 See also Rom 8:15, 23; 9:4; Eph 1:5. On the religious concept of adoption, see Eduard Schweizer, "υἱοθεσία," *TDNT* 8.398; Bauer, *s.v.* υἱοθεσία; Leopold Wenger and Albrecht Oepke, "Adoption," *RAC* 1.99–112; C. F. D. Moule, "Adoption," *IDB* 1.48f.

71 Dieterich (*Mithrasliturgie*, 152) assumed that Paul took the concept over from the mystery religions. See the collection of passages in Wenger and Oepke, ibidem, 105ff. Differently Schweizer, ibidem, 399 n. 15.

72 Gal 3:26f. See also Mark 1:9–11 par. Cf. *Odes Sol.* 7.4 (tr. Charlesworth: "He became like me, that I might receive Him. In form, He was considered like me, that I might put Him on").

73 See Gal 3:2, 14; 4:6; Rom 8:14–16.

74 In Gal 3:26–28 Paul speaks of baptism, but not of the Spirit; where he speaks of the Spirit, he does not mention baptism. Cf. also Rom 6 with Rom 5:5; 7:6; 8:2ff.

75 So most ancient and modern commentaries; see the lists in Sieffert, p. 246; Schlier, p. 197 n. 3; Oepke; Bonnard; Eduard Schweizer, "πνεῦμα, πνευματικός," *TDNT* 6.426 n. 624; Mussner, p. 274 n. 145.

76 To be sure, Schlier (p. 197) stands in a long line of tradition, to which he points by quoting Johann Albert Bengel (*Gnomon of the New Testament* [2 vols.; tr. Charlton T. Lewis and Marvin R. Vincent; Philadelphia: Perkinpine & Higgins; New York: Sheldon, 1864]) on Gal 4:6: "Filiorum statum sequitur inhabitatio Spiritus sancti, non hanc illa"

("The indwelling of the holy Spirit follows the status of sons, not the other way around"). See also Oepke (p. 133) who quotes Luther (1519); Mussner (pp. 274f) who follows Blank (*Jesus und Paulus*, 276) and (without saying it) Schlier. However, the principle problem is that this impressive consensus may be based upon the dogmatic tradition rather than upon Paul.

77 Lietzmann's line of antecedents includes Ambrosiaster, Pelagius (see the list in Sieffert, p. 246), Zahn (pp. 202f), Loisy, Lagrange, *et al.*

78 This is in agreement with Paul's argumentation in 3:1–5, where the experience of the Spirit is used as "evidence." See Lightfoot (p. 169): "The presence of the Spirit is thus a witness of their sonship." Also Eduard Schweizer, "πνεῦμα, πνευματικός," 420–28 (above, n. 75).

79 The parallel Rom 8:15f, to which commentators go for help, speaks of the "spirit of sonship" (πνεῦμα υἱοθεσίας) which has been given to the Christians; this notion eliminates any priority of one or the other. Baptism is not mentioned in Rom 8:15f, while in Rom 6 no reference is made to either sonship or spirit. See also the expression "sons of the divine spirit" (υἱοὶ τοῦ θείου πνεύματος) in *CMC* 62.21f.

80 This position agrees mostly with Lightfoot, while Burton remains undecided. See also Antoine Duprez, "Note sur le rôle de l'Esprit-Saint dans la filiation du Chrétien: A propos de Gal. 4, 6," *RechSR* 52 (1964) 421–31.

back to 3:26, without thereby making "sonship" a principle prerequisite for receiving the Spirit. It is only the categories of "objective/subjective" or "reality/recognition" or "legal/spiritual" which introduce the problem. (2) Paul bases his argument with the Galatian readers upon the fact that they too have experienced the Spirit (3:2–5); what they are in doubt about is whether or not they are "sons of God" already now, although they are not part of the Sinai Covenant. (3) The parallel Rom 8:15–16 does not presuppose a status of sonship prior to the gift of the Spirit. (4) In terms of the phenomenology of religion, the ecstatic experience of the Spirit should be called "objective" evidence, and this coincides with Paul's argumentation, while the concept of sonship is a matter of "subjective" self-understanding.

A number of problems in the text may point to pre-Pauline tradition, perhaps from a baptismal context.[81] Paul names God as the sender of the Spirit, but it is "the Spirit of his son." Not only because of the possible contradiction but also because of later christological

considerations, the manuscript tradition is full of attempts to correct the situation.[82] The expression "Spirit of his son" is unique in Paul, but similar expressions occur elsewhere in his letters,[83] indicating that both are identical: the Spirit "of his son" in effect means the present reality of Christ.

When given, the divine Spirit takes up residence in the human heart ($\kappa\alpha\rho\delta\acute{\iota}\alpha$). This idea is traditional;[84] the heart was considered the organ responsible for the control of the will, and therefore the appropriate place for the indwelling of the Spirit.[85]

Finally, it is not accidental that Paul changes from the second person plural to the first person plural. Since 3:26 he has addressed the Galatians as "you," but now—perhaps because of the traditional phrase "in our hearts"[86]—he speaks about all Christians.

The mentioning of the Spirit also connects Paul's argument again with his prime evidence: the Galatians' experience of the Spirit.[87] It is the Spirit which "cries out" ($\kappa\rho\hat{\alpha}\zeta o\nu$)[88] the acclamation[89] $\dot{\alpha}\beta\beta\grave{\alpha}$ $\dot{o}$ $\pi\alpha\tau\acute{\eta}\rho$ ("Abba! Father!"). '$A\beta\beta\acute{\alpha}$ ("Abba") is the Greek

---

81 See the Introduction, § 6. The origin of Gal 4:6 in baptismal tradition was proposed by Alfred Seeberg, *Der Katechismus der Urchristenheit* (Leipzig: Deichert, 1903; rep. edition, with an introduction by Ferdinand Hahn, Munich: Kaiser, 1966) 225, 240–44; Georg Braumann, *Vorpaulinische christliche Taufverkündigung bei Paulus* (BWANT 82; Stuttgart: Kohlhammer, 1962) 62ff, 73f.

82 $\dot{o}$ $\theta\epsilon\acute{o}\varsigma$ is omitted in B 1739 t sa Tertullian; P⁴⁶ and Marcion (cf. Tertullian *Adv. Marc.* 5.4: "misit spiritum suum in corda nostra…"; cf. Harnack, *Marcion*, 74f*) omit $\tau o\hat{v}$ $v\acute{\iota}o\hat{v}$ $\alpha\mathring{v}\tauo\hat{v}$.

83 Cf. Rom 8:15: $\pi\nu\epsilon\hat{v}\mu\alpha$ $v\iota o\theta\epsilon\sigma\acute{\iota}\alpha\varsigma$ ("spirit of sonship"); Rom 8:9: $\pi\nu\epsilon\hat{v}\mu\alpha$ $X\rho\iota\sigma\tauo\hat{v}$ ("spirit of Christ"); 2 Cor 3:17: $\pi\nu\epsilon\hat{v}\mu\alpha$ $\kappa\upsilon\rho\acute{\iota}o\upsilon$ ("spirit of the Lord"); Phil 1:19: $\pi\nu\epsilon\hat{v}\mu\alpha$ '$I\eta\sigmao\hat{v}$ $X\rho\iota\sigma\tauo\hat{v}$ ("spirit of Jesus Christ"). Elsewhere in Gal, $\pi\nu\epsilon\hat{v}\mu\alpha$ ("Spirit") is used always in the absolute. See Eduard Schweizer, "$\pi\nu\epsilon\hat{v}\mu\alpha$, $\pi\nu\epsilon\upsilon\mu\alpha\tau\iota\kappa\acute{o}\varsigma$," *TDNT* 6.419 n. 570.

84 See also Rom 5:5; 2 Cor 1:22. On the concept of "heart" see Friedrich Baumgärtel and Johannes Behm, "$\kappa\alpha\rho\delta\acute{\iota}\alpha$," *TDNT* 3.605–14; Bauer, *s.v.*; Bultmann, *Theology*, § 20; Conzelmann, *Outline*, 183f; Jewett, *Paul's Anthropological Terms*, 305ff (322f on Gal), with further bib. See Erich Dinkler, "Die Taufterminologie in 2. Kor 1, 21f," in *Neotestamentica et Patristica: Eine Freundesgabe, Oscar Cullmann zu seinem 60. Geburtstag überreicht* (NovTSup

6; Leiden: Brill, 1962) 173–91; rep. in *Signum Crucis*, 99–117, esp. 113. Dinkler assumes that Paul has taken up a formula from "baptismal language."

85 Different is Rom 8:16, where the divine Spirit is associated with the human spirit. See Schweizer (ibidem, 433–35) and Käsemann (*Römer*, 220) who refuse to admit the strange fact. Again different is Gal 2:20, where Paul speaks of the "Christ in me" without mentioning the Spirit. Cf. Schweizer, ibidem, 434–36.

86 The *Textus Receptus*, following several later uncials (Dᶜ E K L Ψ) and minuscules, harmonizes and reads $\acute{\upsilon}\mu\hat{\omega}\nu$, but the stronger evidence favors $\acute{\eta}\mu\hat{\omega}\nu$ (P⁴⁶ ℵ A B C D* *al*). See Metzger, *Textual Commentary*, 595.

87 See Gal 3:2, 5.

88 See especially Luther's long interpretation of this term in his commentary of 1535. Cf. Rom 8:15: $\kappa\rho\acute{\alpha}\zeta o\mu\epsilon\nu$ ("we cry out"). The term has the ring of ecstasy (in Paul only Gal 4:6; Rom 8:15; 9:27). For a gnostic parallel, cf. especially the inspired hymn to the Father in *Corp. Herm.* 13.21, also 13.17–20. For Jewish parallels see Str–B 2.134ff; Walter Grundmann, "$\kappa\rho\acute{\alpha}\zeta\omega$," *TDNT* 3.898–903; Bauer, *s.v.*; Dieterich, *Mithrasliturgie*, 32ff; Betz, *Lukian*, 64 n. 2; Bonnard; Schlier, p. 198 n. 2. For the connection of the term with acclamations (see n. 89), see Erik Peterson, $EI\Sigma$ $\Theta EO\Sigma$ (FRLANT NF 24;

transliteration of אבא, *status emphaticus* of אב (Aramaic: אב), which also serves as vocative.[90] ὁ πατήρ ("Father") is the Greek translation of it, a nominative in place of a vocative.[91] The reason for keeping the double expression is not clear; at any rate, the "Abba" was taken over from the Aramaic–speaking Palestinian church by Greek–speaking Christians.[92] Luther (1535), following Augustine (*PL* 35.2126f) observes "that Paul purposely wanted to use both because of the two–fold nature of the church as gathered from Gentiles and Jews; and that Gentiles and Jews do indeed call God 'Father' in different languages, but the cry of both is the same, since both cry 'Father'." The doubling of the invocation "Father" seems to reflect the bilingual character of the early church. There is no reason to assume that Paul had in mind the "Lord's Prayer," although sever-

al scholars have suggested it.[93] The evidential value for Paul's argument in Gal 4:6 is that the inspired acclamation "Abba! Father!" shows both the inspiration of those who pray and their self–understanding as sons by those who address him "Father."[94]

■ **7** Paul[95] now draws the conclusion from the section 4:1–6 and thereby reaffirms 3:26–29, that is, 3:1–29. If this whole argument is true, then "you are no longer a slave but a son" (οὐκέτι εἶ δοῦλος ἀλλὰ υἱός).[96] The "no longer" has been part of the argument since 3:25 (cf. also 2:20; 3:18). Since Christ's coming, slavery for the Christian of Jewish or Gentile origin is over. Paul has demonstrated this by pointing out the significance of the coming of Christ (3:23–25), by referring to the "baptismal macarism" (3:26–28, and the conclusion 3:29), by discussing the illustration from law (4:1–2)

Göttingen: Vandenhoeck & Ruprecht, 1926) 191–93; Schweizer, "πνεῦμα, πνευματικός," *TDNT* 6.422–24, 425–28.

89 Form critically, "*Abba*! Father!" is an "acclamation" (cf. the acclamation εἷς θεός in Gal 3:20). On the form see Theodor Klauser, "Akklamation," *RAC* 1.216–33; Ernst Käsemann, "Formeln, II. Liturgische Formeln im Neuen Testament," *RGG*³ 2.993–94.

90 On "Abba" see Str–B 2.49f; Gerhard Kittel, *TDNT* 1.5–6; Gottlob Schrenk, "πατήρ," *TDNT* 5.984–85; Bauer, *s.v.*; S. Vernon McCasland, "Abba, Father," *JBL* 72 (1953) 79–91; T. M. Taylor, "'Abba, Father' and Baptism," *SJTh* 11 (1958) 62–71; Lietzmann, *Römer*, on 8:15; Joachim Jeremias, "Abba". *Studien zur neutestamentlichen Theologie und Zeitgeschichte* (Göttingen: Vandenhoeck & Ruprecht, 1966) 15–67; idem, *Theology* 1.61–68, 197; Witolt Marchel, *Abba, Père! La prière du Christ et des chrétiens* (AnBib 19A; Rome: Biblical Institute, ²1971) esp. 170ff; Käsemann, *Römer*, 219f.

91 See BDF, § 147, 3; BDR, § 147.

92 The same form occurs Rom 8:15; Mark 14:36; cf. πάτερ μου Matt 26:39; πάτερ Luke 22:42. The vocative πάτερ alone is found also Matt 11:25; John 17:1; *1 Clem.* 8.3; *Did.* 10.2. See Gottlob Schrenk, "πατήρ," 984ff (above, n. 90).

93 See Gerhard Kittel, "ἀββᾶ," *TDNT* 1.6; Walter Grundmann, "κράζω," 903–04 (n. 88 above); Cullmann, *Christology*, 208f; Jeremias, *Theology* 1.191ff; Oepke, p. 134. Critically, Schrenk, ibidem, 984f, 1006; Schlier, p. 199 n. 1; Käsemann, *Römer*, 220. For a critique of Jeremias' attempt to trace the "Abba" back to the historical Jesus, see Ernst Haenchen, *Der Weg Jesu* (Berlin: Töpelmann, 1966) 492 n. 7a.

94 Cf. Rom 8:15f. See also Ernst Käsemann, "The Cry for Liberty in the Worship of the Church," in his *Perspectives*, 122–37. It has been suggested that Gal 4:6 and Rom 8:14f, 26f provide starting points for a doctrine of a "paraclete." See Nils Johansson, *Parakletoi* (Diss. Lund; Lund: Ohlssons, 1940) 268–73; Rudolf Bultmann, *The Gospel of John: A Commentary* (tr. G. R. Beasley–Murray; Oxford: Blackwell, 1971) 552–55, 566–72; Georg Kretschmar, *Studien zur frühchristlichen Trinitätstheologie* (BHTh 21; Tübingen: Siebeck 1956) 122 n. 4; Johannes Behm, "παράκλητος," *TDNT* 5.813; Schweizer, "πνεῦμα, πνευματικός," *TDNT* 6.425–34, 442–44; Otto Betz, *Der Paraklet* (AGSU 2; Leiden: Brill, 1963).

95 Luther (1535) calls the statement a "rhetorical exclamation" (*epiphonema*), for which Pelikan in his translation rightly refers to Quint. 8.5.11. Differently Luz (*Geschichtsverständnis*, 282), who assumes that also v 7 is "an old (baptismal?) tradition." For previous conclusions, cf. Gal 3:9, 14, 24, 29; furthermore 4:28, 31.

96 Paul changes to the second person singular. This is somewhat surprising, but may be a rhetorical device of the diatribe style. Cf. Epict. *Ench.* 51.1: οὐκέτι εἶ μειράκιον, ἀλλ' ἀνὴρ ἤδη τέλειος ("You are no longer a lad, but already a full–grown man"). See for this and other parallels, Conzelmann, *1 Corinthians*, 226 n. 84; also Schlier (p. 199): "The matter applies to everyone individually." G omits the εἶ. For οὐκέτι, see on 3:25.

and its doctrinal application (4:3–5), and finally by reminding the readers of the inspired acclamation "Abba! Father!".[97] If all of this proves that they are sons of God, than they also must regard themselves as heirs: "if you are a son (then) also an heir through God" (ϵi $\delta \dot{\epsilon}$ $\upsilon i \acute{o} s$, $\kappa a \dot{i}$ $\kappa \lambda \eta \rho o \nu \acute{o} \mu o s$ $\delta i \dot{a}$ $\theta \epsilon o \hat{v}$).[98] The last two words, "through God,"[99] are a reminder of Paul's insistence since the beginning of the letter that the entire process of redemption is the work of God.[100]

---

97 For Schlier (p. 200) Paul's argumentation coincides with the Aristotelean–Thomistic categories of the "objective, general possibility" (4:4f), the "objective, individual actuality" (3:26f), and the "subjective experience" (4:6). This system he then merges with Heidegger's existentialist categories of "being" (*esse*) and "existence" (*existere*).

98 The term $\kappa \lambda \eta \rho o \nu o \mu i a$ ("inheritance") was introduced in 3:18 (cf. 3:22f, 29; 4:1, 28, 30).

99 $\delta i \dot{a}$ $\theta \epsilon o \hat{v}$ is well supported by early and diverse witnesses (P[46] ℵ* A B C*[vid] 33 it[g, r] vg cop[bo] Clement *al*). Other readings stress Christ as the mediator, but this is due to later christological developments. See Metzger, *Textual Commentary*, 595f. For the meaning, cf. the discussion of $\delta i \dot{a}$ $\tau o \hat{v}$ $\theta \epsilon o \hat{v}$ in Philo *Cher*. 124–130, also the gnostic parallel in *Corp. Herm.* 13.21, where $\delta i \dot{a}$ $\tau o \hat{v}$ $\Lambda \acute{o} \gamma o \upsilon$ ("through the Logos") is added at the request of Hermes.

100 For this emphasis, see Gal 1:1, 3, 4, 10, 15, 24; 2:6, 19, 21; 3:6, 8, 11, 17, 18, 20, 21, 26; 4:4, 6, 9, 14; 6:7, 16.

4

8   But formerly, when you did not know
     God, you were enslaved to beings that
     in nature are no gods.[1] 9/ Now,
     however, since you have come to know
     God, or rather to be known by God—
     how can you turn back again to the
     weak and impotent "elements of the
     world,"[2] whose slaves you want to
     become once more? 10/ You observe
     days and months and seasons and
     years. 11/ I am afraid for you, lest I
     might have spent my labor on you in
     vain.[3]

Analysis

Having laid down the argumentative foundations in
3:1–4:7, Paul has now reached the point at which he
can turn to the attack. His goal is, of course, to change
the Galatians' mind and to reverse their present plans.
To accomplish his goal, Paul uses various rhetorical
and argumentative strategies in the following sections.
In 4:8–11 he returns to the method of *interrogatio* which
he had employed at the beginning of the *probatio* section
(see 3:1–5). This passage is followed in 4:12–20 by an
argument based on the friendship theme, and concluded by an allegory 4:21–31.

Interpretation

■ **8** If the previous argument holds, Paul contends[4],
then the present plans of the Galatians must be self-
contradictory. In v 8, he states what he and the Gala-

tians agree to be their pagan past:[5] "formerly, when
you did not know God you were enslaved to beings
which in nature are no gods"—or: "which in reality do
not exist":[6] τότε μὲν οὐκ εἰδότες θεὸν ἐδουλεύσατε τοῖς
φύσει μὴ οὖσιν θεοῖς. It is noteworthy that Paul has
nothing to say about the religions to which the Galatians adhered in the past. Were they worshippers of the
older Celtic Gods? Or did they come from a variety of
cults? Differently from his treatment of Judaism, Paul
avoids references to details of the former religion of the
Galatians. He prefers to lump them all together under
the heading of "the elements of the world" (τὰ στοιχεῖα
τοῦ κόσμου).

Seen in this light, two characteristics mark the Galatians' past paganism: (1) they "did not know God."[7]
This idea, identifying "pagans" as "ignorant of God"

---

1   The translation of the last part of the sentence fol-
     lows *RSV*. Cf. Vg: "iis, qui natura non sunt dii."
     NEB: "beings which in their nature are no gods,"
     and as an alternative: "'gods' which in reality do
     not exist." *JB*: "'gods' who are not really gods at
     all."
2   See the note on the translation of 4:3.
3   So Bauer, *s.v.* φοβέω, 1, a. *NEB* paraphrases: "You
     make me fear that all the pains I spent on you prove
     to be labour lost."
4   ἀλλά ("but") marks the turning point.
5   τότε ("then") refers to the period before conversion
     (cf. Rom 6:21) and corresponds to οὐκέτι ("no lon-
     ger" Gal 2:20; 3:25; 4:7). Cf. Rom 6:20; 7:5;
     1 Cor 12:2; 13:11; 1 Thess 1:9; etc. On the juxta-
     position of τότε/νῦν ("then/now") see Peter Tachau,
     "Einst" und "Jetzt" im Neuen Testament (FRLANT
     105; Göttingen: Vandenhoeck & Ruprecht, 1972)
     12, 80, 81, 86, 87, 113, 127.
6   *NEB* gives both translations (see above, n. 1), but

     translates εἰδότες by "acknowledge," seemingly a
     harmonization with Rom 1:21.
7   See also 1 Thess 4:5 (Ps 78:6 LXX); 1 Cor 15:34;
     Rom 10:3; also somewhat differently 1 Cor 1:21;
     Rom 1:18–23; furthermore Eph 4:18; 2 Thess 1:8
     (Jer 10:25 LXX); Tit 1:16; Acts 17:23, 30; etc.;
     also *Kerygmata Petrou* (ps.–Clem. *Hom.* 2.15; tr. in
     HSW, *NT Apocrypha* 2.117); *Kerygma Petrou* Frag. 2a
     (HSW, *NT Apocrypha* 2.99f); *CMC* 17.1–4. See the
     passages and bib. in Rudolf Bultmann, "ἄγνοια,
     ἀγνωσία," *TDNT* 1.116–21, idem, "γινώσκω,"
     TDNT 1.689–714; idem, *Theology*, § 9; Tachau,
     "*Einst*" und "*Jetzt*," 99, 105; *PECL*, 8–9 and the
     index, *s.v.* "ignorance."

and the converts as "those who know God"[8] comes from missionary language; its roots are in the Old Testament and in Hellenistic Judaism.[9] (2) The Galatians' "enslavement" has its analogy in the Jews' enslavement "under the Torah" (cf. 3:22–24; 4:5). In fact, in one way or another they were all enslaved by the "elements of the world" ($\tau\grave{\alpha}\ \sigma\tau o\iota\chi\epsilon\hat{\iota}\alpha\ \tau o\hat{\upsilon}\ \kappa\acute{o}\sigma\mu o\upsilon$, cf. 4:3). Strangely, Paul goes on to call these "elements of the world" beings which are "in nature no gods."

This expression raises the question[10] whether Paul makes use here of an ancient theory of religion which goes under the name of Euhemerism.[11] Reportedly, this theory goes back most likely to the sophist Critias.[12] He distinguished between two kinds of "divine beings": those $\phi\acute{\upsilon}\sigma\epsilon\iota$ ("in reality") and those $\theta\acute{\epsilon}\sigma\epsilon\iota$ ("by human convention"). The former are "in reality" the astral bodies of sun, moon, and the stars, while the latter have

come about merely "by human convention." Later, this theory merged with the ideas of Euhemeros of Messene, forming a conglomerate of ideas which served to criticize Greek mythology and religion.[13] Long before Paul, Hellenistic Judaism had adapted this theory in its fight against polytheism.[14] Most likely, Paul inherited this polemic from Hellenistic Judaism, either directly or indirectly through primitive Christianity, where it is found as part of its missionary language. Primitive Christian missionaries carried on the same campaign as the Jewish missionaries, when they converted polytheistic pagans to the "one God" (cf. 3:20).[15]

If we assume that this theory lies behind Paul's words, there are two possibilities for understanding them. For Paul as a Christian there can be no doubt that only the "one God" ($\epsilon\hat{\iota}s\ \theta\epsilon\acute{o}s$: 3:20) and "our

---

8   Of particular interest with regard to this concept see 1 Cor 8:1–6 and Rom 1:18–23. See Conzelmann, *1 Corinthians*, 139–50; the material collected by Bultmann (see n. 7 above); Albrecht Oepke, *Die Missionspredigt des Apostels Paulus* (Leipzig: Hinrichs, 1920) 82, 88f; Ulrich Wilckens, *Weisheit und Torheit* (BHTh 26; Tübingen: Mohr, Siebeck, 1959) 29ff; Jacques Dupont, *Gnosis: La connaissance religieuse dans les épîtres de saint Paul* (Paris: Gabalda, ²1960) 51ff and *passim*; Bertil E. Gärtner, "The Pauline and Johannine Idea of 'to know God' against the Hellenistic Background," *NTS* 14 (1968) 209–31; Heinrich Schlier, "Die Erkenntnis Gottes nach den Paulusbriefen," in *Gott in Welt, Festgabe für Karl Rahner* (Freiburg: Herder, 1964) 515–35; Claus Bussmann, *Themen der paulinischen Missionspredigt auf dem Hintergrund der spätjüdisch-hellenistischen Missionsliteratur* (Bern: Lang, 1971) 57ff.

9   See Horst D. Preuss, *Verspottung fremder Religionen im Alten Testament* (BWANT 92; Stuttgart: Kohlhammer, 1970); Juda Bergmann, *Jüdische Apologetik im neutestamentlichen Zeitalter* (Berlin: Reimer, 1908) 11ff and *passim*; Str-B. 3.48–62.

10   Cf. Oepke, p. 138: "sounds almost Stoic." Similarly Schlier, p. 201; cf. Mussner, p. 291; Bauer, *s.v.* $\phi\acute{\upsilon}\sigma\iota s$.

11   On this subject, see Carl Langer, "Euhemeros und die Theorie der $\phi\acute{\upsilon}\sigma\epsilon\iota$ und $\theta\acute{\epsilon}\sigma\epsilon\iota$ $\theta\epsilon o\acute{\iota}$," *ΑΓΓΕΛΟΣ* 2 (1926) 53–59; Nilsson, *Geschichte* 2.283–89; Klaus Thraede, "Euhemerismus," *RAC* 6.877–90, with further bib.

12   Frag. 25 (Diels–Kranz 88 B 25 [II, 386–89]); cf. Plato's critique, *Leg.* 10.889E: $\theta\epsilon o\acute{\upsilon}s, \ldots\ \epsilon\hat{\iota}\nu\alpha\iota\ \pi\rho\hat{\omega}$-

$\tau\acute{o}\nu\ \phi\alpha\sigma\iota\nu\ o\hat{\upsilon}\tau o\iota\ \tau\acute{\epsilon}\chi\nu\eta,\ o\grave{\upsilon}\ \phi\acute{\upsilon}\sigma\epsilon\iota\ \grave{\alpha}\lambda\lambda\acute{\alpha}\ \tau\iota\sigma\iota\ \nu\acute{o}\mu o\iota s \ldots$ ("the first statement . . . which these people make about the gods is that they exist by art and not by nature—by certain legal convention . . ."). See also Menahem Stern, *Greek and Latin Authors on Jews and Judaism, 1: From Herodotus to Plutarch* (Jerusalem: The Israel Academy of Sciences and Humanities, 1974) 53f.

13   In addition to Nilsson (see n. 11 above), see Guthrie, (*Sophists*, 235–47) on Critias (243f); Eric R. Dodds, *The Ancient Concept of Progress* (Oxford: Clarendon, 1973) 8ff.

14   See the Samaritan Anonymous, falsely attributed to Eupolemus (Eusebius *Praep. ev.* 9.17, 18.2 [*FGH* III. C, No. 724]); for a discussion of these texts, see Ben Zion Wacholder, *Eupolemus: A Study of Judeo-Greek Literature* (Monographs of the Hebrew Union College 3; Cincinnati: Hebrew Union College–Jewish Institute of Religion, 1974). See also *Sib. Or.* 3.110–155, 545–560, 721–723; Artapanus (Euseb. *Praep. Ev.* 9.18.1 [*FGH* III. C, No. 726]); Wis 13–15; Add Esth 3:21–22; *Ep. Arist.* 135–137; *Joseph et As.* 13.11; Josephus; Philo; etc. For references, see Bousset–Gressmann, *Religion*, 305f; Hengel, *Judaism and Hellenism* 1.88f, 266; 2.138 n. 638; 176 n. 57; 177 n. 58; idem, in *Pseudepigrapha, Entretiens sur l'antiquité classique* (Fondation Haardt 18; 1972) 323; Edgar W. Smith, *Joseph and Aseneth and Early Christian Literature* (Ph.D. dissertation; Claremont Graduate School, 1974) 162.

15   See 1 Cor 8:4 and the material in Conzelmann, *1 Corinthians*, 142 n. 26; also 2 Cor 6:16, and on this passage Betz, "2 Cor 6:14–7:1," 92.

214

Father" (1:1, 4, 5; 4:6), who raised the Lord Jesus Christ from the dead (1:1), is "in nature God."[16] By contrast, then, those beings which are worshipped in paganism as gods are "gods" only "by convention." This can mean (1) that they do not exist "in reality" (φύσει), but only as human projections. In this case, Paul would conform to the atheist interpretation of the Euhemerist theory.[17] Or it can mean (2) that the beings worshipped by the pagans do not exist as "gods" but are "in nature" (φύσει) "demons". If Paul held this interpretation he would conform to the demonological interpretation, which we find also in Hellenistic Judaism.[18] The identification of the beings which "in nature are no gods" with the "elements of the world" (τὰ στοιχεῖα τοῦ κόσμου)[19] speaks in favor of the latter, the demonological interpretation.[20] This interpretation would mean that those beings do have an existence, but only as inferior demonic entities (v 9).

More can be said when 1 Cor 8:4–6 is brought into the picture.[21] In that passage Paul agrees with the Corinthians "that no idol exists in the world, and that there exists no god except the 'One'." Besides Him, there are only "so–called gods" (λεγόμενοι θεοί). These "so–called gods" do exist and have power, but only to the extent that they are being worshipped. In other words, Paul does not deny that these "so–called gods" exist, but their "existence" consists merely of the superstitious imaginations and projections of the worshippers. This theory about the existence of gods was held not only by Paul, but also, e.g., by Plutarch. Plutarch discusses both the atheist and the demonological version of Euhemerism and shows that they are not mutually exclusive.[22]

■ **9** In contrast to their past pagan ignorance of God, the Galatians are told that they, as Christians, now[23] "know God": νῦν δὲ γνόντες θεόν, μᾶλλον δὲ γνωσθέντες ὑπὸ θεοῦ ("now, however, you have come to know God, or rather to be known by God").

Again Paul provides a description of the "indicative" of Christian existence (cf. 3:26–28, 29; 4:3, 7). The statement appears to have a "gnostic" flavor.[24] To be sure, Paul speaks of "knowing God" elsewhere,[25] also of "being known by God,"[26] but the identity of sonship, liberation from the slavery under the "elements of the world," and acquiring the knowledge of God

---

16   So correctly Richard Reitzenstein, *Poimandres* (Leipzig: Teubner, 1904) 80 n. 4.

17   See also 1 Thess 1:9; 1 Cor 12:2; Rom 1:18–23; Aristides *Apol.* 8–11, 13; *Kerygmata Petrou* (ps.–Clem. *Hom.* 3.23, cf. HSW, *NT Apocrypha* 2.117). The result was that Christians were accused of "atheism" (cf. *Mart. Pol.* 3.2, 9.2; Justin *Apol.* 1.6.1, 13.1; etc.). When K d m Irenaeus [1at] Ambrosiaster omit φύσει, they also prefer the "atheist" position.

18   It is of course found mostly in apocalyptic Judaism; see the material collected in Bousset–Gressmann, *Religion*, 305f; Str–B 3.47–60; Hengel, *Judaism and Hellenism* 1.266f, with notes.

19   Gal 4:3, 9.

20   So also Helmut Koester, "φύσις κτλ.," *TDNT* 9.272.

21   See also 1 Cor 10:19–20, and Conzelmann, *1 Corinthians*, 137–45, 172f.

22   Plutarch takes the "atheist" position in *Superst.* and the "demonological" especially in *Is. et Osir.* (esp. 359F–360A); see *PECL*, 52, and index, s.v. Atheism, Demonology. Another interesting parallel is the discussion in ps.–Heraclitus *Ep.* 4, which is Cynic in character; see the edition by Rodolfo Mondolfo and Leonardo Tarán, *Eraclito: Testimonianze e Imitazione* (Florence: La Nuova Italia, 1972) 315–22.

23   For the meaning of νῦν ("now") cf. Gal 1:23; 2:20; 3:3; 4:29. See Tachau, "*Einst*" und "*Jetzt*," *passim* (n. 5 above). For the *epidiorthosis*, a "figure of thought," see BDF, § 495, 3; BDR, § 495, n. 12; already Luther (1535) notes it.

24   Cf. Pyth. *Sent.* 9 (Chadwick, *Sextus*, 85): βούλει γνωσθῆναι θεοῖς; ἀγνοήθητι μάλιστα ἀνθρώποις ("You want to become known to the gods? Foremost become unknown to men!"). Cf. also 145, and Chadwick's note, p. 169.

25   Paul uses the terminology in Rom 1:21; 1 Cor 1:21, but nowhere else does he define Christian existence as "knowledge of God." Cf., however, 1 Cor 2:6–16; Phil 3:10.

26   1 Cor 8:2f; 13:12; cf. 2 Cor 4:6; also Acts 1:24; 15:8. The language of being known by God appears already in the OT (e.g. Ps 139; 1:6; 37:18; 44:21; 94:11; etc.). See Johannes Behm, "καρδιογνώστης," *TDNT* 3.613.

strongly point toward "gnostic" ideas.[27] Paul assumes also that his readers agree with his assessment, or at least that they did previously agree with it. Having reached this point, Paul addresses to them a question which is the analogy to the dilemma presented to Cephas in 2:14: πῶς ἐπιστρέφετε πάλιν ἐπὶ τὰ ἀσθενῆ καὶ πτωχὰ στοιχεῖα, οἷς πάλιν ἄνωθεν δουλεύειν[28] θέλετε; ("how can you turn back again to the weak and impotent elements of the world, whose slaves you want to become once more?").

Polemical as the question is, it puts a dilemma before the Galatians. If they have followed Paul's argumentation up to this point, there is no satisfactory answer they can give.[29] The two–fold πάλιν ("again")[30] as well as the technical term ἐπιστρέφειν ("turn around")[31] show that in his view they are about to reverse their conversion and return to paganism. Paul reveals at this point that he considers it possible indeed to switch from Christianity back to paganism. But this possibility is in reality an impossibility! It is interesting to see what Paul has to say about a post–Christian religious life. The enlightenment gained by coming to the know-

ledge of the true God cannot simply be shaken off. Return to the worship of the pagan deities would include the knowledge that these deities are "weak" and "impotent"[32] and they are not "in nature" what they are said to be. Therefore, a return to paganism would be more than a taking up again of the "old slavery."[33] Such an act would be irrational, an absurdity. This suggests that for a post–Christian existence Paul leaves open only atheism or superstition.[34] However, this, he tells the Galatians, is what they want.[35]

One will have to emphasize that from the Galatians' point of view things may have looked considerably different. By accepting Torah and circumcision they did not by any means intend to return to paganism. They only wanted to switch from Pauline Christianity to a form of Jewish Christianity which repuired circumcision and obedience to the Torah. In their mind, and no doubt in the mind of the opponents of Paul, such a move was an improvement over the present situation.[36] On the contrary, they might have come to the conclusion that, unless they became part of the Sinai covenant, they never really left paganism. If they had

---

27 But see also Philo *Cher.* 115: "Even now in this life, we are the ruled rather than the rulers, known rather than knowing. The soul knows us, though we know it not . . ." (cf. the context 113–118). Cf. also *Post.* 13; Plut. *Sera num.* 551D (*PECL*, 200); *Corp. Herm.* 10.15; 13.22, also 1.31: ἅγιος ὁ θεός, ὃς γνωσθῆναι βούλεται, γινώσκεται τοῖς ἰδίοις ("Holy is God who wants to become known, and becomes known to his own"); *Odes Sol.* 41.1f: "Let all the Lord's babes praise Him, and let us receive the truth of His faith. And His children shall be acknowledged by Him. . . ." For material and discussion, see Eduard Norden, *Agnostos Theos: Untersuchungen zur Formengeschichte religiöser Rede* (Leipzig and Berlin: Teubner, 1913) 87ff, 287f; Reitzenstein, *Mysterienreligionen*, 66f, 284ff; Bultmann, "γινώσκω," *TDNT* 1.709f; Schlier, p. 202 n. 4, 5; Jacques–E. Ménard, *Evangile de Vérité* (NHS 2; Leiden: Brill, 1972) 28f; Conzelmann, *1 Corinthians*, 141 n. 21; 229 n. 106–08.

28 Text according to Nestle–Aland; B ℵ have δουλεῦσαι.

29 See for the same argument, Gal 2:14; 3:3.

30 Cf. Gal 2:18; 4:19; 5:1.

31 The term belongs to the language of conversion. See 1 Thess 1:9; Luke 1:16; Acts 3:19; 9:35; 11:21; 14:15; 15:19; 26:18, 20; etc.; also Bauer, *s.v.*; Georg Bertram, "ἐπιστρέφω, ἐπιστροφή, μετα-

στρέφω," *TDNT* 7.722–29. In effect, the term in Gal 4:9 means "apostasy" (so also 2 Pet 2:21–22). For the pleonasm, see BDR, § 484.

32 Cf. on Gal 4:3: τὰ ἀσθενῆ καὶ πτωχὰ στοιχεῖα. The expression here seems to come from the context of demonology. Plutarch has extensive discussions about the question, why the demons are inferior compared with the gods. His main reason is that they are subject to passions and even death. See for weakness in demons, *Is. et Osir.* 373D; 393F (*PECL*, 71, 101), and the index, *PECL*, *s.v.* "demonology." A similar case can be made for Jewish angelology; see the material in Betz, *JTC* 6.139ff. In the Pauline tradition, the demonic powers are inferior because they are subjected to Christ (Phil 2:11; 1 Cor 15:20–28; Col 2:10, 15; 1:13, 16; Eph 1:10, 21f; etc.).

33 πάλιν ἄνωθεν ("again anew"). Cf. for this expression Bauer, *s.v.*, 3. On the concept of "slavery" cf. Gal 2:4; 3:28; 4:1, 3, 7, 8, 24, 25; 5:1.

34 See the essay on Plutarch's *Superst.* by Morton Smith, in *PECL*, 1–35. Similar is the position of the *Kerygma Petrou*, Frag. 2 (HSW, *NT Apocrypha* 2.99 f), calling the idolatry of the Greeks atheism, and the worship of the Jews superstition, and advocating Christian worship as a new religion.

35 Cf. Gal 1:7; 4:21; 5:17.

listened to Jewish Christians of the type speaking in 2 Cor 6:14–7:1, they would have understood that obedience to the Jewish Torah, even as part of Christianity, is the only protection against the evil forces of the "elements of the world."[37] Paul's argument holds only if one shares his view that being "under the Torah" equals being "under the 'elements of the world'."

The struggle between Paul and his opponents is really one between two concepts of religion: Paul favors a concept of "enlightened" religion, which is free from cultic and ritual requirements and observances, but is based upon the knowledge of the one true God; the opponents understand their religion as a cultic–ritualistic system of protection against the forces of evil. This kind of struggle is known to us also from other quarters in antiquity, both Jewish and Greek.[38]

■ **10** Paul submits a test which demonstrates that his evaluation of the Galatians' intent is correct. The sentence is descriptive: [39] "You observe days and months and seasons and years" (ἡμέρας παρατηρεῖσθε καὶ μῆνας καὶ καιροὺς καὶ ἐνιαυτούς). The meaning of this statement depends upon the argumentative context. The present tense seems to indicate that the Galatians are already performing those cultic rituals, but this is unlikely.[40] In v 9 Paul had just stated that the Galatians are considering acceptance of Torah and circumcision, but it is clear from the letter that they have not yet done so. Also, the cultic activities described in v 10 are not typical of Judaism (including Jewish Christianity), though they are known to both Judaism and paganism.[41] Therefore the description cannot be a summary of activities in which the Galatians are presently engaged, but in which they would be engaged once they took up Torah and circumcision. In fact, Paul describes the *typical* behavior of religiously scrupulous people.[42]

The description itself is typical and part of a literary topos well–known in antiquity. It portrays the Galatians as conforming to the religious character of the δεισιδαί-

---

36 Schlier (p. 203) does not distinguish clearly enough between Paul's evaluation and what the Galatians really want. As he sees it, the Jewish–Christian propagandists pressure the Galatians to subject themselves again to the powers of the world. The "foolish Galatians" (3:1) do not comprehend the grotesque nature of such an undertaking. It is interesting that in the strange ceremony described in the anti-Pauline *Contestatio* from the *Kerygmata Petrou* (see below, Appendix 3) the elements heaven, earth, water, and air are invoked as witnesses to the vow. Cf. also ps.–Clem. *Hom.* 11.30.2 (HSW, *NT Apocrypha* 2.126): "If you hesitate to do this [i.e., ritual washings], recall to mind how you observed a portion of the purification instructions when you observed inanimate idols. Be ashamed that you now hesitate when you ought to commit yourselves, . . ." Cf. 11.31.1–2.

37 See on this point the Introduction, § 2. C.

38 Cf., *e.g.*, the definition of religion Plutarch gives in *Is. et Osir.* 2 (351E): "For this reason the longing for truth (θειότητος ὄρεξις), particularly for truth about the Gods, is a yearning after divinity, since it involves in its training and intellectual pursuit an acquirement of sacred love which constitutes a holier task than all ceremonial purification and temple-service . . ." (tr. Griffiths, *Plutarch*, 119, with the commentary, 256); see also *PECL*, 38. Judaism's

similar position begins with Hos 6:6: "For I desire loyalty, not sacrifice; the knowledge of God instead of burnt offerings." See Hans Walter Wolff, *Hosea* (Hermeneia; Philadelphia: Fortress, 1974) 120; for the Rabbinic interpretation, see Str–B 1.499f (of special interest is *'Abot R. Nat. A*, chap. 4). In the NT, see Matt 9:9–13; 12:1–8.

39 The majority of the witnesses have a statement of fact. P[46] reads the participle παρατηροῦντες and therefore regards the sentence as part of the question, depending upon θέλετε. This solves the problem created by the contradiction between v 9 ("you want") and v 10 ("you [presently] observe"). Cf. BDR, § 316 n. 3.

40 So correctly Eckert, *Die urchristliche Verkündigung*, 92f, 126ff; followed by Mussner, pp. 301f; differently most commentaries, especially Schlier; Harald Riesenfeld, "παρατηρέω, παρατήρησις, διατηρέω, συντηρέω," *TDNT* 8.146–51; Bornkamm, *Paul*, 82.

41 So Bultmann, *Stil*, 103; see also *Kerygma Petri*, Frag. 2a (HSW, *NT Apocrypha* 2.61; and for parallels Ernst von Dobschütz, *Das Kerygma Petri* [Leipzig: Hinrichs, 1893] 31ff); Käsemann, *Perspectives*, 151; Eckert, ibidem, 93.

μων ("religiously scrupulous" or even "superstitious"). One must read Theophrastus' "Character"[43] or Plutarch's diatribe *De superstitione*[44] to fully realize the power of Paul's argument. Within this context, religious observances such as Paul lists make up the behavior pattern characterized by δειλία πρὸς τὸ δαιμόνιον ("a fearful cowardice with regard to the divine").[45] According to Plutarch, this attitude of fear "utterly humiliates and crushes a man," corrupts his mind and emotions, and disables him, so that he fails to take care of his daily needs and problems.[46] For Plutarch, who speaks for a certain philosophical world–view, this life of the superstitious is even worse than slavery.[47]

The terminology is technical: παρατηρεῖν ("observe") denotes the activity of cultic observances in a general sense.[48] The other terms, "days and months and seasons and years," describe the intricacies of calendar observation, that is, the constant preoccupation with idle questions as to what day, month, season, or year it is, and what that has to say about what one should or should not do. Bultmann was right in claiming that this description is highly sarcastic (*höhnische Konsequenzmacherei*).[49] It is also clear that the statement gives us no clue to what the Galatians are presently doing. The cultic activities apply both to their pagan past[50] and to their future life in Judaism, if they so choose. But these activities are not exclusively Jewish, as some commentators suggest, even if a wealth of material illustrating the attitude of intensive cultic scrupulosity can be found especially in Jewish apocalypticism and Qumran.[51] In any case, a religious behavior such as

---

42 So already Bultmann, ibidem, 103.

43 *Charact.* 16. See Hendrik Bolkestein, *Theophrastos' Charakter der Deisidaimonia als religionsgeschichtliche Urkunde* (RVV 21.2; Giessen: Töpelmann,1929).

44 See Morton Smith's essay on this treatise in *PECL* 1.1–35. In his *Tannaitic Parallels to the Gospels* [SBLMS 6; Philadelphia: SBL, 1951] 74 n. 11) Smith refers to *Sifre Num.* 15.31, "He who despises the set times," and suggests that it is said against Paul or one of his followers.

45 Theophr. *Charact.* 16.1. See the commentary by Peter Steinmetz, *Theophrast, Charaktere* (Munich: Hueber, 1960–62) 2.179–87.

46 Plut. *Sup.* 165 B/C.

47 Ibidem, 166 D/E. See *PECL*, 30, 48, 54, 58, also 100.

48 In early Christian literature the terminology occurs only here, Luke 17:20; *Diogn.* 4.5 (cf. 1.1). See for references Bauer, *s.v.*, Harald Riesenfeld, "παρατηρέω, παρατήρησις, διατηρέω, συντηρέω," *TDNT* 8.146–51; *PGL, s.v.* παρατήρησις. See also Plutarch *Is. et Os.* 363B (*PECL*, 58).

49 See n. 41, above.

50 If the Galatians were former worshippers of the old Celtic religion, Paul's characteristic is certainly fitting. But the same can be said with regard to other cults in Asia Minor. On the Celtic religion, see Jan de Vries, *Keltische Religion* (Die Religionen der Menschheit 18; Stuttgart: Kohlhammer, 1961); Maartje Draak, "The Religion of the Celts," in *Historia Religionum* (Leiden: Brill, 1969) 1.629–47; Françoise le Roux–Guyonvarc'h, "Keltische Religion" in *Handbuch der Religionsgeschichte* (Göttingen: Vandenhoeck & Ruprecht, 1971) 1.245–76.

51 See Smith, in *PECL*, 30: "*Jewish* δεισιδαιμονία was

proverbial, Josephus *C. Apion.* i.205ff, etc.; Ac xvii 22 puts a reference to it into the mouth of a pagan (probably irony); it begins its career as a Christian cliché in Dg i 1." Very close comes the anti–Jewish polemic in *Kerygma Petrou* Frag. 2a (HSW, *NT Apocrypha* 2.100): "Neither worship him (*sc.* God) in the manner of the Jews; for they also, who think that they alone know God, do not understand, worshipping angels and archangels, the months and the moon. And when the moon does not shine, they do not celebrate the new moon, etc." Cf. Tertullian (*Adv. Marc.* 5.4.6) who continues "and sabbaths, I suppose, and meagre suppers, and fasts, and great days." Justin (*Dial.* 46) has given this summary of Jewish Torah obedience: "To keep the Sabbath, to be circumcised, to observe months, and to be washed if you touch anything prohibited by Moses, or after sexual intercourse." Schlier (pp. 204–07) has collected a large number of passages from Jewish apocalyptic and Qumran literature, which illustrate that the cliché is not unfounded. But it is unclear whether the opponents of Paul have already introduced these specific ideas into the Galatian churches. Cf. also Mussner (pp. 293–303), who provides a good survey of the immense material and recent secondary literature. In addition, see Meinrad Limbeck, *Die Ordnung des Heils* (Düsseldorf: Patmos, 1971) *passim*.

218

Paul describes is the very opposite of what the "sons of God" ought to do.[52]

■11 Paul concludes his attack of 4:8–10 with another ironic remark, seemingly an expression of *dubitatio*: φοβοῦμαι ὑμᾶς μή πως εἰκῇ κεκοπίακα εἰς ὑμᾶς. ("I am afraid for you, lest I might have spent my labor on you in vain").[53] In fact, this is self–irony, not resignation,[54] when he admits to his own fear after having made fun of the fear of the superstitious.[55] Of course, he is not afraid for himself, but for the sake of the Galatians.[56] The term κοπιάω ("work hard") is taken from missionary language.[57] Paul contrasts his very real, hard work as a missionary which he had done[58] on behalf of the salvation of the Galatians with the seemingly idle activism of the superstition in which the Galatians want to engage.[59] If they engage in such superstition, his work and the salvation of the Galatians will come to nothing (εἰκῇ).[60]

---

52 Cf. the descriptions of religious scrupulosity in 1 Cor 8:7ff; 10:23ff; Rom 14:1ff. That the anti–Pauline opposition itself was religiously rigorous should not be doubted. See Betz, "2 Cor 6:14–7:1," 88–108; Col 2:16–23 (on this, see the commentary by Lohse, *Colossians and Philemon*, 114ff). For the later position, see Justin *Dial.* 47 (Appendix 4).

53 See the n. on the tr. above, and also BDF, § 370 (1); BDR, § 370.

54 So Mussner, p. 304.

55 Cf. for similar remarks 2 Cor 11:3, 12:20.

56 So correctly Sieffert, Lietzmann, Schlier (p. 207). Cf. Burton (p. 235) who takes it proleptically, anticipating the "you" at the end. Cf. BDF, § 476 (3); BDR, § 476.

57 See Rom 16:6, 12; 1 Cor 4:12; 15:10; 16:16; Phil 2:16; 1 Thess 5:12; Col 1:29; Eph 4:28; etc. See on the term Bauer, *s.v.*; Friedrich Hauck, "κλάω," *TDNT* 3.827–30.

58 κεκοπίακα stresses the ongoing work, perhaps including the writing of the letter; ἐκοπίασα read by P46 1739 regards the work a matter of the past.

59 They do not plan, however, to *return* to the law, as Schlier has it (p. 207).

60 Cf. 2:2 (εἰς κενόν); 3:4 (εἰκῇ); 1 Cor 15:2 (εἰκῇ), 10, 14, 58; 2 Cor 6:1; Phil 2:16; 1 Thess 2:1; 3:5 (κενός).

4

Probatio: The Fifth Argument

12 **Remain as I am because also I have become as you are,[2] brothers, I beg you. You did me no wrong. 13/ You remember[3] that it was because of an illness of the flesh that I originally preached the gospel to you. 14/ Also you [resisted any] temptation through my flesh,[4] and did not despise and reject [me], but you welcomed me as if I were an angel of God, as if I were[5] Jesus Christ [himself]. 15/ What then has become of your praise?[6]—For I bear witness to you that, if it had been possible, you would have plucked out your eyes and given them to me! 16/ Is the result of it all that I have become your enemy for telling you the truth? 17/ They[7] pay zealous court to you not in a good way, but they intend to exclude you, in order that you court them. 18/ Yet, good is always to be courted in a good way and not only when I am present with you. 19/ My children, with whom I am in travail again until Christ takes shape in you[8]—20/ I wished I were present with you now, and I were able to alter my voice because I am perplexed about you.[9]**

Analysis

All commentators point out that the section 4:12–20 presents considerable difficulties. The style seems erratic. Paul seems to be jumping from one matter to the next, without much consistency of thought. Traditionally this situation was interpreted as having been the result of Paul's emotional irritation. Psychological interpretations take it as such; Paul was finally overwhelmed by his emotions, so that he lost control over the argument, ending up in passionate pleas to the Galatians to remain loyal to him. Oepke,[10] who makes the most of this, goes so far as to even deny all ration-

---

1   The translation of this section is extremely difficult. Most translators resort to paraphrasing. This translation tries to stay close to the text; for a better paraphrase, cf. *NEB*.

2   Or: "Be as I am because also I am as you are." Cf. *RSV*: "Brethren, I beseech you, become as I am, for also I have become as you are." *NEB*: "Put yourselves in my place, my brothers, I beg you, for I have put myself in yours." *JB*: "Brothers, all I ask is that you should copy me as I copied you."

3   Literally: "you know."

4   Cf. *RSV*: "and though my condition was a trial to you, you did not. . . ." *NEB*: ". . . you resisted any temptation to show scorn or disgust at the state of my poor body" (or: "at the trial my poor body was enduring").

5   So *NEB*. Cf. *RSV*: "you . . . received me as an angel of God, as Christ Jesus."

6   Cf. *NEB*: "Have you forgotten how happy you thought yourselves in having me with you?"

7   That is, Paul's opponents.

8   Or: "among you."

9   Cf. *NEB*: "I wish I could be with you now; then I could modify my tone; as it is, I am at my wits' end about you."

10 Typical of this psychological interpretation is Oepke (pp. 140ff) but also Burton (p. 235) assumes that Paul has "dropped argument" and has turned to begging and appealing. Understanding the text requires primarily an "intuitive grasping of the meaning and supplementing what is missing" (Oepke, p. 141). Mussner (pp. 304f) agrees. Luther (1535) also notes that the passage "is filled with feelings" but recognizes this as a tool of rhetoric (on 4:12, *Luther's Works* 26.412f).

ality to the section. Schlier[11] calls it "an argument of the heart." What has not been recognized is the rhetorical character of the passage. This does not mean that the observations made by the commentators mentioned are entirely wrong. What Paul offers in the section is a string of topoi belonging to the theme of "friendship" ($\pi\epsilon\rho\grave{\iota}\ \phi\iota\lambda\acute{\iota}\alpha\varsigma$). This theme was famous in antiquity, as the large number of works on "friendship", many of which are extent,[12] demonstrate. By the time of Paul, the subject was treated also in the diatribe literature[13] and in epistles. In the epistolary literature it was even a standard topic.[14] Thus, it cannot be a surprise that Paul also makes use of it. Even before him, Hellenistic Judaism, especially Sirach[15] and Philo,[16] treated the subject, so that it may have come to the Apostle by way of Hellenistic Judaism.[17]

This means that the section in Galatians is neither inconsistent nor lacking argumentative force. It is, to be sure, a lighter section compared with the heavy arguments in the preceding sections. A personal appeal to friendship is entirely in conformity with Hellenistic style, which calls for change between heavy and light sections and which would require an emotional and personal approach to offset the impression of mere abstractions. The argumentative force lies in the topic itself, the marks of "true" and "false" friendship.[18] These topoi were, of course, known to the Galatians, and the content belonged to the common wisdom agreed upon by everyone. At the same time, the section anticipates the major parenetical section beginning with 5:1.[19]

Interpretation

■ **12** The section begins with a gnomic paradox: $\gamma\acute{\iota}\nu\epsilon\sigma\theta\epsilon$ $\dot{\omega}\varsigma\ \dot{\epsilon}\gamma\acute{\omega},\ \ddot{o}\tau\iota\ \kappa\dot{\alpha}\gamma\grave{\omega}\ \dot{\omega}\varsigma\ \dot{\upsilon}\mu\epsilon\hat{\iota}\varsigma$. This gnome can be translated in several ways: "become as I am, because also I

11 Schlier, p. 208. Restating the words of Estius, he emphasizes the "strong pathos" and "erratic train of thought."

12 The importance of the concept of friendship is reflected in the long history of its treatment in Greco–Roman literature. In the Greek literature, works on friendship were written by Xenophon (*Mem.* 2.4–10), Plato (*Lysis*), Speusippus, Xenocrates, Aristotle, (*EN* 8–9, p. 1155a1–1172a15), Theophrastus, Clearchus, Praxiphanes, Epicurus, Cleanthes, Chrysippus, Panaitius, Poseidonius—to mention only the most important ones. For surveys and bib. see Gustav Stählin, "$\phi\acute{\iota}\lambda o\varsigma\ \kappa\tau\lambda$.," *TDNT* 9.146–71; Kurt Treu, "Freundschaft," *RAC* 8.418–34; P. A. Brunt, "'Amicitia' in the Late Roman Republic," *Proceedings of the Cambridge Philological Association* 191 (1965) 1–20; Brunt points to the importance of the concept in Roman politics.

13 See especially the works by Isocrates: *To Demonicus, To Nicocles, Nicocles* (LCL, 1); Epictetus *Diss.* 2.22; Plutarch *Adulat.*; *De amic. mult.*; *De amicitia*; Lucian *Toxaris*; Maximus Tyr. *Diss.* 14, 35; Dio Chrys. 3.86ff, 4.42, 34.76, 44.1ff. Most important are Cicero *Laelius de amicitia* and Seneca *De beneficiis*. See Fritz–Arthur Steinmetz, *Die Freundshaftslehre des Panaitios: Nach einer Analyse von Ciceros "Laelius de amicitia"* (Palingenesia 3; Wiesbaden: Steiner, 1967).

14 Beginning with Seneca's *Epistulae ad Lucilium*? See Ulrich Knoche, "Der Gedanke der Freundschaft in Senecas Briefen an Lucilius," *Arctos*, NS 1 (1954) 83–96; Wolfgang Brinckmann, *Der Begriff der Freundschaft in Senecas Briefen* (Philos. Diss. Köln, 1963);

Hildegard Cancik, *Untersuchungen zu Senecas Epistulae Morales* (Spudasmata 18; Hildesheim: Olms, 1967); and the review by Gregor Maurach, *Gnomon* 41 (1969) 472–76. On the whole subject see Koskenniemi, *Studien*, 115–27; Klaus Thraede, *Einheit–Gegenwart–Gespräch: Zur Christianisierung antiker Brieftopoi* (Diss. Theol. Bonn, 1968); idem, *Grundzüge griechisch-römischer Brieftopik* (Zetemata 48; Munich: Beck, 1970) with a large bib.

15 See esp. Sir 6:5–17 and *passim; Vita et sententiae Aesopi–Achiqari* 109–110 (ed. Albert–Marie Denis, *Fragmenta Pseudepigraphorum quae supersunt Graeca* [Leiden: Brill, 1970] 138–40) and on "Friendship in the OT and Judaism," Stählin, "$\phi\acute{\iota}\lambda o\varsigma\ \kappa\tau\lambda$.," *TDNT* 9.156–59.

16 On Philo see Stählin, ibidem, 158–59; Treu, "Freundschaft," *RAC* 8.424–25.

17 Still useful because of its vast collection of material is Gottfried Bohnenblust, *Beiträge zum Topos ΠΕΡΙ ΦΙΛΙΑΣ* (Diss. Bern; Berlin: Schade, 1905). Cf. also Thraede, *Brieftopik, passim*.

18 Thraede (ibidem, 95–106) deals with the *parousia* motif in 1 Thess 2:17; 1 Cor 5:3f; Col 2:5; but Gal has escaped him.

19 It is imprecise to call it, as Schlier does (p. 208), "eine Mahnung zur Nachfolge," an "exhortation to discipleship;" Paul never employs the concept of discipleship. See Betz, *Nachfolge*, 137.

20 So *RSV* (1973).

have become as you are";[20] or: "be as I am, because also I am as you are."[21] It is, however, not necessary to choose between these translations, for it is the nature of a gnome that it can be understood in several ways. The underlying idea is the topos from popular philosophy that "true friendship" is possible only among equals. The familiar terms in Greek thought are ἰσότης ("equality"), ὁμόνοια ("unanimity"),[22] and ὁμοιότης ("likeness").[23] Most important is the definition of friendship given by Cicero and reflecting common opinion: "for friendship is nothing else than an accord in all things, human and divine, conjoined with mutual goodwill and affection."[24]

The implications of this doctrine of friendship were widely discussed in antiquity. Especially illustrative is Lucian's *Toxaris*, a collection of narrative examples showing why "becoming like the friend" is a sure sign of true friendship; his stories about friends uniting in shipwreck, poverty, prison, even in death illustrate

that "true friends must share all their fortunes."[25] In Gal 4:12a this topos is applied to Paul's relationship with the Galatians.[26] He can appeal to them, in fact he can order them,[27] because as their apostle he is not only a good friend, but a true friend.[28] As an apostle, he can demand imitation: μιμηταί μου γίνεσθε ("become my imitators").[29] At this time, this means: "*remain* as I am." For at present the Galatians are still "like Paul," Christians outside of the Jewish Torah and therefore "like Isaac" (4:28), but they will no longer be "like him" when they accept circumcision and Torah (cf. 1:6–7).[30] Therefore, Paul's appeal means concretely: "remain free from the Law!" This appeal corresponds to the second part of the gnome. The ὅτι is certainly causal ("because"); it refers to what Paul had become, and thus, to his present situation. At least two ideas underlie this statement. It is presupposed, but not expressly stated, that "true friendship" must be based upon reciprocity.[31] One friend must be to the other

---

21 Modern translations vary greatly. Cf. the notes on the tr. above; a variety of possible renderings are discussed in the commentaries, especially Jerome, Luther (1519). See also Burton (p. 236): "Become as I am (or have become), because I am as ye are . . ." (also his discussion, pp. 236f).

22 Paul does not use this term, but the Apostolic Fathers begin to make full use of the doctrine (cf. Ign. *Eph.* 4.2; Ign. *Trall.* 12.2; *1 Clem.* 9.4; 11.2 and often) for more passages see Bauer, *s.v.* In Paul, cf. μία ψυχῇ ("with one mind") Phil 1:27 (also Acts 4:32); ὁμοθυμαδόν ("with one mind") Rom 15:6 (also Acts 1:14; 2:46; 4:24; 5:12, etc.). See Thraede, *Brieftopik*, 122f; Bohnenblust, *Beiträge*, 40.

23 Cf. Ign. *Eph.* 1.3. For the basic definition see Aristotle *EN* 8.8.5, p. 1159b2f: ἡ δ' ἰσότης καὶ ὁμοιότης φιλότης, καὶ μάλιστα μὲν ἡ τῶν κατ' ἀρετὴν ὁμοιότης ("Friendship is equality of rights and values, especially the equality of those who are alike in virtue"). In Gal, this is expressed esp. Gal 2:9; 3:26–28; 5:6; 6:15. Cf. also 2 Cor 8:13f; Col 4:1, etc. See Bohnenblust, ibidem, 42; Gustav Stählin, "ἴσος." *TDNT* 3.345ff, idem, "φίλος κτλ.," *TDNT* 9.152.

24 *De amicitia* 20: Est enim amicitia nihil aliud nisi omnium divinarum humanarumque rerum cum benevolentia et caritate consensio (tr. William A. Falconer, LCL). For a collection of parallel passages see Bohnenblust, ibidem, 27, 42.

25 Lucian *Toxaris* 5: . . . χρὴ τοῖς φίλοις ἁπάσης τύχης κοινωνεῖν. See Bohnenblust, idem, 11; Stählin,

"φίλος κτλ.," *TDNT* 9.153–54.

26 The topos occurs also in Justin *Oratio ad Graecos* 5.7: γίνεσθε ὡς ἐγώ, ὅτι κἀγὼ ἤμην ὡς ὑμεῖς. Thraede (*Brieftopik*, 5–8) rightly states that using *topoi* does not exclude creativity.

27 Cf. Gal 5:26; Rom 12:16; 1 Cor 7:23; 10:7, 20, 32; 14:20, 25, 26, 40; 15:58; 16:14; Phlm 6.

28 This is not at all inconsistent with the friendship *topos* because "true friends" should serve as each other's *custos* ("guardian, advisor"). See Knoche, "Freundschaft," 86ff; Ilsetraut Hadot, *Seneca und die griechisch-römische Tradition der Seelenleitung* (Quellen und Studien zur Geschichte der Philosophie 13; Berlin: de Gruyter, 1969) 164ff.

29 See 1 Cor 4:16; 11:1; 1 Thess 2:14; Phil 3:17; for ὡς ἐγώ 1 Cor 7:7, 8, 40; 10:33. On the concept of "imitation" see Wilhelm Michaelis, "μιμέομαι κτλ.," *TDNT* 4.659–74; Betz, *Nachfolge*, esp. 143f, 152, 169.

30 Gal 4:12a is a parallel to Phil 3:17, which is part of a similar polemic. See Helmut Koester, "The Purpose of the Polemic of a Pauline Fragment (Philippians III)," *NTS* 8 (1962) 317–32; Betz, *Nachfolge*, 145–53. For the opposite parenesis, see 2 Cor 6:14; and on the interpretation, Betz, "2 Cor 6:14–7:1," 89f; Appendix 2, below.

31 Cf., esp., Cicero *Amic.* 22f, 45–48, 56–61.

like "his other I" (ἕτερος ἐγώ, *alter ego*).[32] The other idea presupposed is a strange "missionary doctrine" expressed elsewhere in Paul. It was for the sake of the Galatians that Paul became like them, a Christian outside of the Jewish Torah.[33] He had left the Jewish Torah in order to save them.[34] Commentators usually and correctly refer to the parallel 1 Cor 9:19–23.[35] As one who is "free" Paul is free to be a Jew to the Jews and a Gentile to the Gentiles for the purpose of saving them all.[36] This adaptability was also, although with regret, practiced by Cephas at Antioch (2:11–14). It is, of course, limited by purpose and should not be mistaken as characteristic of the antitype of the "true friend"—the "false apostle," the "flatterer" (κόλαξ).[37] Certainly, Paul does not wish to say that he became what the Galatians *were*,[38] i.e., pagan sinners, but he became what they are *now*. When he lived among them,

he did so as a Christian, neither as a Jew nor as a pagan. This equality and reciprocity is also emphasized by the repetition of the address "brothers" (ἀδελφοί).[39]

The connection of δέομαι ὑμῖν ("I beg you") with the context is not immediately clear. As an epistolary phrase[40] especially connected with the friendship topos[41] it does not need a firm connection with the preceding or following. Asyndetic is also the following statement: οὐδέν με ἠδικήσατε ("you did me no wrong"). The implication is that the fellowship between Paul and the Galatian churches has up to now not been disturbed by any injustice or wrongdoing on the part of the Galatians.[42] The remark, certainly puzzling, is unique in Galatians,[43] but it can be understood as an epistolary cliché belonging to the friendship topos.[44] Among "true friends" there is confidence that they do not do each other wrong.[45]

---

32 Cicero *Amic*. 23: Verum etiam amicum qui intuetur, tamquam exemplar aliquod intuitur sui ("Again, he who looks upon a true friend looks, as it were, upon a sort of image of himself"). On this idea see Bohnenblust, *Beiträge*, 39f; Stählin, "φίλος κτλ.," *TDNT* 9.152; Steinmetz, *Freundschaftslehre*, 32, 139, 143, 202. Already Theodor Beza (see Sieffert, p. 257) and Hugo Grotius (*Annotationes in Novum Testamentum* [Erlangen: Tetzchner, 1756] 2.566) refer to the "alter ego."

33 Gal 1:12–2:14, 15f; cf. Phil 3:6ff.

34 Rom 11:13f; 1 Cor 9:19–23; 10:33; 2 Cor 2:14–17; 1 Thess 2:14–16.

35 Cf. Lightfoot, p. 174; Sieffert, pp. 256–59; Zahn, p. 215; Burton, p. 236; Schlier, pp. 208f; Mussner, pp. 305f.

36 On the passage see Conzelmann, *1 Corinthians*, 158–61; Henry Chadwick, "All Things to All Men (I Cor IX. 22)," *NTS* 1 (1955) 261–75; Betz, *Nachfolge*, 143f; Georg Eichholz, *Die Theologie des Paulus im Umriss* (Neukirchen: Neukirchener Verlag, 1972) 48–55.

37 For a vivid description of the "flatterer" see Plutarch *Adulat*. 51E–54B. The literary *topos* of the all-conforming and endlessly adaptable "flatterer" is widely attested. See Philo *Mig*. 111; *L.A.* 3.182, etc.; in Paul 1 Thess 2:5. See Johannes Schneider, "(κολακεύω) κολακία," *TDNT* 3.817–18. The basic study is still Otto Ribbeck, "Kolax," *Abhandlungen der philologisch-historischen Classe der Kgl.- Sächsischen Gesellschaft der Wissenschaften* 9 (1884) 1–114; cf. Bohnenblust, *Beiträge*, 31ff; Ernst Wust and August Hug, "Parasitos," PW 18 (1949) 1381–1405.

38 Cf. Gal 2:15–17; 1 Cor 9:21. Schlier's interpretation is unclear when he says that Paul became a pagan as *they were*. For a survey of this line of interpretation see Sieffert (pp. 256f). The correct understanding is now found in Mussner, p. 306.

39 For this address, see Gal 1:11; 3:15; 4:28, 31; 5:11, 13; 6:1, 18.

40 For examples, cf. ps.–Libanius *Charact. epistol.*, *Demetrii et Libanii qui feruntur ΤΥΠΟΙ ΕΠΙΣΤΟΛΙΚΟΙ et ΕΠΙΣΤΟΛΙΜΑΙΟΙ ΧΑΡΑΚΤΗΡΕΣ* (ed. V. Weichert; BT, Lipsiae: Teubner, 1910) nos. 17 and 18 (p. 27); *Ep. Phalar.* 130 (ed. Rudolphus Hercher, *Epistolographi Graeci* [Paris: Didot, 1873]) 449.

41 Cf. Knoche ("Freundschaft," 86) who points to the frequent occurrence of *te hortor, te rogo, te admoneo, iubeo te, suadeo te*, etc. in Seneca's epistles. Also Cicero (*Amic.*, 104) concludes with such an exhortation. In Paul, cf. 2 Cor 10:2; 1 Thess 3:10. See also Terence Y. Mullins, "Petition as a Literary Form," *NovT* 5 (1962) 46–54.

42 So correctly Schlier, p. 209; differently Sieffert.

43 Cf. 1 Cor 6:7, 8; 2 Cor 7:2, 12; Phlm 18; also 1 Cor 13:6; 2 Cor 12:13.

44 For other possibilities of interpretation, cf. Burton, pp. 237f.

45 Cf. Plato *Lysis* 208 E; Aristotle *EN* 8.4.3, p. 1157a 23f: καὶ τὸ πιστεύειν ἐν τούτοις, καὶ τὸ μηδέποτ' ἂν ἀδικῆσαι ("and with them there is the mutual confidence, the incapacity ever to do each other wrong"); Plutarch *Adulat*. 37F; Dio Chrys. 3.113, 34.41; Cicero *Amic*. 76–78. See Steinmetz, *Freundschaftslehre*, 134–36; Bohnenblust, *Beiträge*, 43.

■ **13–14** At first puzzling, this statement corresponds to the theme of friendship also. Luther (1535) is right in calling it "a great commendation of the Galatians." Paul reminds the Galatians of their great favor at the beginning of their life as Christians; when he came to them bringing to them the gospel, they had accepted him without any reservations, like an "angel of God" or even like Jesus Christ himself. They did so in spite of the illness from which the Apostle was suffering at the time. Although the language is Paul's, the statement as a whole expresses the theme of friendship. It is the sign of real friendship to provide unlimited help at the moment of great need, in particular in illness;[46] true friendship may begin with an experience of pain and trouble;[47] true friends may remind each other of the "bushel of salt" they have eaten together.[48] It is this background that makes Paul turn (δέ ["but"]) to his and the Galatians' past experiences. As the first words "you know (=remember)" (οἴδατε) indicate, Paul

wishes to remind his readers of the past experience they have had with him.[49] The term ἀσθένεια τῆς σαρκός ("weakness" or "illness of the flesh")[50] in all probability points to a real illness of Paul,[51] from which he was suffering at the time when he first[52] came to the Galatians. Why this illness became the cause[53] for the mission among them,[54] the Apostle does not say. Perhaps, Mussner (p. 307) is right: "for a man like Paul everything became a καιρός ["a good opportunity"], when the gospel was to be proclaimed."
■ **14** Instead of rejecting him, Paul says the Galatians successfully passed their first test: καὶ τὸν πειρασμὸν ὑμῶν ἐν τῇ σαρκί μου οὐκ ἐξουθενήσατε οὐδὲ ἐξεπτύσατε ("and you [resisted any] temptation through my flesh, and did not despise and reject [me]").[55] The translation of the sentence is difficult because of its idiomatic language, but the meaning is clear. There are textual problems as well: ὑμῶν ("your temptation") is a better reading than μου ("my temptation") because it is the

---

46 For examples see Xenophon *Mem.* 2.4.3, 2.7.1ff, 10.1ff; Aristotle *NE* 8.1.2, p. 1155a12ff; 8.3.8, p. 1156b 25ff; *EE* 7.2.9ff, p. 1236a16ff; Plutarch *Adulat.* 68F–69A; Epictetus *Diss.* 2.22.12; Lucian *Toxaris* 18; Dio Chrys. *Or.* 3.100.

47 Plutarch *Amic. mult.* 6; Lucian *Toxaris, passim.*

48 Cf. Cicero *Amic.* 67: ". . . as in the case of wines that improve with age, the oldest friendships ought to be the most delightful; moreover, the well-known adage is true: 'Men must eat many a peck of salt together before the claims of friendship are fulfilled.'" See also 78, 103f; Plutarch *Amic. mult.* 3; and already Aristotle *EN* 8.3.8, p. 1156b 27–28.

49 Cf. Gal 1:6–9; 3:2–5; for the rhetorical term οἴδατε ("you know") see also Rom 6:16; 11:2; 1 Cor 3:16; 5:6; 6:2, 3, 9, 15, 16, 19; 9:13, 24; 12:2; etc.

50 See the extensive discussion of the problems in Luther (1519, 1535). Cf. the parallel in 2 Cor 12:7–10. For the interpretation of this passage, see Hans Dieter Betz, "Eine Christus-Aretalogie bei Paulus (2 Kor 12, 7–10)," *ZThK* 66 (1969) 288–304; idem, *Paulus* 92ff; C. K. Barrett, *A Commentary on the Second Epistle to the Corinthians* (New York: Harper & Row) 314–18.

51 See Bauer, *s.v.* ἀσθένεια, 1; Schlier, p. 210; Güttgemanns, *Apostel*, 170ff; and most modern commentaries (Burton, Oepke, Lietzmann, Mussner [also pp. 314–16]); older works often understood Paul to refer to the wounds from persecution, unimpressive appearance, timidity, sexual desire; etc.

(see Jerome; Luther [1535]; Sieffert, pp. 261f; Schlier, p. 210 n. 3). But the literal and the metaphorical meaning of the phrase must be kept separate (cf. 1 Cor 2:3; 2 Cor 10:1, 10; 1 Thess 1:5; 2:1f); see Betz, *Paulus*, 44ff.

52 τὸ πρότερον should be rendered "originally," "the first time" (see BDF, § 62; BDR, § 62; LSJ, *s.v.*, A, IV; Bauer, *s.v.* 1, b, β; also the commentaries by Burton, pp. 239–41; Schlier, p. 209; Mussner, p. 307). Paul refers to the Galatian beginnings also 1:8, 9, 11; 3:2–5; cf. also Acts 16:6, but nowhere is his illness mentioned again. It is not at all likely that 4:13 supports the notion of two visits of Paul in Galatia (cf. Acts 16:6; 18:23) before he wrote the letter (see the Introduction, § 3.A).

53 Διά + accus. expresses the occasioning cause (Latin: *propter*), not a limiting condition (vg: *per* infirmitntem). See BDR, § 222 n. 2; also Lightfoot, Burton, Schlier, Mussner, Bauer (*s.v.*, διά II, 1 with references), Oepke.

54 For the term εὐαγγελίζομαι ("preach the gospel") see on Gal 1:8, 9, 11, 16, 23.

55 *NEB*: the rather free translation brings out the meaning very well. See the note on the tr. above.

more difficult.[56] Indeed, Paul's illness would have been a good reason for the Galatians to reject him. As 2 Cor 12:7–10 shows, illness was likely to be interpreted by common people as demon possession, a fact which would be incompatible with the claims of an apostle.[57] The temptation therefore was to let superstition and prejudice judge the matter of the gospel.[58] The phrase ἐν τῇ σαρκί μου ("in my flesh"), difficult as it is, can best be illustrated by the parallel in 2 Cor 12:7 σκόλοψ τῇ σαρκί ("a thorn in the flesh"), a metaphor describing Paul's illness as caused by an evil demon residing in his body.[59] The precise nature of this illness is unknown to us. A mass of studies which has been produced on the subject remains mostly speculation.[60] In speaking about his illness Paul does not use medical, but metaphorical and demonological language. The term ἐξουθενέω ("despise") is used with regard to Paul also 2 Cor 10:10, where it describes the negative reaction of Christians towards Paul, who appeared to them as a "charlatan"[61] rather than an apostle. The originally apotropeic term ἐκπτύω ("spit out") describes not merely a gesture of disrespect, but that of averting a

demon. While the term originated in primitive superstition, it later became more or less identical with "despise."[62]

Temptations of this kind are the test of "true friendship." Cicero (Amic. 62f) formulates it in this way: "we ought, therefore, to choose men who are firm, steadfast and constant, a class of which there is a great dearth; and at the same time it is very hard to come to a decision without a trial, while such trial can only be made in actual friendship. . . . Hence it is part of wisdom to check the headlong rush of goodwill as we would that of a chariot, and thereby so manage friendship that we may in some degree put the dispositions of friends, as we do so of horses, to a preliminary test."[63] The hardest of such tests were those of a friend's illness, disfiguration, or ugliness.[64] Luther (1535) points out correctly that the temptation is identical with the "stumblingblock of the cross," which Paul represents.[65]

The Galatians had passed their test with excellence: ἀλλὰ ὡς ἄγγελον θεοῦ ἐδέξασθέ με, ὡς Χριστὸν Ἰησοῦν ("but you welcomed me as if I were an angel of God, as you might have welcomed Jesus Christ himself").[66]

---

56   ὑμῶν ("your") is supported by ℵ* A B C² vid 33 D* G itᵈ· ᵍ· ʳ vg Ambrosiaster. P⁴⁶ it⁶¹ al read μου ("my"), but this reading eliminates the grammatical awkwardness of the sentence. See Metzger, Textual Commentary, 596; Mussner, p. 307 n. 71.

57   Cf. the expression "angel of Satan" in 2 Cor 12:7.

58   In Paul's view, Christians are not exempt from temptations by Satan. See Gal 6:1; 1 Cor 7:5; 10:9, 13; 2 Cor 2:11; 11:14; 1 Thess 3:4; etc.; differently 2 Cor 13:5 (see Betz, Paulus, 89, 134–37). On the whole concept in Paul see Heinrich Seesemann, TDNT 7.161–62; Karl–Georg Kuhn, "Πειρασμός—ἁμαρτία—σάρξ im Neuen Testament und die damit zusammenhängenden Vorstellungen," ZThK 49 (1952) 200–22; Güttgemanns, Apostel, 176f.

59   For the concept of σάρξ (here "body") see the passages and bib. on Gal 2:16.

60   See the collection of material in Güttgemanns, Apostel, 162–65, 173–77.

61   See on this Betz, Paulus, 44–69. The term ἐξουθενέω ("despise") occurs also Rom 14:3, 10; 1 Cor 1:28, 6:4, 16:11; 1 Thess 5:20. See Bauer, s.v. BDR, §§ 33 n. 2; 108 n. 2.

62   The term is found only here in early Christian literature (P⁴⁶ omits it). But cf. Mark 7:33; 8:23; John 9:6; Barn. 7.9. See Heinrich Schlier, "ἐκπτύω," TDNT 2.448–49; Bauer, s.v. ἐκπτύω, πτύσμα; PGM

IV 2299; Betz, Lukian, 150f; PECL, 226. Both terms together occur in Jos. et As. 2.1; see Edgar W. Smith, Joseph and Aseneth and Early Christian Literature: A Contribution to the Corpus Hellenisticum Novi Testamenti (Ph.D. diss. Claremont 1975) 55.

63   "Sunt igitur firmi et stabiles et constantes eligendi, cuius generis est magna penuria; et iudicare difficile est sane nisi expertum, experiendum autem est in ipsa amicitia. . . . Est igitur prudentis sustinere et cursum, sic impetum benevolentiae, quo utamur, quasi equis temptatis, sic amicitia, aliqua parte periclitatis moribus amicorum." See on this point Steinmetz, Freundschaftslehre, 116–19; Bohnenblust, Beiträge, 32–34; Theodor Middendorp, Die Stellung Jesu ben Siras zwischen Judentum und Hellenismus (Leiden: Brill, 1973) 14f; Middendorp mentions Sir 6:6 as an instance of Greek influence.

64   Lucian's Toxaris contains a series of narratives about such tests of true friendship (see for the theme 5f; on illness 18, 19, 53, 60, 61; on ugliness 24, 30f).

65   Luther also refers to the theme in the passion narratives, especially to Luke 22:28: "You are those who have remained with me in my temptations," and to the macarism Matt 11:6 (Luke 7:23): "Blessed is he who takes no offense at me."

66   NEB tr.

Again, the brevity of expression leaves several options for interpretation and translation. The concept of ἄγγελος θεοῦ ("angel of God") which has no precise parallel elsewhere is Paul,[67] can simply refer to a messenger of God, or indeed to an angelic being sent by God.[68] Although the meaning of the term as messenger occurs often enough in the New Testament, "angel of God" seems the more likely translation.[69] To be sure, in antiquity there was not a great difference between the two, because one could never be sure whether one was encountering a divine angel or a human messenger.

The expression "angel of God," however, was used before in Gal 1:8 ("angel from heaven") and it stands in contrast to "angel of Satan" (2 Cor 12:7). For the ancients, the sudden appearance of a divine, or in the Jewish context, of an angelic being, brings good fortune to men, if they welcome the appearance regardless of the human disguise. This was a familiar religious and literary motif.[70] The ὡς ("as if")[71] expresses a distinction, since Paul does not intend to say that he actually came as an angel. No doubt, as an apostle of Christ he considers himself *the* messenger sent by God to the Galatians for the sake of their salvation.[72] Indeed they did welcome him[73] as if he were Jesus Christ himself. This statement is also more than a simple exaggeration, since Paul, as the apostle and "imitator" of Christ,[74] represents Christ.[75] Those who welcome him welcome Christ.[76] And yet, the statements Paul makes about himself are exaggerations. They amount to a praise of the Galatians,[77] corresponding to the common "praise among true friends."[78]

■ **15** The rhetorical question in 15a, ποῦ οὖν ὁ μακαρισμὸς ὑμῶν; ("what then has become of your praise?") can be taken in several ways, depending upon the meaning of the expression ὁ μακαρισμὸς ὑμῶν ("your praise"). If ὑμῶν ("your") is to be taken as a subjective genitive, with most commentators, it would refer to a "self–praise" which the Galatians would have pronounced about themselves when Paul brought the gospel to them. He would now ask with some irony, "what has become of that self–glorification of yours?"[79] This interpretation is possible, and v 15b could support

67   Cf. the usage of the concept of "angel" with reference to human beings in 1 Cor 13:1; 2 Cor 11:14.

68   For the literature on "angel" see on Gal 1:8.

69   So most modern commentaries: Zahn, Burton, Lietzmann, Oepke, Schlier, Mussner.

70   See for this motif esp. Acts 12:15; 14:11ff; Heb 13:1f. For OT parallels see the narratives in Gen 18–19; the Rabbinic material in Str–B 3.707f; *Jos. et As.*, *passim*; for the Hellenistic literature see Conzelmann, *Apostelgeschichte*, on 14:11ff; Betz, *Lukian*, 116 n. 1; 132 n. 4; Nock, "'Son of God' in Pauline and Hellenistic Thought" in his *Essays* 2.936–39; David L. Tiede, *The Charismatic Figure as Miracle Worker* (SBLDS 1; Missoula: SBL, 1972).

71   Cf. 2 Cor 11:16; Phlm 17. See BDR, § 453.

72   On the concept of apostleship see the excursus on Gal 1:17.

73   On δέχομαι ("receive, welcome") cf. Matt 10:14 par., 40, 41; Mark 9:37 par.; 2 Cor 7:15; 11:4, 16; Phil 4:18; 1 Thess 1:6; 2:13, etc. See Bauer, *s.v.*, 1; Betz, *Lukian*, 132.

74   See, esp., 1 Cor 11:1; 1 Thess 1:6. On the whole concept of the apostle as "imitator" of Christ and further literature, see Betz, *Nachfolge, passim*.

75   Cf. 2 Cor 2:14–17; 5:18–20; 13:3–4; also Col 1:23–2:5; Eph 3:1–19; 1 Tim 1:12–17. See also Karl Martin Fischer, *Tendenz und Absicht des Epheserbriefes* (FRLANT 111; Göttingen: Vandenhoeck & Rup-

recht, 1973) 104–08; Martin Dibelius and Hans Conzelmann, *The Pastoral Epistles: A Commentary on the Pastoral Epistles* (tr. Philip Buttolph and Adela Yarbro; ed. Helmut Koester; Hermeneia; Philadelphia: Fortress, 1972) 27–31.

76   The concept is found also in Luke 10:16; Matt 10:40, 41; 25:40; *Did.* 11.2, 4; etc. On the whole concept see Gerd Theissen, "Wanderradikalismus. Literatursoziologische Aspekte der Überlieferung von Worten Jesu im Urchristentum," *ZThK* 70 (1973) 245–71; Bernd Jaspert, "'Stellvertreter Christi' bei Aponius, einem unbekannten 'Magister' und Benedikt von Nursia," *ZThK* 71 (1974) 291–324).

77   Cf. 4:15 on μακαρισμός.

78   On this topos see, e.g., Plutarch *Adulat.*, chaps. 12–17; and the collection of material in Bohnenblust, *Beiträge*, 34f; Thraede, *Brieftopik*, 139f.

79   Translations are very free at this point. Cf. the n. on the tr. above; also *RSV*: "What has become of the satisfaction you felt?" *JB*: "What has become of the enthusiasm you had?" Burton: "Where, then, is that gratulation of yourselves?" Cf. also other translations in the commentaries, and Bauer, *s.v.* μακαρισμός: "Where, then, is your blessing? i.e. the frame of mind in which you *blessed* yourselves" (taken up by Mussner).

it.[80] If, however, we have an objective genitive, someone else,[81] namely Paul, would make a statement of praise about the Galatians. This statement would be his descriptive judgment in regard to their initial wave of enthusiasm (v 15b).[82] He could also refer to his own praise as part of the friendship theme and in juxtaposition to "your temptation" (v 14). In this case we should translate: "what then has become of your praise?" Perhaps Paul's ironical tone operates on several levels at the same time. In any case, the term μακαρισμός ("praise") is used here in its original, secular sense,[83] and not in the Christian sense.[84] Also, Paul's question[85] is one of ironical astonishment: what happened to that praise? Has it vanished?[86] The present inclination of the Galatians to accept Torah and circumcision does render their initial enthusiasm premature. It is also at least a possibility that Paul refers to the previous passage 3:26–28, which we have shown to be related to the literary form of the macarism. Therefore, what seems to be a merely rhetorical question turns out to be the Galatians' real problem.

Verse 15a implies that a sharp contrast has arisen between the Galatians' past and present evaluation of Paul and his gospel. This contrast is pointed out by Paul in another familiar topos from the theme of friendship in v 15b. It is sheer irony when Paul somewhat solemnly begins with the oath formula of assurance: μαρτυρῶ ("I bear witness").[87] "Formerly," he says, "if it had been possible you would have plucked out your eyes and given them to me." Usually, commentators correctly point to the ancient belief that the eyes are man's most delicate and costly organ.[88] Paul then is taken to say: "they would have given him what was most valuable to them, and therefore would have done everything for him."[89] In addition, however, Paul refers to a literary topos. True friendship, teaches the friendship doctrine, requires the readiness of the highest sacrifice.[90]

---

80 Any form of self–glorification was suspect to Paul as well as to much of the ancient literature. See the literature on Gal 6:15 and Betz, *Paulus*, 70ff.

81 Cf. Luther (1535): "In this way Paul tries to temper and sweeten the bitter drink, that is, the sharp rebuke. . . ." Sieffert (p. 266) names Jerome, Theodoretus, Theophylactus, and Oecumenius as proponents of this interpretation.

82 See Oepke (p. 143) who seems to lean in this direction.

83 A good parallel is Plutarch *Solon* 27.6–7, the discussion of Solon with Croesus about whether he is the happiest of all men. Solon advances this opinion: "For the future which is advancing upon everyone is varied and uncertain, but when the Deity bestows prosperity on a man up to the end, that man we consider happy [εὐδαίμων]; to pronounce anyone happy [μακαρισμός], while he is still living and running the risk of life, is like proclaiming an athlete victorious and crowning him while he is still contending for the prize; the verdict is insecure and without authority." Cf. the anecdote about the friendship of Aristippus and Aeschines in Plutarch *Cohib. ira* 462 DE.

84 Cf. Acts 26:2; Rom 4:6, 9. On the whole concept see Friedrich Hauck and Georg Bertram, "μακάριος," *TDNT* 4.362–70; Bauer, *s.v.*

85 Ποῦ οὖν is well-attested by ℵ A B C F G P 33 104 *al.* The alternative reading by 𝔎 D *al,* of τίς οὖν ἦν or ἐστίν seems to attempt a compromise between the two options. For a fuller discussion see Zahn, p. 220 n. 11; Burton, p. 243; Schlier, p. 211 n. 4; Mussner, p. 308 n. 79. See also the parallels in Rom 3:27: Ποῦ οὖν ἡ καύχησις; ("Where, then, is the boasting?"); 1 Cor 1:20; 12:17, 19; 15:55; Luke 8:25; 2 Pet 3:4.

86 It would in fact turn into the curse of Gal 1:8–9; cf. 6:16.

87 The formula occurs in various forms in Paul—μαρτυρῶ ("I bear witness"): Rom 10:2; 2 Cor 8:3; also Col 4:13; θεὸς μάρτυς ("God is my witness") or similar forms: Rom 1:9; 2 Cor 1:23; Phil 1:8; 1 Thess 2:5, 10. Cf. also Gal 1:20. See Theodor Klauser "Beteuerungsformeln," *RAC* 2, *s.v.*; Gustav Stählin, "Zum Gebrauch von Beteuerungsformeln im Neuen Testament," *NovT* 5 (1962) 115–43. In Lucian's *Toxaris*, stories about true friendship are often accompanied by oaths (cf. 9, 11, 12, 18, 19, 20, 38, 42, 56).

88 Cf. *Barn.* 9.19: "You shall love as the apple of your eye all who speak to you the word of the Lord." Other parallels from ancient literature, including the Bible, are collected in Wettstein 2.227f; Oepke; Schlier, p. 211 n. 5; Bauer, *s.v.* ὀφθαλμός, 1; Wilhelm Michaelis, "ὀφθαλμός," *TDNT* 5.376–78; *PGL, s.v.*, B, 6.

89 So Schlier, p. 211. On εἰ δυνατόν see BDR, § 127, 2; 128, n. 4; 360 n. 2; 495 n. 5.

90 Cf. Plato *Lysis* 219D; Aristotle *EN* 9.8.9, p. 1169a 20ff.

Lucian in his "Toxaris" tells the story of the friendship between the Scythians Dandamis and Amizoces. When the Sauromatae made his friend a prisoner, Dandamis went straight to the leader of the enemy, negotiating for a ransom to get Amizoces released. Since all of Dandamis' possessions had already been taken by the Sauromatae, he had nothing else to offer but himself. But the enemy refused since he also was now in their hands. When he asked what he still would have to give, Dandamis was told to give his eyes. He immediately ordered them to be put out, and the friends were allowed to leave. This great demonstration of friendship so encouraged the Scythians and so frightened the Sauromatae that the latter broke off and slipped away during the night. Amizoces, however, could not bear the sight of his blind friend and blinded himself with his own hands.[91] This story seems to illustrate what Paul had in mind. He alludes to a literary motif which must have been almost proverbial in his time.[92] There is, therefore, no reason to assume that Paul had been inflicted with a disease of the eyes,[93] as New Testament commentators often have speculated.

The term ἐξορύσσω ("dig out, tear out") occurs in this connection only here in the New Testament;[94] the meaning of ἐδώκατέ μοι ("you would have given to me") is best explained by the story in Lucian's "Toxaris."[95]

■ **16** This verse introduces a question which also belongs to the friendship theme: ὥστε ἐχθρὸς ὑμῶν γέγονα ἀληθεύων ὑμῖν; ("is the result of it all that I have become your enemy by telling you the truth?").[96] The connection of ὥστε ("therefore") is certainly loose.[97] The question is rhetorical[98] in the sense that Paul throws it at his readers, letting them answer it for themselves. It is an allusion to the friendship topos of "frankness of speech" (παρρησία).[99] Among true friends it is possible to speak the truth with frankness without becoming enemies; telling the truth in this way distinguishes the "true friend" from the "flatterer", while turning against those who speak the truth is the

---

91   *Toxaris* 40–41. Wettstein (2.227) had quoted the parallel, but later commentaries failed to understand its importance. Lietzmann lists it, but Oepke, Schlier, and Mussner do not; Burton (p. 244) is unclear.

92   Cf. Xenophon *Mem.* 2.4.7: "Of all that a man can do with his hands, see for himself with his eyes, hear for himself with his ears or accomplish with his feet, in nothing is a friend backward in helping." Plato *Lysis* 209E–210A; Plutarch *Adulat.* 53 C–F (the parasites of Dionysius go so far to even imitate his failing sight!); 69A (frankness of speech to a friend is compared with supplying an inflamed eye with vision); similarly 72B; Dio Chrys. *Or.* 3.104f (also 3.118). See Bohnenblust, *Beiträge*, 38f.

93   The extensive but mostly fanciful literature on Paul's illness is collected in Bruce M. Metzger, *Index to Periodical Literature on the Apostle Paul* (New Testament Tools and Studies, 1; Leiden: Brill, 1960) nos. 242–57; Güttgemanns, *Apostel*, 174 n. 18; Schlier, p. 211 n. 1; Otto Kuss, *Paulus* (Regensburg: Pustet, 1971) 300 n. 2. The speculation is continued even by Schlier, Bonnard, Mussner.

94   See Bauer, *s.v.;* the verb in Matt 5:29; 18:9 is ἐξαιρέω.

95   For other views see the report in Sieffert, pp. 266f. Cf. Luther (1535): "And surely the Galatians did give their lives for him. For when they accepted and supported Paul, whom the world regarded as the most dangerous, accursed and damnable of all, they earned for themselves, as the partisans and defender of Paul, the displeasure and the hatred of both Gentiles and Jews."

96   Translations vary greatly. *RSV:* "Have I then become your enemy by telling the truth?" (alternative: "by dealing truly with you"). *NEB:* "And have I now made myself your enemy by being frank with you?" *JB:* "Is it telling you the truth that has made me your enemy?" Lightfoot: "Can it be that I have become your enemy?"

97   ὥστε ("therefore") introducing a question is odd. It draws a conclusion from the preceding, but leaves open whether that conclusion is true or not. Cf. Lightfoot: "'therefore' ought naturally to be followed by a direct assertion; but shunning this conclusion and hoping against hope, the Apostle substitutes an interrogative. . . ." Cf. also Sieffert, Burton, Schlier.

98   So Nestle–Aland, Lightfoot, Lietzmann, Oepke, Schlier, Mussner. Differently Zahn, Sieffert, Burton.

99   Cf. Luther (1535): "It is a friend's responsibility, if his friend is in the wrong, to admonish him freely. . . ." See Bohnenblust, *Beiträge*, 35; Heinrich Schlier, "παρρησία, παρρησιάζομαι," *TDNT* 5.871–75, 882–84. Very important for this *topos* is Plutarch *Adulat.*, *passim*; Cicero *Amic.* 89–104 (on this cf. Steinmetz, *Freundschaftslehre*, 148ff).

way of the uncivilized masses.[100] This matter has even become proverbial.[101] The term ἐχθρός ("enemy") refers here simply to the alienated friend;[102] ἀληθεύω ("tell the truth") is to be understood in the common sense of the word,[103] as the opposite of κολακεύω ("flatter"). It is not clear, however, whether or not there is a relationship between this passage and the strongly anti–Pauline *Kerygmata Petrou*, which calls Paul the "inimical man."[104]

■ **17** Rather unexpectedly, it seems, Paul launches a biting polemic against his opponents: ζηλοῦσιν ὑμᾶς οὐ καλῶς, ἀλλὰ ἐκκλεῖσαι ὑμᾶς θέλουσιν, ἵνα αὐτοὺς ζηλοῦτε ("they pay zealous court to you not in a good way, but they intend to exclude you, in order that you might court them").[105] Again making use of the friendship theme, Paul caricatures the efforts made by his opponents to win over the Galatians. Originally, ζηλοῦν ("pay zealous court") belongs to the erotic vocabulary

describing the stratagems of the lover to gain control over the beloved. This language is also found in connection with the friendship theme, where it is used to describe the sincere and deep concern one friend has for another. Not surprisingly, the language can also describe the relationship between the teacher and his students.[106] Standing in this tradition, Paul identifies the efforts of the opponents with the wrong kind of ζηλοῦν, done for egotistic purpose or for material gain.[107] In contrast to the principle of reciprocity which Paul had called for in 4:12, the opponents are said here to be speculating for a good return of their "courtship," a behavior which Cicero denounces as the confusion of a friendship relationship with shrewd business practice: "if we base our friendship on its profit to ourselves, and not on its advantage to those whom we love, it will not be friendship at all, but a

---

100 It is the character of the *"amicitia vulgaris."* Cf. Lucian *Abdic.* 7: "all are angry at those who speak the truth in frankness" (ὀργίζονται γοῦν ἅπαντες τοῖς μετὰ παρρησίας τἀληθῆ λέγουσιν).

101 Cf. the proverb "Obsequium amicos, veritas odium parit" ("Subservience makes friends, truth hatred"), which was often quoted in various forms (Terence *Andria* 1.1.41; Sophocles *Ajax* 1345; Herodotus 7.101, 104; Lucian *Abdic.* 7; Cicero *Amic.* 89). See Michal Swoboda (*De Proverbis a Cicerone Adhibitis* [Towarzystwo Naukowe w Toruniu. Prace Wydzialu Filologiczno–Filozoficznego, 14.3; Toruń 1963] 105f), who mentions also the quotation by Jerome (*Ep.* 116.31 [*PL* 22.951]); Archer Taylor, The *Proverb* (Copenhagen: Rosenkilde & Bagger, 1962) 146 (with later variations); *Corpus Paroemigraphorum Graecorum* (eds. E. L. Leutsch & F. G. Schneidewin; Göttingen: Vandenhoeck & Ruprecht, 1839–51) 2.433, no. 24e; Hans Walther, *Lateinische Sprichwörter und Sentenzen des Mittelalters* 2.5 (Göttingen: Vandenhoeck & Ruprecht, 1967) no. 33 157 k–1; August Otto, *Die Sprichwörter und sprichwörtlichen Redensarten der Römer* (Leipzig: Teubner, 1890) 368.

102 Cf. Ammonius *De adfinium voc. diff.* (ed. Klaus Nickau; Leipzig: Teubner, 1966) no. 208: ἐχθρὸς μὲν γάρ ἐστιν ὁ πρότερον φίλος ("the 'enemy' is the one who was formerly a friend").

103 So also Luther (1535), Sieffert. For a different view see Rudolf Bultmann, "ἀληθεύω," *TDNT* 1.251; Schlier, Zahn, Lietzmann, Mussner. Others are undecided, e.g., Burton, Oepke.

104 Ps.–Clem. *Hom., Ep. Petr.* 2.3: ἐχθρὸς ἄνθρωπος; ps.–Clem. *Recog.* 1.70.1: homo quidam inimicus. See the introduction, § 2.C, the commentary on 2:17, and Appendix 3.

105 Cf. Lightfoot: "True, they pay court to you: but how hollow, how insincere is their interest in you! Their desire is to shut you out from Christ. Thus you will be driven to pay court to them."

106 So correctly Lightfoot, who also points to Plutarch *Virt.* 448E; following a statement about courtship between man and woman, Plutarch says: "So again, when young men happen upon cultivated teachers, they follow them and admire them (ἕπονται καὶ ζηλοῦσιν) at first because of their usefulness; but later they come to feel an affection for them also, and in place of familiar companions and pupils they are called lovers and are actually so."

107 In works dealing with the topic of friendship, the issue is discussed as that of "friendship" and "utility." See especially Cicero *Amic.* 26–32 (on this, see Steinmetz, *Freundschaftslehre*, 36ff; Bohnenblust, *Beiträge*, 29f). Examples are also found in the NT, where the prototype of the false friend is Judas Iscariot who betrayed Jesus for money (see esp. Matt 26:49f; 27:3–10; Acts 1:15–20). Cf. also the political friendship between Herod and Pilate (Luke 23:12).

mere bartering of selfish interests."[108] Instead of reflecting the ideals of friendship, such behavior reflects the "low interests of the crowds": "but the majority of men recognize nothing whatever in human experience as good unless it brings some profit and they regard their friends as they do their cattle, valuing most highly those which give hope of the largest gain."[109] When Paul employs this kind of language, he does so for the purpose of discrediting his opponents in the eyes of the Galatians. He portrays them as nothing but shallow, hollow, and grabby "flatterers."[110] This caricature, of course, should not be taken uncritically as reality itself; it means next to nothing in regard to the question as to who the opponents really were and what they really had in mind.[111]

This uncertain state of things seems to make it even more difficult to determine what Paul may have meant by the term ἐκκλείω ("shut off") in v 17b.[112] The term most probably has a figurative meaning,[113] and thus can have political[114] or legal[115] overtones; in that context it may refer to exclusion from political activities, to conspiracies, deprivation from rights or even from philosophical teaching.[116] All these possibilities may play a role in Paul's usage of the term, but it is interesting that it turns up in the context of the friendship theme—even if only in its Latin equivalent[117]—where it seems very closely related to what Paul wants to say. Cicero says true "friendship embraces innumerable ends; turn where you will, it is ever at your side; no barrier shuts it out; it is never untimely and never in the way."[118] Conversely, the tyrant is, according to this doctrine, unable to make true friends because his many so–called "friends" possess, as it were, too much power, and this is "a bar to faithful friendships."[119] Exclusion, therefore, is the very opposite of true friendship, as it is also the opposite of a fruitful student-teacher relationship.[120]

If this is the background for Paul's statement, one

---

108 Cicero *Nat. deor.* 1.22: "quam si ad fructum nostrum referemus non ad illius commoda quem diligimus, non erit ista amicitia sed mercatura quaedam utilitatum suarum." The idea is widespread and at least as old as Aristotle (*EN* 8.7.2, p. 1158a21); cf. the commentary by Arthur Stanley Pease, *M. Tulli Ciceronis de natura deorum libri III* (Darmstadt: Wissenschaftliche Buchgesellschaft, 1968) 1.532f; also Steinmetz, *Freundschaftslehre*, 55ff.

109 Cicero *Amic.* 79; see Steinmetz, *Freundschaftslehre*, 136ff, 148ff.

110 Cf. Luther (1535): "Now Paul attacks the flattery of the false apostles." For parallels, cf. Plutarch *Adulat.* 54C: contrary to the flatterers, "between true friends there is neither emulation nor envy" (ζῆλος, φθόνος). The combination of ἔρως, ζῆλος, φθόνος is found as early as Plato *Phileb.* 47E. Paul uses this language also elsewhere: cf. 2 Cor 7:7, 11; 9:2; 11:2; the combination of ζῆλος and ἔρις Rom 13:13; 1 Cor 3:3; 2 Cor 12:20; Gal 5:20; furthermore 2 Cor 11:28f; 12:14. By contrast, see 1 Cor 13:4: ἡ ἀγάπη . . . οὐ ζηλοῖ ("love is not jealous"); Gal 5:26. For similar ideas see Xenophon *Mem.* 2.4.6. On the whole, see Albert Stumpff, "ζῆλος, ζηλόω," *TDNT* 2.877–88; Bauer, *s.v.*

111 Cf. Gal 1:7, 10; 2:4, 11–14; 3:1; 5:7–12; 6:12f.

112 The difficult term occurs only here in the NT; cf. *Herm. Sim.* 1.5; *Vis.* 3.9.6. For the great variety of possible interpretations, see Sieffert, pp. 269f; Mussner, pp. 310f.

113 Bauer's treatment is not satisfactory, even if he guessed more or less the right meaning: "in the sense of withdrawal of fellowship"; so also Mussner, p. 311. Cf. also F. R. Montgomery Hitchcock, "The Meaning of *EKKΛΕIEIN* in Galatians IV 17," *JTS* 40 (1939) 149–51; LSJ, *s.v.*

114 Cf. Aeschines 2.85, 3.74; Josephus *Vita* 294.

115 Cf. *Herm. Sim.* 1.5; Preisigke, *Wörterbuch* 4/4, *s.v.*

116 Cf. Aristotle *Magna Mor.* 1.34.31, p. 1198b16; Cicero *Fin.* 3.36; Seneca *Vita beata* 23.3; *Gnomol. Vatic.* 25.

117 The Latin equivalent of ἐκκλείω is *excludo*. See the *Oxford Latin Dictionary* (Oxford: Oxford University 1971), *s.v. excludo*.

118 Cicero *Amic.* 22: "amicitia res plurimas continet: quoque te verteris praesto est, nullo loco excluditur, numquam intempestiva, numquam molesta est."

119 Ibidem, 54: ". . . mores veros amicos parare non potuerunt, sic multorum opes praepotentium excludunt amicitias fidelis." It should be noted that Cicero's work is most likely based on lost Greek sources; on the problem see Steinmetz, *Freundschaftslehre*, esp. 97f. In the NT, cf. the notion of "friend of the emperor" in John 19:12 (cf. Gustav Stählin, "φίλος κτλ.," *TDNT* 9.166–67).

120 It is the opposite of the concept of "sharing with friends" (*amicis impertio*); cf. Cicero *Off.* 1.92: the "Socratic debate" does not "exclude" others (*excludat alios*) from participating.

must be cautious with regard to a theological interpretation as Schlier offers: "this would mean that the opponents of the Apostle supplement their push for circumcision by threatening to exclude [*sc.* the Galatians] from the church. Perhaps, one must also think of the separation from Paul and 'all other influences'."[121] In Paul's view, one would take this as the inevitable consequences of the intentions[122] of the opponents, if the Galatians would opt for them. But it is a question of interpretation whether, in saying what he says, Paul always speaks with utter sincerity and theological profundity. In Gal 4:17 at least, the surface of the language indicates that he uses rhetorical topoi and devices to discredit his opponents emotionally rather than "theologically." He points out that the opponents are false friends and bad teachers who are out to "monopolize" the Galatians, in order then to exploit them for their own interests (cf. 6:12–13).

The same tendency appears in the last statement in v 17c: ἵνα αὐτοὺς ζηλοῦτε ("in order that you may court them").[123] Rather than this being a caricature, Schlier[124] takes it to mean: "in order that you may open yourselves up to their doctrine and care for them as your teachers." Certainly this would be the result of the Galatians' "switching."[125] Paul's use of the friendship topos, however, suggests irony. Has the search for

their security of salvation made the Galatians so blind that they can no longer distinguish between a good old friend and new false friends, and that they end up as victims of one of the oldest games of human manipulation?

■ **18** A kind of definition[126] supports Paul's polemic in v 17: καλὸν δὲ ζηλοῦσθαι ἐν καλῷ πάντοτε ("yet, good is always to be courted in a good way").[127] Formally, this statement is a *sententia*[128] containing a definition of one of the principles of true friendship: good courtship must be done in a good way and continuously. This principle is, of course, the opposite of ζηλοῦσιν οὐ καλῶς ("courting in a bad way") described in v 17. The "always" refers to the principle of βεβαιότης ("firmness") in the friendship doctrine, as it was pointed out as early as Aristotle.[129] In Cicero's *De amicitia* it is represented by *stabilitas* and *constantia*: "now the support and stay of that unswerving constancy, which we look for in friendship, is loyalty."[130] Similarly, Plutarch says: "for friendship draws persons together and unites them and keeps them united in a close fellowship by means of continual association and mutual acts of kindness—'Just as the fig–juice fastens the white milk firmly and binds it', as Empedocles puts it (for such is the unity and consolidation that true friendship desires to effect) . . ."[131] "But friendship seeks for a

---

121 Schlier (pp. 212f) with reference to Gal 5:4.

122 θέλω ("will") indicates the opponents' goal: cf. Gal 1:7; 6:12, 13.

123 D* G it Ambrosiaster add, and thereby change completely the meaning of the sentence, these words based upon 1 Cor 12:31: ζηλοῦτε δὲ τὰ κρείττω χαρίσματα ("but you should seek the greater gifts of grace").

124 Schlier, p. 212.

125 Interestingly, Luther (1519) interprets Paul's words to mean "to shut you out from Christ and from trust in Him. . . ." In 1535, he emphasizes that the opponents want to shut Paul out, just as the sectarian enthusiasts of his day want to shut him, Luther, out.

126 𝔐 D G *pm* read τό before ζηλοῦσθαι, a stylistic improvement; B ℵ *pc* Vg Origen read the present ζηλοῦσθε turning the *sententia* into a compliment.

127 Modern translations often resort to guesswork. Cf. *RSV*: "For a good purpose it is always good to be made much of. . . ." *NEB*: "It is always a fine thing to deserve an honest envy" (alternative: "to be honorably wooed"). *JB*: "It is always a good thing

to win people over [alternative: Be won over to what is good]—and I do not have to be there with you—but it must be for a good purpose." Burton: "But it is good to be zealously sought after in a good thing, always. . . ." See also Moule, *Idiom Book*, 25f, 210.

128 *Sententiae* beginning with καλόν ("It is good . . .") are found elsewhere in the NT; cf. Mark 9:42, 43, 45, 47 par.; Rom 14:21; 1 Cor 7:1; Heb 13:9. Cf. also *PECL*, 86. See Graydon F. Snyder, "The *Tobspruch* in the New Testament," *NTS* 23 (1976) 117–20.

129 On this subject, see Steinmetz, *Freundschaftslehre*, 116–23.

130 *Amic.* 65: "Firmamentum autem stabilitatis constantiaeque est eius quam in amicitia quaerimus fides est. . . ."

131 Cf. Plutarch's *Amic. mult.*, esp. 95 A/B. He contrasts this with the instability of the "flatterer." The *topos* is found already in Aristotle *EN* 8.8.4, p. 1159 a/b; also Plutarch *Adulat.* 52A–53B; *Aquane an ignis* 955F; Epictetus *Diss.* 2.22.25.

---

fixed and steadfast character which does not shift about, but continues in one place and in one intimacy."[132] The phrase ἐν καλῷ ("in a good way") most probably alludes to the doctrine that a good friend should serve his companion only in a good way: "the true friend is neither an imitator of everything nor ready to commend everything, but only the best things . . .".[133] Cicero has a whole discussion about the possible conflict between friendship and justice. He as well as Plutarch condemn all forms of συναδικεῖν τῷ φίλῳ ("committing lawless acts with the help of a friend"). This has had, of course, political implications, particularly in Rome.[134] Cicero even formulates a *prima lex amicitiae*: "ask of friends only what is honorable; do for friends only what is honorable and without even waiting to be asked; let zeal be ever present, but hesitation absent; dare to give true advice with all frankness . . .".[135]

Verse 18b states the opposite of what v 18a has defined: καὶ μὴ μόνον ἐν τῷ παρεῖναί με πρὸς ὑμᾶς ("and not only when I am present with you"). Rather than openly accusing the Galatians of becoming disloyal to him, Paul suggests that they might be that type of person whose style of life follows the rule "out of sight, out of mind." It is interesting that Paul's statement is again a topos in connection both with the friendship theme and with epistolography. According to the friendship theme, temporal separation is one of the severe tests of friendship. Cicero states it as a mark of a weak friendship (*infirmus est mollisque natura*), if the partner "cannot easily bear his grief at the absence of his friends."[136] Plutarch shows it to be one of the symptoms of πολυφιλία ("having many friends"), that people who crave for many friends are unable to maintain those friendships: ". . . we cannot keep our hold on our earlier associates, who are neglected and drift away." "So it is with all of us: because anything new attracts us but soon palls on us, it is always the recent and freshly blooming friend that allures us and makes us change our minds, even while we are busy with many beginnings of friendship and intimacy at the same time, which go but little further, since, in our longing for the person we pursue, we pass over the one already within our grasp."[137] Of course this is not the manner of a true friendship, but only that of "cattle and crows that flock and herd together, and to look upon one's friend as another self and to call him 'brother' as though to suggest 'th' other'."[138] To be sure, true friendship does not change even when the friends are separated.[139]

At this point the conventions of friendship and of epistolography meet.[140] Paul's phrase "when I am present with you" reminds us of the epistolary formula ἀπὼν τῷ σώματι, παρὼν δὲ τῷ πνεύματι ("physically absent, but mentally present")[141] or "having been separated from you for the time being—in face but not

132 Plutarch *Amic. mult.* 97B: . . . ἡ φιλία στάσιμόν τι ζητεῖ καὶ βέβαιον ἦθος καὶ ἀμετάπτωτον ἐν μιᾷ χώρᾳ καὶ συνηθείᾳ.

133 Plutarch *Adulat.* 53C, again in contrast with the "flatterer;" cf. *Virt. prof.* 84F in connection with "imitation."

134 *Adulat.* 64C; Cicero *Amic.* 36–44. See Steinmetz, *Freundschaftslehre*, 62–76.

135 Ibidem, 44, cf. 40. See Steinmetz, *Freundschaftslehre*, 75f.

136 Ibidem, 75; cf. 62ff, 76ff, where he discusses ways in which to handle broken friendships. See Steinmetz, *Freundschaftslehre*, 134ff for a discussion of the subject.

137 *Amic. mult.* 93D.

138 Ibidem, 93E. Plutarch's *Amic. mult.* should be read entirely for the subject. See Steinmetz, *Freundschaftslehre*, 82f; Wolfgang Brinckmann, *Der Begriff der Freundschaft in Senecas Briefen* (Philos. Diss.: Köln, 1963) 10, 94f; also Bohnenblust, *Beiträge*, 36f, 37f.

139 See the final definition in Plutarch *Amic. mult.* 97B (cited above, n. 132).

140 On the connection between epistolography and the friendship theme, see Koskenniemi, *Studien*, 115ff. For examples, see ps.–Libanius *Charact. epistol.* (ed. Weichert), no. 50 (p. 35); also nos. 1 (p. 21f); 14 (p. 25f); 15 (p. 26); 19 (p. 27).

141 1 Cor 5:3; cf. also Col 2:5.

142 1 Thess 2:17. The formulae have been analyzed by Robert W. Funk, "The Apostolic *Parousia*: Form and Significance" in *Christian History and Interpretation: Studies Presented to John Knox* (ed. William R. Farmer *et al.*; Cambridge: Cambridge University, 1967) 249–68; Thraede, *Brieftopik*, 95–106; Gustav Karlsson, *Idéologie et cérémonial dans l'épistolographie byzantine* (Acta Universitatis Upsaliensis, Studia Graeca Upsaliensia 3; Uppsala: Almqvist & Wiksell, ²1962) 34ff, 40ff.

in heart."[142] It is the letter itself which, as a substitute for physical presence, overcomes the distance and serves to continue the friendship.[143] Hence, we understand the enormous importance of the genre of the "friendship letter" in antiquity. Therefore, to a limited extent his letter to the Galatians makes Paul present to them, urging them in this way to maintain their old relationship.[144]

■ **19** Seemingly abruptly, Paul turns to another theme, appealing to the Galatians as his "children." The grammar is difficult, and one should (with Schlier, Bonnard, and Mussner) assume that the sentence in v 18 is anacoluthic. Paul's appeal sounds somewhat pathetic to us, but it has its proper place in epistolography and contains some of Paul's most important soteriological doctrines: τέκνα μου, οὓς πάλιν ὠδίνω μέχρις οὗ μορφωθῇ Χριστὸς ἐν ὑμῖν ("my children, with whom I am in travail again until Christ takes shape in you").[145] The address "my children" is not unique in Paul,[146] but elsewhere he also regards himself as the "father" of the congregations he had founded.[147] In

1 Thess 2:7 he compares himself with a nurse cherishing her children.[148] Apparently Gal 4:19 is peculiar because here Paul speaks about himself as a mother giving birth to a congregation of spiritual children.[149]

In regard to the question of the background of this strange concept, several matters must be taken into account. First, the comparison with the loving mother was part of the friendship theme.[150] But it is also clear the Paul wants to say more than merely *compare* himself with a mother. He understands his own mission as actually giving birth to Christian churches. In Gal 4:19 a number of different concepts must be distinguished: (1) The concept of Paul "giving birth" to a community like a "mother" seems to have parallels only in gnosticism.[151] In Codex VI, Tractate 6 of the Nag Hammadi texts (*Disc. 8–9*), Hermes Trismegistos, acting as the father, explains rebirth and sonship to his "son." The son asks (53, 15ff): "my father, do they also have mothers?" Whereupon Hermes Trismegistos answers: "my son, they are spiritual [mothers]. For they are potencies; they let the souls grow. Therefore I say,

143 See Gustav Karlsson ("Formelhaftes in Paulus-briefen?" *Eranos* 54 [1956] 138–41) for an interpretation of Col 2:5 and 1 Cor 5:3.

144 Cf. also Gal 4:20; 2 Cor 10:2, 11; 11:9; 13:2, 10; Phil 1:27; Col 1:6.

145 Translations reflect the uncertainty of the meaning. *RSV*: "My little children, with whom I am again in travail until Christ be formed in you!" *NEB* takes the address as part of the preceding sentence and repeats it in v 19: "For my children you are, and I am in travail with you over again until you take the shape of Christ." *JB*: ". . . my children! I must go through the pain of giving birth to you all over again, until Christ is formed in you." Burton: "Oh, my children with whom I travail again in birth pangs till Christ be formed in you."

146 Cf. 1 Cor 4:14, 17; 2 Cor 6:13; Phlm 10; also Gal 4:28. See Albrecht Oepke, "παῖς," *TDNT* 5.636–54; Pedro Gutierrez, *La paternité spirituelle selon Saint Paul* (Paris: Gabalda, 1968) 213–23. τέκνα is read by B ℵ* D* G *pc* it Marcion; it is to be preferred against τεκνία (A C 𝔐 *pl* Clement *al*), which is nowhere else found in Paul. For grammatical problems, see BDF, §§ 192 n. 1; 296 n. 3. Tischendorf, Schlier, Mussner take the address as the beginning of a new sentence, putting a period after v 18 and leaving v 19 anacoluthic. Differently Lightfoot and Burton (pp. 248f).

147 1 Cor 4:15; 1 Thess 2:11; Phlm 10. On the concept of "spiritual fatherhood" see Str–B 3.340f; Reitzenstein, *Mysterienreligionen*, 40f; Gottlob Schrenk, "πατήρ," *TDNT* 5.958–59; Gutierrez, *ibidem, passim*; Pieter A. H. De Boer, *Fatherhood and Motherhood in Israelite and Judean Piety* (Leiden: Brill, 1974).

148 See on this passage Abraham J. Malherbe, " 'Gentle As a Nurse': The Cynic Background to I Thess ii," *NovT* 12 (1970) 203–17; furthermore, the concept of "spiritual parenthood" in 2 Cor 12:14; also *CMC* 63. 11.

149 Commentators sometimes confuse "motherhood" and "fatherhood." See e.g., *RSV*, n. on 4:19.

150 See as instances Plato *Lysis* 207E; Aristotle *EN* 8.1.3 p. 1155a15–20; 8.8.3 p. 1159a28–34; 8.12.2f p. 1161b17–34; 9.4.1 p. 1166a6f; 9.7.7 p. 1168a 25–27; Plutarch *Amic. mult.* 93F–94A; Cicero *Amic.* 27. For the history of the *topos*, see Steinmetz, *Freundschaftslehre*, 48f.

151 Cf. the remark about Paul in Pol. *Phil.* 3.2–3: "when he was absent he wrote letters to you, from the study of which you will be able to build yourselves up into the faith given you, which is the mother of us all . . . (. . . πίστιν· ἥτις ἐστὶν μήτηρ πάντων ἡμῶν . . .)." The last sentence is virtually identical with Gal 4:26b. Since Polycarp seems to know Gal (cf. Pol. *Phil.* 3.3; 5.1, 3; 9.2; 12.2), this may even be a quotation.

they are immortal."[152] In the mystery cults, where one might hope to find parallels,[153] "spiritual fatherhood"[154] is well–attested—not, however, spiritual "motherhood".[155] Therefore, many of the parallels referred to by commentaries do not apply here. In the *Hôdāyôth* from Qumran (1QH 3.1ff), the author compares himself with a mother giving birth under great pains, but the image is not used to include the community as the object born.[156] Thus, it remains but a possibility that the concept of "spiritual motherhood" belonged to the complex of "rebirth." The lack of references may be accidental. If this hypothesis is accepted, Paul would have received the concept from this background.

Οὕς is a *constructio ad sensum*;[157] πάλιν ("again") points to the founding of the congregation. In the case of the Galatians' apostasy, the whole act would have to be done again. The verb ὠδίνω is figurative ("give birth to someone amid throes"),[158] a usage found elsewhere. In this metaphorical sense, however, the concept has parallels in the Old Testament and in Judaism,[159] especially Philo,[160] and in the magical papyri.[161]

(2) The concept of "rebirth" is implied in Paul's words, even if it is not clearly expressed.[162]

(3) Paul's "birth pangs" are said to continue "until Christ takes shape within you" (or: "among you").[163] Traditionally, this phrase was believed to contain the concept of Christ's birth in the hearts of the believers, a concept well–known to later Christianity, and in particular to mysticism[164] and gnosticism.[165] Outside Christianity, we find the concept of "rebirth" as the

---

152 I follow the tr. of Karl–Wolfgang Troeger *et al.*, "Die sechste und siebte Schrift aus Nag Hammadi-Codex VI," *ThLZ* 98 (1973) 495–503, 498f. See also *Corp. Herm.* 13.1–2 (and on that passage Nock, *Essays* 1.298, 342; William C. Grese, *Corpus Hermeticum XIII and Early Christian Literature* [Ph.D. diss., Claremont, 1977]). In the NT see John 3:4 (and on that passage Bultmann, *John*, 136–38).

153 See Lietzmann, Oepke, Güttgemanns (*Apostel*, 185–94).

154 See above, n. 147.

155 Cf., however, Dieterich (*Mithrasliturgie*, 138, 256) with reference to Hippolytus *Ref.* 5.8.40–45; Joseph Dey, *ΠΑΛΙΓΓΕΝΕΣΙΑ* (Münster: Aschendorff, 1937) 60f, 128f; Nilsson, *Geschichte*, 2.688f.

156 See Otto Betz, "Die Geburt der Gemeinde durch den Lehrer," *NTS* 3 (1956/57) 314–26; idem, "Das Volk seiner Kraft" *NTS* 5 (1958) 67–75; for a critique, see Johann Maier, *Die Texte vom Toten Meer* (Munich: Reinhardt, 1960) 2.72ff; Braun, *Qumran* 1.211; Georg Bertram, "ὠδίν," *TDNT* 9.670–71.

157 See BDF, § 296, 3.

158 Bauer's tr. See LSJ, *s.v.*; Georg Bertram, "ὠδίν," 667–74; *PGL*, *s.v.*

159 See Str–B 3.340f; Bertram, ibidem, 668–72; H.–J. Fabry, "חכל," *TWAT* 2.716–20.

160 Philo uses the imagery mostly to describe the destiny of the soul: *Sac.* 3, 102; *Det.* 127; *Cher.* 42, 57; *Post.* 135; *Deus* 14, 137; *Conf.* 21; *Agr.* 101; *Mig.* 33; *L.A.* 1.74f. Cf. Bertram, ibidem, 671. See furthermore Clemens Alex. *Quis dives* 16.2 (3.170, ed. Stählin).

161 Cf. *PGM* 2.92. Cf. the concept of "creator of rebirth" (γενεσιουργὸς τῆς παλιγγενεσίας) which is identical with that of the formation of the Logos in the initiate (*Corp. Herm.* 13.5, 9); see Grese, *Corpus Hermeticum. XIII* (above, n. 152); the notion of spiritual "parent" (*parens*) in Apuleius *Met.* 11.257. See Richard Reitzenstein, *Poimandres* (Leipzig: Teubner, 1904) 216; Dey, *ΠΑΛΙΓΓΕΝΕΣΙΑ*, 100 (above, n. 155).

162 See Gal 3:27; 6:15; and also Dey, ibidem, 158, 173; Nock, *Essays* 1.101ff; Widengren, *Religionsphänomenologie*, 217ff.

163 There is no parallel for this concept of μορφοῦσθαι in early Christian literature before Justin. See Bauer. *s.v.*; Johannes Behm, "μορφόω," *TDNT* 4.753–54. The passage is Justin *Apol.* 1.5.8: τοῦ λόγου μορφωθέντος καὶ ἀνθρώπου γενομένου ("when the Logos took shape and became man"). Cf. also Bousset, *Kyrios Christos*, 164ff; Reitzenstein, *Mysterienreligionen*, 77.

164 See Hugo Rahner, "Die Gottesgeburt. Die Lehre der Kirchenväter von der Geburt Christi im Herzen des Gläubigen," *ZKTh* 59 (1935) 333–418; Rudolf Hermann, "Über den Sinn des *Μορφοῦσθαι Χριστὸν ἐν ὑμῖν* in Gal .4, 19," *ThLZ* 80 (1955) 713–26; Johannes Haussleiter, "Deus Internus," *RAC* 3.794–842; Gerhard Binder, "Geburt II," *RAC* 9.153–55. This interpretation is also maintained by Calvin: "he is born in us, in order that we live his life" (nascitur in nobis, ut vivamus eius vitam).

"birth" of the deity in the faithful.[166] If Paul means his words in this sense, *ἐν ὑμῖν* would have to be rendered as "within you": Christ "takes shape" in the Christians like a foetus and is born in the hearts of the believers; simultaneously they are reborn as "children." But *ἐν ὑμῖν* can also refer to the creation of the Christian community as a living organism, the "body of Christ."

There appears to be no need to favor one of the possibilities above the other. Paul probably maintains both concepts at the same time. He does express his belief that Christ is living in the believer;[167] the tradition of the church has understood it also in this way.[168] On the other hand, he holds the view that the Christians are members of the "body of Christ."[169] The ambiguity has led to confusion among interpreters. Understandably, the tendency often prevailed to take the concept in the individualistic sense of "Christ in us."[170] But throughout his letter Paul emphasizes the aspect of the unity and community of the church.[171]

Therefore, Gal 4:19 should be dealt with as a conglomerate of concepts[172] all belonging to the complex of "rebirth." Paul does not clarify precisely how these concepts are related to each other.

Perhaps he can presuppose that the readers are familiar with these concepts. Also, the misunderstandings which later demanded clarification have not yet occurred. It is no doubt true that rebirth for Paul is a very complicated matter. At any rate, in this conglomerate of ideas the Apostle plays the decisive role of the founder "giving birth" to a Christian community. The one "born" is Christ, and his "birth" is his epiphany; his "birth" also coincides with the "rebirth" of the Christians as the "children" of Paul as well as the "sons of God." All this occurs through the gift of the Spirit,[173] "in" the individual Christians, as well as "among" them, because as members of the "body of Christ" they are one "in Christ."[174]

■ 20 The concluding sentence of the section again

165 Cf. the Naassenes, according to Hippolytus *Ref.* 5.7.40; 5.8.37, 41–45; the Perates, according to Hippolytus *Ref.* 5.17.4; "Exegesis on the Soul" (*NHC* II, 134 lines 5, 29; 137 line 8); "Unbekanntes altgnostisches Werk," chap. 14 (in *Koptisch-gnostische Schriften* [GCS 13] 1.355 lines 26ff); *Exc. ex Theod.* 34.1; 59.1, 68, 79, 80; Hippolytus *Ref.* 6.31.7f; 32.2f; 42.8; 46.2; 7.18.1; 8.9.4; Clemens Alex. *Strom.* 7.14.88.3 (3.62, ed. Stählin); *Paed.* 3.1.1.5 (1.236, ed. Stählin).

166 Cf. *Corp. Herm.* 13.7: "Draw into yourself, and it will come; be willing, and it happens; suspend the perceptions of the body, and there will be the generation of divinity" (*ἐπίσπασαι εἰς ἑαυτόν, καὶ ἐλεύσεται· θέλησον καὶ γίνεται. κατάργησον τοῦ σώματος τὰς αἰσθήσεις, καὶ ἔσται ἡ γένεσις τῆς θεότητος*). Cf. 13.9: *εἰς συνάρθρωσιν τοῦ Λόγου* ("for the formation of the Logos"). See the discussion of the passage in Grese, *Corpus Hermeticum XIII* (above, n. 152).

167 See Gal 1:16; 2:20; 3:5; 4:6; Rom 8:9–11; 2 Cor 13:3, 5; Phil 1:20.

168 Cf. Col 3:15f; Eph 1:18; 3:17; 5:19; 2 Tim 2:22; 1 Pet 3:15; *Did.* 10.1; Ign. *Mag.* 12; *Barn.* 6.15, 16.8; *Diogn.* 11.4. See, furthermore, the material collected by Rahner, "Gottesgeburt" (n. 164, above).

169 See Gal 3:26–28, 29; also 2:4; 3:14; 5:6, where the formula "in Christ Jesus" (*ἐν Χριστῷ Ἰησοῦ*) occurs; this is identical with the concept of "body of Christ" (*σῶμα τοῦ Χριστοῦ*), which is not attested in Gal. See 1 Cor 12:12f, 27; etc. See Conzelmann,

1 Corinthians, 210ff; and for further bib. Robert H. Gundry, *SŌMA in Biblical Theology, with Emphasis on Pauline Anthropology* (SNTSMS 29; Cambridge: Cambridge University, 1976) 223ff; Murray, *Symbols*, 69ff.

170 Cf. Rom 14:4f; 1 Cor 1:12f; 3:18; 4:6; 7:40; 8:2; 10:12; 11:21; 12:11; 14:37; Gal 6:3. See Schmithals, *Gnosticism*, 166ff.

171 See Gal 3:28; 5:13–15, 26; 6:2–10; Rom 12:4f; 15:6; 1 Cor 1–4; 10:16f; 11:17ff; 12:4ff; Phil 1:27; 2:2; 1 Thess 2:11; 5:11; etc.

172 See also Luther (1535) who treats the passage as an "allegory." Differently Schlier (p. 214) who prefers "in you" or "through you" as the "body of Christ," although he does not deny the existence of Christ in individuals. Most older commentaries prefer the individualistic interpretation (esp. Zahn, Sieffert, Lietzmann, Burton, Oepke). Bonnard ("with you" in the sense of "a reality to you"), Lagrange, Hermann ("Über den Sinn," n. 164, above), and Mussner (pp. 312f) think of the right christological doctrine as over against heresy.

173 Cf. Gal 4:6.

174 It should be noted that in Gal the concept of rebirth is not expressly connected with baptism.

presents serious problems. For many commentators, interpretation here becomes merely guesswork.[175] But things should become clearer when we look at the statement as an epistolographic topos:

ἤθελον δὲ παρεῖναι πρὸς ὑμᾶς ἄρτι
καὶ ἀλλάξαι τὴν φωνήν μου,
ὅτι ἀποροῦμαι ἐν ὑμῖν

("but I would wish to be present with you now, and to exchange my voice [or: change the tone of my voice], because I am perplexed about you").

The particle δέ ("but") seems to have the force of concluding something.[176] The form ἤθελον ("I would wish") is imperfect de conatu, expressing the fact that the wish is at present not fulfillable and that the letter must suffice as a substitute.[177] This wish to be present with the reader instead of having to resort to a letter is a commonplace of letter–writing: the so–called πόθος ("yearning") motif.[178] If this is so, it is almost certain that the next phrase ἀλλάξαι τὴν φωνήν μου ("to alter my voice") is another epistolary topos, to be translated as "exchange my voice," i.e., for the letter.[179] According to Hellenistic epistolography, the letter is a substitute for the oral conversation (littera pro lingua).[180] The expression "exchange the voice" would then indicate Paul's suggestion that he could talk to the Galatians better orally than by the poor substitute of the letter.[181] In addition, he might allude to the rhetorical expolitio ("refinement"): "refinement" refers to the modulations of the voice for the purpose of persuading the audience.[182] The phrase would then have to be translated "to change the tone of my voice." The last remark is also rhetorical. Confessing that "I am at a loss because of you," Paul pretends to be at the end of his wits—a rhetorical device well–known by the name of dubitatio.[183] Thus, the strongly emotional plea ends

175 On a number of interpretations proposed, see Schlier, pp. 214f; Gerhard Wilhelmi, "ἀλλάξαι τὴν φωνήν μου? (Galater 4:20)," ZNW 65 (1974) 150–54.

176 Cf. Mussner who, with reference to Mayser (Grammatik, 2/3, 125–27) speaks of a "copulative" meaning.

177 Cf. Acts 25:22; Rom 9:3; BDF, §§ 326, 359; BDR, §§ 326, 359; Schlier, p. 214 n. 4; Moule, Idiom Book, 9; Mussner, p. 313 n. 110.

178 Paul also uses this motif in Rom 1:11; 15:23f; 1 Cor 16:7; Phil 2:26; 1 Thess 2:17, 18; 3:6, 10; cf. also 2 Tim 1:4; 2 Cor 12:20; Phil 1:27. See Koskenniemi, Studien, 169–72; Karlsson, Idéologie, 48ff (above, n. 142). Thraede, Brieftopik, 97, 165ff; Terence Y. Mullins, "Visit Talk in New Testament Letters," CBQ 35 (1973) 350–58; Mussner, p. 313 n. 110.

179 See Bauer (s.v. ἀλλάσσω, 1) who translates "change my tone" and refers to Artemidorus Oneirocr. 2.20 (s.v. φωνή, 2, b; he refers to Artemidorus Oneirocr. 4.56). Both passages speak of crows (see also 4.32). More important is Wettstein's citation of Apuleius Met. prooem., where the literary–rhetorical term vocis immutatio is found. See on this Lausberg, Handbuch, 2, index, s.v. immutatio; Martin, Rhetorik, 353–55.

180 Cf., as examples, Demosthenes Ep. 1.3–4; Isocrates Ep. 1.2–3; Philip. 25–26. See Thraede (Brieftopik, 39ff, 149f), followed by Mussner (p. 314 n. 115).

181 Already Jerome (Commentarius, 413, and Ep. 53.2) and esp. Luther (1519, expanded 1535) explain the epistolary topos. See Sieffert, pp. 276f. Cf. 1 Cor 4:21; 5:3f; 2 Cor 10:2, 11; 13:2, 10. On the subject, see Gustav Karlsson, "Formelhaftes in Paulusbriefen?" 138–41 (n. 143 above); Thraede, Brieftopik, 97ff.

182 See Rhet. ad Her. 4.42.54–58, with the definition in 54: "Refining [expolitio] consists in dwelling on the same topic and yet seeming to say something ever new. It is accomplished in two ways: by merely repeating the same idea, or by descanting upon it. We shall not repeat the same thing precisely—for that, to be sure, would weary the hearer and not refine the idea—but with changes. Our changes will be of three kinds, in the words, in the delivery, and in the treatment." See also Lausberg, Handbuch 1. §§ 830–42; cf. Otto Betz, "φωνή κτλ.," TDNT 9.293.

183 This is well–stated by Luther (1519, referring to Erasmus, Jerome; also 1535) where he paraphrases: "I am so distraught in my mind that I do not know what and how to deal with you in a letter from far away." Cf. also Acts 25:20; Herm. Sim. 8.3.1; 9.2.5, 6; in a gnostic dialogue Corp. Herm. 13.2. On the dubitatio (ἀπορία) see Lausberg, Handbuch 1. §§ 776–78. Differently Schlier (pp. 214f) who interprets with the help of 1 Cor 13:1; 14:10f: Paul wishes he could change his language into a heavenly one, in order to dispel the magic charm that has taken possession of the congregation.

236

with a confession of helplessness and the admission of defeat in the argument.[184] Paul acts as if he has run out of arguments. Of course, this rhetorical device must be seen for what it is.[185]

Paul had started out in 3:1 by addressing the Galatians as "simpletons" (ἀνόητοι). So far, chapters 3 and 4 contained heavy argumentative and deeply felt emotional sections. The arguments all went overwhelmingly in favor of the Apostle. According to the psychology of ancient rhetoric, however, people who are to be persuaded should not be left in such a low situation. By confessing his own perplexity in 4:20 Paul removes himself from the haughty position of one who has all the arguments and all the answers. This strategy leads to the next section, in which he provides an opportunity for the Galatians to discover the truth by themselves (4:21–31).

---

184 ἐν ὑμῖν refers to the Galatians. On the peculiar usage cf. 2 Cor 7:16. Mussner (p. 314 n. 111) takes it to be a substitute of the accusative of relation and refers to Mayser, *Grammatik* 2/2, 398.

185 Cf. Luther (1535): "He does not miss anything; he scolds the Galatians, beseeches them, soothes them, commends their faith with wonderful words, and as a genuine orator presents his case with great care and faith—all in order to call them back to the truth of the Gospel. . . ."

4

Probatio: The Sixth Argument

21 Tell me, you who want to be under [the] Law, do you not hear the law? 22/ For it is written that Abraham had two sons, one from the slave woman and one from the free woman. 23/ The one from the slave woman was born "according to [the] flesh," however, while the one from the free woman "through the promise." 24/ These things have an allegorical meaning. For they are[1] two covenants: one from Mount Sinai, giving birth into slavery— this is Hagar. 25/ Now Hagar is Mount Sinai in Arabia, but it also corresponds to the present Jerusalem, for she lives in slavery together with her children. 26/ By contrast, the Jerusalem above is free—this is our mother.

27/ For it is written:

> "Rejoice, O barren one who does not bear;
> break forth and shout, you who are in travail;
> for the children of the desolate one are more than the children of the one who has a husband."

28/ But you, my brothers, are children of promise, like Isaac.[2] 29/ And just as in those days the one born "according to [the] flesh" persecuted the one "according to [the] Spirit," so it is today. 30/ Yet what does Scripture say?

> "Drive out the slave woman and her son; for the son of the slave woman shall not share the inheritance with the son of the free woman."

31/ In conclusion, my brothers, we are not children of a slave woman, but of the free woman.

Analysis

The section 4:21–31[3] contains the concluding proof from Scripture. This argument demonstrates by allegorical interpretation of Scripture that Gentile Christians, such as the Galatians, are the offspring of Abraham's freeborn wife Sarah rather than the slave woman Hagar. It has been suggested that the section is out of

---

1   *NEB:* "stand for."

2   Literally: "according to Isaac," parallel to "the one according to the Spirit" (v 29). *RSV, NEB, JB* render: "like Isaac."

3   On this section, see (apart from the commentaries) esp. Pieter A. van Stempvoort, *De Allegorie in Gal. 4:21-31 als hermeneutisch Probleem* (Nijkerk: Callenbach, 1953); Robert M. Grant, *The Letter and the Spirit* (New York: Macmillan, 1957) 47ff; Luz, *Geschichtsverständnis*, 57, 64, 130, 185, 283–85; idem, "Der alte und der neue Bund bei Paulus und im Hebräerbrief," *EvTh* 27 (1967) 318–36; Herbert Ulonska, *Die Funktion der alttestamentlichen Zitate und Anspielungen in den paulinischen Briefen* (Diss.: Münster, 1963) 64–73; Richard P. C. Hanson, *Allegory and Event* (London: SCM, 1959) 80ff; Philipp Vielhauer, "Paulus und das Alte Testament" in *Studien zur Geschichte und Theologie der Reformation, Festschrift für E. Bizer* (ed. L. Abramowski *et al.*; Neukirchen: Neukirchener Verlag, 1969) 33–62; Klaus Berger, "Abraham in den paulinischen Hauptbriefen," *MThZ* 17 (1966) 47–89, esp. 59–63; Klein, *Rekonstruktion*, 168, 216f, 222f.

place[4] or simply repeats[5] what has been said before, but these assumptions turn out to be unfounded. Paul's method of interpretation is stated clearly in v 24a.[6] What he calls "allegory" is really a mixture of what we would call allegory and typology.[7] It should be admitted that both methods are closely related. Typology[8] interprets historical material commonly used in primitive Christianity. Persons, events, and institutions of Scripture and tradition are taken as prototypes of present persons, events, and institutions, which are explained as their fulfillment, repetition, or completion within a framework of salvation history.[9] In distinction to typology, allegory takes concrete matters mentioned in Scripture and tradition (mythology) to be the surface appearance or vestige of underlying deeper truths which the method claims to bring to light. Thereby concrete matters in the texts are transposed into general notions of philosophical or theological truth. Paul's text consists of quotations from LXX and Jewish haggadic material in Greek translation; he does not make

any distinction between the two.[10] In a general sense, Paul's interpretation of the Abraham tradition and of the figures of Hagar and Sarah is part of a history of such interpretations. Paul, however, does not simply take over this interpretation, but at the same time he gives it his own imprint.[11]

In regard to the composition of the Galatian letter, Paul's allegory in 4:21–31 poses two questions: why does he insert this allegory at the end of the *probatio* section? and: what argumentative force does he attribute to it? Quintilian has some advice to offer in regard to the distribution of arguments in the *probatio* section.[12] He favors the opinion that the strongest argument should come either at the beginning, or it should be divided between the beginning and the end. He clearly rejects an order "descending from the strongest proofs to the weakest."[13] Yet allegory does not seem to be a strong proof, if we examine what some of the rhetoricians have to say about it. Since it is related to the *exemplum* and to the metaphor, allegory is included

---

4   Oepke, p. 147; Luz, "Der alte und der neue Bund," *EvTh* 27 (1967) 319; Mussner, pp. 316f.

5   Schlier (p. 216) who follows Luther (1535); Burton and others regard it as an "afterthought." Oepke (p. 147) assumes Paul did a little more thinking since he wrote 4:20 or read more in the Septuagint. Like Oepke, Erich Stange ("Diktierpausen in den Paulusbriefen," *ZNW* 18 [1917] 115) has Paul take a break in dictating before starting afresh in v 21.

6   See also below on 4:24a.

7   See James Barr, *Old and New in Interpretation* (London: SCM, 1966) 110ff.

8   See Rudolf Bultmann, "Ursprung und Sinn der Typologie als hermeneutischer Methode," in his *Exegetica*, 369–80; Geoffrey W. H. Lampe and K. J. Woolcombe, *Essays on Typology* (SBT 22; London: SCM, 1957). For further literature, see Leonhardt Goppelt, "τύπος κτλ.," *TDNT* 8.246–60; Luz, *Geschichtsverständnis*, 52–64, 283ff.

9   See Bultmann's definition in *Exegetica*, 369; also 377. Cf. Lausberg, *Handbuch*, § 901.

10 On the whole question see Vielhauer's excellent discussion (see n. 3 above).

11 There is no indication that Paul knows the Philonic type of allegory of Sarah and Hagar; cf. Brandenburger, *Fleisch und Geist*, 200ff; Alfred Stückelberger, *Senecas 88. Brief* (Heidelberg: Winter, 1965) 61f; see the review by Karlhans Abel, *Gnomon* 38 (1966) 455–60.

12 Quint. 5.12.1ff.

13 Quint. 5.12.14: "The further question has been raised as to whether the strongest arguments should be placed first, to take possession of the judge's mind, or last, to leave an impression on it; or whether they should be divided between the commencement and close of the proof, adopting the Homeric disposition of placing the weakest in the center of the column, so that they may derive strength from their neighbours. But in the disposition of our arguments, we must be guided by the interests of the individual case: there is only one exception to this general rule in my opinion, namely, that we should avoid descending from the strongest proofs to the weakest" ("Quaesitum etiam, potentissima argumenta primone ponenda sint loco, ut occupent animos, an summo, ut inde dimittant, an partita primo summoque, quod ut Homerica dispositione in medio sint infirma, ut ab aliis crescant? Quae prout ratio causae cuiusque postulabit, ordinabuntur, uno, ut ego censeo, excepto, ne a potentissimis ad levissima decrescat oratio" [ed. Harold E. Butler, LCL]).

among the *figurae per immutationem.*[14] Its argumentative force is weakened by its ambiguity.[15] One could, therefore, come to the conclusion that the allegory in 4:21–31 is the weakest of the arguments in the *probatio* section. In this case, Paul's composition would be subject to a criticism like the one offered by Quintilian.

It is interesting, however, that a more positive evaluation becomes possible if we follow the advice of ps.–Demetrius.[16] This author argues that "direct" (ἁπλῶς) arguments are not always the most effective ones. "Any darkly–hinting expression is more terror–striking, and its import is variously conjectured by different hearers. On the other hand, things that are clear and plain are apt to be despised, just like men when stripped of their garments."[17] As evidence the author refers to the mysteries: "hence the Mysteries are revealed in an allegorical form in order to inspire such shuddering and awe as are associated with darkness and night."[18] When we consider that in the Christian context the Abraham tradition holds the place which is occupied in the Mysteries by their own holy tradition, Paul's argument here becomes highly forceful.[19]

There may be also another rhetorical strategy at work; ps.–Demetrius follows the opinion of Theophrastus in saying "that not all possible points should be punctiliously and tediously elaborated, but some should be left to the comprehension and inference of the hearer. . .".[20] The effect upon the hearer is this: ". . .when he perceives what you have left unsaid [he] becomes not only your hearer but your witness, a very friendly witness too. For he thinks himself intelligent because you have afforded him the means of showing

his intelligence. It seems like a slur on your hearer to tell him everything as though he were a simpleton."[21]

In the light of such rhetorical considerations the place and function of the allegory 4:21–31 becomes explainable. Paul had concluded the previous section in 4:20 with a confession of perplexity (. . .ὅτι ἀποροῦμαι ἐν ὑμῖν). Such a confession was a rhetorical device, seemingly admitting that all previous arguments have failed to convince. Then, in 4:21, he starts again by asking the Galatians to give the answer themselves: "tell me,. . . do you not hear the Law?" In other words, the allegory allows Paul to return to the *interrogatio* method used in 3:1–5 (cf. 4:8–10) by another route. There this method was employed to force the Galatians to admit as eye–witnesses that the evidence speaks for Paul, an admission that had left them in the situation of "simpletons" (ἀνόητοι). However, people who are to be persuaded should not be left in a situation of inferiority. Paul makes two moves to raise the Galatians to a higher level of understanding. In 4:20 he had removed himself from the haughty position of the one who possesses and provides all the arguments. Through the allegory 4:21–31 he then lets the Galatians find the truth for themselves. Thus, by convincing themselves they also clear themselves of the charge of being mere "simpletons."[22]

The conclusion in 4:31, stated in the first person plural, includes the readers among those who render judgment. In formulating not merely the conclusion to the "allegory" but to the entire *probatio* section (3:1–4:31) Paul anticipates that the whole argument has convinced his readers.

---

14 Cf. the definition in *Rhet. ad Her.* 4.34.46: "Permutatio [ἀλληγορία] est oratio aliud verbis aliud sententia demonstrans" ("Allegory is a manner of speech denoting one thing by the letter of the words, but another by their meaning"). See also Lausberg, *Handbuch*, §§ 421, 564, 894, 895–901.

15 Because of its ambiguity, allegory can easily go over into enigma. See Lausberg, *Handbuch*, § 899.

16 See *De eloc.* 2.99–101, 151, 222, 243 (ed. W. Rhys Roberts, LCL).

17 Ibidem, 100.

18 Ibidem, 101: Διὸ καὶ τὰ μυστήρια ἐν ἀλληγορίαις λέγεται πρὸς ἔκπληξιν καὶ φρίκην, ὥσπερ ἐν σκότῳ καὶ νυκτί. ἔοικε δὲ καὶ ἡ ἀλληγορία τῷ σκότῳ καὶ τῇ νυκτί.

19 For the literature on allegory, see below on 4:24a.

20 *De eloc.* 4.222: . . . ὅτι οὐ πάντα ἐπ' ἀκριβείας δεῖ μακρηγορεῖν, ἀλλ' ἔνια καταλιπεῖν καὶ τῷ ἀκροατῇ συνιέναι, καὶ λογίζεσθαι ἐξ αὐτοῦ.

21 Ibidem: συνεὶς γὰρ τὸ ἐλλειφθὲν ὑπὸ σοῦ οὐκ ἀκροατὴς μόνον, ἀλλὰ καὶ μάρτυς σου γίνεται, καὶ ἅμα εὐμενέστερος. συνετὸς γὰρ ἑαυτῷ δοκεῖ διὰ σὲ τὸν ἀφορμὴν παρεσχηκότα αὐτῷ τοῦ συνιέναι, τὸ δὲ πάντα ὡς ἀνοήτῳ λέγειν καταγινώσκοντι ἔοικεν τοῦ ἀκροατοῦ.

22 Cf. Luther (1535): "The common people are deeply moved by allegories and parables; therefore Christ also used them often. They are like pictures of a sort, which show things to simple people as though before their very eyes and for this reason have a profound effect on the mind, especially of an uneducated person."

Interpretation

■ 21 The section 4:21–31 is doctrinal in nature. This is clear from the initial question to the Galatians: "tell me, you who want to be under [the] Law, do you not hear the law?" Stylistically, this kind of address corresponds to the conventions of the Hellenistic diatribe literature.[23] Paul assumes a dialogical situation, an assumption made possible by the ancient understanding of the letter as one half of a dialogue.[24] In a somewhat ironic tone, Paul addresses the Galatian Christians[25] as people who are about to submit to the Jewish Torah.[26] The answer to his question is self-evident: if they would only listen[27] to the Torah itself and understand what it says,[28] the absurdity of their plans would become obvious to them. This type of interrogation is familiar to us from the diatribe literature.[29] It also presupposes the Apostle's allegorical hermeneutic: to understand the Torah means to understand its allegorical mean-

ing.[30] In this sense his call is different from the prophet's call in the Old Testament to "hear the word of the Lord."[31] Paul also intentionally uses the term νόμος ("law") ambiguously:[32] the first time it refers to the Jewish Torah, the second time to "Scripture" or, more precisely, to Scriptural tradition, interpreted allegorically.

■ 22 Although Paul uses the quotation formula[33] "it is written that . . ." (γέγραπται γὰρ ὅτι . . .), he does not really cite Scripture verses, but provides a kind of summary of Gen 16:15; 21:2–3, 9(LXX) and calls it νόμος ("law") (cf. Gal 4:21). That is to say, he simply quotes the tradition. This tradition also includes an interesting interpretation: "Abraham had two sons, one from the slave woman, and one from the free woman" (᾿Αβραὰμ δύο υἱοὺς ἔσχεν, ἕνα ἐκ τῆς παιδίσκης καὶ ἕνα ἐκ τῆς ἐλευθέρας). Paul is not interested in giving an historically accurate account of the Genesis narra-

---

23 See also Gal 3:1–5; 4:8f. For examples in the diatribe literature, see Epictetus *Diss.* 1.11.12; 2.1.23; 2.2.22; 2.5.18; 2.11.10; 2.19.18; 2.7.6f, and often. Cf. Bultmann, *Stil*, 10ff, 64ff.

24 Cf. the definition of the letter by Artemon, the editor of Aristotle's letters, in ps.–Demetrius *De eloc.* 4.223: ". . . a letter ought to be written in the same manner as a dialogue, a letter being regarded by him as one of the two sides of a dialogue." Ps.–Demetrius adds: "There is perhaps some truth in what he says, but not the whole truth. The letter should be a little more studied than the dialogue, since the latter reproduces an extemporary utterance, while the former is committed to writing and is (in a way) sent as a gift." On this theory, see Thraede, *Brieftopik*, 17ff.

25 The addressees are the same as in 3:1 and not—as Lütgert (*Gesetz und Geist*, 11, 88) had proposed—only that group in the Galatian churches which followed the "judaizers." So also most commentaries; see esp. Oepke, Schlier (p. 216 n. 3), Mussner; differently Ulonska (*Zitate und Anspielungen*, 65, n. 3 above), who has Paul address the opponents.

26 Cf. Gal 4:9. Presently the Galatians are not yet "under the Torah" (cf. n. 30, below), but the opponents urge them to take that step (cf. 1:6f; 4:17; 5:1–4; 6:12f).

27 Cf. Rom 10:18; Matt 13:13; Mark 8:18; etc.: ἀκούω means both "listen" and "understand." See Bauer, *s.v.*, 1, a; 7; Schlier, p. 217 n. 1; Mussner.

28 Instead of ἀκούετε D G *pc* lat sa have ἀναγινώσκετε ("read") which excludes "understanding." But Paul no doubt presupposes that the Galatians have

read the Scriptures, while they did not understand their meaning which he is going to develop in the following.

29 See also Mark 12:10 par.; Matt 12:5; Luke 10:26; 24:25f; John 7:19; 10:34; 12:34; Rom 4:3; 11:2; 1 Cor 9:8. For an example from Epictetus see *Diss.* 3.24.9: "Shall we not . . . call to mind what we have heard from the philosophers?" (Οὐκ . . . μεμνησόμεθα ὧν ἠκούσαμεν παρὰ τῶν φιλοσόφων;).

30 Cf. the question by Philip in Acts 8:30: "Do you understand what you read?" (ἆρά γε γινώσκεις ἃ ἀναγινώσκεις;). For the opposite, see Justin *Dial.* 10.3, where Trypho holds against the Christian: "Have you not read that that soul shall be cut off from his people who shall not have been circumcised on the eighth day?"

31 Cf. Mussner (pp. 317f) who sees Paul's call more in line with that of the OT prophets. However, the prophet's call to "hear the word of Yahweh" was the call to obey while Paul refers to the meaning of scriptural tradition.

32 Paul intentionally vacillates between νόμος as "Jewish Torah" and "Scripture" (cf. 3:8, 22; 4:30). The phrase ὑπὸ νόμον εἶναι ("be under [the Jewish] law") seems to be technical; it is also found in 3:23; 4:4, 5; 5:18, and refers to the commitment to and observance of the Torah (cf. 5:3; 6:13).

33 For this formula see Gal 3:10; Rom 12:19; 14:11; 1 Cor 1:19; 3:19.

tives. He does not consider the fact that Abraham had more than two sons (cf. Gen 25:1–6).[34] Nor does he bother to reconcile this tradition with his own argument in 3:6–14, where he envisages only one kind of son of Abraham. What concerns Paul here in 4:22 is the dualistic contrast between Hagar's son Ishmael and Sarah's son Isaac.[35] We can easily see why the tradition comes in handy at this point. That Ishmael's mother was a "slave woman" ($\pi\alpha\iota\delta\iota\sigma\kappa\eta$),[36] while Isaac's mother was a "free woman" ($\dot{\epsilon}\lambda\epsilon\upsilon\theta\dot{\epsilon}\rho\alpha$),[37] fits Paul's argument very well. He had already branded the pre-Christian situation as "slavery" under the Torah and under the "elements of the world," while "freedom" in Christ had at least been mentioned (2:4; 3:26–28; cf. 1:10). In fact, the concept of "freedom" will provide the major topic in the following sections of the letter (see 4:31; 5:1, 13).

■ 23 Paul pushes his interpretation of the Abraham tradition a step further. What is important to him is not merely the different social status of the two mothers, but the contrast between their sons. The birth of the sons, however, must be seen in the light of the theo-logical concepts applied to them and represented by them. If the contrast between the "slave woman" and the "free woman" is applied to the sons, the difference is that between "flesh" and "promise": "however, the one from the slave woman was born 'according to [the] flesh,' while the one from the free woman was born 'through the promise.'" The conjunction $\dot{\alpha}\lambda\lambda\dot{\alpha}$ ("but") does not introduce a point different from the preceding, but marks the transition to the following, on account of which the preceding was told. The particle $\mu\dot{\epsilon}\nu$ ("on the one hand") is missing in some important witnes-ses,[38] so that the rules of textual criticism would favor its elimination in spite of the fact that the majority of witnesses has it. But the new editions have removed the sign of caution.[39] The concepts of $\kappa\alpha\tau\dot{\alpha}\ \sigma\dot{\alpha}\rho\kappa\alpha$ ("according to [the] flesh")[40] and $\delta\iota\dot{\alpha}\ \tau\hat{\eta}\varsigma\ \dot{\epsilon}\pi\alpha\gamma\gamma\epsilon\lambda\dot{\iota}\alpha\varsigma$ ("through the promise")[41] are no doubt Paul's. They conform to the context in Galatians,[42] yet also fit the Genesis narratives.[43] Interestingly, Paul does not here contrast "according to [the] flesh" with "according to [the] Spirit" ($\kappa\alpha\tau\dot{\alpha}\ \pi\nu\epsilon\hat{\upsilon}\mu\alpha$), but stays with "through the promise" because it fits his argument in chapters

---

34   Cf. also Rom 4:19; 9:7ff. For the grammatical problem of $\epsilon\hat{\iota}\varsigma\dots\epsilon\hat{\iota}\varsigma\dots$ see BDR, §§ 247, 3; 250 n. 2; BDF, § 247 (3).

35   Paul mentions the name of Hagar in Gal 4:24f; Sarah in Rom 4:19; 9:9; Isaac is mentioned in Gal 4:28; Rom 9:7, 9. Ishmael is not mentioned by name.

36   That Hagar was a slave–woman is stated only in Gal 4:22, 23, 30, 31, not in Rom; it agrees with Gen (LXX Gen 16:1ff; 21:10ff; 25:12). In Philo, Hagar is interpreted as the "lower education of the schools" while Sarah represents philosophical wisdom and virtue. For this interpretation, see the index in LCL Philo, 10.317–19. On $\pi\alpha\iota\delta\iota\sigma\kappa\eta$ ("female slave"), see Bauer, s.v.

37   That Sarah was a "free–woman" is not mentioned in the LXX; in Philo her name is taken to mean "sovereignty" ($\dot{\alpha}\rho\chi\dot{\eta}$). See the index in LCL Philo, 10.413–19. Paul has gained the meaning as "free–woman" either by juxtaposing it with Hagar, or from the tradition where this contrast was already found; if the latter is true, it is an indication that Paul's tradition was different from Philo's.

38   P46 B f vg.

39   Nestle–Aland, 25th edition: [$\mu\dot{\epsilon}\nu$], 26th edition: $\mu\dot{\epsilon}\nu$ (=Aland, Greek New Testament).

40   The expression $\kappa\alpha\tau\dot{\alpha}\ \sigma\dot{\alpha}\rho\kappa\alpha$ ("according to [the]

flesh") is found in Gal 4:23, 29, and more often in Rom (1:3; 4:1; 8:4, 5, 12, 13; 9:3, 5; 1 Cor 1:26; 10:18; 2 Cor 1:17; 5:16; 10:2, 3); cf. also Col 3:22; Eph 6:5. The "abbreviation" (cf. the Intro-duction above, § 7, 4) has a range of meanings, from "according to human standards" (see Bauer, s.v., 6) to a distinctively negative, dualistic "according to the ungodly flesh" (cf. Rom 9:8: the "children of the flesh" [$\tau\dot{\alpha}\ \tau\dot{\epsilon}\kappa\nu\alpha\ \tau\hat{\eta}\varsigma\ \sigma\alpha\rho\kappa\dot{o}\varsigma$]). The perfect form $\gamma\epsilon\gamma\dot{\epsilon}\nu\nu\eta\tau\alpha\iota$ in Gal 4:23 denotes the continuing effect in the present (see BDF, § 342; BDR, § 342 n. 6). It is noteworthy that in Philo, Ishmael represents inferior "sophistry" in contrast with "self–taught wisdom" (Isaac); see the index in LCL Philo, 10.331–33. Differently Schlier, pp. 217f; see also Eduard Schweizer, "$\pi\nu\epsilon\hat{\upsilon}\mu\alpha$, $\pi\nu\epsilon\upsilon\mu\alpha\tau\iota\kappa\dot{o}\varsigma$," TDNT 6.429; idem, "$\sigma\dot{\alpha}\rho\xi$," TDNT 7.125ff, 131.

41    $\delta\iota'\ \dot{\epsilon}\pi\alpha\gamma\gamma\epsilon\lambda\dot{\iota}\alpha\varsigma$ occurs in Gal 3:18; P46 ℵ A C al read this also in 4:23, while the majority of witnesses prefers $\delta\iota\dot{\alpha}\ \tau\hat{\eta}\varsigma\ \dot{\epsilon}\pi\alpha\gamma\gamma\epsilon\lambda\dot{\iota}\alpha\varsigma$ (Nestle–Aland). $\delta\iota\dot{\alpha}$ ("through") in 4:23 identifies God's promise to Abraham as the primary cause for his birth; cf. Rom 4:16–21.

42   For the concept of "promise" ($\dot{\epsilon}\pi\alpha\gamma\gamma\epsilon\lambda\dot{\iota}\alpha$) see Gal 3:14, 17, 18, 19, 21, 22, 29; 4:1–7; 4:28; also Rom 4:13, 14, 16, 20; 9:4, 8, 9.

43   Cf. Gen 16:1–4a; 17:15–19; 21:1–7.

3–4.[44] In general Paul is in conformity with the Jewish tradition which often dealt with Isaac's miraculous birth, but here he gives this tradition his own distinctive twist.[45]

■ 24 Having set forth the allegory about the two sons of Abraham in vv 22–23, Paul now adds a further allegorical interpretation. This interpretation is introduced in v 24a by a statement of method: "these things have an allegorical meaning" (ἅτινά ἐστιν ἀλληγορούμενα). Ἅτινα summarily refers to the content ("these things") of vv 22–23. The term ἀλληγορέω ("interpret allegorically")[46] is a *hapax legomenon* in primitive Christian literature.[47] However, we know quite well from other sources which method Paul intends to apply.[48]

The term ἀλληγορέω comes from ἄλλο ἀγορεύω ("say something else").[49] The so-called allegorical method was well developed by Paul's time.[50] We must distinguish between the usage of the concept in Hellenistic rhetoric generally, and the allegorical interpretation of literary sources (especially Homer) and mythological traditions in particular. The method rests upon the assumption that the material to be interpreted contains a "deeper meaning" not visible on the surface. The allegorical method was believed to be able to bring this deeper meaning to light. The fact is, however, that for the most part the deeper meaning is secondary to the material which it claims to explain, and that the deeper meaning has its origin in the interpreter and his ideas and frame of reference. Judaism[51] had adopted the method long before Paul and had applied it to the Jewish tradition. Paul must have inherited it from Judaism,[52] but his use of it presupposes that primitive Christianity shared it at least to some extent.

Paul's allegorical interpretation itself is contained in vv 24b–26 (27). It is accomplished by conceptual identifications.[53] First, we learn that the two mothers, Hagar and Sarah, represent two diametrically opposed covenants: "for these are two covenants." Paul is not interested in the two women as historical persons, but in the two worlds they represent.[54] The two covenants amount to two diametrically opposed systems: an "old covenant" (ἡ παλαιὰ διαθήκη)[55] and a "new covenant" (ἡ καινὴ διαθήκη).[56]

The term διαθήκη is difficult to translate. The mean-

44 Cf. Gal 3:29; 4:28, 31; see also Luz, "Der alte und der neue Bund," *EvTh* 27 (1967) 321; idem, *Geschichtsverständnis*, 283–85.

45 For the Jewish tradition, see Str-B 3.216f; and the index in LCL Philo, 10.324–31.

46 See LSJ, *s.v.*

47 See Bauer, *s.v.*; Joseph C. Joosen and Jan H. Waszink, "Allegorese," *RAC* 1 (1950) 283–93.

48 Cf. 1 Cor 10:1–13; 2 Cor 3:14–18.

49 For a rhetorical definition, see Quint. 9.2.46: ἀλληγορίαν facit continua μεταφορά ("a thoroughgoing usage of metaphor produces allegory"). See Lausberg, *Handbuch*, §§ 895–901.

50 For the present state of research, see Felix Buffière, *Les mythes d'Homère et la pensée grecque* (Paris: Les belles lettres, 1956); Jean Pépin, *Mythe et allégorie* (Paris: Aubier, 1958); Reinhold Merkelbach, *Roman und Mysterium in der Antike* (Munich: Beck, 1962); John G. Griffiths, "Allegory in Greece and Egypt" *JEA* 53 (1967) 79–102; idem, *Plutarch*, 100f; Irmgard Christiansen, *Die Technik der allegorischen Auslegungswissenschaft bei Philo von Alexandrien* (Beiträge zur Geschichte der Biblischen Hermeneutik 7; Tübingen: Mohr, Siebeck, 1969).

51 See Nikolaus Walter, *Der Thoraausleger Aristobulus* (TU 86; Berlin: Akademie–Verlag, 1964) 124ff; Hengel, *Judaism and Hellenism* 1.164f; 246f, with notes.

52 On Paul and allegory, see Joseph Bonsirven, *Exégèse rabbinique et exégèse paulinienne* (Paris: Beauchesne, 1939) 309–11; Schoeps, *Paul*, 234f, 238 n. 3; Brandenburger, *Fleisch und Geist*, 200ff; Luz, *Geschichtsverständnis*, 61ff; Richard P. C. Hanson, *Allegory and Event* (London: SCM, 1959); Leonhard Goppelt, *Typos: Die typologische Deutung des Alten Testaments im Neuen* (Darmstadt: Wissenschaftliche Buchgesellschaft, ²1966); idem, *TDNT* 8, *s.v.* τύπος; Philipp Vielhauer, "Paulus und das Alte Testament," in *Studien zur Geschichte und Theologie der Reformation, Festschrift für E. Bizer* (ed. L. Abramowski *et al.*; Neukirchen: Neukirchener Verlag, 1969) 33–62; Barnabas Lindars, *New Testament Apologetic* (Philadelphia: Westminster, 1961).

53 Cf. e.g., 1 Cor 10:4: "The rock was Christ"; *Barn.* 8.2–3; 9.8 and often.

54 See *Barn.* 8.7: "And for this reason the things which were thus done are plain (φανερά) to us, but obscure (σκοτεινά) to them, because they did not hear the Lord's voice."

55 2 Cor 3:14.

56 2 Cor 3:6; 1 Cor 11:25; cf. Rom 9:4; 11:27.

ing here goes beyond that in Gal 3:15, 17, where it refers to a legal testament. The Hebrew ברית, for which διαθήκη is the Greek equivalent, amounts to a world order decreed by divine institution; it contains God's definition of the basis and purpose of human life.[57] Paul's aim is clearly to discredit the "old covenant" as the pre-Christian condition before salvation came. What he offers as proof, however, has strained the credulity of the readers beyond what many people can bear. Often quoted is Nietzsche[58] who called it "*jenes unerhörte philologische Possenspiel um das Alte Testament*" ("this unheard-of philological farce in regard to the Old Testament"). At least Paul's intentions are easy to detect: "one from Mount Sinai, bearing children for slavery; this one is Hagar." The Apostle's statement is extremely abbreviated: the "one from Mount Sinai" refers to the "Sinai covenant."[59] It is represented by the slave woman Hagar,[60] whose child-

ren's destiny is slavery (εἰς δουλείαν).[61] Those who belong to this covenant, the Torah covenant of Judaism, are in the situation of "slavery under the Law" (cf. Gal 3:22–25, 28; 4:1–10; 5:1; also 2:4).

■ 25 In v 25a the text contains a real *crux interpretum*.[62] It is contained in the brief statement: τὸ δὲ Ἁγὰρ Σινᾶ ὄρος ἐστὶν ἐν τῇ Ἀραβίᾳ ("now Hagar is Mount Sinai in Arabia"). The textual tradition at this point shows a large number of variant readings, no doubt most of them due to the problem of the meaning of the sentence. Since the variants appear to be attempts to clarify or correct the text,[63] Nestle–Aland, 26th edition, is right to favor the *lectio difficilior*.

If this text is presupposed as the most original, the statement provides geographical information intended to support the allegorical argument.[64] Paul must have thought that the name[65] Hagar refers to the mountain in Arabia commonly known as Mount Sinai.[66] The

57 On the concept of διαθήκη see Gottfried Quell and Johannes Behm, "διατίθημι, διαθήκη," *TDNT* 2.106–34; Hans Pohlmann, "Diatheke," *RAC* 3 (1957) 982–90; Bauer, *s.v.*; Willem C. van Unnik, "La conception paulinienne de la Nouvelle Alliance," in *Littérature et Théologie Paulinienne* (Bruges: Desclée de Brouwer, 1960) 109–26; Ceslaus Spicq, *L'épître aux Hébreux* (Paris: Gabalda, 1953) 2.285–99, with bib.; George E. Mendenhall, "Covenant," *IDB* 1.714–23; Ulrich Luz, "Der alte und der neue Bund bei Paulus und im Hebräerbrief," *EvTh* 27 (1967) 318–36; idem, *Geschichtsverständnis*, 283ff. On the OT, see M. Weinfeld, *TWAT* 1.781–808; Ernst Kutsch, *Verheissung und Gesetz* (BZAW 131; Berlin: Töpelmann, 1972); idem, "'Ich will euer Gott sein': bᵉrît in der Priesterschrift," *ZThK* 71 (1974) 361–88.

58 Friedrich Nietzsche, *Morgenröte*, in *Werke* (Darmstadt: Wissenschaftliche Buchgesellschaft, 1963) 1.1068, quoted by Schoeps, *Paul*, 235.

59 The name of Mount Sinai is mentioned by Paul only Gal 4:24, 25; cf. also Acts 7:30, 38; *Barn.* 11.3; 14.2; 15.1. While the mountain plays an important role in the OT and in Judaism, its precise location is not clear. For the problem see Str-B. 3.572f; Siegfried Herrmann, "Sinai," *BHH* 3.1801–02; George E. Wright, "Mount Sinai," *IDB* 4.376–78; Eduard Lohse, "Σινᾶ," *TDNT* 7.282–87.

60 Hagar is mentioned only here and v 25 in the early Christian literature; see above, on 4:22. Verses 24, 26: ἥτις = ἡ τοιαύτη (cf. Rom 16:7; 1 Cor 3:17;

Phil 1:28; 1 Tim 3:15; see BDF, § 293, 4; BDR, § 293 n. 9).

61 Cf. Gal 4:22f.

62 Apart from the commentaries, see Franz Mussner, "Hagar, Sinai, Jerusalem," *ThQ* 135 (1955) 56–60; Eduard Lohse, "Σινᾶ," *TDNT* 7.282–87; Hartmut Gese, "Τὸ δὲ Ἁγὰρ Σινὰ ὄρος ἐστὶν ἐν τῇ Ἀραβίᾳ (Gal 4:25)," in *Das ferne und nahe Wort. Festschrift für Leonhard Rost* (ed. Fritz Mass; Berlin: de Gruyter, 1967) 81–94; (also in *Vom Sinai zum Zion* [Munich: Kaiser, 1974] 49–62); G. I. Davies, "Hagar, El-Ḥeǧra and the Location of Mount Sinai," *VT* 22 (1972) 152–63.

63 This could have been done by omitting one of the two names. Zahn (p. 230) has suggested that "Hagar" could have originated in a dittography of a preceding γάρ, in which case the oldest reading would be τὸ γὰρ Σινᾶ, found in ℵ C G Origen; for a fuller discussion, see Zahn, pp. 230ff, 298–301; Burton, pp. 258–61; Schlier, pp. 219f; Mussner, pp. 322–24. However, δέ is now better attested than γάρ (P⁴⁶ A B Dᵍʳ syrʰ copˢᵃ, ᵇᵒ). See Metzger, *Textual Commentary*, 596.

64 This would be true even if, as Burton (p. 259) suggests, v 25 is a gloss.

65 The neuter article τό associated with the female Hagar makes it a certainty that Paul is considering the name.

66 The term "Mount Sinai" is taken as the known, while "Hagar" is new information.

problem is how we understand Paul could have justified the equation. Although his information may be inaccurate, he at least must have believed it to be correct. This information could be of two kinds:[67] (1) merely geographical information—"the word Hagar points to Mount Sinai in Arabia." Such information would add nothing to the argument, but would stand as it is. Or, (2) "the word Hagar is the name for Mount Sinai in Arabia," whereby "in Arabia" would have to be taken to almost mean "in Arabic." It has been suggested that Paul, who spent some time in Arabia (Gal 1:17), may have thought of Arabic ḥadjar ("rock"), a word used in references to mountains in the Mount Sinai area. That the Arabic ḥ does not correspond to Hebrew ה,[68] not to mention the Greek, would not bother a man who is absorbed with "allegory" and who would be guided even by the most superficial similarities.[69]

This explanation is still the most probable, if one assumes as the original the *lectio difficilior*.[70] On the other hand, this assumption is considerably weakened by that part of the textual tradition which does not have "Hagar" at all.[71] The name Hagar itself can easily be interpreted as a later insertion, trying to help the argument by connecting more visibly Sinai with Jerusalem.[72]

The equation of Hagar with Mt. Sinai is followed by a second equation in v 25b: συστοιχεῖ δὲ τῇ νῦν Ἰερουσαλήμ ("it also corresponds to the present Jerusalem")[73] This equation is connected with the previous one by δέ and should, therefore, be rendered as "also." The term συστοιχέω originally means "stand in the same line" or, more generally, "correspond." In primitive Christian literature, the term is a *hapax legomenon*.[74] In Gal 4:25 it could be used in the more superficial sense of an association of terms, or as the category denoting the allegorical logic which justifies the association of the concepts.[75] Lietzmann has pointed out most clearly that in Gal 4:22–30 we do have a kind of συστοιχία ("correspondence") of concepts, subjected to the names of Hagar and Sarah:[76]

Hagar	*Sarah*
son of the slave woman (Ishmael)	son of the free woman (Isaac)
"according to the flesh"	"through the promise"
old covenant	new covenant
Sinai	
present Jerusalem	heavenly Jerusalem
slavery	freedom
"according to the flesh"	"according to the Spirit"
Judaism	Christianity

---

67 See the discussions in Lightfoot, Lagrange, Lietzmann, Schlier, Oepke, Bauer (*s.v.* Ἀγάρ), Lohse "Σινᾶ," *TDNT* 7.285–86), Mussner.

68 For this objection, see Lagrange, Lietzmann, Schlier.

69 Cf. Oepke (p. 150): "Aber das sind Zwirnsfäden, über die die Allegorese nicht stolpert" ("But these are spider–webs which cannot halt the pace of allegory"). Similarly Mussner.

70 Lagrange believes Paul may have thought of Hagar as the mother of Ishmael, of whom the Arabs were believed to be the descendants (cf. Ἀγαρηνοί, הגרים Ps LXX 82:7; MT 83:7; 1 Chron 5:19). But the Galatian readers would have to understand this historical detail and would have to supply the missing link (Hagar ancestor of the Arabs), which is hard to imagine. See also R. F. Schnell, "Hagrite," *IDB* 2.511.

71 Important witnesses do not have the name "Hagar": P⁴⁶ ℵ C G *al*, it vg Origen Ambrosiaster *al*. For a more complete account of the evidence see Aland, *Greek New Testament*; Metzger, *Textual Commentary*, 596; Mussner, p. 322.

72 See for this interpretation Mussner, pp. 322–24.

73 D* G lat connect the female Hagar with the female city: ἡ (D* without the article) συστοιχοῦσα.

74 See LSJ, *s.v.*; Bauer, *s.v.*; Gerhard Delling, "στοιχεῖον," *TDNT* 7.669.

75 In Pythagorean philosophy συστοιχία means "pair of coordinates" or "parallel columns" of notions; in a similar way, also the grammarians used it. For references, see LSJ, *s.v.*

76 See Lietzmann, Burton, Oepke, Delling ("στοιχεῖον," *TDNT* 7.669). Lagrange and Lietzmann have shown that the attempts to explain the connection by Gematria (i.e., by the numerical value of the letters) have failed.

Because it is based upon the Sinai covenant, the "present Jerusalem," [77] i.e., the political–religious institution of Judaism for which the Holy City stands as a symbol, can be associated with "Sinai/Hagar." Paul's intention is clear; he wants to create a dualistic polarity between "Judaism" and "Christianity," in order to discredit his Jewish–Christian opposition: δουλεύει γὰρ μετὰ τῶν τέκνων αὐτῆς ("for she lives in slavery together with her children"). [78]

This conclusion is one of Paul's sharpest attacks upon the Jews. He uses the self–understanding of the Jews in order to reject it. This self–understanding is well expressed by R. Jehoshua ben Levi (c. A.D. 280) in his interpretation of Exod 32:16 ("and the tables were the work of God, and the writing of God graven on the tables"): "read not ḥaruth (graven) but ḥeruth (freedom), for none is your freeman but he who is occupied in the study of Torah." [79] There is no evidence, however, that the Jerusalem Christians specifically operated with the slogan "Jerusalem is our mother." [80]

■ **26** The opposite of the "present" Jerusalem (v 25),

i.e., the political and religious institution of Judaism, is "the Jerusalem above" (ἡ ἄνω Ἰερουσαλήμ). Assuming that the readers are familiar with it, Paul introduces without further explanation this famous Jewish concept. While in his letters he uses it only here, it is found elsewhere in the New Testament (Heb 12:22; 13:14; Rev 3:12; 21:2, 9–22:5; see also *Herm. Sim.* 1.1.2). The concept is more prominent in Jewish apocalypticism. [81] In Jewish apocalypticism we can distinguish between various types of the concept. An older type expects the historical city to be rebuilt in the eschatological age. [82] Or, the "earthly" Jerusalem is to be replaced by a new Jerusalem, descending from heaven. [83] This replacement may be regarded as the fulfillment of the old or its destruction by the "new aeon." [84] Paul's concept is still different: his "heavenly Jerusalem" is pre–existent and remains in heaven; those who are to dwell in it must ascend to it. [85] This concept is found, e.g., in *2 Apoc. Bar.* 4.1–6 (tr. Charles, *APOT* 2.482):

---

77 For the form of the name see on Gal 1:17, 18; 2:1. For the attributive position of νῦν see Gustav Stählin, "νῦν," *TDNT* 4.1108, 1114; BDR, § 261 n. 3. The Jewish concept of Jerusalem (Zion) as "our mother" is found since Isa (49:14–21; 50:1; 51:18; 54:1; 60:4; etc.): see the material in Str-B 3.573; cf. also Joachim Jeremias, *Jerusalem in the Time of Jesus* (Philadelphia: Fortress, 1967) 351 n. 32; Pieter A. H. de Boer, *Fatherhood and Motherhood in Israelite and Judean Piety* (Leiden: Brill, 1974).

78 See on Gal 3:22.

79 *'Abot* 6.2 (tr. Travers Herford). The passage is probably late, but it expresses well the Rabbinic understanding of the matter. Cf. the Jews in John 8:33: "We are Abraham's seed, and we have never been enslaved to anyone." For further material, see Str-B 1.116–21.

80 So Eckert, *Die urchristliche Verkündigung*, 217; Mussner, p. 26 n. 121b; p. 325 (following Heinrich Julius Holtzmann). Cf. Irenaeus *Adv. haer.* 1.26.2, about the veneration of Jerusalem by the Ebionites: "... Hierosolymam adorent quasi domus sit Dei" ("adoring Jerusalem as if it were the house of God"). See furthermore Epiphanius *Pan.* 19.3.5–6, and on the subject, Schoeps, *Theologie und Geschichte*, 140f.

81 On the concept of the "heavenly Jerusalem" and extensive bib. see Georg Fohrer and Eduard Lohse, "Σιών κτλ.," *TDNT* 7.292–338; W. D. Davies, *The*

Gospel and the Land (Berkeley: University of California, 1974) 138ff, 140ff, 142ff, 162, 196ff; Lietzmann, on Gal 4:26; Oepke, pp. 150f; Schlier, pp. 221–26; Mussner, pp. 325f. On Jewish literature, see Str-B 3.573; Bousset–Gressmann, *Religion*, 283ff; Moore, *Judaism* 2.341f; Paul Volz, *Die Eschatologie der jüdischen Gemeinde im neutestamentlichen Zeitalter* (Tübingen: Mohr, Siebeck, 1934) 371ff; Gert Jeremias, *Der Lehrer der Gerechtigkeit* (SUNT 2; Göttingen: Vandenhoeck & Ruprecht 1963) 244–49 (on Qumran); Brandenburger, *Fleisch und Geist*, 200ff (on Philo). On the concept of a "heavenly city" in Hellenistic literature, see Betz, *Lukian*, 92ff.

82 See, e.g., Isa 54:10ff; 60–66; Ezek 40–48; Tob 13:9–18; 14:7; *Jub.* 4.26; *2 Apoc. Bar.* 4.2–7; 32.2–3; *Orac. Sib.* 5.420ff. For references see Bousset–Gressmann, ibidem, 38, 238f, 283, 285; Eduard Lohse, "Σιών κτλ.," *TDNT* 7.324–38.

83 See, e.g., 4 Ezra 7:26; 10:40ff; *1 Enoch* 90.28f.

84 See Rev 3:12; 21:2ff.

85 See *2 Enoch* 55.2 (*APOT* 2.463): "For to-morrow I shall go up on to heaven, to the uppermost Jerusalem to my eternal inheritance."

"and the Lord said unto me: 'This city shall be delivered up for a time, and the people shall be chastened during a time, and the world will not be given over to oblivion. [Dost thou think that this is that city of which I said: "On the palms of my hand have I graven thee?" This building now built in your midst is not that which is revealed with Me, as that which was prepared beforehand here from the time when I took counsel to make Paradise, and showed it to Adam before he sinned, but when he transgressed the commandment it was removed from him, as also Paradise. And after these things I showed it to my servant Abraham by night among the portions of the victims. And again I also showed it to Moses on Mount Sinai when I showed him the likeness of the tabernacle and all its vessels. And now behold, it is preserved with Me, as also Paradise…'"][86].

Schlier (pp. 224f) has pointed out correctly that Paul's concept of the "heavenly Jerusalem" is similar to the gnostic adaptation of this concept. Yet there need not be a contradiction between this and its apocalyptic origin. As in Jewish apocalypticism, for Paul the "heavenly Jerusalem" is virtually identical with the "new age." But he differs from Jewish apocalypticism by the radical dualism separating the two cities as the representatives of Judaism and Christianity. Although he calls only Judaism the "present Jerusalem," its counterpart, the "heavenly Jerusalem," is also "present." The

language does not precisely match: "the present Jerusalem" [87] is juxtaposed with "the Jerusalem above." [88] It is also noteworthy that the concepts do not really say what Paul means: for him the two cities represent the sphere of the "flesh" ($\sigma\acute{\alpha}\rho\xi$) and the "Spirit" ($\pi\nu\epsilon\hat{\nu}\mu\alpha$). Had he used his own terminology, Paul would call the "present" Jerusalem "Jerusalem according to the flesh" ($\kappa\alpha\tau\grave{\alpha}\ \sigma\acute{\alpha}\rho\kappa\alpha$), and the "heavenly" Jerusalem "Jerusalem according to the Spirit" ($\kappa\alpha\tau\grave{\alpha}\ \pi\nu\epsilon\hat{\nu}\mu\alpha$). [89] The former represents the "world," "Law," "sin," and "death"; the latter God, Christ, Spirit, and all the benefits of salvation. Schlier notes the close parallels of this dualism in gnosticism, where, according to Hippolytus (*Ref.* 5.7.39 [88, 16ff]), the exodus from Egypt through the Red Sea was interpreted as the liberation "from the lower mixture to the upper Jerusalem, which is the mother of the living" ($\mathring{\alpha}\pi\grave{o}\ \tau\hat{\eta}\varsigma\ \kappa\acute{\alpha}\tau\omega\ \mu\acute{\iota}\xi\epsilon\omega\varsigma\ \mathring{\epsilon}\pi\grave{\iota}\ \tau\grave{\eta}\nu\ \mathring{\alpha}\nu\omega\ \text{'}I\epsilon\rho\sigma\nu\sigma\alpha\lambda\acute{\eta}\mu,\ \mathring{\eta}\tau\iota\varsigma\ \mathring{\epsilon}\sigma\tau\grave{\iota}\ \mu\acute{\eta}\tau\eta\rho\ \zeta\acute{\omega}\nu\tau\omega\nu$). [90] By contrast, $\mathring{\eta}\ \kappa\acute{\alpha}\tau\omega\ \text{'}I\epsilon\rho\sigma\nu\sigma\alpha\lambda\acute{\eta}\mu$ ("Jerusalem below") represents "the lower, perishable generation" ($\tau\grave{\eta}\nu\ \kappa\acute{\alpha}\tau\omega\ \gamma\acute{\epsilon}\nu\epsilon\sigma\iota\nu\ \tau\grave{\eta}\nu\ \phi\theta\alpha\rho\tau\acute{\eta}\nu$). [91]

In contrast to Hagar (= the "present" Jerusalem) the "heavenly" Jerusalem "is free" ($\mathring{\epsilon}\lambda\epsilon\nu\theta\acute{\epsilon}\rho\alpha\ \mathring{\epsilon}\sigma\tau\acute{\iota}\nu$). [92] It is also "our mother" ($\mathring{\eta}\tau\iota\varsigma\ \mathring{\epsilon}\sigma\tau\grave{\iota}\nu\ \mu\acute{\eta}\tau\eta\rho\ \mathring{\eta}\mu\hat{\omega}\nu$). [93] In reaching this conclusion Paul takes up, no doubt polemically, a famous dictum of Jewish theology, "Jeru-

---

86 Cf. *T. Dan* 5:12f. For the rabbinic material, see Str–B 3.573, 795f; 4.883–85, 919–31; Davies, *Gospel and the Land*, 148ff.

87 The expression is found only here in Paul. Cf. $\acute{o}\ \nu\hat{\nu}\nu\ \alpha\mathring{\iota}\acute{\omega}\nu$ ("the present age") 1 Tim 6:17; 2 Tim 4:10; Tit 2:12; $\acute{o}\ \nu\hat{\nu}\nu\ \kappa\alpha\iota\rho\acute{o}\varsigma$ ("the present time") Rom 3:26; 8:18; 11:5; 2 Cor 8:14; *Barn.* 4.1. See Bauer, *s.v.* $\nu\hat{\nu}\nu$, 3, a; Str–B 3.573; Gustav Stählin, "$\nu\hat{\nu}\nu$," *TDNT* 4:1106–23.

88 Also this expression is unique in Paul; cf. Phil 3:14; Col 3:1f; John 8:23; Acts 2:19; also $\mathring{\alpha}\nu\omega\theta\epsilon\nu$ ("from above") John 3:3, 7, 27 (*v.l.*), 31; 19:11; Jas 1:17; 3:15, 17; *Herm. Mand.* 9.11; 11.5, 20, 21. On corresponding Rabbinic notions see Str–B 3.573; furthermore Bauer, *s.v.* $\mathring{\alpha}\nu\omega$; $\mathring{\alpha}\nu\omega\theta\epsilon\nu$. Cf. also Phil 3:20; Eph 2:6, 19; 5:29. Similar to Paul (dependent on him?) is *2 Clem.* 14.2: "And moreover the books and the Apostles declare that the church is not [simply] present ($o\mathring{\upsilon}\ \nu\hat{\nu}\nu\ \epsilon\mathring{\iota}\nu\alpha\iota$) but from above ($\mathring{\alpha}\nu\omega\theta\epsilon\nu$).

89 Cf. the concepts $\acute{o}\ \text{'}I\sigma\rho\alpha\grave{\eta}\lambda\ \kappa\alpha\tau\grave{\alpha}\ \sigma\acute{\alpha}\rho\kappa\alpha$ ("Israel according to [the] flesh") 1 Cor 10:18, and $\acute{o}\ \text{'}I\sigma\rho\alpha\grave{\eta}\lambda\ \tau\sigma\hat{\upsilon}\ \theta\epsilon\sigma\hat{\upsilon}$ ("Israel of God") Gal 6:16.

90 Cf. the tr. in Foerster–Wilson, *Gnosis* 1.270. Schlier quotes also Hippolytus *Ref.* 5.8.37 (96, 1ff); Irenaeus *Adv. Haer.* 1.26.2; and of the Mandaic literature, *Right Ginza* 29.33; 30.13; 51.9ff; 181.27ff, 338ff; 410.10ff; *Mandaic Liturgies* 211; *Book of John* 75ff, 191ff. See also Foerster–Wilson, *Gnosis* 2, indices, 333; 346, *s.v.* "Jerusalem."

91 Hippolytus *Ref.* 5.8.37 (96, 1ff). Cf. the tr. in Foerster–Wilson, *Gnosis* 1.277.

92 Cf. Gal 4:22, 23, 30, 31.

93 $\aleph^c$ A C^2 K P 81 614 arm *al* read $\pi\acute{\alpha}\nu\tau\omega\nu\ \mathring{\eta}\mu\hat{\omega}\nu$. But the stronger evidence speaks against this variant (P^{46} $\aleph^*$ B C* D G Ψ 33 1739 it vg *al*). See Zuntz, *Text*, 223; Metzger, *Textual Commentary*, 596.

salem [or: Zion] is our mother,"[94] and claims it for the Christians.[95] We do not know whether or not the Jewish–Christian opponents of Paul paid any specific attention to this concept, but at any rate Paul's inclusion of the Gentile Christians must have been offensive to them.[96]

Finally, there are equations which Paul does not make: he does not reconcile his concept of "our mother Jerusalem" with his previous concept of himself as the "mother" of the congregation (4:19).[97] Against Schlier (p. 223) Paul does not equate the "heavenly Jerusalem" with the church. The Christians are called her "children of promise" (v 28), but the present members of the church are not declared simply identical

with the "inhabitants of the heavenly Jerusalem."[98]

■ 27 Paul concludes his allegory by quoting Isa 54:1 according to the LXX,[99] introduced by the quotation formula γέγραπται γάρ ("for it is written"):[100]

εὐφράνθητι, στεῖρα ἡ οὐ τίκτουσα,
ῥῆξον καὶ βόησον, ἡ οὐκ ὠδίνουσα·
ὅτι πολλὰ τὰ τέκνα τῆς ἐρήμου μᾶλλον ἢ τῆς ἐχούσης
    τὸν ἄνδρα

("rejoice, O barren one who does not bear;
break forth and shout, you who are in travail;
for the children of the desolate one are many more
    than the children of the one who has a husband.")

This oracle[101] from Isa 54:1 plays a very important role in Jewish eschatological expectation.[102] Paul, no

---

94 See for passages above on 4:25 (n. 77). See the study by Joseph C. Plumpe, *Mater Ecclesia: An Inquiry into the Concept of the Church as Mother in Early Christianity* (The Catholic University of America, Studies in Christian Antiquity, no. 5; Washington, D.C.: The Catholic University of America, 1943); also Wilhelm Michaelis, *TDNT* 4.642–44; Murray, *Symbols*, 143–50.

95 Brandenburger (*Fleisch und Geist*, 200f) has tried to show that the equation "heavenly city of God" and "wisdom" was known to Paul. There is, however, no visible connection of the two concepts in Paul, as there is in Philo and in gnosticism. See Foerster–Wilson, *Gnosis* 1.191 (Hippolytus *Ref.* 6.34.3–4).

96 Cf. on Gal 4:25 (n. 80).

97 This connection is made in a later prophecy regarding Paul, contained in *Ep. Apost.* 33 (tr. HSW, *NT Apocrypha* 1.214): "That man will set out from the land of Cilicia to Damascus in Syria to tear asunder the Church which you must create. It is I who will speak (to him) through you, and he will come quickly. He will be (*ms. C:* strong) in his faith, that the word of the prophet may be fulfilled, where it says, 'Behold, out of the land of Syria I will begin to call a new Jerusalem, and I will subdue Zion and it will be captured; and the barren one who has no children will be fruitful and will be called the daughter of my father, but to me, my bride; for so has it pleased him who sent me.'"

98 On this element of Schlier's "Catholic" interpretation, see Siegfried Schulz, "Katholisierende Tendenzen in Schlier's Galater-Kommentar," *KD* 5 (1959) 23–41, 40. Schlier (pp. 223f) is able to claim a good number of Protestant exegetes as supporters. Very significant is Luther's extensive discussion in his commentary of 1535. He identifies the heavenly

Jerusalem with the church upon earth, but he restricts the identity to "*generatio*": "Generat tamen in spiritu ministerio verbi et sacramentorum, ... non in carne" ("She gives birth in the Spirit, by the ministry of the Word and of the sacraments. ... not physically."). Note that Mussner (p. 326) also warns against reading a "triumphalist ecclesiology" into Paul.

99 Cf. the editions by Rahlfs; Joseph Ziegler, *Isaias* (Septuaginta: Vetus Testamentum Graecum, Auctoritate Societatis Litterarum Gottingensis editum XIV; Göttingen: Vandenhoeck & Ruprecht, 1939) 323.

100 See on Gal 3:10; 4:22.

101 On the literary form of Isa 54:1, see Claus Westermann, *Das Buch Jesaja, Kapitel 40–66* (ATD 19; Göttingen: Vandenhoeck & Ruprecht, 1966) 218f; Dieter Baltzer, *Ezechiel und Deuterojesaja* (BZAW 121; Berlin: de Gruyter, 1971) 170f, and 162–75 for the whole Zion–Jerusalem ideology in Deutero-Isa.

102 Cf., e.g., the *Tg. Is.* (ed. and tr. John F. Stenning, *The Targum of Isaiah* [Oxford: Clarendon, 1949] 182): "Sing praises, O Jerusalem, who wast as a barren woman that bare not; break forth into a song of praise and rejoice, thou who wast a woman that conceived not; for more shall be the children of desolate Jerusalem than the children of inhabited Rome, saith the Lord." *Pesiq. R.* 32.2 cites Sarah in the context of the eschatological rebuilding of Jerusalem, and quotes Isa 54:1. For a collection of passages see Str–B. 3.574f. Philo quotes the passage in *Praem.* 158f, but applies it to the soul (ἐπὶ ψυχῆς ἀλληγορεῖται). See Martin Dibelius, *Botschaft und Geschichte* (2 vols.; ed. Günther Bornkamm; Tübingen: Mohr, Siebeck, 1953, 1956) 1.25–31.

doubt, received the tradition from Judaism; after Paul it gained prominence elsewhere in Christian literature.[103] In his view, the quotation refers to Sarah, who was at first incapable of bearing children and then became the mother of so many. Paul has applied this prophecy to the (Gentile) Christians whose mother is the "heavenly Jerusalem" (4:26). This conclusion completes the συστοιχία ("parallel columns of concepts") of Sarah = heavenly Jerusalem = Christianity.[104]

■ 28 Paul spells out the consequences of the Scripture proof (4:22–27) for the Galatians: ὑμεῖς δέ, ἀδελφοί, κατὰ Ἰσαὰκ ἐπαγγελίας τέκνα ἐστέ ("but you, my brothers, are children of promise, like Isaac"). The context and the argument clearly require the second person plural.[105] Once again, the proofs from Scripture have shown that the Gentile–Christian Galatians belong to the "heirs" of the divine promise made to Abraham.[106] They are represented by Isaac[107] and not by Ishmael. Therefore, they are "like Isaac" and can be called "children of promise": God's promise to Sarah has become true also for the Galatians.[108] Hence, they are "brothers."[109]

■ 29 The truth of v 28 is confirmed by experience: ἀλλ' ὥσπερ τότε ὁ κατὰ σάρκα γεννηθεὶς ἐδίωκεν τὸν κατὰ πνεῦμα, οὕτως καὶ νῦν ("but just as in those days the one born 'according to [the] flesh' persecuted the one 'according to [the] Spirit', so it is today"). The ἀλλά ("but") provides a transition to the next argument rather than an indication of contrast.[110] The argument is now typological: "just as back then . . . so it is now."[111] It is important to see that Paul no longer uses the names of Isaac and Ishmael, but now merely speaks of the types they represent.[112] These types constitute the dualism of flesh and Spirit[113] as it pertains to the two kinds of people, those who are "according to [the] flesh" (κατὰ σάρκα)[114] and those who are "according to [the] Spirit" (κατὰ πνεῦμα).[115]

Because this dualism underlies the whole of Galatians it must be Paul's goal to arrive at this polarity here too. The tradition that Ishmael "persecuted" (ἐδίωκεν) Isaac is not found in the Old Testament. But we find traces of it in the Jewish haggadah, where Gen 21:9 מצחק ("he jested, played, teased") was interpreted in a

---

103 See *Ep. Apost.* 33 (quoted above on 4:26, n. 97); *2 Clem.* 2.1–3; Justin *Apol.* 53; the "Naassene Sermon" (Hippolytus *Ref.* 5.8.34; tr. in HSW, *NT Apocrypha* 1.276); *Gos. Phil.* 36 (*NHC* II, 59, 31–60, 1, tr. in Foerster–Wilson, *Gnosis* 2.84). See Karl P. Donfried, *The Setting of Second Clement in Early Christianity* (NovTSup 38; Leiden: Brill, 1974) 82f, 107f, 192–200.

104 See on Gal 4:25 above. It should be noted that for Luther (esp. in his commentary of 1535), Hagar represents the Law and Sarah the Gospel. This juxtaposition of Law and Gospel, which became so influential in Protestantism, is a conclusion justifiedly based upon Paul but not identical with his theology. When the juxtaposition of Law and Gospel is read into Gal, difficulties result because of Paul's *positive* understanding of Law in Gal 6:2.

105 This text is strongly supported by early and diverse witnesses: P⁴⁶ B D* G 33 1739 it^{d, g} syr^{pal} cop^{sa} *al.* The *Textus Receptus*, following ℵ A C D^c K P Ψ 614 *al*, read the first person plural ἡμεῖς . . . ἐσμέν ("we . . . are") in vv 28, 31, and also 26. See on this Zuntz, *Text*, 107 n. 2; Metzger, *Textual Commentary*, 597.

106 The conclusion restates 3:26, 29; 4:7; cf. also 4:31.

107 Cf. Rom 9:7, 10.

108 Gal 4:23. The fulfilment of God's promise to Sarah

was preceded by the fulfilment of the promise to Abraham (3:14, 16, 17, 18, 19, 21, 22, 29; 4:7). This also shows that 4:21–31 is not out of context, as commentators have sometimes assumed (e.g., Ulrich Luz, "Der alte und der neue Bund bei Paulus und im Hebräerbrief," *EvTh* 27 [1967] 319).

109 See also 4:12. For the address "brothers" see 1:11; 3:15; 4:31; 5:11, 13; 6:1, 18.

110 See on this Bauer, *s.v.*, 3.

111 See also Rom 5:12, 19; 6:4, 19; 11:30; 1 Cor 15:22.

112 For the background of this interpretation, see the introduction to the section 4:21–31, above; on Qumran see Braun, *Qumran* 2.301–25.

113 Cf. Gal 3:3; 5:16f, 19–23, 24f; 6:7–8.

114 Cf. Gal 4:23.

115 Cf. Gal 5:1, 5, 16, 18, 25; 6:1: "You are the 'pneumatics'".

hostile way.[116] According to Paul, this persecution repeats itself in the present persecution of Christians by the Jews. Once he himself had been a persecutor of the church (cf. 1:12, 23), but now he shares the lot of the persecuted (cf. 5:11, 12).[117] The Galatians know this as a fact of history, but in the past they regarded it as a confimation of the truth and not as a reason for doubt (cf. 4:14; 6:17).[118]

■ 30 Another proof from Scripture follows. It is announced by a forceful ἀλλά ("yet"; cf. v 29) and introduced by a quotation formula in form of a question: "what does Scripture say?" (τί λέγει ἡ γραφή;).[119] Paul quotes Gen 21:10, but his text seems to have been slightly different from the LXX:[120] ἔκβαλε τὴν παι-δίσκην καὶ τὸν υἱὸν αὐτῆς· οὐ γὰρ μὴ κληρονομήσει ὁ υἱὸς τῆς παιδίσκης μετὰ τοῦ υἱοῦ τῆς ἐλευθέρας ("drive out the slave woman and her son; for the son of the slave woman shall not share the inheritance with the son of the free woman").

The last two words "of the free woman" (τῆς ἐλευθέ-ρας) are not found in the LXX and must be regarded as Paul's own interpretation, which he includes in the quotation.[121] This suggests that we should read Gen 21:10 in the light of Gal 4:28–29: if God has given the inheritance to the Gentile Christians (cf. 3:14, 29; 4:1, 7), the Jews are excluded from it, and the Christians constitute "the Israel of God" (6:16). Hence, the term "exclude" (ἐκβάλλω)[122] must be taken seriously;

---

116 The material in Str–B. 3.575f, shows that this could be done in several ways. *t.Soṭa* 6, 6 (304) attributes to R. Yishmael (+ ca. 135): "מצחק means nothing but bloodshed." He arrived at this meaning with the help of the similar word שחק ("perform a fight"). 2 Sam 2:14: "This teaches that Sarah has seen how Ishmael took arrows and shot, with the intention to kill Isaac." Similarly *Gen. Rab.* 53 (34a). The method used is *gezerah shavah* ("comparison of similar words"). *Tg. Ps.-J.* Gen 22:1 has a "dispute" (using the *syncrisis* motif) between the two brothers; see John Bowker, *The Targums and Rabbinic Literature* (Cambridge: Cambridge University, 1969) 224ff; Roger le Déaut, "Traditions targumiques dans le corpus paulinien?" *Bib* 42 (1961) 28–48, esp. 37–43; Louis Ginzberg, *The Legends of the Jews* (tr. Henrietta Szold; Philadelphia: Jewish Publication Society, 1909–38) 1.264, 5.246 n. 211. Josephus also knows of the tradition (*Ant.* 1.215), but Philo apparently does not (cf. *Cher.* 8). On Isaac cf. also Martin McNamara, *The New Testament and the Palestinian Targum to the Pentateuch* (AnBibl 27; Rome: Pontifical Biblical Institute, 1966) 164–68.

117 Schlier (p. 227; see also Oepke, Lietzmann, Bonnard, Mussner). Schlier is right in distinguishing between persecution by Judaism (cf. Gal 1:13, 23; 1 Thess 2:14–16) and the activities of the opposition (cf. Gal 1:7; 2:4; 3:1; 4:17; 5:7–10; 6:12f). Differently Sieffert, Zahn, Lagrange, Burton.

118 See also Luther (1535): "We are learning this today from our own experience. We see that everything is filled with tumults, persecutions, sects, and offenses." He discusses this point at length, including the accusation against him: "It is especially saddening when we are forced to hear that before the Gospel came everything was tranquil and peaceful, but that since its discovery everything is in an uproar,

and the whole world is in tumult and revolution. When the nonspiritual man (1 Cor 2:14) hears this, he is immediately offended and comes to the conclusion that the disobedience of subjects toward their magistrates; sedition, war, pestilence, hunger; the overthrow of states, regions, . . . have all arisen from this teaching. We must strengthen and support ourselves against this great offense with this sweet comfort, that in the world the godly must bear the name and reputation of being seditious, schismatic, and troublemakers."

119 For this formula, see Rom 4:3; cf. 11:2; 9:17; 10:11; 1 Tim 5:18. It is of no interest to Paul that in Gen 21:10 it is Sarah who speaks; for him it is all the utterance of ἡ γραφή "Scripture" (cf. Gal 3:8, 22).

120 The reading of οὐ γὰρ μή and the omission of ταύτης agrees with *A* (LXX). The variant μου Ἰσαάκ instead of τῆς ἐλευθέρας (D* G it Ambrosiaster) is harmonization with the LXX. See on the text Kautzsch, *De Veteris Testamenti Locis*, 62f; John W. Wevers, *Genesis* (Septuaginta: Vetus Testamentum Graecum, Auctoritate Academiae Scientiarum Gottingensis editum I; Göttingen: Vandenhoeck & Ruprecht, 1974) 207f.

121 On this method see Michel, *Paulus*, esp. § 4; Betz, "2 Cor 6:14–7:1," 94, 97f.

122 The term could even be used technically ("expel someone from a group"), as in John 9:34f ("from the synagogue"); 3 John 10 ("from the church"). See Bauer, *s.v.*, 1; cf. also the interpretation given by Philo *Cher.* 9–10.

Paul does the same with the Jews as his Jewish–Christian opponents want to do with him.[123] It should be noted that at this point there is a decisive difference between Galatians and Romans: in Galatians there is no room or possibility for an eschatological salvation of Judaism as in Rom 11:25–32.[124] Romans 9–11, therefore, means that Paul had revised his ideas as compared with Galatians.[125] According to Galatians, Judaism is excluded from salvation altogether, so that the Galatians have to choose between Paul and Judaism. If they decide to follow Paul's Jewish–Christian opponents, together with the acceptance of circumcision and observance of the Torah, they have in fact opted for Judaism, have excluded themselves from grace, and have placed themselves "under the curse."[126] Therefore, the citation of Gen 21:10 not only recommends what the Galatians should do about Paul's opponents, but also makes clear what they do to themselves if they do not carry out the divine order.[127]

■ **31** Contains the conclusion not only of the section 4:21–30, but also of the entire *argumentatio* 3:1–4:30: διό, ἀδελφοί, οὐκ ἐσμὲν παιδίσκης τέκνα ἀλλὰ τῆς ἐλευθέρας ("in conclusion, my brothers, we are not children of a slave woman, but of the free woman"). After the preceding argument, this conclusion can hardly be a surprise. The conclusion restates and sums up the previous conclusions in 3:9, 14, 24, 29; 4:7. The introductory διό ("therefore," "in conclusion"),[128] which stands for the more common ὥστε ("therefore")[129] or ἄρα ("therefore"),[130] may also be an indication that the *argumentatio* section is coming to an end. Conspicuous, and not merely a formality, is the repetition of the address "my brothers";[131] it is made in contrast to the exclusion (cf. 4:30) of the "false brothers" (ψευδάδελφοι).[132] Speaking in the first person plural the Apostle now includes himself among the Gentile Christians (cf. 4:3–6) as those who seek justification before God "through faith in Jesus Christ" as opposed to "through works of the Law."[133] As the various "proofs" in chapters 3 and 4 have demonstrated, these are indeed the heirs of the promise God made to Abraham.[134] They are Abraham's offspring,[135] the sons of the freeborn Sarah.[136] They are "all one in Christ Jesus."[137] The first person plural also assumes that the readers of the letter approve of Paul's final conclusion and, therefore, recognize the proofs as valid. The last two

123 Besides Gal 4:17 (ἐκκλείω), cf., 1:6–9; 6:16; 1 Cor 5:13; 16:22; also 2 Cor 6:14–7:1 and the interpretation by Betz, "2 Cor 6:14–7:1," 88–108. Schlier (p. 227) denies this on the ground that Paul's opponents are Jewish Christians, but not Jews; however, for Paul the valuation of the Torah decides whether or not he regards Jewish Christians as Jews in the religious sense. Cf. also Luz, *Geschichtsverständnis*, 285; Mussner (p. 332) who sees the connection with the present situation in Galatia.

124 Schlier (p. 227) sees the problem but then smooths out the differences, claiming that Gal 4:30 "confirms" Rom 9–11. In Gal, however, there is no consideration of a "mystery of Israel's redemption" (Rom 11:25ff). Another harmonization is presented by Luz (*Geschichtsverständnis*, 285f): because of different circumstances, Paul may say one thing in Gal and another in Rom but still says the same.

125 So rightly Oepke, p. 152. Cf. Mussner, p. 332 n. 79: It "borders on schizophrenia, if the Apostle could present such contradictory doctrines on such important subjects in such a short time."

126 See Gal 1:6–9; 2:4, 11–14, 21; 5:1–2; 6:16.

127 See the comment by Estius: "Terret hac sententia Galatas, ut intelligant se excludendos ab haereditate, si legem recipiant" ("by this sentence he

frightens the Galatians, so that they understand that they exclude themselves from the inheritance, if they accept the law"). Others (Zahn, Lagrange, Mussner) understand that Paul orders the opponents to be expelled.

128 It occurs only here in Gal; see Bauer, *s.v.* The textual tradition supports it well (ℵ B D* *al*), although the variants are also well attested: ἄρα (P46 Dc K L *al*, syrh d g vg Chrysostomus Theodorus Marius Victorinus Hieronymus Ambrosiaster); ἄρα οὖν (G sa [?] go *al*); ἡμεῖς δέ (A C P min sype bo Augustin Hieronymus); ἡμεῖς οὖν (sy Ephraem). See on this Zahn, p. 246 n. 56; Schlier, p. 228 n. 1; Mussner, p. 333 n. 82.

129 At the end of an argument: Gal 3:9, 24; 4:7.

130 At the end of an argument; Gal 2:21; 3:29 (cf. 3:7); 5:11; 6:10.

131 See also Gal 1:11; 3:15; 4:12, 28; 5:11, 13; 6:1, 18.

132 Gal 2:4; see also 1:7; 4:17; 6:12f.

133 See Gal 2:15–21.

134 Gal 3:6–4:7; 4:30.

135 Gal 3:6–29.

136 Gal 4:21–31.

137 Gal 3:28; cf. 5:5f; 6:15.

words τῆς ἐλευθέρας ("of the free woman") repeat the end of the preceding v 30, and also point forward to the beginning of the new section of the exhortation (5:1). They indicate that the entire new section beginning in 5:1 is guided by its leading concept of "freedom" (ἐλευθερία).[138]

---

138 So with Schlier, p. 228; Mussner, p. 334; Bonnard, p. 100; following Lietzmann, Steinmann, Oepke, Burton, Sieffert. Differently, Zahn, Lagrange, Bousset, and others who regard v 31 as the beginning of the paraenetical section. See on this Lightfoot, pp. 185, 200–202; Sieffert, p. 296.

5

Exhortatio: A Warning against
Acceptance of the Jewish Torah

1 Christ has set us free for freedom. Stand firm, therefore, and do not get yourself loaded with a yoke of slavery again. 2/ Look, I, Paul, tell you that if you become circumcised, Christ will be of no benefit to you. 3/ I testify again to every man who has become circumcised, that he is obliged to do the whole Law. 4/ You have become estranged from Christ, you who are justified by Law; you have dropped out of [the] grace.[1] 5/ For through [the] Spirit, by faith, we are expecting [the] hope of righteousness.[2] 6/ For in Christ Jesus neither circumcision nor uncircumcision means anything, but faith working[3] through love. 7/ You were running well. Who got in your path toward obeying the truth? 8/ Such persuasion does not come from him who calls you. 9/ A little yeast leavens the whole dough. 10/ I have confidence in you, in the Lord, that you will take no other view. He who stirs you up will bear his judgment, whoever he is. 11/ But if I, my brothers, still preach circumcision, why am I still persecuted? Then, the 'stumbling block of the cross' has been removed. 12/ As for those agitators, they had better go the whole way and make eunuchs of themselves![4]

Analysis

The last part of the body of the Galatian letter (5:1–6:10) consists of exhortation, parenesis. This much can be said in spite of the difficulties arising from a discussion of the matter.[5]

It is surprising that there exist only a few investigations of the formal character and function of epistolary parenesis.[6] Martin Dibelius' definition is clearly too

1 Cf. *RSV*: "you have fallen away from grace." *NEB*: "you have fallen out of the domain of God's grace."
2 Cf. *NEB*: "For to us, our hope of affirming that righteousness which we eagerly await is the work of the Spirit through faith."
3 Or: "made effective" (given as an alternative by *RSV*). *NEB* renders: "active in love" (with the alternative "inspired by love"); *JB*: "what matters is faith that makes its power felt through love."
4 So *NEB*. See the commentary on 5:12.
5 See Betz, "Composition," 375–77. Differently Otto Merk ("Der Beginn der Paränese im Galaterbrief," *ZNW* 60 [1969] 83–104) who provides a useful survey of the various opinions with regard to the beginning of the parenetical section. However, his own conclusions are not based upon an analysis of the composition and are, therefore, not convincing.
6 Investigations are usually aimed at elements of parenesis, but not at the parenetical sections of letters as a whole. For bib. see William G. Doty, *Letters in Primitive Christianity* (Philadelphia: Fortress, 1973) 49ff; for the larger question see Konrad Gaiser, *Protreptik und Paränese bei Platon* (Tübinger Beiträge zur Altertumswissenschaft 40; Stuttgart: Kohlhammer, 1959); Paul Rabbow, *Seelenführung* (Munich: Kösel, 1954) esp. 270f; Hadot, *Seelenleitung*; also Peter, *Brief*, 225ff.

vague: "*Paränese nennt man eine Aneinanderreihung verschiedener, häufig unzusammenhängender Mahnungen mit einheitlicher Adressierung*"[7] ("we call parenesis a series of different and often unconnected exhortations with a common address"). Hildegard Cancik,[8] utilizing the method of language analysis, distinguished between two forms of argument in Seneca's epistles, that of "descriptive" and that of "prescriptive" language This distinction corresponds to the two means of argument, the "rational" and the "emotive." Cancik points out that the scholarly argument is facilitated not only by "descriptive" language but by "prescriptive" as well, so that parenesis cannot be regarded as a *Kümmerform* (reduced form) which is deficient of logic and merely applies the result of rational argument and theory.[9] She also distinguishes between simple elements of parenesis (series of prescriptions, prohibitions, exhortations, warnings, etc.) and combinations of these with descriptive elements. In addition we have to take into account *exempla*, comparisons, etc.[10]

It is rather puzzling to see that parenesis plays only a marginal role in the ancient rhetorical handbooks, if not in rhetoric itself.[11] Consequently, modern studies of ancient rhetoric also do not pay much attention to

it.[12] On the other hand, parenesis was characteristic of the philosophical literature, especially of the diatribe of the Hellenistic period.[13] In this material we find that rhetoric is denounced with regularity as nothing but concoctions of lifeless syllogisms.[14] The philosophical letters, which are most interesting to the student of Paul's letters, and of which a large number are extant, very often have at the end a parenetical section.[15] Striking as this phenomenon is, these letters have been the subject of only a few studies, none of which, to my knowledge, specifically investigates the parenetical material. But in one of Seneca's epistles (*Ep* 85.1) we read what may be the major reason for including parenesis in the philosophical letters: " . . . I declare again and again that I take no pleasure in such proofs [*sc.* dry syllogisms]. I am ashamed to enter the arena and undertake battle on behalf of gods and men armed only with an awl."[16]

The parenetical section of Galatians can be subdivided into three parts. Each of these parts is recognizable by its restatement of the "indicative" of salvation:[17] (1) 5:1–12 begins with this restatement (5:1a) and contains a warning against taking up the yoke of the Jewish Torah and accepting the ritual of circum-

---

7   Martin Dibelius, *Geschichte der urchristlichen Literatur* (Munich: Kaiser, [2]1975) 140. His treatment of the subject is little more than a random collection of diverse material from a wide range of authors. See also idem, *Die Formgeschichte des Evangeliums* (Tübingen: Mohr, Siebeck, [3]1959) 234–65, esp. 239ff; Wolfgang Schrage, *Die konkreten Einzelgebote in der paulinischen Paränese* (Gütersloh: Mohn, 1961); Victor P. Furnish, *Theology and Ethics in Paul* (Nashville and New York: Abingdon, 1968); Vielhauer, *Geschichte*, 49–57, 69, 120f, and index, *s.v.* Paränese.

8   Hildegard Cancik, *Untersuchungen zu Senecas Epistulae morales* (Spudasmata 18; Hildesheim: Olms, 1967). See also the review of this important work by Gregor Maurach, *Gnomon* 41 (1969) 472–76; idem, *Der Bau von Senecas Epistulae morales* (Bibliothek der Klassischen Altertumswissenschaft, NF 2.30; Heidelberg: Winter, 1970) *passim*.

9   Cancik, ibidem, 16ff.

10 Ibidem, 17.

11 Ibidem, 23.

12 Even Quint. has no special treatment of it, but only incidentally refers to other orators as having a related doctrine (see 3.6.47; 9.2.103). According to Aristotle there are two kinds of deliberative speech,

προτροπή and ἀποτροπή (*Rhet.* 1.3.3, p. 1358b). This doctrine is also found later (cf. *Rhet. ad Her.* 1.2.2; Quint. 9.4.130) but has no apparent connection to parenesis. See Lausberg, *Handbuch*, §§ 61, 2; 1109; 1120; Johann C. G. Ernesti, *Lexicon Technologiae Graecorum, Latinorum Rhetoricae* (Leipzig 1795, 1797; rep. Hildesheim: Olms, 1962) *s.v.* προτροπή, *suasio* (παραίνεσις, etc. is not even listed).

13 See André Oltramare, *Les origines de la diatribe romaine* (Lausanne-Geneva–Neuchâtel: Payot, 1926); Wilhelm Capelle and Henri–Irenée Marrou, "Diatribe," *RAC* 3, esp. 990–1009.

14 For futher literature see Betz, *Paulus*, 57ff.

15 Cf. Cancik's analysis of Seneca *Ep.* 76 (18ff).

16 *Ep.* 85.1: "Illud totiens testor, hoc me argumentorum genere non delectari. Pudet in aciem descendere pro dis hominibusque susceptam subula armatum" (ed. and tr. Richard M. Gummere in LCL). I am indebted for the passage to Cancik, 22f. See also Winfried Trillitzsch, *Senecas Beweisführung* (Berlin: Akademie–Verlag, 1962) 69ff.

17 The restatements refer to 4:31 (conclusion of the *probatio* section) and, by implication, to the entire preceding argument. Cf. the κανών ("rule") in 6:16.

cision. (2) 5:13–24 begins again with this restatement (5:13) and contains a warning against corruption by the "flesh." (3) 5:25–6:10 begins with a final restatement of the "indicative" of salvation (5:25a) and contains a series of gnomic sentences[18] forming the positive exhortation. It concludes with an eschatological warning (6:7–9) and a summary of the whole parenetical section (6:10).

Interpretation

■ **1** The beginning of the parenetical section (5:1–6:10) is marked by an abrupt new start. There is no transitional phrase or particle, a fact that looks strange to modern commentators and most likely was the cause of the confusion already in the textual tradition.[19] However, there is no real reason to conclude, as Oepke (p. 117) does, that this is an "abrupt beginning" and "looks strange." The *probatio* section (3:1–4:31) now concluded, a new section is expected to begin, and its beginning should be clearly indicated. Part of the textual tradition has tried to smooth over the transition from 4:31 to 5:1, but these attempts are secondary.

In 5:1a Paul restates the "indicative" of Christian salvation: τῇ ἐλευθερίᾳ ἡμᾶς Χριστὸς ἠλευθέρωσεν ("for freedom Christ has set us free"). Paul had introduced the concept of freedom before,[20] but now he emphatically places it at the beginning of the section on ethical exhortation and thus in the center of the argument. The centrality of the notion of freedom became clear already in the *narratio* section, when the apostle claimed that the sole purpose of his struggles was the preservation of Christian freedom.[21] The christological passages[22] do not use the concept of freedom, but contain Jewish cultic language; this language, however, is interpreted in terms of liberation from the present conditions of "the evil age" (1:4). This tendency comes to the surface fully in 3:26–28.[23] As a result, ἐλευθερία ("freedom") is the central theological concept which sums up the Christian's situation before God as well as in this world. It is the basic concept underlying Paul's argument throughout the letter.[24] The dative τῇ ἐλευθερίᾳ is peculiar. It is not a dative of cause and instrumentality, but one of "destiny" and "purpose." and it must be interpreted in parallelism with ἐπ' ἐλευθερίᾳ

18   For the gnomic sentences in Gal, see below on 5:25–6:10.

19   The text translated is that of Nestle–Aland, 26th edition, and Aland, *Greek New Testament*; it is supported well by B A ℵ C* D* H P 1739 *al*. Other readings include τῇ ἐλευθερίᾳ οὖν, ᾗ ἡμᾶς... (D^bc E K L min syr^s,pes, etc.). See the discussion of the textual problem in Burton, pp. 270f; Oepke; Sieffert, p. 296 n.; Zahn, p. 244 n. 57; Schlier, p. 229; Karl Heinrich Rengstorf, "Zu Gal. 5, 1," *ThLZ* 76 (1951) 659–62; Metzger, *Textual Commentary*, 597.

20   See Gal 4:22–31.

21   See Gal 2:4–5.

22   See 1:4; 2:20; 3:13; 4:4–5.

23   Note, however, the different usage of ἐλεύθερος ("freeman") in 3:28.

24   See also 5:13. The significance of the concept of "freedom" is evident also from other Pauline letters: cf. Rom 6:18, 20, 22; 7:3; 8:21; 1 Cor 7:21, 22, 39; 9:1, 19; 10:29; (12:13); 2 Cor 3:17; also Col 3:11; Eph 6:8. It is interesting that the Pauline concept of "freedom from the law" was appropriated by the *Cologne Mani Codex* (*CMC* 17.1ff) and applied to the laws of the Elchasaites. Luther, esp. 1535, applies the concept to his monastic experiences (see Luther's commentary on 5:3). On the Pauline concept and for further literature, see Bultmann,

Theology, §§ 38–40; Conzelmann, *Outline*, 275ff; Heinrich Schlier, "ἐλεύθερος," *TDNT* 2. 487–502; Dieter Nestle, *Eleutheria : Studien zum Wesen der Freiheit bei den Griechen und im Neuen Testament* (Tübingen: Mohr, 1967); idem, "Freiheit," *RAC* 8. 269–306; Hans Jonas, *Augustin und das paulinische Freiheitsproblem* (FRLANT NF 27; Göttingen: Vandenhoeck & Ruprecht, ²1965); Jean Cambier, "La liberté chrétienne selon saint Paul," *Studia Evangelica* (TU 87; Berlin: Akademie–Verlag, 1964) 315–53; Ernst Käsemann, "The Cry for Liberty in the Worship of the Church," in *Perspectives*, 122–37; Bonnard, pp. 110–12; Kurt Niederwimmer, *Der Begriff der Freiheit im Neuen Testament* (Berlin: Töpelmann, 1966); Rudolf Schnackenburg, *Christian Existence in the New Testament* (Notre Dame: University of Notre Dame, 1969) 2. 31–53; Karl Hermann Schelke, *Theologie des Neuen Testaments* (1–4.1–2; Düsseldorf: Patmos, 1968–76) 3.10; Franz Mussner, *Theologie der Freiheit nach Paulus* (Freiburg: Herder, 1976).

("to freedom") in 5:13.[25] The whole sentence states in a very concise form both the "indicative" and the "imperative" of Christian salvation in the Pauline sense.[26] Christian freedom is the result of Christ's act of having liberated those who believe in him (the "indicative"), but this result is stated as a goal, purpose, and direction for the life of the Christian (the "imperative"). Thus, the sentence sums up the "logic" which relates the argumentative section of the letter (in principle including the whole of 1:6–4:31) with the parenetical section (5:1–6:10). Theologically, Paul states that there can be no existence in freedom unless man is first given the opportunity of freedom, but that the opportunity of freedom is given only as the task for freedom. This task is then defined as the *preservation* of freedom.

According to Paul's anthropology, man's primordial potential of freedom was corrupted and lost when Adam, through his transgression, introduced sin into the human world.[27] Since then mankind has been living in the state of imprisonment through the power of sin, a state which can be identified with the deprivation of the primordial freedom. In Galatians[28] Paul uses various concepts to describe mankind's situation outside of the Christ–event as one of slavery by the evil elements dominating the world (τὰ στοιχεῖα τοῦ κόσμου).[29] The freedom which the Christian is granted is based upon God's redemption in Christ. However, freedom is not merely a theory but an experience of that freedom. It was the gift of the Spirit which enabled the Galatians, as all Christians, to experience freedom (cf. 3:2–5). This experience amounted to a liberation from the "elements of the world" and their tyrannical regime of evil (1:4, 4:1–10), and included the libera-

tion from slavery under the Law and sin (cf. 2:19; 3:13, 25; 4:5), from death (cf. 2:20; 3:11; 5:25; 6:8), from ignorance of God (4:8–9), from superstition (4:8–10), and from social oppression and religious–cultural discrimination (3:26–28). When Paul describes "the fruit of the Spirit" (5:22–23), freedom is conspicuously absent from the list of the benefits of the Spirit. The reason is that freedom is both the basis of them all and the result of them all. In fact, 2 Cor 3:17 makes clear that for Paul Spirit and freedom are one and the same thing:[30]

ὁ δὲ κύριος τὸ πνεῦμά ἐστιν·
οὗ δὲ τὸ πνεῦμα κυρίου, ἐλευθερία

("the Lord is the Spirit;
where the Spirit of the Lord is, there is freedom").

It is characteristic of Paul's theology that theory and experience cannot be separated; every item of doctrine is at the same time reflection of experience, and every experience is accompanied by reflection and theory. When the Galatians, therefore, experienced the Spirit, it was the Spirit of Christ, sent out by God (cf. 4:6). This made it possible for the Christians to participate in Christ's redemptive act of liberation, his crucifixion and his resurrection (cf. 1:1, 4; 2:20; 3:13; 4:5). Those who have become partakers of Christ and have "put on Christ" (cf. 3:27) share his crucifixion; thus the sharing of the resurrection of Christ, through the gift of the Spirit, leads to the sharing of his crucifixion. This includes the liberation from the Law (cf. 2:19; 3:25; 5:18), from the flesh and its "passions and desires" (cf. 5:24), and from the world as a whole (cf. 6:14). The "new creation" which the Christian existence is called (cf. 6:15) is certainly the recreation of the primordial freedom of man—but it is more than that: it

---

25 So correctly Mussner, pp. 342f. On the "dative of goal" see Mayser, *Grammatik* 2.2, 243f. Cf. the parallels Rom 8:24: τῇ ἐλπίδι ἐσώθημεν ("for hope we were saved"), taking up ἐφ' ἐλπίδι Rom 8:20; εἰς τὴν ἐλευθερίαν Rom 8:21. See the discussions in Burton, p. 271; Oepke; Schlier, p. 229; Moule, *Idiom Book*, 44 n. 2.

26 On this terminology, see Rudolf Bultmann, "Das Problem der Ethik bei Paulus," *ZNW* 23 (1924) 123–40 (also in *Exegetica*, 36–54); Betz, *Nachfolge*, 169ff; Furnish, *Theology and Ethics*, 208ff. Formally, 5:1a uses *figura etymologica* (*Polyptoton, paronomasia*).

27 See esp. Rom 5:12ff. Paul does not say expressly that originally man was free, but this can be concluded from the idea that "sin" and "death" which constitute man's "imprisonment" (cf. 6:22f; 7:24–25a) enter only at the moment of Adam's transgression. Gal is different from Rom in that it does not contain reflection on man's primordial state of existence.

28 See Gal 1:4; 2:20; 3:13, 22–25; 4:1–10.

29 For a collection of passages, see above on Gal 4:3.

30 Contrary to Schmithals (*Gnosticism*, 315ff) we regard 2 Cor 3:17 as a genuinely Pauline passage.

is that freedom which is the result of Christ's act of liberation, and the sharing in this act.

In the Pauline sense, "to be free" means to participate in Christ's crucifixion and resurrection.[31] The gift of the Spirit enables the Christian initially and continually, and therefore freedom and Spirit are the principal concepts of Paul's ethics. As Christian ethical existence is existence "in freedom," it is identical with existence "in and by the Spirit" ("walk in the Spirit [πνεύματι περιπατεῖν],"[32] "be led by the Spirit [πνεύματι ἄγεσθαι],"[33] "follow the Spirit [πνεύματι στοιχεῖν])."[34] These terms describe what Paul expresses in 5:1a by the dative τῇ ἐλευθερίᾳ ("for freedom"). One could also say that freedom is another term for "the fruit of the Spirit" (ὁ καρπὸς τοῦ πνεύματος).[35] For this reason, the statement in 5:1a is not only identical with 5:13a, but also with the paradoxical gnome 5:25: "if we live by the Spirit, let us also follow the Spirit."[36] This concept of freedom is the basis and the content of Christian "ethics."

In v 1b the Apostle defines the general task of Christian ethics in regard to the present situation of the churches of Galatia: στήκετε οὖν καὶ μὴ πάλιν ζυγῷ δουλείας ἐνέχεσθε ("stand [firm], therefore, and do not get yourself loaded with a yoke of slavery again"). The imperative στήκετε ("stand firm") sums up the ethical consequences[37] of the liberation through Christ as Paul had defined it in v 1a. It should be understood as saying: "stand firmly in that freedom, and preserve that freedom."[38] If Christ has brought the Christian freedom, this freedom exists only if it is lived by those who have been enabled to exist in it. The constant danger is to lose that freedom and to fall back into slavery. Therefore, the task of Christian ethics can be defined as "to preserve" freedom. This means that Paul does not share the Jewish concept of "ethics" as the prevention of transgression and the fulfillment of the demands of a ritual code of Law (Torah).[39] Nor does Paul share the general Hellenistic concept of ethics as the improvement of raw human nature by παιδεία, i.e., by the training and gradual acquisition of virtues (ἀρεταί).[40] For the Apostle there is no longer any Law, and therefore there are no transgressions: Christ is "the end of the Law."[41] On the other hand, there is nothing to be achieved by man which has not already been given to him "in Christ."[42] Human nature as such cannot be improved by the acquisition of virtues, because man has to be enabled in regard to his nature—and this individually by special divine acts of redemption.

Paul's ethics is also different from the Jewish and the Greek concepts in that ethics for him is not the achievement of something not yet achieved. What had to be achieved was achieved by the divine redemption in Christ. The danger which conditions the ethical task is, for Paul, that the redemptive achievement might be lost again. From this it follows that the ethical task is the *prevention* of the loss of salvation. In this

---

31 The concept of Christ as liberator occurs only here in Gal. It is not repeated in Rom, where Paul expresses himself with caution (cf. Rom 6:18, 22; 8:2, 21). Interestingly, Gal comes close to John (8:32, 36: ἐὰν οὖν ὁ υἱὸς ὑμᾶς ἐλευθερώσῃ, ὄντως ἐλεύθεροι ἔσεσθε ["If then the Son sets you free, you will be really free."]). Cf. also *Acts Thom.* 142 (p. 249,1) where Christ is called ὁ ἐλευθερωτὴς τῆς ἐμῆς ψυχῆς ἐκ τῆς τῶν πολλῶν δουλείας ("the deliverer of my soul from the slavery of the many"); Alfred Resch, *Agrapha: Ausserkanonische Schriftfragmente* (Leipzig: Hinrichs, ²1906) 128f (No. 88). For later christology, see the passages in *PGL*, s.v., 2.

32 Gal 5:16.

33 Gal 5:18.

34 Gal 5:25.

35 Gal 5:22f.

36 Cf. also Gal 5:5.

37 οὖν ("therefore") is often used by Paul to introduce the parenetical section. See Wolfgang Nauck, "Das οὖν–paraeneticum," *ZNW* 49 (1958) 134f.

38 So Bauer, *s.v.* στήκω. Mussner (p. 343) thinks of grace as including freedom.

39 Paul uses the concept of ἁμαρτία ("sin") in Gal only in regard to the pre–Christian (Jewish) situation of the Christian: 1:4; 2:17; 3:22; the term παράπτωμα ("transgression") in 6:1 is the general legal one.

40 Cf., however, Eph 6:4; 2 Tim 3:16; Heb 12:5, 7, 8, 11.

41 See Gal 2:17f, 19; 3:21–25; 5:18; cf. Rom 10:4; 4:15; 6:14f; 7:4–6, 8, 10.

42 This is implied by the concept of "grace" (χάρις) in Gal 1:6, 15; 2:9, 21; 5:4 (1:3; 6:18); grace does, of course, include eschatology: 5:4f, 10, 21; 6:7–10, 16. Related is "new creation" (6:15).

sense one must say that Paul does not have an ethic in the ordinary meaning of the term.

The danger which the Galatians are in is that they will lose their freedom in Christ if they do not exercise it. Therefore, Paul's warning "stand firm" in effect means "protect your Christian freedom by exercising it."[43]

Paul also names in a general way what he regards as the loss of salvation in Christ: it is the return under the yoke of slavery.[44] This "yoke of slavery"[45] can, of course, take various forms. In the following sections Paul will develop two concerns relative to the situation of the Galatians: the taking up of the yoke of the Jewish Torah (5:2–12) and the corruption by the flesh (5:13–24). The term ἐνέχω (passive) means "be subjected to" and "loaded down with."[46] Both meanings recall the imagery of cruel subjection of the slaves under their masters, and the heavy burden of suppression which the enslaved have to bear.[47]

■ 2 As Paul sees it, there are two dangers threatening the Christian freedom of the Galatians: (1) the acceptance of the Jewish Torah (5:2–12), and (2) the corruption of their life by the "flesh" (5:13–24). The most immediate danger is dealt with first. In v 2 the Apostle begins his "apostolic testimony" (5:2–4) by pointing out the christological and soteriological implications of the Galatians' submitting to the Jewish ritual of circumcision: "Ἴδε ἐγὼ Παῦλος λέγω ὑμῖν ὅτι ἐὰν περιτέμνησθε Χριστὸς ὑμᾶς οὐδὲν ὠφελήσει ("look, I, Paul, tell you that if you become circumcised Christ will be of no benefit to you"). The emphatic way in which Paul introduces this statement shows that he mobilizes his whole authority as an apostle.[48] "To become circumcised" is what the Galatians are presently considering.[49] Of course they have more in mind than merely a physical operation; "circumcision" is the external ritual symbolizing the acceptance of Judaism,[50] even if it takes the form of a Christian Judaism.[51] Paul rejects this step as incompatible with the Galatians' existence as members of the Christian church.

---

43 For this imperative see also 1 Cor 16:13; Phil 1:27; 4:1; 1 Thess 3:8; furthermore 2 Thess 2:15; Rom 14:4. On the whole concept see Walter Grundmann, "στήκω," *TDNT* 7.636–38; Karlheinz Müller, *Anstoss und Gericht* (SANT 19; Munich: Kösel-Verlag, 1969) 110f; Mussner, p. 343 n. 7. Paul himself stood firmly all the time (2:4–5, 11–14), but Cephas did not (2:11–14); now the Galatians themselves are in danger of "falling" (cf. 1:6–7; 3:1, 3; 4:11f; 5:4, 7–10) and becoming like Cephas, Barnabas and other former colleagues of Paul (cf. 2:11–14).

44 πάλιν ("again") does not mean that the Galatians were under the "yoke of the Torah" before (cf. 2:18); they were, as pagans, under the στοιχεῖα τοῦ κόσμου ("elements of the world"); see Gal 4:1–10; 2:4f.

45 On the concept of "yoke" see Matt 11:29f; Acts 15:10; 1 Tim 6:1; *Did.* 6.2; *Barn.* 2.6. See Georg Bertram and Karl Heinrich Rengstorf, "ζυγός, ἑτεροζυγέω," *TDNT* 2.896–901; Michael Maher, "Take my yoke upon you (Matt xi. 29)," *NTS* 22 (1975) 97–103. For the interpretation of 2 Cor 6:14 in connection with Paul's opponents, see Betz, "2 Cor 6:14–7:1," 89f; also below, Appendix 2.

46 Cf. 2 Thess 1:4 v.l. For the term see Bauer, *s.v.*, 2; Preisigke, *Wörterbuch* 4.4 (1971) 795.

47 Paul uses the language figuratively. Deissmann (*Licht vom Osten*, 274ff) and Lietzmann (on Gal 5:1) tried to show that Paul makes use of the legal institution of the purchasing of slaves for freedom which existed at the temple of Apollo at Delphi. This institution allowed a slave owner to "sell" a slave to the god and receive the purchase price from the temple treasury. The freedom of the former slave was then protected since he was "owned" by the god, while socially free. In a similar way, Rengstorf (see above n. 45) tried to make a case for Rabbinic law regarding slavery. However, the language used here by Paul does not include the terms of purchase, purchase price, or "slave of Christ." See also Mussner (pp. 344f) and above on Gal 3:13, 26–28.

48 ἴδε ("behold," "look"), an original imperative which has become a mere particle. See Bauer, *s.v.*; BDF § 144. Paul does sometimes refer to his own name in his letters (1 Cor 1:12f; 3:4, 5, 22; 1 Thess 2:18; Phlm 9; cf. Col 1:23; Eph 3:1), but this emphatic plea has a parallel only in 2 Cor 10:1 (most likely also the beginning of the parenetical section of the letter, the beginning of which is lost; see Betz, *Paulus*, 1ff). On the emphatic "I" in the diatribe literature, see Gustav Adolf Gerhard, *Phoinix von Kolophon* (Leipzig and Berlin: Teubner, 1909) 65–68.

49 That is, the practice of circumcision from here on; see Oepke, Schlier (p. 231 n. 2).

50 On the ritual of circumcision and for further bib. see above on Gal 2:3.

Before we ask for the reasons for his position we recall that he has discussed the issue in previous sections of the letter: (1) Titus, the Gentile Christian, did not have to submit to circumcision (cf. 2:3); (2) the mission to the Gentiles had been separated from that to the Jews, which for Paul implies that the Christian Gentiles become partakers of God's salvation without having to submit to the Jewish Torah and circumcision (cf. 2:7–9). If the Gentile Galatians, after having been Christians for some time, *now* accept circumcision,[52] they would violate what Paul presents as the practice of the church in the past. Moreover, they contemplate introducing circumcision now because they regard it in some way *necessary* for salvation.[53] In so doing, Paul considers that they would render their previous salvation in Christ alone insufficient and thereby invalid. If Christ alone were insufficient, which Paul reminds them by citing the christological formulae in the prescript (1:1, 4) and throughout the letter they would deny that he is their Saviour. They would deny their status as "believers in Christ," and thereby their "justification by faith"[54] which would save them in the eschatological judgment.[55] They would deprive themselves from all the redemptive benefits which the name Christ includes.[56] Why this is the case the Apostle goes on to explain in the next few sentences.

■ 3 It is no doubt with some irony that the former Pharisee Paul informs the Gentile Galatians about the implications of receiving the Jewish ritual of circumcision: μαρτύρομαι δὲ πάλιν παντὶ ἀνθρώπῳ περιτεμνομένῳ ὅτι ὀφειλέτης ἐστὶν ὅλον τὸν νόμον ποιῆσαι ("I testify again to every man who has become circumcised, that he is obliged to do the whole Law").

The formula of oath[57] seems to be in place because of the stubbornness of the Galatians who, in spite of what they have been told before, remain naive with regard to the implications of becoming circumcised. Paul can so testify because as a Pharisaic Jew he knows while they as Gentiles do not. The word πάλιν ("again")[58] suggests that the Galatians continue failing to grasp the meaning of what they are about to do. It appears that Paul displays here the attitude of the Pharisee he has been, over against the typical converts such as the Galatians would become if they received circumcision. To the Pharisaic Jew the implication is self–evident, as it is not self–evident to them that the external ritual makes sense only if one goes all the way and keeps all of the Torah.[59]

The meaning of this statement, however, is beset with a number of difficulties. What was the connection between Torah and circumcision in Judaism? First century Judaism was not unanimous in its answer.[60] Paul's own view can be seen from his discussion in Rom 2:25: circumcision makes sense only if the circumcised person keeps the Torah; if he does not, he is like one who is uncircumcised.[61] This indicates that Paul be-

---

51 The opponents have demanded of the Galatians that they become circumcized (Gal 6:12f, cf. 2:3–5). See also the interesting information in Acts 15:1–5. Jewish Christianity continued the ritual in later times; see below on Gal 6:12.

52 For these plans, cf. Gal 1:6f; 5:3, 6, 11; 6:12, 13, 15.

53 Cf. the request of the "Jews" Acts 15:1, 5.

54 See Gal 2:16, 20; 3:2–29; 5:5f; 6:14–16.

55 The future tense of ὠφελήσει most likely points to the Last Judgment (cf. 5:5; 6:7–9; see also Rom 2:25ff).

56 Gal 2:21: If righteousness before God comes through the Torah, Christ's death did not achieve what the christological formulae say he achieved (cf. 1:4; 2:20; 3:13; 4:4–5), and therefore would be "in vain."

57 See also Gal 4:15; cf. Eph 4:17; Acts 20:26.

58 It is omitted in D* G 1739 *pc* it goth arm, probably because Paul did not make the same statement be-

fore in his letter. As it stands it can simply mean "furthermore," or refer to an earlier communication apart from the present letter. Cf. also Mussner, p. 347.

59 It is interesting that the same doctrine is mentioned in Jas 2:10; ps.–Clem. *Hom.* 8.5–7. On the term ὀφειλέτης ("debtor") see Rom 1:14; 8:12; 15:27; also 13:7, 8; 15:1; 1 Cor 5:10; 7:3, 10; 11:7, 10; Phlm 18; Eph 5:28. See Friedrich Hauck, "ὀφείλω, ὀφείλη, ὀφείλημα, ὀφειλέτης," *TDNT* 5.559–66; C. F. D. Moule, "Obligation in the Ethics of Paul," *Christian History and Interpretation, Studies Presented to John Knox* (Cambridge: Cambridge University, 1967) 389–406.

60 In Judaism itself the question of requiring circumcision of converted pagans was disputed. See above on Gal 2:3, and below, Appendices 1 and 4.

61 See Rom 2:25–29, and the discussions in Kuss, *Römerbrief*, 88–98; Käsemann, *Römer*, 66–72.

longs to the rigorist wing in Judaism, for which the external ritual of circumcision is not enough to ensure salvation. The real basis for hope in the final judgment is rigid obedience to the demands of the Torah.[62] This, of course, means the *whole* Torah.[63] There can be little doubt that by the time of Paul this view was the generally accepted one in Judaism. Still, there was wide-ranging debate as to what constituted "the whole Torah." There were the 613 prescriptions and prohibitions which made up the Torah according to the rabbis. But there were also various attempts made by the rabbis to reduce the number of demands to their common denominator, in order to make it possible to keep the whole Torah.[64] Another approach was taken by the Qumran community; keeping the whole Torah meant for them additional requirements, which made their observance more radical than that of ordinary Jews.[65] Just how one was required to do the whole Torah was not clear.[66] It is not clear which one of the various Jewish positions Paul has in mind. It is apparent that in 5:3 he does not talk of his own view of "fulfilling the whole Law" (cf. 5:14), but of a Jewish view diametrically opposed to his own. The question is, why does Paul have to insist on this consequence, that accepting circumcision makes sense only when one "does" the whole Torah? Does the Galatians' stubbornness have any connection with the theology of the opponents, and if so which connection?

There are several possibilities for an answer: (1) the Galatians *do* know what Paul tells them, so that his remark is a reminder. (2) The Galatians intend to accept circumcision, but they intend to keep only a "special" law, perhaps even calling it "the law of Christ" (cf. Gal 6:2). Paul then would correct this assumption, insisting that there is no such "special" law but only the whole Torah. (3) Walter Schmithals[67] has contended that the gnostics, which form the anti-Pauline opposition, have introduced to the Galatians the ritual of circumcision as a magic ritual, but they do not demand the observance of the Jewish Torah. Combining 5:3 with the equally puzzling statement in 6:13 (the opponents do not keep the Law themselves),[68] Schmithals concludes that the opponents were interested only in the magic ritual, but so far as the Jewish Torah was concerned they were libertines. Schmithals' thesis is attractive because he can explain two difficult passages at the same time.[69] The problem is that we have no evidence that there ever were Jewish–Christian gnostics who practiced circumcision alone, without subscription to the Jewish law. The texts which Schmithals uses as evidence do not in fact support his thesis.[70] There is in the texts no indication

---

62 Str–B. 3.119 suggests that the rabbis would have rejected a statement as found in Rom 2:25. However, this is by no means obvious, since there was no uniformity of opinion even among the rabbis; the view critical of a merely external circumcision goes as far back as Jer 4:4 and is shared by Qumran (1QS 5.5). See Braun, *Qumran* 1.172f.

63 The concept occurs in Gal 5:3 and Jas 2:10; cf. also Gal 3:10; 5:14, and furthermore Matt 5:17–20; 22:40; 23:23; Mark 10:20 par; Acts 21:21ff. See Karl Georg Kuhn, "προσήλυτος," *TDNT* 6.739. Cf. also the interesting discussion of the problem in Justin *Dial.* 46f, which shows that various Jewish-Christian groups took different attitudes with regard to the Torah. The Ebionites were opposed to sacrifices (Frag. 5 [ed. Klostermann, *NT Apocrypha* II, p. 14; also Frag. 6 in HSW, *NT Apocrypha* 1.158]; cf. Schoeps, *Theologie und Geschichte*, chap. 3–4).

64 See the material in Str–B. 1.357ff. The problem is well illustrated by the famous story in Šabb. 31a (tr. of the Soncino edition): "On another occasion it happened that a certain heathen came before Sham-

mai and said to him, 'Make me a proselyte, on the condition that you teach me the whole Torah while I stand on one foot.' Thereupon he repulsed him with the builder's cubit which was in his hand. When he went before Hillel, he said to him, 'What is hateful to you, do not do to your neighbor: that is the whole Torah, while the rest is the commentary thereof; go and learn it.'" See Neusner, *Rabbinic Traditions* 1.322–24.

65 See Braun, *Radikalismus*, index, s.v. כל; idem, *Qumran* 2.229ff; idem, *Studien*, 327f.

66 Paul insists upon the "doing" (cf. 3:10, 12; also 5:17, 21; 6:9). The reading πληρῶσαι ("fulfill") by 440 *pc* sy^h Marcion is a harmonization with Gal 5:14 and Matt 5:17.

67 Schmithals, *Paul and the Gnostics*, 13ff.

68 In Gal 6:13 Paul states that the opponents are themselves circumcized, but do not keep the law. For the interpretation of the passage see on 6:13.

69 It is, however, a questionable method to solve one puzzle with the help of another.

70 See on this point Betz, *Nachfolge*, 148f.

that the opponents kept circumcision only as a "special" law. 2 Cor 6:14 presupposes observation of the Torah, although there is no emphasis on the "whole Torah;" in fact, neither circumcision nor Law are specifically mentioned.[71]

Reasonably certain, therefore, is only the first option of interpretation. From his own ("Pharisaic") point of view Paul reminds the new "converts to Judaism" of what they are getting themselves into: that receiving circumcision makes sense only if they take up the yoke of the Torah seriously, i.e., observe all its requirements, in order to be acceptable to God at the Last Judgment.[72] "Doing" the whole Torah means doing every one of the requirements, because the transgression of even one may endanger the whole effort.[73]

■ **4** After having explained the Jewish dogma in 5:3, Paul leaves no doubt about the Christian consequences of the move the Galatians are presently considering. Speaking in terms of Pauline theology, they are seeking "justification by Law" ($\dot{\epsilon}\nu$ $\nu\acute{o}\mu\omega$ $\delta\iota\kappa\alpha\iota o\hat{v}\sigma\theta\epsilon$).[74] This means they have "dropped out of [the] grace" ($\tau\hat{\eta}s$ $\chi\acute{a}\rho\iota\tau os$ $\dot{\epsilon}\xi\epsilon\pi\acute{e}\sigma\alpha\tau\epsilon$),[75] and this again means they "have become estranged from Christ" ($\kappa\alpha\tau\eta\rho\gamma\acute{\eta}\theta\eta\tau\epsilon$ $\dot{a}\pi\grave{o}$ $X\rho\iota\sigma\tau o\hat{v}$).[76] For the Apostle, "grace" and "Christ" stand in opposition to "Law." This does not, however, *a priori* exclude any other arrangements. On the contrary, one can safely assume that in Jewish Christianity both concepts, that of "grace" and "Christ" and that of "Law" must have peacefully gone hand in hand.[77] If the anti–Pauline opposition had persuaded the Galatians to switch from Pauline theology to their Jewish–Christian theology, they did not mean to "drop out of grace" or to forsake Christ; in fact, we must assume that switching to the opposition in their view did not include the giving up of Christianity in favor of Judaism. It was more a case of changing "denominations,"[78] and the Galatians must have received assurances from the opposition to that effect.[79]

Does Paul then make up artificially extreme consequences in order to keep his churches in line? Is the whole argument merely a matter of church politics? He argues that the case of the Gentile Galatians is different from the case of those who are "Jews by birth" (cf. 2:15). Christians who are Jews by birth and are thus circumcised may remain as they are and continue to do what they do as Jews, since by becoming Christians they have demonstrated that being Jewish does not ensure salvation before God. But Gentiles who have become Christians and who wish to become Jews in addition demonstrate that for them "grace" and "Christ" (i.e., the salvation through Christ outside of the Torah) are not sufficient and that to come under the Torah is necessary for their salvation. By implication, then, "Christ" is no longer a savior and "grace" is no longer grace. As a result, such people do not merely change "denominations," but become real converts to non–Christian Judaism.[80] This conversion, then, also sets in motion the curse of excommunication issued in 1:8–9.

■ **5** Following the negative statements in vv 3 and 4, Paul now defines positively and antithetically to the opponents what characterizes the existence of the Christian (Jewish and Gentile!). The peculiar form of the sentence is due to the fact that the Apostle simply

---

71 Cf. Betz, "2 Cor 6:14–7:1," 89f.

72 Cf. Paul's pre–Christian position reflected in Gal 1:13f; Phil 3:6.

73 Cf. *'Abot* 4.2 (tr. Herford): "Ben Azzai [c. 110] said: Be swift towards a light precept, and flee from transgression; for precept leads to precept and transgression to transgression. For the reward of a precept is a precept and the reward of a transgression is a transgression."

74 Cf. Gal 2:16f; 3:8, 11, 24; also 2:21; 3:6, 21; 5:5.

75 Cf. Gal 1:6; 2:21; also 1:15; 2:9. It is the situation which Paul avoided at Jerusalem (2:4–5) and because of which he had criticized Cephas at Antioch (2:11–14). On the terminology cf. 2 Pet 3:17, and Bauer, *s.v.* $\dot{\epsilon}\kappa\pi\acute{\iota}\pi\tau\omega$, 3a.

76 Cf. Gal 2:21; 4:11, 19; 5:11; also 3:17; Rom 7:2, 6. See Gerhard Delling, "$\kappa\alpha\tau\alpha\rho\gamma\acute{\epsilon}\omega$," *TDNT* 1.452–4; Bauer, *s.v.*, 3.

77 Cf. the $\nu\acute{o}\mu\mu o\nu$ $\kappa\acute{\eta}\rho\upsilon\gamma\mu\alpha$ of the *Kerygmata Petrou, Ep. Petr.* 2.3 (see below, Appendix 3). See also the anti–Pauline fragment 2 Cor 6:14–7:1, in which Torah and Christ harmonize; the term "grace" does not occur. See Betz, "2 Cor 6:14–7:1," 89–99, and below, Appendix 2.

78 Cf. 1:6–7. An instance of such change of allegiance is also Gal 2:11–14.

79 By $o\check{\iota}\tau\iota\nu\epsilon s$ Paul does not address here only a group within the Galatian churches, but those churches as a whole (against Zahn; Lütgert [*Gesetz und Geist*, 11f]).

sets forth a series of dogmatic abbreviations which had been used before in the letter: ἡμεῖς γὰρ πνεύματι ἐκ πίστεως ἐλπίδα δικαιοσύνης ἀπεκδεχόμεθα ("for we, through [the] Spirit, by faith, are expecting [the] hope of righteousness").

This sentence is admittedly almost impossible to translate, but its structure becomes clear once we realize that it consists of a series of dogmatic formulaic expressions, which function as abbreviations of dogmatic statements. Πνεύματι ("by [the] Spirit")[81] comes first because it is the primary *datum* of Christian existence; ἐκ πίστεως ("by faith")[82] has been discussed extensively in chapter 3, especially; ἀπεκδέχεσθαι ("wait eagerly")[83] is what the Christian does as long as he is "in the flesh";[84] finally, ἐλπὶς δικαιοσύνης ("hope of righteousness") spells out the eschatological character[85] of the Christian salvation—"justification by faith" is a matter of "hope" in God.[86] In the last statement Paul is in agreement with Judaism, including his Jewish-Christian opponents, in the sense that righteousness before God will be granted only at the Last Judgment, while presently it is a matter of hope.[87] The question, however, is whether this hope is to be based upon man's "works of the Law" or God's "promise to Abraham" that those who believe will be saved.[88] Paul does not

spell out here, as he does in Rom 8:18–39, what he means by this "hope." It is the eschatological nature of the gift of salvation. It is not visible and obtainable now, but because of the gift of Spirit which the Galatians have experienced, and the "arguments" which the readers have read in chapters 3–4, this hope could and should be a matter of certainty even in this life.

■ **6** Continuing to restrict himself to brief formulae, Paul now states the ethical (or: ritual) consequences of v 5 with regard to the issue of circumcision in the church: ἐν γὰρ Χριστῷ Ἰησοῦ οὔτε περιτομή τι ἰσχύει οὔτε ἀκροβυστία . . . ("for in Christ Jesus neither circumcision nor uncircumcision means anything . . ."). Paul's statement recalls what he had stated before in 3:26–28. "Circumcision"[89] and "uncircumcision"[90] belong together as technical terms of Jewish cultic law. In Judaism the terms symbolize the dividing line between those who belong to the Torah Covenant, and thus are insured of their salvation, and those who are outside of that Covenant.[91] For Christians these Jewish concepts have lost their meaning, because in Paul's view the Christians' salvation is grounded in God's promise to those who "believe in Christ."[92] If that faith has become the decisive basis of salvation, the Jewish cultic symbols

---

80 This is meant by the term "judaize" (ἰουδαΐζω) in Gal 2:14.

81 See Gal 3:2, 3, 5, 14; 4:6; 5:16, 18, 22f, 25; 6:1. For a list of such "abbreviations," see the Introduction, § 5.

82 See Gal 2:16; 3:2, 5, 7, 8, 9, 11, 12, 22, 24; cf. 3:14, 26.

83 The eschatological term occurs only here in Gal, but see Rom 8:19, 25; 1 Cor 1:7; Phil 3:20; cf. Heb 9:28.

84 See Gal 2:20; 5:7, 25f.; 6:7–10, 16.

85 Cf. Rom 5:19. The term ἐλπίς ("hope") occurs here only in Gal, but see Rom 4:18; 5:2, 4, 5; 8:20, 24f; 2:12; 15:4, 13; 1 Cor 9:10; 13:13; 2 Cor 1:7; 3:12; 10:15; Phil 1:20; 1 Thess 1:3; 2:19; 4:13; 5:8. See on the concept in Paul also Rudolf Bultmann, "ἐλπίς," *TDNT* 2.530–33; idem, *Theology* § 35,3; Conzelmann, *Outline* § 22. For further literature, see below on Gal 6:7–9.

86 Cf. Gal 2:16; 3:8, 11, 24.

87 See Gal 5:10; 6:7–10, 16. On the subject of "justification by faith" and "Last Judgment" in Paul see above on 2:15f. Stuhlmacher (*Gerechtigkeit Gottes*, 228ff) and Jürgen Becker (*Das Heil Gottes*:

Heils- und Sündenbegriffe in den Qumrantexten [SUNT 3; Göttingen: Vandenhoeck & Ruprecht, 1964] 267ff) both rightly reject the notion that there is a "double justification" in Paul, one given with baptism (1 Cor 6:11; Rom 6:7) and one given at the Last Judgment (Gal 5:6). The thesis of a "double justification" was proposed by Joachim Jeremias, "Paul and James," *ExpTim* 66 (1954/55) 369. 1 Cor 6:11 at least raises the question whether or not the Apostle was always consistent in thought and formulation.

88 The position against which Paul is arguing is found in Jewish Christianity. See Jas 2:14–26; Matt 7:21–23, and programmatically, *Ep. Petri* (ps.–Clem. *Hom.*) 1.5 (see Appendix 3): εἷς θεός, εἷς νόμος, μία ἐλπίς ("One God, one Torah, one [eschatological] hope").

89 On the concept of περιτομή ("circumcision") see Gal 2:3, 7–9, 12; 5:2, 11; 6:15.

90 On the concept of ἀκροβυστία ("uncircumcision") see 2:7; 6:15.

91 Cf. Rom 2:25ff; 3:1ff. See above on Gal 2:3.

92 On the formula ἐκ πίστεως ("by faith") see Gal 5:5.

and their implications must become a matter of ir-relevance.[93] The symbol of circumcision (or its ab-sence) no longer has any power.[94] This is true for the Gentile Galatians because they are "in Christ,"[95] so that their concern for circumcision is without theo-logical foundation. One will have to say that from the perspective of comparative religion Paul seems correct. Religious symbols and practice make sense only if they correspond to and are integrated with the doctrinal presuppositions of a particular religion. This applies to the Galatian problem insofar as Paul separates Gentile Christianity from Judaism and establishes it *de facto* as a new religion. To be sure, this runs counter to his opponents' intention to keep them both together through the Torah covenant. However, Romans 9–11 shows that Paul also wishes to maintain the kinship of Judaism and Christianity. He struggles hard to keep them both together, and not to subject one to the other. Paul's position in Romans 9–11 represents reflection later than Galatians; in Galatians he does not yet foresee their alienation, while in Romans he regrets it.

But in Romans he does not wish to just lose the Jews, though he cannot accept circumcision for Gentiles either (cf. also Rom 15:8).

The negative judgment in v 6a is followed by its positive counterpart: what matters to those "in Christ Jesus" is instead ἀλλὰ πίστις δι' ἀγάπης ἐνεργουμένη ("but faith working through love"). Again, we have before us formulaic abbreviations. "Faith" is of course "faith in Jesus Christ." While this can be taken for granted after the extensive discussions in chapters 3–4,[96] its new definition as "power" comes as a sur-prise.[97] In Paul's view the Christian is not merely an individual who has belief in Jesus Christ, but by being such a believer, he becomes a channel for the divine power of ἀγάπη ("love"). Paul's introduction of the notion of ἀγάπη ("love")[98] as a concept of ethics is new at this point. From here on this concept will dominate the parenetical section.

How does the believer become a person expressing love? The christological formula in 2:20 explained that Christ's death on the cross was an act of love. Thus,

---

93   The formulation of the κανών ("rule") in 6:15 takes up the sentence almost verbatim and thereby shows that it is the cutting edge of the whole letter. The "rule" is also cited in a different form in 1 Cor 7:19: ἡ περιτομὴ οὐδέν ἐστιν, καὶ ἡ ἀκροβυστία οὐδέν ἐστιν, ἀλλὰ τήρησις ἐντολῶν θεοῦ ("Circumcision is nothing, and uncircumcision is nothing, but keeping the commandments of God").

94   It does not have the power to achieve (ἰσχύει τι) salvation and righteousness before God (cf. Gal 2:16, 21; 3:11, 21; 5:4) or "eternal life" (3:21). Cf. Rom 3:30: εἷς ὁ θεὸς ὃς δικαιώσει περιτομὴν ἐκ πίστεως καὶ ἀκροβυστίαν διὰ πίστεως ("It is 'the one God' who will justify circumcision [i.e., the Jews] by faith and uncircumcision [i.e., the Gentiles] through faith").

95   For this formula, see Gal 2:4, 17; 3:14, 26, 28. Some textual witnesses do not read Ἰησοῦ ("of Jesus"): B Marcion Clement. Cf. Gal 2:17.

96   See Gal 1:23; 2:16, 20; 3:22, 26.

97   The term ἐνεργεῖν has occurred already in Gal 2:8 and 3:5; in 5:6 it is used in the middle ("become effective," "come to expression"). For its meaning, see Gal 5:21–23. For other usage of the term see Rom 7:5; 2 Cor 1:6; 4:12; 1 Thess 2:13; also Bauer, *s.v.*, 1,b. See furthermore 1 Cor 12:6, 11; Phil 2:13; 3:21; 1 Thess 2:13; Phlm 6. Later Paul-inists have elaborated on this concept of faith as

"energy" (cf. Col 1:29; 2:12; Eph 1:11, 19, 20; 3:7, 20; 4:16. For bib., see also above on Gal 2:8.

98   For the important ethical concept of "love" see Gal 2:20; 5:13f, 22; Rom 12:9; 13:8–10; 14:15; 15:30; 1 Cor 8:1; 13; 14:1; 16:14; 2 Cor 2:4, 8; 6:6; 8:7, 8, 24; Phil 1:9, 16; 2:1, 2; 1 Thess 1:3; 3:6, 12; 4:9; 5:8, 13; Phlm 5, 7, 9. For bib. of the great number of studies, see Harald Riesenfeld, "Étude bibliographique sur la notion biblique d' ἀγάπη, surtout dans 1 Cor 13," *ConNT* 5 (1941) 1–32; Bauer, *s.v.*; Ceslaus Spicq, *Agapè dans le Nouveau Tes-tament* (3 vols.; Paris: Gabalda, 1958–9); ET *Agape in the New Testament* (3 vols.; St. Louis: Herder, 1963–66); Robert Joly, *Le vocabulaire chrétien de l'amour est-il original? Φιλεῖν et Ἀγαπᾶν dans le grec antique* (Brussels: Presses Universitaires, 1968); Bultmann, *Theology*, § 39,3; Schelkle, *Theologie*, 3, § 8–9 (n. 24 above); Victor P. Furnish, *The Love Command in the New Testament* (Nashville: Abingdon, 1972); Regi-nald Fuller, "Das Doppelgebot der Liebe" (in *Jesus Christus in Historie und Theologie, Neutestamentliche Festschrift für H. Conzelmann* [Tübingen: Mohr, Sie-beck, 1975] 137–29); Luise Schottroff, "Gewalt-verzicht und Feindesliebe in der urchristlichen Jesus-tradition (Mt 5, 38–48; Lk 6, 27–36)" [ibidem], 197–221; for Gal 5:6 as a prototype of 1 Cor 13:13 cf. Conzelmann, *1 Corinthians*, 229, esp. n. 114.

when the Christian "believes in Jesus Christ" he believes that the Son of God died on the cross because he "loved me and gave himself up for me." When the Christian receives the Spirit of the Son of God (4:6) he also receives the divine power of love which enabled Christ to do what he did. Love is named first in the list (5:22–23) called "the fruit of the Spirit." Love becomes manifest in the individual Christian as well as in the community (2:20; 5:13). It is this love that fulfills the Torah (5:14). Nothing but this love is the basis of the Christian eschatological hope (5:25–6:10).

In Paul's theology faith and love complement each other in many ways. It is too simple to say: "in having faith, love has that which makes love possible; in having love, faith has that which makes faith effective and, therefore, real." [99] True as this may be, one must at the same time consider Christ's love and God's sending of the Spirit of Christ as agents which empower the Christian to have faith and to love. To this we must add the effect of the Apostle's love and the Christian community's love upon each other and upon the world outside. Hence it is not possible in Paul's theology to separate "faith" and "love" as "theory" and "practice." [100] Rather, Christian existence is manifest in faith and love. Both must be seen as inter-related; both are potentials of receiving and enabling. [101]

■ **7** The section vv 7–12 is set up in the style of the diatribe. Contrasted with the highly condensed section vv 1–5, the new section is freer, appearing like a rambling collection of pointed remarks, rhetorical questions, proverbial expressions, threats, irony, and, climaxing it all, a joke of stark sarcasm. Verse 7 introduces the "*agon* motif" which is well–known from the diatribe literature: $\dot{\epsilon}\tau\rho\dot{\epsilon}\chi\epsilon\tau\epsilon\ \kappa\alpha\lambda\hat{\omega}s$ ("you were running well"). [102] Paul compares the past performance of the Galatians with the runners in the stadium. [103] While they were running so well, however, something irrational happened: $\tau\acute{\iota}s\ \acute{\upsilon}\mu\hat{\alpha}s\ \dot{\epsilon}\nu\dot{\epsilon}\kappa o\psi\epsilon\nu\ [\tau\hat{\eta}]\ \dot{\alpha}\lambda\eta\theta\epsilon\acute{\iota}\dot{\alpha}\ \mu\dot{\eta}\ \pi\epsilon\acute{\iota}\theta\epsilon\sigma\theta\alpha\iota;$ ("who got in your path toward obeying the truth?") [104] The first words still seem to be preoccupied with the situation in the stadium, suggesting something like "who got in your path . . .?" [105] The amazement expressed is, of course, a rhetorical device. [106] So is the question itself. Parallels from other Pauline letters make it probable that Paul is thinking of Satan. [107] This allusion indicates that in the second part of the sentence we shift to figurative language: [108] Paul speaks of the irrational phenomenon that people may know the truth, but for inexplicable reasons they decide

99 So Schlier, p. 235.

100 Contra Stanislas Lyonnet (*Les Epîtres de Saint Paul aux Galates, aux Romains* [Paris: Cerf, 1953] on Gal 5:6), who stands for many defining faith as the *principle* of justification and salvation; as a "living faith" it works through the *medium* of love. See also idem, "Foi et charité d'après Saint Paul," *Foi et Salut selon S. Paul* (*AnBib* 42; Rome: Pontifical Biblical Institute, 1970) 211–24.

101 In his commentary of 1535, Luther has a long and incisive discussion of the phrase "faith working through love," in which he argues against "sophists" who base a new works-righteousness upon this passage. This is done when the concept of justification is connected with love rather than faith, so that the act of love becomes the justification of faith.

102 For the "*agon* motif" see also Gal 2:2; Rom 9:16; 1 Cor 9:24–26; Phil 2:16; 3:14; 2 Thess 3:1. See Otto Bauernfeind, "$\tau\rho\acute{\epsilon}\chi\omega,\ \delta\rho\acute{o}\mu os,\ \pi\rho\acute{o}\delta\rho o\mu os$," *TDNT* 8.226–35, esp. 231f; Victor C. Pfitzner, *Paul and the Agon Motif* (NovTSup 16; Leiden: Brill, 1967) esp. 136–38.

103 For the Galatians' past performance, cf. also Gal 4:12–20.

104 The text is that of Nestle–Aland. The article $\tau\hat{\eta}$ is read by P⁴⁶ C 𝕸 D G *pl*.

105 Cf. Hesychius, *Lexicon* (Hauniae: Munksgaard, 1966) 2.104: $\dot{\epsilon}\mu\pi o\delta\acute{\iota}\zeta\omega\nu,\ \delta\iota\alpha\kappa\omega\lambda\acute{\upsilon}\omega\nu$. See also LSJ, *s.v.*; Bauer, *s.v.*; Gustav Stählin, "$\dot{\epsilon}\gamma\kappa o\pi\acute{\eta},\ \dot{\epsilon}\gamma\kappa\acute{o}\pi\tau\omega$," *TDNT* 3.855–60; Preisigke, *Wörterbuch* 4/3 (1966) 648f, quoting Pap. Mich. 56.4 (3rd c. B.C.): $\gamma\acute{\epsilon}\gamma o\nu\epsilon\nu\ \alpha\acute{\iota}\tau\iota o\nu\ \tau\grave{o}\nu\ \dot{}A\rho\acute{\iota}\sigma\tau\alpha\nu\delta\rho o\nu\ \dot{\eta}\mu\hat{\iota}\nu\ \dot{\epsilon}\gamma\kappa\acute{o}\psi\alpha\iota$ ("the reason is that Aristandros got in your way").

106 Cf. Gal 3:1.

107 Cf. 1 Thess 2:18: $\dot{\epsilon}\nu\dot{\epsilon}\kappa o\psi\epsilon\nu\ \dot{\eta}\mu\hat{\alpha}s\ \dot{o}\ \sigma\alpha\tau\alpha\nu\hat{\alpha}s$ ("Satan hindered me"); Rom 15:22; 1 Cor 9:12.

108 Perhaps this is the reason why part of the manuscript tradition (G it vgˢ) concludes the sentence with a question mark. See the discussion of the point by Stählin, "$\dot{\epsilon}\gamma\kappa o\pi\acute{\eta},\ \dot{\epsilon}\gamma\kappa\acute{o}\pi\tau\omega$," *TDNT* 3.856 n. 6; Rudolf Bultmann, "$\pi\epsilon\acute{\iota}\theta\omega$," *TDNT* 6.4 n. 11.

against it.[109] The matter may be proverbial in origin,[110] but Paul interprets it in relationship to the "truth of the gospel."[111] At any rate, it is the mark of foolishness not to obey the truth when one knows it, since "we cannot do anything against the truth, but only for the truth" (2 Cor 13:8).[112]

■ 8 Playing with words of similar root and sound, Paul adds another, rather sarcastic remark: ἡ πεισμονὴ οὐκ ἐκ τοῦ καλοῦντος ὑμᾶς ("the persuasion does not come from him who calls you"). The term ἡ πεισμονή is attested here for the first time in the Greek language; since it remains a rare word, its meaning is difficult to establish.[113] It can mean "persuasion" as an activity or as an accomplished fact ("conviction"), or "obedience." The last option would require adoption of the textual variant in v 7 read by G it Vgs which, however, is not advisable.[114] The first meaning, "persuasion," can be supported by several considerations: (1) it is apparently meant to be something negative[115] in contrast to "truth" (cf. 5:7), as it comes from God and through Paul; (2) in the dualistic thought of Paul, persuasion must have its place opposite to God;[116] (3) later parallels associate it with "empty rhetoric."[117] Therefore, the term seems to belong to Paul's anti-rhetorical arsenal and must be seen in association with statements of similar kind.[118] Calling the present theological position of the Galatians a "persuasion" amounts to throwing it together with the "rhetorical gimmickry" characteristic of the opposition.[119] Such gimmickry is, of course, incompatible with the "truth of the gospel." If that persuasion does not come from God who, through Paul, has called the Galatians,[120] it must come from another source which is easy to guess.[121] Apart from his acid rhetoric Paul is correct; the present tendency of the Galatians is not a well-founded, defensible position in which they firmly believe.

---

109 G it vgs form a new sentence, a maxim, using *paronomasia*: τῇ ἀληθείᾳ μὴ πείθεσθαι μηδενὶ πείθεσθε ("Obey no one in such a way as to disobey the truth"). Cf. also Gal 4:16; Rom 2:8. On *paronomasia* see BDF, § 488,1; BDR, § 488,1.

110 Cf. Hans Walther, *Lateinische Sprichwörter und Sentenzen des Mittelalters* (Göttingen: Vandenhoeck & Ruprecht, 1963) no. 33, 157: Veritas paucis amatur: fabulam plures colunt ("Truth is loved by a few; the many pay attention to fiction"). And no. 33, 157f: Veritas vulgo semper odiosa ("Truth is always offensive to the crowd").

111 For the notion of the "truth of the gospel" see Gal 2:5, 14.

112 Cf. Acts 4:20; 5:29. For a similar proverb cf. Livy 22.39.19: Veritatem laborare nimis saepe aiunt, extingui numquam ("Truth, they say, is all too frequently eclipsed but never extinguished"). For other versions, see August Otto, *Die Sprichwörter und sprichwörtlichen Redensarten der Römer* (Leipzig: Teubner, 1890) 367f; also Bauer, *s.v.* πειθαρχέω.

113 Vg: *persuasio*. See LSJ, *s.v.*; Bauer, *s.v.*; Rudolf Bultmann, "πεισμονή," *TDNT* 6.9; *PGL*, *s.v.*; and the discussions in Burton, p. 283; Lietzmann; Schlier, 236 n. 5.

114 See above on 5:7, n. 109. Bultmann (ibidem) seems to favor this.

115 It should be noted that the witnesses omitting οὐ ("not") take it in the positive sense (D* pc it Origen Ephraem).

116 Cf. Ign. *Rom.* 3.3: οὐ πεισμονῆς τὸ ἔργον, ἀλλὰ μεγέθους ἐστὶν ὁ Χριστιανισμός ... ("Christianity is not the work of persuasion, but of greatness ...").

117 Cf. Epiphanius *Adv. haer.* 30.21.2 (p. 361,19); Chrysostom *Hom.* 1.2 in 1 Thess (*PG* 11.427 D), where the term is associated with κολακεία ("flattery") and where we find this contrast: οὐ πεισμονὴ ἀνθρωπίνη, ἀλλὰ θεοῦ δύναμις ("not human persuasion, but God's power").

118 Cf. 1 Cor 2:3–5; 2 Cor 10:1, 10; 11:4, 13–15, 19f. See Betz, *Paulus*, 57ff.

119 Cf. Gal 1:10; 3:1; 5:7b. See also Justin *Dial.* 47 (Appendix 4).

120 On the "call" see Gal 1:6, 15; 5:13. The preposition ἐκ stands for the *gen. auct.*; see Mayser, *Grammatik* 2/2, 344, 382.

121 According to Hellenistic Jewish apologetics, heresy is the work of the devil. See the material in Juda Bergmann, *Jüdische Apologetik im neutestamentlichen Zeitalter* (Berlin: Reimer, 1908) 32ff. Cf. 2 Cor 11:14; 1 Tim 1:20; 5:15; Rev 2:9; etc. According to *NHC* VI.4, p. 45 lines 14ff, the Antichrist leads the apostates who introduce circumcision; and it is the Antichrist who "will pronounce judgment upon those who are from the uncircumcision who are the (true) people" (lines 20–22, according to the tr. by Frederik Wisse; cf. Karl-Martin Fischer *et al.*, *ThLZ* 98 [1973] 174).

■ **9** As it is customary in letter writing[122] and in the diatribe material, Paul throws in a proverb: μικρὰ ζύμη ὅλον τὸ φύραμα ζυμοῖ ("a little yeast leavens the whole dough"). This proverb is only attested in Paul—here and in 1 Cor 5:6.[123] But there can hardly be any doubt that it comes from popular wisdom, perhaps even from the poets, or both.[124] The symbolic interpretation of leaven is also known from the gospel tradition,[125] Philo,[126] and Roman poets;[127] the negative symbolism of leaven is well documented in Philo and Plutarch, who also interprets it as "spoiling the dough."[128] In Gal 5:9, the proverb[129] is stated without any further interpretation;[130] in context it speaks for itself.[131]

■ **10** The proverb in v 9 is followed here by a conventional epistolary phrase, an expression of confidence: ἐγὼ πέποιθα εἰς ὑμᾶς ἐν κυρίῳ ὅτι οὐδὲν ἄλλο φρονήσετε ("I have confidence in you, in the Lord, that you will take no other view"). The sentence is without real connections to the preceding or the following. Parallels in other letters of Paul[132] as well as in Hellenistic

---

122 See ps.-Demetrius *De eloc.* 4.232: Κάλλος μέντοι αὐτῆς αἵ τε φιλικαὶ φιλοφρονήσεις καὶ πυκναὶ παροιμίαι ἐνοῦσαι· καὶ τοῦτο γὰρ μόνον ἐνέστω αὐτῇ σοφόν, διότι δημοτικόν τί ἐστιν ἡ παροιμία καὶ κοινόν, ὁ δὲ γνωμολογῶν καὶ προτρεπόμενος οὐ δι' ἐπιστολῆς ἔτι λαλοῦντι ἔοικεν, ἀλλὰ μηχανῆς ("Ornament, however, it may have in the shape of friendly bits of kindly advice, mixed with a good few proverbs. This last is the only philosophy admissible in it—the proverb being the wisdom of a people, the wisdom of the world. But the man who utters sententious maxims and exhortations seems to be no longer talking familiarly in a letter but to be speaking *ex cathedra*"). See on proverbs in letter-writing Peter, *Brief*, 20f, 27; Thraede, *Brieftopik*, 24f, and index, *s.v.* "Sprichwort."

123 In 1 Cor 5:6 it is even marked by the "quotation formula" ὅτι.

124 Already Luther (1519, 1535) calls the sentences "proverbial." Cf. Anton Schön ("Eine weitere metrische Stelle bei St. Paulus?" *Bib* 30 [1949] 510–13) who wants to take it as a post-classical iambic trimeter. See Hans Windisch, "ζύμη," *TDNT* 2.902–06; Conzelmann, *1 Corinthians*, 98f.

125 Luke 13:21 ∥ Matt 13:33; *Gos. Thom.*, log. 96; cf. also Mark 8:15 ∥ Luke 12:1 ∥ Matt 16:6; Ign. *Mag.* 10.2; Justin *Dial.* 14.2,3; ps.-Clem. *Hom.* 8.17. On the negative sense of "leaven" see Joachim Jeremias, *The Parables of Jesus* (tr. S. H. Hooke; rev.; New York: Scribner's, 1963) 148; Robert W. Funk, "Beyond Criticism in Quest of Literacy: The Parable of the Leaven," *Int* 25 (1971) 161f. For the usage in rabbinic literature, see Str-B 1.728f, 3.359f; and by the Church Fathers *PGL*, *s.v.* ζύμη, ζυμόω.

126 Philo *Spec.* 1.293; 2.184f; *QE* 1.15. See Windisch, "ζύμη," *TDNT* 2.905.

127 Cf. Plautus *Cas.* 2.5.326; *Mercat.* 5.3.959; Petronius *Sat.* 76. The references are taken from Otto, *Sprichwörter*, 133 (see n. 112 above).

128 Plutarch *Quaest. Rom.* 289F: "Yeast is itself also the product of corruption, and produces corruption in the dough with which it is mixed; for the dough becomes flabby and inert, and altogether the process of leavening seems to be one of putrefaction; at any rate, if it goes too far, it completely sours and spoils the flour."

129 Several witnesses (D* it^d vg goth Marcion Marius Victorinus Ambrosiaster *al*) read here and 1 Cor 5:6 δολοῖ ("falsifies"), instead of ζυμοῖ ("leavens"). See Zuntz, *Text*, 114f; Metzger, *Textual Commentary*, 597; Mussner, p. 356 n. 91: "'But the *lectio difficilior* is ζυμοῖ." These witnesses carry the negative interpretation into the proverb itself, a direction which is reflected in 2 Cor 4:2: δολοῦν τὸν λόγον τοῦ θεοῦ ("falsify the word of God").

130 Schlier (p. 237) and Mussner (pp. 356f) allegorize the proverb by identifying the leaven with the doctrine of the opponents who, if allowed to introduce the one demand of circumcision, may ruin the entire truth and the whole faith of the Galatians. This interpretation stands in a long tradition, beginning perhaps in Ign. *Mag.* 10.1 and including Chrysostom, Theophylactus, Luther, Calvin, Cornelius a Lapide, Lipsius, Sieffert, Schäfer, Kuss, Burton, Lietzmann, Oepke, etc. However, Paul does not take this step, but simply cites the proverb.

131 To this extent, it has a parallel in 1 Cor 15:33, where Menander's *Thais* is quoted: φθείρουσιν ἤθη χρηστὰ ὁμιλίαι κακαί ("Bad company spoils good habits"). It is interesting that a medieval proverb is related to both Gal 5:9 and 1 Cor 15:33: Fermentat celebres numerosa pecunia mores ("A lot of money ferments [corrupts] respectable habits."). The quotation is taken from Walther, *Lateinische Sprichwörter*, no. 9339 (see n. 110 above); see also Prudentius, *Liber Apotheosis* (CChr 126; ed. Mauritius Cunningham, 1966) 353ff.

132 Cf. Rom 14:14; 15:14; 2 Cor 2:3; Phil 1:6, 25; 2:24; Phlm 21; also 2 Thess 3:4; 2 Tim 1:5, 12; Ign. *Trall.* 3.2; Pol. *Phil.* 9.2; *Barn.* 1.4.

epistolary literature[133] show that the Apostle makes use of an epistolary topos. The question is, however, how he can have such confidence if the Galatians have almost deserted him and gone over to the opponents.[134] We may have before us a conflict between a weighty epistolary phrase and the concrete situation which Paul is addressing. The concrete situation may be the reason Paul qualifies his confidence in the Galatians by adding ἐν κυρίῳ ("in the Lord").[135] Such qualification is justified also[136] by Paul's general belief that there can be no confidence "in the flesh."[137] On the other hand, it would be absurd even to use a conventional phrase if the Apostle did not have some real hope that the churches will remain loyal Paulinists.

The situation is apparently one of wavering and undecidedness on the part of the Galatians; bad as it is, there is at least the chance to say what Paul feels needs to be said. This then must be the *Sitz im Leben* of the

epistle: the Galatian Christians have been sufficiently dislodged from their Paulinist position, but they have not yet made up their mind finally and have not yet closed the door to Paul irreversibly.[138] Still, one wonders how much of Paul's optimism is due to convention[139] and how much due to reality. Ignoring that the Galatians may have already taken another view, his hope can only be that having read his letter they may change their mind again.

In v 10b a threat follows: ὁ δὲ ταράσσων ὑμᾶς βαστάσει τὸ κρίμα, ὅστις ἐὰν ᾖ ("but he who stirs you up will bear his judgment, whoever he is"). Without naming anyone, Paul addresses the opponents.[140] Their leader or the whole group will come under the divine judgment,[141] and of course they fall under the curse of 1:8–9. It is difficult to speculate whether Paul has a specific person in mind and, if so, who it might be.[142] Avoiding the naming of people was done as a matter of

---

133 Rudolf Bultmann ("πείθω," *TDNT* 6.3) mentions 2 Macc 9:27 as a parallel. Others are *Ep. Petr.* (ps.-Clem. *Hom.*) 1.2 (see Appendix 3); Pap. Flind. Petr. II, 11, 1: πέπεισμαι ῥᾳδίως με τῶι βασιλεῖ συστασθήσεσθαι ("I am convinced that you will readily introduce me to the King." [*Epistulae privatae graecae*, ed. Stanislaus Witkowski, BT, Leipzig: Teubner, 1911, no. 3]); *Demetrii et Libanii qui feruntur Τύποι ἐπιστολικοί et Ἐπιστολιμαῖοι χαρακτῆρες*; ed. Valentin Weichert (BT, Leipzig: Teubner, 1910) no. 41 (p. 33 line 21); no. 62 (p. 39 line 23); *Ep. Phalarid.* 130 (ed. Rudolphus Hercher, *Epistolographi Graeci* [Paris: Didot, 1873] 449).

134 Cf. Gal 1:6; 3:1; 4:9–11, 15a, 16, 19, 21; 5:4, 7; 6:12–16.

135 This Pauline formula is found only here in Gal, but is more frequent in other letters; cf. Rom 14:14; 16:2, 8, 11, 12, 13, 22; 1 Cor 1:31; 4:17; 7:22, 39; 9:1, 2; 11:11; 15:58; 16:19; 2 Cor 2:12; 10:17; Phil 1:14; 2:19, 24, 29; 3:1; 4:1, 2, 4, 10; 1 Thess 3:8; 4:1; 5:12; Phlm 16, 20. Cf. also Col 3:18, 20; 4:7, 17; Eph 4:1, 17; 5:8; 6:1, 10, 21, etc. See Ernest Best, *One Body in Christ* (London: SPCK, 1955) 1ff, 29, 31; and for further bib., Conzelmann, *Outline*, 208–12.

136 Notably, it is part of the epistolary phrase also in Rom 14:14; Phil 1:14; 2:24; 2 Thess 3:4. In Gal 5:10a, B does not read it.

137 Cf. Phil 3:3f; 2 Cor 10:2; also Rom 2:19; 2 Cor 3:4; Gal 1:10.

138 For the phrase "you will not take another view" cf. Phil 3:15; *2 Clem.* 17.3; Ign. *Smyr.* 5.2. See also

Georg Bertram, "φρήν κτλ.," *TDNT* 9.232–33.

139 For the epistolary *topos* cf. ps.-Libanius *Charact. epistol.* (cf. n. 133, above) no. 10 (p. 24 lines 7–8). Most likely it is related to the theme of "unity in the spirit" (for which see Thraede, *Brieftopik*, 110ff, 125).

140 Paul names a group in 1:7; 4:17; 5:12; 6:12f, so that the sing. in 5:10b should be taken as generic; so also Sieffert, Burton, Oepke, Bonnard, Schlier, Mussner. Or is an allusion to Satan included (see on 5:8)? For the term ταράσσειν ("stir up") see on 1:7.

141 Cf. the direct parallels in 1 Thess 2:16; 2 Cor 11:15, where Paul predicts the fate of the opponents: "their end will be according to their works." This statement agrees with Jewish and primitive Christian eschatology, that everybody will be judged by God according to his deeds. Cf. also Gal 5:5; 6:5, 7–10; Rom 2:2f, 6; 3:8; 13:2; 14:10; 1 Cor 5:5; 11:29, 34; 2 Cor 5:10. See on the whole question Gillis P. Wetter, *Der Vergeltungsgedanke bei Paulus* (Göttingen: Vandenhoeck & Ruprecht, 1912) 56ff; Luz, *Geschichtsverständnis*, 313ff.

142 For speculations about who the person might be, see Zahn, p. 244; Sieffert, p. 309; Oepke; Lietzmann; Bligh; Mussner, p. 358 n. 104. For the phrase ὅστις ἐὰν ᾖ ("whoever he might be") cf. the parallel Gal 2:6.

rule, so as not to give free publicity to the opposition.[143]

■ 11 Without preparation, Paul confronts the readers with a rhetorical question and statement on his own behalf: Ἐγὼ δέ, ἀδελφοί, εἰ περιτομὴν ἔτι κηρύσσω, τί ἔτι διώκομαι; ("but if I, my brothers, still preach circumcision, why am I still persecuted?") What the Apostle has precisely in mind will in all likelihood always be hidden from our knowledge. Presumably, he refers to matters known to the Galatians as well as to himself, but unknown to us. Equally puzzling is the fact that Paul, after bringing up the matter so suddenly, drops it instantly without further comment.

In analyzing the sentence, we recognize that Paul makes a statement about himself: "he speaks on his own behalf."[144] The ἐγώ ("I") is emphatically placed at the beginning of the sentence.[145] Then the address "my brothers" is repeated.[146] The statement then reports two facts: (1) Paul admits that he is still being persecuted,[147] but he does not reveal why and by whom.[148] (2) He denies that he "still" (ἔτι)[149] preaches circumcision, using the first statement as evidence. The undeniable fact of his being persecuted disproves the supposition, by rendering it absurd and thus impossible, that he is still engaged in the propagation of circumcision. Is this a hypothetical and in essence false construction by Paul (cf. 2:21b)?[150] Who could have actually held and advocated such a view?

Some scholars have speculated that the opponents must have spread a rumor. They knew too well the fact that Paul preached the opposite, freedom from the Law, and so did the Galatians. It would make better sense if the opponents had said the opposite about Paul's mission, and this is what they did according to Acts.[151] If the Galatians had been told by the opponents that Paul preached circumcision, how could they believe it?[152] Is "preaching circumcision" what the opponents held against Paul, or is it Paul's construction of what they attributed to him?

The language suggests that κηρύσσειν περιτομήν

---

143 Cf. the remark by Chrysostom on 5:10: "And observe that he never mentions the name of these plotters, that they might not become more shameless." A similar reason is given by Ign. *Smyr.* 5.3 (cited above on Gal 1:7).

144 Oepke, p. 161; Schlier, p. 238.

145 Cf. Gal 6:17; 1 Cor 9:15; 2 Cor 12:11, 15; Cf. 2 Cor 12:13, 16; Phil 3:4, 13 also.

146 Cf. Gal 1:2, 11; 3:15; 4:12, 28, 31; 5:13; 6:1, 18.

147 Instances of such persecution are Gal 2:4f, 11–14; 4:29; cf. 6:17; one should also mention the "catalogs of dangerous situations" (1 Cor 4:10–13; 2 Cor 4:7–10; 6:4–10; 11:23–27; 12:10; 1 Thess 2:14–16; see Wolfgang Schrage, "Leid, Kreuz und Eschaton. Die Peristasenkataloge als Merkmale paulinischer theologia crucis und Eschatologie," *EvT* 34 [1974] 141–75). Equally important are the references in Col (esp. 1:24ff) and Eph (esp. 3:1ff); 1 Tim 1:12ff; 2 Tim 2:12ff; Acts 13–28, etc.

148 See on the whole problem Philipp Seidensticker, *Paulus, der verfolgte Apostel Jesu Christi* (Stuttgart: Katholisches Bibelwerk, 1965); Morton Smith, "The Reason for the Persecution of Paul and the Obscurity of Acts," in *Studies in Mysticism and Religion presented to Gershom G. Scholem* (ed. E. E. Urbach *et al.*; Oxford: Oxford University, 1967) 261–68. On the background see Odil H. Steck, *Israel und das gewaltsame Geschick der Propheten* (WMANT 23; Neukirchen: Neukirchner Verlag, 1967); Güttge-

manns, *Apostel, passim*; Betz, *Nachfolge*, 173ff.

149 ἔτι ("still") is not read by D G it arm goth Ephraem *al.* It was probably believed redundant because of the second occurrence of the particle in the same sentence. Cf. Mussner, p. 359 n. 112.

150 This conclusion was drawn by Chrysostom: "Observe how clearly he exonerates himself from the charge, that in every place he judaized and played the hypocrite in his preaching." But the conclusion is based most likely upon Acts 16:3, where Paul is said to have circumcised Timothy, and it must be seen in connection with the variant readings in Gal 2:3–5 (see above). On the problem see the discussions in Lütgert (*Gesetz und Geist*, 22ff), Sieffert, Zahn, Oepke, Mussner. Paul's statement here has a strange parallel in the *Ep. Petr.* (ps.-Clem. *Hom.*) 2.4–7, where Peter denies rumors claiming that he preaches the abolishment of the Torah (see Appendix 3).

151 See Acts 21:20–26, 28. Cf. 18:13; 25:18f.

152 Perhaps the Galatians themselves thought it would make no difference to Paul whether they were circumcised or not, because to him circumcision and uncircumcision have lost their meaning (cf. 5:6; 6:15; and the rule 1 Cor 9:19–23). However, what makes no difference to him as a Jewish Christian, makes all the difference for them as Gentile Christians!

("preach circumcision") is Paul's language,[153] formulated in contrast to κηρύσσειν Χριστόν ("preach Christ"), his usual concept.[154] It is, therefore, uncertain that the opponents ever attributed "preaching circumcision" to him. However, Paul seems to *restate* in his own words something which in fact was held against him. Commentators have suggested that Paul may refer to his pre-Christian times, when he in effect did preach circumcision. Or he refers to an earlier period in his Christian life, when he held a Jewish–Christian view on circumcision, which was contrary to his present position.[155] Schlier (p. 239) correctly sees that the statements made by Paul in Gal 3:28; 5:6; 6:15 can in fact be interpreted *pro* or *contra* circumcision. Paul deals with circumcision differently when he deals with people who are Jews or Gentiles by birth. In his view, Jews by birth, if they want, continue to practice circumcision because it is "irrelevant" and not a condition for salvation. Perhaps the opponents "misunderstood" his position either by mistake or by intention. We will probably never know whether Paul denies simple "slander" or an allegation which in part was true.

The uncertainty about v 11a carries over into v 11b: ἄρα κατήργηται τὸ σκάνδαλον τοῦ σταυροῦ ("then, the 'stumbling block of the cross' has been removed"). This statement can be taken either as the conclusion to the section 5:2–11a (12), or simply as the reason for v 11a,[156] or both. Paul does conclude entire sections elsewhere by a sentence beginning with ἄρα ("therefore"): cf. 2:21; 3:29; 6:10 (differently 3:7). Also, 5:11b is a parallel of 2:21c, the conclusion of the *propositio* (2:15–21). Therefore, we may best take v 11b as the end and conclusion to the discussion on circumcision (5:2–12); v 12 would add a joke, and v 13 goes on to another matter.

Paul comes back to the issue of circumcision in the postscript (6:12–16), when he sums up the main concerns of the letter. Paul's conclusion points out that, if the Galatians submit to circumcision and obedience to the Torah, the "stumbling block of the cross" is removed (cf. 5:2). By this he means that—as far as the Galatians are concerned—"Christ has died in vain" (2:21), they have been cut off from Christ and have fallen out of grace (5:4), the "truth of the gospel" has been falsified (cf. 2:5b, 14) and exchanged for "another gospel" which is no gospel at all (1:6–7), and Paul's work among the Galatians was "in vain" (cf. 3:4; 4:11, 19; also 2:2). The concept of the "stumbling block"[157] is used only here in Galatians. Paul's concern is that the "stumbling block of the cross" not be eliminated from the Christian gospel and Christian existence.[158]

The term σκάνδαλον ("stumbling block") originally refers to something which turns out to be a trap, a source of embarrassment and offense, a provocation which arouses resentment and resistence.[159] The

153 The expression occurs only here and is taken by most exegetes as an *ad hoc* formulation by Paul; see especially Karlheinz Müller, *Anstoss und Gericht* (SANT 19; Munich: Kösel-Verlag, 1969) 114f; Mussner, p. 359 n. 114, 116. Perhaps this is correct; but cf. the expression in Gal 2:8 "the gospel of circumcision" (for which see on 2:8); and Rom 2:17–29.

154 See 1 Cor 1:23; Phil 1:15; also Gal 2:2; Rom 10:8; 1 Cor 15:11f; 2 Cor 1:19; 11:4; 1 Thess 2:9; Col 1:23.

155 Following a suggestion by Barnikol (*Zeit des Paulus*, 18–24) Schoeps thinks that Paul refers to his pre-Christian activity as a missionary (*Paul*, 219; cf. Schlier, p. 238 n. 4).

156 This is Schlier's (p. 239) and Mussner's (p. 360) interpretation. Cf. also Müller, *Anstoss und Gericht*, 115f; Thrall, *Greek Particles*, 36.

157 Most important is the parallel in 1 Cor 1:23: ἡμεῖς δὲ κηρύσσομεν Χριστὸν ἐσταυρομένον, Ἰουδαίοις μὲν σκάνδαλον, ἔθνεσιν δὲ μωρίαν ... ("But I preach Christ the crucified, to the Jews a stumbling-block and to the Gentiles foolishness ..."). On σκάνδαλον ("stumbling-block") see Rom 9:33 (Isa 8:14); 11:9 (Ps 69:23); 14:13; 16:17; the verb is found in Rom 14:21; 1 Cor 8:13; 2 Cor 11:29. For the meaning of the term and bib. see Gustav Stählin, *Skandalon* (Gütersloh: Bertelsmann, 1930); idem, "σκάνδαλον κτλ.," *TDNT* 7.339–58; Müller, ibidem, 113–21; Mussner, pp. 360–63; Heinz–Wolfgang Kuhn, "Jesus als Gekreuzigter," *ZThK* 72 (1975) 36–37.

158 For the meaning of καταργέω see Gal 3:17; 5:4; also 2:21; 1 Cor 1:18–31; Rom 1:16f; etc. See Müller, ibidem, 116.

159 The term can be associated with παγίς ("trap"); cf. Josh 23:13; Ps 141:9 (140:9 LXX); 1 Macc 5:4; Rom 11:9 (Ps 69:23 [68:22 LXX]). For more material see Bauer, *s.v.*

phrase "the stumbling block of the cross" is another instance of Paul's formulaic language. This phrase sums up several essential aspects of his theology of the "cross" (cf. 3:1; 5:24; 6:12–14). The "stumbling block" of the Christian message is, according to Paul, that salvation is proclaimed on the basis of Christ's crucifixion and death. This is an offense to the Jews because salvation is promised "through faith in Christ Jesus" (cf. 2:16) and, by implication, renders the Jewish concept of salvation through observation of the Torah invalid. It is also a "stumbling block" to the Greco-Roman culture because by implication the Christian concept of salvation denies any validity to the way of Greek *paideia*.[160] Therefore, the Christian message presents the unbeliever[161] with a central and indispensable element of "provocation" and "alienation." Without this element, the Christian message has lost its integrity and identity, i.e., its truth.[162]

■ **12** As an after-thought Paul adds a sarcastic and indeed "bloody" joke:[163] ὄφελον καὶ ἀποκόψονται οἱ ἀναστατοῦντες ὑμᾶς ("as for these agitators, they had better go the whole way and make eunuchs of them-selves!" [*NEB*]).[164] Paul is conforming here to the practice of diatribe preachers, when he salts his arguments with this joke.[165] The ridiculing of eunuchs was a standby of the diatribe preacher.[166] This joke does not imply that the Galatians were in fact under the influence of the γάλλοι (castrated priests) of the cult of Cybele–Attis,[167] but Paul uses the public disgust with regard to these rituals in order to discredit his opponents and their ritual of circumcision, which, it must be said, has nothing to do with castration. Ὄφελον with the future indicative expresses, in contrast to its usage in classical Greek, an attainable wish;[168] it may also be that the term refers to the similar language in 5:2–3. The term ἀποκόπτω is used here in a specific sense ("castrate") as a caricature of the Jewish ritual of circumcision.[169] The opponents themselves are called οἱ ἀναστατοῦντες, a term describing ordinary political "agitators" or "rabble–rousers."[170] This term is, of course, used with the intention to caricature and thus discredit the opponents.[171]

160 See on this point especially 1 Cor 1:18–31.

161 Ign. *Eph.* 19.1 stands in the Pauline tradition when he says that the "cross is a stumbling-block to the unbelievers" (i.e. non-Christians).

162 On the theological implications, see Rudolf Bultmann, "Das Befremdliche des christlichen Glaubens," *ZThK* 55 (1958) 185–200 (also in his *Glauben und Verstehen* [4 vols.; Tübingen: Mohr, Siebeck, 1952–65] 3.197–212).

163 See Hans von Campenhausen, "Ein Witz des Apostels Paulus und die Anfänge des christlichen Humors," *Neutestamentliche Studien für Rudolf Bultmann zum 70. Geburtstag am 20. August 1954* (BZNW 21, 1954) 189–93.

164 Translations sometimes tend to avoid the obscene language Paul is using; e.g., vg: utinam et abscindantur, qui vos conturbant; Luther, *Heilige Schrift* (1545): "Wolte Gott das sie auch ausgerottet würden die euch verstoren." The correct interpretation is found in Luther's commentary of 1519, following Jerome. *JB*: "Tell those who are disturbing you I would like to see the knife slip."

165 On the ironic challenge to do the wrong thing, a diatribe *topos*, see Bultmann, *Stil*, 32ff, 66, esp. 62; he lists Gal 4:9f; 5:12; Phil 3:19; 1 Cor 11:6 as examples of "false and ridiculous presentation" of oppositional views (103, 105).

166 See, e.g., Epictetus *Diss.* 2.20.17–20, 1.2.25; Lucian *Eunuch.*, esp. 8; Dio Chrys. 79.11; Philo *L.A.* 3.8; *Spec.* 1.325. See Betz, *Lukian*, 78.

167 So Oepke (pp. 163f) following Lütgert (*Gesetz und Geist*, 81ff). Cf. Lightfoot, on Gal 5:12; Burton, pp. 288f; Betz, *Lukian*, 77–79.

168 See BDF, § 384; BDR, § 384. P⁴⁶ reads ἄρα ("therefore") instead; P⁴⁶ D G read the subj. ἀποκόψωνται.

169 ἀποκόπτειν and ἀποκόπτεσθαι ("castrate themselves"); cf. BDF, § 317; BDR, § 317. This interpretation was proposed by Chrysostom and Ambrosiaster. On the meaning of the term see Gustav Stählin "κοπετός, κόπτω," *TDNT* 3. 853–5; Bauer, *s.v.*; *PGL*, *s.v.* Most important is the parallel in Phil 3:2: βλέπετε τὴν κατατομήν ("Beware of those who insist on mutilation—'circumcision' I will not call it" [*NEB*]).

170 Cf. Acts 17:6; 21:38 (ὁ ἀναστατώσας—"the man who caused a revolt"). The language is political; cf. Dan 7:23 LXX; ps.–Clem. *Hom.* 2.15. See LSJ, *s.v.*; Bauer, *s.v.* Preisigke, *Wörterbuch* 4/1 (1944) 141, *s.v.*; *PGL*, *s.v.*

171 Stählin, *TDNT* 3.854, perhaps following vg, goes on to connect the castration with the prohibition in Deut 23:2, in order to conclude that Paul recommends "self–excommunication" to those who in fact are already excommunicated. This theologizing of a joke is itself amusing.

5   *Exhortatio:* A Warning against Corruption by the Flesh

13   For you, my brothers, were called to freedom. Only do not let this freedom become an opportunity for the flesh,[1] but through love become slaves of one another. 14/ For the whole Law is fulfilled in one word: 'you shall love your neighbor as yourself.' 15/ If, however, you bite one another and tear each other to pieces, see to it that you are not consumed by one another. 16/ But I say, walk by the Spirit, and you will not carry out [the] desire of the flesh. 17/ For the flesh sets its desires against the Spirit, and the Spirit against the flesh, since they are opposed to each other, so that you do not do the things which you intend. 18/ If, however, you are led by [the] Spirit, you are not under [the] Law. 19/ The works of the flesh are evident,[2] such as: sexual immorality, impurity, licentiousness, 20/ idolatry, sorcery, hostilities, strife, jealousy, outbursts of rage, quarrels, dissensions, factions, 21/ outbreaks of envy, cases of drunkenness, excessive banquets, and things like these. In regard to these I forewarn you as I have forewarned [before]: 'those who do such things will not inherit [the] Kingdom of God.' 22/ But the fruit of the Spirit is: love, joy, peace, forebearance, kindness, goodness, 23/ faithfulness, humility, self-control. No law is against such things! 24/ But those who belong to Christ [Jesus] have crucified their flesh together with its passions and desires.

Interpretation

■13 At the beginning of this section Paul restates the principal definition of the Christian 'indicative' of salvation: ὑμεῖς γὰρ ἐπ' ἐλευθερίᾳ ἐκλήθητε, ἀδελφοί ("for you, my brothers, were called to freedom"). In distinction to 5:1a the indicative[3] of salvation is stated here in the passive, in the second person plural. However, there is no great shift in meaning between vv 1a and 13a, except that v 1a focuses on the work of Christ done for us, while vv 2–18, focussing on God's work, addresses the Galatians in the second person. The intention of both statements is the same:[4] the liberation

---

1   Cf. *NEB:* "only do not turn your freedom into license for your lower nature . . .".

2   Cf. *NEB:* "Anyone can see the kind of behaviour that belongs to the lower nature . . .".

3   On this terminology see the introduction to the Exhortation, above.

4   Against Schlier (pp. 241f) who sees here a major shift: the liberation through Christ occurred "potentially for all" (5:1a), but the Galatians take part in it through God's call. Apparently, Schlier applies the categories of *potentia* and *actualitas* to express the difference, but these categories are not in Paul's mind. Schlier (p. 242) states that he sees God's call to have been fulfilled in baptism, thus identifying the *actualitas* with the sacrament. This conforms to Schlier's Roman Catholic theology, but it certainly is absent from Paul. Mussner (pp. 366f) follows Schlier.

by Christ[5] and God's call[6] are part of the same process of salvation. Another problem is that of the meaning of the conjunction γάρ ("for"). Many commentators assume that it is intended to connect v 13 with v 12, providing the reasons for it.[7] But this is by no means evident. Parallel to other instances in the letter, the term γάρ may indicate another step in the argument, and this usage is most likely the one we have here.[8]

Between the 'indicative' (v 13a) and the 'imperative' (v 13c) Paul has inserted (v 13b) a statement which in all probability is the clue to the concrete problem the Galatians must face: μόνον μὴ τὴν ἐλευθερίαν εἰς ἀφορμὴν τῇ σαρκί ("only [do] not [let] this freedom [become] an opportunity for the flesh"). Beginning with μόνον μή ("only not")[9] and lacking a verb,[10] the statement adds a significant qualification to the preceding. "On this word, as a hinge, the thought of the epistle turns from freedom to a sharply contrasted aspect of the matter, the danger of abusing freedom."[11] Up to v 13 Paul had consistently defended the freedom to which the Galatian Christians are entitled. The question is whether at this point he now turns away from that defense, or whether the following is its continuation.

The Apostle admits that "this freedom" (τὴν ἐλευθερίαν)[12] can become an "opportunity for the flesh" (ἀφορμὴ τῇ σαρκί). The term ἀφορμή is originally a military term ("starting point, base of operations"), but it is used here more generally ("opportunity, pretext").[13] The enemy to whom no opportunity should

be given is the "flesh" (σάρξ). Hence the whole phrase amounts to what Paul elsewhere calls "temptation."[14] The concept dominating the entire following section is that of σάρξ ("flesh"). Paul had mentioned it before in the sense of "the merely human" (1:16; 2:16, 20; 4:13, 14), or as that which is opposite the Spirit (3:3; 4:23, 29). As a result, the whole statement in v 13 b–c amounts to a definition of the ethical task as preservation of freedom.

In the following this task of preserving Christian freedom is described as the task of dealing effectively with the power of the "flesh."[15] In Galatians flesh as an anthropological concept describes (1) man as a being of "flesh and blood," his physical body, mortality, and frailty; and (2) the Christian as a battlefield of the opposing forces of flesh and Spirit.[16] Having been given the Spirit (3:2, 5) and having been granted freedom from sin (1:4; 2:15–17; 3:22), Law (2:16, 19; 3:13, 24–25; 4:4–5; 5:18), and the "elements of the world" (4:3, 9), the Christian in this life still exists ἐν σαρκί ("in the flesh": 2:20; 4:14; 6:7–10). This "flesh" has a life of its own; it produces "desires and passions" (5:16–17, 19–21) which are at work against the Spirit. Although the Christian has "crucified" his "flesh, together with its passions and its desires" (5:24), this flesh has not been altogether eliminated but continues to be a potential threat.

How can Christian freedom become an "opportunity to the flesh"? Freedom itself, being the result of the

---

5   For the concept of "freedom" see on 5:1. For the expression ἐπ᾽ ἐλευθερίᾳ ("to freedom") and this usage of ἐπί with the dative see 1 Thess 4:7; Eph 2:10; 2 Tim 2:14; and Bauer, s.v. II, 1, b, ε; BDF, § 235 (4); BDR, § 235, n. 6; Moule, Idiom-Book, 50: "You were called to (or with a view to) freedom." Almqvist, Plutarch, 111 no. 234.

6   For the meaning of καλέω ("call") see 1:6, 15; 5:8.

7   Against Schlier, p. 241; cf. Mussner, p. 366.

8   For this usage of γάρ see Bauer, s.v., 4.

9   For the usage of μόνον ("only") see Gal 4:18; 1:23; 2:10; 3:2; 6:12. See Bauer, s.v. μόνος 2,c.

10   For the use of μή with omission of the verb, see Burton, p. 292; Oepke; Schlier, p. 242 n. 2; Mussner, 368 n. 14; Bauer, s.v. μή, A, III, 6 (with parallels); BDF, §§ 190 (4); 481; BDR, §§ 190 (4); 481.

11   Burton, p. 291.

12   The article has a demonstrative force, as Burton (p. 292) points out.

13   Cf. the use of the concept in Rom 7:8, 11; 2 Cor 5:12; 11:12; 1 Tim 5:14; Ign. Trall. 8.2. See LSJ, s.v.; Bauer, s.v.; Georg Bertram, "ἀφορμή," TDNT 5.472–74.

14   Cf. Gal 4:14; 6:1; also 1 Cor 7:5; 10:9, 13; 1 Thess 3:5.

15   Cf. Gal 5:16, 17, 19, 24; 6:8, 12, 13.

16   Compared with Rom 7–8 the concept of "flesh" is rather simple in Gal; it is the anthropological concept describing the aspect of man which is juxtaposed with the divine Spirit. This simple dualism must not be confused with the more complex situation in Rom, and Gal should not be read "through Rom" at this point. For the concept and bib., see Bultmann, Theology, § 22–23; Eduard Schweizer, "πνεῦμα, πνευματικός," TDNT 6. 428ff; idem "σάρξ," TDNT 7.125ff; Brandenburger, Fleisch und Geist, 42ff; Jewett, Paul's Anthropological Terms, 101ff.

liberation from sin, Law and "the elements of the world," is an opportunity. Freedom means that the Christian has the option whether henceforth his existence is made up of the "fruit of the Spirit" (5:22–23) or of "the works of the flesh" (5:19–21). The choice is no longer made by the "elements of the world," but it is not made by the Spirit either. Freedom can only mean what it says if the Christian has a choice; he can allow his existence to become a base of operations for the flesh or for the Spirit. If the Christian allows the flesh to get the upper hand, the loss of his freedom is the immediate result, because this freedom is a gift of the Spirit. Therefore, "Christian ethics" can be defined as the exercise of freedom, or as the preservation of freedom; the corruption and loss of that freedom is then identical with the return under the slavery of "the elements of the world."[17]

The question is, furthermore, how these doctrines are related to the Galatian situation. Paul's parenesis is so general that there seems no room for "concrete issues." Yet, Gal 6:1 shows that his parenesis was not without a concrete *Sitz im Leben*. The phrase "if someone is discovered in a transgression" no doubt refers to a concrete instance or instances, not to merely hypothetical possibilities. Flagrant misconduct by Christians must have been one, or even the major, problem of the Galatians. We do not know, unfortunately, whether such misconduct was the result of human failure or of "libertinism."[18] One cannot escape the conclusion that it was related to emancipation (cf. 3:26–28) and to the lack of a new code of law which would specify for the Christian what is right and what is wrong. The

abolishment of the old rituals and conventions implies that the concepts of sin and guilt no longer apply.

In such a situation, the occurrence of failure and misconduct is to be expected; in addition, confusion about these experiences cannot be a surprise. In the absence of a code of law, how should one deal with transgression? This dilemma seems to have been the reason the Galatians opened their doors to the anti-Pauline opposition, in order to submit to circumcision and obedience to the Torah. There is no reason to believe that the Galatians took transgression lightly. On the contrary, they must have been quite concerned that such instances would destroy their hope of salvation in Christ.[19] It also becomes understandable why the anti–Pauline opposition was attractive in their eyes: they needed concrete help, and the opponents of Paul could provide it. Entering into the Sinai covenant and obedience to the Torah would provide them with the means to deal with human failure and misconduct in a way which would not endanger their salvation.

The significance of the section 5:13–24 is that Paul realizes that mere polemic against accepting circumcision and law (5:2–12; especially 2:15–5:12) does not do justice to the Galatian trouble. There has to be a positive and viable proposal as to how to deal effectively with misconduct and failure, that is, with the "flesh."

How, then, can the loss of freedom be prevented without introducing the Law? Paul's principal answer is set forth in the second part of the definition of the ethical task, v 13c: ἀλλὰ διὰ τῆς ἀγάπης δουλεύετε ἀλλήλοις ("but through love become slaves of one an-

---

17 For a different interpretation cf. Schlier (pp. 242f) who associates the Galatian "nomism" with "self-righteousness" and contrasts it with "antinomianism;" this antinomianism, by turning against the law, turns into "egocentrism" ("Selbstsucht"). Although this interpretation may be correct in regard to 1 Cor and Rom, in Gal we have no indication of an "antinomian" tendency except Paul's own opposition to the Jewish Torah.

18 The easiest way to solve the problem is to read the situation of 1 Cor into Gal. A good example of this interpretation is Luther (1535). But the slogan πάντα μοι ἔξεστιν ("I am free to do anything") is not attested in Gal, and there is no evidence that it was practiced among the Galatians. Cf. 1 Cor 6:12;

10:23.

19 The whole question of ethics and asceticism in the mystery cults and in gnosticism should be compared. Cf. as an example my analysis of the "system" in Plutarch's *Is. et Osir.* 351E–352A: Hans Dieter Betz, "Ein seltsames mysterientheologisches System bei Plutarch," *Ex Orbe Religionum, Studia Geo Widengren oblata* (Leiden: Brill, 1972) 1:347–54; also Jan Bergman, "Decem illis diebus. Zum Sinn der Enthaltsamkeit bei den Mysterienweihen im Isisbuch des Apuleius," ibidem, 332–46; *PECL*, 36ff; Griffiths, *Apuleius of Madauros*, index, *s.v.* "Abstinence." For the development of sexual asceticism in Jewish Christianity and in Paul, see Niederwimmer, *Askese*.

other").[20] In other words, the only way to preserve and exercise Christian freedom is to exercise ἀγάπη ("love"). The principal significance of the concept of love has been pointed out before (see on 5:6). The freedom to which the Galatians were called (cf. 5:13a) and to which Christ has liberated them (cf. 5:1a) is the same as that which Christ himself had practiced: it is the freedom to love (cf. 2:20). Hence Paul equates the exercise of love and the exercise of freedom. Paradoxically, the exercise of freedom and love means becoming one another's δοῦλος ("slave", "servant"). Obviously, this juxtaposition of terms is intended. Paul contrasts the slavery under the Law and the "elements of the world," which is a one–sided relationship of submission, suppression, scrupulosity, and fear,[21] with the other "slavery", which is the free and voluntary act of love. The practice of love includes of course the freedom of accepting the love of others. Still, this leaves the question why Paul goes so far as to call the mutual love a form of slavery. There can hardly be any doubt that he does so intentionally. Love is voluntary and reciprocal, but it involves commitments to be maintained even under difficult and strained circumstances.[22] It is the necessity of commitment and the difficulties of maintaining human relationships that cause Paul to describe the free exercise of love as a form of mutual enslavement.[23] The following section 5:14–6:10 provide further discussion and examples of this issue.[24]

■ 14 Surprisingly Paul returns to the subject of the Law (cf. 3:19–25). This raises a number of questions: what are his reasons for this return to the questions of the Law (Torah), which he had answered before in chapters 3–4? Why does he deal with the Law in the parenetical section again? How is the entirely negative view of the Law, expressed up to 5:12, related to the positive interpretation of the concept in 5:14–6:10? Does Paul have two concepts of the Law: the Jewish Torah, which he rejects, and the Christian commandment of the law of the love, which he accepts? Is this love command identical with the "law of Christ" in Gal 6:2? Is the love commandment "law" in the same sense as the Torah is for the Jews?

In v 14 we can distinguish between two matters of concern: (1) in v 14a Paul advances a thesis about the Law in general, while (2) in v 14b he quotes a specific passage from the LXX. The statement in v 14a is a Jewish legal formula of *reductio in unum*: ὁ γὰρ πᾶς νόμος ἐν ἑνὶ λόγῳ πεπλήρωται ("for the whole Law is fulfilled in one word"). The conjunction γάρ ("for")[25] connects the statement with the preceding (v 13c), but also indicates a new matter to be introduced. The concept of the "whole Law" had been discussed before (cf. 5:3; 3:10); it refers to the Torah as a whole. However, the question here is whether Paul has in mind the total number of prescriptions and prohibitions of the Jewish Torah, or whether he is thinking of a principle (the rabbinic כלל) which sums up and contains the whole of the Torah.[26] In Judaism we find the same ambiguity, so that we must stay with Paul's text in order to find his own answer to the problem.

---

20 Instead of διὰ τῆς ἀγάπης ("through love") a number of witnesses (D G 104 it vg^el sa goth Ambrosiaster) read τῇ ἀγάπῃ τοῦ πνεύματος ("through the love of the Spirit"). This is certainly good Pauline theology (cf. Gal 5:22; Rom 5:5; 15:30, where the phrase also is found). But the majority of witnesses support the Nestle–Aland text. See the discussion in Zahn, p. 262.

21 Cf. Gal 2:5; 3:28; 4:1, 3, 7, 8, 9, 24; 5:1; also Rom 6:6, 17, 20; 8:15.

22 It is in this positive sense that Christ became a "slave" (Phil 2:7), that Paul is Christ's slave (Gal 1:10; Rom 1:1; Phil 1:1; 2:22; 1 Cor 9:19; 2 Cor 4:5; see n. 23 below), and that the Christian in general is living a life of slavery (Rom 6:16ff; 7:6; 12:11; 14:18; 16:18; 1 Cor 7:21–3; 1 Thess 1:9; etc.). See Bultmann, *Theology*, § 39.

23 Cf. esp. 2 Cor 4:5: οὐ γὰρ ἑαυτοὺς κηρύσσομεν ἀλλὰ Χριστὸν Ἰησοῦν κύριον, ἑαυτοὺς δὲ δούλους ὑμῶν διὰ Ἰησοῦν ("For we do not proclaim ourselves, but Christ Jesus [the] Lord; ourselves, however, as your slaves because of Jesus").

24 Again, we differ from Schlier's interpretation (p. 244). He takes the Christian's "slavery" to imply the voluntary *giving up* of this freedom in analogy to Christ's sacrifice; this leads to the "placing of oneself at the disposal of God and the other people." One can see how easily Paul's concept of freedom can be misunderstood as a new form of non-freedom.

25 See on Gal 5:1a above, where γάρ is missing.

26 For this point of rabbinic theology see Str–B 1.907f; Daube, *NT and Rabbinic Judaism*, 63–66; Davies, *Sermon on the Mount*, 401 n. 2.

Two reasons indicate that Paul thinks of a principle rather than the sum–total of individual prescriptions and prohibitions: (1) he gives his explicit formulation in v 14b;[27] (2) the "whole Law" is not to be "done" ($\pi o\iota e\hat{\iota}\nu$), as individual laws have to be done (cf. 3:10, 12; 5:3), but is rather "fulfilled." This latter term, stated as a gnomic passive perfect ($\pi e\pi\lambda\acute{\eta}\rho\omega\tau\alpha\iota$), needs special attention.[28] In Judaism the term "fulfilling the Torah" can be identical with "doing" it,[29] but the peculiar thing about Paul is that he wants to distinguish between the two.[30] According to him, the Jew is obliged to do the Torah (cf. 3:10, 12; 5:3; also 6:13), while the Christian fulfills the Torah through the act of love, to which he has been freed by Christ (5:1, 13). This points to a decisive difference between law and love: the prescriptions and prohibitions of the Jewish Torah stand before the Jew as demands "to be done" by him, while love is the result of liberation and the gift of the Spirit. The Jew does the "works of the Torah," while the Christian does "the good" (6:9–10). The occurrence of love is a gift—from God, through Christ, in the Spirit—and also mutually between people. About this gift one can also say that it is the fulfillment of the Torah: in loving, the Torah is always fulfilled also, but such a statement is made in retrospect.[31] Hence the commandment to love functions in Paul's theology in a different way compared with the commandments to do the Torah in Jewish theology.

Why then does Paul bring up the matter of the Law again at this point? As far as his own theology is concerned, he could do well without it. Apparently, however, he cannot avoid the matter, because the Galatians are so preoccupied with circumcision and Torah. If he wants to win his churches back, he cannot ignore the issue that looms largest in their minds and that is central to the theology of his opponents. It may be that they are fascinated by a Christian concept of "Torah," which they may even call "the Torah of Christ" (cf. on 6:2). Therefore his argument in the parenetical section must integrate the concept of Torah in such a way that the Jewish (Jewish–Christian) concept of the opposition is eliminated, while the concern of the Galatians in regard to the ethical problems is taken care of.

Paul accomplishes these goals by: (1) carefully distinguishing between the "doing" and the "fulfilling" of the Torah—the "doing" of the Jewish Torah is not required for Christians, but the "fulfilling" is; (2) by distinguishing between Torah and Scripture and by giving the latter a very positive role in salvation history —Scripture "foresees" and thereby contains and inaugurates the Christian way of salvation (cf. 3:6–14, especially 3:8, 22; 4:21–31); (3) by conceiving of Christian existence as the "fruit of the Spirit" which, far from being against the Torah (cf. 5:23), is in fact the fulfillment of the Torah (5:19ff). Consequently the Galatians do not need the Torah obedience propagated by the Jewish–Christian opposition in order to fulfill the Torah; they need neither circumcision nor Sinai covenant. Instead they simply should lead a life in accordance with the Spirit, because such a life is

---

27 $\dot{\epsilon}\nu$ $\dot{\epsilon}\nu\dot{\iota}$ $\lambda\acute{o}\gamma\omega$ ("in one word") refers to the quotation of Lev 19:18 LXX. A strong effort to completely reserve the fulfillment of the Torah for Christianity is reflected in variant readings, no doubt secondary: Marcion has simply $\dot{\epsilon}\nu$ $\dot{\upsilon}\mu\hat{\iota}\nu$ ("among" or "in you"); D* G it Ambrosiaster read: $\dot{\epsilon}\nu$ $\dot{\upsilon}\mu\hat{\iota}\nu$ $\dot{\epsilon}\nu$ $\dot{\epsilon}\nu\dot{\iota}$ $\lambda\acute{o}\gamma\omega$ ("among [or: in] you in one word"); 1611 syr[h] Ephraem read $\dot{\epsilon}\nu$ $\dot{o}\lambda\acute{\iota}\gamma\omega$ ("in brief"). See Zahn, p. 262 n. 90.

28 $\mathfrak{M}$ D G pm read $\pi\lambda\eta\rho o\hat{\upsilon}\tau\alpha\iota$. But the parallel speaks for the perfect, Rom 13:8: $\dot{o}$ $\gamma\grave{\alpha}\rho$ $\dot{\alpha}\gamma\alpha\pi\hat{\omega}\nu$ $\tau\grave{o}\nu$ $\dot{\epsilon}\tau\epsilon\rho o\nu$ $\nu\acute{o}\mu o\nu$ $\pi\epsilon\pi\lambda\acute{\eta}\rho\omega\kappa\epsilon\nu$ ("for he who loves the other [person] has fulfilled the law"). Cf. also Gal 6:2. On the problem see Walter Gutbrod, "$\nu\acute{o}\mu o\varsigma$," TDNT 4. 1071; Käsemann, Römer, 344ff.

29 The concept of "fulfilling" the law must be inter-
preted contextually. Cf. Matt 3:15; 5:17. See Str–B 1.241; Henrik Ljungman, Das Gesetz erfüllen (Lund: Gleerup, 1954); Bauer, s.v. $\pi\lambda\eta\rho\acute{o}\omega$ 4,b; W. D. Davies, Christian Origins and Judaism (Philadelphia: Westminster, 1962) 32ff; Gerhard Delling, "$\pi\lambda\eta$-$\rho\acute{o}\omega$," TDNT 6.286–98.

30 Elsewhere Paul implies the distinction; cf. Rom 3:3ff; 8:4, 8, 10; Phil 1:11, etc. Cf. Schlier (pp. 244f) who does not make the distinction; Burton, pp. 295f; Sieffert, pp. 316f.

31 See esp. Rom 13:8–10, where Paul provides a more extensive discussion; in v 10 he states: $\pi\lambda\acute{\eta}\rho\omega\mu\alpha$ $o\hat{\upsilon}\nu$ $\nu\acute{o}\mu o\upsilon$ $\dot{\eta}$ $\dot{\alpha}\gamma\acute{\alpha}\pi\eta$ ("therefore love is fulfillment of the law").

de facto the fulfillment of the Torah.[32]

Paul then quotes Lev 19:18 according to the LXX,[33] which does not mean that he quotes directly from the LXX; it is more likely that he takes the quotation from primitive Christian tradition, where it is widely attested.[34] The quotation formula[35] also seems to indicate that the verse is known to the Galatians: ἐν τῷ· ἀγαπήσεις τὸν πλησίον σου ὡς σεαυτόν ("[namely] in the [word]: 'you shall love your neighbor as yourself'"). The formulation of the essence of the Torah as contained in Lev 19:18 is by no means a Christian *proprium*, but is also attributed in Jewish tradition to R. Hillel.[36] However, the tradition may be legendary;[37] later it was also attributed to R. Aqiba.[38] Even if R. Hillel did the same thing as Paul, one should not conclude that Paul was a "Hillelite."[39] Rather primitive Christianity as a whole was in some way related to

that branch of Rabbinic Judaism which tried to explain the essence of the Torah by referring to Lev 19:18. Paul's interpretation of Lev 19:18 is universalistic, taking the command to include fellowman in general, not just the fellow Jew (and full proselyte).[40] Paul's interpretation is spelled out clearly at the end of the section in 6:10: "let us do good to all men, but especially to those who belong to the household of the faith."[41]

■15 The addition of a sarcastic warning follows the style of the diatribe: εἰ δὲ ἀλλήλους δάκνετε καὶ κατεσθίετε, βλέπετε μὴ ὑπ' ἀλλήλων ἀναλωθῆτε ("if, however, you bite one another and tear each other to pieces, see to it that you are not consumed by one another"). Such "beastly" behavior stands, of course, in sharp contrast to the love of one another just described in v 14.[42] Comparisons of bad conduct with the behavior

---

32 So also most commentaries. See Schlier, pp. 245f; Mussner, p. 370.

33 The same quotation appears in Rom 13:9. See Kautzsch, *De Veteris Testamenti Locis*, 14.

34 Lev 19:18 is often quoted in primitive Christian literature (Matt 5:43; 19:19; Mark 12:31 // Matt 22:39 // Luke 10:27; Rom 13:9; Gal 5:14; Jas 2:8; *Did.*1.2; *Barn.*19.5[cf. 2]; Justin *Dial*. 93.2). See Davies, *Sermon on the Mount*, 370, 373, 402, 405 n. 1; Victor P. Furnish, *The Love Command in the New Testament* (Nashville: Abingdon, 1972) *passim*; Klaus Berger, *Die Gesetzesauslegung Jesu* 1 (WMANT 40; Neukirchen: Neukirchener Verlag, 1972) 80ff; André Feuillet, "Loi ancienne et Morale chrétienne d'après l'Epître aux Romains," *NRTh* 42 (1970) 785–805, 798.

35 The quotation formula ἐν τῷ (sc. λόγῳ) is found only here in Paul; cf. 1 Cor 15:54; Rom 9:9; esp. 13:9.

36 *b Šabb*. 31a. For a discussion of the material see Str–B 1.356ff; Davies, *Sermon on the Mount*, 401 n. 2; Neusner, *Rabbinic Traditions* 1.322f.

37 Cf. Neusner, ibidem, 3.331, 359.

38 *Gen. Rab*. 24.7. Cf. for this and other passages, Str–B 1.357f.

39 Joachim Jeremias has tried to show that "Paul was a Hillelite": "Paulus als Hillelit," in *Neotestamentica et Semitica, Studies in Honour of M. Black* (eds. E. E. Ellis and M. Wilcox; Edinburgh: Clark, 1969) 88–94. However, the sources do not allow to connect Paul with this particular teacher.

40 In Judaism, "neighbor" (רֵעַ, ὁ πλησίον) was usually interpreted as fellow Jew (including the full-proselyte), while the universalist interpretation, taking

the term to refer to all men, appears only in the sources we have from a later time. It is possible, however, that the later interpretation is older than our sources allow us to believe. On the problem, see Str–B 1.353ff, 907; 3.306; Johannes Fichtner and Heinrich Greeven "πλησίον," *TDNT* 6.311–18; Bauer, *s.v.*; Berger, *Gesetzesauslegung*, 81ff (see n. 34 above); Hugh Montefiore, "Thou shalt love thy Neighbour as thyself," *NovT* 5 (1962) 157–69; Mussner, pp. 370–2; Andreas Nissen, *Gott und der Nächste im antiken Judentum* (WUNT 15; Tübingen: Mohr, Siebeck, 1974).

41 Gal 6:10; 1 Thess 3:12; Rom 15:2; etc. See also Luther's comment (1535): "Finally, no creature toward which you should practice love is nobler than your neighbor. He is not a devil, not a lion or a bear or a wolf, not a stone or a log. He is a living creature very much like you. There is nothing living on earth that is more pleasant, more lovable, more helpful, kinder, more comforting, or more necessary. Besides, he is naturally suited for a civilized and social existence. Thus nothing could be regarded as worthier of love in the whole universe than our neighbor" (WA 40/2.72; also in *Luther's Works* 27.58).

42 The contrast is expressed by δέ ("but", "however").

276

of wild animals were a commonplace in the diatribe literature.[43] The protasis is stated as a *realis* (εἰ with the indicative),[44] but this does not mean that Paul has concrete instances of such behavior in mind.[45] By intention, the language is hyperbolic.[46] From δάκνω ("bite")[47] we move to κατεσθίω (Bauer: "something like 'tear to pieces'").[48] The climax continues in the apodosis: ἀναλίσκω ("consume," "annihilate").[49] The comparison describes mad beasts fighting each other so ferociously that they end up killing each other.[50]

■16 Paul's own ethical theory now focuses upon the central issue with which the Galatians have to come to grips: how to deal effectively with the powers of the "flesh." Λέγω δέ, πνεύματι περιπατεῖτε καὶ ἐπιθυμίαν σαρκὸς οὐ μὴ τελέσητε ("but I say, walk by [the] Spirit, and you will not carry out the desire of [the] flesh"). The introductory λέγω δέ ("but I say") marks the fact that Paul is about to make an important statement.[51] This statement contains two parts:

(1) The imperative πνεύματι περιπατεῖτε ("walk by [the] Spirit") sums up the Apostle's parenesis, and therefore defines Paul's concept of the Christian life.

The concept of περιπατέω ("walk") describes this life by one of the more important terms of ancient anthropology and ethics, both Jewish and Greek.[52] The term expresses the view that human life is essentially a "way of life." A human being must and always does choose between ways of life as they are presented in history and culture. For ancient man, ways of life are more than "styles of life": they are not only different in their outward appearance, but their different appearance is the result of different underlying and determining factors. These factors influence human behavior by providing the "way" in which human beings "walk". Therefore, the way of life of human beings determines the quality of their life. More than merely a matter of outward style, the way of life provides continuity, guidance, and assistance for the task of coping with the daily struggle against evil.[53]

As far as the Galatian Christians are concerned, they had chosen the way of life that is based upon the Spirit.[54] The dative πνεύματι ("by the Spirit")[55] which is so typical for Galatians expresses the origin as well as

43   See on this type of comparison Gerhard, *Phoinix*, 22–30, 48–54; Bultmann, *Stil*, 36f, 91; Ernst Weber, *De Dione Chrysostomo Cynicorum sectatore* (Leipzig: Hirzel, 1887) 108ff, 173ff; Betz, *Lukian*, 188; for further literature see Victor Pöschl (ed.), *Bibliographie zur antiken Bildersprache* (Heidelberg: Winter, 1964) 569–71. NT examples include Gal 5:15; Phil 3:2; Matt 7:15; Luke 13:32; 2 Pet 2:22.

44   See BDF, § 372; BDR, § 372.

45   So also Oepke; Mussner, pp. 373f; against Schmithals (*Paul and the Gnostics*, 43ff), who, following Lütgert, assumes polemic against "libertinists." Similarly Schlier (pp. 246f), who takes v 15 as a psychological analysis of the inner lack of freedom, false piety, lack of humor, etc., of the wrong kind of enthusiasts.

46   See for this Lausberg, *Handbuch*, §§579, 894, 909–10.

47   See Hab 2:7 LXX; Teles (ed. Hense) 9 line 3; Epictetus *Diss.* 2.22.28; 2.1.17; 3.2.8; 3.24.108; 4.1.122; 4.5.21; 4.8.23; 4.10.23; *Ench.* 46.2; Philo *L.A.* 2.8; Lucian *Revivesc.* 36; *Gnomol. Vatic.*, n. 19; Porphyry *De abst.* 2.8; etc. See also Karl Jöel, *Der echte und der xenophontische Sokrates* (Berlin: Gaertner, 1893–1901) 2.933; Gerhard, *Phoinix*, 38; Bauer, *s.v.*, 2.

48   Cf. Plutarch *Adv. Colot.* 1124E: "For if someone takes away the laws, but leaves us with the teachings of Parmenides, Socrates, Heracleitus, and Plato, we shall be far from devouring one another and living the life of wild beasts (ἀλλήλους κατεσθίειν καὶ θηρίων βίον ζῆν)." In the NT see also 2 Cor 11:20, and for further material Bauer, *s.v.*, 2.

49   For the figurative use, cf. 2 Thess 2:8 *v.l.* and Bauer, *s.v.*, with parallels.

50   Cf. also the parallel in Gal 5:12.

51   Cf. Gal 1:9; 3:17; 4:1; 5:2.

52   For this concept see Georg Bertram and Heinrich Seesemann, "πατέω," *TDNT* 5.940–45; F. J. Helfmeyer, "הלך," *TWAT* 2.415–33; Gustav Wingren, "'Weg,' 'Wanderung' und verwandte Begriffe," *StTh* 3 (1951) 111–23; Betz, *Nachfolge*, 76ff; Furnish, *Theology and Ethics*, 227ff.

53   The concept of περιπατέω ("walk") is used often by Paul: Rom 6:4; 8:4; 13:13; 14:15; 1 Cor 3:3; 7:17; 2 Cor 4:2; 5:7; 10:2,3; 12:18; Phil 3:17, 18; 1 Thess 2:12; 4:1, 12. Synonymous is στοιχέω: Gal 5:25; 6:16; Rom 4:12; Phil 3:16.

54   See Gal 3:3: ἐναρξάμενοι πνεύματι ("you have begun by the Spirit"); also 3:2, 5; 4:6; 5:5.

55   Gal 3:3; 5:5, 16, 18, 25; furthermore Rom 8:13, 14; 12:11; 1 Cor 14:2; 15; 2 Cor 3:3; 12:18; Phil 3:3; 1 Pet 4:6. See also Brandenburger, *Fleisch und Geist*, 193 n. 2.

the quality of that way of life.[56] Paul's advice, therefore, amounts to the rather laconic "continue to do what you have been doing." The Galatians owe their present way of life to the Spirit; it is based upon the Spirit; it depends upon the Spirit. Consequently, defending this life against the forces of evil can only mean letting the power of the Spirit do its work[57] against its opposite force, "the flesh" ($\sigma\acute{\alpha}\rho\xi$). If the Galatians have problems with the flesh, they are advised to seek assistance from the very power that gave them this life, rather than its opposite, that same flesh.[58]

(2) Verse 16 contains a promise: "you will not carry out the desire of the flesh." This promise[59] depends upon the preceding imperative and is its result. In order to understand the promise, one must realize the implicit presuppositions. It is understood that the statement presupposes the radical dualism of $\pi\nu\epsilon\hat{\upsilon}\mu\alpha$ ("Spirit") and $\sigma\acute{\alpha}\rho\xi$ ("flesh").[60] The flesh is active, a force which carries out intentiosn—of course, evil intentions. This is what the Apostle means by $\dot{\epsilon}\pi\iota\theta\upsilon\mu\acute{\iota}\alpha$ $\sigma\alpha\rho\kappa\acute{o}\varsigma$ ("desire of [the] flesh").[61] If the "desire of the flesh" is permitted to be carried out, the result is manifest in the "works of

the flesh" ($\check{\epsilon}\rho\gamma\alpha$ $\tau\hat{\eta}\varsigma$ $\sigma\alpha\rho\kappa\acute{o}\varsigma$) which are listed in 5:19–21. As these "works of the flesh" happen, the goals of the flesh are fulfilled.

The term $\tau\epsilon\lambda\acute{\epsilon}\omega$ ("'carry out")[62] is complex: its grammatical subject is the human individual who carries out the "desires of the flesh."[63] But in reality the human subject is manipulated by the flesh which is the logical subject fulfilling its own intentions. The conclusion is that if the human subject allows the Spirit to completely influence and fill out his life, then the opposite force, the intentions of the flesh, will be prevented from accomplishing their goal, so that the "works of the flesh" cannot happen.[64]

■ 17 Paul submits an anthropological–soteriological theory which underlies not only v 16, but his entire parenesis: $\dot{\eta}$ $\gamma\grave{\alpha}\rho$ $\sigma\acute{\alpha}\rho\xi$ $\dot{\epsilon}\pi\iota\theta\upsilon\mu\epsilon\hat{\iota}$ $\kappa\alpha\tau\grave{\alpha}$ $\tauο\hat{\upsilon}$ $\pi\nu\epsilon\acute{\upsilon}\mu\alpha\tau\varsigma$, $\tau\grave{o}$ $\delta\grave{\epsilon}$ $\pi\nu\epsilon\hat{\upsilon}\mu\alpha$ $\kappa\alpha\tau\grave{\alpha}$ $\tau\hat{\eta}\varsigma$ $\sigma\alpha\rho\kappa\acute{o}\varsigma$ ("for the flesh sets its desires against the Spirit, and the Spirit against the flesh . . ."). Clearly we have before us in a very concise form one of the fundamental anthropological doctrines of Paul.[65] It is stated as a principle in chiastic form,[66] but it also

---

56   Bauer, *s.v.* $\pi\nu\epsilon\hat{\upsilon}\mu\alpha$, 5, d, β, renders "in the Spirit" or "through the Spirit." See also Schlier, pp. 247f.
57   Cf. Gal 5:18.
58   Cf., esp., Gal 3:2, 3, 5; 5:18, 24; 6:13.
59   The promissory character of the statement is rightly emphasized by Schlier, p. 248. Cf. Gal 6:7–10. For $o\grave{\upsilon}$ $\mu\acute{\eta}$ with subjunctive as "the most definite form of negation regarding the future" see BDF, § 365; BDR, § 365.
60   Cf. Gal 5:17.
61   The concept must not be misunderstood as restricted to sexual desires(Vg: *desideria carnis*), but it describes the "flesh" as goal–oriented energy, not as substance (cf. Gal 5:17, 24; and esp. Rom 7:7–11; also 1:24; 6:12; 13:14; 1 Thess 4:5; Eph 2:3; 4:22; Col 3:5; etc.). See on the whole concept Friedrich Büchsel, "$\dot{\epsilon}\pi\iota\theta\upsilon\mu\acute{\iota}\alpha$, $\dot{\epsilon}\pi\iota\theta\upsilon\mu\eta\tau\acute{\eta}\varsigma$, $\dot{\epsilon}\nu\theta\upsilon\mu\acute{\epsilon}ο\mu\alpha\iota$, $\dot{\epsilon}\nu\theta\acute{\upsilon}\mu\eta\sigma\iota\varsigma$," *TDNT* 3.168–72; Bultmann, *Theology*, § 23, 3; Bauer, *s.v.*, 3; Käsemann, *Römer*, 184.
62   On the meaning of $\tau\epsilon\lambda\acute{\epsilon}\omega$ in 5:16 see Bauer, *s.v.*, 2; Gerhard Delling, "$\tau\epsilon\lambda\acute{\epsilon}\omega$," *TDNT* 8.59.
63   Cf. Gal 3:3: $\nu\hat{\upsilon}\nu$ $\sigma\alpha\rho\kappa\grave{\iota}$ $\dot{\epsilon}\pi\iota\tau\epsilon\lambda\epsilon\hat{\iota}\sigma\theta\epsilon$; ("now do you 'complete' it through the flesh"). Paul ridicules the goals of the opponents; perhaps 2 Cor 7:1 contains what the opponents really had in mind: $\dot{\epsilon}\pi\iota\tau\epsilon\lambda\epsilon\hat{\iota}\nu$ $\dot{\alpha}\gamma\iota\omega\sigma\acute{\upsilon}\nu\eta\nu$ $\dot{\epsilon}\nu$ $\phi\acute{o}\beta\omega$ $\theta\epsilon\hat{o}\hat{\upsilon}$ ("achieving holiness through the fear of God"). See Betz, "2 Cor 6:14–

7:1," 98, and below, Appendix 2.
64   What should happen, according to Paul, is formulated for a different context in 2 Cor 12:9: $\dot{\eta}$ $\gamma\grave{\alpha}\rho$ $\delta\acute{\upsilon}\nu\alpha\mu\iota\varsigma$ $\dot{\epsilon}\nu$ $\dot{\alpha}\sigma\theta\epsilon\nu\epsilon\acute{\iota}\alpha$ $\tau\epsilon\lambda\epsilon\hat{\iota}\tau\alpha\iota$ ("For the power [of Christ] comes to perfection in weakness"). Scholars have often pointed to the great similarity between Gal 5:16ff and the anthropological passage in 1QS 3.13–4.26; however, the differences are more striking and illuminate Paul's theology only by way of contrast.See Davies, *Paul and Rabbinic Judaism*, 169ff; Braun, *Qumran* 1.213ff; Peter von der Osten-Sacken, *Gott und Belial* (SUNT 6; Göttingen: Vandenhoeck & Ruprecht, 1969) 116ff.
65   For the dualism of "flesh" and "Spirit" see Gal 3:3; 4:29; 5:19–24; 6:8; Rom 2:28; 8:4ff: etc. A survey of the material is found in Eduard Schweizer, "$\pi\nu\epsilon\hat{\upsilon}\mu\alpha$, $\pi\nu\epsilon\upsilon\mu\alpha\tau\iota\kappa\acute{o}\varsigma$" *TDNT* 6.428–30; idem, "$\sigma\acute{\alpha}\rho\xi$, *TDNT* 7.125–35; Bultmann, *Theology*, § 22–23, 38–40. Basic studies are Brandenburger, *Fleisch und Geist, passim*; Jewett, *Paul's Anthropological Terms*, esp. 49ff; Schottroff, *Glaubende*.
66   On chiasmus see BDF, § 477; BDR, § 477; Joachim Jeremias, "Chiasmus in den Paulusbriefen," *ZNW* 49 (1958) 145–56.

assumes common knowledge.[67] This statement of principle creates serious problems for Paul's theology as a whole and raises the question of its origin and background in the history of religions. The fact that the Apostle submits this theory here does not mean that he himself has created it; it is not simply his own hypothesis.[68] He shares it with other varieties of the same doctrine in Judaism[69] and the Hellenistic religions.[70] He shares it also with other Christian authors, especially the Gospel of John.[71] One of the disputed questions in present Pauline research is the question of the origin of the dualism of Spirit and flesh.[72] Another problem is raised by the fact that the discussions in Galatians and in Romans do not seem to harmonize. In Romans, it is the power of sin ($\dot{\alpha}\mu\alpha\rho\tau\dot{\alpha}$) which produces desires in the body through the law (6:12; 7:7–8), while the flesh looks more like a passive victim and tool of sin. In Galatians the flesh is the active power which generates the desires, while the power of sin is not part of the picture at all. In both Romans and

Galatians however, the dualism of Spirit and flesh is retained. How do we account for the differences and the agreements?

In v 17a the dualism is set up in a rather simple form: flesh and Spirit are named as opposite forces, both agitating against each other. The flesh and its "desiring" ($\dot{\epsilon}\pi\iota\theta\nu\mu\dot{\epsilon}\omega$) are human agents of evil, while the Spirit is the divine agent of the good. Verse 17b spells out the anthropological consequences of this dualism:[73] $\tau\alpha\hat{\nu}\tau\alpha\ \gamma\dot{\alpha}\rho\ \dot{\alpha}\lambda\lambda\dot{\eta}\lambda\omega\iota\varsigma\ \dot{\alpha}\nu\tau\dot{\iota}\kappa\epsilon\iota\tau\alpha\iota,\ \dot{\iota}\nu\alpha\ \mu\dot{\eta}\ \dot{\alpha}\ \dot{\epsilon}\dot{\alpha}\nu\ \theta\dot{\epsilon}\lambda\eta\tau\epsilon\ \tau\alpha\hat{\nu}\tau\alpha\ \pi\omega\iota\hat{\eta}\tau\epsilon$ ("for these are opposed to each other, so that you do not do the things which you intend"). The neuter $\tau\alpha\hat{\nu}\tau\alpha$ ("these things") identifies flesh and Spirit as impersonal forces acting within man and waging war against each other.[74] Man is the battlefield of these forces within him, preventing him from carrying out his will. The human "I" wills, but it is prevented from carrying out its will ($\tau\alpha\hat{\nu}\tau\alpha\ \pi\omega\iota\hat{\eta}\tau\epsilon$) because it is paralyzed through these dualistic forces

---

67 Despite the new studies the whole problem of its origin has not been sufficiently investigated. Hildebrecht Hommel ("Das 7. Kapitel des Römerbriefs im Licht antiker Überlieferung," *ThViat* 8 [1961/62] 90–116) has shown that the theory is related to the philosophical critique of the Socratic idea of *paideia*. But Hommel does not pay attention to Gal 5:17. The background in Hellenistic philosophy would then provide an explanation for the many parallels between Rom 7/Gal 5:17 and Hellenistic writers, among them Hellenistic Judaism including Philo. It is the weakness of Brandenburger's study of the problem that he neglects the wider background. For further parallels see Wettstein on Rom 7:15; Lietzmann, *Römer*, on Rom 7:15.

68 Against Eduard Schweizer, who has argued that Paul is responsible for the formulation. See his articles mentioned above n. 65; also idem, "Die hellenistische Komponente im neutestamentlichen $\sigma\dot{\alpha}\rho\xi$-Begriff," in his *Neotestamentica* (Zurich: Zwingli-Verlag, 1963) 29–48; idem, "Röm. 1, 3f und der Gegensatz von Fleisch und Geist vor und bei Paulus," *Neotestamentica*, 180–89; idem, "Gegenwart des Geistes und eschatologische Hoffnung bei Zarathustra, spätjüdischen Gruppen, Gnostikern und den Zeugen des NT," *Neotestamentica*, 153–79. For a critique of Schweizer, see Brandenburger, *Fleisch und Geist*, 18ff and *passim*.

69 Besides the previous studies see esp. Davies, *Paul and*

Rabbinic Judaism, 17ff; idem, "Paul and the Dead Sea Scrolls," in his *Christian Origins and Judaism*, 145–77 (n. 29 above); Braun, *Qumran*, 2, § 15; other studies are discussed and evaluated by Jewett, *Paul's Anthropological Terms*, 82–95.

70 See Reitzenstein, *Mysterienreligionen*, 71, 282, 284ff, 308ff, 333ff, 377ff, 420; Bousset, *Kyrios Christos*, 172ff; Goodenough, *By Light, Light*, esp. 370–413; idem, with Alf T. Kraabel, "Paul and the Hellenization of Christianity," in *Religions in Antiquity, Essays in Memory of E. R. Goodenough* (Leiden: Brill, 1968) 23–68, esp. 53f.

71 Cf., esp. John 3:6. On the problem of the dualism of flesh and Spirit in John see Bultmann, *John*, 62f, 138–43; Schottroff, *Glaubende*, 273ff; cf. also Jas 4:1ff.

72 See the reviews of the history of research in Brandenburger, *Fleisch und Geist*; Jewett, *Paul's Anthropological Terms*, 49ff.

73 The majority of witnesses relate the sentence to the preceding by $\gamma\dot{\alpha}\rho$ ("for"): P[46] B ℵ* D* G lat; others by $\delta\dot{\epsilon}$ ("but"): A C 𝔐 *pl*.

74 $\dot{\alpha}\nu\tau\dot{\iota}\kappa\epsilon\iota\mu\alpha\iota$ ("be opposed") is used here as elsewhere in the early Christian literature in the figurative sense ("spiritual warfare"). See Friedrich Büchsel, "$\kappa\epsilon\hat{\iota}\mu\alpha\iota\ \kappa\tau\lambda.$," *TDNT* 3.655; Bauer, *s.v.*; LSJ, *s.v.*; *PGL*, *s.v.*

within.[75] As a result,[76] the human "I" is no longer the subject in control of the body.[77]

This description of the anthropological situation raises a number of questions: (1) does Paul want to say that *both* powers prevent man from carrying out his will?[78] Or is it only the flesh that frustrates the will, while the divine Spirit tries to cooperate with it?[79] The answer to these questions depends to a good deal on another question: (2) what is the relationship between Gal 5:17 and Rom 7:15–24? Clearly, Gal 5:17 deals with the Christian man, while in Rom 7:15–24 Paul evaluates the pre–Christian situation from the Christian perspective.[80] At least this is the common opinion in present New Testament scholarship. But if Gal 5:17 applies to the Christian and Rom 7:15–24 to the pre-Christian situation, what is the difference? Are we methodologically allowed to interpret Gal 5:17 on the basis of Rom 7:15–24? Can we assume that Paul had his anthropology all worked out and that we can piece it together from the various letters? Or do we have to assume changes and development in Paul's thinking itself? Are these changes simply reflections of changed situations, so that the expression of Paul's positions could be different while his essential position would remain the same? Or are the changes indications that Paul has modified his position in substance, in order to respond to problems in a more constructive way as they occur in new situations?[81]

In Romans 7 Paul makes a distinction between the "inner man" (ὁ ἔσω ἄνθρωπος)[82] who wills the good, but must witness as through a prison window how "his other will," which is the power of sin (ἁμαρτία), not only wills but also carries out evil. Thus, Romans seems to have two "wills" set against each other: "the inner man" and the power of sin. Even the "I" is split up into two, while the role of the Spirit is left out of the picture. In Gal 5:17, on the other hand, we have three "wills": the "I," the "Spirit," and the "flesh." This arrangement seems to ignore the cooperation between the Spirit and the "I," which we would expect to take place in Christian existence, but in v 18 we do have a clarification of this point. It appears that in v 17 Paul submits his anthropological presuppositions in rather simple terms, but he leaves open the question how his soteriology affects this anthropology. In v 18 the soteriological presuppositions are brought in, but the theory in v 17 is left untouched. This situation forces us to conclude that the theory in v 17 is basically "pre-Pauline." It states the common anthropological doctrine on the basis of which Paul works out his own doctrine, but his own doctrine is much more complex.

In Romans 7–8 we find an even more developed and more complex reworking of the elements which occur also in Galatians 5. This means that Gal 5:17 is not simply an abbreviated and simplified form of what we have in Romans 7. Nor does it mean that in describing Paul's anthropology one should replace the statements in Galatians as insufficient and preliminary, and substitute as more adequate the formulations of Romans 7. But we should assume that Paul's theological thinking did not stop between the letters, that because of new situations he encountered and new insights he gained, new efforts were required to state his position.

The theory in Gal 5:17 must be taken for what it says: the human body is a battlefield on which the powers of the flesh and the Spirit fight against each

---

75 The "I" as the subject of willing is not identical with either flesh or Spirit. This problematization of the will is carried further in Rom 7:15–24.

76 The ἵνα ("in order that") can be taken in a final or consecutive sense (see BDF, § 391, 5; BDR, § 391; Bauer, *s.v.*, II, 2; Schweizer, "πνεῦμα, πνευματικός," *TDNT* 6.429 n. 641). If it is taken in the final sense, it would express the view that each of the opposing powers tries to impose its will upon the human will. See Schlier, p. 249; Mussner, pp. 376–78; Paul Althaus, "'. . . Dass ihr nicht tut, was ihr wollt' (Zur Auslegung von Gal. 5, 17)," *ThLZ* 76 (1951) 15–18.

77 That is, in control of the "doing" (ποιεῖν).

78 So Schlier (p. 250) with most exegetes.

79 The problem was clearly pointed out by Althaus (see n. 76 above).

80 See Rudolf Bultmann, "Römer 7 und die Anthropologie des Paulus," in his *Exegetica*, 198–209; Käsemann, *Römer*, 188ff.

81 There is no investigation which pays adequate attention to these problems. See for the present state of research Ernst Käsemann, "On Paul's Anthropology," in his *Perspectives*, 1–31; Jewett, *Paul's Anthropological Terms, passim.*

82 See on this concept the material and bib. in Jewett, *Paul's Anthropological Terms*, 394ff.

other, so that the human will is disabled from carrying out its intentions.[83] This is true of Christian existence, since only there we can assume the Spirit is present.[84]

■ **18** This adds the soteriological presuppositions which were missing in v 17. The protasis states a reality (εἰ with the indicative),[85] in fact reminding the readers of the "indicative of salvation": εἰ δὲ πνεύματι ἄγεσθε ("if you are led away by [the] Spirit . . ."). The foundation of the Galatians' existence as Christians is that they are possessed by the Spirit.[86] This experience of the Spirit is "enthusiastic" in nature, and it is an experience of "being carried away" (ἄγεσθαι). In the battle between the forces of flesh and Spirit there is no stalemate, but the Spirit takes the lead, overwhelms, and thus defeats evil.[87] How this is to be imagined Paul explains in the following passage 5:19–24. The apodosis reminds the reader of another "indicative": οὐκ ἐστὲ ὑπὸ νόμον ("you are not under [the] Law").[88] If they are driven by the Spirit, they do not need to be under the Torah.[89] Why this is true and how the

Spirit defeats evil, without committing the Christian to the Torah, is explained in the next section, 5:19–24.[90]

Excursus:
A Catalogue of Vices and Virtues

In Gal 5:19–23 Paul employs a literary genre which scholarship has come to call a "catalogue of vices and virtues."[91] The catalogue includes ethical conceptuality which has its origin in Hellenistic philosophy. Some of the concepts indicate that the material has passed through Hellenistic–Jewish adaptation.[92] In addition, v 21 bc shows that the original *Sitz im Leben* of the whole passage was primitive Christian catechetical instruction, most likely in connection with baptism. We can, therefore, assume that Paul quotes the passage here for the purpose of reminding the Galatians of what they have been told initially, when Paul had taught them the Christian faith. With the exception of "love" (ἀγάπη, v 22) all concepts are common in Hellenistic philosophy. But also the form

---

83 Against Mussner (pp. 377f) who interprets Paul in the opposite sense: the fact that both powers oppose each other neutralizes their impact and provides for man a situation for freedom of choice. "The freedom to which Christ has liberated the baptized (5:1, 13) is a real freedom of choice between good and evil" (p. 378). In his view, Gal 5:17 is the basis for ethics: the Christian has the freedom of will to do the good. Mussner tries to avoid a Pelagian interpretation of Paul and quotes Bonnard on the point, but he inevitably makes Paul a Pelagian when he states: "The Pneuma assists him [*sc.* the Christian] to fulfill the will of God, but it does not compel him."

84 It should be noted that Paul does not consider here, but only in the next section, what he had stated in 2:19f.

85 See BDF, § 372; BDR, § 372.

86 See Gal 3:2–5, 14; 4:6, 29; 5:5, 16. On the "indicative" of salvation, see above on 5:1a, 13a, and below on 5:25.

87 Cf. Rom 8:14, where the "sons of God" are defined as those who are led by the Spirit of God (πνεύματι θεοῦ ἄγονται). See also 1 Cor 12:2; Luke 4:1, 9. On the term see LSJ, *s.v.*; Preisigke, *Wörterbuch*, 4/1 (1944) 23, *s.v.*; Bauer, *s.v.*, 3; Betz, *Lukian*, 40 n 10.

88 See Gal 3:2, 5, 23–25; 4:21; 5:1.

89 On the phrase "under the law" see 3:23; 4:4f, 21.

90 It should be emphasized against most commentaries that Gal 5:18 should *not* be interpreted in the light

of Rom 7:7ff and Phil 3:2ff, where the "law" stimulates man to seek his own righteousness (ἰδία δικαιοσύνη), which is "sin." Not even in Gal 3:22–25 does Paul say that the "law" stimulates "sin"; according to Gal, it is the "flesh" that produces its evil works.

91 For other catalogs in primitive Christian literature, see Rom 1:29–31; 13:13; 1 Cor 5:10f; 6:9f; 2 Cor 12:20f; Eph 4:31; 5:3f; Col 3:5, 8; 1 Tim 1:9f; 2 Tim 3:2–5; Titus 3:3; 1 Pet 2:1; 4:3, 15; Mark 7:22; Matt 15:19; Rev 21:8; 22:15; *Did.* 2.1–5.2; *Barn.* 18–20; Pol. *Phil.* 2.2, 4.3; *Herm. Mand.* 5.2.4, 6.2, 8.3–5; *Sim.* 6, 9.15, etc.; *Apoc. Pet.* 21–34; etc. Cf. Jas 3:13–18. Especially interesting for Paul is the doctrine of baptism which includes catalog material in the *Kerygmata Petrou* (ps.–Clem. *Hom.* 11.27–28). For the usage in the liturgy of Chrysostom, see Hugh M. Riley, *Christian Initiation* (Washington, D. C.: The Catholic University of America, 1974) 165ff.

92 On the individual concepts and for bib., see below.

of the catalogues is traditional.[93] There is no parallel in the Old Testament, but the history of the catalogue form can be traced back at least to Plato's Hades myth (*Gorg.* 525A); perhaps an origin in ancient Iran has to be assumed.[94] In New Testament times ethical lists of this kind were enormously popular. Without much difficulty they could be adapted to the various philosophical and religious schools of thought. Therefore, we find them in various forms and contexts, and with various functions.[95] In Judaism we find them especially in Wisdom and in Philo; clearly these catalogues have been taken over from Hellenistic philosophy.[96] A special problem is presented by the long double catalogue in 1QS 4.3–11, since it shows no influence of Greek philosophy.[97] Recently, catalogues have turned up in gnosticism, especially in the Nag Hammadi texts.[98]

Early Christianity seems to have been fond of the catalogues, which served in the largely unknown process of instruction. In the many catalogues which we find in the New Testament and in the Apostolic Fathers little effort to introduce specifically Christian concepts can be detected. The catalogues differ greatly in length, in the order of concepts, and in their transmission in the textual tradition. There was apparently little interest in completeness, systematization, or creativity. The reason was probably that the catalogues sum up the conventional morality of the time. Christianity was interested in that morality to the extent that Christian existence should not be "against the conventions" (cf. Gal 5:23b). As Paul

shows, the Christian interest did not concern itself with the concepts themselves and their relationship to a theory of ethics; the concepts can be changed at will, without indication of the reason why. The primary function was to make clear that Christian ethical life should roughly conform to the moral conventions of the time. This function was of course preliminary and confined to the life in this world, although the eschatological dimension should not be denied. The limited propaedeutic character of the catalogues is also clear. As such they do not contain all the concerns early Christianity had with regard to the life of the Christian. To be sure, Christian life went beyond common morality, and it certainly included a critique and even a replacement of conventional morals. At this point a tension is to be noticed between the forces of change, implicit in the preaching of the Christian message, and the weight of convention which the catalogues of vices and virtues exert. This conflict has become part of Christian ethics ever since.

As far as the catalogues in Gal 5:19–23 are concerned, several matters should be kept in mind: (1) the individual concepts are not in any way specifically "Christian," but represent the conventional morality of the time. (2) They do not represent vices and virtues in the sense of Greek ethics, but describe phenomena or manifestations of the powers of evil ("the works of the flesh") and of the Spirit ("the fruit of the Spirit"). In this respect the Pauline catalogues are remarkably close to gnosticism. (3) Only

93 See the basic studies by Anton Vögtle, *Die Tugend- und Lasterkataloge im Neuen Testament* (NTAbh 16.4–5; Münster: Aschendorff, 1936); Lietzmann, *Römer*, 35f; Burton S. Easton, "New Testament Ethical Lists," *JBL* 51 (1932) 1–12; Siegfried Wibbing, *Die Tugend- und Lasterkataloge im Neuen Testament und ihre Traditionsgeschichte* (BZNW 25; Berlin: Töpelmann, 1959); Erhard Kamlah, *Die Form der katalogischen Paränese im Neuen Testament* (WUNT 7; Tübingen: Mohr, Siebeck, 1964) esp. 14–18; Schlier, pp. 251ff; Johannes Thomas, "Formgesetze des Begriffskatalogs im Neuen Testament," *ThZ* 24 (1968) 15–28; Lohse, *Colossians and Philemon*, 136ff; Conzelmann, *1 Corinthians*, 100f; M. Jack Suggs, "The Christian Two Way Tradition: Its Antiquity, Form, and Function," in *Studies in the New Testament and Early Christian Literature, Essays in Honor of A. P. Wikgren* (Leiden: Brill 1972) 60–74; Mussner, pp. 379–89; Vielhauer, *Geschichte*, 50, 54, 120f.
94 See on this point Kamlah, ibidem, *passim*.
95 Large collections of material from the Hellenistic and Roman literature are found (apart from literature in n. 3) in the following studies: Bultmann, *Stil*, 19 n. 3; *SVF* 3.377–490 (Stoics in general); Betz, *Lukian*, 185–94, 206–11; *PECL*, 31, 33, 40, 157, 208, 209, 227; Gerd Petzke, *Die Tradition über Apollonius von Tyana und das Neue Testament* (SCHNT 1; Leiden: Brill, 1970) 220–27; Mussies, *Dio Chrysostom*, 67–70, 172–77, 184f.
96 Cf. esp. also Justin *Oratio ad Graecos* 5.7–9. See the material collected in Kamlah, *Die Form der katalogischen Paränese, passim*; Conzelmann, *1 Corinthians*, 100 n. 66.
97 See the study of Wibbing (cf. n. 93 above); Kamlah, ibidem, 39ff; Osten-Sacken, *Gott und Belial*, esp. 150ff; Braun, *Qumran* 1.214.
98 Cf. *Corp. Herm.* 13.7ff; also 1.22f, 25. See Richard Reitzenstein, *Poimandres* (Leipzig and Berlin: Teubner, 1904) 231f; Albrecht Dieterich, *Nekyia: Beiträge zur Erklärung der neuentdeckten Petrusapokalypse* (Leipzig: Teubner, ³1913) 163ff; Kamlah, ibidem, 115ff. Parallels from Nag Hammadi texts have been collected by Mussner, p. 379 n. 32.

the catalogue of virtues is related to the divine Spirit; this marks both the similarity and the difference in comparison to the catalogues in 1QS 4, where both catalogues are related to the two spirits opposing each other. (4) It seems intentional that the catalogue of vices contains a chaotic assemblage of concepts, while the catalogue of virtues is well ordered; thus the catalogues represent the dualism between the chaotic multitude of evils and the unity of the Spirit.[99]

■19 Paul now proceeds to demonstrate how in his view evil comes into existence, in order then to show how it can be defeated. First of all, he explains in greater detail what he means by evil. While he had spoken in 5:16–17 of the "intentions of the flesh" ($\dot{\epsilon}\pi\iota\theta\nu\mu\dot{\iota}\alpha\iota\ \tau\hat{\eta}s\ \sigma\alpha\rho\kappa\acute{o}s$), he now states that the result of such intentions is the "works of the flesh" ($\tau\grave{\alpha}\ \check{\epsilon}\rho\gamma\alpha\ \tau\hat{\eta}s\ \sigma\alpha\rho\kappa\acute{o}s$). These "works of the flesh" are "evident" ($\phi\alpha\nu\epsilon\rho\acute{\alpha}$)[100] in the sense that they can be easily observed. This seems to include another important assumption. Considering what the Apostle had stated in v 18b, it is strange that in v 19 he fails to describe "the works

of the flesh" as the result of transgressions of law.[101] In fact, "evident" seems to imply "without Law"; one does not need to transgress a law in order to do evil. Rather than defining evil as transgressions of existing law, Paul treats evil as *manifestations*. Of course, evil deeds are done and therefore called "works."[102] They are done by man, but in reality they are the work of the flesh,[103] which dominates man and dictates his activities (cf. 5:16–17).

Also typical of the phenomena of evil is that they occur without order or system.[104] When Paul makes use of the form of the "list of vices" he puts together a random collection of terms, describing the ordinary occurrences of evil among men.[105] The seemingly chaotic arrangement of these terms is reflective of the chaotic nature of evil; this chaos is to be contrasted with the oneness of the "fruit of the Spirit" and its orderly arrangement (v 22–23). Verse 19 contains the first[106] three of the concepts: "illicit sexual activities" ($\pi o\rho\nu\epsilon\acute{\iota}\alpha$),[107] "moral impurity" ($\dot{\alpha}\kappa\alpha\theta\alpha\rho\sigma\acute{\iota}\alpha$),[108] and "licentiousness" ($\dot{\alpha}\sigma\acute{\epsilon}\lambda\gamma\epsilon\iota\alpha$).[109]

99 Cf. Luther's comments (1535, on Gal 5:15): "According to the mathematicians, beyond the unit there is an infinite progression of numbers. Thus if the unity of the Spirit is injured and destroyed, ... errors will go on arising into infinity." On 5:20 Luther states: "Paul does not enumerate all the works of flesh, but he uses a certain number in place of the infinite number of such works."

100 For the meaning of this term cf. 1 Cor 3:13; 11:19; 14:25; 2 Cor 5:10; 1 John 3:10; *2 Clem.* 16:3; *Barn.* 8.7; *Herm. Sim.* 4.3f; *Mand.* 11.10; Ign. *Eph.* 14.2. See Bauer, *s.v.*, 1; Rudolf Bultmann and Dieter Lührmann, "$\phi\alpha\nu\epsilon\rho\acute{o}\omega$," *TDNT* 9.3.

101 Cf. Gal 6:1.

102 Cf. Rom 13:12 "the works of darkness" ($\tau\grave{\alpha}\ \check{\epsilon}\rho\gamma\alpha\ \tau o\hat{\upsilon}\ \sigma\kappa\acute{o}\tau o\upsilon s$) and similar expressions in Eph 5:11; Col 1:21; John 3:19; 7:7; 8:41; etc. See Bauer, *s.v.* $\check{\epsilon}\rho\gamma o\nu$ 1, c, β. The terminology in the Qumran texts is similar, but not the same; cf. מעשי רשע (1QS 2.5), מעשי רמיה (1QS 4.23); see Braun, *Qumran* 1.185; Kamlah, *Die Form der katalogischen Paränese*, 16 n. 2 (see n. 93 above).

103 Cf. the term "bring about, produce" ($\kappa\alpha\tau\epsilon\rho\gamma\acute{\alpha}\zeta o\mu\alpha\iota$) in Rom 7:8, 13, 15, 17, 18, 20.

104 Attempts to find some systematic order in the catalog have failed. Cf. Schlier, p. 251; Johannes Thomas, "Formgesetze des Begriffs–Katalogs im Neuen Testament," *ThZ* 24 (1968) 15–28, 25f. Correct is

Mussner's statement that an order is not recognizable (p. 381).

105 For this use of the relative pronoun $\ddot{o}\sigma\tau\iota s$, see BDF, § 293; BDR, § 293.

106 $\mathfrak{R}$ D (G) *pl* it sy^h Irenaeus have first "adultery" ($\mu o\iota\chi\epsilon\acute{\iota}\alpha$). Zahn (p. 264 n. 98) is probably right in assuming this order is the result of a harmonization with Matt 15:19; Mark 7:21f.

107 The term is used by Paul also 1 Cor 5:1; 6:13, 18; 7:2; 2 Cor 12:21; 1 Thess 4:3; it is part of lists in Matt 15:19 ∥ Mark 7:21; 2 Cor 12:21; Eph 5:3; Col 3:5. See for further material Bauer, *s.v.*; Friedrich Hauck and Siegfried Schulz, "$\pi\acute{o}\rho\nu\eta\ \kappa\tau\lambda$," *TDNT* 6.579–95; Petzke, *Apollonius*, 225.

108 For this term, cf. the lists in Rom 1:24; 2 Cor 12:21; Eph 5:3; Col 3:5; furthermore Rom 6:19; Eph 4:19; 1 Thess 2:3; 4:7. See Bauer, *s.v.*, 2; Friedrich Hauck, "$\dot{\alpha}\kappa\acute{\alpha}\theta\alpha\rho\tau o s,\ \dot{\alpha}\kappa\alpha\theta\alpha\rho\sigma\acute{\iota}\alpha$," 3.427–29; Wilfried Paschen, *Rein und Unrein* (SANT 24; Munich: Kösel, 1970); Mussies, *Dio Chrysostom*, 70.

109 For this term see the lists Matt 7:22; Rom 13:13; 2 Cor 12:21; Eph 4:19; 1 Pet 4:3; furthermore 2 Pet 2:2, 7, 18; Jude 4. See Bauer, *s.v.*; Otto Bauernfeind, "$\dot{\alpha}\sigma\acute{\epsilon}\lambda\gamma\epsilon\iota\alpha$," *TDNT* 1.490; Betz, *Lukian*, 199 n. 3.

■ 20 The concept of "idolatry" (εἰδωλολατρία) is Hellenistic–Jewish in origin;[110] it points to the history of religions background of the entire catalogue. Then comes "sorcery, magic" (φαρμακεία),[111] "hostile feelings and acts" (ἔχθραι),[112] "strife" (ἔρις),[113] "jealousy, envy" (ζῆλος),[114] "outbursts of rage" (θυμοί),[115] "quarrels" (ἐριθεῖαι; Bauer: "disputes" or "outbreaks of selfishness"),[116] "dissensions" (διχοστασίαι),[117] and "factions" (αἱρέσεις).[118]

■ 21 The list concludes with three concepts: "outbreaks of envy" (φθόνοι),[119] "cases of drunkenness" (μέθαι),[120] and "excessive banquets" (κῶμοι).[121] The final phrase "and things like these" (καὶ τὰ ὅμοια τούτοις) makes sure that the list should not be taken as exhaustive. Evil occurs in innumerable forms, and only some examples are provided in the list.

The following remark in v 21b is puzzling: "in respect to which I predict to you as I have predicted [sc. in the past]" (ἃ προλέγω ὑμῖν καθὼς προεῖπον).[122] The parallels show that we have before us a quotation formula indicating a set style of quoting what the individual himself has stated previously. What Paul quotes is a prediction and a warning of an eschatological nature. The term προλέγω ("I predict") refers to the sentence quoted in the following, but καθὼς προεῖπον ("as I have predicted") recalls a past event. This past event must have been one when Paul provided the Galatians with basic instruction. Therefore, we can also assume that his remark includes the material in vv 19–21, 22–23a which can be related to primitive Christian catechetical instruction. Though we do not know precisely at which occasion this instruction was given, the parallels from Gal 1:8–9; 3:26–28, and from other early Christian sources make it highly probable

---

110 It or εἰδωλολάτρης occurs in lists also 1 Cor 5:10, 11; 6:9; Col 3:5; 1 Pet 4:3; *Did.* 3.4; 5.1; *Barn.* 20.1; cf. furthermore 1 Cor 10:7, 14; *Barn.* 16.7. See Friedrich Büchsel, "εἰδωλολάτρης, εἰδωλολατρία," *TDNT* 2.379–80; Bauer, *s.v.*; Betz, *Lukian*, 194; Mussies, *Dio Chrysostom*, 70; Betz, "2 Cor 6:14–7:1," 92; Horst D. Preuss, *Verspottung fremder Religionen im Alten Testament* (BWANT 92; Stuttgart: Kohlhammer, 1971).

111 The term is found in lists *Did.* 5.1; *Barn.* 20.1; cf. also Rev 9:21; 18:23. See Bauer, *s.v.*; Betz, *Lukian*, 201 n. 7; Petzke, *Apollonius*, 217; Mussies, *Dio Chrysostom*, 70; ps.–Phocylides *Sent.* 149 (ed. Denis).

112 Cf. Rom 8:7; Eph 2:14, 16; Jas 4:4; Luke 23:12; see Werner Foerster, "ἔχθρα," *TDNT* 2.815; Bauer, *s.v.*; Petzke, *Apollonius*, 227; Mussies, *Dio Chrysostom*, 184f.

113 Cf. the list in Rom 1:29; 13:13; 1 Cor 3:3; 2 Cor 12:20; Phil 1:15; 1 Tim 6:4; Titus 3:9; also 1 Cor 1:11. See Bauer, *s.v.* The textual tradition is divided: the sing. is read by ℵ A B D* 1739 syrᵖ, while 𝔐, following C, Dʰᶜ F G K L N P *al* have the plur. The sing. is the more difficult and hence the more probable reading. See for more evidence Metzger, *Textual Commentary*, 597.

114 Cf. the term in lists Rom 13:13; 1 Cor 3:3; 2 Cor 12:20; Jas 3:14, 16. See Albert Stumpff, "ζῆλος, ζηλόω," *TDNT* 2.877–82; Bauer, *s.v.*; Mussies, *Dio Chrysostom*, 185. The plur. ζῆλοι is read by ℵ C 𝔐 *pl*.

115 Cf. the term in the list 2 Cor 12:20; *1 Clem.* 46.5. See Friedrich Büchsel, "θυμός," *TDNT* 3.167–68; Bauer, *s.v.*, 2.

116 The term is rare, the meaning probably political

(cf. in lists 2 Cor 12:20; Phil 2:3; Jas 3:14, 16; also Rom 2:8). For the problem of interpretation see Friedrich Büchsel, "ἐριθεία," *TDNT* 2.660–61; Bauer, *s.v.*

117 The term is political (cf. Plutarch *Adulat.* 20C; *Fort. Rom.* 321C; *Praec. gerend.* 788E; *Pyrrh.* 397C); ps.-Phocylides *Sent.* 151 (ed. Denis); see Rom 16:17; 1 Cor 3:3 *v.l.*; *1 Clem.* 46.5; 51.1, etc. For further references see Bauer, *s.v.*

118 Cf. 1 Cor 11:19; see Heinrich Schlier, "αἵρεσις," *TDNT* 1.180–83; Bauer, *s.v.*

119 Cf. in lists Rom 1:29; Phil 1:15; 1 Tim 6:4; Titus 3:3; 1 Pet 2:1. Cf. also the verb in Gal 5:26. For further material see Bauer, *s.v.*; Ernst Milobenski, *Der Neid in der griechischen Philosophie* (Klassisch–philologische Studien 29; Wiesbaden: Harrassowitz, 1964), and the review by A. W. H. Adkins, *ClR* NS 21 (1971) 293f.
A large number of witnesses read the word–play φθόνοι φόνοι ("murders") which is known since Euripides *Tro.* 766ff. and which was often quoted in antiquity; since it also occurs Rom 1:29 (in the list) it may come from there. See Metzger, *Textual Commentary*, 597f.

120 Cf. the term in the lists Rom 13:13; *1 Clem.*. 30.1; also Luke 21:34. See Bauer, *s.v.*; Herbert Preisker, "μέθη κτλ." *TDNT* 4.545–48.

121 Originally, the term referred to the festivities of Dionysos. See the term in the lists Rom 13:13; 1 Pet 4:3. See for further material Bauer, *s.v.*

122 A similar formula occurs Gal 1:9; cf. also 2 Cor 13:2; 1 Thess 4:6; *Did.* 7.1.

284

that we have before us baptismal instruction.[123]

The somewhat archaic language of the quotation is also confirmation of its origin in pre–Pauline catechetical instruction:[124] "those who do such things will not inherit the Kingdom of God" (οἱ τὰ τοιαῦτα πράσσοντες βασιλείαν θεοῦ οὐ κληρονομήσουσιν). The language contains a number of non–Pauline terms and, therefore, is in some tension with Paul's theology. "Kingdom of God" (βασιλεία θεοῦ) here refers to the eschatological realm of heaven or paradise.[125] "Inherit" (κληρονομέω)[126] stands for "enter into"[127] and does not completely harmonize with other instances of the term in

Galatians.[128] Also "doing" (πράσσω)[129] is traditional and in tension with the concept of "works of the flesh" and other instances of the verb in Galatians. Form-critically, v 21b is an eschatological warning and in this sense a statement of eschatological law.[130] It is related to the catalogues of vices and virtues[131] because they contain the conditions for entering into the Kingdom of God. Parallels show that this whole complex was part of baptismal instruction,[132] but of course could also function separately.[133] In Galatians we have such an instance where the instruction is recalled for the purpose of a parenetical argument. Paul argues

123 *Did.* 7.1 is most important for the possible *Sitz im Leben* of the passage: "Concerning baptism, baptize in this way: Having first repeated all of these things [*sc. Did.* 1–6], baptize in the name of the Father and the Son and the Holy Spirit. . ." (Περὶ τοῦ βαπτίσματος, οὕτω βαπτίσατε· ταῦτα πάντα προειπόντες, βαπτίσατε εἰς τὸ ὄνομα τοῦ πατρός . . .). Cf. also Justin *Apol.* 1.61.

124 See Alfred Seeberg, *Der Katechismus der Urchristenheit* (Leipzig: Deichert, 1903; rep. Munich: Kaiser, 1966) 11, 43; Weiss, *Der erste Korintherbrief*, 153f; Hans Windisch, "Die Sprüche vom Eingehen in das Reich Gottes," *ZNW* 27 (1928) 163–92; Johannes Schneider," εἰσέρχομαι," *TDNT* 2.676–78; Vögtle, *Die Tugend- und Lasterkataloge*, 38–45 (see n. 93 above); Philip Carrington, *The Primitive Christian Catechism* (Cambridge: Cambridge University, 1940) 17f; Kamlah, *Die Form der katalogischen Paränese*, 14f, 21–3 (n. 93 above); Johannes S. Vos, *Traditionsgeschichtliche Untersuchungen zur paulinischen Pneumatologie* (Assen: van Gorcum, 1973) 26ff.

The earlier *Sitz im Leben* of the quotation most likely was in Jewish instruction. See on this Davies, *Paul and Rabbinic Judaism*, 118 n. 1; Str–B 4/2.1183–92; John Gager, "Functional Diversity in Paul's Use of End–Time Language," *JBL* 89 (1970) 325-37, 333ff.

125 The term is rare in Paul: Rom 14:17; 1 Cor 4:20; 6:9f; 15:24, 50; 1 Thess 2:12. See Kamlah, ibidem, 14 n. 2; Joachim Jeremias, "Flesh and Blood cannot inherit the Kingdom of God (1 Cor 15, 50)," *NTS* 2 (1955/56) 151–59; rep. in his *Abba*, 298–307.

126 Cf. esp. 1 Cor 6:9f; 15:50; Matt 25:34; Ign. *Eph.* 16.1; Ign. *Philad.* 3.3; furthermore Eph 5:5f; Col 3:24.

127 Cf. the sayings dealing with "entering into the Kingdom of God" (e.g., Mark 10:15 par.; Matt 7:21; 18:8f; 19:17; etc.). For a collection of passages, see

the articles by Schneider and Windisch (n. 124, above).

128 Cf. Gal 3:18, 29; 4:1, 7, 30.

129 The term is connected with catalogs Rom 1:23 (cf. 2:1–3); 2 Cor 12:21; also Ign. *Eph.* 16.2; John 3:20; 5:29; Rom 9:11; 13:4; 2 Cor 5:10. In Gal, πράσσω occurs only here, but cf. ποιέω 3:10, 12; 5:3, 17; 6:9.

130 The term προλέγω ("tell beforehand") indicates that the quotation is a warning. Cf. 1 Thess 3:4; part of the textual tradition (A C 𝔐 D *pl* Marcion Irenaeus Clement) adds καί ("and") before προεῖπον ("I forewarned, predicted").

An impressive parallel from the Qumran texts is the eschatological warning following the catalog of "the ways of the spirit of falsehood" (1QS 4.11–14): "And the visitation of all who walk in this spirit shall be a multitude of plagues by the hand of all the destroying angels, everlasting damnation by the avenging wrath of the fury of God, eternal torment and endless disgrace together with shameful extinction in the fire of the dark regions. The times of all their generations shall be spent in sorrowful mourning and in bitter misery and in calamities of darkness until they are destroyed without remnant or survivor" (tr. Geza Vermes, *The Dead Sea Scrolls in English* [Baltimore: Penguin, 1962] 77). Cf. Osten–Sacken, *Gott und Belial*, 160–63.

131 Rom 1:32; 1 Cor 6:9f; Eph 5:5; Col 3:6; Herm. *Sim.* 9.15.2, 3; *Did.* 6.1; *Barn.* 21.1; also Matt 25:34.

132 The connection with baptism is made in *Did.* 7.1; Herm *Sim.* 9.16.2–4.

133 Matt 5:20; 7:13f // Luke 13:23f // *Did.* 1.1; Matt 7:21; 18:3; 25:34; Mark 10:23–5 // Matt 19:23f // Luke 18:24f; John 3:5; Acts 14:22; Ign. *Eph.* 16.1; *Philad.* 3.3; Pol. *Phil.* 2.3; 5.3; *2 Clem.* 9.6; 11.7; 12.1; Herm. *Sim.* 9.12.3, 4, 5, 8; 9.20.2, 3; etc.

that he considers his view of Christian ethics to be part of the tradition of the church, a tradition in which the Galatians themselves stand. Paul's present recommendation as to what to do about the flesh does not intend to bring in new ideas hitherto unknown to the Galatians, but consists of a restatement of the original agreement upon which the churches were founded by Paul.

■ 22 The catalogue of vices (v 19–21a) is followed by the catalogue of virtues (v 22–23a). However, the nine concepts of this list are not virtues in the Greek sense of the term. They do not represent qualities of personal behavior which man can elect, cultivate, and appropriate as part of his character. Nor are they "good deeds" in the sense of Jewish ethics: they do not come from or constitute a code of law which must be obeyed and which can be transgressed. Although it may sound strange, the catalogue is *not* simply to be identified with the "law of Christ" mentioned in Gal 6:2. Compared with the catalogue of vices the catalogue of

virtues is peculiar for several reasons. Paul does not call it "works of the Spirit,"[134] in analogy to v 19, nor does he attribute to it the quality of "evidentness" (cf. above, on 5:19).

It is certainly with intention that the open–ended and unstructured list of vices[135] is contrasted by a *unity*[136] called "the fruit of the Spirit" (ὁ καρπὸς τοῦ πνεύματος),[137] a unity consisting of three sets of three concepts, the most important of which are at the beginning and at the end. The expression "fruit of the Spirit"[138] means that the nine concepts should be taken as "benefits" which were given as or together with the Spirit.[139] In other words, when the Galatians received the Spirit, they were also given the foundation out of which the "fruit" was supposed to grow.[140] At this point the question arises whether Paul thinks that the "fruit" was simply given, so that the concepts of the list became the possession of the Galatians, or whether by receiving the Spirit they were enabled and motivated to bear that fruit themselves. In the present

---

134 So rightly Schlier, p. 255; Mussner, p. 384.
135 See above, the introduction to 5:19–23.
136 See above, on 3:20. Cf. esp. *Corp. Herm.* 13.12: the 10 "virtues" are called a "decade," a unity (ἡ ἑνάς) originating from the Spirit: the unity contains the decade, and the decade the unity. An interesting contrast parallel is the "Midrash on the Steps to Perfection," attributed to Pinchas ben Jair (c. 200); see Felix Böhl, *Gebotserschwerung und Rechtsverzicht als ethisch-religiöse Normen in der rabbinischen Literatur* (Frankfurter Judaistische Studien 1; Freiburg: Schwarz, 1971) 109–17. Marcus Aurelius 6.30.4: "One is the fruit of earthly life, a religious disposition and social acts" (εἰς καρπὸς τῆς ἐπιγείου ζωῆς, διάθεσις ὁσία καὶ πράξεις κοινωνικαί).
137 The concept is unique in Paul. Cf. Eph 5:9: ὁ καρπὸς τοῦ φωτός ("the fruit of light"); *Herm. Sim.* 9.19.2: καρπὸς ἀληθείας ("fruit of truth"); also Rom 6:21f; 15:28; Phil 1:11, 22; 4:17; John 15:2ff; Jas 3:12, 17f. Related is the term καρποφορέω ("bear fruit"): Rom 7:4f; Col 1:6, 10; Mark 4:20 par; cf. Ign. *Eph.* 14.2; Ign. *Trall.* 11. 1, 2; Ign. *Smyr.* 1.2; Pol. *Phil.* 1.2; *2 Clem.* 1.3; 19.3; 20.3; *Barn.* 11.11. See Friedrich Hauck, "καρπός, ἄκαρπος, καρποφορέω," *TDNT* 3.614–16; Bauer, *s.v.*; *PGL s.v.*; Kamlah, *Die Form der katalogischen Paränese*, 181ff; Harald Riesenfeld, "La langue parabolique dans les épîtres de S. Paul," in *Littérature et théologie pauliniennes* (Bruges: Desclée de Brouwer, 1960) 47–59

(tr. in his *The Gospel Tradition* [Philadelphia: Fortress, 1970] 187–204).
138 The closest analogies to the concept are found in Stoic philosophy (cf. esp. the notion of ethics as the "fruit of a garden": *SVF* 2.38) and, esp., in Philo. In this context, the "fruit(s) of the soul" refer to the "virtues" (cf. Philo *L.A.* 1.22f, 3.93; *Mig.* 140, 202, 205; *Deus* 166; *Mut.* 74, 98, 192; *Post.* 171; *Det.* 111; *Agr.* 9; *Mos.* 2.66; *Cher.* 84). They can also be called ὁ διανοίας καρπός ("the fruit of intelligence"): *Plant.* 138; *Somn.* 2.272; Epictetus *Diss.* 1.4.32; cf. 1.15.7, 8; 2.1.21; 4.8.36; Cicero *Tusc.* 1.119. Typical is Philo's definition (*Fug.* 176): καρπὸς δ' ἐπιστήμης ὁ θεωρητικὸς βίος ("The contemplative life is a fruit of knowledge.") Cf. also Marcus Aurelius 9.10.1; for gnosticism, cf. *Corp. Herm.* 13.22: The "good fruit, the immortal produce" is identical with the "decade" of powers constituting "regeneration."
139 See esp. Philo *Sacr.* 19–42, where the two women "Pleasure" and "Virtue" are described; they are "followed" (συνείποντο) by catalogs of vices and virtues.
140 Cf. *Barn.* 11.11: . . . ἡμεῖς μὲν καταβαίνομεν εἰς τὸ ὕδωρ γέμοντες ἁμαρτιῶν καὶ ῥύπου, καὶ ἀναβαίνομεν καρποφοροῦντες ἐν τῇ καρδίᾳ τὸν φόβον καὶ τὴν ἐλπίδα εἰς τὸν Ἰησοῦν ἐν τῷ πνεύματι ἔχοντες (". . . we go down into the water full of sins and foulness, and we come up bearing the fruit of fear in the heart and having hope in Jesus in the Spirit").

context of ethical exhortation we can conclude that a simple possession of the "fruit of the Spirit" cannot be what Paul means. Contrary to, e.g., the gnostic concept which we find in *Corpus Hermeticum* 13,[141] the "fruit of the Spirit" presupposes man's active involvement (cf. 5:25).

As mentioned before, the structure of the catalogue is such that three sets of three concepts[142] follow each other, the most important of which are placed at the beginning and the end.[143] The first three notions are different from the rest in that they can be attributed to God, Christ, and man. "Love" ($\dot{\alpha}\gamma\dot{\alpha}\pi\eta$) is the love of God,[144] Christ,[145] and the Spirit,[146] and it is required of the Christian.[147] "Joy" ($\chi\alpha\rho\dot{\alpha}$) is not clearly attributed to God or Christ, probably because of its emotional overtones, but its character as a divine gift is strongly emphasized.[148] The third concept is that of "peace" ($\epsilon\dot{\iota}\rho\dot{\eta}\nu\eta$): the peace of God,[149] Christ,[150] and

the Spirit, given to man.[151] Christian existence is characterized by peace.[152]

The three concepts have in common the fact that they represent "spiritual powers" of the first order. In man they come close to being psychosomatic dispositions which must first be created in him before they can be required as deeds. This structure reveals an important aspect of Paul's ethics: people cannot be expected simply to act in an ethically responsible way, but they must first be enabled, empowered, and motivated before they can so act. Now since the Galatians *did* receive the Spirit of God, the love, joy, and peace of God and of Christ were made present to them, and on the basis of this gift they can be expected to act ethically as Christians.

The second set of concepts takes us further in the direction of human action. "Forbearance" ($\mu\alpha\kappa\rho o\theta\nu\mu\dot{\iota}\alpha$)[153] can be attributed to God[154] and required of

---

141 On the catalog in *Corp. Herm.* 13, see above, n. 136. Cf. Epictetus *Diss.* 4.8.40: "Allow us at least to ripen as nature wishes. Why do you expose us to the elements, why force us? We are not yet able to stand the open air. Let the root grow, next let it acquire the first joint, and then the second, and then the third; and so finally the fruit will forcibly put forth its true nature, even against my will" (... $\epsilon\dot{\iota}\theta$' $o\ddot{\upsilon}\tau\omega\varsigma$ $\dot{o}$ $\kappa\alpha\rho\pi\dot{o}\varsigma$ $\dot{\epsilon}\kappa\beta\iota\dot{\alpha}\sigma\epsilon\tau\alpha\iota$ $\tau\dot{\eta}\nu$ $\phi\dot{\upsilon}\sigma\iota\nu$, $\kappa\ddot{\alpha}\nu$ $\dot{\epsilon}\gamma\dot{\omega}$ $\mu\dot{\eta}$ $\theta\dot{\epsilon}\lambda\omega$).

142 Schlier (p. 256) points to this "triadic pattern" and feels reminded of 1 Cor 13:4–6.

143 Cf. 1 Cor 13:13: $\nu\upsilon\nu\dot{\iota}$ $\delta\dot{\epsilon}$ $\mu\dot{\epsilon}\nu\epsilon\iota$ $\pi\dot{\iota}\sigma\tau\iota\varsigma$, $\dot{\epsilon}\lambda\pi\dot{\iota}\varsigma$, $\dot{\alpha}\gamma\dot{\alpha}\pi\eta$, $\tau\dot{\alpha}$ $\tau\rho\dot{\iota}\alpha$ $\tau\alpha\ddot{\upsilon}\tau\alpha\cdot$ $\mu\epsilon\dot{\iota}\zeta\omega\nu$ $\delta\dot{\epsilon}$ $\tau o\dot{\upsilon}\tau\omega\nu$ $\dot{\eta}$ $\dot{\alpha}\gamma\dot{\alpha}\pi\eta$ ("But now remain faith, hope, love, these three, the greater of them being love").

144 Rom 5:8; 8:35–39; 2 Cor 13:11, 13; 1 Thess 1:4; cf. Eph 1:4; 2:4; Col 3:12; 2 Thess 2:13, 16; 3:5; Col 1:13; Eph 1:6.

145 Gal 2:20; Rom 8:35, 37; 2 Cor 5:14; Eph 3:19; 5:2, 25.

146 Rom 15:30; it is "poured out into our hearts" (Rom 5:5).

147 Gal 5:6, 13, 14; in catalogs it is found 2 Cor 6:6; Eph 4:2; Col 3:14; 2 Pet 1:7, and often in the Apostolic Fathers. See for further references above, on Gal 5:6.

148 Cf. Rom 14:17: $\delta\iota\kappa\alpha\iota o\sigma\dot{\upsilon}\nu\eta$ $\kappa\alpha\dot{\iota}$ $\epsilon\dot{\iota}\rho\dot{\eta}\nu\eta$ $\kappa\alpha\dot{\iota}$ $\chi\alpha\rho\dot{\alpha}$ $\dot{\epsilon}\nu$ $\pi\nu\epsilon\dot{\upsilon}\mu\alpha\tau\iota$ $\dot{\alpha}\gamma\dot{\iota}\omega$ ("righteousness and peace and joy in the Holy Spirit"); 15:13, 32; 1 Cor 7:30; 2 Cor 1:15, 24; 2:3; 7:4, 13; Phil 1:4, 18, 25; 2:2, 28f; 4:1; 1 Thess 1:6; 2:19, 20; 3:9; Phlm 7. For further references see Bauer, *s.v.*; Hans Conzelmann,

"$\chi\alpha\dot{\iota}\rho\omega$ $\kappa\tau\lambda$.," *TDNT* 9.359–72, esp. 369f.

149 Rom 15:33; 16:20; 1 Cor 14:33; 2 Cor 13:11; Phil 4:7, 9; 1 Thess 5:23; 2 Thess 3:16.

150 Col 3:15; Eph 2:14f.

151 Rom 8:6; 14:17; 15:13; cf. Gal 1:3; 6:16; Rom 1:7; 2:10; 5:1; 1 Cor 1:3; 2 Cor 1:2; 13:11; Phil 1:2; 4:9; 1 Thess 1:1; 5:23; Phlm 3; etc.

152 Rom 5:1; 12:18; 1 Cor 7:15; 2 Cor 13:11; 1 Thess 5:3, 13; etc. See Burton, 424–6; Bauer, *s.v.*; Gerhard von Rad and Werner Foerster, "$\epsilon\dot{\iota}\rho\dot{\eta}\nu\eta$ $\kappa\tau\lambda$.," *TDNT* 2.400–20; Gerardo Zampaglione, *The Idea of Peace in Antiquity* (Notre Dame: Notre Dame University, 1973); Erich Dinkler, "Friede," *RAC* 8.434–505, with bib.

153 The concept is prominent in Hellenistic and Roman ethics. See LSJ, *s.v.*; Bauer, *s.v.*; Johannes Horst, "$\mu\alpha\kappa\rho o\theta\upsilon\mu\dot{\iota}\alpha$, $\mu\alpha\kappa\rho o\theta\dot{\upsilon}\mu\omega\varsigma$," *TDNT* 4.374–87; *PGL*, *s.v.*; R. A. Gauthier, *Magnanimité. L'idéal de la grandeur dans la philosophie païenne et dans la théologie chrétienne* (Paris: Vrin, 1951), esp. 202ff.

154 Rom 2:4; 9:22; cf. 1 Pet 3:20; Ign. *Eph.* 11.1.

155 2 Cor 6:6; cf. 1 Cor 13:4; 1 Thess 5:14; Eph 4:2; Col 1:11; 3:12; etc.

man.[155] The same is true of "kindness" (χρηστότης).[156] The concept of "goodness" (ἀγαθωσύνη) represents a late development in the Greek language; it may come from Hellenistic Judaism.[157]

■ 23 The last group of concepts includes three famous virtues from Hellenistic ethics: πίστις (this concept is usually regarded as still being part of v 22) in the sense of "faithfulness";[158] πραΰτης ("humility", "meekness");[159] and finally ἐγκράτεια ("self–control").[160] Especially important is the last term: Socrates had introduced it into Greek ethics, and by the time of Paul it was a central concept of Hellenistic ethics, whence it was taken up by Jewish and Christian writers. In Paul, it appears in the context of radical asceticism.[161] Its place at the end of the list in v 23[162] is conspicuous, and this is certainly intended; it stands in juxtaposition to love (v 22). The concept of self–control in the present context implies the claim that Christian ethics is the fulfillment not only of the Torah (cf. 5:14), but also of the central demand of Greek ethics. The gift of the Spirit and the "fruit of the Spirit" reach their climax in the fulfillment of the old Greek ideal of self–control. This outstanding position of self–control is unique in Paul and may indicate that he quotes the entire passage from a source.

What is the relationship of the "list of virtues" to the Law? Paul's statement immediately following brings some clarification: κατὰ τῶν τοιούτων οὐκ ἔστιν νόμος ("no law is against such things"). Two things are implied: (1) the "list of virtues" is not itself "law"; (2) the virtues do not violate any law; they are all "lawful." It is not certain[163] whether τῶν τοιούτων is masculine[164] or neuter,[165] but the latter is more likely because of the analogy in v 21b.

---

156 Of God: Rom 2:4; 9:23 v.1.; 11:22; cf. Eph 2:7; Col 3:12; Tit 3:4; 1 Pet 2:3, and often in the Apostolic Fathers. See Bauer, s.v., 2, b. Of man: 2 Cor 6:6; Gal 5:22; Col 3:12; cf. Eph 4:32. See Bauer, s.v.; Konrad Weiss, "χρηστός, χρηστότης, χρηστεύομαι, χρηστολογία," TDNT 9.483–92; Mussner, p. 387 n. 85.

157 It occurs first in LXX (Jud 8:35; 9:16; 2 Chr 24:16; Neh 9:25, 35; 13:31; Ps 37:20; 51:5; Ec 4:8; 5:10, 17; 6:3, 6; 7:15; 9:18; 2 Ezra 19:25, 35; 23:31). It is attributed to God Barn. 2.9; to man Rom 15:14; Gal 5:22; Eph 5:9; 2 Thess 1:11. See Burton, p. 316; Walter Grundmann, "ἀγαθωσύνη, φιλάγαθος, ἀφιλάγαθος," TDNT 1.18; LSJ, s.v.; PGL, s.v.; Schlier, p. 259 n. 3.

158 It is generally agreed that the term does not refer to the Christian faith specifically, but to "faithfulness" (cf. of God Rom 3:3; also 2 Thess 1:4; 2 Tim 4:7; Tit 2:10). In this sense also 1 Cor 13:7: (ἡ ἀγάπη) πάντα πιστεύει ("love believes everything"). See Bauer, s.v., 1, a; Rudolf Bultmann, "πιστεύω κτλ.," TDNT 6.204, 206–07.

159 Cf. esp. Gal 6:1; 1 Cor 4:21; 2 Cor 10:1; also Eph 4:2; Col 3:12; 2 Tim 2:25; Tit 3:2; etc. See Bauer, s.v.; Friedrich Hauck and Siegfried Schulz, "πραΰς, πραΰτης," TDNT 6.645–51; Klaus Winkler, "Clementia," RAC 3.735–78; Schlier, p. 260 n. 3.

160 The term is rare in the NT (only Acts 24:25; Gal 5:23; 2 Pet 1:6) but becomes more frequent in the Apostolic Fathers (Barn. 2.2; 2 Clem. 15.1; Pol. Phil. 4.2; Herm. Vis. 2.3.2; 3.8.4, 7; Mand. 6.1.1; 8.1; Sim. 9.15.2). See Walter Grundmann, "ἐγκράτεια," TDNT 2.339–42; Bauer, s.v.; Henry Chadwick, "Enkrateia," RAC 5.343–65.

161 The verb ἐγκρατεύομαι ("control oneself") occurs 1 Cor 7:9; 9:25; cf. Tit 1:8.

162 Several witnesses have a longer list: D* F G it[d,g] goth Cyprian Irenaeus[lat] Ambrosiaster al add ἁγνεία (castitas "chastity"). This concludes the list with a religious rather than a philosophical concept. Vg has 12 terms, rendering μακροθυμία by patientia and longanimitas, and πραΰτης by mansuetudo and modestia. It is interesting that the "Midrash on the Steps to Perfection" (see above, n. 136) differs in the traditions between 10 and 12 steps. Cf. the 12 "vices" in Corp. Herm. 13.7. See Schlier, p. 262 n. 2, 5; Metzger, Textual Commentary, 598. ἁγνεία ("chastity") is found also at the end of the list 1 Tim 4:12; cf. 1 Clem. 64.1 (following ἐγκράτεια); 21.7; Ign. Eph. 10.3; Ign. Pol. 5.2; etc. See Bauer, s.v.

163 See the discussion in Oepke, p. 183; Schlier, pp. 262f; Mussner, p. 389.

164 In this case we would have a parallel in Aristotle Pol. 3.8, p. 1384a14: ... κατὰ δὲ τῶν τοιούτων οὐκ ἔστι νόμος, αὐτοὶ γάρ εἰσι νόμος· ("but there can be no law against such men, for they are themselves a law"). I am indebted to Helmut Koester for this suggestion. Lütgert (Gesetz und Geist, 18), following de Wette, takes the reference to point to the "pneumatics" who are free of the law (cf. Gal 6:1). See also the list of commentators in Sieffert, pp. 327f.

How do we have to understand this concluding remark?[166] It corresponds to v 19: as one does not need to transgress a law in order to do evil, one can "do good" (cf. 6:10), that is, one can be ethically responsible without "obeying law." In view of the situation which the Galatians have to face, Paul suggests that it is more important to be enabled to act with ethical responsibility than to introduce a code of law which remains a mere demand. In other words, the introduction of the Torah into the Galatian churches would not lead to ethical responsibility, so long as the people were not motivated and enabled ethically. If they were motivated and enabled, however, the Torah is superfluous.

■ 24 The purpose of this concluding statement is to spell out the connection between christology/soteriology and the dualism of the "flesh" and the "fruit of the Spirit": οἱ δὲ τοῦ Χριστοῦ ['Ιησοῦ] τὴν σάρκα ἐσταύρωσαν σὺν τοῖς παθήμασιν καὶ ταῖς ἐπιθυμίαις ("but those who belong to Christ [Jesus] have crucified their flesh together with the passions and the desires").[167] In form, the statement is dogmatic, a definition of Christian ethical existence with specific reference to the "flesh." It is related to 2:19–20, but it is an expanded and interpreted form of what was said briefly in the *propositio*. The *propositio* had stated the basic components: the Christian is "crucified together with Christ," and "Christ lives within him."

In 5:24 the Christians are further defined as "those who belong to Christ."[168] Christ is their "Lord" (κύριος)[169] who redeemed them.[170] They are "in Christ" (ἐν Χριστῷ);[171] they have "put on Christ" (3:27: Χριστὸν ἐνεδύσασθε); they were given the Spirit of Christ (4:6). It is this overwhelming presence of Christ, the crucified and resurrected Lord, his Spirit, the "fruit of the Spirit," which prevents the intentions of the flesh from accomplishing the "works of the flesh" (cf. 5:16, 19–21a). Therefore, Paul can say that "the flesh has been crucified".[172] The presence of the crucified Christ as the "fruit of the Spirit" means the crucifixion of the flesh together with its "passions" (παθήματα)[173] and "desires" (ἐπιθυμίαι).[174]

We find a remarkably close parallel to Paul's teaching at this point in Philo: "but thanks be to the victorious God who, however perfect in workmanship are the aims and efforts of the passion–lover, makes them to be of none effect by sending invisibly against them winged beings to undo and destroy them. Thus the mind stripped of the creations of its art will be found as it were of headless corpse, with severed neck nailed

---

165 So most commentators, including Burton, Schlier (pp. 262f), Mussner (p. 389).

166 For the opposite anti–Pauline doctrine, cf. *Ep. Petr.* (ps.–Clem. *Hom.*) 2.3–5 (Appendix 3).

167 Text according to Nestle–Aland, 26th ed. P⁴⁶ ℵ D G lat syᵖ Marcion Clement do not read 'Ιησοῦ ("of Jesus"), which because of the parallels (see following n.) may be original.

168 Cf. Gal 3:29; 1 Cor 1:12; 3:23; 15:23; 2 Cor 10:7. See the remark by Schmithals (*Paul and the Gnostics*, 53 n. 120): "The Χριστοῦ εἶναι ["belonging to Christ"] is the exclusive self–designation of the Corinthian Gnostics (I Cor 1:12; II Cor 10:7). That in Gal 5:24 Paul is taking up the same–sounding designation of the Galatian Gnostics is of course unlikely, since this originally Gnostic–mythological formula is familiar to Paul himself for designation of the Christian status (Rom 8:9; I Cor 3:23; 15:23)."

169 See Gal 1:3, 19; 5:10; 6:14, 18.

170 See Gal 1:4; 2:20; 3:13; 4:4f; 5:1.

171 See Gal 2:16f; 3:26–28; 5:6.

172 See Gal 2:19; 3:1; 5:11; 6:12–14. Following Lagrange, Schlier (pp. 263f) interprets the aorist of ἐσταύρωσαν ("they have crucified") and the whole sentence on the basis of Rom 6:6 as "sacramental": the aorist, in his view, refers to the "decision" to accept baptism (similarly also Burton; Oepke; Wilhelm Michaelis ["πάσχω," *TDNT* 5.930 lines 23ff]); Kamlah, *Die Form der katalogischen Paränese*, 15f (n. 93 above); Jewett, *Paul's Anthropological Terms*, 105. But this "sacramental" interpretation is as artificial here as it is elsewhere in Gal; cf. Schulz, *KD* 5.36ff; Betz, "Spirit, Freedom and Law," 148 n. 10; Mussner, pp. 390f; questionable also is Johannes Schneider ("σταυρόω," *TDNT* 7.583), who thinks of the moral–religious decision ("sittlich–religiöse Entscheidung") which the Christians have made *after* their baptism.

173 The term is technical in Hellenistic anthropology and used by Paul only here and Rom 7:5. See Bauer, *s.v.*, 2; Michaelis, ibidem, 930–35; *PGL, s.v.*; Jewett, *Paul's Anthropological Terms*, 102ff.

174 Here in the plural; cf. Gal 5:16.

like the crucified to the tree of helpless and poverty-striken indiscipline."[175] Both Paul and Philo share the assumption that the "flesh" (σάρξ) has a powerful life of its own which expresses itself in its "passions and desires."[176] "Crucifixion" of the flesh results in its neutralization: having lost its life it is no longer capable of producing the "works of the flesh."[177]

In terms of Paul's theology, this means that the Christian who continues to live "in the flesh" (ἐν σαρκί) can now "live to God."[178] With this argument, the section vv 16–24 is concluded.

---

175 *Som.* 2.213, tr. Colson and Whitaker in LCL. The decisive words are: . . . ὥσπερ τὸν αὐχένα ἀποτμη-θεὶς ἀκέφαλος καὶ νεκρὸς ἀνευρεθήσεται, προσηλωμέ-νος ὥσπερ οἱ ἀνασκολοπισθέντες τῷ ξύλῳ τῆς ἀπόρου καὶ πενιχρᾶς ἀπαιδευσίας. Cf. Clitarchus *Sent.* 86 (Chadwick, *Sextus*, 80): οὐκ ἔστιν ἐλεύθερον εἶναι κρατούμενον ὑπὸ παθῶν. For further passages, see Brandenburger, *Fleisch und Geist*, 216ff.

176 Cf. Brandenburger (*Fleisch und Geist*, 19, 51, 55, 117f, 177ff), who corrects Eduard Schweizer, "σάρξ," *TDNT* 7.121ff; idem, "Die hellenistische Kompo-nente. . ." (see above on Gal 5:17, n. 68) 40–55.

177 Cf. Philo *Cher.* 8: "Then too there shines upon them the light of Isaac—the generic form of happiness, of the joy and gladness which belongs to those who have ceased from the manner of women . . . and died to the passions. . ." (ἀποθανόντων τά πάθη). See also the parallels *Gig.* 33; *Agr.* 17; *Ebr.* 69; *L.A.* 3.131, 190.

178 See Gal 2:19f (*propositio*), and the beginning of the next section 5:25. Important is the parallel Rom 8:13b: "If, then, through the Spirit you kill the acts of the body you shall live" (εἰ δὲ πνεύματι τὰς πράξεις τοῦ σώματος θανατοῦτε, ζήσεσθε).

5

Exhortatio: Recommendations in Form of *sententiae*

25	If the Spirit is the source of our life, let the Spirit also direct our course.[1] 26/ Let us not become boastfully vain—provoking one another, envying one another.
6:1	Brothers, if a person is detected in a transgression, you who are endowed with the Spirit[2] shall restore this person in a gentle spirit. Look to yourself that you are not tempted too. 2/ Bear one another's burdens, and in this way you will fulfill the "law of Christ." 3/ For if anyone thinks he is something when he is nothing, he deludes himself. 4/ Each person should examine his own conduct, and then his reason to boast will be with regard to himself alone, and not in comparison with someone else. 5/ For everyone has his own load to bear. 6/ Let him who is taught the word share all good things with the one who teaches. 7/ Do not be fooled: God is not to be sneered at. For one will also reap whatever one sows. 8/ For whoever sows into one's own flesh will reap a harvest of corruption from the flesh; but whoever sows into the Spirit will reap a harvest of eternal life from the Spirit. 9/ So let us not grow weary of doing what is good, for in due season we shall bring in the harvest, if we do not give out. 10/ Consequently, as we have time,[3] let us work for the good of all humanity, but especially for those who belong to the household of the faith.

Analysis

The parenetic section of the letter which begins in 5:1 ends with a collection of *sententiae*[4] in 5:25–6:10. At first sight the collection appears confused, but it is not without organization and structure. Most likely Paul himself is the composer of the individual *sententiae*, a fact which demonstrates his abilities as a gnomic poet.[5] Although there are close parallels to the form, collection, language, and function of the *sententiae* in the letter, nevertheless extensive research has not turned up *verbatim* parallels. Furthermore, the section seems well-integrated into the present context of the letter. Com-

---

1   So *NEB*; cf. *RSV*: "If we live by the Spirit, let us also walk by the Spirit."

2   So *NEB*; cf. *RSV*: "You who are spiritual," following Vg: "*vos, qui spirituales estis.*" Luther (1545) has: "*die jr geistlich seid.*"

3   Cf. *RSV*, *NEB*: "opportunity".

4   For definitions and forms of the *sententia* ("sentence"), see Lausberg, *Handbuch*, §§ 872–9, and

Index, *s.v.*; Martin, *Rhetorik*, 122–24, 257f.

5   The investigation of Paul's gnomic sentences remains a *desideratum* of New Testament scholarship. See Johannes Weiss, *Beiträge zur paulinischen Rhetorik* (Göttingen: Vandenhoeck & Ruprecht, 1897) *passim*; Bultmann, *Stil, passim*; Norbert Schneider, *Die rhetorische Eigenart der paulinischen Antithese* (HUTh 11; Tübingen: Mohr, Siebeck, 1970).

posing such *sententiae* was common practice among philosophers, especially those in the Cynic–Stoic diatribe tradition.[6] Long before Paul, this tradition had been adopted by Hellenistic Judaism, the type of Judaism from which Paul came.[7] This explains why Paul's *sententiae* are so similar to the ones found among the philosophers; in fact, many of them could well have been formulated by Menander or Epictetus.

The *form and composition* of Paul's *sententiae* show signs of careful work. It was part of the epistolary style to use gnomic *sententiae* individually or in groups. The arrangement here is *seriatim*. The sequence is neither uncoordinated nor overly systematized; some connection is provided by language and inner logic. This arrangement corresponds to that of other collections in the philosophical literature. It is loose enough that the reader is not bored, but has room for reflection and enjoyment. There are enough paradoxes, contradictions, and gaps to make him think and wonder. The frequent references to self–inquiry show the direction in which reflection is intended to go. Among Paul's *sententiae* there is considerable variation. We find a maxim in the third person singular (6:3), maxims in the second person singular (6:1c) and plural (6:2a), maxims using the imperative (6:2a, 4, 6) or the form of an appeal (5:25, 26; 6:9, 10). The maxims include a recommendation (6:1a–b), proverbs (6:7, 8), allegory (6:8), and an abundance of metaphorical language.

With regard to the content of the *sententiae*, there is little that is specifically Christian. By definition the gnome must be general ("infinite"). It must contain generally recognized principles dealing with the issues of human life, the life of the individual and of the community. The gnomic style provides critical observations about what is wrong behavior and advice on how to correct it. The effect, therefore, is provocative, corrective, demanding, and advisory.

The result of this form of exhortation is that Paul does not provide the Galatians with a specifically Christian ethic. The Christian is addressed as an educated and responsible person. He is expected to do no more than what would be expected of any other educated person in the Hellenistic culture of the time. In a rather conspicuous way Paul conforms to the ethical thought of his contemporaries. He does not prescribe anything concrete, nor does he describe absolute ethical ideals. His expectations are modest, taking into account the relativity of standards as well as human weakness. If one realizes this, the consequences become clear: Paul's ethical teaching implies not only a radical critique of the Jewish Torah observance, but also of the older Socratic Paideia, the latter being implicit in the teachings of the Cynic–Stoic diatribe. "Ethical" conduct means doing justice to the values of the culture, values which are named here in a very general sense and are only exemplaric. The purpose of the parenesis is not to exhort the readers to do what they cannot do or would fail to do. Rather, Paul assumes that his readers are already doing what they are expected to do. His goal is to induce self–examination and self–criticism, in order to keep the level of ethical awareness high.

On the other hand, Paul does not share the older ideal that, if man only examines himself critically, he will learn to act responsibly and ethically. For Paul self–examination has only a secondary function: it maintains awareness, flexibility, and readiness to

6   For bib. see Konstantin Horna, "Gnome, Gnomendichtung, Gnomologien," PWSup. 6 (1935) 74–87; and the additional notes by Kurt von Fritz, ibidem, 87–90; Jürgen Mau, "Gnome," *KP* 2 (1967) 823–30; Gerhard, *Phoinix*; Leo Sternbach and Otto Luschnat, *Gnomologium Vaticanum e Codice Vaticano Graeco* 743 (Texte und Kommentare 2; Berlin: de Gruyter, 1963); Chadwick, *Sextus*; James M. Robinson, "*Logoi Sophon*: On the Gattung of Q," (in Robinson and Koester, *Trajectories*, 71–113, esp. 100ff); Vielhauer, *Geschichte*, 316f.

7   This tradition had influenced Judaism long before Paul. See Bousset–Gressmann, *Religion*, 497; Heinemann, *Philons Bildung*; Bo Reicke, "Sprichwort, Spruch," *BHH* 3.1837–38; Gerhard von Rad, *Wisdom in Israel* (Nashville and New York: Abingdon, 1972); Hengel, *Judaism and Hellenism*, 1.115, 129f, 149ff. On the *Sententiae Aesopi-Achiqari* see Albert-Marie Denis, *Fragmenta pseudepigraphorum quae supersunt graeca* (Leiden: Brill, 1970) 137–40; idem, *Introduction aux pseudépigraphes grecs d'Ancien Testament* (Leiden: Brill, 1970) 201–14; Gotthard Strohmaier, "Ethical Sentences and Anecdotes of Greek Philosophers in Arabic Tradition," *Actes du V*e *Congrès international d'arabisants et d'islamisants* (Correspondence d'Orient, 11; 1970) 463–71; Henry Fischel, *Rabbinic Literature and Graeco-Roman Philosophy* (SPB 21; Leiden: Brill, 1973).

change. But first, man must be enabled by the divine Spirit "to do good." This enabling occurs when the "fruit of the Spirit" is allowed to grow (5:22–23). It is only because of the gift of the Spirit that the "good" happens. The Christian is asked merely to let it happen and to share in it when it happens. This is what is meant by the expression "to follow the Spirit" (5:25). Therefore, there is an implicit connection between the "possession of the Spirit" (cf. 5:18), the "fruit of the Spirit" (cf. 5:22–23), and the self–examination which the *sententiae* provoke. Paul's ethic is neither a work ethic (doing good deeds produces the good), nor a call for the realization of ethical ideals. His ethic is of another type. Believing in God's redemption means, according to Paul, that "the good" happens through divine grace. Man, however, must be enabled by an overwhelming experience of the Spirit to see it and to share in it. The "fruit of the Spirit" is an image which describes what happens when man shares in the manifestations of the "good." Self–examination is an intellectual activity, to be sure, but Paul's usage is different than that in Greek philosophy. According to Paul, self–examination prevents the Christian from falling back to where he was before his salvation, and it keeps him from becoming an obstacle to God's grace. This would occur if the Christian vainly attempts to accomplish the "good" by "doing works of the Law" or by allowing the "works of the flesh" (cf. 5:19–21) to corrupt the Christian community. This ethical theory underlies Paul's parenesis in 5:25–6:10. The self–examination which Paul urges the Galatians to undertake is of course carried out in a principal way by Paul himself in his letter addressed to the churches in Galatia.

■ **25** Paul begins this part of his parenesis with a *sententia* of principal importance because it contains his entire ethic in a nutshell: Εἰ ζῶμεν πνεύματι, πνεύματι καὶ στοιχῶμεν ("if we live by the Spirit, let the Spirit also direct our course" [*NEB*]). The saying is in the form of a paradoxical gnome, composed chiastically.[8] Because of its function in the context, the emphasis is upon the last word, while the first part of the sentence sums up what the reader has been told since 3:3. In fact, although in 3:3 Paul had begun the argumentative section by the ironic question, "having begun 'in [the] Spirit,' are you now finishing up 'in [the] flesh'?" he now provides his own answer to that ethical question. Brief doctrinal statements in 5:5, 5:16, and 5:18 have kept the reader informed about the origin of the Christian's life: πνεύματι ("through the Spirit"). Thus the protasis in 5:25a sums up again the "indicative" of salvation,[9] parallel to 5:1a, 13a—now, however, including the discussion of 5:1–24 as a whole. Especially in 5:22–24 Paul has set forth, according to his understanding, how the Christian has access to the divine life: he has such access in the present without doing "works of the Torah," but in effect fulfilling the Torah "through the fruit of the Spirit." However, "to live by the Spirit" cannot possibly mean one's idle possession of it or exclusion by it from the daily struggle of life.[10] Hence the appeal made in the apodosis becomes understandable: if the Christian has been made a participant in the divine life, this life must become manifest in his daily life.[11]

Paul's choice of the term στοιχέω ("follow") is certainly intentional,[12] although we can interpret its meaning in several ways. After ἐξάρχομαι ("begin") 3:3, περιπατέω ("walk") 5:16, ἄγομαι (be carried away")

---

8 Variant readings, by changing the word order, destroy the form; cf. Nestle–Aland, critical apparatus, and Zahn, p. 26 n. 4. On chiasm see BDF, § 477, 2; BDR, § 477, 2.

9 So Zahn, p. 267; Lightfoot; Burton; Schlier; Mussner; Moule, *Idiom-Book*, 44.

10 Cf. 2:19f; 3:11f; and, by contrast, 2:14. See Rom 6:2–14; Col 3:1f; Eph 4:30.

11 Cf. Philo *Det.* 60: "For happiness consists in the exercise and enjoyment of virtue, not in its mere possession" (χρῆσις γὰρ καὶ ἀπόλαυσις ἀρετῆς τὸ εὔδαιμον, οὐ ψιλὴ μόνον κτῆσις·). Philo continues:

"But I could not exercise it, shouldst Thou not send down the seeds from heaven to cause her [*sc.* Virtue] to be pregnant, and were she not to give birth to Isaac, i.e. happiness in its totality, and I have made up my mind that happiness is the exercise of perfect virtue in a perfect life." Cf. Sevenster, *Paul and Seneca* (NovTSup 4; Leiden: Brill, 1961) 153f.

12 Paul uses the same term again in the summary of his ethic 6:16.

293

5:18, he now seems to borrow a military term ("be drawn up in line").[13] If this is the meaning, Paul would be calling upon the Christians of Galatia to all march in line following the Spirit as the leader. The term is used in this sense by Hellenistic philosophers to mean "follow someone's philosophical principles."[14] Another possibility is the meaning "conform" ("agree," "act in harmony").[15] The difference between these may not be great, but "follow" places the accent upon the priority of the Spirit as well as upon concrete ethical behavior.[16]

■ 26 The negative contrast to v 25 is stated in the next gnome: the failure to "follow the Spirit" results in empty pretentiousness. Verse 26 enters a strong plea against such deceptive behavior by Christians:

26a: μὴ γινώμεθα κενόδο-ξοι,	"Let us not become boast-ful,
26b: ἀλλήλους προκαλούμε-νοι,	provoking one another,
26c: ἀλλήλοις φθονοῦντες.	envying one another."

The saying is an extremely concise, independent composition of three parts: an appeal (26a) and two parallel[17] participial clauses (26b, c). The appeal (26a) is in the first person plural, stated negatively.[18] This form is used by Paul elsewhere in the second person plural only.[19] The term κενόδοξος ("conceited, boastful") is well-known from Hellenistic philosophy, where it is used to describe all kinds of intellectual and moral charlatanism.[20] Apparently first coined by Epicurus,[21] it became a synonym of ἀλαζών ("braggart") and was taken up by Hellenistic Judaism[22] and primitive Christianity[23] as part of their polemic weaponry. The two participial clauses describe ways in which a group of people, here Christians, can become an assemblage of such impostors. Probably using a topos from the diatribe tradition, Paul compares unethical conduct with sports or the military. The comparison presupposes two contestants who engage in hostilities (1) by "provoking one another" (v 26b); (2) by "envying one another" (v 26c). While the first describes the hostile

---

13 Cf. also the use of the term in Rom 4:12; Phil 3:16; Acts 21:24; *Mart. Pol.* 22.1; cf. συστοιχέω ("correspond") Gal 4:25. For the meaning and history of the term see LSJ, *s.v.*; Bauer, *s.v.*; Gerhard Delling, "στοιχέω," *TDNT* 7.666–9. Cf Resch, *Agrapha*, 199f (no. 173), where a "saying of Jesus" from Ephraem Syr. is quoted: "Qui spiritu Dei ambulant, hi sunt filii Dei" ("Those who walk by the Spirit of God, are sons of God").

14 See the passages collected by Delling, ibidem, 667.

15 This meaning is preferred by Delling (ibidem, 667–69) followed by Mussner, p. 391. Cf. Lightfoot: "let us also walk by the Spirit."

16 See also Bultmann's repeated treatment of this passage: "Das Problem der Ethik bei Paulus," *ZNW* 23 (1924) 123–40; also in *Exegetica*, 36–54; ET "The Problem of Ethics in the Writing of Paul" in *The Old and New Man* (tr. Keith R. Crim; Richmond: John Knox, 1967) 7–32; idem, *Theology* 1.333, 337; Conzelmann, *Outline*, 282–86.

17 The parallelism is strengthened by those witnesses which read ἀλλήλους also in v 26c (B G* *pm* Clement).

18 For the use of γίνομαι in positive form, see Gal 4:12; 1 Cor 4:16; 10:32; 11:1; 14:20; 15:58; Phil 3:17; cf. Eph 4:32; 5:1; Col 3:15; Jas 1:22.

19 Rom 12:16; 1 Cor 7:23; 10:7; 14:20; cf. 2 Cor 6:14; Eph 5:7, 17; *Did.* 3.5 (singular).

20 For passages, see LSJ, *s.v.*; Albrecht Oepke,

"κενόδοξος," *TDNT* 3.662; Bauer, *s.v.*, *PGL*, *s.v.*; Betz, *Lukian*, 183, 201 n. 5; *PECL*, 263; also Plut. *De coh. ira* 457B; Adolf Bonhöffer, *Epiktet und das Neue Testament* (RVV 10; Giessen: Töpelmann, 1911) 120.

21 Epicurus *Sent.* 30 (p. 78,8 Usener). See also below on Gal 6:3.

22 LXX has the verb (4 Macc 5:10; 8:24) and the noun (Sap 14:14; 4 Macc 2:15; 8:19); the adjective is found *Ep. Arist.* 8; Philo *Som.* 2.105; cf. *Mut.* 96, 226; *Jos.* 36; *Leg. Gai.* 114; Josephus *BJ* 6.172, 395; *Ant.* 8.264.

23 The adjective occurs *Did.* 3.5; the verb *Mart. Pol.* 10.1; the noun Phil 2:3; Ign. *Phld.* 1.1; Ign. *Magn.* 11.1; *1 Clem.* 35.5; *Herm. Man.* 8.5; *Herm. Sim.* 8.9.3.

turning against each other, the latter implies the turning away from one another.[24] The term προκαλέω ("provoke, challenge") is used only here in the New Testament,[25] but occurs in diatribe texts.[26] The verb φθονέω ("envy") also occurs only here in the New Testament,[27] while the noun is part of the catalogue of "vices" in Gal 5:21.[28] Again the conceptuality is very prominent in the diatribe material and in other Hellenistic philosophy.

Such behavior as Paul describes is the very opposite of what befits the "pneumatics" (6:1). It is the opposite of "love" and of "serving one another."[29] Such corruption of love leads to the corruption of the community (cf. 5:13).[30]

■1 The repetition of the address ἀδελφοί ("brothers")[31] indicates that Paul will now present an important matter to the readers. Indeed, it seems as if Paul now

turns from the general exhortation to concrete events in the Galatian churches. But this is only partly true. Paul does make a recommendation on how to proceed in a case of actual wrongdoing by a member of the church, but there is no indication that he has a specific case in mind.[32] Although made for a specific instance, the recommendation remains general.[33] There are three parts to the recommendation: (1) a description of the condition which would precipitate the procedure (v 1a); (2) the procedure for handling the case (v 1b); and (3) a warning to those who administer the procedure (v 1c).

The conditional clause v 1a describes a "case" as it could and most likely did happen in the life of the community: ἐὰν καὶ προλημφθῇ ἄνθρωπος ἔν τινι παραπτώματι... ("if someone is detected in a transgression..."). The statement presupposes a legal or quasi-

---

24 For rabbinic parallels, see 'Abot 4.23: "R. Simeon ben Eleazar said: Soothe not thy associate in the hour of his anger, and console him not in the hour when his dead lies before him; and question him not in the hour of his vow, and seek not to see him in the hour of his disgrace." See also 'Abot 4.23 (Prov 24:17f); 'Abot R. Nat. A, chap. 29; for Hellenistic Judaism, see Philo Agr. 112 (cf. n. 26 below): "I have been vanquished, and this man is the victor, and has proved himself so vastly superior, that even we, his antagonists, who might have been expected to grudge him his victory, feel no envy." Cf. Agr. 121; the anecdote about a philosopher in Prob. 128–30; about Flaccus Flacc. 30: "And the unhappy Flaccus was again stirred up by his companions with incitement and appeals calculated to make him...envious..." (καὶ προκαλούμενοι φθόνον). Epict. Diss. 1.9.20: διὰ τί ἄλλος ἄλλῳ φθονήσει; ("Why should one man envy another?"); 1.27.8; 2.12.7–9; 2.19.25; 2.21.12; 4.4.10; 4.12.20. For Hellenistic Judaism, cf. furthermore Tob 4:7, 16; Josephus Ant. 4.235; Cont. Ap. 2.268; Ep. Arist. 224; T. Sim. 2.14; 3.3,6; T. Gad 3.3; 7.2; T. Benj. 4.4; Sententiae Aesopi-Achiqari, 109 (ed. Denis, Fragm. pseudepigr. gr., 138 lines 26–30; 139 lines 4–8); etc.

25 The term is common in Hellenistic philosophical literature; cf. Plutarch Apophth. 181C; Quaest. Rom. 272F; Glor. Athen. 346C; An vitiositas 499B, and often. See further LSJ, s.v.; Bauer, s.v.

26 Cf., esp., Philo Agr. 110: "This explains what was meant by one of the ancients when challenged to a reviling match (προκληθεὶς ἐπὶ λοιδορίας). He said he would never come forward for such a contest, for

in it the victor is worse than the vanquished." The whole following section Agr. 111ff develops the topos in the diatribe style. Cf. also 2 Macc 8:11; Josephus Ant. 7.315; 18.369.

27 Cf. Jas 4:2 v.1.; 2 Clem. 15.5.

28 See furthermore Bauer, s.v.; Mussies, Dio Chrysostom, 185. On the background, cf. Pfitzner, Agon Motif, passim; Ernst Milobenski, Der Neid in der griechischen Philosophie (Wiesbaden: Steiner, 1964); Willem C. van Unnik, "De ἀφθονία van God in de oudchristelijke literatuur," Mededelingen der Koninglijke Nederlandse Akademie van Wetenschappen, Afd. Letterkunde (N.R., Deel 36, No. 2, 1973).

29 Cf. Gal 5:13; 6:2; for the opposite also 5:15; Rom 1:27. See also Rom 13:8; 14:13; 1 Cor 7:5; Col 3:9; Titus 3:3; Heb 10:24; Jas 4:11; 5:9; 1 Pet 4:9, etc.

30 Cf. Schlier, who emphasizes the "self-love" of the individual rather than the disintegration of the community.

31 Cf. Gal 1:2, 11; 3:15; 4:12, 28, 31; 5:11, 13; 6:18.

32 Some witnesses try to make it more concrete: P reads: τίς ἐξ ὑμῶν ("one of you"); Ψ (69) pc sy: ἄνθρωπος ἐξ ὑμῶν ("a person from your midst").

33 To this extent, the case of Gal 6:1 is different from the one in 1 Cor 5:1ff. On the whole problem of the "concreteness" of Paul's paraenesis, see Wolfgang Schrage, Die konkreten Einzelgebote in der paulinischen Paränese (Gütersloh: Mohn, 1961).

legal context.[34] The term προλαμβάνομαι is not clear;[35] it can be taken as "be detected, overtaken, surprised" (Bauer, *s.v.* 2,b), or the meaning can be: "a fault into which the brother is betrayed 'unawares,' so that it is not intentionally wrong" (so Delling, *TDNT* 4. 14). But the general term παράπτωμα ("transgression")[36] suggests that one should not interpret the whole statement too specifically. In the present context the wrong-doer would certainly be a Christian, and his offense would fall into the kinds of things listed in 5:19–21.

It is important to realize that this is the only passage in Galatians where Paul openly admits that there can be and presumably were "transgressions" done by members of the churches.[37] Most notably Paul does not use the term ἁμαρτία ("sin") to name the offense,[38] but he uses instead a general legal term. Since he regards "sin" as applying to the pre–Christian situation, one should not speak of the offense as "sin"—at least not without explaining what Paul may mean by Christian "sin." The fact that Paul admits transgressions at all is evidence that he touches upon the heart of the Galatian troubles.[39] There is no reason to assume that the recommendation had been given before. Apparently, the Galatians had not been prepared to deal with offenses in their midst. Only now, it seems, are regulations called for, and Paul provides one. This leads to the conclusion that concrete instances of wrong-doing by Christians had unexpectedly occurred in the Galatian churches and that this fact caused Paul to spend so much time discussing the corruption of the "flesh". This conclusion would also explain why the Galatians considered introducing the Torah. When we look at Paul's recommendation, on the other hand, he suggests a way of dealing with the offense, which does not require the introduction of law at all. Surprisingly, Paul does not seem overly concerned with the offense itself, but his concern is more with the possibility that the handling of such a case might become a source of evil for those who administer it. For this reason, severe restrictions are set up, not so much for the offender, but rather for those who deal with him: a case can be made only if someone is "caught in the act" of a real "transgression." This legal language excludes offenses which the courts would not recognize as such.

Verse 1b prescribes the procedure: ὑμεῖς οἱ πνευματικοὶ καταρτίζετε τὸν τοιοῦτον ἐν πνεύματι πραΰτητος ("you, the 'pneumatics,' shall restore this person in a spirit of gentleness"). In short: the case should be dealt with in a manner which befits "spiritual people." What does this imply? It is, of course, intentional that Paul addresses the Galatians as οἱ πνευματικοί ("the spirit–filled, pneumatics").[40] There is no hesitation or irony in Paul's use of this loaded term, and we have every reason to believe that the Galatians themselves

---

34 Gal 1:8; 5:2; Rom 2:25; 7:2f; 1 Cor 5:11; etc.; also Matt 5:23f, 32; 12:11; 18:17; Jas 4:1–12; 5:13, 19f.

35 The term is found in this meaning only here in the NT. LSJ, *s.v.*, II, 6 lists Gal 6:1 ("detect") without parallels. See also Bauer, *s.v.*, 2, b, with references; Gerhard Delling, "προλαμβάνω, προσλαμβάνω, πρόσλημψις, ὑπολαμβάνω," *TDNT* 4.14–15; Burton; pp. 326f; Schlier, p. 270 n. 4; David Daube, "To Be Found Doing Wrong," *Studi in Onore di Edoardo Volterra* (Pubblicazioni della Facoltà di Giurisprudenza dell' Università di Roma 41; Milan: Giuffrè, 1971) 2.1–13.

36 The term is general, indicating any kind of immoral act. Paul uses it also Rom 4:25; 5:15, 16, 17, 18, 20; 11:11, 12; 2 Cor 5:19. See Bauer, *s.v.*; Wilhelm Michaelis ("παραπίπτω, παράπτωμα, περιπίπτω," *TDNT* 6.170–73) who, however, takes it in the theological sense of a "disruption of the relationship to God" (p. 172).

37 Cf. Gal 2:17f.

38 The term refers to the pre–Christian situation in Gal 1:4; 2:17; 3:22. The problem recurs in Rom, where Paul deals with it at greater length. See Rom 6:1; also 14:23.

39 See on this point Betz, "Spirit, Freedom, and Law," 153–55, esp. also Paul Wernle, *Der Christ und die Sünde bei Paulus* (Freiburg and Leipzig: Mohr, 1897) 72–90; Hans Windisch, *Taufe und Sünde im ältesten Christentum bis auf Origenes* (Tübingen: Mohr, Siebeck, 1908) 154–63.

40 The concept occurs only here in Gal, but more frequently in 1 Cor. See 1 Cor 14:37 (with "prophet"); 2:15; 3:1; also 2:13; 12:1; furthermore *Barn.* 4.11; Ign. *Eph.* 8.2. On the subject see Conzelmann, *1 Corinthians*, on 2:13; 12:1; Bauer, *s.v.*; Eduard Schweizer, *TDNT* 6, *s.v.*; Birger Pearson, *The Pneumatikos-Psychikos Terminology in 1 Corinthians* (SBLDS 12; Missoula: Scholars, 1973); Martin Winter, *Pneumatiker und Psychiker in Korinth* (Marburger Theologische Studien 12; Marburg: Elwert, 1975).

approved of it and used it as a self–designation.[41] The title befits them best because of Paul's constant emphasis upon the Spirit ($\pi\nu\epsilon\hat{\upsilon}\mu\alpha$) which they possess.[42] What they should do with the transgressor is described by Paul as $\kappa\alpha\tau\alpha\rho\tau\acute{\iota}\zeta\epsilon\iota\nu$ ("to restore"), another highly significant concept from Hellenistic philosophy, where it describes the work of the philosopher–"psychotherapist" and educator. This work is summed up by Cato's charge to the philosophers: "it is your task to reduce this man's swollen pride and restore him to conformity with his best interests."[43]

Paul does not use the Stoic language of Cato, but the more general terms of Hellenistic popular philosophy.[44] This language must then be understood in the context of Pauline theology, where it is integrated with a radical Spirit/flesh dualism and the self–understanding of the Christian as a "pneumatic." This language and Paul's theological context also make the whole statement different when compared with the Qumran texts, where we find an analogous regulation for the treatment of "transgressors" in that community.[45] When Paul recommends to "restore" the "transgressor," this implies, as Chrysostom has seen, limitations in that the procedure does not include punishment or condemnation.[46] Paul's apparent leniency[47] is also shown by his concern that the "restoring" be done "in a spirit of gentleness": "in a spirit"[48] because this befits the "pneumatics," and in "gentleness"[49] be-

---

41 So also Mussner; cf. Schlier (p. 270), who thinks Paul uses the term ironically. Lütgert (*Gesetz und Geist*, 12) and other commentators dependent upon him assume that Paul here addresses only the group of enthusiasts within the churches, not all of the Christians. Cf. also Schmithals,*Gnosticism*, 166ff.; idem, *Paul and the Gnostics*, 46ff.

42 See Gal 3:2, 3, 5, 14; 4:6, 29; 5:5, 16, 17, 18, 22f, 25; 6:8, 18.

43 Plutarch *Cato minor* 65.5: Ὑμέτερον... ἔργον οἰδοῦντα τοῦτον μαλάξαι καὶ καταρτίσαι πρὸς τὸ συμφέρον. See also Plutarch *Alex.* 7.1; *Them.* 2.5–6; Anton Elter, *Gnomica homoeomata* V (Bonn: Kaiserprogramm, 1904) 39* No. 27 (Plutarch); Epictetus *Diss.* 3.20.10; 4.9.16; Philo *Agric.* 122; also *Ep. Arist.* 191, 281; Lucian *Demon.* 7: Demonax considered it the task of God and the "divine man" to restore what has gone wrong: "he considered that it is human to err, divine or all but divine to set right what has gone amiss" (ἡγεῖτο γὰρ ἀνθρώπου μὲν εἶναι τὸ ἁμαρτάνειν, θεοῦ δὲ ἢ ἀνδρὸς ἰσοθέου τὰ πταισθέντα ἐπανορθοῦν). Wettstein, *ad loc.*, cites Pliny (*Ep.* 8.22), who interprets the rule of Thrasea: Qui vitia odit, homines odit ("Anyone who hates faults, hates mankind."). On the background of these ideas see Hadot, *Seelenleitung*; Heinz G. Ingenkamp, *Plutarchs Schriften über die Heilung der Seele* (Hypomnemata 34; Göttingen: Vandenhoeck & Ruprecht, 1971).

44 Cf. the rendering in LSJ, *s.v.* See also Luke 6:40; 1 Cor 1:10; 2 Cor 13:9, 11; 1 Thess 3:10; Eph 4:12; 1 Pet 5:10; Ign. *Eph.* 2.2; Ign. *Phld.* 8.1; Ign. *Smyrn.* 1.1. See Gerhard Delling, "ἄρτιος," *TDNT* 1.475–76; Bauer, *s.v.*; *PGL*, *s.v.*

45 See '*Abot* 1.1: "Be deliberate in judging." See also '*Abot* 1.8, 9; 2.5; 4.9, 10; 6.1, 6; '*Abot R. Nat.* B, 3 (tr. Anthony J. Saldarini, *The Fathers According to Rabbi Nathan* [Leiden: Brill, 1975] 28f): "Be deliberate in judgment means that a man should not be short tempered and should not interrupt his fellow man because everyone who is short tempered ends up forgetting what he was going to say..."; 1QS 5.24–6.1; 10.26–11.1; CD 13.9f; and on the problem of interpretation Braun, *Qumran* 1.214; for further parallels, see Str-B 1.441–46.

46 Chrysostom, *ad loc.*: οὐκ εἶπε κολάζετε οὐδὲ καταδικάζετε ἀλλὰ διορθοῦσθε ("he does not say 'punish,' nor 'condemn' but 'set right'").

47 Cf. Pliny *Ep.* 8.22.1: "You must know people who are slaves to the very sort of passion while they display a sort of jealous resentment against the faults of others, and show least mercy to those they most resemble; though there are other people who need no man's forgiveness but whose greatest virtue is their tolerance [*lenitas*]." The latter is recommended by and to the philosopher. For a different interpretation, see Schlier, p. 270 (adopted by Mussner, p. 398): "The Church acts in a motherly way even with the sinners."

48 The expression "in a spirit of gentleness" is found only here in Gal; it refers both to the divine and to the human spirit. Cf. 6:18.

49 On πραΰτης ("gentleness"), see the list in Gal 5:23; also 1 Cor 4:21; 2 Cor 10:1; Eph 4:2; Col 3:12; 2 Tim 2:25; Jas 1:21; 3:13; 1 Pet 3:4, 16, etc. *Herm. Man.* 11.8 has this to say about the prophets: "In the first place, he who has the spirit which is from above is meek..." (πρῶτον μὲν ὁ ἔχων τὸ πνεῦμα τὸ ἄνωθεν πραΰς ἐστι...).

cause one is dealing with the shortcomings of a fellow "pneumatic."[50]

The last part of 6:1 consists of a maxim which can be taken by itself: σκοπῶν σεαυτόν, μὴ καὶ σὺ πειρασθῇς ("look at yourself that you are not tempted"). Switching from the second person plural to the second person singular, the Apostle addresses and warns the individual Christian whose task it is to administer the "case." He demands self–examination.[51] The term σκοπέω ("examine critically, keep an eye on") has its background in Hellenistic philosophy[52] and ıs employed by primitive Christian writers at several places.[53] The first part of the maxim comes from the Socratic tradition and no doubt goes back to Socrates himself.[54] The second part of the maxim is an interpretation of the first. Its content, however, does not transcend similar maxims in Hellenistic literature. Paul must have taken the maxim from the tradition of popular philosophy[55] in order to apply it here. The "temptation" he sees here is of two kinds: (1) there is a temptation to develop self–righteousness and arrogance with regard to the wrongdoer;[56] (2) such a temptation presents a threat to the community in that it provides an opportunity for the "works of the flesh." Paul seems keenly aware that a self–righteous posture of prosecutors can cause greater damage to the community than the offense done by a wrongdoer.[57]

■2 This verse contains another maxim which shows quite clearly how Paul worked as a gnomic poet. The maxim has two lines:

v 2a: ἀλλήλων τὰ βάρη βαστάζετε,
      "bear one another's burdens,
v 2b: καὶ οὕτως ἀναπληρώσετε τὸν νόμον τοῦ Χριστοῦ
      and in this way you will fulfill the law of Christ."

The two lines of the maxim are: v 2a the maxim proper and v 2b its Christian (Pauline) interpretation. Variants of the first part are known to us from the Socratic tradition and the Greek doctrines about "friendship."

---

50 Chadwick (*Sextus*, 170) quotes a saying from Basilidian gnosticism (Clement *Strom.* 7.82.1) which comes strangely close to Paul: "If the neighbour of an elect person sins, it is the fault of the elect; for if he had conducted himself as reason dictates, his neighbour's reverence for such a life would have prevented him from sinning." See also the rule in 1 Cor 2:13: πνευματικοῖς πνευματικὰ συγκρίνοντες ("interpreting the spiritual by the spiritual"—the tr. is uncertain).

51 Note the characteristic difference from Matt 18:15–17; Jas 3:19f, and the Qumran community; the latter exercises mutual examination of their spirits (1QS 5.21, 24; CD 13.11). See Braun, *Qumran* 1.38–40.

52 See, e.g., Epict. *Diss.* 1.11.20; 1.18.13; 2.5.25; 2.10.2 (also *Ench.* 30); 3.5.2; 3.15.1–2; (also *Ench.* 21.1–2); 3.22.75; 4.1.163; 4.3.3; Philo *Post.* 174; *Her.* 22; *Som.* 1.191; 2.48; etc. See Bauer, *s.v.*: Ernst Fuchs, "σκοπέω," *TDNT* 7.414–16.

53 The participle σκοπῶν has an imperative meaning, parallel to καταρτίζετε. See on this Daube, *NT and Rabbinic Judaism*, 97–99; Davies, *Paul and Rabbinic Judaism*, 329. See also Rom 16:17; 2 Cor 4:18; Phil 2:4; 3:17; Luke 11:35; *1 Clem.* 51.1.

54 See the famous passage about the Delphic maxim "Know yourself" in Plato *Phaedr.* 230A: "And so I dismiss these [*sc.* irrelevant] matters and accepting the customary belief about them, as I was saying just now, I investigate not these things, but myself, to know whether I am a monster more complicated and more furious than Typhon or a gentler and simpler creature, to whom a divine and quiet lot is given by nature." The important words in Greek are σκοπῶ οὐ ταῦτα ἀλλὰ ἐμαυτόν. Cf. also *Phaedr.* 232 D; *Euthyphr.* 9C. On the subject, see Hans Dieter Betz, "The Delphic Maxim ΓΝΩΘΙ ΣΑΥΤΟΝ in Hermetic Interpretation," *HTR* 63 (1970) 465–84; *PECL*, 85f, 90, 128, 194; Pierre Courcelle, *Connais-toi toi-même de Socrate à saint Bernard* (2 vols.; Paris: Etudes Augustiniennes, 1974) 1.43–47.

55 Similar maxims, also standing within the Socratic tradition, are found, e.g., in Menander (ed. Siegfried Jaekel, *Menandri Sententiae* [BT; Leipzig: Teubner, 1964]) 629: Πράττειν τὰ σαυτοῦ, μὴ τὰ τῶν ἄλλων σκόπει ("Do your own task, don't look at the task of others."). See also 98, 255, 400; Chadwick, *Sextus*, 93; Gerhard, *Phoinix*, 39f. An example of this is Luke 4:23: ἰατρέ, θεράπευσον σεαυτόν ("Physician, heal yourself."). Cf. Matt 27:42a.

56 Cf. Gal 4:14; 5:13.

57 Cf. the interpretation by Schlier, p. 270: "The church knows of the moral frailty of her members." Schlier (p. 271 n. 1) is right against Karl Georg Kuhn, "Πειρασμός–ἁμαρτία–σάρξ im Neuen Testament," *ZThK* 49 (1952) 200–22 (ET: "New Light on Temptation, Sin and Flesh," in *The Scrolls and the New Testament* [ed. Krister Stendahl; New York: Harper and Brothers, 1967] 213f) that Paul's position is quite different from that of Qumran; he does not share Qumran's rigorous observance of the Torah nor its concept of "sin."

The most interesting parallel is a long anecdote about Socrates and Aristarchus, told by Xenophon,[58] in which Socrates says: χρὴ δὲ τοῦ βάρους τοῖς φίλοις μεταδιδόναι· ἴσως γὰρ ἄν τί σε καὶ ἡμεῖς κουφίσαιμεν ("one must share one's burden with one's friends, for possibly we may do something to ease you"). Similar maxims are found among the sentences of Menander, e.g., 534:[59] νόμιζε πάντα κοινὰ τῶν φίλων βάρη ("accept all burdens among friends as common"); and 370: ἰδίας νόμιζε τῶν φίλων τὰς συμφοράς ("accept the misfortunes of your friends as your own").

No doubt Paul has taken over the first part of the saying (v 2a) from the Hellenistic philosophical tradition.[60] He finds it useful because it sums up his teaching in Gal 5:13–14 and is also related to 6:1. The language is metaphorical: τὰ βάρη refers to the "burdens" of human life;[61] βαστάζω is more than "tolerate" and includes effective assistance and relief.[62] Applied to 6:1 the maxim means that "failure" by Christians should

be regarded as part of the "burden of life" and should be shared and borne by the Christian community.[63]

The second line of the maxim (v 2b) is Paul's interpretation of the first line: καὶ οὕτως ("and in this way") means that by doing what the first line demands "you will fulfill[64] the law of Christ." The concept ὁ νόμος τοῦ Χριστοῦ ("the law of Christ") is strange, since it occurs only here[65] and seems to advocate what Paul had repeatedly rejected in his letter—that the Christian is obliged to do the Law.[66] Now, unexpectedly, in the parenetical part of the letter, the readers are told that they must do the Law after all. The problem—one of the most crucial problems in the whole letter—is to explain this seeming contradiction. The following can be stated as facts: (1) Paul has consistently rejected the idea that the *Gentile* Christians must accept circumcision and obey the Jewish Torah in order to become partakers in the divine salvation. For the Gentile as well as for the Jewish Christians the Jewish Torah is

---

58 Xenoph. *Mem.* 2.7.1–14. Another version is cited by Aristotle in a chapter discussing the obligations of friendship (Aristotle *EN* 9.11.1–6, p. 1171a21–1171b28, with the maxim in 1171a29: κουφίζεται γὰρ οἱ λυπούμενοι συναλγούντων τῶν φίλων ("Sorrow is lightened by the sympathy of friends"). Interestingly, a similar demand is among the 48 duties of the student of the Torah, '*Abot* 6.5f: נושא בעול עם חברו ("He carries the same yoke with his fellow-student [or neighbor]"). See Str-B. 3.577.

59 No. 534 is an interpretation of the old maxim πάντα κοινὰ τῶν φίλων ("Friends share everything in common"), Euripides *Or.* 735; Plato *Phaedr.* 279C; *Men.* 71E; *Polit.* 449C; *Leg.* 5.739C; *Lys.* 207C. Because it was part of the friendship theme, it was taken up by Judaism (see, e.g., Philo *Abr.* 235; *Mos.* 1.156) and Christianity (Acts 4:32; cf. also Gal 4:12ff). On the subject see Bohnenblust, *Beiträge* (cf. on 4:12–20, n. 17, above), 41.

60 A close parallel is Rom 15:1 and its interpretation, parallels to which are found in Hellenistic Judaism and Hellenistic diatribe material (cf., e.g., Maximus Tyr. 12.3); for Christianity see Ign. *Pol.* 1.2; *Diogn.* 10.6. Differently Käsemann, *Römer*, 365.

61 The metaphor is common; see LSJ, *s.v.*, V; Gottlob Schrenk, "βάρος," *TDNT* 1.553–56; Bauer, *s.v.* The "burdens" are not those of the Torah, nor limited to sins, but include the whole struggle of daily life (cf. for different views, Mussner, p. 399). Matt 20:12: "bear the burden of the day and its heat" is a good illustration; cf. also 1 Thess 2:7; Acts

15:28; Rev 2:24; *Diogn.* 10.6. For the philosophical background, cf. Epict. *Diss.* 1.9.11; 2.9.22; Philo *Mos.* 1.14; 1.39; *L.A.* 2.2.

62 This metaphor is also common; see LSJ, *s.v.*; Friedrich Büchsel, "βαστάζω," *TDNT* 1.596; Bauer, *s.v.*, 2, b, β; Str-B. 3.673. For other instances, see Rom 15:1; Ign. *Pol.* 1.2; Matt 20:12; Acts 15:28; Rev 2:3; *Did.* 6.2. For the diatribe material, see Epict. *Diss.* 2.9.22; 3.15.9 (*Ench.* 29.5).

63 I do not agree with Schlier, who thinks that Gal 6:2 presupposes the doctrine of imitation of Christ. Similarly Mussner (p. 399): "The Church loves the sinners, as Christ loved them."

64 The reading of the future tense ἀναπληρώσετε is attested by (P[46]) B G lat sy[p] Marcion. It has early and diverse attestation and it fits Paul's thought. The aorist ἀναπληρώσατε, attested by ℵ A C D[gr] *al*, is also possible. See Metzger, *Textual Commentary*, 598.

65 Similar expressions, equally problematical, occur in 1 Cor 9:21: ἔννομος Χριστοῦ ("obedient to the law of Christ" [?]; cf. the discussion in Bauer, *s.v*, ἔννομος); Rom 8:2: ὁ νόμος τοῦ πνεύματος τῆς ζωῆς ("the law of the Spirit of life"), cf. Eduard Lohse, "Exegetische Anmerkungen zu Röm 8, 2" in *Neues Testament und christliche Existenz, Festschrift für Herbert Braun . . .* (Tübingen: Mohr, Siebeck, 1973) 279–87; Rom 3:27: διὰ νόμου πίστεως ("through the law of faith"); 1 Thess 4:2.

66 See Gal 2:16, 19, 21; 3:2, 5, 10, 11, 12, 13, 17, 18, 19–24; 4:4–5, 21; 5:3–14, 18, 23; 6:13.

eliminated as a way to salvation. (2) The Christian is now already made a partaker in divine salvation through the gift of the Spirit.[67] He partakes in this salvation "through faith"[68] without doing the "works of the Law." "Faith" then expresses itself in "love" and this "love" in effect fulfills the Law.[69] Therefore the Christian's relationship to the Law is this: he is not required to earn his salvation by doing the "works of the Law," but by being part of the divine salvation, "through faith," he also fulfills the Law. Strictly speaking it is the Spirit which fulfills the Law, and the Christian shares in the fulfillment by "following the Spirit" (5:25).

Even if all of this is clear in the letter, the expression "the law of Christ" remains a puzzle.[70] The question is whether it is an *ad hoc* formulation, a mockery of the Galatians' obsession with the Torah. Or did Paul make it up in order to demonstrate that his gospel is not antinomist? Is the concept *basic* to Paul's theology? Did the Galatians know it before, or is it now introduced to them for the first time? Did Paul adopt the concept from his opponents, who would have interpreted it in quite a different way, in order to subject it polemically to a "Paulinizing" interpretation? Nothing definite can be said. A number of reasons, however, make it appear probable that Paul took over the notion from the opponents:[71] (1) because of the singularity of the notion in Galatians, and in Paul for that matter; (2) because the notion of the "law of Christ" played a considerable role in other Christian traditions apart from Paul; (3) because of the high probability that the Jewish–Christian opponents of Paul in Galatia combined in some way obedience to the Jewish Torah with obedience to Christ;[72] and (4) because Paul is compelled to defend himself against the accusation of "lawlessness."[73] If the hypothesis holds true, Paul would have taken a key concept from the theology of the opponents in order to make it fit his theology. These opponents would have associated "Torah" and "Christ" in a different but also positive way. This could have been done by associating the Mosaic Torah with Christ, or by regarding Christ as the bringer of a

---

67 See Gal 3:26–28.

68 See Gal 2:16, 20; 3:2ff; 5:5–6.

69 See Gal 5:6, 14, 22. For an analogy in gnosticism, see *Corp. Herm.* 13:9: "See how the good is completed...."

70 For the concept of "law of Christ" see Bultmann, *Theology*, § 27, 39. The older literature is found in Walter Gutbrod, "νόμος," *TDNT* 5.1022–85 (on Paul, section D, II, 2–3). See C. H. Dodd, *Gospel and Law* (New York: Columbia University, 1951) 64–83: "The Law of Christ"; idem, "*ΕΝΝΟΜΟΣ ΧΡΙΣΤΟΥ*," in *Studia Paulina in honorem J. de Zwaan* (Haarlem: Bohn, 1953) 96–110 (rep. in his *More New Testament Studies* [Manchester: Manchester University, 1968] 134–48); Ernst Bammel, "Νόμος Χριστοῦ," *Studia Evangelica* 3 (TU 88; Berlin: Akademie–Verlag, 1964) 120–28; Schoeps, *Paul*, chap. 5, § 5; Irene Beck, "Altes und neues Gesetz," *MThZ* 15 (1964) 127–42; Kertelge, "*Rechtfertigung*", 223f; Andrea van Dülmen, *Die Theologie des Gesetzes bei Paulus* (Stuttgart: Katholisches Bibelwerk, 1968) 66–68, 218–25 (with extensive bib.); Schlier, pp. 176–88, 264–67; Mussner, pp. 284–87; Heinz Schürmann, "'Das Gesetz des Christus' (Gal 6, 2). Jesu Verhalten und Wort als letztgültige sittliche Norm nach Paulus," in *Neues Testament und Kirche, Festschrift für R. Schnackenburg* (Freiburg: Herder. 1974) 282–300.

71 The hypothesis was first presented by Dieter Georgi, "Exegetische Anmerkungen zur Auseinandersetzung mit den Einwänden gegen die Thesen der Bruderschaften," in *Christusbekenntnis im Atomzeitalter* (ThExh 70; Munich: Kaiser, 1959) 111f; idem, *Kollekte*, 35f. See also Betz, "2 Cor 6:14–7:1," 107.

72 An example is the pre–Matthean Sermon on the Mount (Matt 5:3–7, 27); also see the notion of "the perfect law of freedom" (Jas 1:25). How such a theology would look is also exemplified by 2 Cor 6:14–7:1 (for the interpretation see Betz, ibidem, 89–99). Cf. also the christological epithet νόμος καὶ λόγος in *Kerygma Petrou*, Frag. 1 (ed. Erich Klostermann, *Apocrypha* 1 [KlT 3; Bonn: Marcus & Weber, 1921] 13; cf. Ernst von Dobschütz (*Das Kerygma Petri* [Leipzig: Hinrichs, 1893] 28f) who notes further parallels, esp. *Herm. Sim.* 8.3.2; Klaus Wengst (*Tradition und Theologie des Barnabasbriefes*) [Arbeiten zur Kirchengeschichte 42; Berlin: de Gruyter, 1971] 82ff) discusses *Barn.* 2.6 and its background.

73 Cf. Gal 2:17: "Christ a servant of sin." Also 2:21; 3:20c; 5:23b; Rom 6:1; 1 Cor 9:21.

"new" or "Messianic" Torah.[74] Paul, to be sure, gave the notion a completely different interpretation: since the love command is the fulfillment of the whole Torah (Gal 5:14), he who loves fulfills the Torah; and since such love is Christ's love (Gal 2:20), that Torah can be called "Christ's Torah."

In addition, one can argue that if the concept of the "law of Christ" were fundamental to Paul's theology,[75] Paul would have introduced it at the beginning of the letter and the concept would play a more prominent role in his other letters. In the beginning of Galatians (1:6–7) Paul would have argued against "another law of Christ" and not against "another gospel." The unique position of the notion of "law of Christ" makes it most likely that it is used here polemically.

■ **3** The next *sententia* is stated in the 3rd person singular: εἰ γὰρ δοκεῖ τις εἶναί τι μηδὲν ὤν, φρεναπατᾷ ἑαυτόν ("for if anyone thinks he is something when he is nothing, he deceives himself").

The form as well as content of this *sententia* are known from the diatribe literature, and even from Plato.[76] Two examples from Epictetus may suffice as illustrations: κἂν δόξῃς τις εἶναί τισιν, ἀπίστει σεαυτῷ ("and if you think you are somebody for some, distrust yourself");[77] and δοκεῖς τις εἶναι, μωρὸς παρὰ μωροῖς ("you think you are somebody—fool among fools!").[78] Another example from Lucian shows the anti–rhetorical background of the saying: σκόπει γοῦν ὁπόσοι τέως μηδὲν ὄντες ἔνδοξοι καὶ πλούσιοι καὶ νὴ Δία εὐγενέστατοι

ἔδοξαν ἀπὸ τῶν λόγων ("just look how many who previously were nobodies have come to be famous and rich, and by God, even noblemen, all from their eloquence").[79]

The contrast between what one "appears to be" and what one "really is" was a standard topic of diatribe philosophy,[80] from which the language used here comes. Paul sees in the "pneumatics" this very danger of believing oneself to be something of importance, while in reality one is "nothing." It is probably no accident that we find similar sayings at several places in 1 Corinthians (3:18; 8:2; 10:12; 14:37).[81] There is nothing wrong with being "nothing" or a "nobody," because that is what one actually is. It is wrong, however, to be deluded into thinking one is "somebody." The anthropological tradition in which Paul stands goes back to early Greek thought. Usually we find it in the diatribe tradition[82] in connection with the interpretation of the Delphic maxim "know yourself." Human beings must learn to accept that they really are "nothing."[83] Applied to 6:1, Paul tells the Galatians: if you think you are "pneumatics" but are not, you are caught up in a dangerous and preposterous illusion. The verb φρεναπατάω ("deceive") is a *hapax legomenon* in primitive Christian literature.[84] Hesychius[85] gives as a synonym χλευάζω ("scoff at somebody"), but the meaning here might not be much different from 1 Cor 3:18: μηδεὶς ἑαυτὸν ἐξαπατάτω ("let no one deceive himself"); or from Jas 1:26: ἀπατῶν καρδίαν ἑαυτοῦ

74 See for this hypothesis Davies, *Paul and Rabbinic Judaism*, esp. 69–74, 142–45, 174–76; idem, *Torah in the Messianic Age and/or the Age to Come* (SBLMS 7; Philadelphia: SBL, 1952) 91f; Bammel (see n. 70, above).

75 See Davies, *Paul and Rabbinic Judaism*, esp. 73f, 142–5; Schlier, pp. 272f.

76 See Plato *Apol.* 21B/C, 41B, E, and often.

77 *Ench.* 13; cf. also the anecdote about Socrates *Diss.* 2.8.24f; 4.6.24; *Ench.* 33.12; 48. 2–3. Cf. R. Hillel, "Do not trust yourself until the day you die" ('Abot 2.5).

78 *Diss.* 4.8.39.

79 Lucian *Rhet. praec.* 2; cf. *Merc. cond.* 16; *Dial. mort.* 12.2, and often.

80 See Teles' diatribe Περὶ τοῦ δοκεῖν καὶ τοῦ εἶναι ("About appearing and being") in *Teletis Reliquiae*, Frag. 1 (ed. Otto Hense [Tübingen: Mohr, ²1909]);

Chadwick, *Sextus*, 64. A similar saying in *Midr. Qoh.* 9.10 (42ᵇ) [see Str–B. 3.578] from the 3rd. c. A.D. could point to diatribe influence upon the rabbis.

81 The closest parallel is 1 Cor 3:18, but contrast Phil 3:4; cf. Jas 1:26.

82 See the bib. above; also Chadwick, *Sextus*, 97ff.

83 Cf. Paul's "confession" 2 Cor 12:11: οὐδέν εἰμι ("I am nothing"); for the interpretation of this doctrine, see Betz, *Paulus*, 118ff. For more references see Wettstein on Gal 6:3.

84 For later instances in Christian literature, see *PGL*, *s.v.* The noun φρεναπάτης (LSJ, *s.v*: "soul–deceiver") occurs in Titus 1:10. Cf. also Bauer, *s.v.*

85 *Lexicon* (ed. Mauricius Schmidt, vol. 3; Jena: Sumptibus Frederici Maukii, 1861) 257, no. 57.

("deceive one's own heart").[86]

■ **4** Another maxim follows, perhaps connected with v 3 by the catchword (δοκ-). The saying itself, however, is independent. It contains a warning against another form of illusion about oneself. This illusion comes about through comparing oneself with others.[87] In form the maxim is composed of two parts: (1) the maxim proper (v 4a), and (2) an explanation of the consequences of the advice and, implicitly, a reason for the formulation of the maxim itself (v 4b). The maxim v 4a τὸ δὲ ἔργον ἑαυτοῦ δοκιμαζέτω ἕκαστος . . .[88] ("each person should examine his own conduct . . .") is again based upon the Delphic maxim "know yourself" and is an application of it. Similar sayings are found in the diatribe literature.[89] Paul's maxim contains, implicitly as well as explicitly, a number of ethical doctrines which are shared by Greek philosophers and the Apostle: (1) δοκιμάζειν ("examine critically") was regarded as the foremost duty of the philosopher,[90] and now in Paul as

a duty of the Christian; (2) "self–examination" was the primary objective, and Paul approves of that too;[91] (3) one's entire "conduct of life" had to be examined, not merely one's words;[92] (4) self–examination meant scrutinizing of one's own conduct of life (τὸ ἔργον)[93] exclusively, not a comparison with others.[94] All of these ethical doctrines are common in Hellenistic philosophy. Paul approves of them here as well as elsewhere.[95] There was no need to change the language, since it could be interpreted without change by relating it to the context of Paul's theology.[96]

Verse 4b states the reason for the warning: καὶ τότε εἰς ἑαυτὸν μόνον τὸ καύχημα ἕξει καὶ οὐκ εἰς τὸν ἕτερον ("and then his reason to boast will be in regard to himself alone, and not in regard to someone else"). It is understood that the goal of self–examination is ἔχειν τὸ καύχημα, an expression which means "to be able to show an achievement as a basis for boasting."[97] The term καύχημα here refers to the "object of boasting,"

---

86   Cf. also Epicurus' phrase ταῖς κεναῖς δόξαις ἑαυτὸν ἀπατᾶν ("deceive oneself by empty opinions") 298, 29 Usener; and the term κενόδοξος ("boastful") in Gal 5:26.

87   For the *syncrisis* motif and its background, see Betz, *Paulus*, 118ff.

88   ἕκαστος is not read by P[46] B sa.

89   See the literature noted above, n. 5.

90   See Epict. *Diss.* 1.20.7; also 1.1.6; 2.12.20; 2.23.5ff; 8; 3.2.5ff; 4.5.16; 4.6.13. Chadwick, *Sextus*, 540: παίδευε σαυτόν, εἶτα τοὺς ἄλλους ("Educate yourself, then the others").

91   Cf. e.g., Epict. *Diss.* 4.7.40: σκέψαι τί μοι ποτ' ἔχεις τοῦτο καὶ πόθεν ἐλήλυθός, τὸ πᾶσιν τοῖς ἄλλοις χρώμενον, πάντα τἆλλα δοκιμάζον, ἐκλεγόμενον, ἀπεκλεγόμενον ("Consider what this thing is which you possess, and where it has come from, the thing which utilizes everything else, submits everything else to the test, selects and rejects"). The "thing" is, of course, "reason."

92   Cf. Menander *Comp.* 1.63f: Δοκίμαζε πρῶτον τὸν τρόπον κοὐ τὸν λόγον, σεμνὸς τρόπος γὰρ διαφέρει καλῶν λόγων ("First of all, examine the conduct of life, but not the speech, because a respectable conduct of life is different from elegant language"). See also the collection of references in Schenkl's edition of Epictetus, and Chadwick, *Sextus*, index, *s.v.* ἔργον.

93   Cf. Philo *Det.* 129: ἑκάστῳ γὰρ τὸ ἴδιον ἔργον ποθεινότατον ("For each one his own work is the most

important object of desire" [auth.]).

94   Cf. Epict. *Diss.* 3.2.9–18; Philo *Det.* 126ff; also Gerhard, *Phoinix*, 39f, 262, 269f.

95   Cf. the parallels in Paul: 1 Cor 11:28: δοκιμαζέτω δὲ ἄνθρωπος ἑαυτόν...("Man must critically examine himself..."); 2 Cor 13:5: ἑαυτοὺς πειράζετε, ...ἑαυτοὺς δοκιμάζετε...("Test yourselves, ...examine yourselves..."). See Bauer, *s.v.* δοκιμάζω; Betz, *Paulus*, 132ff; Gérard Therrien, *Le discernement dans les écrits pauliniens* (Paris: Gabalda, 1973) 118–25.

96   Therefore, τὸ ἔργον ("the work, activity") must not be confused with τὰ ἔργα νόμου ("the works of the law"), for which see above on Gal 2:16; 3:2, 5, 10; 5:19. Cf. also Rom 15:18; 1 Cor 3:13–15; 2 Cor 9:8; 10:11; Gal 6:10.

97   The phrase occurs also Rom 4:2; cf. 1 Cor 5:6; 9:15, 16; 2 Cor 1:14; 5:12; 9:3; Phil 1:26; 2:16. For the whole concept of "boasting" see Rudolf Bultmann, "καυχάομαι," *TDNT* 3.645–53; idem, *Theology* 1.242f, 264, 267, 281; Jorge Sanchez Bosch, *'Gloriarse' según San Pablo: Sentido y teologia de καυχάομαι* (AnBib 40; Rome: Pontifical Biblical Institute, 1970); cf. the review by Robert J. Karris, *JBL* 92 (1973) 144–46.

98   Cf. Plutarch *Aem. Paul.* 27 (270A): "...he sent the young men away with their vainglorious insolence (τὸ καύχημα) and pride (τὴν ὕβριν) well curbed by his trenchant speech, as by a bridle." See also Bauer, *s.v.* καύχημα.

that is, the achievement that entitles one to be proud.[98] Paul shares with antiquity the view that man is incessantly trying to show himself to be "somebody."[99] This "showing" was often done though comparisons with one's fellow men. Antiquity was all too aware of the dangers of self–illusion in showing contrived "achievements" which in reality were worth nothing. It was recognized that the most widespread illusions occur because of comparison of oneself with others.[100] In playing this game, one can manipulate things at will so that the comparison always turns out in favor of oneself and to the disadvantage of the person with whom one compares oneself. The philosophers, however, constantly pointed out the hypocrisy and worthlessness of this approach. They called for self–examination, in order to discover whatever "true" achievements one might have. Paul agrees with Hellenistic philosophy in that a "true" achievement is one which exists only εἰς ἑαυτόν ("with reference to oneself"),[101] i.e., not as a result of comparing oneself with others.

The New Testament here and elsewhere regards the matter to be highly important because of its implications for one's self–understanding and the resultant behavior towards one's fellowmen. The most impressive examples of this concern in the New Testament are Matt 7:3–5 and the story of the Pharisee and the publican (Luke 18:9–14), in which self–illusion is represented by the figure of the Pharisee,[102] and "true achievement," that is, the admission of the absence of any such achievement, is represented by the figure of the tax collector.[103] Paul himself has developed a complete doctrine of "boasting,"[104] and gives examples of the "right" boasting, e.g., in 1 Cor 15:10: χάριτι θεοῦ εἰμι ὅ εἰμι ("by God's grace I am what I am").[105] Paul is in agreement with Hellenistic philosophy when he does not reject boasting as such, but asks what the basis for that boasting is. Of course, he goes his own way when it comes to the definition of the καύχημα ("object [basis] of boasting"); for him it is divine grace, and not reason, as it is for the philosophers.

■ 5 Another maxim is added: ἕκαστος γὰρ τὸ ἴδιον φορτίον βαστάσει ("for everybody will [or: must] bear his own load"). It is unclear if there is any connection between v 5 and v 4, and if so, what the connection is. Some commentators take γάρ ("for") to indicate that v 5 is supposed to provide a reason for v 4.[106] But the conjunction could also be taken as simply marking the addition of a similar statement.[107] The form of the maxim presupposes that it can stand on its own, and sometimes γάρ ("for") occurs in such maxims without any connection to a context.

Among the similar maxims in the diatribe literature,[108] one of the most interesting comes from Epictetus, even though the form is different from that of Paul's maxim: οὕτως οὐδὲ τὴν τοῦ ἀνθρώπου ἐπαγγελίαν πληρῶσαι δυνάμενοι προσλαμβάνομεν τὴν τοῦ φιλοσόφου, τηλικοῦτο φορτίον, οἷον εἴ τις δέκα λίτρας ἆραι μὴ δυνάμενος τὸν τοῦ Αἴαντος λίθον βαστάζειν ἤθελεν ("so, al-

---

99   Cf. Gal 6:3.

100 See on this point Betz, *Paulus*, 118ff.

101 This expression is unique in Paul; cf. καυχάομαι with εἰς ("boast with regard to") 2 Cor 10:13, 15, 16; see also 13:3; Bauer, *s.v.* καυχάομαι 1; Moule, *Idiom Book*, 70. Cf. also the title of Marcus Aurelius' *ΕΙΣ ΕΑΥΤΟΝ*.

102 Cf. Luke 18:11: ὁ θεός, εὐχαριστῶ σοι ὅτι οὐκ εἰμὶ ὥσπερ οἱ λοιποὶ τῶν ἀνθρώπων…ἢ καὶ ὡς οὗτος ὁ τελώνης ("I thank you, God, that I am not like the rest of mankind, nor even like this tax collector"); also Luke 15:29–32.

103 Note that the comparison is lacking in Luke 18:13.

104 See also 1 Cor 3:21; 2 Cor 11:18; 12:1–10. On the subject see Bultmann, "καυχάομαι," *TDNT* 3.648–52.

105 Paul's rule is set forth 1 Cor 1:31; 2 Cor 10:17; Gal 6:14. It is applied esp. in Rom 8:31–39. For the false kind of boasting, see Rom 2:1ff; 1 Cor 4:6–8.

See also Philipp Haeuser ("Jeder prüfe sein Werk, und er wird alsdann Ruhm nur für sich haben [Gal 6:4]," *BZ* 12 [1914] 45–56), who interprets this passage in accordance with 2 Cor 12:9f; Rom 5:3ff.

106 So Schlier, following many others.

107 For this meaning of γάρ, see Bauer, *s.v.*, I, c, 4.

108 Cf., esp., Teles' diatribe Περὶ αὐταρκείας (ed. Hense, 10 line 7, cf. p. *XXIII*f.): ἀσθενὴς πάλιν· μὴ ζήτει τὰ τοῦ ἰσχυροῦ [φορτία βαστάζειν καὶ διατραχηλίζεσθαι] ("again a weak person: do not seek to carry the loads of the strong person [and put your neck under a yoke]"). Menander *Sent.* 459, 660; *Comp.* 1.312; *Pap.* 1.36, 18.3.9; Antiphanes Comic., Frag. 329 (ed. John M. Edmonds, *The Fragments of Attic Comedy* 2 [Leiden: Brill, 1959] 308); Anaxandrides Comic., Frag. 53 (ed. Edmonds, ibidem, 74); Secundus *Sent.* 9 (ed. Friedrich W. A. Mullach, *Fragmenta Philosophorum Graecorum* [Paris: Didot, 1860] 1.513); Chadwick, *Sextus*, 335.

though we are unable even to fulfill the profession of man, we take on the additional profession of the philosopher—so huge a burden! It is as though a man who was unable to raise ten pounds wanted to lift the stone of Aias").[109] In the gnomic literature the phrase τὸ φορτίον βαστάζειν ("bear the load") plays a significant role and can refer to a variety of different matters, such as the general difficulties of daily life,[110] or specific burdens like old age,[111] wife,[112] or poverty.[113] It is the mark of the fool to take on too big a load, whereas the wise man takes on no more than he is able to handle.[114] The ideal is αὐτάρκεια ("self-sufficiency"),[115] i.e., the ability to "carry one's own load." While the philosopher is made self-sufficient by philosophy,[116] the Christian, according to Paul's theology, is made self-sufficient through the Christian faith and the guidance of the Spirit (5:25).

There can be no doubt that Paul's maxim must be interpreted from within the context of gnomic literature.[117] In these terms, "the load"[118] would refer to the daily struggle of life and is little different from βάρος ("burden") in Gal 6:2.[119] The future tense is gnomic ("one must bear"),[120] not eschatological.[121] It does not point to the final judgment, but to the inevitable pressures of life: everybody has his load to bear, and he had better learn to bear it. The relief comes when one realizes that he must bear only one burden, his own.[122] By this Paul means that one should avoid taking on more than one can handle. There is no contradiction between this statement and that in 6:2, because "sharing the burdens of life" does not eliminate the fact that everybody must learn how to live with himself. A comparison with Phil 4:11–13 confirms that Paul shared this Hellenistic concept of "self-sufficiency."[123]

■ 6 The final maxim is certainly one of the most puzzling in the whole letter: κοινωνείτω δὲ ὁ κατηχούμενος τὸν λόγον τῷ κατηχοῦντι ἐν πᾶσιν ἀγαθοῖς (RSV: "let him who is taught the word share all good things with him who teaches"). The δέ ("but") provides a loose connection with the preceding, simply indicating that this saying follows v 5. The meaning of the saying must, therefore, be established first on its own terms. Opinions of commentators can be divided into two groups: those who take the statement as a recommendation to the student to share his material goods of life with his teacher,[124] and those who take it in a broader sense as including both "material" and "spiritual" goods.[125]

First of all, however, the form, the present function, and the background of the saying must be investigated. In regard to its form, the saying is another maxim

109 Epict. *Diss.* 2.9.22.

110 Cf. Epict. *Diss.* 4.13.16, where it is identical with the περιστάσεις ("crisis situations of life"); similarly Plutarch *De exilio* 599 CD.

111 There is a genre of sayings which defines what one should regard as the greatest burdens of all. On old age as the greatest burden, see the frag. from Anaxandrides (above, n. 108).

112 See again Anaxandrides (above, n. 108); also Menander *Sent.* 459: μεστὸν κακῶν πέφυκε φορτίον γυνή ("A woman is a load full of evils").

113 So Menander *Sent.* 660: πενίας βαρύτερον οὐδέν ἐστι φορτίον ("There is no heavier load than poverty").

114 Cf. Antiphanes Comic., Frag. 3 (ed. Edmonds, 2.164); Demosthenes *Or.* 11.14; Teles, 9f (ed. Hense); Epict. *Ench.* 43.

115 Cf. Teles, 3ff. (ed. Hense); also the anonymous Pythagorean in Stobaeus *Ecl.* 85.15 (5, p. 681, ed. Wachsmuth–Hense).

116 Diog. L. 7.170 tells that Cleanthes was called "the ass" by his fellow students because he alone was considered to "carry the load of Zeno" (βαστάζειν τὸ Ζήνωνος φορτίον). Cf. also Menander *Pap.* 18.3.9 (ed. Jaekel, 23).

117 For Rabbinic parallels, see '*Abot* 1.10, 2.2. Cf. Lietzmann, *ad loc.*, who (following Cramer), suggests a "proverbial" background.

118 Originally, φορτίον is a diminutive form; in Paul it occurs only here. For the metaphor see also Matt 11:30; 23:4; Luke 11:46; *Herm. Sim.* 9.2.4, cf. above n. 110. See LSJ, *s.v.*; Bauer, *s.v.*; Konrad Weiss, "φορτίον," *TDNT* 9.84–86.

119 So correctly Schlier; differently Mussner, p. 401: "the burden of one's own sins."

120 So correctly Burton, p. 334; Sieffert, p. 337.

121 Contra Schlier; Oepke; Mussner, pp. 401f; see also the list in Sieffert, p. 337.

122 Cf. Rom 14:5, 12; 1 Cor 3:8b; 7:7b; 1 Thess 4:11.

123 On αὐτάρκεια ("self-sufficiency") see Joachim Gnilka, *Der Philipperbrief* (Freiburg: Herder, 1969) 174–6; Paul Wilpert, "Autarkie," *RAC* 1.1039–50.

124 So Theodore of Mopsuestia, Theodoret, Chrysostom, Ambrosiaster, Jerome, Lightfoot, Bousset, Loisy, Lietzmann, Lagrange, Kuss, Hauck ("κοινωνός, κοινωνικός, κοινόω," *TDNT* 3.808–09), Lyonnet, Schlier, Mussner.

125 So Meyer, Lipsius, Sieffert, Burton (pp. 338f, covering both), Oepke (pp. 150–2).

stated as an imperative; its function, like that of the other sayings, is parenetical. Again, the content is not specifically Christian, but can be understood on the basis of its parallels in Hellenistic diatribe literature. The Christian meaning, therefore, is secondary and must be concluded on the basis of the present context.

The maxim assumes some form of association of students and teachers "in all good things." Most probably this recommendation is a variation and adaptation of Pythagoras' πάντα κοινὰ τῶν φίλων ("friends share everything in common").[126] This doctrine had an enormous influence upon the philosophical schools in antiquity.[127] The Pythagorean sect, at least for a time, practiced "common property." By the time of Paul, "communal living" was a widely held ideal. Various movements, among them Judaism[128] and Christianity,[129] claimed to have realized it. The ideal also became associated with the ideal of friendship[130] as well as with the student–teacher relationships of the philo-sophical schools.[131] Attempts to institute communal living are reported to have been made in the Academy of Plato, the Peripatos, and Epicurus' "Garden." Most interestingly, the Hippocratic "Covenant" includes this provision: ἡγήσασθαί τε τὸν διδάξαντά με τὴν τέχνην ταύτην ἴσα γενέτῃσιν ἐμοῖσιν καὶ βίου κοινώσασθαι καὶ χρεῶν χρηίζοντι μετάδοσιν ποιήσασθαι ... ("to hold him who has taught me this art as equal to my parents and to live my life in partnership with him, and if he is in need of money to give him a share of mine...").[132] The Cynic–Stoic diatribe also handed down the tradition,[133] and the gnomic literature contains sayings similar to Paul's, e.g. Menander.[134] Finally, it seems to have been a convention of letter writing to mention one's teacher with praise,[135] to recommend someone as teacher, or to request or arrange for the support of an educator.[136]

Given this background, Paul's maxim may indicate some kind of educational institution as part of the life

---

126 See above on Gal 4:12ff; 6:2; furthermore 2:10; Rom 12:3; 15:27.

127 See Kurt von Fritz, "Pythagoras," PW 24 (1963) 220f; also Friedrich Hauck, "κοινός," TDNT 3.791–96; Gustav Stählin, "φίλος κτλ.," TDNT 9.151–54.

128 Cf. Sententiae Aesopi-Achiqari 109 (ed. Denis, Fragmenta [see above, n. 7], 138 lines 7–8): τὸν κατηγητήν σου τίμα ἴσα γονεῦσι· τούτους γὰρ εὖ ποιεῖν χρὴ διὰ τὴν φύσιν, τῷ δὲ ἐκ προαιρέσεως στέρξαντι διπλασίους δεῖ ἀποδιδόναι χάριτας ("Honor your teacher like your parents; for one must treat the latter kindly because of nature, but to him who has shown affection by choice one must return double thanks"). See also the description of the "Essenes" by Philo, Josephus, and Pliny. For references and bib., see Braun, Radikalismus 1.77–80; cf. Hengel, Judaism and Hellenism 1.245f. Cf. 'Abot 1.6, 6.3.

129 Acts 2:44; 4:32. Cf. Sextus Sent. 227; and Chadwick's n., p. 172.

130 See Eurip. Andr. 376f.; Xenoph. Mem. 2.6, 22, 23. On the subject, see Bohnenblust, Beiträge, 41f; Stählin, "φίλος κτλ.," 151–52 (n. 127 above).

131 See Erich Ziebarth, Das griechische Vereinswesen (Preisschriften herausgegeben von der Fürstlich Jablonowski'schen Gesellschaft zu Leipzig 34; Leipzig: Hirzel, 1896) 69ff.

132 Text and tr. Ludwig Edelstein, The Hippocratic Oath: Text, Translation and Interpretation (Supplements to the Bulletin of the History of Medicine, No. 1; Baltimore: Johns Hopkins, 1943). Edelstein has shown convincingly that the "Oath" is strongly influenced by Pythagoreanism. Walter Burkert Lore and Science in Ancient Pythagoreanism [Cambridge: Harvard University, 1972] 179f) refers to the common practices in the mystery cults. The parallel of the "Oath" is mentioned by Oepke.

133 See, e.g., Bion in Diog. L. 4.53; Diogenes in Diog. L. 6.37, 72; Musonius, Frag. 13a (p. 67, ed. Hense); Sextus Sent. 226, 378, 382; Pyth. Sent. 70 (ed. Chadwick).

134 Menander Comp. 1.85; cf. 2.173; Sent. 534 (cited above, on Gal 6:2). Cf. also Epicurus in Gnomologium Vaticanum Epicureum (ed. Peter von der Mühll, Epicurus [BT], nos. 34, 39, 67).

135 See Peter (Brief, 12), who mentions Pliny Ep. 2.18, 3.3, 4.13.

136 Most interesting is Pliny Ep. 4.13, a request to organize a school in Pliny's native town: "Surely it is a matter of great importance to you fathers...that your children should study here on the spot?... If you put your money together, what would it cost you to engage teachers? And you could add to their salaries what you now spend on lodgings, travelling expenses, and all the things which cost money far from home...." See also the letter by the priest Philosarapis to his former teacher Apion, asking him whether he needs anything from home and promising to supply it (POxy. 1664, from the 3rd cent. A.D.).

of the Galatian churches. We do not know how many teachers they employed because Paul uses the exemplaric singular. The "teacher" was called ὁ κατηχοῦν,[137] the "student" ὁ κατηχούμενος, terms familiar to us from later Christian literature.[138] The subject taught is called ὁ λόγος ("the Word"),[139] that is, in this context, the Christian "message." If this is assumed, Paul is speaking of the education of adult Christians, rather than that of children. To say more is only speculation. There is nothing to suggest that the Galatians have any *concrete* problems in regard to the support of their teachers.[140] It is not an oblique appeal of Paul on his own behalf, nor a complaint that the Galatians have not responded well enough to his financial campaign for Jerusalem.[141] As the general maxim would suggest, Paul advises the Galatians to continue what they have been doing. Most likely, the phrase "in all good things" points to the material necessities of life,[142] but taken in a general sense.[143] Although this reference to the sup-

port of teachers is unique in Paul, it is an epistolary convention, a fact which does not exclude its agreement with the principles of Christian living.[144]

■ **7** The section vv 7–9 contains an eschatological warning and is introduced by μὴ πλανᾶσθε ("do not be deceived").[145] This phrase is known to us from elsewhere in the Pauline letters[146] and from the Cynic–Stoic diatribe literature.[147] The reason for the warning is expressed in what appears to be a "proverb":[148] θεὸς οὐ μυκτηρίζεται ("God is not to be treated with contempt").[149] The extremely concise form of the sentence[150] together with its content suggest a proverb. The term μυκτηρίζω ("treat with contempt") has an interesting background in Greek literature: μυκτηρισμός ("mockery") is a rhetorical device for expressing utter contempt for someone;[151] it belongs together with "irony"[152] but is basically "cynical." It can also be associated with χλευάζω, a rude form of scolding

---

137 They are identical with οἱ διδάσκαλοι ("the teachers") 1 Cor 12:28, 29; cf. Eph 4:11; etc.

138 Cf. Rom 2:18; 1 Cor 14:19; Luke 1:4; Acts 18:25; 21:21, 24; *2 Clem.* 17.1. See Hermann Wolfgang Beyer, "κατηχέω," *TDNT* 3.638–40; Bauer, *s.v.*

139 The use of the term without any further definition is rare in Paul (only here and 1 Thess 1:6), but more common in later NT texts (e.g., Col 4:3; 2 Tim 4:2; see the passages in Bauer, *s.v.* 1, b, β).

140 Cf. Lütgert (*Gesetz und Geist*, 20f), Schmithals (pp. 41f), Schlier, who assume that the Galatian "pneumatics" regarded themselves "free" from such obligations.

141 Other commentators, e.g. Lightfoot, Borse (*Standort*, 37f), Mussner, take this position.

142 See the usage of the term τὰ ἀγαθά ("the good things") in Luke 1:53; 12:18f. Cf. Bauer, *s.v.* ἀγαθός 2, b, β.

143 Cf. Xenophon *Mem.* 2.6.22f.; Diog. L. 6.37, 72.

144 Cf. Rom 12:13; 15:27; 1 Cor 9:11; 2 Cor 9:12–14; Phil 4:15–17; *Did.* 4.8; *Barn.* 19.8. See furthermore Oepke, pp. 150f.; Friedrich Hauck, "κοινωνός, κοινωνικός, κοινόω," *TDNT* 3.807–08.

145 Cf. *NEB*: "Make no mistake about this." Marcion's text omits the negation, but the phrase is common.

146 1 Cor 6:9; 15:33; cf. also Jas 1:16; Luke 21:8; Ign. *Eph.* 16.1; Ign. *Mag.* 8.1; Ign. *Phld.* 3.3.

147 See the references in Herbert Braun, *TDNT* 6, *s.v.* πλανάω κτλ., 228f, 242f; idem, *Qumran* 1.191; Bauer, *s.v.* 2, c, γ; differently Mussner, p. 404.

148 See Lightfoot's note *ad loc.*; Burton (p. 341) notes

the gnomic present; Schlier recognizes the "proverbial" character, pointing to 1 Cor 15:33 as a parallel. The proverb is also quoted in Pol. *Phil.* 5.1 (from Gal 6:7?); it does not seem to be attested elsewhere. Cf. Gerhard, *Phoinix*, 78–85; Chadwick, *Sextus*, 186, 224, 325; *PECL*, 143, 215.

149 Literally: "turn up the nose." Bauer, *s.v.*, renders: "he is not to be mocked, treated with contempt, perhaps outwitted." The term is found only here in the NT, but cf. ἐκμυκτηρίζω (Bauer: "ridicule, sneer") in Luke 16:14; 23:35, which provide vivid descriptions of what the term means; furthermore, Rom 2:2ff.

150 θεός ("God") is anarthrous, cf. BDF, § 254, 1; BDR, § 254.

151 Lucian (*Prom. es in verb.* 1) mentions the "attic sneer" of the intellectual snob of the day. See also Longinus *De subl.* 34.2; Plutarch *Adulat.* 57A; *Herod. malig.* 860E; Athenaeus 5.182A, 187B; Quint. 8.6.59. One of the funny names for Socrates was μυκτὴρ ῥητόμυκτος ("sneerer, nose–blowing like the rhetoricians"): Timon Phlisius, Frag. 25 (ed. Hermann Diels, *Poetarum philosophorum fragmenta* [*Poetarum graecorum fragmenta* 3.1; Berlin: Weidmann, 1901] 190). See also Herbert Preisker, "μυκτηρίζω," *TDNT* 4.796; Georg Bertram, "ἐκμυκτηρίζω," *TDNT* 4.796–99; LSJ, *s.v.*; PGL, *s.v.*

152 See Lausberg, *Handbuch*, § 583; also index, *s.v.* "ironia."

("scoffing").[153] Jewish literature adopted the form, usually with a negative tone, chiefly in order to describe the figure of the "godless" and the enemy of the Israelites.[154]

Paul must have received the "proverb" from the Hellenistic–Jewish tradition, within which he stood; but there is no reason why the "proverb" could not have been common in the Hellenistic world. The fact that it is not widely attested could be accidental.[155] The idea of God expressed in the "proverb" was common in antiquity; he was thought of as the inescapable and dangerous deity who relentlessly destroys those who rebel against him. Any cynical attempt to reject his redemption in Christ will bring down God's wrath upon the rebels. This is true even for the "pneumatics," and God would deal with them as if they had never

been part of his love.

Verse 7b, which serves as a reason for v 7a, is also proverbial: ὃ γὰρ ἐὰν σπείρῃ ἄνθρωπος, τοῦτο καὶ θερίσει ("for whatever man sows, that he will also reap").[156] The metaphors of sowing and harvesting are common in all ancient literature.[157] The same can be said of the idea of divine retribution, whether it is understood in the sense of immanent life experience or of eschatological judgment.[158] In Gal 6:7 Paul thinks, of course, of the divine retribution at the Last Judgment,[159] where "man" [= "everyone"] (ἄνθρωπος)[160] will have to appear, in order to be judged according to his deeds.[161] The correspondence of "sowing" and "harvesting" implies that Paul approves of the eschatological law of reciprocity (ius talionis)[162] even for the

---

153 Hesychius *Lex.* no. 1841 (ed. Latte); cf. Pollux, *Onomasticon* (ed. Erich Bethe; Lexicographi Graeci 9; Leipzig: Teubner, 1900) 2.78.

154 See esp. LXX Prov 1:30 (quoted *1 Clem.* 57.5); 11:12; 12:8; 15:5, 20; 23:9; 1 Kgs 18:27; 2 Kgs 19:21; 2 Chr 36:16; LXX 1 Esdr 1:49; Job 22:19; Ps 44:13 (43:14 LXX); 80:6 (79:7 LXX); Isa 37:22; Jer 20:7; Ezek 8:17; 1 Macc 7:34; *Orac. Syb.* 1.171; *Ps. Sol.* 4.8 (7); *T. Jos* 2.3; '*Abot* 2.1. On the subject of ridiculing the gods, see the extensive study by Preuss (see above on 4:8, n. 9). Cf. also the definition of true piety (εὐσέβεια) in *Ep. Arist.* 210.

155 Cf. *1 Clem.* 39.1 (diatribe style); *Prot. Jas.* 3.1.

156 P⁴⁶ reads the objects in the plural: ἃ and ταῦτα.

157 See the material collected by Lightfoot; Friedrich Hauck, "θερίζω, θερισμός," *TDNT* 3.132–33; Siegfried Schulz and Gottfried Quell, "σπέρμα κτλ.," *TDNT* 7.536–47; Victor Pöschl (ed.), *Bibliographie zur antiken Bildersprache* (Heidelberg: Winter, 1964) *s.v.* "Säen und Ernten;" Harald Riesenfeld, *The Gospel Tradition* (Oxford: Blackwell, 1970) 194f; *PECL*, 76f, 90.

158 The eschatological understanding is found both in Judaism and in Plutarch. See Str–B 3.578; *PECL*, 76f.

159 See esp. '*Abot* 1.7: "Be not doubtful of retribution;" 4 Ezra 4:28ff; *2 Bar.* 70.2ff; *Midr. Cant.* 8.14; in the NT: Matt 3:12; Luke 3:15; Matt 13:30, 39; John 4:36–38; Rev 14:15ff; cf. Jas 5:7. For a different meaning, cf. 1 Cor 9:11; 2 Cor 9:6.

160 For this use of the term, see Gal 1:1, 10, 11, 12; 2:6, 16; 3:15; 5:3; 6:1. Without the article, the term means almost "one"; see Bauer, *s.v.*, 3, a, γ;

PECL, 18.

161 See, esp., Rom 14:10; 1 Cor 3:12–17; 4:4; 6:9ff; 9:24–27; 2 Cor 5:10; 11:15; Phil 2:12. Cf. 2 Cor 7:1 (cf. on this Betz, "2 Cor 6:14–7:1," 98f); Jas 1:12–16.

162 See on this subject Klaus Koch, "Gibt es ein Vergeltungsdogma im Alten Testament?" *ZThK* 52 (1955) 1–42; and the material and discussion in Wolfgang Harnisch, *Verhängnis und Verheissung der Geschichte* (FRLANT 97; Göttingen: Vandenhoeck & Ruprecht, 1969) 198–210; Daube, *NT and Rabbinic Judaism*, 255–59.

Galatian "pneumatics".[163] This implies, furthermore, that the gift of the Spirit is not thought of in terms of deification, which would lift the Galatians above the law, but as an enabling power which makes them fulfill the divine law (cf. 5:14, 22–23; 6:2). If the Christian is not accepted by God at the Last Judgment, the reason must be that he has forfeited his salvation in Christ (cf. 5:19–23; also 1:8–9; 6:16, etc.).

■ 8 Paul adds his own interpretation to v 7, thus explaining in terms of his own theology how his eschatological warning in 6:7–10 is motivated.[164] He uses the metaphors of "sowing" and "harvesting" which he had introduced in v 7b and interprets them in terms of the dualism of σάρξ–πνεῦμα ("flesh"–"spirit"). This dualism, stated in 5:17, underlies the entire theology of Galatians. The result is formulated as an eschatological "rule,"[165] in a two-line antithetical, chiastic[166] parallelism:

ὁ σπείρων εἰς τὴν σάρκα ἑαυτοῦ ἐκ τῆς σαρκὸς θερίσει
    φθοράν,
ὁ δὲ σπείρων εἰς τὸ πνεῦμα ἐκ τοῦ πνεύματος θερίσει
    ζωὴν αἰώνιον

("he who sows into his flesh, from the flesh will reap corruption;
he, however, who sows into the Spirit, from the Spirit will reap life eternal").

The metaphors are now taken as an allegory:[167] the sower sows "into his flesh" or "into the Spirit" as if they were fields,[168] and he harvests "from the flesh" or "from the Spirit,"[169] a harvest which is either eternal "corruption" or "eternal life." While the association of πνεῦμα ("divine Spirit") and eternal life is familiar from other passages in Galatians,[170] the association of σάρξ ("flesh") with φθορά ("corruption") is a new idea.

Previously Paul had associated "flesh" with circumcision[171] and "the works of the flesh,"[172] but in 6:8 he goes further. "Sowing into the flesh" is done by placing one's hope for salvation upon circumcision and obedience to the Jewish Torah, a move which would result in missing salvation altogether (cf. 5:2–12). But the same harvest can be reaped by letting the "works of the flesh" flourish (cf. 5:19–21). A life thus corrupted by the "flesh" cannot "inherit the Kingdom of God" (5:21). In this sense, "sowing into the flesh" means nothing less than "giving an opportunity to the flesh" (5:13), and the very opposite of "crucifying the flesh" (5:24).

163 Paul takes over the traditional Jewish parenesis (cf. the eschatological parenesis at the end of 'Abot 1–4 in 4.29). However, the purpose is not to motivate "works of the Torah," but to "follow the Spirit" (5:25). On the problem of Paul's integration of this Jewish parenesis, see Herbert Braun, *Gerichtsgedanke und Rechtfertigungslehre bei Paulus* (UNT 19; Leipzig: Hinrichs, 1930); Lorenz Nieder, *Die Motive der religiös-sittlichen Paränese in den paulinischen Gemeindebriefen* (MThS 1.12; Munich: 1956); Henry M. Shires, *The Eschatology of Paul in the Light of Modern Scholarship* (Philadelphia: Westminster, 1966); Lieselotte Mattern, *Das Verständnis des Gerichtes bei Paulus* (AThANT 47; Zurich and Stuttgart: Zwingli, 1966); Anton Grabner–Haider, *Paraklese und Eschatologie bei Paulus* (NTAbh NF 4; Münster: Aschendorff, 1968); Franz Laub, *Eschatologische Verkündigung und Lebensgestaltung nach Paulus* (BibU 10; Regensburg: Pustet, 1973) esp. 63–66. It should be noted, however, that divine retribution was used also by pagans to encourage morality; see Chadwick, *Sextus*, 14 and n., p. 163; ps.–Phocylides, 229–30 (ed. Denis, *Fragm. pseudepigr. gr.*, 156); Gerhard, *Phoinix*, 19f, 78–103.

164 The ὅτι is causal (cf. Bauer, *s.v.* 3) or declarative (cf. Mussner).

165 See the parallels in Rom 6:20–23; 8:6, 13; Eph 4:22–24.

166 See for this figure of speech BDF, § 477, 2; BDR, § 477, 2.

167 On "allegory" see above, on 4:24.

168 Cf. Mark 4:13–20; Matt 13:18–23; Luke 8:4–15; *Herm. Sim.* 9.20.1; *Odes Sol.* 11.1, 18–24; 38.16–21.

169 For the use of the preposition ἐκ ("from") see Gal 2:16; 3:2, 5, 7, 8, 9, 10, 11, 12, 18, 21, 22, 24; 5:5; cf. 1:4; 3:13.

170 See esp. 5:25, but also, without the term πνεῦμα ("Spirit"), 2:19, 20; 3:11 (cf. 12, 21). The concept of ζωὴ αἰώνιος ("eternal life") occurs only here in Gal; see also Rom 2:7; 5:21; 6:22f. On the concept, see Rudolf Bultmann, "ζάω, ἀναζάω, ζῷον, ζωογονέω, ζωοποιέω," *TDNT* 2.832–75; Bauer, *s.v.* ζωή, 2, b, β, with further bib.

171 See Gal 3:3; also 6:12f.

172 See Gal 5:13, 16f, 19–21, 24; also Brandenburger, *Fleisch und Geist*, 45.

In either case, the end will be φθορά ("eternal annihilation").[173]

■ 9 Paul concludes the eschatological warning (6:7–9) with an "appeal." It has two parts: (1) the appeal in the precise sense of the word (v 9a), and (2) an eschatological promise to undergird it (v 9b).

The appeal (v 9a) presupposes the previous discussion (vv 7–8), as is indicated by δέ ("then"): τὸ δὲ καλὸν ποιοῦντες μὴ ἐγκακῶμεν ("let us, then, not become tired of doing what is good"). The phrase τὸ καλὸν ποιεῖν ("do the good") includes everything the Christian is responsible for doing. Thus, it is identical with the concepts of the "fruit of the Spirit" (5:22–23) and of "following the Spirit" (5:25; cf. 5:16). The language comes from Hellenistic philosophy,[174] so that τὸ καλόν and τὸ ἀγαθόν[175] mean the same thing ("the good"). This and the following verse are the only places in Galatians where we are told that the "good" must be "done"; elsewhere "doing" is associated with "the works of the Law."[176] But "doing the good" is different from "doing the works of the Law" in that the former amounts to a participation in the "fruit of the Spirit." Paul assumes that at the moment the Galatians are in fact doing the good.[177] The problem is, however, that they are in danger of getting tired of it. The Apostle does not supply any specific reasons for this "weariness," but the term is familiar, especially from apocalyptic texts,[178] and points to the cardinal problem of all enthusiasts: time. As time goes on, enthusiasm fades away, boredom sets in, and in this situation "the flesh" gets its chance (cf. 5:13).

The promise in v 9b undergirds the appeal in v 9a: καιρῷ γὰρ ἰδίῳ θερίσομεν μὴ ἐκλυόμενοι ("for in due season we shall reap, if we do not give out"). Again, the metaphor of θερίζω ("harvest") is employed to describe the eschatological reward.[179] The phrase καιρῷ ἰδίῳ ("in due season") points to the eschatological crisis.[180] The condition for this eschatological reward is that "we do not give out" (ἐκλύομαι)—clearly an eschatological topos.[181] Compared with the term ἐγκακέω ("become tired") in v 9a, ἐκλύομαι ("give out") seems the stronger. It sums up what Paul regards

---

173 This eschatological concept is found only here in Gal, but see Rom 8:21; 1 Cor 15:42, 50; 2 Pet 1:4; 2:12, 19; also 1 Cor 3:17. See Bauer, s.v.; Günter Harder, "φθείρω κτλ.," TDNT 9.93–106; PECL, 63, 97, 150, 270.

174 It occurs also in Gal 4:18. For the whole phrase τὸ καλὸν ποιεῖν ("do the good") see Rom 7:21; 2 Cor 13:7; furthermore, Walter Grundmann, "καλός," TDNT 3.536–50; Bauer, s.v. καλός, 2, b; cf. Corp. Herm. 13.15.

175 See Gal 6:10.

176 See Gal 3:10, 12; 5:3; cf. also 5:17, 21. In the positive sense, the term is used only in 2:10, while on the whole Paul seems to avoid it (cf. 5:13f, 23; 6:2). See Herbert Braun, "ποιέω κτλ.," TDNT 6.480–81.

177 Cf. Gal 5:7a.

178 See the parallel in 2 Thess 3:13, and the parenesis in Eph 3:13; Luke 18:1; Rev 2:3; 2 Clem. 2.2; Herm. Man. 9.8; Resch, Agrapha, 138 (no. 96); furthermore, 2 Cor 4:1, 16. See Walter Grundmann, "καλός," TDNT 3.486; Bauer, s.v. Bauer also discusses the variant reading ἐκκακῶμεν (read by C 𝔐 (G), pl), s.v. ἐκκακέω; it seems more common, occurring in Symmachus' LXX (cf. Hatch–Redpath, s.v.); T. Job 24; Menander Comp. 1.42.

179 Cf. Gal 6:7b, 8.

180 For this eschatological topos see 1 Thess 5:1; 1 Cor 4:5; 7:29; Mark 13:33; Matt 16:3; Luke 21:8;

Eph 1:10; 1 Pet 5:6; Rev 1:3; 22:10; Did. 16.2, etc. It should be noted, however, that καιρῷ ἰδίῳ ("in due season") can be interpreted also in a thisworldly way, as in Sententiae Aesopi-Achiqari 110 (ed. Denis, Fragm. pseudepigr. gr., 139 lines 8–11). See Bauer, s.v. καιρός, 4; Gerhard Delling, "καιρός," TDNT 3.455–62; Erich Grässer, Das Problem der Parusieverzögerung in den synoptischen Evangelien und in der Apostelgeschichte (Berlin: Töpelmann, 1957) 84ff.

181 Paul uses the concept only here, but cf. Mark 8:3 // Matt 15:32; Heb 12:3, 5 (v 5b = Prov 3:11); Did. 16.1 (at the beginning of the eschatological parenesis!). See Bauer, s.v. ἐκλύω. See the gnostic prayer for perseverance in NHC VI.6, pp. 64–65; PGM 3. 607–10; Asclepius 41 (eds. Nock and Festugière 2.353–55; with nn. 356, 357). In Hellenistic diatribe literature, the concept appears in an ethical context: cf. Epict. Diss. 2.18.13 (of anger); 2.19.20 of "philosophers without backbone"; Lucian Nigr. 36; similarly Philo Sacr. 81; Det. 167, 168; Cher. 82; differently Virt. 88; also Plutarch Non posse 1099A. Cf. also Jas 5:7–11; and the Rabbinical warnings in 'Abot 2.5: "Hillel said: '...say not when I am at leisure I will study—perchance thou wilt not be at leisure'." 'Abot 2.19: R. Eleazar: "The work is not upon thee to finish, nor art thou free to desist from it."

as the ethical task: to *maintain* the life of freedom in Christ. Such freedom was made possible by the gift and the "fruit of the Spirit" (see on 5:22–23), and is to be practiced by "following the Spirit" as recommended in the maxims (5:25–6:6). If the Christian tires of this "life for God" (2:19) and if he slackens in his ethical responsibilities, the "works of the flesh" will break through again and destroy the Christian's existence in freedom, thereby destroying his salvation. Therefore, *maintaining* that freedom is the condition for reaching the fulfillment of salvation in the hereafter (cf. 5:1, 13).

At this point the question must be raised whether there is a real difference between reaching salvation through "doing the works of the Law" and reaching salvation by maintaining the Christian existence "through doing the good." There is no difference, as far as the eschatological reckoning is concerned: man is responsible for fulfilling the will of God, i.e., the Torah. Without such fulfillment there can be no salvation. The question is, however, how is man able to fulfill God's will? According to Paul, man cannot do it by scrupulously observing the prohibitions and prescriptions of the Jewish Torah. It is this "doing of the works of the Law" which leads man to eternal death.[182] The Christian, on the other hand, is enabled by God's grace, through Christ's sacrificial death on the cross and his resurrection, through the gift of the Spirit and the "fruit of the Spirit," to fulfill the Law. This is accomplished by letting the "fruit of the Spirit" fill out the life of the Christian community so that, although

being in the "flesh," the individual Christian "lives for God."[183]

However, the gift of the Spirit does not mean that the Christian is brought to a kind of "new Christian legalism," in which new "works of the Law" replace the old Jewish demands.[184] The Christian is asked, in this passage, to not let himself get bored with and tired of the "good" as it happens around him, with him, and to him. He is asked to welcome it, further it, and participate in it. If he does this, he also "does the good," and in this way fulfills the Torah (cf. 5:14, 23b; 6:2).

■ **10** This sentence summarizes and concludes the parenetical section (5:1–6:10); it also concludes the letter, except for the handwritten postscript (6:11–18). As the conclusion[185] to the parenetical section, the statement sums up in a general way, and in the form of a final appeal, what the Apostle regards as the ethical task of the Christian community. Hence, it serves also as a definition of Christian ethics.

The appeal itself is prefaced by a temporal clause: ὡς καιρὸν ἔχομεν ("as we have time," i.e. opportunity).[186] The clause means that in Paul's view the Christian's ethical responsibility is limited[187] to the time in which he lives ἐν σαρκί ("in the flesh").[188] The point is that only while being "in the flesh" is the Christian in danger that "the works of the flesh" might again regain their power over him. The limitation, therefore, is not motivated by the relativity of ethical values or by the impending apocalyptic end of the world, but by the anthropological potency of "the flesh." Christian

---

182 See above, on Gal 2:15–21; 3:10–14; 21.

183 See above, on Gal 2:19f; 3:11; 5:25; 6:8.

184 The Galatian opponents of Paul regarded rigid obedience to the Jewish Torah as a prerequisite for salvation through Christ. Cf. 2 Cor 6:14–7:1, and Betz's interpretation in "2 Cor 6:14–7:1," 88–108.

185 The conclusion is introduced by ἄρα οὖν ("consequently"). Cf. ἄρα in Gal 2:21; 3:7, 29; 5:11. ἄρα οὖν occurs Rom 5:18; 7:3, 25; 8:12; 9:16, 18; 14:12, 19; 1 Thess 5:6, etc. See Bauer, *s.v.* ἄρα, 4; Thrall, *Greek Participles*, 10f.

186 For the phrase καιρὸν ἔχω ("have an opportunity") see Heb 11:15; *2 Clem.* 16.1; Ign. *Smyrn.* 9.1; Ign. *Rom.* 2.1; furthermore Col 4:5; Eph 5:16. Cf. also *Sententiae Aesopi-Achiqari* 110 (ed. Denis, *Fragm. pseudepigr. gr.*, 139 lines 8–10); *Gnomologium Vaticanum* (eds. Leo Sternbach and Otto Luschnat

[Berlin: de Gruyter, 1963] no. 449): Ὁ αὐτὸς πρός τινα τῶν μαθητῶν αὐτοῦ ἔφη· "ἐὰν καιρὸν ζητῇς πρὸς φιλοσοφίαν, καιρὸν οὐχ ἕξεις" ("He [Plato] said to one of his students: If you seek an opportunity for doing philosophy, you will not have any").

187 ὡς with the present or imperfect can mean "as long as"; see Bauer, *s.v.*, IV, 1, b. This understanding is represented by the readings in P⁴⁶ A C 𝔐 D G *pm* lat Marcion Clement. The variant reading ἔχωμεν (B* ℵ 69 *al*) assumes ὡς = ἕως with a subjunctive, also meaning "as long as" (so BDF, § 455, 2.3; BDR, § 455; Schlier). The evidence is almost equally divided between the two possibilities. See Nestle–Aland, 26th edition, *apparat. crit., ad loc.*

188 Cf. Gal 2:20; 4:13f; 5:13, 16; 6:8. Differently Schlier; similarly Mussner, p. 407: "until the parousia comes"; but the parousia plays no role in Gal.

ethics is not merely an afterthought to the redemption in Christ, an *addendum* of man to the work of God, but it is a necessary part of that redemption itself. Without the ethical response, "the works of the flesh" will with necessity regain their former power and corrupt the "life for God."

The appeal itself is formulated very generally: ἐργαζώμεθα τὸ ἀγαθὸν πρὸς πάντας . . . ("let us do the good to all mankind . . ."). The term ἐργάζομαι ("do")[189] must not be misunderstood as another kind of "doing the works of the Law."[190] This misunderstanding should be impossible because of the singular τὸ ἀγαθόν ("the good").[191] The term points to the *one* "fruit of the Spirit" (cf. 5:22) and stands in opposition to the plurality of "the works of the Law" and of "the flesh."[192] The oneness of the good also corresponds to the universality of its application: the Christian is expected to do good to all mankind. The universal character of God's redemption corresponds to the universality of Christian ethical and social responsibility.[193] If God's redemption in Christ is universal, the Christian community is obliged to disregard all ethnic, national, cultural, social, sexual, and even religious distinctions within the human community.[194] Since before God there is no partiality,[195] there cannot be partiality in the Christian's attitude towards his fellow man.[196]

Remarkably, the universalistic appeal is appended by what seems a qualification: μάλιστα δὲ πρὸς τοὺς οἰκείους τῆς πίστεως ("but especially towards those who belong to the household of the faith"). This final remark[197] is a typical Pauline paradox.[198] It is not intended to revoke the preceding high–flying universalism, but to direct the attention of the readers to the concrete historical reality of the Christian community. The phrase "members of the household of faith" certainly refers to fellow Christians.[199] Compared with the universalism the "household" seems a rather tiny entity. Perhaps this contrast is intended. One should be cautious in using the well–known metaphor, however, in order to conclude that these Christians most likely had "house churches."[200] The term ἡ πίστις ("the [Christian] faith") appears here as the common name for the Christian movement.[201]

---

189   The term occurs only here in Gal, but see Rom 2:10; 13:10; Eph 4:28; *Herm. Man.* 2.4. See also Bauer, *s.v.*, 2, a.

190   See above, on Gal 6:9, also 6:4.

191   Cf. τὸ καλόν ("the good") Gal 6:9.

192   Cf. Gal 2:16; 3:2, 5; 5:19. On the issue of "one" vs. "many" see above, on 3:20. For an analogous doctrine in gnosticism, cf. *Corp. Herm.* 13.15.

193   Cf. the emphasis on πᾶς ("all") in Gal 2:16; 3:8, 22, 26–28. See also Sevenster, *Paul and Seneca*, 173 (n. 11 above).

194   Cf. Gal 3:26–28. Cf. R. Hillel, '*Abot* 1.12: "Be of the disciples of Aaron, one that loves peace, that loves mankind and brings them nigh to Torah" (tr. Herford).

195   Cf. 2:6.

196   Paul has demonstrated this in his *narratio* section Gal 1:12–2:14. See also Rom 12:17f; 14:18, 20; Phil 4:5; 1 Thess 5:15.

197   It is an epistolary cliché. Henry G. Meecham (*Light From Ancient Letters* [London: Allen & Unwin, 1923] 116) mentions POxy. 293, 16; 294, 31; 743, 43. See also *Treat. Res.* (*NHC* I, 50 line 15, tr. in Foerster–Wilson, *Gnosis* 2.75: "I salute you and those who love you [pl.] in brotherly love"). Str–B 3. 587 notes a Jewish parallel (*Mek.* Exod. 22, 24 [102a]).

198   Cf., e.g., 1 Cor 6:12; 7:38. For the form, cf. Chadwick, *Sextus*, 165f, 277, 382, 395.

199   The metaphor occurs also in Eph 2:19; *CMC* 63.8–9. See Otto Michel, "οἰκεῖος," *TDNT* 5.134–35; Bauer, *s.v.*; *PGL, s.v.*; Schlier, p. 278 n. 3; furthermore Willem C. van Unnik, "Die Rücksicht auf die Reaktion der Nicht-Christen als Motiv in der altchristlichen Paränese," in *Judentum, Urchristentum, Gnosis, Festschrift für Joachim Jeremias* (BZNW 26; Berlin: Töpelmann, 1960) 221–34.

200   The genitive defines the type of kinship; cf., e.g., Polybius 5.87.3: τῆς ἡσυχίας οἰκεῖος ("inclined to peace"); Strabo 1.1.11: οἰκεῖοι φιλοσοφίας ("people familiar with philosophy"); the opposite is ἀλλότριος ("alien"). Cf. Borse (*Standort*, 38f, followed by Mussner), who wants to understand the phrase primarily referring to the Christians in Judaea and the money collection (cf. 2:10), but this combination is forced upon the text.

201   Cf. the use of the term in Gal 1:23; 3:2, 5, 7, 8, 9, 11, 12, 14, 23, 24, 25, 26; 5:5, 6.

6

Epistolary postscript: *conclusio*

11 See with what large letters I am writing
to you with my own hand.
12/ It is those people who wish to make a
nice appearance in the flesh that
compel you to be circumcised—only so
that they may not be persecuted
because of the cross of Christ. 13/ For
not even the circumcised themselves
keep the Law, but they want you to be
circumcised, in order that they may
boast in your flesh. 14/ But far be it
from me to boast—except in the cross
of our Lord Jesus Christ, through
which[1] the world has been crucified to
me and I to the world.
15/ For neither circumcision nor
uncircumcision is anything but [a] new
creation.[2] 16/ As for those who will
follow this rule—"Peace be upon them
and mercy, and upon the Israel of
God!"
17/ Henceforth let no one cause me
trouble, for I bear the marks of Jesus
branded on my body.[3]
18/ The grace of our Lord Jesus Christ
be with your spirit, brothers. Amen.

Analysis

In 6:11–18 Paul adds a postscript in his own hand-writing. This conforms to the epistolary conventions of the time.[4] An autographic postscript serves to authenticate the letter, to sum up its main points, or to add concerns which have come to the mind of the sender after the completion of the letter. Paul's handwritten postscript[5] raises several questions in regard to the authorship of the letter,[6] for the postscript presupposes that the preceding letter was written by an amanuensis, a professional secretary. This amanuensis could have been a simple copyist who merely rewrote what Paul had dictated or given to him as a draft. However, the question must be raised whether the amanuensis had any influence upon the composition of the letter itself. It is apparent that the very employment of an amanuensis rules out a haphazard writing of the letter and suggests the existence of Paul's draft and the copy by the amanuensis, or a sequence of draft, composition, and copy. The highly skillful composition of the letter leaves us the choice of attributing this high degree of epistolographic expertise to Paul, to the amanuensis, or to both. I am inclined to attribute the composition to Paul himself, because the letter does more than simply

---

1   Or: "through whom."
2   The sentence is well paraphrased in *NEB*: "Circumcision is nothing; uncircumcision is nothing; the only thing that counts is new creation."
3   So *NEB*.
4   On the epistolary postscript see Karl Dziatzko, "Brief," PW 3 (1899) 839; Ferdinandus Ziemann, *De epistularum Graecarum formulis sollemnibus quaestiones selectae* (Diss. Halle/Wittenberg; Halle: Karras, 1910) 362–65: "De clausulis autographis"; Carl G. Bruns, *Die Unterschriften in den römischen Rechtsurkunden* (Abhandlungen der königlichen Akademie der Wissenschaften zu Berlin, philol.–hist. Kl. 1876) 41–138; Deissmann, *Licht vom Osten*, esp. 132 n. 6,

136–41, 166f; Otto Roller, *Das Formular der paulinischen Briefe* (BWANT 4.6; Stuttgart: Kohlhammer, 1933) 69f, 489–93; Franz Dölger and Johannes Karyannopulos, *Byzantinische Urkundenlehre 1: Die Kaiserurkunden* (Handbuch der Altertumswissenschaft 12.3.1.1; Munich: Beck, 1968) 54–56; Gordon J. Bahr, "The Subscriptions in the Pauline Letters," *JBL* 87 (1968) 27–41; Joseph A. Fitzmyer, "Some Notes on Aramaic Epistolography," *JBL* 93 (1974) 201–25, 217.
5   For other Pauline postscripts, cf. 1 Cor 16:21; Phlm 19; furthermore Col 4:18; 2 Thess 3:17.
6   On the following see also Betz, "Composition," 356–59.

conform to convention. While making use of convention, it is nevertheless a highly original creation. Nowhere in it is there any indication of a separation of form and content. This is even true of the personal postcript, which is well composed in itself and fully integrated with the rest of the letter. Yet, given the employment of an amanuensis and the common practices in letter writing in Paul's time, the problem of authorship may be more complicated than we have previously imagined.

As a rhetorical feature,[7] the postscript of Galatians serves as the *peroratio* or *conclusio*,[8] that is, the end and conclusion of the apologetic speech forming the body of the letter. The general purpose of the *peroratio*[9] is twofold: it serves as a last chance to remind the judge or the audience of the case, and it tries to make a strong emotional impression upon them. The three conventional parts of the *peroratio* carry out this task: the *enumeratio* or *recapitulatio* (ἀνακεφαλαίωσις) sharpens and

sums up the main points of the case,[10] the *indignatio* arouses anger and hostility against the opponents,[11] and the *conquestio* stimulates pity.[12] In an actual case, the *peroratio* can, of course, take many different forms, but it must conform to the case at issue, and it must be concise. It also must be clearly related to the individual parts of the speech, especially to the *exordium*.[13]

Seen as a rhetorical feature, the *peroratio* becomes most important for the interpretation of Galatians. It contains the interpretive clues to the understanding of Paul's major concerns in the letter as a whole and should be employed as the hermeneutical key to the intentions of the Apostle.

Interpretation

■ **11** Paul directs the readers' attention to the fact that the following words are written in his own handwriting: ἴδετε πηλίκοις ὑμῖν γράμμασιν ἔγραψα τῇ ἐμῇ χειρί ("see with what large letters I am writing to you with my

---

7   The "greeting" (ἀσπασμός) which usually comes at the end of Paul's letters is missing in Gal. See Bauer, *s.v.* ἀσπάζομαι 1, a, for bib.

8   For a treatment of this subject, see Aristotle *Rhet.* 3.19, p. 1419b; *Rhet. ad Alex* 20, p. 1433b29ff; *Rhet. ad Her.* 2.30.47–2.31.50; Cicero *De inv.* 1.52.98–1.56.109; the longest discussion is found in Quint. 6.1.1ff.

9   See Volkmann, *Rhetorik*, § 27; Lausberg, *Handbuch*, §§ 431–42; Martin, *Rhetorik*, esp. 147–66.

10   See Quint. 6.1.1–2 (ed. Winterbottom): "Rerum repetitio et congregatio, quae Graece dicitur ἀνακεφαλαίωσις, a quibusdam Latinorum enumeratio, et memoriam iudicis reficit et totam simul causam ponit ante oculos et, etiamsi per singula minus moverat, turba valet. In hac quae repetemus quam brevissime dicenda sunt et, quot Graeco verbo patet, decurrendum per capita" ("There are two kinds of peroration, for it may deal either with facts or with the emotional aspect of the case. The repetition and grouping of the facts, which the Greeks call ἀνακεφαλαίωσις and some of our writers call the enumeration, serves both to refresh the memory of the judge and to place the whole of the case before his eyes, and even though the facts may have little impression on him in detail, their cumulative effect is considerable. This final recapitulation must be as brief as possible and, as the Greek indicates, we must summarize the facts under the appropriate heads" [LCL 2.383]). For other references see Lausberg, *Handbuch*, §§ 334–5; Martin, *Rhetorik*, 147ff.

11   See Cicero *De inv.* 1.55.106: "Indignatio est oratio per quam conficitur ut in aliquem hominem magnum odium aut in rem gravis offensio concitetur" ("The *indignatio* is a passage which results in arousing great hatred against some person, or violent offense at some action" [LCL 2.151]). See also Lausberg, *Handbuch*, § 438.

12   See Cicero *De inv.* 1.55.106: "Conquestio est oratio auditorum misericordiam captans" ("*Conquestio* [lament or complaint] is a passage seeking to arouse the pity of the audience" [LCL 2.157]). See also Lausberg, ibidem, § 439; Martin, *Rhetorik*, 162ff.

13   See Lausberg, ibidem, § 432. That the final section of Gal conforms to the *enumeratio*, *indignatio* and *conquestio* and that Paul was influenced here by Greek rhetoric was proposed already by Carl Starcke, "Die Rhetorik des Apostels Paulus im Galaterbrief und die 'πηλίκα γράμματα' Gal. 6, 11" *Programm Stargard in Pr.*, 1911); Β. Π. Στογιάννου, "'Η ὑπὸ τοῦ Παύλου ἰδιόχειρος ἀνακεφαλαίωσις τῆς πρὸς Γαλάτας," *ΔΕΛΤΙΟΝ ΒΙΒΛΙΚΩΝ ΜΕΛΕΤΩΝ* 1 (1971) 59–79; differently Bahr, "The Subscriptions..." (cf. n. 4 above).

own hand"). Why he writes his postscript with "large" [14] letters is not immediately clear. Deissmann thought that Paul was making fun of his handwriting which looked clumsy because he was a hard–working craftsman.[15] Although Deissmann can refer to an analogy,[16] $\pi\eta\lambda\acute{\iota}\kappa\alpha\ \gamma\rho\acute{\alpha}\mu\mu\alpha\tau\alpha$ means "large letters" and not "clumsy letters." [17] It is more probable, therefore, that Paul wants to underscore the importance of what he has to say in these last words.[18] This practice would be comparable to the variation in letters (italics, capitals, bold face) in modern printing.[19] The aorist $\check{\epsilon}\gamma\rho\alpha\psi\alpha$ ("I am writing") is an "epistolary aorist" and points to 6:11–18 of the present letter.[20] As has been said above,[21] the phrase "with my own hand" [22] indicates that the letter up to 6:10 was written by an amanuensis. The remark serves to authenticate the whole letter and emphasizes the points made in the following section of the postscript.

■ **12** In vv 12–13 Paul delivers a sharp attack against his opponents. The attack is supposedly descriptive and is intended to disclose the real goals of the adversaries. But, like every polemic, this one is also a mixture of objective facts and subjective judgments, both of them hard to separate. Paul denounces his opponents not only as heretics, but also as morally inferior and despicable. Such a polemic is, in terms of rhetoric, clearly an expression of *indignatio*, with a good dose of *amplificatio*.[23] Its relation to the *causa* (1:6–7) is equally obvious.[24] As in 1:7 the opponents are not named;[25] only their actions are identified: $\check{o}\sigma o\iota\ \theta\acute{\epsilon}\lambda o\upsilon\sigma\iota\nu\ \epsilon\dot{\upsilon}\pi\rho o\sigma\omega\pi\hat{\eta}\sigma\alpha\iota\ \dot{\epsilon}\nu\ \sigma\alpha\rho\kappa\acute{\iota}$ ("those people want to make a good showing in the flesh"). This looks very much like a caricature, and we must be cautious in assuming that this is what the opponents really have in mind.[26]

The term $\epsilon\dot{\upsilon}\pi\rho o\sigma\omega\pi\acute{\epsilon}\omega$ ("make a good showing") is rare, but it is now attested in the papyri.[27] Paul does

---

14   $\pi\eta\lambda\acute{\iota}\kappa o\varsigma$ means "how large." Cf. Plato *Meno* 82D: ...$\pi\eta\lambda\acute{\iota}\kappa\eta\ \tau\iota\varsigma\ \check{\epsilon}\sigma\tau\alpha\iota$...$\dot{\eta}\ \gamma\rho\alpha\mu\mu\acute{\eta}$... ("how long will be the line" [of a drawing]). See LSJ, *s.v.*; Bauer, *s.v.*, 1. P[46] B* read $\dot{\eta}\lambda\acute{\iota}\kappa o\iota\varsigma$ which is the classical form (cf. BDF, § 304; BDR, § 304; Burton, pp. 348f; Schlier, p. 280 n. 1.). Minuscule 642 has $\pi o\iota\kappa\acute{\iota}\lambda o\iota\varsigma$ ("diversified").

15   Adolf Deissmann, *Bibelstudien* (Marburg: Elwert, 1895) 262–64; idem, *Licht vom Osten*, 132 n. 6; against Deissmann: W. K. L. Clarke, "St. Paul's 'Large Letters,'" *ExpTim* 24 (1912–13) 285; J. S. Clemens, "St. Paul's Handwriting," ibidem, 380; Starcke, *Die Rhetorik* (see above, n. 13); Lietzmann; Oepke.

16   A good example is the photo of a letter from the Oxyrynchus Papyri (2, no. 246, plate VII) in *Licht vom Osten*, 140.

17   $\gamma\rho\acute{\alpha}\mu\mu\alpha$ means here the "letter" of the alphabet (Rom 2:27, 29; 7:6; 2 Cor 3:6, 7), not "epistle" for which Paul has $\dot{\epsilon}\pi\iota\sigma\tau o\lambda\acute{\eta}$ (1 Cor 5:9; 16:3; 2 Cor 3:1ff; 10:9f). See Bauer, *s.v.* $\gamma\rho\acute{\alpha}\mu\mu\alpha$, 1.

18   So Burton, pp. 348f; Lagrange; Oepke; Schlier, p. 280; Mussner, p. 410.

19   Almqvist (*Plutarch*, 111) refers to the parallel in Plutarch *Cato maior* 20.5 (348B): "His History of Rome, as he tells us himself, he wrote out with his own hand in large characters ($\dot{\iota}\delta\acute{\iota}\alpha\ \chi\epsilon\iota\rho\grave{\iota}\ \kappa\alpha\grave{\iota}\ \mu\epsilon\gamma\acute{\alpha}\lambda o\iota\varsigma\ \gamma\rho\acute{\alpha}\mu\mu\alpha\sigma\iota\nu$), that his son might have in his own home an aid to acquaintance with his country's ancient traditions."

20   See also Phil 2:28; Phlm 12, 19, 21; Col 4:8. The term can also refer to an earlier letter (1 Cor 5:9; 2 Cor 2:3f, 9; 7:12; 3 John 9), or to the preceding

portion of a letter (Rom 15:15; 1 Cor 9:15; Phlm 21; 1 Pet 5:12; 1 John 2:14, 21, 26). See Burton, p. 349; Schlier, p. 279 nn. 2, 3; Moule, *Idiom Book*, 12.

21   See the introduction to this section, above.

22   The same phrase is found also 1 Cor 16:21; Phlm 19; Col 4:18; 2 Thess 3:17. For the meaning of $\chi\epsilon\acute{\iota}\rho$ ("handwriting") see the references in LSJ, *s.v.*, VI; Preisigke, *Wörterbuch*, 4.2 (1958) *s.v.* $\gamma\rho\acute{\alpha}\phi\omega$ 3; Bauer, *s.v.* $\chi\epsilon\acute{\iota}\rho$, 1. Cf. Philo *Spec. leg* .4.160: "....the lawgiver bids him write out with his own hand this sequel to the laws which embraces them all in the form of a summary. He writes hereby to have the ordinance cemented to the soul" [LCL 8.109]. Furthermore 162, 163.

23   Cf. *Rhet. ad Her.* 2.30.47: Amplificatio est res quae per locum communem instigationis auditorum causa sumitur." In 2.30.48 ten *loci communes* to be applied are listed; similarly Cicero *De inv.* 1.53.101ff. See Lausberg, *Handbuch*, § 438.

24   Cf. Gal 2:4–5, 11–14; 3:1; 5:7, 10–12.

25   See above on 1:7.

26   On $\theta\acute{\epsilon}\lambda\omega$ ("will") as referring to the plans of the opponents, see 1:7; 4:17; 6:13. It must be distinguished from what the Galatians "want": 4:9, 21.

27   It is a *hapax legomenon* in the NT. See LSJ, *s.v.*; Bauer, *s.v.*; Eduard Lohse, "$\epsilon\dot{\upsilon}\pi\rho o\sigma\omega\pi\acute{\epsilon}\omega$, $\pi\rho o\sigma\omega\pi o\lambda\eta\mu\psi\acute{\iota}\alpha$ $\kappa\tau\lambda$.," *TDNT* 6.779; *PGL*, *s.v.* See also Gal 1:10; 2:6b–c; 2:13; 4:13f; 6:13b; Matt 23:27. Cf. '*Abot* 1.15, 3.16.

not indicate whether "in the flesh"[28] refers to the opponents' "flesh" (i.e. their own boasting),[29] or to the Galatians' "flesh" (cf. 6:13b). Verse 12b seems to report a fact: οὗτοι ἀναγκάζουσιν ὑμᾶς περιτέμνεσθαι ("these people compel you to become circumcised"), but how exactly this "compulsion" was achieved we are not told. One should, however, remember the earlier instances of it (cf. 2:3, 14). Rather than by physical force (cf. Paul's own persecution of the church 1:13, 23), the compulsion was probably achieved by putting the pressure on persuasion and conviction of the Galatians (cf. 2:5, 12–13; 3:1a; 5:8).[30] The goal of the adversaries was to get the Gentile Galatians ready to accept circumcision voluntarily.[31]

Paul's next remark in v 12c poses an extremely difficult problem: μόνον ἵνα τῷ σταυρῷ τοῦ Χριστοῦ μὴ διώκωνται ("only that they may not be persecuted because of the cross of Christ").[32] Again the statement is descriptive, disclosing the real intentions of the opponents. To this extent v 12c is parallel to v 12a, but it is difficult to say whether it represents Paul's own evaluation of the goals of the opponents or an objective description of their intentions. Formally, at least, the statement represents Paul's own conclusion; the restrictive μόνον ("only") is argumentative and not

simply informative.[33] On the other hand, the Apostle's words suggest that his argument is based on observation: the opponents do recommend circumcision, and they do so with a purpose in mind. If that purpose is to avoid persecution, their goal is merely tactical.[34] This may be so, or it may be Paul's conclusion; the same question must be raised here as was raised in regard to the episode at Antioch (2:11–14).

We are also left in the dark in regard to other questions. Who were those persecutors Paul was thinking of, and how could such a persecution take place in Asia Minor?[35] Why should Jewish Christians be persecuted? Paul's words leave two basic options for answering these questions: (1) the opponents did preach the cross of Christ, but in order to avoid persecution they recommended circumcision in addition; (2) the opponents did not preach the cross of Christ, but instead preached circumcision for the purpose of avoiding persecution. Parallel passages suggest that the opponents did not preach the cross of Christ as the salvation event,[36] but this judgment may be Paul's own conclusion. In any case, they did not proclaim the cross in the same way Paul did. But why would they be persecuted? Most likely the opponents would be persecuted for the same reason Paul was persecuted, namely because he

---

28   For this expression, see Gal 2:20; 4:14; 6:13.

29   Cf. Gal 6:4; Phil 3:2ff, 17–19; 2 Cor 11:12–15, 18, 30; 12:1–10. See Betz, *Paulus, passim*.

30   Cf. the term ταράσσω ("disturb") in Gal 1:7; 5:10.

31   See the use of περιτέμνω in Gal 2:3; 5:2, 3; 6:13. An interesting parallel is the conversion of King Izates of Adiabene to Judaism (see below, Appendix 1); Justin *Dial.* 47.5 (below, Appendix 4); *NHC* VI.4, p. 45 lines 14–24 (cf. Karl Martin Fischer *et al.*, "Der Gedanke unserer grossen Kraft [Noēma]," *ThLZ* 98 [1973] 169–75, 174). For the continuation of the ritual of circumcision in Jewish Christianity, see Schoeps, *Theologie und Geschichte*, 137ff; idem, *Jewish Christianity*, 19, 75, 113f, 137.

32   The text is that of Nestle–Aland, 26th ed. P⁴⁶ B 69 1175 add Ἰησοῦ ("of Jesus"), but the expression "the cross of Christ" is Pauline (cf. 1 Cor 1:17; Phil 3:18; also Gal 5:11; 6:14; furthermore 3:1; 5:24). The dative is causal (cf. BDF, § 196; BDR, § 196). Moule (*Idiom Book*, 45) renders: "to avoid persecution *for* the cross."

33   Cf. the use of the term in Gal 1:23; 2:10; 3:2; 4:18; 5:13.

34   This is the view of Schmithals, *Paul and the Gnostics*, 39f. However, he does not explain how this tactic is related to the opponents' ritualistic interest in circumcision which Schmithals believes to be one of their characteristics (cf., ibidem, 37ff). See also Willi Marxsen, *Introduction to the New Testament* (tr. G. Buswell; Philadelphia: Fortress, 1968) 53ff; Eckert, *Die urchristliche Verkündigung*, 33; Jewett, "Agitators," 203ff.

35   Cf. Gal 1:13, 23 referring to the non-Christian Jew Paul as a persecutor of Christian Jews; 4:29; 5:11 referring to law-free Christianity being persecuted; furthermore 1 Thess 2:14–6; Rom 8:35; 1 Cor 4:12; 15:9; 2 Cor 4:9; 11:23ff; 12:10; Phil 3:6; etc.

36   See esp. Gal 5:11; and, by implication, the whole *narratio* 1:12–2:14. Braun (*Studien*, 181) points to the "stumbling-block" of the cross. On the cross as salvation event, see Bultmann, *Theology*, § 33; Conzelmann, *Outline*, 199ff.

preached freedom from the Jewish Torah.[37] In other words, the Jewish–Christian opponents recommended that the Gentile Christians of Galatia undergo circumcision, because otherwise Jewish Christians can and would be accused of admitting converts without subjecting them to the Torah. From the Jewish point of view, the Galatians were potential proselytes of Judaism and had to be treated as such. But on the other hand, for Paul the "cross of Christ" and the "Law" are mutually exclusive as ways to salvation, and indeed he can say that his Jewish–Christian opponents are trying to avoid the persecution "that comes because of the cross of Christ."[38]

The whole statement, therefore, is a conclusion in terms of Paul's theology, based upon certain observable facts. If his opponents regarded themselves and the whole Christian movement as still a part of Judaism, their push for circumcision may indeed have been motivated by their fear of being excommunicated from Judaism—a fear which was justified, as events later showed. From this perspective, the voluntary acceptance of circumcision by the Galatians would indeed have solved the problem because the Christian Galatians could have been counted as Jewish proselytes.[39]

■13 Paul's second[40] statement about the opponents is again both descriptive and polemical, and presents again the problem of separating between the facts and the evaluation of the facts. The first problem is the identity of the people Paul calls οἱ περιτεμνόμενοι ("the circumcised"). Are they the same people whom he discusses in 6:12 ("the circumcized" = the Jews)[41]— this is the most probable solution—or are they those Gentile Christians who have accepted circumcision[42] and are now "in the state of circumcision"?[43] Paul's Jewish–Christian opponents could have been Jews "by birth" (cf. 2:15) or "by conversion" (as Titus would have been, had he been subjected to the ritual of circumcision [cf. 2:3]). A decision on this problem is impossible.

Equally difficult is Paul's further assertion that "these people themselves do not keep the Law" (οὐδὲ... αὐτοὶ νόμον φυλάσσουσιν). It could be a citation by Paul of an older anti–Jewish argument, since we find it in a very similar context at the end of Stephen's speech in Acts 7:53.[44] It is conceivable that Jewish Christians would insist on circumcision but would not observe the Torah. In his discussion of the episode at Antioch (2:11–14) Paul in fact deals with Jewish Christians, first of all Peter, who insist on Jewishness without keeping the Law themselves. Peter is said to have "compelled" Gentile Christians to "Judaize" while he himself lives ἐθνικῶς ("as a Gentile"). We do not know whether those Jewish Christians at the Jerusalem meeting who insisted on the circumcision of Titus (see 2:3–5) also would have demanded the scrupulous observation of the Torah. Even if we allow for these

---

37 See Gal 5:11; also 2:4–5, 11–14. On the problem, see Morton Smith, "The Reason for the Persecution of Paul and the Obscurity of Acts," in *Studies in Mysticism and Religion* (presented to G. G. Scholem; Jerusalem: 1967) 261–68.

38 Cf. Gal 5:11; also 2:2, 5, 21; 3:1; 4:11, 9; 5:2, 4; 6:14–17.

39 See also Betz, "2 Cor 6:14–7:1," 88–108.

40 Even if γάρ ("for") indicates that v 13 presents the reason for v 12, we have in fact a second statement. But the term may simply mark a sequence; cf. Bauer, *s.v.*, 4.

41 Cf. Gal 5:3. Usually Paul uses ἡ περιτομή ("the circumcision," i.e., the Jews): Gal 2:7–9, 12. In 6:13 Paul refers to his Jewish-Christian opponents. So also Rudolf Meyer, "περιτέμνω," *TDNT* 6:82–83; Schlier, p. 281; Mussner, p. 413.

42 This view is held by Emmanuel Hirsch, "Zwei Fragen zu Gal 6," *ZNW* 29 (1930) 192–97; Wilhelm Michaelis, "Judaistische Heidenchristen,"

ZNW 30 (1931) 83–89; Lietzmann, *ad loc.*; Schoeps, *Paul*, 65, 77; Munck, *Paul*, 87–90. Against this view are Peter Richardson, *Israel in the Apostolic Church* (Cambridge: Cambridge University, 1969) 85ff; Eckert, *Die urchristliche Verkündigung*, 34f.

43 This may be the interpretation of the variant reading περιτετμημένοι by P⁴⁶ B Ψ 614 *al.* The present tense is read by ℵ A C Dᵍʳ K P 33 81 *al.*; see Metzger, *Textual Commentary*, 598. Cf., however, 1 Cor 7:18.

44 The same accusation is made not only against the Jews in Stephen's speech (Acts 7:53, cf. above on 3:6, excursus on Abraham) but also against Elchasai in Epiphanius *Pan.* 9.1.5. The technical expression νόμον φυλάσσειν ("keep the Torah") occurs in Rom 2:26; Acts 7:53; 21:24; cf. 16:4. See Bauer, *s.v.* φυλάσσω 1, f; Georg Bertram, "φυλάσσω," *TDNT* 9.236–41.

possibilities, Paul's flat statement that the circumcised do not themselves keep the Torah is strange. If this is not merely polemic but is indeed fact, we would want to know why they were not observing the Torah. Were they libertines,[45] or were they interested only in circumcision as a magical ritual?[46] Did they keep only part of the Torah,[47] or a special Torah?[48] All of these questions indicate possibilities, but none can be proven by evidence.

Verse 13b is certainly polemic: ἀλλὰ θέλουσιν ὑμᾶς περιτέμνεσθαι ἵνα ἐν τῇ ὑμετέρᾳ σαρκὶ καυχήσωνται ("but they want you to become circumcised, in order that they may boast in your flesh"). The adversative ἀλλά ("but") makes little sense because v 13b is not really in contrast with v 13a. That the opponents want[49] the Galatians to be circumcised has been reported as a fact throughout the letter.[50] But is the reason Paul gives other than polemic?[51] "Boasting in the flesh" is an attitude repudiated elsewhere by Paul as incompatible with the Christian faith.[52] Does Paul allude to the meritorious value of making converts, a doctrine held by Judaism?[53] Does he assume that his Jewish–Christian opponents held that view? If they did share that doctrine, did they intend to boast "in the flesh?"[54] We do not know with any degree of certainty. We do know that Paul allows only for a "boasting in the Lord."[55] What he means by this he defines in the next sentence (6:14)—an indication, perhaps, that this doctrine was not shared by all Christians.

■ 14 Paul contrasts what he considers false "boasting" (6:13) with his own definition of appropriate "boasting." The rather awkward sentence structure of v 14 corresponds to the doctrinal difficulty with which Paul sees himself faced. In general, ancient anthropology views man as a being who is proud of himself and of his achievements. This anthropological assumption was also widely discussed by philosophers and theologians.[56] Paul himself has developed his doctrine about what is proper and improper "boasting."[57] Verse 14 contains that doctrine in an extremely concise form. There are two lines, the first of which is a strong denial, to which in the second line an exception is added: ἐμοὶ δὲ μὴ γένοιτο καυχᾶσθαι εἰ μὴ ἐν τῷ σταυρῷ τοῦ κυρίου ἡμῶν Ἰησοῦ Χριστοῦ . . . ("but far be it from me to boast—except in the cross of our Lord Jesus Christ . . .") The problem with this statement is its ambiguity. On the one hand, the Apostle emphasizes that, in contrast to what he says the opponents are doing,[58] for him

45 See for this view esp. Lütgert, *Gesetz und Geist*, *passim*; also Morton Smith, *Clement of Alexandria and a Secret Gospel of Mark* (Cambridge: Harvard University, 1973) 180–183, 245, 258–63.

46 Schmithals (*Paul and the Gnostics*, 37ff), following others, assumes that the opponents rejected the Torah, but kept the ritual of circumcision, and that Paul must inform the Galatians of this fact, because they do not understand the implications. Cf. Eckert, *Die urchristliche Verkündigung*, 34 n. 6.

47 Such an interpretation would have to be based upon 5:3. Interesting in this regard is the discussion in Justin *Dial.* 46, where the Jew Trypho admits that he can no longer perform the sacrificial rites in the temple at Jerusalem and therefore cannot keep "all the Mosaic institutions." Asked what one can do, he replies: ". . .keep the Sabbath, . . .be circumcised, . . .observe months and . . .be washed if you touch anything prohibited by Moses, or after sexual intercourse." Epiphanius *Anaceph.* 28.1.1 reports that the Corinthians adhered to Judaism "partially" (ἀπὸ μέρους). On Justin *Dial.* 46 see below, Appendix 4.

48 The further question would then be whether the opponents called this "special Torah" the "Torah of Christ"? For this concept see on Gal 6:2. Cf. the discussions on the "Apostolic Decree" Acts 15:23–29 in the commentaries on Acts (but cf. also above, on 2:1–10).

49 On the meaning of θέλω ("will") see on 6:12.

50 See, esp. Gal 2:3; 5:2–12; 6:12, 15.

51 Cf. Gal 6:12a; also 2:4; 4:17.

52 Cf. Gal 6:14a; 1 Cor 1:29–31; 3:21; 4:7; 2 Cor 11:18; etc.

53 See Paul's interpretation of "boasting": Rom 2:17, 23; 5:3, 11; Phil 3:2ff. On the subject see Oepke, pp. 201f; Schlier, p. 281; Bultmann, "καυχάομαι," *TDNT* 3.649; Kuss, *Römerbrief*, 219–24.

54 Does this refer concretely to the "flesh of circumcision"? Cf. Eduard Schweizer, "σάρξ," *TDNT* 7.129–30; Alexander Sand, *Der Begriff "Fleisch" in den paulinischen Hauptbriefen* (BU 2; Regensburg: Pustet, 1967) 133f.

55 Except for the meaning of the term in 6:4.

56 See my analysis of Plutarch's treatise "On Self-praise" in *Plutarch's Ethical Writings and Early Christian Literature* (Leiden: Brill, 1978) 367ff.

57 See also Gal 6:4, 13 and the literature on the subject above, n. 97.

58 The δέ ("but") points to the rejected matter in 6:13.

there is no possibility whatsoever of "boasting". On the other hand, he admits that there is a possibility for "boasting." Not all forms of "boasting" are excluded. As long as man lives "in the flesh" there will be some form of "boasting." In 2 Corinthians he can even agree, though ironically, that "boasting is necessary" (καυχᾶσθαι δεῖ).[59] Paul's concern is the basis for human boasting. He sees non–Christian boasting as always based upon "the flesh," i.e., man's own achievements (cf. 6:13). This type of "boasting" is strictly excluded for the Christian: μὴ γένοιτο.[60] What are the "achievements" the Christians can and should be proud of? They can only be his salvation—but this was not achieved through his own efforts but through Christ's death and resurrection.[61] The Christian "boasting" would then have to take the form of a glorification of the cross of Christ and would have to correspond to the rule Paul formulates in 1 Cor 1:31; 2 Cor 10:17: ὁ δὲ καυχώμενος ἐν κυρίῳ καυχάσθω ("he who boasts should boast in the Lord").[62] This rule also conforms to Pauline ethics in general: while we still live "in the flesh," we must not live "according to the flesh" (κατὰ σάρκα) but "according to the Spirit" (κατὰ πνεῦμα).[63] This means, of course, that strictly speaking such "boasting in the Lord" is not boasting at all. "Boasting" is a form of "self–praise," while "boasting in the Lord" would call for literary forms like "doxology" or "hymn." The incompatibility of the literary forms seems to match the strange sentence structure of the

strong denial coupled with the subsequent exception, which in effect cancels the denial and calls for a reformulation of the entire sentence.[64]

Verse 14b explains the meaning of the preposition ἐν ("in") in the expression "in the cross of our Lord Jesus Christ." How can this cross count as an "achievement" justifying boasting? Paul's answer to this question is contained in a summary of his soteriology:[65] δι᾽ οὗ ἐμοὶ κόσμος ἐσταύρωται κἀγὼ κόσμῳ ("through which [or: through whom] [the] world has been crucified to me, and I to [the] world"). The whole difference between an improper "boasting" and Paul's "boasting in the Lord" is expressed by the replacement of the emphatic ἐμοί ("to me")[66] in v 14a by the even more emphatic δι᾽ οὗ ἐμοί ("through which [or: through whom] to me"). This means that for Paul "my boasting" cannot simply be based upon "what happened to me," but must be based upon "what happened through Christ to me." Whether δι᾽ οὗ refers to the cross of Christ,[67] or to the person of Christ[68] is of no consequence, since for Paul "Christ" is always the crucified redeemer Christ.[69]

More important is what Paul regards as the Christian "achievement." It is formulated as a chiasmus, a soteriological paradox. In order to understand this paradox we must take apart its components. By presupposing[70] the "rule" of 1 Cor 1:31; 2 Cor 10:17, Paul has interpreted the ἐν κυρίῳ καυχάσθω ("he should boast in the Lord") by καυχᾶσθαι ἐν τῷ σταυρῷ τοῦ κυρίου ἡμῶν

---

59   2 Cor 11:30; 12:1. See Betz, *Paulus*, 72ff, 90, 95f, 140.

60   For this form of denial see Gal 2:17; 3:21.

61   For Paul's christology in Gal, see 1:4; 2:19f; 3:13; 4:4–6; 5:24.

62   See Betz, *Paulus*, 96.

63   Cf. Gal 5:16; Rom 6:4; 8:4; 1 Cor 3:3; 2 Cor 10:2f.

64   Cf. Gal 1:5; where Paul cites a doxology. In Rom 8:31–39 the Apostle has actually carried out how "boasting in the Lord" is to be done in an adequate, hymnic form.

65   On Paul's soteriology in general, see Bultmann, *Theology*, §§ 28–40; Conzelmann, *Outline*, § 24; Käsemann, "The Saving Significance of the Death of Jesus in Paul," in *Perspectives*, 32–59.

66   The first person sing. points to Paul in contrast to the opponents (cf. 6:12f), and to the exemplaric "I" which stands for every Christian (cf. 2:19–21).

67   So most exegetes, among them Lightfoot, Sieffert, Burton, Lietzmann, Lagrange, Oepke, Schlier, Mussner.

68   It would be identical with the christological formula διὰ Ἰησοῦ Χριστοῦ ("through Jesus Christ") which occurs Gal 1:1 (cf. 1:12, 15). Cf. also the formulae διὰ πίστεως Ἰησοῦ Χριστοῦ ("through faith in Jesus Christ") in 2:16; 3:14, 26; διὰ θεοῦ ("through God") in 4:7 (cf. 3:18). The opposite is διὰ νόμου ("through law") in 2:19, 21; δι᾽ ἀγγέλων ("through angels") in 3:19; δι᾽ ἀνθρώπου ("through [a] man") in 1:1.

69   Cf. Gal 2:20; 3:1, 13; by implication also 4:5; 5:24. See also Tannehill, *Dying and Rising*, 62–65.

70   The "rule" is not quoted in Gal, but certainly presupposed.

Ἰησοῦ Χριστοῦ ("boast in the cross of our Lord Jesus Christ"). Such "boasting in the cross of Christ" is possible only for those who are ἐν Χριστῷ ("in Christ"), i.e., those who are members of the "body of Christ."[71] The result is that the relationship between the Christian and the κόσμος ("world") has been "crucified."[72] It has been changed from being a slave under the στοιχεῖα τοῦ κόσμου ("elements of the world")[73] to being a free "son of God."[74] This new situation of those who are "in Christ" in regard to "the world" constitutes the "achievement" on account of which "boasting" is justified.[75]

■ **15** Paul adds the consequences[76] of v 14 for the Galatian controversy: οὔτε γὰρ περιτομή τί ἐστιν οὔτε ἀκροβυστία, ἀλλὰ καινὴ κτίσις ("for neither is circumcision anything nor uncircumcision, but [a] new creation").[77] Again the statement is extremely concise. In v 16 Paul calls it "the rule" (ὁ κανών). This rule consists of several definitions and represents the cutting–edge of the letter. These definitions are:

(1) The basis upon which the Christian "boasting" (cf. v 14) stands is called καινὴ κτίσις ("new creation"). This concept sums up Paul's soteriology, as far as it is related to Christian existence. Why is the Christian existence "new creation"? The answer is, in short, because the Christian is "in Christ" (ἐν Χριστῷ), i.e., he is a member of the "body" of Christ, the redeemer, who was crucified and resurrected from the dead (1: 1).[78] Those who are now "in Christ" (cf. 3:26–28) have been given the "Spirit of Christ" (cf. 4:6) and have, in baptism, "put on" Christ (3:27); they "belong to Christ" (5:24), enjoy the "new life" (2:19f; 5:25), and as such are "new creation."[79]

This concept is not merely exaggerated imagery, but it interprets Paul's anthropology. The "old creation" is referred to in Galatians simply as ἄνθρωπος ("man")

---

71 This concept is found in Gal only implicitly; see 1:22; 2:4, 17; 3:26–28; 4:19; 5:6.

72 Cf. Gal 2:19f, on the relationship to the Law; 5:24 to the "flesh."

73 Cf. 4:1–11; also 1:4: "this present evil age."

74 See 3:7, 26–28, 29; 4:4–6, 7, 22ff; cf. also 5:1, 13.

75 Cf. the "macarism" of Jesus from the First Book of Jeû, quoted in HSW, *NT Apocrypha* 1.261: "Blessed is he who has crucified the world (κόσμος), and has not allowed the world (κόσμος) to crucify him." The saying is followed by an exegesis. See also the reference in *Gos. Eg.* III, 65, 18 eds. Alexander Böhlig and Frederik Wisse, *Nag Hammadi Codices III, 2 and IV, 2: The Gospel of the Egyptians (The Holy Book of the Great Invisible Spirit)* (NHSt 4; Leiden: Brill, 1975) 152: "...Jesus, who possesses the life and who came and crucified (σταυροῦν) that which is in the law (νόμος)." Gal 6:14 was used in Valentinian gnosticism, for which see Foerster–Wilson, *Gnosis* 1.132f; Pagels, *The Gnostic Paul*, 112.

76 The γάρ ("for") is ambiguous: it indicates that v 15 is the reason for v 14 because it is presupposed there, but v 15 is at the same time the consequence of v 14.

77 The reading of 𝔐 (following ℵ A C D F G K L P, most minuscules it^d. g vg sy^h with* cop^sa bo eth^pp *al*) is probably influenced by the parallel Gal 5:6: ἐν γὰρ Χριστῷ Ἰησοῦ οὔτε περιτομή τι ἰσχύει οὔτε ἀκροβυστία ("for in Christ Jesus neither circumcision nor uncircumcision means anything..."). The shorter reading is supported by P⁴⁶ B Ψ 33 1175 *al*. See Metzger, *Textual Commentary*, 559.

78 See on Gal 6:14.

79 The brevity of the expression makes it almost a certainty that it was known to the Galatians. Strangely, the sentence appears later (?) as a quotation from the *Apoc. Mos.*; usually, however, it is believed to come from Paul. Cf. Resch, *Agrapha*, 301 logion 11; Albert-Marie Denis, *Introduction aux pseudépigraphes grecs d'Ancien Testament* (Leiden: Brill, 1970) 137f, 160; Lightfoot; Burton, p. 356f n. The conceptuality of "new creation" has parallels in Judaism, while the mystery cults prefer "recreation" and "rebirth." For the Jewish parallels, see Str–B 2.421 no. 2; 3.519; Werner Foerster, "κτίζω," *TDNT* 3.1000–1035; Erik Sjöberg, "Wiedergeburt und Neuschöpfung im palästinensischen Judentum," *StTh* 4 (1950) 44–85; idem, "Neuschöpfung in den Toten–Meer–Rollen," *StTh* 9 (1955) 131–36; Heinz Schwantes, *Schöpfung der Endzeit* (Stuttgart: Calwer, 1963) 26–29; Bernard Rey, *Créés dans le Christ Jésus* (Paris: Editions du Cerf, 1966) 28–35; Nils A. Dahl, "Christ, Creation, and the Church," in *The Background of the New Testament and its Eschatology: Studies in Honour of C. H. Dodd* (Cambridge: Cambridge University, 1956) 422–43; Peter Stuhlmacher, "Erwägungen zum ontologischen Charakter der καινὴ κτίσις bei Paulus," *EvTh* 27 (1967) 1–35; Anton Vögtle, *Das Neue Testament und die Zukunft des Kosmos* (Düsseldorf: Patmos, 1970) 174–83; Gerhard Schneider, *Neuschöpfung oder Wiedergeburt?* (Düsseldorf: Patmos, 1961); idem, "Die Idee der Neuschöpfung beim Apostel Paulus und ihr religions-

and σάρξ ("flesh")—human existence apart from God's redemption in Christ.[80] Through the Christ–event the Christian is enabled to participate in the new human existence "in Christ" which in Galatians is described as "the fruit of the Spirit" in all its manifestations.[81] It is significant that Paul does not use the terminology of "recreation" or "rebirth," which is often found in this religious context. In fact, for him the "new creation" amounts to a replacement of the old world; God did not simply "recreate" man, but he has sent his Son, Christ, into the old creation (1:4; 4:4–5), in the middle of which he accomplished salvation. The Christian has "put on" the body of the crucified and resurrected Christ (3:27) who now "lives in him" (2:19–20). God has, in addition, sent the "Spirit of Christ" (4:6) who has taken hold of the Christian in ecstatic experiences of that Spirit. All of these concepts are used to show that the "new creation" takes place in the middle of the old world, "in the flesh."[82]

(2) "New creation" determines also the relationship of the Christian to the world of religion.[83] Cultic distinctions characteristic of the old religions such as "circumcision" or its counterpart, "uncircumcision," have lost their meaning and function.[84] Since they belong to the κόσμος ("world"), these religious distinctions mean nothing any more to the Christian.[85] Paul does not spell it out, but in fact he announces the establishment of a new religion. Applied to the Galatian controversy, Paul's definitions function as "cult criticism." The present attempt by the Galatians to accept circumcision would then amount to an act of apostasy in regard to the new religion.[86] It is also significant that both Judaism and paganism are viewed on the same level as a part of the "old world," but Judaism is singled out here because circumcision is the concrete issue among the Galatian churches. There is, in Paul's view, no basis in Christianity for taking over this ritual form from Judaism, because Christianity does not share the same doctrinal presuppositions.[87]

■16 The concluding part of the postscript (v 16–18) is also carefully composed. The Apostle introduces in v 16 a conditional blessing[88] upon those who follow or

geschichtlicher Hintergrund," *TThZ* 68 (1959) 257–70; Heinz–Wolfgang Kuhn, *Enderwartung und gegenwärtiges Heil* (SUNT 4; Göttingen: Vandenhoeck & Ruprecht, 1966) 48–52, 75–78. For the mystery religions, see Hans Dieter Betz, "The Mithras Inscriptions of Santa Prisca and the New Testament," *NovT* 10 (1968) 62–80, 71f; Widengren, *Religionsphänomenologie*, 217ff, with many references.

80 See, esp. Gal 1:1, 10, 11, 12; 2:16; 6:1, 7. See furthermore, 2:15–3:25; 4:1–11, 21–31; 5:3–12, 19–21.

81 Gal 5:22f; cf. 2:4f, 15–21; 3:13, 26–29; 4:4–8, 22–31; 5:1, 5f, 13, 18, 25.

82 Cf. the definition in 2 Cor 5:17: εἴ τις ἐν Χριστῷ, καινὴ κτίσις ("If someone is 'in Christ,' [he is a] new creation"). Cf. also Rom 6:1–8:39, where the doctrine is fully developed.

83 Cf. esp. Gal 4:8f.

84 Cf. esp. on Gal 5:6, where the terminology is more fully discussed. See also 1 Cor 3:7, where the same principle is applied to a different situation.

85 See also the parallel 1 Cor 7:19; cf. Rom 2:25–29.

86 Cf. Gal 1:6–9; 2:1–10, 11–14, 21; 4:11, 19; 5:4, 10b, 11; 6:8.

87 Cf. Gal 2:14. Paul does not go on to say that as a "new creation" Christianity must have altogether new rituals. His assumption is rather that whatever rituals Christianity has, they must be in conformity with its doctrinal presuppositions. Paul does not discuss the situation of his Jewish–Christian opponents who might have had a different set of doctrinal presuppositions which allowed the continuation of the old rituals. That such a possibility existed I have tried to show in my article, "2 Cor 6:14–7:1," 88f; cf. also Jas 1:18 and Dibelius–Greeven, *James*, 103–07.

88 Form–critically, v 16 includes a "blessing" but not a "macarism." Contra Mussner, p. 416.

conform[89] to the κανών ("rule")[90] set forth in v 15: καὶ ὅσοι τῷ κανόνι τούτῳ στοιχήσουσιν ("and those who will follow this rule").[91] This conditional blessing implies a threat[92] against those who, after having read the letter, do not intend to conform to Paul's rule and, consequently, fall under the curse (1:8–9).[93] This means that the body of the letter (1:6–6:10) stands between the conditional curse and this conditional blessing. The whole argument in the letter leads up to the rule in v 15. Paul shows in the *narratio* (1:12–2:14) that he has consistently followed the rule, while the opponents followed either another or no standard (cf., especially, 2:14). The *probatio* (3:1–4:31) no less than the parenesis (5:1–6:10) has implicitly and explicitly (5:6) made the point that Paul's rule is to be followed. In fact, conforming to Paul's rule and following the Spirit (5:25) are one and the same. Paul is consistent when he limits his final blessing to those of the Galatian Christians who, after reading the letter, decide to re-main loyal to his gospel; those who decide against Paul and in favor of his opponents come under the curse automatically. Hence, the conditional blessing, like the conditional curse (1:8–9), amounts to a potential excommunication from the church, at least in the Pauline understanding.

The benediction is unique in Paul and has given rise to considerable discussion among scholars: εἰρήνη ἐπ᾽ αὐτοὺς καὶ ἔλεος, καὶ ἐπὶ τὸν Ἰσραὴλ τοῦ θεοῦ ("peace upon them and mercy, and upon the Israel of God"). This benediction is not only different from other benedictions Paul uses,[94] but it is also remarkably similar to Jewish benedictions, especially to the 19th, the Birkat ha–Shalom ("Blessing of Peace") of the Shemoneh Esreh (Babylonian Recension):[95] שים שלום טובה וברכה חן וחסד ורחמים עלינו ועל כל ישואל עמך ("bestow peace, happiness and blessing, grace and loving–kindness and mercy upon us and upon all Israel, your people"). There is no certainty how old this benediction is, but

---

89   The indicative future is read by A C* D G *pc* it; P⁴⁶ has the aor. subj. στοιχήσωσιν—probably not original. For the meaning of the term, see on 5:25.

90   The quasi-legal term has a long history in Greek philosophy. See, esp., Epictetus' definitions of philosophy, *Diss.* 2.11.13: ἔρευνα δέ τις περὶ τὸ δοκοῦν εἰ ὀρθῶς δοκεῖ καὶ εὕρεσις κανόνος τινός ("a kind of investigation to determine whether the opinion is rightly held, together with the invention of a kind of standard judgment"), and 2.11.24: καὶ τὸ φιλοσοφεῖν τοῦτό ἐστιν, ἐπισκέπτεσθαι καὶ βεβαιοῦν τοὺς κανόνας ("and the task of philosophy is this—to examine and to establish the standards"). See Adolf Bonhöffer, *Epiktet und das Neue Testament* (RVV 10; Giessen: Töpelmann, 1911) 119f. The concept has come to Paul most likely through Hellenistic Judaism. For passages and literature, see Hermann Wolfgang Beyer, "κανών," *TDNT* 3.596–602; LSJ, *s.v.*; Bauer, *s.v.*; *PGL*, *s.v.*; Betz, *Lukian*, 103 n. 3. The major studies are: Herbert Oppel, "ΚΑΝΩΝ," *Philologus Sup.* 30.4 (Leipzig: Dietrich, 1937); Leopold Wenger, *Canon in den römischen Rechtsquellen und in den Papyri*, Sitzungsberichte der Akademie der Wissenschaften in Wien, philos. hist. Kl. 220.2 (1942).

91   I differ here from Mussner (p. 416) who interprets the term too generally. There is not much help to be gained from the other instances where Paul uses the term: 2 Cor 10:13, 15, 16; Phil 3:16 (cf. *t.r.*). Another, opposite "rule" is found in the anti–Pauline *Ep. Petr.* (ps.–Clem. *Hom.*) 1.5: "one God, one Torah, one hope" (εἷς θεός, εἷς νόμος, εἷς ἐλπίς). See Appendix 3 a, below.

92   Quint. recommends the inclusion of a threat in the *peroratio*, as he does for the *exordium* (6.1.13): "Metus etiam, si est adhibendus, ut facit idem, hunc habet locum fortiorem quam in prooemio." Cf. also 4.1.20–22.

93   Cf. 1 Cor 16:22: εἴ τις οὐ φιλεῖ τὸν κύριον, ἤτω ἀνάθεμα ("If anyone does not love the Lord, cursed be he"). See also 2 Cor 13:10; Phil 3:17–19; 4:8–9.

94   For other blessings in Paul, see Rom 15:33; 16:20; 1 Cor 16:23f; 2 Cor 13:11, 13; Phil 4:7, 9, 23; 1 Thess 5:23, 28; Phlm 25. In the Pauline tradition also Eph 6:23f; Col 4:18; 2 Thess 3:16, 18; 1 Tim 6:13; 2 Tim 4:22; Tit 3:15. On the "blessing" generally see Brun, *Segen und Fluch*; Schenk, *Segen*. See also on Gal 1:8–9.

95   The text according to Willy Staerk, *Altjüdische liturgische Gebete* (KlT 58; Berlin: de Gruyter, 1930) 19. On the Shemoneh Esreh, see Elbogen, *Gottesdienst*, 27ff, 232ff; Kaufmann Kohler, "The Origin and Composition of the Eighteen Benedictions With a Translation of the Corresponding Essene Prayers in the Apostolic Constitutions," *HUCA* 1 (1924) 387–425; rep. in Jakob Petuchowski (ed.), *Contributions to the Scientific Study of Jewish Liturgy* (New York: KTAV, 1970) 52–90. Recent literature is listed in *EncJud* 2 (1971) 838–46, *s.v.* "Amidah." See also Str–B 3.578f; 4.1, 208–49 (excursus 10).

in all likelihood it is at least as old as the time of Paul. The variant forms of the benediction in the Palestinian recension and in other prayers show that different forms were in use.[96] There can be little doubt that the Apostle is dependent upon one of the forms of the benediction, if not on the Shemoneh Esreh itself.[97] This does not exclude the fact that he must have altered the words to make them fit his context. Looking at the components, the formula $\epsilon i \rho \eta \nu \eta$ $\kappa a i$ $\ddot{\epsilon}\lambda \epsilon o s$ ("peace and mercy")[98] looks more Jewish than Christian; this short form, in this order, looks even older than the more expanded form in the Shemoneh Esreh, but nothing definite can be said at this point. The phrase $\epsilon \pi$' $a \upsilon \tau o \upsilon s$ ("upon them") must be Paul's own formulation; it is required by the context, limiting the blessing to those who follow the Pauline rule.[99] The expression looks like an adaptation of the "upon us" of the Shemoneh Esreh. Due to this change, the following line becomes ambiguous: the phrase "Israel of God" now seems to refer to another group of people, while in the Shemoneh Esreh the second line is also common and extends the blessing to all the members of the Jewish community, thus transcending the present group of worshippers.[100] Therefore, the Christian Galatians loyal to Paul must be the same group as the "Israel of God."

This conclusion, however, has anticipated a decision upon an enormously difficult question of New Testament scholarship, the question of the meaning of the term "the Israel of God." This term is found only here

in the New Testament and never in Judaism. Where does the expression come from? To whom does it refer? Why does Paul use it here? The usual interpretation of equating "the Israel of God" with the Christian church has been challenged in recent years by several scholars. Gottlob Schrenk[101] argued that the term must refer to "Jewish Christianity" but Nils A. Dahl[102] rightly questioned this hypothesis because it would render Paul's argument in Galatians invalid. Why should he, after having argued against the Judaizers throughout the letter, bless them in the end? Most recently, Peter Richardson[103] has proposed another solution. He agrees with Schrenk that "Israel of God" cannot refer to the church, but must be connected with the original Israel (= Judaism), while he also agrees with Dahl that Paul cannot have extended the blessing to Judaism. He solves the problem, therefore, by repunctuation: "may God give peace to all who will walk according to this criterion, and mercy also to his faithful people Israel."[104] Richardson contends that Paul has made use of the Shemoneh Esreh by giving it "an ironical twist."[105] The problem with this *tour de force* is that the readers of the letter would never have understood Paul's cleverness because repunctuation does not show in the original, and there is no linguistic reason to assume that Paul used the term "mercy" in an ironic way.[106] Richardson's main argument,[107] that the church did not identify itself with Israel before A.D. 160, does not carry weight either, because Paul already

96   Str–B 3.579 refer to the blessings at the end of the *qaddish*; see for the texts Staerk, ibidem, 30–32.

97   See also Peter Richardson, *Israel in the Apostolic Church* (Cambridge: Cambridge University, 1969) 79.

98   It is unique in the NT; cf. other forms in 1 Tim 1:2; 2 Tim 1:2; 2 John 3; Jude 2; also Ign. *Smyr.* 12.1; *Mart. Pol.*, prooem. See $\ddot{\epsilon}\lambda \epsilon o s$ $\kappa a i$ $\epsilon i \rho \eta \nu \eta$ in the *salutatio* of the letter ps.–Bar 78.2; in the wedding context Tob 7:11 (א); also *Ps. Sol.* 4.29; 6.9; 7.9; 9.20; 13.11. See Rudolf Bultmann, "$\ddot{\epsilon}\lambda \epsilon o s$," *TDNT* 2.484; Richardson, ibidem, 77f.

99   For this meaning of $\epsilon \pi i$ with the accus., see Bauer, *s.v.*, III, 1,b,γ.

100 So also Richardson, *Israel*, 79.

101 Gottlob Schrenk, "Was bedeutet Israel Gottes?" *Judaica* 5 (1949) 81–94, with a survey of the history of exegesis; idem, "Der Segenswunsch nach der

Kampfepistel," *Judaica* 6 (1950) 170–90.

102 Nils A. Dahl, "Der Name Israel, I: Zur Auslegung von Gal. 6, 16," *Judaica* 6 (1950) 161–70; idem, *Das Volk Gottes* (Darmstadt: Wissenschaftliche Buchgesellschaft, 1963) 209ff.

103 Richardson, *Israel*, 70ff, esp. 81–84 (n. 97, above).

104 So the paraphrase of Richardson, ibidem, 84.

105 Ibidem.

106 Paul uses $\ddot{\epsilon}\lambda \epsilon o s$ ("mercy") only sparsely, but never in an inferior way. Cf. Rom 9:23; 11:31; 15:9. See also Rudolf Bultmann, "$\ddot{\epsilon}\lambda \epsilon o s$, $\epsilon \lambda \epsilon \eta \mu \omega \nu$, $\epsilon \lambda \epsilon \eta \mu o \sigma \upsilon \nu \eta$, $\dot{a}\nu \epsilon \lambda \epsilon o s$, $\dot{a}\nu \epsilon \lambda \epsilon \eta \mu \omega \nu$," *TDNT* 2.477–87, esp. 484–85.

107 The main passage is Justin *Dial.* 123.7; cf. 124.1ff. See Richardson, *Israel*, 83 n. 2 and *passim*. Cf. the review by J. C. H. Lebram, *VigCh* 26 (1972) 148–52; and Davies' remark, *Gospel ... Land*, 171 n. 18.

identifies the church with the "true" Israel[108] and Judaism with the "Israel according to the flesh" (Ἰσραὴλ κατὰ σάρκα).[109] However, Richardson is right in insisting that Paul does not use the term "Israel of God" elsewhere, when he refers to the church.

Taken as it stands, the expression "Israel of God" is redundant: it makes no sense to speak of an Israel which is not "of God." Yet such an expression does make sense as a critical distinction between a "true" and a "false" Israel. There is no doubt that Paul makes such a distinction, even if he uses other terminology. Analogous genitive qualifications are found elsewhere in Galatians, e.g., in terms like "the church of God"[110] or "the law of Christ."[111] But the Qumran texts have shown that such distinctions could be made very well within Judaism.[112] Although admittedly there is no proof, the suggestion can be made that Paul took over this expression from his Jewish–Christian opponents, in whose theology "Israel of God" would identify them as the true Judaism vis–à–vis official Judaism.[113] Just as Paul transfers Jewish prerogatives to the Gentile–Christian Galatians elsewhere in the letter, he would pick up another concept here and apply it, rather provocatively no doubt, to the readers of the epistle, that is, to those who will remain loyal Paulinists. However, one must also include in the blessing that part of Jewish Christianity which had approved and still approves, perhaps, of the agreements of the Jerusalem Council related to the Pauline mission (cf. 1:22–24;

2:1–10). Clearly excluded and under the curse are the "false brothers" back then (cf. 2:4–5) and now (cf. 1:6–9).

In conclusion, the meaning of the term "Israel of God" presupposes that at the time of Galatians the borderline between Christianity and Judaism was not yet clearly drawn, that a diversity of Christian and Jewish movements and groups tried to come to grips with the issue of Christ, and that the claim expressed in "Israel of God" could be made by different groups at the same time.[114] Thus, Paul extends the blessing beyond the Galatian Paulinists to those Jewish–Christians who approve of his κανών ("rule") in v 15.[115]

■ 17 Apparently approaching the end of the letter, Paul adds another remark, admittedly a strange one:[116] τοῦ λοιποῦ κόπους μοι μηδεὶς παρεχέτω· ἐγὼ γὰρ τὰ στίγματα τοῦ Ἰησοῦ ἐν τῷ σώματί μου βαστάζω ("henceforth, let no one cause me trouble, for I bear the marks of Jesus branded on my body"). Paul concludes the peroratio with an apostolic order in regard to the future coupled with his self–description as a representative of the crucified Christ.[117] The reason for making this remark at this point may become understandable, if we are anticipating the conquestio. Although reduced to a minimum, 6:17 does have the appearance of a conquestio. Among the examples mentioned by Quintilian as having been employed most effectively by Cicero is one that points out the defendant's "worth, his manly pursuits, the scars from wounds received in battle..."

---

108 Of course, Schrenk ("Israel," 87f [n. 101, above]) is right in saying that Paul never uses the concept Ἰσραὴλ κατὰ πνεῦμα ("Israel according to the Spirit"). But Gal 4:21–31, esp. 4:29, and Rom 2:17–29; 9–11 show that he could have used the term if he wanted. On the whole problem, see Gösta Lindeskog, "Israel in the New Testament—Some Few Remarks on a Great Problem," SEÅ 26 (1961) 57–92; Christian Müller, Gottes Gerechtigkeit und Gottes Volk (FRLANT 86; Göttingen: Vandenhoeck & Ruprecht, 1964); Luz, Geschichtsverständnis, 268ff; Käsemann, Römer, 241ff.
109 This term occurs 1 Cor 10:18; cf. Rom 9:3ff. See also Gal 1:13f; cf. 2:13–15.
110 Gal 1:13.
111 Gal 6:2.
112 The Qumran texts employ similar terminology with "of God": names designating the community of

Qumran (קהל אל, עצת אל, יחד אל, but not "Israel of God"). See on the evidence from Qumran, Braun, Qumran 1.214f; 2.146, 326.
113 Cf. the concept of ναὸς θεοῦ ("temple of God") in 2 Cor 6:16 and the interpretation by Betz, "2 Cor 6:14–7:1," 88–108, esp. 92.
114 See also D. W. B. Robinson, "The Distinction Between Jewish and Gentile Believers in Galatians," ABR 13 (1965) 29–48.
115 So also Richardson, Israel, 82f. Mussner (p. 417 n. 61) wants to connect it instead with Rom 11:26 πᾶς Ἰσραήλ ("the whole Israel"), but one does not necessarily exclude the other.
116 So Schlier, p. 284.
117 Cf. Gal 1:1, 12, 16; 2:19f; 4:14; 5:24; 6:14.

as a recommendation to the judge.[118] Gal 6:17 is such a *conquestio*, for it points to the στίγματα τοῦ Ἰησοῦ ("marks of Jesus") with which Paul has been inflicted as a result of his apostolic mission, which is identical with the case presented.[119]

However, it is also clear that Paul does not openly appeal for pity. Perhaps the lack of such an emotional appeal is due to the fact that, as Quintilian reports: "the majority of Athenians and almost all philosophers who have left anything in writing on the art of oratory have held that the recapitulation is the sole form of peroration. I imagine that the reason why the Athenians did so was that appeals to the emotions were forbidden to Athenian orators, a proclamation to this effect being actually made by the court–usher. I am less surprised at the philosophers taking this view, for they regard susceptibility to emotion as a vice, and think it immoral that the judge should be distracted from the truth by an appeal to his emotions and that it is unbecoming for a good man to make use of vicious procedure to serve his ends. Nonetheless they must admit that appeals to emotion are necessary if there are no other means for securing the victory of truth, justice, and the public interest."[120] Paul's restraint at this point with regard to the emotional appeal may reflect the same kind of caution which, according to Quintilian, was characteristic of the philosophers.[121] When the Apostle presents his order in v 17a ("henceforth let no one cause me trouble") he does so in hopeful anticipation that the problems have been solved and that there is no basis for further trouble.[122] The phrase κόπους παρέχειν ("cause trouble") is found only here in Paul.[123] We may not fail in assuming that the troubles are those which caused him to write the letter. Part of the burden of missionary work[124] is the threat of apostasy to those churches which had been founded with so many sacrifices.[125]

As a reason for his demand Paul adds in v 17b the statement "for I bear on my body the marks of Jesus." The term τὰ στίγματα ("the stigmas") originally refers to the marks of religious tattooing which was widely used in the Hellenistic world.[126] This term is qualified by a genitive "of Jesus,"[127] indicating a spiritualizing of that concept. What are the "tattoo–marks of Jesus?" It is possible that Christians at that time had themselves tattooed with symbols of their faith, perhaps the cross.[128] More probably, however, Paul refers to his troubles of all sorts stemming from his "suffering with Christ" during his missionary campaigns.[129] The language should be connected with that describing

---

118 Quint. 6.1.21, tr. H. E. Butler, LCL. Its connection with the catalog of περιστάσεις should be noted (see Betz, *Paulus*, 97ff).

119 Cf. Gal 1:23; 4:29; 5:11; 6:12.

120 Quint. 6.1.7.

121 The refusal to ask for mercy was foremost attributed to Socrates (cf. Xenophon *Mem.* 4.4.4), and subsequently became part of the Socratic tradition. This tradition has influenced Paul, as I have shown in *Paulus*, esp. 15ff.

122 τοῦ λοιποῦ ("from now on, in the future"). See Bauer, *s.v.*, 3, a, β; Moule, *Idiom Book*, 39, 161; BDF, § 186, 2; BDR, § 186, 4.

123 Cf. the occurrence of the term in Matt 26:10; Mark 14:6; Luke 11:7; 18:5; *Herm. Vis.* 3.3.2.

124 κόπος ("work, labor, toil") is specifically that of the missionary. See 2 Cor 10:15; 1 Thess 1:3; 2:9; 3:5. Cf. also the verb κοπιάω in Gal 4:11. See Friedrich Hauck, "κόπος," *TDNT* 3.827–30; Bauer, *s.v.*, 2.

125 Cf. Gal 4:11, 19; also 2:11. Schlier believes Paul points to the hostilities of the opponents and the weakness of the Galatians.

126 The concept is unique in the NT. For the material in ancient religions, see Bauer, *s.v.*; Otto Betz, "στίγμα," *TDNT* 7.657–64; Betz, *Lukian*, 79f; Mussies, *Dio Chrysostom*, 185; Philo *et.* 9 *D*(27–29); *Spec.* 1.58. See also Udo Borse, "Die Wundmale und der Todesbescheid," *BZ* NF 14 (1970) 88–111.

127 Instead of the simple Ἰησοῦ ("of Jesus"), supported by P⁴⁶ A B C* 33 *al*, other witnesses substitute Χριστοῦ ("of Christ") or longer christological formulae. See Metzger, *Textual Commentary*, 599.

128 This hypothesis was proposed by Erich Dinkler, "Jesu Wort vom Kreuztragen," in *Neutestamentliche Studien für R. Bultmann* (BZNW 21 [1954] 110–29); rep. in his *Signum Crucis*, 93. Dinkler believes that Paul's body was marked by an "X" for "Christos," received in Baptism. See also Resch, *Agrapha*, 226, n. 1.

129 Cf. 2 Cor 4:10: "we always carry about in our body the putting to death of Jesus" (Bauer's tr.); 1:5; 4:16; 13:3f; Phil 3:10f; (Col 1:24). So also Borse, "Die Wundmale," 93ff (n. 126 above); Mussner, pp. 418–20.

him as an "imitator of Christ" (μιμητὴς τοῦ Χριστοῦ),[130] which Paul had alluded to at several places earlier in the letter;[131] the term μιμητής ("imitator"), however, does not occur in Galatians.[132] The term βαστάζω ("bear") seems to allude to the "bearing of the cross."[133] That Paul emphasizes the physical nature of the marks is shown by the phrase "on my body," but he does not indicate what these marks really were.[134]

It is important to see that Paul in his final statement speaks again of himself as the apostle of Christ who was sent by his Lord to proclaim the gospel to the Gentiles, and thus also to the Galatians.[135] Not only did he bring the gospel to them, but as the "slave of Christ" (1:10) he represents Christ as in a christophany (4:13-14). Christ lives in him (2:20) and speaks through him (cf. 2 Cor 13:3). In making this remark in the end of the letter, Paul reminds the Galatians of the beginning of their existence as Christians, when he came to them (cf. 4:13-14) hoping as he does now that they will not despise him and reject him, but that they will again overcome the temptation and welcome him as "an angel of God, even as Christ himself."

Thus the letter to the Galatians reenacts the apostolic parousia[136] and the Christianization of the Galatians. The difference is that at the beginning they were confronted as to whether or not they should accept the "gospel of Christ," while now they are asked to re-main loyal to it and not bring upon themselves the curse of apostasy.[137]

■18 The final benediction differs to some extent from other Pauline epistles: ἡ χάρις τοῦ κυρίου ἡμῶν Ἰησοῦ Χριστοῦ μετὰ τοῦ πνεύματος ὑμῶν, ἀδελφοί ("the grace of our Lord Jesus Christ be with your spirit, brothers").[138] Peculiar is the address "brothers" which is so important in the letter,[139] but occurs in no other Pauline benediction. The preposition μετά ("with") with the genitive is common in all benedictions, but the object "with your spirit" is found only here and in Phil 4:23; Phlm 25 (cf. 2 Tim 4:22).[140] In contrast to the letter itself, where it always refers to the Spirit of God or Christ, the term "spirit" here refers to the human spirit.[141] These peculiarities originated in the fact that the benediction is traditional and not made by Paul himself. The term "grace"[142] is also traditional but in Paul's interpretation it has become the all-inclusive concept for salvation.

The closing liturgical acclamation ἀμήν ("amen") is well supported by the manuscript tradition.[143] However, it was probably not part of the original letter, but was added by the church, when the letter was used in the liturgy. This must have happened rather early, and may be the reason why the letter was preserved. In liturgy the "amen" would be spoken by the congregation as a response to the letter.[144]

130 For this concept see Betz, *Nachfolge*, 183 and *passim*; idem, "Eine Christus-Aretalogie bei Paulus (2 Kor 12, 7-10)," *ZThK* 66 (1969) 288-305.
131 Cf. Gal 2:19f; 4:13f; 5:24; 6:14.
132 Cf. 1 Cor 4:16; 11:1; Phil 3:17; 1 Thess 1:6; 2:14.
133 Cf. Luke 14:27; John 19:17; but see Gal 6:2, 5; Rom 15:1. For the meaning of the term, see Bauer, *s.v.* 2.
134 Cf. 2 Cor 4:10; 10:10; Phil 3:21, and on the whole matter Güttgemanns, *Apostel*, 126-35.
135 Cf. Gal 1:1f, 6, 7, 11f; 2:2-10; 3:1-5; 4:12-20.
136 See the Introduction to this commentary, § 5 and § 7.
137 See on Gal 1:6-9.
138 ℵ P 69 *pc* do not read ἡμῶν ("our"), but the benedictions Rom 16:20; 1 Thess 5:28 do read it, while it is missing in 1 Cor 16:23; 2 Cor 13:21; Phil 4:23; in Phlm 25 it is disputed. For literature on "blessings" generally, see on Gal 1:8-9; 6:16.
139 Cf. Gal 1:11; 3:15; 4:12, 28, 31; 5:11, 13; 6:1; also 1:2.
140 Rom 16:20; 1 Cor 16:23; 1 Thess 5:28 have μεθ' ὑμῶν ("with you"); 2 Cor 13:13 (also 2 Thess 3:18; Tit 3:15) has μετὰ πάντων ὑμῶν ("with you all"). The Galatian blessing is used by the ps.-Pauline letter to the Laodiceans (see HSW, *NT Apocrypha* 2.138).
141 On the meaning of "spirit" in Gal, see above on 3:2, 5.
142 Cf. Gal 1:3, 6, 15; 2:9, 21; 5:4. See Brun, *Segen und Fluch*, 36f; Gerhard Delling, "Zusammengesetzte Gottes- und Christusbezeichnungen in den Paulusbriefen," in his *Studien zum Neuen Testament und zum hellenistischen Judentum* (Berlin: Evangelische Verlagsanstalt, 1970) 421.
143 It is omitted by a few witnesses (G it⁸ Marius Victorinus Ambrosiaster). See Metzger, *Textual Commentary*, 599.
144 See also Rom 15:33; 16:24, 27; 1 Cor 16:24, and the endings of other letters, where the amen is supported only by part of the tradition. On the meaning of "amen" see on Gal 1:5.

**Appendices
Bibliography
Indices**

1. Josephus, *Jewish Antiquities* 20.38–48[1]

38   When Izates had learned that his mother was very much pleased with the Jewish religion, he was zealous to convert to it himself; and since he considered that he would not be genuinely a Jew unless he was circumcised, he was ready to act accordingly.[2] When
39 his mother learned of his intention, however, she tried to stop him by telling him that it was a dangerous move. For, she said, he was a king; and if his subjects should discover that he was devoted to rites that were strange and foreign to themselves, it would produce much disaffection and they would not tolerate the rule of the Jew over them. Besides this advice
40 she tried by every other means to hold him back. He, in turn, reported her arguments to Ananias.[3] The latter expressed agreement with the king's mother and actually threatened that if he should be unable to
41 persuade[4] Izates, he would abandon him and leave the land. For he said that he was afraid[5] that if the matter became universally known, he would be punished, in all likelihood, as personally responsible because he had instructed the king in unseemly practices. The king could, he said, worship God even without being circumcised if indeed he had fully decided to be a devoted adherent of Judaism, for it was this that counted more than circumcision.[6] He told
42 him, furthermore, that God himself would pardon him if, constrained thus by necessity and by fear of his subjects, he failed to perform this rite.[7] And so, for the
43 time, the king was convinced by his arguments. Afterwards, however, since he had not completely given up his desire, another Jew, named Eleazar, who came

44 from Galilee and who had a reputation for being extremely strict when it came to the ancestral laws, urged him to carry out the rite.[8] For when he came to him to pay him his respects and found him reading the law of Moses, he said: "In your ignorance, O king, you are guilty of the greatest offence against the law
45 and thereby against God. For you ought not merely to read the law but also, and even more, to do what is commanded in it. How long will you continue to be uncircumcised?[9] If you have not yet read the law concerning this matter, read it now,[10] so that you may know what an impiety it is that you commit."
46 Upon hearing these words, the king postponed the deed no longer. Withdrawing into another room, he summoned his physician and had the prescribed act performed. Then he sent for both his mother and his teacher Ananias and notified them that he had per-
47 formed the rite. They were immediately seized with consternation and fear beyond measure that, if it should be proved that he had performed the act, the king would risk losing his throne, since his subjects would not submit to government by a man who was a devotee of foreign practices,[11] and that they themselves would be in jeopardy since the blame for his action would be attributed to them. It was God who was to prevent their fears from being realized. For
48 although Izates himself and his children were often threatened with destruction, God preserved them, opening a path to safety from desperate straits. God thus demonstrated that those who fix their eyes on Him and trust in Him alone do not lose the reward of their piety.[12]

---

1   Text and tr. Louis H. Feldman, *Josephus*, LCL 9 (1965). See also Feldman's notes LCL 9.409–15, and for bib. his Appendix R (LCL 9.586).

2   ... ἔσπευσε καὶ αὐτὸς εἰς ἐκεῖνα [τὰ Ἰουδαίων ἔθη] μεταθέσθαι, νομίζων τε μὴ ἂν εἶναι βεβαίως Ἰουδαῖος, εἰ μὴ περιτέμοιτο.... Cf. Gal 1:6f; 2:3–5; 5:2f; 6:12f.

3   The Ananias of the story is a Jewish meschant, acting also as a missionary. See Feldman's n. b, p. 406.

4   The term πείθω ("persuade") seems almost technical in the context of Jewish missionary language (see also §42; 43). Cf. Gal 1:10; 5:7f.

5   For the motif of fear see also §41; 42; 47; 48 and Gal 2:12. On persecution, cf. Gal 1:13, 23; 4:29; 5:11a; 6:17b.

6   ... δυνάμενον δ' αὐτὸν ἔφη καὶ χωρὶς τῆς περιτομῆς τὸ θεῖον σέβειν, εἴγε πάντως κέκρικε ζηλοῦν τὰ πάτρια τῶν Ἰουδαίων· τοῦτ' εἶναι κυριώτερον τοῦ περιτέμνεσθαι· Ananias' position comes close to Paul's with regard to circumcision (cf. Gal 5:6; 6:15; Rom 2:25–29). The pre-Christian Paul would have disagreed with Ananias (cf. Gal 1:13f); the Christian Paul would refer to his doctrine of justification by faith (see Gal 2:15f).

7   For this argument, see Feldman's n., p. 410. Cf. Gal 2:1–10, where no reason is given for the decision of the Christian leaders in Jerusalem not to require circumcision of the converted Gentiles. They in fact agreed with Ananias' position against the position of the "false brothers."

8   ... περὶ τὰ πάτρια δοκῶν ἀκριβὴς εἶναι προετρέψατο πρᾶξαι τοὔργον. Cf. Gal 1:13f; 2:4; 6:12f.

9   Cf. Gal 1:6.

10   Cf. Gal 4:21.

11   τῶν παρ' ἑτέροις ζηλωτὴς ἐθνῶν. Cf. Gal 1:14; 4:3, 8–10.

12   This tendency of the Izates story, which assumes persecution because of the preaching of circumcision, is directly opposed to Paul's theology (cf. Gal. 5:11a).

2. 2 Corinthians 6:14–7:1

6:14a	μὴ γίνεσθε ἑτεροζυγοῦντες[1] ἀπίστοις·	6:14a	Do not get misyoked[1] with unbelievers!
14b	τίς γὰρ μετοχὴ δικαιοσύνῃ καὶ ἀνομίᾳ,[2]	14b	For what partnership have righteousness and lawlessness,[2]
14c	ἢ τίς κοινωνία φωτὶ πρὸς σκότος;	14c	or what fellowship has light with darkness?
15a	τίς δὲ συμφώνησις Χριστοῦ[3] πρὸς Βελιάρ,	15a	What harmony is there between Christ[3] and Beliar,
15b	ἢ τίς μέρις πιστῷ μετὰ ἀπίστου;[4]	15b	or what common lot has a believer with an unbeliever?[4]
16a	τίς δὲ συγκατάθεσις ναῷ θεοῦ μετὰ εἰδώλων;[5]	16a	What agreement is there between God's temple and idols?[5]
16b	ἡμεῖς γὰρ ναὸς θεοῦ ἐσμεν ζῶντος·	16b	For we are [the] temple of the living God.
16c	καθὼς εἶπεν ὁ θεὸς ὅτι[6]	16c	As God has said:[6]
16d	ἐνοικήσω ἐν αὐτοῖς	16d	"I will dwell in them
16e	καὶ ἐμπεριπατήσω,	16e	and walk among them,
16f	καὶ ἔσομαι αὐτῶν θεός,	16f	and I will be their God,
16g	καὶ αὐτοὶ ἔσονταί μου λαός.[7]	16g	and they shall be my people.[7]
17a	διὸ ἐξέλθατε ἐκ μέσου αὐτῶν[8]	17a	Therefore come out from their midst[8]
17b	καὶ ἀφορίσθητε,[9]	17b	and separate,"[9]
17c	λέγει κύριος,	17c	says the Lord,
17d	καὶ ἀκαθάρτου μὴ ἅπτεσθε·[10]	17d	"and touch nothing unclean.[10]
17e	κἀγὼ εἰσδέξομαι ὑμᾶς,	17e	Then I will receive you,
18a	καὶ ἔσομαι ὑμῖν εἰς πατέρα,[11]	18a	and I will be a father to you,[11]
18b	καὶ ὑμεῖς ἔσεσθέ μοι εἰς υἱοὺς καὶ θυγατέρας,[12]	18b	and you shall be to me sons and daughters,"[12]
18c	λέγει κύριος παντοκράτωρ.	18c	says the Lord Almighty.
7:1a	ταύτας οὖν ἔχοντες τὰς ἐπαγγελίας,[13] ἀγαπητοί,	7:1a	Since we have these promises,[13] beloved,
1b	καθαρίσωμεν ἑαυτοὺς[14] ἀπὸ παντὸς μολυσμοῦ σαρκὸς καὶ πνεύματος,[15]	1b	let us cleanse ourselves[14] from every defilement of flesh and spirit,[15]
1c	ἐπιτελοῦντες[16] ἁγιωσύνην ἐν φόβῳ θεοῦ.[17]	1c	making holiness perfect[16] in [the] fear of God.[17]

1 The *anti*-Pauline character of the passage was first demonstrated in my article "2 Cor 6:14–7:1," 88–108.

2 This parenesis is in line with the theological position of the "false brothers" at Jerusalem (see Gal 2:4f) and the "men from James" (see Gal 2:11–14). Since Paul regards these opponents as precursors of his present Galatian opponents, the position will also conform to their theology. They would call "misyoking" what Paul had done when he brought the Galatians into the church without subjecting them to the Torah covenant. For the concept of the yoke, see Gal 5:1, and Paul's opposite, the concept of "freedom."

3 Gal defends the opposite; cf. esp. 2:15–21.

4 The crucifixion of Christ plays no role in the passage. Cf. Gal 2:20f; 3:1, 13; 4:5; 5:2, 4, 11, 24; 6:12–14, 17b. For the juxtaposition of Christ and the Devil, cf. the Ebionite theology as reported by Epiphanius *Anaceph.* 30.16.2.

5 The concept of "faith" is not related to Christ as "faith in Christ." Cf. Gal 2:15f, esp.

6 Cf. Gal 4:8–10.

7 The following conflation of Scripture quotations is a highly articulate summary of the Sinai Covenant understood as the divine "promises" (7:1a). Cf. Gal 3:19–25. By contrast Paul bases salvation entirely upon the promise (sing.!) made to Abraham (Gal 3:6–18, 22, 29; 4:23, 28).

8 Cf. the notion "the Israel of God" Gal 6:16.

9 Cf. the term "exclude" Gal 4:17.

10 See the same term Gal 2:12. Cf. Peter's defense of his separation from the table of the Gentiles in ps.–Clem. *Recog.* 2:71f; 7:29; *Hom.* 13.4; see also Epiphanius *Anaceph.* 30.2.3.

11 The subject of purity and impurity is absent from Gal. Paul's view is expressed in Rom 14:20. Cf. the great interest in purity in ps.–Clem. *Hom.* 11.28–30.

12 Note the future tense, and by contrast the present tense in Gal 3:26–28, 29; 4:1–10, 21–31.

13 Cf. Gal 3:28: "neither male nor female."

14 See above, n. 7.

15 By contrast, Paul's parenesis is not concerned with ritual purity, but is strongly influenced by Hellen-

6:16b: ὑμεῖς... ἐστε P⁴⁶ C Dᶜ G K Ψ 614 Byz Lect itᵍ, ⁶¹ vg syrᵖ,ʰ goth arm *al.* So Metzger, *Textual Commentary*, 580. Cf. 1 Cor 3:16.

ναοί ℵ* 0243 1739 Clement Augustine

7:1b αἵματος instead of πνεύματος is read by Marcion

7:1c P⁴⁶ reads ἐν ἀγάπῃ θεοῦ

The manuscript tradition shows several attempts to "Paulinize" the text, thus sensing its non–Pauline character. 6:16b is made to conform with 1 Cor 3:16 (cf. 6:19), so that it reads: "For you are [the] temple of God." Marcion replaced "spirit" by "blood" in 7:1b; "flesh and blood" is a Pauline phrase (cf. Gal 1:16). In 7:1c the non–Pauline "in [the] fear of God" is "Paulinized" to read: "in [the] love of God."

Analysis: A Jewish-Christian Cultic Parenesis

6:14a   I. A concrete parenesis

6:14b–7:1   II. Theological foundations

6:14b–16a   A. Major premise: an ontological orientation, in the form of five rhetorical questions, in the order of *ab, ab, a,* functioning as reminders

14c, 15a   1. Of the radical cosmological dualism

14c   a. Second question: "light" versus "darkness"

15a   b. Third question: "Christ" versus "Beliar"

14b, 15b   2. Of the radical anthropological dualism

14b   a. First question: "righteousness" versus "lawlessness"

15b   b. Fourth question: "believer" versus "unbeliever"

16a   3. Of the "religious" situation

         a. Fifth question: "temple of God" versus "idols"

6:16b–18c   B. Minor premise: an ecclesiological orientation, in the form of a quotation of the "covenant"

6:16b   1. A confessional self–definition of the church, using the language of v 16a

6:16c–18c   2. Scripture proof: quotation of the divine promises (cf. 7:1)

16c–g   a. The first promise

16c   (1) Quotation formula

16d–g   (2) An adapted citation of Lev 26:12 (LXX)

17a–d   b. Cultic ordinances

           (1) An adapted citation of Isa 52:11 (LXX)

           (2) Quotation formula

18a–b   c. The second promise

           (1) An adapted citation of 2 Sam 7:14 (LXX)

18c   (2) Quotation formula

7:1   C. Conclusion: the general parenesis

1a   1. A restatement of the premises ("indicative")

1b–c   2. A definition of the ethical task ("imperative")

1b   a. As cultic–ethical purification

1c   b. As perfection of eschatological holiness

---

istic philosophical ethics (cf. Gal 5:1–6:10).

16   The concept of purification of flesh and spirit is clearly non-Pauline. The purity of the heart (or soul) was, however, highly valued in the anti-Pauline tradition of the ps.–Clem. literature, esp. *Hom.* 2.2; 11.28f; *Recog.* 6.11.

17   Cf. the sarcastic use of the term in Gal 3:3; see also 6:7f, 12, 13.

18   The concept of the "fear of God" is non-Pauline. The concept is, however, highly important to the anti-Pauline tradition in the ps.–Clem. literature, esp. *Hom.* 10.5; *Recog.* 9.15.

3. The *Kerygmata Petrou*[1]

A. The Epistle of Peter to James (*Epistula Petri*)

1.1. Peter to James, the lord and bishop of the holy church: Peace be with you always from the Father of all through Jesus Christ.
2. Knowing well that you, my brother, eagerly take pains about what is for the mutual benefit of us all, I earnestly beseech you not to pass on to any of the Gentiles the books of my preachings which I (here) forward to you, nor to any one of our own tribe before probation.[2] But if some one of them has been examined and found to be worthy, then you may hand them over to him in the same way as Moses handed over his office of a teacher to the seventy.[3] 3. Wherefore also the fruit of his caution is to be seen up to this day. For those who belong to his people preserve everywhere the same rule in their belief in the one God and in their line of conduct,[4] the Scriptures with their many senses being unable to incline them to assume another attitude. 4. Rather they attempt, on the basis of the rule that has been handed down to them, to harmonize the contradictions of the Scriptures, if haply some one who does not know the traditions is perplexed by the ambiguous utterances of the prophets. 5. On this account they permit no one to teach unless he first learn how the Scriptures should be used. Wherefore there obtain amongst them one God, one law, and one hope.[5] 2.1. In order now that the same may also take place among us, hand over the books of my preachings in the same mysterious way to our seventy brethren that they may prepare those who are candidates for positions as teachers. 2. For if

we do not proceed in this way, our word of truth will be split into many opinions.[6] This I do not know as a prophet,[7] but I have already the beginning of the evil before me. 3. For some from among the Gentiles have rejected my lawful preaching[8] and have preferred a lawless and absurd doctrine *of the man who is my enemy*.[9] 4. And indeed some have attempted, whilst I am still alive, to distort my words by interpretations of many sorts, as if I taught the dissolution of the law[10] and, although I was of this opinion, did not express it openly.[11] But that may God forbid! 5. For to do such a thing means to act contrary to the law of God which was made known by Moses and was confirmed by our Lord in its everlasting continuance. For he said:[12] The "*heaven and the earth will pass away, but one jot or one tittle shall not pass away from the law*". 6. This he said *that everything might come to pass*. But those persons who, I know not how, allege that they are at home in my thoughts wish to expound the words which they have heard of me better than myself who spoke them. To those whom they instruct they say that this is my opinion, to which indeed I never gave a thought. 7. But if they falsely assert such a thing whilst I am still alive, how much more after my death will those who come later venture to do so?[13]
3.1. In order now that that may not happen I earnestly beseech you not to pass on the books of my preachings which I send you to any one of our own tribe or to any foreigner before probation, but if some one is examined and found to be worthy, let them then be handed over in the way 2. in which Moses handed over his office of a teacher to the seventy, in order that they may preserve the doctrines of faith and hand on

---

1 The text is according to Bernhard Rehm, *Die Pseudo-klementinen, I. Homilien* (second rev. ed. Franz Paschke; GCS; Berlin: Akademie–Verlag, 1969). The tr., with some alterations, is taken from HSW, *NT* Apocrypha 2.111f. For bib., see the Introduction above, § 2.C.

2 The *Ep. Petr.* sees itself confronted by two opposi-tional Christian groups, the Gentiles (οἱ ἀπὸ τῶν ἐθνῶν) and certain fellow Jews (ὁμόφυλοι).

3 The theology of the *Kerygmata Petrou* regards Moses and his chain of traditions as the prototype for Chris-tianity. Cf. Gal 3:19–25 and Paul's independence stated in Gal 1:1, 12ff. In stark contrast to Paul's openness to the Gentiles, stands the "ordination" ceremony told in the *Contestatio*, another fragment from the *Kerygmata Petrou* (see the tr. in HSW, *NT Apocrypha* 2.112–15).

4 τὸν γὰρ αὐτὸν οἱ πανταχῇ ὁμόεθνοι τῆς μοναρχίας καὶ πολιτείας φυλάσσουσι κανόνα. . . . Cf. the κανών ("rule") Gal 6:15f; for the term φυλάσσω ("ob-serve"), cf. Gal 6:13.

5 εἷς θεός, εἷς νόμος, μία ἐλπίς. This is the "canon" of the *Kerygmata Petrou*. For εἷς θεός see Gal 3:20; for εἷς νόμος cf. Gal 3:19–25; 5:14; 6:2; for ἐλπίς cf. Gal 5:5.

6 . . . εἰς πολλὰς γνώμας ὁ τῆς ἀληθείας ἡμῶν διαιρε-θήσεται λόγος. The statement no doubt reflects ex-periences with regard to the Pauline mission.

7 Peter's "title" προφήτης ("prophet") is noteworthy here.

8 τινὲς γὰρ τῶν ἀπὸ ἐθνῶν τὸ δι' ἐμοῦ νόμιμον ἀπεδο-κίμασαν κήρυγμα. Cf. the "other gospel" Gal 1:6f; 2:7.

9 τοῦ ἐχθροῦ ἀνθρώπου ἄνομόν τινα καὶ φλυαρώδη προσ-ηκάμενοι διδασκαλίαν. The statement no doubt reflects the knowledge of Paul and his gospel. Cf. Gal 4:16; also Matt 13:28.

10 εἰς τὴν τοῦ νόμου κατάλυσιν. Cf. Gal 2:18.

11 Cf. Gal 2:11–14.

12 Cf. Matt 5:18; 24:35; and Gal 3:19–25.

13 Cf. Paul's and Peter's agreement up to the conflict at Antioch (Gal 2:11–14). See also Acts 10:45; 11:3.

331

the true rule everywhere, interpreting everything in accordance with our tradition and not being dragged into error through ignorance and through conjectures of their own minds to bring others into the like pit of destruction.

3. What seems to me to be necessary I have now indicated to you. And what you, my lord, deem to be right, do you carry fittingly into effect. Farewell.

B. Pseudo–Clementine Homilies 11.35.3–6[14]

Our Lord and Prophet who has sent us declared to us that the Evil One, after having disputed with him for forty days[15] and having accomplished nothing against him, promised to send apostles from among his subjects, for the purpose of deception.[16] Therefore, above all, remember to accept no apostle or teacher or prophet who does not first compare his preaching[17] with [that of] James who was called the brother of my Lord[18] and to whom it was entrusted to administer the church of the Hebrews in Jerusalem. Even when [such a person] comes to you with witnesses [do not simply accept him], so that the Evil which had disputed with the Lord for forty days and had achieved nothing may not afterwards, like lightning falling from heaven upon the earth, send a messenger against you, just as he has now pushed upon us this Simon[19] who preaches under the pretense of truth[20] in the name of our Lord, but sows error. Because of him the one who has sent us said: "many shall come to me in sheep's clothing, but inwardly they are ravening wolves; by their fruits you shall recognize them."[21]

C. Pseudo–Clementine Homilies 17.13–19[22]

13.1. When Simon[23] heard this, he interrupted with the words: "...You have stated that you have learned accurately the teaching of your master because you have heard and seen him directly face to face, and that it is not possible for any other to experience the like in a dream or in a vision.[24] 2. I shall show you that this is false: the person to whose hearing something comes is by no means certain of what is said. For he must check whether, being (only) a man, he has not been deceived by appearances. On the other hand, a vision creates together with the appearance the certainty that one sees something divine. Give me an answer first to that."

16.1. And Peter said: "...2. We know...that many idolators, adulterers, and other sinners have seen visions and had true dreams,[25] and also that some have had visions that were wrought by demons.[26] For I maintain that the eyes of mortals cannot see the incorporeal being[27] of the Father or of the Son, because it is enwrapped in insufferable light. 3. Therefore it is a token of the mercy of God, and not of jealousy in him, that he is invisible to men living in the flesh. For he who sees him must die. 6. ...No one is able to see the incorporeal power[28] of the Son or even of an angel. But he who has a vision should recognize that this is the work of a wicked demon.[29]

17.5. ...For to a pious, natural, and pure mind the truth gushes forth; it is not acquired through a dream, but is granted to the good through discernment.[30]

18.1. For in this way was the Son revealed to me also by the Father.[31] Wherefore I know the power of revelation; I have myself learned this from him. For at the very time when the Lord asked how the people named him—although I had heard that one called him one thing, others another—it rose in my heart to say, and I know not how I said it, 'Thou art the Son

---

14 Tr. auth. The speaker of this warning against the "heretics" is Peter, the place is Tripolis in Phoenicia (*Hom.* 11.36.3).

15 Cf. Matt 4:1–11 // Mark 1:12f // Luke 4:1–13.

16 This information goes beyond what is reported in the NT. Cf. 2 Cor 11:14f.

17 ...μὴ πρότερον ἀντιβαλόντα αὐτοῦ τὸ κήρυγμα Ἰακώβῳ.... Cf. Gal 2:2.

18 Cf. Gal 1:19.

19 Simon stands for Paul.

20 Cf. Gal 2:5, 14; 5:7.

21 Πολλοὶ ἐλεύσονται πρός με ἐν ἐνδύματι προβάτων, ἔσωθεν δέ εἰσι λύκοι ἅρπαγες· ἀπὸ τῶν καρπῶν αὐτῶν ἐπιγνώσεσθε αὐτούς. The logion is close to Justin *Apol.* 1.16.13 (see also *Dial.* 35.3) and does not depend directly upon Matt 7:15f. Cf. Leslie L. Kline, *The Sayings of Jesus in the Pseudo-Clementine Homilies* (SBLDS 14; Missoula: Scholars, 1975) 56–58.

22 The tr., with some alterations, is taken from HSW, *NT Apocrypha* 2.122f.

23 Peter's defense against Simon (the name is not to be confused with the name Simon Peter in the NT!), who serves as a stand-in for Paul, is no doubt a fiction by a later author. It is not clear, however, whether the strongly anti-Pauline author depends upon the NT for information, or upon independent tradition which is also reflected in the NT.

24 διὰ τὸ παρόντα ἐναργείᾳ ὁρᾶν καὶ ἀκούειν αὐτοῦ, καὶ ἑτέρῳ τινὶ μὴ δυνατὸν εἶναι ὁμάματι ἢ ὀπτασίᾳ ἔχειν τὸ ὅμοιον. Cf. Gal 1:12, 16.

25 ὁράματι καὶ ἀληθεῖς ὀνείρους ὁρῶντας.

26 δαιμόνων ὀπτασίαι.

27 ἄσαρκος ἰδέα.

28 ἄσαρκος δύναμις.

29 εἰ δὲ ἤδη τις ὀπτασίαν, κακοῦ δαίμονος ταύτην εἶναι νοείτω.

30 τῷ γὰρ εὐσεβεῖ ἐμφύτῳ καὶ καθαρῷ ἀναβλύζει τῷ νῷ τὸ ἀληθές, οὐκ ὀνείρῳ σπουδαζόμενον, ἀλλὰ συνέσει ἀγαθοῖς διδόμενον.

31 οὕτως γὰρ κἀμοὶ ἀπὸ τοῦ πατρὸς ἀπεκαλύφθη ὁ υἱός. Cf. Gal 1:16.

of the living God'.[32] ...6. You see now how expressions of wrath have to be made through visions and dreams, but discourse with friends takes place from mouth to mouth, openly and not through riddles, visions, and dreams as with an enemy.[33] 19.1. And if our Jesus appeared to you also and became known in a vision and met you as angry with an enemy, yet he has spoken only through visions and dreams or through external revelations. But can any one be made competent to teach through a vision?[34] 2. And if your opinion is, 'That is possible', why then did our teacher spend a whole year with us who were awake? 3. How can we believe you even if he has appeared to you, and how can he have appeared to you if you desire the opposite of what you have learned? 4. But if you were visited by him for the space of an hour and were instructed by him and thereby have become an apostle,[35] then proclaim his words, expound what he has taught, be a friend to his apostles and do not contend with me, who am his confidant; for you have in hostility *withstood*[36] me, who am a firm rock, the foundation stone of the church.[37] 5. If you were not an enemy, then you would not slander me and revile my preaching in order that I may not be believed when I proclaim what I have heard in my own person from the Lord, as if I were undoubtedly *condemned*[38] and you were acknowledged. 6. And if you call me '*condemned*',[39] then you accuse God, who revealed Christ to me, and disparage him who called me blessed on account of the revelation.[40] 7. But if you really desire to cooperate with the truth, then learn first from us what we have learned from him and, as a learner of the truth, become a fellow worker with us."[41]

---

32 This allusion to the episode at Caesarea Philippi comes close to the Matthean version (Matt 16:13ff), but the characteristic differences should not be overlooked.

33 ὁρᾷς πῶς τὰ τῆς ὀργῆς δι' ὁραμάτων καὶ ἐνυπνίων, τὰ δὲ πρὸς φίλον στόμα κατὰ στόμα, ἐν εἴδει καὶ οὐ δι' αἰνιγμάτων καὶ ὁραμάτων καὶ ἐνυπνίων, ὡς πρὸς ἐχθρόν. Cf. Gal 1:13, 23.

34 Cf. Gal 1:12.

35 εἰ δὲ ὑπ' ἐκείνου μιᾶς ὥρας ὀφθεὶς μαθητευθεὶς ἀπόστολος ἐγένου.... This information goes beyond what is reported in the NT. Cf. 1 Cor 15:8; Acts 9:3ff.

36 ἐναντίος ἀνθέστηκάς μοι. Cf. Gal 2:11: αὐτῷ ἀντέστην.

37 Cf. Matt 16:17; 1 Cor 3:11 (anti-Petrine?); also Matt 7:24, 25.

38 ὡς ἐμοῦ καταγνωσθέντος. Cf. Gal 2:11: ὅτι κατεγνωσμένος ἦν.

39 ἢ εἰ "κατεγνωσμένον" λέγεις.

40 Cf. Matt 16:17.

41 This is precisely what Paul refused to do (see *Hom.* 17.20.1). Cf. Gal 1:12.

4. Justin Martyr, *Dialogue with Trypho* 46–47[1]

46.1. Ἐὰν δέ τινες καὶ νῦν ζῆν βούλωνται[2] φυλάσσοντες[3] τὰ διὰ Μωυσέως διαταχθέντα[4] καὶ πιστεύσωσιν ἐπὶ τοῦτον τὸν σταυρωθέντα Ἰησοῦν,[5] ἐπιγνόντες ὅτι αὐτός ἐστιν ὁ Χριστὸς τοῦ θεοῦ καὶ αὐτῷ δέδοται τὸ κρῖναι πάντας ἁπλῶς καὶ αὐτοῦ ἐστιν ἡ αἰώνιος βασιλεία, δύνανται καὶ αὐτοὶ σωθῆναι; ἐπυνθάνετό μου.

46.2. Κἀγὼ πάλιν· Συσκεψώμεθα κἀκεῖνο, εἰ ἔνεστιν, ἔλεγον, φυλάσσειν τὰ διὰ Μωυσέως διαταχθέντα ἅπαντα νῦν.[6]

Κἀκεῖνος ἀπεκρίνατο· Οὔ.[7] γνωρίζομεν γὰρ ὅτι, ὡς ἔφης, οὔτε πρόβατον τοῦ πάσχα ἀλλαχόσε θύειν δυνατὸν οὔτε τοὺς τῇ νηστείᾳ κελευσθέντας προσφέρεσθαι χιμάρους οὔτε τὰς ἄλλας ἁπλῶς ἁπάσας προσφοράς.

Κἀγώ· Τίνα οὖν ἃ δυνατόν ἐστι φυλάσσειν, παρακαλῶ, λέγε αὐτός· πεισθήσῃ γὰρ ὅτι μὴ φυλάσσων τὰ αἰώνια δικαιώματά τις ἢ πράξας σωθῆναι ἐκ παντὸς ἔχει.

Κἀκεῖνος· Τὸ σαββατίζειν λέγω καὶ τὸ περιτέμνεσθαι[8] καὶ τὸ τὰ ἔμμηνα φυλάσσειν[9] καὶ τὸ βαπτίζεσθαι ἁψάμενόν τινος ὧν ἀπηγόρευται ὑπὸ Μωυσέως ἢ ἐν συνουσίᾳ γενόμενον.

47.1. Καὶ ὁ Τρύφων πάλιν· Ἐὰν δέ τις, εἰδὼς ὅτι ταῦτα οὕτως ἔχει, μετὰ τοῦ καὶ τοῦτον εἶναι τὸν Χριστὸν ἐπίστασθαι δῆλον ὅτι καὶ πεπιστευκέναι καὶ πείθεσθαι αὐτῷ,[10] βούλεται[11] καὶ ταῦτα φυλάσσειν,[12] σωθήσεται; ἐπυνθάνετο.

Κἀγώ· Ὡς μὲν ἐμοὶ δοκεῖ, ὦ Τρύφων, λέγω ὅτι σωθήσεται ὁ τοιοῦτος, ἐὰν μὴ τοὺς ἄλλους ἀνθρώπους, λέγω δὴ τοὺς ἀπὸ τῶν ἐθνῶν διὰ τοῦ Χριστοῦ[13] ἀπὸ τῆς πλάνης περιτμηθέντας,[14] ἐκ παντὸς πείθειν[15] ἀγωνίζηται ταῦτα αὐτῷ φυλάσσειν, λέγων οὐ σωθήσεσθαι αὐτοὺς ἐὰν μὴ ταῦτα φυλάξωσιν, ὁποῖον ἐν ἀρχῇ τῶν λόγων καὶ σὺ ἔπραττες, ἀποφαινόμενος οὐ σωθήσεσθαί με ἐὰν μὴ ταῦτα φυλάξω.

46.1. "But if some even now wish[2] to live in the observance[3] of the institutions given by Moses[4] and also believe in this Jesus who was crucified,[5] recognizing that he is the Christ of God and that it is given to him to judge all in fairness and that to him belongs the eternal kingdom—can even these people be saved?" He asked me this.

46.2. I replied: "Let us consider also this together, whether it is possible now to observe all of the institutions given by Moses."[6]

He answered: "No.[7] For we know that, as you said, it is not possible either to sacrifice the passover lamb anywhere else [than in Jerusalem], or to offer the goats ordered for the fast, or simply all of the other sacrificial offerings."

Then I said: "Tell me then yourself, I ask, some ordinances which it is possible to observe. For you will be persuaded that someone, although he does not observe or perform the eternal demands of the law, has full salvation."

He replied: "I name the keeping of the sabbath, circumcision,[8] observation of months,[9] and ritual ablutions if one has touched anything prohibited by Moses, or if one has had sexual intercourse."

47.1. Trypho asked again: "But if someone, knowing[10] that this is so, wishes[11] also to observe[12] these [ordinances given by Moses] after he has come to recognize this man [= Jesus] to be the Christ and has become a believer and obeys him—will he be saved?" This he asked.

I replied: "As far as my opinion is concerned, Trypho, I say that such a person will be saved, except when he strives with all his power to persuade[15] other people—I mean of course those from the gentiles who have been circumcised[14] from error through the Christ[13]—to observe the same [ordinances] as he himself, declaring that they shall not be saved unless they observe them. This was the way in which you yourself acted at the beginning of our debate when you stated that I will not be saved unless I observe these [ordinances]."

---

1   Text according to Edgar J. Goodspeed, *Die ältesten Apologeten* (Göttingen: Vandenhoeck & Ruprecht, 1914); tr. auth.
2   Cf. Gal 4:21.
3   Cf. Gal 6:13.
4   Cf. Gal 3:19.
5   Cf. Gal 2:16.
6   Cf. Gal 5:3, 14.
7   Cf. Gal 6:13.
8   Cf. Gal 2:3–5, 12; 5:2f, 6, 11; 6:12f, 15.
9   Cf. Gal 4:10.
10   Cf. Gal 2:16.
11   The term is used frequently in this passage. Cf. Gal 4:21.
12   The term occurs frequently in this passage. Cf. Gal 6:13.
13   Cf. Gal 1:1.
14   Cf. Rom 2:28f; Col 2:11; Eph 2:11.
15   Cf. Gal 5:7f; 1:10.

47.2. Κἀκεῖνος· Διὰ τί οὖν εἶπας· Ὡς μὲν ἐμοὶ δοκεῖ, σωθήσεται ὁ τοιοῦτος, εἰ μήτι εἰσὶν οἱ λέγοντες ὅτι οὐ σωθήσονται οἱ τοιοῦτοι;[16]

Εἰσίν, ἀπεκρινάμην, ὦ Τρύφων, καὶ μηδὲ κοινωνεῖν ὁμιλίας ἢ ἑστίας τοῖς τοιούτοις τολμῶντες·[17] οἷς ἐγὼ οὐ σύναινός εἰμι. Ἀλλ' ἐὰν αὐτοὶ διὰ τὸ ἀσθενὲς τῆς γνώμης[18] καὶ τὰ ὅσα δύνανται[19] νῦν ἐκ τῆς Μωυσέως, ἃ διὰ τὸ σκληροκάρδιον τοῦ λαοῦ νοοῦμεν διατετάχθαι, μετὰ τὸ ἐπὶ τοῦτον τὸν Χριστὸν ἐλπίζειν[20] καὶ τὰς αἰωνίους καὶ φύσει δικαιοπραξίας καὶ εὐσεβείας φυλάσσειν βούλωνται καὶ αἱρῶνται συζῆν[21] τοῖς Χριστιανοῖς καὶ πιστοῖς,[22] ὡς προεῖπον, μὴ πείθοντες[23] αὐτοὺς μήτε περιτέμνεσθαι[24] ὁμοίως αὐτοῖς μήτε σαββατίζειν μήτε ἄλλα ὅσα τοιαῦτά ἐστι τηρεῖν, καὶ προσλαμβάνεσθαι[25] καὶ κοινωνεῖν ἁπάντων, ὡς ὁμοσπλάγχνοις καὶ ἀδελφοῖς, δεῖν ἀποφαίνομαι. 47.3. Ἐὰν δὲ οἱ ἀπὸ τοῦ γένους τοῦ ὑμετέρου πιστεύειν λέγοντες ἐπὶ τοῦτον τὸν Χριστὸν, ὦ Τρύφων, ἔλεγον, ἐκ παντὸς[26] κατὰ τὸν διὰ Μωυσέως διαταχθέντα νόμον[27] ἀναγκάζουσι ζῆν τοὺς ἐξ ἐθνῶν πιστεύοντας[28] ἐπὶ τοῦτον τὸν Χριστὸν ἢ μὴ κοινωνεῖν αὐτοῖς τῆς τοιαύτης συνδιαγωγῆς αἱροῦνται,[29] ὁμοίως καὶ τούτους οὐκ ἀποδέχομαι. 47.4. Τοὺς δὲ πειθομένους[30] αὐτοῖς ἐπὶ τὴν ἔννομον πολιτείαν μετὰ τοῦ φυλάσσειν τὴν εἰς τὸν Χριστὸν τοῦ θεοῦ ὁμολογίαν καὶ σωθήσεσθαι ἴσως ὑπολαμβάνω. Τοὺς δὲ ὁμολογήσαντας καὶ ἐπιγνόντας τοῦτον εἶναι τὸν Χριστὸν καὶ ἡτινιοῦν αἰτίᾳ μεταβάντας[31] ἐπὶ τὴν ἔννομον πολιτείαν, ἀρνησαμένους ὅτι οὗτός ἐστιν ὁ Χριστός, καὶ πρὶν τελευτῆς μὴ μεταγνόντας, οὐδ' ὅλως σωθήσεσθαι ἀποφαίνομαι.

47.2. Upon this he asked: "Why then did you say 'as far as my opinion is concerned', unless there actually are some who say that such people will not be saved?"[16]

"There are such people, Trypho," I answered. "They do not dare have fellowship with such people, be it in form of social intercourse or meals.[17] With these people I am in disagreement. But if they, because of the weakness of their understanding,[18] wish to observe what at present is possible for them to observe of the laws of Moses[19]—which we think were ordained because of the people's hardness of heart—and, after having put their hope upon this Christ,[20] [if they wish to perform] them as what they are by nature, eternal acts of morality and religion, and [if] they choose to live together[21] with the [other] Christian believers,[22] as I have stated before, and do not persuade[23] them to be circumcised[24] as they themselves are or to keep the sabbath or to observe any other such [rituals], then I declare that they should be accepted[25] into the fellowship of all as [Christian] kinsmen and brothers. 47.3. But those of your [Jewish] race, Trypho," I said, "who say they believe in this Christ, but compel the gentiles who believe in this Christ[28] to live completely[26] according to the law ordained by Moses,[27] or do not choose to have close fellowship with them,[29] likewise men such as these I do not accept. 47.4. But I suppose that even those [Gentiles] who were persuaded[30] by them [=Jewish-Christians] to join the legal community [=Judaism], together with observing the confession of the Christ of God, that those will be saved likewise. I do declare, however, that those will never be saved who have confessed and come to know this man [=Jesus] to be the Christ, but have for some reason switched[31] and joined the legal community [=Judaism], now denying that he is the Christ and not changing their mind before their death."

---

16 Cf. Gal 5:2; Acts 15:1.
17 Cf. Gal 2:11–14.
18 Cf. Rom 14:1f; 1 Cor 8:7ff.
19 Cf. Gal 6:13.
20 Cf. Gal 5:5.
21 See n. 9.
22 Cf. 2 Cor 6:14 (above, Appendix 2); Gal 3:9; Acts 10:45; 16:1.
23 See n. 13.
24 Cf. Gal 2:3–5, 12; 5:2f, 6, 11; 6:12f, 15.
25 Cf. Rom 14:1; 15:7.
26 The adverbial ἐκ παντός is peculiar; see Bauer, s.v. ἐκ, 6, Cf. Gal 5:2; 6:13.

27 Cf. Gal 3:19.
28 Cf. Gal 2:3, 14; 6:12.
29 See n. 9.
30 See n. 7.
31 Cf. Gal 1:6f.

1. Commentaries

The list of commentaries given here is selective. From the large number of works written on Galatians those have been selected which have made important scholarly contributions or are still of value to scholars today. Sermons, paraphrases, and devotional works, of which there is an even greater number, have been left out. For a more extensive list, see Mussner, xi–xvii.

Older Works:

Cramer, John A.
Catenae graecorum patrum (vol. 5; Oxford: Oxford University, 1844).
Souter, Alexander
The Earliest Latin Commentaries on the Epistles of St. Paul (Oxford: Clarendon, 1927). Contains:
Marius Victorinus
Ambrosiaster
Jerome
Augustine
Pelagius
Staab, Karl
Pauluskommentare aus der griechischen Kirche aus Katenenhandschriften gesammelt und herausgegeben (NTAbh 15; Münster: Aschendorff, 1933). Contains:
Eusebius of Emesa (+ 359)
Severianus of Gabala (+ after 409)
Gennadius of Constantinople (+ 741)
Oecumenius of Tricca (6th c.)
Photius of Constantinople (c. 820–891)
Ephraem Syrus (+ 373)
S. Ephraemi Syri commentarii in epistolas D. Pauli, nunc primum e Armenio in Latinum sermonem a patribus Mekitharistis translati (Venice: Ex Typographia Sancti Lazari, 1893).
Chrysostom, John (354–407)
S. Joannis Chrysostomi Interpretatio omnium Epistolarum Paulinarum per Homilias facta (ed. Frederick Field; Oxford: Parker *et al.*, 1852).
PG 61.611–82.
Commentary of St. John Chrysostom, Archbishop of Constantinople, on the Epistle of St. Paul the Apostle to the Galatians (The Oxford tr. revised, with additional notes by Gross Alexander; NPNF 1.13; Grand Rapids: Eerdmans, 1956) 1–48.
Ambrosiaster (4th cent.)
Ambrosiastri qui dicitur commentarius in epistulas Pauli-

nas (pars III: in epistulas ad Galatas, etc., recensuit Henricus Iosephus Vogels; CSEL 81.3; Vienna: Hoelder, Pichler, Tempsky, 1969).
Ps.–Augustine [Ambrosiaster?], *Quaestiones Veteris et Novi Testamenti CXXVII* (recensuit Alexander Souter; CSEL 50; Vienna: Tempsky & Freytag, 1908).
Marius Victorinus (+ after 362)
Marii Victorini Afri Commentarii in Epistulas Pauli ad Galatas, etc. (edidit Albrecht Locher; BT; Leipzig: Teubner, 1972).
PL 1.1145–98.
Augustine (354–430)
Aurelius Augustinus, *Epistulae ad Galatas expositio* (*PL* 35.2105–48).
Jerome (347–420)
PL 26.331–468.
Pelagius (+ after 418)
Pelagius' Expositions of Thirteen Epistles of St. Paul (ed. Alexander Souter; TextsS 9.1–3; Cambridge: Cambridge University, 1922–31) 2.306–43.
Theodorus of Mopsuestia (+ 428)
Theodori episcopi Mopsuesteni in epistolas Beati Pauli Commentarii. The Latin version with the Greek fragments (2 vols.; ed. Henry B. Swete; Cambridge: Cambridge University, 1880–82) 1.1–111.
Theodoretus of Cyrus (+ c. 460)
PG 82.459–504.
Cassiodorus (+ c. 580)
PL 70.1343–46.
John of Damascus (+ c. 750)
PG 95.775–822.
Stegmüller, Friedrich
Repertorium Biblicum Medii Aevi (7 vols.; Madrid:
Consejo superior de investigaciones científicas, Instituto Francisco Suárez, 1950–61).
Theophylactus (c. 1050–1108)
PG 124.951–1032.
Lombardus, Petrus (+ 1160)
PL 192.93–170.
Aquinas, Thomas (+ 1274)
Expositio in omnes S. Pauli Epistolas, in his *Opera Omnia* (vol. 13; Parma: Fiaccador, 1862) 383–442.
Commentary on Saint Paul's Epistle to the Galatians (tr. F. R. Larcher; intro. R. T. A. Murphy; Albany: Magi, 1966).
Nicolaus of Dinkelsbühl (c. 1360–1433)
Der Galaterbriefkommentar des Nikolaus von Dinkelsbühl (Textkritische Ausgabe von Rudolf

Damerau; Studien zu den Grundlagen der Reformation 7; Giessen: Schmitz, 1969).

Die Quästionen zur Galaterbriefvorlesung des Nikolaus von Dinkelsbühl (Textkritische Ausgabe von Rudolf Damerau; Studien zu den Grundlagen der Reformation 9; Giessen: Schmitz, 1970).

Erasmus, Desiderius ([1466] 1469–1536)

In Epistolam Pauli ad Galatas Paraphrasis. 1519 (first edition), in his *Paraphrases in Novum Testamentum*, ex recognitione Io. Clerici (vol. 3; Berlin: Haude & Spener, 1780) 517–61.

Lefèvre d'Etaples, Jacques (c. 1460–1536)

Commentarii in Epistolas Pauli (Paris: Estienne, 1512, ²1515).

For this and other commentaries, see Eugene F. Rice, *The Prefatory Epistles of Jacques Lefèvre d'Etaples and Related Texts* (New York: Columbia University, 1972) 558f;

Guy Bedouelle and Franco Giacone, *Jacques Lefèvre d'Etaples et ses disciples: Epistres et Evangiles pour les cinquante et deux dimenches de l'an* (Leiden: Brill, 1976).

Luther, Martin (1483–1546)

Luthers Vorlesung über den Galaterbrief 1516/17 (ed. Hans von Schubert; AHAWPH 5; Heidelberg: Winter, 1918).

Divi Pauli Apostoli ad Galat⟨h⟩as Epistola, WA 57.I–XXVI (intro. K. A. Meissinger); 5–49 (glosses); 51–108 (scholia). First lecture on Galatians 1516/17.

In epistolam Pauli ad Galatas M. Lutheri commentarius, WA 2.443–618. Second lecture on Galatians 1518/19, ¹1519, ²1523.

Lectures on Galatians 1519 (ed. Jaroslav Pelikan; *Luther's Works* 27; St. Louis: Concordia, 1964) 151–410.

In epistolam S. Pauli ad Galatas Commentarius ex praelectione D. Martini Lutheri collectus; WA 40/1–2. Third lecture of 1531, collected 1535.

Lectures on Galatians 1535 (ed. Jaroslav Pelikan; *Luther's Works* 26–27; St. Louis: Concordia, 1963–64).

A Commentary on St. Paul's Epistle to the Galatians (edited on the basis of the "Middleton" edition by Philipp S. Watson; London: Clark, 1953, 1956).

Calvin, Jean (1509–1564)

Commentarius in Epistolam ad Galatas (Corpus Reformatorum 78; Brunsvick: Schwetschke, 1893).

The Epistles of Paul the Apostle to the Galatians (tr. T. H. L. Parker; Calvin's Commentaries II; Grand Rapids: Eerdmans, 1965).

Bullinger, Heinrich (1504–1575)

In D. Apostoli Pauli ad Galatas, etc., epistolas Heinrychi Bullingeri Commentarij (Tiguri: apud Christophorum Froschouerum, 1535).

In omnes apostolicas, divi videlicet Paul xiiii, et vii canonicas, commentarii Heinrychi Bullingeri, ab ipso iam recogniti & nonnullis in locis aucti (Tiguri: apud Christophorum Froschoverum, 1537).

Modern Works:

Cornelius a Lapide (Van den Steen, Corneille Cornelissen)

Commentaria in omnes D. Pauli epistolas (Antwerp: apud heredes Martini Nutii, Ioannem Meursium, 1614, ²1617).

Locke, John

A Paraphrase and Notes to the Epistle of St. Paul to the Galatians, etc. (London: Awnsham & Churchill, 1705–07).

Wet(t)stein, Johann Jacob

ʹΗ Καινὴ Διαθήκη. *Novum Testamentum graecum.* . . . *Tomus II, continens epistolas Pauli, etc.* (Amsterdam: Ex officina Dommeriana, 1752).

Grotius, Hugo

Annotationes in Epistolam Pauli ad Galatas, in his *Annotationes in Novum Testamentum* (Editio nova recensuit Ch. E. de Windheim; tomus 2, pars 1; Erlangen: apud I. C. Tetzschnerum, 1756), 544–82.

Winer, Georgius Benedictus

Pauli ad Galatas epistola latine vertit et perpetua annotatione illustravit (Leipzig: Reclam, 1821, ⁴1859).

Rückert, Leopold Immanuel

Commentar über den Brief Pauli an die Galater (Leipzig: Köhler, 1833).

Usteri, Leonhard

Commentar über den Brief Pauli an die Galater (Zurich: Orell Füssli, 1833).

Schott, Heinrich August

Epistolae Pauli ad Thessalonicenses et Galatas (Leipzig: Sumtibus Joannis Ambrosii Barthii, 1834).

Meyer, Heinrich August Wilhelm

Kritisch–exegetisches Handbuch über den Brief an die Galater (KEK; Göttingen: Vandenhoeck & Ruprecht, 1841, ⁵1870).

ET: *Critical and Exegetical Handbook to the Epistle to the Galatians* (tr. from the 5th edition of the German by G. H. Venables; Critical and Exegetical Commentary to the New Testament; Edinburgh: Clark, 1873).

de Wette, Wilhelm Martin Leberecht

Kurze Erklärung des Briefes an die Galater und der Briefe an die Thessalonicher, in *Kurzgefasstes exegetisches Handbuch zum Neuen Testament* (Leipzig: Weidmann, 1841, ³1864) 2/3.1–91.

Hilgenfeld, Adolf

Der Galaterbrief übersetzt, in seinen geschichtlichen Beziehungen untersucht und erklärt (Leipzig: Breitkopf & Härtel, 1852).

Ellicott, Charles J.

St. Paul's Epistle to the Galatians (London: Longmans, 1854).

Bisping, August

Erklärung des zweiten Briefes an die Korinther und des Briefes an die Galater, in *Exegetisches Handbuch zu den Briefen des Apostels Pauli* (Münster: Aschendorff, 1857, ³1883).

Estius, Wilhelm

In omnes Divi Pauli Apostoli Epistolas commentariorum tomus prior, posterior (Dvaci: Ex Officina Typographica Baltzaris Belleri, 1614–16; editio secunda curavit Joannes Holzammer; 3 vols.; Moguntiae: Sumptibus F. Kirchhemii, 1858–59).

Wieseler, Karl

Commentar über den Brief Pauli an die Galater (Göttingen: Dieterich, 1859).

Bentley, Richard

Epistola Beati Pauli Apostoli ad Galatas, in *Bentleii critica sacra*. Notes on the Greek and Latin text of the New Testament (ed. A. A. Ellis; Cambridge: Deighton & Bell, 1862) 93–117.

Lightfoot, Joseph Barber

Saint Paul's Epistle to the Galatians (London: Macmillan, 1865, [10]1890).

Holsten, Carl

Das Evangelium des Paulus (Teil 1.1, 2; Berlin: Reimer, 1880, 1898).

Sieffert, Friedrich

Der Brief an die Galater (KEK 7; Göttingen: Vandenhoeck & Ruprecht, [6]1880, [9]1899).

Bengel, Johann Albert

D. Joh. Alberti Bengelii Gnomon Novi Testamenti (Stuttgart: Steinkopf, [8]1887).
ET: *Gnomon of the New Testament* (2 vols.; tr. Charlton T. Lewis and Marvin R. Vincent; Philadelphia: Perkinpine & Higgins; New York: Sheldon, 1864; rep. as *New Testament Word Studies*; Grand Rapids: Kregel, 1971).

Schaefer, Aloys

Erklärung der zwei Briefe an die Thessalonicher und des Briefes an die Galater, in *Die Bücher des Neuen Testaments erklärt* (Münster: Aschendorff, 1890) 181–361.

Lipsius, Richard Adelbert

Briefe an die Galater, Römer, Philipper (Freiburg: Mohr, Siebeck, [2]1892) 2/2.1–69.

Ramsay, William M.

A Historical Commentary on St. Paul's Epistle to the Galatians (London: Hodder & Stoughton, 1899, [2]1900; Grand Rapids: Baker, 1965).

Zahn, Theodor

Der Brief des Paulus an die Galater (KNT 9; Leipzig: Deichert, 1905, [3]1922).

Bousset, Wilhelm

"Der Brief an die Galater," in *Die Schriften des Neuen Testaments* (Göttingen: Vandenhoeck & Ruprecht, [2]1908) 2.28–72.

Lietzmann, Hans

An die Galater (HNT 10; Tübingen: Mohr, Siebeck, 1910, [2]1923, [4]1971 [mit einem Literaturnachtrag von Philipp Vielhauer]).

Lake, Kirsopp

The Earlier Epistles of St. Paul: Their Motive and Origin (London: Rivingtons, 1911, [2]1914).

Loisy, Alfred

L'Epître aux Galates (Paris: Nourry, 1916).

Lagrange, Marie-Joseph

Saint Paul, Epître aux Galates (Paris: Librairie Lecoffre, J. Gabalda, 1918, [2]1925).

Burton, Ernest de Witt

A Critical and Exegetical Commentary on the Epistle to the Galatians (ICC; New York: Scribner's, 1920).

Rylands, L. Gordon

A Critical Analysis of the Four Chief Pauline Epistles, Romans, First and Second Corinthians, and Galatians (London: Watts, 1929).

Duncan, George S.

The Epistle of Paul to the Galatians (MNTC; London: Hodder & Stoughton, 1934).

Steinmann, Alphons

Die Briefe an die Thessalonicher und Galater, in *Die Heilige Schrift des Neuen Testaments* 5 (Bonn: Hanstein, [4]1935) 77–170.

Oepke, Albrecht

Der Brief des Paulus an die Galater (ed. Joachim Rohde; ThHK 9; Berlin: Evangelische Verlagsanstalt, 1937, [2]1957, [3]1973).

Beyer, Hermann Wolfgang

Der Brief an die Galater. Neu bearbeitet von Paul Althaus, in *Die kleineren Briefe des Apostels Paulus* (NTD 8; Göttingen: Vandenhoeck & Ruprecht, 1949, [8]1962).

Bonnard, Pierre

L'Epître de Saint Paul aux Galates (Commentaire du Nouveau Testament 9; Neuchâtel and Paris: Delachaux & Niestlé, 1953, [2]1972).

Lyonnet, Stanislas

Les Epîtres de Saint Paul aux Galates, aux Romains (Paris: Cerf, 1953).

Ridderbos, Herman Nicolaas

The Epistle of Paul to the Churches of Galatia (tr. Henry Zylstra; NICNT; Grand Rapids: Eerdmans, 1953).

Stamm, Raymond T.

The Epistle to the Galatians (IntB 10; Nashville: Abingdon, 1953) 427–593.

Bring, Ragnar

Commentary on Galatians (tr. Eric Wahlstrom; Philadelphia: Muhlenberg, 1961).

Viard, André

Saint Paul: Epître aux Galates (Paris: Librairie Lecoffre, J. Gabalda, 1964).

Bligh, John

Galatians: A Discussion of St. Paul's Epistle (Householder Commentaries 1; London: St. Paul, 1969). See the review by Hans Dieter Betz, *JBL* 89 (1970) 126–27.

Schlier, Heinrich

Der Brief an die Galater (KEK 7; Göttingen: Vandenhoeck & Ruprecht, [14]1971, [10]1949, [12]1962 rev.).

Grossouw, Willem K.

De Brief van Paulus aan de Galaaten (Bussum: Romen, 1974).

Mussner, Franz

Der Galaterbrief (HThK 9; Freiburg: Herder, 1974). See the review by Hans Dieter Betz, *SEÅ*

40 (1975) 145–46.

Becker, Jürgen
Die Briefe an die Galater, Epheser, Philipper, Kolosser, Thessalonicher und Philemon (NTD 8; Göttingen: Vandenhoeck & Ruprecht, 1976).

2. Studies

Barrett, C. K.
"The Allegory of Abraham, Sarah, and Hagar in the Argument of Galatians," in *Rechtfertigung, Festschrift für Ernst Käsemann zum 70. Geburtstag* (Tübingen: Mohr, Siebeck; Göttingen: Vandenhoeck & Ruprecht, 1976) 1–16.

Belser, Johann Evangelist
Die Selbstvertheidigung des heiligen Paulus im Galaterbrief (1,11–2,21) (BibS(F) 1.3; Freiburg: Herder, 1896).

Betz, Hans Dieter
"2 Cor 6:14–7:1: An Anti-Pauline Fragment?" *JBL* 92 (1973) 88–108.

Idem
"Spirit, Freedom, and Law: Paul's Message to the Galatian Churches," *SEÅ* 39 (1974) 145–60. German: "Geist, Freiheit und Gesetz: Die Botschaft des Paulus an die Gemeinden in Galatien," *ZThK* 71 (1974) 78–93.

Idem
"The Literary Composition and Function of Paul's Letter to the Galatians," *NTS* 21 (1975) 353–79.

Idem
"In Defense of the Spirit: Paul's Letter to the Galatians as a Document of Early Christian Apologetics," in *Aspects of Religious Propaganda in Judaism and Early Christianity* (ed. Elisabeth Schüssler Fiorenza; Notre Dame: University of Notre Dame, 1976) 99–114.

Idem
"Galatians, Letter to the," *IDBSup* (1976) 352–53.

Borse, Udo
Der Standort des Galaterbriefes (BBB 41; Bonn: Hanstein, 1972).

Bronson, David B.
"Paul, Galatians, and Jerusalem," *JAAR* 35 (1967) 119–28.

Bruce, F. F.
"Galatian Problems: 1. Autobiographical Data," *BJRL* 51 (1969) 292–309.

Idem
"Galatian Problems: 2. North or South Galatians?" *BJRL* 52 (1970) 243–66.

Idem
"Galatian Problems: 3. The 'Other' Gospel," *BJRL* 53 (1970/71) 253–71.

Idem
"Further Thoughts on Paul's Biography: Galatians 1:11–2:14," in *Jesus und Paulus: Festschrift für*

Werner Georg Kümmel zum 70. Geburtstag (Tübingen: Mohr, Siebeck; Göttingen: Vandenhoeck & Ruprecht, 1975) 21–29.

Brun, Lyder and Fridrichsen, Anton
Paulus und die Urgemeinde (Zwei Abhandlungen; Giessen: Töpelmann, 1921). Contains: Brun, Lyder, "Apostelkoncil [sic] und Aposteldekret;" Fridrichsen, Anton, "Die Apologie des Paulus Gal. I."

Buck, Charles H.
"The Date of Galatians," *JBL* 70 (1951) 113–22.

Crownfield, Frederick R.
"The Singular Problem of the Dual Galatians," *JBL* 64 (1945) 491–500.

Dinkler, Erich
"Der Brief an die Galater," *VF* 1–3 (1953/55) 175–83; also in his *Signum Crucis*, 270–82 (see Short Title list, above).

Eckert, Jost
Die urchristliche Verkündigung im Streit zwischen Paulus und seinen Gegnern nach dem Galaterbrief (Münchener Universitäts-Schriften, Katholisch-theologische Fakultät; Regensburg: Pustet, 1971).

Faw, Chalmer E.
"The Anomaly of Galatians," *BR* 4 (1960) 25–38.

Foerster, Werner
"Abfassungszeit und Ziel des Galaterbriefes," in *Apophoreta: Festschrift für Ernst Haenchen* (BZNW 30; Berlin: Töpelmann, 1964) 135–41.

Grant, Robert M.
"Hellenistic Elements in Galatians," *ATR* 34 (1952) 223–26.

Grosch, Hermann
Der im Galaterbrief Kap. 2,11–14 berichtete Vorgang in Antiochia: Eine Rechtfertigung des Verhaltens des Apostels Petrus (Leipzig: Deichert, 1916).

Grundmann, Walter
"Die Häretiker in Galatien," *ZNW* 47 (1956) 25–66.

Idem
"Die Apostel zwischen Jerusalem und Antiochia," *ZNW* 39 (1940) 110–37.

Häuser, Philipp
Anlass und Zweck des Galaterbriefes: Seine logische Gedankenentwicklung (NTAbh 11.3; Münster: Aschendorff, 1925).

Hawkins, John G.
The Opponents of Paul in Galatia (Ph.D. diss.; Yale University, 1971).

Hilgenfeld, Adolf
"Zur Vorgeschichte des Galaterbriefes," *ZWTh* 27 (1884) 303–43.

Holl, Karl
"Der Kirchenbegriff des Paulus im Verhältnis zu dem der Urgemeinde," in his *Gesammelte Aufsätze* 2.44–67 (see Short Title list, above).

Idem
"Der Streit zwischen Petrus und Paulus in An-

tiochien und seine Bedeutung für Luthers innere Entwicklung," in his *Gesammelte Aufsätze* 3.134–46.

Jewett, Robert
"The Agitators and the Galatian Congregation," *NTS* 17 (1971) 198–212.

Kertelge, Karl
"Zur Deutung des Rechtfertigungsbegriffs im Galaterbrief," *BZ* 12 (1968) 211–22.

Knox, John
"Galatians, Letter to the" *IDB* (1962) 2.338–43.

Linton, Olof
"The Third Aspect: A Neglected Point of View, a Study in Gal. I–II and Acts IX and XV," *StTh* 3 (1949/50) 79–95.

Lönning, Inge
"Paulus und Petrus: Gal 2,11 ff. als kontrovers-theologisches Fundamentalproblem," *StTh* 24 (1970) 1–69.

Lütgert, Wilhelm
Gesetz und Geist: Eine Untersuchung zur Vorgeschichte des Galaterbriefes (BFCTh 22.6; Gütersloh: Bertelsmann, 1919).

Manson, T. W.
"The Problem of the Epistle to the Galatians," *BJRL* 24 (1940) 59–80; also in his *Studies in the Gospels and Epistles* (Philadelphia: Westminster, 1962) 168–89.

Mussner, Franz
Theologie der Freiheit nach Paulus (Quaestiones Disputatae 75; Freiburg: Herder, 1976).

O'Neill, John C.
The Recovery of Paul's Letter to the Galatians (London: SPCK, 1972).

Overbeck, Franz
Über die Auffassung des Streits mit Petrus in Antiochien (Gal. 2,11ff.) bei den Kirchenvätern (Programm Basel, 1877; rep. Darmstadt: Wissenschaftliche Buchgesellschaft, 1968).

Ropes, James Hardy
The Singular Problem of the Epistle to the Galatians (HTS 14; Cambridge: Harvard University, 1929).

Sanders, Jack T.
"Paul's 'Autobiographical' Statements in Galatians 1–2," *JBL* 85 (1966) 335–43.

Schmithals, Walter
"The Heretics in Galatia," in his *Paul and the Gnostics*, 13–64 (see Short Title list, above).

Schulz, Siegfried
"Katholisierende Tendenzen in Schliers Galater-Kommentar," *KD* 5 (1959) 23–41.

Stählin, Gustav
"Galaterbrief," *RGG* (³1958) 2.1187–90.

Steck, Rudolf
Der Galaterbrief nach seiner Echtheit untersucht, nebst kritischen Bemerkungen zu den paulinischen Hauptbriefen (Berlin: Reimer, 1888).

Steinmann, Alphons
Der Leserkreis des Galaterbriefes: Ein Beitrag zur urchristlichen Missionsgeschichte (NTAbh 1.3–4; Münster: Aschendorff, 1908).

Stogiannou, Basileiou P.
"Ἡ περὶ Νόμου διδασκαλία τῆς πρὸς Γαλάτας ἐπιστολῆς τοῦ Ἀποστόλου Παύλου," *ΔΕΛΤΙΟΝ ΒΙΒΛΙΚΩΝ ΜΕΛΕΤΩΝ* 1 (1972) 312–28.

Strobel, August
"Das Aposteldekret in Galatien: Zur Situation von Gal. I und II," *NTS* 20 (1974) 177–90.

Tyson, Joseph B.
"Paul's Opponents in Galatia," *NovT* 4 (1968) 241–54.

Idem
"'Works of Law' in Galatians," *JBL* 92 (1973) 423–31.

Viard, André
"Galates (Epître aux)," *DBSup* fascicle 36 (1961) 211–26.

Vielhauer, Philipp
"Gesetzesdienst und Stoicheiadienst im Galaterbrief," in *Rechtfertigung: Festschrift für Ernst Käsemann zum 70. Geburtstag* (Tübingen: Mohr, Siebeck; Göttingen: Vandenhoeck & Ruprecht, 1976) 543–55.

Watkins, Charles H.
St. Paul's Fight for Galatia (London: Clarke, 1941).

Weber, Valentin
Die Adressaten des Galaterbriefes: Beweis der rein südgalatischen Theorie (Ravensburg: Kitz, 1900).

Indices*

1. Passages

a / Old Testament and Apocrypha

Gen

b / Old Testament Pseudepigrapha and other Jewish Literature

*Numbers in parentheses following page citations for this volume refer to footnotes.

3:2	270(169)
3:17	222(30)
4:11–13	304
Col	
1:23	48(57)
3:3–4	123(88)
3:11	182, 191(82)
1 Thess	
2:7	233
2:13	98(392)
2:16	267(141)
2:17	232
2:18	264(107)
5:5	183
2 Tim	
2:15	111(483)
Jas	
1:25	148
1:26	301
2:21–23	139

d / Early Christian Literature and the Ancient Church

Acta Pauli et Theclae	98(390)
Acts Thom.	
110.44	185(27)
142	257(31)
Ap. Jas.	
p. 16 l. 17–18	48(58)
p. 13 l. 23–25	150(120)
Apost. Const.	
8.12.23	166(41)
Barn.	
8.7	243(54)
9.4	169(65)
11.11	286(140)
Benedict	
Regula	
2.20	195(110)
2 Clem.	
12.5	196(121)
Clemens Alex.	
Exc. ex Theod.	
80.1	207(55)
Paed.	
1.7.60.1–2	172(85)
3.1.2.1	171(84)
Strom.	
3.2.6.2	194
3.92.2	196(119)
4.13, 89.2–3	184(22)
7.82.1	298(50)

Disc. 8–9	
53, 15ff	233
Did.	
7.1	285(123)
Ephrem	
Epiphany Hymns	
13.14	184(25)
Epiphanius	
Anaceph.	
28.1.3	149(109)
Adv. haer.	
2.2	134(57)
21.4	170(85)
30.16	68–69(124)
Epistola apostolorum	
33	248(97)
Eusebius	
De eccles. theol.	
2.14	170(85)
H.E.	
5.16.3	156(26)
Epistle to the Laodiceans	38(15)
Firmicus Maternus	
De errore prof. rel.	
22.1	184(20)
Gos. Eg.	
2	196(119)
Gos. Phil.	
49	3(12)
73	196(120)
78	196(120)
101	189
112	184(22)
Gos. Thom.	
22	196(120)
Gos. Truth	
32.32	184(22)
Hermas	
Mand.	
11.8	297(49)
Sim.	
8.3.3	169
Hippolytus	
Ref.	
5.7.15	196(118)
5.7.39	247
Ignatius	
Eph.	
19.1	270(161)
Mag.	
10.3	112(497)
Phld.	
1	39(21)
Pol.	
4.3	195(113)

Rom.	
3.3	55(107), 265(116)
Smyrn.	
5.3	49(65)
Irenaeus	
Adv. Haer.	
1.26.2	246(80)
Justin	
Apology	
1.5.8	234(163)
1.16.13	332(21)
Dial.	
10.3	241(30)
46	218(51), 260(63)
46–47	260(63)
116.3	200(158)
Ps.-Justin	
Oratio ad Graecos	
5.7	222(26)
Kerygma Petrou	
Frag. 1	300(72)
Frag. 2	216(34), 218(51)
Mani-Codex (CMC)	
62.21f	209(79)
69.17–20	149(113)
71.1–20	99(394)
71.1–72.7	65
87.19–21	98(393)
"Marcionite Prologues"	3–4
Odes Sol.	
7.4	209(72)
10.2	124(93)
10.5	120(66)
41.1f	216(27)
Polycarp	
Phil.	
3.2–3	233(151)
Ps.-Clem. Hom.	
2.17.3	9(57)
3.2.2–3	172(85)
11.30.2	217(36)
11.35.3–6	332
11.35.4	88(282)
17.7.3	98(392)
17.17–18	65–66
17.18	93(339)
17.18.2–3	62(70)
Ep. Petr.	
1.1–3.3	331
1.5	321(91)
2.1	173(93)

2.3	9, 49(65), 229(104)
2.4–7	268(150)
Ps.-Clem. Recog.	
1.70.1	229(104)
1.70.2	47(41)
4.34–35	88(282)
Sextus	
Sent.	
85	215(24)
201	122(83)
Tertullian	
Adv. Marc.	
5.4.6	218(51)
De praescr. haer.	
23	96(371)
Treat. Res.	
50, 15	311(197)
Tri. Trac.	
132, 16–28	182

e / Greek and Latin Authors

Aeschylus	
Eum.	
218	176(125)
Alcidamas	
Frag. 1	193–94
Ammonius	
De adfinium voc. diff.	
208	229(102)
Aristotle	
EN	
3.12.8, p. 1119b13	177
1155a34	173
1157a23f	223(45)
1159b2f	222(23)
1165b17	173
1171a29	299(58)
περὶ φιλοσοφίας	
15	134(66)
Pol.	
1.2.3, p. 1253b20–24	193(95)
3.8, p. 1384a14	288(164)
Chrysostom	
Hom.	
1.2 in 1 Thess	265(117)
Cicero	
Amic.	
20	222
22	230
44	232
54	230

65	231
67	224(48)
75	232
79	230
De inv.	
1.19.27–31.30	58–59
1.24.34	128(10)
1.31.51, 53	129(19)
1.32.53	130(22)
1.55.106	313(11, 12)
De leg.	
1.4.14	162(10)
Nat. deor.	
1.22	230
Clitarchus	
Sent.	
86	290(175)
Corp. Herm.	
1.31	216(27)
13.5	234(161)
13.7	235(166)
13.8	184(22)
13.9	234(161), 235(166), 300(69)
13.12	286–87
Demosthenes	
De corona, Or. 18.17	60(36), 67(104)
Dio Chrysostom	
11.1	130(29)
75.2	164
75.10	164
Diodorus Sic.	
15.7.1	149(114)
Diog. L.	
1.3	197
2.68	164(27)
6.11	164(25)
7.170	304(116)
9.2	164(22)
Dionysius Halic.	
3.60.1	132(42)
Dittenberger	
Sylloge	
958, 5–7	185(26)
Epictetus	
Dissertationes	
1.9.20	295(24)
2.9.20	110
2.9.22	303–04
2.11.13, 24	322(90)
2.18.13	309(181)
2.23.3	135(72)
3.24.9	241(29)

4.7.40	302(91)
4.8.39	301
4.8.40	287(141)
51.1	211(96)
Encheiridion	
13	301
33.12	87(278)
Epicurus	
Frag. 530	164
Euripides	
Iph. Taur.	
493	132(42)
Med.	
21	100(411)
Gnom. Vatic.	
7	55(110)
427	163(19)
449	310(186)
507	164(19)
Homer	
Il.	
6.167ff	25(125)
Lucian	
Abdic.	
7	229(100)
Demon.	
7	297(43)
Prom. es in verb.	
1	306(151)
Rhet. praec.	
2	301
Toxaris	
5	222
40–41	228
Livy	
22.39.19	265(112)
Marcus Aurelius	
6.30.4	286(136)
7.9	173(92)
Menander	
Comp.	
1.63f	302(92)
Sent.	
370	299
459	304(112)
534	299
629	298(55)
660	304(113)
Pindar	
Frag. 169	164
Pap. Flind Petr.	
II, 11, 1	267(133)
Pap. Mich.	
56.4	264(105)
479.4f	47(40)

2. Greek Words

ἀββά
210–11

ἀγαπάω
125, 276

ἀγάπη
33, 263, 273–74, 287

αἰών
42(58)

ἀκοή
133(50)

ἀκυροῦν
158

ἀλληγορεῖν
243

ἀμήν
43, 325

ἀναγκάζειν
88, 112, 315

ἀνάθεμα
53

ἀνθίστημι .
106(443)

ἀποκαλύπτειν
71, 176(121)

ἀποκάλυψις
63, 85

ἀπόστολος
38, 74–75, 77–78, 98

αὐτάρκεια
304

ἀφορίζειν
70, 108

ἀφορμή
272

βασκαίνειν
131

Γαλάται
2, 3

γέγραπται
144, 151, 241, 248

γινώσκω
99, 141, 215

γνωρίζειν
56, 59–60

γράφειν
79, 313–14

γραφή
143, 174–75, 250

δεισιδαιμονία
217–18

διαθήκη
155–56, 243–44

δικαιοσύνη, δικαιοῦσθαι
116, 118–20, 126, 141,
142, 146, 173–74, 177

δοκιμάζειν
302

δοκοῦντες
86–87, 92, 99

δύναμις
135(78)

ἐγκράτεια
33, 288

ἐγώ
121–23, 221–23, 280

ἐθνικῶς
112

εἶδον
96–97, 99, 111

εἰκῇ
134, 219

εἰρήνη
40–41, 287, 321–22

εἰς
157, 171–73, 198, 200,
241, 274

ἐκκλείν
229–30

ἐκκλησία
40(38)

ἐλευθερία
29, 90–91, 271–72

ἐλεύθερος
194, 241–42, 247,
250–52

ἐλευθεροῦν
255

ἐμμένειν
144(60)

ἐνάρχεσθαι
133(53, 57)

ἐνεργεῖν
135(78, 79), 263(97)

ἐν Χριστῷ
90–91, 119, 152, 186,
200, 262–64

ἐπαγγελία
152, 156, 159–60, 163,
168, 173, 175, 201,
242, 249

ἔπειτα
76, 79, 83

ἐπίτροπος
203

ἐπιχορηγεῖν
135(77)

ἔργα νόμου
116, 126, 130, 133,
136, 141–42, 143–44,
283

εὐαγγελίζεσθαι
52, 53, 56, 71–72, 81

εὐαγγέλιον
48, 49, 56, 92, 96, 111

θαυμάζειν
46–47

θέλειν
50, 132, 216, 229, 236,
241, 279, 314, 317

ζηλοῦν
229

ζηλωτής
68

ζωοποιεῖν
174(104)

ἰουδαΐζειν
112

Ἰουδαϊκῶς
112

Ἰουδαϊσμός
67

καινὴ κτίσις
320–21

κανών
263, 319, 321

καρδία
209–10

καταγινώσκειν
105

καταλύειν
121(70)

καταργεῖν
158(47)

καταρτίζειν
296–97

κατασκοπεῖν
90

καύχημα
302–03, 317–19

κενόδοξος
294

κηρύσσειν
86(269), 268–69

κληρονομία
159, 201, 202, 212,
250, 285

κληρονόμος
201, 202

κοινωνία
100

κόλαξ, κολακεία
223, 265(117)

κοπιᾶν
219

κόσμος
204, 216–17, 318–19

κύριος
40–41, 78, 266–67,
317–19, 325

μακαρισμός
183, 226–27

μεσίτης
170–71

μεταστρέφειν
50

μετατίθεσθαι
47

μιμητής
325

μνημονεύειν
101–02

μορφοῦσθαι
234(163, 164)

μυκτερίζειν
306

νήπιος
203

νόμος
116, 121–22, 126, 133,
136, 144, 146, 147,
149, 158(45), 159, 162,
164, 166, 173, 175–77,
207, 208, 241, 259–61,
274–75, 281, 288,
298–300, 316

ξύλος
151(132)

οἰκοδομεῖν
121(72)

οἰκονόμος
203–04

ὅμοιος τῷ ὁμοίῳ
173, 222

ὀρθοποδεῖν
111

παιδαγωγός
177

παιδεία
33, 177–78, 257, 270

παραβάτης
121(71)

παραλαμβάνειν
54(97)

παρατηρεῖν
217–18

παρείσακτοι
89–90

παρεισέρχεσθαι
90

παρρησία
228

πάσχειν
134

πείθειν
54

πεισμονή
265

περιπατεῖν
277

πιστεύειν
96(367), 117, 141, 175

πίστις
81, 117–18, 125, 133,
136, 141–43, 146–48,
152–53, 175, 177, 178,
186, 262–63, 288, 311

πιστός
143

πληροῦν
275

πνεῦμα
8–9, 25, 29, 33, 132–33,
135, 152, 209, 249,
262, 277–78, 281, 286,
293, 296, 308, 325

πνευματικός
8–9, 25, 29, 33, 132,
296–98

πόθος
236

ποιεῖν
144, 146, 147–48, 259,
279, 309

προγράφειν
131(39)

προευαγγελίζεσθαι
143

προθεσμία
204

προκυροῦν
157–58

προλέγειν
284

προσανατιθέναι
72, 95
προστιθέναι
164, 166
πρόσωπον λαμβάνειν
95

σάρξ
8, 72, 118, 124–25,
133–34, 224–25, 242,
249, 272–73, 278–79,
283, 289–90, 308,
314–15, 317
σκάνδαλον
269–70
σκοπεῖν
298
σπέρμα
156–57
σπουδάζειν
102
σταυρός
269, 315–16, 317
σταυροῦν
131–32, 289, 318
στίγματα
324
στοιχεῖα τοῦ κόσμου
42, 148, 176, 178,
204–05, 213–16
στοιχεῖν
293
στῦλοι
86–87, 99
συναπάγεσθαι
110
συνεσθίειν
107
συνιστάναι
121(73)
συνυποκρίνεσθαι
109–10
συστοιχία
245, 249

ταράσσειν
49, 267
τελεῖν
277–78
τρέχειν
87–88

υἱοθεσία
208

υἱός
69, 125, 141, 186,
206–07, 209, 211–12,
241, 250
ὑπόκρισις
110
ὑποστέλλειν
108

φύσει θεοί
205, 213–15

χάρις
40, 48, 70, 99, 126,
160, 261, 325

ψευδάδελφοι
89–90

3. Subjects

Abraham
31, 137–44, 146, 152–53, 156–60, 241–42, 251

Acclamations
172, 210–11

Addressees
1–3

Adiaphoron
94

Adoption
186–87, 208–09

Allegory
31, 203–04, 239–40, 243, 307–08

Amanuensis
1, 312–14

Androgyny
196–200

Angel(s)
53, 168, 198, 224–26

Anthropology
28, 118–19, 121, 195–200, 207–08, 256–58, 272–73, 277–80, 283–90, 296–97, 301–04, 307–08, 310–11, 315–20

Anthropos myth (see Anthropology)
197–99

Antioch
82, 85(254)

Antioch-on-the-Orontes
103–06

"*Agon* Motif"
88, 264

Apologetic Letter
14–15, 24

Apology (see also Episto-lography, Rhetoric)
14–15, 24, 28, 30

Apostle(s)
38–39, 40, 54, 62–63, 69–72, 74–75, 77–78, 83–102, 99(395), 105–12, 121–23, 225–26, 235, 265, 317, 319–20, 322, 324–25

Apostolic Council
81–83, 85–88, 94–95

Apostolic Decree
95(363)

Arabia
73–74, 244–45

Atonement
151

Author
1

Baptism
26, 28, 32, 33, 123, 181–82, 186–89, 195, 285

Baptismal Liturgy
181–82, 184, 285

Barnabas
84, 85(254), 100, 103, 110

Beatitudes
183–85

Beliar
9

Benediction
321–22

Blessing
40, 50, 142–43, 152–53, 320–23, 325

Boasting
67, 68–69, 71, 81, 93, 302–03, 317–19

Body of Christ
119–20, 187, 235

Catalogue of Vices and Virtues
281–83

Celtic Religion
218(50)

Cephas (see Peter)

Chiasm
39

Christological Formulae (Christology)
26, 30, 41–42, 125, 149–51, 205–08

Christology
Crucifixion: 131, 149–52, 269–70, 289–90, 315–16, 318–19; Lord: 40, 78, 266–67, 317–19, 325; Resurrection: 39; Self-Sacrifice: 41–42, 123–25, 151; Son of God: 70–71, 125, 185–86, 206–07, 209–10

Chronology
76, 83–84

Chrysostom
193(92)

Church, Doctrine of
3–5, 26, 30, 32, 33, 40, 67, 74, 76, 78, 80, 83–120, 130–36, 141–43, 146, 148–53, 156–60, 177–80,

185–201, 208–09, 211–12, 214–17, 233–35, 242, 246–49, 251–52, 255–58, 262–64, 271–74, 281, 283–90, 293–306, 310–11, 319–23, 325

Cicero
44–46, 58–60

Cilicia
79–80

Circumcision
6–7, 9, 83–89, 91, 96–97, 100, 134, 216, 258–61, 262–63, 268–70, 315–17, 319–20, 328, 334–35

Collection
101–03

Conversion
64–66, 69–70

Covenant
156–57

Cross
317–19

Cultic Rituals
217

Curse
50–54, 144–46, 148–52, 251, 261, 267, 321, 323

Damascus
73–74

Demons
204–05, 213–16, 226

Diatribe
111–12, 130–36, 213, 241, 264, 266, 270, 291–93, 295, 298, 301–06, 309

Digressio
163

Doxology
43

Dualism
29–31, 32, 42, 132–34, 141–53, 164–68, 173–80, 205, 215–16, 241–52, 256–61, 264, 268–70, 277–90, 308, 315–23, 325

Education
33

Elements of the World
25, 42, 91, 148–49, 169, 204–05, 213–14, 216–17

Emancipation of Women
196–97, 200

Epistolography
xiv, xv, 14–15, 24, 26–28,

37, 53–54, 223, 232–33, 236, 255–56, 266–67, 305–06, 312–13

Eschatology
42, 122–25, 169–70, 175–80, 206, 219, 259, 261–62, 267, 284–85, 306–10, 320, 322–23

Ethics
7–9, 32–33, 55, 67–68, 79, 86, 90–92, 106–12, 119–20, 122–25, 166–80, 190–201, 255–58, 272–76, 277–90, 292–93, 319–20

Euhemerism
214–15

Exempla
154

Exordium
44–46, 58, 313

Expositio
121

Faith
8–9, 29, 32–33, 81, 97–98, 100, 112, 115–27, 132, 135–36, 141–44, 147–48, 152–53, 175–79, 185–86, 262–64, 287, 310–11, 320, 322–23

"False Brothers"
89–90, 107–08, 111–12, 329(2)

Fate
205

Father
210–11

Fellowship
100, 106

Flesh
6–9, 29, 118–19, 133–34, 242, 247, 249, 272–73, 277–80, 283, 289–90, 308, 310–11, 317

Freedom
8–9, 32–33, 90–91, 255–57, 271–74

Friendship
32, 221–33, 298–99, 305

Galatia, Galatians
1–9, 40, 130–32

Gallio Inscription
10(63)

Gentiles, Gentile Christians
71–72, 81–83, 89–91,

349

97–98, 103–05, 106, 115, 142, 185–86

Gnosticism
7–9, 196

Gods (see also One God)
3, 39, 41–43, 54, 67, 69–70, 79, 81, 92–95, 98, 121–27, 140–41, 142, 146, 157–60, 171–74, 185–86, 206–07, 209–12, 213–15, 225–26, 285, 300–01, 307–08, 321–23

Gospel
7–9, 26–27, 28, 30, 48(57, 58), 49–50, 56, 64–66, 71–72, 85–88, 92, 325

Grace
31, 40–41, 48(48), 99, 126–27, 261, 325

Guardianship
202–04

Hagar
238–39, 242, 244–47

Heavenly Letter
25

Hellenists
90(303), 139–40

Hellenization
2, 139, 167, 191

Hippocratic Oath
51, 185(26), 305

Hope
262

"I"
123–24, 277–78, 318(66)

Ignatius of Antioch
105, 106(441)

Illness of Paul
224–25

"In Christ"
181–82, 235

"Indicative" and "Imperative"
255–56, 271–72

Inheritance
157, 159–60, 203

Interrogatio
130, 213, 240

Isaac
242, 249

Ishmael
242, 249

Israel of God
321–23

Ius talionis
307

James, Brother of the Lord
7, 78–79, 92, 94, 99, 104, 106–08

Jerusalem
7, 30–31, 73, 75, 76–77, 83–88, 245–48

Jerusalem Conference (see "Apostolic Council")

Jewish Christians, Jewish Christianity
5–9, 26, 28–31, 42, 82–83, 103–06, 110–12, 115, 185, 216–17, 315(31), 315–16, 322–23

Jews
4–5

John
99, 101

Joke
270

Judaism
6–9, 26, 28, 29, 31, 32, 66–69, 89, 316, 321–23

Judaizers
6–7, 112

Judea
80–81

Justification by Faith
8–9, 31, 115, 119–20, 262

Knowledge of God
215

Last Judgment
307–08

Law (see also Torah)
148–51, 163–66, 170, 177–80, 261, 274–76, 288, 299–300, 316

Law of Christ
298–301

Life
124–25, 174

Love
32–33, 263–64, 273–74

Magic, Magical Letter
25, 32–33

Mani Biography
6

Marcion
173

Meals
107

Mediator
170–73

Moses
170, 332(3)

Mother
233–34

Narratio
46, 58–62, 66, 83, 114, 321

Neighbor
276(40)

Neo-Platonism
197

New Creation
319–20

"North Galatian Theory"
4

Oath
79, 227, 259

One God
3, 28, 30, 31

Onesimus
195

Opponents
5–9, 30–31, 49–50, 89–92, 174, 229–31, 248, 251, 268–69, 273, 300, 314–17

Orphism
197

Orthodoxy
111

Parenesis
24, 25, 27, 32–33, 253–55, 291–92

Peace
40–41

Peroratio
313, 323

Persecution
67, 268, 315–16

Peter (Cephas)
7, 75, 76–77, 93, 96–98, 99, 104–12

Pharisee
259–61

Philemon, Letter to
193

Philo
166–67

"Pillar" Apostles
82, 86–87, 99(404)

Poor, the
101–02

Postscript
1, 312–13

Probatio
115, 128–30, 181, 213, 239–40, 321

Promise
152–53, 156–57, 173–74, 242

Prooemium
44–45

Proof from Scripture
31

Prophet
38

Propositio
114–15, 126, 289

Proverbs
26

"Putting on Christ"
186–89

Pythagoras
305

Quintilian
44–46, 58–62, 114

Qumran Community
260

Rebirth
233–35

Refutatio
114

Revelation
62–66, 70–71, 85

Rhetoric
xiv, xv, 14, 16–23, 24–25, 30

Sacred Law
50–51

Salvation
31–33, 39, 41–43, 70, 71, 81, 88, 92, 97, 98–100, 111, 115, 117–18, 120, 122, 125–26, 132–36, 141–53, 159–60, 173–80, 185–201, 205, 206–12, 215–17, 219, 227, 234–35, 249, 251–52, 255–59, 261–62, 277–81, 286–90, 292–95, 295–301, 308–10, 317–23, 325

Sarah
242, 243–45, 249

4. Commentaries and Modern Authors